CAPITALISM

Also by Sven Beckert

Empire of Cotton

The Monied Metropolis

Global History, Globally (coauthor)

American Capitalism (coauthor)

Slavery's Capitalism (coauthor)

The American Bourgeoisie (coauthor)

Plantation Kingdom (coauthor)

CAPITALISM

A GLOBAL HISTORY

Sven Beckert

PENGUIN PRESS

NEW YORK

2025

PENGUIN PRESS
An imprint of Penguin Random House LLC
1745 Broadway, New York, NY 10019
penguinrandomhouse.com

Illustration credits appear on pages 1,255–1,265.

Designed by Amanda Dewey

LIBRARY OF CONGRESS CATALOGING-IN-PUBLICATION DATA
Names: Beckert, Sven, author.
Title: Capitalism: a global history / Sven Beckert.
Description: New York: Penguin Press, 2025. |
Includes bibliographical references and index.
Identifiers: LCCN 2024049068 (print) | LCCN 2024049069 (ebook) |
ISBN 9780735220836 (hardcover) | ISBN 9780735220843 (ebook)
Subjects: LCSH: Capitalism—History.
Classification: LCC HB501 .B37387 2025 (print) |
LCC HB501 (ebook) | DDC 330.12/209—dc23/eng/20250528
LC record available at https://lccn.loc.gov/2024049068
LC ebook record available at https://lccn.loc.gov/2024049069

Printed in Canada
1 3 5 7 9 10 8 6 4 2

The authorized representative in the EU for product safety and compliance is
Penguin Random House Ireland, Morrison Chambers, 32 Nassau Street,
Dublin D02 YH68, Ireland, https://eu-contact.penguin.ie.

For Noah and Pascal

CONTENTS

Part III

GLOBAL RECONSTRUCTIONS

Part IV

THE FUTURE OF CAPITALISM?

PREFACE

The capitalist revolution and its travails: David Teniers the Younger (1610–1690), The Rich Man Being Led to Hell.

We live in a world created by capitalism. The ceaseless accumulation of capital forges the cities we inhabit, determines the way we work, allows an extraordinarily large number of people to engage in unprecedented levels of consumption, influences our politics, and shapes the landscapes around us. It is impossible to look at Earth and miss the world-historical force of capitalism.

This is true as much for the greatest structures we inhabit as for the most intimate parts of our lives, as much for the world's geology as for the ways we think about ourselves. To start, we acquire almost all goods and services we consume through markets, something that would have been unimaginable for most of human history. We sell our labor through markets—again, unimaginable for most of human history. Some of us might trade in stocks, either as a full-time vocation or to safeguard something called retirement; most people at most times would have considered this trading deeply sacrilegious, more like sorcery than a legitimate way to gain wealth. New technologies and economic growth are mundane certainties, and we know that our children will live in a world quite different from the one we ourselves were born into—a novelty. Our consumption connects us to people in far-flung corners of the world—again, unimaginable for most of human history. The T-shirt you may be wearing right now might have been stitched in Cambodia, the steaming cup of coffee before you grown in Brazil, the TV you have switched off to read this book assembled in South Korea, and the iPhone that lies temptingly next to you designed in California and assembled by women laboring in massive sweatshops in the southern Chinese city of Shenzhen. While trade is much older than capitalism—indeed, ancient—what is new is the intensity of global connections that capitalism has given rise to, a world economy.

The capitalist revolution has imprinted itself on your way of thinking about the world too: When you hear or read about economic affairs in the news, you learn about "the economy" as an active subject that did something or needs us to do something. Most people throughout human history considered questions of production, consumption, and trade, just as we do now, but they would have found it strange to make sacrifices to a human-created god called "the economy." Along the same lines, you might speak to friends about how you "spend" your time, talk about what someone is "worth," and recall the last time you enjoyed some leisure—again, concepts alien to most humans of the past. Or you might passionately debate capitalism in a university seminar: You might listen to extolments of the enormous increase in human productivity that it has made possible, to sum-ups of the technical progress it has generated, and to assertions that it has enabled many of us to live longer, healthier, more satisfying lives. On the flip side, you might listen to equally fervent accounts of exploitation, of environmental destruction, of society-structuring inequities, and of grave imbalances between the parts of the world that are fabulously rich and those that are shockingly poor. You might celebrate capitalism as the best of all possible worlds or blame it for the devastations it has wrought and envision its end.

No matter your beliefs, you probably agree that there is no escaping capitalism—neither the debate on it nor its impact on our lives. Capitalism is what one scholar—in a different context—has called a "hyperobject," referring "to entities of such vast temporal and spatial dimensions that they defeat traditional ideas about what a thing is in the first place."[1] It is thus unsurprising that almost everyone has thought about capitalism in some way or that people have strong opinions about it.

Despite, or perhaps because of, capitalism's ubiquitous presence, many take it for granted; it seems unremarkable, even natural. It has imprinted our world so deeply that it is even possible not to notice it. But what seems natural is very recent and wholly human-made. If you live in Cairo, Guangzhou, or Florence, you live in a place where the sprouts of capitalism stretch back a long time, perhaps a millennium. But such places are truly exceptional. Almost everywhere else, the capitalist revolution is, at most, a few centuries old, often much less. From a global perspective, even as recently as 1800, much of capitalism was confined to just a few islands in a vast sea of economic life organized around other principles—subsistence production, tributary rule, and almost no economic growth. If you live outside the capitalist heartlands, especially in the world's countryside, the capitalist revolution may be as recent as the millennium we are living in right now. Capitalism is very new, and even after it emerged, it was spread thinly across the world for most of its life.

Perhaps more surprisingly, the capitalist revolution is recent in terms of not just its spatial spread but its expansion into many spheres of our lives. Even in the world's most capitalist societies, our grandparents, and perhaps our parents, probably grew some of the food they consumed. They almost certainly did all the cooking and might have produced some of the clothing they wore. They found love at the village dance, not on a subscription dating app. These examples remind us that in addition to being newly arrived, the capitalist revolution was, for a very long time, fairly weak and left large swaths of life, even economic life, unaffected.

Yet what is common and seemingly natural—the way things are—has a history. We can ask how and why such a radically new way of economic life evolved. How did we get from a world in which the logic of capital was limited to only a few spaces to one in which it determines almost everything? How did we ever give such superpowers to something created by but also external to us? Even if we take it for granted, see it as natural, this explosion of capitalism is one of the greatest puzzles in human history. And we need to grapple with it, not just to satisfy our curiosity about how we got to where we are but to gain a better foothold in the present and think creatively about our future. As a Chinese proverb puts it, we need to "learn truth from facts."[2]

Yet sometimes the most difficult things to grasp are the most familiar. Capitalism is one of them. This book grew in part out of my urgent sense that we need to understand this almost geological force shaping our lives. But it also grew out of a deep frustration that so many of the stories we tell about capitalism are incomplete and sometimes just plain wrong.

To find ourselves now, we need to journey through one thousand years of capitalism's history. The road—full of twists, turns, and dead ends—will circle the world to explain how we got here and to perhaps suggest the levers by which we might plot out a course for our future. I have spent my career studying capitalism; this book is a wager that its history—all of it—might be understood, if not wholly contained, between two book covers.

While this book is a serious history of a serious topic, I have tried to make it readable for everyone, because no matter where you live or what you do, you live in capitalism. If I have done it right, you should find here a surprising diversity of protagonists—from ocean-traversing eleventh-century Yemeni merchants to young women working in Cambodian textile factories in 2023. You should encounter a globe-spanning range of places—some you know well and might even call home, others so distant you might never have heard of them—that demonstrate that capitalism, despite our proclivities to think in local or (at most) national contexts, can only be understood globally. And you should find answers to a wide range of questions raised by this revolutionary recasting of economic life. Like capitalism itself, it will be a dizzying ride.

CAPITALISM

INTRODUCTION

Elisabeth Voigt, Der Maschinenmann
(The Machine Man), 1932.

I t was in the fall of 1639 that Robert Keayne found himself in front
of the General Court of Massachusetts, the colony's legislature
and its court of appeals. A recent immigrant to the freshly established British colony, he traded in English manufactured goods. By all
accounts, he was a faithful Puritan, having "come over . . . for the advancement of the gospel," but in that fateful year, he found himself
accused of the "very evil" and "corrupt practice" of overcharging his
customers and placing profit above the community's needs. Convicted
and ordered to pay a fine of £200 (equivalent to 2,857 days' worth of
wages for a skilled English worker), he was called before the elders of

Boston's First Church, the "Old Brick," and narrowly escaped excommunication. When John Winthrop, the colony's governor, sat down to write about the case in his journal, he remembered that Keayne, "with tears, acknowledge[d] and bewail[ed] his covetous and corrupt heart."[1] Keayne had confessed to the congregation that he had embraced "false principles," including these:

- That a man might sell as dear as he can, and buy as cheap as he can.
- If a man lose by casualty of sea, etc., in some of his commodities, he may raise the price of the rest.
- That he may sell as he bought, though he paid too dear, etc., and though the commodity be fallen, etc.
- That, as a man may take the advantage of his own skill or ability, so he may of another's ignorance or necessity.[2]

Keayne later complained about the "unkindness" with which he was treated in New England, and about the "deepe and sharpe censure that was layd upon me . . . and carried on with so much bitterness and indignation." He wrote his 158-page last will and testament to vindicate his deeds, arguing that God was best served by accumulating riches that could later be given away to serve the community. He also asked the "overseers of this my will . . . [t]o move the General Court . . . to recall or repeal that sentence and to return my fine" and added that "what is so returned by them may be given to Harvard College at Cambridge."[3]

THE ACTS KEAYNE confessed to were, to many of his contemporaries, wrong prima facie. To our modern ears, they seem commonsensical. "That a man might sell as dear as he can, and buy as cheap as he can"— the logic Keayne embraced in his business dealings—structures almost all economic life today. It appears unexceptional, even natural. Yet such ideas, as Keayne painfully experienced, were seen by his peers as a radical departure. He argued that the "covetous" accumulation of wealth actually served his community—prefiguring Adam Smith's invisible hand. But to his fellow Puritans, Keayne's single-minded pursuit of profit violated long-established norms. It would take another two centuries before the new form of economic life that people like Keayne helped usher in even acquired a name—capitalism. Two more centuries passed before capitalism emerged as the world's predominant form of organizing economic life, such that one economist could describe the world in 2019 as "capitalism, alone."[4]

THIS BOOK INVITES you to explore this vast change: the emergence and spread of capitalism. How did the capitalist revolution begin? How did a form of economic life that was such a breakaway from previous history spread around the world and into ever more spheres of life? How did we move from a society in which markets were embedded in social relations to one in which social relations are embedded in markets? By what mechanism has capitalism evolved and changed over time? And where are we in its history today?[5]

These are big and urgent questions. Debated for several centuries, they retain their force and vitality. As recently as the 2007–2008 Great Recession, discussions on capitalism moved into the mainstream across a wide political spectrum in many parts of the world. In its wake, even conservative newspapers began debating what they called the "future of capitalism," and Paul Polman, then Unilever's CEO, deliberated in the *McKinsey Quarterly* about capitalism's prospects, a topic that also worried the rich and powerful at the 2012 World Economic Forum in Davos as they probed: "Has capitalism got a future?"[6] For Pope Francis, capitalism's impact on the world was so consequential that he made it a significant concern of his papacy. Museum exhibitions dedicated to capitalism opened in New York, Berlin, and Brussels. And even in the 2020s, with the crisis in the rearview mirror, the debate continued: In 2020, Japanese philosopher Kohei Saito published *Slow Down: The Degrowth Manifesto*, arguing that growth—capitalism's fundamental dynamic—has run its course. He sold a remarkable half million copies in Japan alone. That same year, a survey found that only one in eight Germans believed that the form of economic organization they lived under—capitalism—benefited them, while a full 55 percent thought that capitalism, on balance, was more damaging than beneficial. In the United States, young adults found socialism just as appealing as capitalism. In some parts of the world, bookstores were filled with works that predicted, in one way or another, the imminent end of capitalism.[7] In the spring of 2023, fifteen years after the crisis, Albert Edwards of the French banking behemoth Société Générale even said, "We may be looking at the end of capitalism."[8]

With ups and downs, such animated discussions about capitalism have been going on for more than two centuries. While only specialists care to argue about different interpretations of feudalism or hunter-gatherer societies, capitalism provokes visceral reactions. Differences in interpretation of seemingly obscure chapters in its history can bring rhetoric to a boiling point. These passions reflect the importance of capitalism and the ease with which two diametrically opposed stories can be told. One story focuses on increasing wealth and rising output. A revolution in human productivity began in the eighteenth century and was causally linked to the rise of capitalism. The planet now supports a vastly expanded population of people (roughly eight billion, compared with one billion in 1800) who live longer lives and enjoy living standards unimaginable as recently as a century ago. They are healthier, wealthier, and taller. Poverty persists, to be sure, but what is most remarkable is the production of such unbelievable wealth and the breadth of its beneficiaries in such a short time.[9]

The other story of capitalism, just as easily told, focuses on exploitation, violence, and unfathomable misery—it highlights desperate factory workers, brutalized plantation slaves, starving farmers in once self-sufficient countrysides, expropriated Native peoples, and all the victims of colonialism, war, and displacement. Capitalism's forward march then becomes a story of satanic mills, the transport of millions of enslaved Africans to the Americas, the vast theft of land and raw materials during colonialism, and a rapacious system's unprecedented assault on our natural environment. In this story, capitalism is an insatiable demon on a planet-threatening trajectory with staggering social costs.

Capitalism, these diametric stories make clear, is a Janus-faced socioeconomic system, so much so that both the celebration and the condemnation of it have come from all political directions. Most know about the left condemning it and the right celebrating it, but few are aware that conservative critics of capitalism have been common throughout its long history, or that both Karl Marx and the Chinese Communist Party hailed the emancipatory economic possibilities of the capitalist revolution.[10]

This book absorbs the warmth of these vibrant discussions but is ultimately not interested in contributing to the debit and credit columns of the opposing stories. Instead, it examines capitalism from a global and long-term perspective to grasp its core: a radical departure and discontinuity in human affairs. I invite you, the reader, to embrace its study with a sense of wonder, surprise, and astonishment—not because it is "good" or "bad" but because of its world-shaping power, and because understanding it is crucial to navigating our shared future.

To embark on this journey, we must denaturalize capitalism by viewing it as peculiar, even bizarre. It was a fundamental break in human history not just because it revolutionized economic affairs but because it turned human relations upside down; infiltrated our politics, societies, and cultures; altered the natural environment we inhabit; and made revolution a permanent feature of economic life. The capitalist revolution is the only revolution whose fundamental core is that it is ongoing, that it qualifies as a state of permanent revolution. In this and other ways, it is, in sociologist Marcel van der Linden's words, "a pattern of qualitatively novel experiences in social life."[11] Capitalism is often seen as "conservative," but its emergence and spread constituted the most impactful revolution the world has ever seen; historian Joyce Appleby has aptly called it a "relentless revolution."[12] The Puritan ministers of Boston, concerned with maintaining social order, certainly agreed. No other event in history has impacted societies—and the world—as deeply as the expansion of capitalism. A product of human agency, it has increasingly emancipated itself from its creators to become both the Anthropocene's handmaiden and its driving force. So profoundly impactful has the capitalist revolution been that some observers call the period in which we live the Capitalocene. For the first time, a human-made order can be considered as powerful as the geological forces that have shaped our Earth. Many revolutions in world history have been hailed or condemned and their effects debated. Capitalism was the most impactful revolution of them all. The importance of the advent of capitalism can only be compared with the advent of sedentary agriculture during the Neolithic Revolution many millennia ago.[13]

To understand capitalism, we need to be able to see it. This is difficult. Many people believe we can understand capitalism from our own experiences, which makes sense, considering how powerfully it structures our individual lives. Unfortunately, our own experience is a terrible guide. We see only a tiny part of capitalism at any given moment, and we miss the vast story in time and space in which it is embedded. Understanding capitalism from our own experience is like taking a movie frame and looking at one detail, then trying to deduce the movie's plot from that particularity. While such a strategy might lead to some insights, even good ones, it is highly unlikely to help us understand the whole. Capitalism as a planetary phenomenon is not graspable from a biographical, local, or even national perspective.

Another problem is that most of us live in capitalist societies: We are immersed in capitalism like fish in water. We cannot look at capitalism from a distance. As the French sociologist Pierre Bourdieu observed in a different context, "a successful institution is forgotten."[14] Because capitalism is all around us, we often miss its peculiarities and its radicalism. It is easier to look at the Stone Age, Europe, or Song-era China, because those economic orders are so different from our own that we immediately perceive them as strange and in need of explanation. In the twenty-first century, however, when capitalism looks so normal, it is difficult to fathom that it has a history. All of this makes it hard to see that capitalism is not simply the way that economic life works, and to realize that it makes up a very small part of the totality of economic life over centuries.[15]

To see capitalism, we need to understand, first and foremost, that it is a distinctive economic order with a unique logic. We will aim for a fuller definition momentarily, but for now it is important to note that capitalism is distinctive for many reasons, among them its dependence on our acquiring almost everything we need through markets, using money. Almost all inputs and all outputs have been turned into commodities, bought and sold on such markets. Even labor power is a commodity, with almost everyone on the planet hiring out their labor power and a vastly smaller number purchasing it. Moreover, much of the wealth produced is immediately redeployed to produce still more wealth. Capitalism is also distinctive for the particular kinds of social inequalities and global hierarchies it creates. And it is distinctive because it sparked a vast increase in human productivity, making it the most dynamic economic order in human history. How long people live is a good gauge of material well-being. And life expectancy has skyrocketed: It has been estimated that, globally, the average life expectancy in 1820 was twenty-six years; in 2020, it was seventy-two years (largely because of significantly reduced infant mortality rates). Almost unfathomable productivity advances are at the core of that story: Just to make enough in wages to put bread on the table, a French worker in 1830 had to labor for fifteen hours a week; by 1970, just one hour and ten minutes sufficed.[16]

To *see* capitalism, we also need to place it in its proper time frame. Little can be understood from a purely contemporary perspective, from which capitalism can appear natural—an almost universal state of the world, if perhaps with perplexing shifts from West to East. Just as limited is a view from the vantage of geological time, from which the history of capitalism seems like a supernova suddenly bursting onto the scene, leading to explosive growth in productivity, resource use, and human populations but ultimately remaining invisible within that big bang. Going back to the moment modern industry emerged about 250 years ago would be a more reasonable alternative, yet it would equate capitalism with industry, a problematic choice that leaves out how merchants and the countryside shaped the capitalist revolution. Instead, I have taken a middle-of-the-road time frame, focusing on the past millennium, capitalism's millennium. In this time frame, capitalism appears neither natural, as a purely contemporary perspective suggests, nor like a supernova, as a geological perspective suggests. Instead, its history becomes visible as the ongoing unfolding of a new economic logic marked by constant contestation. We can observe its historical development: how islands of capital emerged in cities across the world, became connected, changed shape, extended into the hinterlands—and eventually turned into a capitalist civilization.

There is still another obstacle to seeing capitalism: the politics of our times. For more than a century, some of the deepest ideological divisions in the world have centered on capitalism. This debate was one of the Cold War's central battlegrounds. Over most of the twentieth century, relentless condemnation and uncritical celebration of capitalism permeated the conflict between the Soviet Union and the United States. So violent was that dispute that when Soviet historian Mikhail Pokrovsky published a 1931 book arguing that commercial capital—merchants—was central to the development of Russia (a seemingly innocuous statement), Stalinists forced him to recant his blasphemous interpretation. On the other side of the great divide, when Antonio Gramsci, one of last century's most creative thinkers on capitalism, wrote his *Prison Notebooks* while incarcerated by Benito Mussolini, he used cryptic language to fool his captors. Books have been outlawed—even burned—because of what they say about capitalism; authors have been exiled, imprisoned in camps, disappeared, and executed. This overheated atmosphere has severely compromised our understanding of capitalism, not just by repressing views but by all too often calcifying our ability to really analyze it. On one side, Marx's writings became sacred texts through which to filter the politics du jour; on the other side, scholars read capitalism's history through the equally sacralizing lens of Adam Smith's writings. This book strives to avoid either idolatrous extreme.[17]

Finally, there is one last hurdle to understanding capitalism, depending on where you are reading this book. Living among the rich and powerful has many advantages, but it brings a crucial disadvantage as well: It radically skews your perspective of life on Earth and its history. If you're reading this book in Europe or North America, many of the places and people you'll encounter in the following pages may surprise you: merchants in the Yemeni port of Aden, enslaved sugar growers in Barbados, nationalist industrialists in twentieth-century India. While you might initially find this disorienting, as you read, the problems caused by Eurocentric tellings of the story of capitalism will become all too clear.

To allow us to see capitalism, this book embraces a historical and global perspective. First and foremost, this work is an effort to reclaim capitalism as a territory for historical investigation, eschewing static, essentializing, excessively abstract, or presentist approaches. It takes us across a millennium of change, through, among other tableaux, medieval merchant houses, long-distance dhows, tropical plantations, weaving sheds, stock exchanges, working-class homes, slave cabins, the offices and households of colonial bureaucrats, the production floors of twentieth-century industrial behemoths, labor union meetings, and the conventions of anticolonial capital owners. I trace how trade, agriculture, and manufacturing were transformed, how production intensified, how a new kind of state emerged and participated in managing economic life, how the least powerful staged massive collective mobilizations, how hierarchies emerged and changed, how political regimes shifted, and how forms of labor became more varied. This history will show that capitalism is neither a state of nature nor a process whose internal logic determines its eventual outcome in more than the most general way. Engaging with capitalism's eventful history over the past millennium and seeing its many twists allows us to see it as contingent and eminently historical. Such a sense of its past in turn opens new pathways for its future, restoring a sense of possibility to our political and economic horizons.[18]

Just as important, I analyze capitalism as the quintessentially global economic order that it has always been. Much of our understanding of the history of capitalism has been impoverished because we have studied places in isolation, looking to explain their development or lack thereof in terms of their resource endowment, politics, or cultures. Yet as Jawaharlal Nehru already saw in 1961, "the old idea of writing a history of any one country has become progressively out of date. . . . It is quite impossible today to think of . . . history . . . in terms of any one nation or country or patch of territory; you have inevitably to think of the world as whole."[19] I agree. This book understands capitalism as, above all, a global development whose local articulations can *only* be understood globally. The economic dynamics of a given place are inescapably shaped by its connections to the outside world. There is no "French capitalism" or "American capitalism"; rather, there is capitalism in France and America, which have contested and complicated relationships with capitalism elsewhere, indeed everywhere. I agree with the Brazilian historian Caio Prado Júnior, who as early as 1945 pointed out that "there is really no longer an economic history of this or that country, but only that of the whole of humanity."[20]

Since the capitalist revolution in any one locality was always tied to global connections, the long-running quest to pinpoint capitalism's origin to one specific location has always been futile. As this book will demonstrate, capitalism originated not in any one place but in the connections between various places. While places and states mattered greatly to this history, at no point was capital completely confined to a locality or fully enclosed by states. Capitalism's mainspring was its capacity to connect distant places and draw unprecedented power from a connected diversity spanning continents and oceans. I focus on the whole globe because it is the space where capitalism emerged and developed. As I will show, it is the condition of its possibility. Unlike earlier forms of organizing economic life, which were local or perhaps regional, capitalism was born global—it was always a world economy.

This reality makes a Eurocentric history of capitalism impossible. This bears saying because, regrettably, writing on the history of capitalism remains one of the most Eurocentric realms of scholarship, even in the twenty-first century, when a cursory familiarity with the state of the world should underscore the limits of this perspective. The way the history of capitalism is still told all too often follows nearly perfectly, and certainly conveniently, the world's distribution of economic power until quite recently. Such a narrative marginalizes most of humanity, serving as the ultimate "victor's history"—one in which much of the world features as a "failure" whose missteps amplified European accomplishments. Indeed, the task that many histories of capitalism set for themselves is to explain either that "failure" or European success, frequently by cultural references that go all the way back to antiquity. The Western example is often naturalized: Capitalism *should* work, and the rest of the world must, in light of this, suffer from various kinds of pathologies. The varieties of Eurocentrism are stunning. Some focus on ideas, others on cultures, geographies, innovations, or institutions. Whatever their focus, they always end up in the same place: Europeans were (and are) categorically different from everyone else. Some of these accounts read aggressively, depicting those outside the West as lesser people who, for cultural, religious, or even biological reasons were incapable of competing with their European counterparts.[21]

Eurocentric blinders lead to a narrow telling of the history of capitalism as a regional story rather than a global one. They are not very surprising, considering that the disciplines that study economic life, the social sciences, developed in the nineteenth and twentieth centuries, when much of the world was shaped by colonial rule. This book, however, enters these debates at a new historical juncture, a moment when it has become much less certain that the North Atlantic will continue to hold the exalted material and political position it enjoyed over the past two centuries. The Chinese, Japanese, Korean, Brazilian, Indian, and Nigerian roads to capitalism deserve much greater attention today than they received during the past two hundred years of Eurocentric conversations.[22]

To be sure, Europe and its offshoots (like the United States) were one important center of capitalism's unfolding. There was a divergence in development. This book aims to explain that divergence even as it insists on capitalism's globality, with a key strand of the explanation focused on how Europe's seeming exceptionalism was less intrinsic than embedded in its particular connections to other parts of the world and how actors in other parts of the world influenced European developments. So-called successes in some parts of the world were deeply related to so-called failures elsewhere. The book will show that modern capitalism, even at its most hierarchical and unequal moments, was always a global production and can only be understood as such. Capitalism, we will see, is a totality whose origins and ongoing dynamics are rooted in integrating trade, production, and consumption on a world scale.[23]

This global and long-term approach to the history of capitalism lets us see many things that might otherwise remain hidden, including, for one, the countryside. Discussions of capitalism have been dominated by a focus on cities and industry, but this book will demonstrate the vital importance of the countryside as a source of labor, raw materials, and markets, placing peasants, sharecroppers, and enslaved people alongside artisans, manufacturers, and industrial workers. Moreover, this attention to the countryside allows us to see the ecological dimensions of capitalist development. An unrelenting series of new commodity frontiers propelled the capitalist revolution forward, drawing on ever new reservoirs of ecological resources that were consumed but not priced. We will encounter some of them in these pages—including sugar, indigo, coffee, and cotton—to examine how capitalism developed a predatory relationship to nonhuman nature. Feeding on gifts of nature, its environmental impact has been dramatic; indeed, so much so that scientists believe it might threaten the very survival of our species.[24]

The book also foregrounds what has been called "commercial capitalism," the merchant-driven political economy that dominated capitalism's history until well into the nineteenth century. In contrast to histories that divorce merchants from production and from capitalism, this one demonstrates that the categorical distinction between circulation and production has never been pure, as from its earliest incarnations, merchant capital entered the sphere of production, and merchants were important protagonists of the capitalist revolution.[25]

To make capitalism visible is to make it understandable globally and historically. I will chart how capitalism emerged, spread in space and society, and changed shape along the way. There was nothing preordained about its trajectory; its emergence and development were always contingent on environmental, social, political, and technical factors. The political structures in which capitalism was embedded, the diverse forms of labor mobilization that it required, and the great differences in territorial configurations that it inhabited (from city-states to empires), to cite just three important elements, combined and recombined, with a great variety of actors wittingly or unwittingly shaping them at particular moments and in particular places. The book will explore and explain these configurations.[26]

I will show that capitalism is a global order, but not one determined by frictionless circulation. Local, regional, and national contexts, as well as social movements, produced the fragmented and hierarchical spaces that structured the capitalist revolution, in turn creating an almost fantastic variety of local but always connected outcomes: In the pages that follow we will see that while private property rights strengthened in Europe, massive dispossessions shaped European expansion into the wider world. While enslaved workers toiled on US cotton plantations, wageworkers spun and wove that cotton in Europe's textile mills. Political and social rights expanded in some parts of the world, while categorical hierarchies—between colonizers and colonized, enslaved and free, white and Black—structured life in much of the colonial world. As we will observe, the territorial organization of capitalism was equally dynamic and varied, ranging from a global economy structured by vast colonial empires to one populated by independent nation-states. There were moments in which commodity chains were nationalized and others in which global trade took center stage. Massive territorial states like the United States incorporated labor, raw materials, and markets into their national territories, while small city-states like Singapore and Hong Kong emerged as important nodes of global capitalism. We will encounter a panoply of political regimes: Though fundamentally liberal political structures shaped twentieth-century Britain, authoritarian, even fascist, states partnered with capital owners elsewhere. In contrast to some strands of modernization theory that argue there is a straight line from capitalism to liberal democracy, this book shows that capitalism has been embedded in a diversity of political forms, including a range of illiberal variants.[27]

The diversity in capital, labor, territorial, and political forms that emerged in different regions and times that we will encounter in the book was partly the result of the capitalist revolution colliding with and co-opting older social and cultural systems and distributions of power—from gendered divisions of labor to older inequalities that structured tributary regimes. Consequentially, this stunning diversity is not just a colorful facet of capitalism's history but one of its essential dynamics—capitalism thrives not on homogeneity and consistency through time and across space but on variety. Capitalism is, in historian Kenneth Lipartito's words, "a many-headed hydra."[28] Unlike many of its most vocal apologists and critics, capitalism is undogmatic. Great diversities at any given moment speak to what German philosopher Ernst Bloch called the "simultaneity of the non-simultaneous," the structuring of capitalism at any given moment by a plurality of historical times. Yet as the book will demonstrate, capitalism across these differences remained a totality; there were no "capitalisms" in the plural, only changing and varying articulations of one differentiated and hierarchical structure.[29]

As capitalism unfolded on a global scale, its structures emerged from distributions of power in specific locations. *Capitalism*, therefore, does not tell the story from an orbital perspective alone; it finds capitalism in the local and bottom-up experience as well. Family relations in the English countryside help explain labor mobilization in early factories, the social structure of Indian agriculture has implications for the spread of plantation slavery in the Americas, and the geography of La Réunion Island helps explain the particularities of labor regimes in the post-slavery French Empire.

This wide-ranging perspective makes for an important argument: Capitalism is not just about the working out of ahistorical economic laws that can be analyzed abstractly, even mathematically. Capitalism, instead, is the result of a panoply of political choices and social conflicts, structured in myriad ways by society and the state. Because capitalism is just as much an ecological, cultural, social, and political order as it is an economic one, it can only be understood through an analysis embedded in politics, nature, the distribution of social power, and cultures and institutions.[30]

This book emphasizes these factors. I show that viewing capitalism as an exclusively market-based society is misguided. First, markets have existed in noncapitalist societies as well. Second, nonmarket forces are integral to capitalism. To understand capitalism as primarily a market society would be akin to understanding feudalism as a godly order—a notion that would have rung true to feudal lords and churchmen of the time but would satisfy few hoping to make sense of the feudal order today. Just as the feudal order was partly maintained by its protagonists' success in convincing many that it was godly, so, too, is the naturalizing of the market not incidental to capitalism but a condition for its very existence. Yet this does not explain it.

By showing that economic life under capitalism is deeply entrenched in nonmarket structures, the book joins a broader tradition of political economy, from Karl Polanyi to Melinda Cooper, from Joseph

Schumpeter to Nancy Fraser. The "props made of extra-capitalist materials," in Schumpeter's words—including family structures, beliefs, distributions of social and political power, nature, and categorical hierarchies constructed by sexism and racism—will feature centrally.[31]

No noneconomic institution mattered more than the state, that ensemble of institutions that govern, tax, wage war, regulate society, and adjudicate conflict in myriad ways. Because the state set and enforced rules and allocated resources that helped create novel political economies (and itself emerged from them), it is a fundamental part of my analysis. Capitalism, this book argues, is an extraordinarily statist form of economic life. Though that state changed over time; developed different institutional forms; grew in scale, scope, and territorial extent; and occupied more or less powerful positions within an international system of states, it always remained an essential ingredient in the capitalist revolution. It is impossible to think about capitalism as only an economic order—it has always been a political economy as well.

To be sure, capitalism is a powerful structure that has enabled but also constrained people's interactions with the world. Yet, like everything with a history, capitalism is made by people. The problem with many histories of capitalism is that they start with *capitalism* and *the economy*, as if these structures and processes are actors in themselves, draining the agency and indeterminacy of history and thus radically impoverishing our understanding of the world. By contrast, this book is an actor-centered history. It uses the tools of social history, with its focus on a variety of people, often in conflict, to understand global capitalism as a state of permanent contestation. Some of these actors wielded capital. Whether you call them capitalists, businesspeople, merchants, industrialists, or entrepreneurs (all of these words are used herein), they greatly influenced the capitalist revolution. People such as Aden merchant Madmun ben Hasan ben Bundar, Surat trader Mohammad Chelebi, Augsburg merchant Jakob Fugger, Dutch salt trader Maria Jacoba Daemen, Chinese merchant Wang Zhi (汪直), Barbados plantation owner James Drax, Bordeaux merchant Johann Jakob Bethmann, Glasgow cotton manufacturer Kirkman Finlay, Saar steel industrialist Hermann Röchling, Turin automobile innovator Giovanni Agnelli, Indian serial entrepreneur (and adroit politician) Ardeshir Godrej, and Chinese internet entrepreneur Jack Ma stride across these pages. And while they navigated very different worlds—and found their niches in specific economic, social, and political configurations—they all sought the most profitable ways to invest their capital.[32]

But a history of capitalism requires much more than a history of capital and capitalists. Other actors, both at the level of production and exchange and at the level of local, national, and global political economies, affected the dynamics of capitalism and need to be foregrounded. Indigo-growing peasants (such as Digambar Biswas), enslaved men and women on sugar plantations (such as Jumpeter and Carlota Lucumí), wageworkers in cotton mills and on railroads (such as Elizabeth Brown and Souleye N'Dour), and women binding dynastic fortunes (such as Mary Woodbridge Tiffany) appear prominently in this book, as their individual and collective actions helped channel capitalism's development. These actors' sources of social power were very different from those that capital owners could muster. Yet they impacted the capitalist revolution and moved it in often surprising directions.

Furthermore, and in line with the argument that capitalism is a highly state-centric economic order that needs to be understood primarily as a political economy, statesmen, politicians, and intellectuals—from Kuroda Kiyotaka to Margaret Thatcher, from Rosa Luxemburg to Friedrich von Hayek—appear frequently in the narrative as well.

Last but not least, the perspective of this book allows readers to see the development of capitalism for what it was: a difficult, often unlikely venture that encountered enormous resistance from both elites and commoners. Against these long odds, the capitalist revolution entailed an astounding amount of coercion and violence. Although capitalism's history is often told as a story of contracts, private property, and wage labor—that is, stylized as a history of the realization of human freedom—there is another story, equally important, about vast expropriations, huge mobilizations of coerced labor, brutality in factories and on plantations, fierce destructions of noncapitalist economies, and massive extractions of resources for private gain. Capitalism rested, as we will see in the chapters that follow, not just on productivity gains but on enormous appropriations—dispossessions, really—ranging from land to labor to lives to technical knowledge.[33]

Once we understand capitalism as a difficult, unlikely, but revolutionary project whose essence was a globe-spanning creep that produced a connected diversity, a new view emerges. We see capitalism as a process whose origins spanned centuries and arose in many parts of the world. Importantly, we can grasp that capitalism is still emerging, still becoming, its logic still infiltrating new places and new aspects of human life. There is not one transition to capitalism but many, and those transitions continue. Capitalism is not one thing or one event. Any monocausal explanation, any fragment—an institution, a technology, a nation—does not explain much. As British historian Herbert Butterfield so aptly writes, it is "the whole of the past" that produces the present.[34] Embracing a historical, global, and multicausal approach helps us understand something that is in some ways puzzling—namely, capitalism's staying power. And it lets us see capitalism's great strength: flexibility on a world scale.[35]

⸺

Before we embark upon a journey into capitalism's history, we should clarify what we are talking about when we talk about capitalism. The word itself is recent—it was first used in the 1830s, but people spoke about the phenomenon before that. Is this novel economic order, as Adam Smith argued in 1776, at its core built upon an almost natural "propensity to truck, barter, and exchange one thing for another," which thrives principally thanks to people's "regard to their own interest"? Or, as Marx proposed in the mid-nineteenth century, is it a form of economic life in which surplus-extracting capitalists exploit a vast proletariat, enabled by and enabling the development of the "forces of production"—that is, the combination of tools, materials, scientific knowledge, and human labor—to produce a crisis ending in proletarian revolution? Was Max Weber right when he called it a rational and calculative culture and behavior favored by certain religious beliefs? Or is capitalism, as economic historian Larry Neal, a more recent student of such matters, puts it in his *Cambridge History of Capitalism*, primarily an economic order characterized by "private property rights, contracts enforceable by third parties, markets with responsive prices, and supportive governments"?[36]

The enormous diversity in definitions of this novel economic order is, despite some overlap, confusing. Some have concluded that it is best to discard the word.[37] I instead take a leaf from medievalist Marc Bloch, who, when he tried to grapple with the many definitions of feudalism, the political and economic order he studied, concluded that "the mere existence of the word attests the special quality which men have instinctively recognized in the period which it denotes."[38] Just as Bloch did with feudalism, we can take "the mere existence of the word" as an invitation to "analyze and explain" what concerns us here: capitalism.

When we do so, we see that certain features are unique to capitalism, first and foremost that it is an organization of economic life defined by the ceaseless accumulation of privately controlled capital. In capitalism, capital is productively invested, wealth is principally deployed to generate more wealth—it is invested in undertakings that combine labor, machines, technical knowledge, and raw materials to generate further investable capital. Capital is thus not every and any claim or resource (these have existed throughout human history), but a claim or resource embedded within particular social relations that allows for ongoing accumulation. Its core impetus is therefore the reproduction of conditions that allow such accumulation to continue; the "power of generation," as Marx puts a common insight most memorably, is not just a feature of capitalism but its very essence.[39] Capitalism is a form of economic life in which owners of capital organize the production of commodities not because they need or want them but because they hope to produce more capital. Because such relentless accumulation is the fundamental animating force of capitalism, it always seeks to colonize new geographic spaces and new spheres of life. In this way, it is a radically different form of economic life than, say, European feudalism or precolonial Indigenous communities in North America. Schumpeter may have summed it up best when he observed that "[c]apitalism, then, is by nature a form or method of economic change and not only never is but never can be stationary."[40]

To enable that ceaseless expansion, capitalism can unfold only in a society where both inputs and outputs are sold on markets, that is, commodified, which is capitalism's second defining characteristic. Everything needed to make capital work—land, labor, raw materials, technical knowledge—needs to be available for purchase for money, and everything made, all outputs, must be salable on markets. The "production of commodities by means of commodities," in the words of Italian economist Piero Sraffa, is a defining feature of capitalism.[41]

One of the core commodities is labor: Without the ability of capital owners to buy labor power on markets, there is no capitalism. Across the ideological spectrum, scholars have taken wage labor to be the quintessential form in which capitalism commodifies labor power, seeing it, correctly, as capitalism's most important form of labor mobilization. As this book shows, however, capitalism has been perfectly compatible with other forms of labor commodification, including, at key historical moments, slavery. What defines capitalism, therefore, is the commodification of labor across a spectrum of forms.[42]

The accumulation of privately controlled capital in a world of commodities in turn depends on the powerful presence of the state in economic life. Because capitalism is conceptually unimaginable without the state (while at the same time producing states of unprecedented scale and scope), the state itself is part of the very definition of capitalism, even though the precise forms the state takes have shifted quite dramatically over the past centuries and also vary between different countries.

Last but not least, capitalism is demarcated, as scholars like Maria Mies, Nancy Fraser, and Melinda Cooper have discerned, by the constant redrawing of the boundaries between the spheres of life seen as subject to capitalist logic and those seen as outside it: production and reproduction, economy and polity, human activity and nature. Capitalism subsumes other logics into its reproduction (for example, a deeply gendered organization of economic life), feeds on them, and at times even reinvigorates them. Capitalism rests on, and continually produces, spaces of non-accumulation.[43]

Capitalism, as this definition suggests, is a process, not a thing or an event that can be precisely dated or located. The "transition to capitalism" happened not in one moment but every day, ongoingly. Ultimately, capitalism is best defined as a global process in which economic life is fundamentally driven by the ceaseless accumulation of privately controlled capital, is structured by the state, and propels the ever expanding commodification of inputs and outputs, including labor, creating constantly shifting boundaries between its outside and inside. Despite never-ending quarrels about its precise definition, "eschewing" the term capitalism, as British historian R. H. Tawney once stated, would mean ignoring "a fact."[44] This book will look that "fact" in the eye and trace capitalism's history—not with the goal of offering another impossibly fine-tuned definition of capitalism's essence but with the intent of tracing what I call "capitalism in action." The book aims to look at capitalism not as what it should or could have been but as what it was and is.

Needless to say, any discussion of capitalism encounters a voluminous literature. Indeed, analyzing capitalism has been one of the key projects of the social sciences since their inception in the nineteenth century, and scholars, ideologues, and laypeople have been battling over how to understand it ever since. A book, perhaps even a multivolume study, could be written just about these debates. This is not that book. I follow Marc Bloch, who introduced his study on European feudalism by saying that "[n]o survey will be made here of those paper wars in which scholars have sometimes engaged. History, not historians, is my concern."[45]

That said, two great works of the eighteenth and nineteenth centuries bear mention for their reach: Adam Smith's 1776 *An Inquiry into the Nature and Causes of the Wealth of Nations* and Karl Marx's 1867 *Capital: A Critique of Political Economy*. Max Weber's 1905 *The Protestant Ethic and the Spirit of Capitalism* comes in at a distant third. The staying power of these works testifies to their brilliance, but they are also products of their times. Smith wrote when people—even in more industrialized Britain—still manufactured goods almost exclusively by hand and got around in carriages or on foot; Marx wrote when automobiles, the welfare state, and China's emergence as the world's manufacturing superpower were not even distant dreams. These thinkers theorized a historical formation, capitalism, that was still emerging. Brilliantly, both Smith and Marx (and Weber) understood capitalism as the revolutionary force it is, but they could not anticipate where the revolution would go. Smith naturalized what he called "barter" because he lived in a society where the commodity form was still unusual; naturalizing it made gaining political support for it easier. Marx denaturalized the commodity form to overcome it; to do this, he naturalized class conflict. As much as Smith and Marx disagreed, both tended to universalize from the European experience. And both were certain about the "laws" of this strange new form of economic life, a confidence not shared by this book.

Still, *Capitalism* draws inspiration from the vibrant debates these scholars have spawned and the eclectic mix of authors who have contributed to those debates. It also draws inspiration from the rich and often very specialized studies of economic life that have been published during the past century, many of them quite recently, as bookshelves are again full of fresh studies of merchant communities and financial markets, of slavery and "the Great Divergence," among many other topics.[46] I build upon this flourishing literature to understand global capitalism, ranging from the studies on the activities of Jewish merchants in the medieval Muslim world to the neoliberal "thought collective" of the twenty-first century.[47] My global perspective is, in turn, encouraged by a vibrant strand of recent historical scholarship, global history, that has enabled my rethinking of the history of capitalism, inspiring me to join these scholars in the emancipation of historical writing from national cages.[48] And while this book dispenses with the fundamentally ahistorical and naturalizing readings of capitalism that gained particular force with the rise of neoclassical economic theory in the twentieth century (which clamored for mathematical precision more akin to the claims of physicists by imagining a fictional perfect market along the way), I am inspired by the many economists—among them Thomas Piketty, Ha-Joon Chang, Denis Cogneau, Isabella Weber, and Jeffrey D. Sachs—who have rediscovered history and connected their ideas to some of the discipline's most distinguished but largely forgotten traditions, such as the German Historical School.[49] They all seem to agree with another economist, Schumpeter, who, when looking back at his career, found a historical perspective to economics crucial:

> I wish to state right now that if, starting my work in economics afresh, I were told that I could study only one of the three [history, statistics, and theory] but could have my choice, it would be economic history that I should choose. And this on three grounds. First, the subject matter of economics is essentially a unique process in historic time. Nobody can hope to understand the economic phenomena of any, including the present, epoch who has not an adequate command of historical *facts* and an adequate amount of historical *sense* or of what may be described as *historical experience*. Second, the historical report cannot be purely economic but must inevitably reflect also "institutional" facts that are not purely economic: therefore it affords the best method for understanding how economic and non-economic facts *are* related to one another and how the various social sciences *should* be related to one another. Third, it is, I believe, the fact that most of the fundamental

errors currently committed in economic analysis are due to lack of historical experience more often than to any other shortcoming of the economist's equipment.[50]

If I had to single out one author who has most influenced my thinking about the history of capitalism, it would be the French historian Fernand Braudel, whose monumental work has allowed us to *see* capitalism within economic life by emphasizing its radical departure and slow unfolding, understanding its global condition of possibility, and appreciating merchants as central actors in the capitalist revolution.[51]

Importantly, for my analysis of the history of global capitalism, I also draw heavily on the holdings of archives and libraries around the world, among many others from records on typewriter production in the Godrej Company Archives in Mumbai to fascinating depictions of a rail workers' strike found in the National Archives of Senegal, from technical reports written by 1910s Fiat engineers and kept in that company's archive in Turin to the diary of an anarchist sugar worker stored at James Cook University in Townsville, Australia. At the National Archives of the United States in Washington, DC, I read about economic policymaking in 1970s Chile. At the University of Glasgow archives I found the employment contracts of eighteenth-century children working in cotton mills. In Völklingen, Germany, I was hosted by a steel company with voluminous archives. In Aix-en-Provence, I examined the records of French colonial officials to understand post-slavery labor in La Réunion. I also spent a productive week at the National Archives of Barbados to better understand that island country's seventeenth-century slavery complex; consulted records in Rio de Janeiro to observe the culture of its nineteenth-century economic elite; visited sites of medieval commerce in Florence and Samarkand; and interviewed textile workers in Phnom Penh. Information gleaned from these and other sources helped me grasp global capitalism.

The book is divided into four parts, each representing a moment in capitalism's history, reflecting the fact that capitalism unfolds not linearly but as a process of punctuated change, jelling at times into distinct regimes. After two opening chapters that trace a world of capitalists before capitalism during the first half of the second millennium, part 1 takes the story from the fifteenth century, when commerce intensified throughout the world, to the verge of the Industrial Revolution in the late eighteenth century. It charts the enormous dynamism of merchant capital and the new forms of economic life and global hierarchies that this merchant capital enabled, showing how intensifying trade, recast agrarian production, and manufacturing under the aegis of ever more powerful European capitalists and states redistributed the world's resources and skills, creating new global hierarchies. This was a moment in capitalism's history in which much accumulation materialized from extraction. The second part of the book focuses on the Industrial Revolution and its aftermath, chronicling the rise of industrial capital and the new civilization it created, both in its industrial heartlands and in the world's countryside; the tensions that emerged with the old political and economic order in which it was embedded; and the way those tensions culminated in a series of rebellions. The third part, covering the century after 1870, examines capitalism's reconstruction in the wake of the mid-nineteenth-century rebellions and traces the painful emergence of a fundamentally new ensemble of economic, political, and social institutions. It is here where we encounter the technical innovations of the Second Industrial Revolution, the reorganization of capital, the emergence of new labor regimes, the birth of the modern labor movement, a recast state, and a novel fusion of national capital with that state. Part 4 delineates the post-1970s crisis of this reconstructed capitalism and probes the still-emerging new order that structures our contemporary moment.[52]

W hile I leave the future to others more expert in such matters, or more confident in their prophetic abilities, I hope this book provides you with tools to think about possible futures and to find your place and role in them. It shows that capitalism's history was deeply contingent—and thus it encourages you to expect that the future, like the past, is open-ended, even if at any given moment it feels like we live with insurmountable constraints. This future, the book demonstrates, will also be what we make of it. The book lays out the astonishing effects of human creativity—the scientific, technical, engineering, and organizational expertise that has altered human life in ways that would have seemed fantastic to our ancestors. It also shows that the seemingly weakest protagonists have made some of the greatest changes. If enslaved sugar growers in 1790s Saint-Domingue—mostly illiterate, uneducated, and dirt poor—could topple the well-funded and well-defended institution of slavery, then we can make history as well.

Despite its often grim account of human affairs, this book is optimistic—not just because it is a record of enormous human creativity but because it shows that the world, including capitalism, is historical, a product of our politics, ideas, and collective actions. Our ability to shape history means we can and should think about how we can shape better, more just, and more sustainable worlds.

Viewed from an almost unimaginably distant future, capitalism might turn out to have been a supernova, appearing suddenly in the night sky, shining bright and burning hot—and violently impacting its cosmic neighbors. Supernovas do not end well for the stars involved, but unlike a supernova, capitalism is human-made. We are not just subjects of capitalism; we are its architects.

This book seeks to uncover the historical traces that capitalism has left behind in order to grasp its history. The Italian writer Italo Calvino was talking about cities, but he could have been describing capitalism when he wrote that "[t]he city, however, does not tell its past, but contains it like the lines of a hand, written in the corners of the streets, the gratings of the windows, the banisters of the steps, the antennae of the lightning rods, the poles of the flags, every segment marked in turn with scratches, indentations, scrolls."[53] Capitalism, too, "does not tell its past, but contains it like the lines of a hand." I invite you to join me on a journey of tracing these lines.

We start in a place and time you may have never encountered: the port of Aden in the year 1150. And we begin with the world's earliest capitalists—merchants.

1.

ISLANDS OF CAPITAL

Swahili and Arab merchants on a thirteenth-century
Indian Ocean ship. Page from Al-Maqamat al-Hariri
(The assemblies of al-Hariri), *a collection of fifty*
illuminated tales, or maqamat, *crafted by poet*
and philologist Abu Muhammad al-Qasim ibn
ʿAli al-Hariri (1054–1122).

It is impossible to pinpoint an exact place or moment when capitalism began. Capitalism is a process, not a discrete historical event
with a beginning and an end, and it did not drop fully formed into
a particular location. Even today, no society is organized along fully
capitalist lines, and some have argued that a fully capitalist world is a
theoretical impossibility. Efforts to isolate one patch of soil as capitalism's

place of origin—Florence, Barbados, Amsterdam, Baghdad, the southern English countryside, or Manchester, for example—have all proved
insufficient. That is because the capitalist revolution had always been a
process that drew energy from myriad sources. The first springs fed
into rivulets that over time became meandering and ever more powerful streams. As these streams moved through time and space, they encountered a world often hostile to their further development—rivulets
dried out; brooks met sandbanks and evaporated; and even the mightiest streams encountered mountain ranges that stopped their flow and
forced them to take on new contours. Shape-shifting through the centuries, and against all odds, this novel logic of economic life—one that
centered less on markets as such and more on the growth of capital,
that is, money and goods dedicated to the production of more money
and thus more capital—gained power.[1]

Given capitalism's winding course, one reasonable place to start is
with the first capitalists—merchants—who played a critical role in
propelling capital's revolutionary recasting of economic life on Earth
and personified its logic. While we do not know precisely when and
where merchants of this particular bent emerged first, there surely was
an unusually vibrant and early community of traders who, in the
twelfth century, plied their business in the port of Aden, a port that
became, according to its most important historian, Roxani Margariti,
the heart of Indian Ocean trade.[2] Capitalism did not "break out" in
Aden in 1150, but the city was one among a number of notable places
that linked together to form the stream that became the river and ultimately the flood.

Today a teeming Yemeni city of about half a million inhabitants in
a terribly poor and war-ravaged country, Aden was then, nine hundred
years ago, one of the world's greatest commercial hubs, the center of a
trade network that spanned three continents. Its merchants sent ships
to distant ports across dangerous oceans, brought the riches of Asia,
Africa, Arabia, and Europe back to their storage sheds, then distributed them to the far reaches of the known world, buying low and selling dear, providing shipping services, exchanging currencies, offering

credit, and sometimes financing and even organizing the production of agricultural commodities and manufactured goods.

Aden's principal claim to fame was its pivotal role in the trade between the Arab world and India. When North African scholar Ibn Battuta visited in early 1330, he observed the arrival of "great vessels from" throughout South Asia.[3] He said of Aden, then under the control of the Rasulid dynasty, that "[t]he merchants of India live there, and the merchants of Egypt also," and he added that its inhabitants "have enormous wealth; sometimes a single man may possess a great ship with all it contains, no one sharing in it with him, because of the vast capital at his disposal, and there is ostentation and rivalry between them in this respect."[4] Protected by rock formations as well as walls and citadels, Aden was "completely surrounded by [the sea]"; it was, quite literally, a fortified node of capital, an island of capitalists.[5] Capitalism originated on such islands.

For several centuries, Aden was a bustling port, "the commercial centre of the countries of the Ta-shï [Arabs]," even according to far-off observers like the twelfth-century Guangzhou port official Chau Ju-kua, also known as Zhao Rukuo.[6] From the sparse textual and archaeological information that scholars have painstakingly assembled, we have an idea of what this world must have been like. The tenth-century Arab geographer al-Muqaddasi deemed Aden "a source of good fortune to those who visit it, a source of prosperity to those who settle in it." "It is the corridor of al-Sīn [China], the seaport of al-Yaman," he wrote in his *Best Divisions for Knowledge of the Regions* (985 CE), "the granary of al-Maghrib, an entrepôt of various kinds of merchandise, the depot of all kinds of merchant goods. There are many mansions in it."[7]

The city's pulse was the wind: Ships sailed from Aden to India in the late summer, shortly after another set of ships had arrived from Egypt via the Red Sea. The return journey took place from November to March, when winds shifted. Over the year, according to a contemporary document by the rabbinic court of Aden, these winds brought "ships from every sea," including "ships from India and its environs, ships from the land of Zanj [Africa's Swahili coast] and environs, ships from Berbera [Somalia] and Habash [modern-day Ethiopia and Eritrea]," as well as "ships from al-Ashhar [al-Shihr, Yemen] and al-Qamr [Yemen]."[8] Passage to and from Aden was dangerous and often frightening: Merchant Halfon ha-Levi ben Nethanel noted "the suffering I endured" when he sailed from Aden. Central Asian traveler (and perhaps also merchant) Ibn al-Mujāwir claimed that "[a] man landing from the sea is like one coming out of the grave."[9] Linking the Mediterranean to the Indian Ocean (and beyond) by sea and land, Aden was a world city constructed by people whose mundane activities, majestic in their sheer scale, included assembling cargoes, inspecting wares, haggling over prices, supervising the construction of ships, observing remote markets, gathering information, and, not least, raising capital.[10] As unlikely as it may seem, these banal activities, performed intensively, showed qualitatively new, emergent abilities—early, scattered sparks of the revolution to come.

Traders were surely attracted to Aden by the strong fortifications that provided security for them and their wares, a critical precondition in a world in which a multitude of rulers and strongmen lived off predatory warfare and tribute. But just as attractive were the diversity and density of the city's market connections. Flourishing trade begot more trade. At the height of the trading season, dhows—narrow wooden boats that had up to three triangular or trapezoidal sails and carried merchandise as well as crews of up to thirty sailors—crowded Aden's harbor, watched by merchants in their telltale Arab, Persian, Swahili, and Indian dresses and wrangling over goods.[11]

Aden's port was a well-oiled machine. Upon arrival, each merchant ship (between seventy and eighty annually during the 1220s) moored just off the coast to be met by *mubashshirun* (messengers) who, according to Ibn al-Mujāwir, would "ask him [the captain] where he has come from and [the captain] asks them about the town, who the governor is and about the prices of goods."[12] The ship's clerk would hand the messenger a list of the goods and people on board, and the messenger would take that roster to the governor before informing other traders and relatives of the passengers of the ship's arrival.[13] While the traders could disembark immediately (after having been thoroughly searched for contraband), their goods remained aboard for about three days before being taken to the customs house, painstakingly inspected, and assessed for duties.[14]

Commercial structures crowded the port, befitting a city single-mindedly dedicated to trade. There was the Dār al-Saʾāda—a wholesale market of imported goods sold for either local consumption or re-export. There was the customs house, the storage rooms, and the merchants' dwellings, some multistoried wooden structures built from African and Indian wood brought from distant shores on one of the aforesaid ships. The cityscape was dominated by markets, with most things produced and consumed, bought and sold, as commodities, including food and water.[15]

While most of the records produced by Aden's merchant community perished through time and neglect, the sources that remain document the names and activities of several hundred merchants—Muslim, Jewish, Hindu, and, possibly, Christian. In the first half of the twelfth century, for example, there was Rāmisht, a fabulously wealthy merchant and shipowner, most likely of Persian heritage, whose family owned at least three large ships that sailed to India and China. Merchants originating from India, such as Tinbu, Buda, and Fatan Swami, sailed their ships to Aden, as did Maʾsud al-Habashi from Africa. There was Abu al-Barakat, who acquired dyestuffs like lac, a resinous substance produced by insects, and textiles, among other things, in India and sold them in Aden or transshipped them up the Red Sea to Cairo along with the goods he bought in Aden, such as "brazilwood, cinnamon, and rhubarb."[16] His counterpart, Abu al-Hasan ʿAli ibn al-Dahhak al-Kufi, operated a quarry outside of town and traded in African slaves. There were Jewish merchants from Cairo, such as Joseph Lebdi and Jekuthiel Abū Yaqub al-Hakīm, who conducted much business at Aden (for example, importing lac), with Lebdi also journeying to India. Then there was Joseph ben Abraham, a local shipowner who traded with family members based in India. Ibn Abī al-Kataʾib and his son ran a family business, with the father staying in Aden while his son accompanied their goods to distant ports. And then there was the powerful Madmun ben Hasan ben Bundar, a shipowner who not only served as superintendent of the port and the customs house but also represented the city's mercantile community to the local ruler and headed the Jewish community of "the Land of Yemen."[17] Like many merchants in the city, he traded with India: Abraham ben Yijū, his associate on India's Malabar Coast, sent him pepper, ginger, cardamom, and betel nuts to sell at Aden, receiving in return copper, lead, gold coins, writing paper, sugar, and dates. Some of these traders coordinated their businesses from Aden by working with agents and associates in other ports; others traveled with the goods they sold and bought. These trade missions were often partnerships in which several merchants owned shares.[18] By the twelfth century, these capitalists of different creeds and homelands predominantly conversed and corresponded in Arabic, a sort of lingua franca.[19]

Aden's great merchants focused on long-distance trade. They exported horses to India but also madder (a red dye), metals, sugar, and, especially, gold currency. They brought Southeast Asian pepper from India to forward it to Cairo and beyond; they shipped ivory and gold from East Africa. Dhows arrived from Gujarat full of textiles. Each merchant traded a range of goods: In one of his letters, Madmun ben Hasan ben Bundar mentions iron, copper, lead, dates, hides, mats, and a carpet. To the best of our knowledge, the merchants focused on certain trade routes. Some traded between Aden and India; others between Aden and the ports of the Red Sea, in particular Cairo, the commercial hub of Egypt. From those cities, other merchants ferried merchandise to the Mediterranean. The Indian Ocean trade, with Aden as its pivot, flowed into these two great channels, but its connections spread much farther, through Swahili traders' mercantile centers along East Africa's coast and beyond India to the South China Sea. Remarkably, some merchants in Aden invested in local production of textiles, glass, and, most notably, ships, anticipating by several centuries one of the most crucial developments in the evolution of capital.[20]

The correspondence of Aden merchants writing to Cairo or India

evinces a strikingly familiar day's work. They carefully monitored supply and demand; they were concerned with transport; they worried
about payments and hoped that the investment of their funds would be
profitable. For instance, Madmun ben Hasan ben Bundar, writing to
Abraham ben Yijū, his business partner on India's Malabar Coast,
confirmed on September 11, 1149, that "[e]verything you sent . . . arrived." "As for iron," he added, "this year it sold [well] in Aden—all
kinds of iron—and in the coming year there will also be a good market, because there is none at all left in the city."[21]

Aden's richest merchants built their dwellings along its waterfront,
creating a cityscape of dense business activity and social interactions.
They conducted their commercial lives at their residences, hinting at
the intrinsic connection between business and social life, as they negotiated with business partners, sealed trade deals, planned future investments, and hosted friends and business partners from other parts of the
world. They invested singly and formed partnerships—we know, for
example, that they entered partnerships to send ships to the island of
Sri Lanka. Many of these partnerships were informal, but Islamic law
also afforded a long-established and secure framework in which such
arrangements could be contractually agreed upon.[22]

Seeking worldly riches, repute, and power, Aden merchants nurtured a dense network of institutions and relationships that facilitated
their exchanges. Trade was never just private; it was always also public.
These institutions—some shaped by rulers, others by the merchants
themselves—were part of what made the city attractive to them in the
first place.[23] From the onset, capitalist activities, there and elsewhere,
were structured by an institutional order, the channels through which
capital most efficiently flowed.

The least formal institution, but perhaps the most resilient and
consequential, was the dense network that merchants spun within
their ocean-spanning community. Kinship, religious identities, and a
never-ending stream of correspondence that linked traders to one another and kept them abreast of market developments constituted these
networks. There were also more formal institutions built by merchants

themselves, sometimes in connection with the state. Evidence suggests that in Aden, representatives of the mercantile community—people known as *wakīl al-tujjār* in Arabic and as *peqīd ha-sōharīm* in Hebrew (both terms roughly translate to "trustee" or "representative of the merchants")—facilitated the articulation of merchant interests and conflict resolution. These titles designated individuals who represented foreign merchants in an official or semiofficial capacity. Madmun ben Hasan ben Bundar, for example, was one, legally representing foreign merchants in the local court, storing and selling their goods, and resolving conflicts among them. Adeni merchants settled their disputes in both rabbinic and Muslim courts, part of a system of marketplace regulation that brought together the merchant community and the state in a flexible and informal arrangement.[24]

Despite its severely narrow capacity and limited personnel on the ground, the premodern state defined the riverbed, however improvised, in which trade flowed. That state, ever shifting, proved constitutive to the new economic logic embraced by merchants and remained so for all capitalists who followed. It provided for traders' security, regulated the marketplace, and made possible the enforcement of contracts. To finance all this, a shifting set of local rulers taxed the traders by charging customs fees. In Aden, these payments were modest; they probably hovered around 20 percent of the goods' value. Export taxes were even lower, however, to encourage merchants to buy at Aden. And whatever the rates, payments came due only at the point when the merchants departed—another reason Aden was so attractive.[25]

Adeni merchants turned themselves into important players in an "archipelago of world cities" that stretched across the Indian Ocean and beyond.[26] From a modern perspective, their trade was modest and slow. A typical dhow carried goods that could comfortably fit into two modern-day containers; compare that with the world's largest container ship, the *Ever Ace*, which in 2022 carried twenty-four thousand such containers. The round trip from Cairo to India via Aden took about two years.[27] Yet despite the obvious differences in scale and speed, Aden's merchants inhabited a strikingly modern world, one that is, broadly speaking, familiar to many of us today. Even if we do not trade goods, send ships to distant locales, or advance moneys, we recognize the logic of these merchants' economic life. This familiarity tells us something important about the history of capitalism.

As we embark upon a journey through a millennium of global history, however, we need to remember that in the twelfth century, most people lived on the land, produced their own subsistence with their own tools, or appropriated the resources they desired through extra-economic pressures, often backed by violence. Unbeknownst to themselves, these Adeni merchants were at the vanguard of a world whose ultimate form would have been unimaginable to them—the world we inhabit today. With the passage of time, the Adeni merchants have become less, not more, anachronistic.

I n the first half of the second millennium, merchant communities such as the one in Aden expanded in many corners of the world— from Cairo to Kilwa, Genoa to Changzhou. This was when a new kind of trader rose to prominence—traders who did not travel with their goods but stayed put and traded at a distance. These traders, called sedentary merchants, became the world's first capitalists.[28] Uniquely reliant on the investment of capital for their power, they embodied its logic of ever continuing expansion. Their wealth and power depended on accumulation, which they kept pushing into disparate realms of life and an ever wider swath of the world. These merchants demonstrated that large profits could be had from controlling flexible, fungible capital, that significant resources could be captured by market-based exchanges, not just by systems of mutual obligation, taxation, or violence. Unlike landed elites, they were nimble; they could easily shift to different regions of the world and change commodities and activities. They were at the forefront of opening new avenues to wealth, new forms of power, and a new economic logic. In a few extraordinary and initially marginal locations, they set in motion a transformation of stunning impact.

As merchants deployed their capital to connect producers and consumers, and as agricultural production and manufacturing expanded in many parts of the world—thanks also to merchants' investments—creating a tradable surplus, interregional trade of the kind that made Aden rich accelerated.[29] Those who organized that trade spoke myriad languages, dressed distinctively, held a panoply of religious beliefs, enjoyed a variety of relationships to local rulers, and traded in diverse commodities. Despite these differences, however, they would have recognized one another. They shared a principal aim of amassing profit by buying cheaply and selling dearly, often far from their homelands. They organized the transportation of goods along rivers, on rugged roads traversing mountains, across seemingly insurmountable deserts, and over the seas. Since such transport was expensive and time-consuming, much of what they exchanged was precious—porcelain, silver, gold, dyes, spices, textiles, and furs. As time went by, though, staple goods such as flax and wheat became more important.

These merchants led economic lives based upon a truly exotic principle: They deployed capital to produce more capital. The accumulation of capital was the linchpin of their worldly endeavors. Unlike almost everyone else in the world, they did not produce their subsistence with their own hands; they did not plow, fish, or weave. Moreover, though they were rich, they did not primarily do what other rich and powerful people did: deploy noneconomic power to extract wealth from dependent rural cultivators. They were neither raiders nor collectors of tribute. Instead, they bought and sold; they provided credit, and some of them invested to facilitate expanded production for markets. These merchants lived by the logic of capital, a logic that did not yet dominate economic life. Yet as they invested capital to gain more capital, something strange happened: Capital developed its own powers, including over its owners, a truly extraordinary development of self-mystification in which a human-created social relationship seemed to move beyond human control, making ever more people act on its logic—a kind of rogue artificial intelligence.[30]

The history of capitalism thus begins with the world's first capitalists—long-distance merchants in places such as the Islamic world, China, western India, East Africa, and southern and northwestern Europe. They constructed islands of capital, the sorts of places that sixteenth-century Italian scholar Giovanni Botero called "havens of the sea in the middle of the earth to render it communicable."[31] As their numbers grew, they became an entire "capitalist archipelago."[32] To build each island, merchants forged connections to other, often remote, islands of capital. Unlike different ways of organizing economic life, capitalism was born global. Global connectedness and the attendant hierarchies that such connections produced were the very essence of this strange new world—and one source of its dynamism. Capitalism's origins cannot be explained by finding a kernel from which it sprouted. Its history is a globally networked process that sprang from the building of islands of capital that by their very nature, their raison d'être, were always linking to one another.[33]

Tracing these "sprouts" of capitalism across the globe reveals the rising merchants as revolutionaries in a world still almost exclusively dominated by rural cultivators, subsistence production, systems of mutual obligation, inherited social status, and the powerful regulation of economic life by religious beliefs. Despite the merchants' energetic efforts, their impact on the lives of most of the world's people was small. Outside a very few areas, agricultural production and manufacturing remained almost entirely embedded in noncapitalist structures. And economic growth was exceedingly slow, even imperceptible.[34]

When and where we begin our journey into capitalism's history will always be controversial. Generations of scholars have battled over this question, and while there are very good reasons to start well before the Industrial Revolution, which began around the 1780s, there will never be a date that is beyond contention.

We start in the new millennium, around the year 1000 CE, because it was then, as we saw in Aden, that trade intensified and intercontinental connections became stronger and denser. We start in the Islamic world because trade and merchant communities flourished at an unusually early date there. From the vantage point of 1000 CE, we can observe how, over the next five hundred years, new nodes of capital—geographic spaces with an unusually significant concentration of capital and capitalists—came into being in different places. In each of these nodes, there emerged merchant communities that forged novel institutions and reorganized trade. They thought about capital in fresh ways and began to develop different relations to rulers, or even to become rulers themselves. Economic life in these nodes was characterized by exceptional vitality and complexity.[35] Even though we can delve into only a few of these communities and will leave our explorations of them radically incomplete, we can see the decisive impact of their emergence and flourishing.

To be sure, there had been islands of capitalists and capital before the year 1000, and some of the activities we have chronicled for the port of Aden could have been observed elsewhere earlier. Thousands of years ago, humans in some regions began to produce more than they needed for survival, and as they specialized their labor, partly motivated by the ecological niches they inhabited, they began exchanging goods.[36] As these exchanges expanded, specialists in trade emerged. Once that trade expanded even more, some traders grew wealthier and started specializing in a small niche of the mercantile business: long-distance trade. It was the rise of such long-distance trade that made some merchants rich and, when the conditions were right, created a wealthy class that was distinct from those who derived their wealth from being at or near the top of the social pyramid created by tributary states. This position was unusual in a world in which almost all wealth came from agriculture and in which riches usually accumulated in the hands of those who owned land and who could confiscate, tax, and coerce their subordinates.

There were sprouts of such trade and of merchant communities in many different parts of the world. Already in the ninth century, exchanges between Muslim and Russian traders had intensified to such a degree that tangible traces of them still exist today in the form of hoards of Islamic silver coins from that period, found recently along old trade routes in Russia.[37] Trading cities rose to prominence: Circa 875, the Arab geographer al-Ya'qūbī called Abbasid-ruled Baghdad, his birthplace, "the harbor of the world," while Chinese trade official Chau Ju-kua described it as "the general mart of the natives of the Western Heaven, the place where the foreign merchants of the Ta-shï assemble."[38] So vibrant was Baghdadi trade that the anonymous Afghan author of *The Regions of the World: A Persian Geography, 372 A.H.–982 A.D.* (*Ḥudūd al-ʿĀlam*) said the city was "situated near to the centre of the world," "a haunt of merchants," and a "place of great riches," indeed "[t]he most prosperous town in (*andar miyān*), the world." European trade accelerated as well around the year 800, driven by increasing demand from the Islamic world for furs, timber, war materials, and, most importantly, slaves. Muslim merchants had expanded into the Indian Ocean as early as the eighth century, trading as far as China.[39]

Despite these and many other precedents, however, something new emerged around the turn of the millennium, in part because of changes brought about by trade itself: As new species of plants and agricultural techniques spread—cane sugar in the Islamic world, for example—agricultural output increased and with it a tradable surplus. Cutting down forests and irrigating lands expanded agrarian frontiers, further facilitated by social change in the countryside, such as the emergence of more secure private property rights in the Islamic world and escalating peasant taxation in Europe. Increased agricultural productivity also gave rural cultivators time to devote themselves to manufacturing. Climate change further amplified output, with a warming period lasting through the thirteenth century. As production increased, more goods could be traded, further enabled by the institutional framework and embryonic long-distance connections that linked Asia, Africa, and Europe to one another in unprecedented ways, thanks to the consolidation of Islam. Long-distance trade got faster and more regular.[40] New trading communities burgeoned across the globe.

SOME OF THE most consequential nodes of capital—and one of the earliest, most dynamic, and farthest-reaching nodes within the archipelago of trade—emerged in the Islamic world. For several centuries, it constituted itself as the center of the global economy, its heartland.[41]

This centrality of the Islamic world arose from several factors, including, first and foremost, the urban bias of Islamic civilization itself. Unlike Christian rulers in feudal Europe, who usually ensconced themselves in the countryside, Islamic political and economic elites congregated in cities, and a network of metropolises soon dotted the landscape from North Africa to the Middle East. The need to supply these cities encouraged trade, which benefited from the religious and linguistic unity of the rapidly expanding Islamic world. Urban rulers supported trade too, for it could be taxed.[42]

As Islam spread rapidly, and sometimes violently, from its points of origin on the Arabian Peninsula into West Asia, North Africa, Central Asia, and South and Southeast Asia, then eventually into southern Europe, parts of sub-Saharan Africa, and China, it created an ever larger "zone of unification."[43] Communities were linked across vast distances, and trade grew alongside religious and political ties. Traders could travel freely and communicate across immense swaths of land and sea. Islamic writers considered the logic and legitimacy of profit and capital, with a tenth-century source describing a "passion for the accumulation of capital"—a phrase that would not be out of place to sum up Wall Street today.[44] To make trade easier, Islamic rulers tended to guarantee the stability of currency, striving to issue gold or silver coinage (dinars and dirhams) of reliable weight and fineness. A legal framework based on Islamic jurisprudence made exchanges, even far-flung ones, more secure and predictable, as did a set of shared institutions. Trade derived partly from this integration, with merchants and others coming to feel that they inhabited a common space, a feeling furthered by family connections across great distances, even across continents. But strangers could access the benefits of this trading community as well. Trade begot more trade—not just because of capital's core logic of self-expansion but because trade created an institutional landscape that facilitated further commerce.[45]

Islamic merchants created a known-world economy, connecting across a thin but extensive network stretching from the Middle East to Asia, much of Africa, and Europe. They bought, sold, and transported porcelain, silk, sandalwood, ivory, pepper, horses, and metal goods. Merchants in Siraf on the Persian Gulf sent ships as far as China, India, and East Africa. Central Asian, Chinese, Indonesian, Indian, as well as Adeni traders, and their counterparts from Jeddah all lived in the city of Hormuz. When Arab chronicler Ibn Battuta traveled in the first half of the fourteenth century throughout the then-known world, he journeyed to China, India, Central Asia, the Middle East, East Africa, Spain, North Africa, and the Black Sea, as well as the Maghreb. Wherever he went, he encountered communities of Muslim merchants. The eleventh to thirteenth centuries were an especially golden age for these merchants, as their influence stretched from the Maghreb in the West to China in the East. This rapidly expanding archipelago of capital was, in the apt words of historian K. N. Chaudhuri, an "[e]mpire of Islam."[46]

The dynamic core of this Islamic trade world—and thus of the world economy—was trade with Asia generally and with Indian Ocean cities in particular. The Indian Ocean was ringed by cities, each connected to its own hinterland and the ecological resources that could be mobilized there. They were connected by a middle sea route via Baghdad, Basra, and Hormuz; a northern land route via Samarkand and Bukhara; and a southern sea route via Aden.[47]

The middle route via the world city of Baghdad was the earliest, the longest-lasting, and, for a great stretch of time, the most important. Its hinges were several small states in the Gulf, including Basra,

Caravan of Arabic traders: miniature from the intricate maqamat presented in Al-Maqamat al-Hariri.

Oman, Hormuz, and Siraf, where ships arrived loaded with the riches of Asia. Traders assembled goods in lots and transported them by huge desert-crossing camel caravans to cities in the Arab world, many—Tripoli, Aleppo, Alexandria—on or near the shores of the Mediterranean. The city of Aleppo in what is today Syria was at times one of the largest markets in the world, its souks displaying the riches of the East and attracting merchants from throughout the Mediterranean region.[48]

As Mongol power strengthened in the second half of the thirteenth century (the Mongols captured and devastated Baghdad, for example), this middle route deteriorated, and another trade route, this one entirely land-based, arose. The northern route let merchants travel along a huge, unified area stretching from China to Hungary and cross the Mongol heartland in the Central Asian steppes. The Mongols guaranteed a relatively safe passage through the vast area they controlled and provided basic trade infrastructures, including roads, waypoints, and water sources, while limiting extortion along the route. Traders could access credit, transfer money, and exchange currencies at important nodes along the way, which, much later (in 1877) came to be known as the Silk Road. It was, in the Swedish writer Sven Hedin's words, "the longest . . . [and] most significant connecting link between peoples and continents that has ever existed on earth."[49] Traders congregated in cities such as Bukhara—not only a renowned center of Is-

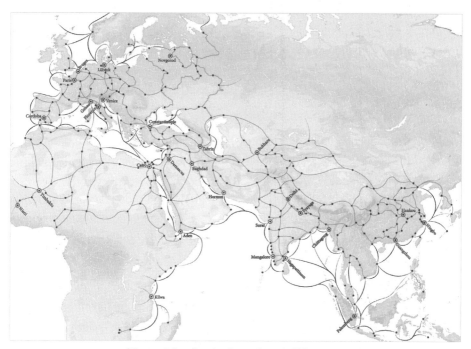

The conduits of trade, eleventh to twelfth century.

lamic learning, a hot spot of the Islamic Renaissance, and a home to philosopher Ibn Sina, but also a source of markets, credit, and water. The city rose like a mirage from the brown soil of what is today Uzbekistan, offering shelter and trade to visiting merchants. Caravansaries (such as the one at Lyabi-Hauz), mosques, synagogues, and madrassas (often financed by merchants) dotted the cityscape, testifying to the massive caravans that passed through, at times several thousand camels strong. Some Europeans—most famously, the Venetian merchant Marco Polo—traveled along this route and through Bukhara in the 1260s and 1270s; for Polo, it was a "large and splendid city, the finest . . . in all Persia."[50]

The greatest meeting place along this route, however, was the city of Samarkand, the "Rome of the East," which in the 1390s counted within its huge city walls 150,000 inhabitants. Traders, believers, and

Nodes of capital in Central Asia:
caravansary in Bukhara.

scholars, including one of the world's most important astronomers, Ulugh Beg, walked its dense cityscape. It was a major destination for Chinese exports. Thousand-camel caravans loaded with silk, tea, and cottons, among other goods, stopped here to trade. When Mongolian statesman Yelü Chucai visited the city in 1218, he concluded that it was the most beautiful he had ever seen. Spanish ambassador Ruy González de Clavijo concurred in 1403, describing the city as "a little larger than . . . Seville," with "much merchandize, which comes every year from Cathay, India, Tartary, and many other parts," and well "supplied with judges."[51] The city also produced its own silk textiles, an example for early merchant-formed manufacturing enterprises.[52]

Farther south, another route had flourished since the eleventh century, connecting Cairo, via the Red Sea, to India and places beyond. Merchants known as *karimi* organized this trade, selling to both India (where many had agents) and China, often operating, as we have seen, out of the port of Aden. They dealt in many different goods, owned shops, and operated as bankers; some even owned mines and factories.[53]

In this Islamic archipelago of capital, some cities stood out for their wealth and power. Baghdad was one, but its fortunes declined rapidly in the eleventh and twelfth centuries. A new commercial entrepôt—Fustat (now Cairo)—emerged farther west. Driven by the rise of the Fatimids in North Africa around 900, the city boomed by 1000. The Persian geographical work *Ḥudūd al-ʿĀlam* considered the Nile city the "wealthiest city in the world, extremely prosperous," while Ibn Battuta, as late as the fourteenth century, called it "the mother of cities."[54] Most eloquently, al-Muqaddasi described Cairo as "a metropolis in every sense of the word." For him, "it has effaced Baghdad and is the glory of Islam and the centre of the world's commerce. . . . It is the treasure-house of the West and the emporium of the East."[55]

Cairo was for some time the world's most important node of capital. It grew rapidly and by 1325 had an estimated six hundred thousand inhabitants, making it the second-largest city in the world, after Hangzhou in China. Cairo's merchants were renowned for their wealth and the reach of their commercial undertakings. They exported precious metals, cloth, copper, and glass beads to South and Southeast Asia. They returned with spices, porcelain, indigo, and, especially, cotton cloth. Their connections to India were so profound that some lived there for extended periods, such as the Cairo merchant Joseph Lebdi, who made his home in India from 1078 to 1097. While most merchants were well off but not rich, some accumulated true fortunes, allowing them to compete with the wealth of rulers. It has been estimated that by the 1450s, Cairo counted two hundred merchants with two million pieces of gold each.[56]

One such trader, Ibn ʿAwkal, rose to prominence around the turn of the millennium. He inherited his business from his father and was probably of Persian origins. He and his business partners, the Tustari brothers, had close relations to Persia and Iraq, but he also traded with North Africa, Spain, and Sicily. From Cairo, his agents in distant locations kept him informed about prices, arrivals, departures, and demand in local markets. Usually he traded on his own, but sometimes he joined short-term partnerships. His diversified business undertakings dealt in at least eighty-three distinct commodities—he exported madder, indigo, brazilwood, lacquer, pepper (from the East), spices, sugar, and a variety of goods, some made in China.[57] He also shipped significant quantities of flax that his agents bought in the Egyptian countryside and that he then processed and packed for shipping. In one year, he exported a staggering fifty-four tons of it.[58]

Collectively, in the second half of the eleventh century, Egyptian merchants annually traded more than five thousand tons of raw flax from Alexandria, and they worked hard to gain exclusive control over local suppliers. They soon involved themselves in its production, too, financing the cultivation and processing of flax. They linked to manufacturing in other ways as well—for example, by investing in the burgeoning Egyptian textile industry. Cairo merchants also invested in sugar, including the 66 sugar refineries found in their city by the early fourteenth century. Ceramics was another product that interested them: Historian Maya Shatzmiller's massive study of Egypt's surviving records of that industry identified 418 distinct firms. While merchants in the Islamic world and elsewhere focused on buying and selling, they also became involved in production early on through loans to producers or direct ventures. Such vibrant economic life also encouraged thinking about its mechanisms, with Ibn Khaldun, one of the world's earliest political economists, developing theories about economic growth, the division of labor, and the labor theory of value (an early version of it), observing in the fourteenth century that "human labor is necessary for every profit and capital accumulation."[59]

As TRADE INTENSIFIED and traders from the Islamic world moved with their goods into new regions, their islands of capital connected to islands of capital elsewhere—for example, in South Asia, to merchants on the Indian subcontinent, which Muslims called al-Hind. By the second millennium, Indian merchants brought gold, silver, ivory, and slaves from the West, spices (such as pepper) from the maritime world of Southeast Asia (especially towns and cities in the Strait of Malacca), and Chinese goods such as tea and porcelain from the East. A fourteenth-century Arab source listed a stunning array of goods traded at Gujarat on the subcontinent's western coast, mentioning all of the above as well as diamonds, teakwood, textiles, precious stones, and perfumes. Merchants kept some of these goods for domestic consumption and transferred others to remote markets, shipping them alongside the products of Indian industry. The most important was cotton cloth, which was spun, woven, painted, and dyed in ample quantities and with high-quality craftsmanship by India's spinners, weavers, and printers. If trade was asymmetrical (as with Christian Europe, East Africa, and the Arab world), treasure—gold and silver—made up for the difference. Indian goods were shipped to Arab ports such as Aden (and ultimately to the massive center of Cairo), but they also ended up farther afield; by this point, Europe had consumed Indian goods for more than a millennium. While Muslim expansion helped intensify India's trade, Indian vessels also landed at Malacca and the ports of the East African coast.[60]

It is difficult to fully understand the world of Indian merchants because they left very few sources behind. To the best of our knowledge, almost none of their no doubt voluminous business accounts, letters, and books have survived. From the sources we have, mainly accounts by Arab, Chinese, and European chroniclers, we know that a wealthy, sophisticated, and powerful community of merchants emerged in port cities across the subcontinent—in places such as Bharuch, Mangalapura, and Cambay, as well as in Calicut (from which the word *calico* is derived), farther south on the Malabar Coast. Many Indian merchant families remained prominent for generations. Niccolò dei Conti, a fifteenth-century Venetian merchant who knew of such places, reported that "the merchants [are] very rich, so much so that some carry on their business in forty of their own ships, each of which is valued at fifty thousand gold pieces."[61]

The intercontinental trade with South Asia, however, was dominated by Chinese and Arab merchants, with Arab dhows and Chinese junks far outnumbering Indian sailing vessels in Malabar ports. Arabs, mostly Muslims, had settled in western India as part of a trade expansion before the year 1000, and in Bharuch, according to the Cairo Geniza records, there was a Jewish community of traders as well. Arab merchant Mithqual of Calicut was said to have possessed "[g]reat riches in many ships" going to China, Yemen, and Fars (in modern-day Iran). Another trader, Abraham Ben Yijū, born in what is now Tunisia, operated from various ports on India's western coast for seventeen years, including, for a long time, from the city of Manjrur (present-day Mangalore), sending pepper, brass, and other goods to Aden in exchange for Egyptian cloth.[62]

Merchants of western India had robust connections elsewhere too. They traded gold, slaves, and ivory with East Africa. Arab geographer Ibn al-Wardî reported in his 1240 treatise of geography and natural history that "[t]he Indians visit [the Sofala coast] and buy iron for large sums of silver."[63] There was also a vibrant trade with Malacca, which was particularly important to Indian merchants, not just because they could acquire nutmeg, cloves, and mace through exchange of Indian textiles but also because they could trade with resident Chinese merchants who had porcelain and silks on offer. Over years of trading, as many as one thousand Gujarati merchants settled in Malacca.[64]

No port, however, was as consequential, rich, and central as Cambay. Rising to prominence in the tenth century, its merchants traded in one direction with Aden and in the other with Malacca, creating enormous wealth. For Ibn Battuta, Cambay was outstanding "in regard to the excellence of its construction and the architecture of its mosques. The reason is that the majority of its inhabitants are foreign merchants, who are always building their fine mansions and magnificent mosques and vie with one another in doing so."[65] Trading in Indian cotton textiles, Chinese silks and porcelain, Southeast Asian spices, and Arabian horses, among many other things, its merchants controlled a large fleet.[66]

Cambay, like other ports in South Asia, was a multiethnic city, with Muslim, Jewish, Parsi, and Hindu merchants living in notable harmony. Ibn Battuta reported on the early fourteenth-century Cambay merchant Taj al-Din ibn al-Kawlami (who was probably from Egypt), mentioning that the ships he sent to Malabar and Ceylon made him "enormously wealthy."[67] We know the names of a number of other merchants: Bohra Ibrahim owned six ships. Jain merchant Vastupala was exceptionally wealthy (in the first half of the thirteenth century), and Jagadu, also a Jain, had business interests in Persia.[68]

The intensification of trade in a port such as Cambay was bolstered by an expansion of local industry, especially the production of cotton textiles. This massive industry was aided by the infusion of capital from Hindu merchants who linked spinners and weavers to the largely Muslim overseas traders. Surviving historical sources attest to some investments in production as well: Abraham Ben Yijū owned a brass factory in the western Indian port city of Manjrur in 1132, employing wage-workers alongside slaves producing for the Arab market.[69]

ARAB AND INDIAN traders also met on the eastern shores of Africa, where they encountered yet another thriving trading community—coastal Swahili merchants who specialized in bringing resources from their own, often very distant, hinterlands to the coast to exchange for highly desired textiles and Chinese pottery.[70]

The Swahili coast of East Africa was punctuated by nodes of capital and capitalists. There was Mogadishu, which Ibn Battuta called "a town of enormous size" populated by "merchants possessed of vast resources." Farther down the Somali coast, merchants congregated in Merca, Barawe, and Kismayo. In what is today Kenya, islands of trade emerged in Malindi and Mombasa, "a place of great traffic," according to Ibn Battuta.[71] And then there was Kilwa, located in what is now Tanzania, which Ibn Battuta described as "a large city on the seacoast, most of whose inhabitants are Zinj."[72]

In these cities and towns, a dense network of traders—some

Swahili, some Arab, some Indian—exchanged the goods of the East (especially spices, textiles, and porcelain) for the riches of Africa (especially termite-resistant mangrove wood, gold, ivory, and slaves). A Portuguese seafarer who arrived in Mombasa somewhat later, in 1505, when it had perhaps ten thousand inhabitants, saw "quantities of cotton cloth from Cambay" and observed that "all this coast [is] dressed in these cloths and has no others."[73] Indeed, the Portuguese reported frequently, and with some amazement, on the presence of Indian goods along these coasts, on the Indian merchants and vessels in the port, and on the "great profits" these merchants accumulated.[74]

The vibrant trade here, as elsewhere in the Indian Ocean, was built upon the shifting directions of the monsoon winds, which made travel across the Indian Ocean to ports as far south as Zanzibar fast and predictable. And while "[t]he Zanj [Africans] of the East African coast have no ships to voyage in," according to the twelfth-century traveler al-Idrisi, they "use vessels from Oman and other countries which sail to the islands of Zanj which depend on the Indies. These foreigners sell their goods there, and buy the produce of the country."[75]

The Swahili merchants, Muslims all, served as brokers, who secured trade goods from Yao merchants who brought gold and lumber to the coastal trading towns. They also brought such fabulous amounts of ivory onto the market that ivory carving was already common throughout the Mediterranean by the eleventh century. They engaged in a flourishing slave trade as well, with Basra (in present-day Iraq) merchants acquiring large numbers of slaves as early as the ninth century. In turn, the *waungwana* (as the Swahili merchants were known in Kiswahili) accumulated substantial wealth, becoming an urban ruling elite who mingled in the port cities with merchants from the Arab world and South Asia (mostly Muslims but also Hindus), some of whom settled in East Africa to profit from the burgeoning trade. Some Africans also journeyed up north to Arab ports with their goods. For these communities, as for others in the orbit of the Muslim world, the tenth to the fourteenth century was truly a "golden age."[76]

African tusks travel north: Arab and European ivory carvings. On the left: *plaquette, Egypt, eleventh to twelfth century.* On the right: *left panel of* Diptych with Scenes from the Life of Christ, *circa 1275–1300.*

DURING THE FIRST centuries of the new millennium, the emergence of thriving nodes of capital and capitalists extended beyond the Indian Ocean: On the far eastern edge of this trading system centered on the Islamic world were the merchants of China. In the 1270s, Venetian traveler Marco Polo observed China's great contribution to long-distance trade, describing the ships and caravans that carried raw Chinese silk, porcelains, tea, and other goods throughout Asia, East Africa, the Middle East, the Mediterranean, and as far as northwestern Europe.[77]

Not surprisingly, the world's "most extensive, populous, and technologically advanced region" (in historian Abu-Lughod's words) hosted one of the world's most vibrant communities of merchants. As agricultural productivity improved and the tradable surplus expanded, new opportunities arose for people who specialized in moving goods across long distances. In key regions such as South Fukien, the use of new rice varieties and new plows enabled by the infusion of outside capital led to expanded output, which in turn stimulated commerce. The intensifying interregional trade supplied cities with food and moved luxury goods around the empire and far beyond its borders. Cities such as Guangzhou, Fuzhou, Wenzhou, Mingzhou, and Hangzhou expanded. More than two centuries ago, Scottish Enlightenment philosopher Adam Smith recognized that "China has been long one of the richest, that is, one of the most fertile, best cultivated, most industrious, and most populous countries in the world." Though he knew little about China and was wrong to call it "stationary" (which to him meant unchanging), he understood an important fact about China that most nineteenth- and twentieth-century Europeans chose to forget:[78] It was among the world's most complex and resilient economies—and it may well have been the world's largest at the time of Smith's writing.[79]

Chinese trade had a long history. During the Tang dynasty (618–907), China had attracted foreign merchants from Southeast Asia and the Muslim realm who carried its wares around the known world. Commerce expanded rapidly during the Song dynasty (960–1279). Though most domestic trade had been handled by the state in the past, by the later eleventh century, private merchants took charge. As the size and seaworthiness of Chinese ships saw significant improvements in the twelfth century, they replaced Arab dhows as the backbone of Chinese overseas trade. Long-distance trade, including overseas to Southeast Asia, India, and the Arab world, began flourishing. As trade volume grew in the first half of the millennium—ships from China could contain cargo worth up to half a million dinars (at a time when a metric ton of wheat fetched perhaps fifteen dinars)—a variety of trade routes developed. International ports at Guangzhou, Quanzhou, Mingzhou, Banqiao, and Hangzhou sprang up, building on the active regional trade within China and on the increasing sophistication of the Chinese economy at large. Cities thrived. Hangzhou counted up to one million inhabitants in 1300, the world's largest city at the time, including a prosperous group of traders. Under Ming rule (1368–1644), commerce contracted, as the Mongol invasions of the fourteenth century put an end to Song economic expansion. Yet some Song achievements persisted, including the infrastructural and technological advances that gave rise to projects such as the Grand Canal, a waterway system that from 1415 onward linked cities such as Beijing, Linch'ing, Tsining, Kaoyu, Yangzhou, and Kuchou.[80]

Like their Indian counterparts, Chinese merchants had a panoply of things that rich consumers across the world desired. China's manufactures were of high quality and outstanding utility, and the country's merchants were eager to serve the enormous demand they commanded. An early fifteenth-century European observer commented on this global craze for things "made in China," asserting that they were "the richest and most precious of all . . . for the craftsmen of Cathay are reputed to be the most skillful by far beyond those of any other nation."[81] Ibn Battuta agreed wholeheartedly: "The Chinese are of all peoples the most skillful in crafts and attain the greatest perfection in them."[82] Everywhere, people of means sought access to these wares, and Chinese trade kept expanding. One of China's most prominent trade goods—porcelain, on which Chinese producers had a monopoly— has been uncovered by archaeological digs throughout the known world of the time, even in places on the periphery of the world economy, such as northern European towns, African cities, and the island world of Southeast Asia. Such monopolies enriched merchants, such as Shen Wansan from Zhouzhuang, who was described in 1429 as the "wealthiest man under Heaven."[83]

Chinese merchants like Shen congregated in port cities and inland towns, but their greatest concentration was in the port city of Guangzhou, once known in the West as Canton. In what would become by the twenty-first century the center of the world's most industrialized area, Guangzhou hosted a community of traders of exceptional wealth and scope as early as the seventh century. Silks, porcelains, and teas left the port according to a predictable rhythm, while rhinoceros horns, pearls, spices, medicinals, perfumes, incense, and—most importantly— silver arrived on its shores.[84]

Like Aden, Cambay, and Mombasa, Guangzhou was a quintessentially cosmopolitan city, attracting Arab, Indian, Malay, and even a sprinkling of European merchants. Chinese traders focused their business on trade within China itself and on shipments to the

Strait of Malacca, but they also sailed to India. A twelfth-century book, *Pingzhou ketan*, written by the son of the port superintendent of Guangzhou, reveals that Chinese merchants were traveling and staying abroad. This guidebook to the trade of the world describes the raising of credit for a ship's journey and how the superintendent of mercantile shipping disbursed loans. So global were Guangzhou's trade links that in 1225, Chau Ju-kua, the inspector of foreign trade, was able to describe the known world based solely on information he had gleaned from the seamen and traders he encountered in Guangzhou, producing an amazingly detailed account of India, Southeast Asia, the Arab world, and East Africa.[85]

In addition to the enormous wealth and the growing fleet of Chinese-owned ships, foreign merchants played an important role in Guangzhou's overseas trade as well. Some might have settled there as early as the seventh century, and by the ninth century, they had forged a substantial community. Merchant Sulayman al-Tajir from Siraf (in present-day Iran) reported on Guangzhou's mosque and the presence of an imam and a qadi (an Islamic judge) who put their stamp on the city. Indian merchants built Hindu temples. Chau Ju-kua remarked on "the foreign quarter," where "all the people from beyond the seas" lived, adding that "[a] foreign head-man [Muslim] is appointed over them and he has charge of all public matters connected with them."[86] That community of Muslim traders grew in the first centuries of the new millennium as they connected the Chinese economy to those of South Asia and the Arab world. In the process, they became rich, with a seventeenth-century Chinese scholar looking back to the Song period describing foreign merchants as having "great wealth"—"in their personal adornment everything was of gold, pearls, and fine silk."[87]

Encouraged by both domestic and foreign demand, Chinese merchants sought to gain direct control of production as well. As early as the eleventh century, they invested in textile manufacturing, tea growing, and salt mining, among other industries. As a result, such production expanded, as did the manufacture of porcelain. Coal mining, metalworking, shipbuilding, and papermaking also increased in the twelfth and thirteenth centuries. Some Chinese historians have considered these developments the "sprouts of capitalism."[88] Whether one agrees or disagrees, we can certainly see merchant capital pushing into production, as it did in other parts of the world.

As Chinese trading communities grew, accumulated wealth, and traded ever more intensively, craftsmen created significant technical innovations. China was, in many ways, the world's technology leader, realizing important advances in papermaking, weaponry, gunpowder, and iron and steel manufacturing (with total iron output reaching 150,000 tons around the year 1000, or as much as all of Europe produced in 1700), not to mention in unique industries such as silk spinning and porcelain making. Chinese merchants also built the world's largest ships. With a maximum carrying capacity of more than one thousand tons, the standard Chinese ship of the time was about eight times the size of the *Santa Maria*, the nao that brought Columbus to the New World, and about twice as big as the day's largest European ships. To navigate these vessels, Chinese captains used yet another technical innovation—the compass; in use since at least 1119, it guided them as far as the Cape of Good Hope.[89]

Just as important for accelerating the commercialization of economic life and promoting the role of merchants was another innovation—paper money. An early eleventh-century Chinese invention, the *jiaozi*, a form of promissory note, came about on the initiative of Chinese rulers—two hundred years before similar developments took place in Europe, when Genoa, Florence, and Venice began using bills of exchange for similar purposes. The invention of paper money was directly related to commercial expansion, which created shortages of bronze coins and thus a need for an alternative medium of exchange.[90] It was difficult to get people to accept paper currencies, and the notes caused inflation, leading to various reforms over the next two hundred years. Yet the Chinese Empire successfully maintained a monetary system based on paper currency up until the 1350s, when it

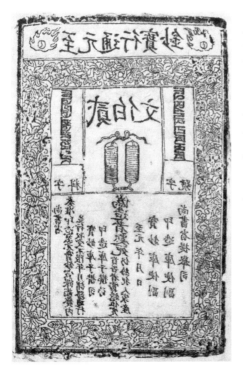

The world's first paper money, yuan banknote, thirteenth to fourteenth century. The string of coins at the bill's center indicates its value.

was replaced by silver coins. Ibn Battuta was astonished when he observed that Chinese merchants "buy and sell with pieces of paper the size of the palm of the hand which are stamped with the Sultan's stamp."[91] Eventually, that buying and selling with "pieces of paper" became a defining characteristic of capitalism.

NOT COINCIDENTALLY, merchant communities flowered, too, at the opposite end of the Islamic world—Europe. Prior to the thirteenth century—and looked at from the centers of global trade in China, India, and the Muslim world—the Europeans who inhabited the far western and northern fringes of the Islamic trading universe were unimpressive in terms of agriculture or manufacturing. European traders were late bloomers compared with their Middle Eastern or Asian counterparts, their trading prowess, institutional infrastructure, and urban life no match. European cities were minor affairs next to Baghdad, Aden, Cairo, Hangzhou, and Cambay.

Europe remained a relative backwater of the global economy. Until well into the twelfth century, Arab merchants did not even bother distinguishing between the various people living on the fringes of their world. They called them, collectively, the *Rūm*—Romans. The Rūm exported timber, gold, silver, slaves, linens, furs, cheese, and honey to cities such as Damascus, Tripoli, and Cairo. Later, they added woolens to their offerings, an industry in which they would eventually lead the world. The European traders' position was so weak that they had to accept inferior goods in exchanges with their Eastern counterparts. Even as their economy commercialized, Europeans looked in awe at the Islamic world: its magnificent cities, its riches, and its political might.[92]

After two centuries of urbanization and incremental growth of local trade, however, this began to change by about 1200. The shift was partly a result of the Crusades. As European merchants grew in wealth and power, they sought new trading opportunities in the Islamic world, India, and China. This would come, they thought, not just from more ships sent out to trade, but from a physical presence. Establishing this presence required military means. The Crusades—which one scholar described as "an enormous plundering enterprise if there ever was one"—were crucial in this process.[93] Eight crusades, starting in 1096 and running intermittently until 1291, used military campaigns to establish, with mixed success, a Christian presence in the Muslim world. To be sure, the crusaders were religiously motivated, but to succeed they needed the infrastructures and the materials, the ships and the money of the Genoese, Florentines, and Venetians, who translated their support for Christian zealotry into more direct commercial access to the commodity trades that they knew could bring them so much wealth. The Crusades marked a tipping point for Venetian and Genoese power in the eastern Mediterranean, where their domains now included eastern Mediterranean islands (like Rhodes), the Levant, and the Caspian and Black Seas. By the second quarter of the thirteenth century, between 41 and 71 percent of all Genoese trade was with crusader ports, such as Tripoli and Acre, testifying to the impact of that military expansion.[94]

As a result of not only such expansion but also intensified agriculture and wealthier and growing merchant communities, European cities, especially Genoa and Venice, became globally significant by the thirteenth century. Merchants in these cities (and a few others) were drawn to the riches of the East, journeying to Alexandria, Constantinople, Beirut, and Aleppo to acquire goods, typically in exchange for woolens. From there, they distributed the goods across the European continent. All Italian city-states relied on these links to the East. They eventually built a multicontinent-spanning network that connected them to agricultural and industrial producers as far away as Flanders, England, the Near and Far East, and western Africa. They were middlemen whose raison d'être was providing commercial ties to the Islamic world and farther east. Even some of the industries they financed relied on raw materials imported from the East: cotton from the Levant, flax from Egypt, silk from Persia, and dyes from throughout the world.[95]

Merchants from Genoa, for example, specialized in trading with the eastern Mediterranean: Byzantium, the Muslim world, and, from there, South and East Asia. The city on the Ligurian coast had been just a "big village" in the tenth century, but after its local elites found their niche in organizing long-distance trade, it grew rapidly. In the 1090s, its population was about ten thousand inhabitants; during the twelfth century, that figure expanded to between twenty thousand and forty thousand; and in the fourteenth century, the population grew from fifty thousand to one hundred thousand people. They imported grain (largely to feed their own people) from the Black Sea; wool, gold, alum (a material required in woolen manufactures), and indigo from North Africa; and spices, silks, cotton, and porcelain from Asia. Their trade was significant, with one historian estimating that its value in 1293 equaled triple the tax revenue of the Kingdom of France. To facilitate all that trade, Genoese merchants traveled to an enormous archipelago of port towns that stretched across the entire Mediterranean and the Black Sea. There were Genoese merchants in Alexandria, Valencia and Ceuta, and towns along the Black Sea's coastline. They inhabited a liminal space between the northern and southern Mediterranean, between Christianity and Islam. Genoese merchant Segurano-Sakrān Salvaygo, for example, was a resident in Cairo; the

Muslim king of Mallorca, Abu Muhammad Abd Allah, provided an entire special residential quarter for his Christian neighbors from northern Italy. By 1430, it was said that "[i]t is not possible for anyone to go to some hidden lands, to reach such distant regions without, wherever you go, finding many Genoese merchants there."[96] Genoese merchants created colonies along the Black Sea (the city of Caffa on the Crimean coast, for example) that gave them access to a thriving trade in wheat and slaves, as well as in Eastern goods that traversed the "silk roads" of the Mongol Empire from India and China. By the late thirteenth century, they also increasingly sailed as far as the North Sea to reach Bruges and London.[97]

Genoa's rival Venice first grew rich by exporting slaves from Europe to the Middle East and bringing back luxuries like spices, dyestuffs, and textiles. It then greatly benefited from trading privileges granted by the Byzantine emperors and ultimately ascended to international prominence after taking part in the conquest and plunder of Byzantium's capital, Constantinople. Having attained a position of political and economic strength, Venice invested heavily in domestic industries, developing workshops for manufacturing a range of luxury goods, including textiles, glass, maps, books, and silver. Andrea Barbarigo (1418–1449), a fairly typical fifteenth-century Venetian merchant, imported spices and raw cotton from the Levant (some of which came from much farther east) and transferred them to Bruges in northern Europe, returning woolens as well as silver to the East. Also increasingly important were cotton imports from the eastern Mediterranean, as Europeans began to experiment with turning that fiber into thread and then into cloth—that is, to engage in import-substitution manufacturing.[98]

The traders of Florence, who built yet another important European node of capital, followed a different trajectory; lacking a port until 1406, they had to interact with intermediaries in other cities, usually Venice. Local merchants made their riches first in the European and Arab cloth trade and then, eventually, from banking services. The Bardi and Medici families were among dozens of prominent Florentines whose capital resources facilitated a quickening of the European economy, less beautiful but as important as the great outpouring of artistic work that launched the European Renaissance, which they funded as well, just as their Muslim counterparts funded the Islamic Renaissance in Cairo, Bukhara, and elsewhere.[99]

From the ninth to the eleventh century, Florence was part of the March of Tuscany, "a small city . . . its history unremarkable," with a few thousand inhabitants living in a town that "obscurely vegetated in slow, uninterrupted decay."[100] When that territory fragmented, the Republic of Florence (1115–1494) arose on parts of its ruins. Unlike its predecessors', that small republic's economy grew rapidly and with it the number of its inhabitants: from about 10,000 in 1175 to 60,000 in 1250 and 120,000 by the 1320s, a massive urban agglomeration, almost as large as contemporary Samarkand. Its market supplied "the whole world," said poet, bellfounder, and town crier Antonio Pucci in the fourteenth century, and Florentine banker Giovanni Villani celebrated its "many beautiful houses."[101] The republic progressively conquered neighboring territories and cities, gaining Arezzo in 1384, Pisa in 1406, and Volterra in 1474 (along with its hinterland—the *contado*—rich in alum).[102] Yet Florence, just like Genoa and Venice, remained fundamentally a city-state, akin to twenty-first-century Singapore.

The fortunes of Florentines were initially rooted in the city's manufacturing and trade of wool and woolen clothing. From the end of the twelfth century, its merchants brought raw wool from England, cloth from Flanders, and dyes from France and the Arab world. At first, they acquired these goods at large trade fairs held in towns such as Troyes, in France's Champagne region. There, Flemish traders offered textiles, while Italian merchants sold spices and other Asian goods. Massive annual affairs, the fairs thrived from about 1150 to 1250 under the watchful eyes of local lords, who protected the traders in return for duty payments. The scale of these gatherings guaranteed that there were both ample supplies and eager markets. By 1300, political changes made travel more difficult for Flemish merchants. Italian traders abandoned the fairs and began accessing Flemish textiles by sailing into the

The Florentine Bourgeoisie in Bruges: Maria Portinari (Maria Maddalena Baroncelli, born 1456), circa 1470.

Atlantic and then up the southern edge of the North Sea to Bruges. By 1350, as a result of such shipborne trade, the coastal backwater of Bruges was well on its way to becoming a vibrant node in the archipelago of capital. Large numbers of Italian traders moved there and gradually came to dominate its trade. When Bruges's harbor silted up, the traders relocated to nearby Antwerp, soon to be the central node in Europe's North.[103] Eventually, the capital amassed by Florentine families in these businesses was invested in financial ventures from the Middle East to western Europe, and it generated an immense return.[104]

Florentine merchants traded with Europe and parts of the Middle East. Tellingly, the Bardi banking family had representatives not just in such Christian cities as Bruges, Constantinople, and London but also in Islamic Seville, Tunis, and Jerusalem. Florence's Medici rulers had long-lasting ties to the Mughals. By the end of the fifteenth century, Florentine merchants had also made their home in Constantinople, selling Florentine cloth and securing raw silk for Florentine industry. So close were their ties to the Islamic world that they helped shape the city's fabled artistic production. The use of perspective in Renaissance paintings caused a stir in Europe, but the theory that informed that departure had been developed in Baghdad by the eleventh-century mathematician Ibn al-Haytham.[105]

Most crucially, Florentines used their position in the woolens trade to move into finance—the trade in money—including bills of exchange, public debt (the Monte Comune), banking, and insurance. At first, they conducted their business over a bench they brought with them—a *banco*, whence we get the word *bank*. As they acquired ever more wealth through investments and trade, they began financing the many worldly and ecclesiastical rulers across the European continent who frequently declared war on one another.[106] For the Italian merchants, money dealings and credits, though always bound up with trade in commodities, became as important as trade in goods. Banking activities made the fortunes of many Florentine families: In the twelfth and thirteenth centuries, a few super-companies (associated with rich families, such as the Bardi and Peruzzi) dominated Florence's economic life. Later, the Medici Bank, established in 1397, used its huge international networks to dominate Florence's and much of Europe's financial sectors, organizing a system of partner banks as semi-independent branches or independent correspondents as far away as Egypt and Syria.[107]

The expansion of northern Italian capital eventually also linked it to the distinct trading network that existed in the North Sea between England, northern Europe, and Scandinavia. England, despite the destruction wrought by the eleventh-century Norman conquest, soon recovered and became a significant exporter of raw wool, which it sent to Flemish and Italian manufacturing towns in exchange for velvets, linens, spices, and fine cloth. The Company of Merchant Adventurers of London undertook much of this trade, regulated by a royal charter granted by Henry IV in 1407. In addition to wool, it exported agricultural produce, tin, and lead to Portugal and Spain in exchange for iron and warhorses, and to France in exchange for wine.[108]

Southern Europeans also began to dominate Mediterranean trade. While a trove of eleventh-century Judeo-Arabic commercial letters found in Cairo's Geniza contain references to Mediterranean shipping as controlled by Arab traders, such epistolary references began to wane in the twelfth century, when ships from Genoa and Pisa were mentioned and soon became a frequent sight in the eastern Mediterranean. By the thirteenth century, European traders were notably present in all the Levant ports. As power in the Mediterranean shifted slowly but surely, Arab merchants swung their activities toward the Indian Ocean, inaccessible to European ships until Vasco da Gama sailed around the Cape of Good Hope in 1497. Until then, geography and Islamic power prevented Europeans, much to their chagrin, from direct access to the riches of the East.[109]

ON THE SOUTHERN edges of the Sahara, another nexus of concentrated capital emerged as cities such as Kano and Katsina—in what is today Nigeria—became hubs of trade, with powerful merchants sending camel caravans on the long, arduous journey across the desert. In 1526—the tail end of our period but applicable to earlier times as well—visitor al-Hasan ibn Muhammad al-Wazzan al-Fasi (also known as Leo Africanus) reported that "[t]he inhabitants are rich merchants and most [civil] people."[110] On major routes to what is now central and eastern Algeria, across a distance of approximately twelve hundred miles, merchants traded gold, slaves, leather goods, ivory, and textiles northward, then brought salt, steel weapons, copper, chain mail, horses, textiles, glass beads, silk, semiprecious stones, and cowrie shells south. The trade networks these merchants spun connected to producers and consumers in a vast swath of western Africa that spanned what is now Mali, Senegal, Gambia, Guinea, Guinea-Bissau, the Ivory Coast, Burkina Faso, Ghana, Benin, and, of course, Nigeria. These trade networks connected people in Central Africa's forested regions in the South to people on the shores of the Mediterranean in the North, to the Arab world in the East, and eventually all the way to the Silk Road (and thus to China). Archaeological digs have uncovered a great diversity of goods traded from distant locations; some of the copper that traveled across the Sahara was mined as far away as present-day Belgium and Germany. So large were these networks that archaeologists unearthed a piece of porcelain produced during China's Song dynasty in the city of Tadmekka, in present-day Mali.[111]

In a sense, these urban centers on the edge of the Sahara were port cities, except that the sea they faced was made of sand. They were large, rich, vibrant, and important urban agglomerations by global standards. Tadmekka, facing the Sahara, was one such trade (and gold-processing) center. By the twelfth century, that city had probably one hundred thousand inhabitants, many more than Florence at the time. It was by all accounts a "cosmopolitan center" with strong connections to many remote places, including faraway Andalusia.[112] Around 1500, the cities of Gao, Timbuktu, and Djenne, all of which engaged in the trans-Sahara trade, each had between fifteen thousand and eighty thousand inhabitants. Gao, the center of what became the powerful Songhai Empire in the fifteenth century, was rumored to house one hundred thousand people.[113]

Two groups of traders converged in these towns: the Wangara from the South and Arabs from the North. Wangara merchants specialized in long-distance trade, bringing gold (often produced by enslaved workers and secured from undisclosed locations) farther south to the edge of the Sahara. Historians estimate that they carried between 340 and 1,000 kilograms annually, the value of which would have been equivalent to somewhere between $21 million and $62 million in 2024 US dollars.[114] That gold lubricated trade: It was used, for example, to mint the Florentine florin, and it enabled Europeans to acquire superior goods from Asia.[115]

This trade produced fabulous wealth: The Mali emperor Mansa Musa (pictured below), who reigned from circa 1307 to circa 1332 and was strategically positioned to tax the gold trade, has been called "the richest man who . . . ever lived." While we cannot possibly know how rich he was, his wealth was undoubtedly stunning.[116] Merchants also became rich. When Arab writer Ibn Hawqal came to Sijilmasa—"the city of gold" and the terminus of the trans-Sahara trade on the northern edge of the desert (in what is today Morocco)—he was amazed at what he saw: "[T]here is . . . an uninterrupted trade with the land of the Sudan and with other countries, abundant profits, and the constant coming and going of caravans," he reported.[117] He noted a letter of credit between two traders that allegedly provided credit in the form of a staggering forty-two thousand dinars, which contemporaries in far-

West African trade networks: Mansa Musa, as pictured in a circa 1370s atlas showing the known world, by Abraham and Jafudà Cresques.

away Persia considered a "remarkable" sum.[118] Manufactured goods from the Arab world and Europe were for sale, as was the salt so highly desired south of the Sahara.[119] The city also had a significant slave market; some slaves were forced into local domestic and agricultural toil, while others were traded as far as the Arab world and Europe.[120] There was, too, a substantial industry focused on minting gold coins.[121] So much gold flowed out of this trade that it would affect the art made in far-off cities such as Florence and Venice, whose artists had, by the thirteenth century, begun to use more gold leaf in their work.

The trade networks these African merchants built were sophisticated. African economies were highly monetized, using gold, cowries, and commercial papers. As Ibn Battuta observed in 1352, during the reign of Mansa Sulayman, trade was generally low-risk: "There is no need to travel in a caravan for the road is safe."[122] He was impressed by the well-ordered system of trade, adding that "[a]mong their good practices are their avoidance of injustice; there is no people more averse to it, and their Sultan does not allow anyone to practise it in any measure." He lauded "the universal security in their country, for neither the traveller nor the resident there has to fear thieves or bandits: they do not interfere with the property of white men who die in their country, even if it amounts to vast sums; they just leave it in the hands of a trustworthy white man until whoever is entitled to it takes possession of it."[123] In 1324, when Musa traveled to Cairo on a pilgrimage to Mecca, he brought sixty thousand people and as much as eighteen tons of gold. The journey became renowned throughout the world and intensified European desires to find the source of that gold.[124]

═══

The Islamic trading world—stretching from Kano to Seville, from Fez to Cairo, from Aden to Guangzhou—sat at the center of the web of the world economy in the first centuries following the turn of the millennium. Its trade reached into three continents, and as we have seen, African, European, Indian, Southeast Asian, Central Asian, and Chinese merchants comprised this globe-spanning web that supported the flourishing of what were hundreds of nodes of capital. As time went by, some regions rose and others fell, a pattern that repeated itself for centuries to come.

Few merchant communities, no matter how peripheral, escaped some contact with this world economy: Khmer merchants in what is today Cambodia brought in goods from China.[125] The Srivijaya traders of Java commodified the wet-rice agriculture of their hinterland to participate in distant markets, while other Javanese merchants traded with the Banda Islands, exchanging nutmeg and mace for rice and Indian textiles, a trade relationship that motivated the Bandanese to give up on subsistence agriculture and focus on commerce long before Europeans ever arrived on their shores.[126] And the traders of the Malay Peninsula boosted their transactions in the twelfth and thirteenth centuries.[127]

The archipelago of capital did, however, have one commercial network unconnected to this world: the vast continents of the Americas. In South America, state bureaucrats managed much of the Inca Empire's production and exchange, keeping marketplaces (and thus merchants) on the fringes. Farther north, however, in Central America, specialized traders emerged within Mayan societies. The most significant mercantile communities emerged even farther north, in the Aztec Empire, which maintained long-distance trade connections from present-day Mexico City to present-day Nicaragua, Honduras, and the Yucatán, about two thousand miles away, a stunning distance considering that much of the trade was land-based and the goods were carried on the backs of people.[128]

Indeed, the Aztecs forged some of the largest markets anywhere in the world. We get some sense of their scale and scope from sources produced after the European conquest: In 1519, when Hernán Cortés saw the marketplace at Tlatelolco (next to the metropolis of Tenochtitlán, with its half a million inhabitants), he observed what has been estimated to be a stunning sixty thousand buyers and sellers congregating in a huge square. "We were astounded at the great number of people and the quantities of merchandise, and at the orderliness and good arrangements that prevailed," remarked Bernal Díaz del Castillo, another conquistador, "for we had never seen such a thing before."[129] "You could see every kind of merchandise to be found anywhere in New Spain."[130] The realm of the Aztecs was filled with such markets, some more important than others.

Like elsewhere in the world, a distinct group of people organized the Aztec trade: the *pochteca*. These merchants sold goods and created the market's institutional infrastructure, including special courts where they served as judges, deliberating "on all cases arising in the market and [passing] sentence on evildoers."[131] Protected by their tutelary god, Yacatecuhtli, and organized in guilds, the pochteca managed long-distance trade in such things as cotton goods, precious stones, and metals. Diego Durán, a Dominican friar, described the pochteca as "[b]uying and selling, going forth to all the markets of the land, bartering cloth for jewels, jewels for feathers, feathers for stones, and stones for slaves, always dealing in things of importance, of renown, and of high value. These men strengthened their social position with their wealth."[132] A drawing of an Aztec market found in Durán's narrative,

*Trade in the Americas: a precolonial Aztec altar depicting a
marketplace, including the sale of two enslaved workers,
Diego Durán,* Historia de las Indias de Nueva España
e islas de la tierra firme *(1579).*

pictured above, depicts four vendors and three customers mid-
transaction. There are two slaves for sale, a man and a woman; the
woman is spinning cotton as if to show her skills.[133]

The ubiquity of trading communities, the ubiquity of nodes of
capital, and their presence even in areas of the world not connected to
the beating heart of the world economy—which remained the Islamic
world well into the fourteenth century—demonstrate powerfully that
the archipelago of capital was rooted in forces and mechanisms independent of specific cultures, religions, and habits. Of course, not all
trade was about accumulation—indeed, most exchanges were purely
local or regional at most, enabling a feeble division of labor but no capitalists.[134] Yet above this layer of mundane exchanges, there emerged a
small but impactful set of merchant communities driven by another
motive: accumulation. They found ways to encourage or coerce agricultural producers to create more ample surpluses. These merchant
communities at times found support from rulers who saw in intensifying trade a means to increase their revenues.

In the first half of the second millennium, those tradable surpluses increased significantly. As we will see later, however, there were limitations to these changes. Capitalism did not emerge from these merchant communities inevitably; in fact, it had not yet emerged. But the growing reservoir of global capital, with skillful, inventive, often ruthless capitalists ready to unleash and direct its floodwaters, presaged the fundamental conditions necessary to the emergence of capitalism. Its global reach and society-altering power remained embryonic, but these merchants, unbeknownst to themselves, had crafted its possibility.

2.

CAPITALISTS WITHOUT CAPITALISM

Trade in Asia: portrait and biography of a merchant from Tangtou Village in Qimen County, Huizhou Prefecture.

As the Shens, Bardis, Vastupalas, Madmuns, and pochteca merchants bought, sold, shipped, and financed, they intensified links between distant producers and consumers—a Gujarati weaver and a Swahili trader, a Chinese potter and a Brugesian housewife, a Muranese glassblower and a Damascene bride, an Oaxacan cotton grower and a Tenochtitlán weaver. At a time when most people never left the confines of their villages and held a knowledge of the world that was severely limited by their geography, the realm of traders was radically different. In that realm, an Arab dhow took goods to Malabar and Coromandel, where they were transferred to a junk traveling the eastern Indian Ocean and South China Sea to Guangzhou. In that realm, an unknown wealthy person in the Gujarati port city of Bharuch placed their hoard in a vessel and buried for safekeeping, but never recovered, a global potpourri of almost two thousand thirteenth- and fourteenth-century coins from Genoa, Venice, Cairo, Damascus, Armenia, Persia, southern Arabia, and the Delhi Sultanate.[1]

Although these networks remained thin rivulets of capital and goods far removed from the economic life of most of the world's people, they would grow to become the great tributaries upon which a radical new world emerged. Traders connected producers and consumers across vast distances, and in the process, they built a layer of economic life fundamentally different from the world in which their reservoirs of capital found themselves. To be sure, they traded goods and labor in and out of this world, but their essential work of building connections followed its own logic and business organization. Some gained a level of riches that had previously been largely reserved for emperors, tribute-extracting lords, religious authorities, and others who appropriated their subjects' resources through taxation, obligations, coercion, and warfare. While risky, these merchants' work could be extraordinarily profitable, allowing them to build thriving communities and vibrant cities; patronize artists, writers, and scientists; and influence rulers or even, occasionally, become them.

Economic life began to change—and the first inklings of capitalism began to emerge—on these islands of capital. As communities of traders concentrated in emerging cities across the globe, they forged a world of striking similarities. Despite immense distances and distinct cultures, Cantonese, Gujarati, Adeni, Genoese, Swahili, and Bukharan merchants would have been broadly recognizable to one another. Everywhere, these traders shaped themselves into a distinct social group, and their ways of conducting business would have been familiar across geographic and cultural divides.[2]

Their lives were different from both those below them in the social hierarchy and those above. They resided in towns and cities, not countrysides. They connected to people living at great distances from them. And unlike almost everyone else, they neither produced things, as rural cultivators and artisans did, nor gained a living by plunder and taxation, as most rulers did. Instead, by investing their capital to accumulate more of it, they took to global extremes the hoary trading logic of buying cheaply and selling dearly, an ancient and seemingly banal technique that—when married to new institutions and, as we soon will see, strengthening states—became deeply consequential. It was a world of surprising resemblances across enormous expanses, partly because they learned from one another and partly because merchants faced similar pressures and opportunities that called for, broadly speaking, similar responses.[3]

Merchants' public presence and growing strength stemmed not least from their ability to self-organize. Long-distance trade, as they constructed it, was not just a contractual relationship between isolated economic subjects; it was deeply embedded within an expanding panoply of private and public institutions, including family, religious, and place-of-origin networks. It was these networks that made possible exchange on a global scale. Eventually, they also made it possible for the swelling nodes of capital to gain political support for imposing their logic beyond their fortified islands.

Wherever they lived, merchants formed tight-knit communities out of business necessity. Long-distance trade was risky, as personal supervision was difficult, if not impossible. Agents could abscond; captains could disobey orders; ships could sink; and pirates, predatory rulers, and bandits could siphon off goods. Trade depended on mechanisms to ensure trust, perhaps a merchant's most valuable asset, and one not provided by the market as such. For Chinese traders, *xinyong* (trustworthiness) was a matter of survival; in India, merchants depended on their *nanayam* (probity, honesty, honor). The Wangara merchants of Kano likewise relied on a powerful system of trust, just as Genoese merchant bankers did. When historian Jessica Goldberg analyzed the networks of two Jewish merchants from Cairo—Ibn 'Awkal (active

circa 990–1030) and Nahray ben Nissim (1042–1095)—she emphasized the importance of reputation to their business enterprises, a reputation forged by letter writing, co-religiosity, and deep-rootedness
within a shared community.[4]

Some of that trust emerged from the routinized interactions of
merchants across long distances. But family connections were important to forging trust as well, with merchant women laboring tirelessly
to build the material and emotional ties that held trading communities
together: inviting family friends and strangers for meals, finding suitable spouses for their children—and running the businesses in the absence of their husbands. The letters of Jewish traders that survive in
the Cairo Geniza show a sophisticated system for extending credit and
sharing risk that was predicated largely on ties of kinship and personal
repute. Just after the turn of the millennium, when Nahray ben Nissim, the teenage son of a Jewish family from Qayrawān, first arrived in
Fustat, he had already been tasked with trading on behalf of several
senior merchants, all relatives. This was the start of a long career in
which he would operate as a crucial node in a dense, interlacing network of family and business connections.[5]

From the very beginnings of the European commercial revolution,
Italian merchants practiced this same blurring of family and business
relationships. The merchants of medieval Amalfi administered their
affairs in the eastern Mediterranean largely by sending relatives to set
up bases in the cities of Byzantium and the Levant. The Comitemau-
roni family dominated the city's overseas trade between the eleventh
and thirteenth centuries, with several brothers eventually obtaining
land and rights to collect tariffs in the Peloponnese. In Venice, some of
the earliest business records show that the mechanics of trade were already defined by ties of kinship. In his old age, Romano Mairano, the
twelfth-century Venetian merchant, delegated much of his business to
his sons. Centuries later, Andrea Barbarigo relied on his brothers-in-
law for his London trade. Genoese overseas trade also saw a shift away
from reliance on a wider pool of unrelated investors toward eventual
domination by a select number of elite families in the later Middle

Ages—families who had risen to prominence through commerce and consolidated their status through intermarriage and inheritance. In Florence, this process gave rise to the Renaissance family firms.[6]

Women played a crucial role in such family-centric firms. The archives of medieval merchants such as those of Francesco Datini preserve correspondence that reveals women's routine handling of crucial administrative and social tasks to keep the family business afloat. Marriage, the documents show, was one of the main means merchant families employed to establish and maintain successful companies. In the Low Countries town of Douai, women routinely ran family businesses and administered transfers of property. Genoese and Venetian women enjoyed considerable financial agency throughout the medieval period as well, participating in commerce in a full legal capacity as widows and somewhat more informally as merchants' wives and daughters. Strasbourg economic elites frequently married off their daughters to members of the same guild, braiding business and kinship ties.[7]

Maintaining family relations was important both internally and externally: Families served as a reservoir of personnel to extend the firm, while the propriety of a trader's family was subject to scrutiny by business partners. The Genoese trader Giovanni Brignole is remembered for his role in building deep familial connections and friendships. Should ties by birth or marriage be lacking, kinship relations could also be established in other ways: In Portugal, *compadrazgo*—godparenthood—enlarged kinship networks, while in China adoption was common among merchant families.[8]

Familes were one important foundation for expanding trade networks, but just as important were networks based on places of origin, shared religious beliefs, and caste. Such ties allowed merchants to regulate their trades, settle disputes, and secure their positions in relation to both competitors and sovereign authorities. In China, as increased long-distance trade required greater capital intensity and more personnel, merchants formed alliances of traders from the same area—a proto-corporate form of business organization. Those alliances led to the formation of influential trading empires (for example, of Huizhou silk merchants). Throughout the port cities of South, Southeast, and East Asia, Muslim merchants built such communities as well, including by constructing urban quarters in which they lived near other believers, spoke Arabic, and had access to mosques and Muslim courts.[9]

Guilds and guildlike institutions also became important to regulating trade; they gave merchants a more powerful voice. Chinese merchants such as the aforementioned merchants of Huizhou organized guilds based on hometown solidarities embodied and reflected in extensive guildhalls for trade and socializing. In the thirteenth century, northern European merchants created the Hanseatic League, a guildlike network that drew upon the merchants' institutional links to regulate their trade. It was governed by a Hanseatic diet known as the Hansetag, which met at the German-speaking city of Lübeck every three years. This setup allowed the league to reduce the commercial risks of long-distance trade and lower transaction costs. Venetian merchants followed suit, creating in 1507 the Cinque Savi alla Mercanzia, a board of trade that regulated the city's commerce. Tamil merchants along the Coromandel coastline also built guild organizations that protected their local and regional interests. Florence and other Italian cities were home to a panoply of guilds, or *arti*, that supported particular groups of capital owners, including the Arte di Calimala, the guild of cloth merchants, and the Arte della Lana, the guild of raw wool importers and wool weavers. Ottoman merchants also organized guilds across the empire.[10]

When abroad, traders often settled into communities of compatriots, solidifying networks. Merchants from the Hanseatic League enjoyed their own residential quarter in London that boasted a chapel, countinghouses, warehouses, and scales—a shared foundation for expanding trade in England. The Republic of Venice provided spaces to particular groups of foreign merchants, among them the Fondaco dei Tedeschi for merchants from German lands and the Fondaco dei Turchi for Ottoman merchants. Italian merchants, meanwhile, organized their own guilds in cities such as Bruges and Constantinople. These organized commercial diasporas became almost extraterritorial, often

Rakish revolutionaries:
merchants in medieval Yemen, Italy, and China.

enjoying their separate judicial systems. Italian city-states created so-called consulates in places where their merchants settled and traded, with the Venetians opening them in Alexandria and Aleppo. Muslim merchants enjoyed access to similar institutions, which provided for legal representation in foreign places, the storage of goods, and conflict resolution. South Asian merchants built networks based on caste loyalties to handle social, ritual, political, and economic issues. The Bania—a caste central to trade—exerted collective power based on caste solidarities and their ability to manage their internal affairs, amplifying these ties by building *mahajans*, or merchant guilds, that regulated their trade for many centuries. Beyond such place-of-origin and guild-like organizations, religious networks enforced trust as well: Armenian merchants relied on such networks, as did Muslim and Jewish merchants.[11]

To discerning observers, merchants' distinct position in society—and their sense of community—was visible in their style of dress. As Portuguese traveler Duarte Barbosa observed, wives of Swahili merchants in Mombasa were recognizable because "they wear many jewels of fine Çofala gold, silver too in plenty, earrings, necklaces, bangles, and bracelets, and they go clad in good silk garments." Merchants often signaled their success and immersion in far-reaching networks by wearing conspicuously imported garments. The merchant in Chaucer's

Canterbury Tales is introduced as having "[u]pon his heed a Flaundryssh [Flemish] bever hat," along with a litany of other luxurious garments and accessories.[12] Donning foreign garb could signal not only worldly sophistication but also political allegiance, as in the case of the merchants of late Byzantium, who could be seen in the streets of their own cities wearing Persian or Venetian fashions. The extravagance of merchants' fashion was not always uncontroversial. Sumptuary laws aimed at restricting the wearing of luxury dress to the political elite and the aristocracy were repeatedly passed in many cities, targeting the families of newly wealthy merchants and businessmen whose lavish spending was thought to represent a threat to the social order. The very frequency of this legislation, however, hints at its repeated failure: More than three hundred sumptuary laws survive from Italy alone from the period 1200 to 1500. Somewhat similar tensions played out in China, where from the Song dynasty (960–1279) on, merchants were subject to a system of sumptuary laws enforced with variable rigidity yet never fully repealed. Merchants broke social norms and laid claim to a new, and exalted, position within society—one often regarded with suspicion by commoners and elites alike.[13]

As capital-rich merchants the world over fashioned more powerful islands of capital and intensified the networks that connected them, they produced not just more of the same but the seedlings of a qualitatively different world. That departure, with its novel economic logic, was the sprout of the capitalist revolution.

The burgeoning archipelago of capital did, to be sure, put unprecedented wealth in the hands of leading merchants. Yet wealth alone was hardly new—many a tributary chief and landowning noble had amassed much greater fortunes. More consequential, arguably, a set of innovations sprang from such intensified trade—conventions, rules, and institutions that transcended individual exchanges. They mattered because trade—the market itself, in fact—was a complex system of collectively forged structures that belied simplistic notions of economic life being founded on individualized barter. From the moment of its inception, the market was an institutional ensemble—both produced by and the product of a collective politics. These institutions were foundational to capitalism's eventual global ascendancy, and some of its oldest and most consequential elements emerged on these islands of capital starting in the first half of the second millennium.[14]

Almost always, the forging of such institutions was a response to immediate needs emerging from the changing nature and opportunities of trade. Collectively, merchants solved problems: They found ways to conduct exchanges over great distances, gauge the trustability of distant partners, enforce agreements, raise substantial sums of capital, secure their goods on long voyages, and create needed infrastructure. Trade—though undoubtedly motivated by a merchant's desire for profit—was fundamentally a collective undertaking.

But there were many other problems that required different kinds of institutional solutions: Merchants who did not personally travel with their goods, for example, needed to find ways to transfer payments across distances measured in weeks, even months, of travel. As long-distance trade surged, traders everywhere invented systems that made such transfers possible. Japanese merchants carried bills of credit—known as *kaezeni*, *saifu*, or *kawase*—to limit the risks of travel. South Asian merchants utilized so-called *hundis*, a financial instrument deployed to direct payment from one person to another. These were also used in East Africa to connect local trade networks to both India and the Arabian Peninsula. In West Africa, such commercial paper helped transfer funds across the central Sudan. In China, since at least the eighth century, merchants had used *feitsyan*, a similar financial instrument, to transfer money over long distances; at the same time, the *hawāla*, a transfer of debt, an order to pay, and the *suftaja*, a letter of credit, a demand note equal to a bill of exchange, spread throughout the Islamic world. These bills of credit allowed merchants to transact without carrying cash.[15]

The Islamic world was particularly innovative in constructing the institutional foundations of long-distance trade—hardly surprising, given its central place in the global archipelago of capital. When Muslim rulers conquered parts of Europe and Arab merchants traded with their Christian counterparts, their innovations traveled with them. By the tenth or eleventh century, they had influenced practices in Italy and on the Iberian Peninsula; by the late fourteenth century, in England. Northern Italian merchants, in turn, created *lettere di cambio*, which allowed for the cashless transfer of money across space while simultaneously facilitating currency exchange. These bills of exchange became foundational to long-distance trade, as they allowed buyers to pay sellers either "on sight" or at an agreed-upon future date.[16]

As their trade expanded, merchants also sought ways to mitigate losses from *forces majeures*, unavoidable catastrophes. Ships laden with valuable merchandise could sink, traders could fall victim to attacks, and stores of goods could burn down. To limit the impact of disasters, merchants collectivized risks. The most important form of risk sharing was spreading one's investments by sharing the investment for a voyage with several traders. Chinese merchants pooled risks and diversified their investments in this way. Indian merchants developed their own risk-mitigating institutions, mediated by religious bodies. Insurance for long-distance trade was another way to limit risk: Islamic commercial law had regulated risk-sharing arrangements for long-distance trade since the Middle Ages, with the sharia (a religiously grounded system of law) specifying the institution of *daman* to transfer liability to a third party. Insurance as a business completely separate from a specific trade is documented first for Genoa in 1347; it came into common use in Italy and northern European ports soon thereafter. Such insurance was also present (somewhat later) in the Indian Ocean; caravans traveling from Surat to Agra carried it, and insurance contracts protecting South Asian seaborne trade were almost mandatory. The Bania of Gujarat insured their cloth- and ivory-laden ships for voyages to and from East Africa with so-called *jokhmi hundis* at a rate of between 7 and 10 percent of the insured value. We also have evidence that merchants in the Ottoman Empire used insurance contracts no later than the fifteenth century.[17]

As trade became increasingly intricate and the time horizon of transactions lengthened, merchants developed new forms of taking stock. Accounting became a crucial tool. Though few account books have survived, we know that eleventh-century Jewish merchants in Cairo used sophisticated accounting methods. They entered the details of each transaction—accounting for the debtor, creditor, weight of goods, customs duties, transportation costs, supplier names, and so on—in a *daftar al-mu'ayyama* (daily notebook). These details were transferred daily into a final ledger (an *al-daftar al-kabīr*), composed of what letter writers referred to as *awrāq ṭiwāl* (long sheets). Accounts were also drawn up at the time of the sale of merchandise or when currencies were changed. Muslim merchants kept elaborate accounts too. Chronological cross-referenced accounts were most likely maintained throughout the Indian Ocean world. When Dutch trader Jan Huyghen van Linschoten reported on his travels in late sixteenth-century Southeast Asia, he remarked that the merchants there "are most subtill and expert in casting of accounts," a skill that most likely went a long way back.[18]

As early as 1211, Italian merchants faced with the ever greater complexities of their businesses engaged in "paragraph accounting"—a system of bookkeeping that listed credits and debits in chronological fashion. Over the next two centuries, Genoese, Florentine, Milanese, and Venetian merchants improved that system, which slowly morphed into double-entry bookkeeping, with its characteristic multiple account books, its cross-referencing and categorization of all transactions, and its insistence that each transaction be listed twice—as a credit and a debit. Requiring merchants to continually do math, double-entry bookkeeping allowed them to understand their businesses in new ways, giving them a sense of how profitable each of their undertakings was. In 1494, Venetian Luca Pacioli famously formalized that system in his *Summa de arithmetica, geometria, proportioni et proportionalita.* Double-entry bookkeeping migrated to other parts of the world (or was invented there separately). We know, for instance, that Armenian merchant Hovhannes Joughayetsi used it at Surat in the seventeenth century and that Chinese merchants deployed it during the Ming era.[19]

In the same period, expanding trade volumes and longer distances meant greater capital requirements and more time before trades settled. To mobilize capital beyond their own individual resources, merchants entered into partnership agreements, another crucial institutional innovation. Such partnerships, regulated in a voluminous corpus of law, had been common in the Islamic world since before the turn of the millennium. The *fiqh*, Islamic jurisprudence, outlined these agreements in detail. *Shirka* (or *sharika*) connoted a contract between partners who pooled investments and shared the attendant risks and proceeds. Even limited liability partnerships were known. To pool capital, Islamic merchants used so-called *mudaraba* as early as the eighth century, with principals providing capital for a single venture (such as a sea journey) to an agent who would employ that capital in trade and return it with a profit (a very early example of the division of ownership and control). Investors benefited from their ability to profit from the trades and from their limited liability; agents, in turn, received some of the returns.[20]

In the eleventh century, merchants in Italian commercial cities increasingly used the commenda, a risk-sharing contract that combined elements of the mudaraba with Roman, Jewish, and Byzantine risk-sharing forms in order to draw on capital beyond that of the immediate family. The earliest such Italian commenda to survive, signed in 1073 between Giovanni Lissado of Luprio and Sevasto Orefice in Venice, stipulated how the *habere* (the capital) was to be used (for a sea voyage to Thebes) and how the two partners were to share the proceeds. Genoese archives reveal that similar contracts appeared in Genoa by the twelfth century, and throughout the northern Mediterranean (in cities such as Barcelona) by the thirteenth century, when they became the dominant form of cooperation. In Holland, this mechanism for mobilizing capital was known as *partenrederij*—a type of fractional ownership of a merchant vessel by which each owner, functioning as an equity partner, shared proportionately in the proceeds and the corporate debt of the voyage. These contracts enabled further innovations—for example, by making it easier for people of modest means to invest small funds with a wealthy traveling merchant who was happy to take any contribution he could get to increase his operating capital overseas. Partners could also enter into various commendas simultaneously, and the shares of these contracts could change hands and operate as a kind of currency.[21]

Mudaraba/commenda arrangements traveled into the Indian Ocean, including its eastern parts. As Malay-speaking traders interacted with their Muslim counterparts, they learned about Islamic commercial law—including its detailed and standardized body of partnership law. Indeed, in the first half of the fifteenth century, Malayan maritime law (codified in the Undang-undang Melaka) appropriated core elements of the mudaraba/commenda.[22]

Other ways of organizing capital emerged as well, though they were less common. The Islamic *mufawada* created more permanent relationships between groups of investors in which all partners carried unlimited liability. The *compagnia*—a form of pooling capital—emerged in European cities such as Venice, Florence, and Ravensburg; its literal translation, "with bread," hinted at the familial nature of a partnership in which meals would be shared. Then, in fourteenth-century Florence, a new system of organizing businesses emerged: the so-called partnership system. It meant that one person, or a small number of partners, controlled multiple legally distinct companies, thus limiting their respective liability should any one of them fail. The first known (and prolific) merchant to institute what amounted to a medieval holding company was the merchant and banker Francesco Datini of the Tuscan city of Prato. By the early fifteenth century, limited liability partnerships flourished in Florence as well.[23]

Banking provided another method of pooling capital. Forms of banking itself, of course, were old, with merchants having for centuries acted as financiers, providing loans to traders and rulers. In the Islamic world, the provision of credit for business undertakings can be traced to the eighth century. In China, landlords, eunuchs, and others who possessed wealth but lacked the desire to engage in risky mercantile undertakings had long lent money to merchants, backed by existing communal bonds and commercial law. Pawnshops linked to Buddhist monasteries had been especially prominent in the provision of such credit since the fifth century. Eventually, these "banks" also provided loans and kept deposits. European merchants had provided credit for centuries as well, an industry that was particularly strong in northern Italian cities—for example, in Florence, which saw an explosive expansion of its banking sector around the year 1300. In nearby Genoa, an institution developed that foreshadowed the future in many ways: the Casa di San Giorgio. Established in 1407, this body of creditors was first meant to control the commune's debts (*compere*) as a single debtor. By the mid-fifteenth century, it owned almost all compere—and therefore tax collection and other rights, like minting. What pointed most toward the future was that the Casa di San Giorgio became a sovereign power, taking charge of virtually all the Genoese colonies abroad, including the island of Corsica and the Black Sea city of Caffa—an early example of state and capital growing symbiotically and of capital owners enjoying sovereign rights.[24]

As communities of merchants around the world developed these tools and strategies in the first half of the millennium, their institutional innovations flourished inside a global network, with the medieval Islamic world at its center. The mechanisms of the businesses they built and the ways that they organized their economic lives are still largely with us many centuries later, and the logic that propelled them feels familiar.

But we need to pause here to remind ourselves that we have focused so far on a very small group, a minuscule percentage of the human population, really: those who organized their economic lives around growing their capital, not around growing crops or extending their land holdings, the number of vassals under their control, or the size of their armies. The revolutionary importance of this vanguard is visible only in retrospect. In their time, they occupied an ambivalent position. Although rulers appreciated their ability to secure goods and sell the things produced by their subordinates, and although some came to rely on them to finance state growth and operations, nascent capitalists were nevertheless often viewed with suspicion—hostility, even—by both commoners and elites who considered the idea of capital multiplying itself unethical and illegitimate. For many onlookers, making money from money seemed closer to sin, sorcery, or plain theft than to productive engagement with the earth, which was generally considered the proper form of economic life.

The mercantile avant-gardes dispersed around the world were droplets in a sea of economic life whose main currents flowed by fundamentally different logics. Yet attention to these numerically negligible and often not even particularly rich merchants highlights those elements of economic life that were harbingers of the coming capitalist revolution and sharpens our appreciation for the radicalism that burst forth in the second half of the millennium.

While economic life in the first half of the millennium featured enormous diversity and significant change, for most of humanity it took place in the countryside. Merchants made their homes in towns, but in 1391, 90 percent of Chinese lived in the countryside (that is, outside centers of more than two thousand inhabitants); even in China's most urbanized region, the Yangtze Delta, 81 percent of the population lived outside towns. In Europe in 1300, 95 percent of people lived in the countryside (in this case, outside centers with more than ten thousand inhabitants). In Italy, the continent's most urbanized region, "only" 85.3 percent lived in the countryside. In England, that figure was a staggering 98.8 percent. Not much had changed by 1500, when 94.4 percent of Europe's people (including those in eastern Europe) still dwelled in the countryside, though a new node of significant urbanization had emerged in the Netherlands. Even in the Middle East and

North Africa, which held some of the world's largest cities, the vast majority of people still lived in the countryside. It has been estimated that around the year 1100, only 8.5 percent of people there were city dwellers.[25]

While merchants—not least because they lived in cities—generally acquired everything they needed at markets and made a living by selling their services (and so had much in common with most readers of this book), almost everyone else on Earth labored primarily for their own and their immediate community's subsistence, not for exchange. Those outside the world of merchants and cities were members of "use-oriented societies," part of the "vast world of self-sufficiency" that Fernand Braudel has identified. And there was a colossal gap between the structures of their economic lives and those of the merchants, whose modus operandi was the accumulation of capital.[26]

Producing for one's own use was timeless. For millennia, the world had been structured by an immense sphere of what Braudel has called "material life"—the plowing, herding, fishing, and manufacturing that largely took place in households to fulfill personal needs. Some goods had always been traded, both to allow for pooling of resources and to account for environmental diversity, but most exchange remained small in scale and purely local. The Greeks called it *oikonomia*—the management of the household. More than two thousand years ago, in his *Politics*, Aristotle insisted on the contrast between production for use and production for the market, with the former both dominant and superior: "There are two sorts of wealth-getting," he said. "One is a part of household management, the other is commerce: the former necessary and honorable, while that which consists in exchange is justly censured; for it is unnatural, and a mode by which men gain from one another." Efforts to maximize money were, to Aristotle, "a hazard to the moral well-being of the individual."[27] In India, to cite one example of such oikonomia, production primarily took place within traditional village structures (the so-called *jajmani* system), catering primarily to the needs of the local community. Exchanges were mediated by custom, not markets: Specialized workers such as carpenters would work for the village in return for food, land to cultivate subsistence crops themselves, or cash—all set by convention. This organization of economic life, as one political scientist noted, provided no "possibilities for profits, capital accumulation, technical innovation, or upward mobility." In Gujarat, inhabited largely by tribal groups that also combined settled agriculture with pastoralism and gathering, the merchants' sphere of influence was severely limited. These kinds of structures, preferences, and resistances were not peculiar to India—they were common throughout the world.[28]

For centuries, if not millennia, economic life, far from being seen as an autonomous sphere, was embedded in such a framework of social norms. Indeed, as Karl Polanyi, one of the twentieth century's most perceptive observers of capitalism, argued, "[A]ll economic systems known to us up to the end of feudalism in Western Europe were organized either on the principle of reciprocity or redistribution, or householding, or some combination of the three." Even though it sounds counterintuitive to most people living in the twenty-first century, Polanyi was right when he emphasized that "previously to our time no economy has ever existed that, even in principle, was controlled by markets." Marc Bloch, one of the most brilliant analysts of this order, agrees: "Nothing could be more misleading than to dwell exclusively on the economic aspects of the relationship between a lord and his men, however important they may seem." Economic life was "submerged [in] social relationships."[29]

Merchants' economic lives were categorically different—not just from those of commoners but from those of the privileged. In the first half of the last millennium, the world's rich and powerful generally gained access to the ample resources they controlled through taxation, tribute, and plunder, not through capitalist accumulation. Their extraction of wealth was almost always non-market-based—that is, they were able to command people to part with labor, goods, or (in monetized societies) their money. Even when more substantial bulk trade made inroads into rural cultivation, tributary—nonmarketized forms of surplus extraction—remained the primary driver of economic life.

Tributary rule: ambassadors bearing gifts
in seventh-century Samarkand.

War booty was also crucial: To cite an extreme example, when Central Asian ruler Timur (also known as Tamerlane) spread his power from Central Asia into Afghanistan and India in the late fourteenth century, millions of people died in the ensuing wars, yet his plunder so enriched him that he could construct magnificent mosques and madrassas that glisten in the sun of Samarkand to this day. Like Timur, these elites could be very rich—but in ways essentially different from capital owners. Confirming these hierarchies, tributary elites' social status and wealth were so pronounced that many merchants aimed to leave the world of trade behind and join the ranks of the landowning, rent-extracting aristocracy.[30]

Tributary economic systems, with rulers collecting rents, tributes, or taxes from the populace, were present across the globe. The appropriations that made these rulers rich and powerful were almost always strikingly visible: Rural cultivators could be forced to work without wages on the fields of local potentates, part with food they had grown to meet the demands of the rulers' collectors at harvesttime, or supply provisions for warring armies. Lords gained control of nonwage labor by custom, and in return, rural cultivators gained certain rights to their protection. It was a system of mutual obligations, not markets, its mechanisms of extraction extra-economic and inscribed in custom or law. Unlike under capitalism, there was nothing mysterious about the reshuffling of resources. To anyone who cared to look, it was blatantly visible how elites became rich. Not until capital came to rule economic life did the sources of inequality become obscured.[31]

Though this general principle held true for tributary systems across time and space, the precise workings of each system differed from location to location. European feudalism was one important tributary regime among many, and pausing to look at its dynamics will give us a sharper sense of how radical a departure the economic rationality of merchants—and eventually capitalism—was. While there were regional specificities and divergent trends in different parts of Europe, they all shared certain attributes. Feudal economic life was propelled by landowning elites who kept everyone else in personal dependence. Hardly any land or labor entered markets as a commodity, as both were attached by right and custom to lords. Rural cultivators were forced to give up a portion of their production in the form of tax, tribute, labor, or, increasingly, rent. This organization of economic life could and did witness innovation, development, and significant urban and rural commercialization, but although merchants could take advantage of markets created by lords' luxury consumption, the tributary regime's core principle was extra-economic exploitation of the peasant by the lord. At the same time, since landowners usually did not get involved in production itself, rural cultivators enjoyed considerable autonomy and an ability to maintain, and even at times increase, their share of the product. Many modern-day readers may see property rights as naturally mediated by markets, but in tributary societies and throughout most of human history, they were not.[32]

Within this world of tributary regimes, manufacturing followed its own distinct logic. As with agriculture, most manufacturing took place within the domestic sphere for subsistence purposes. Women spun, men wove; women churned butter and stitched clothing. In cities, where manufacturing was increasingly concentrated, it generally fell under the control of urban artisans organized in guilds. These associations aimed to regulate production and set prices; they controlled certain crafts, limited entry, regulated training, and created rituals to forge solidarity among their members. They constructed monopolies, restricted production, stipulated the shape and size of production sites, and constrained investment. And even though their efforts were not always successful, their world was a far cry from the organization of manufacturing under a market.[33]

These economic relations—in cities and countrysides—were both enabled and curbed by rulers who had an ambivalent relationship with the merchants in their midst. On the one hand, landowners' and rulers' dependence on merchants was limited, as much of their power and most of their resources derived not from taxing trade but from extracting wealth from the countryside. In South India, to cite one of many possible examples, the state never relied on the taxation of commercial capital because the tax basis in agriculture was sufficient. In the same way, Byzantine rulers drew almost all of their income from rural cultivators, which explains why trade and the merchants who plied it were not central to the functioning of the state. As a result, capital owners found themselves in a politically subordinate position. In the first half of the millennium, power rested with those who controlled land. Merchants, of course, built some alternative nodes of power and wealth alongside the dominant system, creating an unorthodox road to riches and articulating a different set of interests. While these merchants could potentially challenge rulers, they did not, with a few exceptions (the Italian city-states), usurp political power or become rulers themselves.[34]

At the same time, merchants provided some important services and resources to tributary rulers, which, in turn, encouraged these rulers to provide the merchants with support and institutional scaffolding. Merchants were embedded within the tributary order, and they benefited from it. They extended loans, distributed surpluses, and supplied crucial materials for industries, as well as enriched the rulers more directly, since their private wealth and transactions or activities could be taxed. Merchants could also help extract wealth from the countryside and infuse capital into production; they could organize trade that promoted the expansion of markets and provided goods to the rulers' realms. Moreover, thanks to their control of important infrastructures such as ports, ships, and navigational knowledge, merchants could be exceedingly important to warfare: To maintain the integrity of their power, the Arab Ayyubids, for instance, needed soldiers. They bought enslaved soldiers from Venetian and Genoese merchants who had acquired them from Central Asia and the Caucasus—a clear example of how useful merchants could be. Islamic rulers as early as the ninth century also supported merchants because commercializing parts of the countryside, especially in agriculturally prosperous provinces such as Egypt, enabled rural cultivators to pay their taxes in coins, an important resource for rulers. In similar ways, China's Song emperors supported trade after the turn of the millennium, not least because the dynasty drew an increasing share of its tax revenues from trading activity. At the beginning of the twelfth century, trade taxes amounted to only 1.7 percent of its total revenues; they increased to 20 percent in 1128, then stabilized at around 5 percent in the second half of the century. Taxing trade gave the Song emperors a new way to mobilize revenue and keep up the empire's military without burdening peasants with ever higher levies. "[T]he people from distant lands should be encouraged to come and trade," argued Chinese emperor Gaozong (r. 1127–1162), because "the profits of maritime trade contribute much to the national income."[35]

For these and related reasons, tributary elites at times encouraged trade and the resulting commercialization of the economy. When it suited their interests, Chinese rulers actively promoted commerce, provided infrastructure, and encouraged agricultural surplus production. Forging the world's most extensive and cohesive empire, they furthered the commercialization of the economy. Domestically, the state provided security, as Ibn Battuta observed in the fourteenth century: "China is the safest and best country for the traveller. A man travels for nine months alone with great wealth and has nothing to fear."[36] China's significant navy also projected power into Southeast Asia, supporting Chinese trade in the region, with Admiral Zheng He's massive armadas traveling all the way to Arabia. In Kano and Katsina, in western Africa, the fifteenth-century expansion of trade was equally connected to the formation of new state institutions. Rulers such as Sarki Kanajeji (r. 1390–1410), Sarki Abdullahi Burja (r. 1438–1452), and Sarki Muhammad Rumfa (r. 1463–1499) secured trade routes, established trade connections with faraway territories, and set up local markets. Most rulers also set trade rules and provided mechanisms for their enforcement. Merchants were in and of the old order. Still, the logic of tributary rulers' road to wealth and power conflicted with that of capital-investing merchants. To break out, capital owners needed an external shock.[37]

Finally, and like virtually everyone else in human history, merchants lived in a world of slow economic growth, which was a constraint in and of itself. It has been estimated that annual average economic growth rates per capita in the entire world amounted to just 0.05 percent between 1000 and 1500, which means that it would have taken 1,387 years for per capita output to double. Compare that with the annual 2.92 percent per capita growth in the world during the boom years of 1950 to 1973, or to China's 10-plus percent growth rates in the 2000s. These numbers are rough and controversial, yet no one questions their basic message: In the first half of the second millennium, economic growth was almost imperceptible. To be sure, Aden, Cambay, Guangzhou, Kano, and Venice experienced very significant economic change, but they were islands in a sea of economic life that transformed at a turtle's pace. They encountered huge barriers to change, from the very small scale of markets, to the disincentives to engage in technical innovation, to the peculiar structures of the state. But as these barriers began falling away, one key effect of the capitalist revolution was that growth rates rose steeply.[38]

Wherever they lived during the first half of the millennium, merchants operated within a political, social, and economic order that was not of their making. They nestled in its nooks and crannies, at times drawing great profit from it, not least because rulers everywhere resorted to them to supplement the tributes they collected. But they also met resistance. They pushed against it, sometimes gaining traction, often stumbling back. The level of resistance—some structural, some contingent on the politics of particular moments—made it strikingly clear that the logic of this strange group of people who claimed wealth and authority based on their control of capital was not the natural or necessary outcome of the division of labor. And this limitation, this hedging in of capital and capitalists by elites and commoners, helps explain, as we will see later, the often violent nature of the expansion of capital as it unfolded in subsequent centuries.[39]

Most basically, capital owners encountered ecological constraints: An economy that relied almost exclusively on human and animal muscle power could produce only so much beyond the subsistence needs of producers. With severe limits on production and thus on tradable surplus, the frontiers of commodification lacked sufficient volume or force to push into new spaces or social realms. Nature itself, under the conditions of the prevalent technologies of the first half of the second millennium, acted as a powerful dam on the ability of capital owners to break out of their radically constricted economic spaces.

Social and political constraints also made it hard for the logic of capital to make deeper inroads into economic life. As we have seen, most of the world's people produced first and foremost for their own and their immediate communities' subsistence, and safeguarding that subsistence was of overwhelming, even existential, importance. Because rural cultivators the world over protected as best as they could the crucial resources they needed for their subsistence—most prominently, their labor and access to land—capital owners often failed to wrest control from them.

Such boundaries were deeply ingrained in even some of the fundamental workings of markets: In the towns of late medieval England, one could make a living from trade and buy all necessities at the marketplace—and yet the prices of food were determined not by supply and demand but, rather, by a complex set of laws and a shared sense of morality. In the markets of medieval Italy, the newly wealthy merchants had to contend with an increasingly virulent moral and theological backlash to their activities—one driven as much by popular religious sentiment as by the institutional church. The marketplaces of Japan and China in the first half of the millennium were the foci of the tightest forms of social control, achieved through both legal and informal means. In Islamic societies, the market inspector, the *muhtasib*, served as the guarantor of the morality of exchange in the marketplace. Indeed, the morality of making a profit from trade and from investing capital was negotiated in myriad ways across societies, but a common throughline was the idea that profiteering and greed were reprehensible and should be prevented.[40]

As cultivators and craftspeople defended the sphere of production and consumption against market inroads, they radically limited the sphere of capital. As we will see, that resistance, much weakened and muted, continues to the present day. Because rural cultivators the world round produced almost everything they consumed, the market's scope was extremely limited. As a result, capital owners had a difficult time inserting themselves into production. It was not impossible to do so (merchants, for example, sometimes provided advances to weavers), but most production remained outside capital's umbrella. Traders typically purchased goods from independent producers (some of them small peasant operators, others feudal lords with thousands of vassals) that they then sold elsewhere—a profitable undertaking but one that palisaded the spheres of both subsistence production and tributary regimes.[41]

Moreover, rural cultivators resisted the impositions of landowning elites bent on extracting surplus to spend on the wares peddled by the merchants, further limiting the reach of capital owners. A wave of mass risings that escalated into wars rolled across Europe during the fourteenth and fifteenth centuries. But even before this, peasant rebellions were not uncommon. The Jacquerie in France, the Peasants' War in England, the Flemish Coast Uprising, and many others were fueled by the resistance of the rural population to lordly and government impositions.[42]

Another limiting factor was the structural constraints that elites put on capital owners' ability to expand their interests and logic. After all, elites in tributary regimes drew their surplus from the people they dominated through extra-economic means, and they had little interest in seeing the logic of the market interfere too deeply with these repressive but rewarding relations. European feudal lords, Chinese bureaucrats, Muslim rulers, and religious authorities of all kinds were fiercely invested in taxing, seizing, and expropriating the little surplus that rural cultivators managed to produce, and they were not inclined, if they could help it, to share that surplus with merchants.[43]

Rulers did at times provide support to merchants. But they did just the opposite as well: By the 1370s, political authorities in China had constrained the important Muslim merchants who conducted much of the trade with the Middle East. By the fifteenth century, the Chinese empire had, more broadly, severely limited overseas trade in all its forms. In Europe, popes issued prohibitions against trade with the Muslims they called "infidels," a move motivated by religious and military conflict but one that also had economic effects. In Japan, the Kamakura shogunate, or *bakufu*, issued, in 1297, a *tokusei* decreeing that all the outstanding debts of its vassals, known as *gokenin*, were to be forgiven. These vassals could even reclaim some of the lands they had lost earlier when they had defaulted on their debts. The judiciary would no longer hear any cases brought against government retainers that concerned nonpayment of debt—an effort by rulers to limit a commercializing economy that could threaten not only established landholders but also the traditional ties of loyalty and gift giving that bound landholders, warriors, and the bakufu to one another. Such opposition to the logic of capital meant that capitalists the world over often failed to gain the support of rulers and states. But, as we will see later, capitalism without the state was impossible, indeed unimaginable.[44]

These ecological, social, and political boundaries formed the background conditions for capital owners' position in society, effectively limiting their sway to their often heavily fortified islands—some real, some metaphorical. When the logic of capital did succeed in entering new spheres of society and new parts of the world, capital owners faced powerful rebellions. These revolts came as much from the top of the social hierarchy as from the bottom—showing, in a roundabout way, that the logic of capital lacked the support (the legitimacy, even) and political muscle to force its further expansion.

Some grassroots uprisings responded to urban capital's efforts to dominate production; some elite rebellions mobilized tributary rulers against merchant power. When Florentine traders, for example, pushed into the Flanders woolen industry, workers staged multiple rebellions, among them uprisings in Valenciennes in 1225, Ghent in 1272 and 1274, and Flanders as a whole in 1280. In Florence itself, proletarianized workers, especially the thirteen thousand women and men in the city's textile industry, along with small artisans and shop owners, frequently rose against the city's mercantile elite. Historians have chronicled forty-three riots and rebellions from 1343 to 1385, a particularly rebellious period. Most consequentially, the famous Ciompi Revolt, which began in 1378, shook Florentine society to its roots, as the rebels—principally lower-tier wool carders known as *ciompi*—captured the city's government. It took four years for the capital-rich elite to regain control over the city. Genoa, too, was riven by a constant stream of rebellions, ranging from conflicts with the city's lower classes to confrontations with the nobility, as when the marchesi of Gavi rebelled, in 1197, against the growing power of the Genoese commune.[45]

The resistances faced by capital and capitalists become most visible when we look at ideas and ideology—which, in the first half of the millennium, means religion. All the world's major religions expressed severe doubts about capital owners and the logic they represented. Many religious injunctions aimed to constrain the reach of capital. Almost everywhere, merchants were looked down on; almost nowhere did they rise to the top of the social pyramid. They were detested, disliked, made into scapegoats, and at times expropriated, expelled, or even killed.

It would be wrong to explain capitalism's history as the result of these religious injunctions. Max Weber famously argued that religious beliefs could be an insurmountable barrier to capital owners' interests and inclinations and that they could explain different historical trajectories in different areas of the world. Yet looking at the flourishing of trade in the Islamic and Catholic world and the entrepreneurial talents of people in South Asia and China puts such arguments into question. Worldly and religious authorities, moreover, were always more ambivalent about the economic activities and logic of merchants for the simple reason that they needed them. The Catholic Church, to cite just one example, became utterly dependent on loans and a variety of banking services provided by northern Italian merchants.[46]

Throughout Asia, the social position of the trading communities was never particularly high, certainly below that of bureaucrats, soldiers, and even farmers. In Aztec society, to give another example, merchants enjoyed a privileged status but were considered inferior to the nobility, even though they might have been richer. In the Cham polity (today's Vietnam), merchants were feared and "kept isolated, away from the Cham state's capital in the north." In an 875 inscription, merchants are described as people "who were likely to abscond with a temple's wealth"; they were "demonic," "vicious," and "stupid."[47] In the Islamic world, too, trade was considered "a transient means of living (ma'ash), and the accumulation of wealth for its own sake was thus condemned." Islam also had strong prohibitions against usury. In the Quran, the prohibition against riba—usury, interest—is absolute. The fundamental principles of Muslim trade ethics found a classical expression in al-Ghazali's Ihya' 'ulum al-din. To engage in commerce, this important eleventh- and twelfth-century Islamic philosopher said, merchants needed to remember that "trade was a social duty." They had to execute "transactions with good faith and intention" and "not be distracted from fulfilling religious duties and rituals." He saw the accumulation of money as legitimate if it allowed the accumulator to acquire necessary goods, support his family, aid the poor, and live a pious life, but as illegitimate if it focused on the display of wealth and excessive consumption. He cited Mohammad as saying that "unfortunate is the slave of the dirham," of silver. Merchants were "just" in seeking gain but should be satisfied with moderate profits; they should serve society, avoid fraud and price gouging, fear Allah, be trustworthy in their operations, and observe a sense of equity and leniency in their dealings. Such teachings set clear boundaries to the sphere of capital accumulation: When the sultan of Delhi, Muhammad ibn Tughluq (r. 1325–1351), gave loans to peasants to enable them to plant, a Muslim theologian accused him of usury.[48]

In China, Confucian thought placed merchants on the lowest rung of society, below state officials, peasants, and artisans, with a Huizhou trader characteristically seen as a "grasping pawnbroker who sued anyone he disagreed with and spent vast amounts of money on commercial sex." Chinese elites' ideas about the proper ordering of society and the primacy of agricultural pursuits made them suspicious of the road merchants took to wealth and social prominence. Confucianism condemned profit-making and moneymaking, especially if they came from nonphysical work. In the fifteenth century, one Chinese commentator warned of "fellows who aim for profit." Commercial activities and trading (particularly long-distance trading) were seen as economic activity that did not fit into the agrarian ideal (and its social order) that many rulers, officials, and other elites had in mind.[49]

Christian religious sentiments were full of injunctions against the logic of capital and its bearers as well. Charging interest was considered a sin. As is said in the Old Testament: "Hath given forth upon usury, and hath taken increase: shall he then live? he shall not live . . . he shall surely die." Profit-making, especially making money from money, was generally suspect. In another familiar Bible passage, the condemnation is even broader: "[I]t is easier for a camel to go through the eye of a needle, than for a rich man to enter into the kingdom of God."[50] In Christian thought, the prohibition and condemnation of usury and inflated profit were manifested in the canon law and recurrently appeared in stories, sermons, and church frescoes. A tenth-century monk described a community of merchants as "wicked and lawless men, who habitually pooled their resources to pay for unbridled orgies." For thirteenth-century French philosopher William of Auxerre, usury was an illegitimate business undertaking and not "a proper business or way of gaining a living," as it was selling something that was common to all and only God's to give: time.[51] To this day, the cathedral in the French city of Reims features a stone-carved merchant begging the Virgin to show him mercy for his deceptive trade practices. The Christian Gospels of Mark, Matthew, and Timothy observe that "the love of money is the root of all evil." At the Sorbonne, it was taught that those who charged interest were "attenuated robber[s]." When Giovanni Boccaccio sat down to write his *Decameron*, the first story that spilled from his head is about two traders who welcome into their home a Prato merchant of ill repute. When their guest falls sick, they fear that he might die and be denied a church burial, that he "will

Begging for forgiveness: A "dishonest" cloth merchant kneels before a statue of the Virgin Mary. Northern transept of Reims Cathedral, France, thirteenth century.

be cast out into some ditch like a dog. . . . In which case the folk of these parts, who reprobate our trade as iniquitous and revile it all day long, and would fain rob us, will seize their opportunity, and raise a tumult, and make a raid upon our houses."[52]

On their deathbeds, several of the Medici, Florence's wealthy rulers, feared they had committed a sin by engaging in usury; they worried more about the theological consequences of their day-to-day business activities than about their many children born out of wedlock. Cosimo de' Medici (1389–1464) was so anxious about his afterlife that he paid for the rebuilding of San Marco's monastery to get a papal bull clearing him of all his sins, which he then had prominently placed on the portal to the sacristy of the monastery's church.[53]

D espite religious injunctions and other evidence of resistance to the logic of capital, capitalists flourished in the first half of the millennium. Capitalism did not. Though its underground springs were there, the world that would burst forth from capitalist activities centuries later was still unknowable. Despite their hard work and enormous creativity, merchants remained on the periphery. They were few in number, and the relative importance of their trade paled in comparison to the age-old exchanges occurring at local and regional levels. Even in the fifteenth century, their presence in the everyday lives of almost all the world's people was minimal. Nearly all production (and much exchange) went on outside their purview. They did not enjoy much— or any—control over the people who produced the things they traded. They connected producers and consumers to one another without revolutionizing much of the world's patterns of production or consumption. This strategy made sense: first, because it was in long-distance trade—in the sphere of capital—that they enjoyed their peculiar advantage, and second, because it meant that they did not need to upset local social and political structures. It was the very resistance against

*To atone for the sin of usury, Cosimo de' Medici rebuilt
a run-down monastery in Florence, San Marco.*

their logic that drove them into the one sphere they could dominate, even monopolize: long-distance trade.[54]

Given the environmental, epidemiological, social, cultural, ideological, and political resistances (at times rising into open rebellion), it is not surprising that the logic of capital and the place of its bearers—merchants—in the social order were restricted to well-defined and often rather marginal spheres. The self-propagating thrust of capital led to an expansion of trade and the accumulation of riches among merchants in Aden, Cambay, Florence, Guangzhou, Sijilmasa, and many other cities, but that capital and these merchants also bounced off the seemingly impenetrable walls of the existing order. The entire archipelago of capital was hemmed in behind walls both figurative and literal.

Half a millennium, if measured in human lifespans, is a very long time. It seems even longer at a time when visible historical change on multiple dimensions has become part of life for most people, an unexceptional reality. In the 2010s, to cite an almost banal example, one million rural Cambodian cultivators turned into industrial workers at a speed and scale of change truly unimaginable in the age of the Hasans, Bardis, Vastupalas, and Shens. Change happened during the first half of the second millennium, of course—empires rose and fell, diseases decimated human populations, new technologies arose, knowledge accumulated, the climate changed, and merchant communities came and went. But the prime revolutionary force of our lives today—capital—left only modest traces. It continued to exist only on the margins. Its revolutionary potential did not become obvious.

Capital owners could have puttered on languidly as they were. Communities of merchants and nodes of capital waxed and waned—in one part of the Arab world, then another; in India, China, Africa, and Europe. The core of economic life across the world, however, remained ordered around lords coercing rural cultivators to give up some share of the things they produced, a logic that showed enormous persistence. These rural cultivators retained access to the land and enjoyed considerable power vis-à-vis the lords, especially after the Black Death killed so many potential workers. Commercialization expanded, only to retreat again, with rural inhabitants reverting time and again to subsistence production. Yet the tributary logic, even in this commercializing world, remained dominant and astounding in its obduracy.[55]

The five-hundred-year history of the archipelago of capital reveals that its extension was extremely unlikely. Merchant communities had prefigured some institutions and embraced a logic that would become important to the capitalist revolution, but there was no unbroken line from Aden, Surat, Florence, or Kano to modern capitalism. Capitalists were unable to create capitalism; they needed allies to break through the boundaries that hedged them in.[56] And by far the most powerful ally they would acquire was the state.

Part I

Building Capitalism

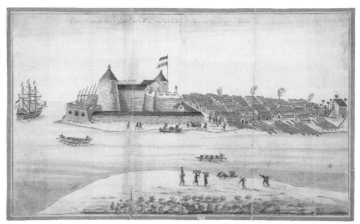

A new island arises in the archipelago of capital:
Elmina Castle (in today's Ghana).

THE GREAT CONNECTING,
1450–1650

*Accumulating capital: merchant in Cambay, as painted
by Ludovico di Varthema, early sixteeth century.*

Poised on the banks of the Tapti River in western India, Surat
today is a buzzing metropolis of almost five million inhabitants. It was already a major center of trade by the fifteenth
century, its merchants situated at the confluence of the markets of
Asia, Africa, Europe, and Surat's own fertile hinterland. By 1663, this
chief entrepôt of the Mughal Empire counted one hundred thousand
inhabitants, making it one of the largest cities in the world.[1] A German
traveler who reached its shores in 1658 commented on its "glorious castle," its large market square, its "exceptionally beautiful gardens," and
the abundant fertile soil on its outskirts. It was, he said, one of the
"noblest trade cities in all of India."[2] When British missionary Edward
Terry arrived around the same time, he remarked that the area was a

"very goodly, large, and exceedingly rich province," with its merchants trading "to the Red Sea, to Achin, and to divers other places."[3]

Surat was a city of merchants. Traders crowded in its narrow lanes, purchasing textiles brought from rural producers near and far; dealing in diamonds, rubies, and manufactured wares made of iron and copper; selling wheat, indigo, tobacco, lentils, sugar, and opium; acquiring silver; and sending ships to Mocha and Mombasa, Java and the Moluccas, England and Japan. By the seventeenth century, it was said, dozens of ships traveled each year just between Surat and Mocha in today's Yemen. Gujarati traders provided cottons and silks to Arabian and East African markets; cloves and pepper came from the Moluccas. Others dealt in Persian rose water, pickles, and runa (a colorant). Malabar teak was in constant demand in Bahrain, used to expand and sustain pearl-fishing fleets. When pilgrims on their annual hajj to Mecca stopped in Surat, they exchanged vast amounts of silver for Indian textiles, providing a critical source of liquidity for traders. Surat's merchants had made the city a vital link in the trade between Southeast Asia and the Middle East. And by 1625, Surat was also the main center for trade between Gujarat and Europe.[4]

Surat's merchants were diverse: Gujarati, Persian, Ottoman, Portuguese, Armenian, French, English, and Arab traders mingled on its streets. Parsi merchants, such as broker and shipowner Rustom Manock, were an important presence as well. In 1612, the English opened a trading post there (a "factory," as it was then called) and were followed soon after by the Dutch and French, but trade remained largely under Muslim and Hindu control. In 1630, East India Company clerk Richard Booth complained that "base Banian [one merchant-heavy caste] brokers and zarofes [bankers] . . . governe the Companies affairs at their pleasure."[5] Fledgling European factories had little choice but to build on the trade networks that had existed long before their arrival. Gujarati merchants made the rules of trade.[6]

Fortunes accumulated. Surat merchant Mulla Abd al-Ghafur owned no fewer than twenty ships that plied the Indian Ocean. "There are People vastly rich in Surat," observed French traveler Jean de

*An island of capital: panoramic copper engraving of Surat in 1672 (variously
attributed to Philippus Baldaeus, Johan Nieuhof, and Jacob Koppmayer).*

Thévenot during his 1666 stay, "and a Banian a Friend of mine, called
Vargivora [Virji Vora], is reckoned to be worth at least eight Millions
[rupees]."[7] With their palatial dwellings and many ships, Surat's
wealthiest families compared favorably with their Cairene and Genoese counterparts. One of them, the Chalebis, were Ottoman Turks
who arrived at Surat when merchant-scholar Sidi Ali Reis Chelebi dis-
embarked on its shores in 1553, and they quickly established themselves as one of the richest families in the city—part of a large and
influential trading diaspora that dealt in ever increasing quantities of
sugar and tobacco, among other commodities. Mohammad Chelebi,
who led the family in the late seventeenth century, joined with other
Ottoman merchants to dominate not just Surat's trade but also its lavish civic life. Building extravagant mansions on the outskirts of the
city, the family excelled at creating exquisite gardens meant to impress
their guests, not least of whom were Mughal government officials.[8]

A s we have seen, islands of capital-rich merchants, epitomized by places like Surat, had dotted the globe for centuries. In the sixteenth and seventeenth centuries, they grew in size, wealth, and power and spread to new regions. After a harvest-limiting little ice age and a fourteenth-century plague epidemic that swept across Eurasia, populations and tradable surpluses rebounded. Gujarati, Arab, European, African, and Chinese merchants led yet another global acceleration of trade, exchanging ever more goods over ever longer distances. The rapidly expanding top layer of merchants focused as before on long-range trade and finance. While the value of goods traded across long distances remained, in quantitative terms, much less than that of things produced and consumed locally, it allowed for flexibility and large, concentrated investments, and, as a result, unprecedented accumulation, none of which was yet possible in agriculture or industry.[9] To be sure, the vast majority of humans continued to dwell and work in the world's countryside, bound in unequal vassalage to local lords, chiefs, and religious authorities or living in self-sufficient communities of subsistence farmers. Yet despite their relatively small numbers, the Chalebis and traders like them marked a notable uptick in the expansion rate of the archipelago of capital created over the prior five hundred years.

Wherever we look, we find evidence of such intensifying trade. As in earlier centuries, Muslim traders, now often Ottomans, plied old trade routes to enlarge their businesses. In Cairo, merchant Abu Taqiyya expanded his sugar trade with cities such as Istanbul, Mecca, and Jeddah. In the Iranian city of Isfahan, Persian, Indian, and Armenian merchants traded with renewed vigor. By the mid-sixteenth century, merchants in Damascus imported ever more coffee from Yemen, shipped to the city by camel caravan. Nearby Aleppo expanded as an important trading hub that connected the Ottoman Empire to India, and a French merchant told of caravans up to fifteen thousand camels

Intensifying commerce: Baghdad on the Tigris River, 1690.

strong, all crossing the desert loaded with the riches of the East: spices, cottons, and silk. Arab merchants in Ottoman lands became wealthy from organizing such trade, as showcased by the fact that some of the world's largest cities were still there: not just Damascus and Aleppo but Cairo and Baghdad. In that latter city, a visiting London merchant observed in 1583 the "great traffike of strangers," while German physician and botanist Leonhard Rauwolf marveled at "all sorts of merchandizes, whereof many ship-loads are brought in daily . . . thither by sea as well as by land from several parts, chiefly from Anatolia, Syria, Armenia, Constantinople, Aleppo, Damascus, &c. to carry them farther into the Indies, Persia, &c."[10] He recounted how, "on the second day of December, in 1574 there arrived twenty five ships with spice and other precious drugs here, which came over sea from the Indies, by the way of Ormutz to Basara . . . where they load their goods into small vessels, and so bring them to Bagdat, which journey, as some say, taketh them up forty days."[11] Basra, down the Tigris from Baghdad, was again a major trading city, and when French merchant Jean-Baptiste Tavernier arrived there in the mid-seventeenth century, he described it in terms that would have rung familiar to any merchant:

The Prince of Balsara has entered into leagues with several strange Nations, so that whencesoever you come, you may be welcome. There is so much liberty and so good order in the City, that you may walk all night long in the streets without molestation. The Hollanders bring spices thither every year. The English carry Pepper and some few Cloves. . . . The Indians bring Calicuts, Indigo, and all sorts of Merchandize. In short, there are merchants of all countries, from Constantinople, Smyrna, Aleppo, Damascus, Cairo, and other parts of Turkie, to buy such Merchandizes as come from the Indies, with which they lade the young Camels which they buy in that place; for thither the Arabians bring them to put them to sale.[12]

Caravans made up of as many as seven hundred camels frequented the city from Syria, freighted with gold, currency, textiles, and spices.[13]

Farther east, merchants like those we visited in Surat flourished too. As Scottish writer and geographer John Ogilby observed in 1673, the world's greatest trading communities continued to be found in Asia, a continent he considered "ennobled with several grand Prerogatives over the rest."[14] South Asian traders experienced a significant expansion of their business, their wealth, and their position in society, sending manufactured goods, especially cotton textiles, to the Red Sea, the Persian Gulf, Southeast Asia, East Africa, and Europe.[15]

Chinese commerce also prospered. As agriculture and manufacturing expanded, a growing merchant class distributed goods within the empire and beyond. Some of China's merchants became rich and powerful. As the official Xie Zhaozhe reported in 1616:

If we were to name those recognized as the richest families of all, one would have to propose the Huizhou merchants in the south, and the Shanxi merchants in the north. The great merchants of Huizhou trade in fish and salt, amassing fortunes measured in the millions of silver taels; those worth 200,000–300,000 taels could only be considered merchants of middling rank. Shanxi merchants deal in salt and silk, some traveling afar to peddle their goods while others pile up stocks of grain. Their wealth exceeds that of the Huizhou merchants, because while the latter are spendthrift, the Shanxi merchants are frugal.[16]

The salt merchants of Yangzhou became the empire's leading capitalists. Their monopoly on salt was broken up into sectors, with some controlling salt mines and the labor to work them, some controlling the salt trade, and some controlling both. East central China had about thirty such capitalists. The truly large operators became very rich, with some earning 1.5 to 2 million taels per year (the equivalent of between 555 and 740 kilograms of silver, worth between $560,000 and $750,000 in October 2024). And like their Florentine or Samarkand counterparts, they supported scholars, poets, and artists. The significant expansion of trade and commercialization made cities grow and swelled merchant communities. Maritime trade also picked up again, especially after the Qing reopened ports to private trade. Between 1684 and 1724, more than one thousand Chinese vessels went to Nagasaki alone. In short, China was perhaps more commercialized than any other country.[17]

On the far eastern edge of Asia, Japanese merchants also experienced growth. Profits from silver mining allowed for the consolidation of a

Ma Yueguan, leader of the salt merchants from Anhui Province who did business in Yangzhou. Portrait by Fang Shishu (1692–1751).

thriving community of merchants and the creation of a highly commercialized economy. Especially during the seventeenth-century Genroku era (1688–1703), newly powerful merchants emerged, among them Mitsui Takatoshi and the Sumitomo and Konoike families. Concentrated in Kansai and Edo (present-day Tokyo), they traded in rice, salt, fabrics, and hardware. The city of Osaka boomed as a rice market, with its merchants financing trade and making loans to local rulers.[18]

African merchants intensified their trade as well. Their far-flung networks intersected with a greater European presence on the coast but just as often had nothing to do with Europeans. When Soninke women produced cottons dyed in indigo, merchants traded them across the Sahara and into the Atlantic world.[19] African merchants catered to the tastes and needs of local consumers as much as they sold African-made goods such as gold objects—and enslaved people—into global markets.

Many more examples for such intensifying trade could be cited—but the central point is this: the sphere of capital and capitalists remained global. When Tomé Pires, the first European ambassador to the Chinese emperor, traveled to India in 1511 and then wrote his

Detail from a portrait depicting merchant Zheng Chenggong, also known as Koxinga (1624–1662).

Suma Oriental, he aptly captured this broadening circuit of commodities and the traders who made it possible:

> The merchants from Cairo bring the merchandise which comes from Italy and Greece and Damascus to Aden, such as gold, silver, quicksilver, vermillion, copper, rosewater, camlets, scarlet-in-grain, colored woolen cloth, glass beads, weapons, and things of that kind. [The merchants of] Aden bring the abovementioned goods with the addition of madder, raisins, opium, rosewater, quantities of gold and silver, and horses that Aden gets from Zeila and Berbera and the islands of Suakin, in the Strait, and from Arabia, and they come to do business in Cambay. They take back with them all the products of Malacca: cloves, nutmeg, mace, sandalwood, brazilwood, silks, seed pearls, musk, porcelain, and other things which may be found in the [list of] merchandise from Malacca, as well as the following from the country itself: rice, wheat, soap, indigo, butter [and lard], oils, carnelians, coarse pottery like that from Seville, and all kinds of cloth, for trading in Zeila, Berbera, Sokotra, Kilwa, Malindi, Mogadishu, and other places in Arabia. And this trade is carried out by ships from Aden and ships from Cambay, many of one and many of the other.[20]

One of the vectors through which this great connecting deepened was the global mobility of merchant communities themselves. As merchant networks expanded, they did not just trade with distant places—they moved to them. Chinese merchants were particularly mobile, creating mercantile diasporas throughout North, East, and Southeast Asia—in Manila, Jakarta, Nagasaki, Batavia, Banten, Ayudhya, Malacca, and Makassar. The island of Taiwan became such an important destination for mainland merchants that the powerful Zheng family—which controlled many ships and produced massive annual profits (between eighty-five and one hundred tons of silver in the mid-seventeenth century, equivalent to between $75 million and $86 million in 2024 US dollars)—relocated their business to the island, expelling the Dutch in the process. From there, they traded to ports all over East Asia.[21]

After 1500, diasporic communities began cropping up across the

Islands of capital, East Africa: Suaquem (Suakin) and its islands, as seen by Portuguese naval officer and navigator João de Castro in the early 1500s.

world. Ottoman merchants settled not just in Surat, as we have seen, but in Diu and Calicut, on Sumatra and Java, and in Florence and Venice. South Asian merchants spread out as well: Having traded with Africa since the fourth century, they settled in Mombasa and all along Africa's east coast, as well as in Iran, the Ottoman Empire, and across Southeast Asia and the Red Sea, using inventive financial tools—ranging from mortgages to futures contracts—to convey goods and treasure across vast distances. Later, Banian traders from Diu Island on the Gujarati coast settled on Mozambique Island, where they built dynamic exchanges around Indian textiles, African elephant tusks, and enslaved women, men, and children. Other merchant communities scattered too: Persian merchants formed trading diasporas across the Indian Ocean—from South to Southeast Asia and into Eastern Africa. In West Africa, Dyula merchants built new commercial hubs, for example, in Bitu, a center of trade for the Abron (Brong) people in what is now Ghana. With an environment that stimulated trade, Kano attracted foreign traders, especially Bagauda and Wangara immigrants from the kingdoms of Borno and Mali.[22]

European merchant communities migrated within the archipelago of capital as well: Venetian traders congregated throughout the eastern Mediterranean, from Istanbul to Alexandria. In 1555, English merchants organized the Muscovy Company and established communities in Russia. English merchants also built trading communities in various parts of Africa: The Company of Merchants Trading to Guinea established trading stations in Komenda, Kormantin, and Winneba in the 1630s. By 1650, three additional "factories" were established in Anomabu (1639), Takoradi (1645), and Cabo Corso (1650), all places with long-established African merchant communities. As Portuguese traders expanded into Atlantic Africa in the second half of the fifteenth century, they founded entrepôts in places such as Axim, Mouri, Accra, and along the Volta River. They dealt with local merchants and married into the most influential trading families from Senegambia to Sierra Leone. There, women played a crucial role in connecting merchant communities across cultural barriers and, in the process, secured access to waterways linking the coasts to the hinterlands.[23]

Everywhere, dense multinational nodes formed as a result of these diasporic communities. When European merchants struck out for Asia, they met communities of equally expansive Chinese, South Asian, and Ottoman merchants. Portuguese and Chinese merchants met in Malacca; Surat, as we have seen, facilitated exchanges between Gujarati, European, and Ottoman traders, and Mombasa was a meeting ground for Gujarati, Swahili, and European merchants.[24]

Without this vast pool of capital and capitalists that had coalesced over centuries across the globe, the energy that was about to revolutionize the world would have been absent.[25] Like a gathering hurricane whirling across the warm waters of the Caribbean, capital gained energy in the great connecting. Yet even then, it was not enough to break out of the old order.

The global intensification of trade was impressive, as was the mobility of merchant communities within this archipelago of capital. Yet it leaves us with a sense of déjà vu. After all, how different was sixteenth-century Surat from twelfth-century Aden? There was more trade, to be sure. There were more merchants. But trade structure and merchant activities were much like what had existed before. At first glance, this was a change in quantity, not quality. If things had kept changing in this way, the archipelago of capital might have continued to expand and contract on the margins of economic life for a long time, changing cast and stage without escaping its subordinate place, dammed up by popular and elite resistance and its fateful collision with some of the most fundamental pillars of the ideological—that is, religious—order. The merchants of sixteenth-century Surat, Cairo, Florence, and Guangzhou had little reason to assume that economic life was on the verge of its most dramatic shape-shift since the advent of sedentary agriculture.[26]

Yet this is exactly what happened. In the fifteenth century, a small subset of capital owners burst out of their island fortresses. They altered the archipelago of capital not just by doing more of the same but by moving in radically different directions. Although these changes were at first slow, across three centuries, capital owners made capital ever more central to economic life, until one day it was no longer relegated to outsider islands—it constituted the whole sea.[27]

At the core of this departure was a small slice of the world's merchants in a few European cities. They built new nodes of capital that were dramatically different from what had been forged before. They integrated these nodes with one another in hierarchical ways, and in the process, they created a world economy. Enabled by this great connecting, they pushed, as we will see later, their capital into production—both agriculture and manufacturing. By the nineteenth century, they had changed the world so drastically that when contemporaries sought to name the form of economic life these merchants had created, the obvious choice was *capitalism*. Its roots, however, predated by centuries most of what we associate with it—its name, the beginning of modern machine production, the emergence of massive factories, and the mobilization of millions of wage laborers.

The capitalism that we know originated in the great connecting during what scholars have called the long sixteenth century, the period between about 1450 and 1640.

Let us begin with the great connecting itself before moving on to its impact on agriculture and industry. At the heart of the emergence of capitalism were dozens or hundreds of new islands of capital scattered across the globe: Cape Verde and Potosí; Santo Domingo and Calcutta; the southern English countryside; and Salvador, Danzig, and Gorée. Clustered throughout the Atlantic world (and more modestly in Asia), they were created by adventurous capitalists and European states that—first tentatively, then voraciously—pursued a breakout strategy centered on spreading the archipelago of capital and, by doing so, accessing new hinterlands, new commodity frontiers, and new pools of labor.[28] As we will see, these novel islands of capital emerged from a peculiar intersection between merchants escaping their fortresses and states wishing to escape the crisis of tributary (feudal) rule by expanding into new areas of the world—an intersection of interests and inclinations that materialized only in a few parts of the world.[29]

It began with the expansion of Europe's most developed nodes of capital—the Italian city-states. Genoese merchants built the model that others followed: Like other European merchants, they had made their riches in the East, trading with the Muslim world. Yet as early as the thirteenth century, Venetian trade prowess excluded them from this profitable realm and forced them to turn west and south, intensifying their presence on the Iberian Peninsula and in North and West Africa. Two Genoese sailors, Ugolino and Vadino Vivaldi, journeyed far down the African coast as early as 1291. (They were never heard from again.) In trying to bypass powerful Muslim merchants in the Sahara, Genoese merchants traveled farther into the Atlantic and down the western coast of Africa. The extremely wealthy Centurione family exemplifies this reorientation: They started out trading on the eastern Mediterranean islands of Chios and Cyprus before moving some of their capital into the African gold trade. As they and other Genoese traders pushed into the Atlantic, they settled in Madeira and the Canaries, island groups off Africa's western coast. From these outposts, they traded African gold, sugar, slaves, and other commodities.[30]

One key to the Genoese merchants' success was the way they came to draw on state power. They dominated their small Italian city-state—not only did they rule Genoa's formal colonies directly, but they also enjoyed privileged access to the offices of the state, a position they continued to hold more informally even after the constitutional reforms of 1528. As they began dominating European finance from this basis, they built coalitions with larger but less capitalized territorial states, especially the Portuguese crown. It was this alliance between Genoese capital and Portuguese state power that pushed down the West African coast in search of easier access to the gold that Muslim traders had been bringing north through the Sahara for centuries. By the 1470s, they arrived at what Europeans came to call the "Gold Coast," today's Ghana. They built a permanent outpost there, Elmina, the first of sixty forts that Europeans constructed over the next three centuries along the African coast, where they exchanged textiles and metals for gold. Genoese traders gained access to massive amounts of gold, which in turn helped to commercialize the European economy. Portugal minted a new gold coin, the cruzado, in 1457, and between 1480 and 1500, the money from the trade at Elmina alone doubled Portugal's royal revenues. As this "river of gold" flowed in, Portugal imported massive amounts of grains from the Baltic states via Dutch intermediaries. The newfound wealth also financed ship construction in Portugal that made further exploration possible.[31] So significant was African gold that the Portuguese king of the time, João II (1455–1495), was called "João the African."

Quickly, yet more opportunities emerged: In 1460, Antonio de Noli, a Genoese businessman traveling to the west coast of Africa to trade Portuguese horses for enslaved workers, spotted a group of islands that came to be known as Cape Verde. It was a fateful encounter: As these islands were uninhabited, controlling the dry, rugged lands was straightforward and inexpensive. Immediately, they struck some traders as ideal places to begin planting high-demand commodities such as sugar and cotton. To secure labor and provide collateral for the loans that had made the project possible in the first place, these settlers ratcheted up the trade for enslaved workers from Africa's coast—about 350 miles distant—with as many as one thousand slaves arriving annually by the 1490s. A plantation complex emerged on Cape Verde with particular ease, because neither the commercialization of land nor that of labor met resistance from local commoners or elites, who elsewhere would have certainly tried to erect roadblocks. Unsurprisingly, by 1485, the Genoese sugar complex expanded to yet another island, São Tomé.[32]

But then even greater riches beckoned on the horizon: As the Genoese and Portuguese kept moving farther down the African coast, they hoped to find a way to circumnavigate the continent, to locate a hidden sea route to Asia that did not depend on Arab intermediaries. And when they succeeded, in 1498, it became access to "the most memorable thing that has happened in the world for many centuries," in the words of sixteenth-century Florentine historian Francesco Guicciardini.[33]

The riches generated by this alliance between the Portuguese crown and wealthy Genoese merchants did not go unnoticed. Forging novel islands of capital became infectious. Spain, Portugal's competitor (and sometime partner, as between 1580 and 1640) on the Iberian Peninsula, quickly followed suit, with Italian and southern German mercantile support. Like their Portuguese counterparts, the Spaniards pushed into Atlantic Africa, accessing gold, growing sugar, enslaving people, and seeking novel routes to Asian trading ports. To further the latter project, the Spanish crown took a decisive new step, pointing its ships, captained by Genoese merchant Christopher Columbus, westward. The vessels, a carrack and two caravels, left Seville in 1492, looking for more direct access to the rich Asian trade but instead finding a

Departure of a Portuguese fleet from Lisbon to India (1592).

continent that was entirely unknown to Europeans. Riding the coattails of a potent new mix of concentrated capital and nascent territorial
statehood on a large scale, Columbus and his imitators captured more
and more of the Americas for the Iberian monarchs, a breakthrough
moment if ever there was one. European control of the Atlantic, this
"great ocean," was what gave the capitalist revolution its European flavor and made possible Europe's global ascendance.[34] The Iberian empires and Italian merchants were central to that rise.[35] It was not
coincidental that the continents themselves came to be named for an
Italian trader—Amerigo Vespucci, who departed from Cádiz for South
America in 1497 on behalf of the Spanish crown.

In Spain, as in Portugal, imperial expansion produced immense
wealth. At the same time, Iberian trade with Africa and the Americas
stimulated northern European economies that provided high-demand
textiles, metal goods, and wheat, eventually propelling their capital
owners and states to build new islands of capital as well.

First came the Netherlands: By the late sixteenth century, this

Liaison dangereuse: *Capital and state power merge. Christopher Columbus, around 1520.*

province of the Spanish Empire was already unusually urbanized, combining commercialized domestic agriculture and vibrant proto-industry with a dynamic trade sector. Its merchants skimmed substantial margins off the Iberian bounty of gold, silver, and sugar coming into its ports, exchanging them for Baltic grain and goods produced in its manufacturing sector, especially textiles. Strengthened by trade, Dutch merchants revolted against their Spanish overlords in 1566. Though the war lasted until 1581, the Dutch eventually created a small but powerful independent republic principally characterized by merchants' control of political power. Already by 1600, trade exploded, as nineteen hundred Dutch ships sailed the oceans. That global presence motivated and enabled merchants to build new nodes of capital across the world, from the southern cape of Africa to Guyana in Latin America, from the Caribbean to Batavia in today's Indonesia. So precocious and impressive was that expansion that Karl Marx described the seventeenth-century Dutch Republic, with its leading city, Amsterdam, as the "model capitalist nation."[36]

Other European merchants and states followed suit, albeit less spectacularly. By the end of the sixteenth century, following the collapse of the Venetian Empire, English merchants, who had been mostly marginal to the empire of capital, began visiting the Greek isles and the Levant. In 1592, the British Levant Company began acquiring raw silk, cottons, woolens, currants, nutmeg, pepper, indigo, galls, camlets, maroquins, and soda ash, much of it from South and Southeast Asia. In

New European islands of capital in Asia: Dutch East India Company
(VOC) factory in Hooghly (now Hugli), West Bengal, 1665.

return, the English traded shortclothes, kerseys, tin, pewter, lead, and, later, cochineal, and American silver. Learning from Dutch successes, English merchants in the beginning of the seventeenth century struck out to more distant locations as well, trading with Asia beginning in the late sixteenth century. Aided in 1603 by the Union of the Crowns of Scotland and England, Britain also moved into the Atlantic. The first doomed attempts, exemplified by the famously (and mysteriously) failed Roanoke Colony, were unsuccessful, but a more lasting outpost followed in 1607 in Jamestown, Virginia, followed by settlements throughout what came to be known as New England, the Bahamas, Bridgetown, Barbados, and other places in North America. Even though the British expansion was at first marginal and weak compared with its Iberian counterparts, it grew in scale and importance. In the first three decades of the seventeenth century, roughly fifty thousand British subjects migrated to new settlements along the eastern coast of North America and in the Caribbean.[37]

Throughout the long sixteenth century, the archipelago of capital metastasized as island after island was added: Santo Domingo (by Spain) in 1516, Macau (by Portugal) in 1557, Batavia (by the Dutch) in

Peopling the great connecting, colonial trade opens new opportunities. Aelbert Cuyp, VOC Senior Merchant with His Wife and an Enslaved Servant, *circa 1650–1655. The merchant is probably Jakob Martensen.*

1619, Manhattan (also by the Dutch) in 1624, Barbados (by the British) in 1627, Saint-Louis, Senegal (by the French) in 1659, and many, many more.[38] Much more can be said about European expansion, but the main point for our purposes is that this new archipelago was different—not just because of its size but because within it, merchant communities were more influential than the forces that had historically counterbalanced their economic logic: the religious authorities who belabored the corrupting effects of commerce; the cultivators who defended their subsistence production and access to the commons; and the agrarian elites who protected their privileges, including their ability to extract revenue from their subordinates. Crucially enabled by "the discovery of America, and that of a passage to the East Indies by the Cape of Good Hope," which Smith called "the two greatest and most important events recorded in the history of mankind," European merchants could push their capital and power ever deeper into the vast hinterlands of subsistence production and independent producers and their dependents.[39] They defeated resistances and some of the ecological constraints that had previously inhibited economic life.[40] And, as we will see later, in this new formulation of capital, a select few merchant communities also concentrated unprecedented amounts of capital on a radical series of gambles that revolutionized production.

As European capital owners put all their chips—their fortunes, ships, and networks—behind this emergent form of economic life, they upset ancient global hierarchies. Their ability to break out was not the outcome of unbridgeable divergences of skills, beliefs, quantities of capital, or technological prowess. Europe instead owed its development to a state-facilitated set of mutually reinforcing connections between islands of capital and the often violent transfer of resources (including human beings) from many corners of the world. In the process of building these new islands of capital, merchants redoubled their connections, creating a network of trade and capital unlike anything the world had seen before and playing a key role in the emergence of a new kind of state. It was in that cauldron that capitalism emerged.

⸻

The torrential breakout of European capital was extraordinary— both from a historical perspective and as measured against other parts of the contemporaneous world. It was also surprising. After all, merchant communities with equally functional institutions and just as much dynamism—both earlier (twelfth-century Cairo) and contemporaneously (sixteenth-century Guangzhou)—saw nothing like the economic revolution unfolding in the European-dominated archipelago of capital. Why did it happen there and then? There are three main reasons, all rooted, ironically, in the prior relative weakness of European nodes of capital and the relatively fractured nature of European states. Europeans, as one group of scholars has put it, enjoyed the "privilege of historic backwardness."[41]

First, European capital owners forged new islands of capital because they had great incentives to do so. When the Ottomans defeated the Byzantines in 1453 and made Constantinople the capital of the empire, Italian merchants saw diminished access to the lucrative trade routes to India and China, the world's most dynamic economies and the source of much of the wealth of Europe's first generations of capitalists. To get around increasingly assertive Islamic middlemen, these merchants sought new trade routes to the East—a step made more urgent because their rivals, especially in England and the Dutch Republic, received so-called capitulations that gave them trading privileges in the Ottoman sphere of influence. The northern Italians rechanneled their mercantile energies to the Atlantic to access African gold as well as Asian spices and textiles, agreeing with seventeenth-century English political economist Charles Davenant that to control trade with Asia was to "give law to all the commercial world."[42]

Second, these capital-rich merchants were ruled by states facing a seemingly intractable crisis in the system of tributary rule they had constructed over the past millennium. As early as the thirteenth century, feudal lords who had to support retainers and engage in warfare had amped up the pressure on peasants, resulting in widespread desertion and frequent rebellions. Then, the devastating effects of the fourteenth-century plague and the resulting sharp population decline (about one-third of the European population died) brought labor shortages that exacerbated the decay of the feudal order. As lords were forced to pay wages to get access to labor, they further undermined their ancient prerogatives of drawing resources based on custom rather than market exchanges. Higher labor costs (wages almost doubled) and lowered feudal rents, combined with feudal society's wasteful use of resources and inability to increase productivity, meant that feudal society commercialized, with market production becoming more prominent, further undermining the dynamics of this ancient economic organization. Efforts to shore up the old order actually weakened it even more. Towns—islands of capital and capitalists—acted as a solvent for feudalism, as lords drew on their support in a rearguard action to save the system of rule and exploitation that they had crafted.[43]

Third, European feudal elites urgently sought new resources to fund the escalating costs of widespread warfare. They could see the advantages of access to new sources of income, ecological resources, labor, and precious metals from other regions of the world—a "fix" that drove them straight into the arms of merchants, giving traders new economic, social, and political sway. Some aristocrats even began engaging in trade to fill their coffers: In Spain and England, they embraced the wool trade, developing overlapping interests with merchant communities. As labor shortages made it harder to control rural producers or extract revenue, feudal elites also capitalized the countryside (by converting forests into pastures, for example).[44] Another response to feudal crisis was imperial expansion. The trade with Asia loomed especially large: More direct access to India and China via a new sea route would allow European rulers to capture more of that wealth—and thus support their system of rule.

As a result of these mutually reinforcing dilemmas, the drive to expand the archipelago of capital and state power joined capital-rich European merchants and states in a union of mutual dependence. As European states expanded into new areas of the world, they intersected with the interests of capital owners, for whom expansion brought not only new opportunities for accumulation but also a way to circumvent the resistances they had long encountered. The relative weakness of European states and capitalists on the global stage drove them closer to one another and toward a consensus on projecting their power and capital into novel spaces and constructing entirely new islands of capital. They were greatly aided in this project of conquest by the fact that the resistance they encountered in the Americas was easily overcome by a combination of more advanced weaponry and introduced European viruses, which devastated Indigenous populations and their empires.

Among these new European-built islands of capital, few were as consequential as Potosí, which was not an island at all but a mountain high in the Andes. Located in what is today Bolivia, Potosí became one of the world's most significant sources of silver, "the richest [silver mine] which [has] been known in the world," according to Adam Smith.[45] Having plundered the gold and silver of Incan, Aztecan, and other Indigenous rulers, European colonists in Latin America turned toward mining. By 1600, Potosí had become the biggest city in the Americas and one of the largest in the world, more populous than London, Milan, or Seville. One hundred and sixty thousand Andean, African, and European inhabitants labored in what has been called the "first city of capitalism," mining huge quantities of silver that made the city's market so opulent that it offered costly sugar, spices, and wine, despite the difficulty of transporting them twelve thousand feet above sea level. Potosí soon saw a kind of premature flowering of a capitalist society, in which everything that was produced or consumed was exchanged on markets. Wealthy Potosíans could buy Ceylonese diamonds, Neapolitan stockings, Venetian crystal, and Chinese porcelain—and attend services at ostentatious churches and shows at an opulent theater, the Coliseo de Comedias, which had its grand opening in 1716. Potosí was, according to Emperor Charles V, the "treasury of the world."[46]

Huge quantities of silver—more than 151 million pesos' worth from 1556 to 1783—flowed out of the mountain and into the smelters, then onto huge packtrains that lumbered the heavy, valuable loads to the Peruvian ports of Callao and what is now known as Buenos Aires, a city whose adjacent river was, for good reason, called Río de la Plata—river of silver. By the second half of the sixteenth century, Potosí produced perhaps 60 percent of the world's silver: seventeen thousand tons in that century (the equivalent of $13 billion in 2024 US dollars), thirty-four thousand tons ($27 billion in 2024 US dollars) in the seventeenth, and fifty-one thousand tons ($40 billion in 2024 US dollars) in the eighteenth.[47]

As in almost all the new islands of capital, laboring in Potosí was extraordinarily brutal: Gains from silver mining were quite literally achieved by killing the miners. As many as 25 percent of the workers drawn into the mines died there. Laborers were recruited to the remote

*High tech in a sky-high city, Potosí, 1585: Andean miners digging
for the silver that greased the wheels of the world economy.*

Andean highlands via a peculiar system of forced labor—the *mita*,
which intersected with and built upon an older Incan system of taxation and workforce mobilization. Up to fifty thousand workers came to
Potosí annually, creating huge financial gains for mining entrepreneurs
and the Spanish crown. Miners carried hundred-pound loads of ore up
dangling rope ladders, climbing both sides of the ladders at once. After
mercury amalgamation—a chemical process that separated the silver
from the rocks in which it was embedded—revolutionized the mining
industry by allowing for the profitable processing of large amounts of
low-grade ore, the already horrific working conditions worsened. The
two hundred tons of mercury that were used annually between 1580
and 1640 to extract silver from ore poisoned the workers, causing their
hair and teeth to fall out and bringing on uncontrollable trembling. In
the mercury mines of Huancavelica, Indigenous Peruvian miners
hauled ore through cramped tunnels with almost no ventilation, while
the internal heat of the mines vaporized the mercury and slowly poisoned them. Even in cooler areas, miners created a fog of mercury,

sulfur, arsenic, and silica just by hacking at ore with their picks. Not surprisingly, Potosí came to be known as "the mountain that eats men," with tens or even hundreds of thousands of Indigenous people dying there to fund Europeans' new, exalted position in the archipelago of capital. The mountain that ate men provided one of the essential fuels that powered capitalism's emergence.[48]

———

Potosí, Cape Verde, Manila, Santo Domingo, Malacca, Gorée, Batavia, Rio de Janeiro, Mexico City, and New Amsterdam, among others, became new islands within the now sprawling archipelago of capital. While these places all engaged in trade and production under the auspices of merchant capital and European states, they were diverse: Some focused on mining, some on the production of agricultural commodities, mobilization of enslaved workers, and trade in precious metals, manufactured goods, or crops and fibers sold by local merchants. As merchants and states expanded their archipelago, these islands strengthened one another, each one infusing energy into the entire network. However disparate and distant, these profit foundries heralded a fundamentally new state of things. Their very diversity created the dynamic that came to characterize the revolution in economic life.

A closer look at Cape Verde shows some of these complementarities. As the island drew on slave labor from the nearby African mainland to grow sugar, local merchants discovered that they could also deliver that labor to far-flung places in the Americas, which suddenly had an extensive need for workers. The first shipment of enslaved workers was requested by Santo Domingo authorities as early as 1517. Fatefully, slaving quickly became more profitable than planting. In the following years, merchants established a regular trade with their West African counterparts for Wolof and Serer captives who were trafficked to New Spain and Cartagena. After 1540, the trade accelerated, and between 1541 and 1594, Cape Verdean merchants traded seventy-five thousand enslaved Africans to the Americas, mostly to work in the emerging sugar industry. Trading in humans became a specialized business dominated by Portuguese and Spanish merchants—a hideous frontier of capital that delivered the living labor used to make other new islands of capital in the Americas profitable. Some families became big players in this labor commodity frontier: Florentine merchant Cesare de Barchi, for example, sold thousands of Wolof people into slavery in the late 1400s, with his agents organizing the business from bases on Cape Verde. A few decades later, merchant (and Cape Verdean governor) Fernam de Mello became one of the most prolific slave traders. The Bento Rodrigues family received a royal privilege to enter the slave trade in 1550, and it stayed in the family for at least three generations. As merchants turned Cape Verde into a "[g]igantic holding pen," they helped power the unprecedently dynamic new commodity frontiers throughout the Atlantic world. Trading in workers allowed for significant accumulation of wealth and made slave traders the elite of Cape Verde. By the 1550s, that cluster of islands played a central role in Atlantic commerce, attaining one of the fastest ascents of any node in the archipelago of capital, and it kept this role until 1600, when larger ships skipped over Cape Verde and transported captives directly from Africa to the Americas.[49]

The experience there taught capital owners a new and sinisterly consequential lesson: In zones from which escape was difficult and where no competing political authorities existed, a small number of Europeans could control large numbers of enslaved Africans. Imprisoning laborers, in fact, enabled entirely new forms of the productive uses of capital, sundered from worldly and religious authorities and from the common autonomies of rural cultivators the world over. And slavery was profitable enough to capitalize Atlantic expansion more generally. This fateful application of the merchants' basic logic to labor would become a crucial factor in the capitalist transformation of the world's countryside.[50]

Another set of complementarities, just as important, comes to light when taking a closer look at Potosí. This mining complex mattered not just for the wealth it produced but for the boost it gave to trade. So important was it that the entire period of its influence has been characterized as the era of "silver capitalism." American silver, which became a sort of lingua franca for capitalism, quickened European trade, thereby transforming Europe's countryside and its manufacturing sector. As Spain used the silver extracted from the Americas to acquire wheat, copper, tin, wood, hemp, linen, and high-quality woolens from northern Europe, it stimulated agriculture and industry, and American silver accumulated in northern European markets such as Antwerp. Silver payments for grain linked eastern European wheat producers to western European cities. Moreover, by the late 1550s, Genoese banking had expanded because Genoa's merchants controlled so much of the silver flowing from Latin America. Silver also enabled European merchants to intensify their trade with Asia, which had little interest in most European-made products. The Spanish crown became completely dependent on the precious metal for its ever more ostentatious state, its colonial adventures, and, not least, for paying the interest on its loans from Italian and German bankers.[51] Silver, in short, enabled Spain's trade with the rest of Europe, not to mention its spectacularly intense and long-lasting warfare with France, the Dutch provinces, the Ottoman Empire, and many others.

The impact on Asia was just as momentous: More than one-third of all silver mined in Latin America ended up in Asia. As the French writer Guillaume Thomas François Raynal (known by his clerical title, Abbé Raynal) observed in the eighteenth century, "India has always swallowed the world's resources. . . . Silver still takes the same route at present. It flows continuously from the Occident to the heart of the Orient. . . . It is thus for the Indies that the mines of Peru are opened. It is thus for the Indians that the Europeans have sullied themselves with so many crimes in America."[52] By the middle of the fifteenth century, moreover, the depreciation of Ming China's paper money prompted Emperor Jiajing to require that silver be used in international trade and the payment of taxes. The burgeoning Chinese population

Gorging on silver: the custodia del Corpus Christi *(monstrance) at* Catedral de la Santa Cruz *in Cádiz, Spain.*

also created a huge demand for silver, making it worth twice as much there as elsewhere.[53]

Demand for silver in South Asia, as Raynal had suggested, was almost as insatiable. As in China, the new availability of silver resulted in rapid commercialization of large sectors of South Asia's economy. Silver even became central to the expansion of Gujarati trade on the East African coast: Cotton cloth could be sold in Africa for silver, which was in high demand in India and thus attractive to South Asian merchants. The African merchants had acquired that silver as payment for the captives they sold to Portuguese and other slave traders. As it fed the global economy, the silver-based Spanish peso became a universal currency—the dollar of the sixteenth century—replacing the formerly dominant Arab dinar. Silver lubricated commercial exchanges seemingly everywhere. It created the monetary basis—the lifeblood—that sped up trade in Europe, Africa, and Asia, as well as between Europe and Asia (especially the three centers of the world economy: the Levant, India, and China). It was the availability of silver (and African gold) that eventually allowed commercial capital to penetrate the countryside.[54] These complementarities, of which there were many, show that capitalism was a coproduction between various regions of the world, between various social groups, and between state and capital.

Potosí and Cape Verde, although consequential, cannot alone explain the economic sea change that became visible in the long sixteenth century. But, cumulatively, the new and diverse nodes that emerged from the great connecting were crucial to launching the capitalist revolution, not least because these new islands of capital throughout the Atlantic world—and, to some extent, Asia—greatly strengthened islands of capital within Europe as well.

Consider Amsterdam, smack dab in the middle of the Amstel delta in the northwestern reaches of continental Europe. When Frenchman Charles Ogier arrived there in 1636, the city had about one hundred thousand inhabitants (fewer than Potosí), but the "plethora of artists and craftsmen, foreign and local merchants who flock here together" amazed him.[55] The port, he observed, was the "busiest of the entire ocean," and "everywhere one encounters curiosities and treasures from India, which either were bought from the Indian peoples or forcibly wrested from them."[56] In this city, he concluded, "one can buy anything"—a sentiment shared by diarist David Beck, for whom Amsterdam in 1624 "presents the world on a small scale."[57] In Amsterdam, almost all wealth derived from trade, the metropolis's merchants not just rich but powerful.[58]

In many ways, Amsterdam was the European counterpart to Surat. Like that city, its trade spanned the world. By the mid-seventeenth-century zenith of Dutch trading prowess, Amsterdam's merchants imported wood, iron, and copper from Scandinavia; shipped Brazilian and Caribbean sugar to European ports; and brought in spices and textiles from Asia. They imported much of the wheat harvest of eastern Europe, especially Poland, for reexport to Spain in return for American silver.[59] They reconstituted the Dutch countryside and built a dynamic manufacturing complex.

Like merchants everywhere, Dutch traders succeeded by connecting to remote producers and consumers across sharply divergent societies.

The city was marked by its dedication to trade, yet the absolute number of merchants at the top of its social hierarchy was small, perhaps as few as three hundred across the seventeenth century. These merchants monopolized lucrative trade connections and used their economic and political power to build an infrastructure conducive to trade. In the center of town, Dam Square, they constructed their city hall and put in its basement the safe of the Wisselbank, the world's first central bank, founded in 1609. Nearby were the Stadsbank van Lening, the Amsterdam Exchange, the corn exchange, and the navy headquarters, all facilitating trade. A global mindset suffused the city: When master carpenters Willem Ruysch and Isaac Lieuwens thought of names for an ensemble of four houses they had built, what came to mind were Africa, America, Asia, and Europe. The Dutch had built islands of capital on five continents, islands that were exceedingly consequential for the city. The fast-growing "rich trades" of high-value items (in contrast to the "bulk trades") with West Africa, the Caribbean, and Asia were integral to the most important merchants. Freedom of religion enhanced Amsterdam's ability to attract traders from everywhere; like their business partners in Surat or Aden, Amsterdam's were a cosmopolitan lot.[60]

Together, they made Europe's Surat into a quintessentially capitalist city, dominated by merchants, dedicated to trade, and drawing on wage labor. The government they built was responsive to their interests. Consumption was almost exclusively mediated by the market and not, as almost everywhere else on Earth, by subsistence production. Asian products—spices, textiles, porcelain, furniture—played a big role in how the Amsterdam elite presented themselves. The use of money in exchange (instead of in-kind transfers, driven by custom) was unexceptional and almost universal, a sign of how capital owners had broken through previously powerful barriers. Clocks became common. Not coincidentally, the concept of leisure time emerged alongside more exact working hours and with it the popping up of commercial venues where that time could be "spent."[61] Amsterdam's merchants, like their

Forging islands of capital: Amsterdam traders amass vast fortunes,
as seen by Rembrandt, 1662.

Potosí counterparts, had commercialized life so much that in 1668, Dutch author Adriaan Koerbagh lamented how "all the time spent differently from making money, no matter how it is spent, is (it seems) considered by people to be lost time."[62]

As these islands of capital multiplied and as the process of the great connecting quickened and the velocity of capital accelerated, European nodes within the archipelago of capital were vastly strengthened. This had enormous implications. Parts of Europe tightly connected to the Atlantic and Asia grew faster than places less connected to these geographies. From 1340 to 1850, European urbanization rates tripled in Atlantic-connected economies, while increasing by only 1.7 times in unconnected parts of western Europe. Colonial expansion of European capital did indeed make a definite difference, as Max Weber argued more than a century ago: "The acquisition of colonies by the European states led to a gigantic acquisition of wealth within Europe for all of them."[63] It was out of this breakthrough that global capitalism emerged.[64]

The reordering of global economic life had yet another major consequence: It encouraged the development of novel institutions. Pooling capital, transmitting it over long distances, and regulating trade through mercantile organizations were common practices; as we have seen, *hundis* and commendas helped merchants the world over. But as the archipelago of capital evolved in the sixteenth century, new institutions arose that helped European merchants break out of their island fortresses and laid the foundations for a politics that served their interests.[65]

To cite one of the most consequential departures: In the early seventeenth century, merchants in a few key European cities constructed a new way to pool capital—the joint-stock company. With their expansion into Africa, Asia, and the Americas, they created this new institutional form as a direct response to the unusual opportunities they glimpsed. Joint-stock companies first appeared in the United Provinces and England with the express purpose of initiating and organizing trade in new markets. They were so effective that they became a vehicle through which traders and rulers forged new islands of capital, solving a key limitation of all other forms of merchant capital's risk management by institutionalizing the integration of capital and state.[66]

Operating on the basis of shared trading capital, the English East India Company (EIC) and the Dutch East India Company, the Vereenigde Oost-Indische Compagnie (VOC), were established in 1600 and 1602, respectively. These competitors in the lucrative Asian spice trade both adapted the sixteenth-century Dutch *partenrederij* form of legal partnership to attract investors and accumulate capital. Queen Elizabeth I granted a royal charter to "George, Earl of Cumberland, and 215 Knights, Aldermen, and Burgesses" on December 31, 1600, under the name "Governor and Company of Merchants of London Trading with the East Indies," awarding the company a monopoly on trade with all countries east of the Cape of Good Hope and west of the Strait of Magellan for a period of fifteen years. Following on the trail of the Muscovy (1553) and Levant (1592) companies, the EIC at first attracted investors who had dealt in spices via the Arab world but had seen their businesses threatened by increasing European trade around the Cape of Good Hope. Initially, these merchants pooled their resources for single voyages, as the feasibility and profitability of such risky ventures had to be established before the merchants would commit to a more long-term use of their capital. The EIC expanded rapidly, with total imports and exports growing 2.2 percent annually between 1660 and 1760. It began in the spice trade—pepper, cloves, mace, and nutmeg. Later, Indian textiles became an ever more important part of the company's business; it sold them in the East Indies (to buy spices), throughout Africa, and in Europe. In 1685, the EIC also arrived in China, where it exchanged spices for tea. Eventually, it came to dominate almost half of the world's trade and assumed territorial control in parts of its trading empire; according to Edmund Burke, it became "a state in the guise of a merchant."[67] In time, this model spread to other groups of English traders, among them the Hudson's Bay, South Sea, and Royal African Companies, creating similar pools of capital to trade with still other parts of the world.[68]

The Dutch followed suit. Just two years after the creation of the East India Company, the Estates General of the United Provinces, the Dutch Republic's highest governing body, chartered the VOC and granted a twenty-one-year monopoly on the spice trade. The company, just like the EIC, was empowered to retain its own military forces, and to engage in diplomacy with Asian rulers. So successful was the VOC that it became "permanent" in 1610, gaining, like the EIC, legal personhood; these agglomerations of capital thus had a "life" divorced from that of any human being, a consequential innovation that would remain at the center of global capitalism into the twenty-first century. The VOC's dividend payments did not disappoint investors: 57.7 percent in 1612, 42.5 percent in 1613, and 62.5 percent in 1618—paid in cash or in goods such as cloves and nutmeg.[69]

As chartered companies pooled capital and mobilized it for the great connecting, stock exchanges began to emerge. For centuries,

Amsterdam Stock Exchange, 1634.

merchants had met to exchange goods at markets and trade fairs in Aleppo, Lyon, and Tenochtitlán, but now the world's first exchange dedicated to trading in financial instruments emerged in Amsterdam. Shares in the VOC began to be traded there in 1602, at first in the open air and then, in 1611, inside a building designated as a place to transact such business—what came to be known as a stock exchange. For its first century, this institution focused on the stock of just two companies: the VOC and the Geoctroyeerde Westindische Compagnie (West India Company), established in 1621. With a registered capital of more than six million guilders (equivalent to about $120 million in 2024 US dollars), the VOC issued both bonds and shares in the world's first public subscription, a way of selling securities in which the investors acquire shares directly from the company.[70]

By 1608, another momentous financial innovation, the forward selling of shares, had emerged in Amsterdam, modeled after the ancient practice of the forward selling of grain. This practice of forward selling (when a buyer and seller agree on a price at some future date) solidified Amsterdam's position as the world's most important exchange and the only place where a significant business in derivatives (financial instruments based on underlying assets) occurred. Not surprisingly, it attracted capital-rich traders from around Europe. The London Stock Exchange became significant about a century later, when the newly founded (1694) Bank of England began issuing transferable governmental debt notes, and joint-stock companies became more widespread. A formal Paris stock exchange, the Paris Bourse, emerged another generation later, in 1724.[71]

Stock exchanges were important institutional innovations, enabling traders to raise more capital. And they had further effects: Interest rates in Amsterdam decreased as creditors accepted the VOC shares as collateral for loans.[72] They also made plain a qualitative difference of the emergent institutions of capitalism: Their primary impetus was to generate more capital, not to increase particular trade or production streams. Slowly but consequentially, capitalists severed their age-old attachment to specific forms of economic activity, a step that symbolized capitalism's future.

Though rarely mentioned in literature focused on the importance of institutions to capitalism, another institution was just as pivotal to the capitalist revolution: the bourgeois family. While families varied in scale and scope (some were tightly focused on the nuclear family, others more extended), the family—economically, socially, and ideologically—became constitutive of capitalism. Families were important vehicles for raising capital, forging trust, hedging risks, ensuring continuity of enterprises, establishing the social standing of merchant firms, and simply feeding, clothing, and housing merchants. Family alliances through marriage helped secure capital and enlarge firms, and family inheritances facilitated continuity in the world of business—an intricate system of economic relations not primarily mediated by the market. In Europe, the dominance of nuclear families had roots in the early Middle Ages and was amplified by church regulations: Marriages between relatives were increasingly restricted, culminating in a decree issued by

The bourgeois brood: Abraham van den Tempel, David Leeuw and Cornelia Hooft with Their Children, *1671.*

the Fourth Lateran Council in 1215 that forbade marriage between anyone related within seven degrees of affinity—that is, if any of the couple's ancestors in the previous four generations had married. The church also imposed rules mandating monogamy and limiting inheritance to children born of legitimate marriages. Between the eleventh and thirteenth centuries, primogeniture gradually became standard, replacing the previous practice of equal division between heirs and further narrowing the economic family unit. This strictly limited nuclear family came to be the dominant model throughout Europe.[73]

Families were intricate institutions, more complex in many ways than the stock exchange or the joint-stock company. Women played a key role in building and managing them, not just by running households and raising the next generation to take over the family business but by maintaining affectionate relations with distant relatives, imposing specific ethical and religious standards, finding marriage partners for their offspring, and even managing the family business itself. Think of Maria Jacoba Daemen (1658–1733), the daughter of a Limburgish salt trader who had settled in Amsterdam in 1640, who worked closely with her father, keeping up his account books and cultivating the relationships that undergirded the trade network. She corresponded with a factor in Setúbal, Portugal, to assure him of the quality

The Haarlem artist Maarten van Heemskerck produced a series of prints titled Praise of the Virtuous Wife *to illustrate the morally responsible commercial household, 1555.*

of a shipment, but more importantly, she heavily intervened in the affairs of her brother and cousins in Cologne and inserted herself into questions about which family members would control the business and who married whom. Unlike in aristocratic court cultures, bourgeois women were barred from participating in "the theater of public power" by a strict ideological separation of the household and the public sphere.[74] Yet they were crucial to maintaining the family, one of the most basic institutions of emerging capitalism. As a result, women became ever more associated with domesticity and the realm of consumption, not production. As the Italian poet Torquato Tasso wrote in 1580:

> It is well ordered that . . . the office of acquiring should be attributed to the man and that of preserving to the woman. The man struggles to acquire and carries out farming or operates in commerce in the city . . . but the woman looks after that which has been acquired and her virtues are employed inside the house, just as the man demonstrates his outside.[75]

Tasso's trope was a powerful ideological one that helped propel the bourgeois revolution for many centuries. But unnoticed by him (and many others), it was the family unit that enabled "the office of acquiring."

These constantly evolving institutions emerged from a particular historical juncture, the spread and integration of nodes of capital—the great connecting—and came to play a crucial role in the unfolding of capitalism; indeed, they are still important today.[76] Yet the most important institution to rear its head was not the joint-stock company or the stock exchange or the bourgeois family but a new kind of state.

Despite Smith's claims that capitalism was self-generated by utility-maximizing individuals organizing their economic relationships through specialization and exchange, the state emerged as *the* crucial institution in capitalism's history. From his study in the Scottish seaside town of Kirkcaldy, Smith rightly critiqued the corrupt and powerful British state, yet asserted wrongly that "the profusion of government must, undoubtedly, have retarded the natural progress of England towards wealth and improvement."[77] His emphasis on the "nature of man" as the foundation of capitalism led him to miss that the capitalism of his time and beyond was unimaginable without the state. There was no "freedom" of trade to be corrupted by government: Political authorities controlled every aspect of economic life.[78] The "free market" that eventually emerged in the collective consciousness as a potent force was nothing more than a figment of scholars' and ideologues' imaginations, an ideal type unrelated to capitalism's actual history but appealing for its seeming ability to make sense of economic life and its promised conjunction of freedom and prosperity.

As we have seen, the archipelago of capital had always been a co-production of merchants and rulers, of capital and states, and the great connecting cannot be explained without understanding that connection.[79] The state had a critical hand in the creation of this new way of organizing economic activities everywhere; at the same time, the state was one of its products. This is because, as the great mercantilist Thomas Mun observed in 1621, "[t]he Trade of Merchandize is the verie Touchstone of a kingdomes prosperitie."[80] Fernand Braudel said this even more directly more than three centuries later, when he observed that "[c]apitalism only triumphs when it becomes identified with the state, when it is the state."[81]

Most, if not all, private institutions emerging out of the great connecting were backed by state power—in Europe and everywhere else too. The stock exchange in Amsterdam was wholly reliant on public authority: The town regulated it, stipulating that all traders congregate at certain times and conduct their business in a particular location. Insurance contracts in the Ottoman world relied on state regulations that required the keeping of particular sets of shipping records—the cargo book—and provided legal sanctions against those who defrauded insurers. The emergence of banking and financial institutions was also deeply connected to the state, especially the financing of warfare's escalating costs. Joint-stock companies such as the EIC, the VOC, and the Royal African Company were just as much creations of the state. Even the most "private" institutions—contracts, for instance—were under the check of public authorities, as the state (in the Islamic world as much as in Europe) defined and enforced the laws backing each and every contract. Private contracting alone did not suffice.[82] Markets themselves were deeply institutionalized and politically constituted entities, not spontaneous creations. From the very inception of the archipelago of capital, it was, across the world, the state that made the market.

Even property rights were not a fact of nature but something that the state constantly defined and redefined.[83] They were neither "secure" nor "insecure" in the abstract; they were subject to shifting state interventions, deeply fungible, and deeply political. Even for England, which some have upheld as the epitome of "secure" property rights, historians have charted plentiful expropriations for infrastructural development and the ending of thousands of heritable jurisdictions.[84]

There was nothing peculiarly European, or particularly new, about states' role in the archipelago of capital. How universal the state's importance was becomes clear when we look at its role in building the essential infrastructure of trade: roads, ports, canals, postal networks, and the military institutions charged with their protection. Sixteenth-century

Making markets, opening up trade:
Dutch warships, 1665.

Japanese rulers improved transportation networks; Chinese government investments built canals, roads, and postal services (the mounted imperial courier service, I-chan, for example, eventually connected 1,936 relay stations to one another, allowing information to travel swiftly across the empire); and sixteenth-century Mughal ruler Akbar expanded already sophisticated irrigation systems. States also fashioned the infrastructure of financial systems—and money itself. As mentioned, in 1609, Amsterdam built a kind of central bank—the Wisselbank—that created a stable currency by guaranteeing the silver and gold content of coins and acted as a clearinghouse for bills of exchange, enabling merchants to significantly cut transaction costs.[85]

The state also mattered because it created one of capital owners' favorite and most important institutions: the monopoly—that is, the ability to, as the leaders of the VOC put it, "enjoy privately, to the exclusion of all others, the fruits of the trade conferred to her alone."[86] Almost all long-distance trade veered toward monopolization, and merchants the world over strove for monopolistic markets—a temptation of capital owners ever since. The most durable monopolies were a function of political authority, as only the state could reinforce such restrictions over a given territory in the long term. The Wangara in Kano, for example, enjoyed a monopoly on western African trade routes, while Huizhou merchants had a salt monopoly in 1617. In Portugal, too, long-distance trade had been attached to government-enforced monopoly since Vasco da Gama opened a sea route to India in 1497. The Casa da Índia organized and dispatched annual armadas to Goa and Cochin, present-day Kochi, managing all aspects of the trade. The Spanish crown, in similar ways, provided merchants with *asientos*, a particularly profitable monopoly to trade enslaved people to overseas territories.[87]

Capitalism—to Smith's chagrin—found its mainspring not in competition but in the novel and fabulous wealth enabled by state-backed monopolies. And in global markets, monopoly rights necessarily entailed protecting a nation's merchants from foreign competitors, such as through the 1660 English Navigation Acts (requiring that all tobacco from the colonies be shipped to England) or China's confinement of foreign merchants to the city of Guangzhou.

Military force, that epitome of state power, proved critical in the great connecting as well. By the late seventeenth century, Britain, to cite only the most prominent example, maintained the world's largest navy, and its military forces captured and held not only huge territories in the Americas, Africa, and Asia but also protected trade routes. By 1710, that navy could launch 180 ships and employed 48,072 seamen. Such commitment to naval power was crucial to facilitating English merchants' prominent role in global trade. Despite Enlightenment thinkers' hopes that trade would bring about peace, it went along with an almost uninterrupted state of global war. Between 1689 and 1815, Britain and France were at war for sixty-four years.[88] Other states also deployed military power for commercial advantage: Dutch, French, Chinese, Ottoman, Malian, and Mughal military forces shaped local, regional, and global markets. Wherever we look, warfare was almost the default mode of the great connecting.

Considering this history, it is hardly surprising that many contemporaneous political economists—scholars whom modern historians have called mercantilists or cameralists—saw the connections between the archipelago of capital and the state so clearly, what Thomas Hobbes described in 1651 as the link between wealth and power: "The wealth and riches of all the particular members, are the strength [of the state]," he observed.[89] Indeed, Western political economy, as a concept and a science, emerged in the seventeenth century, and its primary obsession was examining how state power and economic wealth related to one another and how one could generate the other. Perceptive observers of the world they lived in, these early modern political economists shared none of their modern-day counterparts' preoccupation with allegedly "free" markets; they sought instead to understand how wealth could make nations powerful and reasoned that an activist state was the root cause of economic development. As Napoli's Gaetano Filangieri observed, "[C]ommerce [had become] essential to the organization and to the existence of political bodies."[90] Trade, to David Hume, was "an affair of state," as the "greatness of a state and the happiness of its subjects" are "inseparable with regard to commerce."[91] This viewpoint was almost the necessary result of a way of thinking about the world that had not yet separated "the economy" as a distinct sphere of society and life, a separation that emerged only in the nineteenth century.[92] If this generation's contributions to political economy have been largely forgotten by modern economics, it is not because they lacked influence in their own times but because their theorizing goes so strongly against the mythical story the West tells about its rise.

As states played a crucial role in the expansion of trade, rulers everywhere became more dependent on the fortunes and whims of the capitalists whose expansion they had enabled. In Japan, they drew on merchant wealth to build up cities and towns, including Edo, modern-day Tokyo. As merchants and bankers financed the territorial expansion of European states, the states taxed the resulting profits. Britain's tobacco trade with the Americas, for example, became an important part of the Crown's revenue, with 25 percent of its customs revenue and 5 percent of its total income coming from that tax alone in the 1660s. In India, too, connections between merchants and rulers were important, setting in motion a process that would produce both more powerful states and more powerful capital owners after 1500.[93]

As a result, the sixteenth and seventeenth centuries were characterized by the political ascendancy of traders. Their power increased in particular vis-à-vis the landed interests that had for so long dominated global politics. In the West African city of Kano, for example, traders and rulers became closely interconnected; the *Ta:rikh Mandinka de Bijini*, a Wangara text, describes the Wangara merchants as "gifted political mediator[s]."[94] In Japan, as many merchants learned that extending loans to *daimyo*—feudal lords—could be extremely lucrative, they gained power, even though some thinkers, such as Sato Shin'en, believed that "merchants should be ordered to build markets [but] they should be strictly forbidden to be in the fields" advancing loans and speculating in crops.[95] On the east coast of Africa, Indian merchant capital and the revenues that could be derived from it were central to sustaining Portuguese colonial rule. And in the Dutch Republic, merchants gained significant political power after the revolt that ended in 1648; in fact, they came to constitute the state itself. Everywhere, rulers and capital owners bargained for power. The Mughal Empire was not the example of "Oriental despotism" that Marx described; there was political competition in South Asia, just as in Europe. The sultan and his advisers constituted only "a loose layer of authority" above the power of local authorities. Even in Spain, the quintessential absolutist state, the monarchy was, in practice, an assembly of overlapping sovereignties and different institutional regimes in different locations, all engaged in continual bargaining. Indeed, beneath the pomp and circumstance, all the so-called absolutist states survived by constantly negotiating with various groups for funds and materials for warfare.[96,97]

As the great connecting unfolded, the interests of states and capital owners continued to intertwine across the world—from the Mughals to the Ottomans to the French. Yet precisely how they were

entangled took different forms in different places, with drastic consequences for the emergence of capitalism.

China, probably the world's largest economy, reveals one variant of
that relationship. There, as elsewhere, the state played crucial roles in
facilitating commercial activity and the emergence of merchant communities. Its state was rich and capable; in 1683, one European looking
at China observed "that the Court of Peking does not yield in magnificence to any other Court in Europe."[98] China's great territorial expanse secured a much larger free-trade area than anything available to
European merchants, lowering transaction costs. In this way, the Chinese institutional setting was arguably superior to its European equivalents. Indeed, long-distance trade within the empire between 1500
and 1800 was more extensive than on the European continent.[99]

Yet fundamental difficulties hemmed merchants in, setting China's political economy on a very different trajectory from those of its
European counterparts. Most important was the balance of power between the merchants and the state: Chinese merchants confronted a
rich, powerful, extensive, and increasingly sophisticated centralized
state that made it difficult for them to exert influence. Moreover, because the Chinese state derived much of its revenue from agrarian
production—not from merchant loans or trade taxes—it did not depend on merchants to any great extent. This radically limited merchants' sway. The state's centralization and relative stability meant that
it had little need to bargain with them.[100]

Because of China's size and lack of serious competitors, governance
was both complex and cheap—a far cry from the situation in Europe.
The Chinese bureaucracy was well developed but also inexpensive.
The Pax Sinica rested, as elsewhere, on military power, yet the empire's relative security kept it from having to spend significant resources
on warfare, allowing state revenues, and thus taxation, to remain lower.
With less sway vis-à-vis the state, merchants had to live with a power
that was not especially attuned to their interests. This became particularly noticeable in the arena of overseas trade: Chinese rulers did not

think it important to the empire. The state did not embolden merchants to invest abroad, did not facilitate the construction of chartered companies, and did not dole out monopoly rights—all things European states did. Ming rulers instead tightly circumscribed both the scale and scope of trading voyages, so much so that by the mid-sixteenth century, little private overseas trade had survived.[101] When merchant and pirate Wang Zhi (汪直) developed a thriving overseas business with Japan and Southeast Asia in the 1540s, circumventing Ming prohibitions, the Chinese authorities had him arrested. As Wang Zhi told the emperor: "I conduct maritime business and trade in Fuzhou and Zhejiang Province. I defend the country's border while sharing benefits with locals. I swear to heaven and earth, celestial beings, and the world that there was no treason or harassment."[102] His plea fell on deaf ears. He was executed in 1560. And in 1567, when private trade was again allowed, the state still mistrusted merchants and did not lend its support to their undertakings. China's traders were indeed, in the words of one scholar, "merchants without empire."[103]

Other heavily commercialized parts of Asia with vibrant merchant communities followed similar trajectories. In Mughal India, like China, taxes on agricultural production funded the state; before 1700, land revenue amounted to 99 percent of expenditures, limiting merchants' political power. Even in a highly commercialized part of the subcontinent such as Gujarat, only 6 percent of state income derived from maritime trade. Moreover, South Asian merchants, like their Chinese counterparts, did not succeed in turning their loans to rulers into marketable bonds, as happened in England. As a result, Gujarati merchants could not translate their economic might into political power.[104]

Things were similar in West Asia: Throughout the Muslim world, capital owners remained distant from rulers and did not have much influence over the state. In the territorially extensive Ottoman Empire, traders could not rely on the state to support their interests, not least because the state was not dependent on them. The Ottoman sultan taxed rural cultivators directly, and his dependence on tribute extracted from the countryside meant that he could be less solicitous of merchants.[105]

In Europe, things were fundamentally different: While the state mattered as much to merchants as it did elsewhere, merchants mattered more to the state. European states were less stable and more resource-hungry than their Asian counterparts: Their constant need for allies and resources kept them dependent on merchants. Europe's dispersed nobility controlled fewer resources than, say, Ottoman rulers. Sultan Suleiman, for example, assembled twice as much state income as even Europe's richest ruler, Charles V, resulting in the Habsburg ruler—but not his Ottoman counterparts—being dependent on merchant loans.[106] The archives of the Bethmann Bank in Frankfurt hold evidence for a huge bouquet of loans to both local and more distant rulers, from nearby Hesse-Darmstadt to those of faraway Sweden.[107] As state debts grew stratospherically, moreover, they provided capitalists with a secure place to invest their funds, binding their fate to the state's might.

Moreover, because Europe was divided into a large number of competing states, rulers were constantly jockeying for advantage, which, first and foremost, meant military advantage. But technical changes, especially the spread of firearms, undermined medieval forms of warfare and made it more costly. Vast numbers of soldiers had to be raised and equipped; between 1500 and 1700, the size of European armies grew tenfold. At the same time, war became an almost constant feature of European states: During the sixteenth and seventeenth centuries, European countries fought wars almost always, and even in the eighteenth century they were at war 78 percent of the time.[108]

Warfare drove rulers into the arms of merchants because so much coercive capacity—ships, guns, and soldiers—required the mobilization of vast resources. In the first half of the sixteenth century, France and Spain both raised the equivalent of about 100 to 150 tons of silver per year in taxes—three times more than England and about as much as the Ottoman Empire. In 1700, England and France each raised 600 to 900 tons of silver; by the 1750s, 800 to 1000 tons; and in the 1780s, 1,600 to 1,900 tons. Almost all of it went to the ever rising costs of warfare. In the eighteenth century, Britain spent between 75 and 85 percent of its revenues on the military and war-related debt—a stunning figure. Not surprisingly, between 1670 and 1815, the British government managed to increase tax extraction by a factor of seventeen, even though the national income only tripled during those same years. (Whoever associates capitalism with low taxation has not studied history.) Over the same period, Ottoman tax revenue remained almost unchanged. As states made war, war made states.[109]

To raise the needed revenues, European rulers had to forge states of a different kind, along with territorial political economies to sustain them. Inadvertently, this helped capital owners carry their revolutionary logic into ever more parts of society. It favored, for example, the monetarization of the economy, as rulers preferred taxing people in fungible money rather than goods. Moreover, as political leaders aimed to find novel ways to raise resources, they built an entirely new form of state— what has been called the "fiscal-military state." They invented new kinds of taxation and bureaucratic structures to collect taxes and administer expenses. As rulers became dependent on merchants and bankers, these innovative administrative methods eventually influenced business practices as well.[110]

Resource-hungry states also fostered the broader development of financial institutions and money itself. One of the most significant innovations in this context came from a European upstart, England. With a shortage of gold and silver, English political elites sought ways to "re-engineer money" and expand the country's supply of it. In the process, they built a financial architecture that is still evident today. Most far-reaching, in 1694, the government permitted the newly chartered private Bank of England to issue notes that the government would borrow and use to pay its bills, thus making them redeemable for tax obligations. Money itself was far from being a neutral facilitator of exchange; it was an eminently political construction, with coin minting tellingly the prerogative of the sovereign. Public borrowing enabled a simultaneous increase in the money supply, which was now divorced from the highly constrained stock of silver and gold. This borrowing also created a market in government securities that was so large and liquid it enabled a broader securities market. The interests of capital owners and the state became aligned in a fundamentally new way—the Crown was dependent on the stream of revenue coming from trade and production, while capital owners swam in the institutional waters created by political authorities and, importantly, received interest payments from the state.[111]

Capitalism was thus a coproduction—admittedly inchoate and at times at cross purposes—between states and capitalists. It was, as one scholar pointed out, a "series of *liaisons dangereuses*."[112]

As European states became dependent on merchants, merchants moved into new political roles, in comparison both with medieval Europe and with their Asian and African contemporaries. Of course, they were not the first merchants to possess political power. In Venice, Florence, and Genoa, the state and merchant communities had already fused in what Weber called "political capitalism"—the "memorable alliance between the rising states and the sought-after and privileged capitalist powers." During the sixteenth and seventeenth centuries, that alliance moved from city-states to territorial states as well. To be sure, these states differed—the Dutch Republic of bourgeois notables was quite different from the British constitutional monarchy—yet they all provided European capitalists with unique political influence.

As capital owners formed into a powerful new elite and shaped states, they could combine their capital with new forms of state power and carry that power into new global configurations, building new African, Asian, and American islands of capital and integrating them into a newly Eurocentric archipelago. As a result, the state became deeply vested in enabling catpital owners to access further resources so as to better draw those resources in, while capitalists became deeply vested in the successes of the state. Though rulers often believed

Turning westward: The Medici envision the world. Map of the Caribbean and Venezuela, 1563.

that capital-driven expansion would reinvigorate feudal rule, it actually strengthened urban capitalists and their interests. The very efforts to stabilize tributary rule further undermined it. Moreover, the creation of new islands of capital led to conflicts between European powers, further increasing states' dependence on merchant resources. Portuguese power in India was (successfully) contested by Dutch and English warships; the Dutch, English, and French battled over the control of Caribbean islands for centuries; and competing claims for North American and Asian trade also led to almost constant warfare.[113]

Spreading the archipelago of capital helped states stabilize, grow, and raise further funds, while military power supported European merchants' expansion into Asia, Africa, and the Americas, a move that relied on force and violence as much as or more than on the "classic" institutions beloved by economists—rule of law in general and property rights in particular. The more powerful the capital-owning elites, the more the state used its powers to protect and expand mercantile interests. Expansion was inherently lawless, putting states at odds with rival territorial authorities. It focused on monopoly and caused vast dispossessions. Violence was everywhere, from the grandest sea battles to petty cruelties on the trading frontier. When Captain John Engleduc traded in the 1750s on the coast of Gambia and his ship was "attacked by the damned villains in the Cassinka country," he spread gunpowder across the ship's deck, inviting the "natives to come on board," then gave an enslaved boy a match to light the gunpowder: "Above 30 of the barbarians perished by the explosion."[114]

Indeed, the meshing of trade and rule points to a crucial aspect of the great connecting: Much of it was based on force. Trade did not bring the peace that Immanuel Kant prophesied from his study in Königsberg and that Thomas Paine mused about in Philadelphia when he claimed that "commerce . . . is a pacific system, operating to cordialize mankind by rendering nations, as well as individuals, useful to each other."[115] Such ideas were common wisdom among European Enlightenment thinkers in the mid-eighteenth century, but Montesquieu's (and others') notion of *doux* commerce (gentle commerce)—"it is almost a general rule, that wherever we find agreeable manners, there commerce flourishes; and that wherever there is commerce, there we meet with agreeable manners"—was wishful thinking, not reality.[116]

Dutch commerce, for example, drew its strength from both the goods it had on offer and the power of the state. When the VOC arrived in the Banda Islands (in today's Indonesia) to get access to their nutmeg, warfare and trade did not just go hand in hand—they were the same thing. As Jan Pieterszoon Coen, a two-time governor-general of the VOC, remarked in the early seventeenth century: "It is not possible to wage war without trade, nor to keep up trade without waging war."[117] This was not a Smithian market, as the VOC made clear when it instructed its emissaries in Asia,

[I]n the principal places where you conclude friendships and alliances, we recommend that you establish fortresses with the consent of the Indians, in order that we may secure these places and defend them as our possessions, keeping their trade for ourselves alone and excluding the Portuguese and all others.[118]

As much as the VOC was a private venture of merchants eager to expand the archipelago of capital, the company was also tightly linked to the state and, in many places, became the state.[119]

The peculiar relationship between European capitalists and rulers found its clearest expression in their interest and ability to create new islands of capital—Cape Verde and Potosí among them. Such interests and abilities were not distributed evenly across the globe. As we have seen, Asian and African merchant communities broadened as well, but they did so less rapidly and radically than their European counterparts. The capacity to create new islands of capital during the long sixteenth century was largely limited to European merchants, and it was this ability that allowed them—over several centuries—to forge new kinds of links that recast global hierarchies. While the state was strong enough to support their interests, it was simultaneously weak enough to depend on their uniquely liquid and fast-growing fortunes. This combination allowed for the emergence of a connected diversity of labor regimes, political institutions, and sets of rights—a core feature of capitalism's dynamism.

Few families illustrate the new connection between capital and state power more effectively than the Fuggers, who were so important from the late fifteenth century to the mid-sixteenth century that some historians have called these years the "Age of the Fuggers." The family grew rich in trade, yet what made it so significant was its ability to construct new islands of capital and link these to strengthening states, making it a true capitalist trailblazer.[120]

It all started in 1367, when weaver Hans Fugger migrated from the small town of Graben in Lechfeld to the city of Augsburg, twelve miles distant, in search of opportunities. Hans and his sons, Andreas and Jakob, quickly turned profits from weaving into the acquisition of property, and the family married into Augsburg's mercantile elite. Increasingly focusing on commerce, a move facilitated by Augsburg's deep connections to Venice, they pursued opportunities in the textile trade, then moved into spices and mining—primarily silver, copper, and mercury but also brass, tin, lead, and coal—before turning to the trade in metal goods (such as arms); luxury goods and provisions; and banking and credit services to European sovereigns. They rose to great prominence; Hans Fugger's grandson Jakob II, "the Rich" (1459–1525), might have been the wealthiest person to ever live, and under the control of Jakob II's nephew Anton (1493–1560), the company's commercial stock comprised a staggering five million guilders in 1546, when the average craftsman made about one hundred guilders annually.[121]

The Fuggers, like all expanding mercantile venturers, were embedded within familial connections, with control of the business remaining entirely in the hands of the Augsburg family. They took pains to prepare their sons for roles as managers of great accumulations of capital: In 1473, for example, at the tender age of fourteen, Jakob II was sent to Venice, the capital of eastern Mediterranean trade, to learn the ins and outs of the mercantile and banking businesses. His brother Markus, who worked at the same time as a clerk at the papal registry in Rome, initiated the first Fugger money transfer with the Papal States in 1476, marking the beginning of the family's involvement in banking, which became an important source of income.[122]

While focused on Augsburg, the Fuggers built an extensive network of factories across Europe to coordinate their trading activities. These factories—perhaps as many as seventy-five—were not the modern production sites familiar to us; they were places where goods were stored and trade conducted. Antwerp, Königsberg, Lisbon, and Madrid all held Fugger factories, as did Goa at a later point and perhaps Santo Domingo on the Caribbean island of Hispaniola. It was the flows of information from these factories to the head office in Augsburg that permitted the Fuggers to coordinate and control their business.[123]

As the Fuggers' information and trade networks stretched across the European continent and eventually into South Asia and the Americas, the firm intersected in myriad ways with the kings, emperors, and local potentates—rulers who, in turn, became increasingly dependent upon the Fuggers' resources. On the most basic level, the Fuggers married strategically into noble families, particularly families who served the Habsburgs. This social prominence, largely forged by women's labor, helped the Fuggers become among the most prominent financiers to many of Europe's rulers, including its popes. Already close to the Habsburgs, the Fuggers became a "superpower of money" when they financed the dynasty's warfare and received monopolies in return for providing these existentially important services. Leases gave them exclusive access to subsoil resources such as silver, copper, and mercury. They gained noble titles, privileged access to overseas markets, and exemptions from tax payments and customs. The most awe-inspiring example of the Fuggers' power came in 1519, when they financed the bribes needed to secure the election of Charles V as the emperor of the Holy Roman Empire, receiving in return monopoly access to Spain's mercury deposits. It was win-win: The Fuggers became the main bankers of the Habsburgs, and the Habsburgs became a global power.[124]

This connection propelled the Fuggers across the Atlantic. Their capital had helped finance Spanish and Portuguese voyages in the first place, including some of the earliest colonial expeditions. With Spanish and Portuguese power extended into the Americas, the Fuggers now rode on its coattails: They supplied the mercury that was used in the exploitation of the silver deposits in the Spanish colonies of New Spain and Peru. In exchange, the Fuggers received precious metals extracted there. The May 1552 asiento between the Fuggers and Charles V, for example, included a huge loan at 12 percent interest paid with gold and silver stock from the Casa de India in Seville. A September 1552 report of the Consejo de Hacienda—the Spanish Treasury—stated that almost 80,000 ducats from ten silver shipments amounting to 158,000 ducats in total were used to amortize outstanding debts owed to the Fuggers and other merchants. The Fugger factory in Seville played a key role in that silver trade: It was the place where precious metals were received and then transferred to Antwerp. The Fuggers, who had learned much of their trading skill set from the Venetian trade in the eastern Mediterranean, now helped move the European economy, including their own business, around the Atlantic, the flow of resources enabling them to accumulate unprecedented riches while strengthening the House of Habsburg, which had made that expansion possible.[125] It was an almost symbiotic relationship.

The Fuggers were not alone in creating links between capital, state power, and the expansion of the archipelago of capital. Their Augsburg compatriots and competitors—the Welsers—followed suit. In business since 1411, the Welsers moved overseas in 1505, when they cofounded and outfitted (with the Fuggers and other south German mercantile families) the Seventh Portuguese India Armada. That expedition was the Welsers' breakthrough—it gave them access to the Portuguese island of Madeira and, by 1509, the sugar plantations on the Castilian-controlled Canary Islands. A decade later, the Welsers were the second-biggest financier of Charles V's election as emperor of the Holy Roman Empire. In return, they were allowed to establish a factory in Seville in 1525 and a trading post in Santo Domingo in 1526. Between 1526 and 1535, the Welsers invested in ninety-three voyages from Seville to Santo Domingo, giving them an interest in a staggering 10 percent of the total trade with the Americas. Besides sugar, they brought gold, pearls, indigo, and drugs (such as balsam) to Europe and sold African slaves to Spanish America. An asiento that concluded between the Welsers and Charles V in 1528 allowed them to import four thousand enslaved Africans in return for the payment of a license fee.[126]

As the stories of the Welsers and the Fuggers demonstrate, one central feature of the great connecting was the emergence of a new relationship between rulers and merchants, between state and capital. At their most radical, traders took on statelike functions, and the boundaries between state and business—between "private" and "public"—became fuzzy or nonexistent, even though, ideologically, these (imagined) boundaries later became hugely important to capitalism's self-understanding. Even warfare was often privatized. Examples abound: The Genoese Casa di San Giorgio, a bank, became a territorial ruler of Corsica in 1453. In the 1520s, when Spanish emperor Charles V set his sights on subduing and colonizing parts of present-day Venezuela, he counted on private efforts and private resources; at the same time, the south German banking house of the Welsers sought a territorial trading base in continental America to exploit natural resources and trade. In similar ways, the Dutch VOC directly governed growing territories in Southeast Asia, enjoying a panoply of sovereign rights such as waging war, negotiating treaties, and minting coin. Similarly, the English East India Company ruled overseas territories, taxing local populations and using those revenues to purchase goods (opium, for example) to ship to China in exchange for tea. The English Royal African Company asserted statelike functions as well, building heavily guarded forts and engaging in treaty making and military combat. Its ships provisioned the Royal Navy, and the Royal Navy shipped the company's gold. All the international trade routes of the British Empire indeed depended on this "contractor state" and its ability to win wars. When the British king mobilized soldiers in the Caribbean in 1692, he promised "plunder," including slaves, to white Barbadians who were willing to join his troops.[127] French-chartered private companies—monopolies, all—also took on statelike functions. The Compagnie des Indes received land in northern France (at Lorient) as a base for its trading missions, and its successor company owned territories abroad (such as the Mascarene Islands), where it enjoyed sovereign rights such as taxing the local population, making treaties, and conducting military operations. This was very much "the colonization of the state by economic elites," and this intermixing of the public and the private infused the entire fabric of the capitalist revolution.[128]

This peculiar relationship between state and capital, rulers and

War capitalism in action: armed forces equipped by Augsburg's Welser family on their way to capture territories in Latin America.

capitalists, becomes clearest when we look at the expanding archipelago of capital: While these new islands were clearly the result of state
power, capital owners enjoyed near-total sway there. Not only were
they unconstrained by the state, but they often represented and even
embodied the state itself, especially in the newly constituted islands of
capital in Africa, Asia, and the Americas. In Barbados, a small elite
of planters dominated the executive, legislative, and judicial branches
of local government—that is, everything. The Barbadian state was an
assembly of capital owners—hardly surprising considering that the island was a private venture, with its owners appropriately called "lord
proprietors."[129] European monarchs did not always appreciate this organization of power. In 1682, the British king bitterly complained that
Barbadians did not keep him informed of the island's revenue, which
he considered "derogatory to our Right of Sovereignty and not fit to be
allowed by us."[130] Nonetheless, planters still kept the Crown at bay,
delivering as little information as possible to London. Elsewhere in the
archipelago of capital, the situation was similar: In Saint-Domingue,

constant conflicts about taxation pitted planters and merchants against the French state.[131]

The blurring of rulers and capitalists came into clearest relief during mobilization for war—that core state activity. Throughout Europe, as mentioned, a peculiar kind of contractor state emerged in which many military services were provided by private actors—military entrepreneurs. Some of their operations were small: merchant privateers who captured foreign cargo ships to gain a bounty. Others were gigantic: The VOC counted between ten thousand and fifteen thousand soldiers and two hundred ships under its command by 1700. The first multinational corporation was thus also one of its most significant fighting forces, a distant precursor to such twenty-first-century merchants of violence as Blackwater in the United States and Wagner in Russia. Indeed, much of European states' military power rested on these armed traders, as states lacked the capability or resources to send large armies to far-flung places. Even in the Americas, the focal point of European conquest, most military power was held by private armies and individuals—a peculiar intersection between state power and private capital that lay at the core of the great connecting and the prominent position of European capital owners within it.[132]

One of the remotest new nodes in the archipelago of capital illustrates some of these possibilities. In Saint Helena, a small island in the South Atlantic that even today requires a days-long boat journey from Cape Town, capitalists and statesmen created new forms of overlapping sovereignties that characterized the great connecting and became crucial building blocks of the capitalist revolution. Controlled by the EIC since 1657, when English military leader and politician Oliver Cromwell granted the company a charter, Saint Helena's settlers, upon the orders of the company, grew plantation crops such as indigo, cotton, and cloves. As in Cape Verde, slavery quickly became central. When the EIC began to issue licenses for private traders to send ships to Madagascar, off the coast of East Africa, it required them to return with nine slaves for every 500 pounds of British goods traded.

Consequently, in 1722, of the 924 people recorded as living on Saint Helena, about 400 were enslaved Africans, of whom the company owned half.[133]

What made Saint Helena noteworthy, however, was not the size of its economy or the number of its enslaved workers but its distinct form of rule. Saint Helena was a company-state. EIC leaders were not just Saint Helena's merchants but its sovereigns. In 1673, the company created the offices of governor and deputy governor for "the good Government of the said island," who "[were] under us to have and Exercise the Chief Command and Authority in the said Island in all matters whatsoever."[134] By decree, the company could "Constitute Laws, Orders, and Ordinances for the Government of St. Hellena . . . as they shall think fitt and Convenient," with the only constraint that they were "consonant to Reason, and not repugnant or Contrary But as Near as may be a Greeable to the Laws of England."[135]

Ultimate sovereignty rested with the Crown, but both the EIC and the Saint Helena council operated outside its purview. This privatized form of political rule suggested a novel merging of public and private power, of a company as state and a state as a company, which the EIC would later apply to much larger places like Bombay, Madras, and Calcutta.[136] Such company-states were indeed "hybrid entities," statelike businesses that gained sovereign rights because states lacked sufficient resources to power their global expansion.[137]

So crucial were these businesses to early capitalism that they became a core characteristic of the emerging capitalism of the long sixteenth century. They were also one element of several that made the capitalism that emerged in these centuries distinct from the more familiar industrial capitalism that would arise two hundred years later. Indeed, it was so distinct that this moment in the history of capitalism deserves its own name: war capitalism.

War capitalism rested on a peculiar structure of state power. It was built on imperial expansion and armed trade, as we have seen, and on violent domination of labor and vast dispossession of collective re-

War capitalism in action as seen from West Africa: A Benin bronze portrays a sixteenth-century Portuguese gunman.

sources, as we will discuss later. In this system, colonialism was crucial to trade. War capitalism forged huge territories in which property, both human and landed, was for the taking. Europeans could as often as not expropriate with impunity; workers could be robbed of their personhood by their masters' fiats; and any traders trying to compete were blown out of the water by state-financed navies. As Smith observed, the countries creating this world "advanced more rapidly to wealth and greatness than any other human society."[138]

Capitalism thus emerged in the world as war capitalism, a unique configuration that enabled something implausible: economic growth without significant technical change or productivity gains. Per capita economic growth, to the best of our knowledge, amounted to an annual rate of perhaps 0.41 percent in Holland (between 1500 and 1850) and about 0.3 percent in England (between 1600 and 1750). A reconstruction of Portugal's per capita GDP growth reveals long stretches of impressive development as well—between 1630 and 1755, it grew by about 0.44 percent. Compared with the world after 1800, this was not much, but at this preindustrial moment, it was extraordinary. Later, accelerating growth would be fundamental to capitalism's enormous wealth generation. Now, in the long sixteenth century, it was largely the vast redistribution of the world's wealth under the auspices of the coercive expansion of European nodes of capital that generated wealth. At this point, access to the resources of the new archipelago of capital made an outsize difference, not least because this was still a world of small populations and modest production.[139] But unlike in all previous moments of violent expansion (such as Timur's terrifying assault on India), this time the redistributed wealth went not just to tributary rulers but into the coffers of merchants, who then applied their age-old logic to it: Invest and accumulate.

A s capital owners, in conjunction with states, spread the empire of capital, forged the institutional framework of war capitalism, redistributed the world's wealth, and made capital's logic more central to economic life, they, too, came to be seen in new ways. Not surprisingly, the mercantile elite increasingly bucked against centuries of religious and worldly injunctions against them. Catholic merchants in the Italian city-states wrote in their ledgers such statements as "In the Name of God and of Profit." Dutch Calvinists argued that economic success was evidence of virtue, of God's favor, rather than of sin, and theologians found ways around the faith's doctrinaire hostility toward accumulation. There emerged pragmatic workarounds to bypass religious prohibitions on charging interest (for example, so-called dry exchanges, in which the interest on loans was hidden in bills of exchange).[140]

Most tellingly, however, religious attitudes themselves began to shift, balancing hostility toward capital accumulation with more welcoming positions, not least because religious authorities—like their worldly counterparts—depended on the work that capital owners undertook and the resources they raised. All major religious traditions changed their stances on interest, profit, and trade. Taking up some of the ideas of thirteenth-century Franciscan theologists Peter John Olivi and Thomas Aquinas (a Dominican friar), fifteenth-century Italian friar Bernardino of Siena began distinguishing between "fruitful and sterile" commerce, declaring the fruitful variety legitimate. In 1514, theologian Johann Eck of Ingolstadt declared that interest charges of 5 percent or less were unproblematic, an argument that found great favor (and financial support) with the Fuggers. Theologians drew new lines between what they called "legitimate profits derived from sales or the employment of others and the stigmatized category of usury"—in other words, between good and bad commerce.[141] Sometimes theological reorientation and mercantile interest fed upon each other: When papal envoy Cardinal Bernardino López de Carvajal arrived in Augsburg in 1507, he was wined and dined by Jakob the Rich, who in return received his "mercy and indulgences."[142]

To be sure, religious injunctions against mercantile endeavors continued. English preachers still proclaimed the sinfulness of excessive profit, with theologian Thomas Cartwright, for example, reminding his London audience at St. Paul's Cathedral in 1562 once more of the biblical injunction that "[i]t is easier for a Camel to go through the eye of a Needle, than for a rich man to enter into the Kingdom of God."[143] Others continued to criticize the merchant class as well; in Japan, for example, influential philosopher Motoori Noringa (1730–1801) saw the corrupting influence of money and demanded restrictions on commerce. Sumptuary laws still dictated the dress code for wealthy merchants reflecting the belief that exuberant self-presentation violated godly commands. As is not surprising, given the radicalism of the shift, it took many centuries for the capitalist revolution to become as naturalized as it is in most of the world today.[144]

⸺

As the great connecting progressed over several centuries, and as commercially minded European states and armed traders slowly but consequentially altered the connections between remote islands of capital, giving rise to new institutions, European merchants and states also created new kinds of global hierarchies. Hardly perceptible at first, these small differences cumulatively made for a truly momentous divergence by the eighteenth century. What was so significant about the building of new islands of capital, especially in the Americas, was not just the capture of new forms of wealth, ecological resources, and physical and institutional infrastructures, important as those were, but the forging of new forms of power by a small number of European states and a subset of European capital owners. As this group gained strength, it reordered economic space on a global scale—first statesmen and capital owners from Portugal and Spain (along with their Italian partners) and then, somewhat later, from England, France, and the Dutch Republic. These shifts created a set of deeply consequential new hierarchies and led to a truly epic transfer of ecological, technical, and human resources.[145]

As the great connecting allowed European traders and states to develop new wealth and new institutional capacities, it increasingly undermined such capacities elsewhere. While differences in wealth between the advanced parts of Europe and Asia were still small, European traders and states weakened competing nodes of capital and centers of political power, limited the range of their activities, and, especially, destabilized links between non-European centers of power and sources of capital, links that were, as we have seen, the central condition of the European breakthrough. Global hierarchies were thus a function not of "failures" by non-European peoples but of a novel kind of integration.[146]

Examples of the creation of differential hierarchies abound. When islands of capital in Africa, Asia, and the Americas encountered armed European traders and commercially minded states, the consequences were often devastating. In the Americas, Aztec merchants—prosperous, highly organized in guilds, and closely linked to state power—had greatly impressed the Spaniards. Yet the overwhelming violence of conquistadores and the diseases they brought with them left the Aztecs unable to prevent an almost complete transfer of political authority and wealth to newly arriving Europeans—a transfer that gave a huge human, social, and ecological gift to a distant continent and effectively shut out the possibility of forging links between Indigenous state power and capital in the Americas themselves. Unlike in the Chinese, Indian, and Arab worlds, American trading systems collapsed almost entirely, not least because the conquistadores destroyed Indigenous cities and thus the ability to maintain trade infrastructures.[147]

In Africa and Asia, European power was much more limited, and local merchant communities remained more vibrant. In 1700, to cite two telling examples, seven-eighths of the trade at Surat was still conducted by Gujarati and Ottoman merchants, while at Diu the vibrant exchanges with Mozambique Island expanded almost entirely under the control of Banian merchants. In Asia, Africa, and the Americas, local traders continued trading, artisans continued manufacturing, and peasants continued to grow food and fiber.[148] Revolutionary capital owners wielding capital and guns appeared there too, of course, but their importance was almost always confined to the scattered islands of capital.

Yet even there, the arrival of European capital owners and their states was consequential. As European merchants in Asia strove for monopolies, they aimed to marginalize deeply rooted and capital-rich local merchant communities. Sometimes they succeeded: In the Indonesian archipelago, for centuries an important trading base for Indian merchants, disrupters—first the Portuguese and then, in the second half of the seventeenth century, English and Dutch trading companies—tried to dislodge Gujarati traders from the profitable trade in Indian-made textiles, one of the core links of the Indian Ocean economy. In the spice-producing Banda Islands in the early seventeenth century, the Dutch VOC issued orders for native spice traders who traded with "foreign nations" to be "rigorously punished." By 1680, the Dutch had succeeded in replacing Gujarati spice traders in Southeast Asia. Another century later, in 1750, the number of large Gujarati ships had decreased by 82 percent and the value of trade at Surat by about 70 percent.[149]

The once thriving merchant community of the East African city of Mombasa met a similar fate. The Portuguese plundered Mombasa in 1507, 1528, and 1589, disrupting its trade networks. They sought to impose a commercial monopoly by introducing regulations that would require all Indian Ocean commerce to be carried on Portuguese ships, breaking the power of long-established Gujarati traders. Due to the impossibility of policing such a policy given limited military resources, the power grab ultimately failed, but not before eroding the prosperity of the East African cities and traders involved in Indian Ocean trade. By 1667, an English trading captain observed that "Mombaza . . . is a place of noe great traffiq, the evidean of which I imagine is the poverty of the inhabitants. . . . Mombaza its selfe seldome sens anything considerable, their onely trade consisting in their small boates, with which the Governor sends downe to Quilo, Pembah, and Zanzebar, and oft times to Musembeque."[150] With the arrival of the Portuguese in the sixteenth century, the influence of Swahili merchant communities diminished. Even when non-European trade networks remained vibrant, as they did for the Banian traders on Mozambique Island, the context in which their trade unfolded—the world economy—was increasingly dominated by Europeans.[151]

The new integration of the world economy also weakened non-European mercantile activities elsewhere. The once lively merchant communities of the Muslim world, already enfeebled by the devastating impact of the fourteenth-century plague, declined even further as they lost their central position in the east-west trade to the new European-dominated maritime routes. Egyptian merchants, who had been key actors in global trade, saw many of their businesses fail. As soon as the Portuguese reached India, spice exports to Europe from cities such as Beirut, Cairo, and Alexandria collapsed. The number of boats arriving in Jeddah from the west coast of India fell by about 60 percent after the Portuguese opened direct trade. As Arab merchants lost some of their core business, their cities shrank. When theologian and historian Shaykh Zainuddin Makhdum wrote his 1583 *Tuhfat al-Mujahidin*, he documented the destruction of the world of Muslim merchants on the Malabar Coast by "the cruel and wicked Portuguese Europeans."[152] He spoke of the "atrocities and cruelties" that left local Muslim communities "impoverished, weak and powerless."[153] He chronicled the theft of their wealth and reported how Muslim traders were hindered in their business undertakings, how their wealth was confiscated, their boats raided, their businesses destroyed:

> Their trade was flourishing in these ports, and elsewhere, while the Muslim merchants in these places were humbled and made to submit to the Portuguese as slaves. The Muslim merchants were not permitted to trade in all merchandise except in goods for which the Portuguese had a little interest. The commodities in which the Portuguese had interest yielded large profits. They assumed the right of exclusive possession of the trade in such commodities. . . . Their monopoly started at pepper and ginger but gradually added in the list cinnamon, clove, spice and other such things. . . . The journey by sea was not possible for the Muslims except under the protection of the Portuguese and with their passes.[154]

The fortunes of Muslim capital owners reversed—and not because of any essential characteristic of their communities. There was a basic but deeply consequential reason: Trade routes had changed.[155]

Some of that change in trade routes was the result of Europeans' great willingness to deploy military might, what Smith perceptively called the "superiority of force," which "happened to be so great on the side of the Europeans that they were enabled to commit with impunity every sort of injustice in those remote countries."[156] When da Gama sailed into the Indian Ocean in 1497, he brought heavily militarized trade with him. While pirates had attacked shipping in pre-European times, states had generally left one another's ships alone. The Portuguese, by contrast, attacked peaceful traders and seized their ships and cargoes. Da Gama's cruelest act was the 1502 plundering and sinking of a pilgrim ship, the *Miri*, in the Red Sea, during which he coldly watched the slow drowning of hundreds of passengers. In 1509, the Portuguese destroyed the joint naval forces of Gujarat and Mamluk Egypt at Diu. A year later, Portuguese sailor Afonso de Albuquerque wrested Goa from its Muslim rulers in an orgy of violence, massacring its Muslim population. In 1511, he and his troops attacked Malacca, with ruinous consequences for the resident Indian merchants. The city was so important that Portuguese traveler Tomé Pires, who stayed there from 1512 to 1515, concluded that "[w]hoever is lord of Malacca has his hands on the throat of Venice."[157] They also blocked the Red Sea trade by destroying the Egyptian fleet guarding entry, an approach that one historian aptly calls "trade-cum-plunder."[158]

For several centuries, Islamic, Indian, and Chinese capital owners had been important riverbeds of the fledgling capitalist archipelago. But these channels eventually trickled out and sometimes even went dry, as their European counterparts, once peripheral and weak, strengthened. Despite their access to capital and their ability to intensify trade, Asian and African merchants failed to build hierarchical connections spanning the globe—not least because they did not have the backing of their states. Europeans, by contrast, gained strength vis-à-vis their African and Asian counterparts—in part because of the resource bonanza from the Americas. What counted was not just the ability to forge new islands of capital but the ability to connect these islands in entirely new ways. Though military power (when aimed at capturing, holding, and exploiting territory) was still fairly evenly distributed around the world (the Ming, Mughals, and Ottomans continued to control much larger lands than any European powers), and though conquering distant hinterlands outside the Americas was still beyond the capacity of European military power, Europeans had clear advantages on the seas, a field of conflict of limited interest to the larger, land-based empires of Asia but crucial for enabling Europeans to dominate the networks between old and new islands of capital and to create a connected diversity of institutions—with far-reaching consequences.[159]

—————

European capital owners extended the archipelago of capital, intensifying trade, creating new hierarchies, fashioning new kinds of connections, and forging and refashioning powerful new institutions, especially states, in the process. The result of their efforts was a world economy. All islands of capital, without exception, were linked to other islands of capital, and their dynamic depended on these links—that is, on the world economy. In the first half of the sixteenth century, world trade grew by an astonishing 2.4 percent annually. In a significant departure, that trade expansion moved markets, especially long-distance markets, closer to the center of economic life. And the expansion of the global archipelago of capital fertilized trade, especially on the European continent. It was the soil from which capitalism sprang.[160]

Capitalism was thus both product and producer of a continent-connecting world economy; it was global in a way that no other form of organizing economic activity had ever been. Capitalism's condition of emergence was the world economy, a framework of possibility that stamped its every facet and forever foreclosed the possibility of understanding this new form of economic organization from a local, regional, or national perspective. By squeezing accounts of capitalism into the frame of states and empires and assigning these capitalisms (a plural preferred by some scholars) certain roles in the playbook of capitalist revolution, we miss something crucial: Capitalism is a global production in which states play an enormously important role, but in every case it transcends these states. Capital was fungible, and its loyalty to particular rulers and particular states was weak: Capital that accumulated in Italian city-states like Florence and Genoa, for example, was crucial to Iberian explorations along the coast of West Africa, the early slave trade, and the Spanish and Portuguese push into the Americas. Gujarati capital helped finance the expansion of Portuguese merchants, as did East African ivory production. Dutch capital funded the transformation of the countryside in English-controlled Barbados, and the Augsburg-based Fuggers and Welsers funded Spain and Portugal's expansion into the Americas. The Habsburgs depended on capital raised in Genoa (35 percent), Augsburg (35 percent), Spain (18 percent), and Antwerp (10 percent). Both the VOC and the EIC drew on Prussian, French, Danish, and Swedish investment in addition to local sources.[161] Investors in various East India Companies were deeply embedded in transnational networks and often financed companies of more than one nationality. Though their commerce rested on the power of states, "in many senses," as one historian notes, "these capitalists had no country."[162]

At the same time, it is important to remember that despite the spread and intensification of connections between these islands of capital in the long sixteenth century, the world economy was still quite weak, as indicated by the fact that islands of capital were so often literally located on islands—that is, places more easily defended, places conducive to protecting the new logic of capital. Even in the Americas, where territorial control made the deepest inroads and power imbalances were at their starkest, capital owners' clout had limits. Pushing commodity frontiers into the South American Atlantic rainforest in Brazil often failed, thanks to Indigenous resistance. And in North America, Indigenous fur traders retained control over resources, political power, and great bargaining might vis-à-vis their European counterparts. While Europeans succeeded in extracting minerals, produce, and labor from existing and reconstituted communities in the Americas, they never completely dominated them.[163]

Yet despite these limits and these islands' fortresslike appearance, they clearly pointed to the future. As the archipelago of capital grew, a spatial expansion that would slowly undermine the traditional economy in many parts of the world became visible. Historically, it had been difficult for capital owners to bust through the walls of fortified cities and move beyond islands, but now, as some states depended ever more on their resources, they gained political leverage to leapfrog over local resistances and break out of the constraints that had hedged them in.[164] Finding themselves at great distances from their rulers as they settled in areas where their power outmatched potential local opponents and resistances, they realized that they could produce a world in their image. They built islands of freedom (for capital), where they could overcome some of the constraints and resistances they had encountered in Europe, then reinvented the world in these places, recreating it almost from scratch. Along with their newfound wealth and power, they brought back to Europe some of the lessons they learned in this process, enabling their revolutionizing agenda to take root there as well.

In doing so, capital owners created a world of great diversity—of institutions, forms of rule, and labor regimes. That diversity was often a sign of weakness that forced them to adjust to certain local institutions, ecologies, and distributions of power. Yet in the end, it was this connected diversity—and not the homogeneity of the world they helped erect—that best explains the enormous dynamism of the emergent capitalism. While some property rights got a hearing in English courts, the property rights of Indigenous peoples in the Americas were ignored. Even as some people gained certain protections vis-à-vis the state in England, millions could be enslaved in the New World. As much as law came to structure relationships between cultivators and landowners and between workers and employers in parts of Europe, the personal dominance of the planter over his workers still ruled on the newly forged islands in the archipelago of capital. There is no reason to remember just one set of these institutions when we think about modern capitalism; instead, it was their connected diversity that explains much of capitalism's unfolding dynamic—a diversity that nonetheless turned into hierarchy wherever it touched ground.[165]

In this connected and hierarchical archipelago, capital owners could break into production on a massive scale for the first time, opening new vistas for accumulation. The Fuggers and Welsers, as we have seen, had already moved their money into mines and plantations, a testament to the revolutionary potential of merchant capital.[166] Genoese capital was at work organizing intensified production in Cape Verde and Sao Tomé. As merchants connected to one another in new ways, they also began to push into the countryside, into agriculture and eventually manufacturing—transforming the archipelago of capital into capitalism. Indeed, what might have been most consequential about this archipelago of capital was that it provided the incentive, the conditions of possibility, and perhaps even the necessity to push the revolutionizing agenda of urban capitalists into the sea—that is, into the vast stretches outside their often heavily fortified cities and islands.

4.

TRANSFORMING THE
COUNTRYSIDE, 1550–1750

*The plantation machine at work: sugarcane making,
Jamaica, circa 1747.*

There has never been an event so interesting to the human race
in general, and to the peoples of Europe in particular, as the
discovery of the New World and the passage to the Indies by the
Cape of Good Hope. Then began a revolution in commerce, in
the power of nations, in the manners, industry, and government
of all peoples. It is at this moment that men from the most distant
countries have become necessary: The productions of the climates
placed at the equator are consumed in the climates near the pole;
the industry of the North is transferred to the South; the fabrics
of the East dress the West, and everywhere men have
communicated to each other their opinions, their laws, their
customs, their diseases, their virtues, and their vices.[1]

— Guillaume Thomas François Raynal, 1770

In 1646, London merchant Thomas Noell and his brother Stephen boarded a ship bound for the West Indian island of Barbados to "manage . . . island investments."[2] Thomas and his three brothers had been deeply embroiled in economic policymaking in London. Chief among them, Martin Noell had been an intimate adviser to King Charles I, a member of the Board of Trade and Plantations and the Privy Council. From these posts, he had profitably channeled convict laborers to the Caribbean, especially Irish and Scottish prisoners of war, and, as a shareholder in the Royal African Company, invested in slaving voyages.[3] When the brothers' political position deteriorated in the 1640s as a result of the English Civil War that pitted Royalists against the Parliament, they decided to seek their fortunes in the Caribbean, in territories only recently connected to the global economy.

The Noells, like many, sensed the opportunities for capital-rich merchants from the great connecting in general and in the recently acquired Caribbean islands in particular. Immediately after landing in Bridgetown, Thomas and Stephen began purchasing property, and in March 1647, they joined a group of the largest landowners by buying a quarter share of the 270-acre Spring Plantation from fellow London merchants turned planters. The brothers quickly added adjacent land and more plantations. By late 1647, they owned 600 acres, an investment of almost 10,000 pounds sterling. Three years later, Thomas bought another huge plantation, Mount Clapham, at 510 acres one of the island's largest. The land, which came "with all the negroes, men, women, children, horses, cattle, ass . . . and all and every other thing," cost 380,000 pounds of muscovado sugar, the unit of value in Barbados in the 1650s.[4] The transaction provided the Noells with everything they needed for a profitable enterprise: land, tools of production, and labor—including Jumpeter, Pailnah, Mingo, Sutto, Joyce, Bessey, and twenty-four other enslaved women and men.[5]

For visionary merchants in the 1640s, sugar—the first of the "planetary commodities"—was an exciting avenue to profit.[6] The Noells were wealthy even before traveling to Barbados. Yet in three short years, they were among the world's most important planters. They owned dozens of enslaved workers, and their sugar fed New England farmers as well as British aristocrats. Thanks to their capital and the labor of their enslaved workers, Barbados became one giant sugar plantation—and the site of some of the most terrifying labor exploitation in the world.[7] True revolutionaries, the Noells fused capital and state-supported coercion to transform the island's countryside, in the process deepening connections within the capitalist archipelago and building one of the first recognizably capitalist societies.

Nothing was foreordained about this step on Barbados or elsewhere. When the first English "warrior entrepreneurs" arrived in 1627, the island was densely forested and uninhabited. A few pioneers began clearing the land to grow tobacco, then cotton, and eventually indigo, none of which proved particularly profitable. One contemporary author could only "mourn the decaying and improvised island."[8]

The crucial moment in Barbadian history—and the history of capitalism—came in the 1640s, when an assortment of planters, including the Noells, began to focus on sugar. Noting the thriving global market in the sweetener—and the profits that early producers in Madeira and Brazil generated from growing cane and extracting its sweet juices—this new crop of adventurers saw war-torn Brazil's diminishing exports as an opportunity to put their resources into growing sugarcane on Barbados. In 1647, when English traveler Richard Ligon arrived on the island, he observed that "the great work of Sugar-making, was but newly practiced by the inhabitants there."[9] Impressed by "how much the land there hath been advanced in the profit since the work of Sugar began," he anticipated that sugar would "make Barbados 'one of the richest Spots of earth under the Sun.'"[10] And by the 1650s, sugar was the dominant crop—exports averaged fifteen thousand tons annually, a full 65 percent of Caribbean production.[11] Cane soon covered half the island's surface. More capital was invested in Barbados and more trade conducted with the island than in "all the other English colonies put together," including New England, New York, and Pennsylvania.[12]

IN 1650S BARBADOS, the theoretical possibility that markets might one day structure all aspects of economic life came to fruition: Land, labor, supplies, food, and, of course, sugarcane all had a price and could be bought and sold—an almost perfectly Smithian economy, with utility-maximizing individuals creating a newly productive division of labor. At the heart of that nightmarish dream was a new kind of business—what has been called the "plantation machine"—a "revolutionary form of social and economic organization."[13] That "machine" generated enormous profits: Barbadian sugar estates returned between 40 and 50 percent on their invested capital annually during their 1650s boom. It also created great poverty, making Barbados one of the most unequal places ever in world history.[14]

Ecologically rich, unsettled, and secure from outside aggression because of its location, Barbados allowed merchants and planters to use the magic of capital to forge a new world in their own image. Unlike almost anywhere else, nothing muddled the picture—no historically ossified social structures, no customs, no feudal dependencies, no family-centered subsistence production, no systems of mutual dependence, no entrenched uses of the land and labor, and no hostile rulers who claimed authority over their subjects. Capital owners could reinvent the world, and the enormous profitability of sugar gave them a reason to. Barbados, the cutting edge of the capitalist revolution, pointed to the future, to how capital could be inserted into production on an entirely novel scale.[15]

The radicalism of Barbados was the result of planters' determination to rethink agriculture, to create an industrialized form of cultivation, and—crucially—to commodify everything. Instead of re-creating European societies, as the Puritan migrants to New England did, the planters made markets and control of capital the nexus around which all social relations revolved. Anything and everything had a price; anything and everything could be acquired or disposed of by the highest bidder. Capital and capitalists, as we have seen, had existed for centuries—Madmun ben Hassan ben Bundar in Aden, the Medici in Florence, the Chalebis in Surat, the Rumfas in Kano, and the Zhengs in Guangzhou, to name a few—but now they began to deeply immerse themselves in production. In so doing they participated in the world-altering project of building capitalism, and, crucially, they pursued the revolutionary edge of this project in a part of the world where their still-fledgling powers went largely unchallenged.

L ike the Noells in Barbados, merchants in Amsterdam and Surat, in Cairo and Guangzhou, pushed out of cities and commerce, and moved into the countryside and into production. No longer satisfied with connecting islands within the archipelago of capital, they increasingly strove to colonize the countryside, connecting it to distant places and, whenever possible, transforming it from a site of subsistence to one of market production. Presented with new opportunities emerging from the radically widened and deepened scope and scale of the connections they had forged and the inability of older social structures in some parts of the world to withstand this intervention, their capital flowed outward—into the fields, vineyards, rice paddies, and plantations beyond their towns' gates and across the world.[16]

Capitalists emerged in cities, but capitalism was born in the countryside, where almost all the world's people lived.[17] Geographic islands (Venice, Cape Verde, Surat, Amsterdam, Baghdad, Guangzhou, and Mombasa among them) and social islands (the small group of capital-rich people focused on trade) began a centuries-long expansion of turning ever more of the natural world—land, forests, raw materials, even labor—into commodities that could be bought and sold. Centuries before industrial capital took charge of production, generations of merchants did the same, with the countryside a particular focus of

their attention, making merchants the revolutionary vanguard of capitalism.[18]

Capitalism emerged as the result of this epic struggle—still ongoing in some parts of the world—between capital-rich elites' efforts to
transform the countryside and lords, peasants, slaves, and ecclesiastical
authorities trying to protect their own resources, autonomies, freedoms, and privileges. As traders aimed to secure supplies, realize
profit, and increase productive efficiencies, they used capital to control
ever more aspects of agriculture. At critical times they found allies
among modernizing tributary rulers, feudal elites, and enterprising
peasants. In the sixteenth and seventeenth centuries, the revolutionary
sparks were still almost imperceptible from a planetary perspective,
barely visible against an entire constellation of quotidian rituals and
practices. Yet from Barbados to Burgundy, from the Banda Islands to
Sussex, from Fujian to Pomerania, glimpses of a radically restructured
social order began to appear.[19]

Superficially, capitalist ventures into the world's rural regions had
great similarities: As merchants gained riches, they began investing
some of their capital in the country. They bought increasing quantities
of wool, wheat, rice, cotton, and other agricultural commodities and
sold goods to rural cultivators. They acquired cottages and villas to escape crowded cities, grow food, and invest in agricultural production,
advancing capital to producers and, most consequentially, engaging in
production themselves.[20] Goods that commanded large markets—
wool, sugar, wheat, tea, and grapes—were particularly attractive. This
was a global development, but it unfolded most intensely among European merchants, who, by drawing "their livelihood from the whole
universe," as Montesquieu wrote in 1748, burst out of their nearby hinterlands.[21] As European colonial expansion created an extended agrarian hinterland, these merchants built new commodity frontiers in the
world's countryside.

But however similar their goals and tools were, merchants around
the globe confronted infinitely diverse countrysides. Landowners en-

joyed specific rights and different positions within distinct social and political structures. Rural cultivators grew different crops and worked the land in a variety of ways—as freeholders, wageworkers, slaves, serfs, nomads, sharecroppers, or indentured servants.[22] Almost everywhere urban capital went, it adjusted to these conditions, its very flexibility proof of its revolutionary potential to reorganize economic activities against the great power of older social and economic structures.

Capital owners entered the countryside in distinct ways. Sometimes, they bought land outright and inaugurated new forms of agricultural production. In Tuscany as early as 1363, the plague instigated a significant increase in urban investment. Village proprietors, lacking the capital to pay for agricultural laborers needed to replace their recently deceased dependent producers, were forced to sell their holdings to Florentine merchants, already rich from trading and banking. Former landowners became *mezzadri* (sharecroppers) on land that had been theirs, growing olives and grapes (and producing what we think of as the classic Tuscan landscape). The new urban landowners, in turn, drew rents from their investments, often half of the harvest, with some, the *scioperati*, living entirely off their rural properties.[23]

In Venice, the demands of a growing city encouraged Venetian merchants to expand into the Domini di Terraferma (the mainland) and purchase rural properties. While this expansion began in the early fifteenth century, when the Republic of Venice captured its surrounding territories, it was not until the late sixteenth and early seventeenth centuries that urban capital moved inland to establish commercial agriculture. Texts like the 1651 treatise *L'economia del cittadino in villa* (The economy of the city dweller in his country house) instructed Venetian merchants on how to acquire and manage rural estates. Large-scale investment in irrigation systems increased viable pastoral and arable land and farms specializing in the production of meat, rice, mulberries, wheat, and hemp were established. Such commercialized agriculture often resulted in rural cultivators losing access to the commons, the lands used jointly by villagers.[24]

In New Spain, across the Atlantic, capital owners followed suit. In the late sixteenth century, they invested in agricultural estates, acquiring huge stretches of land—where they grazed animals or grew cereals and agave. In the Bajío of central Mexico, they built one of the world's earliest capitalist societies. Similar to Barbados, this sparsely populated land with weak social and political structures gave them a free hand to reinvent the world, as they warred against, settled, or removed the nomadic Chichimecas who had once controlled these territories.[25]

Acquiring land was one way that urban capital moved into the countryside. In East Africa, merchants on the coast off Mozambique Island purchased landed estates and built a small commercial agricultural sector. Mombasa traders invested in nearby fields to produce grain, using some to feed the city itself and some to supply their long-distance trade. Japanese merchants acquired land for agricultural production, often through funding land reclamation projects; it has been estimated that eventually these traders owned almost a third of Japanese agricultural land. In mid-seventeenth-century China, population growth, the commercialization of the economy (thanks to the greater availability of American silver), and the increased demand for food and raw agricultural materials encouraged urban capital to move into the countryside as well. Jiangnan merchants acquired rural holdings that they managed from the city with the help of local overseers. Tea traders in Jianyang and Chong'an bought large holdings too; in Fujian, urban capital enabled the "opening up of the mountains" for commercial tea production. In the sixteenth century, merchants pushed the age-old sugar frontier into southern Fujian. Chinese traders, aligned with local landowners, transformed agriculture in southern Xinjiang as well, producing cotton, wheat, and livestock for long-distance trade; as landowners consolidated their holdings, cultivators turned into wageworkers. Everywhere merchants acquired land they put sharecroppers, wageworkers, slaves, or serfs to work, producing rice, wheat, olive oil, millet, and more—not for the merchants' or growers' sustenance, but to be traded.[26]

Another common way merchants gained greater control over agricultural production was by advancing capital to rural producers without taking ownership of the land. In sixteenth-century Gujarat, urban merchants provided funds to rural traders—*sahukars*—who offered credit to agricultural cultivators. The resulting indebtedness tied these producers to merchants, giving these traders more secure access to trade goods. Older trends of merchant capital infusing the countryside accelerated as well: As the Mughals consolidated their power, commercial relations intensified, as some merchants became tax farmers (that is, they acquired the rights to revenue from certain groups of people in return for advancing moneys to government). Similarly, early seventeenth-century Cairo traders expanded their control over agricultural production, with leading merchants—Isma'il Abu Taqiyya, al-Ruwi'i, and Jamal al-Din al-Dhahabi among them—investing in their region's fledgling sugar, flax, and rice industries. Abu Taqiyya advanced loans to landowners, receiving preferential access to the sugar they harvested in return. This move often unfolded in collaboration with local tax collectors—*multazims*—who advanced capital to local peasants to allow them to dig canals, buy seeds, and focus on cash crops. Since at least the seventeenth century, Japanese merchants had also been making such advances to rural cultivators to secure their harvests; the *ton'ya* (traders) of Osaka funded the equipment of fishermen to secure their catch, while other merchants financed cotton production around the city. Urban capital also entered the Hokkaido fishing industry, as merchants provided credit and tools to herring fishermen for access to their catch. And in the northern Chinese province of Henan, merchants advanced loans to cotton growers, enabling a commercialization of local agriculture that would create cotton farms bigger than sixteen hundred acres in size.[27]

Everywhere, the great connecting enabled this accelerating but initially modest move of urban capital into the countryside. While encroaching merchants used a variety of methods, weak rural social structures were almost always a necessary precondition. Often, they had been weakened by epidemiological catastrophes. In the Americas, perhaps most dramatically, the rapid spread of diseases brought by

European arrivals killed a large portion of the Indigenous population, devastating their complex societies and undermining their capacity to significantly resist the commercializing agenda of foreign merchants. The Black Death had had similar effects in Europe: It killed between one- and two-thirds of all Europeans, leaving feudal landowners starved of labor and more dependent on urban moneyed elites, creating the conditions for the commercialization of the countryside. Two centuries later, when rural smallholders and village communities on the outskirts of Paris faced famine, plague, epidemics, war, and indebtedness, many had to sell their lands to survive, prompting the French jurist Charles Loyseau to comment in his 1610 *Traicté du déguerpissement et délaissement par hypothèque* (Treatise on abandonment and desertion of property by mortgage) that "debts have increased with the interest of the past, creditors are more pressing and debtors poorer."[28] These debts provided an opening to capital-rich Parisians, who bought land, remained in Paris, and collected rents from tenant farmers, who in turn hired local agricultural labor to meet the expanding city's ever increasing demand for food.[29]

The history of Burgundy, the French region south of Dijon famous today for its wine, was similar: First, the civil wars of the late sixteenth century raised tax burdens on villages. Then, for the decade after 1634, Swedish and other troops ransacked these towns during the Thirty Years' War. Survivors trying to rebuild their communities either took loans from merchants in the nearby city of Dijon or unloaded common lands. In previous centuries, common lands could be sold only under exceptional circumstances, but in December 1604, the Dijon judiciary decided that communities under its jurisdiction could sell these lands to cover their debts, decreeing that common lands "belonged to the community as a legal person, and just as properties belonging to any person could be sold, leased, or willed, properties belonging to communities could be alienated."[30] To pay its debts, the village of Pasques, for instance, sold 825 acres of its communal forest in 1614.[31] And this was not exceptional: When the village of Barjon fell into debt in the last decade of the sixteenth century, it contracted at least eight loans totaling 2,190 livres tournois, the French currency of the time. When it defaulted on these loans in 1602, it ceded common fields to one of its principal creditors, Dijon merchant Jean Vauthereau. Twenty years later, the village tried to reclaim the property, alleging before Dijon's parliament that Vauthereau's heirs had usurped it. Vauthereau's son denied the allegation but offered to return the property if the village repaid the original loans along with back interest. The village agreed, and in July 1623, the *parlement* ordered Barjon to reimburse all of the principal plus 6.125 percent interest for twenty years. The reclaimed commons were partitioned and repartitioned to service this communal debt. As a result, in some parts of Burgundy, private property rights in land spread by the mid-seventeenth century, and much of the land around Dijon moved into the hands of its urban economic elite.[32]

In the Low Countries, too, social crisis—the collapse of feudalism—gave urban merchants a newly prominent role in the countryside: As early as the thirteenth century, regions of the Low Countries saw the disintegration of feudal manors. Labor shortages forced landowners, who had for centuries drawn on labor tied by feudal dependencies, to lease their holdings to rural cultivators. When the Black Death made that labor increasingly scarce, land leasing accelerated, bringing opportunities for urban investments. Rich burghers purchased lands and leased them out, and as farming became more oriented toward markets and rich farmers rented ever larger units of land, agriculture became more capital-intensive, providing yet another outlet for merchants' trade profits.[33]

The investment of capital changed agriculture. The Beaujolais region near Dijon, for example, began growing wine grapes in the late sixteenth and seventeenth centuries under the initiative of outside capital, with three-quarters of its land passing into nonresident hands. In Catalonia, family farmers and sharecroppers converted more land to producing wine for distant markets as well. In the Dutch Republic, land ownership concentrated and tenant farmers began specializing in capital-intensive production of crops and livestock for the market. Some areas of the Dutch Republic, including the Guelders river area and coastal Frisia and Flanders, transitioned to concentrated commercial farming dominated by rich farmers employing wage labor. The Dutch countryside became an adjunct to the country's thriving cities.[34]

Beneath all the variations in form, the catalyst for urban capitalists' conquest of the countryside was the same: the heretofore unparalleled profits and the potential for long-distance trade. Markets for agricultural production grew as cities expanded and fewer people produced their own subsistence. In the Low Countries, trade with the Baltic states brought increasing quantities of grain to Dutch ports, allowing local agricultural production to focus on higher-value products like dairy products and beef, much of which in turn went into the expanding export markets forged by Dutch merchants. So attractive an investment was agriculture that in the first years of the seventeenth century, rich Amsterdam traders invested almost 1.5 million guilders (about $130 million in 2024 US dollars) in a huge land reclamation project, creating seven thousand hectares of new agricultural land. The 10 million guilders that flowed into drainage projects in the Noorderkwartier between 1590 and 1650 exceeded the capitalization of either the East or the West India Company. Accelerated by the confiscation of church lands, urban influence on the Dutch countryside deepened, and by the eighteenth century, more than two-thirds of rural lands were controlled by merchants. Manorial territory, with all its adjacent rights, was now a commodity like any other, and Dutch agriculture, once feudal and focused on provisioning manor lords and peasants, was now overwhelmingly oriented to local and global markets.[35]

The Dutch example demonstrates the tight links between the expansion of trade and the transformation of the countryside. Narratives that frame the Dutch push into the wider world as separate from the rearrangement of domestic agriculture or cast the expansion of the Dutch economy as a last gasp of an old mercantile regime miss the deep connections between the interior and the exterior, between trade and the transformation of the countryside, and, as we will see, between different systems of labor at the heart of the capitalist revolution. Merchant capital's transformation of agrarian production—though distinct from industrial capital—was nonetheless its foundry, generating not just the initial stake for capitalism but also some of its core legal, social, and financial mechanisms.[36]

A look at the English countryside further amplifies this point. For centuries, England's rural society was shaped and defined by lords who claimed sovereignty over rural cultivators, but in the fifteenth and sixteenth centuries, economic distress forced many feudal landowners to part with their property and others to incur heavy debts, allowing rising urban capital owners to gain new footholds.[37] As in the Low Countries, urban capital pushed into agriculture from a burgeoning trade sector. As the feudal system slowly disintegrated, and landlords failed to reestablish old dependencies after the plague, property owners leased their holdings to enterprising peasants who employed wage laborers, inserting commercial competition and free labor into the countryside in what has been termed "agrarian capitalism."[38]

Partly necessitated by the greater capital intensity of new agricultural techniques—particularly the Norfolk System, a four-course crop-rotation scheme—urban capital streamed into the countryside. Landowners took out mortgages, and merchants began purchasing manors. So significant was the redistribution of peasant property that a 1514 petition to the king critiqued merchants and artisans for their too-frequent land purchases. Investments in land were also motivated by the decline of other economic sectors, as when Essex textile manufacturer Thomas Griggs (1701–1760) moved his capital into agrarian production. New market opportunities, like supplying the needs of growing cities or raising sheep to supply the booming wool trade, were also motivations. At the same time, formerly feudal landowners became capitalist entrepreneurs, leasing their land to tenant farmers.[39] "The new society," observed economist Maurice Dobb, "had to be nourished from the crisis and decay of the old order."[40] The old system of servile labor and peasants' access to common lands slowly gave way to a system whose signal innovations were private property in land and wage labor.

Cotesbach, in the south of Leicestershire, sat in an area at the center of England's open field system. For centuries, eighteen to twenty households had worked the eleven hundred acres of the manor, which had no boundary markers and included meadows and other lands used by all, with shared rights among various users. Change came slowly, but in the early sixteenth century, the local lord enclosed one-fifth of the land. As the lord's sheep and cattle began grazing on the grass covering now fallow fields, five farming households with about thirty members lost access to the land. But the most drastic change came about a hundred years later. In 1606, John Quarles, a London drapery merchant, bought the manor for six thousand pounds. To maximize profits, he enclosed the rest of the land, despite protests by local cultivators. As the open fields disappeared and farmers could no longer graze their sheep and cows on the commons, about half of the population left the village, while Quarles almost doubled his income. So drastic a change was the infusion of urban capital that, in 1607, thousands of farmers revolted.[41]

A s capital moved outward from the cities and into the nearby countryside, the distances it traveled were usually modest—from Dijon to Beaune, from Surat to Tadkeshwar, from Amsterdam to Frisia, from Cairo to the Nile Delta. But sometimes urban capital traveled far greater distances to gain control over agricultural production, although only a few capital owners had the ability to do so. Only in rare cases did non-European merchants participate in this process—mostly Chinese traders who invested in sugar production in various parts of Asia. Much later, by the eighteenth century, Gujarati merchants brought capital into the East African countryside, enabling an expansion of the elephant hunt, as Banian merchants traded up to 310 tons of ivory from Mozambique Island to Gujarat yearly. Even later, Omani capital transformed the Zanzibar countryside by building there a thriving spice plantation economy, much of it fueled by slave labor.[42]

But the most significant streams of capital moving over long distances into agricultural lands were Italian, Spanish, Portuguese, Dutch, and English traders' prominent positions in the great connecting now translated into an equally prominent role in the transformation of the countryside. Among the most prevalent participants were Dutch capitalists, who moved tentatively into the Polish countryside as early as the fourteenth century, drawing timber and grain into western and southern Europe. By the sixteenth century, a quarter of the total wheat consumption in the Netherlands came from Poland, while Dutch merchants also made money passing on huge quantities of wheat to the Iberian Peninsula.[43]

Danzig became the hub of that great trade, an impressive spectacle described in 1636 by German traveler Kurt Schottmueller, who observed that "as soon as the Poles and Prussians bring their wheat into storage, the Dutch have arrived with their ships, to load the wheat with enormous zeal in large quantities and to distribute it around the world."[44] In 1642, 2,052 Dutch vessels called at the port, making Danzig by far the most important trading city in the Baltic.[45] Almost 80 percent of Danzig's overseas trade rested in the hands of Dutch merchants, who settled there in ever larger numbers: Between 1558 and 1709, 456 Dutch merchants moved to Danzig, often relatives of merchants in the Netherlands. (Amsterdam trader Cornelius Pietersz Hooft sent two of his brothers there in 1584.) This export boom was possible, as we will see, because of the territorial extension of wheat production in Danzig's rapidly expanding hinterland and the sharpening of labor coercion there.[46]

Dutch merchants, flush with highly liquid American silver, channeled capital to Polish nobles, providing credit by contracting for future wheat deliveries. The merchants also funded Danzig's financial institutions, which then invested even more in agriculture. Sometimes

Danzig merchants gained direct control of farms, as when King Casimir IV Jagiellon of Poland granted them the right to purchase lands in 1466.[47] Maximilian Transsylvanus, the imperial emissary to Hamburg for the governor of the Netherlands, described this system in detail in 1534:

> [T]he Dutchmen come once or twice a year to Danzig with two or three hundred ships, to buy and to raise in fourteen days all the grain that one finds in said city of Danzig. For all the great lords and masters of Poland and Prussia have found, for the last twenty-five years, the means of sending, by some rivers, all their grains to Danzig, and having them sold to that city. And for these reasons the kingdom of Poland and the great lords became very rich and greatly increased. For in the past they did not know what to do with their grains, and left the lands uncultivated, and the town of Danzig, which was no more than a village, is at this time the most powerful and richest city in the whole Baltic.[48]

So influential were these investments that by the seventeenth century, eastern European grainlands were practically a Dutch economic colony. As we will see in detail later, this created further beneficial links for Dutch merchants. They invested in a thriving shipbuilding industry to transport all that wheat and acquired Silesian linens to trade into Atlantic markets. Dutch merchants also plowed some of their profits into the protoindustrialization of the Low Countries. They also sold a range of luxury goods to Danzig, including colonial products, fueling the conspicuous consumption of Polish nobles. But at the heart of it all was grain export.[49]

THE MOVE OF Dutch capital into eastern European grainlands and Norwegian forests rearranged the economic and social landscape of Europe. Yet the truly revolutionary potential of urban capital was elsewhere—namely, in the incursions of Italian, Portuguese, Spanish, Dutch, English, French, German, Swiss, and Scandinavian merchants into the American countryside. There, modest investments were amplified by the

Merchants in Danzig: Detail of a map made by German cartographer Johann Baptist Homann (1664–1724), Nuremberg, circa 1720.

outsize resources of the dominated peoples and lands. Through violent dispossession, merchants created opportunities for capital accumulation, clearing the way for commercial domination.

As we have seen, in the sixteenth century, European merchants were already a powerful presence in the world, trading in Asia and Africa and subduing the Inca and Aztec Empires and appropriating their rich stores. Increasingly, however, Europeans broadened their original focus on exchange and theft and launched production on distant continents. Indeed, it was these new islands of capital in Africa, Asia, and, most importantly, the Americas that unlocked the radical potential of urban capital to transform the countryside, and with it, the world economy.[50]

Fortunes accumulated in trade were now invested into the transformation of the American countryside. From the fifteenth century on, many a Genoese family invested in sugar plantations on islands off the coast of Africa, in the slave trade, and then in the Americas. The Florentines were not far behind, with the Medici investing in the slave trade and the Bardis financing the Spanish move into the Americas. Giannotto Berardi, a Florentine living in Seville, invested heavily in transatlantic expansion, and when he died in 1494, Amerigo Vespucci, the executor of his will, took over much of his business, including financing voyages to the Caribbean and the associated dealings in enslaved people. The American continent is named for a slave trader.[51]

The first crucial commodity pushed by these traders into the Atlantic world was sugar, a voracious consumer of capital. Sugar had ancient origins in India, the Arab world, and places like Cyprus, but in the fifteenth century, Italian merchants moved its cultivation into the Atlantic: first to the islands of Madeira, Cape Verde, and São Tomé, then across the ocean to Pernambuco and Bahia in Brazil. It was in these places that modern sugar cultivation emerged, with its crucial trifecta of monoculture, slave labor, and domination by distant European capitalists. As early as 1555, twelve thousand slaves worked on São Tomé alone.[52] By the 1640s, as mentioned, the sugar frontier arrived on Barbados.

That Caribbean island, as we have seen, prototyped the coming capitalist utopia of markets becoming the sole arbiter of human affairs. Almost from the outset, Barbadian land was turned into private property. The colonial government gave land grants to tobacco, indigo, and cotton planters, and the recipients immediately pressed for the rights of freehold ownership. Sugar plantations needed much larger units of land, and incipient sugar lords purchased the holdings of small farmers and evicted tenants. Real estate values soared, increasing ten times between 1640 and 1646 alone. A feverish land market emerged: Between March and December of 1647, prospective sugar planters bought ten thousand acres of land, almost 10 percent of all the island's cultivatable land. While some smaller cotton and indigo planters successfully transitioned to sugar, the sugar boom's entirely new scale pushed many recently established smallholders off their properties. Men of modest means had to either work on larger plantations, in the capital of Bridgetown, or, more commonly, leave Barbados. The number of immigrants living on the island dropped by almost half in the years between 1655 and 1712, as at least ten thousand people left. A tiny elite of just seventy-four planters came to dominate the newly forged sugar island, each holding plantations of between two hundred and one thousand acres. The sugar frontier devoured the Barbadian countryside. By 1680, 80 percent of its arable land was used for sugar, 90 percent of its workers labored in sugar, and 90 percent of its export earnings came from sugar. The island had become a sugar-producing slave labor camp, with thousands worked to death every year to feed Europeans' appetite for profit and sweetness. Bridgetown had become one of the most important cities in British America.[53]

Significant investments of Dutch and English capital made this revolutionary mobilization of land, labor, and technology possible. In the first half of the seventeenth century, Dutch merchants redirected some of their capital, expertise, slaves, and technology to the island, as Portuguese conquest threatened their earlier investments in Pernambuco, Brazil. The English moved capital as well: In 1647 alone, English merchants invested 150,000 Barbadian pounds, equaling about one-tenth of the entire revenue of the English government. Between 1640 and 1660, the English capital invested in Barbados totaled 1.5 million pounds, much of it accumulated in trade—in the Atlantic, Asia, Africa, and the Mediterranean, but also in the woolen trade within Europe itself. Such investments showcased almost perfectly the connection between the great connecting and the transformation of the countryside. The world economy and the plantation created each other.[54]

European capital combined with coerced labor to fuel the explosive growth of Barbados sugar production. In 1665, the island exported 11,529 metric tons of muscovado sugar, 919 tons of refined sugar, 529,943 liters of molasses, and 567,827 liters of rum—with nearly half going to North America and half to England. By the early 1650s, the value of that sugar was more than three million pounds, or twice the annual income of the English government, making the island itself the richest part of the New World."[55] By the 1660s, sugar imports into England were of greater value than all other colonial imports combined.[56] As historian David Eltis has argued, "Barbados was probably exporting more, proportionate to its size and population, than any other colony or state of its time or, indeed, in the history of the world up to that point."[57] Its planters were wealthier than anyone else in English America.[58] The sugar exports from Barbados and elsewhere in the Americas, moreover, massively accelerated global trade; in the two centuries after 1600 they were significantly more valuable than any other international commodity trade.[59] Contemporary observer Richard Ligon was awed by the "vast Revenue this little spot of ground can produce," and that all this wealth had been accumulated "without the help of Magic or Enchantment."[60]

Indeed, as the capitalist revolution unfolded in Barbados, it could seem as if magic were at play. Certainly, significant change had occurred elsewhere, but the speed with which a wave of the wand of capital had recast a Caribbean island was spectacular and, to keen observers, hinted at the nascent powers of capital and its seemingly limitless opportunities.[61]

A peculiar and novel kind of society, Barbados showed how combining American lands, African labor, and European capital could produce agricultural commodities for distant consumers. It was one of the first times in human history that capital owners controlled production on a massive scale and built an entire society around the single-minded pursuit of the production and consumption of commodities. Elements of this new world, as we have seen, also emerged in the Dutch, Egyptian, Gujarati, English, and other countrysides, but more slowly and less dramatically. Tellingly, European capital owners had been able to forge this new society only by going abroad, since at home, such radical moves would have entailed an unceasing struggle with feudal lords and deeply rooted rural cultivators, a struggle that had broken out in some parts of the continent and had by no means been resolved.[62] Unpopulated Barbados was remote, but the challenges involved were tiny compared to the difficulties of effecting such a transformation in the world's settled countrysides. Barbados demonstrated the enormous profit possibilities that came from combining trade and production, commodified land and labor. So important was this lesson that over the next two centuries the lesson spread across the world, not least to Europe, whose weaknesses in global trade and ossified social structures had sent its adventurers into the Atlantic expanse in the first place.

Barbados became a beacon of capital's ability to revolutionize production and, more tangibly, a profitable outlet for large accumulations of capital, which was not easily found in the early modern world. Sugar planters came to control some of the largest businesses of the age. And the plantation itself, with its labor discipline, tight workforce organization, and focus on productivity and time control, was arguably the first modern industry. It was yet another mode of the transition to agrarian capitalism.[63]

European migrants flooded to these ventures: Of the 378,000 Europeans migrating to the English Americas between 1630 and 1700, 59 percent went to the Caribbean. While citizens of the modern-day United States tend to imagine New England as the core of the New World, it was much less economically important than Barbados. Barbados was the center, Boston the periphery. Boston mattered primarily as an important supplier of food and capital goods (wood, horses, candles) consumed by dynamic Caribbean economies, including Barbados.[64] It became, from the perspective of London, the hinterland's hinterland.

One of the greatest attractions of this plantation machine was that it was portable, its intrinsic radicalism and disregard for local peculiarities allowing for the integration of ever more land and labor. It arrived in Guadeloupe in the 1660s, spread to Martinique and the Leeward Islands in the 1670s, moved on to Jamaica in the 1680s, and then, most consequentially, came to Saint-Domingue in the 1690s. European merchants converted island after island into monocultural factory-style plantations powered by slave labor; Martinique counted 6,582 enslaved workers in 1671, but by 1719 that number had exploded to 35,478. Jamaica produced twenty thousand tons of sugar in 1754; twenty years later, that production had doubled. Slavery was the driving force; the vast majority of Jamaica's population was enslaved, with 106,592 women, men, and children by 1752. Barbadian sugar experts transferred their expertise as far as Saint Helena and Sumatra.[65] Adam Smith, no friend of the planters, explained the rationale behind these moves straightforwardly: "The profits of a sugar-plantation in any of our West Indian colonies are generally much greater than those of any other cultivation that is known either in Europe or America."[66]

Among the most powerful transformations was that of Saint-Domingue, modern-day Haiti. Sugar cultivation emerged there in the 1690s, thanks to the Compagnie de Saint-Domingue. Backed by France's highest echelons of merchants and bankers, including royal financier and slaver Samuel Bernard, merchant and financier Antoine Crozat (who later controlled Louisiana), and financier Pierre Thomé, and boosted by wartime booty from Jamaica (sugar-making equipment and thousands of slaves), these massive investments from France (needed not least because of the time lag between the first investments in slave labor and the first sugar harvests), allowed 450 plantations to produce forty thousand tons of sugar by 1739, more than the entire British Caribbean. As always, with the expansion of sugar came the expansion of slavery: In 1715, Saint-Domingue housed 158 sugar plantations; 38,723 people lived there, of whom 30,651 were enslaved. By 1786, 340,000 slaves worked across 4,820 plantations—910 for sugar, 3,000 for coffee, 700 for indigo, 60 for cacao, and 150 for cotton.[67] In 1789, that number was 450,000. They worked alongside 40,000 whites and 28,000 *affranchis* (free people of color). By the 1780s, the island's agro-industry sucked in 4 out of 10 Africans traded across the Atlantic, with 40,000 enslaved women, men, and children arriving in 1790 alone. Enslavement unfolded on a tremendous scale: Traders transported twice as many Africans to Saint-Domingue as to the entire United States and its colonial antecedents.[68] France built one of the world's most important production complexes by combining military protection and preferential customs treatment with what Saint-Domingue's first French governor, Jean-Baptiste du Casse, called in 1698 the "natural" propensity of people "to want to increase their wealth."[69] When US commission merchant Samuel Gardner Perkins traveled to Saint-Domingue in 1791, he observed that "the flourishing state of trade and the prosperity of [its] inhabitants were without a parallel perhaps in the world."[70]

Financing slavery's expansion in Saint-Domingue: portrait of Samuel Bernard (1651–1739).

Léogâne, a parish just west of Port-au-Prince, was at the forefront of the plantation revolution on this French outpost, remaining for years under the direct sovereign control of the Compagnie de Saint-Domingue. In 1696, Léogâne counted several tobacco farms, fifty-four indigo plantations, and one sugar mill, worked by 973 white laborers and 675 Africans. In 1730, fifty-nine sugar mills dotted the landscape, along with thirty-one indigo plantations. And while the number of white farmers dropped to 706, the number of enslaved workers stood at 7,646—Léogâne had become a murderous but immensely productive vortex that funneled unprecedented sugar and profit into metropolitan France.[71]

The profitable investments in the transformation of the Saint-Domingue countryside attracted many a French merchant and aristocrat. The Chaurands, one of the richest families in the Atlantic port city of Nantes, with an estimated personal fortune of three million livres tournois, moved some of their capital to the Caribbean. Founded in 1771 by Honoré Chaurand, their business specialized in loans to West Indian planters, usually used to expand the enslaved labor force. During the 1780s, they got more directly involved in the slave trade, financing seven slaving voyages to Africa. Between 1771 and 1792, they dispatched fifty-three ships to Saint-Domingue to retrieve sugar, as contractual arrangements with thirty-eight Saint-Domingue planters provided them with a constant stream of commission trades. The Chaurands—contra supposedly neat divisions between merchants and planters—also purchased sugar and coffee plantations outright, drawing as needed on the capital of additional Parisian investors. Though they never set foot in Saint-Domingue, their fortunes depended on a fine-tuned sense of the island's topography and its opportunities. Their plantations were remarkably profitable; their Fleurau estate, for instance, returned an eyebrow-raising 15 percent annually between 1775 and 1784.[72]

With such profits, it is no surprise that the Chaurands had company. In 1768, banker Jean-Joseph de Laborde invested his proceeds from government loans made during the Seven Years' War into sugar plantations in Saint-Domingue. Jean-Baptiste Hosten, the son of a Bordelaise sugar merchant, held a large sugar plantation near Port-au-Prince, along with 216 enslaved workers. When he retired to Paris in 1788, he invested massively in the city's real estate.[73]

So much capital moved to Saint-Domingue that in the grim accounting after the Haitian Revolution, traders in Nantes estimated their losses at 93 million livres tournois. In 1828, when a French commission investigated the economic damage sustained by French investors as a result of Saint-Domingue's emancipation, it found that the island was "as rich . . . as three or four *Départements* in France."[74] A full ten thousand French families claimed indemnities for their lost properties—investing them into real estate and industry, while the Haitian people paid for their freedom with reparations and debt service on loans that shackled them to France until 1947.[75] State and public support for the indemnities showed how deeply involved capital-rich France was in the slave economy, a depth and breadth of involvement matched by England and the Dutch Republic.

Plantations powered emerging Atlantic capitalism, and sugar was its single most important engine.[76] Contemporaries were aware of the great significance of the plantation revolution, not just because of its radicalism, but because of its reverberations in many other parts of the world. In 1760, British colonial official William Burke wrote from occupied Guadeloupe: "[I]t is by Means of the *West-Indian* Trade that a great Part of *North America* is at all enabled to trade with us. . . . [I]n

*Reshaping the countryside: a map of plantation lands in Saint Croix,
Danish West Indies, 1754.*

Reality the Trade of these *North American* Provinces . . . is, as well as
that of *Africa*, to be regarded as a dependent Member, and subordinate
Department of the *West-Indian* Trade; it must rise and fall exactly as
the *West-Indies* flourish or decay."[77] Guillaume Thomas François Raynal and Adam Smith agreed with him that this uniquely revolutionary
use of slave labor for the production of sugar in the Caribbean countryside fueled as nothing else could a further intensification of the great
connecting.[78]

And it was not just sugar. Enslaved workers produced other commodities in great quantities as well. Other commodities poured out of
the Americas: In Dutch-controlled eighteenth-century Surinam, capital
owners funded vast slave-powered coffee plantations that played a major
role in establishing the Dutch Republic's trade position in Europe.[79]

In Virginia, on the North American mainland, English settlers
discovered another crop—tobacco—that could be profitably grown for

world markets. Europeans had first encountered tobacco in the New World as a medicine and narcotic, and they had planted it in various parts of the world before eventually concentrating production in the English North American colonies, where it became the economic waterwheel for the small Virginia settlement. In 1616, Virginia exported 1,250 pounds of the addictive substance; twelve years later it had jumped to 370,000 pounds; in 1672 it was 10.5 million pounds. Virginia became a boom country, dedicated so heavily to tobacco that early tobacco farmers often failed to produce sufficient foodstuffs to feed themselves.[80]

This radical transformation of the Virginia countryside was enabled by British merchants moving their capital to the New World. Scottish capital, in particular, flowed into Virginia tobacco, and by the eighteenth century all three major Glasgow banks were controlled by tobacco lords. Glasgow firms posted salaried agents in the colonies, where those agents purchased cargoes in advance for their employers' ships, reducing the turnaround time in the Chesapeake.[81]

The colony's success depended on acquiring land—of which there was plenty—and, more importantly, workers. Tobacco would grow almost anywhere, so planters rushed to stake claims to laborers. At first, they focused on indentured servants. Eventually, however, just as on the sugar islands, slavery emerged as the dominant labor system.

The opportunities for profit in tobacco and sugar not only recast agriculture, they also produced important innovations crucial to the capitalist revolution.[82] Planters developed new accounting practices and ways of organizing work. The overseers at the Saint-Domingue plantations of the Marquis de Paroy, for example, produced extremely detailed accounts of their expenses and income, affording the marquis an unprecedented grasp of his enterprise's profitability. And Barbados planter Henry Drax demonstrated a keen understanding of management in his early eighteenth-century manual, which recorded in excruciating detail how to run a plantation—from how to punish slaves so as "to terrify others" to exactly how to apply fertilizer to cane seedlings— an early effort to "manage at a distance."[83] That such innovations came from plantations should not come as a great surprise, since these places were among the world's largest worksites. Mines in northeast England employed a maximum of one hundred people, and the few existing "manufactories" typically employed just a handful of workers. Only state-owned enterprises—such as the Royal Plate Glass Company of Tourville, France, with its one thousand workers in 1750—were larger than sugar plantations.[84]

Plantations also provided new forms of storing capital. Slaves were the most fungible form of collateral for loans; in fact, the relative security of property rights in enslaved workers was a necessary precondition for the vast infusion of capital. About one-third of capital assets owned in the British Empire in 1788 was in slaves: Their value in 2024 currency was a substantial 3.5 billion pounds. "Capitalized captives" were one of the catalysts that allowed European merchants to take center stage in an emerging global capitalism.[85]

Even more important, the plantation economy innovated long-distance trade, laying the groundwork for a new kind of global integration that would later enable other trade and capital flows. The transformation of the Caribbean countryside created a world economy: In the Americas, enslaved African workers supervised by Europeans grew sugar for global markets; and these workers had been purchased with Indian textiles acquired thanks to ample supplies of American silver generated by the European domination of the Americas. Never before had so many continents been drawn so deeply into the networks of interconnected capital as in the new Atlantic-focused world economy.

That world economy was crucial to capitalism's extraordinary new dynamic. As the sphere in which capital moved, it was both the condition of capitalism's emergence and its offspring. Even as states strengthened and built world-spanning empires, capital consistently transcended these boundaries. Think of Dutch merchants: While they operated in both the Dutch countryside and the Dutch Empire, they were crucial to the Caribbean sugar revolution on all islands, to the global trade in slave-produced agricultural commodities, and to the financing of their greatest adversary, the British state.[86] (In 1716, Dutch investors held

59 million of the 143 million pounds of British state debt.)[87] Later, Dutch capital was crucial to the young United States. It makes no sense to think of the Dutch Empire as an enclosed economic space, since Dutch capital and trade continually crossed these boundaries. To cite another telling example: When English merchant and planter Gedney Clarke ran up against the spatial limitations of Barbados, he bought thousands of acres of plantation land in the Dutch colony of Demerara.[88] Capitalism has just one history—a world history, with one of its key sparks in the forests, barrens, and swamps of Caribbean islands and the American mainland.

Most important, plantations demonstrated how capital could dominate and control land and labor, putting them into the vanguard of a new kind of production. As the Americas became critical to the forging of a world economy, they demonstrated that creating the new order—a world in which markets dominate almost everything, where almost anything can be bought and sold—took great effort, energy, creativity, and coercion. There had been markets for millennia; people have forged debt relations and traded for as long as there have been communities. But now something entirely novel began emerging as capital owners combined new forms of labor with new forms of land ownership and new ways of organizing production, often across vast distances. The struggle to bring forth this new world unfolded on a global scale, even if its reverberations looked different in disparate locations. In Barbados, on the new order's cutting edge, capitalism rested on enormous violence, massive dispossessions, and coerced labor that let capital owners "solve" the problem of production by reinventing social structures almost from scratch. This was possible because there were no meddlesome feudal lords, rebellious peasants, or obstructionist states—because capital owners distant from their homelands could step outside the established order to extract unprecedented riches.[89]

Given this, it is puzzling that most scholarly treatments of the history of capitalism have left the Caribbean on the margin of their analysis. Many either ignore the importance of the Caribbean or, alternatively, write about it as if the Caribbean were a precapitalist, premodern remnant destined to be overcome by a spontaneously generated, modern capitalist revolution. Smith saw the ever more elaborate division of labor and the freedom of producers as the crucial animating force of capitalism. Marx wrote that slavery enabled the "rosy dawn of the era of capitalist production," an argument that some Marxists have used to relegate slavery to capitalism's prehistory.[90] Weber took the religious imperatives of European Protestantism as decisive. Violence, slavery, and dispossession have played only a tiny role in the stories Europeans told themselves about their newfound wealth. Only equally marginalized Caribbean intellectuals—Eric Williams and C. L. R. James prominent among them—kept alive the reality of the Caribbean's importance to the modern world and for capitalism's rise.[91]

The greater Caribbean's unique importance becomes clearer when we look at other parts of the world. In Virginia, Surinam, Saint-Domingue, and Barbados, among other places, European capital owners rapidly transformed huge swaths of the countryside. But that model did not travel easily to other continents. To be sure, Europeans had built a presence in Asia and in Africa as a crucial part of the great connecting. But there, they usually traded with Indigenous capital owners who were more locally powerful than they were, came to mutually beneficial arrangements with local rulers, and engaged with rural

Trade without controlling production: a Dutch merchant acquiring cotton on the Coromandel coast, Gable Stone, Amsterdam, circa 1700–1720.

cultivators who retained control over their labor and land. A meaning-ful transformation of the countryside of the kind seen in the Caribbean lay in the future.

━━━━━

But in exceptional circumstances, the Caribbean model took root in Asia—for example, in the Bandas, a small group of islands in to-day's Indonesia. When Jacob van Neck arrived there in 1599 from Amsterdam, he saw an opportunity to take control of the local nutmeg trade, a sought-after spice grown only on these islands. Local rulers, the *orang kaya* (rich men), controlled the trade, selling nutmeg to trad-ers from Gujarat, China, Bengal, Persia, Japan, and Portugal in a com-petitive market with multiple producers and purchasers and limited regulation or interference. The Dutch entered the fray, but the orang kaya retained control.[92]

But the Dutch East India Company was not interested in free and competitive markets. In Europe, nutmeg was a luxury good thought to have medicinal properties, and importing it was extraordinarily profit-able: For Dutch traders, profits on nutmeg exports could add up to 400 percent per journey. Consequently, they sought a monopoly. When the orang kaya refused to stop trading with other merchant groups, the Dutch applied ever increasing military pressure. Following a series of wars, the orang kaya signed a treaty obliging them to sell their entire harvest to the Dutch, and not, as the treaty said, to "the English, French, Javanese, Malay, Makassarese, Butonese and other European and black nations."[93]

In 1621, as local merchants continued to trade with non-Dutch merchants, the governor-general of the VOC, Jan Pieterszoon Coen, moved to completely subdue Bandanese society. He first depopulated the island and then repopulated it with enslaved workers from else-where. The VOC captured and executed the island's elite, beheading and quartering thirty-six elders, then shipped survivors to Batavia, to-day's Jakarta, where they were forced into slavery. That genocide de-

Transforming the countryside through genocide: Jan Pieterszoon Coen depopulates the Banda Islands to secure a monopoly in nutmeg and maize, 1627.

stroyed local society. Only eighteen hundred of the fifteen thousand people who had once lived on the Banda Islands survived. Land was distributed among European settlers, who used enslaved labor brought from other islands—Seram, Timor, Borneo, Buru, Papua, Bali, and South Sulawesi—to grow nutmeg for European markets. And so arrived the Caribbean revolution in Asia, albeit initially in a small outpost.[94]

Yet this "Caribbean cuckoo in an Asian nest" (in the apt words of historian Vincent C. Loth) remained the exception that proved the rule.[95] Plantation slavery and far-reaching European control arrived in some parts of Asia in the seventeenth and eighteenth centuries (about 26,000 slaves grew sugar around Batavia in 1688, for example, and by 1700 there were about 68,000 slaves in VOC-controlled territories). In the 350 years after 1500, between 500,000 and 750,000 slaves—some Asians but mostly African—were deported by Europeans to Asia. Still, enslaved workers never dominated production. Asian social and political structures remained deeply entrenched, and Europeans remained dependent on local resources: capital, access to labor, social structures, and even military prowess. Further testifying to the relative weakness of European traders and imperial bureaucrats outside the Americas, islands continued to remain at the center of Indian Ocean slavery wherever it reared its ugly head: in the Bandas, as we have seen, but also in the Mascarene Islands of Isle de France (Mauritius) and in Île Bourbon (La Réunion). It was only centuries later, in the second

Tabula rasa in Asia: nutmeg plantations on Neira, one of the Banda Islands.

half of the nineteenth century, that European capital owners dominated production in larger parts of Asia and Africa.[96]

Many European merchants, like the Noells on Barbados, saw the allure of the wealth-producing machine emerging in the world's countryside. They pushed commodity frontiers—sugar, tobacco, spices, labor—across vast swaths of the globe, integrating ever more territories and labor into the emerging capitalist world economy. Just as capitalism was "frontier-making," frontiers created capitalism by providing access to inputs of land, labor, and raw materials.[97]

As this merchant capital spread into the world's countryside, it began to transform all that it touched. While that revolution looked different depending on where it manifested (Burgundy or Barbados, Saint-Domingue or Surat, Poland or the Nile Delta), what these places all had in common was merchants at the fore. Indeed, merchants were hardly the conservative force that many nineteenth- and twentieth-century observers perceived them to be. For Marx, merchant capital had a purely external relationship to the "mode of production," siphoning off some of the profits of agricultural production, leaching from but not altering a panoply of different "social relations of production."[98] Economist Maurice Dobb, writing in the 1930s, agreed: Merchants were first and foremost "parasites on the old economic order," they were "a conservative rather than a revolutionary force; . . . [they] retard[ed] rather than . . . accelerate[d] the development of capitalism as a mode of production."[99] Historian Róbert Brenner even saw "merchant capitalism as an integral part of feudal society."[100] But this reading overlooks the crucial links between the intensification of trade—the arguably parasitical activity for which merchants are known—and the less understood merchant-led transformation of the countryside.[101] At a minimum, this lacuna in the history of capitalism is Eurocentric, missing the import of merchants' drastic recasting of the countryside in the Americas.

This revolutionizing infusion of merchant capital into the countryside required the mobilization of land and labor—whether on wheat farms in Europe's East or Ottoman cotton fields or nutmeg gardens in the Bandas. And often it was dispossessions that provided capital owners with claims to both. The colonization of the countryside by capital owners from Scotland to Virginia, from the Banda Islands to Gujarat, entailed the destruction of communal land tenure systems, the dispossession of rural elites, the forced removal of Indigenous peoples, and widespread expropriation of the land of rural cultivators. Dispossession and the creation of private property went hand in hand. The frontiers of commodification were zones of simultaneous dispossession and property making, enabling what Adam Smith called "previous," and Karl Marx "primitive," accumulation.[102] Capitalism's initial great stake was the spoils of a massive redistribution of social wealth—just as much between social groups as between different regions of the world.

Waves of dispossession in Europe itself affected elites and commoners alike. English King Henry VIII (1509–1547) expropriated church properties after the Reformation—a process that one historian has called the "naked plunder of the monasteries." That plunder was valuable: In 1535, English church properties produced perhaps as much as four hundred thousand pounds a year in revenue, while Crown lands yielded just forty thousand pounds. After 1536, 60 percent of these profitable church properties passed to the Crown, a massive transfer. As 825 monasteries in England and Wales were expropriated, 20 to 30 percent of England's real property was transferred, often to the gentry, but lawyers, government officials, and merchants also benefited.[103]

Expropriations from elites occurred elsewhere too. The Dutch Revolt (against Spanish rule) in the 1560s caused a violent reordering of the Dutch countryside, with the state expropriating monasteries and their ample land holdings. When the state leased the land to farmers, it furthered a rapid commercialization of agriculture that let urban capitalists purchase large estates.[104] Elite dispossession was not limited to Europe. Like the orang kaya in the Bandas, the enormously wealthy rulers and elites of the Inca and Aztec Empires lost their properties as part of genocide on a truly massive scale.

But it was commoners who felt the real brunt of dispossessions. As urban capital entered the countryside, rural cultivators the world over lost rights to the land or were displaced entirely. The forceful eradication of the commons took crucial resources away from rural cultivators; enclosures pushed peasants off soil tilled for generations; farmers lost grazing rights and the right to collect wood and berries; nomads lost access to grazing and hunting grounds; and rural cultivators from Virginia to the Banda Islands were expelled from their lands at shocking speed. It was, as Karl Polanyi succinctly observed, "a revolution of the rich against the poor."[105]

The pace and extent of these dispossessions stood in direct proportion to rural cultivators' ability to resist. By 1600 in Spain, one-fifth of rural cultivators were landless. The greatest expropriations of all time, however, took place in the Americas, where over the course of a few centuries the continents' Indigenous inhabitants lost almost all their land, all their natural resources, and, often, their lives. Two million Taino people lived on the Caribbean islands, but a century after the arrival of Europeans, almost all of them were dead.[106] Dominican friar Bartolomé de las

Casas observed this depeopling of the Americas and urged the Spanish to "remember that we found the island full of people, whom we erased from the face of the earth, filling it with dogs and beasts."[107]

Dispossessions also played a crucial role in areas where the balance of social power was less skewed than in the Caribbean. Perhaps the most well-known case among these dispossessions involved cultivators in the British Isles—first in England, then in the Irish colony and Scotland. Beginning in the early sixteenth century, English landowners—both the old feudal elite as well as new wealthy merchants—turned common lands into private property. The balance of power shifted toward these new capitalist landowners, including landowning merchants. By 1550, almost half of all English land was enclosed; by 1760, three-quarters. After Oliver Cromwell's reconquering of Ireland in the mid-sixteenth century, Catholic rebels had their land confiscated en masse, while Protestant land ownership doubled.[108]

In Scotland, the Parliament passed a series of acts between 1661 and 1685 to enable the enclosure of arable land and the improvement of Scottish farming practices. In 1684, Sir David Dunbar of Baldoon used these new mechanisms to construct a cattle park that could hold one thousand animals, expelling resident tenants in the process.[109] Landowners dispossessed subtenants of the land they had used for subsistence farming and transformed arable land into pasture. In June 1723, when landowners founded the Honourable Society of Improvers in the Knowledge of Agriculture, their goal was expressed in the title of one of their publications: *Directing the Husbandry of the Different Soils for the Most Profitable Purposes*.[110] Profit meant enclosing ever more land and expelling tenant farmers from that land.

Enclosures dramatically altered the English, Irish, and Scottish countryside and society. They transformed fields into sheep pastures, encouraging the wool trade and demonstrating once again how transforming the countryside also accelerated the great connecting. As peasant families lost access to land, they had to sell their labor to the highest bidder. Aided by laws penalizing vagrancy and the use of wood from the commons, the countryside became less thickly settled and agricultural cultivators' incomes declined. Without access to land, workers now became available for other pursuits. Because of the superior agricultural techniques of new farmers, productivity improved, with the resulting wealth captured almost exclusively by landowners, which increased inequality but also doubled agricultural output between 1520 and 1739.[111]

The vast wave of dispossessions that capital owners caused in their effort to commercialize the countryside created societies unlike any that had ever existed. Never before had there been a place that produced solely or mostly for markets. Whether we look at the rolling hills of England, the plantations of Saint-Domingue, the *çiftlik* of Istanbul, the vast estates of eastern Europe, the tea plantations of China, or the vineyards of Burgundy, we see places characterized by production for markets—and the incomplete but far-reaching commodification of land, inputs and outputs, and labor. And once merchants remade the countryside in one place, they remade it somewhere else: moving from colony to home country and from home country to colony. Moreover, thanks to the great connecting, these places were all linked to one another—that is, to the world economy.

They were different from what had come before, but, equally important, they were different from one another, and this heterogeneity came to define capitalism. Most striking, perhaps, was the diversity of labor systems. Sometimes peasant producers worked the commercializing countryside, sometimes slaves. Sometimes sharecroppers produced goods for markets, at other times wage laborers or serfs. The reason for this diversity is obvious: As capital owners pushed into the countryside, they encountered different social structures, polities, legal traditions, and distributions of power; by adapting to this diversity, they produced different outcomes. Such diversity characterizes capitalism to the present day and is no small part of its extraordinary dynamism. From its very beginning, capitalism was dogmatic only about profits.

Access to labor was one of the most crucial variables, as the transformation of the countryside rested on mobilizing large numbers of workers. Throughout history, it has been difficult to persuade people to work willingly for the benefit of others. Tributary societies solved this problem by rulers taxing independent producers in goods as well as labor. In this world, supervision over production was almost nonexistent, and rulers skimmed the largely independent strivings of the people they controlled. As urban capital began streaming into the countryside, however, new forms of labor mobilization and control emerged.

Indigenous slavery was one of them. Upon reaching the New World, Europeans enslaved Indigenous peoples. Columbus was eager to trade them, even bringing hundreds of them to Spain.[112] "The Indians of Española," he said, "were and are *the greatest wealth of the island*, because they are the ones who dig, and harvest, and collect the bread and the supplies, and gather the gold from the mines, and do all the work of men and beasts alike."[113] This enslavement, however, became ever more difficult, as white settlement caused the Indigenous populations to collapse, with de las Casas observing that Europeans killed "anyone and everyone who has shown the slightest sign of resistance."[114]

Indentured workers were another source of labor: poor Europeans who agreed to several years of agricultural service in return for passage to the New World. In Barbados, as we have seen, much of the early production of tobacco, cotton, and indigo had been done by such workers. But there were limits to this form of labor as well. Sugar could be produced in larger quantities only with a larger, more stable, and better supervised group of workers. Such labor was not forthcoming— indentured servants did not arrive in sufficient numbers, nor did people volunteer to work for low wages.[115]

Planters quickly found another source of workers: African cultivators and artisans who could be forced into the holds of ships and transported to the Americas from some of the newly constituted islands of capital that dotted the African coast. In Barbados, kidnapped Africans dominated sugar labor from the beginning. Even in the pre-sugar years, one thousand enslaved Africans were sold on the island each year to power the growing of tobacco, indigo, and cotton. This relatively small number established a pattern of labor mobilization that could be expanded without creating social upheaval. Slavery, political economists believed, was also advantageous because it relieved pressure on the labor supply back home.[116]

By the 1640s, European traders had brought an additional 23,000 slaves to Barbados, with a further 90,000 arriving between 1664 and 1688. By 1700, the population of enslaved women and men laboring on the island had exploded to 50,000, who made up a full 75 percent of its inhabitants. This brutal mobilization of labor continued into the new century: During the 1710s, almost 4,000 enslaved workers arrived, on average, annually. This constant stream enabled the production of ever more sugar backed by ever more violence. The supposed industriousness that some scholars see as decisive for European economic takeoff was, in the Caribbean, forced upon workers. Before 1760, European traders transported 4.38 million enslaved Africans to the New World—about twice the number of European migrants who arrived in the Americas in the same period. Perhaps capitalism could have developed differently, but, as economist Barbara Solow pointed out long ago, the reality is that it developed based on slavery.[117]

The great connecting that brought European merchants to the coast of Africa to traffic the continent's people made possible the mobilization of labor for plantations in the Americas. When du Casse traveled to the coast of West Africa in 1687, he negotiated a trade agreement with the king of Ardra, securing French access to a share of the more than 20,000 enslaved workers who were exported annually from West Africa. To put the massive commodification of labor into perspective: In 1750, roughly 1.73 million enslaved cultivators, artisans, and miners labored on sugar, tobacco, rice, indigo, and cotton plantations and in silver mines in the Americas—at a time when the entire population of England was 5.74 million people, with a workforce of about 2.9 million people. By 1800, the total slave population in the Americas had increased to 3.35 million.[118]

With the increasing reliance on enslaved workers, securing labor from Africa became an urgent matter to merchants investing in the Americas. An early trading place emerged on the Cape Verdean islands, one of the first sites where Europeans concentrated capital in Africa. Cape Verdean merchants built trading bases in the West African aquatic forests bordering the Atlantic Ocean, with some migrating there. They connected to African merchants and African political authorities in their quest to secure workers. The persistent warfare between Muslim Wolof and ancestor-worshiping Serers, conflicts that produced a steady stream of captives and were fueled by the demand for enslaved labor, made merchants' efforts to secure enslaved workers easier. In later decades, Portuguese and Cape Verdean ships penetrated some of the rivers adjacent to Cacheu (in today's Guinea-Bissau), further expanding the trade in human cargo.[119]

Merchants exchanged slaves for European and South Asian textiles, metals, manufactured goods, wines, brandy, beads, paper, silver from Spanish America, and Cape Verdean products such as raw cotton, cotton cloth, salted goat meat, horses, and cattle. Already in the sixteenth century, they were bringing the production of Asia, Africa, the Americas, and Europe to the western coast of Africa—pointing to complementarities that developed among the islands of capital.[120]

Thanks to this efficient trade in workers, with enough money, any labor needs could be met almost instantaneously. In Barbados and elsewhere, the concentration of landownership went hand in hand with the concentration of ownership in labor. By 1680, two hundred planters owned more than sixty enslaved workers each, with another two hundred planters owning between twenty and sixty. Sugar plantations typically extended over about two hundred acres of land and were worked by one hundred enslaved cultivators, a much larger workforce than those on typical English farms. Barbados had become a huge labor camp, turning the living labor of enslaved Africans into sugar for world markets and killing workers at startlingly high rates in the process. Sugar planter James Drax, who created in 1654 what might have been the first integrated sugar plantation (combining growing and processing) in Barbados, had two hundred slaves at work on his 850 acres of land.[121]

Planters could acquire and murderously exploit all that labor because sugar was so extraordinarily profitable. Buying a slave could pay off in just eighteen months, after which extracting her or his labor power was almost pure profit. Further, as labor hunting in Africa became more efficient, and the labor commodity frontier itself became more productive, the price of slaves fell by about 50 percent between 1627 and 1680, providing an almost unprecedented elasticity of labor supply and a clear price advantage over indentured workers. As a result, sugar and slavery expanded hand in glove. Two-thirds of all Africans sold into the Americas ended up in sugar colonies. "[T]he Planters buy them out of the Ship, where they find them stark naked," Richard Ligon observed about the workings of this dynamic labor market in the 1640s. "They choose them as they do Horses in a Market."[122] Nowhere else was the rapid mobilization of labor as simple as in Barbados and analogous places in the Americas.[123]

Slavery powered a vast wealth-creating machine throughout the Caribbean and the Americas, and also—in less numerous but still significant ways—in Asia and Africa. It provided avenues to prosperity for planters and merchants alike. To cite just one example, the Marquis de Paroy owned three plantations in Saint-Domingue in 1755—Bellevue, Du Clos, and La Grande Place—with a total of 245 enslaved workers. Twenty-eight years later, Paroy owned 484 slaves on five plantations, among them fifty-five-year-old Alexis, working in the sugar mill; Antoine, a forty-five-year-old Congolese domestic servant in the "Big House"; and Milhridatte, also from Congo, who at age thirty-seven was in charge of the banana gardens. Their labor paid to decorate Paroy's estate with several mahogany beds, ample silverware, eighteen paintings with golden frames, a marble table, and a "big" mirror, among other furnishings. With expanding wealth, a new capitalist mentality emerged on the sugar frontier as well. As planter G. Lerond wrote in 1769: "All fashions are found in the colony today: plays, concerts, libraries sumptuous parties where gaiety and wit oppose irksome boredom. . . . Pirates have given way to dandies with embroidered velvet jackets. . . . A love of learning accompanies this love of luxury."[124] The sugar islands were the first place in the world where social status depended almost exclusively on wealth, where capital owners could liberate themselves from ancient hierarchies and display their gains with unchecked abandon. After Saint-Domingue's enslaved workers staged a successful revolution and emancipated themselves, Paroy claimed compensation. Pleading for a speedy settlement, he appealed to the commission as the "protecteur des malheureux colons," and in 1827 he received 292,496 livres tournois from the French state, which forced the Republic of Haiti to foot the bill. That staggering sum was equivalent to the cost of building about six spinning mills in Alsace, the most cutting-edge industrial undertakings of their time.[125]

Slavery did more than just solve the problem of securing labor to work the new sugar plantations; it enabled new forms of labor control in which the entire production process took place directly under the planters' watch. Effective labor control had usually been out of the reach of capital owners, but conditions of extreme subjugation made it possible. It took planters some time to figure out how best to manage the labor process, but by the 1680s, plantations were worked by gangs of slaves who hoed, seeded, and harvested under the overseer's close watch, their efforts and movements continually monitored. Such a surveillance-based labor system did not come to Europe for another two hundred years. Indeed, Ligon, the seventeenth-century traveler to Barbados, was impressed by both the complexity of the enslavers' task and their ability to innovate.[126] A Barbadian sugar planter, he observed, "feeds daily two hundred mouths, and keeps them in such order, as there are no mutinies among them. . . . All these are to be employed in their several abilities, so as no one be idle."[127]

Managing labor became more systematized. The Drax plantation in Barbados kept accounts enumerating the labor force, distinguishing age cohorts, divisions of labor by sex, and jobs. While a few enslaved workers had skilled occupations, such as "carpenter" or "boiler," most were listed as "field" and assigned to particular "gangs." They were categorized as "very good," "good," "infirm," "indifferent," or "worthless," and any annual "increase" or "decrease" of the labor force was precisely accounted for.[128] Paroy's plantations in Saint-Domingue kept similarly detailed accounts. In the aptly named "Journal d'exploitation de l'habitation Bellevue Paroy," the plantation's administrators listed, for each day in October 1784, the temperature, exact locations where various slaves worked, their output, and observations about the work done—a strikingly modern form of tracking labor.[129] Paroy's "Regulations for the Negroes of my plantations," which he penned in Paris in 1777, formulated rules for every possible scenario, including the unconscionably cruel stipulation that if an enslaved woman's baby died "due to his mother's fault, she will be forced to carry her dead child in her arms for 3 consecutive days, and will receive 30 lashes two days in a row," hinting at a particularly cruel form of commodification that women under slavery had to endure.[130]

Carrying the burden of Venetian civilization: Four barefoot Africans dressed in rags stoop from carrying the weight of Venetian wealth, mid-seventeenth century.

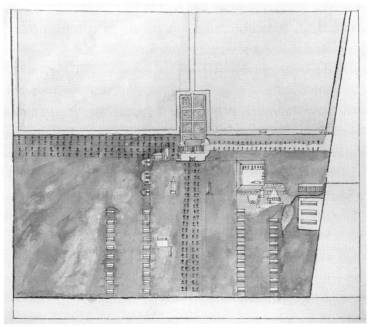

Military-style agriculture: one of the Marquis de Paroy's
plantations in Saint-Domingue.

Due to Europeans enslaving millions of Africans, labor was transformed from a social relation mediated by religious and worldly authorities to a commodity market almost entirely soluble to capital—enabling vast mobilizations of workers and thus deploying capital (and not just in trade) on a much-extended scale.

This computability of capitalism and slavery was specific to this moment in capitalism's history, allowing for capitalism's greatest breakthrough. Capital owners preferred to enslave their workers under very particular conditions, namely, when there was cheap and ample land, labor was hard to come by in other ways, and there was a huge imbalance in power between capital owners and everyone else. Some contemporaries perceived slavery as necessary: "It is impossible to achieve anything in Brazil without slaves," argued Johan Maurits van Nassau-Siegen in his 1638 "Brief Report on the State of the Four

Captaincies . . . in the North of Brazil."[131] Embracing slavery also helped establish European territorial claims, as it helped European powers make a particular territory economically useful, speedily creating new commodity frontiers in new countrysides.[132]

Enslaved workers were exploited to an extraordinary degree. In the late seventeenth century, planters typically worked their laborers to death in seventeen years.[133] As many as one in three slaves died within three years of stepping on American soil. The average life expectancy was as low as twenty-three years. In 1688, about twenty thousand slaves needed to be imported to the Caribbean just to keep the labor force level, testifying to what can only be described as genocide for profit.[134] Indeed, a bestselling 1792 pamphlet in Britain compared eating sugar to cannibalism.[135]

Slavery and other, slightly less coercive forms of labor mobilization that emerged from capital's march into the countryside sharpened notions of difference between humans as well. Early labor regulations on capitalist frontiers focused on creating tightly policed boundaries between different groups of workers and on policing and limiting contacts across those boundaries. Early sixteenth-century petitions in New Spain appealed to the government to keep poor Spaniards out of the view of Indigenous people to maintain the illusion that Spaniards across the board were better off and keep them separated.[136] Enslaved workers were especially targeted for complete separation. While white workers' freedom was greatly limited by indentures and labor laws, their status was above that of the enslaved. This diversity of rights used to marshal and control workers was naturalized in notions of difference that later ossified into what was called "racial science." Influential European Enlightenment thinkers sought to bury the bloody origins of their ascendant civilizations by, essentially, dehumanizing the African people whom they enslaved. For Immanuel Kant, Africans "received from nature no intelligence." For Voltaire, differences between Europeans and Africans make "Negroes . . . thus slaves of other men." And for David Hume, Africans were "naturally inferior."[137] Such notions of difference became crucial to capitalism's forward march.

Since plantation slavery required particular conditions that were—with few exceptions—unique to the Americas, capital owners elsewhere did not have the power to remake society as radically or quickly. Eastern and central Europe were examples of places where different forms of labor mobilization emerged. As Dutch merchants demanded ever more grain to feed their burgeoning cities and to supply Iberian markets, landowners in grain-producing regions like Livonia, Bohemia, Moravia, Pomerania, Poland, and eastern Prussia recast agriculture toward production for distant markets. This was possible because of Dutch capital—and because landowners mobilized massive numbers of workers by increasing pressure on rural cultivators and taking greater control of their labor and time. The outcome of these combined traditions and pressures was the rapid spread of serfdom, a system of labor that, like slavery, had deep historical roots, but was now recast and harnessed to the great capitalist project of transforming the countryside.[138]

This new serfdom departed from previous regional forms of labor mobilization in two ways: It curtailed the relative freedom many peasants had enjoyed since the fourteenth-century weakening of feudalism, and it was embedded in a very different economy. Feudal dependencies had mainly supplied the manors and the feudal lords themselves; now production was oriented toward distant markets.[139] This "second serfdom," as Braudel has called it, was thus not a return to feudalism—just as plantation slavery in the Americas was different from ancient forms of slavery.[140]

The Polish-Lithuanian Commonwealth was one region where serfdom spread. As the sixteenth century progressed, land fell into the hands of fewer and fewer individuals, empowering owners and disempowering laborers. By 1569, the nobility owned approximately 60 percent of the Commonwealth's territory, with the church 25 percent and the Crown the remaining 15 percent. Profit-driven landlords, presented with a newly dynamic exterior market, deemed coercion necessary to mobilize workers. They quickly circumscribed the rights of rural cultivators: In 1496, the Polish Parliament limited peasant mobility; in 1501, it attached peasants firmly to the lands of their lord; in 1518, gave nobles complete legal control over peasants; and in 1520 more than quadrupled the annual statutory labor rent (corvée). Serfs became dependent on their lords—not only legally and economically but also socially, requiring, for example, permission to marry, go to school, or travel off the land. The more a particular area specialized in the production of grains for export, the more extensive landowners' demands on serfs' unpaid labor became. By the eighteenth century, lords expected from their serfs as many as six days of unpaid weekly labor on the manor, increasingly pushing the boundaries of exploitation toward what one historian has called their "physiological limit." This transformation of the countryside moved eastern Europe toward a "colonial destiny" not unlike that experienced in the Caribbean at the same time. Despite significant regional variations, serfs were universally deprived of personal freedoms, becoming ever more dependent on the manor for their survival.[141] No less than Montesquieu described how eastern European feudal lords "possess whole provinces, they oppress the plowman in order to have a greater quantity of grain to send to foreigners and procure themselves the things their luxury demands."[142]

The *folwark*—a form of manorial estate associated with serf labor— developed to maximize grain production, transforming traditional strip holdings into large demesne fields and significantly reducing the peasants' individual plots that were supposed to let peasants support themselves. Wealthy families often operated multiple folwarks: In 1739, the Lubomirski family controlled 1,050 properties, including 213 folwarks, spread all across the southern lands of the Polish-Lithuanian Commonwealth.[143]

This rural economy was churned both by the growing strength of western European merchants and European expansion into the Americas. Indeed, they were part of the same process. It was the pressures on feudal incomes and the new opportunities arising from the ever increasing commercialization of the European economy that suggested to landowning nobles that they should immobilize their laborers anew by enserfing them and pivot away from the reproduction of the manor to retool production for the world market. Like their counterparts in the Caribbean, they were leading rather than resisting the capitalist revolution. Serfdom was a catalyst to greater commercialization, forcing cultivators to focus their labor power on producing commodities for markets.[144] This system, Montesquieu memorably observed, subjugated the peasants and "made [them] slaves"; indeed, scholars have determined that it made them worse off than their Indian and Japanese counterparts.[145]

ULTIMATELY MOST CONSEQUENTIAL for the history of capitalism, however, was yet another form of labor mobilization: wage labor. Like serfdom and slavery, wage labor was a response to the constraints and opportunities owners of capital faced. Wage labor had existed for centuries, even in ancient Mesopotamia. But it had never been a prevalent mode of labor mobilization or at the core of organizing the productive activities of entire societies. It was, in some ways, strange.[146] Yet in the sixteenth and seventeenth centuries, it grew by leaps and bounds along with the spread of urban capital into the world's hinterlands. It became so important that analysts of capitalism as different as Smith and Marx saw the prevalence of wage labor as the very definition of what the capitalist revolution was all about—it became to them almost capitalism's most essential trait.[147]

One countryside where wage labor arose at an early juncture was New Spain's Bajío, in what is today central Mexico. As silver mining intensified, and as cattle ranging and agriculture expanded, huge new labor needs emerged. With the discovery of silver at Zacatecas in 1546, Europeans enslaved Indigenous peoples. When the Spanish crown declared Indigenous enslavement illegal, capital owners found new ways to bind labor to the mines and farms, including acquiring enslaved Africans on the markets of Veracruz. By 1640, about one thousand enslaved Africans worked in the mines at Zacatecas, a substantial presence among the town's eighty-five hundred inhabitants.[148]

But in the vast spaces of the Bajío, enslaved people could easily run away, making the Bajío less suited for coerced labor. In response, mine owners hired workers for wages; by 1640, about two thousand Indigenous people worked for wages in the mines, in part also because slave owners were reluctant to deploy their valuable human property for this highly dangerous work.[149]

The Bajío was hardly the definitive victory of wage labor as the labor of capitalism; coerced labor and free labor coexisted, and wageworkers often got caught up in some form of debt peonage. But it was pervasive, and though the Bajío was an outlier in the Americas, it was no quirk in the fabric of the wider world. Around Mexico City, which had seen a coexistence of Native "autonomies" and commercial estates, population pressures in the eighteenth century made it increasingly difficult for Indigenous people to do subsistence farming, and economic expansion demanded more labor on commercial estates. Formerly independent farmers became wageworkers on these estates.[150]

In England, the dominant path to the commodification of labor was also through wage labor, which became more common in the countryside, just as it expanded in the rapidly growing cities. That process accelerated as early as 1348, when the labor shortages caused by the Black Death gave surviving rural cultivators new bargaining power. They used it to escape servile status and sell their labor power on markets, a process helped by the peasant revolt of 1381. Workers were still subject to extra-economic compulsion, and wages were just a supplementary form of making a living, but over the centuries, wages became increasingly common. As ideas of contract spread, employers and employees, despite huge power imbalances, became legal equals. In England, a rural proletariat emerged—though one that combined subsistence labor, even ownership of some land, with wage work.[151]

In the Ottoman and Dutch countrysides, wage labor also became important. In the areas around Filibe, Plovdiv (in today's Bulgaria), *waqf* estates, producing rice for long-distance markets, employed wageworkers as early as the 1490s. Dutch landowners who leased their lands to tenant farmers hired additional labor for wages. Indeed, the ability to mobilize labor was the precondition for the emergence of

Dutch commercial agriculture. Here, as elsewhere, dispossessions and the emergence of wage labor fed upon each other—as fewer people had access to subsistence, more had to sell their labor power. A study of the Guelders river area, in today's eastern Netherlands, found that by the late sixteenth and early seventeenth centuries, 55 to 60 percent of the total labor input was in the form of wage labor, what the study's author calls "extreme proletarianization."[152]

Wages did not mean the absence of coercion. Corporal punishment of workers remained common, and their mobility was often legally restricted. Still, the kind of extra-economic pressures that lay at the core of feudal labor relations, as well as modern serfdom and slavery, were increasingly replaced in some regions of the world by economic pressures.

A s merchants accumulated profits, sought access to additional trade goods, and attempted to gain more sway over these goods' production and marketing, they infused the logic of capital into a countryside that for centuries, even millennia, had operated very differently.[153] Merchants advanced credit to rural cultivators, sold supplies, mobilized labor, produced sugar and other such foodstuffs, transmitted them to distant markets, and traded land. Each of these steps made it more likely that another would follow, as ever more of the world's countryside became oriented toward social relations determined by the logic of capital, with inputs, outputs, land, and labor becoming tradable commodities. Most crucially, merchants' mounting ability to connect, and their increasing accumulation of wealth and power, spilled into the realm of production with great intensity. Without the accumulation of capital in cities, there was no transformation of the countryside, but urban economies also increasingly rested on capital's transformation of the countryside into a hinterland. Amsterdam and Surat, London and Cairo, for instance, were coproductions of their hinterlands, both near and remote. Amsterdam, prominently, became a coproduction of the islands of the Caribbean, the manors of eastern Europe, the islands of Southeast Asia, and the Dutch countryside.

The resultant colonization of the countryside by capital owners was a slow process, unfolding over several centuries and continuing today. In the two centuries after 1550, much of the world carried on unaffected by the deepening imprint of the archipelago of capital, even in Europe.[154] As in most of Africa and Asia, it was exceedingly difficult—often impossible—to turn European rural cultivators into wageworkers or commodify the land. Tributary lords and religious authorities, along with peasants, resisted capitalists' revolutionary agenda.

These difficulties help explain the extraordinary degree of violence deployed by states and merchants to further the capitalist revolution in the countryside. After all, most rural cultivators, which included almost all the world's people, did not voluntarily part with their property, rights, and autonomies. The transformation of the countryside initially succeeded only at its most violent and vulnerable edges, where capital owners and states could use concentrated force—and the level of force needed reveals how big a break this was with the past.

Coercion, a common feature of many human societies, was also used by the state, which in many cases deployed its military capacity to enable the penetration of urban capital into this or that countryside. And that coercive capacity itself rested on further violence, since marshaling soldiers and sailors also took enormous physical coercion, from rounding up recruits to punishing the disobedient.[155]

In this process, capital owners had a powerful, even decisive, ally—the state. It was not, as Smith argued, the quasi-natural expansion of networks between utility-maximizing individuals that led to the expansion of capitalism; it was almost the opposite—a state-sponsored anti-market.[156]

The state's role in transforming the countryside was a global phenomenon. Consider South Asia: When the fifteenth-century Gujarat Sultanate consolidated its power by expanding the army, improving tax collection, and strengthening bureaucracy, it gave the sahukar traders a more prominent role in the countryside. They now provided credit to peasants not just to help them engage in production but to pay taxes. This process accelerated with the Mughal assumption of power in 1573, when tax farming became prevalent and merchants became tax collectors.[157]

As in Gujarat, the commercialization of the Dutch countryside was furthered by raising taxes on rural producers. Once farmers had to generate income to pay the levies, cultivators' ability to engage in subsistence farming became more limited—foreshadowing a development that would force millions of rural cultivators in the nineteenth and twentieth centuries into market-oriented agriculture in Asia, Africa, and the Americas.[158]

The Ottoman state also facilitated capital's move into its countryside. Legal transformations in the status of land encouraged investment in farming by urbanites. There were, for one, the Islamic foundations—the waqfs—that came to control large swaths of agricultural lands around the cities of Istanbul, Cairo, and Damascus, and in smaller places like Filibe, where rice growing for markets, financed by urban capital, took off in the sixteenth century. As the state pressured rural cultivators for taxes, it encouraged greater commercial production and provided openings for capital owners to invest. Increasingly, by the mid-sixteenth century, these lands were turned into tax farms, sold to the highest bidder—usually city dwellers, some of whom forged new types of commercially oriented farm enterprises called çiftlik. With urban capital infusing the countryside, rural cultivators faced increasing indebtedness, and the use of the land shifted toward commercial endeavors, with landholders specializing in trade goods such as cotton, grain, livestock, produce, and wine. Pushed off the land, some rural cultivators became wageworkers, whom officials identified as "bachelors" and whose rapidly growing numbers they tried to control, often unsuccessfully. As parts of the Macedonian and Albanian countryside faced enclosures, peasants migrated to distant cities like Istanbul, emerging as a proletariat that could be hired to work on the commercial farms that had emerged around the city or in the service sector as porters or boatmen, much needed due to the rising intensity of trade in the harbors and ports of the city.[159]

In Barbados, merchant capital was tightly linked to the state as well; indeed, the line between the two was often blurry. For one thing, English military forces protected the island's planters. At times, merchants and members of the navy went into joint business, for example, the importation of enslaved workers. Local merchants, in turn, sold so-called prize goods (goods pirated from enemy ships) for the English navy. In 1763, when enslaved workers rebelled in mainland Demerara (where Barbadian planters owned significant plantations), one Barbadian family, the Clarkes, equipped and dispatched five armed ships carrying members of the Barbadian militia as well as the navy to suppress the uprising.[160] The state also played a crucial role in the slave trade: In 1663, the British House of Commons in London chartered the Company of Royal Adventurers Trading into Africa; and, in 1672, its successor, the Royal African Company. By 1680, two of its agents lived in Barbados.[161]

Everywhere, state power infused the countryside in new ways. As warfare demanded ever more ample revenue, rulers looked for new ways to squeeze rural cultivators. They shifted from the familiar practice of payment in kind and forced cultivators to pay taxes to further commercialize the countryside.

The most important tool in all of this was the growing military capacity of many states. Navies played a crucial role in protecting trade routes, while armies allowed states to capture and mold new hinterlands, facilitating first and foremost European expansion in Africa, Asia, and the Americas.

Once secured, the state began building infrastructure to support the more efficient operation of urban capital in the countryside. As we have seen, the Dutch state built dikes and canals; the British Crown laid out new roads and canals; the Chinese emperor built the world's most sophisticated postal system; Ottoman rulers raised camels to power long-distance trade, improving the security of major trade routes; and Egyptians invested in major irrigation projects.[162] This was not yet the infrastructural state of the nineteenth century, but it put producers and consumers into closer proximity.

As important as physical infrastructure was, states also played a role in establishing property rights in land and labor by determining what counted as legitimate and enforceable claims. The land in the Caribbean dedicated to plantation agriculture, for example, had been given by the king to private individuals; the king, in effect, generated private property. In Barbados, at first the Crown gave the land to a company of merchants, and planters were employees of the company. But then the lord proprietors appointed governors who allocated land to settlers, making land into private property.[163] As the state sanctified certain property rights and made them enforceable in court, pacifying the potential war between capital owners, it became instrumental, as we have seen, to massive dispossessions. Property rights emerged hand in hand with expropriation.

While the state helped capital to expand into countrysides everywhere, the deepest alliance emerged in Europe, where it was driven by the intra-state competition born of the political fragmentation that characterized the continent. Since states needed merchants for resources, merchants could push their capital into the far-flung regions of the world on the coattails of expanding states.

The resulting capitalism was highly diverse. On one hand, on the European continent, the state strengthened property rights, subdued violence between capitalists, and removed extreme forms of extra-economic coercion from labor relations. On the other hand, that very same state legitimized massive dispossessions and enslavement outside Europe and violently enforced trading privileges. European states created the conditions for a vast industrialized agriculture to emerge in the Americas, and granted great control, even sovereignty, to the slave traders and plantation owners who launched that transformation.[164]

Philosopher John Locke was one of many who rationalized that diversity. An investor in the Royal African Company and the Company of Bahamas Adventurers, a member of the Board of Trade, the secretary of the Council of Trade and Foreign Plantations from 1673 to

1674, and the secretary of the Lords Proprietors of Carolina, Locke was deeply involved in discussions on mobilizing land and labor for plantation agriculture.[165] In his *Second Treatise of Government*, he argued that when land "lay waste," it could be rightfully taken, adding that when Indigenous peoples violently resisted European settlement, they became a "savage ravenous beast" and lost their natural rights and could be legitimately conquered and enslaved.[166]

Such a disparity of rights and forms of rule was a core characteristic of the war capitalism we saw emerge during the great connecting. It was a direct outgrowth of the character of European states themselves, which had always been shaped by overlapping and competing sovereignties, and thus disparities, even within just one kingdom. This model of weakly integrated and diverse polities came to structure the new empires as well, especially as rulers provided private investors with sovereign powers over distant territories.[167]

These initiatives created and reinforced cycles of revenue: As states channeled capital to the world's hinterlands, wealth-producing frontiers made states more powerful. In 1660, to cite just one example, the British Parliament passed a law requiring all tobacco from the colonies to be shipped to England, making it an important part of customs revenue: The transformation of the Chesapeake countryside directly affected the British state's strength.[168] A more commercialized countryside brought more revenue, and commercialization eased the extraction process at the points of both production and trade. All this made the state increasingly invested in an even further transformation of the global countryside and dependent on those who effected that transformation—the merchants.

We can clearly see how significant the particularities of state power could be in channeling the transformation of the global countryside by comparing the development of two islands: Taiwan and Saint-Domingue. Both were superbly suited for sugar agriculture, and indeed, soon after the Dutch arrived in Taiwan in the 1620s, they began to grow sugarcane, as their French counterparts did a few decades later in Saint-Domingue. Taiwan's sugar production expanded dramatically after the 1640s, when the Atlantic sugar market was disturbed by the Portuguese invasion of the Dutch plantation belt in Brazil, and, by 1660, sugar exports from Taiwan had skyrocketed to more than 2.5 million pounds, or fifteen times the amount grown two decades earlier. In this way, Taiwan and Saint-Domingue had similar histories. Yet when we look more closely, the expansion of Taiwan's sugar frontier was radically different: Failing to convince the Indigenous inhabitants of Taiwan to engage in export agriculture, and unable to enslave cultivators, the Dutch established a network of Chinese smallholders whom they brought from the mainland to Taiwan, beginning in 1624, with Chinese pirate, merchant, and official Zheng Zhilong (1604–1661) shipping "several tens of thousands" of rural cultivators from drought-stricken Fujian to Taiwan. Promised a tax holiday, three taels of silver, and the use of an ox, the mainland immigrants pushed Indigenous people from their hunting grounds and converted land to sugar planting. By 1650, Taiwan was one of the world's leading sugar producers.[169]

But Taiwan's history ultimately diverged from that of the Caribbean isles. After 1655, when the Atlantic sugar market recovered, demand for Taiwanese sugar fell dramatically on European markets. Within three years, almost the entire harvest was being shipped to Japan and Persia. Moreover, the Chinese Empire disrupted established trade relations. In 1662, Zheng Chenggong, Zheng Zhilong's son, chased the Dutch away in a well-orchestrated military campaign, and in 1683 the island was incorporated into the Qing Empire. Its Dutch moment was over. At first, thanks to the huge demand from Chinese consumers, sugar continued its ascent, with Taiwanese sugar production reaching around 54,240 metric tons in the 1720s, far outpacing any sugar island in the Atlantic. But in the 1720s and 1730s, the government began restricting Taiwanese sugar exports and encouraging a diverse economy dominated by small farms producing food crops—rice, beans, military provisions, vegetables and fruit, fish and livestock—and a range of rural handicrafts. As a result, rice, not sugar, became the driving force of Taiwan's economy until the late nineteenth century, when another colonizing power, Japan, returned Taiwan to its sugar roots. In the eighteenth century, however, Taiwan became the rice bowl for food-deficient southeast China, entering a very different trajectory from its counterpart in the Caribbean—with significant long-term consequences, as a comparison between present-day Taiwan and Haiti suggests.[170] Absent state pressure to promote export-oriented sugar production, rice remained the dominant crop.

⸻

As wave after wave of commodification and dispossession crashed over large swaths of the world's countryside, societies were remade on a massive scale, changing how millions lived and subsisted. Capitalists reimagined the ecology of large areas and connected distant societies. The world that they built over two centuries was fundamentally different from any that had shaped human affairs before. This was the moment the familiar framework of the global capitalist economy emerged.

Unsurprisingly, the revolutionary agenda that was shaking up the countryside encountered opposition—from both the top of social hierarchies and the bottom. Many rulers still preferred keeping capitalists at bay, even as they increasingly depended on them, and producers everywhere preferred the commons and subsistence farming. Resistance was powerful in areas where older social and political structures were resilient, including much of the European countryside, the west coast of Africa, almost all of Asia, and indeed much of the world. Global capitalism was neither a natural state of things nor a straightforward undertaking—the restructuring of ever more parts of the world and of social life along a capitalist logic was, in fact, exceedingly difficult and took centuries to unfold. It took even longer to reach a state in which this peculiar way of organizing economic life seemed "natural."

This is why the first significant commercialization of the countryside unfolded on islands—some metaphorical, some real—areas where social and political opposition were least pronounced, areas that were either unpopulated (such as Barbados), occupied by nomadic people who had little ability to resist, as in the Bajío, or where social structures were severely weakened (as in feudal Europe).[171] But even in these places, people resisted dispossession, proletarianization, enslavement, and the commodification of their lives.

The world in which capital owners increasingly ignored the preferences of peasants and tributary rulers was a scene of global social struggle: Capitalism resembled a state of war. As with most revolutions, it rested on an enormous degree of coercion, and even when it succeeded, its offspring, a rapidly growing group of propertyless workers—some enslaved, some indentured, others enserfed or hired for wages—frightened those who drew on their labor.[172] The countryside became the site of struggles, with peasants, indentured servants, feudal elites, wageworkers, and slaves resisting the revolutionizing agenda of early capitalists.

This was true everywhere.[173] Ottoman rural cultivators, for example, threatened with losing control over land as urban capital gained power, sometimes resorted to court battles, but at other times took up arms or turned to banditry to assert their claims and rights.[174] British rural cultivators revolted against enclosures for three centuries. Already in 1548, in an expostulatory tract titled *An Informacion and Peticion Agaynst the Oppressours of the Pore Commons of This Realme*, Robert Crowley had warned land reformers about the consequences of dispossessing farmers of their lands:

> If the impotent creatures perish for lacke of necessaries, you are the murderers, for you have theyr enheritaunce and do minister vnto them. If the sturdy fall to stealeyng, robbyng, & reueynge, then you are the causers thereof, for you dygge in, enclose, and wytholde from the earth out of the whych they should dygge and plowe theyr lyueynge.[175]

A spate of rebellions ripped across the English countryside. In 1549, peasants destroyed hedges and fences in what is remembered as

Kett's Rebellion. Its leader, Robert Kett, demanded "that no lord of no mannor shall comon uppon the Comons." His movement was suppressed, and he was hanged for treason.[176] Half a century later, in 1607, the Midland Revolt (culminating in the Newton Rebellion) announced, "Wee, as members of the whole, doe feele the smarte of these incroaching Tirants, which would grind our flesh upon the whetstone of poverty, and make our loyall hearts to faint with breathing, so that they may dwell by themselves in the midst of theyr heards of fatt weathers."[177] Their rebellion was as forcefully repressed as similar revolts in Lincolnshire, Oxfordshire, Bedfordshire, Derbyshire, and Worcestershire.[178]

Scotland saw peasant revolts against the landowners' commercializing agenda as well.[179] In the Levellers Revolt of 1723, up to a thousand Levellers, also known as "Dykebreakers," knocked down the stone walls enclosing their leased plots, "slaughtering some of the cattle within them"—and quite literally leveled the walls that kept livestock within newly created pastures, which had theretofore served as the cereal fields.[180] As *The Caledonian Mercury* reported in April 1724, "[S]everal hundred armed persons subsequently demolished dykes in the neighbourhood."[181] The manifesto that the Levellers nailed onto church doors in various towns called for an end to the "chain of miseries" and protested against how landowners made "Commonty" (collectively held land) into the property of individuals.[182] The Levellers also published a steering manifesto, *An Account of the Reasons of Some People in Galloway, Their Meetings Anent Public Grievances Through Inclosures*, which highlighted the economic and social consequences of enclosure. They claimed that "depopulating Inclosures" had resulted in rent increases, trade disruption, and the eviction of more than sixty families from parishes in the region, who, they said, either emigrated or committed suicide. Women played a central role in these protests, for example in 1724 when they threw stones at local landowners who tried to arrest a group of rioters. And when Sir Basil Hamilton's dykes were leveled that year, "there were a great many lusty young women among them who yet performed greater wonders than men," as one contemporary wrote.[183]

The Levellers questioned central tenets of the emerging capitalist ethos. Protesting the "extraordinary Profits which return to a few Landlords," they "disagree[d] about the Persons to whom the Profits of the Earth should redound." Opposing the legitimacy of "act[ing] only for my self," the Levellers believed that things "ought not be done" if they violated "the greater Good of humane Society," even if "there be no particular and express humane Law against it." They saw it as "a Sin to hinder the Poor from cultivating the Ground." Owning a piece of land did not, in their view, give the landowner the right to expel the tenant. "[D]efrauding the Poor of the Profits of the Earth, which God hath given to all" was ungodly. They reserved special wrath for "Several of our Landlords [who] are become our Merchants" and concluded that "your Principle, That you may do with, and improve, your own as you please, should not be without Limitation interpreted, as commonly it is; That all the Profits of the Earth do not belong to the Landlords, and that a Man may not, many Times, improve his own Property, to the Prejudice of that Society, whereof he is a Member."[184]

Even in the Americas, where the capitalist transformation of the countryside had its most rapid and radical successes, an almost-constant struggle accompanied the expansion of commodity production. Despite ceaseless declarations of their death or disappearance, Indigenous peoples waged a continual war against their dispossession and exploitation. In the seventeenth-century Lesser Antilles, for example, the Kalinagos resisted English settlement, causing the English to conclude that the Kalinagos "were a barbarous and cruel set of savages beyond reason or persuasion and must therefore be eliminated."[185] Farther north, in the upper reaches of New Spain, in what is today the American state of New Mexico, Spanish settlers and troops plundered, taxed, murdered, and harassed the Pueblo people for almost a century and a half until, according to one Spanish observer, "the Indians fear us so much that, on seeing us approach from afar, they flee to the mountains with their women and children, abandoning their homes, and so we take what we wish from them."[186] In the summer of 1680, however, Pueblo communities under the leadership of medicine man Po'pay rebelled and expelled the Spaniards from their lands, securing a decade-long reprieve—a rare victory in an asymmetrical struggle. At the very southern tip of the Americas, in present-day Chile, conflicts with the Mapuche lasted, with varying degrees of intensity, from 1536 to 1883. The Spanish initially triumphed with relative ease, but in 1598 the tides turned, as 300 Mapuche warriors ambushed and decisively defeated 350 men led by Royal Governor Martín García Óñez de Loyola, then the highest Spanish authority in Chile.[187] The Mapuche victory at Curalaba triggered a general uprising among the Indigenous population that culminated in the destruction of all seven Spanish cities in the Mapuche territories of southern Chile. As the war progressed, the Mapuche's guerrilla tactics led them to emerge victorious from the century-long warring phase of the conflict.

Subduing labor was just as difficult as expropriating land, and it encountered similar resistance. Indentured servants, the first labor force in the Americas, were among the key participants in revolts in Barbados during the mid-1600s, "laying fire so negligently, as whole lands of Canes and Houses too are burned down and consumed," scarring the planters so much that they built their houses "in manner of fortifications, and have lines, bulwarks, and bastions to defend themselves in case there should be any uproar or commotion . . . either by the Christian servants, or Negro slaves."[188] In Virginia, after their indentures ended, landowners pushed tobacco-growing indentured servants to poorer lands outside the prosperous Tidewater regions, areas often still inhabited by Indigenous peoples. Tensions exploded in 1676, when Nathaniel Bacon led these poor white farmers in a three-month-long uprising—Bacon's Rebellion. That uprising improved opportunities for poor white farmers but sharpened the codification of racial categories and entrenched the exploitation and segregation of enslaved workers. Greater white freedom became predicated on the unfreedom of African Americans.[189]

Slavery in the Americas, as we have seen, was a response to the myriad political, social, and economic difficulties of mobilizing indentured labor. But enslaved workers were just as rebellious. They resisted their enslavement by limiting the labor they provided, running away, or even committing suicide.[190] Sometimes they engaged in concerted political action that envisioned the overthrow of their owners and a new kind of polity, striking fear into the hearts of frontier capitalists. As French King Louis XVI observed in 1779, "An unfortunate experience has taught us for a long time that only an exact discipline can maintain order in the colonies of the New World and ensure the tranquility and the life of the Europeans. The slave, who can always revolt against the yoke that is imposed on him, can only be restrained by fear and by his feeling of inferiority."[191]

In seventeenth-century Barbados, actual or preempted uprisings of Black workers occurred in 1633, the late 1640s, 1675, 1683, 1685, 1692, and 1701—so frequently that it suggests a constant state of planning for and executing rebellion.[192] Planters' greatest fear, according to Ligon, was that enslaved workers would "commit some horrid massacre upon the Christians and thereby enfranchise themselves, and become Masters of the Island."[193]

Barbadian revolts, led mostly by skilled Black workers, kept the planter elite on edge. In an effort to maintain their power, planters passed a steady stream of laws aimed to control their workers. So-called slave laws in 1661 Barbados detailed how enslavers should regulate their slaves' lives, but in 1675, "a bloody Tragedy intended against his Majesty's Subjects here in the island by the Heathen Negroes, which was by the Providence of god miraculously discovered," led to the "depressing [of] the Rebels," who were "put to death, and the rest kept in a more strict manner."[194] New laws passed in 1676 regulated slave lives even more, aiming to keep the enslaved from exchanging information and assembling.[195] In 1685, the Barbados Council again urged enslavers to "keep their arms more secure than formerly. . . . [G]ood watches was also necessary to be kept in their plantations, and that they had taken all due care to prevent the Negroes assembling together."[196] In 1692, in response to yet another uprising, new laws were passed to "prevent as much as possible . . . the negroes rebelling."[197]

But violence, not law, was the core of planter response to feared or actual rebellion.[198] When an alleged "conspiracy" was discovered in Barbados, seventeen presumed participants were executed: Six were burned alive while the others were beheaded, "their dead bodies . . . dragged through the streets."[199] In 1683, in response to another feared uprising, slaves "were well whipped for terror to others."[200] And in 1692, when a rebellion led by enslaved workers Ben, Sambo, and Sampson hit Barbados, the rebels were hanged, burned, and executed in gibbets.[201]

The Barbados Council compensated owners for their executed slaves. Its minutes show that nine such owners were compensated on May 12, 1686.[202] In 1692, the planters pleaded to King William for more military protections to "strengthen us against the bold attempts of our numerous slaves, whose present machinations and bloody designs of Cutting all of our Throats we have lately discovered."[203] In 1694, a rebellious slave was punished by "sixty lashes . . . inflicted upon him at ten of the most *puttynge* [punishing] places . . . and to be afterwards branded in the forehead with the letter 'R.'"[204]

Maroonage, that is, running away from the plantation to set up communities in areas inaccessible to the planters, was possible, though that became increasingly difficult as the island grew more densely settled and the forests were razed.[205] In 1657, the Barbados Council asked the governor to "issue commissions for a general hunting of . . . the great number of Negroes that are out."[206]

Other Caribbean islands also faced revolt.[207] In Santo Domingo in 1522, Spanish governor Diego Colón crushed a slave revolt on his own plantation. French Saint-Domingue was characterized by a persistent state of war between enslavers and slaves that became a revolt and then a full-blown revolution in the 1790s. In 1688, Jamaican planter John Taylor described in sadistic detail how a fellow planter, "Collonel Ivey," repressed a slave rebellion, asserting that he "caused all his slaves to be bound and fetter'd with irons . . . and then caus'd them to be severely whip't, caused them to be roasted alive, and others to be torn to pieces with dogs, others he cutt off their ears, feets and codds, and caused them to eat 'em; then he putt them all in iron feters, and soe with sever whipping every day forced them to work, and soe in time they became obedient and quiet."[208] Despite such unspeakable terror, slave rebellions continued. In 1760, slaves rose up en masse during Jamaica's most significant rebellion, Tacky's Revolt, which begat yet more horrifying violence in the name of repression. Some rebels were "burn[ed] by degrees with a Slow fire" or "placed in gibbets hung up in public squares and left to starve to death."[209] Such barbarity was constitutive of what was called "civilization."[210]

—

The capitalist transformation of the countryside was most successful in places that could be defended against the encroachment of powerful competitors—in a word, *islands*. Places of limited mobility—from Cape Verde to Potosí, from the Bandas to Barbados—allowed for much tighter control of labor. Yet these islands were not universes unto themselves; they were connected to other places. And, as islands, they sat in a sea of diverse social relations—places whose economic life followed different logics, which were transformed much later, if ever. Yet through the universal solvent of exchange, the capitalist archipelago remained connected to the sea outside—and soon the one could not thrive without the other.[211]

As merchants and planters began transforming the world's countryside, they drew on the earth's ecological bounty. Around the mines in Potosí, they cut forests to fuel their smelters. In Barbados and other parts of the Caribbean, logging created denuded landscapes ripe for planting sugar. In some corners of the world, coal began replacing the burning of wood from diminishing forests. Capital owners captured nature's energy, embodied in its plants and minerals, building on what sociologist Jason W. Moore has called "free inputs"—the giant store-house of energy forged by geological and biological processes. Increasingly, those inputs accumulated in one part of the world—Europe, which got around its own ecological bottlenecks by accessing calories and industrial inputs from across the Atlantic, Africa, and Asia.[212]

Merchants eager to capitalize the countryside also drew on and began to control the knowledge produced in agricultural societies the world over. Tobacco, for example, had been cultivated by Amerindians for centuries. Within fifty years of Columbus's first voyage, Europeans had learned how to grow the plant, and by 1570 they grew it on a small scale throughout the continent. Three decades later they had transported it to the far reaches of the world, including, in 1614, to North America, where Virginians began to see the possibilities of a colony based on tobacco's profitability. Silver miners in Potosí built upon local mining knowledge and technologies. Many of its miners had worked in the Inca mining center of Porco and had experience using the cone-shaped, wind-blown furnaces called *guayras* to extract silver from ore. Until the introduction of mercury amalgamation in the 1570s, the Spanish relied on these Indian guayras, as their own furnaces did not work in Potosí.[213]

Such capturing and redistribution of the world's accumulated knowledge and resources shows that capitalism rested—and rests—on a huge array of inputs not produced by or exchanged on markets. Wageworkers, indentured servants, and slaves still produced sustenance outside the market—perhaps in small vegetable gardens or on family farms. And in the absence of much wage work, as in New England, the production of goods for Caribbean markets remained embedded within a household-focused subsistence economy all the way into the nineteenth century—indeed, the one was essential to the other.[214]

Most strikingly, this included the provision and social reproduction of labor. To this day, capitalist societies cannot reproduce labor without recourse to noncapitalist forms of reproduction. Wherever we look, we see a reliance on the work of social reproduction outside the market. The starkest form was the slave trade, a form of "producing" labor that rested entirely on the efforts of African peasants, whose children were stolen for their labor power. In wage labor, this reliance on work outside the market was almost as great, as children had to be raised and schooled, housework completed, and communities forged, and most of this work took place outside the market. In fact, much of the labor done in capitalism at its beginnings and today is not embedded in market relationships.

As some labor became commodified, and some not—as a division arose between work and reproduction—this dichotomy created a heavily gendered division of labor. Work under capitalism took on a new set of meanings, as some activities, often by men, were within the market and others, often by women, outside it. Working on the landowner's field was "work," but tending a vegetable garden behind the house was not; tending to someone else's children was "work," but tending to one's own children was not. From the beginning, capitalism rested on resources produced outside its logic. It never existed in a "pure" state—its history was always about the shifting boundaries between the market and the nonmarket.[215] As late as 1751 an estimated half of all transactions in the Italian city of Naples were "outside the market," with local peasants using cash for only about a tenth of their transactions.[216] Then—and now—capitalism was defined as much by the limits of its revolutionary energy as by its transformative powers.

Still, by 1750, vast quantities of commodities poured into cities from the new capitalist frontiers in Europe, Asia, Africa, and the Americas. Serfs, wageworkers, sharecroppers, indentured servants, and slaves labored in the world's countryside to produce wheat, tea, silver, rice, sugar, cotton, and other things. They worked under the direction of capital owners not for their own needs or those of lords but for distant markets, which in turn supplied them with many of the things they needed to make a living. Capital owners gained wealth and power not just from trade but from production. As the islands of capital emerging from the great connecting generated a multitude of islands of production, capital owners accumulated wealth, established new forms of labor mobilization, and built new institutions. They built war capitalism, a novel merging of the power of capital owners and states, the sovereign powers granted to capitalists, and the massive dispossessions and enslavement that characterized the world's countryside. As a result, the archipelago of capital became more extensive, dynamic, and impactful, even though it continued to sit at the margins of economic life.

This archipelago of capital spanned the world—involving Chinese and European capitalists, Indian and African traders. But as the archipelago's connections intensified and stretched into the world's countryside, hierarchies sharpened—hierarchies that increasingly benefited one part of the world: the continent of Europe. It was there, and only there, that capital owners connected across continents and vast differences—the slave economies of the Americas, the wage economy of the Bajío, and the second serfdom of eastern Europe—to cite three prominent examples. Martin Noell, the Barbadian planter, not only added twenty thousand acres of Jamaican plantation land to his holdings in Barbados; when he died in 1665, he also owned agricultural land in England and Ireland, ships, and shares in the Royal African Company.[217] It was also in Europe where the strengthening of state power and capital reinforced each other to an unprecedented degree, unlike in Africa and Asia. As the French Enlightenment philosopher Guillaume Thomas François Raynal observed so insightfully a few decades later, in 1770: "The labours of the colonists settled in these long-scorned islands are the sole basis of the African trade, extend the fisheries and cultivation of North America, provide advantageous outlets for the manufactures of Asia, double perhaps triple the activity of the whole of Europe. They can be regarded as the principal cause of the rapid movement which stirs the Universe."[218]

That "rapid movement" did not stop with the transformation of agriculture. Capital owners the world over pressed further against existing ways of doing things. Pushing against the boundaries of craft production and subsistence-oriented household manufacturing would again take them out of cities and into the world's countryside.

5.

INTENSIFYING INDUSTRY, 1600–1750

Manufacturing intensifies in the countryside:
Indian weavers, early eighteenth century.

Jelenia Góra is a small city in southwestern Poland, a few dozen miles from the modern German and Czech borders. A provincial center that attracts tourists for its picturesque arcaded market square and nearby ski slopes, it was once a bustling center of the global linen industry, one of many places worldwide where manufacturing began to intensify.

Three hundred years ago, impoverished weavers from surrounding mountain villages descended every morning along narrow paths and rough roads toward town, their packs swollen with linens. They converged on Jelenia Góra's square—now filled with ice cream and trinket stalls—and offered the cloth to merchants ensconced under the arcades. US ambassador to Prussia (and later US president) John Quincy Adams observed the scene in a neighboring town: "[We] have had all the forenoon a crowd of peasants under our windows, each of them with one or two pieces of linen in a bag, standing and waiting for a purchaser. The merchant offers his price, and if it is agreed to, marks it upon the piece of linen, which the peasant then carries to the purchaser's store, and receives his money."[1] Once the merchant had bought the bale, he sent it to one of the eighty-two bleaching manufactories on the outskirts of town before forwarding the cloth to traders in Hamburg, Amsterdam, or Bordeaux. They then shipped it to cities such as Rio de Janeiro, Charleston, and Havana to clothe thousands—soon hundreds of thousands—of enslaved workers on sugar, rice, tobacco, and indigo plantations. The transformation of the countryside in the faraway Americas, combined with the great connecting, drew regional producers like those in Jelenia Góra into the vortex of world-altering changes.[2]

By 1750—when the town was known as Hirschberg and its inhabitants spoke German—peasants in surrounding villages operated more than six thousand looms to meet the demands of the new Atlantic markets. Many were desperately poor. Dressed in rags, bodies marked by hunger and unrelenting toil, some worked the land by day and wove at night; others only wove, from childhood to early death. Dealers acquired the yarn from the thousands of women and children (some as young as four years old) who spun whenever they had a free moment, using the flax grown on large estates nearby. Most spinners and many of the weavers were unfree dependents of local nobles, forced to spin and weave to pay feudal labor dues and rent on meager plots.[3]

Hirschberg's bucolic landscape belied the ever more frantic industrious activities inside the peasants' small cottages. Beginning in the seventeenth century, local merchants Christian Mentzel (1667–1748), Johann Martin Gottfried (1685–1737), and Daniel von Buchs (1707–1779) injected new intensity into rural manufacturing. They commercialized and industrialized the adjacent countryside, a process one

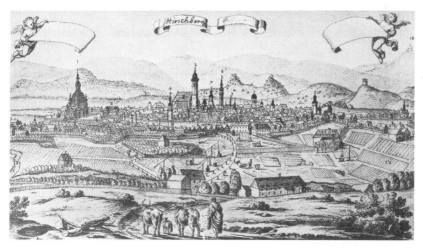

Clothing America's enslaved workers:
Hirschberg emerges as a center of intensified industry, 1752.

observer has called "intensive internal colonialization"—not in the holds of ships but in feudal dependencies and in the paper bondage of urban credit and capital.[4] Coerced labor in the Americas deepened coerced labor in the European countryside, the frontiers of unfreedom expanding alongside the frontiers of capital.

The Silesian linen industry had ancient roots, as peasants had spun yarn and woven cloth for many centuries to satisfy their needs and those of local markets. In response to the rapid expansion of Atlantic trade in the early sixteenth century, Dutch and English merchants searching for inexpensive linens began arriving in towns like Hirschberg. Initially, it was urban artisans, organized in guilds, who expanded their production. By 1550, however, the landowning nobility began to force their dependent peasants to spin and weave as well. English and Dutch merchants forwarded the cloths to England and Holland, then on to Africa, where these flaxen fabrics were exchanged for enslaved workers, and finally to the Americas, where they clothed slaves. Silesian linen production became, in effect, an extension of the Atlantic economy, with Nantes merchant Jean-Daniel Schweighauser informing his Hirschberg counterpart that he had shipped some linens to be "debited only for the slave trade."[5] In just fourteen years (1593 to 1607), Dutch merchants had shipped 180,000 meters of Silesian cloth to West Africa alone.[6]

The Thirty Years' War disrupted that system, but when it was over, in 1648, local Hirschberg merchants replaced Dutch and English interlopers and began acquiring fabrics directly, then forwarding them to Hamburg and other northern European ports for Dutch, English, Spanish, French, Swiss, and other traders. They secured their foothold in these burgeoning markets not only with lower prices but also by enforcing certain quality norms: In 1658, they organized the so-called Kaufmanns-Societät (which, unlike previous guilds, included only merchants and not the actual producers) to regulate production, inspect cloth, and thus collectively create what amounted to a trademark for Hirschberg linens. The town's trade boomed, and at its height, in 1724, more than one hundred merchants exported linens worth 1.45 million thaler (about $18 million in 2024 US dollars). In 1748/49, 66 percent of such Silesian linen was exported to England, Holland, France, Spain, Portugal, and the West Indies; by 1775/76, it was 86 percent. So dynamic was the local industry that, in 1740, when Prussia took over much of Silesia from its previous rulers—the Habsburgs—the linen industry became in one stroke Prussia's most important industry.[7]

To meet the burgeoning demands of the Atlantic markets, these local merchants pressured Silesian peasant workers to produce more linen. When ordinary practices came up short, the nobility—benefiting handsomely from the new system of trade—sought greater control over "their" peasants, intensifying the new system of dependency that later observers called a "second serfdom."[8] Serfs had long been attached to particular pieces of land and thus to particular nobles who could draw on some of their labor. Now these nobles expanded corvée duties—days when the peasant had to produce for the landlord without compensation—to as many as three days a week. In the mountainous areas where it was harder to engage in agriculture, nobles pressed peasants into spinning and weaving. In addition to corvée duties, the nobil-

Lest the visitor forget the source of Hirschberg's wealth: the memorial of a Hirschberg linen merchant, Christian Mentzel, decorated with a linen cloth chiseled into stone.

ity also demanded that rent payments be made in cloth or money tied to linen sales. Merchants and nobles purchased ever more land to acquire access to the valuable corvée labor bound to these properties. Trader Christian von Kluge acquired six villages; Mentzel had 2,481 people living on his estates. This system of labor mobilization was old—it had been at the very heart of European feudalism—but in its scale, intensity, and focus on the control of labor as the primary source of value in trade, it was a radical innovation. In the past, it had slaked the appetites of the manor, but now it also fulfilled the capitalist world market's voracious demands. Rural production was thus qualitatively transformed by the reorganization of labor producing exclusively for sale.[9]

Merchants and nobles became fabulously wealthy because of this coerced labor. They built lavish country houses filled with tasteful furniture and refined entertainments. Some merchants, aping the nobility, bought country seats.[10] Decades later, Silesian writer Gerhart Hauptmann's play *The Weavers* described the home of one of these erstwhile merchant-manufacturers as filled with "mahogany, richly-carved, and upholstered [furniture] in red," "crimson damask curtains," gilded framed pictures, and "the drawing-room, over-furnished in the same style of comfortless splendour."[11] How this contrasted, he went on to lament, with the suffering of the producers, dressed in torn clothing, often hungry and desperate in their miserable homes: "On the left a small window, in front of which stands the loom. On the right a bed, with a table pushed close to it. . . . A winding-wheel and bobbins on the floor between table and loom."[12] Hauptmann depicted an old weaver decrying his fate: "See what they've made of me! Stretched on the rack day after day. [*He holds out his arms.*] Feel that! Skin and bone! You villains all, you brood of hell!!"[13] When Adams traveled to Silesia in 1800 and 1801, he wrote about the region's thriving textile industry, but also about the extreme poverty he encountered and the beggars he passed by in his carriage. "The manufactories of linens, in particular, which raise large fortunes to the merchants who export them from the cities, scarcely give bread to the peasants, who do all the valuable part of the work."[14]

Such exposés were not uncommon and inspired charitable souls, such as one banker from the faraway city of Frankfurt am Main, Moritz von Bethmann, to sponsor a campaign to aid the weavers in 1844.[15] Perhaps not coincidentally, the industry was then in rapid decline. Capital was moving on too.

V iewed from a merchant's parlor in Jelenia Góra, the capitalist revolution had, by 1700, connected the novel capitalism of Caribbean slavery with the ancient flywheel of central European serfdom. It had joined nascent Atlantic markets with hoary manufacturing centers to create an unprecedented machine for profit and power. Urban capital streamed into the countryside, not just intensifying the production of marketable crops but transforming the rural manufacturing sector. Of course, for millennia, people the world round had manufactured things for personal use and for trade. Their workshops continued to thrive, deploying age-old techniques to produce goods for local markets with little need for outside capital: Bakers baked, seamstresses stitched, butchers butchered, cobblers made shoes, ironsmiths forged plows. Manufacturing as such preceded capitalism, and vestiges of small artisanal workshops survive, however much diminished, even today.[16]

Yet in labor-rich areas linked to islands of merchant capital, manufacturing intensified by the sixteenth century and increasingly catered to long-distance markets, jump-starting the transformation of industry. Merchants' investments almost always made that extension possible, as very little capital moved from the traditional sector of wealth—agriculture—into manufacturing. Traders invested this way because the great connecting and transformation of the countryside had vastly expanded markets for things produced at a distance. Manufacturing, though still subordinate to trade, underwent a critical and qualitative transformation, with merchants setting the tempo.[17] Merchants, with few exceptions, did not devote themselves exclusively to manufacturing, but enough commercial capital flowed into industrial production to enable its significant expansion—in Amsterdam and London, Antwerp and Genoa, Cairo and Aleppo, Kano and Bruges, Nanjing and Surat.

First came the cities and towns, places where industry had traditionally been rooted. This was what happened initially in Hirschberg: When demand from Atlantic markets for linens increased, it was in Silesian towns that production, organized in guilds, increased.[18] Even earlier, Florentine merchants had already created a thriving manufacturing sector in high-quality woolens whose roots extended to the thirteenth century. This dynamic and profitable industry drew on English and Spanish raw materials and delivered its goods to domestic, European, and Ottoman markets. Modest workshops usually specialized in one phase of wool processing—washing, combing, spinning, weaving, or dyeing. Each employed a relatively small number of workers paid by the piece. Increasingly, as demand grew, these firms also subcontracted the spinning of their fine wool to rural women—a consequential step, as we will later see.[19]

In Danzig, merchant investment also intensified manufacturing. As the port boomed, thanks to the rising exports of wheat to western Europe in the first half of the seventeenth century, markets for manufactured wares grew rapidly, both in the city itself and among the Polish nobility, flush with wealth pressed from their dependent peasants. New demand energized Danzig's established artisanal manufacturing sector. Dominated by guilds, it was a highly regulated system, with masters training apprentices who lived with them, ate at their tables, and learned the craft before eventually setting out to become masters themselves. When merchants arrived and pushed into manufacturing, they put pressure on such artisanal production. Masters hired more workers to satisfy demand, and apprentices became wageworkers—that is, proletarians without opportunities to become masters. Moreover, new weavers, especially migrants from the Netherlands unattached to guilds, began competing with local artisanal production. Large overseas merchants remained aloof from this production complex, while smaller merchants—with their local knowledge, access to markets, and capital reserves—put their funds into the supplier side of their trade. This led to a manufacturing boom—by 1640, six thousand to seven thousand women and men worked in textiles alone, a stunning concentration of proletarian labor that made Danzig the Polish center of industry.[20]

In commercial cities in the Ottoman Empire, like Cairo, İzmir, Salonika, and Aleppo, both trade and industry underwent significant growth as well. Entrepreneurs produced textiles, leather goods, sugar, and vegetable oils, among other things, for domestic consumption and for export, by the eighteenth century, even to faraway France. As early as 1600, Cairene merchants had invested in manufacturing to such a degree that this moment has been interpreted as the emergence of "artisan capitalism."[21]

This urban manufacturing took root throughout the empire: Fez factories in Tunis and soap factories in Nablus produced for imperial markets. The cotton textile producers of Aintab, a town near the present-day border between Syria and Turkey, copied Indian textiles favored by consumers worldwide to Ottoman and European consumers. Weavers produced silk cloths in many locations, with the most important manufacturing centered around Bursa, Aleppo, and Damascus. Even though most enterprises in the Ottoman Empire, as elsewhere, were small (usually consisting of a master with a few apprentices), by the mid-seventeenth century, dozens of larger-scale enterprises were founded, their tools, labor relations, and productive capabilities transformed by merchant capital. Thus enabled, some manufacturers now employed larger numbers of workers. Bursa, for example, boasted a substantial number of weaving workshops with thirty or even sixty looms. As Aleppo textiles captured favor with consumers, such novel demand forced manufacturers to overcome limits in the local labor supply by attracting skilled weavers from nearby towns such as Mardin and Diyarbakır.[22]

In the Chinese Empire, urban production also expanded. Porcelain manufacturing proved especially dynamic and capable of intensification. In the city of Jingdezhen, between two hundred and three hundred kilns produced the toponymic china, employing up to one hundred thousand wageworkers by the 1740s. They turned out fine porcelain for the empire's ruling elite and increasingly for imperial and then global markets. As merchants invested in kilns and provided credit to manufacturers, they gained access to greater quantities of porcelain. Bolstered by the infusion of commercial capital and the expansion of markets, workers quarried the raw material, prepared it, spun the wheels, painted the porcelain, and fired it. Merchants then shipped the beautifully decorated pieces across the empire and, eventually, over the seas, making these delicate wares among the most prized possessions of elites everywhere while they themselves accumulated wealth. "China" became an almost universal class marker for capital-rich elites from London to Rio de Janeiro, Aleppo to Surat.[23]

Genoese merchants, like their Chinese and Ottoman counterparts, also used their capital and long-distance trade networks to expand manufacturing. That capital enabled the city's artisans to churn out silks, velvets, and damasks, as well as iron goods made from ore mined on the nearby island of Elba. Genoese paper production developed in the seventeenth century as well, and that industry's products were exported as far as the New World. Venetian merchants, on the other side of the Italian peninsula, also facilitated expanded manufacturing,

Chinese manufacturing prowess: porcelain recovered from the VOC trading ship Witte Leeuw, *which sank off the coast of Saint Helena on June 13, 1613.*

with the glass industry on the island of Murano becoming known throughout the Mediterranean for the quantity and quality of its production.[24]

Driven primarily by changes within the archipelago of capital, trade nodes that produced both markets and capital generated new centers of industry as well. They shared certain characteristics: powerful guilds, proximity to markets, and the presence of merchants eager to secure goods to trade.

Perhaps most crucially, guilds or guildlike organizations played a central role. They had a long tradition: As early as 1260, Paris already had 101. By 1670, Cairo seems to have had 262, and they dotted the urban societies of Hirschberg, Danzig, and Venice as well. Damascus and Aleppo each had between 160 and 180 during the seventeenth and eighteenth centuries. Everywhere, they followed certain patterns: They set prices, enforced quality standards, determined the distribution of inputs, and fixed the division of labor within workshops. They structured not just manufacturing but society more broadly, forging at times a uniquely cosmopolitan identity among their members. This becomes strikingly clear if we look at the religious diversity of those organizations: In predominantly Muslim cities such as Damascus, many guilds included Muslim, Christian, and Jewish members.[25]

As much as guilds mediated the expansion of urban manufacturing, they also constricted the pace and norms of the new manufacturing enterprises. They set strict standards about who could be admitted to their ranks; their entire raison d'être was to restrict labor supply and competition. Guilds constrained output by prescribing production processes, limiting price competition, monopolizing access to the trade, setting boundaries on the exploitation of labor, and stipulating strict rules about tools and processes to restrain technical innovation. That drove up labor costs. In 1698, in the French city of Amiens, labor costs were between 50 and 73 percent higher than in the countryside, which was unaffected by such rules.[26] Expanding manufacturing also created labor conflicts and volatile relations in the workshop—strikes, riots, or public demonstrations—that could threaten urban social peace.

Especially after 1650, in Hirschberg, as elsewhere, such limits on urban manufacturing pushed capital, and manufacturing with it, into the countryside. A century later, by 1748, only 24 percent of all Silesian weavers could be found in cities. Around Ghent, the number of looms increased from 4,976 to 8,868 between 1730 and 1792, while in the city of Ghent itself, their numbers fell. When merchants in the French city of Nîmes sought to secure supplies of high-quality silk textiles for their booming domestic and colonial markets, they invested heavily in production: In 1735, Nîmes had 503 looms, but that number exploded to 2,200 by 1754. As wages in Nîmes itself increased, however, merchant-manufacturers sought labor elsewhere, increasingly focusing on cottagers in the countryside. In nearby Uzès, silk manufacturers contracted with weavers in the surrounding countryside as well; by the mid-eighteenth century, there were sixty such rural producers. Urban artisans complained about the practice, arguing—to little avail—that the resulting competitive pressures reduced them to the status of pieceworkers.[27]

Everywhere, the pressures of the great connecting and merchants' desire to secure supplies for their trades leapfrogged the boundaries of urban manufacturing. As had been the case in agrarian production, too, the balance of power between various social groups in cities had a direct impact on the structures of emerging capitalism as well: Cities' social structures and the relative power of workers within them pushed manufacturing into the countryside just as the most radical edge of the transformation of agriculture by commercial capital took full shape on the Atlantic islands, the incubators of slavery and war capitalism. Capitalists' revolutionary impetus operated, as often as not, from the outside in. Intensifying industry was, in some ways, like an ocean wave—it surged forward in urban workshops, pulled back into the countryside, and then, by the nineteenth century, as we will see, surged forward again to power industrial concentration in cities.

———

As manufacturing's expansion pressed against the social structures and institutions of towns and cities, merchants in search of a reliable supply of goods to trade increasingly turned to where most of humanity dwelled—the countryside. Rural regions offered plentiful labor not subject to guild restrictions—peasants, serfs, and slaves. And merchants could draw on a rich stock of experience: In various parts of the world, their counterparts had already infused capital into agrarian production; the additional step to invest in manufacturing was a small one. Moreover, the people in that countryside saw opportunity as well: Many a cultivating family had the skills and desire to supplement their agricultural labor with manufacturing.[28]

Given these opportunities and constraints, merchants in some areas of the world redirected larger and larger portions of their capital into rural manufacturing—what historians call proto-industrialization. As global demand for labor-intensive manufactured goods swelled, the countryside offered a superb reservoir of labor that was cheap and relatively easy to mobilize, often because demographic pressures limited access to land and forced the landless or land-poor to find alternative ways of making a living. This expansion of manufacturing into the countryside only rarely entailed new technologies or new concentrations of workers; rather, it dispersed production along merchant-organized credit and trade arteries. Merchants advanced or sold raw materials to workers in the countryside, who then processed them to return them to merchants for pay. Crucially, production remained within households and was unsupervised by capital owners; workers organized their own labor, often allocating the time of various household members to manufacturing, and they found their own rhythms of work using their own tools.[29] Proto-industrialization did to seventeenth-century manufacturing roughly what Uber did to drivers in the twenty-first century: Workers could sell some of their family's slack labor time on markets (the winters then, the evenings and weekends now) while drawing on their own capital assets (a loom then, a car now). This work has often remained hidden to latter-day observers because it fails to correspond to our ideas about the workings of industrialization.

Driven by a similar set of opportunities and pressures, this rural expansion of industry occurred throughout Eurasia, Africa, and the Americas. It flourished throughout the seventeenth and eighteenth centuries, when the great connecting and the transformation of the countryside opened new markets.[30] Without doubt, the most significant proto-industrial complex emerged in Asia, notwithstanding Marx's 1853 claim that India "has remained unaltered since its remotest antiquity."[31] Indian and Chinese merchant-manufacturers produced better, more varied goods in much greater quantities than anyone anywhere in the world.[32]

There and elsewhere, the largest proto-industrial sector and the one most consequential for the emergence of industrial capitalism was textile production: silks, woolens, linens, and, especially, cottons. Their production was labor-intensive; they were valuable, with large and expanding markets; and they could be transported over long distances. The world's single largest proto-industrial sector, indeed, was the cotton textile industry of India. Many regions of the subcontinent had large numbers of workers dedicated to cotton production alone; the size of the domestic market in 1800 has been estimated at a minimum of 775 million yards of cloth; in addition, there were very substantial export opportunities. The quantity, quality, and diversity of the output of Indian spinners and weavers was unmatched, and they also dominated many of the world's markets—from Southeast Asia to the Middle East, from East Africa to Europe. As early as 1639, each year between twenty thousand and twenty-five thousand camels carried Indian cottons to Persia alone. So eager was the world for South Asian manufactures that one-fifth of the world's silver production in the seventeenth and eighteenth centuries ended up there, spent on cottons. European visitors stood in awe when they got a close-up look at the quantity and quality of Indian textile production, making these centuries, for them, an "age of apprenticeship."[33]

As the merchants of Surat and other South Asian port cities traded ever larger quantities of textiles, they had the means and motive to reorganize cloth production in their hinterlands. They moved some of their capital into manufacturing towns such as Gandevi, Navsari, and Bulsar—all near Surat. Farther away, merchant investors enabled weavers to produce fine cottons to be dyed and printed. Similarly, when the merchants of Diu expanded their trade with Mozambique Island, they required ever greater quantities of textiles to exchange for elephant tusks and slaves, financing a booming weaving industry in the town of Jambusar. African consumer demand encouraged Gujarati merchants to fund the production of textiles.[34]

In seventeenth- and eighteenth-century China, commercial capital also streamed into the countryside to invest in, and control, cotton and silk textile production, especially in the Yangtze and the Pearl River Deltas. The late seventeenth-century gravestone of Hsi She-jen, a cotton merchant, told visitors that "weaving became known and was to be met with in every highway and byway" thanks to his investment in production.[35] Merchants encouraged the expansion of silk textile production to serve a domestic market that had expanded by a factor of ten, along with export markets. One author has estimated that in the Jiangnan region alone, annual output of cotton textiles doubled to one hundred million bolts between the first half of the seventeenth century and the mid-eighteenth century—the result of the labor of about three million workers, mostly rural. In the lower Yangtze, almost every rural household produced textiles for the market, an estimated half million people. As the quantity of textiles increased, so did their quality.[36]

Japan experienced the expansion of its own proto-industry no later than the seventeenth century, and here, too, textiles were at the center. To gain access to cloth, merchants provided raw materials to spinners and

The world's proto-industrial center: India produces the world's highest-quality cotton textiles.

weavers, as a putting-out system took hold in the countryside. Merchants also capitalized rural production of ever larger quantities of pottery, sake, paper, iron goods, metalworks, and processed agricultural wares. Proto-industrial regions popped up across the entire Japanese archipelago. They were partly the response to China's economic dominance: The domestic manufacture of silks and porcelains was to replace Chinese-made wares with those produced in Japan—a form of import-substitution (proto-)industrialization. In Hokkaido, fisheries were an important locus for proto-industrialization, too, as eighteenth-century merchants invested capital to produce fish-meal fertilizer intended for sale elsewhere in Japan, providing both equipment and loans to local fishermen. Farther south, in the Japanese Alps region of Shimoina, the mid-eighteenth century saw the emergence of proto-industry in paper, textiles, and lacquerware. Supported by local rulers, merchants provided advances of materials and money to local producers—some skilled artisans, others underemployed peasants, often women.[37]

On the western edge of the Asian continent, merchant capital also increasingly moved into the countryside to organize manufacturing. The Ottoman Empire had a vibrant cotton cloth industry, especially in western Anatolia and around the Aegean coast, as sixteenth-century merchants began investing in rural production to improve access to the goods they traded. In the western Anatolian city of Denizli, merchants bought undyed cloth from weavers to have it dyed in the Aegean town of Tire; similar transactions occurred in Thrace in today's Greece. Village women worked up mohair wool for merchants in Ankara; manufacturers of camlet (a type of woven fabric) depended for their livelihood on merchants who sold their products in Venetian markets. Rural producers around Uşak knotted carpets for sale as early as the sixteenth century. Bursan silk merchants supplied silk to weavers in the surrounding rural environs, while in seventeenth-century Egypt, merchants infused capital into the countryside to facilitate and control the production of a variety of rural manufacturers. In the eighteenth century, putting-out networks spread into Balkan villages, particularly in the hill districts of present-day Bulgaria. Merchants organized the production of rough woolen cloaks called abas around Bulgaria and Albania; ingots and ironware around Bulgaria and Macedonia; and cotton cloth or yarn from around Bulgaria, Macedonia, and Thessaly, selling it in towns, at regional fairs, and in distant ports, thereby accelerating town-country integration. In eighteenth-century Mosul, when demand for local artisans' products increased, some of them moved their shops outside town, tempted, as elsewhere, to reach beyond guild structures for cheaper raw material and labor. By the 1690s, Mosul cotton guilds protested the growing presence of women in the industry, spinning, as they did, in their homes in the countryside, with little power to improve their status or pay.[38]

Even though proto-industrialization was first and foremost led by Asia, this injection of merchant capital into rural manufacturing affected various parts of Europe as well. Merchant entrepreneurs insinuated themselves into the textile, cutlery, and metalworking industries, among many others, from Catalonia, northern Italy, Sweden, and Poland to France, England, and the German lands. Again, textiles were at the core. The mass production of linens for long-distance markets began in the seventeenth century—not just in Silesia but in Flanders and Ireland. Italian city-states such as Florence and Genoa, as mentioned, had a long tradition of manufacturing, but by the sixteenth century, their merchants, such as woolen merchant-manufacturer

Francesco de' Medici (1450–1528), had moved much of that manufacturing into the countryside. In England, merchants in the clothing industry had organized rural production as early as the fifteenth century, and that production—first in woolens and linens, later in cottons—had subsequently expanded tremendously. In seventeenth- and eighteenth-century Catalonia, clothiers—local putting-out merchants along with urban merchants from Barcelona and Madrid—contracted with peasants to spin and weave woolens, supplying expanding markets on the Iberian Peninsula and in the wider Atlantic world. As their capital flowed into rural hamlets, peasant producers could allocate some of their labor to manufacturing, enabling them to stay on the land. These networks were big business: By 1745, in the Catalan town of Igualada, the largest merchant-manufacturer supplied five hundred people with textile-related work. Most consequentially, merchants financed the spinning and weaving of cotton—in the Black Forest, around Zurich, and across the northern English countryside, among other places.[39]

Expansion of rural manufacturing also took place in parts of sub-Saharan Africa. In 1611, Portuguese traders bought more than one hundred thousand meters of cloth in the eastern Kongo region. If we combine that staggering quantity with production for domestic use and trade elsewhere, we can see that the region's production equaled that of a great European textile-producing center such as the Dutch city of Leiden. As Claude Boucard, a French official, noted in 1729 about one such African city: "The inhabitants [of Bondu] grow cotton there, of which they make very beautiful loincloths that they dye black with the . . . indigo that grows naturally in the country," to sell it for gold.[40] Kano (in modern-day Nigeria), a center of such trade and production as early as the twelfth century, housed weavers and merchants specializing in cotton textiles, leather goods, and ironware. With expanding trade in the fifteenth century, it became a leading production site alongside nearby Katsina and Kebbi, with Wangara merchants investing heavily in the cotton industry in the adjoining countryside. As their financing optimized production, their trade networks opened up cloth markets in western and northern Africa.[41] German traveler

Heinrich Barth, who visited the area much later, observed that the "greatest advantage of Kano is that commerce and manufactures go hand in hand"—an observation that now applied to large swaths of the world.[42]

THIS GLOBE-SPANNING PROTO-INDUSTRIAL complex featured great variety in the goods produced, in the ways production was organized, and in how manufacturing activities were embedded within agricultural and trade systems. The precise ways that merchants accessed goods for their trade differed across place. Sometimes they advanced capital to producers who used it to buy materials for working up, with Gujarati weavers, for example, generally purchasing their cotton, just as Hirschberg weavers purchased the linen yarn that they worked with their own tools before selling the finished products to merchants. Chinese women also usually bought the raw cotton they processed, then sold the finished cloth to whoever offered the best price. At other times, merchants advanced raw materials—cotton, for example—to producers and thereby had a claim on the finished products. The northern English countryside offers a good example of that putting-out system. The power differential between these two systems was substantial: Indian weavers could generally sell their finished goods to the highest bidder, while English weavers generally had to deliver the fabric to the merchants who had advanced the raw materials.[43]

Despite their differences, all these places of intensifying industry drew on the initiatives, services, and resources of urban capital owners. For merchants, such investments made good business sense—indeed, they were crucial to maintaining the vibrancy of their trade networks, as they needed to secure the goods they sold, and to do so, they needed to enable their production. Whenever a proto-industrial complex formed, it was because merchants had moved some of their accumulated riches into manufacturing—riches amassed through long-distance trade and the transformation of the countryside. Smaller merchant intermediaries, in turn, connected larger merchants to rural producers.

No matter how they worked, these ventures gained their dynamism from the great connecting, which had created expanding markets that could not be exclusively supplied by urban producers. Wherever we look, investment was critical, especially for providing circulating capital of raw materials and other inputs. In China, in the early 1600s, an observer from the town of Nanxun commented that "[m]erchants often buy raw cotton from neighboring prefectures and set up shops on our land. The people take what they have produced, cotton yard or cotton cloth, and go to the market early in the morning. They exchange it there for raw cotton which they carry home to spin and weave as before."[44] In Jiangnan, merchants from Huizhou (in Anhui Province) purchased cloth produced in rural households, had it dyed and finished, and sold it throughout the empire, aided by the availability of silver. They provided spinners with raw cotton or credit to buy it. Once rural producers had finished the cloth, merchants purchased it from weavers. By the late seventeenth century, these merchants had even greater control of production and stamped their cloth bundles to certify quality.[45]

Merchants also did so in Japan, where the *ton'ya* provided the input and machinery that enabled rural dwellers to manufacture in their homes. Cotton weaving was the quintessential example of this kind of manufacturing. In Iruma, in Saitama Prefecture, rural traders bought fabrics produced by peasants as sideline work and sold them to local wholesalers at distributing centers, a system similar to the one instituted in Izumo Province, where most of the cotton spinning and weaving took place. Sometimes merchants allotted certain parts of the production process to certain people, an incipient division of labor under the auspices of capital.[46] In Japan and elsewhere, merchants struggled to gain access to predictable supplies, attempted to lock in prices, and strove to have weavers produce to the specifications of distant markets. In crucial ways, the logic of trade, the logic of capital, began to impinge on the logic of manufacturing.

Merchants frequently connected to rural producers through a chain of intermediaries. Wealthy Surat export merchants, for example, acquired their goods from local brokers who, in time, contracted with weavers—just as large Dutch merchants acquired their linens from Hirschberg traders. These chains were often solidified by common religious beliefs, place-of-origin networks, guilds, or other nonmarket identities, such as caste.[47]

Merchants did not just advance capital and raw materials; they also provided market information, arranged for transportation and insurance, and, crucially, provided for the marketing of goods made by dispersed producers. The intensification of production in the countryside was thus rooted in urban developments; cities, with their agglomerations of people and capital, were an important part of proto-industrialization. Sometimes, as in Nîmes, production was integrated across city and countryside.[48] So powerful was the impact of rural manufacturing that, in rare instances, new urban nodes even developed out of proto-industrial networks, as in the case of the English city of Manchester.

There were some surprising resemblances across great distances. Most importantly, manufacturing workers or their families continued to engage in agricultural pursuits. Handicraft producers in Asia almost always combined their manufacturing with subsistence agriculture for a measure of security. In England, spinning and weaving—first of wool, then of cotton—were deeply embedded within agricultural pursuits. When cotton came to the Black Forest in the eighteenth century thanks to the investments of Basel merchants, spinners and weavers continued working their fields and herding their cattle. And in Catalonia, all but the very poorest woolen and cotton workers continued to work fields they rented or owned. Wherever proto-industry emerged, peasants combined working the land with manufacturing for distant markets. Indeed, the low pay they received for their manufacturing labor was made acceptable only by their ability to supply themselves with many of the things they needed for subsistence.[49]

Proto-industrial workers sometimes shifted between manufacturing and agricultural pursuits according to the season, the state of markets, or the division of their family labor supply along gender and age

lines. Even though the forms of connection between industry and agriculture could be quite diverse, the basic pattern—the balance between agricultural and manufacturing activities—was consistent.[50]
Proto-industrial workers' ability to eat, dress themselves, raise their
children, and tend to their elders rested on nonmarket family labor.
Market production encompassed only a part, even a small part, of their
labor time. Like a predatory cuckoo stealthily laying its eggs in the
nests of other birds to be hatched and raised by hosts, merchant capital
incubated itself in social worlds outside its urban milieu, accumulating
its transformational powers from swelling rural populations whose
own reproduction was organized outside the market.

With production taking place in households, the capital intensity
of proto-industry was generally low: concentrated in textiles, mostly
spinning wheels and looms. Yet it would be wrong to assume that production technologies did not change; there was slow but significant
innovation. In the Chinese textile sector, artisans improved on ginning
technology and spinning wheels. Technical innovation also came to
India, with significant improvements in textile production. Highly
skilled Indian artisans communicated and developed technical knowledge. In Europe, too, proto-industry was a source of slow but significant technical change—weaving, for example, was greatly sped up by
the introduction of Kay's flying shuttle in 1733, which doubled weavers' productivity.[51]

By and large, however, innovations focused not on labor productivity but on improving quality and diversifying products to cater to
increasingly complex and varied tastes. The reason for this was simple:
Labor almost everywhere was abundant, and there was little reason to
economize it. In the Indian textile sector, there was a trend toward
greater professionalization and specialization, but there were no significant productivity gains. Tellingly, merchants almost everywhere remained aloof from involvement in the production process itself, which
continued to be organized by peasant workers.[52] Proto-industry principally expanded globally by the simple dynamic of ever more people

doing ever more similar things—what scholars have called an "industrious revolution."[53]

———

Merchants also began to invest with new intensity in sites of concentrated manufacturing: mines, breweries, tanneries, forges, and even textile factories. This was a significant shift, not just in terms of the quantity of output enabled by this infusion of capital but in terms of how production was organized. By the seventeenth and eighteenth centuries, these production sites assembled much larger numbers of workers under one roof than any urban workshops or rural proto-industrial undertakings, which meant that workers would be directly supervised by agents of capital.[54] While still exceptional and typically smaller than Caribbean plantations, these freshly capitalized enterprises pointed to the future.

That future was shaped, in part, by private capital owners, but also by states, which frequently organized and almost always tightly regulated and supervised concentrated manufacturing sites. They did so for a range of reasons: On the most obvious level, these enterprises served their military needs. Monarchs, political elites, and rulers wanted to ensure that the ships, muskets, and other line items dominating their budgets were produced efficiently. Moreover, they were eager to secure their own ample consumption needs. Consequently, even more than in urban production and rural proto-industrialization, states played a crucial role in these proto-factories, showing that the antecedents to modern industry rested significantly on the initiatives of rulers, not just of capitalists. States built complex manufacturing projects, policed the many workers, and helped maintain production methods as "secrets." The willingness, even eagerness, of states to collaborate with capital owners to expand production was truly remarkable.[55]

Many such projects emerged: Louis XIV established the arsenal in Lorient, France, in 1666, declaring that his "vain and vague and useless" land possessions around Port Louis and Faouédic would be transferred to the Compagnie des Indes Orientales. Soon, the company's ships armed themselves and off-loaded their goods there.[56] In 1690, the Marquis de Seignelay, minister of the navy, opened a royal naval base to take advantage of the company's facilities. By 1702, six thousand people lived in Lorient; thirty-six years later, the city had fourteen thousand inhabitants, many of whom worked in vast shipyards. The Venetian arsenal, along similar lines, was one of Europe's most important industrial sites, employing 2,343 workers by 1645, a stunning and truly exceptional concentration of proletarian labor, churning out ships for war and trade—and showing the tight connection between the two.[57]

China had sites of concentrated manufacturing as well, including a very significant shipbuilding industry. Huge state-owned factories built ships for warfare and transport alongside booming privately owned dockyards. The shipyards of Qiantang, Renhe, and Banqiao launched ships for the domestic grain trade, while the Baochuan and Longjiang Shipyards in Nanjing focused on seagoing vessels. With trade intensifying in the seventeenth and eighteenth centuries, the dockyards expanded, becoming some of the largest worksites in the world. At the Longjiang Ship Factory, for example, it

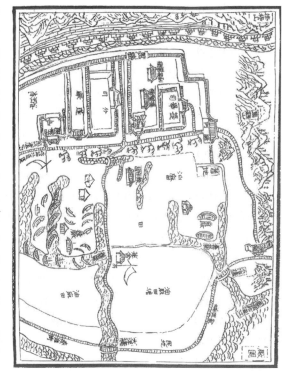

Site of concentrated manufacturing: China's Longjiang Shipyard, 1553.

took almost two thousand workers—both "official workers," or artisans, and "unofficial workers," or unskilled laborers who moved materials around the yard—to build vessels.[58] Chinese artisans did not just build very large numbers of ships; they built much larger ships than their contemporary European counterparts. The industry was notable, too, for the high skills of its artisans, who generated significant technical innovations, including ships with very low clearances and new kinds of sails.[59]

Such concentrated industry not only supplied military requirements; it also served the often outsize material needs of rulers. The royal manufacturers in the Faubourg Saint-Antoine in Paris employed six hundred workers, churning out high-quality mirrors, wallpaper, and other luxury items. Large numbers of French workers also labored in the state-run Parisian Manufacture des Gobelins, creating tapestries for the royal household and other elites.[60] Its Indian counterpart, the *gen* system, expanded the concentrated production of luxury items for the state. In the *karkhana* workshops, the Mughal court employed thousands of "embroiderers, goldsmiths, painters, lacquerwork varnishers, joiners, turners, tailors, shoemakers, armorers and the like" to produce a panoply of goods.[61]

In a handful of exceptional cases, urban capital flows alone were sufficient to spark a major industrial site—almost always the outgrowth of the previous centuries' great connecting and transformation of the countryside: As tobacco flowed into Glasgow and sugar into Amsterdam, processing industries employing large numbers of workers followed. As a torrent of sugar arrived in Britain, the country sported 120 sugar refineries by the 1750s. Expanding Dutch trade led the Nederlandsche Handel-Maatschappij to establish a weaving factory to gain access to a predictable supply of cloth at predictable costs and encourage and improve textile manufacturing for foreign markets in and around the Dutch city of Twente. In Newport, Rhode Island, manufacturing took off thanks to trade with the Caribbean, and by 1780 there were twenty-two rum distilleries in town. As Egypt's sugar harvests grew, Cairo refineries each employed as many as one hundred workers.[62]

Flush with orders both at home and abroad, energy-intensive manufacturing such as papermaking, oven manufacturing, and glassmaking also began benefiting from economies of scale at centralized production sites. By 1780, a French metalworking firm, Dietrich, employed fifteen hundred workers, while the iron production center of Le Creusot had five hundred people on its payroll. Russian capital owners such as the Stroganov family infused capital into ironworking, operating seventy-one iron- and copperworks in 1750, all sites of concentrated production and supervised labor. The North American iron industry also originated from the investments of British and then American-born capital owners—with Virginian planter John Tayloe, for example, channeling some of his tobacco profits into blast furnaces.[63]

Capital owners concentrated industry to better supervise production and workers and improve the quality and consistency of goods. In the late seventeenth century, Chinese silk entrepreneurs, the *zhangfang*, owned looms and ran factories, employing wageworkers to operate them. In Augsburg and Chemnitz, cotton-printing workshops employed large numbers of workers under one roof. Such manufactories were often linked to a wide network of small-scale rural cottage workers, and thus to the expansion of rural manufacturing—securing better and more consistent quantities and qualities by allowing some steps in the production process to take place under the exacting eyes of capital owners while also drawing on cheap rural labor.[64] Yet despite their promise, these sites remained rare compared with artisanal urban production and rural proto-industry; Fernand Braudel estimated that, circa 1700, there were fewer than one thousand manufactories in all of the German lands.[65]

Mining attracted merchant investments as well, turning what used to be a small-scale artisanal industry into another site of concentrated production. While early mining was not particularly capital-intensive, that changed as miners moved deeper underground to access coal, iron ore, gold, and silver. As Wangara merchants invested in the gold trade through the Sahara, they transformed the Akan gold-mining zone in present-day Ghana and the southern Ivory Coast with the credit they provided. In Hungary, Bohemia, the Harz, the Tyrolean Alps, and other such places, merchant investment increased output. The Augsburg Fuggers massively invested in mining, with Fugger-mined copper and silver fueling global trade and generating huge profits. The family declared that "almost all our benefits are derived" from mining.[66] Their mines in Schwaz and Falkenstein in Tyrol employed twelve thousand workers in 1550, while four thousand workers labored in their mines in Anzin.[67]

A walk along Kloveniersburgwal, one of Amsterdam's central canals, features a large mansion built of massive blocks of Bentheimer sandstone that now houses the Royal Academy of Science. Its facade projects wealth and power, which is the impression the building's first owners, Louis and Hendrick Trip, members of one of Amsterdam's richest families in the 1660s, intended.[68] The origins of their wealth are quickly apparent: The roof of the Trippenhuis is decorated with chimneys shaped like large mortars, and the frieze above the top floor shows two cannons. Like almost all the wealthy of that city, the Trips were traders. But they did not limit themselves to investments in the VOC or to supplying the Dutch Republic with weaponry that would help it secure its global trade networks. They chose to plow a significant percentage of their capital into manufacturing.

The Trips were initially iron and copper merchants, but they rapidly expanded, becoming perhaps the most important metal traders on the European continent by 1600, their goods reaching all corners of Europe, West Africa, and Brazil. Flush with profit but frustrated with inconsistent quality, slow technical advances, and competition for scarce

War profits transmuted into stone: The Trip family's wealth is reflected on an Amsterdam canal, 1662.

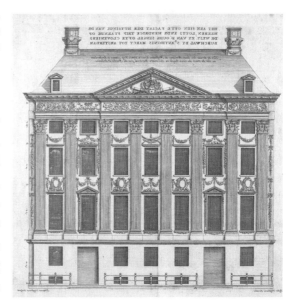

products during a period of many wars, they soon extended into manufacturing, including German munitions foundries in the late 1610s, with Elias Trip purchasing four foundry "huts" in Waldeck, alongside several mines in the area.[69]

When the Thirty Years' War threw into disarray the shipment of iron down the Rhine to the iron-hungry Dutch shipyards, the Trips leveraged the opportunity to expand their trade into capital-poor Sweden. In 1618, they linked up with another iron merchant, Louis De Geer, and invested in an iron concession in Finspång, obtaining a foothold in Swedish weapons manufacturing. They invested heavily in these operations, expanding their company's working capital to four hundred thousand guilders in 1626. As Swedish king Gustavus Adolphus granted them the necessary privileges to consolidate their network of mines, foundries, and ports, the Trips sent relatives to Sweden to manage their holdings.[70] A constant stream of investments followed, with De Geer writing to the Trips in 1627 to say that to "pour weaponry" in greater numbers, "we need more [of your investment] than we would otherwise."[71]

The Trips combined trade with manufacturing for several reasons: For one, the Admiralty of Amsterdam, the family's main client, sought weapons supplies more secure than the vulnerable imports channeled through the southern Netherlands and Westphalia. Since

War as business opportunity:
Louis De Geer, early seventeenth century.

1614, moreover, Elias Trip had been a member of the Amsterdam chamber of the VOC, a crucial customer with an insatiable appetite for metals and weaponry. Swedish iron, thanks to its lower phosphorous content when properly smelted, was of better quality than the Westphalian or southern Netherlandish product. To manufacture it, De Geer and the Trips recruited around five thousand Walloon laborers, skilled in the most up-to-date techniques of iron smelting. In addition, Swedish production was a tempting investment opportunity for the merchants because local wood and labor were cheaper than in Germany or the Low Countries, but the products could be sold at the same price. As a result, Swedish cannon exports increased from 185 pieces in 1622 to 1,319 pieces in 1631. In 1630 alone, De Geer and the Trips sold 2.5 million pounds' worth of cannon iron produced in their factories in Finspång and Nyköping, between 15 and 20 percent of total Swedish production. Their Holmens Bruk industrial complex at Norrköping employed over four hundred workers and boasted a weapons foundry, copperworks, ironworks, lumbermills, a wharf, a brewery, and a fish-processing facility. When three of the Trip brothers—Hendrick, Jacob, and Louis—obtained a stake in De Geer's Juletha Bruk foundry at Nyköping, in 1642, it expanded even farther. That foundry was later painted by Allaert van Everdingen, who depicted the factory in a bucolic landscape, erasing the dangerous conditions its workers faced, as well as the violence and subjugation its products enabled.[72] Juletha Bruk's armaments helped Dutch merchants control Caribbean islands and African forts, Southeast Asian outposts, and spice production in

Concentrated manufacturing meets warmaking: Allaert van Everdingen, Hendrik Trip's Cannon Foundry in Julitabruk, Sweden, *circa 1650–1675.*

the Bandas—a bloody testament to the way the intensification of industry was both a product of the great connecting and an enabler of it.

With thousands of industrial workers, the Trips also encountered another by-product of concentrated production: the strike. Near the end of the Thirty Years' War in 1648, growing competition in the copper trade, interruptions in raw material flows, and mechanization of parts of the production process led to foundry layoffs. In response, workers went on strike. Adriaen Trip was brought in to quell the unrest. He ended the strike by forging compromises with the workers, whose gains were limited in no small part by the threat of repression by the Norrköping authorities—another example of the growing closeness between state and private actors.

In Norrköping and elsewhere, intensification of industry rested on the labor of millions of women, men, and children. As in agriculture, they were mobilized in many ways: as contractors, apprentices, serfs, slaves, or wageworkers. The capitalist revolution—here and elsewhere—was unabashedly willing to draw upon older ways of doing things.

Labor systems have always been embedded within particular social contexts: In seventeenth-century Egypt, manufacturers "rented" boys from their fathers, and Egyptian women produced yarn for their weaving husbands without pay—examples among many of how patriarchal families structured labor markets. In other places, such as the Mexican town of Querétaro, enslaved workers labored alongside wageworkers.[73] Indeed, the combination of heterogenous kinds of labor—family and nonfamily, paid and unpaid—was a norm of emerging capitalism.

The most common labor form, by most accounts, was petty entrepreneurship. With most manufacturing taking place in households and in the countryside, peasants combined cultivation with manufacturing and entered a wide variety of contractual relationships with merchants and their agents. Linen weavers around fifteenth-century Lake Constance spun and wove to supplement the subsistence their agricultural holdings provided. In India, so meager were the cultivators' rewards that some weavers gave up agricultural employment to focus exclusively on weaving. They did the same in Moravia: In 1600, 90 percent of all households were independent peasants, and just 1 percent so-called *Häuslers*—peasants with no landholdings or very small landholdings that were insufficient for their subsistence, thus forcing them to work elsewhere. One hundred years later, only 35 percent of households were independent peasants, while 50 percent had become Häuslers.[74]

In urban areas where manufacturing was almost always organized by masters of small workshops, labor, as mentioned, was bound by a form of apprenticeship where masters instructed young apprentices in the secrets of the craft in return for their labor. Often, apprentices lived in their masters' households, and when they finished their apprenticeships, they set out to become masters themselves. While employment was first and foremost contractual, corporal punishment was not uncommon in this paternalist relationship.

Indeed, extra-economic coercion went hand in hand with the intensification of industry, though not as severely as in agriculture. In Silesia, as we have seen, the linen industry rested to a significant degree on coercion. Local landowners forced peasants to spin and weave and to part with monetary remuneration for these activities. Elsewhere, manufacturing workers were simply enslaved: Yusuf bin Suliman Da'bus, who ran an oil press in Cairo in the mid-seventeenth century, used enslaved workers for some of the tasks that emerged in his large, complex enterprise. Indeed, it seems to have been common for Egypt's larger industrial establishments to employ slaves. Likewise, in New Spain, large-scale textile workshops—the *obrajes*—were dominated by enslaved workers. And many of the Bursan manufacturers who produced silks relied on slave labor as well.[75]

Coerced labor, however, remained the exception rather than the rule in manufacturing. Instead, a distinct form of labor mobilization gradually became common: wage labor. Although it had also begun to spread in agriculture, as we have seen, paying workers for their labor time remained rare. Before the advent of capitalism, most of the world's people worked either under their own direction for their own benefit or were forced by worldly or ecclesiastical authorities to do so—on pain of physical or material sanctions, not wages.

Yet as industry intensified, wage labor spread. Sometimes it developed quite directly from the tensions produced by other systems of labor. As we have seen in Danzig, the expanding demand for manufactured wares could put guild organizations under tremendous pressure. In response, masters supplemented the labor of their apprentices with hired workers who were clearly never going to become masters. At other times, wage labor emerged as the most efficient way to recruit growing numbers of workers, as at the Trips' factories in Sweden, with their Walloon immigrant iron smelters. Similarly, the workers in Ahmedabad's paper manufactories were paid a wage.[76]

Wage labor emerged in a variety of production sites. In Cairo's seventeenth-century factories, wageworkers seem to have been common, with a wide range of annual remunerations: from eight hundred *nisfs* (the smallest silver coin) for a skilled worker in an oil mill to as little as thirty nisfs for a young helper. In the European countryside, independent producers forced to labor under feudal relations could morph into wageworkers. Some of the very large worksites—arsenals, mines, forges, and breweries—drew on wageworkers as well. Naval shipyards often employed several hundred workers, some embedded within the traditional apprenticeship system but most working simply for wages. Wage work on this scale was truly exceptional, which made these sites laboratories for the emergence of new ways of mobilizing and managing labor.[77] They were trailblazers for a labor system central to latter-day capitalism, with labor power (and not workers), like everything else, sold and bought on markets.

Whether manufacturing intensified in cities or in the countryside, whether it was powered by contractors, serfs, slaves, or wageworkers, the state played a crucial role. It was not just the state's direct investment in major production sites, as mentioned, but also its role as a major customer of arms and luxury goods and as an active partner in industrial development—planner, investor, and policeman. The German economist Gustav von Schmoller was exactly right—if somewhat Eurocentric—when he observed in the late nineteenth century that "[w]hat . . . made Milan, Venice, Florence and Genoa, later Spain and Portugal, now Holland, France and England . . . rich and superior: was a state economic policy."[78] The spread of manufacturing and the formation of more powerful polities went hand in hand. Inequalities in state capacity go a long way toward explaining how certain less-developed regions of the world—most importantly, Europe—gained greater manufacturing capabilities and began to catch up with Asian producers.[79]

States around the world immersed themselves in manufacturing in a variety of ways. In 1750s Shaanxi, Governor Chen Hongmou encouraged peasants to raise silkworms and actively sought to spread silk-weaving skills among them. In Kano, rulers secured trade routes and liberally welcomed traveling merchants to encourage industry. In some cases, that encouragement was very direct: As we have seen, rulers and bureaucrats frequently set up and controlled industrial enterprises themselves. Indeed, from England to India, from China to France, they were at the forefront of concentrated industry—often related to military or luxury trades. The state was also an outsize customer for many goods, from the tens of thousands of woolen uniforms that kept soldiers warm to the muskets that subdued domestic and foreign challengers to the ships of naval fleets.[80]

Almost all polities also endeavored to protect their domestic industries from competition with prohibitions and tariffs, not least to secure the tax revenues and prosperity that came with manufacturing. Government officials, laws, and rulers protected and enabled the rapid growth of Britain's coal industry, for example. As coal consumption increased by a factor of as much as ten between 1550 and 1700, the government placed a tariff on coal exports from all English and Welsh ports in 1590, stockpiled coal, and at times regulated its price. The 1651 Navigation Acts went further: Confining trade within the empire, thus forcing goods into the holds of British ships, the domestic shipbuilding industry blossomed. The British state also encouraged iron production by charging import duties. The textile industry benefited from myriad protections as well: In 1701, the British government banned the import of Indian cottons, protecting fledgling British producers against the vastly superior Indian cloth. The Tudor monarchs engaged in "a deliberate infant industry promotion policy," according to economist Ha-Joon Chang.[81] And such prohibitions were equally common elsewhere: German proto-industry developed behind high tariff walls, while China and Japan closed off their domestic economies, sharply limiting trade. These protections also limited domestic competition: Quite a few manufacturers depended on privileges and monopoly rights to make their enterprises sustainable—with European states favoring such import-substituting luxury industries as silk and porcelain.[82]

The state was also deeply involved in other ways. In Hirschberg, the town council stipulated how things were to be produced, inspected the manufactured goods, instituted tariffs on both the export of raw materials and the import of competing textiles, and compelled subjects to spin and weave to preserve the reputation of the area's goods in the marketplace. By the early eighteenth century, state-appointed inspectors increasingly evaluated and branded the cloth brought in by weavers. To guarantee the uniformity of the yarn, they also supervised the manufacturing process itself, requiring spinners to use only certain reels. By 1724, spinners and weavers who flouted these regulations suffered harsh penalties, including public pillorying—with heavy iron collars fastened around their necks, they would be forced to stand in the churchyard during Sunday services. The goal of these regulations and draconian punishments was to create standardized products, a difficult task in preindustrial times with dispersed producers. The French and British governments also played a crucial role in regulating production quality. French minister of finance Jean-Baptiste Colbert, for example, issued a whole series of regulations to guarantee the quality of national silk production, in addition to bringing in skilled foreign workers and granting special privileges to assorted manufacturers.[83]

The state, moreover, played a magnified role in securing access to raw materials and markets. As we have seen, European states—Britain, France, and the Dutch Republic among them—projected military power into many different regions of the world. That power secured a predictable supply of sugar, tobacco, cotton, and other goods coming into European ports—all crucial for the most dynamic proto-industrial sectors of that continent.

Rulers' and bureaucrats' interest in fostering manufacturing brought the state deep into economic life because it was one important source of their power: Industry was taxed, industry increased the wealth of the state, and industry provided the tools of warfare to secure the state itself. This rising importance of manufacturing to the state lent weight to the counsel of capital-rich merchants and producers. State archives brim with petitions and correspondence from capital owners, demanding infrastructure investments, protections, regulations, and troops to control labor. British, Dutch, and French rulers' support for intensifying industry was, in fact, crucially related to the increasing power of capitalists within these states. Capital owners leveraged rulers' dependence on them to reconstitute society along increasingly capitalist lines. The Fuggers and Welsers are just one example among many: In return for revenue for expanding armies, they demanded concessions from the state to enable deeper investments in mining, sugar production, and trade. Such policies were essential to sparking intensifying industry, especially in those parts of the world that were far behind the Asian manufacturing sector. They created the eventual British breakthrough—a theme we will return to in later chapters. It was here, in the realm of the state, that crucial differences emerged between producers in different parts of the world, differences that forged new and long-enduring hierarchies.[84]

The state's central role in the slow emergence of manufacturing shows once more that capitalism was a difficult project. And the opposition that this revolutionary recasting of economic life faced brought the state into the mix again. When workers struck at the royal cloth factory in Abbeville in 1716, a contingent of troops compelled them to return to work. Across Europe, the military was used to keep workers in line. In manufacturing, as in agriculture, coercion was never far away, not least because, as Adam Smith so bluntly observed, "[t]he affluence of the rich excites the indignation of the poor, who are often both driven by want, and prompted by envy, to invade his possessions."[85] The advent of capitalism was not about overcoming the state: Early capitalism was a project of the modernizing, expansionist factions in states worldwide. The great gamble of intensifying industry was no less a gamble by the architects of the state.[86]

In 1700, the world of town-based artisanal manufacturing, proto-industrialization in the countryside, and concentrated industry was still one of striking resemblances. Proto-industrial regions on all continents churned out increasing quantities of textiles, ironware, pottery, and other goods and traded them across ever longer distances—the great connecting providing access to markets. The global manufacturing core remained in India and China, yet producers in parts of Europe had begun to catch up, encouraged by rulers and financed by their capital-owning allies, who had amassed unprecedented wealth and power from a new archipelago of capital that they increasingly dominated.

It is tempting to see this intensification of manufacturing as the precursor to modern industry. Many elements of that industry, after all, became evident in the urban workshops—proto-factories as well as proto-industrial and household-based production sites. Yet the relationship between early intensified manufacturing and later large-scale industrialization is not as straightforward as it may initially seem. There was, of course, often a connection: In Kansai's cotton sector, proto-industrialization led, eventually, to Japanese cotton industrialization, and the same thing happened in Alsace. Lancashire's cotton industry led to the emergence of factories in the late eighteenth century, just as happened with Bohemia's glass industry. Capital accumulation, entrepreneurship, the creation of marketing networks, and the mobilization, disciplining, and skilling of workers all transitioned smoothly into the age of the factory. Indeed, a few decades later, many a putting-out merchant would open a factory and thus launch modern industry.[87]

However, in most cases, industrialization did not follow in situ. Despite its critical role as a site of proto-industrialization, Hirschberg, for example, never industrialized significantly. Its powerful merchant guilds successfully resisted the institutional and technical innovations required to do so. In the nineteenth century, with the onslaught of industrially produced cottons from elsewhere, Hirschberg's weavers were put out of work, and Silesia was transformed from Prussia's most industrial region to its poorest province.[88] Neither India's vibrant proto-industrial sector nor the plentiful urban and rural industries in the Ottoman Empire led to the emergence of factories. It has been argued that Indian proto-industry was, in practice, an "evolutionary cul-de-sac."[89] In East Asia, too, the widespread intensification of manufacturing was not followed by industrialization. Instead, its low-capital but labor-, energy-, and natural-resources-intensive production was idiosyncratic enough to constitute what has been called an "East Asian path of development."[90]

And despite all the industrious activity in seventeenth- and eighteenth-century cities and countrysides, few predicted a breakthrough to something fundamentally new. Even the citizens of Hirschberg, Lancashire, and Surat could not have imagined an industrial society of the kind that emerged only a century later.[91]

What was clearly visible at the time, however, was the revolutionary potential of capital, best expressed by its fungibility: Unlike feudal holdings, attached to particular places and forms of property, capital, as the move into intensified production had shown, could morph from one thing into another. It was a uniquely fluid form of property. Merchants belied their reputation for being unwilling to enter the dirty world of production and pushed into not only intensive agriculture but also urban and rural manufacturing, showing decisively that Karl Marx and many scholars after him were wrong to say that "merchant capital is synonymous to the non-submission of production to capital."[92]

Yet capital's great revolutionary potential—emerging first on islands, pushing into the countryside, and then intensifying industry—had only just begun to be visible. Its greatest transformation lay in the near future. By midcentury—in one part of the world, in one industry—a perfect storm gathered, and that unlikely convergence threw human history onto a fundamentally new course. In the process, it created the world we live in today.

6.

THE PERFECT STORM

Resources pour in from a new hinterland: London's port in the eighteenth century. Painting by Thomas Luny (1759–1837).

Late in 1740, Johann Jakob Bethmann, the twenty-three-year-old scion of a well-to-do Frankfurt mercantile family, boarded a ship in Amsterdam bound for the French port of Bordeaux. Educated in Leipzig and familiar, despite his youth, with markets as far away as Batavia, Bethmann felt drawn to France's fast-growing Atlantic periphery and Bordeaux's reputation as its entrepreneurial epicenter.[1] With his Frankfurt relatives supporting the venture, Bethmann hoped to found a profitable new outpost and make his mark on his storied family's fortune.

By the early eighteenth century, Bordeaux had become a crucial node in the new European economy. As it was located on the Garonne, with easy access to the Atlantic, Bordeaux's merchants had overcome their former dependence on the wine trade by sending ships first to

*Atlantic port cities boom: Bordeaux in the late eighteenth century.
Etching by Yves-Marie Le Gouaz (1742–1816).*

Africa to engage in the slave trade and then eventually to the Americas, from whence they returned richly laden with sugar, coffee, cotton, indigo, and other once exotic goods. By 1750, it counted between sixty thousand and seventy thousand inhabitants, making it France's fourth-largest city. It claimed almost a third of the entire French colonial trade and cornered half of the imports from Saint-Domingue and Martinique, France's most dynamic colonial possessions. Viewed from its docks, the port's dependency on the Caribbean was nearly complete: By the 1750s, three-quarters of all imports came from there; by the second half of the 1770s, that share had surged to 81 percent, with Saint-Domingue the leading supplier. While most of these imports were almost immediately shipped on to northern European ports, some were processed locally, especially sugar and tobacco. "The life of our beautiful port," a merchant reported, rested on "the intimate and numerous relationships that existed between the merchants of Bordeaux and the inhabitants of Saint-Domingue."[2] In 1790, profits extracted from French colonies added about 7 percent to the French national income, with almost half coming from Saint-Domingue.

No mere way station, Bordeaux built on its early lead as one of Europe's principal entrepôts for the American trade to become a sophisticated hub for the distribution of commodities—from the expanding transatlantic French hinterland to the intensifying trade, agriculture, and industry of the Dutch Republic, the Habsburg Empire, and the German lands. These opportunities drew increasing numbers of British, Portuguese, Scandinavian, and Dutch merchants to the city, alongside a sizable enclave of German traders. By the mid-1760s, that German community counted about eighty merchants, including young Johann Jakob Bethmann.[3]

Bethmann soon became a major player in this tricontinental complex of trade, agricultural production, and industry. His rise was accelerated by marrying Elisabeth Desclaux, a strategic match with one of the city's most influential merchant families.[4] Eager to benefit from their newfound Bordeaux connection, his family members put their wealth and global networks behind several joint undertakings. When the Frankfurt Bethmanns needed access to colonial goods, they drew on Johann Jakob, who in turn made his Frankfurt relatives commission merchants for his trades in Germany.[5]

Initially, Bethmann imported sugar, indigo, coffee, cotton, and cacao from the Caribbean. He moved these goods to northern European ports and from there into the central European hinterland. Mostly he worked as a commission merchant—brokering for a fee goods he did not own. But by 1748, he began engaging in shipping, especially of sugar, from Martinique and Saint-Domingue. Over the next thirty-six years, he sent fifty-seven ships to the West Indies and owned shares in other vessels. His trade

Trade, finance, plantation agriculture, and industry combined: portrait of Johann Jakob Bethmann.

expanded rapidly, in part because of his privileged connections to central European markets, which gave him, for instance, a monopoly on supplying sugar to the only Habsburg refinery in the Adriatic city of Fiume and then the chance to invest, with his Frankfurt brothers, in the refinery itself. Such exclusive and vertically integrated trade was, in the words of one historian, a "bonanza."[6]

Engagement in colonial trade led Bethmann, like other Bordeaux merchants, to ever deeper involvement in plantation agriculture, often inadvertently. As planters proved to be voracious consumers of capital, expertise, and market access, they depended on metropolitan merchants. When agricultural enterprises went bankrupt, these merchants became their owners. Bethmann also administered plantations for absentee owners and, once confident in their profitability, purchased plantations outright. In 1777, he partnered with merchant David Gradis to buy a plantation on Saint-Domingue. And in 1787, he began to administer the Saint-Domingue sugar plantation of the Marquis François Jacques René de Fauveau.[7]

From the 1760s on, Bethmann's interests also included the slave trade—hardly surprising considering that labor was the key ingredient for expanding production and thus trade. An estimated 411 slaving expeditions (about 12 percent of the French total) left Bordeaux in the eighteenth century. While this number pales next to the 11,000 voyages organized by British merchants, these trades still represented noteworthy merchant investments: One journey could require more than 200,000 livres, but in 1789, when merchant Jean Dommenget equipped three slaving ships, his total investment amounted to 1.25 million livres—a vast sum. As one of the port's biggest players, Bethmann, now known to most as Jean-Jacques Bethmann, dabbled in this trade as well: In 1767/68, he negotiated a contract with the Danish Guinea Company to invest 800,000 livres in the slave trade, a project he later abandoned.[8] Two decades later, Bethmann took a deeper dive into the trade, albeit in a roundabout way: In 1789, he joined a number of his merchant colleagues to rescue from bankruptcy a business that specialized in slave trading, administering plantations, and trading Saint-Domingue plantation goods: Romberg, Bapst & Cie. With 2.2 million livres from Bethmann and others, Georg-Christoph Bapst, one of the founders, continued to run the firm under the supervision of five merchants, including Bethmann, the house's single largest investor.[9]

Romberg's history elucidates how deeply European agriculture, industry, and finance were entangled with American slavery by the eighteenth century. Bethmann had known the company's founder, Friedrich Romberg, since the 1760s. Born in Sundwig, Germany, in 1729, Friedrich Romberg launched his Bordeaux house in 1783. At this point, he had already lived out an illustrious career: He had formed businesses in Ostend, Bruges, and Ghent, engaged in the manufacturing of printed cottons—*toiles d'indiennes*—in the Austrian Netherlands, and offered maritime insurance. He was also a major banker, providing loans to the Habsburg emperor and to fund canal construction. Those investments made Romberg very rich, enabling this quintessential bourgeois to acquire that quintessential symbol of aristocratic wealth and power—a massive château. Now, in Bordeaux, Romberg added to his portfolio the Atlantic slave trade, as well as the management of indigo, sugar, cotton, and coffee plantations in the French Caribbean. To help him manage these complex operations, he partnered with the young Bapst and put his son Henry in charge.[10]

Henry Romberg and Bapst started their Bordeaux trade boldly, attempting to integrate their trade in labor and plantation products with agricultural production.[11] As an observer retrospectively described the business in 1814:

> This enterprise consisted in dealing with a large number of colonists in Saint-Domingue, making sufficient advances to them to repair and cultivate their plantations, and to provide them with income proportionate to their fortune. A branch house was established in Saint-Marc; it was to receive from the head-house, established at Bordeaux, all the utensils, edibles, effects, and goods necessary for the exploitation and repair of the properties of

Saint-Domingue; it had to receive all the products of these same properties. These products were to be sent to Bordeaux in the ships belonging to the head-house, and sold by it.[12]

The firm transacted with some sixty-three Caribbean sugar, coffee, and indigo plantations, twenty of which it managed directly. It owned six or seven ships. Between 1783 and 1791, the height of Bordeaux's slave-trading boom, Romberg, Bapst & Cie embarked upon as many as fourteen slaving voyages to Africa. In 1789, it dispatched the 142-ton *Aimable Nanon* to the Guinea coast and kidnapped 182 Africans to be enslaved in Saint-Marc. Trading in slaves had become the company's most profitable business.[13] As Bapst bragged, "Our shipments from Europe are sold at their departure, our ships always employed, our negroes always firmly placed and finally our commissions and those of Saint-Marc certain on the returns, without delay."[14]

As trader, creditor, and active investor in Romberg, Bapst & Cie, Bethmann filled his coffers with the proceeds of one of the cruelest labor systems ever invented: In 1791, his profits amounted to a full

A mercantile outpost in the heart of the eighteenth-century slave lands: Saint-Marc in Saint-Domingue.

363,000 livres (about \$4 million in 2024 US dollars). This was at a time when a skilled Parisian mason could make 2.5 livres a day.[15]

These profits were consequential not just for Bethmann personally but for the capitalist revolution more generally. Bethmann's close ties with his Frankfurt-based brothers meant that his gains in turn breathed vital funds into their investments in the centers of early German industrialization—copper mining, metalworking, and textile production. Tellingly, Germany's first mechanized cotton-spinning factory, Johann Gottfried Brügelmann's Textilfabrik Cromford in Ratingen, drew on the Bethmanns' capital.[16]

——

With capitalist islands such as Bordeaux flourishing, merchants' multidirectional ambitions generated new and striking feedback loops. They demonstrated that capitalism's unprecedented dynamism was not a static or insular ensemble of institutions, cultures, coercions, resource endowments, class struggles, and geographies but a revolutionary, often violent mixture of all these elements in the context of novel connections across the globe. Capitalism, Möbius strip–like, created and emerged from within the world economy, whose unprecedented expansion into the Atlantic was its explosive core, the breakthrough departure from all previous ways of organizing economic life, including that of the ancient islands of capital in the first half of the second millennium.

What distinguished these novel links was not their geographic expanse, as long-distance trade preceded capitalism by many centuries, as we have seen. Instead, these links owed their transformational and self-propelling dynamism to the simultaneity of the great connecting, the transformation of the countryside, and the intensification of industry, all further propelled and enabled by the expansion of state power. It was a multidimensional feedback loop; a capital-driven unfolding of circulation, production, and consumption; a multilayered and globally made social process.

The feedback loops were many, showing again that any search for a monocausal and monolocational explanation for this great break-through moment of capitalism is futile.

Crucially, the great connecting helped intensify manufacturing. Across the world, manufacturers in urban workshops and peasant homes benefited from expanding markets made possible by new trade links. Egyptian artisans increased their production of leather goods and textiles as trade within the Ottoman Empire expanded. The silk industry of Lyon expanded vigorously, thanks to Italian investments and access to Spanish markets. Indian spinners and weavers increased their output as the European trading companies connected them, as we have seen, to European, African, and American markets. They also found new markets in East Africa: As the elephant hunt—a particular form of the transformation of the countryside—intensified, Gujarati merchants shipping ivory from East African ports needed more textiles to acquire more elephant tusks. This encouraged Indian weavers to use pattern books that indicated the preferences of their African customers. That trade was voluminous. Around 1750, Zena, a town in the Zambezi Valley, received 120,000 to 160,000 pieces of cloth annually, while 300,000 to 500,000 pieces of Gujarati cloth might have arrived in Mozambique, all under the aegis of Banian merchants, who also provided the credit that lubricated both the expansion of textile production in India and the African elephant hunt.[17] European linen manufacturers, as we have seen, radically augmented their production for Atlantic markets as well, and their brands were now known throughout that world—with customers in Havana or Rio having a precise sense of what to expect when they ordered "Brunswicks," "Hessians," or "Osnaburgs."

The intensification of commerce further expanded markets by encouraging the growth of cities, effectively bringing consumers to the merchant islands of capital and their points of entry—another way in which the great connecting advanced both commercial agriculture and intensified industry. Bordeaux's 70,000 city dwellers not only made a living connected to trade—like their counterparts in Amsterdam and

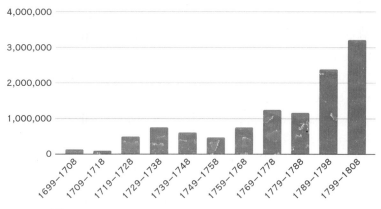

*The great connecting encourages industry, as shown by the value
(in pounds sterling) of Indian cotton cloth imports into West Africa, 1699–1808.*

Surat, London and Guangzhou—but also drew food and manufactured wares from the surrounding countryside. India's growing cities also became important markets for manufactured wares. In Japan, the number of cities with more than 10,000 inhabitants quadrupled between 1500 and 1800; by 1804, 6.4 percent of the Japanese population lived in such cities. China saw slower urban development, about equal to the rate of expansion of its population. Yet this population grew rapidly: In 1500, between 100 and 125 million people lived in the Chinese Empire, but 250 years later, that number had doubled.[18] Large cities emerged, with Nanjing counting perhaps around a million inhabitants as early as the seventeenth century—many more than inhabited the largest European cities.

While urbanization was a global process, its dynamic in eighteenth-century Europe was unique—a direct outcome of the prominent role of Europe in the great connecting, yet another feedback loop. Nowhere did cities multiply and grow more, as a proportion of the population, than in western Europe: London had about 400,000 inhabitants in 1650 and 675,000 in 1750 (a direct outcome of its imperial ambitions); Paris expanded from about 500,000 people in 1700 to about 650,000 in 1790. Twenty-nine percent of Britons lived in cities by 1800, only outdone by the Dutch, 34 percent of whom made their homes in urban centers such as Amsterdam, Haarlem, and Utrecht. Such urbanization was one of the by-products of intensified trade—and it encouraged both the expansion of manufacturing and the commercialization of agriculture, which was particularly important because most people in most of the world still remained entrenched in rural ecosystems and bought few manufactured wares.[19] Urbanization resulted in expanded markets.

INTENSIFIED TRADE HAD another salutary effect: Producers had to compete, often for the first time, with distant counterparts. English cloth manufacturers found themselves fighting for market share with high-quality textiles from South Asia. European crockery makers encountered the finest Chinese porcelains. They responded to these pressures by making production more efficient and improving quality. English potters Sarah and Josiah Wedgwood thrived by imitating the styles of imported Chinese porcelain. Dutch delftware was also an imitation of Chinese porcelain catering to the desire for luxuries among the middling class.[20] The Wedgwoods understood this connection between trade in Chinese porcelain and their own production—named for its main place of manufacture—writing in 1772 to one of their business partners, Liverpool merchant Thomas Bentley, that "[t]he Great People have had their vases in their Palaces long enough for them to be seen and admired by the *Middling Class* of People," making them in turn potential buyers of domestically manufactured porcelain.[21] These competitive pressures mostly affected European manufacturers, since few imported manufactured wares found their way to Asian markets until the late nineteenth century, during which time colonialism gave Asian capitalists and states little ability to respond.

On the most general level, these feedback loops between the great connecting and the intensification of manufacturing were common across the eighteenth-century globe. Yet they took on a particular dynamic on the western fringes of the European continent. This was not caused by Europe's proto-industrial sector, since, as we have seen, proto-industrialization occurred everywhere, especially in Asia, and did not necessarily lead to industrialization. It was, instead, because in these areas, the features of the merchant-driven capitalist revolution— the great connecting, the transformation of the countryside, the intensification of manufacturing, and the burgeoning of state power— interacted with world-altering force. Nowhere else in the world were there businesses like that of the Bethmanns, businesses that drew not just on the transformation of Caribbean agriculture but on connections to new islands of capital along the coasts of Africa and the Americas, the French state's military commitment to protecting these trade connections, and intensified manufacturing in Fiume and Ratingen, among other places. Only in Europe did a political economy take shape that enabled this integration. By the mid-eighteenth century, in fact, the transformations of the previous 250 years had become a powerful brew of mutually reinforcing developments, focused on the continent of Europe.[22]

Just look at the epicenter of this new capitalism—the United Kingdom, where the great connecting had an unmatched impact on manufacturing. Between the 1720s and the 1780s, Britain's fastest-growing trade by far was with Africa, Asia, and the Americas, while the relative importance of its trade with continental Europe declined drastically. Around 1700, extra-European markets on other continents had made up 15 percent of all British exports; seventy years later, that number was 51 percent. Scholars have estimated that half of all additional industrial production between 1688 and 1815 was exported, a stunning number that provided producers with unprecedented markets and new kinds of incentives. As a result, after 1763, every second manufacturing worker in the United Kingdom owed their job to exports. Exports to the Americas, economist Barbara Solow has found, supported the expansion of Britain's core industries. Access to global markets reachable from Atlantic ports almost *solely* accounted for the faster economic growth of western versus eastern Europe.[23]

In eighteenth-century France, a similar story unfolded: Foreign trade developed more rapidly than the domestic market, providing an important outlet for manufactured wares. From 1716 to 1787, colonial imports grew annually by 3.33 percent, exports and reexports by 3.1 percent. In 1786, one-third of French exterior trade was to and from the extra-European world, with two-thirds of that trade made up of imports from the Caribbean. A voluminous study of the eighteenth-century French economy has indeed found that foreign trade was the "heart of growth."[24]

The transformation of the countryside everywhere further expanded markets for manufactured goods, yet another feedback loop. As subsistence production diminished, self-sufficient manors disintegrated, and tributary relations dissolved, rural cultivators began consuming things that had been produced elsewhere: cloth, above all, but also crockery, metal goods, and processed foods such as sugar and beer. This was acutely true in the world's slave lands and areas whose agricultural production was primarily meant for markets. The emergence of highly commercialized islands in the archipelago of capital—Barbados and Saint-Domingue but also Gorée and Potosí, the Chesapeake and Bahia—expanded markets for manufacturers. All tools, much food, and almost all manufactured goods came from elsewhere, unusual in a world in which most families grew their own food and manufactured most of the goods they consumed. The enslaved workers' clothing was spun and woven in distant locations such as Jelenia Góra; the iron chains that controlled them were forged in Birmingham and Nantes; the ships that transported labor, sugar, and supplies were manufactured in massive shipyards in places such as Toulon, Boston, and London. Meanwhile, the small elite of planters ate from plates made in China, wore textiles manufactured in India, and consumed luxury goods coming out of European workshops. Perhaps most surprisingly, even food traveled vast distances, with regions like Bordeaux taking advantage of the extent of their agricultural hinterlands to send their grains and wines as far as the Caribbean. When the *Triomphant* sailed from Bordeaux to Saint-Domingue in 1791, it carried almost forty-five thousand liters of locally produced wine.[25]

The Marquis de Paroy, a planter we encountered earlier, owned a litany of items from the world's expanding proto-industry: tables and chairs; beds and mirrors; "towels in cloth from Brittany" and an "*indienne* from the Provence with red flowers"; rifles and a sword; ceramics and glassware; a clock; and "5 jars from Provence," among other household items.[26] The plantation economy of Saint-Domingue was thus connected to the labor of families, peasants, and artisans who would never cross the seas from Asia, Africa, and Europe to step onto its shores. It was eerily modern, with a degree of market reliance that came to Europe itself only decades, even centuries, later. The unprecedented demand in the hyperconnected Atlantic slave lands from people like the Marquis de Paroy significantly aided the expansion of industry. Slow-moving domestic markets did not suffice.[27]

The merchants, nobles, weavers, and spinners of places like Jelenia Góra all, in turn, depended for their livelihoods on this transformation of the remote countryside, since, as mentioned, almost all the linens they produced went to distant markets. These textiles played a particularly critical role in the African slave trade—historians have estimated that over the course of about 350 years, textiles constituted more than half the value of the products exchanged in Africa for slaves, generating significant new demand for textiles in the Indian and European proto-industrial sectors. Among Bordeaux's slaving expeditions in 1743, textiles—mostly from India, in this case—constituted 60 percent of the value of the cargo. These textiles also flowed into the world's plantation belt to provide inexpensive attire for the enslaved sugar, rice, cotton, and indigo growers.[28]

These markets were important for both urban and rural manufacturers. Eighteenth-century England exported unprecedented quantities of nails, axes, and firearms, with exports to overseas markets increasing much more rapidly than exports to the continent. Likewise, seventeenth-century Dutch textile industrialization thrived because of the demand from Dutch overseas merchants. Iron goods, from plows to machetes to shackles; French silks to dress elites—all found markets in the newly buoyant Atlantic world.[29]

The more incremental transformation of the countryside outside the hard-driven slave lands of the Americas expanded markets as well.[30] As Polish nobles focused single-mindedly on producing wheat for world markets, they procured most of the manufactured wares that they consumed from Danzig, most of which were imported from western Europe. As rural cultivators in Europe lost access to land and became wageworkers, they, too, needed to acquire their subsistence on markets, leading to further expansion of the domestic market.

The transformation of the countryside thus had a direct impact on the world's manufacturing; indeed, it was a prerequisite for its expansion. We can comprehend the significance of these links by looking in some detail at one early European industry: copper production. Before 1650, copper production in England—never very important—had almost disappeared; copper making required expensive charcoal, and its domestic markets were too small and inelastic.[31]

Then the mid-seventeenth century brought the Caribbean sugar revolution and its demand for copper kettles to boil cane sap. About 8 percent of the investment in a sugar plantation went to copper utensils, cumulatively creating a huge demand for the metal. New markets for copper also emerged in the trade-driven shipbuilding industry, as well as on the west coast of Africa, where African merchants took copper as payment for slaves; between 1673 and 1704, copper made up 10 to 15 percent of the value of the Royal African Company's exports. While domestic demand remained lackluster, four times more copper was exported in 1700 than in 1670, with 90 percent sold into the Americas and Africa.[32]

This expanding market encouraged British inventors and investors to search for more efficient production methods. Smelters worked to replace expensive charcoal with coal, a cheaper energy source. As demand for copper ore shot up, English West Country miners searched for ways to pump water out of ever deeper shafts to get to the copper. This encouraged a young engineer, Thomas Newcomen, to build what came to be known as the Newcomen engine, a powerful machine that for the first time succeeded in using steam to propel a piston in a cylinder on a continual basis. While Newcomen built his first engine in the Midlands, he had begun his work near the copper mines. These new techniques demanded hefty merchant investments. Atlantic trade—principally powered by the slave lands—thus had a direct impact on the English copper industry. And that industry was made up not of mere tinkerers, as some might tell us, but of concerted strategies and investments by the same capital-rich merchants who fueled the great connecting and the transformation of the countryside. As a result of these pressures and incentives, England by 1800 produced more copper than anyone else.[33]

As copper exports increased by 11 percent annually between 1750 and 1770—faster than all other metals trades—opportunities for accumulating enormous wealth emerged. Coppersmith William Forbes moved to London in 1771 to start a copperworks with an initial investment of five hundred pounds. Production was so profitable that when he retired from his business in 1783, he bought a country seat in Stirlingshire for one hundred thousand pounds. When he retreated to his estate, he enclosed the land and increased rents for the remaining farm families.[34]

Iron manufacturers also benefited from the great connecting and the transformation of the countryside. The slave trade depended on iron goods, and though it was never iron's most important source of demand in tonnage, the industry felt the stimulus of the mass enslavement and transportation of millions of Africans, because iron bars were exchanged for enslaved workers in Africa. Iron manufacturers also produced the hardware of coercion, with Birmingham emerging as an important production center for shackles and chains, while iron foundries around Nantes produced what the French called "fers à nègres," or "negro irons." When the *Jeune Reine* left the port of Nantes in 1765, embarking first for Gorée and then for Guadeloupe to trade in captives, it had on board "137 negro irons, handcuffs and chains etc." In 1784, the *Jeanne Therese*, sailing from Nantes for the Gold Coast to trade in enslaved Africans, loaded the usual assortment of "negro irons, handcuffs, neck irons, negro brand irons."[35]

———

In yet another feedback loop, proto-industrialization furthered the transformation of the countryside, even in historic industries such as English wool manufacturing. The demand for ever greater quantities of raw wool encouraged English landowners to enclose their fields to raise sheep. In Silesia, linen producers pushed landowners to convert their fields to flax, while African and Indian farmers produced cotton for cloth manufacturing. The transformation of the countryside provided the raw materials for industrial production and the calories necessary to nourish workers who did not produce their own sustenance.

The Americas especially provided ever increasing quantities of food, fiber, and raw material, helping Europe to overcome its resource constraints and escape the Malthusian dynamic that had acted as a brake on past economic development. By the late seventeenth century, sugar, all of it imported, had become part of daily life in Britain. A hundred years later, a rural English family of six purchased two pounds of sugar weekly. Rum—an important by-product of sugar production—provided one-quarter of the caloric intake of adults in British North America. To meet this demand, sugar production in British America almost quintupled in the eighteenth century: By 1805, its annual output—297,400 tons—equaled the total caloric needs of 1,446,200 English workers for a year when the British population numbered just 10.5 million people.[36]

That sugar not only fed Europeans but also made possible entirely new industries such as chocolate manufacturing, which, in turn, encouraged further transformations of the countryside. In port cities and beyond, chocolatiers created small artisanal workshops to produce the increasingly popular concoction of sugar and cocoa, with Nantes and Bristol renowned for the number of their producers. In Bristol, one of

Britain's most important Atlantic ports, Joseph Fry, a Quaker businessman, started manufacturing chocolates in 1760, building the foundation of Fry's, which became one of Britain's largest chocolate manufacturers. In Switzerland, chocolate manufactories spread in the eighteenth century, especially around Lake Geneva.[37] Cacao became an important Atlantic import, laying the groundwork for what became a nineteenth-century symbol of Swiss trading and manufacturing prowess.

Other plantation commodities—cotton, indigo, rice, coffee, tobacco—streamed into European ports as well. The effects were substantial: The plantations meant industrial workers in Europe could be fed by crops without the commitment of local land, and capital owners benefited from cheap labor without risking local social upheaval. Colonial holdings provided significant gifts to Europe's development.[38] A seemingly unlimited quantity of ecological resources from the far ends of the world arrived on Europe's shores as capital owners pushed commodity frontier after commodity frontier into the world's hinterland. European merchants had unique access to huge expanses of what has been called "ghost acres"—lands that were not part of the prior physical reality of Malthusian Europe—a consequential step that set small parts of a small continent on an increasingly exceptional trajectory. In a world in which technology-driven productivity gains were rare, the redistribution of the world's resources was crucial to development. As European wages did not increase either (the leading expert on such matters, Robert Allen, states categorically that "[i]n no case did workers realize real wages above medieval levels"), this reallocation of resources in effect benefited only a tiny number of privileged European capital owners.[39]

Because the great connecting, the transformation of the countryside, and the intensification of industry were self-reinforcing, they created a positive feedback loop on a truly global scale in which people all over the world, wittingly and unwittingly, participated. Indian artisans provided new technologies; African rulers secured labor for plantations on a distant continent, enslaved workers grew crops; central European peasants spun and wove, and Bordeaux and Surat merchants traded. The capitalist revolution was a coproduction that drew on the creativity, hard work, and accumulated wealth of much of the world, sometimes with ferocious violence.

Within that global scope of emerging capitalism, hierarchies hardened, and resources were increasingly transferred across inequalities. European merchants, as we have seen, created a remarkably connected archipelago of capital that let them play increasingly dominant roles in manufacturing networks. In terms of quality and quantity, European proto-industrialization was still more modest than its Asian counterpart. Yet European merchants' agricultural and industrial networks were uniquely global, fusing production, trade, and state power into a powerful new alloy. That amalgam allowed European capital owners and rulers to concentrate resources, capabilities, and institutions in their hands and their region for the next three centuries.

⸻

The radical transformation of the countryside in the Americas was especially crucial in the sharpening of the hierarchies that came to constitute the world economy. No one benefited more from the rapidly expanding Atlantic complex—the beating heart of war capitalism—than merchants and shippers in European port cities. The radical transformation of the countryside was, in fact, crucial to what would become the great leap forward.[40] The real innovation of this moment in capitalism's history was the creation of an institutional politico-economic framework that allowed for massive redistributions of resources across the globe.

Modern scholars have confirmed the insights that Caribbean and African American intellectuals such as Eric Williams, Walter Rodney, C. L. R. James, W. E. B. Du Bois, Aimé Césaire, and Anton de Kom offered nearly a century ago: The great connecting and the radical transformation of the countryside in the Americas shaped virtually every part of the European economy.[41] Despite the affront that the linkage between slavery, dispossession, colonialism, and Europe's economic ascension has provoked among those wedded to the ex post facto assumption that capitalism and freedom are almost synonymous, contemporaries of all ideologies saw these connections clearly.[42] In 1745, British economist Malachy Postlethwayt observed that "the first principle and foundation of all the rest, the mainspring of the machine which sets every wheel in motion," is the slave trade.[43] Bristol merchant John Cary elaborated on this in some detail in 1695:

> The African Trade . . . is a Trade of the most Advantage to this Kingdom of any we drive, and as it were all Profit, the first Cost being little more than small Matters of our own Manufactures, for which we have in Return, Gold, Teeth, Wax and Negroes, the last whereof is much better than the first, being indeed the best Traffick the Kingdom hath. . . . These are the Hands whereby our Plantations are improved, and 'tis by their Labours such great Quantities of Sugar, Tobacco, Cotton, Ginger, and Indigo are raised, which being bulky Commodities imploy great Numbers of our Ships for their transporting hither, and the greater number of Ships imploys the greater number of Handecraft Trades at home, spends more of our Product and Manufactures, and makes more Saylors, who are maintained by a separate Imploy.[44]

This appreciation for the salutary effects of the plantation economy on Europe's economic development was shared on the continent: When in 1787 German chamber assessor J. L. P. Hüpeden discussed the state of the local linen manufactures, whose products disproportionately went to the Americas, he spoke of "Hessian Peru and East India" (to suggest their deep connections) and asserted that the sale of linens constituted "the main channel through which Spanish gold and silver flows into our coffers."[45] "Without that trade," he argued, "the clockwork of the state" would come to a standstill.[46] An anonymous 1830 memorandum in the archive of the mayor of Amsterdam estimated that colonial Surinam contributed more than 2.2 million florins to the city's economy through trade in cotton, coffee, sugar, and cacao, along with their processing, shipping, and provisioning, concluding that "no working man can be found in Amsterdam . . . who does not earn a piece of bread from this colony."[47]

All European economies were deeply entangled with that slavery-driven Atlantic complex. As we have seen for merchants like Bethmann and cities like Bordeaux, French capital owners were inextricably enmeshed with the Atlantic complex, with some sectors almost entirely dependent on the slave economy. Nantes, Rouen, Le Havre, and Honfleur all rested on Atlantic trade—not just through their mercantile sectors but through their sugar, shipbuilding, iron, and textile manufacturing. Profit from French exterior trade was greater than profit from interior trade and therefore important to eighteenth-century capital accumulation. More ships docked at Saint-Domingue in 1789 than in the port of Marseille. Many a French merchant family derived its wealth from this world: The Chaurands of Nantes financed and organized eleven slave-trading voyages between 1782 and 1788, with their average return standing at a very healthy 17 percent. But slave trading specifically, though profitable, was just one small element of a larger story. French merchants, planters, financiers, and others also profited from the Americas through trade, insurance, banking, and the sale of plantation goods. The effects of the Americas percolated throughout the French economy. Even Paris, far removed from the Atlantic, was deeply shaped by it. The city's banks and stock markets took an active role in Atlantic trade. Significant amounts of colonial wealth, moreover, accumulated in that grand ville on the Seine, especially in the form of real estate. Saint-Domingue planter Jean-Baptiste Hosten transferred his sugar profits into the Parisian real estate sector. When Hosten returned to Paris in 1788, he bought multiple elite properties; within three years, he had risen to the pinnacle of Parisian society. When slavery disintegrated in Saint-Domingue, much of his slave-produced wealth was already safely harbored in Paris.[48]

The Dutch Republic, with its expanding Caribbean and Latin

American slave lands, was enriched just as much. Indeed, in 1770, the slave economy added about 5 percent to Dutch GDP and more than 10 percent to that of the province of Holland, as much as the combined contribution of all domestic agriculture and all fisheries.[49] To put this into perspective: In 2018, the automobile industry constituted about 7.7 percent of the German economy, while the "information, communications and technology" industry in the United States added 6.8 percent to the gross value of all American private industry, with the software sector coming to just 3.6 percent.[50]

The Dutch, whose population numbered fewer than two million people in 1795, forced a staggering six hundred thousand enslaved Africans across the Atlantic and profited from the goods that they produced. Additionally, by 1688, sixty-six thousand slaves were at work in Dutch Asia. And while trading in slaves produced significant gains for some, slavery's impact was much more generalized because of its importance to many key Dutch industries, including the mercantile sector, shipbuilding, food (sugar), textile production, commissions, and insurance. In 1770, 19 percent (by value) of all goods traded in Dutch ports were produced by enslaved Africans, with another 4 to 5 percent provisioning plantations and slave ships. After 1770, 40 percent of Dutch economic growth could be attributed to slavery. That year, 13.8 percent of all workers laboring in the Dutch Empire (at home and abroad) were enslaved. When the imports of slave-grown commodities rose rapidly in Dutch ports (from both Dutch and French colonies) during the eighteenth century, they energized Dutch trade into German lands; in 1790, two-thirds of Dutch traffic on the Rhine was in sugar, coffee, indigo, tobacco, and cotton—all grown by enslaved people. Expanding German consumer demand for sugar thus also fueled slavery's expansion. The Atlantic system was crucial to the Dutch economy, and slavery was crucial to that system.[51]

The impact of the slavery complex on European development becomes strikingly obvious when we look at places we would expect to be isolated from it: central and eastern Europe. From the very beginning,

merchants from German lands invested heavily in the Atlantic economy. Already in the 1420s, traders from the southern German city of
Ravensburg had moved capital into the slave-worked sugar plantations
of the Canary Islands. In 1508, the Augsburg Welsers bought one of
the largest sugar plantations in the Canaries; the next year, they purchased one on Madeira. Beginning in the 1530s, they also owned
shares in plantations on Hispaniola. Not to be left behind, the Fuggers
procured textiles for the purchase of slaves in Africa.[52] In the 1500s,
they, along with many others, already profited from the slave economies of the Americas, not least because the transformation of the
countryside provided profitable outlets for large capital stores at a time
when such profitable outlets outside state and war financing were rare.

This involvement continued for the next 350 years. German merchants invested in the Dutch West India Company (WIC) and the
Dutch East India Company (VOC): Banker Marx Conrad von Reh-
lingen owned shares worth fifty-six thousand and eleven thousand
guldens, respectively. German merchants moved to Atlantic port cities
such as Cádiz, Bordeaux, and Lisbon, where they participated in
slavery-related businesses. Some also became plantation and slave
owners. These German investors in the world's slave lands often originated from interior areas, not port cities, testifying to the draw of the
profits that the Atlantic slave economy offered. Abraham Korten, for
example, went from the Rhineland city of Elberfeld to London around
1740 and invested in the East India Company and the South Sea Company. By 1720, John and Francis Baring left Bremen for London, turning themselves into slave dealers, among other things, not least by
investing in the Company of Merchants Trading to Africa.[53] Beyond
such direct relations, trade connections into and out of the slave lands
invigorated central and eastern European agricultural production,
manufacturing, and mercantile communities.

Swiss merchants, though bereft of colonies and far from the sea, also
participated heavily in the Atlantic economy, confirming the insight that
"the entire West was a plantation society," not just the Caribbean.[54]
Swiss money streamed into the slavery complex of Nantes, with 30 per-

cent of the shares in the slave-trading Compagnie des Indes owned by Swiss nationals, who also owned shares in the South Sea Company and the Pernambuco and Paraíba Company. Swiss citizens invested in slave voyages and slave plantations; they participated in the trade and processing of slave-grown agricultural commodities. It has been estimated that Swiss merchants were involved in the shipment of almost two hundred thousand enslaved workers from Africa, a small percentage of the total, to be sure, but remarkable for a landlocked nation with a population of just 1.5 million people in 1750. Indienne producers such as the Basel-based company Christoph Burckhardt & Sohn produced for the slave trade and also directly invested in slaving voyages. The Basel merchant family Faesch was deeply involved in Atlantic trade, including in enslaved people, and one of them, Isaac Faesch, even became governor of Saint Eustache and Curaçao in the early eighteenth century. A historian-created database lists 334 Swiss individuals and institutions involved in the slave trade, a substantial share of the Swiss elite.[55]

The slavery complex of empires such as Spain and Portugal—a complex that was crucial to their sixteenth- and seventeenth-century histories—continued to power large swaths of Europe. To cite just one example: In the eighteenth century, two-thirds of slave-produced Brazilian gold ended up in Britain to pay for imports of British wares, not only fertilizing British industry but also underpinning the value of the British pound, laying the foundations for the gold standard and shoring up British financial institutions.[56]

It was in Britain, indeed, where the interactions between the great connecting, the transformation of the countryside, and proto-industrialization had the most dramatic implications. Britain stood out from all other European countries in the intensity and depth of its commitment to trade as a mainspring of wealth. The Atlantic slavery complex was at the heart of British trade, providing markets for Indian and domestically made textiles, as well as delivering crucial agricultural commodities to the British economy and creating outlets for massive amounts of capital. It has been estimated that the triangular trade, the American plantation economy, and the related industries in Britian were responsible for about 11 percent of British GDP by the late eighteenth century.[57]

All kinds of gains flowed from the slave economy into Britain: The British West Indies alone generated about 2.5 million pounds in annual profit during the 1760s and 1770s. The profits from the slavery complex amounted to between one-quarter and one-third of Britain's gross fixed investment needs—more than from any other British industry. In the slave trade, profits were far from certain, but the average returns were still higher than from investments in land or government bonds. Plantation investments were also profitable: For Barbados in the mid-eighteenth century, it has been estimated that the annual rate of return on invested capital was 11.2 percent; for Jamaica, 14.8 percent. Merchant Joseph Manesty boasted in 1747 that the ships he "fitted in London for Africa are likely to make very advantageous voyages. Negros at Jamaica at 50 to 55 pounds a head bought on the coast of Africa at from 4 to 6 pounds a head."[58] London merchants moved their capital into all aspects of this Atlantic economy: the slave trade; supplying plantations; transporting, insuring, and selling slave-grown agricultural commodities; and owning plantations directly, not least because other opportunities to invest large amounts of capital were limited.[59]

Slavery infused the British economy like no other: Just look at the Drax plantation in Barbados, which expropriated the labor of enslaved workers from the 1650s until emancipation in 1834; in 1803, more than two hundred enslaved workers labored in its fields and sugarhouse. The Drax family transferred its profits to England. In 1827, when Richard Erle-Drax-Grosvenor's daughter, Jane Frances Erle-Drax-Grosvenor, married John Samuel Wanley Sawbridge, whose family also made its fortunes in the slave economy, they "spent money prodigiously," with their luxurious home sporting a "large picture gallery and collections of art, Venetian Towers and garden ornaments, such as a huge fountain at the entrance."[60] A few years later, in 1836, the British government paid them 4,293 pounds, 12 shillings, and 6 pence—about 3 million pounds in 2024 currency—to compensate them for the emancipation of their 189 enslaved workers, while these workers themselves never received any compensation for generations of unpaid labor. Such wealth determined life chances for many generations: The plantation is still in the hands of the Drax family to this very day, with one of its descendants, Richard Drax, born in 1958, also a large landowner in southern England and a former Conservative member of Parliament, following at least six of his ancestors in representing Dorset and Gloucestershire. Slavery did more than just produce wealth in the European heartland—it brought long-lasting power. It created, in fact, many of the domestic and global inequalities that are still with us today.[61]

THE ATLANTIC ECONOMY produced enduring violence-backed wealth, but, perhaps more crucially, it allowed commodity production to break through the resistance of elites and commoners alike and thus become key to capitalism's ascendancy over more entrenched social organizations. How central slavery had become to British economic life became strikingly clear at the moment of its abolition: In 1835, the UK government borrowed on capital markets 20 million pounds sterling (about 2.1 billion pounds in 2024 currency), or 40 percent of its entire budget, to compensate slaveholders for the emancipation of their human property. The loan was so large, in fact, that the final payment on it was made in 2015, offering the remarkable spectacle of modern British taxpayers paying compensation to slaveholders for the loss of their ill-gotten human property.[62] But even these economic facts could not shake Europe's ennobling explanations for its economic ascendancy, cast as rooted in its unique love of freedom; its superior culture, institutions, and enlightenment; its knack for technological innovation. Britain, and other parts of Europe, were distinguished far more consequentially by their slave-powered empires.

The slavery-driven Atlantic economy also upset global hierarchies, enabling, among other things, bolder European interactions with Asians, for so long the masters of the world economy. A recent careful examination of what has been called the East India Company's "drain of wealth" estimates that the company's land tax captured about half of the value of Indian agricultural production, with almost all that revenue spent on the company's military and bureaucracy, and almost none of it spent on improving such things as irrigation systems, as Mughal rulers had done in earlier times. Fiscal capacity thus did not translate into development, unlike in Europe—the development of Europe, in fact, directly undermined the possibility of development elsewhere.[63]

Not only did the unique position of European capital owners and states in the world economy allow for the accumulation of riches and the concentration of wealth in the hands of capitalists (rather than, for example, tributary rulers)—it also allowed for institutional innovations, the accumulation of knowledge, and the emergence of a particularly powerful form of state. As we saw earlier, extraordinary institutional innovations originated in many parts of the world, and new scientific ideas, technologies, and ways of accumulating knowledge had emerged on several continents. In India, historians have found a dynamic culture of technical innovation and contributions to global scientific knowledge in medicine, botany, mathematics, astronomy, and chemistry. Knowledge production in India enjoyed state patronage, and the subcontinent boasted large libraries. Scholars of Chinese history have remarked on that country's vibrant culture of disseminating new knowledge and technologies. In the Ottoman Empire, knowledge production, science, and technological improvements remained significant up through the last third of the eighteenth century.[64]

Europe, too, developed a rich scientific culture during its years of economic ascendancy, often encouraged by capital owners and the state.[65] There was a flourishing of "useful knowledge" by the eighteenth century that culminated after 1750 in a moment termed the "industrial enlightenment," when knowledge was catalogued, techniques were generalized, and connections emerged between theoretical science and on-the-shop-floor engineering.[66] Many of these developments were not uniquely European, and many of the still-incremental improvements of the eighteenth century were rooted less in "pure science" and more in artisanal ingenuity. Nevertheless, amid the heady intoxication of unprecedented profits, there arose a new curiosity about the world, new access points to that world, and new ways of transmitting useful knowledge.[67]

But this inventiveness sprang not from peculiar natural or historical gifts but from the unique challenges that European capital owners faced. The most advanced regions of India, for example, did not encounter the same pressures and thus followed a different path. Unlike Britain, India had plentiful wood resources and was already the world leader in cotton textiles; transitioning to fossil fuels or developing new spinning and weaving techniques seemed much less urgent. In China, labor-saving inventions were less likely to emerge, since manual manufacturing in the countryside was exceedingly productive and profitable.[68]

By contrast, Europeans forged technical innovations and knowledge advancements often in the struggle to overcome formidable obstacles unique to the continent's particular position. The vast number of workers on slave plantations, for example, necessitated the development of new systems of labor management. Transiting immense oceans encouraged the development of new tools—from precision-engineered nautical tools to clocks to cartography. Colonial governance also demanded new techniques: When Oliver Cromwell's adviser William Petty generated the first census of people and agricultural resources from 1656 to 1658 in Britain's newest colony, Ireland, he anticipated a new form of knowledge that would soon become essential to capital owners and their partners in government bureaucracies—specifying the economic potential of this or that resource.[69]

And then there was the direct appropriation of knowledge from other societies that colonialism facilitated. The European cotton industry, as we will see later, depended upon such technology transfers. New crops from the Americas, predominantly potato and corn, both domesticated over many centuries by Indigenous Americans, became crucial to sustaining Europe's growing populations. Consider the role played by the Hortus Botanicus, Amsterdam's botanical garden, established in 1638. This was where the coffee plant was first brought to Europe from the East Indies and then disseminated to the Americas. Colonial expansion enabled that entire chain of knowledge transfer: In 1696, the VOC transported the coffee plant from Arabia to its holdings in Java. In 1706, it carried coffee beans from Java to Amsterdam. In 1714, the Dutch gave a plant to King Louis XIV; France transferred the coffee tree in 1725 to its American colonies. From there, planters brought it to Brazil. The Hortus Botanicus was thus crucial in the dissemination of the coffee plant, even though the plant's domestication rested on the centuries-long labor of rural cultivators in Yemen.[70]

As WE HAVE SEEN, the transformation of the countryside and the intensification of industry also emerged from, and generated, a crucial institutional innovation: a state uniquely positioned to further these processes and facilitate their productive interactions. Despite significant diversity, European states had elements in common, none more important than their responsiveness to the interests of the owners of capital. This was not surprising. With states engaged in ever intensifying forms of warfare that consumed vast resources, encouraging economic activity was no mere emolument but a matter of survival. These states raised their revenues to a significant degree by taxing trade and production. By the 1760s, for example, customs duties and excise taxes made up 80 percent of Britain's total state income. Regulating, encouraging, redirecting, and restricting trade were all tremendously important to European states.[71] These pressures drove rulers closer to capital owners and diminished, however slightly, the influence of aristocratic and landed elites, who for centuries had dominated political life. Long before the "bourgeois revolutions" of 1789, 1830, and 1848, European capital owners had become a significant political constituency, enabling them to forge a political economy that at least partially served their interests. This political economy allowed them to draw upon their states' expanding powers to access resources, markets, labor, and raw materials.

In fact, state power was perhaps the most crucial ingredient in the exceedingly complex project of capitalizing trade, agriculture, and industry. Because capitalism expanded from sharp discontinuities rather than from a natural propensity for trading since time immemorial, it encountered significant resistance from elites and commoners alike, and its expansion rested to a great degree on extra-economic coercion, much of it exerted by the state, including the institutional arrangement that characterized European expansion abroad: war capitalism. The origins of capitalism were thus not the result of the evolutionary expansion of markets but of what Braudel called the anti-market—monopoly, privileges, slavery, and colonialism. Capitalism was not only a process of "civilizing," as the German British sociologist Norbert Elias would have it, but also often of its opposite—barbarism.[72]

As we have seen, this war capitalism was distinctive in that it combined militarized trade, enslavement, dispossessions, colonial rule, and companies that took on statelike functions in some parts of the world with contract, wage labor, private property, and the rule of law in Europe. The latter institutions were certainly much more conducive to economic development, but, importantly, they rested on different arrangements elsewhere; indeed, these seemingly opposite worlds formed a cohesive whole, the one enabling the other. While war capitalism flourished often on an attempted social tabula rasa of a completely remade society, the lawless "outside" provided the foundation for the emergence of what would become, eventually, remarkably liberal and orderly states on war capitalism's "inside." This war capitalism, with its enforcement of different sets of institutions and rules, was perhaps the single most important institutional innovation of this era.[73]

And the war-capitalist expansion of the archipelago of capital created, for the first time, a world economy. As it revolutionized production in the countryside around the creation of commodities sold in markets, it rendered extraneous the oceans separating Barbados from England. With merchants in the vanguard, it emerged from and produced the global.[74] While the capitalist revolution was—at first—much more radical and consequential in Barbados than in England, in São Tomé than in Portugal, in Saint-Domingue than in France, these expansions were all part of capital owners' drive to seek out profitable investments. It was the very radicalism of the transformation of the Americas that helped set Europe in motion on a path unlike any other part of the world. Europe's social relations were reshaped from the outside in. The same thing happened in manufacturing, its recasting enabled by the merchant-fueled expansion of rural industry looking for opportunities beyond the much less malleable social structure of cities and towns. Capitalism, in more ways than one, was produced on what has been called its periphery—not in its presumptive centers.

As the perfect storm gathered on the eighteenth-century European horizon, those same forces increasingly uprooted the sprouts of capitalism elsewhere. The situation was most dramatic for capital-owning elites in the Americas. Diseases, colonial warfare, and plunder, as well as the radicalism of the European colonial project, essentially wiped out local merchant communities and made local producers subservient to Europeans. In Africa, local merchants benefited from the export of enslaved workers, at least in the short run, and intensified trade in coastal communities, yet the long-term impact of removing precious human capital in societies already facing labor scarcity, along with the destructive warfare that resulted, increasingly marginalized these African merchants and rulers as well.

In Asia, the story was more complicated. There, the European presence remained focused on just a few places and unfolded in cooperation with local capital owners and rulers. Prior to the nineteenth century, the Ottoman and Chinese Empires remained powerful, extensive, and well-integrated polities. But Asian state power on the continent's fringes weakened, just at the moment when the power of the fusion between European capital and state power gained tremendous force from their global expansion: The Dutch increasingly became territorial rulers in Southeast Asia, and the British extended their control inward from South Asian port cities—securing their first substantial territorial foothold in Bengal in 1765. Colonial states also erased traditional rights and protections in a solvent of European-controlled legal and market institutions, which were often pushed forward with extraordinary violence. By midcentury, for example, in British-occupied India, indigo cultivators increasingly depended on advances (loans provided by merchants to allow them to grow crops) and thus lost control of their crop. Weavers found themselves bound by new kinds of contracts, no longer able to sell goods to higher bidders.[75] Since capitalism, as we have seen, was a coproduction of capital owners and states, the process of undermining local state power across the globe was deeply consequential. It was at the root of institutional divergence.

As a result of the increasingly skewed balance of state power and the projection of war capitalism into ever more areas by a powerful alliance of European capital owners and states, parts of Europe looked, by 1750, very different from the rest of the world. Europe had unique states, capitalists, and, decisively, relationships between these states and these capitalists. It dominated global networks in the newly emerging world economy and increasingly dominated production in locations remote from its heartland. It was this combination of factors that set the stage for the world-shattering event of the Industrial Revolution.

After breaking through the shade canopy of traditional economic and social systems, capitalism spread with accelerating speed: Accessing the resources of the Americas let European merchants and states eventually weaken their African and Asian counterparts and subordinate both Europe's nobility and its producing masses at home. By the nineteenth century, the resulting differences in manufacturing capacity produced stunning new hierarchies. Hitched to rapid technical change that began in the late eighteenth century, modern manufacturing rapidly marginalized proto-industry worldwide. Soon, huge differences in wealth would characterize the world and become a signal feature of global capitalism.

The new global hierarchies were first established and most visible in the new islands of capital created by European merchants in areas remote from their homelands. One of the most consequential examples of these new islands of capital was the city of Boston, home to Robert Keayne, whom we encountered earlier. Boston emerged in 1630 as a settlement of religious refugees from England, widely known as Puritans. Hoping to build a theocratic society, the small group of settlers engaged in subsistence agriculture and some minor trade with the Massachusett and the Wampanoag peoples who inhabited the area. The location of the town was not promising, the climate harsh, the soil not particularly fertile, and the local population deeply hostile to the European arrivals. So dire was the situation that in the 1640s the grand experiment seemed close to failing, its rulers growing increasingly despondent. As Cromwell put it quite accurately in the 1650s, New England was a "poor, cold and useless place."[76]

But then something surprising happened: Settlers on the faraway island of Barbados began growing sugar for world markets, and the high profits of that undertaking rapidly created a monocultural plantation economy that came to depend on the import of everything needed to sustain its population along with its industry: enslaved workers for labor; fish, grains, and cattle for nourishment; horses for transport; whale oil for illumination; wood to fire the sugar evaporators; ice to preserve foodstuffs; and ships to transport all these things to and from the island. North America in general and New England in particular were well placed to supply many of these articles.[77] When John Banister, merchant of Newport, Rhode Island, sent ships to Barbados in 1745, they carried beef, pork, butter, and hams, but also candles, staves, and casks.[78] As merchant and planter Richard Vines remarked to John Winthrop, first governor of the Massachusetts Bay Colony, Barbadians needed to "trade for provisions for the belly," because in Barbados "men are so intent upon planting sugar that they had rather buy foode at very deare rates than produce it by labour."[79] Despite the approximately one hundred ships arriving in Barbados annually from Holland, England, New England, Virginia, and elsewhere, Richard Ligon lamented in 1647 about "there being a general scarcity of Victuals throughout the whole Island."[80] Food supplies were so tight that Barbadians' diet was at "semi-starvation" levels.[81] Planters did not even prioritize building their homes: "[T]hough the Planters talk of building houses, and wish them up, yet when they weigh the want of those hands in their sugar work, that must be employed in their building, they fall back, and put on their considering caps."[82] Then, in 1651, the Crown proclaimed the Navigation Acts, which stipulated that all the things Barbados needed had to be acquired from within the empire. It was at this intersection of favorable political winds and new opportunities that Boston merchants seized their chance to turn their city and the wider New England region into the Caribbean's most important supplier. Boston began its rise on the back of the sugar complex, which meant on the back of slavery.

The emerging class of Boston merchants saw these new opportunities clearly and built a multitude of links to the center of the new British Empire—the Caribbean. They began supplying these islands with the things they needed most urgently: enslaved workers, dried (cod) fish, cattle, wood, ice, horses, corn, whale oil, and pork. Already by 1680, half the ships in Boston Harbor traded with the West Indies, while half of all arrivals in the West Indies were from New England. That newly emerging commerce was embedded within family connections, with many Boston merchants' sons making their fortunes in the West Indies.[83] Boston merchant Samuel Maverick's son Nathaniel, for example, settled on Barbados, while Henry Winthrop, son of John Winthrop, had been planting tobacco on Barbados for three years before his father became governor-general of the Massachusetts Bay Colony in 1630. Samuel, his brother, also went to the West Indies, reporting back to Boston: "The certainest commodityes you can carry for those parts . . . will be fish, . . . drye fish, beefe porke, . . . linen cloath."[84] Trade with the West Indies rescued the economy of the fledgling Boston settlement, with John Winthrop seeing it in 1648 as a form of divine intervention: "[I]t pleased the Lorde to open to [u]s a Trade with Barbados and other Ilandes in the w[est] Indyes."[85] Salem merchant Gedney Clarke migrated to Barbados in 1733 to trade, speculate in enslaved people, and buy plantation lands.[86] As the English captain Thomas Bredon observed in 1660, New England was "the key of the Indies without w[h]ich Jamaica, Barbados & the Caribee Islands are not able to subsist."[87] New England merchants also supplied, when they could, the French islands: In 1784, for example, local planters on Saint-Domingue requested permission to import salted fish, salted meat, rice, and grains—"objects of premier necessity for the conservation of the Negros"—from British North America to add to the insufficient supplies coming from the French provinces.[88]

This trade, in turn, allowed for the intensification of industry in New England. Thanks to the Caribbean connection, markets for manufactured goods were much larger than they would have been if producers were only supplying the small North American market. In exchange for the supplies sent south, New Englanders received sugar and molasses, turning much of that into rum and building a significant distilling industry. Newport sported twenty-two stillhouses. In 1750, Massachusetts alone consumed more than fifteen thousand hogsheads of molasses to distill rum. Last but not least, sugar helped the development of North American colonies by providing them with a needed leg in the triangular trade system that allowed them access to British manufactured goods.[89]

Such deep involvement in the West Indies trade, and in the processing of West Indian sugar, made it perhaps inevitable that New England merchants would enter a particularly profitable branch of commerce: the trade in human beings. Massachusetts traders developed significant trade routes to the west coast of Africa, though they were outdone by Rhode Island families such as the Browns (the funders and namesake of the university), who made a fortune buying and selling enslaved Africans to power the Caribbean plantation machine.[90]

Unsurprisingly, this participation in the slavery complex brought slavery to New England itself, with the first shipment of enslaved Africans arriving in 1638. Though the number of enslaved workers in

New England remained small compared with the Caribbean, the fifteen hundred enslaved Africans and the additional fifteen hundred Native American slaves laboring in New England had a notable, if relatively small, presence among the roughly ninety thousand people of English origins living in these colonies by 1700.[91]

Enslaved workers' sparse share of the local population should not distract from New England's utter dependence on trade with the slave-based centers of the Caribbean. Boston merchants benefited from the trade in enslaved workers through sugar processing and investing in manufacturing for the Caribbean. Some even invested in West Indian plantations directly. Moreover, institutions that became important to later economic and regional development drew on fortunes made from the violent transformation of the Caribbean countryside. Harvard College, founded in 1636, benefited from the gifts of wealthy Boston merchants: Isaac Royall Jr.'s donation, which created the first professorship in law, came from money made by his father's sugar plantation in Antigua. Israel Thorndike, another Harvard benefactor, made his fortunes in the West Indies trade, including the slave trade, and the Perkinses, yet another family connected to the college, traded slaves and slave-grown agricultural commodities in Saint-Domingue before turning their investments to the China trade and, much later, American railroads and manufacturing.[92] New England styled itself as the "cradle of freedom," but it owed its position just as much to enslavement.[93] The efficient institutions so lauded by latter economists as explanative of the superior economic performance of New England and other such places in the North Atlantic region were built upon the most violent exploitation of human labor and souls elsewhere. And so was Boston's original stock of wealth.

As the great connecting, the transformation of the countryside, the intensification of industry, and the newly emerging capacities of the state fed back on one another, they generated upheavals and new hierarchies. The place where the turbulence produced the most consequential disruptions was, perhaps surprisingly, one of the world's oldest industries: the spinning of yarn and the weaving of cottons. The industry went back at least five millennia and, aside from agriculture, had been the most labor-intensive and valuable of all industries for at least eight centuries. People on all continents crafted cotton fabrics, with the center of production, especially for export markets, located in South Asia.[94]

For a long time, Europe was marginal to that industry, not least because the cotton plant was alien to much of the continent. Yet textile production had slowly expanded there in previous centuries: Cotton spinning and weaving had taken hold in the twelfth century in Italian cities and, a few decades later, in southern German ones; these activities soon spread to France, the Dutch Republic, Britain, and elsewhere. By 1700, tens of thousands of women, children, and men spun and wove cotton all across the European countryside, most of them in remote peasant homes resembling those that housed the linen workers of Jelenia Góra. They received raw cotton from itinerant merchants, spun and wove it, then delivered it back to those merchants for a small profit. The traders then had the fabrics printed and dyed before distributing them to consumers near and far. Areas in Europe, including northern England and the Black Forest, came to specialize in this kind of proto-industrial production. In Catalonia, the woolen proto-industry, which we encountered earlier, increasingly turned to processing cottons, unexpectedly sparking the Catalan Industrial Revolution. By the 1770s, one in ten inhabitants of the German Wupper Valley worked in textiles, mostly operating out of their homes.[95] A Rhenish author reflected on the boom:

> If the Duchy were to have in its midst an old man of 125 years, who in his youth had been intimately acquainted with the area and who now still remembers it, he indeed would be the embodiment of the history of almost all local industry, population and progress. . . . Such an old man would know . . . that about 100 years ago the children of Elberfeld still twisted rope in front of the house

doors and that sixty years ago Barmen seemed quite different from what it is now; there were cow pastures where presently yarn is being bleached.[96]

By the eighteenth century, cotton was a significant European manufacturing activity, but considered globally, the quality and quantity of European cottons was still rather marginal.

Yet this homespun industry eventually brought together the four large processes we have discussed—the great connecting, the transformation of the countryside, the intensification of manufacturing, and the formation and involvement of increasingly powerful states. Cotton manufacturing became the eye of the storm of industrialization—it was at the center of the great leap forward. ·

This taproot at first fed only a very small part of the world and a very small part of economic life. And while this might seem surprising, it should not, because, bluntly put, this root was unlikely to emerge among the ancient and stronger competitors. In a way, what needs explaining is not the absence of this revolution where it did not occur but how this new form of economic life arose at all, and why it would lead to such productive upheavals in such a small part of the world. Like any upstart organism, the fledgling social system drew strength from multiple developments that unfolded separately, and while they all mattered, no one element alone was sufficient to explain its unlikely and revolutionary novelty.

Global trade was the first change to affect the cotton industry. Simply put: Many more people started consuming cottons after 1500, and more cotton was traded all around the world. The great connecting radically altered the structure of the world's cotton markets: Indian textiles found their way to Europe in ever increasing quantities as the various East India Companies flocked to that lucrative trade. Europeans developed a taste for these fabrics, and European traders found new customers for cotton due to the slave trade, whose local suppliers in Africa became an important market for South Asian cottons. The expansion of commercialized agriculture in the Americas further ex-

The perfect storm's quaint beginnings: domestic cotton spinning and weaving in eighteenth-century England.

panded markets for cottons, making export markets ever more important for European cotton manufacturers.[97] Europeans increasingly came to dominate this global cotton trade, even while production remained largely concentrated in South Asia.

Transfixed by rapidly expanding markets for cottons in Europe—for both domestic consumption and export—European producers moved to capture some or even most of the market. They worked to understand how South Asians manufactured their textiles, traveling to India to observe firsthand how they were made and generating books, circulars, and oral reports for budding manufacturers. French cotton manufacturers in particular devoted great effort to copying Indian techniques by closely observing Indian ways of manufacturing. In 1678, Georges Roques, who worked for the French East India Company, wrote what quickly became an invaluable report on Indian wood-block printing techniques, based on his observations in Ahmedabad. Forty years later, in 1718, Père Turpin followed suit, and in 1731, Georges de Beaulieu, the second lieutenant on a French East India Company ship, reached Pondicherry to investigate how Indian artisans produced chintz. By 1743, French manufacturers could copy all but the very finest Indian textiles. Competing with Indian producers—and observing them—sparked tremendous waves of innovation.[98]

The great connecting was a fertile general environment for the growth of the textile industry. But it was not enough: To produce more cotton, Europeans needed access to raw cotton, since the fiber did not grow on the European continent. Fortunately, new opportunities for accessing agricultural resources had emerged, allowing European merchants to get into the raw cotton trade with West Africa, India, and the western shores of Anatolia.

In the eighteenth century, when the limits of distant peasant production stunted the elasticity of supply, cotton growing moved to the Caribbean and Brazil. Planters there had learned from the transformation of sugar agriculture that expropriated land and stolen labor could unleash an agricultural revolution like no other. Already in January 1698, a letter from Versailles had arrived at the Chamber of Agriculture of Cap Français, in Saint-Domingue, suggesting that planters "should also increase their production of cotton, so that more of it can be sold within the Kingdom and to a higher price than the cotton from the Levant."[99] Planters across the American slave lands did exactly that. In almost no time, Saint-Domingue became a major producer of cotton—indeed, the single most important source of cotton for European industry. Such production had another advantage: It insulated the industry from a steep rise in agricultural prices because it did not press against limited land and labor resources in Europe itself.[100]

The rapidly expanding European cotton industry also drew on state policies in its expansion. Industrial policies encouraged manufacturing. We have already encountered British prohibitions against South Asian cottons. Such steps were taken elsewhere as well: In 1676, Dutch linen merchants petitioned the VOC to stop the import of Asian cottons. In 1686, to protect domestic producers of woolens, linens, and silks in France, King Louis XIV banned not only the import of Indian textiles but also the domestic copying of such textiles, whose designs and qualities appeared dangerously popular. The decree remained on the books for seventy-three years. No fewer than two further royal edicts and eighty rulings of the king's council attempted to repress imported cottons, with penalties ranging from imprisonment to death. When the ban was repealed in 1759, it was replaced by a 25 percent tariff on printed fabrics imported into France. Catalonia (in

1717 and 1728) and Prussia (in 1721) followed suit with similar bans. As European states became increasingly concerned with industrial production and favored policies that enabled its expansion, they embraced protectionism.[101]

Supported by the state, and able to access ever larger quantities of raw cotton, European entrepreneurs next looked for ways to compete against the higher quality and cheaper textiles of the market leader— South Asia. Their experiments in developing better ways to spin and weave failed as often as they succeeded but eventually led to breakthroughs. James Hargreaves invented the spinning jenny in 1764, and Richard Arkwright followed up in 1768 with the water frame, a much-improved version of the jenny. From shaded sprouts, the growth of a new kind of capitalism—industrial capitalism—had broken through the canopy and yielded a tectonic and exceedingly unlikely departure in human history.

At midcentury, however, the revolutionary implications of that brewing storm were still on the horizon and hard for contemporaries to detect. To be sure, in some parts of Europe, economic growth had accelerated. Yet technical breakthroughs were few and far between—and productivity remained largely unchanged. Most Europeans—like everyone else on Earth—still dwelled in the countryside and worked on the land. While capital owners inhabited an ever more densely connected archipelago of capital with many new opportunities for profit, these places remained islands within a sea of different societies. Wherever growth happened, it remained slow, including in England.[102] This was not yet an industrial economy nor an economy of rapid technological change. The territorial spread and social intensification of capitalism—the emergence of a capitalist civilization tied to state power in new ways—emerged only later.

The capitalist revolution unfolded ploddingly, not least because it encountered opposition from both elites and commoners. But its peculiar double character—intensely private and intensely public at the same time—allowed it to break through in many places at once, thanks to its thinly spread but nonetheless global root system. All the nodes within its archipelago fed back on one another and strengthened a drawn-out but powerful trunk that might eventually support a more general shift in economic life. In some parts of Europe, economic growth accelerated; not coincidentally, it was at this moment that Bethmann's slave profits found their way to Germany's first modern factory. As capital ignited more dynamic economic development, its logic, which had been just one among many, began to dominate some parts of the world.

Adam Smith observed this moment more perceptively than almost anyone else. His analysis stripped that world of what he perceived to be its contaminants—power, violence, the state, among other seemingly superfluous nutrients—and focused on a nearly divine spark of utility-maximizing individuals spontaneously creating a more productive society by focusing on their self-interests. He loudly dismissed all the historical essence of capitalism's root, trunk, and leaves as blemishes, consigning slavery, state-sponsored monopolies, and colonizing empires to the margins while forcefully condemning them. Smith thus sealed his place as the hero of capitalism's triumphant self-remembrance.

Part II

The Great Leap

*Revolutionaries at home: portrait of the German merchant
family Jacobs by August Dankworth, 1852.*

THE RISE OF INDUSTRIAL CAPITALISM, 1760–1850

Women make an industrial revolution.

For centuries, the capitalist revolution was a meandering river moving across a vast landscape. Nodes of capital multiplied and gained strength, connected in novel ways, and spread the logic of accumulation and commodification in both space and in society, in agriculture and manufacturing.

Between 1760 and 1850, the great connecting, the transformation of the countryside, the intensification of manufacturing, and the construction of new kinds of states together catalyzed a perfect storm. Suddenly that meandering river became a torrent. What latter-day scholars call the Industrial Revolution was the single most consequential offspring of capitalism, its reimagining of manufacturing of such planetary import that it qualifies, in retrospect, as a great turning point in human history. Simply put, there was a world before the Industrial Revolution and an entirely different one after it. The acceleration of change it sparked was not just rapid but self-sustaining. And it continues to this day.

Its humble genesis lay in an initially modest intensification of manufacturing along the rivers and dales of the English and Scottish countrysides. At first there were a few dozen, then hundreds, then eventually thousands of modestly sized stone buildings in which women, children, and men used water-powered machinery to spin cotton yarn—one of the world's oldest and most important industries. For all its world-altering effects, the Industrial Revolution's "rapid advancement in the art of spinning and weaving," as one nineteenth-century expert put it, was, before 1830, inconspicuous and confined to a few localities.[1] One of its contemporaries, Adam Smith, hardly noticed it, and even as eagle-eyed a historian as Fernand Braudel believed it was "barely noticeable at the beginning."[2]

As in all revolutions, a few individuals discerned and harnessed the energies of long-lasting and far-reaching origins—taking advantage of the opportunities created by previous capitalists and state officials—and began to reimagine ingrained ways of doing things. The Scottish city of Glasgow and the west of Scotland more broadly were home to an unusually early and dense concentration of such individuals and favorable circumstances. Up until the eighteenth century, Glasgow had been a small and unremarkable town of twelve thousand inhabitants, its cathedral and university its principal claims to fame. Its fortunes improved somewhat in 1707, when Scotland and England joined to form the Kingdom of Great Britain, which brought its linen and woolen producers unfettered access to the English market and colonial trade. With Caribbean commerce dominated by English merchants and Asian commerce dominated by the East India Company, Scots of moderate wealth looked elsewhere to invest their capital and found opportunities in the recently colonized parts of North America—the Chesapeake colonies of Virginia and Maryland in particular.

The heady but unlikely profits from those colonial ventures made Glasgow not the greatest, but still a significant node in the empire of capital by midcentury.[3] Newly minted Scottish tobacco lords built Palladian-style villas and faux-medieval country seats. But when Americans declared independence from the United Kingdom in 1776, they claimed the tobacco trade, and the Glasgow business model evaporated. Seeking new outlets, some capital-rich Glaswegians moved into the Caribbean sugar trade (sugar imports increased by 400 percent between 1783 and 1800), while a few turned their gazes homeward to an experimental form of local industry: cotton manufacturing. Glasgow tobacco merchant and Jamaica plantation owner Robert Dunmore, for example, invested in building a cotton mill at Balfron in 1780 before partnering with the Buchanans, another rich merchant family, in launching the Ballindalloch Cotton Works in 1789.[4]

Like Dunmore and the Buchanans, dozens of enterprising Scots entered the industry in the last two decades of the eighteenth century. Landowning merchant John Clerk opened the first water-powered mills in 1778 in Penicuik, near the eastern coast of Scotland, just seven years after such mills began operating in England. Kirkman Finlay, who eventually became the leader of the "cotton magnates," invested in

Making an industrial revolution: Ballindalloch Cotton Works, undated.

his first cotton mill at Ballindalloch in 1798, adding a second mill in Catrine in 1801 and a third in Deanston in 1806. In 1802, James Coats started manufacturing canton crepe, modeled after Chinese shawls, in Paisley, the same town where James Clark began mass-producing sewing thread. As these enterprisers rushed for a share of outsize profits, tantalizingly within reach, the Scottish cotton industry expanded at breakneck speed. By 1791, fifty-five Scottish cotton mills employed twenty-five thousand workers, with more than half a million pounds invested in buildings and machinery. While the first generation of mills were located in the countryside and water-powered, by the turn of the century they were increasingly located near Glasgow and used a flexible, mobile, and continual source to power their machinery—the steam engine, lately much improved by another Scot, James Watt, whose experiments had been funded by his sugar-trading family.[5]

The industry's growth was as unprecedented as its margins: The New Lanark Mill, for example, established in 1785 by David Dale and managed by his son-in-law Robert Owen, returned 15 percent annually on its paid-in capital between 1799 and 1810. In the boom years, from 1811 to 1814, payments rose to 46 precent annually, then returned to 15 percent between 1814 and 1825. Between 1799 and 1828, the mill produced total profits of almost four hundred thousand pounds, roughly $50 million in 2024 US dollars. Finlay accumulated wealth just as rapidly, with his firms' balances increasing almost fourteen times between 1789 and 1800.[6] When Richard Arkwright, the inventor of cotton spinning by water frames, visited Glasgow in October 1784, the city's economic elite gave him a "triumphant" reception.[7] For them, cotton manufacturing was the goose that laid golden eggs. Lots of them.

This early flourishing of the industry was possible because budding Scottish industrialists enjoyed extraordinary access to technology, power, cotton, capital, markets, workers, and a supportive state. By the 1770s, access to technology was the least of their hurdles. The machines invented by British artisans just a few years prior—the spinning jenny, the water frame, and eventually the spinning mule—easily traveled north to Glasgow, along with the highly skilled workers needed to install them. At the Ballindalloch Cotton Works, one of Dunmore's partners, Archibald Buchanan, "had been taught the practical parts of cotton-spinning at Cromford in Derby, under the well-known [inventor] Arkwright."[8] Power was also widely available. Scotland was full of streams that could drive waterwheels, and landlords were eager to lease some of their water rights for the construction of cotton mills or to invest in these mills themselves. The state was supportive as well: Trade flourished thanks to the protections offered by the Royal Navy and the interventions of the Navigation Acts, which directed all colonial trade to focus on Britain. Bounties encouraged the production of cheap cloth, and the Scottish Board of Trustees for Manufactures offered technical aid to the cotton industry. Manufacturers understood their dependence on the state quite well. In 1788, for example, they demanded higher import duties on Indian products to better be able to compete with them. In 1803, by contrast, they demanded a reduction in tariffs on imported raw cotton. Thanks to their deep trade connections with the Caribbean and the United States, rising Glasgow industrialists also had no problem accessing raw cotton, even though it had to be imported from distant locations. They began shipping Caribbean cotton as early as the 1750s, and by century's end supplemented that cotton with shipments from the United States. The trade's growth was extraordinary: Cotton imports from all sources skyrocketed by a factor of thirty-two between 1783 and 1801—as good an indicator as any of the explosive growth of the industry.[9]

It was a motley lot of Scots who took advantage of these opportunities. While the capital needed to start a cotton mill in the earliest phase of industrialization was modest, it was still far beyond common reach, which is why most cotton industrialists had previously been engaged in other businesses. Some were major merchants, others marginal operators. An analysis of the wills of fifty-two cotton manufacturers who died between 1787 and 1912 found that the owners of Scottish cotton mills generally came from mercantile and manufacturing families, just like their English counterparts.[10] Of the twenty-eight whose parents' occupations are known, 28 percent of their fathers were "merchants," 25 percent "manufacturers," and 18 percent "farmers."[11] Some of these early industrialists also drew capital from the intensification of manufacturing that had taken place in the eighteenth century, when merchants had organized vast networks of home-based spinners and weavers. Clark, for example, had started out as a weaver and small manufacturer before investing in cotton manufacturing. Dale, the founder of New Lanark's mill, had been a linen merchant, like Finlay had been.[12]

Other cotton manufacturers had accumulated entrepreneurial talent and capital in foreign trade. Of the 163 Glasgow merchants involved in the trade with America between 1740 and 1790, more than half, 85, eventually invested in textile manufacturing, ironworking, mining, glassmaking, and brewing. The most important Caribbean trading house, Alexander Houston & Co., invested about twenty thousand pounds in the cotton industry. The merchant houses of Leitch and Smith and Stirling, Gordon & Co. invested in Finlay's cotton mills. In 1795, of the cotton mills insured (not all were), 17 percent of their total investments had come from tobacco merchants, while among the seventy-six Glaswegian merchants trading to the Caribbean in 1800, twenty-one were partners in cotton-manufacturing enterprises. Capital accrued during the slave-powered transformation of the American countryside flowed into cotton manufacturing.[13]

The great connecting did not just produce some of the capital that kick-started the industry; it also provided access to markets. The local market alone was insufficient (the Scottish population consisted of just 1.6 million people in 1801) to make the kinds of risky industrial ventures that spread around the Scottish countryside worthwhile. Export markets were crucial. And those markets expanded rapidly, not least because of Scottish merchants' long history of selling linens abroad. Exports of cotton goods grew by a stunning 900 percent between 1785 and 1835; in 1825, 86 percent of the industry's workers labored for export. The slave economies of the Americas were a particularly promising market, in no small part because there were more African slaves toiling in those lands than there were people living in Scotland.

Cotton cloth exports to the Americas swelled by a factor of ten in the last decade of the eighteenth century. Enslaved people harvested the cotton, and then, after it was processed in faraway Scotland, it came back to them as cloth. By 1813, a full 65 percent of Scottish exports (by value) went to the Caribbean.[14]

Yet capital owners' greatest constraint in embarking upon the Industrial Revolution was labor. As we have seen, there had been two principal ways of securing labor for the infusion of capital into production: enslavement and the massive expansion of proto-industrialization through outwork in which capital owners developed contractual relations with independent producers. Neither strategy, however, served the interests of cotton manufacturers. The core of manufacturing was investment in machinery that could be operated neither in households nor by single families, making the outwork system unworkable.

Scottish cotton manufacturers thus enticed workers into factories by paying them wages. This, too, was difficult, as a mill manager from Blantyre explained: "[F]ew Scotch families could be prevailed upon to go into a cotton mill, they looked on it as a sort of degradation."[15] Drastic changes in the Scottish countryside came to their aid: In the Lowlands, new enclosures driven by a desire to increase the land's profitability pushed people out of rural villages and into expanding industrial towns, while the so-called Highland Clearances moved rural cultivators, often violently and always forcefully, out of the countryside to make space for sheep runs.[16] Together, they created an industrial proletariat, especially because manufacturers focused on the mobilization of two groups most vulnerable to a move into the factory: women and children.

In this hothouse of favorable factors, the Scottish cotton industry exploded. In 1833, Scotland had 134 cotton mills with about 1.7 million spindles, and cotton manufacturing dominated the Scottish economy. By 1844, Finlay alone employed a stunning twenty-five hundred workers at his mills. Glasgow had metamorphosed from a small port to an urban agglomeration dedicated to manufacturing; its one hundred thousand inhabitants in 1811 and its three hundred thousand in the mid-1840s made it Britain's fourth-largest city. Massive waves of construction and real estate speculation followed, showcasing a novel kind of inequality. On the one hand, elegant neighborhoods of large stone mansions housing the city's new economic elite expanded. On the other, as *The Artizan* reported from the working-class districts in October 1843, so did "an endless labyrinth of narrow lanes" with "ill-ventilated towering houses crumbling to decay, destitute of water and crowded with inhabitants."[17] In the late 1830s, an inquiry into the living conditions of weavers in Glasgow described "human degradation," with the reporter questioning if "so large an amount of filth, crime, misery, and disease existed on one spot in any civilized country."[18] Typhus and cholera epidemics spread.[19] Factory worker turned poet Alexander Smith remembered the bleak scene in one of his 1857 poems:

> We crept into a half-forgotten street
> Of frail and tumbling houses propt by beams. . . .
> With drunken strife, hoarse curses; then the cry
> Of a lost woman by a ruffian felled Made the blood stop.[20]

As this brief look at Scottish cotton industrialization shows, something radically new emerged: Capital owners on a few of the islands of intensified manufacturing that had grown in previous centuries began to locate production in factories, employing wageworkers to operate sophisticated machinery, first powered by water, later by steam. In these places, industrialists gained an entirely novel degree of control over manufacturing, one akin to what they had realized earlier on plantations. The capitalist revolution shifted its cutting edge from commerce and agriculture to industry, thus sparking the Industrial Revolution.

Capitalism, as we have seen, had been a "vast but weak" system.[21] In the late eighteenth century, older forms of manufacturing continued and even intensified, with home-based proto-industrialization

Steam power: The Industrial Revolution transforms Glasgow, 1831.

spreading in the United Kingdom and India, China, and Prussia. In scattered places, however, this proto-industrialization became full-blown industrialization by harnessing the revolutionary energy of capital to the endless possibilities of technology. Industrial capital gained tremendous strength in the process, its distinct interests shifting economic power throughout the world. At the global level, much sharper geographic hierarchies soon emerged in what historians have called the Great Divergence: the moment at which a small part of humanity concentrated in Europe became much wealthier than anyone else.[22]

No single factor can explain the origins of the Industrial Revolution, frustrating the search for one decisive cause—institutions, the climate, labor costs, the shape of Britain's coastlines, its access to colonies, its artisans' inventive spirit.[23] While all these factors mattered, they mattered more in context than on their own.[24]

Rapid, ongoing technical progress in manufacturing was uncontroversially essential to ushering in the Industrial Revolution, which was not the "cause" of capitalism but its consequence. No prior form of organizing economic activity had ever birthed comparable ongoing innovations along with such productivity gains and economic growth.

As we have seen, the capitalist revolution in the three centuries after Columbus's arrival in the Americas brought about only modest economic growth and ordinary technical innovations. But once these changes intersected with one another, they enabled a leap forward into a world fundamentally different from anything that had existed before. And humble cotton was at its forefront as Europeans caught up to more advanced manufacturers in India and China and then moved decisively beyond any existing industry.[25] Just as an archipelago of European cities had become the dominant node of commercial capital in prior centuries, now they became the dominant node of manufacturing too.

The Industrial Revolution was a world event even though it played out in a very local register. It emerged from a globe-spanning network of processes that let a particular set of localized nodes break through to something fundamentally new. And this process confirms once again that capitalism cannot be understood in local, regional, or national terms; it can be understood only by focusing on the permanent combination and recombination of its fragments across the world. Dutch capital, for example, played a crucial role in the Industrial Revolution, even though the Netherlands industrialized comparatively late.[26] Industrial capitalism was a radical departure from the war capitalism of previous centuries but utterly dependent on it for its origins.

It has often been observed that the microprocessor revolution of the late twentieth century started in garages and college dormitories, with Steve Jobs assembling computers, Bill Gates programming operating systems, and Harvard undergrad Mark Zuckerberg dabbling in frivolous social networking software. While this picture is radically incomplete, it can help us understand the Industrial Revolution. Its beginnings are analogous to garage-bound innovations, with tinkerers like James Hargreaves, Richard Arkwright, and Samuel Crompton, allowing for skyrocketing productivity. With little formal education, these skilled craftsmen addressed problems confronted on the job to find new ways of spinning cotton. In 1764, weaver Hargreaves invented his spinning jenny, which was initially used in households and enabled one spinner to operate at first eight and then sixteen spindles simultaneously.[27] In 1771, inventor Arkwright opened the first cotton-spinning mill in Cromford, where his new water frame, powered by waterwheels, radically accelerated the age-old work of making thread from cotton fibers. And in 1779, Samuel Crompton developed the first prototype of the spinning mule, the machine that would come to enable massive cotton industrialization.

This quotidian industry (the spinning and weaving of cotton) with its commonplace products (yarn and cloth) seemed an unlikely spark to light the Industrial Revolution. Localized at first in a tiny part of the United Kingdom, it spread rapidly; in 1860, British cotton expert James A. Mann remarked on the "suddenness of the impulse"—with the share of value it added to the British economy shooting from 2.6 percent in 1770 to 22.4 percent in 1831.[28] In 1788, there had been a modest fifty thousand spindles in British cotton factories; by 1821, there were seven million—140 times as many. (By 1850, Britain counted almost twenty-one million spindles.) As early as 1795, 340,000 people worked in about nine hundred British cotton mills. The industry flourished in a hothouse atmosphere marked by elastic markets, a supportive state, an abundance of available capital, and constant technical innovation. Even people with modest capital were attracted to this industry, as many of the mills were small undertakings: In 1812, two out of three mills operated fewer than ten thousand spindles.[29]

Sustaining a radical reinvention of production only made sense if the growing quantity of goods coming out of newly productive factories was met by demand. Machines, buildings, and wages needed to be paid for on a regular basis (unlike in the proto-industrial sector, where workers were fungible and much of the capital investment was carried by workers, not merchants), which meant that goods had to be sold predictably and at accelerating velocities. The domestic market was an important source of demand, not least because commercialization of

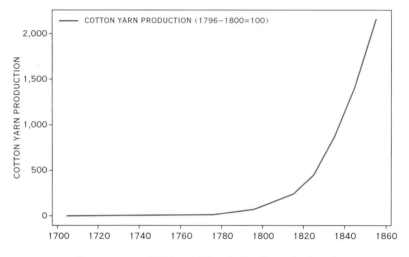

A cotton-powered Industrial Revolution: the production of cotton yarn in the United Kingdom, 1705–1855.

the British economy meant that people increasingly depended on markets for food and manufactured wares. But for continued investments in new machinery to make sense, export markets had to expand just as much. Fortunately for would-be entrepreneurs, these export markets were extremely dynamic. Trade, economists have shown, propelled industrialization just as much as all that new machinery.[30]

Driven by dynamic markets, mechanical innovations, and a tsunami of slave-grown raw cotton imports (mostly from the United States—by the early 1820s, 68 percent of cotton came from there, climbing to between 70 and 80 percent by the end of the 1850s), the industry came to define Britain's position in the world. Exports increased more than sixfold between 1780 and 1815 and made up more than 40 percent of the value of Britain's total exports. As a contemporary remarked, "[W]ithout machinery we could not carry on a foreign trade."[31] At its heart, the industry's expansion was an example of import-substitution industrialization—for the first time, British manufacturers succeeded in undercutting their Indian competitors—at first on price and eventually on quality.[32] As productivity in cottons increased, prices fell, with the cost of yarn declining by about 80 percent between 1779 and 1812. It has been estimated that already by 1787, British-made muslins were between 25 and 33 percent cheaper than their Indian counterparts.[33] Unsurprisingly, when Mann looked back at the early history of the British industry from the vantage point of 1860, he marveled that "those wonderful inventions" gave "the power of almost unlimited production to our people" and "revolutionized that manufacturing world."[34]

THIS STUNNING EXPANSION of the British cotton industry generated notable economic growth and rearranged the hierarchies in one of the world's largest and oldest manufactural undertakings. Yet it was not the first time that economic growth accelerated, new technologies arose, or economic pecking orders shifted, and it is easily imaginable that—except for changes in cotton manufacturing—economic life could have gone on much as before, that, in fact, the revolution could have petered out. Indeed, from the perspective of the early nineteenth century, a large swath of British economic life continued as it had been.

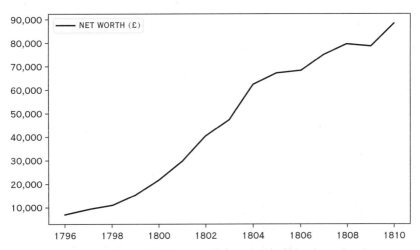

Profits in "white gold": the net worth (in pounds) of Manchester-based cotton manufacturers James McConnel and John Kennedy, 1796–1810.

It was so stable that some scholars have argued that there was no Industrial Revolution at all, that there was, in fact, more continuity than change.[35]

At first glance, such an assessment seems plausible. The British cotton industry's growth slowed almost as fast as it took off: As cotton mills multiplied in Britain and then elsewhere, competition sharpened. Profits declined. As A. E. Speirs of Finlay's cotton mills complained in 1834: "[A]t the present time, cotton spinning is not a beneficial mode of employing capital."[36] Some mills even went bankrupt. By the mid-1830s, Finlay's letter books filled up with complaints about competition: "We know that no one can make the Goods cheaper than we can do, but there are too many competitors to allow the Best to do more than save themselves from loss."[37] Perhaps, he speculated, India would reinvigorate the industry, its consumption of cotton goods increasing thanks to its new opium trade with China. Despite such hopes, he tried to divest from his three cotton mills, selling the one in Ballindalloch in 1844.[38]

But this was not the end of British industrialization. Instead, the recasting of manufacturing migrated, most prominently to the iron, coal, railroad, and machinery industries.[39] Capital that had accumulated in cotton manufacturing found new and profitable outlets, some of which emerged from the broader impact of the cotton industry. After all, cotton had created a market for spinning jennies, water frames, and looms: As everyone went what Watt's business partner and steam engine producer Matthew Boulton called "Steam Mill Mad," cotton mills became the major market for this new machine.[40]

Capital owners moved some of their assets into these new industries. Again, Finlay can serve as an example. In 1835, just when he was ranting about the manifold problems of cottons, he reported that "the making of bar iron is at present a most profitable trade in this part of the Kingdom and new works for the manufacture are erecting to an incredible extent."[41] Predicting that "immense profits" could be made in iron, he radically diversified his portfolio:[42] He also began trading with India in 1816, investing in railroads, banks, government obligations, insurance companies, and canals.[43] Perhaps surprisingly, he also diversified into agriculture, acquiring an estate, Castle Toward, which he considered—revealingly—"our plantations."[44]

For Finlay, as for British capital owners more generally, the cotton industry was but a stepping stone, albeit an important one, to a fundamentally different world characterized by a new kind of capitalism—industrial capitalism. Instead of being just a moment of acceleration, after which things reverted to their prior state, the cotton industry's rapid growth heralded further growth, productivity gains, proletarianization, and capital accumulation. Britain and a handful of other countries launched themselves onto a path of sustained expansion that is with us to this day. By spreading across dozens of industries, the Industrial Revolution became permanent.

The next phase of this revolution focused on producer goods: things sold not to consumers but to other manufacturers who needed them to fabricate something else. Coal was one of them. As it began to power machinery and heat homes, demand skyrocketed—launching the fossil fuel economy that has persisted into the present.[45]

While coal mining had a very long history, it remained largely inconsequential until the mid-eighteenth century. People were reluctant to substitute coal for wood; they did not appreciate the smoke or the smell of coal fires, and transporting coal was expensive. As a result, early coal mines were small endeavors and can best be pictured as peasants digging out coal that rose to the surface. With the rise of intensive coal-consuming industries such as lime preparation, glassmaking, and coke-fired ironworks, the demand for "black gold" increased. British coal output almost doubled in the first half of the eighteenth century, nearly tripled in its second half, and then multiplied by a factor of four in the first half of the nineteenth century, when 80 to 90 percent of British energy use was coal-based. Growing cities, especially London, which thrived through Britain's privileged trade position in the world, demanded coal, in part because traditional sources of fuel, especially wood, were running up against ecological limits. So massive were mining investments in northeast England, Scotland, the Midlands, and Wales that the intensity of Britain's coal production was unrivaled: By

1831, its coal output equaled 31.5 million tons, almost five times as much as its nearest competitors—the United States, France, Germany, and Belgium—combined, principally driven not by new technologies but by more miners using more axes and shovels to loosen the coal from its seams, as they had done for centuries.[46] By 1860, coal expert William Fordyce could argue that "[t]he true source of England's wealth, no doubt, is Coal."[47]

Early coal entrepreneurs were often worldly or ecclesiastical land-owners on whose lands coal happened to be located. With the rise of large-scale and capital-intensive ironworking, these estate mines quickly began to lose their importance, and new kinds of coal enter-prises emerged. Merchants invested some of their capital in coal min-ing. Joint-stock companies emerged as well, bringing together the capital from various investors—a pattern especially pronounced once mines became more capital-intensive thanks to investments in steam engines and large land acquisitions. From his 1860 vantage point, Fordyce observed that in 1829, capital invested in collieries on the Tyne and Wear coalfield amounted to 2.2 million pounds, and by the end of the 1850s, it had reached 14 million pounds. Some individual mines now brought together capital of half a million pounds sterling.[48]

COAL WAS IMPORTANT, but no industry mattered more to making the Industrial Revolution a permanent revolution than the railroads. Pre-cursors to this wheel-and-track-based system of transportation were an-cient, with horse-drawn proto-trains used in Britain's coal mines in the eighteenth century. Mines were heavy users of steam engines (to pump out water), so it was only a matter of time before someone thought to put the steam engine on wheels and use its power to propel wagons, with the first passenger line chugging along at seventeen miles an hour between the cotton port of Liverpool and the cotton-manufacturing center of Manchester in 1830. Naturally, the railway was used early on to facilitate the country's most important industry. Eight years later, London, Birmingham, Liverpool, and Manchester were linked to each other. By 1844, Britain had two thousand miles of railway tracks; by 1850, about six thousand miles. They allowed goods, especially coal, to be distributed on a much greater scale, and let workers move more easily into industrial centers. They enabled an increased velocity of capital, bringing producers and consumers into closer proximity. Railway manias gripped the investment classes at regular intervals, with merchants, industrialists, landowners, clergy, widows, and anyone else with any resources pouring moneys into this or that scheme to build this or that railroad—sometimes producing notable profits, other times only modest returns.[49] So drastic were the changes brought about by the railroad that British writer William Makepeace Thackeray noted in 1860: "We who have lived before railways were made, belong to another world. . . . It was only yesterday; but what a gulf between now and then!"[50] His sense that time itself had accelerated was novel at the time but in industrial capitalism's heartlands became almost commonsensical. It is a sense familiar to all readers of this book.

The iron industry benefited the most from the expansion of railroads, providing yet more outlets for profitable investments. As we have seen, iron manufacturing was ancient and had attracted merchant investment for centuries. It had expanded in the eighteenth century, not least because of the intensifying demand for its products from the plantation economy in the Americas. Like cotton mills, iron drew on capital accumulated through trade. The industry grew rapidly, and by 1804, it could supply the local market; by 1815, one-third of British production was exported. Technical innovations diminished production costs by 66 percent in the early 1830s, expanding output even further. In 1785, Britain had produced 61,000 tons of pig iron; in 1850, it churned out 2.25 million tons, with an additional 2 million tons of bar iron. The industry partly thrived because of protections; the tariff on bar iron was 2.81 pounds per ton from 1782 to 1795, but that rose to 6.49 pounds in 1813.[51]

And then came the machinery industry. Mechanized production needed machines—spinning mules, drills, steam engines, locomotives—all of whose production increased rapidly. But this industry did not grow in the same way that cotton manufacturing, iron production, or coal mining grew. Lacking large-scale demand, machine manufacturers initially operated in small workshops that employed skilled artisans, rather than in large factories that harnessed nonhuman power sources. They produced goods in small batches, often to very exact specifications. Workers were highly skilled. They retained control over their work processes and production techniques, and they were much better paid than cotton operatives. Manufacturers thus could not totally reinvent production processes, as they had in cottons.[52]

Particular clusters of such businesses emerged in and around the English city of Birmingham, with its pronounced concentration of skills and its long tradition of arms manufacture. A "war-driven industrial capitalism" had already developed in Birmingham in the eighteenth century:[53] Between 1790 and 1804 alone, gun production in Birmingham increased by a factor of five to fourteen thousand firearms weekly. Accumulated expertise could be used for engineering other goods. High-precision cannon manufacturing pushed by the Ordnance Office, for example, helped improve steam engines by demonstrating how to bore cylinders more precisely. As state orders poured in, manufacturers escalated the division of labor to improve productivity. Large and small firms contracted with one another in a dense network of expertise and labor, making the city a "virtual factory."[54] Using Birmingham's "tinkering culture," firms also made incremental technical changes. Between 1760 and 1850, Birmingham inventors secured many more patents than their Manchester counterparts.[55] But even in Birmingham, sciences had no real role in early industrialization. *A Descriptive History of the Steam Engine* (1824) observed "that science, or scientific men, never had anything to do in the matter. . . . Indeed, there is no machine or mechanism in which the little that theorists have done is more useless. . . . It arose, was improved, and perfected by working mechanics— and by them only."[56] Yet the many small artisan-driven improvements recast industrial production and led to massive investments in manufacturing, feeding an expansion of industry unmatched in the history of the world.

In a fortuitous coincidence, these industries reinforced one another. Railroads demanded coal, iron, and machinery; cotton demanded steam power, coal, and machines; and mining benefited from the steam engine and the railroad. As a result of these synergies, by 1850, Britain was almost unrecognizable to people who had lived there half a century earlier and shockingly modern to visitors. Half of all Britons now lived in cities and worked in industry. With 1.8 percent of the world's people and 0.16 percent of the world's land, Britain mined two-thirds of all coal and spun and wove half of all cottons.[57] Years earlier, in 1814, Scottish merchant and scholar Patrick Colquhoun had gushed that technical improvements in Britain were "beyond all calculation."[58] It was, according to his breathless testimony, "impossible to contemplate the progress of manufactures . . . without wonder and astonishment. Its rapidity . . . exceeds all credibility."[59] *Chambers's Encyclopedia* agreed in 1849: "In point of national industry England stands unrivalled by any other country on the globe."[60]

As Britain industrialized, capitalists, rulers, and bureaucrats in many different parts of the world hoped to follow its lead. Pressured by an avalanche of increasingly inexpensive British yarn exports, and inspired by British advances, they focused on cottons. At first, they imported machine-made British yarn to weave into cloth. Much of that production continued to take place in the countryside, but in Saxony and the Rhineland, entrepreneurs brought weavers into large workshops to better supervise their labor.[61]

Soon, entrepreneurs embarked upon local yarn production as well, using the new machinery invented in Britain. The industry spread like wildfire. The first modern cotton mills opened in 1771 in France, in 1783 in what became Germany, in 1785 in Catalonia, in 1789 in the United States, in 1792 in the southern parts of the Netherlands, in 1793 in Russia, in 1801 in Switzerland, and in 1808 in what would become Italy. Everywhere, the industry was quite small, not yet comparable to the massive cotton complex found in the United Kingdom. But it exploded after the turn of the century: In Saxony, the number of spindles grew from 3,000 in 1800 to 284,000 in 1815; in Prussia, from 15,000 in 1800 to 150,000 by 1840. Across Germany, the number of cotton textile workers climbed from around 77,000 in 1820 to around 213,000 in 1840, and the number of spindles increased almost a hundredfold between 1800 and 1860. In Switzerland, the number of spindles more than tripled between 1827 and 1857; in France, they increased by a factor of ten between the 1780s and the 1830s; in the United States, by a factor of approximately twenty. In 1810, there were 87,000 mechanized spindles in the United States; by 1860, there were 5 million, and cotton manufacturing was the country's most important industry.[62]

Almost always, these copycat industrial revolutions were based on British technology, British machines, and skilled British workers. Capital owners and government officials intent on embarking upon industrialization went to Britain to learn the secrets of the new industry. Because British policies forbade both exportation of the machinery and emigration of the workers skilled in its construction and use, much of the technology transfer took the form of what today would be called industrial espionage. Belgian cotton pioneer Lieven Bauwens took thirty-two journeys to England in the last decade of the eighteenth century, investigating the new technology and recruiting skilled workers for his factory.[63] Providence merchant Moses Brown induced Samuel Slater, an apprentice at an Arkwright textile mill, to emigrate in 1789 to establish the first mechanized cotton mill in the US.

The transfer of skills, knowledge, and machinery was crucial but not sufficient. Capital was also needed. Initially, however, capital requirements were quite modest, and the wealth accumulated by a putting-out merchant or even a skilled artisan was enough to begin manufacturing cotton. Swiss spinner Heinrich Kunz, to cite an extraordinary example, started in the industry as an operative; when he died in 1859, he controlled eight spinning mills that employed two thousand workers. In Russia, it was often enserfed peasants who started the nation's cotton industry. More typically, merchant capital funded factories—often coming from small-scale merchants who had been involved in aspects of the industry but also from large overseas merchants, such as Francis Cabot Lowell, an extraordinarily wealthy Boston trader who was part of a group that invested $400,000 in the construction of a massive mill in Waltham, Massachusetts, in 1813.[64]

IF ACCESS TO technology and capital combined with a previous history of textile production was all that was needed to embark upon cotton industrialization, the industry would have spread to much of the world. It did not. What set places that experienced early cotton industrialization apart from those that did not was an institutional framework, especially a powerful state that was interested in and able to constitute a novel form of capitalism—industrial capitalism.[65]

Again, Britain showed the way. Not only was the United Kingdom in the vanguard of the Industrial Revolution; it was also in the vanguard of crafting a state that, unbeknownst to its protagonists, was unusually well suited to launching its capital owners onto a world-changing trajectory. Britain's governing elites had constructed a state with great infrastructural, bureaucratic, fiscal, and military reach, an "aggressive and intervening State," as one scholar argued—the very capacity that distinguished places that experienced early cotton industrialization from those that did not. This powerful state had played a crucial role from the beginning, not least by protecting infant industries, as British markets had been largely closed to textiles from continental Europe and India in the seventeenth and eighteenth centuries.[66]

States where industrialization began followed the British example and provided all kinds of incentives to engage in cotton manufacturing, including monopolies, privileges, and subsidies. Even more important was their capacity to protect domestic industries from competition, following up on the British example.[67] The most important bout of such protectionism came about inadvertently, but at exactly the right moment, during the Napoleonic Wars, when a modern cotton industry had already emerged in some parts of the world. From

1806 to 1814, as continent-wide warfare disrupted and then made illegal trade between the belligerents, the continental European cotton industry was insulated from its more advanced British competitors. The effect was immediate: In the Saxon city of Chemnitz, the number of mechanical spindles increased by a factor of seventeen during the wars. While France had counted just 6 mechanized cotton mills in 1789, it hosted 272 by 1812. In 1807, as his industrial investments merged with the postrevolutionary imperial French government's state-making project, textile entrepreneur Guillaume Louis Ternaux announced: "And I also will make war on England!"[68] In the United States, the effects were similar: When trade with Europe froze between 1807 and 1815, the country's domestic cotton industry took off. Between 1808 and 1811, the number of mechanized spindles grew by a factor of ten.[69] As a French prefect reported from Belgium on the effects of such war-induced protectionism: "No industrial progress has ever taken place more rapidly."[70]

When the end of the wars unleashed a vast wave of British exports, cotton manufacturers in some countries had amassed sufficient political clout to demand tariff protections. The United States imposed tariffs as early as 1816; Prussia and Austria followed suit in 1818, joined over the next few years by Russia, France, Italy, Bavaria, and Württemberg. In 1842, France actually outlawed all imports of cotton goods. These measures were in part driven by arguments from economists such as Friedrich List, who stressed that the "value of manufactures [must] be estimated from a political point of view."[71] He opposed the free-trade teachings of British liberals and observed in the 1830s: "It is a common rule of wisdom that when we reach the summit of greatness we should kick away the ladder . . . in order to deprive others of the means of climbing after us."[72] Across the Atlantic, Henry Charles Carey agreed. He was an ardent advocate of protectionism and a believer in the active role of the state in forging a national economy. His 1851 *Harmony of Interests* promoted import duties, which he believed would benefit all Americans and bring about the titular harmony.

For him, free trade secured "to the people of England the further existence of the monopoly of machinery"; therefore, if the United States was to develop, it had to protect itself.[73] His economic nationalism was influential in the emerging Republican Party, and he became a close adviser to President Abraham Lincoln, driven not least by their shared belief that to prosper in a system of competitive states, they needed to foster domestic industrialization. Only in a few parts of the world did states enjoy sufficient power to make these rules. It was in those parts of the world that early cotton industrialization succeeded.[74]

As in Britain, in large parts of Europe and the United States, cotton industrialization translated into a broader industrial revolution. The industries involved were similar—coal mining, iron manufacturing, railways, and machinery, all feeding upon the expansion of the others and all deeply embedded in states favorable to building institutional structures that fostered industrial capitalism. France had 356 miles of railroad lines in 1840 but 2,208 in 1850; Prussia's network increased from 115 miles to 1,851; and the United States' expanded from 2,796 to 8,948. Coal production increased just as rapidly. In the United States, it went from almost 100,000 metric tons in 1800 to 3.6 million metric tons in 1850, while the higher-quality Pennsylvanian anthracite coal rose from about 1,000 metric tons in 1808 to almost 4 million metric tons in 1850. French and German coal production almost quintupled between 1815 and 1850, though their production was less than that of Belgium, which in 1850 produced 10.2 million tons of coal. Iron production expanded just as impressively: in the United States, from 54,431 metric tons of pig iron in 1810 to 572,434 metric tons by 1850. France led pig-iron production in continental Europe, processing some 406,000 metric tons in 1850, a significant increase from the 113,000 tons it produced in 1819. German states, too, saw pig-iron production more than double, from 85,000 tons in 1823 to 210,000 tons in 1850.[75]

Everywhere, states were crucial to the deepening of industrialization. In Germany, the new customs union created free trade between

German states and thus a larger domestic market while simultaneously unifying tariff barriers to outsiders. The postrevolutionary French government introduced crucial juridical reforms, outlawing guilds and freeing up the labor market in the 1790s, as well as elevating private property to a "sacred, inviolable right" in the 1805 civil code. The French state increasingly invested directly in public works or, as in the case of an 1842 law establishing a "demi-concession" regime, lowered investment risks by guaranteeing interest to investors in railway ventures. As with the Zollverein, the state also crafted an integrated national economy by abolishing internal tolls and setting a common tariff policy to aid manufacturers. The French state supported the transfer of technology and educational reforms, not least by actively circumventing British restrictions. Tellingly, when Carl von Clausewitz, that great theoretician of war, wanted to explain how war had changed, he compared it with commerce—a concept that would have been immediately clear to early nineteenth-century European rulers.[76]

Even though their industrial revolutions unfolded at least a generation later than that of the United Kingdom's, by the 1850s, the European continent and the eastern shores of North America were dotted with industrial centers. The German Ruhr saw the emergence of a complex of coal mining, iron production, and heavy industry. Around Liège, a similar interconnected complex of mines and furnaces emerged, along with those in French Lorraine, New England, Alsace, Normandy, Lombardy, Saxony, the Black Forest, the Zürcher Oberland—all filled with centers of mechanized cotton production.

Industrial espionage and cross-border travel remained important to the spread of industry. In the 1790s, English blacksmith and model maker William Cockerill arrived in France, where he set up a metallurgical plant and machine workshop at Seraing, close to Liège. In 1810, Napoleon made Cockerill a citizen, and by 1812, his plant employed two thousand workers. Cockerill would often boast about his capacity to imitate British workshops: "I have all the new inventions over at Liège ten days after they come out of England."[77] In 1824, his metalworks installed Belgium's first iron furnace utilizing coke rather than charcoal, copying British technology. In 1819, the Prussian state sent a locksmith to Britain to study machine manufacturing; upon his return, he established a major plant. Alfred Krupp traveled to Britain in 1838, returning to the Rhineland to establish an important foundry and machine workshop. In that same year, Dutch manufacturer Paul van Vlissingen made trips to London, Birmingham, and Glasgow; his Amsterdam machine workshop, which employed a team of British metalworkers, grew into the Netherlands' largest, with sixteen hundred employees in the 1850s. Bremen merchant Ludwig Knoop visited England, and then, after 1843, he began exporting machinery to Russia, playing a major role in its industrialization. Machine building also boomed in France: In 1775, artillery officer and metallurgist Mathieu Henri Marchand de la Houlière traveled to England to visit iron smelters William and John Wilkinson, whom he persuaded to help him establish a cannon foundry at Le Creusot. Although this initial attempt failed due to the different chemical composition of the metals mined in the Loire Valley, the region became a hotbed of machine manufacturing. By 1828, it boasted eight machine workshops.[78] Yet despite all these advances, by 1830 Britain dominated world manufacturing in ways comparable only to US domination after 1945 and Chinese domination in the first decades of the twenty-first century.[79]

———

As new forms of manufacturing emerged, older forms, such as those organized by guilds or by putting-out merchants, did not disappear; rather, they intensified. Clockmaking in the Black Forest, for example, spread in the eighteenth century, as peasant sons without land sought alternative ways of making a living. But it was in the next century that this industry really took off: There were five hundred clock workshops in the Black Forest in 1800 and fourteen hundred in 1900.[80] Propelled by expanding markets, such intensification of manufacturing without significant technical or organizational change was common.

*Early coal baron
John Cockerill, Belgium.*

Solingen—a town on the outskirts of the Ruhr blessed with charcoal, coal, and iron ore, as well as ample waterpower—was another example. Since the Middle Ages, its highly skilled craftsmen had specialized in the manufacturing of weapons, especially high-quality swords, always in demand due to the unending cycle of warfare. Solingen's iron and steel industry was structured the same way for centuries: highly skilled blacksmiths, grinders, and finishers organized in guilds that regulated all aspects of production, their privileges bestowed by local rulers. Children inherited their positions from their parents, creating almost dynastic structures. The Henckels family, who had worked in the industry since the mid-1400s, registered the Zwilling trademark in 1731. It is still in use today by the namesake company.[81]

By the late eighteenth century, however, things began to change. Opposed by increasingly powerful merchants and faced with competition from English manufacturers and producers outside their organizational structures, guilds saw their influence diminish. The death knell came with Napoleon's expansion into Germany: In 1809, guilds were outlawed. Power shifted to merchants, who became key actors in coordinating production. Blacksmiths, grinders, and finishers still worked in small workshops or at home and still used age-old technologies and age-old knowledge. But they now worked for merchants, who provided them with materials and paid them by the piece.[82] The production of weapons, knives, scissors (a new product that reflected new routine levels of precision), and cutlery increased rapidly during the 1820s and 1830s—without moving into factories or generating technical change.

Rather, a larger number of people worked much as they would have in previous centuries, but in a critical departure, capital owners now enjoyed unprecedented control over them and the industry.

J. A. Schmidt & Söhne, a maker of knives and cutlery, was founded in 1829 by a man from a poor family who had apprenticed as a finisher. Eventually, he began producing his own knives and expanding production, turning from a producer into a putting-out merchant. He bought steel and other supplies from nearby traders and coordinated an expanding network of blacksmiths, grinders, and finishers in the surrounding countryside who produced in their own dwellings with their own tools. Carl Rau, one such worker, delivered his work to Schmidt weekly—on June 12, 1832, for example, Rau brought him three hundred items. In 1832, Schmidt received wares from twenty-three blacksmiths, eight grinders, and thirty-five finishers; he was a major organizer of production but had no employees. This strategy proved profitable: When he died in 1874, his estate was estimated at 133,000 thalers—about $2.5 million in 2024 US dollars.[83]

No longer having to negotiate with producers as a group, thanks to the end of guilds and the legal prohibitions against workers collectively organizing, merchants like Schmidt could cut payments. According to an 1832 observer, payments were low "because of . . . competition everywhere . . . workers can be hired and the putting-out merchant accepts such workers no matter their lesser skills, as the purchaser pays more attention to an acceptable price than its inner quality . . . but also partly because the factory artisan in these parts can live with a low wage, because he often owns some land, which provides him with his immediate needs, a dwelling, fruit and sometimes wheat, and similar things."[84] Workers were often paid in goods instead of money, a truck system that led to a further fall in income. Payments fell so low that workers struggled to secure their most basic subsistence needs. Once-proud artisans had been reduced to semi-proletarians. By 1848, even the Solingen Chamber of Commerce remarked that workers were increasingly impoverished. At the same time, work intensified, with blacksmiths spending ever longer days in front of their forge fires and grinders over their grinding stones. Workers' incomes were so paltry that families depended on women's and children's agricultural activities, especially their tending of fruit and vegetable gardens. Many workers often ate nothing but potatoes for several months a year, as a contemporary noted in 1823. Local parlance spoke of the "grinder's cow"—a goat. Few people had mattresses; entire families slept in one wooden bed and used the same small room to also store food.[85]

As production spread across the countryside, technology stagnated and skills continued to be concentrated in the hands of the workers, output expanded. A local mayor reported in 1836 that the number of workers had doubled in the previous twenty years and production had tripled. Production tripled again between 1832 and 1856. Solingen and its surrounding areas turned into a gigantic virtual factory, coordinated by merchant entrepreneurs, with four thousand workers in the 1830s, all with their own tools.[86] Manufacturing intensified but in ways fundamentally different from manufacturing in contemporary Glasgow.

Expanding markets explain the dynamic development of the industry. The military remained an important customer. The transformation of the countryside in the Americas provided another significant new market, with a report on the state of the industry emphasizing the importance of "plantation knifes, sugar knifes [and] tools for the colonies."[87] Not surprisingly, local merchants frequently traveled to France, Portugal, and Spain; one firm even stationed an agent in Rio de Janeiro. In 1821, Solingen merchants and their counterparts from nearby cities created the Rheinisch-Westindische Kompagnie to sell their products in the Caribbean and the Americas. Carl Joest and Johann Schimmelbusch, two such merchants, engaged deeply with the Brazilian trade. Eventually, they brought sugar back as return freight and invested in a Cologne sugar refinery that became, by 1839, Prussia's largest, helping turn Cologne into one of Europe's leading chocolate producers. A quintessentially local and small-scale production complex was thus deeply embedded in global markets—not least, too, because its workers themselves became consumers of sugar, coffee, tobacco, and chocolate.[88]

Back in Solingen, the intensified manufacturing system that emboldened merchants had constructed reached its limits in an epic battle with producers. The pressure on workers resulted in sporadic outbreaks of resistance, notably in 1826, when Solingen's grinders went on strike. To win greater control, some employers had tried to organize production in factories, focusing on casting (instead of forging) goods, but their efforts had often failed. When incomes fell further in the 1840s, workers rebelled. On March 16, 1848, they gathered to demand an end to the truck system, which had forced them to accept overpriced necessities in lieu of wages. As they marched through the countryside, they destroyed the new factories, making it clear, even to merchant capitalists, that the ever sharper exploitation of workers had reached a breaking point.[89] As we will see, the mobilizations of 1848, in Solingen and elsewhere, would play an important role in yet another recasting of capitalism.

Despite these reversals, by the midcentury, capital owners nonetheless relocated production into factories. Most decisively, Johann Abraham Henckels visited Sheffield in 1851 and was greatly inspired by the concentration of production there. Upon his return, he had a factory built right next to his family's home, and it began operating in 1852, the grinding stones now propelled by steam engines, not waterpower. Yet even in the 1860s, he still rented workstations to the grinders instead of employing them directly—the old social relations of proto-industrialization, in other words, now moved into the factory.[90]

REGARDLESS OF WHAT form industrialization took, it created gobal hierarchies far more radical than anything seen in prior human history, opening a deep divide between those few parts of the world that had undergone industrial revolution and the rest of the planet.

Britain stood out within this divergence. Despite the rapid expansion of continental European and US manufacturing, Britain's behemoth cotton industry was still, in 1840, about three and a half times as large as that of France, four times as large as that of the United States, and seventeen times as large as that of Germany. That same year, Britain's stationary steam engines produced about two hundred thousand horsepower, or about twice as much as the United States, Prussia, France, and Belgium combined.[91]

Beyond Britain's ever competitive neighbors, vast regions of the world did not experience an emergence of modern industry—not in 1800, not in 1850, not in 1900. Considering the Industrial Revolution's radical departure from earlier economic life, such exceptionalism should not surprise us. Yet islands of modern industry did appear outside the heartlands of industrial capitalism. Their trajectory tells us indirectly about the conditions needed to forge industrial capitalism.

Most importantly, outside the emerging industrial heartlands, industry emerged to process raw materials for export—sugar, for example. In 1800, a British-Danish merchant house brought a steam mill to Java, along with eight British engineers, and by the 1850s, many of Java's mills had at least a backup steam engine to generate power when water levels dropped. Hundreds of steam engines were shipped to plantations in the tropics to power plants that extracted juice from cane. The first steam-driven sugar mill in Brazil opened in 1815, and by 1834, the country had sixty-four of them. In Cuba, as mills transitioned from oxen to steam power, the average sugar mill production capacity shot up from 58 tons of sugar per grinding season in 1790 to 1,176 tons around 1860. Cuba's railroad lines, as well as those on other Caribbean islands, expanded from 65 miles in 1840 to 272 miles in 1850, though not to help build an integrated island-wide market but to move sugar to the coast for export.[92]

Mechanized industry advanced in Egypt as well. Understanding the growing importance of industrial power to military strength, Egypt's ruler, Muhammad Ali Pasha, paid European engineers to set up workshops, including sugar refineries, paper mills, and armories. He also had modern cotton mills erected, beginning with one mill in 1818; by the mid-1830s, fifteen thousand to twenty thousand workers labored in thirty cotton mills, operating four hundred thousand spindles. By population, Egypt was the world's fifth-largest cotton power. To the great consternation of the British, Egyptian factories began to dominate their home market and even exported to faraway India.[93]

Other countries followed suit: The Ottoman sultan imported machinery in the 1830s to construct factories that mainly served the needs of the military. In Mexico, as the "silver capitalism" of previous centuries went into terminal decline, Mexican capital owners worked with a proactive Mexican state to embrace industrialization.[94] After Mexico gained its independence in 1821, it saw a wave of textile industrialization, with a first cotton mill established in Puebla in 1832, followed in 1835 by Don Pedro Baranda's steam-powered mill in Valladolid, in the center of the Yucatán Peninsula. By 1843, the country counted fifty-nine cotton mills operating 125,362 spindles.[95]

But industrialization outside Europe and North America did not amount to an industrial revolution. In the first half of the nineteenth century, sites of intensified industry remained rare, and, in purely quantitative terms, unimportant to economic life on planet Earth. They remained islands. Until about 1830, even in the United Kingdom, per capita GNP growth continued to be slow. Productivity growth was focused in only a few sectors: Cotton, woolens, iron, canals, ships, and railways, taken together, saw annual total factor productivity growth of 0.34 percent between 1780 and 1860. Other sectors contributed just 0.08 percent.[96]

But it was that structural change that made the Industrial Revolution, despite its limits, a sea change in human affairs, both globally and from the perspective of the industrial heartland. Like so much of the capitalist revolution, it unfolded in particular circumscribed regions at first, almost undetectable from broad total statistics. Yet in key industries, such as textiles, a fundamentally new dynamic of manufacturing—comparable in its radicalism to the plantation revolution in agriculture—emerged, forging a new kind of capitalism that still stamps our world.[97]

The Industrial Revolution was a moment in the long history of capitalism when manufacturing intensified and a small number of new nodes of capital dedicated to industry arose. We have seen other such nodes take shape—in the linen production center of Jelenia Góra, in western India, and near the clay-rich soils of China. These places had churned out linens, cottons, and porcelain in ever increasing quantities, all produced under the aegis of capital.

Despite these seeming continuities, the intensification of manufacturing—first in the United Kingdom between 1780 and 1830, then elsewhere—was distinguished by four key innovations: the relocation of manufacturing into factories, the recruitment of millions of wageworkers to staff these factories, the intensifying use of fossil fuels, and the historically unprecedented productivity increases that led to not just rapid but continual economic growth.

None of these developments on their own were pathbreaking: Factories emerged much earlier (witness the Venetian Arsenal or the Barbados sugar plantations). Wage labor is also very old, going back at least three millennia.[98] Fossil fuels had been burned earlier, too (in iron production, for example), and there had been moments of economic growth in various societies at various times. What was new now was that all these developments converged simultaneously. Take factories, for example: In previous centuries, manufacturing had been widely dispersed throughout households in the countryside or limited to small artisanal workshops in cities. This changed with the advent of modern cotton mills. Large machines could not be set up in homes, and the complicated organism of production could no longer be coordinated by merchants connecting the activities of small and distant producers. Instead, capital owners erected buildings that housed large numbers of machines and workers to coordinate and control labor.

Inside these factories, the relationship between capital owners and workers changed significantly. Industrialists took on a much more decisive role in supervising labor and coordinating its effort—something that had been unnecessary or impossible in earlier systems of manufacturing. Moreover, manufacturing was newly capital-intensive. Earlier merchant-manufacturers had provided forms of circulating capital (raw cotton, for example), but now fixed capital (machines, buildings) became a large expense and was bound to a particular place and a particular asset in ways new to a world of capital that had for centuries been dominated by exceedingly mobile merchant investments. In the old days, a merchant family in Surat, London, or Cairo could shift their investments easily, swapping one trade route, commodity, or trading partner for another. Not so for the newfangled manufacturers who invested capital for the long term and dealt with issues that earlier merchants could often evade: the consistent flow of raw materials into the factory; the availability of inexpensive, docile, and sufficiently skilled labor; and the securing of markets for the increased output of machine production. Factories were sites of intensified production, and as they congregated in particular places—in Manchester and Lowell, in Chemnitz and Lille—they constituted new nodes of a new form of capital: industrial capital.

THE FACTORY COMBINED, crucially, with new forms of labor mobilization. Investments in new production technology depended on the ability to recruit workers to operate machinery. Capital owners had mobilized large numbers of workers previously (a prime example being the Caribbean sugar plantations with their hundreds of thousands of workers). Yet this form of labor mobilization—slavery—remained marginal to the emerging industrial heartland. Religious sensibilities, Enlightenment ideas, Europeans' ability to resist enslavement, and the great risks of entrusting expensive machinery to workers with little to lose limited the role of slave labor in industrial production to only a few regions of the world—principally, the southern United States and Brazil, where a small number of enslaved workers labored in factories. No industrial revolution emerged in regions of the world dominated by plantation slavery (such as the southern United States), and slavery never played an important role in mobilizing industrial labor.

Industrialists instead drew on another ancient mode of labor mobilization—purchasing labor time by paying wages. In much of the capitalist world today, this is the dominant form of labor recruitment—so much so that it has been mistakenly identified as its only form. Wage labor has become so common and so unexceptional that it is hard for most of us to understand that recruiting millions of workers into factories by paying them wages was a radical break in human history. It was never easy or "natural." But it became the second defining characteristic of the Industrial Revolution. By 1850, there were approximately 873,000 cotton workers and 270,000 coal miners in Europe, all paid wages.[99]

Wage labor needed to be procured, just like any other commodity, an exceedingly difficult process because, as we saw in Scotland, few people voluntarily entered the factory if alternative means of subsistence were available. When an 1825 observer looked back to the earliest history of Finlay's cotton mills in Scotland, he noticed that it "was difficult to find a sufficient number of people with skill and experience to carry out the work. . . . The more respectable part of the surrounding inhabitants was at first adverse to seek employment in the works, as they considered it disrespectable to be employed in what was labeled a public work."[100] They preferred the independence of working at home, retaining control of their labor and their time, however meager their existence.[101] As John Orr, a spinning manufacturer, explained in 1810: "[T]he native people had an objection to work in cotton mills and other work was so plenty they did not require it."[102] At the Deanston mill, things were similar: According to one chronicler, people "were suspicious of the works, especially the Highland people, who regarded them as a kind of prison, the interior sound and sights of the machinery at work being in some degree a terror to them."[103] Wage labor encountered deep resistance because people considered it a form of unfree labor—characterized by prisonlike structures, militarized discipline, workplace violence, and intense, unrelenting work requirements, independent of seasons and communal needs.

Factory work was indeed hard and could be dangerous. Janet Henderson, who worked in one of Finlay's mills, was forty-eight when she was interviewed by an investigator. She had worked in the mill for twenty-three years. Henderson reported that the temperature in the factory ranged from eighty to eighty-four degrees Fahrenheit and that it smelled of sour glue. The fumes, she believed, had "taken away her complexion" and swollen her feet. She was likely right: Recent osteological research (studying the composition and growth of bones) has shown that the Industrial Revolution increased women's workloads to such a degree that its bodily effects can still be seen today in the bones of their exhumed remains. Because conditions were so difficult, workers usually did not stay for long. Labor turnover was high, with more than half of workers staying less than a year. In 1833, when managers at the Catrine Mills looked back on their workforce from two decades earlier, they found that only 189 of the 867 workers still worked at the factory.[104] Everyone else had left.

Because people were reluctant to join the factory proletariat, the first generation of workers came from the most powerless groups: In Scotland, these were migrants from the countryside, especially women and children.[105] Indeed, accessing and intensifying women's labor was one of the Industrial Revolution's conditions of possibility. Parents or husbands sent young women into factories to supplement the family income—to allow the family a respite on the land. This was a pattern that would repeat itself around the world and persists to the present day.

But then, as estates commercialized and were enclosed, tenants were pushed off the land, leaving some families with no other option. When one landowner offered to move families into a factory town, he warned that those who refused his offer would "do well to look out for possessions elsewhere as the Duke is determined not to let his lands again in such small farms."[106] One landowner spoke of factory villages as a "convenient asylum" for those "who have been ejected from their farms."[107] If we look at the employment records of the Catrine Mills in 1813, we can see many individuals working there, but we can also see large family groups, such as six members of the Cummings family, five Cooks, six Hoods, five Millikens, five McClintocks, and seven Orrs. Wage labor was the consequence of, not the precondition for, the development of capitalism.[108]

Dramatic changes in the countryside indeed drove rural cultivators into factories. As cotton manufacturer James Smith observed at Deanston, Perthshire, in the late eighteenth century: "The first supply was chiefly from the Highlands, where, from the introduction of sheep, the farmers and small cotters were forced away to seek employment in such establishments."[109] David Dale, owner of the New Lanark Mill, recruited two hundred workers from the Highlands in 1792, "a year when sheepwalks were being established."[110] A minister described in 1791 how "[f]ew or none have emigrated from this parish, but whole troops of boys and girls go annually to the low country for service and of late to the cotton works, many of whom settle there."[111] We know of Scottish islands where all inhabitants moved to the new industrial centers to work in the mills.[112]

In the Scottish Lowlands, change was just as consequential but slower: With the decay of feudalism, landlords had developed more commercial attitudes toward their land, not least because their expenses rose as they partook in increased consumption. In the seventeenth century, most farms focused on subsistence production and were remote from markets; in the eighteenth century, the countryside became more market-oriented and the relationship between landowners and tenants entirely commercial. By 1700, landlords had converted land rents, once in kind, to monetary payments. These changes accelerated in the second half of the century: As cities grew because of the expansion of trade and industry, merchant capital also commercialized the countryside. By the 1760s and 1770s, landlords invested in the modernization of agriculture and pursued massive enclosures, with land becoming a commercial asset like any other.[113]

Sometimes the commercialization of the countryside was also the direct result of merchants' investments. When traders, flush from their American ventures, bought estates, they altered how the land was worked. Scottish merchant Richard Oswald, for example, bought an estate in 1765 and invested some of his profits in agricultural improvements.[114]

Moreover, as Britain consolidated its rule over Ireland and began enclosing the Irish countryside, rural Irish cultivators fled into newly built factories, becoming low-wage competitors of workers displaced from the Scottish and English countrysides. Indeed, much of Europe's proletarianization occurred first in the countryside, as rural cultivators dispossessed of their holdings were turned into farmworkers or proto-industrial workers before they moved into factories. Once they left for urban centers in the nineteenth century, the countryside, ironically, became more rural and more dominated by cultivators than before.[115]

British cotton industrialization typically unfolded in areas where wages were particularly low. Richard Arkwright, for example, moved production to Cromford in Derbyshire, knowing that local parents, suffering from economic hardship, would be eager to find employment for their children. While some economic historians have explained Britain's early-budding industrialization as an outgrowth of its desire to replace unusually high-wage workers with machinery, others have argued that supplies of cheap labor were elastic, especially as women, children, and the Irish moved into industry.[116]

Children were a massive part of the early factory proletariat. An analysis of the workforce of three Scottish cotton mills in the 1790s showed that of their 1,818 workers, 1,177 (65 percent) were younger than fifteen. When a parliamentary commission investigated child labor in 1833, it chronicled an array of abuses: Elizabeth Brown from Glasgow, nineteen years old when she was interviewed, had worked in the Bartholomew & Co. mill for a year and in other spinning mills for five years prior. She testified that she sometimes got sick at work and vomited due to the heat from the machinery. She and many of her colleagues traveled daily from Rutherglen, a town about three miles southeast of Glasgow, and often felt sick from exhaustion. She earned seven shillings and six pence weekly, the equivalent of thirty-two

British pounds or forty-one US dollars in 2024—that is, sixty cents an hour. A four-pound loaf of bread (in London) at that time cost eight and a half pence; that is, it took Elizabeth Brown more than six hours of spinning labor to buy one loaf.[117]

It can be argued that the Industrial Revolution was made by children. In coal mines, workers started at a young age, characteristically at six or eight. Some entered the factories as bound workers from orphanages and poorhouses. Called "barracks children," they were indentured to the mills for between four and seven years, receiving board and food but no pay.[118] When the Royal Commission on the Employment of Children in Factories inquired about the age of the youngest worker at Finlay's Catrine Mills, a mill manager replied that the youngest was "nine years of age," arguing that work at tender ages benefited both children and their parents.[119] The children, like all the other "hands" (as workers were tellingly called), toiled twelve hours daily on Mondays to Fridays and nine hours on Saturdays. The manager explained why these inhumane working times were necessary: "The inducement to a manufacturer to work long hours is evidently to get a larger produce from a given sunk capital."[120] There was no need for reform, he said, since "[w]e can suggest nothing beyond the

(Scènes dans les mines de houille, en Angleterre. — Le Trapper.)

Children work in coal mining, United Kingdom, 1840s.

self-interest of the parties, which, when well considered, ought to be sufficient in all cases."[121] Glasgow cotton manufacturers mobilized to make their point: In April 1816, they met to oppose any parliamentary interference with child labor, arguing "[t]hat the interference of the legislature between parents and children, and master and free servant, appears to be in all cases inexpedient."[122] They also opposed schooling for children working in the mills, since such education would entail "strangers" interfering in the family relationship between parents and their children.[123] Work, they argued, was beneficial to children—the more hours, the better—a convenient belief, as they knew that to staff their mills, to turn people into factory proletarians, they needed society's weakest members.

Early wage labor, as these examples suggest, was remarkably coercive. Finlay, for example, signed indentures with 155 workers in 1791 that bound them for three years to the factory. The youngest worker, Mary Black, was eight years old; the oldest, Mary Paul, sixteen. "The servants" (as the children were called), though illiterate, signed the contract "voluntarily" and received a weekly payment for their "aliment and subsistence." They agreed to "bind themselves for three years and faithfully serve and obey the orders of the Claud Alexander Company. . . . No wages to be paid during sickness and absences." Workers who stayed home "without leave of absence shall pay to the Master at the rate of six pence Sterl. for each absent day."[124] While the Scottish Parliament's 1606 Act "Anent Coalyers and Salters," which legally bound miners to their "masters," ended in 1799, miners who were paid wages were still sometimes entangled in long contracts, limiting their ability to switch jobs.[125]

Such indentures, both in Europe and on American plantations, were a form of contractual coercion much like earlier forms of unfree agrarian service. Indeed, many modes of unfree agricultural labor relations moved to the factory. As on the estate or the plantation, factory owners supervised all aspects of workers' lives. Employers also often provided (a very basic form of) housing to their workers or permitted, as Finlay did, workers to grow some of their own subsistence. Labor markets were still deeply embedded in the kind of paternalistic struc-tures that had defined relations of dependence for centuries.[126]

While wage labor is frequently conflated with what is called "free labor"—a concept born in the nineteenth century to distinguish the pro-letarian labor of the industrial heartland from slave labor elsewhere—that construction obfuscates the important role played by coercion. Wage labor was enabled by force, with people compelled into factories and noneconomic coercion used to keep them there.[127]

The state played a vital role in creating those conditions. In naval shipyards, huge sites of employment, forced labor remained important, with convict labor crucial to the English docks of Chatham. A variety of laws coerced people into wage work and then forced them to remain with their employers for a certain length of time. Since 1714, the Brit-ish Vagrancy Act targeted the "idle and disorderly poor, whether in their own parishes or wandering outside of them." These "rogues and vagabonds," including "persons wandering and begging," were to be apprehended, forcefully returned to their "settlement," and possibly punished with public whipping or by sending them "to the bridewell for hard labour."[128] In 1824, the revised Vagrancy Act rewrote these laws and stipulated that anyone who was caught "begging and rough sleeping" and "not giving a good account" of themselves could be ar-rested and prosecuted.[129] Immobilizing workers in different ways, the Master and Servant Act of 1823 restricted workers' ability to quit em-ployment and made them criminally liable if they left their employer before the contractual end of employment. Thousands of workers were prosecuted under the law, with many sent to prison for "breach of con-tract."[130] This draconian law was only repealed in 1867.

Britain was hardly an outlier: American workers absconding from their place of employment were sentenced to the payment of pecuniary fines, while in Prussia "[j]ourneymen, helpers, and factory workers, who leave work without permission and without legal justification, or are guilty of shirking or gross disobedience . . . are to be punished with a fine of up to twenty Thalers or prison up to fourteen days," according to the Prussian trade and industry regulations of 1845.[131]

The expansion of wage labor, moreover, went hand in hand with new forms of labor discipline. Outside the plantation economy of the Americas and the few large-scale production sites that had existed earlier (such as shipyards and monasteries), capital owners had enjoyed little direct control over how people worked. The factory made an entirely new form of supervision possible. Indeed, the drive to supervise was one of the reasons capital owners embraced factories in the first place. At factories, workers had to show up on time, consistently tend to their machines, and perform their work in a manner that coordinated with everyone else's activities and the wishes of their managers. Workers, for the first time, became part of the machine that was the factory. As Solingen scissor manufacturer Daniel Peres emphasized in a speech to his workers in 1804, a factory was like "clockwork" and required "order and harmony" to operate.[132]

But how to create this "order and harmony"? Everywhere, the transformation of rural cultivators or outworkers into proletarians was sluggish. The new industrial labor force was difficult to discipline. Workers left the factory after very short stints, drank excessively, and did not subordinate themselves to foremen. They sparred with their employers almost constantly: Skilled, mostly male workers in one Scottish cotton mill reportedly struggled over such things as the provision of "wholesome" drinking water, adequate breaks, and the dismissal of abusive supervisors. One worker demanded that "Robert Craig [a supervisor] should have no power whatever over him," a claim that was seen by his employer as a "dangerous interference with . . . masters."[133] In 1810, these kinds of demands led Glasgow employers to organize a Master Cotton Spinners' Association to oppose spinners' efforts "to raise the prices of labour." The association focused on "protecting the just rights of the Masters," including their right of "hiring and dismissing their workmen."[134] Workers sometimes launched outright rebellions, as when they moved across industrializing areas of Britain and destroyed machinery. To subdue these Luddites, as they called themselves, the state mobilized thousands of soldiers. The struggle to create a factory proletariat was indeed an unending battle in which workers enjoyed some power. This modicum of power in turn brought nonmarket coercions—including an ever more powerful state—into employment relations.[135]

Such "factory discipline" built upon precedents—both the so-called disciplinary revolution in European monasteries three centuries earlier and the military revolution in the seventeenth century—and fed into ideas about how to control the labor of others. There was a close affinity between coercive labor relations and innovations in labor management, with one vector of innovation the model of the Caribbean's slave plantations, whose owners were closely connected to emerging industrial elites. Another vector, an early precursor to scientific management, came from Australia, as Governor Lachlan Macquarie of New South Wales, hoping to control the unruly convict workers of Sydney, produced what were probably the world's first detailed job descriptions. In 1810, building on his military background, he drew up precise rules for the work to be done by the market clerk and his assistants. In 1811, Macquarie outlined the organizational structure of Sydney's police force and stipulated exactly what each worker was responsible for and how the job was to be executed.[136]

From his perspective, Macquarie's project unfolded under ideal conditions: His workers were all convicts, including the police force itself. To scholars, this example demonstrates the extraordinary efforts taken to control the labor power of others, both to get them to part with it reliably and to make sure it was applied in ways that furthered their employer's goals. Yet we tend to forget that these coercions went into constructing the idea of free labor: As abolitionism spread in elite circles, wage labor was increasingly presented as the epitome of free labor; denaturalizing slavery made it easier to naturalize wage labor.[137] This construction, both materially and ideologically, was a core project of capital owners, and it came to define the Industrial Revolution.

As WAGE LABOR in factories became critical to manufacturing, it combined with a third defining characteristic of the Industrial Revolution: fossil fuel use. Previously, all manufacturing in human history had been powered by either muscular strength or the energy provided by water, wind, and the burning of organic matter, such as wood. This has been called an "organic energy regime"—and it was astoundingly flexible, plus potent enough to power almost all the cotton mills erected in the eighteenth and early nineteenth centuries.[138]

That all changed with the rise of the steam engine and the fuel that powered it—coal. After Thomas Newcomen commercialized the steam engine in 1712, it was mainly used to pump water out of mines. Only in the 1780s was it latched to machinery. When James Watt upgraded Newcomen's unwieldy and inefficient engine by inserting a separate condenser and making the movement of the piston connect to a wheel and thus to circular motion, it made steam efficient enough to potentially power all machinery. Very quickly, the first steam engines began moving into the sugar plantations of the Caribbean and the cotton factories of Europe and North America. The first cotton mill was connected to steam power in 1786. In the last quarter of the eighteenth century, Boulton & Watt—the world's leading producer—sold 289 steam engines, 84 of which went into cotton mills, the firm's single largest market.[139]

In the short term, the benefits of steam power versus waterpower were not clear cut, and most manufacturers continued powering their factories with water well into the nineteenth century. In the one thousand textile mills that had been constructed in Britain by the turn of the century, waterpower dominated, with Finlay operating the largest water-powered mill. But waterpower had its limits—not just because it was at times insufficient and seasonal but because it constrained where factories could be built. Industrialists wanted to locate production in cities, and for that they needed steam. Cities housed proletarians who were accustomed to wage work and took charge of their own social reproduction (unlike, say, orphaned children). Indeed, after 1825, there was a "superabundance" of workers in cities, a tempting prospect to capital owners in search of labor.[140]

Another reason was that there were only so many water sites to exploit and so many forests to cut down. As the energy intensity of production increased, resource limitations increasingly dictated a move to fossil fuels. England already faced a shortage of timber and charcoal by the end of the eighteenth century, provoking manufacturers to switch to coal, which had gotten cheaper because of improved canal transportation. In the process, England transitioned to an "inorganic energy regime"—using energy stored in hydrocarbons. By 1800, the coal consumption of England in wood equivalents would have required cutting eleven million acres' worth of trees—about one-third of all English land. In 1815, coal output in Britain saved five million acres of land for wood production, or 88 percent of its arable area. And in 1913, the UK produced so much coal that its embodied energy would have required wood grown on land five and a half times the extent of the British Isles. As Britain inaugurated the fossil fuel age, it provided enormous ecological relief.[141]

But fossil fuels had drastic environmental consequences: Their use inaugurated the age of human-made global warming. They also had more immediate effects: London was notorious for its smog, but in the nineteenth century, pollution intensified so much that it was enveloped in dense coal fog. Despite the 1821 Smoke Nuisance Abatement Act, urban air pollution increased every decade, peaking at the end of the century. Air pollution hampered urbanization and industrial growth by decreasing productivity and making big cities less attractive places to establish new businesses.[142]

WHEN CAPITAL OWNERS combined fossil fuels, wage labor, and factory production, they launched some parts of the world into accelerated and nearly continual economic growth—the fourth characteristic of the Industrial Revolution. As technical improvements increased the productivity of human labor, often drastically, and as people worked harder and longer, it allowed for a much greater output of things and services—ever more cotton cloth, iron beams, railway journeys, and housing, among others. Growth in economic output was not unprecedented, but what was new was the rate of that growth and, even more decisively, its duration. Aside from a few temporary interruptions, economic growth has continued to the present day.

Looked at from the perspective of Germany in the 1890s, the United States in the 1960s, or China in the 2010s, output growth between 1760 and 1830 was modest. But looked at from the perspective of the millennia of economic life before, it was a radical departure. While exact numbers vary, one estimate claims that British output grew by about 1.2 percent per year from 1760 to 1801, then accelerated to an average annual growth rate of 1.7 percent between 1801 and 1831. Humble productivity gains of 0.3 percent annually between 1760 and 1831 increased to 1.1 percent between 1831 and 1873.[143] This was a marked acceleration after many centuries of only minute, or no, economic growth.

Such economic growth was propelled not just by more people doing the same thing but by new ways of production. At first, the contribution of productivity increases to growth was modest: It has been estimated that in Britain, only one-fifth of growth came from total factor productivity increases, with the rest coming from more people doing the same thing longer. Economic historian Nicholas Crafts,

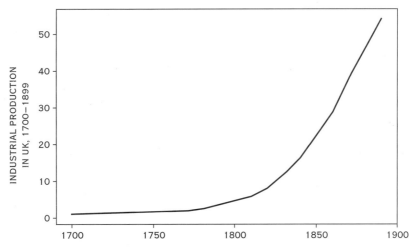

The Industrial Revolution distilled in one graph: indexed industrial production in the United Kingdom, excluding construction, 1700–1709=1.

famous for his downward revision of productivity growth estimates for the Industrial Revolution era, calculated that the total factor productivity in Britain grew 0.3 percent annually between 1780 and 1830, and 0.75 percent between 1831 and 1873. In some specific industries, however, productivity gains were quicker, and it was these industries that pointed to the future: It has been calculated, for example, that the total factor productivity of the pig-iron industry improved by roughly 50 percent between 1800 and 1850, and early jennies allowed for a tripling of output per spinning worker.[144]

As factories, massive proletarianization, and fossil-fuel-powered machinery spread from the dales and valleys of England and Scotland into British cities and then other parts of the European continent and the United States—as cotton gave way to iron, railroads, and machinery, with industry transforming from small, almost quaint sites along fast-flowing rivers into bustling behemoths of noise, smoke, and human masses—industrial capitalism was born. It was as profound a change to its protagonists as it was to elites and commoners who feared its revolutionary impact. Virginian planter Thomas Jefferson warned of the corrupting influences of manufacturing and pledged to "let us never wish to see our citizens occupied at a workbench or twirling a distaff." He wanted to "let our workshops remain in Europe."[145] By the mid-nineteenth century, viewed from the vantage point of the industrial heartlands, it was clear that the world had changed beyond recognition. Industrialists celebrated the new productive powers that they had helped unleash as the first step into a permanent state of abundance. Speaking at the Great Exhibition of 1851, Thomas Bazley—a British cotton manufacturer, a member of Parliament, and president of the Manchester Chamber of Trade—gushed that

> [w]ith raw material abundantly supplied—with mechanical and moral progress—with intelligence, skill, industry, and probity,

combined, and these high qualifications discreetly directed in our sea-girt land, free and unfettered, ages yet to come may witness the growing greatness of honest labour's dignity; and the future historian may record that even more has been achieved than was "dreamt of in our philosophy," still leaving unexplored fields for science, art, and industry, to subdue for the benefit of the human race![146]

Critics saw the new world as an end of history in a different way: For Karl Marx, the Industrial Revolution readied the world for a proletarian revolution that would create a classless communist society. Critics and advocates did not agree on much, but they agreed on this new society's millennial character.

Unsurprisingly, a world so radically altered produced massive resistance at both ends of the social scale. The elites who drew their wealth from land remained politically dominant almost everywhere, and they defended their social and political position in society against the upstart industrialists. And as the rapidly growing working class, those who owned nothing but their labor power, mobilized to demand higher wages and better working conditions, their nearly continual resistance and rebellions became an integral part of industrial capitalism itself. In 1810, the newly founded Association of Operative Cotton Spinners of Glasgow had a motto that sounds contemporary: "United We Stand, Divided We Fall."[147] Two years later, forty thousand Glasgow weavers went on strike, followed in 1837 by a walkout of thirty-two thousand cotton spinners.[148] Workers also rallied against the entire new edifice of industrial capitalism, which they saw as deeply illegitimate, and objected, like agricultural producers the world over, to lives spent at the mercy of implacable market forces.

Industrial capitalism created new social inequalities in the heartlands of the Industrial Revolution and new hierarchies globally. The ancient centers of intensified industry—China and India—experienced almost no industrialization of the kind that characterized the leading economies of the North Atlantic region, despite their iconic backgrounds in manufacturing, their very large proto-industrial sectors, and their significant accumulations of capital. Neither China nor India had built trade networks remotely comparable to those of some European powers; their countrysides remained deeply traditional; and—perhaps most decisively—their states were unwilling to foster, or incapable of fostering, a drastic departure in economic life. In India, of course, the British presence undermined any kind of domestic industrialization, as India became for certain key industries, such as textiles, Britain's most important market. The colonial project drastically weakened the local political authorities that otherwise could have launched industrial activities and created important markets for goods—from textiles to armaments. Industrialization was impossible without the active involvement of the state—and under conditions of colonialism, a national state oriented toward national economic development was absent.[149]

Though these new islands of intensified production were localized, they had radical global implications. As parts of the world industrialized, others deindustrialized. For instance, in Ireland, a British colony, home-based manufacturing quickly declined as cheaper wares from industrial production overwhelmed it, leaving tens of thousands of women unemployed. In the 1821 census, 41 percent of those listing an occupation were employed in "trades, manufactures, or handicraft"; by the 1841 census, three-quarters of all families were "chiefly employed in agriculture." Industrialization in England and Scotland created ruralization in Ireland, a pattern that repeated elsewhere—first in Europe, then almost everywhere around the world as old centers of proto-industry declined. In the Ottoman Empire, as a free-trade treaty went into effect in 1838, Britain swamped Egypt and the rest of the empire with cheaper, high-quality imported textiles. The price of cotton textiles declined by as much as 80 percent over the first half of the nineteenth century, pushing rural textile production into a downturn.[150] Taken together, the impact of such imbalances was drastic: For the first time, the world's manufacturing capacity was concentrated in a tiny part of the globe.

Yet the greatest impact of the Industrial Revolution was its forging of an entirely novel form of capitalism—industrial capitalism, with its new demands on the state, new organization of capital and labor, new forms of economic growth, new patterns of inequality, and a new logic of ever intensifying production. The Industrial Revolution changed fundamentally the conditions of capital worldwide. Fixed capital—machines, buildings, and other assets—became more important. Investments in such fixed assets, in turn, put more pressure on securing labor, raw materials, and markets. As Karl Polanyi observed, the logic of markets now infused everything: "[O]nce elaborate machines and plants were used for production in a commercial society, the idea of a self-regulating market system was bound to take shape."[151] An entirely new class structure emerged, too, as a new elite character—the industrialist—strode onto the scene. Unlike merchants of previous centuries, industrialists made money first and foremost by organizing production. As they accumulated unprecedented masses of capital, and as securing inputs and markets became ever more important to them, new technologies like railways, steamships, and the telegraph connected the world in novel ways, putting further pressures on social structures

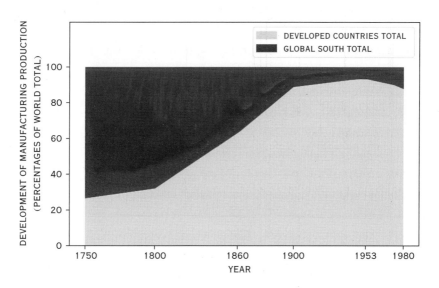

The Industrial Revolution creates new global hierarchies, 1750–1980: Developed countries include Austria-Hungary, Belgium, France, Germany, Italy, Russia, Spain, Sweden, Switzerland, Canada, Japan, the United Kingdom, and the United States, among others. Global South countries include China, British India, Brazil, Mexico, and more.

and nature. At the same time, a few states gained entirely new capabilities from the resources made available by industrial production, and new configurations of class forces made the state a much more important and capable institution within society. Industrial capitalism helped produce a different kind of state:[152] As Charles Tilly, the leading observer of state-making, noted, "[S]tate structures expanded, were centralized and became the dominant organizations within their own territories."[153]

As industrial capitalism emerged, it increasingly jostled with old-regime capitalism—older social and political structures, older distributions of power, and older ideas and mentalities, ranging from slavery as a form of labor mobilization to the overwhelming political clout that the aristocracy still held in much of the world. That old regime had created the conditions for industrial capitalism's emergence, but over a decades-long process, it was devoured by the new regime it had birthed.[154] Industrial capitalism became a new totality.

One of the areas where industrial capitalism's impact was most strongly felt and where it changed the life courses of the greatest number of people was, perhaps surprisingly, the world's countryside. Industrial capitalism had, in fact, sprung forth from the countryside and in turn recast it.

8.

Capturing the Hinterland,
1780–1860

Enslaved workers powering commodity frontiers: Departure for the
Coffee Harvest by Ox Cart, Vale do Paraíba, Brazil, *circa 1885.*

The heavily fortified Château de Joux towers over the valley of the Doubs, a river that for much of its serpentine flow marks the border between France and the Swiss canton of Jura. More than two centuries ago, the life of Toussaint Louverture, an insurrectionary leader, general, and famous statesman, ended there. On August 25, 1802, Louverture arrived from Haiti as a military prisoner. A few harsh winter months later, he died, a grim close to an unlikely career: He had successfully challenged one of the world's most powerful nations, France, and one of the most deeply rooted systems of labor exploitation, plantation slavery, founding out of these ashes the second republic on American soil—the Republic of Haiti. When he was taken from his beloved homeland, he warned his captors that "[i]n overthrowing me you have cut down in Saint-Domingue only the trunk of the tree of liberty, it will spring up again from the roots, for they are many and they are deep."[1]

In the wake of the Industrial Revolution, commodity producers in the world's countryside struggled to meet expanded demand. At exactly this moment, the mostly illiterate and propertyless revolutionaries of Saint-Domingue turned on their enslavers and set in motion not only, as Louverture predicted, a century of political upheaval but also, less obviously though just as consequentially, the transformation of global capitalism itself. By ending Saint-Domingue's world-leading production of sugar, cotton, indigo, and coffee, half a million enslaved workers along with an elite of free Black *gens de couleur* sparked a century-long struggle against slavery, rerouted the production of agricultural commodities away from long-dominant Caribbean islands, and sowed the seeds for what eventually became new systems of labor. Haiti created winds of change nearby (the expansion of cotton production in the United States, sugar production in Cuba, and coffee planting in Brazil) and far away (indigo harvesting in India). These short-term dispersals of commodity production to new regions affected areas and peoples around the globe; in the longer term, they dealt a massive blow to the slavery system that had enabled capitalism's penetration into large swaths of the world's countryside. Together they exemplify how the most consequential changes in capitalism's history originated not only in countinghouses or stock exchanges but with the world's least powerful people. The massive fortifications of the Château de Joux, where Louverture spent his final hours, testify to the grave threat that states and capital owners saw in the economic, social, and political liberation of the world's enslaved workers.

Before Louverture entered the scene in 1791, Saint-Domingue produced more than any other colony in the Caribbean, with a very large enslaved workforce of over half a million people laboring on a sprawl of plantations—three thousand for indigo, twenty-five hundred for coffee, eight hundred for sugar, another eight hundred for cotton, and fifty for cocoa. As elsewhere in the Americas, European entrepreneurs combined unprecedented control of the land with unprecedented control over the labor of the African people they had forcibly transported and enslaved under brutal conditions of toil to clear, seed, tend, and harvest enormous quantities of crops for distant markets.[2]

While virtually all of Saint-Domingue's people were enslaved, a small but growing class of free people of color emerged. By 1790, they were numerically equal to the small white population. Some had become wealthy plantation owners themselves, though they still were not legally equal. Inspired by the French Revolution's ideals of "liberté, égalité, fraternité," these gens de couleur—under the leadership of Vincent Ogé, a wealthy free man of mixed ancestry—rose up to claim these rights. Their rebellion was crushed. Then, in 1791, rumors began circulating among the enslaved that the king of France had promised them three days off a week to cultivate their own subsistence plots. A new insurgency emerged.[3]

In August of that year, enslaved and free Black people rebelled in the fertile northern sugar plain on the estate of the Marquis de Galliffet, notorious for its cruel labor exploitation and low life expectancy: Few of the marquis's enslaved workers were older than forty, and almost none would celebrate their sixtieth birthday. Of the fifty-seven African captives who had arrived there in February 1789, twelve died within the first year. On August 21, enslaved workers woke manager Pierre Mossut "to talk to him."[4] Their rebellion spread rapidly to neighboring plantations, where people assailed overseers and burned equipment and homes. As the owner of one plantation reported to an absentee owner of a nearby property: "Your houses, Monsieur le Marquis, are nothing but ashes, your belongings have disappeared, your administrator is no more. The insurrection has spread its devastation and carnage onto your properties."[5]

Across the ocean, among Bordeaux's merchants, the panic over "these horrors" was just as real.[6] Bordeaux merchant Georg-Christoph Bapst, whom we have already encountered, asserted in 1791 that "[n]o one, as you know, is more interested than we are in the peace and tranquility of the colonies."[7] Ironically, the insurrection had some short-lived but extremely positive side effects for him and other Bordeaux merchants. Prices of sugar, coffee, cotton, and indigo soared to "dizzying" heights.[8] With the part of Saint-Domingue where Bapst traded

Enslaved workers rebel: revolution in Saint-Domingue, an image from 1797.

less affected by the upheaval, he had high hopes that planters would finally pay off their debts: "[L]uckily, for us, the district of Saint-Marc has not felt the effects of the commotion at all," resulting in a "high price of commodities."[9] But in 1792, Bapst received more worrisome dispatches from Saint-Domingue: Madame d'Abnour had taken refuge from her plantation in Petite Rivière, planter Lefèvre de la Paquerie was in a "deplorable" situation, and other planters had had their homes and fields burned, plundered, and destroyed, sometimes with "an unheard-of cruelty," according to one French observer.[10] To the horror of merchants such as Bapst and slave owners everywhere, the workers of Saint-Domingue had shown that they could fight the intense repression that had terrorized generations. Bapst warned "that the commerce of Bordeaux could not forget that its connections with America made its existence," but the French government failed to suppress the revolution.[11] With no effective French countermeasures, Pierre Alexandre de Saint-Martin, one of the co-owners of the company, reported to investor Peter Heinrich von Bethmann in Frankfurt: "[T]he news continues to be very distressing."[12]

By the spring of 1792, insurrectionary workers had carved out an autonomous zone made up of hundreds of former plantations in the northern plain just as Revolutionary France went to war with Prussia and the Habsburgs. No stranger to European geopolitics, Toussaint Louverture, the leader of the rebellion, allied with Spain in exchange for weapons vital to sustain the revolt. Territorial losses and the threat of Spanish encroachments forced the French colonial government to make concessions, for all could see that "the defence of the colony itself depended utterly upon securing the military support of the slaves in the name of revolutionary France."[13] In a series of decrees over the following two years, slavery was abolished, first only for those fighting for the republic in the North and then, eventually, for all. Louverture ended his alliance with the Spanish, but through much of the 1790s, he continued waging civil war against rump elements of the old order, invading British forces and competing leaders among the gens de couleur. By March 1800, Louverture emerged the unequivocal victor. Not trusting France's commitment to emancipation, he drafted a new constitution in 1801. The following year, Napoleon ordered an invasion to reinstate slavery and arrest Louverture. While Louverture was captured, it was a Pyrrhic victory. Backed by a popular uprising in the South, Louverture's successor, Jean-Jacques Dessalines, defeated the invasion, and the Republic of Haiti formally declared full independence in 1804.[14] At a tremendous cost in lives, Haitians had seized on French revolutionary ideals and, as so often in colonial rebellions, assistance from the colonists' European rivals to end slavery and replace it with self-government in what had been the world's most profitable slave society.

The global implications of the revolution were massive. Just as factories were demanding more cotton, workers more calories from sugar, and hardworking capital owners more coffee to stay awake, the world's most important producer stopped producing. Sugar output from Haiti fell from 75,000 metric tons in 1790 to 900 tons in 1795. By 1795, coffee exports plummeted to just 980 metric tons from the 35,000 tons produced in 1790. Indigo production completely collapsed.[15] The most important producer of a crucial set of goods had gone off-line, a move akin to modern Saudi Arabia ending its oil exports at the very moment that the demand for its products rose rapidly. A frantic and global search for new suppliers ensued, recasting the countryside over wide swaths of the earth.

Many white plantation owners had been killed; others had fled to neighboring slave states, such as Cuba or the United States. John Montalet abandoned his Caribbean cotton plantation for Georgia, where he immediately converted a rice plantation to cotton. Former slaves appropriated Haiti's abandoned estates, pillaging their former enslavers' wealth and pursuing a profoundly altered vision for how best to use the fertile lands. Almost everywhere, they quickly expanded their garden plots and, in the face of wartime chaos, produced for themselves or for local markets. Working their own small plots was the ultimate marker of their freedom.[16]

Bordeaux's merchants paid a price: When trader Jean-Jacques Bethmann wrote to his business partner Pierre Desclaux in April 1793, he observed that "[w]e have just done the balance of our books and the result is not very satisfactory. . . . [T]he revolt of the negroes at Saint-Domingue brings an immense loss to our commerce."[17] That revolution also bankrupted Romberg, Bapst & Cie in 1793—not surprisingly, considering that 93 percent of its business was in Saint-Domingue. When the company's accounts were settled in 1807, a staggering thirty-four million livres tournois (about $122 million in 2024 US dollars) had been lost.[18]

The unfolding Industrial Revolution in Europe and North America—itself enabled by prior waves of the great connection, intensification of manufacturing, and transformation of the countryside—exponentially increased pressure on agrarian producers as ever more ravenous machines and consumers fueled new demand for food and fiber, and the need for markets for its ever more ample production. For investment in fixed capital assets like factories to be profitable, capital owners needed a predictable stream of inexpensive inputs. At the same time, a massively growing industrial working class demanded food and stimulants—about 9 percent of calories consumed in the United Kingdom came from abroad in 1800 and 22 percent in 1850. Merchants scouted the world in search of urgently needed cotton, sugar, coffee, tea, and wheat, forging new commodity frontiers— places of freshly commodified land and labor.[19]

As a result of their efforts, by 1800, production elsewhere had replaced Saint-Domingue's exports, with 500 million pounds of sugar, 84 million pounds of cotton, 125 million pounds of tobacco, 120 million pounds of coffee, and 40 million pounds of tea streaming into Europe—a radically accelerated movement of commodities across oceans.[20] Industrial capitalism's enormous appetite for raw materials in Europe and North America pushed capital into the hinterland farther and faster than merchant capital ever had. As the rhythm of machine production now infused the world's countryside, bulk commodity trade replaced the more modest transoceanic commerce of earlier centuries.

As we have seen, by the early decades of the nineteenth century, industrial capital had become the driving force of the capitalist revolution. But that revolution depended on further transformations of the countryside and, at least initially, breathed new life into existing strategies for radical expansion—enslavement and new dispossessions. Factories needed workers, raw materials, markets, and energy, all of which came from where the vast majority of humanity (indeed, almost everyone) still lived—the countryside. To enable low wages, workers required cheap food. The countryside was as much a site of urban capital's massive expansion as the infernal mills we are more familiar with. As new factories, power sources, and machines drew manufacturing out of rural areas and into cities, a counterbalancing surge of motives, tools, capital, and institutional power transformed rural life. This transformation rested on millions of workers; indeed, many more than labored in the fledging industries of the first half of the nineteenth century. The rhythm of industry now, for the first time, began to dictate the rhythms of life in the countryside, not least because the greater importance of fixed capital depended on the velocity of circulation. And as industry expanded, these frontiers also became important markets for industry: By the mid-1840s, for example, India had become the United Kingdom's most important export market for manufactured wares, paid for by India's cotton, indigo, and opium exports.[21]

Industrial capitalism drew into cities the sun, water, and nutrients of the world's countryside as much as it did the mental and physical energies of its agrarian workers. It engaged nature predatorily, drawing on ecological resources as free inputs that were not priced on markets and often leaving ecological devastation behind. Forests were logged to fuel sugar evaporators; water was redirected to allow cotton to thrive; and nutrients were removed from the soil to feed coffee trees until the soil gave out and planters found new territory to exploit. Commodity frontiers always moved, drawing on ecological resources that had yet to be exploited and exhausted, searching for ever more takings from nature, concentrating and transferring not just the world's labor power but also its ecological resources into the emerging industrial heartlands.

Industrial capitalism's new pressure on the global countryside after 1780 generated one last flourishing of war capitalism—the fabulously effective system of redistributing the world's resources by dispossessing land, enslaving workers, and allowing ongoing predation by capital owners who often enjoyed sovereign powers in distant lands. Despite the departures of industrial capitalism, large swaths of the commodity-producing countryside remained within the confines of that old regime. In 1770, one million enslaved people had labored in Cuba, Brazil, and the United States; by 1860, the almost six million slaves in these three countries produced about half the world's coffee, three-quarters of its cotton, and one-third of its sugar.[22]

Land dispossession also took on truly continental scope. Indigenous peoples lost control of more land in the wake of the Industrial Revolution than in the three centuries before 1800 combined—perhaps nowhere more radically than in the United States. At the same time, corporate territorial rule swelled: The Dutch East India Company expanded its holdings, as did French, English, and Danish companies, a testament to private capitalists' continued role in dominating rural cultivators. As in prior centuries, war capitalism's political economy rested as much on physical coercion as on market forces. Tellingly, India went through an "intense militarisation" in the 1830s: Of 42,108 Europeans living in India, a staggering 36,000 were military personnel. During that same decade, British planters, worried about rebellious slaves on the Indian Ocean sugar island of Mauritius, hardened their military installations and kept their troops in a constant state of preparedness.[23] Old-regime war capitalism expanded and radicalized as vast tracts of the world's countryside were newly transformed into a hinterland of the emerging centers of industrial production. At the same time, war capitalism generated new resistances, as we saw in 1790s Saint-Domingue, and eventually also the conditions for its own overcoming.

Textiles, as we have discussed, stood at the center of the Industrial Revolution, and the needs of this rapidly expanding industry had the most dramatic impact on the world's countryside; it generated the tightest connection between industrial and war capitalism. No commodity was in more urgent demand than cotton, not least because fewer people produced their cloth at home. Between 1789 and 1815, cotton imports into the United Kingdom almost tripled, the result of the requirements of machine production.[24] Before 1750, European manufacturers had sourced cotton from places like western Anatolia, West Africa, and India, where local rural cultivators harvested small quantities to feed their own production and sold any surplus to local merchants, who brought it to port cities for shipment to distant manufacturing locations. By the mid-eighteenth century, these sources could no longer meet rising European demand. Planters in the Americas began growing cotton for European markets using the tried-and-true methods of war capitalism—expropriating lands from Native inhabitants and importing enslaved workers. This intense new form of cotton agriculture took hold in parts of Brazil and on almost all Caribbean islands, nowhere more successfully than on Saint-Domingue.

When revolution ended most cotton production there, the United States stepped into the void, soon enlarged by another former French possession: French Louisiana. Drawing on European capital, enslaved labor from the declining tobacco plantations of the Upper South, Indigenous peoples' land, and a novel machine—Eli Whitney's cotton gin—the United States rapidly became the beating heart of world cotton agriculture. Three years prior to Whitney's invention, cultivators in the United States had produced a modest 1.5 million pounds of cotton, compared with 6.3 million pounds exported from Saint-Domingue during its heyday in 1789. In 1800, US cotton exports amounted to 36.5 million pounds; in 1820, 167.5 million pounds. Exports to Britain alone multiplied ninety-three times during the 1790s, only to increase another seven times by 1820. By 1802, the United States was the single largest supplier of cotton to Britain, and by 1860, three-quarters of cotton worked up in European factories came from the United States, harvested by about one million enslaved workers. Some cotton still came from the Ottoman Empire, and its Egyptian province in partic-

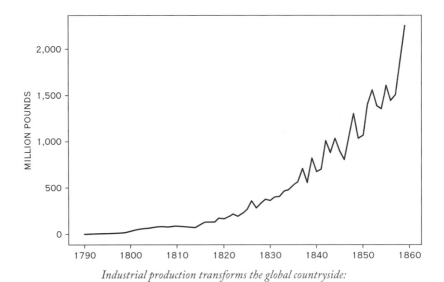

Industrial production transforms the global countryside: cotton production in the United States, in pounds, 1790–1860.

ular produced significant amounts for world markets, with merchants from Palestine to the Nile Delta investing in expanded production.[25] But the proven power of combining enslaved labor with massive new tracts of dispossessed land allowed the United States to quickly capture a majority stake in world cotton markets. "The immense strides made in the cultivation of cotton in the United States; the comparatively cheapened supply . . . gives to it an importance second to none in the world," British cotton expert James A. Mann noted in 1860.[26]

American planters were intensely aware of the critical role that forced labor played in their ascent. In the quarter century before the closing of the international slave trade to the US in 1808 (as stipulated by the US Constitution), traders raced to import 170,000 enslaved women, men, and children; after the ban, traders transported a million enslaved workers from the Upper to the Lower South, mostly to grow cotton, which reinvigorated the institution that some antislavery activists had briefly hoped might die out in the wake of the decline of tobacco agriculture. White family farmers also grew cotton, but their share of the total crop was small. The value of the uncompensated labor time coerced from enslaved workers was very substantial: It has been estimated that between 1776 and 1860, the forcibly forgone wages of the enslaved in the United States amounted to between $5.9 and $14.2 trillion in 2021 US dollars, assuming a modest 3 percent annual interest on the unpaid wages—a huge subsidy of the enslaved to the Industrial Revolution in the North Atlantic.[27]

As more slaves were put to work, the pace and management of their work intensified. American landscape architect and social critic Frederick Law Olmsted noted in 1861 how the organization of work under slavery affected output: Traveling through the American South, he observed the "machine-like manner" in which African Americans were forced to labor.[28] Between 1800 and 1860, their productivity increased by as much as 400 percent. There is disagreement about how that productivity increase was achieved; some scholars argue that it was the result of superior cotton varieties, or "biological innovation," while others contend that it was the result of severe labor exploitation—either through innovations in violence or more intense supervision.[29] Most likely it was both. Broadly similar to the slavery system that unfolded on Caribbean sugar plantations, American cotton plantations also sped things up by marrying industrial techniques to agriculture. The steam engine, for example, enabled the American plantation complex to expand into new territories, with steamships transporting cotton bales up and down rivers and, eventually, railroads carrying them to ports.

The Mississippi Delta was the center of the American cotton industry—it was for cotton what Saudi Arabia was for oil in the twentieth century.[30] Situated in the northwest corner of Mississippi, it extended roughly seventy miles across and almost two hundred miles from top to bottom, from Vicksburg in the south to Memphis in the north, bounded by its namesake river to the west and the Yazoo River to the east. When Mississippi became the twentieth state admitted to the Union in 1817, the Delta was populated by Chickasaw and Choctaw living in as many as fifty villages. They were, according to two 1891 writers, "a large and powerful tribe . . . in possession of an immense territory . . . which embraces the most fertile and productive soil in the world."[31]

Reports of the Delta's amazingly fertile soils drew tens of thousands of settlers. North Carolinian Daniel Jordan set out for Mississippi in the early 1830s, excitedly expressing his hopes for quick prosperity in a letter to his wife: "[H]ere I can make *money*. . . . [I think] I can in this State make as much money in 5 years as [any] man should want and then I can return home to my friends with pleasure."[32] Annual cotton production in Mississippi increased an astounding 146 times between 1811 and 1838—from 884,000 pounds to almost 129 million pounds. No US state produced more cotton by the 1830s than Mississippi.[33] When French engineer Michel Chevalier visited the United States in the mid-1830s, he was awed by how experimentation and the fertility of the soil made for a level of dynamism and change such as he had never seen before:

> If movement and the quick succession of sensations and ideas constitute life, here one lives a hundredfold more than elsewhere; all is

here circulation, motion, and boiling agitation. Experiment follows experiment; enterprise succeeds to enterprise. Riches and poverty follow on each other's traces, and each in turn occupies the place of the other. . . . An irresistible current sweeps away everything, grinds everything to powder, and deposits it again under new forms. Men change their houses, their climate, their trade, their conditions, their party, their sect; the States change their laws, their officers, their constitutions. The soil itself, or at least the houses, partake in the universal instability.[34]

What made this intense dynamism possible was dispossession, slavery, capital, and political power.

First, land: As South Carolinian statesman John C. Calhoun thundered in Congress in 1817, "Let us conquer space."[35] Capital-owning planters like him agitated ceaselessly for the dispossession and removal of the Delta's Native inhabitants. Between 1820 and 1832, the United States government executed three treaties, backed by military force, that resulted in what can only be described as a form of ethnic cleansing: The government deported the Choctaw, Chickasaw, Creek, Cherokee, and Seminole peoples from their ancestral territories, transporting them hundreds of miles west to arid, less fertile lands.[36] When Mississippi's preeminent cotton men gathered at Parker's Hotel in Natchez to celebrate, they toasted President Andrew Jackson: "He found one half our territory occupied by a few wandering Indians. He will leave it in the cultivation of thousands of grateful freemen"—and, of course, their slaves.[37]

The removal of Indigenous peoples allowed the United States government to survey and sell their lands, unlocking a tidal wave of white settlement. In 1833, the United States sold over a million acres of Mississippi lands, double what it sold in any other state. The majority of these lands were purchased not by "thousands of grateful freemen" but by land companies backed by New York, Boston, or European capital owners. The New York and Mississippi Land Company, for example, was incorporated in 1835 by New York merchants and bankers Joseph D. Beers, Benjamin L. Curtis, and Morris Ketchum. Advertising "Cotton Lands for Sale," they made short-term investments designed to bring swift returns and enormous profit. They flipped the land as quickly as they had acquired it, doubling its price in the process. Other companies followed suit, including the Boston and New York Chickasaw Land Company and the New York, Mississippi, and Arkansas Land Company. One company described its goal as to control the land "at the Cost of the poor Aborigines."[38] These speculators, in one historian's estimate, doubled or tripled their capital as they used US and European investments to acquire lands and cheaply empty them of their original inhabitants.[39] For Peggy Scott Vann Crutchfield, one Cherokee observer of this process, the ultimate goal was clear: "Our neighboring white people seem to aim at our destruction," she wrote in an 1818 plea to the government to stop deportation.[40]

Capital flowed to the Delta in other ways as well. Starting out in cotton was capital-intensive: One historian estimated that acquiring the land, clearing it, and buying the labor for a sixteen-hundred-acre plantation cost about $150,000 at the time—more than $4 million in 2024 dollars. Local merchants and bankers provided that capital, secured by mortgaged land, but they drew on the resources of the world's financial centers. When the state of Alabama issued bonds to capitalize its banks, it sold them in New York, Boston, Paris, and London. In 1838, Mississippi capitalized its Union Bank by issuing $15.5 million in state bonds, around a third of which were sold in England. These seemingly neutral, legal financial instruments—deeply embedded in a globe-spanning system of credit—were instrumental in the dispossession of Native peoples.[41] Only with capital could the lands be turned into productive plantations and could their owners afford to purchase armies of enslaved laborers.

Cotton growing was indeed labor-intensive, and in the Delta, almost all of that labor was enslaved. Planters, according to contemporary writer Joseph Holt Ingraham, sold

> cotton in order to buy negroes—to make more cotton to buy more negroes, "ad infinitum," is the aim and direct tendency of all the operations of the thorough-going cotton planter; his whole soul is

wrapped up in the pursuit. . . . [W]ithout slaves there could be no planters. . . . Without planters there could be no cotton; without cotton no wealth. Without them Mississippi would be a wilderness, and revert to the aboriginal possessors. Annihilate them tomorrow, and this state and every southern state might be bought for a song.[42]

It is not surprising, then, that between 1830 and 1840, the number of enslaved people in Mississippi more than tripled to 194,000. In the Mississippi Delta alone, the slave population increased almost sixfold. By 1830, when 1,976 people lived in Washington County, 1,184 of them were enslaved—a concentration reminiscent of Caribbean plantation economies of previous centuries. By 1840, there were more than ten slaves for every free person. Planter Andrew Turnbull owned twenty-six slaves in 1830; by 1835, he controlled the labor power and lives of ninety-six people. On average in 1850, Delta planting families held eighty-two enslaved workers.[43]

Outside capital enabled massive enslavements; as a form of private property, slavery, in turn, enabled outside investments: Slaves were the ultimate hedge against volatile global commodity markets. Cotton factors, slave traders, and bankers secured their business first and foremost on the cotton that enslaved workers would grow. If its value dropped or the crop failed, enslaved workers served as collateral that could be liquated at any time, given the tremendous demand for slaves on the still-legal internal market. By 1827, the Consolidated Association of the Planters of Louisiana (CAPL) created even more leverage by securitizing slaves: allowing stockholders to draw on half their value if they mortgaged them. In 1828, the British merchant bank Baring Brothers bought $1.67 million of CAPL bonds to resell on European securities markets. Baring Brothers sold the bonds in units of $500 and $1,000—not coincidentally roughly the average price of one young enslaved man at the time—which paid 5 percent in annual interest and matured after ten to fifteen years. They would, in effect, generate revenue for investors around the world based on planters' repayment of mortgages taken out on their slaves. For $500, investors around the world could purchase minute portions of the profits reaped through the unpaid labor of thousands of enslaved workers. Such was the explosive alchemy of capital, enslaved labor, and dispossessed lands that even distant investors who never owned an enslaved person and lived in countries where slavery had been abolished could still draw profit from the slavery complex.[44]

⸻

After 1800, the sugar commodity frontier also surged, devouring ever more lands and enslaved workers as sugar changed from a luxury good to a necessity for the burgeoning number of industrial workers who needed calories but did not grow food. In the late eighteenth century, sugar for European markets had mostly been cultivated in Jamaica, Martinique, and, especially, Saint-Domingue. When the latter fell into the hands of its former slaves, and later, when slavery was abolished on the British sugar islands in 1834, production in some of the old sugar colonies, such as Jamaica, plummeted: British colonies had produced 50 percent of the world's sugar in 1815–1819, but their output fell to just 25 percent in 1838–1842.[45] French Caribbean production also declined.

Staggering from these losses, planters and merchants pivoted toward the theretofore lightly exploited Cuban countryside, quickly turning the colony into the world's premier producer of cane sugar, with a production ten times greater that of Saint-Domingue at its height. Cuba, ruled by Spain, had produced sugar for a long time, but as late as 1792, its small sugar plantations had a relatively modest output of only 14,455 tons. After the Haitian Revolution, however, the sugar frontier expanded into Havana's hinterland and then into new areas like Matanzas, about sixty miles to the east.[46] As one observer wrote in 1837:

> Getting towards Macurijes, one passes on the road long stretches of woods and clearings, evident signs of an emerging culture that

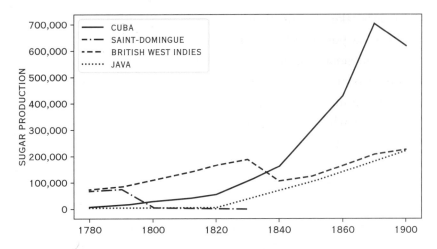

The Cuban sugar revolution: sugar production in metric tons.

extends through those wild terrains. Now here the valleys have ceased; in general a flat soil, lightly undulated in parts, extends to the horizon that the eye can see; next to an already developed farm can be seen an uprooting of woodlands; beyond, the fire consumes a clearing that is going to be converted into an extensive cane field, and indeed everything is here a creation of man and improvement of nature.[47]

After two decades of breakneck clearing and expansion of cultivated land, sugar production had almost quadrupled to 54,906 tons by 1820. A census of Cuban sugar mills taken in 1827 found a staggering one thousand mills producing 76,669 tons of sugar. These mills were also larger and more productive, with the average output six times as large as in 1775. As with cotton, the rhythms, technologies, and dynamics of the Industrial Revolution increasingly set the tempo in Cuban sugar fields, expanding output to 295,000 tons in 1850 (a quarter of global production) and 720,250 tons in 1868.[48] This expansion helped transform sugar into an affordable commodity for Europeans and North Americans.

The spectacular increase was first and foremost the result of the transportation of 780,000 enslaved workers from Africa to Cuba between 1791 and 1867.[49] The control of enslaved labor on an industrial scale launched the flywheel of an industrial boom.

In addition to slavery, other factors enabled the expansion. Legal changes in 1815 allowed planters to cut down Cuba's forests, making virgin territories and land available to the nutrient-hungry cane. By the 1830s, the sugar frontier annually consumed as much as fifty-two thousand acres. The resulting deforestation, a contemporary remarked, brought about the "ruin of our mountains," with a concomitant precipitous loss of biodiversity.[50] Three years after declaring Cuba's forests fair game, the Spanish colonial government tried to appease Cuba's restive elite by letting them trade their sugar freely, and not just with the Spanish imperial metropole. As a result, the United States became the principal market for Cuban sugar, and American capital poured into the modernization of the Cuban industry.[51]

A year later, in 1819, the colonial government broke with centuries of colonial policy and offered its existing land grantees clear ownership title, making land private property—not least to more firmly tether colonial elites to the motherland. At midcentury, Cuba hosted a stunning one hundred land surveyors, as investors sought to document and secure their rights to improvements in perpetuity.[52]

The mass importations of slaves, the deforestation, and the changes in property law encouraged the use of new technologies, intensifying the impacts of all three factors. Vacuum evaporators, a technology perfected on Cuban plantations, and centrifuges improved the processing of the cane sap. Cuba also became a hot spot for the widespread uses of steam power. An observer of the time described the "magic presses, those apparatuses, those trains that are simple and easy to direct, compensating with an astounding economy of fuel all that the machines consume. Large-scale improvements are seen wherever you look. . . . The slaves in a mill were expensive, but also their necessity has been diminished to a considerable extent."[53] No wonder productivity jumped.[54]

Steam also enabled new economies of transport: The first Cuban railroad opened in 1837, making Cuba the second country in the

William Clark, Ten Views in the Island of Antigua, *1823*.

Americas with the technology, ten years ahead of its colonial overlord, Spain. The railroad enabled the inexpensive transport of sugar to Cuban ports, giving "new life to everything like a river."[55]

The radicalism of the Cuban sugar revolution becomes visible when we look at the hamlet of Banaguises, situated about 125 miles east of Havana, near the city of Colón, a newly emerging center of the Cuban sugar industry. The Júcaro Railway connected it to the port of Cardenas, about 42 miles distant, as early as 1847, and soon a full 168 miles of railroad tracks connected local sugar mills to the port. The inflow of capital and workers transformed the Colón area: By 1859, 46.4 percent of its land was dedicated to sugar, and by 1876, cane's share was 71 percent. The average Colón plantation cultivated almost one thousand acres of cane.[56] Contemporary observers were awed: By 1857, "[n]o person who is concerned with the agricultural interests of the island, can ignore the extraordinary development that the plain of Banaguises has experienced, nor fail to be aware of the number of beautiful mills that have been formed in its fertile lands as if by magic."[57]

Some of the world's most modern sugar mills sprouted in Banaguises. Julián de Zulueta's Alava plantation, for example, processed the

Bringing the Industrial Revolution to the world's countryside: steam engines, Narciso Plantation, Banaguises, Cuba, 1857.

Slavery and steam power in the Caribbean:
Ingenio Alava, Cuba, 1857.

rich produce of its flat, fertile black soil with a fifteen-horsepower steam engine and a network of private railroad tracks that went from the fields to the grinding mill and from there met public tracks that went to the port of Cardenas. Its first harvest was in 1847, and by 1853, the plantation produced 7.35 million pounds of sugar. One contemporary described Zulueta as "very inclined to manufacturing advances, [he] was the first who at the cost of great sacrifices established by means of a test the triple-effect apparatus with vertical tubes, the Derosne system."[58] Alava was just one of several plantations that Zulueta owned, a form of horizonal integration that, by 1866, let him maximize his workers' productivity by moving them from one plantation to another.[59]

Alava was surrounded by other large sugar plantations: Ponina, Conchita, San Nicolas, Santa Gertrudis, and Narcisco. The Marqués de Arcos's nearby Ingenio el Progreso was planned like a factory, its layout designed to create the most efficient workflow, one capable of extracting the greatest added value from its 550 enslaved people of African descent and its 40 indentured Chinese workers. The Ingenio la Ponina had a forty-horsepower steam engine manufactured by New York's West Point Foundry.[60] An observer remarked on the "great intelligence and high knowledge[,] both theoretical and practical[,] of its owner who has become the administrator of his property."[61] Also in Banaguises, the Ingenio Purísima Concepción drew on the labor of 989 enslaved workers.[62]

Banaguises, like the rest of the Cuban sugar industry, was strikingly modern. A writer looking at it in 1857 was struck by the "regularity and symmetry" of "[t]he numerous factories . . . [which] offer the traveler from a certain distance the appearance of one of those beautiful European manufacturing towns," and suggested that a visitor would be surprised by the factories' location "in the tropics" rather than where they would be expected—in the old world so distinguished by "order and industry."[63]

A modern sugar industry also emerged elsewhere, albeit on a smaller scale, following the Cuban formula of matching cutting-edge technology with one of the oldest and most violent labor systems. Between 1803 and 1820, the British steam engine producer Boulton & Watt, a technological leader of the early nineteenth century, sold 114 steam engines to what later became British Guiana (now Guyana). Heavy investments by British merchants fi-

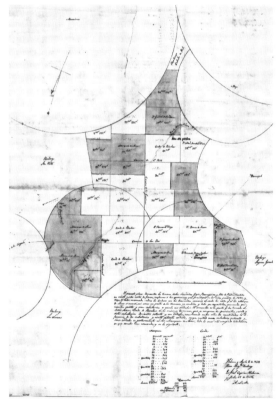

Simplifying nature: plantation lands at the sugar commodity frontier in Banaguises, Cuba, 1837.

Slavery profiteer: Sir John Gladstone, owner of more than two thousand enslaved sugar workers in British Guiana in 1833 and father of future Liberal British prime minister William Gladstone.

nanced slavery's expansion: Half of all plantations exploited more than 200 enslaved women, men, and children, while nearly all—94 percent—mobilized at least 100. Output increased rapidly: Profits rose and investors plowed funds into ever more slaves. Some of these plantations were gigantic: In 1833, John Gladstone, father of future British prime minister William Ewart Gladstone, exploited 2,508 enslaved Africans. Meanwhile, the output per enslaved worker tripled between 1810 and 1834.[64]

British Guiana and Cuba show how the mixture of modern technology and enslavement could vastly increase and cheapen agricultural production. The legal and technical capabilities honed in these war-capitalist zones also flourished where slavery was not the prime mode of labor mobilization, including in Asia, where an export-oriented sugar complex started growing out of its ancient industry. In 1800, Asia still produced as much as 70 percent of global sugar, yet its share of global exports was just 6 percent, a figure that slowly increased to 29 percent in 1900.[65] This expansion was partly the result of a concerted effort at technology transfer from the Caribbean to Asia, as many West Indian planters prepared for emancipation of their workers by diversifying throughout their respective empires.

In India, British colonial authorities did not adopt anything as bold as the Cuban system, instead connecting to precolonial systems of sugar production that aggregated sugar from local producers without dominating production itself. Long-standing patterns of landholding continued to shape huge tracts of land and agricultural activity, making it difficult to drastically recast agriculture. Still, while exports between 1790 and 1813 had amounted to only about eleven thousand tons annually, by 1847, they had grown to sixty thousand tons—one-tenth of Cuban capacity.[66]

The Dutch on Java followed suit, but with a different strategy. While sugar production dominated by Chinese merchants had a storied past, by 1800, it had run out of steam, literally—the forests needed to power the boiling rooms had been cut down and the soil exhausted. The Dutch initially addressed these problems by bringing coal-powered steam engines to the Javanese countryside. While this solved the fuel problem, these expensive machines only turned a profit with a constant flow of cane. Soon the Dutch colonial administration began a concerted campaign to motivate cultivators to produce more cane.[67]

Javanese sugar production really took off after 1830, when Governor-General Johannes van den Bosch introduced the so-called *Cultuurstelsel*—Cultivation System—which lasted until 1870 and guaranteed a flow of inexpensive cane into the modern factories. The transformation of the countryside was something of a hobbyhorse for Van den Bosch: Before traveling to the East Indies, he had set up vagabond work camps and enclosed common pastures in the northern Netherlands. He applied these lessons to Java, arguing that agrarian societies showed a "lack of responsiveness to external [economic] stimuli" and therefore needed strong measures to convert to cash crop production, a common enabling myth among nineteenth-century colonists who sought self-flattering explanations for why the allegedly natural laws of the market did not do their expected work when it came to colonial peoples.[68] Van den Bosch told King William I in 1827 that only compulsory labor would enable Java to compete on the world market:[69]

> Given the circumstances I have presented, and taken in relation to the aforementioned advantageous location and the resultant cheaper transport, more fertile soil and cheaper labor costs in America above Java, I think I can safely deduce that intended

products for Java, namely sugar, coffee, and cotton, cannot be grown by hired workers.[70]

Like so many early nineteenth-century political economists, he had no qualms about the ethics of his proposed system of forced labor, which he defended by claiming that even "free" labor requires coercion:

> I think it pertinent to assume that the basis of labor, above and beyond that which directly satisfies our animalistic needs, is the consequence of coercion; that this coercion often presses most heavily on the laborer's existence when he appears most free, and that when such coercion does not exist or cannot be implemented, man will not work more than that which is necessary to satisfy his most direct animalistic needs.[71]

The Javanese commodity frontier already relied on military power, dispossession, the destruction of local polities, and the coercive appropriation of labor—all core features of war capitalism. What Van den Bosch focused on was making cane available to the mills by forcing cultivators to grow it. He required them to invest in the most modern systems of production—which was possible because he guaranteed them a market—and all sugar produced was automatically acquired by the semi-governmental Nederlandsche Handel-Maatschappij (Netherlands Trading Society), or the NHM, for export. Established in 1824, the NHM was a quasi-monopolistic company in which King William I was the largest investor.[72]

The overarching feature of Van den Bosch's plan was to assign each village a cash crop to deliver to factories for fixed and low "plant wages." The factories did not own the land, but they got exclusive rights to cane harvested in certain areas. Villages were obliged to set aside a portion of their land—about one-fifth—to produce commercial crops for the Dutch. Peasants could also be forced to carry out corvée labor in the factories, on infrastructural projects, or in transportation.[73] Backed by the coercive power of the state, Javanese aristocrats relied on this web of legal obligations to force peasants to deliver cane. The

NHM and the so-called cultivation banks also provided rural cultivators advances to plant sugar, ensuring its delivery on pain of default. As elsewhere, both state and nonstate actors gained new powers in the global countryside.

As a result, sugar production in Java surged from 6,000 metric tons in 1820 to 102,000 in 1850 (that is, many times faster than in India) and continued expanding for decades. In 1820, Javanese sugar represented just half a percent of the global market; in 1850, its share was 4.7 percent of a much larger market. The NHM's fixed-rate purchases of cash crops from factories—a gamble for the Dutch Treasury—paid off handsomely. Between 1850 and 1854, Cultivation System sugar profits stood at 3.4 million guilders; between 1855 and 1859, this had grown to 33.7 million guilders. By this time, almost one-third of the Dutch government's income came from its East Indies profits.[74] The wages of war capitalism accrued not just to private adventurers but also to the state.

Before the system drew its first direct profit, it had another effect: the creation of a consumer market for goods produced by emerging industry in the Netherlands, especially textile mills that had been coaxed to the town of Twente in the eastern (Dutch) part of the country after the Belgian Revolution, which erupted in 1830 and ended with independence in 1831. It was Van den Bosch who then suggested bringing British engineers to the Netherlands to help set up factories so that NHM ships would not be empty on their journeys back to the Indies. Sugar imports also supported the mechanization of sugar refining in Amsterdam and Antwerp—just one of the more obvious ways that the transformation of the countryside continued to feed metropolitan industrialization.[75]

Some of that sugar went into coffee, which was now being grown most intensively in Brazil. Coffee's long history of production and consumption began in the Arab world, especially in Yemen, where small peasant cultivators had a monopoly on coffee production in the two centuries before 1720. Their output was modest, and as late as the 1780s, coffee was a luxury even in the Middle East. Over the nineteenth century, however, its markets expanded in northern Europe and the United States, the stimulating properties of coffee a perfect match for the intensifying work regimes of an industrializing world. In the United States, per capita coffee consumption jumped more than 162 times in the hundred years after 1783, translating to a 2,400 percent increase in total coffee imports. By 1859, Americans consumed nearly one-third of the world's coffee harvest.[76]

Thanks to efforts by European states and merchants to move the coffee plant to other regions of the world in early instances of biopiracy, by the 1780s, this crop had expanded along a global coffee frontier that mobilized peasants through forced cultivation under a VOC monopoly in Java, as well as enslaved workers on plantations in Saint-Domingue and Surinam. As in so many areas, Saint-Domingue quickly surpassed all other producers, displacing Yemeni coffee from even the Cairo market. In that French colony, production costs were uniquely low, with an unprecedented elasticity of output. Though Saint-Domingue had produced just 12 percent of the global coffee harvest in 1755

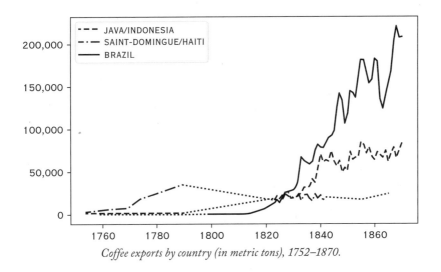

Coffee exports by country (in metric tons), 1752–1870.

(compared with Yemen's 45 percent that same year), by 1790, 158,000 enslaved workers in Saint-Domingue produced 50 percent of world output (compared with Yemen's 17 percent). This was in no small part due to the vast expansion of the Dutch coffee trade into new German markets along the Rhine. Saint-Domingue planters pushed coffee production from five million pounds in 1770 to seventy-six million pounds in 1786, while Yemen's output remained level at twenty-four million pounds, showing that peasant agriculture could not compete with the world's slave lands.[77]

After the Haitian Revolution, the labor-intensive coffee frontier moved yet again: Jamaica saw an upswing in coffee exports in the 1790s, as did Cuba, where the uncle of pioneering Swiss industrialist Alfred Escher—one of the founders of the Swiss Liberal Party, the bank Credit Suisse, the insurance company Swiss Life, and Switzerland's most prestigious university, the ETH Zurich—grew coffee on a slave plantation. Alfred's father, Heinrich, later inherited and liquidated this plantation, an oft-repeated story that reveals the symbiotic connections between the world's slave lands and its industrializing heartlands, between slavery and latter-day national heroes. Despite these efforts by Cuban and Jamaican planters, however, before 1825, global coffee production expanded relatively slowly compared with other high-demand commodities.

But then it exploded. First, Dutch interests in Java pushed coffee deeper and deeper into rural areas, and the Cultivation System enabled ever more coffee to pour out: In 1790, the island had produced 1,678 tons; in 1840, its output was 70,000 tons.[78] Then Brazilian planters used war capitalism's large-scale land appropriation and human enslavement to focus on coffee. Between 1815 and 1830, Brazilian coffee production increased annually by an astounding 22 percent. Whereas Brazil had exported, on average, a meager 374 metric tons from 1807 to 1811, it exported sixteen times as much by 1820. Exports reached 28,800 tons in 1830 and surpassed those of Java in 1840, reaching 78,660 tons. Java's production stayed put thereafter, but Brazil's exploded to 182,850 tons in 1860. That year, it produced 55 percent of the world's coffee.[79]

Brazil became the center of the world's coffee industry for the same reasons that Cuba dominated sugar and the United States cotton: a combination of a lot of suitable land and planters who forced a vast number of enslaved workers into the coffee fields. The transatlantic slave trade with Brazil was the most intense in the entire history of slavery, with 1.2 million enslaved Africans arriving in Brazil during the first half of the nineteenth century, almost all to work on coffee plantations. In addition, between 1850 and 1881, coffee planters bought 220,000 enslaved workers from elsewhere in Brazil. The high fertility of virgin rainforest soil; the ease with which planters could drive Indigenous people, unable to muster much military resistance, off this soil; and the access to a seemingly inexhaustible supply of enslaved labor allowed plantation owners to survive agricultural productivity's age-old nemesis: declining prices.[80]

In the 1820s, the most significant of these new coffee frontiers moved into the Paraíba Valley, just west of Rio de Janeiro, pushing the

War capitalism as fantasy:
coffee harvest in Brazil, 1830s.

Indigenous Coroado and Goitacá peoples out. Coffee planters transformed huge areas into coffee plantations. One Dutch traveler observed that "one may ride for hours through coffee plantations."[81] As coffee production expanded, prospective coffee planters brought ever more slaves into these territories. In 1828, the town of Nova Friburgo counted 2,887 inhabitants, 1,272 of whom were enslaved. By 1872, there were 25,546 people, 11,574 of whom were enslaved. Slave ownership there and elsewhere became ever more concentrated, and in the 1870s, 60 percent of all enslaved workers labored for the 5 percent of planters who owned more than 100 slaves.[82]

Drawing on enslaved labor, British and especially American capital, and state-sponsored infrastructure improvements, such as railroads, the coffee frontier for decades managed to outrun the rapidly depleted soils that resulted from its myopic focus on short-term profits by moving farther west within the Paraíba Valley and then west of São Paulo. With the 1808 arrival of the Portuguese royal family in Brazil (it was fleeing advancing French troops) and then Brazilian independence in 1822, Brazil could trade more freely, opening up the massive US market and importing more enslaved workers. By the 1850s, the D. Pedro II and São Paulo Railways, built largely with British capital, efficiently moved coffee to the ports. As with cotton in the United States, the lack of overlap between economic and political spaces was crucial to the expanding coffee frontiers: British capital could invest in the slavery complex, even though slavery by that time was illegal in the British Empire; American coffee markets could be supplied thanks to the unpaid labor of newly enslaved workers from Africa, even though it was now illegal for the US to participate in the international slave trade.[83]

Coffee planters, like their sugar counterparts in Cuba and the cotton lords in the United States, became politically powerful and used that power to protect slavery and the international trade regime that enabled it.[84] They accumulated vast wealth, often reflected in grand, refined homes and travel to the capitals of bourgeois opulence, such as Paris. They also formed the electoral base of the Conservative Party, Brazil's most important proslavery political force.

The production of the vital commodities that fueled the Industrial Revolution shared common factors: They all experienced extraordinarily fast increases in output, rapidly falling prices, and the infusion of European and, later, US capital. Enslaved workers and machines meant that unit costs often, but not always, dropped ahead of price erosion. And slave labor usually outcompeted peasant production. Coercion depressed prices.[85] As emancipation swept parts of the Atlantic world after 1834, it seemed to confirm British politician Lord George Bentinck's fears about the impact of slavery's end: Looking at the declining state of Jamaican agriculture in the 1840s, he doubted that "free labour could compete with slave labour."[86] In 1848, the editors of the British journal *The Economist* fretted similarly:

> We little dream, when we exult over the manufacturing ingenuity of Birmingham, Manchester, and Leeds, or when we admire, without exultation, the kindred products of Elberfeld, Silesia, Verviers, and Liège, or when we feel grateful for the rich products of the vineyards of the Garonne, which we only share with the planters of Brazil and Cuba, that we are exulting and admiring and grateful for the means of stimulating the slave trade, which we otherwise take so much trouble and are at so much cost to repress.[87]

Slavery's role in transforming the global countryside in the wake of the Industrial Revolution is hard to overstate. Forced workers produced many of the core commodities of the global economy in the nineteenth century. In 1851, the "cottonopolis" Manchester employed 17,771 wageworkers in its textile industry, a concentration of human labor that inspired both celebration and consternation among stewards of European culture, ideas, and mores. Less remarked upon but arguably equally essential to the unfolding of industrial capitalism were the 76,337 enslaved workers in the Mississippi Delta who grew cotton for those mills. Globally at midcentury, about 2.5 million enslaved workers were directly involved in producing coffee, sugar, and cotton—making the slavery complex one of the largest industries of its time. Another million people, as we will see, grew indigo under conditions of debt peonage not far removed from enslavement. This compares with about 873,000 workers in Europe's leading mechanized manufacturing industry—cotton textiles—and about 270,000 coal miners.[88] Even during the Industrial Revolution, some of the frontiers of the capitalist revolution were still located in the world's slave lands.

Many contemporaries recognized slavery's importance. In 1856, German naturalist Moritz Wagner had no doubts about "[t]he commercial importance" of slave labor for "our daily joys and needs."[89] Herman Merivale, a British colonial administrator and professor of political economy, agreed that

> [n]early all our sugar, and the greater part of our cotton, tobacco, and coffee, not to mention other and less important articles, are raised by negro labour; nine tenths of which is that of slaves. About one third of our export trade is now carried on to slave countries, and the products which we receive in exchange for the goods which we send there are raised by slaves. . . .
>
> We speak of the blood-cemented fabric of the prosperity of New Orleans or the Havana: let us look at home. What raised Liverpool and Manchester from provincial towns to gigantic cities? What maintains now their ever-active industry and their rapid accumulation of wealth? The exchange of their produce with that raised by the American slaves.[90]

The Dutch colonial bureaucrat C. F. van Delden Laerne, who traveled to the Paraíba Valley to study Brazilian methods of coffee planting and learn lessons to bring back to Java, had a similar appreciation of slavery. Indeed, he was pessimistic about the possibilities of coffee agriculture without slavery: "[I]f one sets aside the basis on which everything rests viz. the slave labour by which the soil is cleared and planted, everything collapses at once."[91] Wageworkers, he explained, were reluctant to work on coffee estates, except for what he perceived as unsustainably high wages.[92] For *The Economist*, slave-grown produce was a perhaps unwelcome but necessary feature of the global economy: When some called for the embargo of Brazilian coffee imports in the 1840s, the journal pointed out that "if this policy is to be acted upon, on principle, it must extend to the exclusion of *all* articles produced in whatever country by slaves," including "*cotton*, the *rice*, the *indigo*, the *cochineal*, and the *tobacco* of the Southern States of America."[93] That was obviously an unimaginable course of action, not least because, as *The Economist* pointed out, it would "inflict a severe punishment on the millions of hard-working, ill-fed *consumers*."[94] "To refuse slave-grown sugar for the purpose of putting down the slave trade," A. Oswald argued in the British House of Commons, "and then to take slave-grown cotton . . . was to strain at a gnat and swallow a camel."[95]

The golden age of industrial revolution was thus also a golden age of slavery, the "second slavery," as it has been dubbed by scholars. It was characterized by a new emphasis on industrial rhythms and managed productivity in slave production, the infusion into the fields of some of the world's most advanced technologies, and a symbiotic relationship with new, often liberal state institutions. And its importance was not limited to the mobilization of labor power—it also included slaves' role as collateral that secured unprecedented mobilizations of capital.[96]

SLAVERY'S IMPORTANCE IN mobilizing agricultural labor to churn out the foodstuffs and raw materials necessary for industrialization comes into sharpest relief when we look at the many futile efforts to produce these crops using other labor systems. The almost universal failure of these experiments testifies, in a roundabout way, to the tremendous inertial resistance to the revolutionary spread of capitalism and its attempts to convince people in myriad traditional roles to primarily create commodities for distant markets.

Beginning in 1817, for example, the French colonial administration hoped to produce exportable cotton and indigo on the west coast of Africa. Concerned about the stability and reliability of slave labor and eager to make up for lost Caribbean production—Haiti loomed large in the white collective imagination—colonial administrators laid out plantations along the Senegal River near the town of Richard Toll (named for the French governor and the Wolof word for "garden"— *toll*), on land rented from the king of Waalo, Brak Amar Fatim Mborso, not far from the centuries-old trading city of Saint-Louis. They hired wageworkers from surrounding areas and, in a most unlikely scenario, also brought more than two hundred workers from Martinique to toil on the plantations. African wage labor was to make up for the loss of enslaved Africans' labor in the Americas.[97]

Things at first looked good for Governor Julien-Désiré Schmaltz's plans: He built military posts at Dagana to protect these agricultural settlements, Futa landowners provided access to land, and the chief of Dimat agreed to supply the necessary labor. Schmaltz negotiated with Waalo's king, and a first treaty was signed to allow for agricultural colonization as early as January 27, 1817.[98]

As they would soon discover, however, conditions along the Senegal River differed in significant ways from those in the Mississippi Delta, the Colón plains of Cuba, or the Paraíba Valley in Brazil. For one, the French could not unilaterally impose their will—they had to bargain with local rulers, merchants, and aristocrats, many of whom were hostile to agricultural projects that took land and labor away from their own agricultural activities. Indeed, these colonial designs were so controversial that in March 1820, a military confrontation ensued in which fifty Waalo-Waalo warriors died and one hundred were taken prisoner—a terrible toll for the Waalo-Waalo, yet by no means a fatal blow to their continued military, political, and economic power.[99]

Schmaltz's efforts were wrecked on the rocky shoals of active resistance and the refusal of local cultivators to part with their land and labor. But the French did not give up: In 1822, Jacques-François Roger, the new governor, started another, more substantial effort to construct a plantation economy that could overcome dependence on American slavery. That year, French authorities received a long report on the potential for export agriculture in the Senegal River Valley. While the author described the region as a "hot, arid, unpleasant and unwelcoming sandy landscape," he also reported on the cows and goats that rural cultivators raised and on the existence of cultivated lands abutting the river that he deemed suitable for establishing sugarcane, cotton, indigo, and cacao plantations. He observed that there was plenty of food, the local people peaceful, and the area easy to defend in times of war. The problem, as he saw it, was labor: The local cultivators, he alleged, worked only as much as needed to satisfy their needs, caring primarily about pleasure and rest—not, in his eyes, a promising situation.[100]

Despite such concerns, cotton was planted, some by French colonists and some by Indigenous merchants from Saint-Louis. The plantation revolution there and elsewhere was knowledge-intensive, and experts—geologists, agronomists, soldiers, lawyers, and others—advised on how to transform the land. Despite the perceived urgency to secure raw materials for French mills, the emerging cotton sector languished at first, then surged modestly by 1825, when it processed the bolls of almost one million cotton plants from the region's thirty-four small cotton plantations.[101]

Indigo agriculture began that same year, with seeds that the colonial government had shipped from Bengal to Senegal for plantations run by both the colonial administration and French planters. Struggling to understand how to grow indigo, planters requested and received frequent and extensive reports from Indian experts. Nonetheless, the indigo output remained minuscule, amounting to only 763 kilograms in 1827. There seems to have been just six indigo plantations left by 1828. The French colonial administration reported reduced cotton and indigo harvests. Despite the ever more intense and frequent production of reports and statistics, French efforts had essentially collapsed by 1830.[102]

At the root of the French failure lay Senegal's entrenched and powerful social, political, and economic structures, which gave local people the ability to mount an effective resistance. Planters frequently expressed their concerns about the military might of the Waalo-Waalo, and the government was urgently concerned with "eliminating that threat of fundamentally hostile groups."[103] As a French colonial bureaucrat put it: "Our policy must be to reduce, destroy if possible, or at least move away from our establishments, those ferocious neighbors with whom we can never hope to enter into a durable accommodation."[104] Even when local rulers were willing to collaborate, their tenuous hold on power meant they did not have an easy time providing the land and labor that the French required. Moreover, African merchants in Saint-Louis, whom the French hoped would invest in agricultural undertakings, were less than enthusiastic, as their trading activities were much more profitable than agrarian investments. Local rulers were also wary of the spread of wage labor, which they feared would weaken their grasp on workers bound by conditions of hereditary servitude. Local cultivators, meanwhile, refused to work for planters: They saw wage labor as servile—so much so, indeed, that they attacked workers who had agreed to such employment. And when the French could hire workers, their wages were too high to make the projects profitable.[105] Roger observed "a certain discontent among the natives, or rather a vague anxiety at seeing us form agricultural establishments in the African interior."[106]

In such a settled social order, recruiting labor proved an insurmountable challenge. The colonial archive is full of planters' complaints about promised workers never reaching them. In May 1827, for example, the colonial administration bemoaned that the production of indigo still could not begin "because [a planter] lacked the workers," even though "nothing is more urgent to the interests of the colony" than to get these projects underway.[107] In 1828, urgent appeals to transfer desperately needed workers to indigo factories persisted. And even when the French advocated for "peasant agriculture" to provide cotton, rural cultivators refused to provide such harvests. In 1824, Senegal exported 14,386 kilograms of cotton; ten years later, that figure had dropped to just 3,047 kilograms.[108] The different values and interests of local power holders and French colonists eventually led to the complete disintegration of the plantation project.

By contrast, successful transformations of the countryside usually went along with almost complete control over land, labor, and political power, none of which was yet possible on the African continent. After the British had ruled the area around Saint-Louis along the Senegal River for a few years, the colony's then governor, Lieutenant General Charles William Maxwell, reported similar frustrations in 1811:

> Indeed a considerable quantity of cotton is gathered for the manufacture of cloths both in the settlement and in the native villages and is obtained at a very cheap rate. The character of the natives is too indolent to form any reasonable hope of their being ever cultivated by them for exportation.[109]

Only after 1855, when the French military had greater control of the territory, could Waalo cultivation become at least partially geared toward world markets, while the focus of French efforts increasingly moved farther south toward the center of the colony and into peanut production.[110]

FROM THE PERSPECTIVE of European bureaucrats and capital owners, Senegal was just one failure among many: Considering cotton's importance to the British economy, and the obvious instability of slavery, it was hardly surprising that the British also tried to produce cotton without slavery elsewhere. The most significant of these efforts centered on India in the 1840s, when the East India Company helped create experimental farms run by US-born cotton planters. American cotton farmer W. W. Wood had "entertain[ed] the Idea for some time of going to India to cultivate the Cotton plant on my own account," and, supported by the East India Company, he went in 1842 along with other planters, seeds, gins, and implements.[111] Unable to enslave workers, as was possible in the Americas, the EIC hired them for wages or contracted with local cultivators for a share of their cotton harvests.[112]

Yet despite the planters' "zeal and diligence," the project failed. A poorly developed infrastructure and a mismatch between American ways of growing cotton and the requirements of Indian agriculture were two reasons, but more importantly, the project encountered tremendous resistance from rural cultivators: When the American planters wanted to use so-called wastelands to cultivate cotton, local rural cultivators rejected this move, since "they have been able to feed their cattle without expense upon the wastelands." According to the Americans, these cultivators also worked with less care in the planters' fields than in their own. There was also outright opposition: "Mr. Mercer [one of the US farmers], a few weeks ago, had his bungalow burnt down, and the estate and works, together with his whole property, destroyed, except the suit of clothes he had on him."[113] Frustrated that they were "obliged to give way to [their workers'] prejudices," the planters complained endlessly about their laborers' "laziness," the pilfering of cotton, strikes, and their general inability to "succeed in obtaining labor." They concluded that "cultivation by paid labor could, under no circumstances, be profitably applied to Cotton in that part of the country," not least because it was "quite impossible to secure any laborers; the few by whose aid he [one of the American planters] had sown a little patch of ground . . . were driven to work for him only by temporary necessity, and would soon leave him."[114]

So unhappy were the American farmers and the British colonial officials with their Indian workers that they advocated what they called "a little gentle coercion." Orphans were one possible labor source, convicts another. As these efforts failed too, so did the European-run cotton plantations. Unlike in the United States, planters seeking hypergrowth in 1830s India had to deal "with local rulers, . . . power structures, . . . property ownership patterns, and . . . ways of producing things" that made it extraordinarily difficult to transform the countryside.[115]

Indeed, capital-fueled transformations of the countryside provoked resistance almost everywhere. In Ireland, dispossessed rural cultivators violently struck back at their dispossessors. When one British colonial settler tried to take land from an Irish peasant in the late 1830s, the woman took revenge: "It seems it was by an axe his skull was broken, and his brains scattered abroad."[116] In 1820s Java, efforts by the Dutch to increase coffee production failed just as resoundingly, as peasants refused to do wage labor and the Javanese elite pushed back. Rural cultivators in central Mexico engaged in almost constant struggle to keep commercializing capitalists at bay, and they largely succeeded. Estate owners needed laborers to work their lands, but the workers prioritized their own fields before they showed up elsewhere.[117] In the 1840s, when planters tried to privatize communally held Indigenous lands to enable commercial sugar growing around the town of Chalco, southeast of Mexico City, they met dogged resistance from Indigenous peoples and years of often violent strife, with cultivators marching, as one estate manager remarked, "armed with stones and sticks."[118] After unavailing interventions by troops and armed guards, the estate manager contended: "The attack made the indios the masters of the fields and left the authority that is supposed to instill respect in them in a sorry predicament."[119]

People in the countryside throughout much of the world thus still exercised some control over their economic, and often also political, lives. That power rechanneled commodity frontiers into those parts of the world where rural cultivators' sway was, or could be, broken. It also funneled capital into different institutional arrangements that went beyond the tried-and-true forms of war capitalism. Though these novel and varied forms often still depended on some degree of extra-economic coercion—and showed, as often as not, war capitalism's paternity—they demonstrated that commodity frontiers could draw on more than just slavery: Wage labor, indentured labor, sharecropping, tenant farming, and family labor were all possible.[120] They pointed to a future beyond the slave lands, one only dimly perceived by midcentury merchants in their never-ending quest for cheap supplies and by a small subset of industrialists whose experiences with mobilizing labor by paying wages suggested that the labor regimes of industrial capitalism could, perhaps, be deployed in the world's countryside as well. Given the right circumstances, contract could do the work of coercion.

Despite the failures in Senegal and western India, Africa and Asia paved the way. As slavery in the Americas came under new pressure in the wake of the Haitian Revolution and British abolition, commodity-trading European and American merchants looked to these continents to fill gaps in supply—despite encountering wealthy, powerful local capital owners and social structures that were by no means easily dislodged.

One way to do so, however, was to draw on the commodity frontiers organized and financed by the wealthy merchant communities of China and India. Tea was a prominent example. To satisfy demand, both domestically and internationally, Chinese merchants pushed tea growing deeper into the countryside, but in ways that were fundamentally different from its closest equivalent—the coffee frontier. Building upon a more than millennium-long history of producing tea as a cash crop, itinerant merchants (what the Chinese called "guest merchants") purchased tea from independent producers. Some of these traders—the *hongs*—owned tea fields, but most merchants were just brokers or contractors. They provided two-thirds of the tea's value as an advance to growers, canceling the debt upon delivery of the product.[121]

As a result of such efforts, tea was by 1840 the fourth-most-valuable good produced in China, after grain, cotton cloth, and salt. With between 23 and 41 percent of the harvest exported (about eighty-one million pounds), it was also China's most important export; tea, indeed, brought China into the nineteenth-century global economy. Between 1719 and 1833, 70 to 90 percent of all exports from Guangzhou, China's epicenter of trade, consisted of tea. Thanks to energetic military and fiscal machinations, much of the tea exported from China was traded by the East India Company. Between 1792 and 1828, as exports approximately doubled, a quarter of the EIC's profits derived from that trade alone. By the end of the nineteenth century, British workers dedicated no less than 10 percent of their food budget to tea. US consumption grew as well. It is said that by 1860, a ship arrived from China in the port of New York every week, mostly loaded with tea, a business that set a young American entrepreneur, George Gilman, on his path to creating the world's largest food retailer, the Great Atlantic & Pacific Tea Company, later known as A&P.[122]

As demand for tea skyrocketed, the EIC doubled down on its strategy to exchange Chinese tea for Indian-grown opium, making it the world's largest narcotics trader, with a reliable—addicted—and growing consumer base in China. In 1828, opium exports from India to China amounted to $15 million in US dollars (about $476 million in 2024 dollars), a substantial sum even when compared with US cotton exports of $22 million (about $640 million in 2024 dollars) that same year.[123] Eventually, British forces "opened up" the Chinese market, including for opium, in the aptly named First Opium War of 1839–1842. The Second Opium War in the 1850s compelled the legalization of the drug in China.

As a result of such military market opening, tea exports exploded, leading to an expansion of production. Merchants pushed tea agriculture

Making the world safe for drug traffickers: British forces attack and capture Chusan (the largest island in an archipelago of the same name) on July 5, 1840.

Chinese tea warehouse in Guangzhou. Chinese artist, circa 1800.

even deeper into the countryside. Uncultivated terrain at higher altitudes was newly dedicated to tea. Buddhist and Taoist temples lost control of some of their lands to capital owners in the valleys, while small producers turned into tenants and migrants into wageworkers.[124]

Chinese merchants—to enable such expanding output—also pushed for greater control of production, especially of tea-leaf processing. With between one hundred and one thousand workers employed during the processing season at tea-processing plants, owners like Jiang Yaohua of Huizhou increasingly controlled, regulated, and sped up the labor process. When he wrote his manual *An Outline for Making Tea*, he described the tea-making process, focusing on workers' productivity. One way of measuring and increasing output was to burn incense sticks to gauge time and expect workers to accomplish certain tasks within these units of time—a system much like Frederick Winslow Taylor's more widely known efforts to enhance industrial efficiency in the late nineteenth century. Productivity could be increased without the introduction of new machines, a lesson widely applicable to commodity frontiers the world over.[125]

As the tea frontier transformed part of the Chinese countryside,

British capital owners aimed for greater control of tea production as well. Unable to gain such powers in China itself, where they encountered a weakened but still capable state, they transplanted the tea plant to a part of the world where it had not been previously grown—Assam, which the British had turned into a protectorate in 1833. With the transformation of forestlands into large tea plantations, the dream of the tea garden under the auspices of European capital became real. This feat was so significant that members of the Tea Committee, tasked by the British government to set up tea plantations in Assam, reported, perhaps somewhat exaggeratedly, that it was "by far the most important and valuable [discovery] that has ever been made on matters connected with the agricultural and commercial resources of this empire."[126] Kirkman Finlay, whom we previously encountered as a Scottish cotton industrialist, moved some of his capital into exactly such plantations, showing that industrial capital could metamorphose into agrarian production just as much as vice versa. When local laborers, who had access to subsistence outside capital's control, predictably deserted the plantations or rebelled, imported indentured workers from distant areas powered this newly emerging tea complex.[127]

India would also become the site of yet another crucial commodity frontier powered by labor mobilized by contract, not enslavement—that of indigo, as Bengal was turned into the world's most important producer of the blue dye. Ruled by the English East India Company since 1757, Bengal had for centuries been the source of the world's finest cottons, sometimes colored by the brilliant blues of the indigo plant, a leaf locally grown from time immemorial and since at least the thirteenth century exported, in very small quantities, as far away as Europe. For a long time, indigo competed with European woad, a plant that also produced blue dye. French king Henri IV threatened the death penalty against anyone using Asian-grown indigo but failed to protect Languedoc woad growers. By 1750, these prohibitions had ended, and the indigo that dominated European markets was now grown not just in Asia but on the colonial slave plantations of the Americas, with French Saint-Domingue the largest source.[128] No sooner had European manufacturers become dependent on this source, however, than Toussaint Louverture's revolution threw its dominant supplier into turmoil.

As manufacturers struggled to access indigo elsewhere, Bengal emerged, in their eyes, as the best solution, since it was well suited to indigo production and already within the East India Company's territorial purview. Under the company's watch, Bengal's indigo exports to Britain increased by roughly a factor of forty in the last two decades of the eighteenth century. By 1815, Bengal almost exclusively supplied all textile manufacturing regions of the world.[129] Production peaked in 1842, when it accounted for 46 percent of the value of all exports from Calcutta and indigo factories had become "responsible for the welfare of millions of people."[130] This sudden shift was emblematic of the pace and magnitude of the forces unleashed by industrial manufacturing and its supercharged markets for raw materials and finished goods.

Shifts like this were not solely or even primarily caused by the

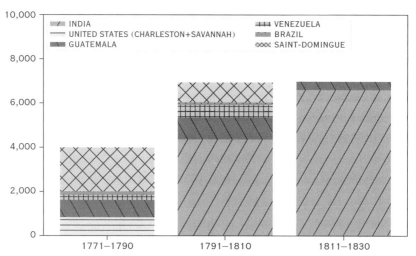

Expansion of indigo production, 1771–1830: annual averages in metric tons.

workings of markets. Indigo came to Bengal largely because of a concerted effort by the East India Company. Tasked with improving the "[r]aw products of British India so as to render them fit for the general Consumption of the Manufacturers of Great Britain," eager to solidify its territorial control over Bengal, and fortified by the migration of Caribbean planters, the EIC rapidly expanded indigo production.[131] It alone enjoyed sufficient political and economic power to move land, labor, and capital onto markets at a sufficient scale.[132]

To make Bengal's rural cultivators produce indigo for world markets, the EIC had to dismantle its earlier social and political structures, a project that succeeded, unlike French efforts on the shores of the Senegal River. One of the most significant actions taken was making changes to tax policies. In prior decades, Bengal weavers had lost export markets for their cottons, leading to widespread impoverishment—a crisis vastly worsened by a famine in 1770 that killed as many as ten million people. To avoid tax payments, suffering peasants left their home villages, which hurt the company's land-based revenue. In 1793, the EIC responded by creating the Permanent Settlement Act, which taxed zamindars—landowners—and not rural cultivators. Intended to simplify collection and encourage these landowners to improve their newly surveyed and assessed land, the act built upon precolonial schemes of extracting resources from the countryside while giving landowners property rights similar to those enjoyed by Europeans. By making land into private property, it undermined traditional social connections and systems of mutual obligation that had long characterized local landownership.[133]

Once land became a marketable commodity, it could serve as security for loans, and in the decades after the new tax law passed, merchant capital poured into indigo production. Much of the capital came from so-called agency houses—firms that pooled the resources of merchants, EIC employees, and wealthy Bengalis. The first indigo factory, as these businesses were called, was built by a Frenchman near Chandannagar in 1777. By the 1830s, there were as many as 829 indigo

Reshaping the global countryside:
Bengal indigo factory, 1857.

firms—some very small, others major concerns—like the British Ear-skin & Co., which owned twenty factories, or the Bengali firm of Joy Chand Palchowdhuri, which owned thirty-two.[134]

Like cotton, coffee, and sugar, indigo was a labor-intensive crop, and the ability to mobilize sufficient numbers of workers proved crucial. Already by the 1820s, more than a million people in Bengal tended and processed the crop. Some undertakings were gargantuan. Almost eight thousand people labored for the Mathurapur factory alone; the Kaliachak factory was said to employ more than eleven thousand people, some as manufacturing workers, others as carters, transport operators, or workers in "indirect employment"—contractually obliged to deliver certain quantities of indigo to the factory for a certain price.[135] The work was revolting, as the fermented urine used to extract the blue dye from the leaves of the plant emanated an overpowering stench. Despite such conditions, it was, according to one colonial official in 1785, "[t]he cheapness of labour in Bengal" that made this part of the world perfectly suited to indigo production.[136]

In the Americas, indigo had been produced by slave labor. In Bengal, a variety of labor regimes took hold. Wage laborers who lived on factory premises processed the raw indigo. But most people who worked in the indigo industry worked in the fields, not in the factories. Two different labor regimes emerged there: Under the *nij* system, indigo planters rented or purchased large tracts of land from zamindars and then contracted with peasants to work it. This system remained marginal because the most fertile areas were densely settled, making it difficult to acquire contiguous pieces of land. The *ryoti* system was far more common. Rural cultivators, known as ryots, rented land from zamindars and then signed contracts with indigo planters. These planters provided the cultivators with cash advances that they could use, for example, to pay the zamindars, and in turn obliged ryots to plant indigo on at least a quarter of their land.[137]

In both systems, the relationship between the peasant and the indigo company was contractual.[138] At first, the contracts were attractive because they offered cash. After 1825, however, when indigo prices fell, it no longer paid to grow indigo—the ryots were obliged to "cultivate at a loss," as a British observer noted in 1861, "compelled to carry on such cultivation" by a system of advances that bound them to the factory.[139] According to the special commissioner to the secretary of the government of Bengal, concerned with peasant protests, "The Report of the Indigo Commissioners has sufficiently proved that the cultivation of Indigo is unprofitable, and that it is a compulsory cultivation."[140] According to a British colonial official, "Indigo cannot be grown at the rate . . . quoted except under the influence of strong compulsion."[141]

Indigo processors and planters did not enslave cultivators, but they did force them to grow the crop; it was, as a British colonial official remarked, a "system of pressure."[142] They threatened to increase rents and expelled recalcitrant tenants at will. Advances they provided to tenants when markets dropped had interest rates so high that cultivators entered a state of debt bondage.[143] Moneylenders, as elsewhere in the global countryside, gained control over agrarian production. In addition to these contractual pressures, labor conditions on indigo plantations were harsh and often included bodily coercion. Considering

Millions of workers labored in the global countryside to churn out commodities for European industry, here harvesting indigo in India.

that many planters started out on Caribbean slave plantations, this is not surprising. Yet there was a deeper reason: Many cultivators quite reasonably refused to grow and deliver the contractually stipulated quantity of indigo once it became unprofitable. At this point, the ways that planters forced their cultivators to produce that indigo were so repressive and violent that the later British secretary at war, Thomas Babington Macaulay, called it "a state not far removed from partial slavery."[144] In letters to his father, indigo factory manager Thomas Machell commented on the "violent nature" of indigo growing; he wrote about "the distress, the poverty, the utter ruin of the labourer" and how many "are driven from their miserable homes to become beggars and robbers over the country."[145] An English writer described in 1861 "the oppressions which the Ryots have really endured under the system of the Indigo planters": working "like slaves, without payment for their labour, by such means of compulsion as imprisonment, flogging, pulling down or burning their houses, ploughing in their crops, rooting up their date trees and gardens, seizing their cattle, sometimes even beating or spearing them to death, in short, by an organized system of oppression."[146] For many British colonists, however, the system was legitimate because it was contractual: Antislavery efforts had laid the groundwork to categorically divorce slavery from all other forms of labor exploitation, including that of Bengal's nominally free ryots. Yet the system was so deeply oppressive that by the 1860s, rural cultivators launched a large-scale revolt that, as we will see later, brought it to collapse.[147]

If the indigo frontier combined contracts with coercion, the wheat frontier moved from coercion to contract. Wheat cultivation expanded in two different ways. For one, production intensified in places where wheat had historically been grown. In England, for example, output rose from 703,000 metric tons in 1800 to 2.9 million tons in 1850; in France, it grew from 3 million tons in 1815 to 6.6 million tons in 1850. This happened even though the area under cultivation expanded only modestly.[148] Though continuing enclosures eliminated common grazing rights to "waste" and fallow lands, most of the increased output was due to improved techniques such as crop rotation and, later, imported fertilizers, first whale blubber and ground-up bones, then manure and guano. Alternate husbandry let more land remain under cultivation, as nitrifying crops and manure replaced the need for fallow land. In Britain, the expansion of wheat production lasted until the repeal of the Corn Laws in 1846, after which cheap imports from Russia brought down prices and replaced domestic producers. In France, enclosures also concentrated lands in the latter half of the eighteenth century, and new husbandry with "English methods" took hold in the early nineteenth.[149]

Grain production also intensified in the German and Italian lands, as well as in China and Japan, but much more radical expansion occurred where plentiful, fertile land became available: Russia and the United States. At the core of both was territorial expansion. While productivity remained at low levels compared with western Europe, Russia's grain exports more than tripled between 1800 and 1860,

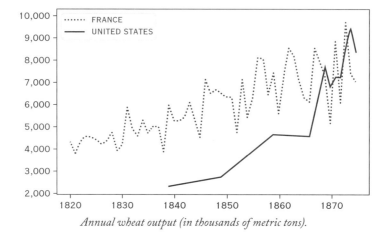

Annual wheat output (in thousands of metric tons).

reaching 1.1 million tons. For decades, the imperial state had encouraged colonists to move into Russia's southern frontier, a frontier that moved as new territory was acquired: Novorossiya from the Zaporozhian Cossacks in 1775, Volhynia from the Polish-Lithuanian Commonwealth in 1793 and 1795, and Bessarabia from the Ottomans in 1812. Already in 1763, Catherine II had published a manifesto declaring that in Russia, "a great many . . . [p]laces for the settlement and Habitation of Mankind . . . remaine yet uncultivated."[150] The manifesto offered encouragements to settle in these new areas, covering foreign migrants' travel costs, allowing foreign landowners to buy Russian serfs, and guaranteeing non-enserfment to foreign cultivators. These efforts at colonization were ramped up in the 1780s, when Prince Grigory Potemkin was given the task of asserting control over the military frontier. The empire granted four-thousand-acre plots to mostly aristocratic elites, who were required to populate them.[151] Poles, Mennonite Germans, Bulgarians, Greeks, and Moldavians settled on state lands, joining serfs, fugitives, and religious outcasts from other parts of the empire, as well as formerly nomadic Cossacks forced to settle on estates. Novorossiya's population ballooned from 600,000 in the early 1780s to 2.4 million in 1850, with many growing wheat. These "frontier" estates, often massive operations cultivating up to one thousand acres, accounted for much of Russia's increased output, and by the late 1850s, more than a third of Russia's exports consisted of wheat. At that point, 700,000 wagons transported grain to Black Sea ports.[152]

While workers on the Russian wheat frontier were not actually enslaved, coercion was still central: Many serfs labored on wheat fields as part of their corvée duties. They worked alongside hired laborers and a class of legally free peasants who lived on landlords' estates but owned movable property and could arrange their own marriages and settle elsewhere. Even enserfed peasants were initially offered more generous terms by frontier landowners, who sometimes allowed them to buy their freedom or limited their *barshchina* (corvée) obligations to two days a week. Landlords, in turn, overcame short-term labor shortages by resorting to imprisoned workers from other regions in Russia. But with population increase on the wheat frontier and the depression in global wheat prices during the third decade of the nineteenth century, terms became increasingly unfavorable for laborers. Many landlords abolished freedom of movement and peasants' right to buy their freedom; over time, barshchina obligations were steadily increased, sometimes up to six days a week. Serfs became ever more like American slaves, while serf owners gained newly strengthened property rights in land and labor. Coercion remained central.[153]

Almost contemporaneous with the southward expansion of the wheat frontier in Novorossiya was the wheat frontier's westward expansion in the United States. The Land Ordinance of 1785 had developed a mechanism to survey and sell massive areas of land west of the Appalachians. More land was added to these holdings through the Louisiana Purchase in 1803, the conquest of Indigenous American lands, and eventually the 1846–1848 Mexican-American War. The federal government sold much of that land at public auction, first with a high minimum acreage and price. But by 1832, the prices and minimum acreage auctioned had dropped so much that a forty-acre farm could be had for as little as fifty dollars. Veterans of the Revolutionary War, the War of 1812, or the Mexican-American War even received free lands.[154]

Early nineteenth-century Indigenous communities in most of the United States could not defend their autonomy over the long term. Given a small but determined state aligned with private capital, dispossession of Indigenous lands paved the way for the expansion of wheat agriculture into the American Midwest, just as it had on the cotton frontier in the South. Infrastructural improvements—first canals and roads, then railroads—undermined the sway of Indigenous peoples and opened markets for farmers engaged in commercial agriculture.[155]

As the wheat frontier pushed farther west, new farms required intensive labor to clear the land and break the prairie soil. Farmers usually relied on their families, hiring and paying additional help when needed. While farms remained owner-operated, increasing input costs over the course of the nineteenth century meant that a greater proportion of farmers found themselves indebted and tenanting their land from larger landowners. By 1880, Great Lakes states had between 9 and 31 percent of their farmers tilling tenanted land—a substantial number, though the majority of wheat-growing land still was owned and worked by the farmers themselves.[156]

The wheat frontier moved through Ohio and into the Mississippi Valley, especially the states bordering the Great Lakes. In 1800, the United States had produced around 660,000 tons of wheat, of which it exported a meager 10,000 to 15,000 tons; in 1850, US wheat production had skyrocketed to 5.2 million tons, of which it exported about 90,000 tons. Expansion was closely tied to the rhythms of the international market: By the 1850s, American wheat was beginning to feed an ever more urban and populous Europe, and the Midwestern states of the US, along with Russia, became the world's breadbaskets.[157]

⸻

As agriculture intensified and commercialized in many regions of the world, rural cultivators and landowners looked for ways to preserve soil fertility. Traditional methods of fertilization by nitrogen fixers such as bones and manure spread. By midcentury, another fertilizer became critically important, generating yet another commodity frontier: guano.

Since before the Spanish conquest, the Inca had gathered guano on the Chincha Islands off the coast of present-day Peru to fertilize their fields. Boobies and cormorants fed on shoals of anchovy and used the resulting guano to build nests; the lack of rain meant that the white powder, which had accumulated over many millennia, remained easily accessible at the surface. Alexander von Humboldt took a sample of guano during his travels in South America, and German chemist Martin Heinrich Klaproth and his French counterpart, Antoine-François de Fourcroy, brought Incan knowledge into European scientific discourse by demonstrating its suitability for European agriculture.[158]

In 1841, the heavily indebted Peruvian state awarded a contract granting the "collection, shipping, marketing and sales" of guano to a consortium of trading houses led by W. J. Meyers of Liverpool and Antony Gibbs & Sons of London, leading wits to say that the "House of Gibbs made their dibs selling the turds of foreign birds."[159] The traders paid fees to the Peruvian government, and by 1869, 80 percent of all Peruvian state revenues came from that contract. Huge quantities of guano were exported: By 1850, 95,000 tons were shipped to Britain annually; by the 1860s, up to 575,000 tons.[160]

When the guano deposits on the Chinchas neared depletion, they had become so important that a frantic search for further deposits ensued: There was a minor guano rush on Ichaboe Island, off the Namibian coast, in the 1840s. When that source was depleted, extraction efforts shifted to Malgas Island off Cape Colony. In 1854, at the high point of guano mania, a group of Americans claimed Aves Island off the Venezuelan coast. They left to gather their guano-digging equipment and upon their return found that the island had been claimed in their absence by a British company. In response, the United States passed the Guano Islands Act of 1856, which allowed investors to claim guano islands in the name of the United States, a form of land grabbing that constituted a core element of war capitalism. Under this

Act, in 1859, a US company claimed the uninhabited Navassa Island, off the coast of Haiti, "over strenuous objections of Haiti."[161] During the next thirty years, at least seventy islands in the Pacific (including Midway Atoll) and the Caribbean were claimed by US entrepreneurs for guano extraction.[162]

Like on all frontiers, labor was crucial. Initially, the operators of the guano mines had relied on a combination of wageworkers and enslaved Africans.[163] When slavery was abolished in Peru in 1854, contractors sought new sources of labor, as waged laborers were difficult to find and often reluctant to remain on the guano islands. As an administrator wrote to the minister of war in 1863, "Experience has shown . . . that it's not easy to find laborers on the Continent." This matched the assessment of Nicolás de Piérola, inspector of the Chinchas in 1853 and future Peruvian finance minister, that "the free workers are very flaky[;] they don't want to work, as we keep seeing on the island. With the free workers the government will not be able to honor its commitments. . . . If the government were to take over the venture, it wouldn't be assured of workers without the use of prisoners."[164]

Prisoners and vagabonds from the mainland were indeed used, but far more significant were the thousands of indentured Chinese workers, derogatorily called "coolies," who came to dominate the guano mines, previewing a system of indentured labor that would become ever more important in the second half of the nineteenth century. Domingo Elías, co-owner of the first concession for Chincha guano deposits, set up a business in Macau to bring Chinese workers to Peru, a trade formalized by the 1849 Peruvian "Chinese Law." In the next quarter century, ninety thousand Chinese laborers came. They signed eight-year contracts that promised them food, housing, and a meager wage. The indentured workers were then packed onto ships, often without knowing their destination, and brought to the Chinchas. The trip—across cold and hot latitudes, in cramped conditions—could take up to 120 days, and one in ten died on the journey.[165] Because of their long contracts and captivity on the islands, these workers were treated as fixed capital, their deaths recorded as "losses."[166]

Workers mining the last remnants of guano
in the Chincha Islands, circa 1870.

Guano mining was extremely taxing, and workers died in large numbers. They were woken up at 5:00 a.m., given some rice and meat for the day, then sent off to work. The guano had to be broken up by picks and gunpowder, packed into sacks by hand, and either loaded onto mule-drawn carts or carried—workers transported eighty full sacks a day, equivalent to four tons of guano. The sacks were brought to wooden silos by the shore that could hold up to one thousand tons. Guano powder, with its intense smell, covered everything, invading eyes and nostrils. As George Washington Peck, a US congressman sailing home from Australia via Peru, wrote in 1853: "Coolies, who are obliged to wear thick bandages over their mouths, push the guano down to the lower ends of the mangueras [hoses], where there are openings connected with 'shutes,' or long canvas pipes, about as large [a]round as barrels, that lead down to the bases of the cliff. Through these the guano is conducted into launches, or directly into the holds of vessels loading."[167] Accidents were common: Operators could be sucked into the chutes or crushed by the guano, and workers were overseen by "corporals" who dished out cane lashes for "indolence" and "insubordination."

Contractors sold opium to their workers to "pacify" them and dull their pain; suicides were an almost weekly occurrence.[168]

T he number of commodity frontiers pushing into the global countryside was awe-inspiring and should be central to our thinking about the moment when capitalism entered its industrial moment. These commodity frontiers constituted an important part of a novel capitalist civilization. And while we have seen glimpses of the guano, wheat, indigo, tea, coffee, sugar, and cotton frontiers, there were many others: Gujarati traders sought ever more ivory from eastern Africa; trading from Mozambique Island, they exchanged Indian textiles for ivory and made loans to caravan traders such as Jairam Shivji and Ladha Damji, who traveled into the African hinterland to acquire elephant teeth with caravans reaching as far as Congo. At the same time, Chinese and Japanese peasants intensified and extended rice agriculture, successfully keeping up with rising populations, making their countries independent of food imports, and producing enough that rural cultivators in China had more calories at their disposal than their English counterparts. In China, the soy frontier broke into new spaces as well, as Manchurian peasants produced the fertilizer upon which intensifying agriculture in Jiangnan increasingly rested. The sultan of Oman pushed the spice frontier into new territories by turning Zanzibar into a major spice-producing island in conjunction with an adventurous Boston merchant; by 1860, about twenty thousand slaves labored on the island. In West Africa, the British abolition of slavery brought about the production of palm oil, dyes, and peanut oil for export.[169]

Despite their great diversity, commodity frontiers had one thing in common: More and more agricultural commodities and minerals were extracted from the global countryside, creating a metabolic flow of ecological resources into the centers of manufacturing, which for the first time in the history of the global economy were almost exclusively concentrated in a very small part of the world.

One of the most significant flows, however, was neither indigo nor cotton, neither sugar nor coffee, but the people who moved from the rural world to industrial jobs in cities, from subsistence agriculture to plantations. Millions were on the move, and as production concentrated, so did workers. Some moved no farther than down the hills and into the valleys—the Lancashire cotton outworkers, for example, who came into Manchester; peasants in the Vosges who relocated to the spinning towns below in the valley of the Thur; and the New England farm girls who left their parents' homesteads to move to Lowell, Massachusetts. Many of these migrations were temporary and did not cover great distances, but emergent industrial capitalism relied on ever more population displacements to secure labor power, both in the world's cities and its countryside. That widespread commodification of labor power, that ability of capital owners to acquire it in a variety of forms on markets, was unique to capitalism—and came close to defining it.[170] This commodification constituted a frontier itself.

Some of these newly emerging labor frontiers were particularly radical, creating more permanent displacements and covering much longer distances. One such frontier was Ireland. Millions of Irish left this British colony in the first half of the nineteenth century, powering

Number of Irish immigrants to Britain and the United States.

with their brains and muscles the industrial mammoths emerging across the Irish Sea to the east and the Atlantic Ocean to the west. In the thirty years after 1815, as many as a million Irish rural cultivators left, mostly for the United Kingdom and North America. During the Great Famine of the 1840s (which produced "excess mortality" of between 1.4 and 1.5 million people), another 2.1 million emigrated.[171]

Irish migrants were disproportionately urban, moving from the countryside into cities. With almost a quarter of its population Irish-born in 1851, Liverpool, for example, became known as the "capital of Ireland . . . in England," attracting the poorest Irish peasants.[172] Those with slightly more means continued on to Canada and the United States, nowhere more so than to New York City, which came to house 13 percent of all Irish-born Americans.[173]

Wherever they went, they typically arrived penniless. Almost half the Irish immigrants were landless laborers before emigrating, and one-third were farmers. Sometimes facing explicit exclusion in the form of notices that read "No Irish Need Apply," they found jobs at the lower end of the labor market. In Manchester, they were drawn into the expanding cotton industry. John Doherty, who would become one of England's early trade union leaders, started off in 1808 as a child cotton spinner in County Donegal before moving to Belfast. He then migrated to Manchester, where millowners were keen to recruit experienced Irish workers.[174]

In Liverpool, Irish immigrants toiled on construction sites and in sugar refineries. In the early 1830s, one in two Irish immigrants labored on the docks as lumpers or porters, lugging the cotton grown by America's enslaved workers. Irish immigrants also worked in the "'slop' and 'sweated' sectors," producing low-quality garments from rags in basement enterprises. The Irish served in similarly low-level jobs in the United States. Women were employed in domestic service and the garment industry—in 1855, three-quarters of all domestic servants in New York were Irish. Men worked as construction workers, dug canals, hauled goods, and peddled wares on the streets. Irish women also worked in the cotton mills of New England, replacing the Native farm women who had been the first generation of proletarians and whose rebelliousness encouraged employers to look for cheaper, more pliant laborers.[175]

The Irish in the United States often worked on infrastructure projects. In the South, they substituted for slaves in dangerous labor such as building levees: As one Virginian planter put it, "[A] Negro's life is too valuable to risk."[176] Irish immigrants also built canals that connected coalfields to industry and industry to markets. In the 1820s, they dug the canals that allowed Pennsylvania's coal to be removed. They also helped construct the Erie, Blackstone, and Farmington canals. The first long-distance railroad in the United States, connecting Baltimore to the Ohio River, was completed by a large contingent of recent Irish migrants. Wherever they went, the Irish were the poorest, most exploited white workers; the cellars of some of New York's most impoverished neighborhoods housed thirty thousand Irish immigrants in 1850.[177]

So many Irish left their homeland and were pushed into industrial labor because of the Irish chapter of the transformation of the global countryside. As British capital entered Ireland in the eighteenth and nineteenth centuries, and as Irish agriculture was increasingly reoriented to supply the nutritional needs of the United Kingdom, the structure of Irish society shifted. As one Irishman recounted in 1836, the British aimed "to change him from a cottier living upon land to a labourer living upon wages."[178] During the Napoleonic Wars, agricultural exports to Britain boomed, with grain and potato exports doubling. An ever expanding road network integrated Irish producers into British markets, now cut off from continental supply lines by war. As a result, by the 1820s, three-quarters of food imports at Liverpool, such as beef, oats, and butter, came from Ireland. With continual growth in population (in 1800, there were about 5 million people in Ireland; in 1845, that number jumped to 8.5 million), labor was abundant.[179]

Landlords and farmers recruited cultivators for this export boom by letting small plots of land for potato farming on one-year leases, so-called conacres, that were payable in labor. While advantageous for landowners, as potatoes cleansed the soil without extracting nitrogen and thus played a role in crop rotation, it was a highly risky form of income for laborers. Since all the perils of a bad harvest lay on their shoulders, they were essentially bonded laborers. In years of good harvests, they were still poor, but access to bog peat and highly nutritious potato plots let them survive in relatively good health, thereby feeding further population expansion.[180] Years of bad harvests, however, put the system under immense stress, as the Great Famine in the late 1840s demonstrated.

Moreover, at the close of the Napoleonic Wars, the export price of agricultural produce plummeted, prompting landlords, often absentee, to switch to cattle raising. They increasingly took direct control over their estates, removing layers of renting and subrenting farmers to ensure themselves a larger share of income. They expanded commercial crops and livestock production by displacing subsistence crops. These shifts were frequently accompanied by evictions from conacre plots, swelling the ranks of landless laborers. In western Ireland, this additionally involved the enclosing of common grazing lands. In the

Mobilizing labor in the Irish countryside: A peasant family gets evicted, 1848.

Mullet Peninsula of County Mayo in the early 1800s, the landlords Denis Bingham and William Carter began a campaign to increase the yields on their lands. They contracted an engineer to construct a road and initiated dividing up "unused" land on their estates into conacres by evicting tenants from commonly held pastureland. As a result, oat and barley production rose from eighty tons in 1822 to eighteen hundred tons in 1835. Evictions also surged: In the Mullet, about one thousand dwellings disappeared, probably burned by the sheriff on orders of the landlords.[181] In Ireland as a whole, half a million cultivators were displaced. Irish diarist Amhlaoibh Ó Súilleabháin described one such cast-out peasant woman in 1828 as a "poor, barefooted, tall, very thin, ragged woman, blackhaired, bleareyed, touselhaired, without hat or fillet, with no clothes to her back but dirty soot-coloured rags . . . weeping bitterly."[182]

The often violent colonization of the Irish countryside by Britain and the massive displacement of poor Irish rural cultivators into burgeoning industrial cities across the Irish Sea and the Atlantic Ocean also frequently brought the kind of racialist thinking that had legitimized the enslavement of Africans to the fore. Thought of as colonial subjects, the Irish were described as having "africanoid" characteristics; indeed, British anthropologist John Beddoe indexed them by a scale of what he called "nigrescence."[183] The Irish were described as primitive, indolent, superstitious, and dishonest, among other "racial" attributes.[184] These attitudes even infected the works of critical thinkers like Friedrich Engels, whose *The Condition of the Working Class in England* (1845) asserted that "Celtic faces . . . one recognises at the first glance as different from the physiognomy of the native."[185]

MEANWHILE, THE ENSLAVED Africans to whom the Irish were compared also continued to arrive in the Americas as the slave labor frontier intensified and shifted. It is a stunning fact that more African slaves were forced into boats bound for the Americas between 1770 and 1860 than in the previous 270 years combined. Slavery, wrote

Marx in a 1846 letter, is "the pivot upon which our present-day industrialism turns."[186] And, indeed, the slave trade reached new dimensions in the wake of the Industrial Revolution: In the 1780s, 868,000 Africans were trafficked across the Atlantic; in the 1790s, 848,000; in the 1800s, 824,000; in the 1810s, 686,000; and in the 1820s, 856,000. The industrialization of Europe and North America did not lead to a diminishment of slavery but to its intensification.[187]

The slave trade opened up new trade networks—for example, in East Africa, a region that had a long history of slaving into the Arab world but that had not been much affected by the Atlantic slave trade before the 1780s. After 1780, however, about half a million East Africans were forced to the Americas on journeys like the one carried out by the *Guteman d'Altona*, chartered by German merchant Jean-Charles Schultz, who sailed in 1802 from Bordeaux to acquire slaves in Mozambique bound for Rio de Janeiro. Many of these newly captured East Africans were sent to grow coffee in Brazil, with almost 150,000 arriving in Rio in the twenty years after 1811 alone. In addition, East Africa now produced labor for the Indian Ocean sugar islands of La Réunion and Mauritius, with about 100,000 transported there between 1770 and 1810.[188] Slaving became what one historian has called the "mainstay of the export economy of northern Mozambique."[189]

The hunt for labor itself became ever more efficient, intense, and brutal. Enslavers used larger and faster ships and more efficient labor-capturing techniques, partly facilitated by new European weaponry.[190] The "production of slaves" in Africa became rationalized—one more downstream impact of the global expansion of a world trade fed by what has been called the African "slave mode of production."[191]

Banian merchants from Gujarat became important players in that expanding East African labor frontier, connecting to Arab traders in the hinterlands. They provided credit to slave traders, *mussambazes*, who conducted their business away from the coast—in the territories controlled by the Yao and Makua; the southern Lunda kingdom of Kazembe; the Rozvi kingdom of Changamira; and north of the Zambezi River. They traded captives for cotton cloth acquired from India.

Packed with this cloth, mussambazes set up caravans to travel from interior town to interior town, setting up slave markets whenever they came across a willing local ruler. The most famous of these interior traders was Hamed bin Mohammed al-Marjebi from Muscat, who, with access to significant credit from the mercantile community of his hometown, could purchase the goods that were in demand in the African interior, especially cloth, and then trade in slaves. These caravans were not averse to directly capturing slaves themselves if they came across lone travelers, but they usually relied on enslavement through wars fought by local rulers, aided by the population displacements following major droughts in the 1760s, 1790s, and 1820s.[192] Portuguese governor-general Joaquim Pereira Marinho described the trade in 1840:

> The main employers asked *baneanes* [Muslim slave traders] for the necessary amount of cloth and clothes to go to the bush and exchange them for slaves. . . . Generally, the ladies of the houses received these goods, gave them to different Blacks who were used to the bush[,] so they could go inland and exchange them for slaves. . . . Once the consignment of slaves comes in from the bush, each of the contractors puts theirs in their backyard where they are fed corn and water, and kept in order and without any other kind of comfort, until the ships from Brazil and Havana arrived.[193]

Once in the port city, enslaved women, men, and children were absorbed into a transoceanic trade vortex. Traders such as Laxmichand Motichand and Shobhachand Sowchand owned their own ships and gathered slaves to send to Portuguese traders like Mozambique's leading slaver, José Henriques da Cruz Freitas. This trade was both high-risk and highly paid—profits of over 100 percent were not unknown—and the workers' labor brought profits for Brazilian coffee planters and Cuban sugar lords, as well as the European and American merchants and manufacturers engaged in the trade and production of these goods.[194] A shirt produced in Manchester might have its origins in the enslaving of African cultivators in Mozambique.

Ever more labor, cotton, coffee, wheat, and other commodities flowed from the global countryside into cities to feed increasingly productive machines and swelling numbers of consumers who no longer grew their own food or produced their own clothing. In all these exchanges, outside capital played a critical role, as urban merchants transmitted the pulse of intensified production into the world's hinterland. Some merchant communities specialized in such connections, an essential task at a time when no industrial enterprise engaged in the kind of vertical integration that was to become common in the second half of the nineteenth century. Merchants thus remained critical to the capitalist revolution even after the onset of industrialization, connecting a diverse set of producers in the global countryside to an equally diverse set of consumers of raw materials in the emerging industrial cities.

These merchants came from all corners of the world—including, as we have seen, Asia and Africa. They formed tight-knit communities. A quintessential example can be found in the Greek merchants who integrated the trade of the eastern Mediterranean and connected the region to the burgeoning economies of northwestern Europe. The Rallis, a Greek merchant family from the island of Chios, came to play a crucial role in the cotton trade, as did the Volkarts from Winterthur in Switzerland. Beirut merchants invested in Palestinian agriculture. Some merchants specialized in the commodity trade itself, gathering products in places like Havana, Mozambique Island, Charleston, Rio, and Guangzhou and organizing shipments to cities near industrializing regions like Liverpool, Le Havre, Hamburg, and New York. Moreover, capital-rich trading communities emerged in places such as Memphis, Bombay, and Rio to infuse capital into the local countryside and build new islands of capital across continental-scale hinterlands. Another set of merchants distributed goods to industrial and private consumers. The Brazilian coffee trade brought together large numbers of very specialized traders, among them local commission agents near the fields who forwarded coffee to merchants in Rio, so-called factors who provided planters with credit and supplies and sold the coffee to so-called sackers, who mixed different kinds of beans and then sold them to export merchants, mostly foreigners, mediated by yet another set of brokers.[195]

As goods flowed from the countryside into industrializing centers, capital flowed the other way. Rio coffee exporters relied on credit from European banks, credit that flowed all the way to the planters themselves. Bankers provided the funds that let planters in Bengal, Mississippi, São Paulo, Cuba, and elsewhere cut down trees, drain swamps, acquire labor, and focus their energies on the production of goods for distant markets. Some investments were small—for example, when Dutch banking house Staphorst & Hubbard provided, in 1796, a mortgage to Thomas Jefferson in the amount of $1,893.21, secured by his enslaved laborers. Others were huge, as when Dutch banking houses bought $5 million of the $12 million in US bonds that the fledgling US government needed to acquire Louisiana from France. In Bengal, by the 1790s, so-called agency houses pooled the capital of British and Indian investors and used it to provide loans to factory operators and to trade the resulting goods, supporting the production of agricultural commodities such as indigo, sugar, opium, and cotton. By the 1790s, there were fifteen such agency houses in Calcutta, none more prominent than Palmer & Co., which dominated indigo production and trade.[196] Commodity frontiers were thus also always capital frontiers.

While European capital was crucial, local capital remained important to commodity production, as Indian, Chinese, African, and Japanese capital owners, among others, profited by investing their ample funds into emerging new opportunities. In Bengal, indigo houses depended on capital from Indian merchants.[197] Muscati capital fueled the East African slave trade, Guajarati capital the ivory trade, and Guangzhou capital the tea boom. While non-European capital owners were slowly pushed to the margins of political decision-making by

European colonial states and capital owners as the century progressed, their capital remained important to the transformation of the countryside, leading to the creation of institutions, networks, knowledge, and additional capital that by the twentieth century proved exceedingly significant to the economic development of these parts of the world.

<hr>

As commodity frontiers pushed into the global countryside, hierarchies between different regions of the world sharpened. Ever bigger areas of the globe became dedicated to providing food, fibers, minerals, and labor to the industrializing centers of the world, which made their economies less diversified, weakened their manufacturing capacities, and increasingly marginalized local capital-rich entrepreneurs and local political structures. Networks became ever more hierarchical, and resources were redistributed in a rapidly accelerating process that concentrated the world's wealth in a few—mostly European—areas. Capital accumulation rested not just on the exploitation of labor but on the extraction of resources from colonial settings and the redistribution of that wealth to colonizers. Mid-nineteenth-century capitalism was still just as much about redistribution as about productivity increases. The global countryside was a huge reservoir of riches that were neither exchanged nor produced on markets—from the fertility of its soil to the minerals deposited in its ground to the labor power reproduced in its subsistence-oriented communities. Agricultural commodities, minerals, and labor, so crucial to the newly industrializing centers, were cheap because their costs were not priced on markets; these off-the-books resources and labor were critical to fueling the emerging centers of global capital accumulation.

Not just capital but institutional capacity accumulated in this small set of places. Property rights, for example, strengthened in a few regions of the world, while massive dispossessions characterized much of the rest. Self-ownership became the norm in western Europe and a few other parts of the world, while massive enslavement continued to characterize the Americas. Most important of all, that institution of institutions—the state—grew in capacity in some parts of the world, while being undermined just as thoroughly in other parts. State power was now more unevenly distributed than ever before in human history. And while that power in Europe was directed toward the accumulation of wealth and power locally, imperial state power in places such as India focused on benefiting the colonizer, not the colonized.[198] Eventually, the forging of such capacities and the lessons of the wheat, tea, and guano frontiers, along with the energy, wealth, and institutional innovations drawn from the world's countryside, allowed capital owners in the last third of the nineteenth century to reenvision the production of cotton, sugar, and coffee as well. But this is a story for a later chapter.

For now, the emerging industrial capitalism drew its newfound dynamic from these sharpening hierarchies and unequal institutional forms. In fact, the world economy depended on and created those inequities. Euphemistically called noninclusive, extractive institutions were the critical enablers of the very inclusive institutions celebrated by many.[199] The "good" institution of secure property rights was built on the "bad" institution of dispossession, the "good" institution of wage labor on the "bad" institution of slavery.

Such connected diversity, best illustrated by the new interactions between industrializing urban centers and a revolutionized countryside, transformed the archipelago of capital. Capitalism left its island fortresses and spread into new social and geographic spaces, creating an emerging capitalist civilization in which the rhythms of urban and rural life, industry and agriculture, the heartland and the colony, increasingly fed on one another, drawing ever more realms of life of ever more people into the circuits of commodity production. Older forms of production and older networks of merchants persisted, of course, but by the mid-nineteenth century, the capitalist civilization, an archipelago no more, reigned as the dynamic core of the global economy.

9.

A Capitalist Civilization, 1830–1880

The Black man's burden I: Lady in the Litter with Two Slaves,
Bahia, Brazil, *circa 1860.*

In late March 1880, New York's economic elite congregated in
Central Park to inaugurate a new venue to house a decade-old and
expanding art collection: the Metropolitan Museum of Art. One
thousand five hundred of the city's most distinguished citizens attended, and the new museum's eastern hall was "thronged" with
well-dressed ladies and gents, "fashionably attired in costumes of various gay colors."[1] A band played "Hail to the Chief!" as the president of
the United States, Rutherford B. Hayes, entered, flanked by "railroad
man" John Taylor Johnston, the president of the museum's board. Joining them on the platform were illustrious and powerful men, including
Secretary of State William M. Evarts, iron manufacturer Peter Cooper,

railroad entrepreneur Cornelius Vanderbilt, merchant William E. Dodge Jr., real estate tycoon William Waldorf Astor, and printing-press manufacturer Robert Hoe Jr.[2] Looking on from the audience, among many other moneyed New Yorkers, May Suydam Palmer represented railroad fortunes; Anne Morgan, J. Pierpont Morgan, Russell Sage, and Jesse Seligman represented the city's dynamic banking sector; and Mary Woodbridge Tiffany and Lewis Comfort Tiffany represented its jewelry industry. Their wealth and splendor competed for attention with the assortment of "Greco-Phoenician antiquities, . . . European ceramics, . . . Dutch and Flemish pictures . . . and other articles of real artistic merit."[3]

Creating the Metropolitan Museum of Art was an audacious move in a city that, for a long time, had been rather provincial. The idea was first floated at a July Fourth dinner hosted by Americans a decade earlier in Paris. Supported by the elite Union League Club, a board of trustees had been formed in 1870.[4] In the beginning, financial support was hard to come by—from Florence, American newspaper editor and art collector James Jackson Jarves wrote somewhat discouragedly that in the United States, not art but "material wealth is the great prize of life."[5] Yet, eventually, the board's aim to "increase the power and influence of the institution" found receptive ears among New York's economic elite and, critically, in the municipal administration that agreed to contribute the land and the building.[6] As New York entered the ranks of world economic powerhouses, the museum came to symbolize both its elite's wealth and its claims to cultural leadership. Many among New York's upper crust saw the Met as "one of the essential elements of a polished civilization," a civilization they aimed to dominate.[7]

That March day in 1880 was a celebration of all they had accomplished. Harvard-trained lawyer Joseph Hodges Choate's keynote set the tone: Pointing to older museums like the Louvre in Paris and the British Museum in London, he professed "that the diffusion of a knowledge of art in its higher forms of beauty would tend directly to humanize, to educate and refine a practical and laborious people."[8]

The museum was not only a class project but a nationalist one, with Choate hoping it would liberate the United States from its cultural dependence on Europe. He lauded the "irresistible inventive genius of America," asking his wealthy compatriots to consider the artistic possibilities:

> Think of it, ye millionaires of many markets, what glory may yet be yours . . . to convert pork into porcelain, grain and produce into priceless pottery, the rude ores of commerce into sculptured marble, and railroad shares and mining stocks—things which perish without the using, and which in the next financial panic shall surely shrivel like parched scrolls—into the glorified canvas of the world's masters, that shall adorn these walls for centuries.[9]

The museum was not without critics, including those who pointed out that its Sunday closings excluded much of the city's working class. The *New-York Tribune* noted that visitors' behavior was closely policed by guards and lambasted the museum as "an exclusive social toy" for the families of the city's elite.[10] While this may have been true, the museum was still meaningful. Its launch demonstrated that a rich, powerful, well-organized, and self-conscious economic elite had emerged in New York City. That elite had accumulated vast wealth from the transformation of the countryside—first the slave lands of the US South, then the rapidly expanding wheat complex of the American West. Moneys from coal, copper, and gold mining flowed into their coffers along with profits from investments in Cuba's sugar fields and Peru's guano deposits. Industry had become increasingly important to them as well, at first in the city itself (the giant sugar refinery of William Havemeyer and the ironworks of John Roach & Sons, for example) and then elsewhere (in Pittsburgh's steel mills and Chicago's railroads); really anywhere markets, materials, labor, and transportation came together profitably. In the wake of the US Civil War, New York had become the headquarters of the United States' economy, and many a banker and financier—in addition to merchants and manufacturers—with continental, even global, visions made their

*Cultural entrepreneurs: the grand opening of the Metropolitan Museum
of Art's first building in New York's Central Park, 1880.*

home there. Expert administrators such as managers and lawyers,
functionaries of capital who themselves now controlled significant
wealth, also joined this buoyant new class.

Members of the new class were connected in numerous ways. Not
only did they trade with one another, but they also gravitated to increasingly segregated neighborhoods, where their architects and interior designers constructed homes quite similar to one another, but
different from "how the other half lives"—to quote the title of a prominent book of the time.[11] They attended elaborate parties, ate fine
foods, and dressed in ways that made them mutually recognizable.
They also married one another; met on journeys to Paris, Florence,
and London; and patterned their lives and ideas in increasingly similar
ways. If need be, they mobilized politically and made their voices heard
in the tumultuous politics of the city and the nation. They also worked
on creating institutional and aesthetic distinctions between high and
popular culture, sacralizing art by removing it from the market. The
Metropolitan Museum of Art was one such project, but there were also
the New York Philharmonic and the newly constructed Metropolitan
Opera. Excluded from the professional opportunities their husbands

enjoyed, women played a particularly important role in the forging of this class: They oversaw domestic workers, raised the next generation, fashioned networks of affection and social bonding, and implemented a rigorous program of cultural policing, enforcing habits and tastes they deemed appropriate. In the process, they made their class.[12]

When women and men of this economic elite met on that 1880 spring day in the newly built museum, the air must have fairly crackled from the dynamism of the dense connections between them. Perhaps most consequentially, their burgeoning confidence in the power and virtue of their class allowed them to embark upon an ideological project to remake the world in their own image. One of its crucial gambits was to compartmentalize the world, presenting as unrelated the violence descending upon enslaved Cuban sugar workers, the backbreaking working conditions in Pittsburgh steel mills, and the long hours and low pay of seamstresses stitching together clothing for Brooks Brothers in the basements of New York tenements—all of which played, among other forms of grueling labor, a critical role in making possible the unprecedented scale and refinement of the museum specifically and their lives more generally.[13] Capitalist civilization, that form of life rooted first and foremost in that novel organization of economic life that we have chronicled, to them, was polite conversation in the parlor, not orders barked on plantations and in factories; the sociability of the club, not cutthroat competition for jobs; and the tastes and habits that could only be absorbed in a bourgeois household, not acquired on markets. It was stunningly different from, yet also deeply contingent on, those aspects of the capitalist civilization that we just chronicled when we looked at the making of the industrial world's rural hinterlands.

B y 1880, when the Metropolitan Museum of Art opened, capital owners in New York City and elsewhere had expanded their sphere of control far beyond the often heavily fortified trade entrepôts and islands of the previous centuries' merchant-controlled enterprises. Expanding in space and penetrating ever deeper into the social order, capitalist ways of organizing economic activity were now dominant in significant parts of the world. The long-term push to connect islands of capital had intensified so much that islands had become continents, large geographic expanses whose economic operations were principally organized around capitalist social relations. A capitalist civilization—an empire of capital—had emerged, characterized by endless accumulation, commodification, and much-accelerated economic growth. It structured economic life in small towns like Saint-Étienne, Lagos, Bochum, Ahmedabad, Birmingham, Mérida, and Turin and in cities like Chicago, Buenos Aires, Paris, Calcutta, Rio de Janeiro, and Hong Kong. Its logic had captured the vast lands of the Midwestern United States and the Argentinean pampas, the coffee plantations of Java and the wheat fields of southern Russia. This new capitalist civilization had spread around the globe, always connected and recognizable across large distances, yet always embedded within deeply consequential hierarchies. It seems paradoxical: As the world became more connected and more similar, it also became more sharply differentiated. It was exactly that connected diversity that propelled the forward march of capitalism. Not seeing that connection was yet another telltale sign of the capitalist civilization.

The signal driver of this capitalist civilization was an unprecedented commitment of capital to production and capital's ability, when applied forcefully and relentlessly, to penetrate agriculture and manufacturing, space and society, in new ways. Whole segments of the economic elite were now primarily oriented toward production rather than, as previously, trade and finance. If the quintessential capitalists of the seventeenth century had been Surat's Mohammad Chelebi, Amsterdam's Isaac Le Maire, and China's Zheng Chenggong—merchants, all—the quintessential capitalists of mid-nineteenth-century New York were steel industrialist Andrew Carnegie, sugar manufacturer William Havemeyer, and banker James Brown. While 1650 Surat

A bourgeois world: Chinese merchant family, Guangzhou, 1860s.

capital owners had focused on trade in a world that—in general—was not organized along capitalist logics, two centuries later, bourgeois elites in New York stood atop a thoroughly capitalist national economy. When Jelenia Góra merchants had moved their capital into manufacturing in 1750, they had engaged the producers as traders, not as employers, in stark contrast with mid-nineteenth-century New York's capital owners, who employed thousands and thousands of workers streaming into the factories they commanded.

By midcentury, it had become clearer than ever before that capitalism was an imperial project that abhorred stasis. Capitalism was not, and cannot be, conservative; it has always been and continues to be a state of permanent revolution. Its expansionary drive came from its innermost logic—its continual need to generate more capital. Making more and better things and services, while clearly an important and impactful outcome of that impetus, was in some ways just incidental. For capital to increase, it had to be productively invested—that is, mixed with labor. What sounds abstract was actually quite concrete: Those who controlled capital had to find new outlets for that capital, new investment opportunities that enabled them to grow their assets.

As more capital accumulated, this process accelerated, integrating more people, territories, and spheres of human life into its circuits of production and consumption. One of the results was that economic output expanded in ways never before seen in human history, becoming both more intensive and more extensive: Unsurprisingly, nineteenth-century world trade grew by a factor of twenty-nine.[14]

As capital infused ever more realms of life, it began to look as if it stood outside human agency. The central organ of nineteenth-century economic liberalism—Britain's *The Economist*—issued a drumbeat of appeals to "natural laws" or even "the great natural law" that allegedly animated capitalist economies. For *The Economist*, capital was a primal, disembodied historical force, and its ongoing need for ever more accumulation, for ever more spatial and social expansion, was fueled by ever more exacting efficiencies. A particular set of human institutions, values, and social relationships—capital—once seen as alien and disrupting, now appeared, in the eyes of not only capital owners but also their critics, to have gained control over people. The "economy" seemed to have separated from the human community that constituted and powered it—to have gained an existence outside and above that community. Markets assumed supranatural powers as arbiters of almost everything.[15] This emergent capitalist civilization exercised unprecedented powers over nature and spawned a global emancipation from centuries-old social orders seen, just as much, as divinely mandated. To critics of the new order—the new working class prominently among them—it created exploitation, misery, and social disintegration. And it did. But equally important, if harder to grasp, was that this revolutionary civilization had made humans—all of them, regardless of how much money they had or lacked—subservient to a new god: capital. The mainspring, the seemingly invisible hand behind nature and human history, might not have been divine, but it was no less powerful. As human-made relationships had gained power over humans, some observers began to think of this new order as outside history itself, as *natural*.

Perhaps no one was more impressed by this extraordinary dynamic civilization than two German-born thinkers, Karl Marx and Friedrich Engels, who saw how "the need of a constantly expanding market for its products chases the bourgeoisie over the entire surface of the globe." Capital owners, they observed, "must nestle everywhere, settle everywhere, establish connections everywhere."[16] By 1853, Marx compared the impact of "trade and industry" to the "geological revolutions [that] have created the surface of the earth."[17] And as they saw clearly, capital did not just expand horizontally and colonize the hinterland; it also burrowed ever deeper into human life.

For centuries, wealthy lords had acquired raw materials and labor power without recourse to market transactions; now, capital owners acquired all inputs to production on markets and then sold the entirety of their production on markets as well. At the same time, a much larger number of people depended on markets for almost all aspects of their subsistence—the foods that sustained them, the clothes that kept them warm, the homes that housed them, and even the entertainments they enjoyed. The capitalist logic that had once been limited to relatively small areas now took root in the centers of the emerging economic hierarchies, moving into wider spaces and expanding within societies.

The cash nexus that became a telltale sign of the capitalist civilization increasingly dominated human relations. Take the northern English city of Manchester. By 1850, in this heart of the global cotton industry, almost all production, consumption, and labor was mediated by markets. Workers sold their labor power, even that of the very youngest members of their families, to employers for wages. Vast spinning and weaving mills churned out cottons for distant markets, not the owners' or workers' clothing needs. Rich and poor women, in charge of household reproduction, acquired food from producers local and distant, self-sufficiency now being both impossible and seemingly unnecessary. Clothing, housing, furniture, and almost everything else was procured on markets. This expansion of market relations allowed for a far more nuanced division of labor and a much more productive organization of labor, generating an ever greater panoply of goods.

To see how this new commodification of life began to take shape, let's consider the family of a silk worker in midcentury Vienna. With both parents working, the family earned 75 kreuzers a day. At a minimum level of subsistence, they had to spend 67 percent of that on food, 12 percent on rent, 8 percent on clothing, and the rest on heating, taxes, schooling, and miscellaneous expenses. Any disruption from sickness or pregnancy would drop the family's income below subsistence levels—a subsistence entirely acquired on markets. Workers in the Prussian Rhineland also depended on markets for their subsistence. It was estimated by contemporaries that in 1845, a factory worker made 120 thalers a year. More than half of that income, 73 thalers, was spent on bread, followed by 26 thalers on potatoes. Even without paying rent or consuming any meat, vegetables, or beer—and without considering the possibility of sickness or extraordinary costs, such as christenings and funerals—the worker's subsistence needs were a third higher than his income, the shortfall presumably made up by the paid and unpaid labor of other members of his family. While wageworkers aimed to limit their dependence on markets whenever possible—by raising vegetables in small garden plots, for example, or keeping rabbits for meat—their ability to do so was restricted. Bourgeois families were just as deeply integrated into markets, albeit at higher levels of consumption and with women rarely taking on paid labor.[18] This degree of market dependence was unprecedented, even if important spheres of life—cooking, cleaning, and raising children, among others—remained outside the market, as reproductive labor continued to remain the unpaid domain of women.

Capitalist social relations expanded everywhere, and as a result, the world most of us live in today came into being. The more people lived in cities, the more they depended on supplies from elsewhere, and to access these supplies, most urbanites had to sell their labor power. By midcentury, some parts of the world had been massively urbanized.

In the United Kingdom, one of the most extreme examples, 56 percent of the country's people lived in cities of 5,000 people or more in 1880, compared with just 19 percent in 1800. In France and the United States, this movement was slower yet still significant: By 1880, one in four people in these two countries lived in cities. In Europe as a whole, urbanization more than doubled between 1810 and 1880. Some cities grew spectacularly: By 1880, London had almost 5 million inhabitants, four times as many as in 1800. Berlin's population had more than sextupled to 1.1 million people, Paris's had quadrupled to 2.3 million, and New York's had grown thirty-two times to almost 2 million. Chicago, which in 1800 was a tiny settlement of a few hundred Indigenous Americans and European traders, now counted more than half a million inhabitants.[19] Outside the North Atlantic region, urbanization proceeded noticeably slower. Yet Hong Kong, Bombay, Rio de Janeiro, and Lima, among others, were also on their way to becoming highly capitalized urban spaces.

Moreover, as the scope and scale of commodification spread, the capitalist logic moved deeper into society. With an eye aimed toward standardizing and organizing work routines for maximum efficiency, capital owners broke down preindustrial work patterns. Efforts pioneered on Caribbean plantations and in Chinese tea-processing plants became common in other fields of production as well. In Brazil, to cite just one of many examples, print media and business associations proselytized what they called the "gospel of work," with the Industrial Association demanding that workers be "subject to a rigorous discipline, which would progressively inoculate ideas of order and the habit of obedience and respect toward superiors."[20] Even Indian palanquin bearers, their labor notoriously difficult to supervise and to fasten to capitalism's logic, faced new regulations: Bearers who disobeyed elite passengers could be imprisoned or lashed.[21]

The effort to control labor found its ultimate expression on plantations and in factories. Indeed, one of the reasons why employers concentrated workers there and made heavy use of women and children was because concentrating them made them easier to control and discipline, as women and children were assumed to be more amenable to such efforts.[22] With mixed success, owners aimed to orchestrate the movements of their workers through the use of bells, rigid timekeeping, and strict minute-by-minute routines. According to the 1825 British Act to Make Further Provisions for the Regulation of Cotton Mills and Factories, and for the better Preservation of the Health of Young Persons Employed Therein, cotton mill workers were allowed a half hour for breakfast between six thirty and ten in the morning and an hour for dinner between eleven o'clock and two in the afternoon. Weavers' memoirs from this time often focus on the sounds of bells. Employers punished violation of these time restrictions, like other infractions such as whistling, singing, and absence from one's post. Still more rules focused on cultivating sobriety and attentiveness, or barring horseplay, drunkenness, looking out the window, and speaking with other employees.[23]

In their quest to control workers, capital owners employed ever more sophisticated methods to capture and harness time, which acquired itself a new prominence in capitalist civilization. Throughout most of human history, people had divided their days, weeks, and years by tasks—harvesting the rice, milking the cows, or sewing pieces of clothing, for example, with the intensity and length of the effort determined by the task and natural conditions. They worked hard at times but were largely idle at others—no one could be expected to plant in the winter, for instance. Capitalism ended this cyclical and flexible sense of time. As employers purchased labor time, they wanted to measure it precisely and to increase output per unit of time, which became much easier with the spread of clocks and, eventually, watches. Iron manufacturers put up huge clock towers next to their forges. Moreover, as expensive machinery became associated with production, employers had an incentive to continually utilize that capital and to seek a predictable and disciplined exertion from workers. Coffee and tea, then novel drugs, helped by enabling industrial workers to "endure exposure and withstand hard work," as a 1920 pamphlet written by the N. W.

Mastering time: clock tower at the ironworks in Forsmark, Uppland, Sweden, constructed in 1813 and photographed in July 1915. The ironworks were established by Louis De Geer, whom we encountered in chapter 5.

Ayer Advertising Agency put it, another characteristic of the capitalist civilization.[24] Work now became sharply demarcated and set apart from all other activities—a novelty.[25]

At the cutting edge, as some people remade themselves to gain the greatest possible valuation on the market, the capitalist civilization moved inward too. For most of human history, the self was not an important object of concern; people were embedded within hierarchies that prescribed their relationships to their parents and children, to their work, and to their larger communities—none of which were mediated by markets. Children followed in their parents' footsteps, working their lands or taking up their manufacturing activities. Dress was dictated by traditions or authorities. With the deepening of capitalism, people had to acquire salable skills, skills "that could be used to advantage," as American author T. S. Arthur put it in his 1860 *Advice to Young Men on Their Duties and Conduct in Life*.[26] For the growing group of white-collar workers, selling one's labor power meant making oneself marketable. To take on "the appearance of a gentleman," English essayist William Hazlitt wrote in 1821, a white-collar worker should display "an habitual self-possession. . . . He should have the complete command, not only over his countenance, but over his limbs and motions. In other words, he should discover in his air and manner a voluntary power over his whole body, which, with every inflection of it, should be under the control of his will."[27] As the capitalist civilization moved inward, it commanded individuals to exercise self-control and focus on the project of self-making—to better market their labor power.[28]

═══

M ost characteristic of the capitalist civilization, however, was the advent of new patterns of inequality. As far as we can tell, inequality has been a feature of all human societies: Imperial China, sixteenth-century Africa, feudal Europe, and other places all had pronounced economic, social, and political inequality. Capitalism did not invent inequality. But it changed its patterns. It created what Thomas Piketty has called a "new inequality regime."[29] Instead of being based on birth, privilege, or inheritance—on an ordered and static idea of society, as had been the case for most of history—status was determined by an individual's position within the stratifications that capitalism fostered, most importantly the distinction between those investing and thus accumulating capital and those who sold the only asset they had: their labor power. Of course, intergenerational wealth transfers—and thus birth—still mattered, as did stratifications based on gender and race. Also, people moved from one side of the great social divide to the other, and some found themselves rather ambiguously situated in the social order—shopkeepers, artisans, and professionals such as doctors and lawyers, for example. Still, the emerging capitalist civilization was gradually characterized by the formation of distinctly modern social groups—what many nineteenth-century observers came to call "classes." People's locations within these inequalities organized their lives, with deep-rooted class cultures and even class politics emerging.[30] By mid-century, that trend had become pronounced. As *The Economist* commented in 1857, almost programmatically: "Each class has its own work, and each should have its own characteristic culture."[31]

Among the people who defined their social positions within these new inequalities was Antonio Clemente Pinto. A Portuguese native, Pinto arrived in Rio de Janeiro, Brazil's capital, in 1821. He embarked

A bourgeois world: With a model of Rio de Janeiro's Palácio do Catete in the background, Laura Clementina da Silva Pinto poses beside her husband, Antonio Clemente Pinto, who holds an unscrolled plan of the Cantagallo Railway, painted in 1867.

upon his career by working for various merchant houses as a *caixeiro*, or minor employee, before starting his own business in the booming trade of enslaved workers. He soon became one of the city's most prominent slave traders, selling 3,647 captives between 1827 and 1830. By the 1830s, now well off, Pinto moved some of his gains into the Paraíba Valley, acquiring and building huge coffee plantations around Nova Friburgo, a town about one hundred miles from Rio. Eventually, he owned sixteen plantations with almost six billion coffee plants worked by 2,180 enslaved women, men, and children. Experiencing the kind of social mobility newly available at the frontiers of capitalism's expansion, he had become the "king of coffee." In subsequent decades, 63 percent of his wealth remained in land and slaves, but real estate eventually made up 18 percent of his holdings— including the Palácio do Catete, a neoclassical palace that later became the seat of Brazil's president. He also invested in railroads and finance, and when he died, his wealth equaled 751,000 British pounds (equivalent to 74 million pounds in 2024).[32]

The stratum of merchants, manufacturers, planters, bankers, and other capital-rich families—the stratum of which Pinto was part— grew worldwide. These "capitalists," as they often called themselves, had a history that went back centuries, as we have seen. Still, their numbers grew, their wealth swelled, their position in society became more prominent, and their claims to economic, social, cultural, and political leadership multiplied. They moved from the margins into the center of many societies.

To remain in Brazil for a moment, let us look at Rio de Janeiro. The empire's prime city counted 245 "capitalists" and another 1,572 "property-holders" among its 250,000 inhabitants, according to its 1870 census.[33] This small but potent group of coffee planters and merchants (who exported that coffee) dominated the Brazilian economy and, increasingly, Brazilian society and politics.[34] Like their counterparts elsewhere, they were—in the apt words of Ida Pfeiffer, an Austrian merchant's daughter—"addict[ed] to money."[35]

Similar patterns of concentrations of wealth and inequality were found in many other cities: In Lima, bourgeois Peruvians made their money not from coffee but from guano. Heinrich Witt, born in 1799 into a merchant family in the then Danish city of Altona (near Hamburg), was educated in his hometown and London. In 1823, he went to work as an accountant for Antony Gibbs & Sons, a substantial London merchant house, whose principal owner sent him, the following year, to work in the firm's southern Peruvian office in Arequipa. Eventually,

Cosmopolitan bourgeois: María Teodora del Patrocinio de Sierra y Velarde and Heinrich Witt, born in Altona, then part of Denmark, in their Lima, Peru, house, circa the 1860s.

Witt became an important merchant in his own right and joined the tight-knit Lima economic elite by marrying the wealthy María Teodora del Patrocinio de Sierra y Velarde. They bought a house near Plaza Mayor and opened a trading business, first exporting precious metals and wool, then guano, which became such an obsession that Witt mentioned the guano-mining Chincha Islands a full sixty-one times in his diaries. Like most of his peers, Witt later diversified, investing in railroad companies, banking, utilities, the insurance industry, and the importation of goods from Europe. The family became wealthy enough to employ five servants.[36] In 1848, Witt described what united all his various economic activities: "Collecting money and lending it out again as quickly as possible, in order not to lose interest on the same, was my sole mercantile operation."[37] And so it was for capital owners the world over.

An identifiable and self-identified group of capital owners emerged everywhere as the capitalist civilization expanded. New York, as we have seen, had a large and mighty economic elite by midcentury. London and Paris became quintessentially bourgeois cities, that is, cities dominated by capital owners primarily engaged in trade and finance but also in urban manufacturing. Manufacturers were at the core of economic elites of industrial cities such as Saint-Étienne, Bochum, Pittsburgh, and Birmingham, and commodity traders were prominent in cities such as Bremen and Le Havre, Liverpool and Genoa. By the mid-nineteenth century, an economic elite, that is, bourgeoisie, also arose in coastal Chinese cities such as Shanghai, Guangzhou, Tianjin, Hankou, and Xiamen. In Japan, a new economic elite, among them Yokohama entrepreneur Shinohara Chuemon, surfaced after the Meiji Restoration of 1868, composed in part of earlier mercantile and proto-industrial elites but also, increasingly, modern industrialists. And in India, trade continued to propel this new class, with rich merchants such as Ramgopal Ghosh, Mutty Lall Seal, Dwarkanath Tagore, and Ashutosh Day setting the tone in Calcutta. In Bombay and Ahmedabad, the first steps toward industrialization were taken, and an Indian manufacturing elite began to take shape: Merchant Cowasjee Nanabhoy

The Bombay bourgeoisie: Jamsetji Nusserwanji Tata, cotton industrialist, late nineteenth century.

Davar opened Bombay's first mechanized cotton mill in 1856, and Ahmedabad's Ranchhodlal Chhotalal soon followed suit.[38]

It was not just their shared economic position that signaled the arrival of a new kind of social class; it was also their ability to develop dense social networks, collective institutions, and a common culture that helped them act politically. The peculiar ways in which capital owners constituted themselves as a class were strikingly similar across vast spaces. The well-trodden paths of the mercantile archipelago centuries earlier were becoming paved roads—highways, really—for the emergence of what scholars have called the mid-nineteenth-century "global bourgeoisie."[39] Their distinct culture spread rapidly—as they produced new economic links that increasingly formed a dense network across the globe, their social class itself became a production of the global. While it is easy to see capitalist civilization as a force spreading outward from Europe, it is important to recognize that many of this capitalist civilization's cultural and social features were shaped by global relations and experiences.[40] Just think, for instance, of the importance of coffee and tea to bourgeois socializing, of the prevalence of Indian textile designs, and of the chinoiserie beautifying bourgeois homes the world over.

Wherever we look, the family was at the center of capital owners' efforts to create a shared culture—just as much in Calcutta and Rio as in New York and Paris. Capital owners made an enormous effort to forge and maintain both nuclear and extended family networks. The reason was straightforward: Families created a high-trust environment conducive to far-flung business undertakings; they united various segments of capital and—perhaps most important—guaranteed firms' long-term stability through inheritance. Relatives could play critical roles that allowed for the opening of new business branches or for a division of labor in the firm's management—and they ensured the continuation of the firm beyond the lifetimes of individuals. Maintaining such family networks was enormously labor-intensive—letters had to be written, dinners planned, weddings organized. Forging these connections was primarily women's work, making women not just central to the process of bourgeois class formation but central to businesses themselves, whose foundations often rested on such webs of kin. Women displayed the family's wealth at dinners and salons, demonstrated mastery of a shared culture (for example, by playing the piano), and coordinated the raising of children, essential for transferring cultural and financial capital to the next generation. They cast the family as an escape from the market—as labor-intensive a project as any and one crucial to the self-definition of capital owners across the world. With the emergence of a "separate sphere" inhabited by bourgeois women, sharpened gender roles became a vital characteristic of the capitalist civilization.[41]

As a result, the marriage market was maybe the most important market of all. Portrayed in countless novels, matchmaking occupied bourgeois women's time, as they looked for a "union beneficial in familial terms."[42] "[O]nly wealth and political power gave weight," one historian of Rio's elite marriage market observed.[43] Economic elites, there and elsewhere, wed their offspring into planting, professional, political, trading, and manufacturing families to secure access to different spheres of power. Matches were carefully managed: When cotton spinner Thomas Mitchell married Ellen Maria Poyser, the daughter of Samuel Poyser of Derbyshire, their marriage contract regulated all eventualities and extended to twenty-nine pages in length, going into excruciating detail about how the money Ellen Maria brought into the marriage was to be invested, and used, including precise rules outlining how the yet-to-be-born children were to be educated and provisioned. Women also often brought fresh capital and business networks into families, as when Johanne Maria Rauh, the daughter of a Solingen cutlery merchant, married the cutlery manufacturer Johann Abraham Schmidt.[44]

Residential segregation increasingly came to define the economic elite's social networks as well. For centuries, merchants, manufacturers, and bankers had lived close to their businesses and often next door to their less well-off neighbors. Merchants often had their clerks board with them in the same house or even household, and manufacturers typically lived on the factory grounds. That all began to change at midcentury, as bourgeois families retreated into their socially homogenous neighborhoods. In Rio, rich and poor lived next to one another for decades, but beginning in the 1820s, the wealthy moved away from their warehouses and into newly built neoclassical homes in new *bairros* on the outskirts of town. As a result, their radius of activity was progressively confined to a very small part of Rio. In New York, similar processes brought bourgeois New Yorkers into ever-changing sets of Manhattan neighborhoods, and by midcentury, an overwhelming majority of them congregated in a small area around Washington Square. This self-segregation continued in the summertime, when large segments of the American economic elite converged on the seaside resort town of Newport, Rhode Island, and a few other fancy places, as exemplified by an 1895 compilation of Newport's "summer residents" that lists members of the Astor, Belmont, Brown, Harriman, Morgan, and Vanderbilt families among 517 names from New York, Boston, Providence, Chicago, Philadelphia, and Baltimore.[45]

Educational institutions came to play a vital role in solidifying these networks. The sons and, especially, the daughters of merchants, manufacturers, and financiers were often educated by tutors at home. Higher education was deemed unnecessary for their future task of managing the household, countinghouse, plantation, or factory. But elite schools and universities began to crop up, creating another level of solidarity among the economic elite. In Rio, the Colégio Pedro II opened its doors in 1837 to train the sons of the elite, building its curriculum on French classical education. In Boston, Harvard University, once primarily a seminary for training ministers, became the training ground of the sons of the city's merchants and manufacturers.[46] Almost every city soon claimed such an elite educational institution, the start of what became an influential pillar of capitalist civilization until today.

Initially, however, smaller, more intimate institutions played the central role in shaping bourgeois networks: associations and social clubs, which multiplied in cities throughout the world, connecting elites with diverse economic interests. In New York City, these clubs included the New York Club, the New York Yacht Club, the Union League Club, and the Century Club. By 1875, Saint-Étienne, a center of coal mining and metalworking near the French city of Lyon, counted twenty-one bourgeois voluntary associations, such as the Cercle des Tisseurs and the Cercle de l'Union. In Calcutta, the Bengal Chamber of Commerce became a central meeting place of that city's economic elite. In Hong Kong and Shanghai, Chinese capital owners came together to engage in, for example, charity activities. In Rio, the Casino Fluminense, founded in 1845, brought together that city's economic elite, its grand building allowing planters, merchants, high-flying professionals, and politicians to mingle with one another. The city's Jockey Club was another such venue, combining horse racing with networking. In Frankfurt, at the same time, bourgeois institutional and cultural life flourished—indeed, it came close to defining the class of capital owners itself. The Bethmanns—noted earlier for their role in Caribbean trade, German state finances, and industrialization—were active in the Frankfurter Kunstverein (Frankfurt Art Association), the Senckenbergische Naturforschende Gesellschaft (Senckenberg Natural Research Society), the Paris Zoo, the Volksbibliothek (People's Library), the theater, the Palmengarten (one of the city's three botanical gardens), the Städel Museum, the Volksküche (to feed the poor), the Verein für Blinde (to support the blind), and the Verein gegen Tierquälerei (to protect animals from cruelty). In Hamburg, the Kunsthalle and the Musikhalle played very similar roles, wresting culture from commercial interests and cultural impresarios and distancing music performances from the vagaries of the market. The Manchester economic elite just as eagerly joined musical societies, the Geological Society, the Medical Society, the Victoria Institute, the Natural History Society, the Phrenological Society, the Botanical and Horticultural Society, and many others. Such a vibrant civil society became a vehicle of bourgeois influence and power—newspapers, museums, zoos, and other such venues projected elite tastemaking and networking. For now, these associations were mostly local. For all their national and even global connections, the mid-nineteenth-century bourgeoisie remained primarily provincial in their institutional engagements. Their associational life solidified their still rather fresh claim to leadership, reaffirmed in their predictable daily routines. When Brazilian engineer André Pinto Rebouças sat down to write his diary, he chronicled an unending pattern of letter writing, business meetings, lunches at various clubs, evenings at the opera, and dinner invitations within the same circle of people.[47]

In the process of establishing social networks, merchants, manufacturers, planters, and bankers developed a shared class culture as well. When Brazilian writer Joaquim Maria Machado de Assis sat down in 1880 to depict the world of Rio's economic elite, he painted a portrait of a self-conscious class whose members drew profits from slavery and the coffee trade and were deeply connected to one another through family networks, institutions, residential segregation, and the cultivation of shared habits and manners.[48] Following the life of a fictitious rentier, Brás Cubas, he described people in frock coats and breeches, their student years spent at the Portuguese University of Coimbra, their homes featuring "tablecloths from Flanders [and] large pitchers from India," enslaved servants nurturing the "little masters." In Machado's Rio, the bourgeoisie dined at the elite Hotel Pharoux (whose chefs were Paris-trained), attended balls and theater performances ("he liked the theater very much"), and led a remarkably "elegant and polished life." In such a world, "public opinion" was exceedingly important, capable of making or breaking careers, and thus something to be "afraid of."[49]

Strict rules applied to public deportment, for example, on that

Bourgeois honor defended:
a set of dueling pistols, Italy,
circa 1850.

most bourgeois of all Rio streets: the Rua do Ouvidor, filled with cafés and stores offering Parisian wares. There, those of the entire "fashionable world" flocked, displaying themselves with their fineries, sipping coffee, and hoping to be seen. That street was so important to Rio's economic elite that author Joaquim Manuel de Macedo published a chronicle about it in 1878, *Memórias da Rua do Ouvidor*, describing the street as a "territory of passion" because of its significant cultural offerings.[50]

Rio's capital owners, like their counterparts elsewhere, created an *alto mundo*—a high society.[51] When one writer nostalgically looked back to the 1870s from his 1911 vantage point, he imagined that society as "supremely distinguished and delicate, with habits of refined sociability."[52] Planters, merchants, investors, and politicians met at their homes, clubs, or theaters. Their sense of what was fashionable was informed by the bourgeois capital of the world—Paris.[53] Elite education focused on acquiring French language skills; French governesses along with French furniture and French architecture were all the rage—even the built environment underwent a thorough "frenchification."[54] Champagne, in Rio and elsewhere, was a favorite drink, and the high-end products of the French economy invaded bourgeois homes to such a degree that French capitalism has been called "champagne capitalism"—its economy, in some ways, focused on exporting class-affirming luxury goods to elites the world over.[55]

Bourgeois culture became a marker of capitalist civilization itself. Tellingly, when Brazil's economic elite presented itself at the world exhibitions—in Paris in 1869, Vienna in 1873, and Philadelphia in 1876—it emphasized not only Brazil's resource abundance and fertile soil but also its "intellectual culture": its theaters, its charitable and benevolent societies. That is, it presented a picture of a fully formed capitalist civilization.[56]

As this self-representation of Brazil's economic elite shows, class formation was a deliberate project. Entertaining and receiving, lunching at elite restaurants, holding memberships in exclusive clubs, and having a particular way of public self-presentation were prerequisites to being recognized as a member of what the *Jornal das Senhoras* in 1854 called "boa sociedade" (good society).[57] Dinners were elaborately choreographed events, with obscene varieties and quantities of food. An obsession with genealogy spread: The Brazilian Werneck family, having grown wealthy from plantation investments, drew up elaborate family trees showing their distinguished familial lineage.[58]

These manners and customs would have been recognizable to visiting merchants, bankers, and industrialists from other parts of the world. Indeed, the emerging bourgeois culture was astoundingly predictable because it addressed the same problems everywhere: forging trust, providing a basis for collective action, bridging the gap between disembodied capital and the impermanent individual, and marshaling family to lubricate the capital and render it immortal. Behaviors, in Rio and elsewhere, were strictly codified. Etiquette manuals such as the *Elementos da civilidade* prescribed a total of 159 rules—how to dress appropriately, how to visit, how to converse "at the table," how to write letters. It urged its readers to show "civility" in dealing with other members of "society."[59] While the bourgeoisie universally aspired to a world governed by markets, it defined itself by networks, rituals, habits, and manners that were not transacted on markets, a seeming contradiction at the heart of capitalist civilization.

Rio was not unique: An ostentatious bourgeoisie emerged elsewhere too. The interiors of elite New York homes were plush and crowded with elaborate furniture; paintings of family members lined the walls, and spaces were filled with an astonishing amount of crystal, sculptures,

Food as a marker of class: excerpt from a dinner menu in Rio de Janeiro, Brazil, 1877.

and mementos brought back from trips around the world. When a member of Glasgow's elite died in 1850, a list of household items and furnishings was drawn up that spanned seven pages at a time when most industrial workers and rural cultivators owned almost nothing.[60]

Bourgeois culture became planetary in scope: Its structure, artifacts, and manners in Indian cities would have looked vaguely familiar to visitors from New York, Glasgow, or Rio. In Calcutta, like elsewhere, sumptuous dress, elaborate social events, and ostentatious consumption became telltale signs of the city's economic elite. Taverns and theaters became spaces of socializing, while carriages drove down fashionable streets so that their occupants could display their finery. As the biographer of one of Calcutta's most important merchants, John Palmer, observed, Palmer lived a "private life . . . so inextricably interwoven with his business career that it is often difficult to ascertain whether decisions were guided by personal or commercial considerations."[61] At the core of that private life was Palmer's extended family. He and his wife, Mary, sent their daughters to England for an education that would prepare them for suitable marriages. Navigating this world was expensive but necessary for displaying his success in business and thus his creditworthiness.

Taste was a matter of class. Wealthy Bengalis were no strangers to this world; Palmer enjoyed, within limits, close relations with Indian merchants such as Ramchunder Mitter—not least because he depended on them for capital, institutional support, and expertise. And just as the Bengali elite sampled some of the trappings of European bourgeois culture, so, too, did the European elite tap wells of local influences: Mughal aesthetics shaped Palmer's household furnishings, a mix of British foods, local ingredients, and his servants' cooking.[62]

Thousands of such stories could be told about capital owners across the globe. This bourgeois culture also took root in cities like Aleppo, Damascus, Beirut, Haifa, Cairo, and İzmir, with capital owners dressing in distinctly Western ways (albeit with the addition of a fez), living in smaller family units than other families, and demonstrating great interest in science, Western literature, and the arts. They organized voluntary associations and charitable societies; balls and theater performances came to play an important role in their social lives.[63]

Soon the cotton-producing Egyptian countryside also saw the emergence of a class of capitalist landowners whose wealth translated into acquiring the artifacts of bourgeois culture. Richly furnished mansions went up in small villages, city homes filled with servants to cater to every whim of the newly rich, and travel to the seats of European bourgeois culture became common. Cotton planter Hassan Fuuda's family was one of many who, in the second half of the nineteenth century, rode the crest of the cotton boom to significant wealth, acquiring several mansions, hiring European tutors for their children, and entertaining at lavish parties.[64]

Broadly speaking, bourgeois life in Lima followed the manners and customs of this class in other parts of the world. The expansive diary of merchant Heinrich Witt, whom we briefly encountered earlier, reveals an obsession with "reputation," the material and moral worth of the members of the city's economic elite, and the ways property moved through inheritances. Tellingly, Witt condemned the marriage of an acquaintance to an "unknown woman" and approved of the groom's mother immediately abandoning the house where she had

An agrarian bourgeoisie: Hassan Fuuda, cotton planter, Egypt, late nineteenth century.

lived with her son. He wrote about people from a "moral point of view" and was deeply immersed in cultural activities.[65] Well educated and fluent in seven languages, he devoured literature and history books and followed the political and economic news on all continents. Deeply embedded in bourgeois cultural networks, he regularly attended operas. He went for walks, rode horses, and visited the seaside, often mixing business and pleasure. To a striking degree, his world was sex-segregated, even at home: After dinner, men would "retire" to a separate space to drink and smoke.[66]

Networking was crucial to Witt's business. Visiting people and writing letters, he created a web of acquaintances, reflected in his habit of spending Christmas Day traveling through Lima to visit important contacts to leave his calling card. To solidify their network, he and his wife, María Teodora del Patrocinio de Sierra y Velarde, frequently attended and organized parties and dinners at which politicians mingled with businesspeople. When the Witts organized a large party in October 1848, 161 guests attended, including many businesspeople and politicians, not least of whom was Peru's president. They ate ample foods and consumed champagne until daybreak.[67]

Like others of his class, Witt understood that his most important network was his family, and he paid enormous attention to marriages. When a young man from Altona asked for the hand of his daughter Enriqueta, Witt turned him down, writing to the suitor's mother to say that his "total lack of capital wherewith to commence business was a weighty reason why we could not sanction his marriage with our daughter. Love, to be sure, was a fine thing, but love without bread did not fill the stomach."[68] A few months later, in May 1848, Enriqueta married Gerald Garland, whom her father considered a better match: "Mr. Garland was continually our guest at dinner. He and my daughter were, of course, excellent friends, but as lovers I rather thought them quiet and taciturn."[69] Yet Witt considered Garland an "excellent counting-house man," and, belying his usual calculating attitude, he was moved to tears during the wedding.[70]

Some of the coherence of bourgeois culture across vast distances stemmed from the economic elite's cosmopolitanism and their emerging penchant for travel. Witt, for example, was an avid traveler, visiting Switzerland, Paris, Prague, Berlin, Munich, Naples, Algiers, Norway, Denmark, Brussels, London, Liverpool, and Manchester, among other places. The grand tour became something of a rite of passage for a new class of young bourgeoisie, with an entire far-flung generation of capital owners consorting in the covered arcades of Paris, the tailories of London, the ancient ruins of Rome, and the Uffizi in Florence. Banker Moritz von Bethmann traveled with his family through Italy for six months in 1864, visiting Venice, Rome, Florence, Bologna, Milan, and Genoa. On that journey, they used a new technology—photography— to document works of art they encountered. They also assiduously collected business cards from clothing, jewelry, and furniture stores, savoring the novelty and luxury of patronizing the icons of high-quality artisanal production, a nostalgic return to the cul-

Touring the bourgeois world: The Bethmann family takes a photograph of the ancient wonders of Venice.

tural repertoire of past ruling classes.[71] Seen sharing elegant meals at such stops along the tour, they made their cosmopolitanism clear, as they did their attachment to world-spanning solidarities.

The spread of bourgeois culture can be best mapped by looking at the spread of Italian opera houses—a quintessentially bourgeois cultural form. The world's first such opera house opened in Venice in 1637. Others like it then sprang up in Italian and other European cities (and Le Cap in Saint-Domingue, whose theater opened in the 1780s). By the midcentury, a global opera boom had ensued. In the 1840s, the Dresden Semperoper opened its doors, followed by the Gran Teatre del Liceu in Barcelona. The next decade saw the inauguration of the Tiflis Imperial Theater; the Staatsoper in Hannover; the Teatro de la Zarzuela in Madrid, modeled on La Scala in Milan; the Teatro Solís in Montevideo; the Academy of Music (with a performance of Verdi's *Il Trovatore*) in Philadelphia; and the Teatro Colón (with a performance of Verdi's *La Traviata*) in Buenos Aires. More theaters followed in the 1860s: the Mariinsky Theatre in Saint Petersburg; the Théâtre du Châtelet in Paris (seating twenty-two hundred people); the Sauto Theater in Matanzas, Cuba; the Apollo Theater on the small Greek island of Syros in 1864; the Teatro Degollado in Guadalajara; the Royal Colosseum and Opera House in Glasgow; the Vienna Court Opera House on the new Ringstrasse (ground zero for the Habsburg bourgeoisie); and the Khedivial Opera House (designed by Italian architects Avoscani and Rossi) in Cairo, with a performance of Verdi's *Rigoletto*. The opera boom continued in the 1870s, with many new standouts opening their doors: the Croatian National Theatre in Zagreb; the Theatro Lyrico Fluminense in Rio (which "enjoyed exceptional social importance," including for Antonio Clemente Pinto, who patronized that house and the Jockey Club, in addition to attending an endless series of balls and parties); the Athenaeum in Cork, Ireland; and the Festspielhaus in Bayreuth (dedicated solely to Wagner performances).[72] Budapest's Hungarian State Opera House followed in 1884. And in 1897, in a city deep in the heart of the Amazon rainforest, far from roads and railroads and reachable only by ship, Brazil's rubber barons opened their own opera house—the Teatro Amazonas of Manaus, with a performance of Amilcare Ponchielli's *La Gioconda*.[73]

As they built networks and a shared culture, capital owners also articulated distinct ideas about the society they played such a crucial role in creating and their place within it. Capitalist civilization became an ideological project in search of legitimacy and coherence. One of the core dogmas uniting economic elites everywhere was the belief that they were part of a historically progressive moment. They believed they were leaving behind a world they described as stagnant, often tyrannical, and beholden to religious and secular convictions based on superstition and aristocratic privilege. Their belief in a progressive future was encouraged by the sparkling technical innovations of the time. Steam engines, railroads, and the like promised a newly unshackled world, a tomorrow in which human energy, intelligence, and determination would overcome the material limitations of all earlier ages. Theirs was an almost boundless optimism, celebrating the material progress unfolding all around them. They saw the dawn of a new age, an age they felt enticed by and called on to steer.[74]

Crucially, theirs was a confidence rooted in the very universalism

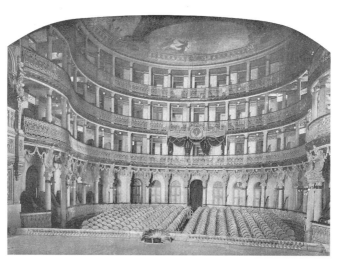

Bourgeois culture spreads its wings: The Teatro Amazonas, an opera house, opened in Manaus, Brazil, in 1897.

of the values of their own class. Conveniently forgetting the significant importance of the nonmarket in the forging of their exalted position and forgetting the importance of such forms of exploitation as slavery and dispossession, they typically ascribed their good fortune not to birth, inheritance, luck, or lineage but to hard work, prudence, intelligence, and a willingness to forgo rewards in the present for future well-being. As *Hunt's Merchants' Magazine and Commercial Review* observed in 1850s New York, "honesty," "[m]utual confidence," "honor," "sincerity," "integrity," "strict morality," and "endurance" were all exceedingly important virtues.[75] Capital owners made the rejection of the very notion of the existence of "classes" a cornerstone of their identity, in contrast, for example, to the unabashed fetish of hierarchies common among the European aristocracy.[76] "[S]uccess," *Hunt's Merchants' Magazine and Commercial Review* declared, "springs from no condition of birth or accident."[77] As the elite Association for Improving the Condition of the Poor (AICP) remarked in 1858, "[N]o one man has rights which are not common to all."[78] This belief in the universalism of the values of their own class lent itself quite easily to an agenda of naturalizing the world they were in the process of building, a move elites throughout history have taken to protect their status.[79]

Despite its all-too-obvious contradictions, this emerging worldview also produced the intellectual tools and political energy needed to oppose forms of dependence and hierarchy that had structured human societies for centuries—from religious justifications for rule to the subordinate role of women, from notions of class-bound rights to slavery. By midcentury, to cite a consequential example, American abolitionism, while mostly a movement of African Americans and less-well-off whites, attracted wealthy capital owners to its ranks, demonstrating the emancipatory thrust embedded within the emerging bourgeois worldview.[80] New York merchant brothers Arthur and Lewis Tappan helped make New York a center of antislavery by establishing the American Anti-Slavery Society. When the clothing manufacturer George Opdyke published *A Treatise on Political Economy* in 1851, he described slavery as "clearly inconsistent with the principles of justice and political equality." Moreover, he forcefully argued that capital tied to slavery could not be invested elsewhere more productively and that economic development depended on the motivation to work hard, which, he observed, was lacking in slaves for whom "the hope of gain and the fear of want are both extinguished by the deprivation of freedom."[81]

Such enlightened beliefs also impacted eonomic elites' ideas about the political order. Having emerged from a world of tributary rule and aristocratic privilege—indeed they were still surrounded by that world—they sought political influence that corresponded to their exalted economic position. They demanded aristocratic power to be reduced, and to get there, they favored the rule of law (a radical departure from the personalistic decision-making of the aristocracy), the freedom of the press, the freedom of opinion, and systems of checks and balances that limited the age-old power relations favored by tributary rulers the world over. Such a liberal worldview, though compromised in multiple ways, was foundational to capitalist civilization.

Yet that fundamentally liberal universalism, driven by the economic elite's sense of the world becoming ever more modern and progressive, was always tempered by a fear of the instability of the civilization they had played such a key part in constructing: the crises, social dislocations, and rebellions by unattached and impoverished "masses" that spread throughout the empire of capital. Even capital owners' antislavery leanings, as far as they were present, were undercut by a deep fear that attacking that peculiar property right—the right to own another human being—might undermine property rights more broadly. Sometimes, the "antagonism between capital and labor" was made sense of through recourse to Darwinism, as when *The Economist* pronounced in 1867 that social differences resulted from "a process of natural selection as certain and rigid as any other part of the mechanism of the world."[82]

There were fears, and then there were outright contradictions. The emancipatory component of bourgeois worldviews had a counterweight in the deeply hierarchical nature of capitalist civilization, which built upon unequal gender relations, as well as upon racist and imperial forms of domination. Gender distinctions were categorical and deeply rooted

*Racial hierarchies central to bourgeois class formation: a white
entrepreneur and his enslaved workers, Brazil, 1870.*

in both custom and law. Imperialism and enslavement, along with
strongly held beliefs in racial and civilizational hierarchies, shaped the
bourgeois world just as much. Racialized thinking—sometimes crass,
sometimes subtle—was virtually everywhere within the capitalist civilization: *The Manufacturer and Builder*, which billed itself as "a practical
journal of industrial progress," once stated: "There is more difference
between a Caucasian and the lowest type of [Indigenous] Australian
than between such an Australian and the highest type of monkey."[83]
The Economist spoke of "indolent and half-savage Malays."[84] Heinrich
Witt in Lima thought that people of African descent were naturally
lazy.[85] For Ida Pfeiffer, the Austrian traveler we came across earlier,
Rio's people of African descent were "truly repulsive."[86] And despite
John Palmer's close interactions with his Indian business partners, racism colored his view: Malays, for example, were "savage and rapacious."[87] The most radical expression of this tendency was the emergence
of what came to be called a "science" of race.[88] Influentially, Louis
Agassiz, a Harvard professor of zoology and geology, elaborated a theory in which he argued for the separate origins of various peoples—
polygenism—and claimed that each race was its own distinct species.[89]

Racist thinking—a prominent, even core, feature of the economic elite's understandings of global hierarchies within the new capitalist civilization—seeped into their understandings of domestic and local economic hierarchies, too, at deep odds with the universalist worldviews simultaneously embraced by bourgeois across the world. By midcentury, merchants, industrialists, and bankers spoke of urban social problems in increasingly analogous term to those in the colony—the "barbaric underclasses" and the dangers they posed became a constant theme within elite discourse, as the bourgeoisie began to draw parallels between colonial subjects and European underclasses. Fear of workers intensified exponentially as they moved into factories and neighborhoods far removed from their "betters." As these workers became less known and more otherized, a market emerged for journalists and writers to report to elite readers on the strange form of life within the cities they painted as lighthouses of the capitalist civilization.[90] In 1871, *The New York Times* reported that "[i]t is very difficult for a journalist who knows the condition and feelings of the working classes throughout the world to make readers of the comfortable classes understand how they regard their relations to capitalists and to society at large."[91] Social segregation, just as in Rio and elsewhere, made large parts of Manchester unknown to its "better sorts."[92] Charles Dickens's writings harped on descriptions of England's poor—a world exotic to the upper crust.[93]

Workers became strangers, the target of various reform movements. In New York, a "home missionary movement" spread the gospel in working-class neighborhoods and advocated temperance, while the Association for Improving the Condition of the Poor provided charity. A "moral imperialism" took root in Manchester as well, with the Manchester and Salford Town Mission wanting to reform the habits and leisure patterns of workers.[94] They established libraries, parks, and temperance societies to "improve" people who they increasingly perceived as the "dangerous classes."[95] Christian economic elites focused on reforming the disorderly working class, a movement explicitly connected to similar "civilizing" efforts in the colonies. When William

Booth, founder of the Salvation Army, sat down to write *In Darkest England and the Way Out* at the end of the nineteenth century, he used "Darkest England" to evoke the "Darkest Africa" that Henry Morton Stanley had just so vividly described.[96] "Darkest England, like Darkest Africa, reeks with malaria. The foul and fetid breath of our slums is almost as poisonous as that of the African swamp."[97] He asserted that one could "discover within a stone's throw of our cathedrals and palaces similar horrors to those which Stanley has found existing in the great Equatorial forest."[98] Engaging in a new civilizing mission, bourgeois activists saw the colony and the home country as "two fronts, however geographically separated, of the same war against savagery."[99] As German reformer Friedrich von Bodelschwingh contended: "[T]he frontiers between the *Heimat* and the world of the heathen did merge" and "the German protectorates [in Africa] were put on par with the German hinterland."[100] Colonized economic elites could be drawn into this discourse, too—for example, as happened when the Indian branch of the Salvation Army gained the support of one of India's preeminent entrepreneurs, the Tata family.

In the end, the bourgeois worldview was much stamped by its encounter with the global working class, whether Black or white, foreign or domestic. Yet the bourgeois program of moral imperialism, despite all the energy spent at home and abroad, was an almost complete failure. Capital owners' power on the shop floor did not translate to effective control of the inner lives and culture of workers.[101]

The capitalist civilization, as imagined in the halls of the Metropolitan Museum of Art and parlors everywhere, was defined by yet another product of the economic transformations that capital owners had helped create: the working class. The "unwashed masses," often racialized, stood in frequent tension with the ideology and interests of the ascendant bourgeoisie. Just as mid-nineteenth-century capital owners increasingly fashioned themselves into a tightly connected, even self-conscious class, manufacturing workers, miners, stevedores, and others who did hard labor also began to develop networks, shared manners, and identities. Sometimes they even engaged in mobilizations and collective politics, hoping, like their bourgeois "betters"—but with their own ideas—to remake the world.

The agrarian working class was centuries old, and we have encountered some of their politics and collective actions already. In a new development, a massive industrial working class emerged as a recognizable social group as well. Their numbers burgeoned. By 1880, millions worked in industry, in mining and construction. They were the first wave of a rapidly growing industrial proletariat. In 1881, 4.5 million workers worked in the manufacturing, construction, and mining sectors of the United Kingdom. In France, the number was 3 million (in 1876); in the United States (in 1881), 4.3 million. This was an astounding increase over a short period—numbers almost doubled in the United Kingdom and more than quintupled in the United States in the preceding four decades. Scholars have estimated that another twenty years later, more than every second family on the European continent was headed by a proletarian wage earner—a social change of staggering radicalism and one that came to define capitalist civilization.[102] The speed of the growth of the working class pointed directly to the future centrality of inequality rooted in wage labor, and the actions of this class—in workplaces, communities, and politics—decisively shaped the future of the capitalist civilization in the twentieth century.

One of the greatest concentrations of manufacturing workers emerged in the textile regions of northern England, particularly in the city of Manchester. In this "great capital of the weavers and spinners of the earth," whose products "will form the clothing and household drapery of half the nations of the east and south," tens of thousands of workers streamed into hulking factories; in 1841, 40,000 people labored in cottons alone, churning out formerly unfathomable quantities of yarn and cloth delivered to markets all over the world.[103] Ten years later, as the city grew to 250,000 inhabitants, it was 57,000 such workers, while another 14,000 women and men labored in engineering and metals, especially textile machinery; a further 22,000 people worked in apparel, 9,520 in textile warehouses, and 20,000 in domestic service.[104] For good reason, future British prime minister Benjamin Disraeli called the city "as great a human exploit as Athens."[105] There, developments that were more subdued elsewhere came to the fore in their starkest form.

Manchester attracted visitors from all over the world who were curious about what this newly emerging capitalist civilization looked like fully formed. What they encountered in the "shock city" of the Industrial Revolution gave them pause.[106] Entering Manchester, British journalist George Jacob Holyoake observed a "town [that] has the appearance of one dense volume of smoke, more forbidding than the entrance to Dante's Inferno."[107] Its industry was such a heavy user of coal—in the 1860s, Manchester burned around six tons of coal per person annually—that people "saw, tasted, and felt" the smoke, according to Reverend John Molesworth.[108] Even after the Manchester Association for the Prevention of Smoke was founded in 1842, French economist Léon Faucher compared the city to an active volcano, while British general Sir Charles James Napier considered Manchester "the chimney of the world . . . the entrance to hell realized."[109]

But it was not just concern about the dire environmental effects of industry and the specter of a once bucolic townscape dominated by mills and warehouses that agitated contemporary observers. It was also the sheer number of workers who powered the mills and filled the streets. From 1851 to 1871, Manchester added another 150,000 people, mostly workers.[110] French traveler Alexis de Tocqueville, seeing a city inhabited by "a few great capitalists, thousands of poor workmen, and little middle class," feared the social implications of this new structure.[111] "Here humanity attains its most complete development and its most brutish; here civilisation works its miracles, and civilised man is turned back almost into a savage," he wrote.[112] There was widespread anxiety among elite observers about the implications of such inequalities. What would happen when, as one priest asked, "the moral sewers of the community—a confluence of the scum and offscouring of society"—came to vastly outnumber everyone else?[113]

As elsewhere, the Manchester working class that attracted so much commentary was quite heterogeneous. However, across these differences its members also shared specific experiences. In return for wages, they spent much of the day working for others, sometimes as long as sixteen hours a day. They were poor. And they encountered sharp social divisions, unleavened by any practical hope of social mobility.[114]

Working-class life in the ever-increasing number of industrializing cities, across industries and levels of skill, was precarious. Jobs could disappear at any moment; household members could fall sick, dropping income below subsistence level; workers could be evicted at any time from their miserable homes. This was perhaps the most unifying experience of the emerging proletariat—that life could take a turn for the worse at any moment; that even in the best of times, hunger, cold, homelessness, and general destitution could set in with almost no warning. In England, the poorhouse always hovered, a place where the work regime of the plantation was alarmingly close to being realized in the newly emerging industrial heartland: There, impoverished workers

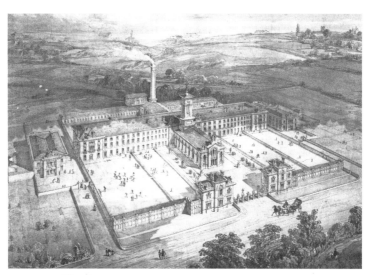

The plantation in the heartland of industrial capitalism:
Withington Workhouse, 1856.

were subject to the most rigorous discipline, all-encompassing supervision, and grueling labor (such as breaking rocks or grinding bones). And at night, they were locked in tiny cells separate from their family members.[115]

Workers also shared a realization that despite such intense work regimes, and partly because of them, their overall well-being did not improve along with the growth of revenue and fortunes among their employers. They were poor in a world of plenty. Until the 1850s, the growth of real wages in the United Kingdom did not exceed the rate of inflation, and working-class living standards did not improve, despite all the new machinery that made human labor so much more productive. Biometric data shows that from the late 1700s to 1860, the average height of British Army recruits, largely drawn from the country's lower classes, decreased by about two centimeters, testifying to worsening nutrition. The high mortality rates characteristic of a city such as Manchester did not decline until the 1860s, while average life expectancy stagnated. In 1870, economist Gustav von Schmoller observed that industrialization had not brought about any improvement in mortality—a finding confirmed by more recent research showing that the new industrial working class experienced such a decline in well-being that by 1870, life expectancy dropped to barely 25.3 years in Manchester.[116] It was a "life-destroying, mind-stunting system of long hours," as a worker noted on a placard addressed to "the Employers and Work People of Mossley."[117]

Working-class communities, identities, and politics emerged from such experiences. They also formed in the dense neighborhoods that workers inhabited, grimly described in 1849 by journalist Angus Bethune Reach during a detailed investigation of Manchester's working-class life. Reach noted "a black, mean-looking street with a black unadorned mill rising over the houses, and a black chimney pouring out volumes of black smoke upon all."[118] Middle-class observers like him went into these working-class communities precisely because their readers considered them exotic and mysterious. Removed from elite quarters, workers lived in derelict and poor areas. Homes were beyond

Working-class housing near a Manchester mill, James Street, 1895.

crowded; it was not unheard of for a cellar of only 144 square feet to house eleven people, along with pigs or even donkeys. When Friedrich Engels, son of a German textile mill owner, joined the parade of middle-class spectators in the early 1840s, he reported on these neighborhoods' "unendurable stench," resulting from an almost complete lack of indoor plumbing.[119] It was, according to Engels, impossible to walk in the district "without sinking into [the mud] ankle-deep at every step."[120]

The catalog of miseries that contemporary observers described was long. Reach remarked that "Manchester, like most great manufacturing and commercial cities, is scantily supplied with water, and that which is to be procured is not by any means universally transparent or tasteless."[121] Workers, he observed, got a "large portion of their nourishment" from the sugar they spooned into their tea, drawing on the cheap calories produced by the enslaved of the Caribbean.[122] Perhaps most disconcertingly to his middle-class audiences, Reach understood that the demands of work were so extreme that the reproduction of families had become almost impossible, with workers resorting to drugs—"Mother's Quietness," "Soothing Syrup," and "Baby's Mixture," all opium derivatives—to calm their children, "with the view to obtaining an undisturbed night's rest."[123] The opium farmers of India thus helped to reproduce Manchester's working class while the East India Company profited from this trade.

Given cramped living conditions, the street was the center of working-class life. People chatted, watched buskers, bought things

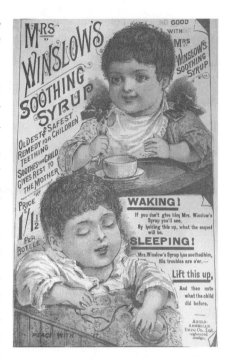

Anglo-American Drug Company advertisement for opium syrup to make children sleep, 1892.

from peddlers, and listened to musicians. Reach described how "itinerant bands bang and blow their loudest; organ boys grind monotonously; ballad singers or flying stationers make roaring proclamations of their wares. The street is one swarming, buzzing mass of people. Boys and girls shout and laugh and disappear into the taverns together."[124] Women played a vital role in street life and over time could assume considerable authority, aided by the depth of their social relationships. Gossip was an important collective activity for both women and men, helping to overcome isolation and forge a sense of community. Newsagents and bookdealers set up shop in these neighborhoods. Serving as working-class libraries, they rented out books for a small fee to the minority of workers literate enough to read them.[125]

Working-class culture was also rooted in formal, often commercial institutions, none more critical than the pub. Boisterous, sometimes violent centers of public life, pubs multiplied in Manchester along with workers; despite efforts to enforce temperance, heavy drinking was unexceptional. In addition to beer, pubs offered entertainments, such as rat-baiting and cockfighting, and plenty of opportunities for gambling, as horse racing and betting became important to male working-class culture.[126]

Other important working-class institutions were the burial societies that organized elaborate and festive wakes, to the intense dislike of the city's economic elite. There were also working-class provident and mutual aid societies, often linked to craft unions. Later, soccer emerged as an important working-class pursuit, with the precursor to Manchester United, today one of the world's most prominent soccer clubs formed in 1878 by workers from a local railroad company at Newton Heath.[127]

Such experiences were not unique to Manchester or the United Kingdom. Poverty and harsh working conditions were common to all sites of industrialization. In the French city of Mulhouse, between 1823 and 1834, one in two working-class children died before reaching the age of two. Émile Zola spent time in the French coal-mining area of Anzin in the 1860s and used his observations to write *Germinal*, a literary monument to the miners' inhumane living conditions and their desperate but violently repressed strike. The working class of Osaka was crammed into impoverished districts haunted by cholera outbreaks (a common feature of working-class neighborhoods everywhere). When as many as twenty thousand migrant workers streamed into Bochum, one of the Ruhr's industrial powerhouses, in the two decades after 1850, many were housed in dormitories, with up to twelve single men to a room.[128]

Just as commonly, a vibrant working-class culture took shape. In Bochum, facilitated by dense working-class housing, workers passed rare idle moments within an ever-growing number of pubs and formed various associations. Like their bourgeois opposites, they also married one another. Osaka workers also managed to build a raucous cultural life outside elite control, including celebrating and defending a huge number of holidays that totaled almost three months a year. Rapidly growing Philadelphia experienced the same: crowded tenements, residential concentration, and shocking poverty among the lowest-skilled workers but also a lively drinking culture and working-class associational life.[129]

YET DESPITE THESE shared experiences, working-class life in Manchester and elsewhere was hardly uniform. Experiences differed significantly between skilled and unskilled workers, women and men, and native-born immigrants. Skilled native-born men could achieve a modicum of respectability (even though durable security escaped them, too), while unskilled immigrant women filled the lowest ranks of the working class and lived lives of great precarity.[130]

Gender divisions were as crucial to the internal structure of the working class as they were to the families of economic elites. Unlike elite women, almost all working-class women worked for wages in one form or another, yet their pay was always less than that of their male counterparts, and they still had to take charge of childcare and household labor. In Manchester, women crowded into the textile industry. By 1861, 75 percent of textile workers were women; ten years later, that figure reached 93 percent.[131] Their working conditions were often dire.

The working class was also ethnically diverse. In Manchester, Irish immigrants became a significant part of the city's working class, resulting from a vast influx after the Great Famine of the second half of the 1840s. By 1851, 13 percent of Manchester inhabitants were Irish-born, many laboring in the city's textile factories, often in the worst-paying jobs. They were often desperately poor: The elite Poor Law Guardians found that "in the streets of Manchester an immense number of Irish stand . . . at the corners of streets begging."[132] Many lived in Angel Meadow, the most densely inhabited neighborhood, where ramshackle tenements stood next to breweries, dyeworks, chemical factories, and warehouses. Living conditions were abysmal: The Irish-born Egans packed seven family members into a cellar basement they shared with a family of eight. Another basement dwelling was said to accommodate twenty-six people.[133] When a doctor laid out the causes of a recent Manchester cholera outbreak, he described the Sharples family of four adults and three children at 52 Back Irk Street as "half starving and half naked, sleeping all on the floor."[134] The density of the dead replicated the density among the living: The parish burial ground, a small plot of land known as St. Michael's, contained perhaps as many as forty thousand graves, with a little less than two square feet per burial on a site that, according to an inspector, also saw "constant gambling and fighting, particularly on the Lord's day."[135]

The Irish entered the labor market from a particularly disadvantaged position and encountered frequent discrimination. They were racialized by the worldwide system of classification that increasingly split the working class along ethnic, religious, and racial lines.[136] In 1847, a visiting journalist dismissed Irish workers as characteristically the type to "lie unscrupulously and with a loud voice."[137] While ethnic and religious diversity was also common among economic elites all around the world, divisions within the bourgeoisie were never as deep or as consequential as they were among workers—partly because the power of economic elites rested on the control of capital, while that of workers rested on a difficult-to-achieve solidarity.

But migration could also foster solidarity. The Manchester Irish were densely networked, not least because they often originated from the same part of Ireland and were related to one another. Networks migrated, not just individuals. These solidarities facilitated collective action. Joseph Sadler Thomas, Manchester's deputy constable from 1833 to 1839, reported that when the police wanted to execute a warrant in Angel Meadow, "[t]he Irish are very easily hurried into violence, even by a single one of their countrymen, and at a moment's notice: five minutes will bring together a thousand people at any time."[138] Midcentury Saint Patrick's Day celebrations in Manchester were boisterous affairs, especially as they became linked to Irish nationalism, challenging authorities' ability to control urban spaces.[139]

Many among Manchester's economic elite, like their counterparts elsewhere, disliked, even feared, this working class of their own creation, just as planters feared the enslaved. They tried at times to reform workers, yet only saw modest success. Middle-class campaigns for alcohol abstinence or against such popular hobbies as pigeon fancying usually failed. Workers instead appropriated whatever benefits they could derive from middle-class eagerness to better them: When elite reformers in Manchester built parks in the city's poorer neighborhoods, working-class people took over these spaces and used them according to their own likings, often at odds with the parks' sponsors.[140]

The economic elite's limited ability to control working-class behavior extended to workers' worldviews. Indeed, a distinctly working-class worldview came to characterize capitalist civilization, fostering and sharpening its most enduring and prominent fault lines. Historians have long debated if mid-nineteenth-century manufacturing workers, like their bourgeois counterparts, exhibited an early form of class consciousness. Regardless of the outcome of this debate, what is incontrovertible is that workers widely questioned the legitimacy of the new order.[141] That outlook was first and foremost manifested by the rebuffing of liberal individualism. As a weaver from the English town of Middleton said: "[C]ompetition . . . [is] undermining, with its selfishness, the morals of the folk."[142] Articulated by a Chartist in 1841, the belief that employers were "greedy, grasping and [had] grinding propensities" was common among industrial workers, who held that the rich had "duties" to the poor that they usually failed to fulfill.[143] When talking about their employers during the 1830s and 1840s, stonemasons in the French city of Bordeaux typically used the words *tyrants* and *despots* to describe them.[144] When masons struck in Manchester in 1837/38, they characterized their employers in similar terms as "the combining despots . . . that they may, with impunity, treat those by whom they are kept in affluence with their wanted barbarity," while their nearby Weedon and Coventry counterparts described them as "men who, after toiling and bleeding to keep a set of lazy and insolent plunderers in luxury, are very frequently doomed to pass their declining years in some accursed Bastille, or in obscurity, starvation and wretchedness!"[145] For French locksmith Achille François, workers like himself "carried chains."[146] A nineteen-year-old textile worker in Aachen, Johann Vandenhirtz, accused "the rich" of "repressing" the poor: If I "would have 100 rifles, every rich person would deserve to be shot with them."[147] This working-class worldview was frequently the foundation for collective action—riots, strikes, and, eventually, a passionate allegiance to trade unions, all of which, as we will see momentarily, were central to the rebellions that eventually brought midcentury capitalist civilization into deep crisis.

S uch thinking about capitalism and the new inequalities it generated showed that workers, just like their bourgeois betters, struggled not just for short-term economic interests—a wage increase here,
shorter working hours there—but also for the construction of what
they considered a just society. From within the working class—and
then also from intellectuals who were not of the working class but associated their beliefs and politics with that working class—there came
a fuller critique of the capitalist civilization, including of its foundational pillars—profits, property, class, inequality, and accumulation.
Such criticism of the new capitalist civilization came to define it as
well. Critics' analysis of the present and their ideas about the future
and how to get there were diverse, but what they had in common was
that they thought about capitalism from the particular perspective
of the nineteenth-century empire of capital—that is, from industry,
from the cities, and from Europe—a way of thinking that would become deeply and lastingly consequential to the very foundation of anti-
capitalist thought.

Across their differences, these thinkers had in common their
lamenting of the severe inequality, the extreme poverty, the squalid
living conditions, the children being forced into mines and factories,
and the early deaths that characterized the new social order. They all
questioned the legitimacy of the freshly arrived capitalist civilization
and saw it as against the natural, human, or religious order of things—
an analysis that was widespread, even commonsensical among ordinary workers the world over as well. They also commonly questioned
the notion of private property as such—the inequalities it generated,
the poverty spreading alongside the accumulation of unprecedented
wealth, and the enormous power that ownership of capital conveyed to
a small group of people over the vast majority of humankind. Yet they
disagreed on the nature of the inner workings of the new order, how to
change it, and what an alternative economic order would look like.

Often, the first generation of critics of capitalism favored frequently a turn to a form of cooperation between producers, with resources that would be collectively managed, owned, and used for the benefit of all. Influential among them was Robert Owen, an ill-educated but skilled draper from Wales who by the late eighteenth century had lifted himself up to become a mill manager and eventually a millowner in New Lanark, Scotland. Even though Owen's career on paper exemplified the novel opportunities generated by the capitalist civilization, he broke ranks and criticized the very notion of private property, that cornerstone of capitalism. In its place, Owen envisioned a society that focused on the cooperative organization of industry, with workers' self-management at its core.[148] French social reformer Henri de Saint-Simon and his followers, often skilled workers, developed a similar critique of the new capitalist civilization. They called for a "scientific" organization of society, held together by a rational new Christianity. Decisions would be made by experts in three "natural" social classes: the "industriel" (those engaged in productive labor), the scientist, and the artist. By replacing "the government of men" with "the administration of things," society's productive capacities would expand to the benefit of the poorest, with "production associations" playing an important role.[149]

A few decades later, in 1829, Charles Fourier, from the French city of Besançon, published *Le nouveau monde industriel et sociétaire*, in which he set out a critique of "civilization" and proposed a utopian alternative. Fourier believed the capitalist civilization had led to disharmony and the repression of natural passions. Industry threatened what he called the "natural order," leading to the creation of redundant work in terrible conditions. His utopian society would instead be organized in communes designed to "conduct the human race to opulence, sensual pleasures and global unity."[150] The division between town and country would disappear, and women would be liberated from the constraints of marriage.[151] Throughout the 1830s and 1840s, workers inspired by Fourier and Saint-Simon established communes and cooperatives.

Another French utopian socialist particularly popular among artisan workers was Étienne Cabet, son of a cooper from the Burgundy capital of Dijon. In 1839, he published *Voyage en Icarie*, a utopian novel depicting a society in which a government elected by men (and men only) would make all production and distribution decisions. This society would place smoky factories outside city limits, provide free education for all, and establish palaces of public entertainment. It would be held together by a civic religion with strict gender roles. In the decade following the novel's publication, the so-called Icarian movement attracted a large following; in 1845, Cabet boasted of one hundred thousand members, most of them male artisans.[152]

In the meantime, Wilhelm Weitling, a German journeyman tailor working in Paris, published his 1838 tract *Humanity as It Is and as It Should Be*, in which he demanded the socialization of property, the forging of an egalitarian order, and democratic governance, all propelled by a rebellion of workers. Influenced by Fourier, Saint-Simon, and Cabet, he established the Bund der Gerechten—the League of the Just—among fellow émigré workers, mostly skilled artisans like himself. His league joined the abortive uprising against the July Monarchy the following year, after which Weitling was forced to flee to Switzerland. Once there, he established Christian communist organizations, soon counting at least thirteen hundred members.[153]

Out of this fertile intellectual soil of early French socialism also came French Peruvian Flora Tristan, who in 1843 published *L'union ouvrière*. She saw capitalism as an organizational imbalance between workers and capitalists and called for the creation of an international workers' union. For Tristan, the emancipation of workers and of women had

A new society: utopian socialist Flora Tristan.

to go hand in hand. In 1849, she was joined by socialist feminist Jeanne Deroin, who took up Tristan's call and drafted the statutes for an overarching "Union of Associations," bringing together three hundred workers' associations with fifty thousand members.[154]

Joining this cacophony of voices, Pierre-Joseph Proudhon, who had been a skilled printer in his hometown of Besançon, became the founder of modern anarchism when he published *What Is Property?* in 1840. Therein he famously declared that "property is theft." He denounced income that did not derive from work, such as rent and interest.[155] He called on workers to form "mutualist" cooperative associations in which they would be remunerated according to labor time. They would subsequently be able to directly trade the products of their labor with one another using vouchers. Proudhon, who did not believe in the capacity of the state to create such mutualist associations, claimed the label "anarchist." After moving to Paris in the winter of 1844, he socialized with revolutionary exiles such as Karl Marx, Mikhail Bakunin, and Alexander Herzen. Here he worked on his *System of Economic Contradictions, or The Philosophy of Poverty*, published in 1846. During the 1848 revolution, he spoke at popular Parisian clubs, founded a newspaper with a circulation of forty thousand, and was elected to the National Assembly.[156]

As the political climate in Europe became more repressive, many of these utopian socialists migrated to the United States, where they set up separatist utopian communities. In 1847, Weitling joined the New York Social Reform Association among German migrants and helped establish the League of Emancipation and the Philadelphia Arbeiterverein.[157] Many Saint-Simonians followed. His movement largely destroyed by police repression, Cabet migrated to Texas to set up a colony that would put his ideals into practice. Increasingly, Weitling and Cabet struggled not to alter the capitalist civilization from within but to secede from it—and nowhere except in the United States did they see such ample opportunity to create what amounted to islands of postcapitalism.

A future world of cooperation, instead of market-based competition, was one of the core themes of early critics of the capitalist civilization, undoubtedly informed by Christian notions of community and fellowship. However, there was another critique of the capitalist civilization that focused more directly on the state. The Chartists in the United Kingdom were prominent among them, combining their critique of capitalism with an agenda of increasing working-class political representation in existing governmental institutions.[158] Louis Blanc, a self-proclaimed French socialist, insisted on the centrality of the state as well. In *The Organization of Labor* (1839), he attacked the system of "unlimited competition" that had led to the "dissolution of family existence," the decay of morals, and the displacement of artisans.[159] Against this, he proposed that the state become the "banker of the poor," providing funds for workers to set up cooperatives that would, in time, become self-regulating.

German philosopher and political activist Ferdinand Lassalle also favored such a state-centric view. In 1861, he published *The System of Acquired Rights,* arguing for the political participation of the working class. From his readings of the Ricardian socialists, Lassalle coined the term "iron law of wages" to describe how wages inevitably descended to the bare minimum; only the state could arrest their fall.[160] Lassalle drew on Blanc's vision of establishing worker cooperatives through state support. In 1864, also inspired by the Chartists, he and others established the Allgemeiner Deutscher Arbeiterverein (ADAV), the world's first mass social democratic party, which demanded universal suffrage and social improvements for workers.[161]

Out of this hodgepodge of ideas that grappled with industrial capitalism and the possibilities of a postcapitalist future came the world's most influential body of thought on the capitalist civilization, birthed by two German radicals: Karl Marx and Friedrich Engels. They regarded Owen, Saint-Simon, Fourier, and Cabet as "utopian socialists" who aspired to a more just future without grounding their analyses in the material realities of the world and in what Marx and Engels considered the objective developmental trajectories of existing societies. However sympathetic they were to some of the early socialists' goals,

Celebrating capitalism, and anticipating its overcoming: Karl Marx, 1875.

Marx and Engels condemned them as idealists lacking an understanding of the laws of motion of capitalist societies and embracing political strategies that were equally misguided.

Midcentury was the pair's most productive moment. Fusing German philosophy (especially that of Georg Wilhelm Friedrich Hegel), English economics (especially of Adam Smith and David Ricardo), and French politics (of the utopian socialists), Marx and Engels grappled with the logic of capitalism, placed capitalism in the long sweep of human history, and believed to have identified the conditions under which a postcapitalist future was imaginable. Their thinking emerged at the exact moment of the birth of the midcentury capitalist civilization, and their oeuvre (unrivaled for its staying power and impact among analyses of capitalism since Adam Smith) was stamped indelibly by this moment of its emergence.[162]

Marx and Engels celebrated capitalism while at the same time seeing it as the last great barrier to the emergence of human freedom. Engels, the son of a prominent textile factory owner in the German city of Barmen, had come into contact with Owenite political economy and the communist thought of German migrants. In 1843, his essay "Outlines of a Critique of Political Economy" attacked private property and competition and, fatefully, convinced Marx of the importance of political economy. Several years later, Marx and Engels authored a collection of essays that would later be published as *The German Ideology*, in which they applied Ludwig Feuerbach's left-Hegelian critique of religion to political economy: They saw not only God but also the state and property as externalized projections of humans' own creative social processes.[163] Marx's and Engels's work charted how capitalism had allowed for the unprecedented development of what they called the "forces of production"—causing an explosion of human productivity and wealth unimaginable to previous generations. To them, capitalism—like other modes of production—was rooted in a particular class structure, with the bourgeoisie and the working-class core actors in what they termed "class struggle." Seen superficially, that analysis was not much different from the one presented in the *Journal des Débats* to explain the uprising of Lyonnais silk workers in 1831, as we will later discuss. For Marx and Engels, however, class and class struggle were not just a set of facts among many having to do with history. They were its very motor, though one deeply embedded within the development of the forces of production—the machines and technical knowledge that circumscribed the productive potential of societies throughout history and thus also defined their class structures. Capitalism, Marx and Engels claimed, was a fundamentally new and exceptionally dynamic order, yet one that, like all orders before, produced its own contradictions, its own antithesis, and thus its own gravediggers. That antithesis was a yet only vaguely imagined "communism," and those gravediggers were the industrial proletariat.

Because Marx and Engels saw the working class as the decisive world-historical subject—the embodiment of capitalism's antithesis—they invested their political energies in the emerging labor movement. In 1846, the pair of social theorists, who were living in Brussels at the time, became key founding members of the Communist Correspondence Committee. A year later, they merged that committee with Weitling's League of the Just to form the Communist League, for which their *Communist Manifesto*, penned in a few weeks in 1848 and published in several European languages, would serve as a founding document. That manifesto charted in bold strokes the capitalist revolution of the previous decades, declared the struggle between the bourgeoisie and the proletariat to be the latest iteration of a long history of class struggle, and called upon workers to organize to supplant that capitalist civilization.[164]

In 1867, Marx began publishing his magnum opus, *Das Kapital*. Therein he developed his critique of political economy more fully. Unlike Proudhon and the Ricardians, he did not see capitalist exploitation as arising from "the unequal exchange between worker and employer," as workers never actually sold their specific labor.[165] Rather, under capitalism, workers sold their potential labor power, implying that exploitation was not a function of incomplete remuneration and therefore could not be remedied with labor vouchers. Marx instead saw exploitation as arising from the production process itself, where the capitalists were responsible for combining labor power, raw materials, and machinery to extract what Marx called "surplus value" from their workers. *Das Kapital* did not go into details as far as the remedy was concerned, but its analysis suggested that only the communization of the factors of production would suffice. Unlike French and British socialism, which usually aimed to elevate workers to the position of full democratic citizens, Marx did not base his appeal to the working class on an appeal to democracy (although he did see suffrage as an important step in building workers' power). The initial print run of the volume was modest, selling just a thousand copies in its first five years. In the 1870s, however, the book was reprinted in Russian and French. By the 1880s, it was being propagated and popularized by several new social democratic parties on the model of the German Sozialdemokratische Partei, the French Parti Ouvrier, the English Social Democratic Federation, the Russian Group of the Liberation of Labor, the Parti Ouvrier Belge, the Swiss and Austrian Social Democratic Parties, and the Italian Socialist Party. Marx's and Engels's works became some of the greatest bestsellers of all time—*The Communist Manifesto* sold an estimated five hundred million copies—competing with only the Bible, the Quran, and the IKEA catalog.[166]

Just as Marx and Engels saw the working class as the decisive historical subject who would bring an end to capitalism, millions of workers would much later come to see Marx and Engels as the most incisive, relevant analysts of this new system that had so powerful a grip on their lives. Part of the attraction of Marx and Engels's analysis was its ability to combine an incisive critique of the social inequalities produced by capitalism with a deeply optimistic account of the future and the role of workers in bringing about that future. Tellingly, when workers and intellectuals from various European countries founded the International Working Men's Association in 1864 in London, they put Marx in charge of writing their organization's platform. His speech at the founding convention condemned the continued stark poverty in the midst of a society that "is unrivaled for the development of its industry and the growth of its commerce." He called upon workers to organize and concluded with what would become the battle cry of a movement that would reshape and contest global capitalism for the next century and a half: "Proletarians of all countries, unite!"[167]

Such critics came to define the empire of capital just as much as the novel patterns of social inequality and the new intensity of the commodification of life. Yet the capitalist civilization was also defined by a newfound global synchronicity in which economic patterns, especially booms and busts, proved contagious, moving at breakneck speed around the world. As American poet Walt Whitman asked, was there now "but one heart to the globe"?[168] Economic life had followed local or perhaps regional rhythms for millennia, with any global trends usually connected to slow-moving changes in the earth's climate. Now, however, economic life pulsated to a new rhythm. No one could agree on what led to these strange regularities and their astonishingly global reach, though some began searching for answers within the new capitalist civilization itself.

Perhaps least mysterious was one kind of synchronicity—the convergence of prices. In previous centuries, prices for goods varied greatly across the world, as producers catered to consumers within limits circumscribed by communication and shipping. The price of grain in Tenochtitlán, for obvious reasons, had no relationship to the price of grain in Rome; copper prices in Edo were unrelated to those in Timbuktu. That began to change around 1800, as markets integrated globally.[169] The price of sugar—or cotton or cloth—moved in the same direction whether in Buenos Aires or New York, Paris or Bombay. What did not converge, however, was the price of labor, leading one French journal to threaten Lyon silk workers in the wake of a strike in ways that seem almost contemporary: "[F]ive hundred leagues from you, in Russia, in Austria, somewhere finally where labor is cheap, a factory of your kind has just been established which delivers its goods at a lower price than you. How can you compete? By lowering the daily rate?"[170]

More mysterious was another synchronicity: the new rhythms of global booms and busts that became commonplace. An example of this global interdependence struck in 1837. The new industrial world relied heavily on cotton exports from the United States, and American cotton farmers depended on European credit. As a result of this highly leveraged arrangement, disturbances in the markets for "white gold" reverberated throughout the world economy. The first signs of this unprecedented global crunch emerged as early as 1835, when New Orleanian cotton factor, banker, and sugar refiner Edmond Jean Forstall traveled to London to secure funding for his Louisiana bank bonds. He was "shocked to discover" that the banking house of Baring Brothers was unwilling to issue the necessary credit, judging the investment too risky in the face of stagnating cotton prices.[171] The following year, the Bank of England tightened credit to keep its gold bullion from leaving the United Kingdom. Cotton prices kept going down, and by early 1837, cotton factors, traders, and banks had begun failing in London and Liverpool.[172] News of these failures reached New York on March 17, leading to further bankruptcies, with *The Herald* reporting that "[c]rowds collected in Wall Street—and that busy avenue was filled with anxious faces through the live long day."[173] As prices fell and credit dried up, planters went bankrupt, and with them many of the middlemen who facilitated the movement of cotton and capital across the Atlantic. Land markets in the cotton-growing areas of the South collapsed. Upon his travels to Mississippi, a North Carolinian traveler reported that "it may probably be said that not one man in fifty are solvent and probably less a number than this."[174] In Vicksburg, the southern border of the Mississippi Delta, squalor "spread like a funeral pall over the young city. . . . Its wealth had taken to itself wings like an eagle, and had fled."[175] As New York lawyer George Templeton Strong wrote in his diary in 1840: "[T]he last three years [are] comparable to nothing but the explosion of a pack of crackers—pop—pop—pop— one after another they go off and all their substance vanishes in fumes."[176]

So far, so bad. But then the crisis spread. On June 5, 1837, after the failure of British trading house Wilson & Co., *The Times* of London observed that "every part of the globe must in succession be visited by [the crisis's] influence."[177] Soon, silk manufacturers in Lyon began suffering from the collapsing North American markets. In Guangzhou and Bombay, the crisis dampened business. Banks in Canada suspended payment. There was a run on Parisian banks in late June 1837. The Banque de Belgique and the Hamburg banks suspended specie payments. Indian indigo production slumped. On October 19, 1837, a partner in the British trading house Jardine, Matheson & Co. reported from Guangzhou: "At present everything is at a stand, in consequence of prices demanded by the Chinese being far too high for the depressed state of the home market."[178] In India, tight cash flow combined with a drought led to a famine. Groups of starving farmers, sometimes numbering more than a thousand, converged on markets to seize food. Java began to feel the financial contraction and the concomitant depression in prices in 1839. By November 13, Amsterdam newspapers reported that the main note-issuing bank in Batavia, the Bank of Java, had suspended specie payments. Following the panic, even food became scarce; in the United States, those of the generation born in the wake of the crisis grew, on average, about five centimeters less in height than their predecessors.[179] American writer Ralph Waldo Emerson wrote in his diary: "The land stinks with suicide."[180]

The Panic of 1837 demonstrated that economic life could no longer be lived in isolation; its rhythms were now global. Just two decades later, in 1857, a similar crisis cascaded through the world, erasing many of the gains of the intervening economic expansion in the second half of the 1840s. Sparked in part by disruptions to crucial trade flows, especially in silver—caused by the Indian Rebellion of 1857 and the Opium Wars in China—a wave of bankruptcies began in France, and then stock market crashes roiled Paris, Berlin, and Vienna. In the United States, land and railroad stock prices fell in the summer of 1857, and the Ohio Life Insurance and Trust Company, heavily involved in railway speculation, failed on August 24. Stock prices declined sharply on the New York Exchange. A few weeks later, the Bank of Pennsylvania suspended specie payments (that is, they did not honor their promises to redeem notes in gold), setting off a nationwide bank run. Early October saw an even larger run on the banks, and by October 12, all but one of "New York's 63 commercial banks had suspended payments."[181] Within a few weeks, the panic spread beyond the financial world, as trading and manufacturing also contracted.[182]

On October 18, 1857, *Der Aktionär*, a finance weekly read by German bankers, commented:

> The crisis is more than a European one, it has become a world issue. . . . World trade is governed by interactions; if the elements of their balancing are missing, a stagnation occurs, which moves from place to place, from country to country, from one part of the world to another and affects the whole organism of trade.[183]

Indeed, merchant houses in Liverpool and Glasgow immediately felt the trouble in New York. Mounting bankruptcies there affected banks, and on October 27, the Borough Bank of Liverpool declared insolvency; on November 9, the Western Bank of Scotland suspended payments. London and Hamburg merchants went bankrupt. The effects of the crisis were truly global: By early 1858, commodity prices in South America had halved, and trading houses collapsed from Buenos Aires to Batavia. In the United Kingdom, wages fell; in the United States, unemployment reached new heights. Between October 1857 and March 1858, one-third to one-half of Pennsylvania's foundries shut down.[184] In November, unemployed workers occupied New York's Tompkins Square, with spokesman George Campbell declaring: "[W]e must not beg, but *demand* work; and if we do not get it *we can do what we please*."[185] The *Preussische Jahrbücher* complained that "[a]ll relationships seem to be topsy-turvy."[186]

Soon, this new pattern of booms and busts was understood and dreaded as an ongoing feature of the new capitalist civilization.

———

B y midcentury, another significant and final sign of the transformation of the archipelago of capital into a distinct civilization emerged: It acquired a label—capitalism. As contemporaries grappled with the radical transformations they encountered, they discerned a set of "special qualities" and gave that complex reality a name.[187]

Capital owners had described themselves, and been seen by others, as "capitalists" since the early sixteenth century, and "capitalist"—a person commanding capital—came into common use across various languages in the seventeenth century.[188] In the Dutch Republic, the term even carried legal weight for certain types of taxes levied on "full- or half-capitalists," while in Rio, calling someone a "capitalist" was precisely pinpointing their position in the social order.[189] In 1807, the *Journal de Genève* spoke of "messieurs les capitalistes," indicating a group of people capable of and interested in purchasing public bonds, while an 1834 publication in Havana noted the "traditional incompatibility between the capitalist and the writer."[190]

But when people talked about more than individual capital owners, when they tried to grapple with the system in which the economic activities played an outsize role, they stumbled. Something new had emerged, but what to call it? One possible answer harked back to the eighteenth century and Adam Smith, who, in his 1759 *Theory of Moral Sentiments*, contrasted "pastoral countries" with "commercial countries," which included Britain.[191] Some in the English-speaking world spoke of "commercial societies," "commercial nations," and "commercial states," others of "political economy," which considered the political preconditions for capitalism—and moved into common usage in the 1820s.[192] As late as the 1870s, Walter Bagehot, the editor of *The Economist*, referred to the system structuring economic life as "political economy."[193] He described England as "a society of grown-up competitive commerce" and claimed that for "very large scenes of our present English life, Political Economy is exactly true."[194] True to the customs of his day, Marx, despite calling his magnum opus *Kapital*, usually used the term "political economy" for the new civilization he was dissecting.

By the early 1840s, as critiques of this new world began to take fuller shape, a variant on the word *capitalist* came to the fore: *capitalism*. It was built upon two older concepts—capital and capitalists, both important facets of the new order—and carried within itself an older meaning of *capitalism* as a centralized (capital-city-centric) polity.[195] This new name took hold in almost no time, reflecting a collective realization—no doubt sped up by the 1837 crisis and its successors—that capital was central to the understanding of this new society and that the owners of capital (capitalists) played a crucial role. The step from *capital* and *capitalist* to *capitalism* was small, given a pervasive awareness that something fundamentally new had emerged. The term first gained traction in France, where, in 1839, the Marquis de Villeneuve spoke of capitalism—"capitalisme"—as an "insinuating and dangerous snake."[196] The oldest dictionary definition of *capitalism* anywhere in the world comes from an 1842 book of "new words" entering the French language: Therein *capitalism* is defined, somewhat circularly, as a "system of capitalization."[197] Four years later, the Académie Royale de Lyon again classified it as a "new word."[198] The first usage of the term to describe a social system might have been by Pierre Leroux, a Saint-Simonian, who wrote in 1848 of "shackled nations, working under the yoke of capitalism."[199] In 1850, Louis Blanc critiqued the "confusion between . . . *capital* and that which I call *capitalism*, that is to say the appropriation of capital by some to the exclusion of others."[200] A year later, Pierre-Joseph Proudhon followed up by calling "the land . . . the fortress of modern capitalism" while lamenting the inequalities engendered by a "centralizing capitalism."[201] And finally, in 1867, the *Grand dictionnaire universel du XIXe siècle* weighed in, defining it as the "power of capital and capitalists."[202] By the 1870s, *capitalism* had come into common usage, mostly to distinguish the new economic order from both the past and possible alternative futures.[203]

By the middle of the 1850s, *capitalism* had also traveled from France to Britain, where it at first popped up in socialist circles. By the 1880s, the word had burrowed deeper into society and was used, for example, by social-reformist Fabians. Then, in 1894, the social liberal John A. Hobson published *The Evolution of Modern Capitalism* to chart the emergence of an industrial society. In the United States, the word initially emerged in socialist circles; by the 1880s, it had been appropriated, for example, by the American Economic Association, whose president, Edwin R. A. Seligman, defined American society in 1900 "as the society of competitive capitalism."[204] By 1914, Thorstein Veblen wrote of capitalism in his *Instinct of Workmanship and the State of the Industrial Arts*. Perhaps more than it did anywhere else, the word *capitalism* became mainstream in American discourse across the political spectrum—a term of both critique and celebration of what was coming to be seen as a crucial defining feature of American society.[205]

Marx, who became the most influential analyst of the system and its fiercest critic, rarely used the word, so even in 1871, it was not surprising when an interviewer from *The Herald* defined the term for him: "[C]apitalism, that is, as you [Marx] would say, monopoly."[206] The earliest German use of the term *Kapitalismus* might have been by a Breslau merchant, F. A. Stilch, who condemned this strange new way of organizing economic activity in an 1848 lecture at the Demokratische Verein zu

Breslau.[207] The term was also picked up by conservative German economists like Johann Karl Rodbertus, who in 1869 wrote that "capitalism has become a social system." Recognizing the historical specificity of that form of economic life, Rodbertus argued that "capitalism was just one phase of a long-range economic development." The following year, liberal-conservative professor of political economy Albert Schäffle argued in his *Kapitalismus und Sozialismus* that "the present economy is characterized by the capitalist mode of production."[208] By the 1870s, German social scientists in particular had begun to look at political economy from a historical perspective, using the term *Kapitalismus* to denote the most recent epoch, influencing, among others, Max Weber's forceful 1904 analysis in *The Protestant Ethic and the Spirit of Capitalism.*[209]

From Germany, the term migrated south: In Italy, one of the first mentions of the word *capitalismo* came in the early 1880s, in economist Gerolamo Boccardo's translation of Albert Schäffle's *Kapitalismus und Sozialismus.*[210] Soon after, two political economists interested in the "social question" took similar approaches in comparing socialism and capitalism as historical economic systems: Achille Loria published *Le basi economiche della costituzione sociale* in 1886, and Salvatore Cognetti de Martiis put out *Socialismo antico* in 1889. Both described capitalism as a historical system.[211]

The word followed a similar trajectory in other languages. In Dutch, *kapitalisme* was used first by critics of the new order before entering the broader political discourse. An unsigned article on the workers' movement used the term as early as 1874. Liberal Jan Stoffel, who campaigned for land nationalization, used the term in 1885.[212] Then, in 1891, the Dutch version of Pope Leo XIII's encyclical on the "Social Question" translated the Latin *usura* as "capitalism" (instead of as "usury") to produce this sentence: "An insatiable and profit-driven capitalism continues to this day."[213]

From Europe, the term spread worldwide: In Japan, a 1902 article in *The Asahi Shimbun* referred to "the history of capitalism."[214] The word soon slid into academic discourse, and *capitalism—shihonshugi* (資本主)—appeared in a 1909 manuscript of technical terms related to sociology.[215] A year later, Abe Hidesuke's "The Age of the Reformation and Capitalism" (*Shūkyō kaikaku jidai to shihonshugi*) appeared in Keio University's *Mita Journal of Economics*.[216] Shortly thereafter, in China, 经济学要览—capitalism—was mentioned in a 1914 economics guidebook as an "era" with particular characteristics.[217] With its naming, the capitalist civilization had finally fully arrived.

———

Yet even after this new civilization had acquired a name, even after it had heightened the importance of markets, forged new patterns of inequality and new rhythms of economic life, and brought a broad array of critics into prominence, it still sat in a world predominantly organized along noncapitalist lines. Limits to commodification remained an indelible feature, even in capitalism's heartlands. While bourgeois elites commodified some elements of reproductive and household labor by hiring domestic servants, and slave women's very bodies were commodified to produce the next generation of enslaved workers, reproductive labor—the cooking, cleaning, and child-rearing—remained largely outside the logic of the market. Market integration, for all its rapid advances, still went only so far: Farmers continued to produce much of the food they ate and the clothing they wore, and even industrial workers grew and manufactured some of their own subsistence. The household of an artisanal watchmaker in the Black Forest town of Neukirch around 1880 had a small landholding that let the family produce about 400 kilograms of potatoes, 300 kilograms of meat, 1,500 liters of milk, 480 eggs, and 50 kilograms of butter per year. While not enough to live on, this arable plot critically supplemented their clock business, whose revenue allowed no more than the purchase of flour, schnapps, coffee, sugar, soap, spices, cooking oils, wood, and nine loaves of bread a week. Only 43 percent of the family's consumption was acquired on markets; the rest was produced at home.[218]

As much as the material limits to capitalism's reach mattered, there was also an ideological one: This new civilization was seen by many as not wholly legitimate; it was too radical a departure from previous patterns of economic life to find widespread acceptance, and despite the best efforts of capital owners who chattered about the "laws" of political economy, it was very far from being naturalized. Workers from urban Manchester to rural Bengal put up ideological resistance. As new religious movements swept Bengal in the nineteenth century, groups like the Baul, Sahebdhani, and Kartabhaja appropriated the language of the market in their songs and writings, infusing them with characters such as Banians (local merchants), brokers, and East India Company men. But the goal was critique, not acceptance, an articulation of hope for the creation of a more equal society.[219] The Bauls ridiculed the Bengali and English economic elite and expressed the "sorrows of their laboring existence."[220] As a Sahebdhani song complained, "the railway has conquered the Bengalis, looted the land, and taken all the wealth!"[221]

However incomplete, capitalist civilization proved dominant and ubiquitous enough to cause and reveal substantial fissures in many regions of the globe. As capitalist social relations spread and deepened, the archipelago of capital morphed into a continent whose conflicts strained its new borders, political and social. Wave after wave of startlingly global crises beat against the existing structures of competitive industry, slavery, the countryside, class relations, the state, and relationships between European and non-European capitalists. The emerging capitalist civilization, it turned out, was socially, economically, and politically unstable—not just because of its boom-and-bust cycles and day-to-day distributional conflicts but because it bounced with increasing force against the still-powerful structures that had given it the power to break through in the first place: a deeply exploited working class, slavery, and a state dominated by aristocratic elites. The revolutionary empire of capital was still embedded within an old regime. As a result, this supremely confident civilization, propelled as it was by a self-conscious economic elite animated by a universalist and world-historical disposition, entered a crisis, one that originated on the periphery—the slave plantations of the Americas—and would end with a global reconstruction of capitalism by century's close.

10.

REBELLIONS:
THE CRISIS OF OLD-REGIME
CAPITALISM, 1830–1870

Revolution in the world's slave lands: Attack and Take of the
Crête-à-Pierrot *(March 4–24, 1802). Original illustration by
Auguste Raffet, engraving by Ernst Hébert.*

The expansion of the empire of capital in space and society created by the mid-nineteenth century, for the first time, a recognizably capitalist civilization not confined to its islands but spread across entire societies. New patterns of inequality—mediated by the market and not by inherited status—were palpable. Its economic rhythms converged around the world. In Manchester and New York, industrialists strode the streets confident that they had unlocked the secret of rapidly expanding output. Economic growth accelerated. In London, Frankfurt, and Calcutta, capital owners weighed the respective benefits of investments in a new railroad between São

Paulo and Santos, a coal mine in the Ruhr, a tea garden in Assam, or state bonds in Louisiana. A swelling river of agricultural commodities rushed into the new industrial heartland, produced by seemingly unending expansions of slavery in some parts of the world and free-labor agriculture elsewhere. Day after day, millions of rural cultivators and industrial workers entered fields and factories to labor under the aegis of capital, not the domination of lords or their own subsistence-oriented self-directed activities. At times, euphoria swept over capital owners, as in December 1851, when the stock market reacted to Louis Napoleon Bonaparte's ascent to power and a Parisian stockbroker saw "the most breathtaking market rally that may ever take place."[1] Claiming cultural leadership from earlier landowning elites, capital owners built opera houses, met in clubs, and confidently asserted that the civilization they had forged bestowed universal benefits upon mankind. Loud, dirty, and often gigantic machines defined this new civilization as much as grand theaters, industrial workers crammed into tenements as much as refined conversations in richly furnished parlors. Powered by both the lash and the contract, this civilization was dizzyingly new and dizzyingly disorienting.

Despite the enormous dynamic, or perhaps because of it, this capitalist civilization was shaken by deep tensions and a steady stream of related, globe-spanning, and mutually reinforcing revolts led by diverse protagonists with distinct and sometimes contradictory goals. The politically ambitious German bourgeoisie wanted a larger share of political power; the enslaved workers in the United States wanted freedom; the colonized economic elites in Bengal demanded a say over the state; and the newly proletarianized workers in Birmingham called for respect, security, and subsistence. Some of these rebellions sought to restore a precapitalist status quo. Others urged a different, only vaguely imagined postcapitalist future in which the productivity miracle of the capitalist revolution was harnessed to a more just, less socially divided society. Still others focused on creating a different kind of capitalism, on leaving behind the old regime—that framework of politics, state power, and labor mobilization that had given rise to capitalism but now seemed to be ill matched with the new world.

For all its novelty, the midcentury empire of capital was still largely embedded in the rules, politics, state structures, business configurations, labor relations, and power distributions that had evolved over previous centuries. Despite its unprecedented global dynamism, the newly industrial capitalist civilization tottered on these preindustrial foundations. By midcentury, it was almost like a cuckoo's egg: It had emerged from and was hatched by a world much different than itself.[2] Even in its newest, industrial incarnation, capitalism was still dominated by this older world: Capital-owning elites shared political power with other, usually landowning elites and inhabited a state that was, to a surprising extent, set up for the interests of these other, much older elites. In much of the world's countryside, planters still controlled agricultural labor through extra-economic coercion. Business enterprises continued to be either state-adjacent and monopolistic—such as the East India Company—or, much more typically, small, run by owners, lacking in significant bureaucracy, and trapped in severe competitive struggles. Capital owners' control of the labor process outside plantations and cotton factories remained superficial in almost all branches of industry, with the essential skills of production still "under the workman's cap."[3] Indeed, the relationship of employers to workers was persistently rooted in preindustrial patterns and laws, such as the British Master and Servant Act, which, as we have seen, brought a heavy dose of noneconomic compulsion to wage labor. And workers themselves embraced strategies and solidarities entrenched in that preindustrial universe—from unruly crowds to disciplined guilds. This old-regime capitalism persisted deep into the nineteenth century. The capitalist revolution, its speed ever increasing, was a train hurtling down rotted track.

Around the globe, tensions and conflicts, sometimes so severe that contemporaries described them as "war," surfaced: *The Economist* referred to "the war between capital and labour." In Bengal, the British special commissioner of Jessore, G. G. Morris, alerted his superiors in Calcutta to "a state of chronic warfare" in the indigo-growing countryside. Louisiana planter James Pitot observed that he lived "in a state of war with his slaves." German economist Franz Hermann Schulze-Delitzsch declared, amid warlike conflict between capitalist elites and aristocratic Junkers, that the Junkers' "future is the grave," while the French socialist Victor Meunier spoke of an "industrial war" of industrial capital against the "disinherited masses."[4]

These globe-spanning "wars" gained intensity in the middle decades of the nineteenth century, pushing against central pillars of the old regime and blossoming precisely where capitalist civilization had met its greatest reach and depth: manufacturing hubs, areas of the countryside subject to capitalist transformation, and the burgeoning cities where the new capital-owning elites lived.[5] Industrial workers rebelled against their employers; slaves rose up against their enslavers; capital owners sought both greater political voice vis-à-vis their aristocratic betters and a new kind of state; and elites in the colonized parts of the world began pushing back, however feebly at first, against their European overlords. Some of these upheavals were spectacular—the European revolutions of 1848, the 1860 rebellions in the Bengali countryside, and the US Civil War, for instance. Others, more muted and local, were still consequential—the 1843 uprising of enslaved workers in Cuba, the rebellion of Silesian weavers in 1844, and repeated peasant uprisings on Java in the middle third of the nineteenth century, to name but a few examples. Often powered by the world's most marginalized people, these revolts fed off the energy of the others, one fire lighting another.

The rebellions occurred in far-flung parts of the world among a diverse cast of actors, leading scholars, often bounded by a regional lens, to understand them as separate. After all, the German Revolution of 1848–1849 seems quite distant from the world of protesting Bengali cultivators. Seen from a global perspective, however, the connecting strands appear more clearly, revealing the profound shifts that rocked the empire of capital. It was, as Italian writer Andrea Giovene observed, the "partition between two eras; . . . the entire Middle Ages (first weakened by the chant of the *Marseillaise*) came to their end; and there began . . . a collective world history of unprecedented proportions."[6]

O n June 3, 1844, about twenty weavers in the Silesian town of Pieszyce, then known as Peterswaldau, moved toward the house of merchant brothers Ernst Friedrich and August Zwanziger to protest a wage cut. The town, today about an hour's drive east of Jelenia Góra, focused on the spinning and weaving of cottons, and the Zwanzigers employed outworkers in the nearby countryside to weave the wares they traded. When the workers arrived at their employers' home to demand respect and a just wage, the Zwanzigers' servants dispersed the crowd with sticks and called on the local police to arrest the weaver they thought was the ringleader, Wilhelm Mäder.[7]

That small demonstration sparked the Weavers' Rebellion of 1844, an uprising that has been memorialized by writers, dramatists, and artists as symbolic of the extreme poverty and desperation of midcentury

Silesian weavers at the gates of a millowner's home, 1844,
as imagined by German artist Käthe Kollwitz, 1897.

workers. A day after the initial confrontation, the weavers returned, this time joined by almost all local outworkers. Finding the Zwanzigers' house deserted, they entered it and destroyed all its furnishings. From there, they moved on to other manufacturers' homes, leaving them intact only if they received a payment in money or goods. When they arrived at the factory of Christian Gottlob Dierig in neighboring Bielawa (then Langenbielau), they broke apart what the workers called a "Brotdiebesmaschine" (bread theft machine)—that is, a mechanized loom. Berlin's *Vossische Zeitung* reported with concern and surprise the "hatred, revenge, destruction, and devastation. That vengeance was carried out completely, everything that was there was smashed, cut, shredded."[8] Troops that were mobilized to control the rebellion killed eleven—women, men, and children—and seriously injured twenty-four workers.[9] Poet Heinrich Heine, in his "Die armen Weber," made his anger palpable:

> A curse on the king of the wealthy, whom often
> Our misery vainly attempted to soften;
> Who takes away e'en the last penny we've got,
> And lets us like dogs in the highway be shot[10]

Mostly small in scale but often violent, these kinds of labor revolts were frequent at midcentury, as workers like the one in Gerhart Hauptmann's play *Die Weber* asked, "Should we eat powder and lead instead of bread?"[11] Rebellions, mutinies, riots, machine breaking, violence against manufacturers and merchants, the public ridiculing of entrepreneurs, the destruction of industrialists' homes—all were common, the exact timing dependent on the stage of economic development. In Britain, this happened earlier (in the 1810s); in Germany, later (in the 1840s).[12] Workers focused on three key complaints: First, old systems of mutual obligation and provisioning, however inadequate, had increasingly broken down with the expansion of the empire of capital, including access to collectively used resources, such as forests. Second, the degree of exploitation in the newly emerging world of industry was staggering. And third, workers were often still subject to extra-economic coercions.

The response did not yet take the form of the large working-class collective actions of later years—the massive strikes, gigantic and bureaucratic trade unions, and tightly organized and highly disciplined socialist parties that populate our imagination of nineteenth-century labor. At midcentury, workers' collective actions remained local, often spontaneous, largely unorganized, and focused on direct action against those deemed responsible for a particular problem or misery. The Silesian weavers illustrate this pattern well: They didn't man picket lines, but they sang insulting songs in front of merchants' homes; they didn't call meetings, but they vandalized their employers' shops. Notions of "just" wages were more common than theories of exploitation rooted in political economy. Workers protested against low pay, high prices, and exploitative working conditions, demanding that customary rights and a modicum of well-being be upheld irrespective of market conditions. They embraced "penalizing actions" against factory owners, such as the destruction of their homes.[13] Their protests occurred not just at sites of production but at points of frustrated consumption, as when grain was exported in times of shortages or high inflation increased food prices. Women, especially, mobilized to force traders to lower prices, sometimes by rioting in markets. In Berlin and Vienna, they plundered bakeries selling bread at what they considered excessive prices.[14] In their eyes, the basic logic of capitalist civilization, the fact that markets determined prices, was wrong.

We can find such rebellious activity among manufacturing workers throughout the industrializing centers of the empire of capital. Workers who dug the canals that accelerated the circulation of goods throughout North America rioted regularly: We know of fifty-one riots in the 1840s alone. These workers threatened to blow up tunnels and locks; they struck, burned down machinery, terrorized contractors for not paying them the wages they had earned, and fought competing workers. In the French mining district of Montrelais, workers resisted the mine owners' seemingly overwhelming power in almost constant and often violent battles. In Paterson, New Jersey, striking cotton workers set fire to one mill and entered another to cut the warps. In 1845, textile workers in Pittsburgh struck for a ten-hour day, and when their employer threatened to replace them with strikebreakers, the mostly female workers rioted, slinging mud and taking up axes to break down the factory's fence, the newest battle in what the *Pittsburgh Daily Gazette and Advertiser* called the "constant warring between employer and employed."[15] In the United States, there were an estimated 735 riots from 1850 to 1870.[16]

Machines were a frequent target of workers' rebellions, often led by outworkers whose spinning wheels and handlooms were threatened by labor-saving contraptions. The quintessential story of machine breaking, which we encountered earlier, was that of the Luddites in northern England—handloom weavers who burned and smashed machinery during the 1810s, only to be met by an 1812 law that made machine breaking a capital crime, resulting in executions and the forced exile of the rebels to various colonies. Similar movements characterized all areas of fledgling factory production. In the early 1840s, workers in Prague and Bohemia broke textile machinery that threatened their jobs. In the Ottoman Empire, machine breaking was an important way that workers made their voices heard, as in 1839, when women in Dobri Zhelyazkov's factory in Sliven, Rumelia, wrecked machinery. In 1851, women in a Samokov textile factory attempted to destroy power looms, and in 1861, workers in Bursa set an entire factory ablaze.[17]

One of the most spectacular uprisings broke out in Lyon in 1831, when thousands of silk workers, protesting their abysmal working and living conditions, confronted wealthy silk merchants. Despite gunfire, the workers prevailed and secured power over the city until they were met with overwhelming military force that left hundreds dead—and left the bourgeois public shocked by the nature of the social tensions that the new capitalist civilization had wrought. The liberal Parisian *Journal des Débats* examined the "secret" of such "sedition" and found it rooted in a society that divided "between the class that owns and the one who does not own."[18] It was a frightening situation, the paper concluded, as "[e]ach manufacturer lives in his factory like the colonial planters in the middle of their slaves, one among a hundred, and the sedition of Lyon is a sort of Saint-Domingue insurrection."[19]

It is telling that in 1831, Saint-Domingue was still very much on the minds of French economic elites, confirming the importance of that revolution to the broader rebellions against old-regime capitalism. Indeed, as the *Journal des Débats*—like many others—saw, the emerging world of industry was one of nearly constant conflict, production disruptions, and outbursts of violence. Industry had irreversibly transformed the world, but it remained unclear if society could withstand the strain this had placed upon it. At midcentury, the balance of power remained decisively in favor of capital owners: Workers had to eat, and generally to do so they had to seek factory employment. Yet everywhere workers battled their employers, and as they did so, they questioned the very legitimacy of the new capitalist civilization.

THERE WAS ONE important variant to this general trajectory: the independence and privilege that highly skilled workers—printers, iron puddlers, skilled miners, machinists, loom fixers, and others—retained vis-à-vis their employers. Skilled workers also organized against the logic of the market, but unlike their unskilled counterparts, manufacturers depended on these workers' specific abilities and deep knowledge of production. This fact let these workers organize more formally, collectively asserting themselves through disciplined activities and, increasingly, institutions: In British mines they retained such prominent control over production that they hired their own unskilled subordinates and paid them from the salary they received from the mine owner, which rewarded them (and their group) for a given output, not the time spent on the job.[20] Skilled workers in other industries—cotton manufacturing, for example, or iron forges—held equally central positions.

Given their intrinsic leverage, it makes sense that these workers built the world's first trade unions and engaged in the first modern

*Skilled workers organize: cotton spinners in Glasgow as depicted on a tray
designed by the Friendly Association of Cotton Spinners, 1825.*

form of strikes, building on their strong occupational solidarities and a
long tradition of organizing in guilds and mutual aid societies. In
France, the years between 1800 and 1880 have been called the
"artisanal" period of that country's labor movement. Because these
skilled workers retained great control and autonomy on the job, their
strikes focused mostly on wages—a full 80 percent of French strikes in
the 1830s had pay raises as their primary demand. Yet even here, in
this more formal sector of labor rebellion, workers' actions were typically isolated from one another, based on close-knit communities in
particular towns, and drew on craft solidarities.[21]

But even when filtered through local circumstances, there was something universal about these skilled workers' insurgencies. In Britain, regional miners' unions emerged in 1824, as soon as they were first
declared legal. As mining expanded rapidly across the empire of capital,
unionization and strikes—typically led by skilled workers—became
common. British craftworkers, moreover, built a powerful social movement in the 1830s—Chartism—that demanded popular suffrage for

men to counter their employers' power over the institutions of the state.[22] In New York, as early as 1831, journeymen printers organized the Typographical Association, and in 1833, skilled workers in nine different trades formed the General Trades' Union of the City of New York. Those unions grew rapidly, organizing a significant share of all New York City craftworkers by the middle of the decade. In Germany, skilled workers also launched the first strikes: in the Wupper Valley in 1857, among book printers in Leipzig in 1865, among construction workers in Berlin shortly thereafter, and among miners in Silesia by 1870. In the Ottoman Empire, even though the Police Regulation Law of 1845 had banned strikes and trade unions, communities of skilled workers developed long-lasting cultures of resistance as well. Istanbul's armaments industry became a hotbed of labor organization: Shipyard workers at the Imperial Arsenal struck four times between 1873 and 1879. Newly booming industries such as coal mining, railways, and telegraphing also saw Ottoman workers lay down their tools—as highly skilled craftworkers rebelled against the burdens of capitalist civilization.[23]

As industrial workers sought ways to improve their often desperate situations, and as employers struggled to gain control over an unruly working class, rural cultivators staged their own rebellions. Just a few years after the weavers appeared at the Zwanzigers' gate to protest, more than four thousand miles to the east, in Bengal, indigo growers revolted against the extreme pressure from planters to grow more of the vegetable dye crucial to expanding European textile industries.

That rebellion began in 1856, when up to one thousand peasants "plundered several large farms and burnt an indigo factory."[24] In response, indigo planters demanded "from the Government of Bengal the immediate distribution . . . of a sufficient Military force to suppress the recent outbreak . . . and to prevent its spreading."[25] Nonetheless, other indigo cultivators joined the rebellion in protest against the injustices brought down upon them, including:

3. *Burning* a house for the purpose of sowing Indigo on its site.
4. Forcibly taking away Ryots' bullocks to sow Indigo and to compel them to fulfil contracts.
5. Duress to compel Ryots to fulfil contracts, &c.
6. Cases of assault and oppression on Ryots to compel them to give Indigo lands or fulfil contracts. . . .
10. Compelling Ryots to sign blank paper.[26]

Rural cultivators protested first and foremost against planters who compelled them to fulfill money-losing contracts for the production of indigo. Even colonial officials worried that the ryots had good reason for the "general dislike to the cultivation of Indigo on the terms offered," reporting that three-fourths of the peasants had signed agreements to cultivate indigo for a period of ten years at fixed prices in return for advances "at a rate which has been decided to be unremunerative."[27] To make matters worse, the ryots had been forced to sign contracts binding not just themselves but also their descendants.[28]

As planters enforced money-losing contracts, cultivators increasingly refused to fulfill them. In 1860, protests broke out in the district of Barasat, only twenty-five miles from Calcutta. From there, they spread quickly. A few days later, just north of Barasat, in Nadia, cultivators Digambar Biswas and Bishnu Biswas refused to grow indigo, despite the pressure of planters and their *lathiyals* (private security guards), backed by police and the courts. Then, on February 23, 1860, three thousand ryots led by Morad Biswas, Sauhaus Biswas, and Lallchand Saha marched on a local indigo factory in Aurangabad Concern to protest, among other things, efforts to survey their lands. The next day, they returned to force "Mrs. Rice and her daughters [the planter's family] to weed indigo."[29] Even when that dispute was settled, the ryots continued to protest the amount of indigo they were supposed to plant, eventually refusing to sow indigo altogether. Special investigator Browne Wood reported to the lieutenant governor that a "regular league was now formed against indigo cultivation, oaths were subscribed to by both Hindoos and Mussulmans, Ryots of one village were called upon, by beat of drum, to assist those of another. . . . [T]he Police were afraid and had been brought over by the Ryots."[30] Testifying to the increasingly violent nature of the conflict, some ryots armed themselves with swords and spears. In turn, planters took village leaders who supported the uprising hostage. In September 1859, cultivators attacked John White's indigo factory in Nadia, leading White to defend himself with the help of more than one hundred lathiyals, some riding elephants. Huge crowds were involved in the disturbances. In the nearby district of Bilaspur, cultivators at the Ratnapur factory refused to grow indigo, and when the owner tried to force them to take advances and enter into contracts, he met with "unexpected resistance"—as arrows, spears, and even plates were launched at him.[31] This military-style mobilization of both women and men broke the owner's power, and no indigo was sown.[32] Bengal's countryside dissolved into turmoil.

In response, planters appealed to the colonial government, asking for a law that made breach of contract a criminal offense. The ensuing Indigo Act, intended to enforce the fulfillment of indigo contracts, sharpened the conflict considerably: Police were sent into the indigo districts to enforce the new policy, as cultivators could now be imprisoned for refusing to sow the crop. Thousands of criminal investigations were launched. By April 25, 1860, just two weeks after the act had come into force, authorities had arrested 279 ryots in Nadia alone.[33]

But the new law failed to quell the rebellion; in fact, further outbreaks resulted. Magistrates tried to force cultivators to grow indigo, jailing and at times brutally abusing them, yet with the help of literate allies, ryots learned how to use the legal machinery to protect their interests, and when that did not suffice, they continued to refuse to plant indigo.[34] When planters ordered the cultivation of indigo, one official reported, "[t]he ryots greeted him with laughter" and said "they would obey no such order."[35] When the lieutenant governor of Bengal, John Grant, went on a tour of the indigo districts in late August 1860 to gain a better understanding of the rebellion, he encountered crowds into the thousands "calling for justice." One indigo planter complained that "the Ryots seized all the lands . . . in the most open . . . defiance of the laws."[36] Peasants drove their cattle onto indigo lands.[37] Cart drivers refused their services. "[T]he combination just now in this quarter appears to me very determined they will do all they can to prevent my manufacturing," wrote an indigo manufacturer.[38] Ryots enforced a kind of moral economy of resistance: In the village of Sahibinuggur, a ryot who agreed to plant indigo "had his house burnt and plundered by . . . members of the combination who were opposed to Indigo cultivation."[39]

These upheavals alarmed planters. In June 1861, indigo planter T. R. Kenny lamented the upheaval in a wide-ranging letter. Rebellious ryots, he complained, "drive me off my Indigo lands," forging a "combination against my interests."[40] Cultivators had refused to sow and deliver sufficient quantities of indigo and had assaulted, plundered, and even beaten to death Kenny's "servants"—the people he employed for wages at the factory.[41] He included an impressive list of thirty-six such attacks that he alleged had taken place within the previous year—testifying to a state of warfare in the countryside in which ryots "cut down and took . . . [t]rees belonging to me," fished in his lakes and reservoirs, attacked his employees on many occasions "because they worked for the Factory," and "broke up my Indigo."[42] These cultivators, a colonial official observed, exhibited "a power of union," as a "formidable combination was organized."[43] He noted protests emerging with "startling suddenness," becoming "rapidly like an epidemic," a "popular movement," creating "a state of chronic warfare."[44]

Charles Canning, India's viceroy, admitted that these mobilizations "caused me more anxiety than I have had since the days of Delhi [the 1857 uprising]. . . . A people who can do this, and do it soberly and intelligently, may be weak and unresistful individually, but as a mass they cannot be dealt with too carefully."[45] For that reason, another official warned sternly, government cannot compromise: "[W]hat security can there be for property, where, because the peasantry combine in murderous assault on their Landlord's servants for the mere exercise of his property rights, the Government of the country proposes to transfer the beneficial interests from the Landowners to the Tenantry? What would now be the condition of Ireland if, whenever an agrarian outrage had been there committed, the Government had proposed forcibly to concede Tenant right to the Cottiers in detriment of the Landlord's rights to ownership?"[46]

The government appointed an indigo commission to look into these matters, and in November 1860, on the basis of that commission's recommendations, it declared that the ryots could not, in practice, be compelled to grow indigo and that all disputes were to be settled legally. It was a victory for the ryots. Most just stopped growing indigo; the others received much better payment for the crop. Bengali indigo cultivation was essentially wiped out.[47] Wherever it persisted, upheaval continued to be its companion: Even as late as 1864, a "factory servant," Rammohun Banerjee, was killed in Nadia when he tried to get a group of wageworkers to plant indigo against the will of a group of rural cultivators.[48] "The Ryots of the village attacked the Coolies in a body and beat them with lathies [wooden sticks]," reported a colonial official.[49]

THE BENGALI COUNTRYSIDE had generated unprecedented quantities of indigo for global markets for almost a century, but now an alarming underside had been revealed. The uprising of indigo growers was one of hundreds of rebellions that shook the foundations of old-regime capitalism globally. In terms of the number of participants, no place witnessed more consequential upheavals than the world's countryside— unsurprisingly, given that it had witnessed some of the most drastic effects of the capitalist revolution, and most people still lived there.

The most sustained, violent, and ultimately successful revolt took place in the world's slave lands, where one of the core pillars of old-regime capitalism—plantation slavery—met its final collapse. This rebellion was a war of attrition, stretching across decades. But the revolution on Saint-Domingue had already shown in the 1790s that rebellion could succeed. Word of that uprising had coursed through the ranks of even the most isolated communities of rural cultivators throughout the American slave lands, striking fear into the hearts of planters, merchants, and industrialists who depended on slave-produced commodities and sending a ray of hope to the enslaved. In 1795 alone, enslaved cultivators emboldened by the Haitian Revolution rose up in Cuba, the Bahamas, Puerto Príncipe, Dutch Demerara, and Pointe Coupée in French Louisiana. Approximately two thousand slaves rebelled in Curaçao. Others rose up on Saint Lucia and in Richmond, Virginia, where the 1800 Gabriel Prosser "conspiracy" led slaveholders to execute twenty-seven slaves.[50]

The continual drumbeat of rebellions that followed failed to bring down slavery, but the sweeping march of resistance weakened slavery's scaffolding. In September 1800, a large revolt occurred in French Curaçao. In early 1802, a slave rebellion in Norfolk, Virginia, resulted in the execution of twenty-five slaves. Hundreds of slaves rebelled in Brazilian Bahia in December 1808, and just weeks later, four hundred slaves revolted in Salvador, also in Brazil. The largest slave insurrection in the United States, involving four hundred to five hundred rebels, began in January 1811 in the German Coast region of Louisiana. That same year, enslaved workers revolted in Martinique, and from 1811 to 1813, Venezuela was riven by far-reaching slave rebellions. In 1812, the so-called Aponte Rebellion broke out in Cuba; almost simultaneously, a widespread revolt unfolded in Puerto Rico. Another large rising rippled through Salvador, with fifty-six enslaved workers killed along with thirteen whites, leading a group of planters to write to the Portuguese king that "the spirit of insurrection" had been brought into the city by "the ideas of liberty . . . communicated by black sailors coming from Saint-Domingue."[51] In April 1816, Bussa's Rebellion in Barbados involved as many as 4,000 enslaved people; planters killed at least 120 outright and executed 144 in its aftermath. It took planters a full two days to regain control of the island—"a rude shock to the whole system of British Colonization in the West Indies," as one contemporary report remarked.[52] The following year, "a great insurrection of Jamaican Negros" broke out.[53] Battered by rebellions and appealing for solidarity among European slaveholding powers, the Spanish royal family insisted on "the importance and necessity of strengthening the military resources in the Caribbean in order to . . . counter the rebellion in the Americas."[54] Then, in October 1822, Denmark Vesey, a carpenter and former slave, was accused of planning a slave uprising in Charleston, South Carolina, which led to the execution of thirty-five alleged participants.[55] A year later, in August 1823, a revolt of between nine thousand and twelve thousand enslaved workers on about sixty plantations took place in Demerara, an event so remarkable that two decades later, in 1848, French colonial officials cited this "grave insurrection" as an important milestone for emancipation in the British Empire.[56]

Everywhere, kidnapped Africans and their enslaved descendants resisted. In the summer of 1825, when news broke of a revolt that swept across twenty estates and involved five hundred enslaved workers among the coffee and sugar plantations around Matanzas, Cuban planters and colonial administrators trembled in fear: "[O]ur slaves

"ON TO ORLEANS": THE NEGRO INSURRECTION.

Andry's Rebellion, or the German Coast Uprising of 1811,
as remembered in the late nineteenth century.

may rise up," Cuban intendant Claudio Martínez de Pinillos warned ominously. And, indeed, on the night of June 14, 1825, Pablo Gangá, a coach driver, and several other enslaved workers gathered on El Solitario, a colonial coffee estate, and walked from plantation to plantation, murdering enslavers, their families, and white overseers. As they marched along the fields and roads, they acquired machetes and guns and began to wear uniforms, beating drums. This ragtag army of about 180 rebels burned and looted estates; their ability to organize, mobilize, and fight was aided by the fact that the leaders—Pablo Gangá, Lorenzo Lucumí, and Federico Carabalí—had been soldiers in Africa. The rebellion lasted for about twelve hours and required intense violence to put down. Some rebels fled into the mountains, as planters enacted harsh retribution, including executions and wholesale massacres. Everywhere in the slave lands, anxious government officials and planters created new slave codes that limited the enslaved's mobility and built prisonlike accommodations to control workers at night.[57]

News from Cuba spread quickly around the world. By August, *The Liverpool Mercury* had reported on the rebellion, driving home the instability of slave commodity production to its merchant audience.[58] Meanwhile, the enslaved, whose information came through less formal channels, could glimpse their power: Maria Dolores, a fifteen-year-old enslaved worker in Cuba, reminded her mistress, who had punished her for rebelliousness, that "[t]here are also blacks who slaughter whites."[59]

Despite the asymmetrical distribution of force and the ferocity of repression, enslaved women and men continued to rebel. Some ran away, at times forming substantial maroon, or refugee, communities. Others saw no recourse beyond withdrawing their labor through suicide. Still others continued to rise up. In February 1827, fear of rebellion swept across half a dozen estates in Maranhão in northeastern Brazil. In August 1831, a rebellion led by Nat Turner succeeded in killing as many as sixty-five white Virginians, driving planters into a general panic. That same year, there were slave insurrections in Martinique, Antigua, Guadeloupe, and Tortola. Three months later, during the Montego Bay Rebellion in Jamaica, British soldiers killed over five hundred rebelling slaves. The following year, another insurrection alarmed colonial authorities across the Caribbean: The Spanish government warned of a plan to "destroy the Antilles through the emancipation of black people."[60] In 1833, the Carrancas Revolt in Brazil further shattered the equilibrium of that country's elites. On March 24 of that year, a "complete insurrection" in Antigua led to martial law, with all white male inhabitants called upon to take up arms in defense. In Guadeloupe, enslaved people poisoned planter families, resulting in "serious devastation in the population of the Whites."[61] In June 1835, a major rebellion in Salvador mobilized 300 slaves and freedpeople.[62] In the summer of 1835, slaves revolted again in Matanzas and in Aguacate, Cuba; the uprising involved four plantations and 130 slaves. In January 1839, a rebellion occurred on the slave ship *La Amistad*.[63] And in 1841, another rebellion took place on the south coast of Puerto Rico, where plotters expected assistance from both Haiti and abolitionists; that same year, colonial authorities in Cuba noted "a concentrated hatred against whites" among the free people of color.[64]

The enslaved certainly had not accommodated themselves to their fate. And while planters and their state sponsors won the major battles, this incomplete list shows that the world's slave lands were in a state of constant warfare. No one doubted that each war might be a turning point. When, in the early morning of January 15, 1843, a fire consumed a Puerto Rican hacienda owned by planter Guillermo Bedlow, the authorities assumed it was arson carried out by rebelling slaves. The local white elite immediately took up arms "to thwart . . . the rebels." A colonial official noted: "[I]t is necessary to act immediately, as much to punish the delinquents . . . as to find out the causes and true instigators of these disorders among the slaves."[65]

To BETTER UNDERSTAND the dynamics of these rebellions, let us look at Cuba in 1843. On March 26, Cuban enslaved workers rose up on a plantation called La Alancía, burning farm buildings, killing the Black overseers and white elite (including an American machine operator),

then "sound[ing] their drums" and marching to another nearby plantation, Trinidad, where they entered the main house, smashing up its
furnishings and taking valuables.[66] The Matanzas countryside was
now suffused with revolutionary energy.[67] While the uprising was immediately repressed, unrest continued on a smaller scale throughout
the summer of 1843, and then, on November 5, "amongst the negros of
the Triumvirato sugar mill," just when the grueling sugar harvest was
about to start.[68] From there, Cristóbal, Santiago, and Eduardo, the
rebels from Triumvirato—as well as Manuel Gangá, Fermina, Carlota,
Adán, Narciso, Zoilo, Cirilo, Agustín Carabalí, and Nicolás Gangá
from other *ingenios* (sugar mills)—moved on to Concepción, San Miguel, and San Lorenzo, where more enslaved workers joined them.
Armed with machetes and fire, they destroyed buildings and machines
and attacked the resident elite.[69] Colonial officials, "discovering new
branches of the insurrection," fretted about the "huge volume of people
engaged in the plot." About three hundred had taken up arms, but
many more had supported the uprising by providing the insurgents
with food, shelter, and intelligence.[70]

As in most slave revolts, leadership was diffuse. Many local organizers emerged, mostly from the ranks of the more privileged and
skilled enslaved workers. Transport workers, who connected plantations to one another and to towns and cities, played a particularly crucial role, enslaved coachman Antonio Abad among them. Free
Afro-Cubans also inspired the rebels and helped link plantations. José
María Mondejar, for example, moved around the plantation world doing various jobs while simultaneously creating communication networks for the rebellion. Free Afro-Cuban poet Diego Gabriel de la
Concepción Valdés, known as Plácido, was similarly critical to organizing an inner circle of associates. On the plantation, enslaved women
played a key role, most prominently Fermina and Carlota. Fermina, a
"troublemaker" who had been "whipped and placed in iron shackles for
five months" before the uprising, was a twenty-four-year-old worker on
the Ácana sugar plantation. She had been kidnapped from the Bight of
Benin.[71] At the onset of the rebellion, fieldworker Carlota attacked her

enslaver's daughter with a machete. The uprising was further buttressed by newly arrived workers from Africa, who brought with them military experience and skills.[72]

Like the others, though, this rebellion collapsed under colonial force. When the rebel army, which numbered more than one hundred, reached San Rafael on the morning of November 6, they were met by a detachment of cavalry. Roughly fifty Afro-Cubans died in this encounter, and sixty-seven were taken prisoner; others escaped to the mountains, where many were later caught and killed. Carlota was found dead in the aftermath; Fermina was executed.[73] As the captain general of Cuba, Leopoldo O'Donnell, remarked with evident satisfaction: "Public order was reestablished."[74]

Yet colonial officials remained troubled by the broad scope of the uprising. O'Donnell later observed with unease that there had been "many branches" of the insurrection, as "these insurrections were neither isolated nor partial," and a "high number of plantations" had been affected. He envisioned a Cuba in which the rebellion had succeeded and found the possibility "horrifying."[75]

As local and imperial anxieties rose, so did the ferocity of the reprisals. In response to the revolt of 1843, Spanish authorities noted with alarm the particularly strong connection between the Matanzas countryside and independence-minded urban abolitionists. Like the indigo rebellion in Bengal, slave rebellions could pose a larger challenge to colonial rule if they were joined by imperial rivals or restive local sponsors in towns and cities. Cuba's Spanish governor "acknowledges that the black race conspiracy was fueled by some whites . . . of this island, promoted by English agents and excited by abolitionist societies."[76] And, indeed, the uprising connected to an emerging anticolonial strain among a small group of white Creoles and free people of color, along with the British ambassador to Cuba, the abolitionist David Turnbull.[77]

As a result of these fears, colonial officials loosed a wave of terror upon Cuba's enslaved and their urban allies. A military council and trial condemned fourteen rebels to death and six to prison. The executions took place immediately, with Black people forced to watch. Rebels "will be executed in the locations where the crime has been committed," wrote the governor to his superiors in Madrid, assuring them of his determination to quell all future uprisings.[78] Dionisio Carabalí, who had participated in the uprising, was shot, "his head subsequently mutilated."[79] Terrible torture was common: The accused "were tied face down to a ladder and beaten"—with the goal "to impose fear."[80] It has been estimated that more than eighteen hundred people were tortured, executed, or displaced, leaving the government confident that its actions had thwarted any future rebellion.[81]

YET DESPITE THIS gruesome repression, tales of resistance and revenge carried over long distances. Rebellions continued throughout the world's slave lands, intensifying further at midcentury: From May to July 1848, revolts in Martinique and Saint Croix accelerated emancipation in the French and Danish Empires. In 1857, freed Africans in Bahia went on strike. In the spring of 1861, deepening tensions over slavery unleashed the US Civil War and with it what W. E. B. Du Bois called the "general strike."[82] As Confederate troops tried to defend the slaveholders' republic in the southern parts of the United States, enslaved workers deserted plantations en masse for Union lines, often joining Union forces to help overthrow the slaveholders' regime. At the same time, partly inspired by news of the war for freedom in the United States, sixty-three slave rebellions took place across Brazil, taxing Brazilian authorities' repressive capacities to the utmost. In 1864, the situation had escalated to such an extent that the Bahian police chief, José Maria Brandão, feared that "a general insurrection" of slaves was about to occur.[83] In 1864, yet another "slave conspiracy" occurred in Matanzas, Cuba. By April 1865, at the cost of more than six hundred thousand lives, the slaveholders' republic in the American South had been defeated, and four million enslaved women, men, and children gained their freedom—"one of the most extraordinary spectacles" in all of history, observed Brazil's minister to the US. In 1864 and 1865, rumors of a Christmas uprising circulated across Cuba and Jamaica, with more than three hundred Afro-Jamaicans killed by British troops sent to quash the rebellion. Inspired by US emancipation, slaves rebelled in Brazil's Pará region, as well as in Maranhão, in 1865 and 1866, again taxing the country's military resources. Beginning in August 1879, Black soldiers led a revolt in Cuba under Afro-Cuban general Antonio Maceo. Then, between September 1887 and May 1888, mass insurrections and slave flights in southeast Brazil accelerated the final abolition of slavery.[84] The planters of the slave lands trembled in fear of their workers' insurrectionary actions right up to the very day that plantation slavery ended in the Americas in 1888. A central pillar of old-regime capitalism had been toppled.

THE REBELLIONS IN the world's countryside were not limited to its slave lands, as we saw in Bengal. Banten, on the western edge of the island of Java, witnessed social upheaval as well. In this Asian outpost of the Dutch Empire, rural cultivators fought against the presence of colonial administrators and tax collectors, and the corvée labor that came with them. As the colonial administration changed land rights, the leasing and mortgaging of lands became common, introducing credit into the newly monetized economy, which concentrated landownership and created a group of rural cultivators without access to land. These novel legal, political, and military structures collided with traditional economic and political configurations, and the friction regularly ignited conflicts. Rural cultivators particularly objected to the aspect of the new regime that was most closely tied to the bottomless demands of industrial capitalism and world markets: coerced labor. The Dutch required peasants to work one day a week on public works projects, a burden that was distributed unevenly and often arbitrarily extended. Already enraged by what they perceived as excessive taxes, the peasants resisted. The decades of rebellions and their sheer number testify to the enormous collective resources that peasants brought to bear: They rose up at least four times in the 1820s, four times in the

1830s, once in the 1840s, twice in the 1850s, and three times in the 1860s. Some were military confrontations directed against the European presence. Others were connected to religious revivals. Social banditry, another form of resistance, was common in Banten too.[85]

These uprisings culminated in 1888, when peasants led by the "great teacher and popular saint" Hadji Abdul Karim captured various villages and marched upon the provincial capital. The well-armed rebels protested against the presence of Europeans, especially tax collectors. After marching through the countryside, the rebels were met by Dutch military forces in the town of Cilegon. There, repeating rifles—a new tool of colonial governance—doomed the insurgents and, for a moment, their capacity to resist Dutch exploitation.[86]

Seven thousand miles to the west, in the Galician provinces of the Austro-Hungarian Empire, peasants rebelled as well. That outbreak, known as the Galician Slaughter, began in the winter of 1846 as an uprising of Polish nobles against their Habsburg overlords. Almost immediately, peasants seized advantage of the turmoil to strike against the hated nobility. While they may have been encouraged to do so by Habsburg administrators, their animosity toward the nobility had deep roots in a decades-long process of ever tightening coercion. Cash-strapped landowners, who saw their last best hope in the rapidly growing long-distance markets for wheat, increasingly pressured their peasants to specialize in this crop and devote an ever more onerous proportion of their working hours to the manor's fields. As usual, large-scale monocultures forced peasants into the cash economy to secure food. With many cultivators living in grinding poverty, a difficult harvest in the region further stoked tensions between cultivators and landlords.[87]

Galician peasants took out their resentment against their loathed landlords in an orgy of violence equal to the most spectacular slave revolts. Under the leadership of Jakub Szela, they moved from estate to estate, laying waste to over five hundred of them and killing at least a thousand Polish nobles, a "social explosion," according to Austrian writer Leopold von Sacher-Masoch, who was a child during the upris-

Szela, Anführer der Bauern in Galizien.

Peasant rebel:
Jakub Szela, 1848.

ing and memorialized it in his novel *Eine galizische Geschichte, 1846*.[88] "It went like wildfire from one to the other, from village to village," he observed, and "the whole country . . . seemed just like a large army camp of peasants."[89] For Sacher-Masoch, Szela was the "Galician Spartacus": "In Szela's clear eyes were revealed great intelligence and energy."[90] His fame spread through Europe; the *Kemptner Zeitung* in faraway Bavaria referred to him as the "peasant king."[91] On February 19, 1846, cultivators congregated with the corpses of their hated nobles in the town of Tarnów, the uprising's epicenter.[92] Vienna's *Österreichischer Beobachter* described "bands of peasants" who carted along "a few wagons filled with corpses . . . landowners, private officials, and estate administrators."[93]

Peasant rebellions sprang up elsewhere too. When rice prices shot up in Sri Lanka (then Ceylon) in 1866, workers on coffee plantations broke into rice storage facilities and assaulted or murdered overseers and planters. The Syrian Peasant Revolt of 1834–1835 erupted on the heels of the Egyptian–Ottoman War in response to the revenue-seeking Muhammad Ali Pasha, nominally the Ottoman governor of Egypt but in fact a formidable ruler in his own right. In a significant challenge to the integrity of the Ottoman Empire, he pushed to expand his imperial demesne into Syria, including the imposition of a newly centralized system of Egyptian-style taxation. Agricultural workers and Bedouin nomads rebelled, seizing parts of Galilee, particularly near the city of Safed. In nearby Mount Lebanon, the commercializing pressure exerted by the demand for the region's silk from the Lyonnais silk industry created deep fissures in the structure of local rural society and resulted in large peasant revolts by the late 1850s. In the Japanese village of Shinano, more than ten thousand peasants rebelled in 1869. In post-famine Ireland, rural cultivators engaged in a decades-long struggle for lower rents and greater security of tenancy, a struggle that found organized expressions in the Tenant Right League of the 1850s and, twenty years later, the Irish Land League. In the 1840s, Mexican peasants went to war against commercial agriculture. On Peru's guano islands, workers, many of whom were prisoners from the mainland, found ways to rebel and escape, despite oppressive conditions, by socializing with their guards at nightly parties, then ultimately bribed their way back to the mainland. At the same island factories, Chinese workers, who were excluded from these social occasions, also rebelled against harsh treatment. On January 25, 1866, they killed four overseers, the uprising eventually put down by troops and the murder of an unknown number of workers. A similar mutiny occurred the following year. Workers on one island had even declared a "guano republic" in 1844, after which the British navy intervened.[94]

India, too, was shaken by upheaval, as we have seen when we looked at the indigo-growing Bengali countryside. One scholar identified more than one hundred peasant rebellions there between 1783 and 1900.[95] Unlike many other slow-simmering rural rebellions, the Indian rebellion of 1857 had a precise start date: May 10, 1857. It began as a rising of Indian soldiers—sepoys—near Delhi, then spread rapidly through the northern Indian countryside. Its twelve-month course confirmed what British Conservative MP George Chesney would observe in 1871: "India was held at present by the sword."[96]

The mutiny gained its staying power and strength from the mobilization of hundreds of thousands of rural cultivators enraged by the ever more direct assertion of British control and the material deprivations caused by its signature reforms of land rights and taxation regimes. Awadh, in present-day Uttar Pradesh, became the uprising's nexus, its rural cultivators offering the rebellion their unstinting support. Soldiers and peasants alike resented the commercialization of the countryside, considering it a grave attack against the moral economy that had structured rural life for generations. As noted, they further

Revolt in the countryside: the Irish Land War, 1881.

opposed the new taxation regimes, especially when combined with tax hikes that threatened their ability to produce their subsistence crops. Peasants frequently gained the support of landowners, who also disliked how market relations replaced older dependencies.[97] Since the British were rightly seen as those responsible for this rapid transformation of the countryside, the rebellion was increasingly directed against British colonialism. One rebel proclamation put the goal plainly: "Put the English to death."[98]

While such uprisings (there were many more) found their way into European papers and the historical record, perhaps the most significant form of rebellion in the world's countryside was its least visible: the mass refusal of millions of rural cultivators to give up their diverse, subsistence-oriented agricultural practices to focus on production for world markets. This "silent" rebellion was the most common, because cultivators usually tried to get around rules instead of taking the riskier path of openly challenging them. We saw traces of this refusal when we looked at the Senegal River Valley and at western India in the early nineteenth century. In much larger areas of the world, capital's penetration of production still floundered. In Assam, whose land the British had begun converting into tea plantations in the 1830s, Indigenous cultivators refused to comply with the impositions of the colonial state. They were successful enough that the colonial power had to recruit labor from distant parts of the Indian subcontinent. In Mexico, as we have seen, Indigenous cultivators successfully defended their autonomies. In Germany, rural cultivators staged collective actions and disobeyed the law to continue accessing arboreal resources in once communal but now privatized forests.[99]

Altogether, a stunning number of rural cultivators rebelled against the capitalist transformation of the countryside. They were hardly "a sack of potatoes," as Karl Marx called them.[100] Quite the opposite: Rural cultivators destabilized old-regime capitalism even as it penetrated ever more deeply into the world's countryside. They had clearly articulated ideas about the importance of subsistence, about securing the economic independence of their families, and through means both mundane and murderous, they claimed their freedom from overbearing landlords or states. Their experiences of the capitalist revolution—with its colonialism, physical violence, ever sharpening global inequalities, absence of liberal rights, and mutating racism—informed these rebellions, undermining yet another fundamental pillar of old-regime capitalism.

In the middle decades of the nineteenth century, rebellions loomed not just among the world's poorest and most marginalized people but among the new elites inhabiting the centers of the newly constructed capitalist civilization—the cities. The rebellion of capital owners was in many ways surprising, even astonishing, considering that the world's merchants, bankers, and manufacturers were the driving force behind the emergence of the capitalist civilization and often its greatest beneficiaries. Yet as their activities increased in scale and scope, their roots sinking and spreading deeper into society, some among this new elite pushed against aspects of the old regime: politically entrenched landholding elites, the power of state-distant capitalists in the agrarian periphery, slavery, personal relations of dependence in labor relations, and state-enforced monopolies. These capital owners had come to believe that the old regime was holding back further development of their revolutionary agenda and limiting their ability to respond to upheavals in the countryside and in the factory. When they felt their political influence to be perilously out of balance with their rapidly expanding economic power, these unlikely revolutionaries rebelled in their own ways in Paris and New York, Calcutta and Rio, Osaka and Frankfurt. Sometimes, their revolutionary vanguard even manned the barricades. More often, their political struggles took the more congenial but still potent form of committees, resolutions, and newspaper articles, such as in Rio, where the genteel business-run Commercial Association took to the pages of the elite *Jornal do Comércio* to advocate for their demands. Although they had a more nuanced repertoire of collective action than did rural cultivators or factory workers, they also fought the old regime passionately and with the conviction that they were a progressive force with history on their side.[101] As English-born German politician and ardent free trader John Prince Smith (deeply rooted in the country's economic elite) argued at an 1861 congress of economists:

> Our governmental institutions and governmental attitudes are at present still derived from the period of economic isolation and weakness, that is to say, from the period before the introduction of steam, engines, railroads, steamships, and the electric telegraph, before the general application of machinery and factory production on a large scale. They are no longer suited to the newly emerging economic life, to the movement of goods growing like an avalanche. In practice they are being driven back on all fronts, they must make daily concessions to the imperative need for economic liberation. The tariff duties separating states are being riddled, the guild barriers are falling, the system of monopoly is declining, freedom of movement is spreading. The economic seed is everywhere breaking through the sod of the old state; the old inveterate attitudes are being forced into a new environment. The traditional antagonism is changing into a force for national unity.[102]

This was a program for revolution. With "governmental institutions . . . no longer suited" to the age, bourgeois self-assertion broke out all over the empire of capital. The German lands were marked by uprisings that demanded both national unification and an end to aristocratic rule. In Calcutta and Havana, local economic elites began challenging their colonial overlords. When revolutionary energy crackled through the streets of Paris with popular uprisings against the monarchy, the Parisian bourgeoisie failed to come to the monarch's rescue. In London and New York, bourgeois elites questioned the underlying mechanisms of old-regime capitalism and began to move the levers of power to alter them.

These bourgeois revolts had many things in common: They took place in cities and towns, not in the countryside, as the nodes of capital became nodes of bourgeois politics.[103] They worked in concert with other social groups—usually the petite bourgeoisie and educated professionals but also at times skilled workers and even rural cultivators. Not coincidentally, they developed a universalist language and supported policies with a universalist thrust: "He who raises his sword against the people will perish by the sword of the people," proclaimed German physician, writer, and rebel Georg Büchner together with Friedrich Ludwig Weidig in *Der hessische Landbote* in 1834. "You have dug in the earth all your long lives; now dig a grave for your tyrants. You have built fortified castles; now tear them down and build a house of freedom."[104] These rebels demanded a new kind of state that was responsive to their interests. As Max Duncker, adviser to the Prussian crown prince, remarked in 1863: "People on all sides misunderstand the true character of the situation. This is no longer a fight over a few articles of the constitution. It is a struggle involving principles, it has become a class struggle, a struggle of the bourgeoisie against Junkerdom."[105]

During this moment of midcentury political assertiveness, capital-owning elites increasingly questioned the political underpinnings of old-regime capitalism, aspired to new forms of political influence, exhibited a newfound desire to rule, and, thanks to their assertiveness, gained considerable new sway over state institutions. In so doing, they had specific policy objectives, most centrally the creation of what came to be called a liberal order. They favored the rule of law, and they wanted strict limits on the arbitrary powers of monarchical states. In the face of a rapidly expanding market-based system of economic life, they found anachronistic the inherited forms of personal domination, hierarchy, and systems of mutual obligation that had structured social relations in many parts of the world for centuries. Not coincidentally, this old regime also disadvantaged them in its relentless favoring of titled landed elites. In the past, inherited status had politically, legally, and socially trumped individual accomplishment, a notion increasingly at odds with the capitalist logic. Lombardian lawyer and political economist Carlo Cattaneo critiqued the old regime and saw great potential in its overcoming: the end of guild restrictions, technical progress, an ever finer division of labor, and increased world trade. When a group of German mining entrepreneurs appealed to the government, one of their core demands was to end surviving feudal traditions, which they called "an insulting violation of the national feeling."[106] Opposing the myriad customs borders that crisscrossed the Italian peninsula— borders created by splintered aristocratic fiefdoms—Cattaneo believed, like most liberals, that "[t]he larger the field and the market for production, the vaster, more varied, more powerful and more ambitious will be industry."[107] Capital, he insisted, had to be absolutely free to produce thriving societies—and the shackles of the old regime shed.[108]

In the German Rhineland (such as in Solingen), bourgeois elites also criticized existing old-regime politics, such as press censorship and a restricted franchise. They complained about high tax burdens, made worse by the fact that the noble Junkers in the east were not taxed by the Prussian state at all. Among their demands were popular militias (instead of a state army), male suffrage, occupational freedom, an end to guild privileges, lower taxes, and the reining in—or even, most radically, the complete abolishment—of the power of the monarchy.[109]

These demands were common throughout the empire of capital. In the German lands, capital owners called for what they considered "industrial freedom"—namely, the removal of the myriad guild and government regulations that controlled their businesses.[110] They demanded unlimited mobility of labor and capital in the Zollverein, the customs union whose steady expansion over the preceding decades had already eliminated tolls on trade within its territory. The Chamber of Commerce of Aachen called for the freedom of "[e]very Prussian . . . to apply his intelligence and labor" everywhere within the Zollverein's territory, as well as for the creation of a central—national—political authority with uniform laws and regulations, a demand frequently articulated by newly created chambers of commerce.[111] Liberals in the southwestern German constitutional monarchies pushed these claims even further: When left-liberals met at Offenburg on September 12, 1847, to draft their demands, they called for freedom of the press, an end to censorship, a progressive income tax, and an end to all privileges. They also demanded the formation of a pan-German parliament to give the Zollverein legislative powers.[112] A month later, more moderate liberals met at Heppenheim to call for not only the creation of a national German state and an end to feudal rights and obligations but also judicial independence. They, too, proposed turning the Zollverein into a political body and fought for new forms of rule, especially parliamentarism, which would check or even replace the crown. Whenever and wherever capital owners rebelled, they wanted greater control over the state. They wanted their political power to match their economic power, which required first and foremost limiting the influence of older, generally landholding elites and developing a program to build a robust state.[113] Imbued with great confidence about the future, tarnished only by a realization of their dependence on the state, these capital owners worked to win political sway.

All of these bourgeois rebellions also saw their political project not as a class undertaking that solely favored their own narrow interests but as an endeavor that drew on Enlightenment ideas to advance the well-being of society more broadly, unleashing economic, scientific, cultural, moral, and political improvements that would better humanity as a whole.[114] The merchant community, argued the president of the Commercial Association of Rio de Janeiro, was "the most dedicated and zealous protector of the common people."[115] In September 1848, Gaulthier de Rumilly, a French deputy, declared: "So let us no longer try to divide the dispersed members of the same family, known as workers and bourgeois. The people is everyone, it is the universality of equal citizens, brothers endowed with the same rights, owing the same duties."[116] This strategy was partly a result of their dependence on building coalitions with other social groups against the deeply entrenched power of older elites. It was also a strategy employed by all economic and political elites throughout history and was in itself a crucial element of capitalist elites' desire to rule.

Urban liberal clubs, a favorite form of bourgeois politicking, spread to cities everywhere, organizing weekly or monthly meetings at which the most prominent and educated members provided commentary on current affairs to a mass following. These clubs shaped political demands, including those of non-elite and non-urban groups, and formed them into political programs. Chambers of commerce also served as political vehicles, with traditionally staid banquets becoming platforms for political protest. At these banquets, speakers followed politically charged toasts with calls to dismiss conservative ministers, secure freedom of assembly, loosen property requirements for voting in national elections, and—at their most radical—create a republic. Capital owners' rebellions tapped into the social and cultural networks that they had built over decades. From this fertile soil of bourgeois associational life sprang forums for more explicitly political mobilizations. The German Rhineland counted almost four hundred democratic clubs in 1848, with a strong contingent of merchants, rentiers, and manufacturers among their leadership.[117] When a mass banquet across the Rhine in France—an event organized by liberal clubs—circumvented an earlier ban on political organizing and was outlawed by conservative minister François Guizot, the February Revolution of 1848 erupted.

A core feature of these bourgeois rebellions was a newly fervent nationalism rooted in the desire to overcome fractured polities. They demanded the refounding of the state as a nation. Capital owners the world over aimed to build strong nation-states to integrate markets, create uniform laws and regulations, and forge a national identity that could help stifle class conflict and prepare a nation to extend its power around the world.[118] In this way, their rebellions were connected to, and at times even motivated by, a desire to contain the rebellions among industrial workers and rural cultivators. They understood that the fragmented and regional political coalitions entrenched in the preference given to one form of property—land—had severely limited the state's capacity to support a new economic civilization. However well they had served old-regime capitalism, including its violent expansion, capital owners now judged these institutions insufficient for the newly emerging world of industrial capitalism. The conditions of accumulation were increasingly national, calling for a state with national— indeed, global—reach, a state with strengthened imperial capabilities.

At midcentury, business elites became more and more adept at using this language of nationalism. At the outbreak of the war with Paraguay in 1864, Brazilian commercial associations loudly proclaimed their patriotism, showing up at rallies and religious festivals. Despite being disproportionately foreign-born, Brazilian manufacturers campaigned against "foreign manipulation" to obtain trade protections.[119] In faraway Italy, Cattaneo touted the importance of "national states" and their ability to create larger communities of law, language, politics, and defense.[120] He celebrated "those glorious days of March and April 1848" during what came to be known as the Milan uprising, not least because they "revealed the people to the people, Italy to Italy."[121] In the German Revolution of 1848–1849, national unification was foremost on the revolutionaries' agenda.[122]

Bourgeois nationalism had a strong anti-aristocratic, liberal, and often democratic thrust and amounted to a crushing critique of the old regime, but it was no better than that old regime at settling claims to territory, which laid the foundation for the twentieth century's most devastating conflicts. But in the 1860s, nationalism had a more innocent, progressive tinge, as it linked itself to national emancipation and liberal freedoms. This was also true in the United States, where it reached a fever pitch among economic elites during the 1860s: Faced with secession—the power play of the slaveholding elites, who many felt had crippled the fledging nation from its founding—northern capital owners unified politically behind a struggle to reconstitute the American Union, with the Republican Party becoming an important vehicle in that fight against the old regime. In 1863, the economically elite founding members of New York's Union League Club spoke loudly in defense of the forceful unification of the nation, emancipation, and the strengthening of the nation-state. An internal circular laid out the club's founding objectives, which were "to cultivate a profound national devotion, . . . to strengthen a love and respect for the Union, . . . to elevate and uphold the popular faith in republican government [as well as] . . . to enforce a sense of the sacred obligation inherent in citizenship."[123]

The rebellious urban bourgeoisie was small (in the German Zollverein, industrialists, merchants, and financiers made up, at most, 1 to 2 percent of the population), but in their embrace of liberal nationalism, their opposition to aristocratic powers, and their hostility toward a society structured by inherited hierarchies, they built what one scholar has called the "most numerous, geographically expansive and violent political movement of nineteenth-century Europe."[124] Unabashedly invoking many of the principles and ideas behind the French Revolution of 1789 (which was to the bourgeois rebellion what the Haitian revolution was to the rebellions of the enslaved), especially its core idea of civic equality, the movement's most outspoken leaders aspired to grasp the levers of power and mold the state in ways conducive to their interests.[125]

The most dramatic moment of these rebellions—which, like the rebellions in the factories and in the countryside, stretched over decades with various degrees of intensity—was 1848. That year saw revolutions, uprisings, and the introduction of new constitutions in France, Ireland, Denmark, Sweden (including its Norwegian possessions), Brazil, Chile, Peru, Costa Rica, the Netherlands, the German Confederation, the Habsburg Empire, various Italian states, and some Balkan possessions of the Ottoman Empire. Over just a few weeks, old regimes in large swaths of Europe collapsed. In Paris, King Louis Philippe of France abdicated in February, ending the reign of the July Monarchy with a revolt by French republicans, during which Amable de Courtais, commander of the National Guard of Paris, asserted that "there should be no elite men, only men elected by all."[126] The provisional revolutionary government enacted a number of reforms, including a massive expansion of the franchise to all adult males, the expulsion of old-regime prefects, and the abolition of slavery. Revolts erupted across Berlin on March 18, as revolutionaries barricaded the streets while urging political reforms, including freedom of the press. When a German national pre-parliament met at Frankfurt's Paulskirche to draft a constitution in March 1849, that constitution abolished seigneurial privileges and capital punishment, enshrined the freedom of travel, and established a customs union throughout Germany by removing any remaining internal tariffs. In Milan, liberal nationalist forces overcame their Habsburg rulers in March 1848. Cattaneo, who played a crucial role in these "five days of Milan," noted that they "propelled all the peoples of Italy" as if by an "invisible superhuman power."[127] In Switzerland, in a brief civil war between forces favoring a loose association of largely independent territories and those who wanted a modern nation-state, the nationalizing forces won out. Backed by a liberal elite of industrialists, bankers, and merchants, they forged an integrated market guaranteed by a constitutional settlement. In Hungary, on March 15, 1848, a crowd of Hungarians who had organized themselves at Café Pilvax (a quintessential bourgeois social spot) marched to the Habsburg governor with twelve demands aimed at transforming Hungary into a constitutional monarchy under the Habsburg king. They demanded the abolition of press censorship, the creation of a Hungarian parliament seated in "Buda-Pest" rather than Pressburg, equality before the law, trial by jury, the creation of a national bank, and the release of political prisoners.[128] News of these uprisings spread far and wide. In 1848 Lima, merchant Heinrich Witt noted in his diary how "the lawyer Tirado . . . was holding forth in a long speech on the subject of the wonderful benefits which not only

France but all the nations of the globe would derive from the last French revolution which had upset monarchy and established a Republic."[129]

The year 1848 was neither a pure and simple class movement nor a "bourgeois revolution" in the caricaturing mold of modernization theories and some forms of Marxism that assert that the politically mobilized bourgeoisie grasped for the levers of state power and pushed aside competing elites to build an unambiguously liberal and democratic state. Yet these rebellions did mobilize capital owners to press against the boundaries of established politics, to overcome their political weaknesses, and to topple the landed elites' grasp on state power.[130] Their demands structured by their upstart status and their weaknesses as much as by their strengths, they opened up a vista toward liberal polities that would become an important element of reconstructed capitalism—and, like antislavery and working-class improvements—a crucial legacy of the nineteenth century.

Merchants, bankers, industrialists, and elite professionals played an important role within these revolutions. In Germany, for example,

Rebellions against the old regime: Frankfurt, September 18, 1848.

financiers created an opening for revolutionary passions when they forced the Prussian monarchy in 1846/47 to convene an all-Prussia legislature that combined the kingdom's various provincial estates as a precondition for a loan that would enable railroad construction in eastern Prussia. When the resulting United Diet of 1847 insisted on its right to approve the monarch's budget, Frederick William IV dissolved it, igniting the fervor that led to the March Revolution of 1848. In the Rhineland, members of the economic elite, such as railroad entrepreneur and banker David Hansemann, banker Ludolf Camphausen, and industrialist Gustav von Mevissen were strong supporters of the liberal cause and active in revolutionary politics. One in ten of the elected representatives who assembled at Frankfurt's Paulskirche to deliberate on a new German constitution was a businessperson, and another one in three was a member of the educated bourgeoisie, with many of the rest civil servants. Bourgeois activists were not only the leaders of these rebellions; they were also important participants, along with their educated offspring who had entered the professions. They sought to create a world in which political structures were more akin to the foundational equality of all people within a market.[131]

This bourgeois political assertiveness was not limited to Europe. Two decades later, economic elites in Japan also sought new forms of political influence and power. Having been marginalized by the formerly governing coalition of samurai—local lords who largely drew their wealth through tributes extracted from the countryside—a small but growing group of merchants and industrialists claimed their share of influence over state policy after the Meiji Restoration of 1868, forging a bourgeois civil society with all its attendant newspapers, political clubs, and associations. Most prominently, entrepreneur Shibusawa Eiichi (1840–1931), whose involvement with up to five hundred banks, textile mills, railroads, and shipping firms earned him the designation "father of Japanese capitalism," had an intense dislike of the old elites, the sort who "revere officials and despise the people."[132] He believed that "it was only right that a person have full possession of his property and be judged on the basis of his intelligence and ability in dealing

Rebel: railroad baron and banker David Hansemann, fighting for the liberal cause in 1848.

with his fellowmen"—not on his lineage.[133] Eiichi strove to liberate Japanese capitalism from the old regime; right after the restoration, he took an official position in the Finance Ministry and set out to shape the economic policies of the new Japan. In 1878, he founded the Tokyo Chamber of Commerce to advocate for the interests of businesspeople, favoring the joint-stock company as a liberal form of business organization. The Meiji Restoration was hardly a "bourgeois revolution," but it was rooted in the new economic elites' desire for power, and it gave them a tangible imprint on Japanese policymaking after 1868.[134] Capital owners pushed liberal demands for basic rights, such as freedom of opinion and support for a market economy. Some of these demands were implemented after the Meiji Restoration, which allowed for the free choice of occupation, the end of autonomous duchies (*dainyo*), the right to private property in land (instead of feudal fiefs), the creation of banks, joint-stock companies, newspapers, schools and universities—and, eventually, a parliament.[135] State-building and bourgeois economic and political aspirations, there and elsewhere, went hand in hand.

And even as many of these rebellions failed, the aspirations of capital owners kept growing, and many of their goals came to fruition in the coming decades. The German bourgeoisie, for example, continued their rebellions against old-regime capitalism, even after their defeat in the Revolutions of 1848, staging what Italian political philosopher Antonio Gramsci called a "passive revolution."[136] Despite setbacks, they gained ever more traction within the state machinery, resulting in what has been termed the *"embourgeoisiement* of German society."[137] They pushed their demands on multiple levels, seeking economic and political reform. They increasingly organized and mobilized through political parties, forming the National Liberal Party—an important vehicle for their politics—in 1867. Instead of catering to a hierarchical agrarian society, they continued to advocate for a political and legal system that favored industrial capitalism's further expansion, protecting private property and newly institutionalizing equality before the law irrespective of one's station in life. The capitalist logic so infused German society that even Junkers began to run their estates along capitalist lines. Remnants of feudal systems of mutual obligation and unfreedom on estates and in guilds weakened; the rule of law was established; the famous German bureaucracy became legally accountable; and laws guaranteeing the private property rights of individuals were established. When economist Viktor Böhmert observed this moment from the vantage point of 1900, he saw that "the entire current of the time . . . drove the German economy to progress in the direction of industrial and commercial freedom."[138] The new legal regime focused on formal equality and was hostile to earlier mercantilist modes of regulating economic activity. It effectively turned the old legal order upside down, undermining age-old protections of systems of mutual obligation within categorical hierarchies and replacing them with the interests of the self-owning individual. These were the successes of the "silent" revolution.[139]

These liberal claims were always connected to a desire for power. And they expressed themselves not just in rebellions and collective action but also in more symbolic claims, as when wealthy New Yorkers in the 1840s began to decorate their homes "in the style of Louis [XIV]," appropriating the culture of earlier ruling classes.[140] Perhaps the most curious expression of the aspirations of this insurgent class and its desire to rule was its newfound obsession with that greatest creature ever to roam the earth: the dinosaur. American steel magnate Andrew Carnegie, born into a family of handloom weavers in Scotland, became deeply invested in acquiring dinosaur bones and eventually built a museum to house them in Pittsburgh. When he acquired a particularly large specimen, he saw to it that the ancient skeleton carried his own name, *Diplodocus carnegii*, and donated casts of its bones to museums in London, Paris, Berlin, and elsewhere—not so subtly expressing his and other industrialists' ambition to be recognized as the rulers of the natural world in the modern era.[141] To rule became foundational to capital owners' self-understanding.

As BOURGEOIS REBELLIONS spread at midcentury, they began to feed into the slow emergence of another consequential revolt: anticolonialism. Colonialism had been a crucial component of old-regime capitalism, but anticolonialism eventually became one of the most powerful shapers of capitalism's twentieth-century history. That history began, albeit in a modest way, in the late eighteenth century. The American Revolution had succeeded in 1783, the Haitian Revolution in 1804, and most of Latin America's revolutions in the early decades of the nineteenth century, all driven in significant ways by nationalist economic elites. By midcentury, the first tentative sprouts of anticolonial rebellion emerged elsewhere, focused principally on creating a state responsive to local interests, not those of a distant metropole.

In South Asia, for example, there was Dadabhai Naoroji. Born into an Indian Parsi family in Navsari in 1825, Naoroji was a scholar, a cotton merchant, a politician (he was the first Indian elected to the British Parliament), and one of the founders of the Indian National Congress. As early as the 1860s, he began to develop an economic critique of British colonialism, formulating what came to be called the "drain of wealth theory."[142] He saw Indian poverty, including its terrible famines, as the outcome of British imperial domination. At first, Naoroji believed the root cause of the drain to be the British civil servants employed in India on the Indian taxpayers' dime. Later he widened his analysis, arguing in his 1876 pamphlet *Poverty of India* that Britain had taken huge amounts of wealth from India, and as a result, "under the present system of administration, India is suffering seriously in several ways, and is sinking in poverty."[143] He critiqued prevalent British economic theorizing that blamed "economic laws" for India's poverty instead of the imperial policies of the United Kingdom. Naoroji received some support, however modest, from Indian industrialists, merchants, and professionals.[144]

Elsewhere, other anti-imperial voices emerged: In the wake of the Opium Wars and China's shock over its defeat by a remote power, nationalist and anti-imperialist voices introduced anticolonial themes to public debates in China as well. Lin Zexu, a central government commissioner, argued that it was "wrong . . . to make profit out of what is harmful to others, to bring opium (which you do not smoke in your own land) to our country, swindle people out of their money and endanger their lives. You have been doing this for twenty or thirty years, accumulating an untold amount of wrongful gain, incurring the universal resentment of man and the certain retribution of Heaven."[145] African elites similarly began formulating a critique of European imperialism, which, in western Africa, began to intersect with an incipient nationalism. The prolific writings of James Africanus Beale Horton (1835–1883)—including *Political Economy of British Western Africa, with the Requirements of the Several Colonies and Settlements: The African View of the Negro's Place in Nature* (1865); *West African Countries and Peoples, British and Native, . . . and a Vindication of the African Race* (1868); and *Letters on the Political Condition of the Gold Coast* (1870)— argued powerfully against notions of racial hierarchies, advocated for Pan-Africanism, and began to imagine political independence, seeking to ascertain "the requirements necessary for establishing that self-government."[146] Edward Wilmot Blyden (1832–1912), born on Saint Thomas but living in Liberia, wrote books demanding "Africa for the Africans" and celebrating what he saw as a budding nationalism among the Mande and Fulbe.[147]

While these anticolonial strains remained marginal outside the Americas, the larger midcentury rebellions of which they were part proved to be the tipping point, bringing old-regime capitalism's forms of rule into a terminal crisis. Just as the rebellions of rural cultivators had brought down slavery, and with it one crucial pillar of old-regime capitalism, the bourgeois rebellions diminished the former centrality of status. Capital owners did not necessarily take control of the state, and indeed their most audacious seizures of power were devastatingly reversed (such as in 1849 Germany), but their policy agenda became ever more influential. States took on many of the liberal attributes that bourgeois activists demanded, and the power of older elites, the nobility and an assortment of landowners, waned. The power of hereditary status diminished, guildlike restrictions on economic freedom were dismantled everywhere, and new kinds of states emerged: Germany, Japan, and Italy consolidated as nation-states in the 1870s, just as the United States reconstituted and sharply strengthened its state in the wake of the Civil War.

The rebellions of industrial workers, rural cultivators, and capital owners destabilized long-established agricultural and industrial production and forms of political rule that had been at the core of capitalism's dynamic for almost three centuries. Sometimes these rebels fought against one another, but just as often, they built coalitions out of their shared antipathy for the constraints of the old regime. The particularities of these interactions played a crucial role in shaping the future of capital's empire.

Rebellions were most successful when they overlapped in propitious ways. This was perhaps most remarkable in the struggle against slavery. No place illustrates such an intersection better than the island of Martinique. By the 1840s, the rebellions of enslaved workers in Martinique and the bourgeois revolutionary politics in France mutually supported one another—and that juncture resulted in abolition in 1848. At the centennial commemoration of that revolution in 1948, French poet Aimé Césaire, speaking in his capacity as National Assembly deputy for Martinique, reminded his audience that among many of its accomplishments, the revolutionary government had also abolished slavery throughout the French Empire, adding that it had done so under pressure from enslaved workers.[148] Although many members of the French provisional government that had been brought about by the urban revolts of February 1848 were abolitionists, the colonial lobby had remained strong and could initially count on the government's support when it came to the slavery question. This changed on March 3, when prominent abolitionist campaigner Victor Schoelcher visited the minister for the navy and colonies, François Arago. Schoelcher argued that any delays in abolition would "cause impatient slaves to rise up in revolt," a frightening specter to French colonial officials.[149]

Schoelcher's warning was soon confirmed by events in Martinique: When news of the Parisian revolution arrived on the island, enslaved workers rose up. By late May, demonstrations in various parts of the island had led to violent confrontations that left several dead. Concerned about the possibility of a Saint-Domingue-style uprising, interim governor General Rostolan declared general emancipation. That news then traveled to nearby Guadeloupe, whose colonial governor declared an end to slavery on May 27, almost two weeks before news of France's emancipation decree, which had been signed in Paris on April 27, arrived on the islands. The rebellions of slaves thus intersected with those of economic elites and brought about abolition. The revolutionary ideas of 1789, which had also informed 1848, fed into antislavery politics worldwide.[150] In the wake of the manumission, when the *Gazette officielle de la Guadeloupe*, beholden to that island's planters, angrily called emancipation "an invasion of communism," its position retained little support in the metropole.[151]

Pressure on slavery also intensified because of industrial workers' rebellions. Sometimes the relationship was direct: Working-class activists frequently understood that their emancipation was related to abolition, with Karl Marx succinctly stating that "[l]abor cannot emancipate itself in the white skin where in the black it is branded."[152] At other times, the working class pressured slavery more indirectly: Intensified social conflicts in Britain—Chartism prominent among

them—suggested to economic elites, especially Manchester millowners, the urgent need to lower subsistence costs for British workers and
open up food markets, which led to the repeal of the Corn Laws and
the Sugar Act in 1846, effectively opening the British market to Brazilian and Cuban sugar producers. This created upheaval in the West
Indies, where planters could not compete on labor costs given the 1834
abolition of slavery. As a result, they put enormous political pressure on
the British government to limit the slave trade and slavery itself
worldwide—committing the state to antislavery politics on a global
scale. In a first, the Royal Navy attacked a Brazilian slave ship in
March 1848, seizing it off the city of Salvador. Working-class mobilization thus intersected in a roundabout way with rebellions among
Brazilian and Cuban slaves, and with the willingness of the British
state to enforce antislavery measures globally.[153]

In the United States, too, it was the confluence of slave rebellions,
a rising industrial elite opposed to the political economy of an Atlantic
trade dominated by the planters of the American South, and politically
mobilized wageworkers that ended slavery in 1865. These intersecting
rebellions were already prominent in the 1850s, when a conflict among
economic elites about the political and economic development of the
young nation shook the foundations of slavery. As the labor lords of the
South saw their interests weakening within the republic, enslaved
Americans pushed against the boundaries of slavery, making their
owners ever more dependent on the national state to maintain the institution. Growing segments of the economic elite disavowed slavery,
or at least its further expansion into the territories of the American
West. Then, after the outbreak of sectional war in April 1861, slaves
fled the plantations in droves and took up arms as soldiers in the
United States Army to militarily defeat the regime of Southern slaveholders. That concatenation of rebellions—of workers, of Northern
capital owners, and of the enslaved—generated an enormous transformational force. Its revolutionary implications were just as powerful as
those of Saint-Domingue a few generations earlier, not least because it
put tremendous pressure on slavery in Cuba and Brazil, ultimately

resulting in the passage of the chillingly named Law of the Free Womb, which stipulated that children born to enslaved mothers in Brazil would be free—a signal of the beginning of slavery's end in that nation.[154] As entangled as old-regime capitalism was with slavery, capitalist development awakened a surprisingly diverse set of rebels that led to the institution's abolition.

Everywhere, these rebellions reinforced one another: In Cuba, slave rebellions at times intersected with anticolonial urban elites, and in Bengal, rebelling indigo cultivators received support from anticolonial elites in Calcutta. There and elsewhere, their combined action eroded old-regime capitalism and revealed through-the-cracks glimpses of a reconstructed capitalism still all but unimaginable in the mid-nineteenth century.[155]

And then there was also an emerging link between working-class rebellions and anticolonial nationalism. The rebellion against English colonialism in Ireland, for example, found eager allies among Irish workers in Manchester. When a well-known Irish nationalist, Thomas J. Kelly, was arrested in Manchester in 1867, about thirty workers liberated him on the way from the courthouse to the jail; during the action, a Manchester policeman was killed. The three participants executed by the state came to be known as the "Manchester Martyrs" and from then on were celebrated annually by Manchester's working class. Irish American workers also supported the struggle of rural cultivators and Irish nationalists: Patrick Ford, editor of the United States–based *Irish World*, argued that "[t]he cause of the poor in Donegal is the cause of the factory slave in Fall River."[156] A few decades later, British workers became the most significant supporters of Indian nationalist Dadabhai Naoroji's successful run for a parliamentary seat. They and others demonstrated that despite a descending fog of "scientific" racism, a lower-class internationalism remained possible.[157]

Yet for all the many important moments in which these midcentury rebellions reinforced one another, they also got into each other's crosshairs. These collisions deeply shaped the reconstructed capitalism that emerged from the rubble of the old regime by the end of the cen-

Intersecting insurgencies: the Manchester Martyrs, 1867.

tury. Perhaps most pivotal was the clash between the bourgeois rebellion and that of the urban working class.[158] Just as the bourgeois rebellion showed significant successes, its instigators became increasingly ambivalent about some of its core tenets, especially its universalist thrust. While their political projects benefited greatly from the political activities and collective actions of other social groups—rural cultivators as much as industrial workers—capital owners increasingly feared them. In 1848 Paris, as the revolution radicalized under the pressure of mobilized workers, capital owners began rallying to defend their property and the new republic against the insurrection.[159] Heinrich Witt expressed these qualms most pointedly in his musings on the Revolutions of 1848. From his remote perch in Lima, he was so preoccupied by these developments that he noted on July 8, 1848, that the "political occurrences in Europe . . . were of such vast importance that I . . . could . . . hardly think of anything else."[160] He worried about the impact these outbreaks would have on commercial life: In June 1848, he reported that "[i]n France mercantile affairs looked extremely bleak. . . . Heavy failures had likewise taken place in Frankfurt, Berlin, Cologne and other mercantile places in Germany."[161] In Germany, indeed, "things look very threatening."[162] He was pleased that in London, where working-class Chartists mobilized, the "police force were more than sufficient to overawe the mob," and he was relieved that "the people of Germany wanted no republic; they had made their legitimate demands, these had been conceded to them, and I was in hopes that peace would be maintained."[163] A year later, in September 1849, he appreciatively reported that "the Democrats, Republicans and socialists were decidedly losing ground, whilst the various governments of Europe, whose stability had been shaken by the events of 48, were gradually regaining their legitimate ascendancy."[164] Fortunately, he concluded, "all such day dreams [of radical change] of the patriots had vanished in the air like soap bubbles."[165]

Such concerns also drove many capital owners, at the moment of their rebellion against the old regime, back into the arms of older elites. Considering the scale of working-class rebellions, it was not surprising that capital owners relied on the powers of the state to contain these challenges, and that dependence on ready state backing often constrained their own restlessness.[166] Bourgeois success in the economic sphere and fear of social conflict made capital owners less focused on the "bourgeois revolution" of securing immediate political ascendancy—especially when confronted by social realities that frightened them.[167] The 1871 Paris Commune stoked the worst fears and brought the tension between the bourgeois and working-class rebellions to the fore. In the wake of the siege of Paris during the Franco-Prussian War, workers and soldiers took control of the city, and on March 18, 1871, these armed workers seized city hall and called for municipal elections under universal suffrage.[168] Witt again worried about these "red republicans" taking control of Paris.[169] Testifying to widespread bourgeois unease, his every diary entry in the following weeks remarked on the Paris Commune, which he called "a system of terror not inferior in atrocity to that of 1793."[170] He was relieved when "[a]t last the Commune had succumbed, and Paris was once more in the hands of the established Government."[171]

Witt's fears were widely shared. The de Goncourt brothers, an inseparable pair of conservative authors, recorded in their shared diary that "workers are what barbarians were to ancient societies, convulsive agents of destruction and dissolution."[172] The Amsterdam merchant Gideon Jeremie Boissevain, patriarch of a wealthy Huguenot family that had fled France in the seventeenth century, closely followed the events in Paris, recording any news he received in his diary. On May 25, he noted with relief how the "rebellious Commune" had been "defeated by the Versailles troops, but only after many atrocities were committed by the villains who run the Commune, after they set Paris on fire."[173] Indeed, after the bloody destruction of the Commune in June, commentators across the bourgeois world drew similar lessons. In New York, *Harper's Weekly* recognized the supposed "ignorance and suffering of multitudes of the Parisian population," which had allowed them to be "swayed by men whose political and social theories are incompatible with those of our civilization."[174] In London, a retrospective by *The Times* declared that "[t]here [was] no reason to believe that the great body of Parisian workmen were suffering at all, except in so far as it is a grievance for any class to be less fortunate than another. . . . In short, the ruling passion was now envy."[175]

In the following decade, the Commune remained a useful image for those wishing to demonize workers' organizing. In 1877, Allan Pinkerton, founder of the infamous Pinkerton Detective Agency, which came to play an important role in the extraordinarily violent suppression of the nascent US workers' movement, declared that the Commune's

> lesson is not one for Paris, or even France alone. It is one for the entire civilized world. . . . The same inveterate hatred of society was shown in the spirit and actions of American Communists. Fire, pillage, murder were their object and aim. Their enlistment of the workingmen of the country has always been for the purpose of securing tools. The continued exciting of their worst passions

against law, order, and society has been merely for the purpose of holding them in hand, bleeding them for their own support, and, in a time of great public excitement, using them for their own desperate purposes.[176]

There was widespread fear among capital owners of the disorder that rebellion, any rebellion, could generate, and thus they saw dangers in the liberal project many espoused. In Brazil, Bernardo Pereira de Vasconcelos, the chief ideologue of the aptly named Party of Order, argued that liberal institutions from the Anglo-American world could not be brought wholesale to Brazil, with "its relative lack of a liberal political culture and citizenry and an educated society."[177] He believed that a strong state, with an emperor and a parliament representing society's elites, was required to keep the country from slipping into chaos. Similarly, New York capital owners mobilized against the municipal suffrage rights of their poor neighbors. They were ambivalent about democracy, and, at times, also about liberal society more generally.[178]

Just as the rebellions of unpropertied workers and rural cultivators led many a bourgeois to wonder about the wisdom of their at times enthusiastic support for their liberal project, European and European-descendant economic elites looked warily at the remaining power of African and Asian economic elites and worked actively to subdue them. The competition between European and rival elites and capital owners and their workers brought new prominence to an ever more racialized view of the world. In fact, the notion of racial difference offered a welcome way for capital owners to reconcile their contradictory belief in universal values and universal rights on the one hand and the establishment of new kinds of hierarchies and inequalities, both domestically and globally, on the other. If Irish workers were indeed of lesser racial stock, or Indian peasants less civilized, then the fact that they were disenfranchised and subject to economic and extra-economic exploitations could be justified. Racism, though it directly contradicted central tenets of the liberal worldview, became constitutive of that liberal order.

By midcentury, old-regime capitalism had weakened but not collapsed. Then came 1873: an economic crisis so severe that it swept away much of what was left of that order. The crisis brought a deep and long-lasting economic contraction, deflation, social conflict, and widespread bankruptcy. Massive labor unrest roiled capital cities. Rural cultivators in Egypt, Brazil, India, and the United States, among other places, rose up. Non-European business elites were just as gravely affected, often losing their influence. Mombasa ivory dealers, for example, saw their exports shrink from about fifty thousand pounds in 1872 to less than half as much a year later, and when the Muscat and Zanzibar governments were unable to enforce the debt claims of countless Indian merchants, many of them then aligned themselves with the British.[179]

The crisis was first felt in Vienna, where the stock market fell so sharply on May 9 that it was closed. When it reopened three days later, panic had subsided, but industrial investments within Austria-Hungary slumped, as did European investments in North American railway bonds, the main source of capital for the previous decade's railway boom. By fall, the tightened borrowing conditions in the United States had started to affect its banking system: September 18 saw the collapse of Jay Cooke & Company, a bank that financed the construction of the Northern Pacific Railroad, which triggered the failures of other New York financial houses. On September 20, the New York Stock Exchange was closed to forestall a panic. It stayed closed for ten days.[180]

The global economy entered an enduring depression from which it would not fully recover until the 1890s. In 1889, the American economist D. A. Wells commented that the preceding decade and a half had been characterized by "unprecedented disturbance and depression of trade," noting with astonishment that "its most noteworthy peculiarity has been its universality."[181] Between 1872 and 1876, US steel production declined by 45 percent, a trend repeated across all iron-producing countries, where almost half of all foundries stopped operating. By

1877, German shares had lost around 60 percent of their value. The Ottoman state entered a debt crisis in 1875 due to decreased revenues and a near end to lending by European banks.[182]

As in previous panics, the decline in manufacturing employment intensified a struggle for survival among workers. In Quebec, a newspaper reported: "It is predicted by all that the financial crisis which is currently occurring in the country is going to worsen. . . . On all sides misery is taking on larger and larger proportions; workers come to complain that they have not had a single day of work for a month."[183]

Increased unemployment among Buenos Aires artisans triggered an eruption of social tensions. In 1875, the Argentinian state embarked on a war against the Indigenous peoples inhabiting its interior to free up land for wheat production and thus ease tensions in its urban centers. In India, the wider global recession coincided with a drought that triggered a deadly famine. The contraction of credit and the simultaneous expansion of Russian and Argentinian grain production prompted a collapse in agricultural prices, bankrupting small farmers from the United States to Germany. Some workers rose up against the slide in living conditions. In the United States, the Great Railroad Strike of 1877, which spread from Pittsburgh's railyards to many other workplaces, was set off by a wage cut triggered by the depression.[184]

Faced with a devastating economic crisis driven by falling commodity prices, rural cultivators in northeastern Brazil, many of them cotton growers, rebelled in 1874 against taxation and merchant exploitation. This revolt, dubbed Quebra-Quilos (Smash the Kilos) by Brazilian officials, brought together hundreds of peasants who targeted tax collectors and destroyed core artifacts of the empire of capital, such as tax records and official commodity market weights (hence the epithet). In 1884, a wave of rural risings—the Chichibu Incident—spread across Japan, culminating in October in Saitama Prefecture, a mountainous region near Tokyo, where peasants, organized as the Freedom and People's Rights Movement, attacked a local district tax office and sought to destroy debt records. The immediate causes of the unrest seem to have been falling rice prices, financial reforms, and deflation.[185]

By the 1870s, it was obvious that old-regime capitalism could no longer reproduce itself. Its major supports, including its war-capitalist palisades, were crumbling. Consequently, the last third of the century became arguably the most monumental turning point in the global history of capitalism. Industrial capitalism, it turned out, had corroded the structural foundations of the old regime, and as the various rebellions undermined the foundations of the old order, they created the basis for a long global reconstruction. But amid the rubble were novel technologies, ideologies, and state capacities that could bear the tremendous load of this new capitalism. As we will see, the capitalism of 1900 would be almost unrecognizable to the generation of the mid-nineteenth century, but broadly speaking, it would be recognizable to us today. Even more than the Industrial Revolution itself, the 1870s were a fundamental breaking point in the five-hundred-plus-year history of capitalism.

The rebellions against old-order capitalism were the critical wedge that opened the cracks these broader transformations rushed in to fill. Of course, rebellions had accompanied the emerging capitalism, just as they had other economic orders, throughout its history—indeed, capitalism is as much the product of rebellions as the product of the logic of capital itself—but in the middle decades of the nineteenth century, they had an unprecedented intensity, scale, and dynamic of mutual reinforcement. The most perceptive contemporaries understood this transformation: "What historic denouements are these we so rapidly approach?" asked Walt Whitman in 1855:

> Years of the modern! years of the unperform'd!
> Your horizon rises, I see it parting away for more august dramas.[186]

The "august dramas" brought a new capitalism into the world. It emerged not fully formed but in a painful, decades-long process of experimentation, struggle, and coincidence. This global reconstruction recast capitalism and created the world of the twentieth century.

Part III

Global Reconstructions

Reconstructing capital: Andrew Carnegie,
steel tycoon, United States, 1878.

RECONSTRUCTING CAPITAL, 1870–1914

Machines to make machines: steam engine at the
Centennial Exhibition in Philadelphia, 1876.

Carl Röchling prized bigness: massive machines, clamorous rolling mills, and ever burning furnaces. He disliked competition and was inspired as much by the Prussian military as by his British industrial counterparts; he admired armies of highly disciplined workers, clear hierarchies with a near-military submission, and the security, wealth, and authority that came with owning iron-ore and coal mines, steelworks, and a network of trading companies. Born into a family of coal traders in 1827, Carl grew to be one of Germany's great steel industrialists, and his family became a pillar of the country's twentieth-century imperial aggressions.

His luckiest break came in 1881, when he purchased a failing wrought-iron mill in the Saar city of Völklingen, a few miles downriver from his hometown of Saarbrücken. Courageous and creative, he turned this factory into a massive steel manufacturing establishment, the epicenter of a continent-spanning business that still generates great wealth. Today a museum and UNESCO World Heritage site, the factory at its peak figured largely in Germany's darkest chapters, after Carl's son Hermann carried out plans that twice brought him into French courts for war crimes. The wealth that these mills produced poured into the Röchling accounts and financed mergers and acquisitions far and wide, including the acquisition of yet another German arms manufacturer, Rheinmetall, known for, among other things, its contributions to the Leopard battle tank, an important player in late twentieth-century arms markets. The site's hulking presence, illuminated at night by the fires from a nearby working steel mill, is a monument to the transformative powers of industrial capitalism. Röchling's family and its mill symbolized a crucial aspect of the reconstructed capitalism that emerged during the last decades of the nineteenth century—the reconstruction of capital itself.

The roots of the Röchlings' imperium stretch back into the eighteenth century. Carl's great-grandfather Johann Gottfried Röchling held clerical jobs for local nobility, advancing in 1764 by becoming the superintendent of a small local ironworks operated by the Duke of Palatanite-Zweibrücken. An innovator, Röchling was among the first to use coal instead of the traditional charcoal to smelt iron ore. He also started investing in the coal and raw iron trade, moves that his grandson Friedrich Ludwig Röchling parlayed into a major merchant fortune in the 1820s. When Friedrich Ludwig died childless in 1836, four nephews inherited the firm, among them nine-year-old Carl.[1]

Under the brothers' direction, the trading firm expanded rapidly: In 1849, as the fires of the German Revolution cooled, business was good enough to start a branch office in the Rhine city of Ludwigshafen—about seventy miles to the east. In the following years, the brothers opened outlets in Rotterdam, Nancy, Mulhouse, Duisburg, Basel, Milan, Middlesbrough, and Antwerp. They bought two river steamships in 1872, then another steamer to cross the English Channel.[2]

As their trade in coal and iron expanded along with the European economy, the brothers grasped a critical fact: The competitiveness of their business rested on reliable access to iron and coal. To secure it, they invested in a coking work in nearby Altenwald in 1855. Two years later, Carl married Alwine Vopelius, who brought into the marriage substantial coal mine shares.[3]

With a grip on coal, the Röchlings tackled the main consumer of that fuel: iron manufacturing. As a young adult, Carl had become infatuated with iron production upon visiting iron mills in the French city of Metz. Now he traveled to Britain to learn about new ironworking technologies. Then, in 1862, he acquired shares in a French iron mill. Even this tentative initial industrial investment quickly exhausted the Röchlings' sources of raw materials. When the 1871 Prussian military victory against France added new iron ore– and coal-rich territories to Germany, the Röchlings pounced. They bought extensive coal and iron-ore mining claims in the newly occupied territories of Lorraine. These bounties of war and expansion of state power and capital, married to growing foundries, proved to be the foundation the family needed for industrial success.[4]

As we have seen, the Röchlings' business strategy—moving from trade into production—was not novel. Done by Caribbean sugar planters, Chinese tea traders, and Silesian linen merchants, this practice had characterized the slow expansion of capitalism for several centuries. But the Röchlings—along with empire builders like Andrew Carnegie in the United States, Friedrich Alfred Krupp in the German Ruhr, Robert de Wendel in France, Arthur Dorman in England, and Sakichi Toyoda in Japan's Nagoya—added a new twist late in the century: They built integrated business emporia that aimed to control industrial production from raw material deposits to final customers. As novelist Robert Musil saw it, these "presidents, chairmen of boards of directors, governors, directors, or managers of banks, concerns, mines and shipping companies" had this in common: "Apart from their very highly developed family sense, the inner reason of their life is money; and it is a kind of reason with very strong teeth and a hearty digestion."[5]

Unlike not only eighteenth-century manufacturers, planters, and traders but also virtually all the early manufacturers of the first half of the nineteenth century, these new industrialists aimed to replace Adam Smith's invisible hand of the market with what has been called the "visible hand" of management. They controlled the flow of raw materials through its entire process, from source to factories to consumer. Their goal, even at this early point, was to gain what one chronicler of the Röchling family has called "independence from market forces"—the driving vector of their lives' work and the critical innovation behind the astonishing reconstruction of capitalism of the late nineteenth century.[6]

When Carl Röchling decided to buy the Völklinger Hütte, an almost new but already failing iron mill, for the steeply discounted

price of 270,000 marks in 1881, it was a big leap, but it did not come out of nowhere. For years, the family had wanted to grow their stake in iron and steel production; now they had that opportunity. Flush with profits from their trading ventures, they put their capital reserves and experience in the commodity market to good use—vastly expanding

Reconstructing capitalism, building an empire: Carl Röchling, iron and steel magnate.

the mill's capacity, upgrading its technology, and changing its product line to meet the needs of their corner of the market. They had started producing raw iron in 1882 and thus no longer needed to acquire that crucial input on the open market. Then they expanded the puddling and rolling mills, one to convert pig iron into steel, the other to shape the steel. By 1891, they had constructed four new furnaces, and that same year, in their most consequential step, they embarked on the production of "Thomas" steel, a way of processing highly phosphorous iron ore—common in the region—invented in 1878 by Sidney Thomas and Percy Gilchrist in England. Further expansions followed: In 1897, they began coke production in Völklingen; in 1915, they inaugurated the even more advanced Siemens–Martin steel production process. A site of concentrated capital investment and integrated production was now also a site of significant technical innovation. And the family learned its lessons increasingly not in Britain, where earlier generations of Röchlings had expanded their technical knowledge, but in the United States, where young Hermann Röchling traveled in 1898 to study new steelmaking technology.[7]

The Röchlings invested sixty million marks between 1881 and

A fossil-fuel civilization: blast furnaces at Völklingen, 1905.

1906, and production in Völklingen grew rapidly. The output of iron girders, crucial to the booming construction industry, exploded, as did the output of rails. By 1890, the Völklinger Hütte had become the largest iron-girder producer in the German Reich. Steel production increased by a factor of ten between 1881 and 1908, and by 1900, the factory produced more than forty-five thousand tons each month.[8]

The number of laborers grew as well: By 1906, forty-five hundred workers powered the works, and by 1913, the Röchlings' various enterprises employed eighty-five hundred men and women. It had taken centuries before sites of industrial production finally matched the numbers of workers on Caribbean plantations and the productive efficiencies that came with such a massive orchestration of human labor. Now it had happened.[9]

The Röchlings' colossal investments in steel production rippled across their entire business. Trade had been the company's financial core well into the 1870s, but the Völklingen factory quickly overshadowed its original capital sources as the family's investments overwhelmingly went into upgrading and expanding production. The Völklingen operations became the linchpin of all the Röchlings' activities—from coal and iron-ore mining to the production of coke, raw iron, wrought iron, and steel, as well as sales. Enormous advantages accrued from this integration: The coke that their workers produced in Altenwald always had a customer in their Völklingen factory, and the beams coming out of their Völklingen factory could be sold through their trading houses. Even the Röchlings' bank, once largely associated with their trade activities, now focused on financing production and later became a general bank.[10] Industrial capital had finally overshadowed its merchant roots as the primary engine of capital accumulation.

As the Röchlings' investments in Völklingen grew, so did their need for more inputs. Further mines needed to be acquired, and thanks to German territorial expansion, the prospects were good. Already in 1881, just days after the family had bought the Völklingen plant, Theodor Röchling told his brother Carl that they should "search for blast furnace ores to free ourselves from the pig iron people and not get strangulated by them." A year later, they acquired an estimated 120 million tons of iron-ore deposits nearby. In 1886, they bought further iron-ore mining claims in the French parts of Lorraine. By 1897, they had built a dedicated furnace in Thionville (then known as Dieden-hofen), near their mines, to produce raw iron for Völklingen. They also bought limestone deposits, another key input for steel production, and invested in coal mining in both France and the Ruhr. As they increased production, they also expanded their trading network, building branch offices in Turin, Genoa, Venice, Glasgow, Munich, Vienna, and Hamburg, whence they exported their goods everywhere, including Mombasa, Bombay, and Dar es Salaam.[11]

The Röchlings' intense dislike of market competition did not stop at vertical integration. They also tried to safeguard themselves from competition vis-à-vis other steel manufacturers too. Their acquisition of competing works made them the only German family simultaneously producing iron and steel on the Saar, the Ruhr, and the Moselle. They joined various trusts, and by the 1910s, they were members of the steel, coal, and limestone syndicates that aimed to control markets and cut down on competition by agreeing on prices and production quotas: The Rheinisch-Westfälische Kohlen-Syndikat was founded in 1893 and by 1904 had ninety-eight member companies that controlled 98 percent of the total Ruhr output.[12]

When Carl died in 1910, he, his family, and his workers had created a marvel of modern technology, an industrial behemoth that transformed huge quantities of coal and iron ore into seemingly unending quantities of steel. Every morning, thousands of workers entered the gates of his giant factory and labored under his personal supervision, patriarch that he was. In technical sophistication, the company's size and structure were unlike anything the world had seen before.[13]

On the strength of its profits, the family arrived socially and politically as well. Carl's brother Fritz even acquired that ultimate symbol of aristocratic power—a *Rittergut*, or rural estate—in Pomerania.

Together, the Röchlings built a business that was both instrumental in the ascent of the German state and dependent on that state for its support of the firm's unprecedented authority over workers, their families, materials, and territories.[14]

━━━

In the last third of the nineteenth century and the first years of the twentieth, capital owners like the Röchlings—but also statesmen, workers, and rural cultivators—reconstructed global capitalism. By the end of this transformation, capital, labor, and the state were fundamentally different, as were global hierarchies. While the influence of capital owners might seem to overshadow the cumulative sway of millions of individual acts on the factory floors and in the fields, the reconstruction of capitalism emerged from a decades-long struggle between these actors in boardrooms and bedrooms, in courts and union lodges, and in the halls of power in Washington, London, and Rio. It was decisively framed by the world's inability to carry on as before. Rebellions, as we have seen, had shaken the empire of capital from Matanzas to Milan. As capital owners had sought to overcome constraints on their political influence and construct a political economy that intersected with their interests, industrial workers had rebelled against the harsh regime in factories. Slaves, serfs, and other rural cultivators had revolted against coercive labor relations. And then, between 1873 and 1896, periodic and severe economic crises convulsed the capitalist world, intensifying that turmoil and making it clear that old-regime capitalism had entered a cul-de-sac.

Less visible to contemporaries, however, were the novel conditions that, if nurtured, might eventually allow capitalism to overcome the impasse, though not without leaving behind many core features of the old regime. New industries and new technologies (which some scholars have called the Second Industrial Revolution), as well as expanded administrative and military capacities, were not just solvents eating away at old ways of doing things but also dynamic catalysts for economic, social, and political power that allowed protagonists across social hierarchies to imagine a break with the past. As this generation of capital owners, workers, rural cultivators, and statesmen emerged with fresh sets of interests, sources of power, and technical, economic, bureaucratic, and military possibilities, they created a different kind of political economy. By reconstructing capital, labor, and the state, they reconstructed global capitalism. Scholars have tended to study these reconstructions as separate events, yet their essential qualities and intensities came as much from how they connected and reinforced one another across borders, industries, and classes as from their intrinsic qualities alone. A true departure, they were part and parcel of a new form of capitalism. One of its core facets—the reconstruction of capital—was indeed so far-reaching that it has been identified as a "metamorphosis of property" itself. The emergence of this new regime confirms once more Fernand Braudel's insight that capitalism is not a stable form, that "creative destructions," as Joseph Schumpeter has called them, are capitalism's heartbeat.[15]

When the dust of this long reconstruction had settled, the new dynamo of global capitalism was heavy industry; the center of gravity had shifted from trade, agriculture, and light manufacturing to steel, rail, coal, electricity, and chemistry. Industrial capital, increasingly allied with finance capital through family-based and legal means, came to dominate the political economy that had been governed by merchants until now. This created, among other things, a new institutional order that, while subsuming the war capitalism of old, was also different from it. New firms, owned by shareholders and managed by a new group of professionals, integrated both vertically and horizontally. Fatefully, fossil fuels began to overtake organic energy sources, creating an energy intensity of economic life that hastened the advent of what some have called the Anthropocene and others the Capitalocene and humans as "a geological force." To be sure, nature and labor had always been crucial to capital's expansion, but now the long period principally characterized by coercive, low-capital-intensive exploitation of ever more workers transitioned to a state-centric, high-capital-intensive capitalism that relied heavily on the exploitation of nature, especially fossil fuels. In the process, a massive expansion of wage labor took place, and this rapidly expanding and permanent industrial proletariat began to embrace socialist politics and organize in huge bureaucratic institutions structured along national lines to challenge capital owners in novel ways. A new globalization driven by industrial capital emerged as well, with massive streams of trade, capital, and migration connecting far-flung regions of the globe with fresh intensity, facilitated by new infrastructures—especially railroads and the telegraph—that enabled unprecedented market integration. These developments were tremendously Eurocentric, as European capital and European state power came to colonize large areas of the world, and as European political and economic elites subdued, with very few exceptions, their Asian and African counterparts. As the Global South was decisively relegated to supplying raw materials to the industrial heartland, global inequalities sharpened, while the postcolonial outlier on the American continent—the United States—embarked upon a journey that in the next century would bring about the Second Great Divergence and the end of British hegemony. The state began playing a radically more prominent role in economic life. In the countryside, new forms of labor—sharecropping, indentured servitude, and wage labor, among others—would come to dominate. And societies changed: 1920s gender norms, family structures, patterns of sociability, and culture would have been almost unrecognizable to someone living in the 1870s.[16]

During the last third of the nineteenth century, these transformations were so pervasive that people from very different stations of life and regions of the world agreed that they were entering a new, and yet uncharted, age. They were in awe: American writer William Dean Howells's protagonists observed the "superb spectacle" of New York's Grand Central Terminal, filled with "fabled monsters" that "would soon be hurling themselves north and east and west through the night!" One of his French contemporaries, Émile Zola, dedicated an entire novel, *L'argent*, to that strange force that was altering life at an astounding speed—money. Zola's protagonists were obsessed with lands to be "conquered" by a steamship company, with the possibility of "a few millions to gain *en passant*" in mining investments. They were enthralled by the "money found in the bowels of the earth and thrown up by the shovelful" and by investments that "would be worth gold when the country should be covered with factories." But Zola also saw the intensifying inequality, the "indescribable dens, some half tumbling down," with the "men, women, and children, rotting like decayed fruit," and the rebellions of the poor. Between 1880 and 1914, the top decile of French, British, and Swedish citizens came to control 80 to 90 percent of all property in their respective nations, with the wealthiest 1 percent alone controlling between 60 and 70 percent.[17]

The reconstruction of capitalism went hand in hand with an enormous expansion of output, as men, women, and children produced previously unfathomable quantities of agricultural and industrial goods. Global GDP grew by a stunning 145 percent between 1870 and 1913, turning into surprising reality the once seemingly fantastic predictions of economists ranging from Adam Smith to Karl Marx. Capitalism seemed to have shattered the shackles on human productivity. Global coal production, as good an index as any in this age of heavy industry, increased by a factor of sixteen between 1850 and 1913. Railroads, equally emblematic, crisscrossed the world, growing globally from 43,299 miles in 1860 to 152,200 miles in 1890. World iron production increased by 447 percent between 1870 and 1910, world steel production by a whopping 11,122 percent. In the United Kingdom, pig-iron output almost doubled, and it increased by three and a half times in France, eight and a half times in Russia, and more than sixteen times in the United States. In Germany as a whole, it swelled by more than ten times, while in the Saar region, home of the Röchlings, production exploded by more than two hundred times between 1850 and 1913. Even older industries kept expanding: The world had roughly 55 million mechanized cotton spindles in 1870 and 143 million in 1913. The output of agricultural commodities skyrocketed, too, with global wheat production increasing by 56 percent between 1885 and 1914. In 1870, merchants traded 6.2 million bales of cotton globally; in 1913, that number jumped to about 16 million. The global coffee harvest almost tripled between those years. Even sugar, by now an ancient plantation crop, expanded drastically, more than doubling in a short thirty years after 1880. Never before had there been such explosive growth in production and productivity, leading Serbian writer Ivo Andrić to describe it in his account of the Bosnian city of Višegrad in *Na Drini ćuprija* (*The Bridge on the Drina*) not just as "relative prosperity" but as a "Fata Morgana of convenience, safety and happiness."[18]

All that production fed and was fed by a quadrupling of world trade between 1870 and 1913. The trade in steel and iron goods grew by 358 percent. The exchange of agricultural products expanded rapidly as well, accounting for approximately half of all trade, with bene-

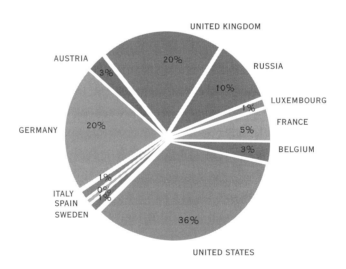

Global steel production, 1910.

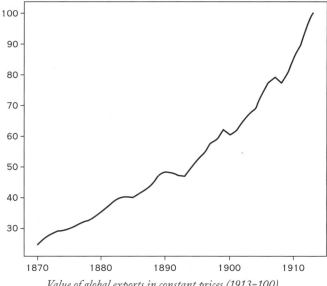

Value of global exports in constant prices (1913=100).

fits and strains felt by rural cultivators from the Veneto in Italy to the Paraíba Valley in Brazil. World trade in cereals more than tripled between 1860 and the end of the century. Between 1870 and 1910, rice exports from Indochina, Siam (now Thailand), and British India (primarily Bengal and Burma, now Myanmar) quadrupled. The new density of economic exchanges was enabled and symbolized by the 252,463 miles of submarine telegraph lines that traversed the world's ocean floors by 1903—almost one hundred times as many as in 1865. The lines connected distant markets almost instantaneously: By 1900, a message from London to New York arrived in just three minutes, one to Bombay in thirty-five minutes, and one to Hong Kong in eighty minutes. By 1902, Britons sent ninety million telegrams annually.[19]

Much of that stunning growth in trade and production, however, was concentrated in just a few regions. In 1870, 80 percent of the world's manufacturing capacity was located in the United Kingdom, the United States, Germany, and France; in 1913, these countries still controlled 72 percent of a greatly expanded output. This was a radical departure from earlier centuries, when the great balance of economic vitality had been distributed more evenly across the globe and anchored in Asia. This moment featured an unfathomable level of North Atlantic economic dominance, one that would last for about a century but now has come to an end.[20]

That expansion of output and trade was even more shocking set against the backdrop of the years between 1873 and 1896, often described as the "Long Depression," when a series of severe economic crashes seemed to point not to capitalism's new birth but to its accelerating instability. In 1873, 1882, and 1893, mass unemployment threatened the social stability of industrial societies, and debt crises ravaged the world's countryside, bringing political and social turmoil. Yet the Long Depression was less a crisis of capitalism than a shedding of the skin of the old regime. It was a crisis not of output but of deflated profit, as cutthroat competition and destabilizing social relations revealed the bankruptcy of older capitalist norms and market relations. After 1896, out of the destruction of the old arose the widespread economic boom of the Belle Epoque.[21]

While not terminal, the Long Depression, along with the rebellions we have chronicled, created some of the key challenges—in particular, the severe, long-lasting deflation—that motivated the reconstruction of global capitalism. In the United Kingdom, prices declined by 40 percent between 1873 and 1896. In Germany, the price of pig iron fell from 145.5 marks per ton in 1873 to 45.7 marks in 1887—that is, almost 70 percent. Everywhere, agriculture suffered the most, decisively weakening agrarian elites and with them old-regime capitalism. Wheat was two-thirds cheaper in Britain in 1894 than it was a quarter century earlier, largely thanks to the vast expansion of prairie agriculture in the United States and Russia. In five short years between 1881 and 1886, wheat prices in Germany declined by 31 percent. This deflationary development put enormous pressure on capital owners to unleash the productive powers of industry and agriculture, producing what Marx, at the cusp of this period, called the newly "feverish velocity" and "Cyclopean scale" of large-scale industry.[22]

The global reconstruction of capitalism was at bottom a reconstruction of western European and North American *capital*. This North Atlantic reconstruction occurred in plain sight; in fact, the in-your-face quality of the change stood out to contemporaries, who marveled at the size of the machines and factories, the teeming masses of workers, and the polluted air. The vast fortunes and expanded reach of its innovations are still etched in cities like Pittsburgh and Dortmund, Liège and Cardiff. The huge factories, tall smokestacks, opulent mansions, and massive working-class neighborhoods of the late nineteenth century left an archaeological record more imposing than that of the Roman Empire.

In the centuries prior, capital had spread beyond the merchant islands, morphing into a capitalist civilization. Now, capital adapted to opportunities and threats on all fronts by focusing decisively on industrial production that featured ever more complex and gargantuan machinery, novel managerial strategies and legal constructions, much larger numbers of workers, and a much more rapid throughput of materials. Dwarfing all prior investments combined, capital-intensive sites of industrial production took shape, all firmly attached to a particular location. This was a radical change from the past, when significant amounts of capital had been bound up only at the highest levels of intercontinental trade and state financing. A steel company simply devoured capital at an incomparably larger scale than cotton mills or sugar plantations. In the early nineteenth century, when Robert Owen and his partners bought the cotton mill in New Lanark, then one of the world's largest, they paid sixty thousand pounds; a century later, the Röchlings invested more than sixty million marks—almost fifty-six times as much—in their Völklingen steel mill. Older forms of businesses and older organizations of capital did not disappear. As always in capitalism's long history, earlier patterns—the artisan workshop, the slave plantation, the family-run microfactory, the merchant house—persisted, yet capitalism's dynamic had shifted from these artifacts of the old regime to the blast furnaces of the new form of creative destruction.[23]

Relentless competition, expanding markets, mass labor resistance, and scientific breakthroughs drove the technical innovations that became crucial to this late nineteenth-century reconstruction of capital. Entirely new industries emerged; older industries like iron and steel production were often recast. Iron had been produced for centuries, as we saw when we looked at Dutch merchant Louis De Geer's ironworks in Finspång in seventeenth-century Sweden, but these workshops usually employed only a few dozen workers, used locally mined iron ore and charcoal, and produced relatively small quantities. Two hundred and fifty years later, iron and then steel production skyrocketed. Things were also produced in very different ways: The gigantic factories at Völklingen sported a new complexity of work processes and drew on new technologies that only an extensive and well-trained managerial corps could direct. The railroad, one of the chief consumers of iron and steel, had emerged a few decades earlier, but in the last third of the century, both the size of its network and the density of its traffic grew exponentially, requiring ever larger capital investments and new forms of management.[24]

Other industries that came to define the age were truly novel. Oil production began its ascent. In 1859, in northwestern Pennsylvania, a onetime train conductor named Edwin Drake became the first prospector to successfully strike oil in America. Other entrepreneurs followed on his heels, drilling wells and putting up small refineries, distilling the oil into petroleum. "So much oil is produced," reported a contemporary observer in 1861, that "it is impossible to care for it, and thousands of barrels are running into the creek; the surface of the river is covered with oil for miles." In Austrian Galicia, too, oil discoveries resulted in a rush of landowners, prospectors, and even peasants getting into the business, at first mostly by digging holes in the ground, then later by drilling, making the province the world's third-largest oil producer by the early twentieth century. As in Pennsylvania, Galician oil towns boomed: One of them, Borysław, saw its population grow by

Oil booms, Galicia.

a factor of twenty-four in the four decades after 1860. Initially a dispersed and small-scale undertaking, by the 1880s, the industry had begun to consolidate and take on some of the characteristic forms of reconstructed capital: Polish economist Stanisław Szczepanowski and Canadian oil prospector William Henry McGarvey, for example, raised larger amounts of capital and integrated their Galician production vertically—combining oil exploration with refining and the production of the equipment necessary for both. In 1895, they founded the Galizische Karpaten-Petroleum Actien-Gesellschaft—the Galician Carpathian Petroleum Joint-Stock Company. The US oil industry soon followed suit with such integration.[25]

The newly emerged electrical industry was another center for the massive concentrations of industrial capital that defined the age, but thanks to its much deeper knowledge base, it developed less chaotically. In January 1882, in London, Thomas Edison opened the first steam-powered electricity-generating station in the world; later that year, he opened another in New York. Edison produced the dynamos, large electric motors, and other components needed for these systems. In 1886, he moved his company to upstate New York, to Schenectady, where he employed 450 workers. Just three years later, banker J. P.

Morgan played a central role in merging Edison's electrical-related companies into Edison General Electric, which soon controlled much of the US market for the electrical lighting business. Edison General Electric not just generated electricity but also manufactured dynamos, large electric motors, batteries, electrical lighting fixtures, sockets, and other electrical lighting devices. As was typical in these new industries, the company grew fast. In 1892, the Schenectady works had 3,800 employees; by 1913, the now reconstituted General Electric had 70,000 people on its payroll.[26]

Elsewhere, the electrical industry was more splintered but just as dynamic. In 1883, one year after Edison opened his first power stations, Emil Rathenau, a member of a well-off Berlin merchant family, founded the Deutsche Edison Gesellschaft, which later renamed itself Allgemeine Elektricitäts-Gesellschaft, or AEG. Starting out in the manufacturing of such things as light bulbs, motors, and generators, it rapidly turned into a global player in the construction of electric transmission systems, with 30,667 employees by 1907. Its principal competitor, in Germany and worldwide, was Siemens, originally founded in Berlin in October 1847 by Werner von Siemens and Johann Georg Halske to manufacture electric telegraphs. In 1848, they built one of the first continental European telegraph lines from Berlin to Frankfurt am Main. The company also opened cable-manufacturing plants in Woolwich (south of London) and Saint Petersburg, then grew further when Werner von Siemens patented an electrical generator in 1867. Perhaps most famously, in the late 1860s, Siemens built a large part of the telegraph line that stretched almost seven thousand miles to connect Britain with India. The company incorporated in 1897 as Siemens & Halske. In 1907, Siemens employed 34,324 workers, more than all but five German companies.[27]

The chemical industry followed this lead, building more integrated, capital-intensive, and market-domineering accumulations of manufacturing capital. Two sources were particularly instrumental: the production of military supplies—principally explosives—and dyes for textiles. The

One of the roots of the world's chemical industry: explosives, 1920.

American company DuPont followed the former trajectory. Éleuthère Irénée du Pont opened a gunpowder mill in Wilmington, Delaware, in 1802. During the Civil War, the Union Army purchased between one-third and one-half of its gunpowder from the company. By the early twentieth century, the firm had diversified into new markets, eventually gaining a major foothold in paints, plastics, and insecticides. In its drive to diversify, it sought surprising synergies: A 1910 pamphlet bore the alarming title *Farming with Dynamite: A Few Hints to Farmers.*[28]

Other companies entered the chemical business to serve textile markets. The British company United Alkali Company Limited was formed in 1890 when forty-eight British chemical companies merged; in 1926, it combined with some of its remaining competitors to create the chemical behemoth ICI, which became Britain's largest manufacturing enterprise, employing thirty-three thousand people that year.[29]

The Swiss chemical and pharmaceutical industry also started out in the textile dye business, in the city of Basel, the heart of a textile-industry nexus that had emerged in the eighteenth century, stretching from the valleys of the Black Forest to the Vosges, and including Mulhouse, one of Europe's most important cotton-printing cities. Ciba-Geigy, which became a leading drugmaker, got its feet wet in the 1850s by developing dyes for that industry. By 1900, it had become Switzerland's biggest chemical company and branched out into pharmaceuticals. Its then competitor Sandoz, founded in 1886 by Alfred Kern and Edouard Sandoz, also began producing dyes for textile manufacturing before transferring some of its knowledge to pharmaceuticals, starting in 1895. A century later, in 1996, the two erstwhile rivals merged and formed the pharmaceutical giant Novartis.

Germany's leading chemical firms developed to serve the textile industry as well. In 1863, Friedrich Bayer and Johann Friedrich Wescott opened a factory to produce dyes in Barmen, the same town where Friedrich Engels's father had his cotton factory. The company's most important products were initially fuchsin (a synthetic magenta dye) and a chemical equivalent to indigo, the blue dye whose production had generated such terrible exploitation (and rebellion) in Saint-Domingue and Bengal. When Bayer died in 1880, the business turned into a joint-stock company, Farbenfabriken vorm. Friedr. Bayer & Co., with a workforce of more than three hundred. Like Ciba-Geigy and Sandoz, Bayer expanded into pharmaceuticals, and between 1897 and 1899, it developed what is probably the world's bestselling drug: aspirin. From 1898 till 1910, it also sold heroin, which it patented as a treatment for a whole range of mostly mild conditions. During World War I, Bayer developed and produced chemical weapons.[30]

Bayer's principal competitor, the Baden Aniline and Soda Factory (BASF), was located a few hundred miles up the Rhine in the city of

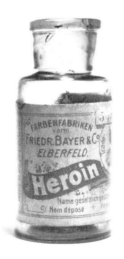

Ludwigshafen. BASF produced aniline-based synthetic dyes beginning in 1865; by 1901, dyes made up 80 percent of its production. BASF later went into fertilizers and in 1925 became part of IG Farben, a corporation that brought together the six major players in the German chemical industry, including Bayer.

From chemicals to pharmaceuticals: Bayer's potent cough syrup, early twentieth century.

From textile dyes to chemicals: BASF, Ludwigshafen, 1881.

F ounded in the wake of the midcentury rebellions and sorely tested during the exigencies of the Long Depression, the interests and demands of these new companies differed fundamentally from those of earlier manufacturing enterprises and merchant houses. These new companies diverged from their predecessors in terms of the quantity and organization of their capital, their relations to their workers, and their connections to the state. Their reconstructed capital was rooted in, and propelled by, a fundamentally different political economy.

First, this new version of capital demanded and enabled new market structures. With markets becoming more integrated and new technologies allowing for the shipment of low-value goods at high speeds across vast distances, goods could be sold over longer distances, making mass production profitable. To cite just one example, Chicago's meatpacking industry, like its Buenos Aires counterpart, depended on a national market linked by the railroad and refrigerated railcars. Eventually, refrigerated oceangoing ships—reefers—would enable the emergence of a global meat market as well. Such new market structures hastened the collapse of the subsistence economy in many parts of the world, as it expanded markets for goods manufactured in distant factories, along with the capital-goods inputs that made such production possible. This kind of market integration went hand in hand with new forms of distribution in some regions; department stores, super-markets, and mail-order businesses took off, nowhere more so than in the United States, creating the infrastructure for mass consumption and thus further mass production. Market integration allowed for economies of scale that undermined smaller-scale production and in-tensified the concentration of economic power in the world's industrial heartlands—both within national economies and across the globe.[31]

Second, capital became much more knowledge-intensive. As these firms represented ever larger agglomerations of capital, they focused unprecedented resources on technical experimentation and productivity increases. In earlier generations, skilled workers had created many, if not most, technical innovations in manufacturing, drawing not on the-oretical science but on skills learned on the job and honed over time. Universities had largely focused on theology and classical education, not engineering. In the vast new undertakings of the Second Industrial Revolution, however, individual workers, even highly skilled ones, increasingly lost the ability to control the production processes they were part of, much less to alter them materially. For the first time, university-based science became a significant partner with industrial production. Tellingly, in 1861, the Massachusetts Institute of Technol-ogy opened its doors. Louis Röchling, Hermann's brother, studied chemistry in Heidelberg, while other family members enrolled at tech-nical and mining schools in Berlin. Eager for security, control, and speed, they brought science into their company, hired university-trained chemists, and created a chemical laboratory in Völklingen that em-ployed a staff of three chemists by 1900. Almost all the new industrial companies created such research labs: BASF in 1868, Edison in 1876, Eastman Kodak in 1893, tire manufacturer B. F. Goodrich (now BFGoodrich) in 1895, and General Electric in 1900. DuPont invested heavily in research and development as well, establishing the DuPont Experimental Station in Wilmington, Delaware, in 1903.[32]

Third, reconstructed capital was much more energy-intensive. Throughout most of human history, productive powers had emerged from human and animal energy—good old brawn, really—along with

A fossil-fuel civilization: Vincent van Gogh,
Women Carrying Sacks of Coal in the Snow, *1882.*

wind and water, but now fossil fuels, almost exclusively coal (as late as 1910, 92 percent of global fossil-fuel usage was in the form of coal), became crucial to production. As machines needed to be powered, ideally without interruption, to amortize their immense capital costs, a fossil-fuel-based manufacturing civilization emerged. Without fossil fuels, there would have been no reconstruction of capital. "Our civilization," George Orwell observed a few years later, "is founded on coal." He added that "[i]n the metabolism of the Western world the coal-miner is second in importance only to the man who ploughs the soil." Fossil-fuel usage expanded almost seven times between 1870 and 1920. A seemingly free gift of nature whose benefits largely accrued in one small part of the world further accelerated global inequalities at a decisive moment in capitalism's history. So great was this new reliance on fossil fuels that in 1896, Swedish scientist Svante Arrhenius concluded that the amount of carbon dioxide in the atmosphere would eventually change the Earth's climate—just as it ultimately did. The gift wasn't really free, of course, but when the bills came due a century later, they were largely shouldered by those who had never received the gift in the first place.[33]

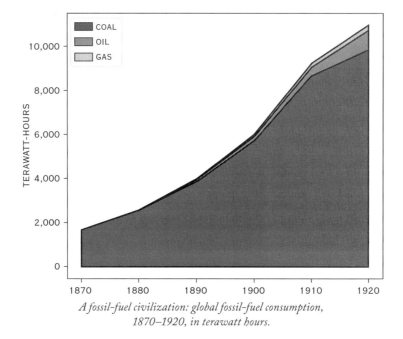

A fossil-fuel civilization: global fossil-fuel consumption,
1870–1920, in terawatt hours.

Fourth, as much larger and more concentrated agglomerations of capital emerged, they called for a different constitution of capital itself. Building a steel furnace was very different from putting up spinning machinery. Operating a railroad network was a challenge quite unlike coordinating a group of linen weavers in the Silesian countryside. Developing new products for Basel's burgeoning chemical industry required significantly more capital than creating a print pattern for Mulhouse's cotton manufacturers. The amount of capital needed to start a steel mill or a railroad was far greater than the capital needed to spin cotton, operate a plantation, or process tea. Such concentrations of capital were partly the result of the new technical requirements of production and partly a response to the crisis of 1873, whose ensuing deflationary spiral forced a generation of business leaders to confront the perils of what they called "excessive competition."[34]

Capital owners, unlike economists, had always disliked competition and favored monopoly. But now this went beyond idle talk and toward what has been termed an "anticompetitive consensus." As Carl

Duisberg, the founder of German chemical cartel IG Farben, re-marked, concentration was necessary to "achieve . . . the highest possi-ble profits by eliminating ruinous competition." John D. Rockefeller agreed: "The day of combination is here to stay. Individualism has gone, never to return." Future US president Woodrow Wilson cele-brated in 1897 "the triumphs of cooperation," which he considered "the self-possession and calm choices of maturity." Scholars have also high-lighted this anticompetitive trend, describing this moment in the his-tory of capitalism as "organized capitalism" or even "monopoly capitalism," attributing the most significant regulatory power not to markets but to the "visible hand" of management. While monopolies were rare and concentrations of capital not unassailable, there is no question that much larger agglomerations of capital emerged, dimin-ishing competition in many industries. The steel, oil, electrical, and chemical industries looked quite different from the cotton industry a century earlier. To secure the profitability of their massive, immovable investments, capital owners in these and other industries worked to limit competition, some via business organization, others via collective action, and still others through politics—all options fundamentally conditioned by the midcentury rebellions that gave capital owners, es-pecially owners of industrial capital, new prominence in the gover-nance of the political economy of the North Atlantic.[35]

In the realm of business strategy, some industrialists focused on commanding entire commodity chains. Most prominently, iron and steel manufacturers like the Röchlings bought mineral interests (coal and iron-ore mines as well as limestone deposits), developed private transportation infrastructures, and sought to create outlets to market their products—all with the goal of making their massive investments in an immobile asset, the steel mill, profitable.[36]

Andrew Carnegie's steel empire in the United States resembled that of the Röchlings. From his background in railroads, Carnegie un-derstood the importance of market power as well as the possibilities that came from internalizing markets and replacing them with the vis-ible hand of management. He strove to control steel manufacturing from the mines to the furnaces to the marketing: In 1881, he partnered with Henry Clay Frick to gain access to coal and coke, bought Minnesota iron-ore mines, and moved into marketing his products. Carnegie Steel gained control of the entire steel commodity chain from the mine to the consumer, becoming one of the world's largest industrial corporations, with twenty thousand people in its employ by 1900.[37]

Other industries followed suit: Henry Osborne Havemeyer built a near monopoly in the US sugar industry, and by 1892, he was acquiring sugar mills in Cuba to further secure a reliable flow of the raw material into his giant New York City refinery. Metallgesellschaft, a German metals trading company, acquired smelting and refining capacities so it could control the making of the products it sold. Even the cotton industry, which was notoriously splintered, made some effort to integrate vertically, with firms investing in cotton plantations. The Saxon Ottos, a cotton-manufacturing family, invested in plantations in German East Africa, and the British Fine Cotton Spinners' and Doublers' Association Limited purchased the Delta and Pine Land Company in Scott, Mississippi, to grow cotton on thousands of acres of land. Other industrial companies sought similar direct control over agricultural inputs: Lever Brothers, the English soapmaker, acquired palm-oil plantations in the Belgian Congo; Goodyear, the American tire manufacturer, opened the Goodyear Orient Company in Singapore to purchase Malaysian and Dutch East Indian rubber in 1908; and Firestone acquired huge rubber plantations in Liberia, Malaysia, and other places, a strategy the Ford Motor Company later pursued in the Brazilian Amazon. European merchants themselves also moved closer to producers; in India, they expanded from their age-old hubs in port cities and moved their capital and trading activities into the hinterland—Swiss cotton traders Gebrüder Volkart, for example, built branch offices in the cotton-growing countryside of Berar.[38]

To further limit competition and stabilize profits, business owners combined these vertical consolidations with horizontal ones—striving for a form of business organization that was as close to monopoly as possible. Among the businesses they merged were railroads and tele-graphs. Both required heavy capital investments that were costly no matter how much traffic they attracted; drumming up business at al-most any price made sense but also created a competitive environment that proved ruinous to many of these companies. As a result, they con-solidated.[39]

A particularly radical example of horizontal combination was John D. Rockefeller's Standard Oil. From the outset of his business career as a grain merchant during the Civil War, Rockefeller had disliked com-petition. After he went into the notoriously fragmented oil business in 1863, he bought as many competing firms as he could; by the 1870s, he controlled many of his former rivals around Cleveland, Pittsburgh, and other cities.[40] When he became president of the newly founded Na-tional Refiners Association, he tried to fix output and prices among its members. But voluntary agreements, he quickly learned, were almost impossible to enforce; they were, as he put it, "ropes of sand." Learning from this experience, Rockefeller's Standard Oil entered secret agree-ments with railroad companies, promising to use them consistently to ship oil in return for lower transportation rates. Rockefeller then of-fered to share this deal with other refiners who abided by his prices. Increasingly, he invited competing refiners to become part of Standard Oil in exchange for shares, and by 1880, he had forty oil producers under his control. In January 1882, these companies formed the Stan-dard Oil Trust, which controlled almost 90 percent of the United States' refining capacity. A Senate committee on interstate commerce concluded in 1886 that "[t]he Standard Oil Company brooks no com-petition; . . . its settled policy and firm determination is to crush out all who may be rash enough to enter the field against it; . . . it hesitates at nothing in the accomplishment of this purpose." Not surprisingly, a scholar considered Rockefeller one of the "Napoleons of the market."[41]

Other "Napoleons" popped up throughout the North Atlantic. In the Ruhr, Friedrich Alfred Krupp, who in 1887 took over his family's steel concern, with its more than 20,000 employees, grew the company through mergers and acquisitions. He acquired minette fields in German-ruled Lorraine as well as coal mines on the Ruhr and the Lahn rivers. He also invested in a longtime competitor, Gruson Ironworks in Magdeburg. In 1896, Krupp acquired the Schiff- und Maschinenbau-Actien-Gesellschaft Germania, a shipbuilder in the Baltic port of Kiel. This gave him control of naval manufacturing—and an ideal outlet for his steel. By 1907, Krupp had grown to 64,354 employees.[42]

The specific forms that such integrations took depended on the political context, demonstrating once more that private property—that crucial institution of capitalism—was a fundamentally political creation. In Germany, as we saw when we looked at the Röchlings, the organization of trusts usually allowed formally independent companies to collude, so companies could remain legally independent while still agreeing on production and prices. This harmonization was made even easier by the growing importance of banks, which played a central role in financing large industrial undertakings and coordinating their activities. As a result, there were 350 such cartels in Germany by 1905. In the United States, by contrast, the Sherman Antitrust Act made pools and trusts illegal; by 1890, US lawyers were advising corporations not to form cartels. Consequently, business consolidation under a holding company was more common in the United States.[43]

Reconstructed capital commanded new legal forms, and the law—and thus the state—played a critical role in its emergence. Perhaps most consequential was the rather sudden reorganization of industrial capital into corporations—a form of business organization in which management was divorced from ownership and property was socialized among many owners. So important was this feature that one historian has defined the entire period as driven by "corporate reconstruction." Corporations received important privileges: They gained legal personhood, existed in perpetuity, could easily disperse ownership, separated management from ownership, and won limited liability, reducing risks for investors. Of course, corporations had long existed (just think of the East India Company), but they had been rare and considered deeply problematic, with Adam Smith worrying in 1776 that "[t]he directors of such companies, . . . being the managers rather of other people's money than of their own, it cannot well be expected that they should watch over it with the same anxious vigilance with which the partners in a private copartnery frequently watch over their own."[44] Early in the nineteenth century, US corporations had been largely grants of privileges by state governments: They served a public purpose and had to be explicitly approved by legislatures.

By the mid-nineteenth century, however, general incorporation laws had spread through the United States, making incorporation a simple bureaucratic procedure. At first, mostly capital-intensive railroads took advantage of this new form of property, but then, in a sudden burst in the 1890s, hundreds of formerly privately owned manufacturing companies merged into corporations. In 1890, there were fewer than 10 industrial corporations; in the decade after 1895, eighteen hundred manufacturers merged to form 157 corporations, including General Electric, American Tobacco, and American Sugar Refining. Some of these companies were gigantic: In 1901, US Steel became the first billion-dollar corporation in the world. In 1896, when New Jersey allowed the ownership of corporations by corporations—that is, holding companies—further mergers ensued. This process of consolidation built upon an existing infrastructure of investment bankers and stock exchanges that propelled financiers like August Belmont, Jay Gould, and J. P. Morgan to prominence. In 1890, the total value of US industrial bonds and stocks was $33 million. In 1903, it was $7 billion.[45]

"Socialized capital," the spread of ownership in the form of corporations, emerged elsewhere as well. In Britain, the Joint-Stock Companies Act of 1844 paved the way, and in 1855, the Limited Liability Act reduced investors' liability. Similar acts were soon passed elsewhere, as general incorporation laws came to France in the mid-1860s, to Germany in 1870, and to Japan in 1899. They were impactful: In Germany, a boom in joint-stock companies saw 843 such companies launched between 1871 and 1873 alone.[46]

China also had a new corporate law code. Written in 1904, the first Company Law self-consciously borrowed from Western examples to construct a legal infrastructure for development. Corporations were not completely alien to China—there had been earlier forms of business organization rooted in guilds or lineages that undergirded complex organizations with great capital needs. In 1914, a more detailed corporate law, the Ordinance Concerning Commercial Associations, was passed, with 251 articles that drew on German commercial law. But the state was too weak to enforce the new laws, and Chinese businesses largely retained earlier forms of organization, with families and regional solidarities remaining central—a tradition, it turned out, that was highly adaptable. Chinese businesses thus retained national characteristics—just as the reconstruction of German capital looked different from its American counterpart.[47]

While much of the reconstruction of capital was in industry, capital in the countryside also consolidated and reorganized: In Portuguese São Tomé, small coffee growers increasingly went under in the late 1870s because of falling world market prices. They were replaced by Lisbon-based investors—including banks and joint-stock companies— who built large cocoa plantations. In the United States, the cotton trade moved away from small-scale factors, exporters, importers, and brokers on both sides of the Atlantic and turned toward giant integrated European and American trading firms. Large commodity dealers also became important in distributing food crops: Cargill, a Minnesota-based company founded in 1865, became a major presence in first American and then global markets for agricultural commodities. Alsatian businessman Léopold Louis-Dreyfus built a European grain-trading juggernaut that was, by 1900, the largest company of its kind in the world. Increasingly, even plantations became part of large corporations. In 1928, the French tire maker Michelin employed forty-eight hundred workers on its rubber plantation in Dâu Tiêng, Vietnam. In Cuba, American investors muscled into the world of sugar, building massive *centrales*, where harvests from multiple plantations were processed, and buying up land, with the United Fruit Company controlling seventy-five thousand hectares and the Cuba

Company forty thousand by 1901. Investments were substantial; British investors put almost three times more money into the rubber plantations of Southeast Asia than into US railroads. The corporate reconstruction of agrarian capitalism had many similarities with the corporate reconstruction of industry.[48]

As they consolidated and grew, capital owners redrew the geography of capital. The Boston economic elite, for example, which for generations had reaped profits from Atlantic and Caribbean trade and then from its deep investments in the American Industrial Revolution and its cutting-edge cotton-manufacturing sector, reoriented its capital. It saw new opportunities in the vast territory of the United States: Michigan copper mines, Colorado silver deposits, meatpacking in Chicago and Kansas, and especially railroads, which would interconnect the new empire of capital. This focus on continental industrialization created a "new geography of capital," as a continentally integrated economy replaced the earlier archipelago. In 1868, Bostonian Thomas Jefferson Coolidge had invested 45 percent of his capital in New England and 26 percent in the American West. Just fifteen years later, investments in the West had increased to 60 percent of his portfolio.[49]

Fifth, as capital owners reconstructed capital, they developed new kinds of social networks, manners, habits, and institutions—another key element in the reconstruction of capital. Most significantly, as their businesses outgrew urban or regional economies, they left their local cultural, social, and political orientation behind for more national visions and networks. At the same time, the once cosmopolitan merchant communities that had inhabited the port cities of the archipelago of capital became more provincial, not less, discovering their own hinterlands and becoming more rooted in national communities. The proud Hamburg and Bremen merchants, to cite an extreme example, joined their independent city-states to the German Reich in 1871. From both ends, capital owners became more national—and often more nationalist—in orientation.

This new national orientation of capital owners was the result of fundamental economic changes: Now even owners of single firms organized production in multiple locations, bought materials from distant places, and sold in national or imperial markets. At the same time, the corporate organization of businesses and the attendant socializing of capital meant that firms began to draw capital from investors across the nation. Most significantly, capital became increasingly invested in immovable assets and fixed in space (unlike earlier mobile mercantile investments).

As the national state became all-important to capital owners, this class became more national in outlook. Rio de Janeiro drew economic elites from all of Brazil's provinces. The city, according to one historian, came to "function like a great lock, rechanneling external flows and accommodating regionalisms in a broader, for the first time truly national, framework." In the United States, Pittsburgh steel industrialists, Cleveland oil refiners, and Southern railroad owners moved to New York, now the headquarters of a newly national American economic elite. US silk manufacturer Milo Merrick Belding oversaw his factories in Massachusetts, Michigan, Connecticut, California, and Canada from Manhattan. He was joined by Chicago meatpacker Philip Danforth Armour, California railroad magnate Collis Potter Huntington, Pittsburgh steel industrialist Andrew Carnegie, Pennsylvania oil entrepreneur John D. Rockefeller, and Colorado mine operator Meyer Guggenheim.[50]

The social networks and cultural institutions of this economic elite also became increasingly national in scope. In the United States, New England private schools such as Phillips Exeter and Andover Academies drew a national elite. Harvard, Yale, and Princeton Universities attracted wealthy sons from throughout the nation, so much so that by 1882, a Harvard alumnus spoke of Harvard as "a great and national university, and the national features and relations of Harvard are now its most striking and attractive ones." These institutions let economic elites abandon their age-old localism, transcend their sectoral economic interests, and build connections to the managers, engineers, and lawyers who would run much of the day-to-day business of their investments.[51]

Sixth, the bourgeoisie expanded to include not just capital owners but those who have been called "functionaries of capital"—lawyers, engineers, and, especially, managers. This broadening was first and foremost the result of economic changes: Up to this moment, capital owners had managed their own firms. By the late nineteenth century, however, the tradition of merchants living above their countinghouses and manufacturers on the factory grounds diminished. Instead, a group of professionals, a "new subspecies of economic man," began running this reconstructed capital. Its arrival was perhaps best marked by the 1908 founding of Harvard Business School, dedicated to training these professionals. A modern-day seminary, yeshiva, or madrassa, it taught both the theology and the practices of capitalism. Managers were now educated like doctors or lawyers, a notion that an eighteenth-century London trader or a Surat putting-out merchant would have found almost surreal.[52]

As these functionaries rose to prominence, they refined tools to cultivate the capital under their control: statistics, accounting, and, increasingly, planning. These tools made reconstructed capitalism and its terrific scale newly legible, deliberate, and abstract. Well into the nineteenth century, economic statistics had been largely "moral," delineating changes in literacy, drunkenness, criminality, and other indicators to chart the progress of communities. By the end of the century, however, the reconstruction of capitalism demanded, and was nourished by, a new lens of economic statistics that looked at people, places, institutions, land, and natural resources first and foremost in terms of their income-generating potential. As money and future earning capacity moved into the center of how progress was measured, they made different industries and interests commensurable. This quantification of growth led economist Simon Kuznets to construct, in 1934, an influential index of economic progress—the GDP.[53]

Within firms, statistical measurements and methods became nearly universal. Well into the nineteenth century, entrepreneurs had had very little sense of the cost and profit structures of their businesses; such economic workings were not a major worry in a world in which productivity, for most entrepreneurs, was not yet an important consideration. By the late nineteenth century, however, competitive pressures had brought an obsession with productivity. Increasingly complex systems of accounting allowed managers and others to see what was happening inside their firms. The number of specialists making the heretofore unseen inner life of capital visible grew so rapidly that they began organizing themselves into professional societies. The first, in 1870, was the Incorporated Society of Liverpool Accountants; it was followed by similar efforts in other British cities before the creation, in 1880, of the Institute of Chartered Accountants in England and Wales. In 1881, the Société Académique de Comptabilité began defining standard accounting practices in France. Across the Atlantic, the Institute of Accountants and Bookkeepers of New York emerged in 1882 to credential accountants; in 1886, the American Association of Public Accountants was founded. Ten years later, the State of New York legally recognized certified public accountants, and German auditors formed the Verband Deutscher Bücherrevisoren.[54]

Empowered with their newfangled statistics and accounts, these bookkeepers and managers made possible new forms of planning within firms. Even though "captains of industry" such as Rockefeller, Röchling, and Toyoda were known for their ability to command and control, it was their willingness to delegate control to bureaucratic structures that made autocrats archaic. The industries of the Second Industrial Revolution released a torrent of paper, with ever more clerical workers plying its streams, as companies were increasingly characterized, in Werner Sombart's incisive wording, as "administration."[55]

In the United Kingdom, there were 91,000 people in "commercial employment" in 1851, while in 1911, that number was 900,000, of whom 17 percent were women. Siemens alone had 12,500 white-collar workers on its payroll in 1912. These workers encountered others within a rapidly forming lower middle class: hundreds of thousands of teachers who taught rudimentary writing and calculating skills to the children of proletarians and rural cultivators, social workers who aimed to stabilize this crucially important working class, and the engineers

Paper administrators come to industry: US typists, circa 1900.

who increasingly monopolized the technical exper-tise that until very recently had been largely held by skilled workers. White-collar workers, teachers, and social workers—like semiskilled machine operators but more likely to be women—became the hall-marks of reconstructed capital.[56]

Seventh, enabled by this greater insight and control over recon-structed capital, one form of business achieved a new and exalted im-portance: finance. This was partly the result of the capital intensity of industrial production. Investment needs were so great that they were beyond the capacity of even the very richest individuals. Even though trading ventures like the East India Company had done so before, in-dustrial undertakings only now, for the first time in history, raised funds on capital markets. The shift gave power and prominence to a new kind of expert who specialized in the allocation of money, financ-ing both horizontal and vertical integrations. In the United States, J. P. Morgan reorganized the US steel industry, convincing Andrew Car-negie to part with his Carnegie Steel, combining it with Morgan's Federal Steel to create US Steel, a true colossus that controlled 60 per-cent of the market.[57]

In Germany, many of the large banks—Deutsche Bank, Dresdner Bank, and Commerzbank among them—took on similar roles and be-came important sources of capital for industrial undertakings. Deutsche Bank, the most prominent among them, was founded in 1870. At first, its shareholders aimed to create an institution that would support Ger-many's increasing foreign trade. Led by Georg von Siemens, a relative of

Werner von Siemens, and Hermann Wallich, these efforts were not particularly successful, and the bankers soon reoriented their focus to domestic manufacturing, especially heavy industry. They started keeping current accounts for industrial companies, with a revolving line of credit attached, and in the aftermath of the crisis of 1873, they purchased failing competitor banks, becoming Germany's richest bank by assets by 1876. By the mid-1870s, Deutsche Bank also expanded into investment banking. In 1879, it floated Krupp bonds worth 22.5 million marks and underwrote bonds and shares for BASF, AEG, Bayer, and Siemens, along with governments and railroads. In the process, German banks built close relationships with industrial firms, solidified by their widespread use of proxy voting rights and the banks' plentiful seats on supervisory boards (221 in 1903). They became, in effect, a "house bank" for many of Germany's large industrial concerns and a coordinating institution for significant swaths of the German economy. In 1913, Deutsche Bank held 10.8 percent of private bank assets in Germany and had arguably risen to the zenith of that country's businesses.[58]

The far-reaching effects of the rise of finance capital still resonate today: The horizons of capital owners broadened past any particular industry or any particular political economy to the process of capital accumulation more generally. When Thorstein Veblen discussed this emergence of "greater businessmen," he observed that their "fortunes are not permanently bound up with the smooth working of a given sub-process in the industrial system. Their fortunes are rather related to the larger conjunctures of the industrial system as a whole." Their perspectives became national in scope, and often imperial, unlike earlier generations of industrialists, who were largely rooted in local systems of power and politics.[59]

Nowhere was this reconstruction more radical than in the United States. The reasons were partly structural, partly political: The US stretched across a vast territory that allowed for the construction of many vertically integrated companies; its resource abundance suited energy- and material-intensive mass production, and its continental scale created the world's largest integrated market, allowing for the early marrying of mass production to mass consumption. Tellingly, in 1910, 43 percent of global iron and steel manufacturing took place in the United States, more than triple the output of mills in Britain. But there was also the United States' unique politics, which had emerged directly out of the rebellions of midcentury. The country's national political system was dedicated to facilitating continental industrialization and prairie agriculture and to a state whose policies did not have to compromise with the political interests of aristocratic (or, more generally, landed) elites. Sociologist Barrington Moore Jr. called the US Civil War the last bourgeois revolution, highlighting its significance in putting the United States on its way to a radically reconstructed capitalism and a formerly unimaginable expansion of its national economy, which would lead to its global ascendancy and the beginnings of the Second Great Divergence.[60]

One of the most striking aspects of this reconstruction of capital, indeed, was the foundational importance of politics. Of course, the state had always mattered to the unfolding of capitalism, and one of this book's core arguments is that capitalism was, and continues to be, a state-driven project. Yet by the late nineteenth century, as investments expanded and capital owners became deeply invested in controlling a vastly enlarged working class (and, eventually, consumers), they engaged in politics with renewed vigor—and secured the spoils of their midcentury rebellions. In *The Man Without Qualities*, Musil depicted the captains of industry, reminding readers that despite all their talk of laissez-faire, "it is well known that they made thoroughly sound use of the advantages to the public welfare offered by customs negotiations backed up by armed force or by using the military against strikers." Indeed, from the naval protection of trade routes to the military raiding or threatening of regimes that did not open up to global trade,

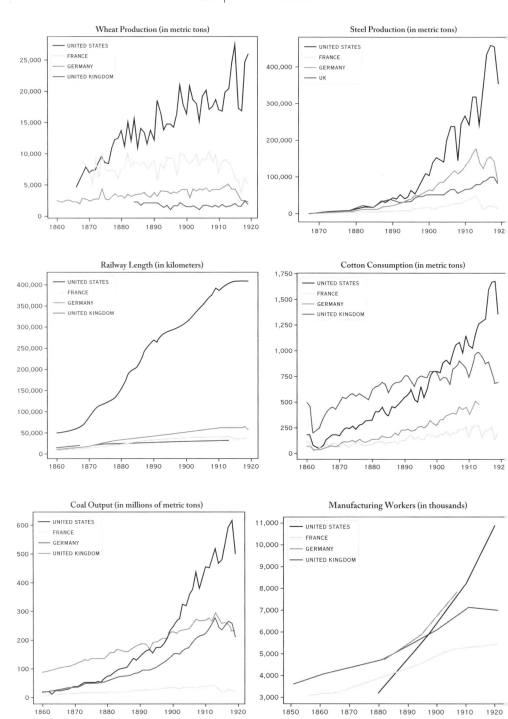

The Second Great Divergence: the rise of the United States in the global economy, 1850–1920.

and from the mobilization and control of workers to the legal reforms that enabled new structures of capital, the state—and thus politics—played a central role in reconstructing capital.[61]

This centrality of politics to business becomes obvious when we look again at the Röchlings. In their business, politics was everywhere and everything, as important to their operations as the organization of production or the management of workers. Consequently, their political activities were wide and deep: On an informal level, they mingled with like-minded elites. For decades before World War I, the Saarbrücken Casinogesellschaft, a social club, brought the economic elite of the Saarland, including the Röchlings, together with military officers, creating tight links within and between the economic elite and military leadership. Several Röchling women married into the military, symbolizing on an intimate level the ties between heavy industry and industrialized warfare that figured so tragically in the twentieth century.[62]

On a more formal but still local level, the Röchlings tried to gain a dominant say in municipal affairs. In Völklingen, they deeply involved themselves with local newspapers to shape public opinion. They funded much of the construction of a new church in the city, ensuring that the ceiling fresco depicted, in addition to Jesus on the Cross, members of their family and their crown jewel—the steel mill. They stayed in close contact with the city's mayor, municipal administration, and council, chiming in on decisions large and small. On the regional level, too—in the Saarland, where most of their facilities were located—they were as interested in the state's surveillance of their workers' politics as they were in infrastructural improvements.[63]

The climax of their political activism, however, took place at the national level. National politics was the lifeblood of their business, as the national state made raw materials and markets accessible, helped repress working-class discontent, improved essential infrastructures, and reimagined Europe's economic geography, all of which were crucial to the firm's business strategy. Carl's son Hermann, born in 1872, was heavily involved in that politics. In the 1912 elections for the Reichstag, he actively campaigned, advocating at crowded rallies for the continuation of protective tariffs for his industry, arguing that they enabled the firm's welfare payments. He was not subtle about persuading his workers to vote the right way: Workers who supported the Zentrum, a centrist Catholic party, allegedly lost their pension payments. And the Röchlings were no outliers. Everywhere, heavy industry owners in particular were intensely involved in politics: Emil Kirdorf, manager of the Ruhr's largest coal company and leading member of the Rheinisch-Westfälische Kohlen-Syndikat, became a founding member of several nationalist, militarist, and pro-colonial organizations, including the Alldeutscher Verband (the Pan-German League), the Kolonialverein (the Colonial Association), and the Flottenverein (Navy League). He also eventually became an early backer of an up-and-coming far-right politician, Adolf Hitler, whom he helped propel into the center of the nationalistic, militaristic, expansionistic, and antisemitic German right.[64]

This kind of political activism gave industrialists and financiers new sway over the state. In the United States, in the wake of the Civil War, the political mobilization of manufacturers in coalition with workers and Western farmers in the Republican Party had produced a political economy that departed from the free-trade, proslavery, and Atlantic agenda that had unified Southern planters and Northern merchants in the antebellum decades. The Republican Party not only fought a war for national unification—and eventually against slavery—but also instituted tariffs to protect industries, built an infrastructure conducive to the development of a continental industrial economy, favored the commercialization of Western agriculture (a huge market for industrial goods), and encouraged immigration to supply workers for that expanding industry. This new political economy of continental industrialization lay at the very core of the reconstruction of American capitalism.[65]

Protectionism there and elsewhere became a hallmark of this new political economy: Everywhere, iron and steel industrialists clamored for tariffs, as did Europe's beleaguered nobility, whose wealth derived from their uncompetitive grain production. At the behest of such entrepreneurs, protectionism spread—the McKinley Tariff of 1890 in the United States, the Méline Tariff of 1892 in France, and a whole slew of tariff legislation in Germany and Italy sought to support domestic industry and agriculture. Only the United Kingdom—still at the center of the world economy—committed to free trade (a departure from its protectionist roots), though even there, some voices demanded protection for domestic industries.[66]

And just as capital owners became deeply dependent on the state and eager to influence its policies, the state became deeply dependent on the reconstructed capitalism. Coal, steel, railroads, chemicals, electricity, and machinery did not just create a vast increase in output that could be taxed to fund an expanded state; they also provided the essential tools for the modern warfare that states, rightly or wrongly, believed to be essential to their very survival. As we will later see, the reconstruction of capital was a project not just of business elites but of government officials who eagerly created the conditions that allowed for market integration, market capture, technical innovation, capital concentration, and access to fuel and workers.

This reconstruction of capital had significant implications for global economic hierarchies as well. New centers of economic power emerged—particularly the United States and Germany—that first competed with and then outcompeted Britain. Japan also began to grow into that industrialized world, and in a step that would have a tremendous impact on global capitalism a century later, merchant capitalists in China, Mexico, India, and Brazil began to sprout industrial offshoots. In 1899, a modern cotton factory, the Dasheng Cotton Mill, started production in Nantong. In 1903, Mexico's earliest integrated steel mill started production. Four years later, Tata Steel followed suit in India. In Argentina and Brazil, stunning industrial growth characterized the first decades of the twentieth century; in Brazil, industry grew by an average rate of 14 percent a year in the 1910s. Globally, however, these were still decidedly minor affairs. In 1913, Europe (chiefly France, Germany, and the UK) and North America controlled almost three-quarters of the world's manufacturing output—a dramatically higher share than a century earlier or a century later. That same year, more than 50 percent of fossil fuels consumed worldwide were burned in Europe and 45 percent in the Americas, while less than 5 percent of global fossil fuel consumption occurred in Africa and Asia—as good an index as any in this age of fossil-fuel-intensive industrialization. And though Britain's once overwhelming leadership of the global economy diminished, it still had countless hidden and obvious advantages such as that in 1900, 72 percent of all telegraph cables in the world were British property. This was also the moment when an unprecedented form of economic specialization emerged. The vast majority of the world's people produced primary materials that, if exported, went to the world's industrial heartlands, while manufactured wares were almost exclusively sourced in these industrial heartlands. Economic and political hierarchies between the so-called core and the so-called periphery had sharpened in ways that would have been unimaginable a century earlier.[67]

Indeed, this was the most Eurocentric moment in the history of the empire of capital. From the perspective of the long-term history of capitalism, it was fleeting, to be sure, yet for the three-quarters of a century after 1870, capital owners and political elites in other parts of the world found themselves marginalized. The effects of concentrated mechanized production in the cities of the North Atlantic demanded and enabled new forms of hinterland integration to meet the needs of the imperial metropoles. New forms of the great connecting—steamships, railroads, and the telegraph most prominently—had a ruinous impact on proto-industrial manufacturing worldwide. Non-European merchant capital was also marginalized: In India in 1861, local merchants still controlled 67 percent of all cotton exports from Bombay; by 1875, their share had fallen to just 28 percent and continued to decline. But perhaps most consequential was the rebalancing of military power enabled by reconstructed capital, which allowed a few states to militarily dominate much of the world's hinterlands—indeed, entire continents. While states in the North Atlantic strengthened, elsewhere they were devastated, often destroyed in a further round of colonial and semicolonial acquisition. The states that succeeded in marrying industrial production—especially heavy industry—to vastly extended state capacities remained matchless for many decades.[68]

This radically Eurocentric moment of reconstructed capital emerged just as the writing of history became institutionalized and professionalized; it thus stamped the worldview of generations, including their perception of capitalism. Material power shaped the world, and just as tectonically, ideas fashioned the world's self-understanding. As the reconstructed empire of capital seeped into radically expanded geographic and social spaces, the stories told about that process became radically Eurocentric as well, reducing most of humanity to no more than extras in the drama of the history of capitalism. That was the case across the political spectrum, from the socialist left to the nationalist right, and this mythologizing has had tremendous staying power. Indeed, it continued to flourish even as the world it purportedly described was gone.[69]

Yet despite the parochial, circumscribed, and often racist self-understanding—and the often nationalist rhetoric and protectionist policies that came along with it—the cathedrals of capital that dotted the North Atlantic retained their essential global characteristics. In the hurly-burly of periodic booms and contractions, discerning observers conceded as much, as when Frankfurt banker Baron Carl Mayer von Rothschild opined that "the whole world has become a city." Not long after the crisis of the 1870s, the global economy itself became an object of focused observation, with economist Franz Xaver von Neumann-Spallart publishing his *Übersichten der Weltwirtschaft* (*Surveys of the world economy*) in 1885. As scholars associated with the German Historical School of economic thought drew maps, compiled statistics, and wrote accounts of economic developments in many parts of the world, they furthered the sense that economic life was essentially global. Four years later, von Neumann-Spallart's American counterpart, Richard T. Ely, spoke of the "world economy," and by 1895, the French *Revue mensuelle de la science économique* was dissecting what it called the "économie mondiale." By 1914, such insights found organized expression, with the launch of the Königliches Institut für Seeverkehr und Weltwirtschaft—the Royal Institute for Maritime Transport and World Economy—in the German city of Kiel. Where earlier global integration had been principally propelled by the merchant-driven dispersal of production, sourcing, and consumption, it was now driven by the industrialization of the heartlands.[70]

While nation-states took center stage, the global reality of capitalism constantly pitted them against one another as they jockeyed for dominance. Indeed, as capitalism expanded, it not only devoured and generated ever more capital but also drew on more land, more raw materials, and many more workers, both in the world's countryside and in its expanding industrial centers. As the rebellions of midcentury undermined slavery, serfdom, and the mobilization of a largely preindustrial proletariat, and as states and capitalists gained new capacities, new forms of labor emerged too. Millions of additional men, women, and children toiled in agriculture, mining, and industrial production to produce commodities for world markets, but how they were mobilized, how they worked, and how they organized their lives shifted radically. This global reconstruction of labor was among the most consequential of the late nineteenth-century reconstructions of capitalism.

Reconstructing Labor, 1870–1920

Steelworkers, Völklinger Hütte, Völklingen, 1890.

A s the shape of global capitalism shifted in the second half of the nineteenth century, the reconstruction of labor moved to center stage. With ever accelerating speed, capital owners had invested in rural and urban production, drawing on steadily increasing numbers of men, women, and children to hoe fields, harvest crops, load ships, mine coal, type letters, and operate elaborate machinery. By choice and necessity, they had, until midcentury, propelled that expansion conservatively, intensifying older work regimes: The patterns of the artisanal workshop had moved into factories, plantation slavery had expanded, and household production had entered more homes. This was an astounding feat, yet the midcentury rebellions—on factory floors, farms, and plantations—had made it clear to all that the old ways had reached their end.

As a result, capital owners the world over sought new ways of recruiting and controlling the great masses of people needed to keep growing capital by meeting the commodity demands of distant markets. Capital owners understood that without the remaking of labor—new methods for its recruitment, control, and retention—there was no reconstruction of capitalism. In this project, however, they predictably encountered highly mobilized workers who sought autonomy, dignity, and a greater share of the fruits of their labor—demands amplified by new modes of thinking about capitalism and new forms of collective organization.

A global social conflict unfolded and produced a fundamentally altered global landscape of labor. Testifying not only to workers' determination to improve their conditions but also to local social, economic, cultural, and political disparities, a vast variety of labor regimes emerged from this conflict. While these reconstructions informed one another—with workers, governments, and capital owners learning from one another's efforts and attentively observing other parts of the world to inform their strategies—they also continued the production of difference that has been such a telltale characteristic of capitalism.

This global social conflict can be viewed from many vantage points. La Réunion is one. The island—the outcrop of a volcano rising from the floor of the Indian Ocean—lies about thirteen hundred miles off the eastern coast of Mozambique. France claimed the largely uninhabited territory in the mid-seventeenth century, as England had Barbados. By the second half of the eighteenth century, the island's sugar fields supported a small community of white planters; by 1848, they numbered just under two thousand. This vanguard of French plantation owners directed the unpaid labor of fifty thousand enslaved workers, predominantly from East and Central Africa. Because most of these workers died young without having children, La Réunion's capital owners needed a constant stream of newly enslaved cultivators: eighty thousand between 1769 and 1794 alone and another forty-five

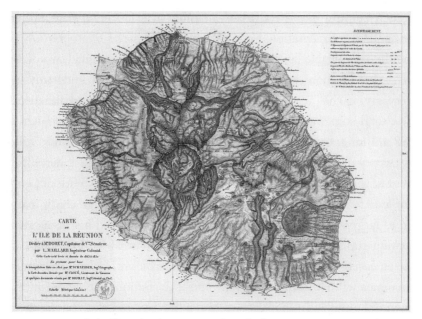

Rebuilding the plantation machine: La Réunion in 1853.

thousand between 1817 and 1835. Sugar ate people. As an early twentieth-century French colonial official noted without qualification or fear of contradiction, it was "slavery that founded the prosperity of the island.[1]

By the early nineteenth century, the slave regime of La Réunion, like those elsewhere, was profitable but unstable. Sugar still had markets, but workers pushed against their enslavement, with some taking off to the mountainous interior to form settlements beyond the reach of planters in so-called maroon communities. New British and then French prohibitions against the slave trade, moreover, made planters realize that slavery might not always secure their labor needs. In the face of manumissions, high mortality, slave self-emancipation, and the compulsion to expand cultivation, La Réunion seemed increasingly unstable as a profitable outpost of European capital.[2]

Then, in 1848, the Martinican and Parisian rebellions abolished slavery throughout the empire, realizing in one stroke planters' long-standing fears. Slave owners and metropolitan investors across the

French empire, like their British counterparts fourteen years earlier, demanded compensation for what they saw as the expropriation of their most valuable assets. Failure to pay them, they argued, would be to "make common cause with the sects who gather now to destroy society, saying that property is theft"—namely, anarchists and socialists.[3] The total sum was open to debate, with some asking for as much as 288 million francs. Eventually, they settled on 120 million francs, paid in twenty annual installments. About 5 percent of these indemnities went to the enslavers of La Réunion, bracing its economy with not only immediate capital but also, just as importantly, a source of credit many times larger, secured by future indemnity payments. This state intervention transformed slave ownership into collateral for loans, just as the enslaved workers' actual bodies had been before. Indemnity money also meant that capital flowed into the Banque de la Réunion, giving planters even more access to credit.[4] Even in the very moment of their emancipation, African workers continued to play the pivotal role in the plantation economy, as a source of not just labor but also credit.

Beyond capital and credit, however, emancipation raised a much bigger question: how to continue, even expand,

Calculating the price of the enslaved and the indemnities to be paid: These are rough calculations by a French colonial bureaucrat, 1848–1849. There were 48,761 enslaved men, women, and children on La Réunion at this point. He estimated their value at 76,488,942.68 francs.

plantation agriculture without enslaving the cultivators. Slavery, as we have seen, had been one cornerstone of capital's expansion into the global countryside. How would coffee be planted, cane sown, and cotton harvested now that slavery was illegal? In the wake of the midcentury rebellions, this question occupied planters and colonial officials the world over. Planters on La Réunion followed the most familiar path: forcing freedpeople to sign one- or two-year labor contracts. As these contracts expired, however, freedpeople left the plantations in droves. Almost 50,000 enslaved women, men, and children had labored on the island in 1848; just four years later, in 1852, only 15,843 remained working for pay on the plantations. These departures confirmed the planter elite's greatest fears: "[H]aving virtually no needs [and] being able with the wage of three working days to live & support his family during the whole week," freedpeople "loath . . . regular labor."[5] In "warm countries" like La Réunion, the planters reasoned, a formerly enslaved worker with a small income happily settles for that and "returns to his house, smokes and rests, or goes fishing."[6] According to lawyer and colonial official Delabarre de Nanteuil (who was somewhat of an expert in such matters, having been born amid the revolutionary upheaval in Saint-Domingue), "[T]he freedmen abandoned the plantations. Most settled in the cities; others retreat[ed] to the corners of isolated lands in the heights of the Isle. . . . [T]he freed have not returned to work."[7] Freedpeople constructed—along with a group of impoverished white settlers—a subsistence-centered economy on the margins of the plantation complex in the island's high plains, which were unsuited to sugar and thus still largely unsettled.[8]

As former slaves retreated from plantation work and the reach of short-term contracts, planters and colonial officials redoubled their efforts to secure workers. A survey of other emancipations appalled them, since, as in the British West Indies, they were often followed by a decline in sugar output. As a French colonial official noted, with "the blacks having in great number deserted the properties to which they were attached, it was necessary to be concerned, to maintain the value of the land, to bring in a certain number of workers from outside and to establish special regulations for those freed slaves who would agree to enter into commitments of limited duration with the owners of rural properties."[9] And, indeed, to better control newly freed workers, Réunionese planters called on the colonial government to limit workers' mobility and coerce them into selling their labor power. In 1852, the state introduced a "labor book" that workers who did not sign yearlong contracts had to carry around. In 1855, legislation against "desertion" was passed: Anyone who had not signed an employment contract was considered a "vagabond" and subject to criminal sanctions.[10]

But freedpeople continued withdrawing their labor. In response, planters pressured the colonial government to revive long-term indentureship. They appealed for permission to recruit workers on the east coast of Africa by purchasing enslaved Africans from local traders, "liberating" them, and then forcing them to sign contracts that committed them to years of labor on La Réunion. Between 1848 and 1860, planters brought over thirty-four thousand Africans under this ploy, facilitating the tripling of sugar production in just eleven years.[11] Just four years after slavery had ended, more indentured workers labored on plantations than freedpeople.

Metropolitan protests against this renewal of something close to slavery ended that system by 1860, and labor became scarce once more. Planters now looked east, to India. Since the 1820s, planters had employed a small number of Indians from the French colony of Pondicherry, men such as Caddy Poulicadow, Gong Patow Palalow, and Chinom Abigadow, who signed three-year contracts. The experience had been mixed from the planters' perspective, not least because these workers had resisted their often terrible conditions: The Réunion newspaper *Le Glaneur* had reported as early as 1833 that indentured workers roamed the countryside as "vagabonds."[12] Moreover, the Indians often refused work orders, "commit[ted] all sorts of disorders"—including moving to find better working conditions—and even organized a union.[13]

Confronted with French public outrage over coercive employment of Africans, planters decided to expand the recruitment of indentured workers from India. They urged the French government to sign a treaty with Britain for tens of thousands of such workers, who began arriving in 1862 for five-year stints. Workers received a salary, food rations, and some clothing—"little more than sacks," according to one reporter.[14] Even though they were formally free and the system was highly regulated, the workers' treatment was characterized by such "extreme brutalities" that a French colonial official called it a form of "disguised slavery."[15] Mortality was nearly as high as under slavery, and some workers were forced to renew their indentures beyond the number of years to which they had originally agreed.[16] Britain demanded greater oversight. Then, in 1882, it terminated the treaty.[17]

When Indian migration ended, planters embarked upon another effort to solve what they called the "question of muscle power."[18] Once more, they "turned their eyes toward Africa" for "docile and robust" workers, demanding that the French authorities negotiate with Portugal for further labor imports from its colony of Mozambique.[19] Such recruitment, they argued, was part of their "civilizing work, full of philanthropy"—and African workers began arriving again in April 1888.[20]

Planters also looked to the nearby island of Madagascar. In 1884, La Réunion's colonial authorities had negotiated an agreement to secure workers from there, and when France took over the island in 1896 after a bloody war against Queen Ranavalona III, a growing number of women and men arrived to work. They experienced significant coercion and violence, inadequate food and clothing provisions, and withheld pay.[21] "[M]any," a French colonial bureaucrat reported in 1924, "claim to be undernourished."[22] A report found "poorly ventilated lodgings without beds," "illegitimate withholdings, beatings . . . insufficient food," "brutality," and "physical abuse."[23] A worker from Madagascar complained of the lack of respect: "[T]hey insult us."[24] One French bureaucrat even concluded that "[t]he way Madagascan workers are generally treated in La Réunion is essentially a form of slavery."[25]

In total, fifty thousand indentured workers arrived from East Africa and Madagascar in the second half of the nineteenth century, but planters still complained about labor shortages. Some invested in labor-saving technologies, hoping these new tools would help them "to arrive by rational manufacturing to extract from the cane all the wealth it contains."[26] Thanks to their efforts, productivity rose: In 1880, La Réunion's planters produced twenty-three and a half tons of sugar per hectare; in 1895, that number more than doubled, reaching sixty tons. Other planters began to move toward sharecropping, paying rural cultivators for their labor with a fixed share of the crop.[27] Their casting around for labor showed, in a roundabout way, that they had to contend with the power, however modest, of their workers.

But sharecropping and agricultural innovations remained insufficient to meet the market opportunity for sugar and the available capital poised to realize it. Planters and colonial officials redoubled their hunt for labor, from the coast of Africa to China, from Madagascar to Somalia, from the Comoros to Vietnam. In the mid-1890s, the Syndicat Central Agricole—an association of planters—requested a reopening of Indian migration. Without such workers, they argued, La Réunion "will be devastated." With 50 percent of sugar lands allegedly uncultivated and sugar output shrinking despite productivity gains, they appealed to the state to address their "profound distress."[28] In 1921, they tried to recruit workers in Egypt and Syria. In January 1924, the colonial governor of La Réunion, Maurice Pierre Lapalud, sent a telegram to the Ministry of Colonies in Paris urging for more workers to be recruited from Madagascar, bemoaning the tendency of Creoles to become smallholders and craftsmen. In 1925, his successor requested workers from Java. And in 1927, his administration tried to recruit Japanese workers.[29]

L a Réunion was a microcosm of a global struggle. For centuries, as we have seen, slavery had been spectacularly successful in enabling the delivery of agricultural commodities to North Atlantic markets. With its abolition, planters, merchants, and industrial consumers of slave-produced wares wondered how labor would be secured. La

Réunion was not the only place where planters worried about this issue; there was widespread dread that freedpeople would retreat into mere subsistence agriculture. In 1883 Cuba, a newspaper writer for *La Tribuna* feared that "the scenes of mass labor desertion that unfolded in Jamaica will repeat themselves, because there are so many uncultivated lands where blacks prefer to establish themselves independently, and where they can work exclusively to satisfy their limited needs."[30] For Charles Victor Frébault, governor of Guadeloupe from 1859 to 1863, the culprit was "wild fruit," which freedpeople could harvest and thus survive on without working for others.[31] *The Times* of London came to the same conclusion: Because freedpeople required "little shelter, less clothing, and scarcely more food than can be found above his head or at his feet," they would not come to work for low wages on plantations.[32] When Dutch colonial bureaucrat Karel Frederik van Delden Laërne traveled to Brazil in 1883 to understand how coffee production was organized in that leading producer nation, he expected to see a decline in production with the impending end of slavery, just as Jamaica had.[33] Indeed: "[A]ll progress is arrested now by a want of labourers," he observed.[34]

These fears were well founded. As in La Réunion, freedpeople everywhere, in a feat of individual and collective determination, moved out of plantation labor. Jamaica was the terrifying example that all planters referred to: Even though the planter-dominated local colonial assembly had done everything in its power to attach freedpeople to plantations by requiring so-called apprenticeships, freedpeople had simply refused that work and developed their own provision grounds for subsistence production. Some seven years after full emancipation, more than 21 percent of the "apprentice" population had become residents on peasant freeholds where they could combine subsistence production with market gardening and wage labor. The effort of freedpeople to eke out an independent living alarmed British policymakers so much that they universally came to denigrate life outside the aegis of capital as a form of "barbarism."[35] Most prominently, Haiti's postrevolutionary historical trajectory was described as a "gradual relapse from comparative civilization to barbarism," and its freedpeople's communities were maligned as having sunk into regression, a state "of small occupiers vegetating in barbarous indolence on their prolific soil."[36]

Such retreats from plantation agriculture occurred throughout the world's former slave lands. In the western parts of Colombia, freedpeople left their former owners and engaged in independent gold mining and peasant agriculture—they became "a rainforest peasantry."[37] The Select Committee on Sugar and Coffee Planting of the British House of Commons lamented the new realities:

> That from the now independent condition of the mass of the people, the command of labour has become exceedingly precarious, often not to be had at all when most wanted; that hardly in any case will the people work on estates for more than five days in the week; that in several districts they refuse to work more than four days in the week; that the average time of field labour is from five to six hours a day; that the labour given for the wages is not only inadequate in quantity, but generally ill performed; that on the anniversary of freedom, and at Christmas, the entire agricultural population spend from one to two weeks in idleness; that in some districts this is also the case at Easter; that at all these periods, even if the canes are rotting on the ground, and the coffee falling from the trees, no rate of wages will induce the people to work; and that labour continues to become more scarce every year by the people withdrawing from the plantations.[38]

A French planter concurred: The world had been turned upside down. A Malagasy worker, he complained, "gives up his job when one does not let him do it completely as he pleases."[39]

In response, planters and their allies embarked upon an effort to reconstruct the world's agricultural working class. Some of the agitation against slavery had been animated by "free labor" arguments: the notion that markets would create incentives for both workers and employers to strike a bargain. Faced with the sheer scale of the challenge imposed by emancipation, however, nearly all planters and colonial officials concluded that markets were insufficient to secure the workers required for the continued production of cheap raw materials and agricultural commodities, especially now that the Second Industrial Revolution was pressing down with its new demands on the world's countryside. Instead, capital owners and their state allies intervened. It was a project of planetary scope. "Europe has definitively taken over the government of the globe," a journalist from the French daily *Le Temps* explained in 1899, to "ensure a better distribution of men over the habitable surface" of the planet: "Some countries are overcrowded, while others are empty; nothing can be more advantageous to each of them, as to what one might call the good administration of our planet, than to bring those who do not have enough [of] the population that the others have in excess. In temperate regions, the white race colonizes itself; in warm regions, it needs the help of races made for the climate and whose migration it must cause."[40] A planetary labor market was to be created—by force, if necessary. The French Commission on Work Regimes in the Colonies concurred in 1873, with one of its members, Michel-Félix Rivet, arguing that former slaves needed to be coerced to work, while another member, Pierre Cuinier, then the governor of La Réunion, supported penal sanctions for workers who did not fulfill their labor contracts.[41] Post-slavery labor, it was widely assumed, would have to rest on coercion and even violence. To trust an "invisible hand" of the market was to court disaster.

Even the post-emancipation rulers of Saint-Domingue, Toussaint Louverture and Jean-Jacques Dessalines, had attempted to coerce freedpeople back onto plantations in order to revive the export economy. Louverture instated internal passports and military discipline on plantations, complaining that young workers who had never experienced slavery "do not want to devote themselves to [plantation] agriculture, because, they say, they are free and spend their days running about, giving a bad example to the other workers."[42] To the revolutionary elites' chagrin, however, many former slaves managed to evade the restrictions and realize their dreams of a small squatter's plot in the Haitian mountains.[43] It was not an easy life, but it was still much preferable to cultivating sugarcane.

———

The search for new laborers and the emergence of new forms of labor control in the world's countryside were products of the combined pressure of the abolition of slavery and struggling to fulfill burgeoning demand from global markets. Everywhere, private and industrial consumers wanted coffee, cotton, tea, sugar, wheat, and other such goods. As urbanites and industrial workers needed calories (as well as drugs like coffee and tea to keep them productive), and as capital-intensive machines demanded continual inputs to turn a profit, capital owners pushed commodity frontiers ever deeper into the world's countrysides.[44]

As a result, for planters, merchants, and industrialists, the reconstruction of labor was not just a question of how to mobilize and control workers on land formerly cultivated by enslaved women, men, and children, but a question of how to recruit agrarian labor in areas of the world where slavery had not played much of a role. The crisis in the slave lands indeed led them to expand the plantation complex to new regions, especially around the Indian Ocean and into the Pacific. Unprecedented numbers of Caribbean planters moved to distant locations in search of fresh labor and land, while some US planters relocated to India and, later, Brazil, where a few thousand former Confederates hoped to re-create their slave-powered cotton kingdom.[45]

Capital owners pushed one commodity frontier after another into the world's countryside. They propelled the tea frontier beyond China to Assam, and then to Ceylon, allowing British capital owners to finally circumvent the Qing government's restrictions on the tea trade and their inability to penetrate deeply into the Chinese tea-producing hinterland by expanding tea production in their colonial holdings. The cotton frontier also advanced, moving beyond the United States. Egypt became a major producer of cotton for European markets: In 1870, it produced 89,000 tons; in 1913, its fellahin produced almost four times as much. Congo, Malaysia, and Dutch Southeast Asia began producing rubber for world markets: Rubber imports into Germany alone increased tenfold from 1880 to 1910. Sugar moved too: Fiji, which produced no sugar in 1860, churned out 100,000 tons in 1913. In 1875, there were 3,260 workers on Hawaiian sugar plantations; twenty-five years later, their number was 37,760. In Manchuria, Japanese capital propelled a massive expansion of soy agriculture. As before, these expansions of commodity frontiers required moving land into commodity production, but they also rested on military capacities, the provision of infrastructure, and the novel use of the state's legal and administrative powers.[46] The spread of such commodity frontiers was part and parcel of the global reconstruction of capitalism.

Whether new commodity frontiers emerged because of additional demand or because older ones had collapsed under social and ecological strains, the question of labor remained paramount. Indeed, the so-called labor question became an obsession of capital owners the world over. When the French journal *La Dépêche* discussed, in 1926, Madagascar's economic potential, it described the island's future in glowing terms, with the only worry "the labor question."[47] Millions of additional workers were needed to produce agricultural commodities and minerals for European and North American markets. The demand was so great that

The tea commodity frontier in China, 1908.

plantation frontiers competed with one another for labor. When La Réunion's planters recruited workers in Madagascar, for example, local planters protested against labor exports. The French governor of Indochina in turn groused about labor exports to Madagascar, saying he could not spare the workers. Cheap labor was a national resource, and access to it motivated many a colonial project, as opening up territories for cheap labor continued to drive capitalism's geographic expansion. Colonialism was also a form of labor mobilization.[48]

Cheapness and control were crucial for many planters across the world who wanted to reconstitute labor to look as close to slavery as possible. The enslavers of the American South had such visions. When they lost their war in 1865, planter-controlled legislatures immediately passed so-called Black Codes to immobilize Black laborers and force them to remain on plantations; vagrancy laws allowed for easy sentencing to forced labor. Yet by and large, these efforts at re-enslavement failed—labor conditions akin to slavery either remained temporary (such as the apprenticeship system in Jamaica) or encountered such determined pushback from the formerly enslaved that they quickly unraveled, as in the United States. Enslavement needed the backing of the state, and with that support uncertain, planters failed to reconstitute it.[49] The rebellions of the enslaved had forever decimated that horizon of heinous possibility.

Instead, a panoply of labor regimes took hold. The striking aspect of the reconstruction of labor was its enormous diversity, sometimes even in the same place. In Peru, for example, with slavery abolished in 1854, capital owners used debt peonage, wage labor, *yanaconas* (Indigenous servants), and Chinese indentured workers. On Manchuria's soy frontier, several million Chinese migrant workers labored as tenant farmers, small proprietors, and wageworkers.[50] The same variety can be observed when we look at single commodities. After emancipation, sugar, coffee, and cotton were produced in different parts of the world by different kinds of workers: in some places by sharecroppers and tenant farmers, in others by peasants, in still others by forced workers, and elsewhere by wage laborers.

This stunning diversity was the outcome of local conditions, especially the uneven political and economic power of capital owners, rural cultivators, and states, as well as the mobilizations and politics of the millions living in the world's countryside. The importance of these local balances of power in the global history of reconstruction can be seen with particular clarity when we look at a kind of natural experiment that occurred on the shores of the Central African Lake Kivu in the early twentieth century. The lake straddled the Belgian Congo on its western shores and German- and then Belgian-administered Rwanda and Burundi on its eastern shores. On both sides, planters and colonial administrators tried to increase coffee production for metropolitan markets. Both succeeded but in very dissimilar ways—on one side's shores, large coffee estates emerged, while on the other side, smallholders produced coffee beans for global markets. The different kinds of societies that had existed on the two sides of the lake before Europeans arrived shaped the distinctive trajectories: On the eastern side, the Rwandan and Burundian side, high population densities left little land uncultivated, with much of it farmed by small independent peasants. On the western side, the Congolese side, land was less densely settled and Indigenous property claims less legible. As a result, the Belgian colonial state and its investors built large plantations on the lake's western shores, drawing on forcefully recruited workers—more than twenty thousand of them. On the eastern shores, however, German colonial officials forced peasants who remained independent smallholders to produce larger coffee crops for export. Both labor systems involved significant coercion, yet they looked drastically different.[51] The global history of capitalism, this example shows, was also always local.

Such local histories, however, were also deeply connected and part of a global conversation on post-slavery labor. Colonial archives of this period overflow with writings on the "labor question." Spanish colonial officials tried to learn from French bureaucrats about their experience with emancipation. The French, in turn, hoped to appropriate lessons from the United States' experience while keeping an eye on British efforts in India just in case. In 1905, the French Foreign

Ministry investigated the expansion of cotton agriculture in both the Bombay Presidency and German Africa. In the process of expanding coffee agriculture on São Tome, Portuguese colonial officials studied Brazilian efforts to recruit and control labor.[52] These global discourses influenced local strategies—without moderating the period's extreme variety of outcomes.

⎯⎯

As labor in the reconstructed countryside took on a kaleidoscopic variety of forms, indentured labor was one important variety, most closely linked to slavery. Over the nineteenth century, tens of millions of workers left their homes for often distant parts of the world under contractual arrangements—so-called indentures—to labor on plantations that produced commodities for world markets. They came from India, China, parts of Africa, Japan, Malaysia, Melanesia, and Southeast Asia, having signed contracts with labor recruiters who provided them transport, subsistence, and cash payments in return for a certain number of years of labor. These workers typically lived in barracks that resembled Caribbean slave quarters, and physical coercion—including kicking, floggings, and beatings—was a regular feature of their lives. Historians have estimated that between the mid-1830s and 1920s, European colonial powers transported 2.2 million such workers throughout the world. The Caribbean isles saw an influx of 259,700 Indian workers, Mauritius received 452,652, and others went to La Réunion, Fiji, and eastern and southern Africa. Labor recruiters transported 500,000 Chinese workers to the Caribbean and South America—120,000 to Cuba alone—while about 14,000 indentured laborers from Melanesia, Micronesia, and China went to work on Samoan coconut plantations. This heavily regulated European system, however, paled compared with the 27 million South Asian workers sent by Indian labor brokers to Burma, Ceylon, and Malaysia to power rapidly growing rice, tea, and rubber plantations.[53] The number of people transported this way was greater than the number bought and sold by the Atlantic slave trade, testifying to the continued globe-shaping dynamism and impact of the plantation sector during the Second Industrial Revolution.

Indentured workers entered the world's countryside in two distinct situations. Most prominently, they replaced formerly enslaved workers; indeed, it was the political pressure of West Indian sugar planters that motivated the turn to indentured labor in the first place. In La Réunion, as we saw, indentured workers powered the plantation complex just a few years after the end of slavery. The same was true in British Guiana: Planter John Gladstone, for example, used compensation he received for the emancipation of his more than 2,000 enslaved workers to transport indentured Indians to his plantations. Similarly, when slavery ended in neighboring Surinam in 1863 and freedpeople left plantations to grow subsistence crops after completing a period of forced contractual labor, the Dutch signed a treaty with Britain in 1870 for the importation of Indian workers. About 35,000 arrived between 1873 and 1916, joined by 31,000 workers from Dutch-controlled Java.[54]

The resurgence of indentured labor was triggered primarily by planters' short-term inability to turn freedpeople into wageworkers. But indentured workers were also transported into regions of the world where capital owners had been able to acquire land, often by force, but had not been able to turn local peasants into workers. As the island of Ceylon fell under British sway, planters used credit from large merchants and banking houses to convert lands into coffee and, after 1880, tea plantations, setting up a "West India system of production."[55] The Finlays of Glasgow, renowned for their massive investments in cotton manufacturing a century earlier, now moved significant capital into such tea plantations—controlling more than thirty thousand acres by 1896, enough to produce ten million pounds of tea annually. Complaining about the "competition for native labour," they and others often failed to recruit labor locally; their plantations remained little more than isolated capitalist islands in places still dominated by peasant agriculture.[56] The planters turned elsewhere for labor—to the severely indebted farmers

Post-slavery plantations: tea gardens in Ceylon
(now Sri Lanka), turn of the twentieth century.

from the Tamil districts of the Madras Presidency. Mobilizing such migrant workers had the added advantage of not disturbing social relations in the Ceylonese countryside, the control of which was a project still beyond the power of British planters and colonial officials. On the tea frontier of Assam, things were roughly similar: When it was impossible to persuade local cultivators to work on plantations, property owners secured indentured laborers from other parts of India. In Burma, the booming rice economy was powered by up to fifteen million indentured Indians, brought by labor brokers called Chettis. And in Samoa, where coconut plantations had begun producing copra for metropolitan markets by the late nineteenth century, the continued strength of the local Samoan economy and polity meant that almost all labor was done by indentured workers brought from elsewhere.[57]

As millions of indentured workers crossed oceans to produce ever more agricultural commodities for global markets, contractual labor relations replaced enslavement. Yet labor relations remained heavily coercive, with workers facing not only criminal sanctions for failing to fulfill their obligations but also confinement, physical and verbal abuse, and, at times, forced extensions of their contracts. As indentures "mobilized labourers only to immobilize them," as one historian has put it, the expansion of capitalism in the countryside continued to produce unfreedom.[58] In Surinam, once workers signed their labor contracts, they were confined to prisonlike structures while their transport to the plantations was arranged. Once there, they retained an inferior legal status, were subject to penal sanctions, and experienced labor conditions so coercive that in 1911, the British consul called indentureship "veiled slavery."[59] When an Indian indentured worker sought legal aid in La Réunion in 1873, he arrived in an iron collar and chains fastened by his employer. In Assam, workers were physically disciplined in ways reminiscent of Caribbean slavery, with planters allowed to make "private arrests." In the tea pluggers' communities of origin, there circulated rumors of workers being burned alive and cannibalized by European colonials. The new regime was really a grim midpoint between slavery and free labor.[60]

Indian nationalists raised their voices in protest—indeed, this was one of the causes that radicalized them.[61] As Mahatma Gandhi pointed out, "An Indian hard-pressed by pangs of poverty . . . can scarcely be called a free agent when he signs the contract of indenture. Men have been known to consent to do far worse things in order to be free from immediately pressing difficulties."[62] Gandhi condemned "the evils of the indenture system," which he compared with a "state of slavery."[63]

IN AREAS WHERE freedpeople's escape from the plantation world that had once enslaved them was more difficult, and where they failed to gain access to land, another system of post-slavery labor became common: sharecropping and tenant farming. Under this system, planters continued to own the land, but they rented it to cultivators for either a share of the crop or a money payment—which they could do because they enjoyed sufficient political power to severely constrain the movement and landownership ability of their workers, even as these workers enjoyed enough power to make it impossible to turn them into full-fledged wageworkers.[64]

This form of agrarian labor was most prevalent in the southern United States. As formerly enslaved workers gained their freedom in 1865, and as planters' efforts to turn African Americans into wageworkers largely failed, sharecropping and tenant farming came to characterize much of the cotton-growing countryside. Former slaves cultivated the land with the help of their families; they got their supplies and sustenance from local stores, which provided them with credit at often exorbitant rates, and they paid their rent at the end of the harvest season in kind or money. In Cuba, too, sharecropping and tenant farming became an important source of sugarcane labor, especially when landowners' efforts to import Chinese indentured laborers ended in 1873. Cuban sugar producers constructed what came to be known as the *colonato* system, in which small landholding peasants and tenant farmers, or *colonos*, and sharecroppers, or *subcolonos*, raised sugarcane to sell to the nearest sugar mill. Similar arrangements emerged in many parts of the world, including Japan, the eastern Mediterranean, Martinique, and Barbados.[65]

SHARECROPPING, TENANT FARMING, and indentured servitude characterized much of the reconstructed countryside. In some areas of the world, agrarian wage labor emerged as well. While most landowners reached for more coercive methods of reconstructing labor, a few held out hope that they could turn rural cultivators into proletarians, creating a free-labor system in which workers would voluntarily sell their labor power for a contractually agreed-upon payment in money or kind. Industry stood as a shining example of that form of labor. In the United States, even before Union victory in the Civil War, manufacturers of New England and New York had written pamphlets, articles, and books celebrating the productive potential and emancipatory effects of wage labor and its putative harmony with human nature.[66]

Eager to associate proletarian labor with the natural order of things, these capitalist revolutionaries little appreciated how drastic a departure their agenda truly was.[67] After all, the world's countryside had been dominated by radically different systems of labor for millennia: On one side were independent producers whose self-directed labor focused on the reproduction of their families and immediate communities. These rural cultivators could be found everywhere—in the mountainous regions of the American state of Georgia, in the tropical rainforests of Central Africa, and on remote Greek islands. On the other side, millions of rural cultivators were deeply enmeshed in systems of personal dependence to enslavers and other worldly or ecclesiastical authorities. So radical a departure was proletarian labor that it could be imposed only in regions where capital owners and states exercised unusual, almost unchecked, power. Even in such places, it often involved decades-long struggles.

Wage labor in the countryside was, of course, not entirely new. For several centuries, many British and Dutch fields had been tilled by wageworkers. But now, in the face of the emancipation of both slaves and serfs and the spread of heavily capitalized commercial agriculture, the practice became more common. Cowboys who herded vast numbers of cattle were quintessential agrarian proletarians paid wages for their labor, but so were southern Russian wheat cultivators and Galician rye growers. Where serfs had once done mostly agricultural labor, as in East Prussia, Poland, and Russia, emancipation increasingly turned them into wageworkers. Lacking the political power to force land reforms or the ability to escape to unsettled lands beyond the reach of the state, they stayed put and labored for wages. In Galicia, emancipated serfs lost access to common grazing land and forests and had to pay taxes, forcing them to work for pay on the same estates that had enserfed them a few years earlier.[68]

This transition to wage labor depended on a lopsided distribution of social, economic, and political power. People did not freely choose wage labor; they were deprived of alternative ways of making a living.

That was as true in Java as on the estates of eastern Europe. In South Africa, changes to landownership laws after 1894 resulted in lost access to land for many people, who thus had to sell their labor power. El Salvador saw similar developments: As European settlers discovered the enormous promise of that small Central American country's volcanic soil, they began to take control of it. An 1882 law abolished communal landownership, privatizing lands once held by local Indigenous peoples. Then, newly arriving European settlers, encouraged by the terminal crisis of coffee slavery in Brazil, replaced the ample food crops that had nourished El Salvador's people for generations with coffee trees. The new coffee lords subsequently made it a crime to settle on land that was now private. Coffee plantations grew by leaps and bounds: In 1860, they had covered a meager 2,100 acres; by 1890, coffee grew on 110,000 acres of land. From the planters' perspective, privatizing the land not only provided them with soil suited to coffee but also produced the labor needed to tend the crop. Land in El Salvador was so fertile that it had been difficult to recruit wageworkers to the plantations, but once planters had systematically destroyed peasants'

Post-slavery workers' housing, Brazil, 1910.

ability to grow food—by chopping down fruit trees, destroying fields of tomatoes and beans, and violently enforcing their newly acquired property rights (in one instance, a ten-year-old boy was beaten to death for picking a mango from a tree)—that quickly changed. In the late 1920s, El Salvadoran journalist Alberto Masferrer reported that "El Salvador no longer has wild fruits and vegetables that once everyone could harvest, nor even cultivated fruits that once were inexpensive. Today there are the coffee estates and they grow only coffee."[69] As early as the 1880s, people had lost their ability to secure their subsistence and were forced to offer their labor to the coffee lords—the 134 families who now owned almost all of El Salvador's land, dominating its economy and its politics.[70]

The inability to make a living off the land also brought wageworkers into Brazil's coffee plantations. Beginning in the 1870s, anticipating the impending end of slavery, the planters of the rapidly expanding coffee frontier of western São Paulo forged a new labor system: hiring wageworkers to tend patches of coffee land. The source of labor for this colonato system was, somewhat surprisingly, Italian peasants. As the price of wheat fell in the wake of the expansion of US wheat production following the Civil War, farmers in the Italian Veneto increasingly lost their ability to make a living.[71] This provided an opening for Brazil's coffee lords, who traveled to Europe to recruit desperate peasants and "reported back . . . that the deep and growing poverty of North Italy was pointing to a promising path."[72] In 1888, coffee lords organized the Sociedade Promotora da Imigração to pressure the government for subsidies to recruit these Italian workers, a project that succeeded not least because, unlike US planters, they controlled the government. As a result, between 1886 and 1896, more Italians migrated to São Paulo than to anywhere else in the Americas. The labor force of about two hundred thousand migrants inserted a new dynamic into the Brazilian coffee frontier: After nearly a complete halt in the planting of coffee trees during the late 1880s, 350 million trees were planted during the 1890s.[73] The Veneto dialect is still spoken in Brazil today.

Whether they labored as wageworkers, tenants, sharecroppers, or indentured servants, rural cultivators found themselves increasingly enmeshed in labor relations that more closely mirrored the ways labor was mobilized in industries and in cities, with contracts at their core. These systems of labor shaded into one another.[74]

As chains and lashes faded as symbols of capital owners' power, debt came to the fore, a contractual relationship that ordered new forms of dependence and new kinds of coercion. Fettering workers to their employers to extract their labor inexpensively and durably, the reconstruction of agricultural labor created a countryside filled with toilers working primarily to pay off their debts. When the freedpeople of the Drax Hall plantation in Barbados had their annual balances drawn up, almost all of them were in the red, despite the year of labor they had just completed. Since they remained indebted to the Drax family, they had no choice but to continue working at Drax Hall.[75] Though they were nominally free and bound by voluntary contracts, the perpetual cost-to-income imbalance, strategically engineered by the Draxes, reduced them to a peculiar form of dependence, even peonage. Unable to serve their debt, they were forced to continue working for the family, leaving them nearly as immobilized as they had been when enslaved.

The millions of indentured servants who newly peopled the world's plantation belt started off in debt, too, as their (often long) journeys to their places of employment, as well as the provisions provided to them upon arrival, had to be paid for. These workers, as one observer proclaimed, were "born in debt, lived in debt and died in debt"—debt that could even pass on to the next generation.[76] Employers everywhere used debt to bind workers to their jobs. In Ceylon, Ordinance No. 11 of 1865 made it a crime for workers to leave their employers without having first settled their debts. But doing so was often impossible, and employers kept it that way. Plantation stores charged inflated prices and high interest—with workers' wages insufficient to cover these subsistence costs. Elsewhere, wages were only paid four or perhaps six times a year, forcing cultivators to secure their subsistence on credit. Moreover, since many workers were illiterate, it was easy for employers to cheat them out of their meager earnings. After serving their original indentures, they often remained snarled in debt and hemmed in by laws against vagabondage. In Burma, as elsewhere, these migrants became so deeply mired in debt that no matter how hard they worked, their low pay made it impossible to get free.[77]

Sharecroppers and tenant farmers also found themselves in this nightmare of debt peonage. Ann Ulrich Evans, a formerly enslaved worker in Missouri, looked back on these years from the vantage point of the 1930s and remembered that "[w]e never did git out of debt. We always git through with fine big crops and owed de white man more dan we did when we started de crop, and got to stay to pay de debt. It was awful."[78] To access provisions, seeds, and implements, Evans, like millions of sharecroppers and tenant farmers, had to obtain credit from local stores and merchants. When she and other sharecroppers settled their accounts at harvesttime, they often found themselves in as much debt as they had been in before the season started.[79] As a result, they remained, according to American agricultural periodical *The Progressive Farmer*, "always only 12 months away from freedom."[80]

Wage labor was no protection against debt peonage either. In the southern Mexican state of Chiapas, a late nineteenth-century transformation of the countryside toward the production of coffee, cocoa, rubber, and tropical hardwoods for global markets resulted in a massive dispossession of Indigenous peoples and their transformation into wageworkers. As land was taken by outsiders, small commodity production and markets in property, goods, and labor increasingly shut down. Claims to communal land were abrogated and church properties privatized. Indigenous cultivators had little choice but to begin working on plantations. As elsewhere, meager wages never sufficed to pay off debts; some cultivators even inherited debts from their parents. By 1900, a full 40 percent of Chiapas's population was indebted to property owners and thus tied to them.[81] Physical violence gave way to economic coercion to mobilize and discipline the world's agrarian workers.

W age work, sharecropping, tenant farming, and indenture were all forms of proletarian labor. Yet in wide swaths of the world's countryside, this transformation to contractual forms of labor, in which the cultivator sold their labor power for money or goods, did not happen. Despite the awe-inspiring advances in wealth, technology, military hardware, and institutional strength, revolutionizing capital owners and governing officials encountered many resourceful rural cultivators who successfully resisted their proletarianization. These rural cultivators retained access to land, mobilized political power to defend their independence, and produced sufficient goods to secure subsistence for their families and communities. While they engaged in markets, selling their surplus production to acquire things grown or manufactured elsewhere, their labor still focused on the reproduction of their families' and immediate communities' livelihoods. This self-sufficiency often remained so powerfully enrooted that planters had to bring workers from elsewhere, as we see when we look at the tea gardens of Assam, the copra producers of Samoa, and the coffee plantations of Ceylon.

But even these peasant-dominated areas saw a great expansion of market production in the second half of the nineteenth century. In part, this was the result of peasants grasping new opportunities offered by a more integrated global economy. The growers of the Gold Coast exported no cocoa in 1890; by 1923, exports had skyrocketed to an almost unbelievable two hundred thousand tons, making them the world's largest growers. Peanut farmers in Senegal grew five metric tons of the legume in 1850 and ninety-five thousand metric tons in 1898. Expanded markets indeed could be advantageous to rural cultivators: In one somewhat extreme case, during the years of the US Civil War, rural cultivators in western India garnered substantial wealth as they took advantage of the disruption in the US cotton trade to produce vastly more cotton for European markets at higher prices. In Upper Galilee in the 1870s, Palestinian peasants drew on family labor to expand their production of tobacco, fueled by demand for the modern, soon-to-be-machine-made cigarette. They planted tobacco alongside food crops as a source of cash revenue that added to their subsistence agriculture. In the Midwestern United States, refugees from the European countryside turned vast prairies into wheat fields and cornfields. In Bengal, where large-scale rebellions had overthrown a deeply repressive indigo-growing regime, peasant producers cultivated expanded quantities of jute, a fiber used to make packaging materials, by the late nineteenth century, responding to rising prices, new demand, the availability of land, and the favorable ecological conditions of the Bengal Delta. Dedicating 20 percent of delta farmland to jute, these peasants drew on household labor (with some wage labor during harvesttime) to combine subsistence with market production. As they could sell their crop profitably, they increasingly shifted their labor away from food crops, especially rice, and started to consume goods produced elsewhere, drawing on new credit networks. In 1829, Calcutta had shipped a meager eighteen tons of jute, but by 1910, thirteen million tons left the port, with much of this expansion occurring in the last decades of the century. As rural cultivators responded creatively to new opportunities presented to them, they generated a modest prosperity.[82]

Urban capital often facilitated this expanded market production. Gold Coast merchants invested in cocoa; Senegalese merchants, peanuts; Chicago commodity dealers, wheat and corn; Assam's Marwari brokers, rubber; and Bombay's merchants, cotton. Collectively, they created a vibrant "Indigenous capitalism" that was related to, but also independent of, European colonialism.[83] But capital also flowed from distant locales into such remade countrysides—from London, Istanbul, Winterthur, and Nantes, among other nodes.

These funds enabled expanded production but entailed new risks, exposing rural cultivators to market fluctuations over which they had little or no control. When commodity prices fell after the crisis of 1873, a whole generation found themselves hopelessly indebted, losing control of their land and livelihoods as a result. In the southern United

States, subsistence-oriented landowning yeomen farmers initially profited by producing cotton for world markets, yet when cotton prices collapsed, those who had borrowed heavily lost their land to local merchants. In Bengal, a similar story played out: Cultivators who had limited their food cultivation to expand jute production became dependent on markets. When prices for jute fell, as they periodically did, these cultivators had a hard time making up for lost income. By the 1900s, "seasonal hunger" became a feature of the Bengali countryside. And when the price of jute collapsed after World War I, highly indebted growers became disastrously impoverished.[84]

As the demand for jute, tobacco, cotton, corn, rice, peanuts, cocoa, and many other commodities flourished, merchants, state officials, and metropolitan industrialists sought to further such production. In Bengal, Upper Galilee, western India, and the Midwestern United States, peasants themselves had been the drivers of export production, but elsewhere, colonial administrators and European capital owners encouraged or even forced landowning peasants to expand into export-oriented production. Unlike earlier in the century, when such efforts had often failed—as in the Senegal River Valley during the 1810s and 1820s—by the end of the nineteenth century, the balance of power had begun to shift. Political, economic, technological, and social changes had coalesced to increase capital owners' ability to insert themselves into peasant-dominated countrysides.

By the late nineteenth century, for example, French colonists and their British, Belgian, Japanese, German, and Portuguese counterparts were at last able to effectively recast the peasant production of cotton for industry. Worried about their continued dependence on the United States for this crucial raw material, French cotton manufacturers organized the Association Cotonnière Coloniale in 1903 to pressure colonial administrators to focus their energies on transforming the colonial countryside. The French diplomatic archives filled with thousands of pages reporting on the cotton-growing potential of various parts of the world, noting that "[t]he cotton question thus appears at the forefront of economic news and we cannot remain indifferent to this movement."[85] Russian, Japanese, German, and British colonial administrators agreed that the most promising path forward was to encourage peasant production of such cotton. After all, rural cultivators throughout the world had grown cotton for centuries, and they continued to cultivate significant quantities of the white gold for their domestic manufacturing, interspersed with food crops like corn and millet.[86]

Colonial officials, metropolitan industrialists, and merchants aimed to reorient this domestic industry toward the production of cotton for global markets. In French West Africa, colonial administrators met with local rulers to communicate their interest in promoting cotton agriculture and worked to make the local cotton more homogenous and thus more suitable to European machine production, introducing exotic seeds, especially US varieties, into local production. They advocated for the monocultural production of cotton. They also tried to regulate the local market—for example, by demanding that growers sell their cotton to European exporters instead of local manufacturers. They built warehouses to store that cotton and infrastructure to transport it, and they invested in military campaigns to stabilize the cotton-growing countryside.[87] According to a French observer, "The formula—great colonization, white leadership, monoculture, black labor—is currently the only one that can be applied immediately" to expand cotton output.[88]

Crucially, these colonial officials aimed to undermine the market power of local cultivators, as they believed that local cotton prices were too high to give European trading companies sufficient profit. "Where does the high price of cotton come from?" asked a colonial administrator in 1910, answering the question by arguing that

> the lazy and carefree African peasant cultivates only for himself, and therefore, having only a small production for a rather strong demand, is master of maintaining high prices. In order to lower the market value of cotton, it is therefore absolutely necessary to provoke overproduction by bringing black people to work not only for their own needs but also for export.[89]

Unable to compete against local manufacturers, French colonial officials forced lower cotton prices on cultivators. The market of Siguiri, Guinea, 1899.

The problem, in the eyes of the French, was that local cultivators "subordinated [cotton] to the development of corn and red millet crops & to consider increasing cotton production beyond certain limits means reducing other food crops at the same time."[90] Colonial administrators thus forced growers to accept lower prices, justifying these market distortions by arguing that "if there was not this paternal constraint that the administration exerts on him [the cultivator], the Cotton Association would only buy a stock of very insignificant cotton."[91]

These efforts produced some results: A colonial official observed a tripling of cotton deliveries in one area from 1909 to 1910. Yet that was not enough. What was called for, colonial bureaucrats argued, was the "profound modification of the psychology of the Negro."[92] Rural cultivators were too attached to their ancient ways of doing things and insufficiently motivated by a desire for gain.[93] The "Noir Soudanais," observed a French official, is not strictly speaking a "producer," because he "works only to satisfy his few and insignificant household needs, a style that exists vestigially within certain parts of France, for example among the linen producers of the Limousin."[94] Because metropolitan interests could not wait for African rural cultivators to "evolve from this naturally," they had to accelerate matters.[95] In short, the version of market rationality that the French preferred had to be forced.

Merchants and colonial officials everywhere recognized that constructing purchasing stations and transport infrastructures was important but insufficient. The coercive powers of the state were needed

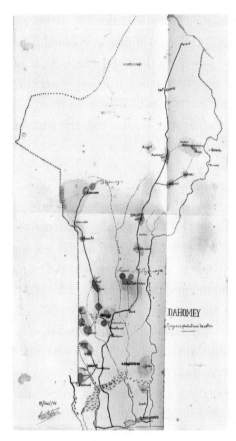

Penetrating the countryside: a map of Dahomey (today's Benin) indicating a railroad line and potential cotton-growing areas, 1905.

as well—what one author described as "precise designs through the reasoned and methodical use of force."[96] One common "use of force" was the imposition of cash taxes that compelled peasants to sell some of their produce on markets. In German Samoa, early twentieth-century taxes on colonial subjects aimed to coerce them into wage labor. In South Africa, colonial authorities required Indigenous peoples to pay high taxes that they had difficulty affording—thus forcing them into contractual labor.[97] As a British prime minster argued when putting forth this tax legislation, it would "help the natives to overcome their idleness, it would teach them the value of work and would give them an opportunity to do something in return for the wise rule of the Europeans."[98]

More immediate coercion was also called for, according to one colonial official: "Rightly impressed by the horrors of slavery, we readily forget that this merciless enslavement has elevated in a few decades the elements of the primitive races which suffered it to the level of the most civilized peoples. . . . Nowadays, the Germans in Cameroon, the Belgians in the Congo, the English in most of their African possessions have exercised or exercise on their nationals measures of constraint implying more or less openly the obligation to cultivate or to work."[99] Africans, argued this official, did "not seek to get rich, [as this desire was] the moral creation of Aryan civilizations."[100] To recast peasant agriculture, to orient it toward distant markets, colonial officials would have to use the coercive powers of the state. The amount of coercion and violence required for the global reconstruction of agricultural labor reveals the relative weakness of capital owners in many areas of the world—and the importance of state aid. Indeed, the plunder of labor often preceded its proletarianization.

THIS LEVEL OF forced labor was also facilitated by the racism that let capital owners legitimize sharply different sets of rights and rewards for different groups of workers. Labor under capitalism was siloed, often along racial lines, walled in by legal tropes, international boundaries, and state-enforced categorical hierarchies, enabling a radically uneven treatment of labor across the capitalist world.[101] Richard Adams's 1921 *Farm Management: A Text-Book for Student, Investigator, and Investor* "helpfully" distinguished different "classes of farm labor": White laborers were "steady, reliable, kind to stock"; Italians, "entirely happy just to be alive and out in the open"; and Mexicans, "somewhat childish, rather lazy, unambitious."[102] Knowledge of "racial characteristics," Adams opined, was crucial for successful farm management.[103] In similar ways, Japanese writer Adachi Kinnosuké explained the dire poverty among abysmally paid Chinese workers on the soy frontier in Manchuria as an artifact of these workers' alleged preference for a bare-bones life, claiming that they sought no more than "cheap, coarse food—such food as is given to cattle in other lands" in return for their hard labor.[104] In El Salvador, too, the extreme exploitation of Indigenous coffee workers was justified by racial difference. Likewise, in British India, poor treatment of local workers was explained in racist terms. It was not the "laws of supply and demand" but asserted racial differences that determined how people got slotted into the labor market. French colonial officials considered cotton a crop to be tended by the "black race": "It's a fact," they reported, that "[t]he American cotton field is a creation of the African workforce led by the European."[105]

The voice of British liberalism, *The Economist*, enthusiastically agreed: Coercive intervention in the African labor market was justified because that continent had "hitherto baffled every attempt to civilise or improve it" and was in a "depraved condition."[106] For that reason, distinct legal regimes seemed appropriate for the colony; ideas of racial differences came to legitimately structure the market. The French commission on colonial labor regimes solidified these notions by creating special labor laws that applied only to the colonies. At the same time, in the United States, institutional racism shaped every aspect of the country's labor market, fostering an ever more elaborate system of political and legal discrimination against African Americans. As reconstructed capital pushed into new areas and spheres of life, as it led to the massive reconstruction of labor, more finely framed hierarchies structured it everywhere. Even Friedrich List, advocate of state-sponsored development, thought that some of the world's people, like the Turks, could not jump into the modern era, as they were held back, in his view, by their "barbarian and only half civilized" conditions.[107]

That recourse to "race" helped address a central contradiction that emerged as part of the capitalist revolution in the countryside: on the one side, its universalist, voluntarist, and contractual character, and on the other side, its reliance on coercion and violence. Capitalism, as we have seen, derived its dynamic, to a significant extent, from its connected diversity—and that diversity revealed itself, too, in the process of constructing racial hierarchies.

RACISM ALSO FACILITATED the pivotal use of forced labor in the expansion of commodity production in not only the Americas but also Africa, Australia, and Asia. In the US South, a vast prison complex incarcerated thousands of freedpeople and their descendants on often flimsy pretexts and then hired them out to local planters and budding industrialists without pay. In the American state of Georgia alone, there were almost fifty thousand such leased convicts between 1873 and 1908, 90 percent of whom were African Americans. Japan used

Undated photo of colonial officials recruiting workers in Korea.

convict labor as well; in the important Miike Coal Mine, the Meiji government forced prisoners to work. When the mine was privatized in 1889 and newly operated by the powerful Mitsui family (which not long after formed a massive *zaibatsu*, or business conglomerate), it continued to draw on such coerced labor. Racism produced pay differentials as well: Korean workers were paid only half as much as their Japanese counterparts.[108]

In Latin America, forced labor, mostly of Indigenous peoples, was ubiquitous. In 1900, 80 percent of Mexico's Indigenous agricultural workers were "debt slaves," especially on tobacco and agave plantations, working off debts that, as we have seen, were a means of shackling them to their employers for life. Farther south, the British-owned Peruvian Amazon Company exploited large numbers of Indigenous peoples. The company literally kidnapped them to tap rubber and then transport it on foot over very long distances. Such forced labor helped Peru increase its rubber exports from about 16 tons in 1900 to 6,450 tons just six years later.[109]

Nowhere was forced labor more common than in Africa, not least because capital's penetration of the continent remained weak. Because rural cultivators showed little inclination to desert their farms, fishing villages, and forests to become wageworkers, sharecroppers, indentured laborers, or peasant producers for world markets, forcing them into commodity production became common. When the French took control of the island of Madagascar in 1896, they abolished "slavery"

A global hunt for workers I: the rubber frontier.

but immediately created a system of coerced labor that obliged all able-bodied men to work. Those who refused to sign contracts were considered vagrants and subject to six months of imprisonment—time mostly spent in hard labor. In Portuguese-controlled Mozambique, a vast expansion of cotton agriculture in the twentieth century drew on the forced labor of hundreds of thousands of peasants who had to leave their food crops to slake metropolitan appetites for raw materials, often with devasting impact on their communities.[110]

The Belgian Congo was ground zero for this turn-of-the-century forced labor, with one author justifiably calling it "one of the most horrifying chapters in the history of the meeting of white and dark-skinned people."[111] At first, the Belgian king, Leopold II, who had taken control of the territory as head of a private investment venture in 1885, focused on exploiting naturally occurring rubber (in high demand in the booming tire industry) and ivory, which was needed for, among other things, the pianos and billiard tables coveted by a growing metropolitan bourgeoisie. As prices for rubber increased at a fast clip, sixty-five trading companies settled in the Belgian Congo to acquire it, first from local middlemen and then from forced workers. In a replay

A global hunt for workers II:
captured workers in the Belgian Congo, 1905.

of the war capitalism of earlier centuries, private company officials taxed locals to force them to work and raided villages to press them into labor.[112]

So stark was the violence in King Leopold's Congo that international protest eventually persuaded the Belgian state to take over its own king's private colony. In 1908, the new colonial authorities began to regulate labor in a colonial charter that outlawed forced labor by private employers. Still, it persisted: While King Leopold had forced people to labor as a direct form of taxation, labor taxes were now replaced by monetary taxes, with those who could not pay imprisoned and sentenced to hard labor—a common system across European-dominated Africa. As "[m]anhunts were undertaken" to collect these taxes, people had no choice but to take on employment.[113] Forcing people into wage work provided a thin legal veneer to conceal continued reliance on coercion. Beginning in 1911, William Lever of the British Lever Company acquired huge concessions in the Belgian Congo for palm-oil plantations and used his private military forces (several hundred so-called *capita*) to secure workers. What emerged was a literal hunt for labor: Local cultivators were rounded up, put into chains, and transported to worksites. Moreover, Belgian colonial administrators instituted a system of military service as another way to force tens of thousands of locals to serve on public building projects, especially the railroads that would allow the Belgian Congo's natural riches to get to the markets of the North Atlantic.[114]

In addition, Belgian administrators instituted a system of forced cultivation in 1917—so-called *cultures obligatoires*—compelling cultivators to produce certain quantities of rice or cotton and provide them to their colonial overlords. When mining for copper took off in the province of Katanga, compulsory labor again came into play, forcing tens of thousands of rural cultivators into the mines to extract a raw material of urgent importance to European industry. They made Katanga the world's third-biggest copper supplier. Unalloyed racism legitimated even the cruelest violence: As King Leopold explained to a US journalist, coercion was necessary because "[i]n dealing with a race that has been composed of cannibals for thousands of years, it is necessary to use methods that best can shake their idleness and make them realize the sanctity of work."[115] The number of people pressed into forced labor in King Leopold's Congo was staggering, and scholars have estimated that between five and ten million Congolese people died as a result.[116]

Congo was an extreme case, but it was not unique. Forced labor was found almost everywhere on reconstructed commodity frontiers. In Liberia, a nation politically and economically dominated by fifteen thousand African Americans from the United States, the ruling elite deployed the country's military to force Native rulers to provide workers for infrastructure projects such as roads and for plantation labor. When a hut tax was instituted in 1916, they forced those who could not pay into wage work or into pawning their children. They sent some of these workers also to European colonies—for example, to the cocoa plantations of the Spanish island of Fernando Pó, where they were subjected to a form of de facto slavery. When, in 1926, the American tire maker Firestone set up the largest rubber plantation in the world in the Liberian town of Harbel (a site that came to employ thousands of workers), it drew on these massive state mobilizations of labor. The Liberian government supplied Firestone with workers, a system so coercive that a few years later, the League of Nations accused Liberia of reinstituting slavery.[117]

In Portuguese Africa, forced labor also continued. After slavery ended on São Tomé in 1875, freedpeople had to sign work contracts and, if they refused, were sentenced to forced labor as punishment for "vagrancy." Slavery thus transitioned into compulsory labor. As colonists transformed São Tomé into a vast cocoa plantation (producing twenty-five thousand tons in 1905), workers had to sign five-year labor contracts to fulfill their legal obligation to work. When local labor reservoirs did not suffice, the administration brought contract workers from Angola, another Portuguese colony, housing them in prisonlike structures, their lives and work under the boot of excruciatingly detailed regulations that were not much different from those of planters who brutally enslaved workers in seventeenth-century Barbados.[118]

Cocoa agriculture on São Tomé became so successful that colonial officials from Germany and Belgium visited the island to study it, especially keen to learn from local planters' ability to gain access to workers and then control them. The German colony of Cameroon applied these lessons, with the Westafrikanische Pflanzungsgesellschaft Victoria (West African Planting Society of Victoria) building the world's largest cocoa plantation—ten thousand hectares of expropriated lands worked by forced labor. Germany's largest chocolate manufacturer sat in the port city of Hamburg, home of the plantation's main investor, Adolph Woermann.[119] That Belgium to this day produces some of the world's finest chocolates owes as much to its violent exploitation of Congolese cocoa plantation workers as to its confectionary talents.

That hunt for labor also shaped Australia, especially its tropical north, where the last third of the nineteenth century saw new cotton and sugar plantations hungering for cheap manpower. During the chaotic years of the US Civil War, Sydney merchant Robert Towns perceived an opportunity to enter the cotton market, so he bought a four-thousand-acre plantation north of Brisbane and hired a labor recruiter. This recruiter and others like him scouted the islands of the

Pacific on what Sydney's *Daily Telegraph* in 1882 called a "savage-hunting expedition."[120] Labor agent Henry Ross Levin advertised workers at seven pounds per head, saying he would be "happy to receive orders for the importation of South Sea natives to work on the cotton and sugar plantations now rapidly springing up in this colony" and that "[p]arties favouring H.R.L. with orders may rely on having the best and most serviceable natives to be had among the islands."[121] When, in late 1870, W. G. Farquhar captained a ship to "obtain labourers for ourselves and the other farmers on the River," he traveled between various South Sea islands, bribing local rulers with muskets, cows, and money to get them to send young workers back with him to Australia.[122] On one island, he told the ruler that he "would give him a musket if he got me 5 men which he did."[123] In 1882, a medical student accompanying a labor merchant observed that they were often greeted with hostility and suspicion—including being shot at—which was not surprising, given the stories the student heard about workers being abducted against their wills and workers returning from Queensland in a "shocking state of filth and disease."[124] Newspapers reported on the ill-treatment of the Pacific Islanders during the recruitment process, on the shootings, kidnappings, floggings, destruction of crops, and burning of villages carried out by the recruiters. The practice came to be known as "blackbirding," and though it was, formally speaking, a contractual form of labor, in reality workers were "recruited" through trickery or kidnapping.[125]

Between 1863 and 1908, blackbirding brought around sixty thousand workers to Australia to toil under abysmal conditions on three-year contracts, powering through their labor the expansion of the Queensland sugar industry. Several smaller islands, including Nukulaelae (part of Tuvalu, a nation of nine isles), lost more than half their populations. Brisbane's *Courier* called these new arrivals "comparatively useless in the land of their birth, they have no industries, they only grow sufficient food for their own needs."[126] Pacific islanders, to the best of their ability, resisted "the white men . . . carry[ing] away their countrymen."[127]

A global hunt for workers III: "blackbirding" in the New Hebrides, circa 1890.

But as early as 1867, missionaries reported that some islands "have been almost entirely stripped of their male population."[128] Some were shipped as far away as La Réunion. The Australian state became ever more deeply involved in regulating this trade, beginning in 1868 with the Polynesian Labourers Act and ending with the Pacific Islands Labourers Act of 1901, leaving behind a voluminous documentary trail. Though the laws regulated the trade, abuses continued into the twentieth century.[129]

In her 1960 book, *Involuntary Labour Since the Abolition of Slavery*, Dutch scholar Willemina Kloosterboer chronicled the enduring role of coercion in rural labor mobilization, showing that the rationale for its widespread embrace was its relative effectiveness in securing cheap and dependable labor. Economists have recently confirmed and elaborated on Kloosterboer's decades-old insights, though they have added little to what colonial officials, planters, and rural cultivators knew a century earlier: Extra-economic coercion moved people into agricultural labor while lowering the costs of mobilizing them by limiting their exit options.[130] It was this novel combination of the "pistol and pen" that brought many cultivators into commodity production, mobilizing workers in order to immobilize them, blocking their escape with a web of debt, contracts, laws, and taxes just at the time when global rebellions had brought plantation slavery to an end.[131]

These reconstructed labor regimes blended into one another, and workers combined various strategies to make a living. Wage labor could be forced, and forced workers could be paid wages. Indeed, too much emphasis on the variety of labor regimes in the countryside obscures what they had in common—namely, the transformation of labor into a worker-owned commodity that could be brought onto the market under contractual agreements. "Capitalist social relations," historian Barbara Fields observed, "were on the march on a world scale," generating what Rosa Luxemburg called the "relentless battle of capital against the social and economic ties of the natives."[132]

Despite its coercion and violence, this world of labor was very different from the one that had characterized the earlier war capitalist moment, not least because it rested to an unprecedented degree on the powers, structures, and interventions of states. While slavery had drawn on the state's powers as well, its core relationship—between enslaver and enslaved—was largely beyond the state's purview. In the reconstructed capitalism of the late nineteenth century, by contrast, the state—sometimes colonial, sometimes national—was present everywhere. On La Réunion, as we have seen, the colonial government played an overwhelmingly large role in securing and regulating labor. At the same time, another state, this one British, supervised the treatment of Indian workers on the island. And if mistreated, immigrants had recourse to the state's *protecteur des immigrants*, however compromised and insufficient, in Saint-Denis, La Réunion's capital.[133]

Indeed, the state and its functionaries came into the countryside and took over many of the functions traditionally held by enslavers and lords. Like in La Réunion, in the Dutch East Indies, a so-called Coolie Ordinance regulated the employment relationships of indentured workers. Portugal also passed a special colonial labor law in 1878, just nine years after the abolition of slavery. When, in 1904, Samoan cocoa planter Richard Deeken beat up Ah Tsung, the overseer of his Chinese indentured workers, a German imperial court sentenced him to four months in prison—a scenario unimaginable during slavery times. Ceylon created the Immigrant Labor Commission in 1858. And in Burma, the Workmen's Breach of Contract Act of 1869 allowed labor contractors to seek state enforcement of their contracts. Everywhere, the law gained ever greater influence over labor relations. At times, it could even be mustered to protect indentured workers: In 1908, China sent a special envoy, Lin Shu Fen, to German Samoa to investigate alleged abuses of its indentured workers.[134]

First and foremost, the state was crucial to tying rural cultivators to the land. In the French Caribbean, a newly instituted head tax forced freedpeople to produce cash income; "domestic passports" after 1850 helped control workers' movements; and another law penalized workers who did not sign a yearlong contract. In 1918, the lieutenant governor of Dahomey (today's Benin) sent a proposed decree to the governor-general of French West Africa to regulate "indigenous manpower."[135] In South Africa, the Native Labour Regulation Act of 1911 required workers to carry passes when they left their worksites and stipulated that a breach of contract was a criminal offense. In the coffee-growing districts of El Salvador, the law was crucial to dispossessing workers of their land, mobilizing them, and binding them to their employers. The military, another state institution, played a role in labor control as well. When El Salvador formed a national guard in 1912, it was mainly stationed on the coffee plantations and charged with controlling labor. In India, the British imperial state regulated both the traffic in "coolies" and their working and living conditions at their destinations, including the provisions provided to them. Criminal sanctions for breach of contract on the part of indentured workers remained common. In Mauritius, leaving one's job or giving the planter cause for dissatisfaction resulted in imprisonment. "Desertion" from work was a crime that could get workers thrown into prison (as forced laborers) for up to three months.[136] State power now enclosed labor just as it enclosed land.

More than any other state measure, vagrancy laws mobilized and controlled labor. While people the world over saw the ability to move about as a mark of freedom, their ability to do so was increasingly curtailed and even declared illegal by political authorities hoping to force people into contractual labor. In Jamaica, these labor enclosures—vagrancy laws—entered the books as early as 1840. Anyone wandering the countryside without a pass could be arrested and imprisoned; "in fact," Kloosterboer noted, workers "were hunted down."[137] In Mauritius, South Africa, the United States, and the Portuguese colonies, vagrancy laws served similar purposes. When French colonists sought to turn people in Madagascar into wageworkers, they used the law: The seminomadic Antandroy, according to French observers, had been proud of their independence and were reluctant to work for others. Yet by the 1920s, many had been forced into wage work, defeated by vagrancy laws that had made their traditional way of life illegal.[138] French colonial administrators delineated a precise strategy, including repressing "vagabondage" by imposing three- to twelve-month jail terms on those who now fit the criteria and forbidding locals from developing rice paddies in the mountains (which, according to administrators, "allows families to settle in difficult and remote locations where they live in tremendous indolence and escape all fiscal obligations").[139] Colonial officials everywhere believed that it was necessary to steer the local population toward embracing the "necessity of work, which in our time dominates the organization of civilized peoples."[140] Criminalizing "vagabonds" became a way to force people to sell their labor power, showing once more how difficult the capitalist project truly was and the depth of the resistance it encountered. Far from free or natural, the labor market was a creation of state coercion. For some capital owners, forcing people to labor under the aegis of capital was an essential part of the work of civilizing that they believed they were doing.

Not surprisingly, given the central role of the state, the distributions of social, economic, and political power in specific places conditioned the diversity of labor regimes.[141] Many African peasants were still deeply embedded in a precolonial, precapitalist political economy and, as a result, successfully resisted the transformation of their lives.

Freedpeople in the United States mustered sufficient collective power to contest their former owners to a stalemate that resulted in the spread of sharecropping and tenant farming, not just wage labor. Dispossessed El Salvadoran farmers, lacking political allies and facing the legal, administrative, economic, and military violence of a state under the sway of a tiny planter elite, had little choice but to embark upon wage work on coffee plantations.

Despite the overwhelming power of states and capital owners, cultivators continued to push against the countryside's reconstruction. As it had during slavery, this resistance mostly manifested in cultivators' everyday interactions with their employers. They often shied away from open rebellion, instead trying to get around rules to the best of their ability.[142] A list of workers' convictions under the indentured servant laws of La Réunion reveals some of that resistance. On January 10, 1923, 39 workers on La Bagatelle, a sugar plantation in the Sainte-Suzanne area, were sentenced for "disorder on the property." Others were convicted for "absence," "desertion," "refusing to work," and "bad service." On July 11, 1923, 13 workers on La Convenance refused to work.[143] That year, 161 workers in total were sentenced for "crimes" such as "flight," "theft of the harvest," and that old standby, "vagabondage."[144]

Workers indeed enjoyed a significant ability to organize and resist. In French Indochina, plantation workers engaged in a wide variety of rebellion, both individually and collectively. On the sprawling Michelin rubber plantation in Dầu Tiêng (which employed forty-eight hundred people in 1928), they slowed down their labor, refused to renew their contracts, engaged in sabotage, and went AWOL. Between 20 and 30 percent of them took off in any given year. Sometimes they murdered particularly cruel and violent managers or overseers. In Ceylon, workers deserted plantations, carried out sabotage and theft, and committed suicide—all to escape the tremendous pressures that bore down upon them. On Assam's tea plantations (whose workers often died just getting there), indentured laborers resisted in a panoply of ways, including running away and building a cultural life outside the purview of managers. Workers in Portuguese São Tomé rebelled as well. In Mauritius, planters continually complained about "absenteeism" and vagabondage, filing some seventy thousand complaints against their workers between 1860 and 1870, with 80 percent of those grievances focused on "desertion." Colonial officials described workers in Madagascar as having a "penchant for indolence."[145] Runaway workers were a crucial feature of labor under capitalism well into the twentieth century, as escaping from the aegis of capital was in itself criminalized. In a society where the control of labor time meant the control of people, fleeing a job was a form of exit.[146]

As pressures on rural cultivators spread and intensified, they also rebelled collectively. In 1865, under the leadership of Ahmed al-Shaqi, rural cultivators in Egypt revolted against the enormous pressures that a commercializing cotton economy put on their lives. In 1875, Indian cotton growers attacked money-lending merchants in the Deccan Riots. In February 1907, tenant farmers rose up violently in Romania, instigated by large landlords' efforts to squeeze more labor from the export-oriented wheat-growing countryside. Six weeks later, with the uprising having gone national, the army suppressed it, using heavy artillery against the peasants, killing thousands. In the United States, a wave of rural discontent swept the countryside in the last decades of the nineteenth century, with the Populists demanding state protections from creditors and price-stabilization mechanisms, among other measures. Around the turn of the century, just south of the Rio Grande in Mexico, cotton workers engaged in banditry and pilferage to protest their exploitation by cotton planters, only to be brutally repressed by federal-troop-backed private armies. The newly proletarianized coffee workers of El Salvador staged an open rebellion in 1932 and met unfathomable depths of state violence. As one historian later reported, "Machine guns made the counterinsurgency so efficient that the revolution itself has been buried in history under the name of its suppression. *La Matanza*, the massacre."[147] The state and the coffee barons who controlled a country turned plantation murdered as many as twelve thousand El Salvadoran campesinos. The strategies that rural cultivators embraced differed, as did state responses, but they all testify to the enormous strains that these workers faced as their labor was mobilized to turn the global countryside—and their lives—upside down.[148]

———

Reconstruction of labor, so prominent in the world's countryside, also spread to the world of industry, with the two informing and enabling each other. In the last third of the nineteenth century, as new industries emerged and industrialization spread, the number of industrial workers exploded: In the United States, there had been 3.5 million industrial wageworkers in 1870; in 1910, this number reached 14.2 million, its growth twice as fast as that of the US population in general. The figure for this vast proletariat is even larger when we include the 1.5 million mostly female domestic servants and the 1.7 million clerical workers. In 1910, 1.7 million Americans labored in metalworking, 1.2 million in clothing, 917,000 in mining, 800,000 in textiles, and 326,000 in iron and steel. Some industries saw explosive growth: In the American chemical, oil, and rubber industries, the number of workers grew by close to 2,000 percent between 1870 and 1910; in the iron and steel industry, by 1,204 percent; and in railroads, by 638 percent. There were many more firms, to be sure, but existing companies also grew to previously unimaginable sizes. By 1900, four factories in the United States employed more than 8,000 workers each, and three of those plants were steelworks—Cambria, Homestead, and Jones and Laughlin. In France, the number of manufacturing workers (including in construction) increased by 64 percent between 1866 and 1911; in Germany, by 72 percent between 1882 and 1907; in Italy, by 29 percent between circa 1880 and 1918; and in the United Kingdom, by 63 percent between 1871 and 1911. In Germany, almost 8 million people labored in industry by 1907 (3 million more than in 1882); by the early

1920s, Germany had more than a million miners alone. Altogether, so rapid was the growth that by 1910, more than 40 percent of British and Belgian workers labored in industry, more than 30 percent of their German and Dutch counterparts, and more than 20 percent of Austrian, Danish, French, Italian, Norwegian, and Swedish workforces. It has been estimated that by 1900, 81 million people worldwide worked in manufacturing, a huge number compared with midcentury, but still many fewer than the 541 million workers in agriculture.[149]

For this mass proletariat to emerge, tens of millions of people had to leave older manufactories, artisan workshops, and, most significantly, the countryside—a quantum leap massively greater in scale and scope than what had happened during the original Industrial Revolution. Indeed, the four decades after 1870 were perhaps the most remarkable in the history of proletarianization until Chinese industrialization took off in the early twenty-first century.

Where did these workers come from? In the Saar, it was mostly rural cultivators who moved into the mines and into the rapidly expanding iron and steel mills. In 1850, only about 1,400 men, women, and children had labored in iron and steel; in 1913, there were more than 31,000 workers in those industries, 6,000 of whom worked at the Röchling family's Völklingen factory. In addition, there were about 55,000 miners. Industrial cities grew at an enormous pace: Völklingen had counted 3,123 inhabitants in 1871; forty years later, it had grown to 18,000. As elsewhere, these new proletarians came almost exclusively from the nearby countryside, as family and village networks connected rural areas to the burgeoning factory towns. Only when labor ran low in nearby villages did Saar employers begin recruiting from farms in neighboring France and faraway Bavaria.[150]

In Völklingen, in the Saar, and in the North Atlantic area more generally, these workers came out of the European peasantry—indeed, this emerging working class has been described as a worker-peasantry. Between 1850 and 1914, the European countryside lost between 120 and 150 million people, many of them moving into industry. Even in the distant United States, the new working class had been born, more often than not, on European farms, as economic refugees from Germany, Italy, and eastern Europe sought their fortunes in American industry. With population pressures and the transformations of the global countryside making peasant agriculture increasingly untenable in some parts of the world, rural areas produced not just agricultural commodities but an urban proletariat. The links were so tight that industrial workers frequently remained rooted in that agrarian world, even after entering factories. Not only did they retain family connections to farms, but they also often continued their agricultural pursuits. When the Röchlings built company housing for some workers, tellingly, they provided small gardening plots and even stables. Enough Röchling workers kept animals that in 1913, the company created a statistical compendium of animal husbandry among its workers, counting their pigs, goats, chickens, and rabbits. Such persistent connections to the countryside were universal; workers on the Senegalese Dakar–Saint-Louis Railway, for instance, also supplemented their income with farming and fishing.[151]

As the world's industrial working class grew, the nature of its labor transformed as well. In much of the history of capitalism, as we have seen, capital owners outside the plantation economies of the Americas had little control over how labor was executed. Many workers contracted for work not as individuals but in groups, organizing work processes and dividing the proceeds among themselves.[152] In iron mills, skilled workers hired their own helpers and passed their jobs from father to son; they enjoyed significant job control.

This changed by the end of the nineteenth century. As owners developed a better understanding of what actually transpired on the shop floor, they took greater control, not least by adopting a finer division of labor.[153] This was the moment that so-called scientific management, associated most closely with American engineer Frederick Winslow Taylor, emerged. Modern-day management scholar Peter Drucker was only slightly exaggerating when he called scientific management "the most lasting contribution America has made to Western thought since the Federalist Papers."[154]

Taylor and his disciples urged managers to study the work process, subdivide it, and make sure that workers executed their jobs exactly as they were told. The goal was to make work more efficient and less skill-intensive, with workers losing all discretion over how they executed their particular jobs. Taylor summarized his project succinctly: In a first step, he said, "managers assume . . . the burden of gathering together all the traditional knowledge which in the past has been possessed by the workmen and then of classifying, tabulating, and reducing this knowledge of rules, laws, and formulae."[155] In a second step, "all possible brain work should be removed from the shop and centered in the planning or laying-out department."[156] Conception was to be separated from execution, mind from hand. As powerful groups like the American Society of Mechanical Engineers popularized these methods, scientific management moved deep into industry.[157] It became an important part of the curriculum of Harvard Business School, founded around this time. Walter Bagehot, editor in chief of *The Economist*, saw that as a result of "the industrial tasks of mankind . . . every day becoming more and more monotonous," it became ever harder for workers to exert "restraining discipline over their passions."[158]

Taylor emphasized that this reorganization entailed a long and protracted struggle, and he remembered his own exertions on his employers' behalf as a "fight."[159] That fight was not just with individual workers who resisted a move that disempowered them but with their organizations: As American companies reorganized along Taylorist lines, they unsurprisingly clashed with their highly skilled and organized workers. Most prominently, in 1892, Andrew Carnegie broke the Amalgamated Union at his Homestead plant using armed private police forces—the Pinkertons—in part to assert his unilateral control over work processes.[160]

The effort to control the industrial proletariat on the shop floor took wings: Ottoman Empire carpet-making factories sharpened supervision over their workers. The Tatas in India used scientific management at their steelworks as early as the 1920s. In Germany, *Rationalisierung* became a buzzword. Steel industrialist Carl Ferdinand von Stumm-Halberg believed that "for an industrial company to thrive, it has to be organized along military lines."[161] The Röchlings concurred and asserted their authority and control over the many stages of production in their ever more complex factory. When Hermann Röchling, who now headed the family firm, issued new "Work Regulations" in 1904, they extended to a full fifty-one articles, aiming to control workers' movements and behaviors in torturous detail. And disciplining workers went hand in hand with reorganizing the production process. In the Röchlings' rolling mill, workers had traditionally rolled steel in batches, with highly skilled workers supported by a team of unskilled workers who were under their personal command. When the company introduced the new Thomas–Gilchrist steel process in 1891, that mill moved to continual rolling, in which the machine did much of the shaping previously done by workers. A further subdivision of labor now allowed unskilled workers to do a lot of the work, with the formerly dominant highly skilled artisanal workers losing control. These workers resisted—they threw down materials, refused to work, and even threatened to kill Hermann, who fired the "agitators" and successfully asserted control.[162] The previously central role of highly skilled workers, and their authority over their subordinates, had been decisively undermined—and with it one critical axis of the midcentury rebellions.

As work was reconstructed, a new intensity of manufacturing labor became ever more common: Workers spent most of their waking hours in the factory. Until 1918, the standard workday in Germany (and elsewhere) was twelve hours. And even that was not a given. At the iron and machinery factory of Eduard Laeis & Cie, "[i]n urgent cases, the workers are obliged to continue working even after the shift is over."[163] Employers like the Röchlings also required workers to labor more than one shift in a row, and workers were occasionally required to stay on the job for an extraordinary thirty-six hours. One historian called this schedule "barbarian work times."[164] The heightened labor intensity affected working-class families as a whole: Even though it was illegal, some of the Röchlings' workers were as young as twelve, while fifteen- or sixteen-year-olds might work for many more hours than was legal.[165] It would take decades of struggle for workers to wrest some of their time back from employers.

Work was physically strenuous. Iron and steel puddlers were exposed to great heat and extremely bright lights that made the job so physically taxing that most of their bodies, even without accident or illness, gave out at around age forty. Throughout the Röchlings' works, machines were noisy, the heat extreme, and the exposure to the elements difficult to endure. Many workers were maimed or killed. On December 30, 1889, a steel plate fell on the head of nineteen-year-old Karl Jakob Klein, killing him instantly. Christian Dries, twenty-five, was crushed between two train cars on March 4, 1884. Nikolaus Schweitzer, thirty-five, suffocated on May 10, 1888, from exposure to "furnace gas." On December 12, 1888, sixteen-year-old Paul Bach died due to a similar cause. In the two decades after 1892, about one and a half in a thousand workers died annually in industrial accidents at the Röchlings' complex. Many more were maimed. For good reason, workers' greatest fear was suffering an on-the-clock accident that left them unable to work and subject to abject poverty.[166]

Conditions outside the factory gates were just as difficult. Families lived in tight quarters: As late as 1923, one Röchling worker reported that he and his wife lived with their seven children in a two-room apartment. That same year, another worker testified that he lived four to a room, and worker Johan Bayer related that he walked forty-five minutes each way to catch the train that took him to Völklingen. Many workers resided with their parents, unable to pay for or find their own apartments. Such conditions led to a high rate of departure from the factory. One historian found that in 1891, at a Luxembourgian steel-works in Dudelange, near Völklingen, 45 percent of all workers had been on the payroll for less than three months, and only 3.1 percent had been employed for more than five years.[167]

This instability affected all aspects of working-class life. Records produced by Völklingen's municipal administration at midcentury reported on working-class youth delinquency, violent abuse of working-class women, and "neglected children." Half a century later, the city, along with the Röchling company, was still trying to chasten workers for these behaviors: the filching of fruit from trees by working-class children (the same complaint that coffee growers filed in El Salvador), the "wandering around in the forest" of large groups of youths, and the nightly small-scale property vandalization carried out by these youths. All were seen as signs of a working class that resisted discipline. Not to mention the fact that family life was often characterized by stress, fights, and frequent physical violence.[168] Holidays in particular were occasions for binge drinking and disorderliness; unsurprisingly, the Röchlings were not "particularly fond of holidays."[169]

Employers like the Röchlings tried to control, pacify, and stabilize this new working class in the interest of securing mass production in capital-intensive facilities and leaving as few openings as possible for the emergence of trade unions and working-class political mobilizations.[170] They extended this desire for control from the shop floor into the homes, relationships, and behaviors of their workers, aiming to mold the industrial proletariat so that its most intimate life was more conducive to the new demands of production. In the volatile vortex of massive agglomerations of capital, workers, machines, and fossil fuel, it was uncertain if they would succeed.

But they tried. One way of doing so was to stabilize working-class life, not least by firmly attaching workers to the factory. The last decades of the nineteenth century saw the beginnings of company welfare policies, usually focused on health, housing, education, income security in illness and old age, and occasional cultural activities.[171] The Röchlings and their counterparts began building an incipient welfare system that would, by the mid-twentieth century at the latest, characterize all industrialized nations and come to be an essential element in the reconstruction of capitalism—especially when the state absorbed these welfare policies into its institutions. They formed a health-insurance scheme for their workers (which became obsolete in 1883 with the introduction of state-sponsored health insurance in Germany) and built a hospital. They supported some of their workers in old age. Moreover, the Röchlings began to provide housing to attract workers to Völklingen, believing that "the solution must aim to enable the worker to find a morally and socially acceptable and healthy home."[172] The apartments were small (about five hundred square feet), and the inhabitants of multifamily dwellings all shared one exterior toilet. Access to such housing was a privilege bestowed on only particular groups of workers, usually especially valuable and highly skilled or pliant workers, and workers and their families could be threatened with expulsion if they violated the company's political or cultural sensibilities.[173]

Not only did the Röchlings aim to stabilize the material conditions of some of their workers, but they also tried to influence working-class culture in a way that built loyalty. In 1912, the company sponsored a Hüttenarbeiter-Verein, or an association of workers, with twelve hundred members that organized cultural events like musical parades and gymnastics competitions. The company also constructed a public swimming pool, provided milk to local schoolchildren, and encouraged students to start saving while in school. Capital owners' (and states') efforts to discipline workers were all-encompassing: In education, for instance, care and coercion were thoroughly blended. When a school opened for the children of local workers in Völklingen, students were granted access to formal education but were also at times subject to terrifying violence. One child was beaten so badly by a teacher that blood gushed from his head, while another child was so severely injured by a teacher that he was no longer able to sit.[174]

One concern for the Röchlings, a concern shared by many employers of industrial labor, was alcohol. Workers the world over drank beer, wine, and spirits. In Völklingen, there was one bar for every 179 inhabitants, and male workers spent much of their free time at these establishments. Upon returning home, those workers who drank heavily were more prone to domestic violence. Hermann Röchling feared alcohol's ill effects not only because of such violence, but because he believed that alcohol reduced worker productivity and played a role in industrial accidents.[175] As

"Attention, Workers: Without Alcohol, Higher Wages!" Controlling labor: Röchling pushes abstinence on his workers through promises of higher pay.

he put it, there is an "increase in working power with complete abstinence."[176] For decades, he fought an almost quixotic battle against his workers' liquor consumption, and by the early twentieth century, he began to reward those who promised not to drink with so-called abstinence payments. Not many workers took him up on the offer: In 1907, only eleven of about six thousand workers received abstinence payments. Paradoxically, while Röchling forbade alcohol use on factory premises, he made one exception that laid bare the continued weakness of his position as an employer of labor: "[B]eer can be enjoyed during the specified breaks. The beer is served by the company."[177]

While the conditions of working-class communities remained difficult, the decades after 1870, unlike during the first Industrial Revolution and unlike for contemporary counterparts in the global countryside, saw significant improvements in workers' standard of living. Between 1870 and 1913, real wages among unskilled workers increased by 47 percent in the United Kingdom, 47 percent in the United States, 57 percent in Belgium, 32 percent in France, and 58 percent in Germany. Literacy, life expectancy, and leisure time increased significantly as well. It was also in the 1880s that the welfare state began its century-long climb, first in Australia, New Zealand, and the Scandinavian countries, then in Germany. Pensions, poor relief, housing subsidies, public health expenditures, and accident and unemployment insurance all increased, albeit slowly. As a result, workers' purchasing power rose, which in due time made the working class itself a significant market for mass-production industries.[178] Living standards for industrial workers in a few areas of the world now improved for the first time in substantial ways. Rising living standards were amplified by falling prices, especially for agricultural commodities such as wheat, coffee, soap, cocoa, tea, and sugar—many of which poured forth in unprecedented quantities, produced largely by ill-paid workers in the world's countryside. The reconstruction of the global countryside shaped the conditions of the reconstruction of labor in the industrial heartland; they were, in fact, bound together.

This amalgam of political and economic forces allowed a small segment of the world's working class to improve its conditions and set itself apart from the vast majority of workers on Earth. As the world became more interconnected, however, these workers also began to enter into direct competition with their lesser-paid counterparts, sometimes because they produced the same things elsewhere and sometimes because they migrated into the industrial heartland. African Americans moved from the US South into the North; Mexicans came to the United States; southern Italians relocated to northern Italian industrial cities; Polish workers rode a wave of migration into the Ruhr; and Chinese workers resettled all over the world. This new labor-market competition was often met by vicious working-class racism.[179] When Clements Kadalie, the general secretary of the Industrial and Commercial Workers' Union of Africa, penciled a letter to his Indian counterpart, Narayan Malhar Joshi, in 1928, he remarked on some of that racism:

> I note from your letters that in the working class Movement of India, you do not make any distinction between the workers of any race, creed or colour and that you certainly desire that the Indian workers in South Africa should work in fullest co-operation with us. The Indian workers up to now have shown very little sympathy with us and we shall be extremely grateful to you if you could arouse them to the realization of the fact that, as workers, we have one common enemy, namely Imperial capitalism.[180]

But even though living standards had improved for a small segment of the world's workers, working-class life was still exceedingly modest: In 1887, the average annual wage at the Röchlings' iron- and steelworks complex in Völklingen was 753.13 marks, and the average family of three to four members needed to spend 478.80 of those marks on food. That left a meager 300 marks for housing, heating, clothing, and all other expenses. Working-class youths were often so marked by the deprivations of their existence, especially in their stunted growth, that they failed to pass muster for service in the armed forces.[181]

WHILE THIS RECONSTRUCTION of industrial labor was largely based on contractual wage labor, which so many liberal and Marxist thinkers have depicted as the very essence of capitalism, some of the repressive mechanisms that characterized reconstructed countrysides moved into industry as well: Bombay millowners paid workers with much delay, forcing them into the hands of moneylenders to secure their subsistence and producing a life of eternal indebtedness. Millowners there, like the Röchlings in the Saar, were often autocratic figures who ruled through deeply embedded hierarchies, control, and coercion. Japanese cotton industrialists went so far as to lock their women workers in dormitories to keep them from fleeing.[182]

Yet largely thanks to the availability of much greater numbers of workers due to demographic expansion, and thanks to the collective mobilizations of workers against remnants of the old regime, the elements of extra-economic coercion that had characterized even industrial labor in the centers of industrialization earlier in the nineteenth century diminished. France, Germany, the United States, and, most prominently, the United Kingdom slowly did away with criminal sanctions for leaving employment relationships, including by Britain repealing the Master and Servant Act in 1875. As these penalties became illegal, economic coercions now remained the sole force behind wage work, coercions that were themselves often created by the elaborate legal machinery of the state.[183]

. . .

THE ACTIONS OF the new working class also shaped the reconstruction of labor. As the proletariat grew, new forms of collective action, organization, and politics became prominent—and decisively altered the face of global capitalism. Improvements in working conditions came not from employers' kindliness but from workers' individual and collective mobilizations.

Workers were no longer the "primitive rebels" of prior decades; like their work, their resistance became more industrial (versus artisanal), institutionalized, and bureaucratized. Earlier in the century, working-class collective action had typically consisted of crowds assembling at the gates of a factory owner's home and pelting it with stones, insulting the owner, and carting off the family's furniture. Now workers joined highly formalized organizations that followed parliamentary procedures as they decided whether to call strikes or organize electoral campaigns. Workers struck, organized in trade unions and political parties, and increasingly built a class-based and institutionalized cultural world far removed from their bourgeois "betters," developing in the process ideas that challenged capital owners' authority—not just in the factory but in society and in politics. Self-educated working-class intellectuals became common, workers who, despite their often minimal schooling, followed the burgeoning left-wing press, read widely (including the dense treatises of the socialist intelligentsia), and even delved into authoring tracts and novels themselves. Salvador Torrents—born in 1885 in the Spanish city of Mataró, as a workers' son who himself entered the factory at age ten—became exposed to anarchist ideas, started reading voraciously, joined Spanish political struggles, and was eventually driven into first French and then, in 1914, Australian exile. Throughout his long life on the Queensland sugar frontier, and despite unrelenting physical labor, he subscribed to left-wing journals from around the world, engaged with global and local struggles, and left behind a corpus of writing in which he analyzed the state of the world and laid out his own political philosophies.[184] Anarchism, the *folies* of the bourgeoisie, war, racism, and women's emancipation all feature in

Working-class intellectual: Salvador Torrents, 1915, as pictured in his passport.

his reflections—a true working-class philosopher.

For activists like Torrents, strikes became the archetypical weapon of working-class collective action. Where they had been illegal, they were now permitted (as in France and Belgium as of 1864, thanks to political elites seeking new popular support), and everywhere, they were deployed to similar ends: better pay, shorter work hours, and safer work environments. Between 1880 and 1884, despite significant government repression, French workers organized an average of 121 strikes annually; this rose to 400 between 1890 and 1894 and to 1,188 strikes between 1910 and 1914. There and elsewhere, miners formed one of the vanguards of organized labor: One in five French strikers between 1880 and 1914 was a miner. In the German Ruhr, large strikes hit the coal and steel industries: In 1872, 20,000 miners struck for six weeks in Essen, and then again in 1889, 1905, and 1912. In Silesia's coal-mining areas, there were 64 strikes between 1889 and 1905. In Germany as a whole, the number of strikes grew from 79 in 1870 to 806 in 1900 to a peak of 2,469 (involving 397,000 workers) in 1912. In Britain, 393,000 workers engaged in 1,040 strikes in 1890. Not only were there more strikes; they were also vastly better organized and sometimes even nationally coordinated.[185] In the United States, massive strike waves broke across the country, with a railroad strike in 1877 and a massive walkout of 350,000 workers in May 1886, with an eight-hour day among the most prominent demands. No wonder British statistician George Phillips Bevan lamented in 1880 that "[s]triking has become a disease, a very grave disease, in the body social . . . [that] shows no sign of having run its course."[186]

*Military might confronts industrial workers: A local militia shoots
at striking workers in Scranton, Pennsylvania, in 1877.*

Unions played a crucial role in these strikes, unlike earlier in the
century, when workers engaged in unorganized and spontaneous rebellions, including walkouts. In Britain, regional miners' unions had
emerged as early as 1824, but only in 1888 did workers create a national organization, the Miners' Federation of Great Britain. In the
1880s, Britain's long tradition of skilled workers' organizations was
supplemented by the organizing of unskilled workers. In 1868, workers
had launched a national umbrella organization of unions—the Trades
Union Congress (TUC)—which counted 250,000 members by 1870
and 1,470,000 by 1890. In the United States, the Knights of Labor
emerged as a powerful collective voice of the American working class,
with around 700,000 members in 1886. The American Federation of
Labor (AFL), founded in 1886 under the leadership of working-class
cigar maker Samuel Gompers, quadrupled its membership between
1897 and 1910, when it organized 2.1 million workers. In France, by
1870, between 250,000 and 300,000 workers had organized themselves into unions affiliated with the First International. By 1900,
there were 500,000 French trade unionists. In Germany, 300,000
workers had joined the Free Trade Unions by 1890; by 1913, that

number had exploded to 2.5 million. In Belgium, too, workers formed unions, federating nationally within particular industries: metalworkers in 1886, cigar makers in 1887, miners and quarriers in 1889, textile workers in 1898, and tobacco workers in 1900. They won important concessions, both in the workplace and in the state's welfare provisions. National trade union federations also emerged in Spain in 1888, Germany in 1890, Austria in 1893, France in 1895, Sweden in 1898, and Italy in 1906. Everywhere, skilled workers took the lead in forging organizations; those run by the highly skilled workers of Solingen, whom we encountered earlier, for example, made the city a center of German socialism.[187]

As these institutions of workers came to be dominated by skilled male workers—"respectable" workers—they increasingly looked down upon the "mob . . . as an inferior mass," as German labor activist Stephan Born put it in 1848.[188] Labor leaders mostly came to distance themselves from the spontaneous, uncoordinated, often violent actions of their lower-skilled counterparts—many of whom were women and children—as we saw, for example, among the Silesian weavers. Karl Marx and Friedrich Engels were, in many ways, at the forefront of separating a "respectable" labor movement—and "respectable" workers—from those whom they defamed as the *Lumpenproletariat*—the ragged proletariat. When German socialist Ferdinand Lassalle formed the Allgemeiner Deutscher Arbeiterverein (ADAV) in 1866 and connected to some of the earlier traditions of rebellion, he was immediately attacked by Engels. Yet Lassalle himself drew a firm line between the new forms of protest, which were to be respectable and legal, and what had come before—the spontaneity and lawlessness of earlier rebellions.[189] Reflecting a shared calculus of risk and reward, most strands of the European and American labor movements became deeply vested in bourgeois morals. This channeling of the dominant value system, the invention of the "respectable worker," was a source of tremendous power, but it also marginalized women, those perceived as the racial "other," and most workers in the world who lacked advanced skills or worked either outside factories (in the countryside) or outside the core industrialized countries. This divide would shape the politics of labor for the next 150 years.

The majority of industrial workers remained unorganized, and there were significant differences in working-class collective actions in different regions of the world, but what was remarkable was that the strike as a form of collective politics and the union as the working class's prevalent institutional form spread anywhere and everywhere that industry took hold. A Lyonnais worker would have felt at home in the class politics of Pittsburgh; a worker from Milan would have understood the working-class politics of Manchester. While strategies and institutional forms sometimes might have been the result of a connected working-class internationalism, they also emerged spontaneously out of local situations. In a world where workers owned little but their own labor, withholding that labor was their most effective—and usually only—weapon, and to be effective, it had to be wielded by large numbers simultaneously.

Collective action and organizations of industrial workers were not limited to the centers of heavy industry in Europe and North America. The almost eighty thousand workers in Bombay's massive textile mills (many Indian-owned) began organizing in 1890 in the Bombay Mill Hands Association; over the next decades, tens of thousands of these workers struck. As work in the mills was informal and work times intentionally kept fluid by management, workers focused their efforts on greater control of time, including the institution of clock time—that is, work schedules defined by a clock visible to all, not by the arbitrary whims of management. In the Ottoman Empire, it has been estimated that between 1891 and 1911, 260 strikes took place. The two thousand Muslim, Jewish, and Christian workers at the Cibali Tobacco and Cigarette Factory in Istanbul, for example, were consistently involved in activism that peaked with a large strike in 1911. Despite serious repression under Sultan Abdülhamid II, unions emerged in the Ottoman Empire, and by 1894, some of the four thousand workers at the Ministry of War's munitions factory in the Tophane quarter of Istanbul secretly created the first Ottoman workers' organization, the

*Labor activists, Istanbul: women rollers at the
Cibali Tobacco and Cigarette Factory.*

Osmanlı Amele Cemiyeti, or the Ottoman Workers' Society.[190] Given all these strikes, it is no wonder that when, in 1890, a government commission in New South Wales looked into the relationship between capital and labor, it found that strikes were "undeniably the great social problem of the age."[191]

In Argentina, too, a vibrant labor movement sprang up in the last decades of the nineteenth century, powered by a working class that emerged on the heels of the genocidal transformation of the Patagonian steppe—the so-called Conquest of the Desert—from an area inhabited by Indigenous people to one that produced wheat and beef for global markets. As almost two million Europeans settled in Argentina between 1880 and 1890, especially in Buenos Aires, to process and ship that meat, a vibrant working class emerged, with butchers, stevedores, leather tanners, and train mechanics. As these foreign-born workers mobilized, they encountered mutual aid societies forged by artisans decades prior, including organizations of shoe menders, construction workers, masons, bakers, tailors, and carpenters. From 1888 onward, they made numerous attempts to federate these unions into larger organizations. In that year, anarchists and socialists met at the

German immigrant club Vorwärts to create a union federation, eventually leading to the short-lived Federación de Trabajadores de la Región Argentina in 1891. Workers established nineteen trade unions between 1880 and 1890, the most significant being the Confederación de Ferrocarriles, whose highly mobile members connected different industrial cities and commanded key logistical points in the export economy. By 1907, that union claimed a membership of 15,000. Cross-industry organization emerged as well, with the Federación Obrera Regional in 1901 (which left *Argentina* out of its name to signal its principled opposition to all forms of nationalism). By that year, its constituent unions had organized 11,000 workers, compared with 7,500 in the socialist Unión General de Trabajadores; by 1919, the newly renamed FORA (now with an *A* at the end of its acronym— standing for *Argentina*) had more than 100,000 members, 60,000 of whom were organized by the federations of railway workers and seafarers alone.[192]

This vibrant Argentinean working class spawned not just unions but organized strikes. While only 12 strikes were recorded between 1881 and 1887, the following three years saw 36 strikes. Between 1903 and 1904 there were 113; and between 1906 and 1909, 775, involving 204,000 workers. At times, they escalated into a general strike. When, in 1902, stevedores at the port of Buenos Aires refused to carry bags that weighed more than one hundred kilograms, they were joined by the national federation of stevedore unions, spreading the strike to other cities. As strikers marched to a warehouse on November 4 to recruit its workers, police intervened; a cascade of other unions then called for strikes, with FORA mobilizing for a general strike on November 22. Similar escalations occurred in what protagonists came to call the Tragic Week of 1909 and 1919, both marked by intense violence.[193]

Such collective actions also spread beyond the workplace. In 1915 Glasgow, women working-class activists battled landlords against rent increases. In Buenos Aires, workers lived in crowded compounds with an average of eleven and a half people per apartment. When a new

Labor activists, Buenos Aires: the March of the Broomsticks, 1907.

municipal tax was introduced in 1907 and FORA called for a rent strike, the housing compounds proved fertile ground for action. Women played a prominent role in the ensuing strike, organizing a march with broomsticks and promising to "sweep away the slumlords." *La Protesta* gleefully reported that whenever landlords visited the tenements, they were greeted by women drenching them with cold water dumped from their windows.[194]

THIS PROLETARIAT ALSO created political parties, hot on the heels of their bourgeois "betters," who had themselves engaged in a pronounced class politics since at least 1848. Workers founded socialist parties in Germany in 1869, Denmark in 1876, France and Spain in 1879, Belgium in 1885, Norway in 1887, Sweden and Austria in 1889, Italy in 1892, the Netherlands in 1894, Argentina in 1896, Finland in 1899, the United States in 1901, and the United Kingdom between 1900 and 1906. Japan's first socialist party, the Shakai Minshuto, came in 1901; Cape Town's Social Democratic Federation, in 1904; and Indonesia's Indies Social Democratic Association, in 1914.[195]

These parties were fractious, often split along sectarian lines, but their emergence signaled a sea change in working-class collective action and the reconstruction of capitalism. Whatever their precise politics, these parties all recruited from their respective country's working class; engaged in abstract discussions on capitalism, revolution, and postcapitalism; created programs summarizing their political demands; engaged in meetings to deliberate and vote on policies and strategies; organized themselves hierarchically; and aimed their reformist or revolutionary agendas beyond the sphere of work, aspiring to change national politics and to reform, if not abolish, capitalism. This reconstructed working-class politics, far removed from the rowdy crowds earlier in the century, created one of the political fault lines that came to structure the twentieth century.

During the late nineteenth and early twentieth centuries, working-class politics emerged from the blatant inequalities of the age, the violent disruptions of the lives of millions of people, and their frequent encounters with great poverty, hardship, and exploitation. Less noted, it also emerged from the optimism generated by the capitalist revolution itself: The great machines, the novel industrial processes, and the enormous productivity increases brought oppression, to be sure, but also made new forms of human emancipation imaginable. Working-class politics retained this paradoxical optimism from the moment of its emergence well into the 1970s, when the likelihood of human emancipation from fossil-fuel-based mass production faded. The modern labor movement, with all its promises and all its limitations, just like the vertically and horizontally integrated manufacturing enterprise, was a child of the Second Industrial Revolution.

During this time, working-class organizations gained major influence on national politics almost everywhere, with their influence often even larger than their (very substantial) memberships: The French Section of the Workers' International, for example, had 76,000 members in 1914 but garnered 1.4 million votes. Germany's Social Democratic Party, the SPD, also won 1.4 million votes in the federal elections of 1890; by 1912, it had more than a million members and won more than a third of the popular vote. In the US presidential elections of 1912, Eugene V. Debs of the Socialist Party of America garnered almost a million votes, capturing 6 percent of the total. Across Europe as a whole, the number of votes for parties claiming to represent workers grew from 431,000 between 1881 and 1885 to 3,513,000 between 1901 and 1905 to 8,399,000 between 1911 and 1915. By the early years of the twentieth century, socialists had won more than 40 percent of the vote in Finland; more than 30 percent in Belgium, Germany, and Sweden; and more than 20 percent in Austria, Denmark, and Italy.[196] Working-class politics, as such numbers suggest, came to shape the state. Indeed, twentieth-century capitalism was, to a significant extent, the result of the stunningly powerful working-class political mobilizations that emerged during the global reconstruction of capitalism in the late nineteenth century.

While many activists found progress slow, viewed from the perspective of the five hundred years of capitalism's history, what is remarkable is how quickly these parties gained significant political power. Belgian socialists, inspired by the success of the SPD, attempted to coordinate disparate workers' struggles on the level of the nation-state, founding the Belgische Werkliedenpartij (Belgian Workers' Party) in 1885. The party, which brought together fifty-nine local co-ops, unions, and mutual aid societies, demanded universal male suffrage, abolition of child labor, tariff removal, and free and compulsory secular education. The Workers Party of Britain (WPB), which first entered Parliament in 1894, had 276,000 members by 1916 and was part of the ruling government, joining a wartime coalition of Catholics and Liberals.[197] By 1919, socialists of all stripes participated in the governments of Germany, Russia, Sweden, Denmark, Hungary, Italy, Australia, and the Kingdom of Serbs, Croats, and Slovenes.

Working-class politics also spread rapidly into less industrialized areas, appealing to those beyond the industrial proletariat. Armenian émigrés established the social democratic Hunchakian Revolutionary Party in Geneva in 1887. Dimitar Blagoev founded the Bulgarian Workers' Social Democratic Party in 1891, and the Romanian Social Democratic Party was started two years later. Bulgarian and Macedonian revolutionaries (including Muslims) who had been in contact with Mikhail Bakunin in Switzerland advocated for a broader liberation movement against the governing Ottoman sultan, and they founded the Macedonian Secret Revolutionary Committee in 1895. The Argentinean Socialist Party was founded in 1896; initially focused on expanding the franchise and passing parliamentary reforms, it elected the first socialist deputy to the Chamber of Deputies in 1904.[198]

Of course, large segments of the working class did not organize in unions or join socialist parties. Völklingen's workers were an example of this. Faced with not only internal divisions about wages and access to welfare benefits but also the determined opposition of their employer, workers had a hard time organizing: Well into the twentieth century, there were almost no unions or socialist organizations in Völklingen.[199] The SPD was so weak there that its leader, August Bebel, admitted in 1891 that "this area is still a complete *terra incognita.*"[200]

But even in Völklingen, there was dissatisfaction and resistance on the shop floor—what one historian has called "micropolitics."[201] At an 1892 meeting in Völklingen, miner Thomas Altenwald argued that wages were falling because of the "disunity and cowardice" of the workers, and another worker pointed out "that only solid cooperation leads to the goal."[202] In March 1890, the *Saarbrücker Gewerbeblatt* reported on the "new interferers of the peace" and on agitators who "sought to hurl the torch of social war into the working masses."[203]

Even in Völklingen, discontent could translate into collective action. In 1906, seven hundred workers at a neighboring iron- and steelworks, the Burbacher Hütte, walked out in a strike organized by the Christian Metalworkers' Association. There were also strikes in nearby coal mines. The first strike in Völklingen itself, a strike to protest wage reductions, took place in 1908.[204] In 1912, about one hundred union activists met in the pub Zum Karlsberg to listen to a Christian unionist who insisted that "if the Saar workers are not man enough now to throw off their slave shackles, they will continue . . . to have to suffer under sad circumstances." For workers, "the time has come," he argued, "to move forward, to free themselves . . . to roll off the pressure that still rests on them today. Without an organization this is not possible."[205]

Everywhere, workers encountered enormous resistance from employers and the state when they tried to improve their fate. As early as 1877, Saar industrialists and mine owners met to discuss how they could prevent their workers from organizing, deciding that none of them would offer employment to SPD members and setting up the Employers' Committee for Combating Social Democracy.[206] So nervous were they about possible challenges that they kept a close watch on any known SPD member, and the mayor of Völklingen reported regularly on "movements in the field of wage labor."[207] The police surveilled all worker collective actions, including every meeting of working-class associations, and reported to their superiors what was said and heard. Officers were particularly attentive to anything having to do with the Social Democratic Party. Even though strikes were legal, the state played a large role in suppressing workers' collective actions, showing capital owners that they depended on the state to enforce order. Many industrialists now moved away from the more emancipatory and liberal ideas that they had embraced as recently as 1848.[208]

It was not just surveillance and talk. At the Röchlings' factories, workers sympathetic to unions and the SPD were designated as "agitators" and fired. In 1899, the Interior Ministry of Berlin recommended that police forces be increased in mining and industrial areas to "secure quiet and order."[209] When workers struck at the Burbacher Hütte, the company asked for and received police protection for strikebreakers. In the Ruhr in 1890, entrepreneurs went a step further and organized an Ausstands-Versicherungs-Verband, a kind of insurance scheme against strikes. So repressive was the climate for Völklingen's working-class activists that they invented a new word to describe their home region: *Saarabien*, a portmanteau of the words *Saar* and *Arabien*, with the Arab word meant to stand for autocratic rule and repression. Hermann Röchling was so concerned about working-class collective action that it even trumped his anti-alcohol crusade. In 1907, when a social democratic teetotalist organization, the Deutscher Abstinenter Arbeiterbund, suggested to Röchling that he offer his abstinence payment to its members, Röchling said that "we have absolutely no intention of promoting any social democratic endeavors in our country."[210] Yet despite all that repression, or perhaps because of it, even in the Saar, even in Völklingen, unions and socialist parties eventually became a powerful presence. By 1922, 23.9 percent of all votes in the Saar went to socialist candidates.[211]

Moreover, islands of postcapitalism—places and institutions that embraced a different economic logic—emerged in industrial centers, just as they had among rural cultivators in places like La Réunion, Surinam, and Jamaica. In 1928, German economist Werner Sombart observed such pre- and postcapitalist economic forms. Some within the industrial labor movement pursued what we might call decommodification—attempts to remove areas of workers' lives from the market. We saw similar efforts earlier, when we covered the midcentury spread of utopian communities, mostly in the United States, and the rebellions in the countryside. Later in the nineteenth century, cooperative markets, cooperative housing, and even cooperative manufacturing and banking became popular as well. In Belgium, labor leader César De Paepe advocated for collectively owned banks, land, and transportation. There was real enthusiasm for cooperatives among Belgian workers: In 1873, bakers in Ghent established a baking co-op called De Vrije Bakkers (the Free Bakers). The co-op grew rapidly, baking 245,000 loaves in 1879, and eventually purchased one of the first steam-driven flour mills in Belgium. In 1880, the bakers were incorporated into a larger cooperative, Vooruit (Forward), and their turnover grew tenfold from 1880 to 1900. For a twenty-five-centime sign-up fee, workers could purchase clothes, food, and "colonial goods"—coffee, for example—cheaply and receive a share of the co-op's profits every three months. Cooperatives sprang up all over Belgium, from the Maison du Peuple (House of the People) in Brussels to the Wallonian Au Progrès (Progress) in Jolimont. They maintained

Islands of postcapitalism: advertisement for the Au Progrès cooperative in Jolimont, showcasing its bakery, steam-driven brewery, pharmacy, general store, relief fund, and old-age pension system, turn of the nineteenth to the twentieth centuries.

huge buildings they called "Fortresses of Socialism" that formed central nodes of working-class sociability, hosting not just bakeries but meeting rooms, party halls, printing presses, theaters, and sporting facilities.[212]

We can find such efforts outside Belgium too: In Germany, the Allgemeine Konsumverein Kiel was founded in 1899, and Swiss consumer-owned businesses spread rapidly in the late nineteenth century. Dutch workers' organizations created cooperative businesses, including in food retail. Workers in Russia and the Habsburg Empire created consumer cooperatives late in the century. Cape Town workers followed suit just before World War I, and by the 1920s, the idea had spread to Korea as well.[213] Islands of postcapitalism began to appear, vaguely reminiscent of the islands of capitalism that had emerged many centuries earlier in a largely noncapitalist, often tributary society.

A world beyond the dominant empire of capital also emerged in the form of an archipelago of working-class cultural activities and institutions. Workers forged a rich cultural life, removed from the market, that often provided underpinnings for collective activity. In 1914, the German Workers' Choral Federation counted two hundred thousand members. Viennese socialists established the Worker Rambling Association in 1895. Founded that same year by British working-class activists, the National Clarion Cycling Club counted 230 chapters, with over six thousand members in 1909. De Stem des Volks (The People's Voice) was a socialist choir founded in Amsterdam in 1898; by 1902, it had united with similar associations in the Bond van Arbeiders Zangverenigingen of the Netherlands. In 1913, the Socialist Physical Culture International brought workers together from five European nations for a kind of working-class olympic games organized by Belgian socialist Gaston Bridoux. Workers even challenged the economic elites' cultural power on their home turf, as in 1886, when 120 labor unions asked the State of New York to force the Metropolitan Museum of Art to open on Sundays so that workers could visit. This request turned into a drawn-out battle that the unions eventually won in 1891—over the strong resistance of elite trustees.[214]

A new kind of capitalism had emerged by the early twentieth century, arising from the ashes of the old regime. These global reconstructions responded not only to the rebellions of industrial workers, rural cultivators, and capital owners but also to economic crisis and the technical and administrative possibilities of the age. They opened entirely novel vistas for the organization of capital, labor, and—as we will see in the next chapter—the state.

By 1900, these global reconstructions had forged a capitalism that would have been almost unrecognizable to midcentury observers. It was characterized by new industries, heavy investments in immobile assets, the emergence of vertically and horizontally consolidated firms, and the marginalization of previously powerful groups of merchants. The world of labor was in turn stamped by the waning of noneconomic forms of coercion, the rise of contractual labor relations, and the strengthening of organized labor, which at the same time led to intensified domination and control by capital, especially on plantations and shop floors. Capital owners were now a hard-hitting political force, decisively setting the course of the political economy. Within their ranks, a new group, financiers, who were invested not in any one form of capital but in broad capital accumulation for its own sake, rose to newfound influence. The reconstruction of capitalism also increased pressures on the Global South—its peasants, rulers, and capitalists. In this reconfiguration, capital owners gained tremendous power, not least on account of their close connections to nation-states. A formative new fusion reshaped the relationship between national capital and national states, each dependent on the other for survival. It was this world that would make Hermann Röchling a war criminal—not once but twice.

13.

ENCLOSURES

*The opening of a new highway in Hokkaido.
Ainu workers are depicted with beards and
geometrically patterned yellow clothes.*

A s capital and labor changed, so did the state. The late
nineteenth-century reconstructions of capitalism focused to
an astounding extent on the state, the institution of institutions. From our modern-day vantage point, this does not seem surprising, but from the perspective of the 1850s, it was unexpected: In the
previous centuries of capitalism, after all, capital had sought to escape
tightly regulated cities. Its dominant merchants had infused capital
into agriculture and manufacturing in an imperial cosmopolitanism

that had in turn forged the archipelago of capital into a capitalist civilization. Capital owners' inclination to trade, cultivate, and manufacture had gone hand in hand with the mounting dominance of ideas prescribing a future in which the "invisible hand" of the market shaped a world where people's supposedly natural inclination to truck and barter would facilitate both private wealth and economic growth. The logic of capital, rather than the imperatives of chieftains, was to govern economic life; to do so successfully, it would have to appear natural and inevitable.

Just the opposite happened. During the turn-of-the-century reconstruction of capitalism, the state in the industrial heartlands grew more powerful, more imperial (penetrating society in novel ways and securing the conditions of accumulation globally), and more able to marshal resources than any institution the world had ever known. In a century-long process, its scale and scope expanded, at first slowly, then explosively. Inequalities between states rapidly sharpened as well, with a few select states gaining disproportionate power while undermining rival polities almost everywhere else. The historical distance between the British state of 1600 and the US state of 1900 was as great as that between the quaint Swedish iron manufacturer at Finspång in 1600 and the giant Röchling iron- and steelworks in 1900. The state, like capital, underwent such dramatic changes that one historian has labeled it "Leviathan 2.0."[1] As French sociologist Pierre Bourdieu summarized the trajectory of his studies into the modern world: "[A]t the beginning, I did not intend to study the state. It imposed itself." The state imposes itself on any student of capitalism's history, and never more so than during the late nineteenth century, when reconstructed states, reconstructed capital, and reconstructed labor constituted one another. At their core, all these reconstructions emerged from the cauldron of the midcentury rebellions of capital owners, rural cultivators, and proletarians—that is, from the crisis of the old order.[2]

Capital's tendency had been to seep out of its islands and into the nooks and crannies of society, causing unprecedented economic growth and social, economic, environmental, and political turmoil. What we see in the late nineteenth-century reconstruction seems like the oppo-site: The state's enclosures accelerated capital's expansion. Strengthen-ing, deepening, and extending state power within a given territory allowed new forms of capital and labor to emerge and spread—indeed, one of the core characteristics of this moment was that these enclosures globalized as never before.[3] They were of the most varied kind. Many were literal and time-honored: Capital owners constructed fences to demarcate their enlarged properties, dissolved the commons, and pro-vided for the legal definitions of new forms of property rights. But some were novel: enclosing capital within more sharply defined eco-nomic spaces (some national, some imperial); defining the rights of new social groups, especially the working class; containing cosmopoli-tan capital within precisely drawn national economic spaces, with the state as key arbiter; organizing diverse legal systems into a more rigid and well-defined legal code; decontextualizing economics from history, class, and society at the apex moment of their politicization; and carrying out the most drastic enclosure of all—vastly expanding the portion of the globe under imperial sway.

Taken together, these state-enabled enclosures, a kind of confine-ment, newly demarcated and policed the ambiguous boundaries of the empire of capital. By late century, they also testified to a new capacity of the state and its new role. It extended its scale and captured a rapidly increasing share of the nation's wealth. It also extended its scope, stretching its tentacles ever deeper into society—from enabling and regulating new forms of capital to inserting itself into the relationships between employer and employed. Its composition changed as well: The landowning elites who had monopolized state power for centuries were in retreat, while capital owners in general and industrialists in particular were in advance, gaining new influence. Increasingly, other social groups also influenced the councils of state—none more so than a massively extended and politically mobilized proletariat. While this general tendency was universal across the industrial heartland, its mo-dalities differed: a centralized state here (in France) and a decentral-ized one there (in the United States). While the social base of state power expanded everywhere, some states remained deeply rooted in autocratic forms of politics (Germany, for example). Others, such as Britain and the United States, followed a more liberal or even democratic path. Everywhere, wars were crucial to making these states—the US Civil War as much as the Italian and German wars of unification. Some of the best-known protagonists of this moment were statesmen—Abraham Lincoln, Benito Juárez, Otto von Bismarck, and Itō Hirobumi.[4]

The fact that the reconstructed state remained a crucial condition for capitalism's viability related directly to the changed nature of capital. Huge investments had flowed into immobile properties, such as coal mines and blast furnaces, not, as before, into highly portable assets, such as goods and ships. A state's capacity to hold sway in the international order or to pacify its newly mobilized and politically empowered citizens and subjects now depended almost entirely on these innovative production facilities. Meanwhile, capital needed state support to control its masses of workers and access materials and markets. Capital thus became newly attached to the nation-state and the nation-state to capital.[5] And because states competed with one another, this process was contagious.[6] In the sixteenth and seventeenth centuries, the state had been important but distant from the frontiers of capital. Now it was everywhere.

⸻

The role of a rapidly evolving nation-state in the reconstruction of capitalism can be observed in many different places throughout the empire of capital. Ezo—the "land of the barbarians" in Japanese parlance, later renamed Hokkaido—was one.[7] Situated about fifteen miles north of the main Japanese island of Honshu, the island of Hokkaido became a training ground for Japanese colonialism, a vast (the size of Ireland) state-driven enclosure that dispossessed Indigenous people of their lands and fishing grounds while it introduced new property rights for others; brought settlers and forced workers onto its construction sites, farms, and mines; and turned the island into one of Japan's most significant agricultural, fishing, timber, and mining frontiers.[8]

For centuries, Ezo had been weakly integrated into the Tokugawa shogunate, with the control of the local lords, the Matsumaes, confined to a few fortified coastal areas from which they traded with local inhabitants, about fifteen thousand Ainu hunter-gatherers who largely controlled the island's bountiful resources. The Matsumaes hoped to extract resources from the island beyond trade, slowly undermining the Ainu subsistence economy, turning many into ill-paid fishery workers or driving those who refused farther inland. Nonetheless, for some decades, the impacts of the Matsumaes' activities were limited to coastal regions.[9]

In the wake of the Meiji Restoration of 1868, however, policymakers' perspective on Hokkaido shifted radically. The national government began integrating the island into the Japanese economy and polity, making it Japan's first colony. Hokkaido was enclosed within the nation, which allowed the legal enclosure of its abundant natural resources and lands as private property. This project, in turn, played an important role in the formation of the Japanese nation-state.[10] The central tool of the project was the Kaitakushi—the commission

charged with "opening up" and developing Hokkaido—directed in 1869 by then twenty-nine-year-old Kuroda Kiyotaka.

Kaitakushi's members were deeply inspired by Anglo-American settler colonialism, with Tsuda Sen, one of the commission members, explicitly comparing Hokkaido with California, a place whose "population and material products," according to him, "grew exponentially"

Recasting the countryside: Kuroda Kiyotaka.

thanks to colonial settlement.[11] He imagined a similar trajectory for Hokkaido. Japanese policymakers' faith in Americans' expertise on colonial transformations led them to bring a group of American advisers to Hokkaido to advise on "opening up a new land and pushing back the frontier."[12] As Kuroda observed, "We must recruit the most talented personnel who are experienced in frontier development."[13] In 1871, he traveled to the United States, that "rising power of the future," and met with President Ulysses S. Grant and Commissioner of Agriculture Horace Capron.[14] Kuroda hired Capron on the spot as a special consultant to the Japanese government.[15]

Kuroda and his advisers aimed to fundamentally transform Hokkaido by surveying the island, building roads, attracting Japanese settlers, creating new property rights, locating and mining minerals, removing timber, erecting modern machinery, creating educational institutions, starting cattle farms, planting fruit trees, expanding fisheries, and building telegraph lines. Capron and other American advisers played a key role. Born in August 1804, Capron had witnessed firsthand the settler colonial transformation of much of the North American continent. His multifaceted career included running textile mills, managing violent labor conflicts, operating large-scale commercial farms, and engaging in Civil War combat. The most significant line on his résumé, however, was his 1852 appointment by President Fillmore as a special agent in charge of Native American affairs—this meant forcibly relocating peoples Capron described as "savages," "wild tribes which roamed over that country [the American West]."[16] Then, in 1868, President Johnson appointed him commissioner of agriculture, the position from which he left for Yokohama in 1871.[17]

Capron's past experiences deeply influenced him on Hokkaido: "The great tidal wave of civilization which . . . was sweeping across the American continent," he asserted, "seems only to have paused upon the western coast to gather strength for its passage over the broad Pacific in its westward progress around the world."[18] Tasked with the "examination of the Island as to its condition, Geological, Vegetable and Mineral, and with a view to a decision where the roads, canals . . .

should be constructed," he hoped to contribute to "opening up" Hokkaido.[19] Capron and his Japanese counterparts set out to remake the island into a new frontier of Japanese state power and capital accumulation. The challenge they faced was figuring out how to create a capitalist economy almost from scratch, a project that reminded Capron of the United States.[20]

As a first step, Capron and his collaborators tried to ascertain the character and shape of the territory, making a "mineralogical and topographical survey of the country as minute and careful as possible."[21] Traveling, often on horseback, under the guidance of the Ainu, they catalogued their new possession, exploring its mineral deposits, seeking out places and crops for agricultural settlements, and taking note of rich fishing grounds. After a few months of exploration, Capron concluded that "[t]his is a splendid Island; the real value of it is not well understood or appreciated. Its mineral resources are great. Its fisheries unlimited, its timber abundant and superior in quality, its agricultural capacity great."[22] Investments, he concluded, "will richly repay."[23] The Japanese state so valued Capron's service that the emperor personally welcomed him, a rare honor for a Westerner.[24]

The most glaring obstacle to unlocking the island's wealth was infrastructure. "The road is so necessary an instrument of development and progress," pointed out the American advisers, "that in every new colony it is one of the first thought of."[25] Indeed, the state sponsored not just roads but canals, bridges, railroads, towns, ports, and new steamship connections. Experimental farms were built as well, suggesting the possibility of sculpting the landscape along North American lines. Accelerating the circulation of biological material, the Kaitakushi brought trees, seeds, and even animals from the United States and Europe. They planted thousands of fruit trees in the center of Sapporo. In 1890, reflecting another instance of agricultural innovation, the Sapporo Sugar Company began to process beets into sugar, making Hokkaido the local center of that industry.[26] Japanese bureaucrats built new institutions, including the Sapporo Agricultural College in 1876.

Legal changes came next: Private control over land, infrastructure, and mining developments, Capron insisted, was essential, notwithstanding its incongruity with Ainu conceptions of land and property. A land reform grounded in the doctrine of terra nullius turned Hokkaido into a "land without a master."[27] The Land Regulation Ordinance of 1872 brought private property rights in land to Hokkaido, important not least because it allowed for tax assessments of the land and a virtuous cycle of raising government revenue to balance infrastructure spending. The Kaitakushi also pushed for private property rights in seafront land, where fish could be sorted, dried, and packaged, forcing the Ainu to give up their communal traditions of landing and processing the catch. Moreover, it abolished the system of merchants contracting with independent fishermen, hastening the emergence of full-fledged sea proletarians.[28]

With these innovations in place, labor became, as always, crucial to the transformation of the countryside. The Kaitakushi recruited a wide variety of workers. Migrants from Japan's main island, Honshu, were among them: As the countryside there became increasingly socially bifurcated, peasants were pressured to pay cash taxes, and many lost their access to land. The government provided support for these cultivators to set up as farmers on Hokkaido. They acquired and cleared land; brought tools, supplies, and seeds; and embarked upon cultivation. Some also became wage laborers on larger properties, where they joined former impoverished samurai, especially those on the losing side of the Meiji Restoration. By 1899, 7,337 households with about 40,000 members had been resettled. Each received sixteen acres of land and the opportunity to purchase another eighty acres cheaply. By 1909, there were 1.5 million Japanese settlers on the island. Those among the Ainu who survived the onslaught of Japanese settlement into the once-safe interiors joined their new coastal neighbors as ill-paid, deeply exploited wageworkers in coal mines and fisheries.[29]

Forced labor became crucial for mining and infrastructure construction. Revolts in the wake of the Meiji Restoration had yielded a large number of political prisoners, some of whom were now trans-

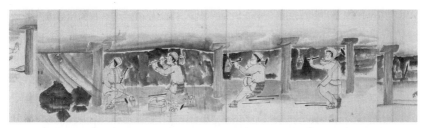

Prison workers digging coal in Hokkaido: detail of an eight-meter-long picture scroll known as the Shūjin rōdō emaki *(囚人労働絵), produced between 1881 and 1889 by an unknown inmate at Sorachi's prison.*

ported to specially built prisons on Hokkaido. Many ended up doing road construction: As five thousand men with ball-and-chain fetters around their ankles labored on a sixty-mile road connecting Date with Satsuporo, hundreds died on what came to be called the "Prisoner's Road of Death." Other prisoners worked in coal mining. For government official Kaneko Kentarō—a graduate of Harvard Law School— these penal laborers could be sacrificed because they were "rough hoodlums by nature," and "if they are unable to bear it [the work] and perish, then the reduction of these persons is, in light of today's situation where reports are made on the extreme difficulty of funding prisons, to be considered an unavoidable strategy."[30]

When the state ended the practice of outdoor prison labor in 1894 for political and ethical reasons, it began importing indentured workers. Recruited among the poor of Honshu, the migrants were housed in labor camps adjoining construction sites and mines. During World War I, they were joined by several thousand Korean forced workers, who experienced even lower wages, worse working conditions, and racial discrimination.[31]

As settlement, industry, and enclosures reached every corner of the island, the impact on the Ainu was catastrophic. The Japanese state dispossessed the Ainu, immobilized them, and devastated their ability to reproduce their families and societies. Ainu livelihood was assaulted from many directions: Japanese hunters killed more than half a million deer, crucial to Ainu subsistence and culture, in just five years between

1873 and 1878—a mass extinction of wildlife akin to the collapse of the buffalo in the American West. The Japanese government further undermined Ainu economies by outlawing the use of poisoned arrows for hunting and then, in 1878, the traditional Ainu practice of night fishing. Borrowing closely from the US model of relocating Native Americans onto reservations and allotting them small parcels of land, Japan passed a law in 1899 that was supposedly meant to protect the Ainu by settling them on specially defined and much reduced lands. By 1901, the Native population had collapsed.[32]

These moves were made easier by the virulently racist ideologies that justified even the most far-reaching policies. Many Japanese people considered the "Ainu as inhuman and the inferior descendants of dogs."[33] They described the Ainu as "hairy men" who hunted and fished, "apparently, very docile and gentle" but also "rude, illiterate and inferior."[34] Chiri Yukie, a female Ainu writer looking back at the devastations of the early colonial period, observed in 1922 that "this land has undergone rapid change . . . progressively turning mountains and fields to villages, villages to towns," in the process ruining Ainu life.[35] So shattering was the Ainu's defeat that in 1904, seven Ainu women, men, and children were exhibited at the St. Louis

Ainu at the Louisiana Purchase Exposition, 1904.

World's Fair in a zoolike setting alongside Indigenous peoples from the Americas and the Philippines—the most radical form of enclosure imaginable.[36]

In the last decades of the nineteenth century, new imperial enclosures under the auspices of powerful states formed around the globe, becoming a defining characteristic of reconstructed capitalism. These enclosures had two forms: As before, they entailed a privatization of the commons—communally owned land redefined as the private property of individuals.[37] But they now also sought to energize reconstructed capital by creating national and imperial spaces that allowed for the envelopment of commodity chains, markets, and labor reservoirs. Capital's imperial thrust—both spatial and social—was a consistent feature, as we have seen, but in the late nineteenth century, it took a specific form shaped by the powers and needs of the most fortified nation-states and the novel demands of capital owners, who had become heavily invested in immobile assets.

To European and Japanese capital owners and state officials, the United States offered a model of how capital's envelopment into nation-states produced a new spatial order conducive to profit and power, something they both admired and feared. Just as many Westerners of the early twenty-first century came to worry about what they called the "Chinese danger"—and tried to brake, learn from, or emulate the Chinese example in response—capital owners and state officials of the late nineteenth century fretted about the "American danger."

This fearful envy of the United States characterized late nineteenth- and early twentieth-century debates in Europe and Japan, where industrialists, public officials, economists, and journalists warned that the United States' "monstrous contiguous economic territories," enormously fertile soil, and wealth of raw materials could undermine European competitiveness.[38] The United States, French economist Louis

Bosc believed, would soon dominate "the universe"; the once juvenile nation had matured into a "grave menace."[39]

As late nineteenth-century European and Japanese observers recognized, the United States had pioneered a new form of integration of its continent-spanning national territory, with railroads, telegraphs, courts, capital, and soldiers acting in concert to consolidate access to minerals, labor, agricultural commodities, and markets. The resulting resource abundance embedded in national commodity chains was one of the primary drivers of the United States' stunning economic performance at the cusp between the nineteenth and twentieth centuries, the era when mining, agricultural production, and industry fed into one another. In the years after the Civil War, US steel output, wheat production, railroad construction, and textile manufacturing reached the top ranks of the world economy. This was the Second Great Divergence, the preamble to not only the "American Century" but also the "age of empire," with Europe struggling to retain its global dominance. Shocked by the discontinuity that American ascendence represented, European and Japanese observers sought to emulate it, just as they had tried to emulate Britain during the original Great Divergence a century earlier. Understanding that this new form of integration was a deeply political undertaking requiring a powerful state, they embraced similar projects. Japanese empire builders understood that the United States' ability to secure raw materials, labor, and markets on its extensive national territory—itself a form of enclosure—was essential to its rapid economic rise.[40] Walther Rathenau, the head of the German engineering conglomerate AEG, tellingly saw the United States as the "happiest country in terms of raw material supplies. . . . The more industry orients itself to the world economy, the more the remotest coasts have to supply the market for raw materials, the more dangerous it becomes that we own only such a minor part of the land of the world."[41]

Territorial expansion had long been a key to the American economy. By 1900, the recently added states west of the Mississippi produced 65 percent of the nation's wheat, 44 percent of its cotton, 51 percent of its corn, 75 percent of its copper, 17 percent of its coal, 38 percent of its iron ore, and 9 percent of its petroleum. The thirteen original colonies, by contrast, produced only 9 percent of the United States' wheat, 28 percent of its cotton, 9 percent of its corn, 1 percent of its copper, 0.04 percent of its cane sugar, 43 percent of its tobacco, 13 percent of its cattle, 11 percent of its iron ore, 37 percent of its coal, and 23 percent of its petroleum. By more than tripling the size of its national territory in the first half of the nineteenth century, the US had made its agricultural and mineral resources extraordinarily abundant. By 1913, the US produced 39 percent of the world's coal, 56 percent of its copper, 65 percent of its petroleum, and 36 percent of its iron ore.[42] As commodity chains broadened and deepened, the country's precocious continental political economy let American entrepreneurs control them with relentless efficiency.

Rising American industries—textile production, steelmaking, oil refining, chemical manufacturing, food processing, telegraphy and telephony, and the new automobile industry—were built around commodity chains that were almost completely confined to the national territory of the United States. This constituted a sharp contrast to earlier eras, when coastal merchants linking American slave plantations to British factories had dominated the US economy. As American

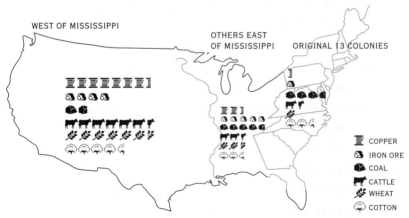

The wages of territorial expansion: geographic distribution of commodity production in the United States in 1900, by three regions—the original thirteen colonies, other states and territories east of the Mississippi, and states and territories west of the Mississippi.

merchants and financiers aligned themselves with domestic industry in the late nineteenth century, the newly integrated national territory became crucial to them as well. The trademark of this expansive capitalism was the intense relationship between nation-states and national capital, a relationship that required a state with new capacities to satisfy the novel demands of its spatially anchored capitalists. In North America, the two integrated and protected a national economy across a vast territory, creating an unprecedented continental economic zone largely independent of the rest of the world. Global trade was of only minor importance to fin de siècle America; between 1890 and 1914, the value of its exports was responsible for just 7.3 percent of GNP on average, and its imports equaled 6.6 percent.[43]

The national integration of so sprawling a territory was aided by the severely lopsided distribution of military power between settlers and the continent's Indigenous inhabitants, as in Hokkaido. Equally crucial was the fact that territorial integration was one of the core missions of the American state from its founding. The government focused its expanding military resources on territorial expansion and then ensured effective administrative, scientific, and bureaucratic integration, a project that the US Constitution had set out in 1787. An important driver here was the 1849 creation of the Department of the Interior, the American counterpart to the British Colonial Office and the French Ministère des Colonies.[44] Instructed to "open up" the continent for private exploitation by "[s]urveying, parceling, codifying, dispossessing, disposing, settling, and utilizing land," the Department of the Interior grew rapidly; its Indian Service branch alone grew fourfold between 1865 and 1885.[45]

Beyond political, legal, and military mechanisms of integration and domination, the United States created an expansive free-trade zone rivaled only by that of the British Empire. The US went far beyond Britain's vaunted navy, however, in its integration of that free-trade zone by ensuring its continuity and connectivity via an extensive continental-scale infrastructure, relentlessly pursued by an activist federal and local state and by abundant private capital—much of it, ironically, of European and Native American origin. While Native Americans nominally received indemnity payments for dispossession of their lands, the federal government held these funds in trust and invested them in further territorial expansion. Canals, turnpikes, and railroads (first local, then transcontinental) allowed goods and people to move into the remotest corners of this territory and transported agricultural commodities and minerals to industrial enclaves and the coasts. This accomplishment was central to the nation's self-understanding, as illustrated by late-century American anxiety over the "closing" of the frontier. By 1898, the United States surpassed its continental home, enclosing Hawaii, Puerto Rico, and, temporarily, Cuba and the Philippines, into its empire.[46]

No other recently colonized region had been as thoroughly integrated into the national and global economy as the territory of the United States. There were other territorially expansive nations (including Russia) and energetic empires (first and foremost the United Kingdom), but none matched the economic dynamism of the United States. "The superiority of England," argued German economist Julius Wolf, "is a matter of the past," and the "superiority of America a matter of the present."[47] Territorializing commodity chains, not free trade, seemed the way to the future. And as Britain's once extraordinary role in the world economy began to diminish, its former free-trade imperialism gave way to ever more imperial enclosures, further amplifying the "territorial" model of national economic development. Even in Britain, empire began to trump trade.[48]

THE NEWFOUND APPRECIATION for the spatial requirements of modern economies and the desire to match American power led influential capital owners, statesmen, and intellectuals in various countries to rethink their national economic strategies. They now believed that access to cheap and reliable sources of raw materials, plentiful labor, and expanding markets were crucial for European and Japanese economies to prosper in a newly industrialized world of heavy capital investments in fixed assets. Risking these prerequisites of industrial prosperity to global markets was unacceptable, not least because thinkers and strategists increasingly saw the global economy as a battleground of competing national units. As US naval officer Alfred Thayer Mahan confidently argued in 1890 in *The Influence of Sea Power upon History*, for a country to be rich, it needed to trade; to trade, it required colonies; and to secure those colonies, it needed a strong navy.[49]

No strangers to the challenges of colonial administration, European nations—like their Japanese counterparts in Hokkaido—turned to securing American-style territorial control over minerals, agricultural commodities, labor, and markets across greater distances and a wider diversity of populations. In the last two decades of the nineteenth century, Europeans captured land on other continents that added up to more than eight times the size of Europe itself. Their new imperialism was truly global. In 1870, only 10 percent of African territory was under European control. Thirty years later, 90 percent was colonized, with only Liberia and Ethiopia still independent. Russia moved at a rapid clip into Central Asia: Uzbekistan in 1866, northern Turkmenistan in 1873, Kyrgyzstan and western Tajikistan in 1876, southern Turkmenistan in 1885, and eastern Tajikistan in 1893.[50] European powers, Japan, and the United States gained substantial spheres of influence in China, albeit without formally colonizing most of it. France colonized Vietnam, Cambodia, and Laos. This new imperialism was significantly different from the chartered companies and trading posts of earlier ages, in no small part because it was principally driven by the state, not by merchants and adventurers.

Much as Japan and the United States had worked to integrate Hokkaido and the huge western territories, respectively, into their economies and polities, the Europeans sought to incorporate Africa as the centerpiece of the territorial reconstruction of their economies. Influential European elites convinced themselves that neighboring Africa could become their continent's *Ouest*, *Westen*, or *Occidente*. "[T]o free our industries from the dangerous yoke of foreigners," wrote a French colonial bureaucrat in Dakar, "we are turning to our colonies."[51] Colo-

Modern industry comes to colonial warfare:
Fiat automobiles in Italy's war in Libya, 1912.

nizing Africa seemed to promise a "powerful promotion of economic independence and prosperity"—the labor, land, minerals, agricultural commodities, and markets needed to compete with the United States.[52] "The right way to look at Africa," editorialized the British journal *African World* in 1905, "is to regard it as another America, lying fallow and ready to yield rich harvests."[53] *La Dépêche* in France agreed: Africa is an "America at our doorsteps."[54] As National Assembly member and sometime prime minister Jules Ferry put it in 1890: "Colonial policy is the daughter of industrial policy."[55]

Ferry was no outlier. One historian has remarked that these opinions were met with "virtually unanimous approval."[56] The first edition of economist Paul Leroy-Beaulieu's *De la colonisation chez les peuples modernes*, which came out in 1874, had advocated a kind of free-trade imperialism; the second edition, released in 1882, stressed the need for territorial expansion, explicitly warning of the "American danger."[57] Sorbonne economist Charles Gide also emphasized the connections between industrial prosperity and export markets, worrying that territorially extensive countries had huge economic and military advantages over small ones like France. France had to extend its territory, and since that was impossible within Europe itself, Africa was the next best option, an idea made even more urgent after France's humiliating defeat by Prussia in 1870/71.[58]

Italian peasants conquering African lands:
a poster celebrating colonial soldiers.

France's Eugène Étienne was a particularly articulate proponent of the colonization of Africa. Born in 1844 in Oran, part of French-controlled Algeria, Étienne was a military officer and, from 1881 to 1919, a member of the National Assembly. In 1887, he became head of the Sous-Secrétariat d'État aux Colonies, where, following in the footsteps of Ferry and others, he expounded tirelessly on the economic importance of colonies.[59] Rapidly expanding industry needed raw materials, labor, and markets, yet access to these essentials was increasingly difficult, as the world had entered a phase in which the last remaining markets were falling under the sway of rivals. In those years, encouraged by Étienne, the slogan "development of the colonies" became central to the French administration.[60] In late November 1889, in response to the protectionist McKinley Tariff Act about to be passed in the United States, he summarized that increasingly popular position:

> There are some facts that old Europe cannot ignore, because they are so obvious: that America, having created her industry behind carefully closed doors, dreams of creating a Zollverein reserved only for American products. Today, therefore, France must take

care to procure her own market, that of her territory, that of her colonies. . . . With the faster and faster production of machines, it is necessary to expand consumption. So France must go outside her own borders. She should go to Africa and to the Indies.[61]

French hopes for the creation of a "new America" in Africa were widespread. Writer Jean-Gabriel Capot de Feuillide compared Algeria with the American West—*l'Ouest africain*—and historian Augustin Bernard called Algeria the "America of France."[62] "Unite! Go South!" proclaimed Victor Hugo, author of *Les misérables*, in 1879, an echo of the American "Go West."[63]

These sentiments convey how, for European imperialists, America's integrated expanses served as a model for the new imperial project they increasingly embraced. For Fiat engineer Bernardino Maraini, the United States' "great development and the enormous production is principally the result of the great potentialities of absorption of the country, because of the extension of its territory, its richness of natural resources and the rapid increase of its population."[64] And while observers often rhetorically posited "Europe" against the United States, much of the politics of the 1880s, 1890s, and nineteen-aughts was nationalist—with countries hoping to expand at the expense of their rivals.

For Europeans, Africa was a potential source of raw materials, the control of which many believed would distinguish "great powers" from minor players in a sort of final reckoning.

Dividing up Africa: scene from the Berlin Conference, 1884.

In the melodramatic style typical of many European futurists, liberal politician Friedrich Naumann's Nationalsozialer Verein argued in 1897 that Germany needed to expand territorially because "to live" required ever more access to "wheat, oil, cotton," and other such materials.[65] The president of the Deutsche Kolonialgesellschaft, Duke Johann Albrecht of Mecklenburg, hoped for minerals, cotton, and cacao from Germany's African possessions.[66] Businessmen agreed, including AEG's Rathenau, for whom it was clear that

> [s]oon we will recognize that every part of the earth has substantial value, because even the least consequential contains or produces some raw materials. . . . [T]he world has been almost completely divided up. . . . The time is rapidly approaching when natural resources will no longer be willingly exchanged on markets. Hotly contested preferential goods such as iron ore deposits will one day be worth more than battleships.[67]

For Rathenau and others, commodity chains were to be nationalized and, ominously, militarized—a direct outcome of the tight embrace between reconstructed capital and reconstructed states.

Advocates for colonial expansion harped on raw materials. When, in 1903, French cotton manufacturers created the Association Cotonnière Coloniale, they positioned it as the solution to the United States' domination of the world's cotton markets.[68] Similar associations emerged in Belgium, Italy, and Germany, where the Kolonialwirtschaftliches Komitee, supported by Germany's cotton industry and the imperial government, encouraged colonial cotton production.[69] The response to the "American danger," argued the Belgian journalist Prosper de Haulleville, was to colonize Africa: "We can soon expect an economic rupture between Europe and America, an intolerable oppression of the Old World by the New," but "[f]ortunately Europe has found in Africa her terrain of defense."[70]

Africa's potential as a consumer market was also important. Africans and European settlers would provide a captive and expanding pool of customers for European-manufactured goods, and unlike the former

European colonies in North America, Africa would remain a subordinate market for ever more productive European industries. By the 1880s, this thinking was orthodoxy.[71] King Leopold believed that Belgium was dependent "on its ability to exploit overseas markets and resources."[72] Without colonial markets, worried Naumann, Germans would "lose our heavy industry."[73] Africa, in the minds of many European capital owners and statesmen, was a new "commodity frontier"—a region of uncommodified land and labor awaiting its integration into a new stage of European capitalism.[74] Africa would be a new "New World," the European response to the powerful emergence of the old "New World."

These concerns played a significant role in the efforts to occupy African territory that unfolded in the last decades of the nineteenth century. For centuries, Europeans had been constrained, with few exceptions, to a few coastal settlements in Africa. "They did not go inland," as the revealingly named *Journal of Race Development* put it, looking back across the entire nineteenth century.[75] But with the partition of Africa by European powers and with the United States at the Berlin Conference in 1884, things began to change. The goal, as stated at the conference, was to "capture the interior."[76] To dominate this hinterland and the people who inhabited it, state structures—including military garrisons and bureaucracies—had to be forged, which required that territory be "nationalized" in ways similar to the incorporation of North America, where territorial control had supplanted informal trade networks with Native Americans. It was not sufficient to traffic with African merchants for the products of African agriculture; rather, production had to be controlled by European capital owners.[77] And, as in the United States, that integration of the hinterland could go hand in hand with differences in rights, political economies, and labor regimes. The Berlin Conference wrote the epitaph for Europe's previous efforts to integrate Africa into the global economy through mechanisms of Smithian trade. As a Lagos newspaper put it in 1891, from the perspective of the considerable African commercial establishment in that city, "[a] forcible possession of our land has taken the place of a forcible possession of our person."[78]

In French West Africa, to cite one prominent example, territorial enclosures became the goal of colonial rule. In what is now Côte d'Ivoire, the French aimed to integrate a vast hinterland just fifty years after taking control of the port city of Grand-Bassam.[79] When colonial administrator Louis-Gustave Binger arrived in 1893, an old-fashioned trading entrepôt was no longer enough: His confidential instructions from the Ministry of Colonies in Paris tasked him with the "methodical penetration of territories . . . under our domination."[80] In nearby Senegal, "penetration" was also the goal: When Louis Léon César Faidherbe, French governor of Senegal in the 1850s and 1860s, looked back on his career in 1889, he asserted that he had been ahead of his time, writing that "I showed myself to be a partisan of penetration." This assessment was confirmed by a fellow colonial bureaucrat who remembered Faidherbe's "tenacity" and "generous ardor which he brought to facilitate, encourage and reward all that could contribute to the development of the wealth of Senegal."[81] Faidherbe transformed a French colonial effort focused on trade to one focused on territorial control, generating, among other things, a vast expansion of peanut production for export.[82]

Military control, infrastructure development, and administrative and bureaucratic diffusion all aimed to facilitate the dispersion of capital into various hinterlands—and, in time, stimulate their fields and mines to churn out commodities for metropolitan markets. This was partly motivated by the perceived failure of the commercial strategy of previous decades. There was a widespread sense among French imperialists that French power in West Africa had been too compromised by the continued influence of local rulers and traders. In an 1850 book that advocated for direct rule, Baron Rodolphe Darricau pointedly asked: "Will Senegal be a colony or a simple trading post?"[83] Émile Pinet-Laprade, who commanded the former slave-trading island of Gorée in 1864 and served twice as governor of Senegal, complained that French merchants "suffered humiliations, violent acts, and abuses of all kinds by native chiefs."[84] Military power would help French merchants secure their trade by limiting local leaders' power. In 1861, upon

The Black man's burden II: making a hinterland,
West Africa, 1898.

the conclusion of a successful military campaign in Senegal's hinterland, Pinet-Laprade celebrated the French triumph: "The arrogant
peoples who dared provoke us into combat are today trembling at our
feet; they beg for peace and the protection of France."[85] The
Waalo-Waalo, who had successfully resisted the plantation experiments of the 1820s, were now ruled directly by the French.[86]

Military power, the result of new inequalities in the capacity to
wage war on land (repeating weapons such as the Gatling gun prominent among them), was important to this newfound ability to control
the hinterland, but so was greater administrative and bureaucratic capacity. As in Hokkaido, accumulating knowledge came first: The land
and its people had to be mapped and surveyed as the colonial state focused on understanding and then expanding its colonies' productive
capacity. Colonial states also devised new administrative structures of
governance, building bureaucracies akin to the vertically and horizontally integrated corporations emerging elsewhere. As the French colonial administration for West Africa asserted, such innovation was
necessary "to maintain the unity of command, the fusion of interest,
the spirit of order, speed, and enterprise."[87] Novel taxation regimes
were usually among the first interventions: Tribute payments, which

had implicitly acknowledged local rulers as independent centers of power, were replaced by direct taxes on subjects, to be paid in cash or labor.[88] New infrastructures were important to this project as well, including not only improvements to the port of Saint-Louis in the northern part of the colony but also the construction of a railroad from Saint-Louis to Dakar, a project that Faidherbe believed was long overdue—as early as 1853, he had complained that "[t]he Americans would have established a railroad here long ago."[89] Although this new phase of colonial rule only came to fruition in the 1880s, Faidherbe was celebrated as a prophet of the new age: "[Y]ou have broken the barriers that barbarity opposes to civilization," a Parisian journalist penned admiringly.[90]

While Europeans focused their colonial enclosure projects on Africa, Japan's efforts at territorially reconstructing its economy focused on East Asia. Hokkaido and Okinawa were its first steps, but more followed: In 1874, Japan started a "punitive" expedition to Taiwan, and in 1876, it sent gunboats to Korea to force the signing of the Treaty of Kanghwa.[91] Following the Sino-Japanese War of 1894–1895, Japan established colonial rule over Taiwan, and after its war with Russia in 1904–1905, the country established a protectorate over Korea and later colonized that country as well. Japan also gained control of the Kwantung Leased Territory and the South Manchurian Railway Zone in China.

Like elsewhere, these colonial enclosures were the result of deliberate planning: Being a properly modern industrial nation, Japanese statesmen believed, meant following the American and European model of continental-scale enclosures to access raw materials and markets. Politician and military leader Kodama Gentarō saw colonial policy as a form of economic warfare, supplying resources necessary for waging wars: "Taiwan cannot ignore the challenge of economic warfare, the trend so prevalent in the world today," he argued.[92] The business journal *Ekonomisuto*, looking back from the vantage point of 1938, confirmed the importance of this move: "[S]ince the 1870s Japan has relied on continental policy for both the survival and the development of Japanese capitalism."[93] Reconstructed capitalism, that journal and others declared, required new forms of territoriality. As Japanese foreign minister Inoue Kaoru contended in 1887:

> The [European] countries are all devoting their power more and more to the colonization and development of overseas territories. . . . In India, Cambodia, Cochin-China, and elsewhere, the weak become prey for the strong. . . . During the past three or four years the European countries have expanded their power into Asia and Africa more than ever before, and they are brandishing their power in the Far East as well.[94]

Like their European and American counterparts, the Japanese rhetorically embraced a "civilizing mission"—earnestly felt, in its way, but ultimately a thin veneer masking self-serving interests.[95] Japanese business analysts believed that territorial expansion—especially the forging of an integrated economic bloc including Japan, Manchuria, Taiwan, Korea, and parts of China—was necessary for Japan's survival. As a result of this focus on lands, peoples, and commodities, Hokkaido became a significant supplier of fertilizer that enhanced agricultural productivity in Honshu, which in turn helped foster Japan's industrialization. Markets for the crucial textile industry were sought and found in colonial settings. Financial penetration followed as well: The Hokkaido Colonial Bank, the Bank of Korea, and the Bank of Taiwan all channeled metropolitan capital into the colonies—sometimes generating significant profits. In Manchuria, as the Japanese aimed to commercialize agriculture, capital flowed into the South Manchurian Railway, which carried millet, sorghum, coal, and, especially, soybeans to Japan and Europe. Its first quarter century was so profitable that its rate of return hovered between 20 and 30 percent annually.[96] By the 1920s, the railroad's revenue equaled a quarter of the Japanese state's tax revenue, making it and other colonial companies among the largest and most profitable of all Japanese enterprises.[97]

Taiwan's sugar industry was another example of enhancement. Encouraged by Taiwan's centuries-long tradition of growing sugar (since at least the beginning of Dutch rule in 1624), Japan transformed its island colony into a supplier of agricultural commodities, hoping to eliminate its need to import sugar. When Japan conquered Taiwan in 1895, rapid sugar growth followed. In 1870, when the island was under Qing rule, total sugar exports had been around 18,500 tons. Just seventy years later, they stood at 1.4 million tons—seventy-six times as much. One-fifth of Taiwan's agricultural lands had been turned into sugar fields. Japan now grew enough sugar in its empire to spur a significant increase in sugar consumption (albeit still much below European levels) and a thriving export business.[98]

As was common in reconstructed capitalism, the Japanese government had cooperated with private investors but taken the lead in building up the sugar industry. Under the management of US- and German-trained agricultural economist Inazō Nitobe, Japan constructed agricultural laboratories and experimental farms and invested in roads, harbors, and railroads. Subsidies, loans, tax benefits, and protective tariffs to encourage Japanese investments in the sugar industry came next.[99]

In typical fashion, the colonial administration started by creating clear-cut private property rights in land. Property rights in Taiwan had been ill-defined, even overlapping—to Inazō, a telltale sign that many of the locals were "savages."[100] The Japanese surveyed the land, and if a farmer could not prove ownership of a particular piece of property, it was confiscated and auctioned off. The result was that large Japanese investors soon owned one hundred thousand hectares of Taiwanese sugar lands—10 percent of the island's farmland. Large investments followed, with the Taiwan Sugar Corporation and the Mitsui family, among others, cutting out local Chinese capital owners to dominate the island's sugar complex.[101]

By 1902, the Japanese government had developed an elaborate system of control, splitting up the country into what it called "cane supply regions." To minimize competition between sugar producers, it gave

Moving sugarcane to the factory: Japanese sugar colonialism in Taiwan.

each company monopoly rights over sugar produced in a given region. Peasants were allowed to deliver cane only to the designated company in their area, thus reducing competition that tended to favor the farmer. There was no market: Companies would instead stipulate a guaranteed (but low) buying price for sugarcane at the beginning of the growing season. While farmers could decide not to grow sugarcane, they were under pressure to do so, not least because access to irrigation water was limited to farmers who produced for factories. The system was hugely profitable for the Japanese companies but not so much for the growers. It has been estimated that a hectare of sugarcane produced a profit of about 722 yen for the company and only 124 yen for the grower. By 1909, the government-supported Sugar Industry Association of Taiwan—a trust—coordinated the industry. Two hundred and fifty years after the end of Dutch rule, sugar production for export was again the mainstay of the island's economy. So successful had the project proved that it became a model for further colonial transformations in Manchuria and Korea, with the South Manchuria Sugar Manufacturing Company (Minami Manshū Seitō Kabushiki Kaisha) created in 1916 and the Korea Sugar Manufacturing Company (Chōsen Seitō Kabushiki Kaisha) two years later. Colonial enclosures—with their imperial control of new territories, their encasement of markets and social groups, and their delimiting of formerly common lands—became an important form of reconstructed capitalism.[102] In a 1912 article in *The Journal of Race Development*, Inazō, who had headed Taiwan's Sugar Industry Bureau, proudly advertised the great skill by which the Japanese had turned Taiwan into a producer of export commodities and concluded that now, the island "is to us a necessity."[103]

By the 1880s, a small subset of states had shaped the global economy in new and deeply hierarchical ways predicated on constructing enclosed, typically imperial economic spaces across different state structures, sets of rights, and labor regimes. Despite superficial similarities, these efforts were fundamentally different from earlier colonial projects, most decisively, as economist Werner Sombart pointed out, because imperialism provided "capitalism [with] the aid of strong state power" to "grow into the formidable force that it has become today."[104]

A good example of this change is Nigeria, first claimed by the (British) Royal Niger Company, chartered in 1886. Much like the East India Company and other earlier private/public partnerships, this company had the right to make treaties and take on statelike functions in the territories it controlled. In a sign that a return to the past had become impossible, however, the British state took over the company's sovereign rights in

King Soap governs Congolese plantations, 1913.

1895. The Royal Niger Company—reduced to a regular business enterprise—became the Niger Company. The Lever Brothers acquired it in 1920 and turned it into the United Africa Company in 1929; it eventually became part of Unilever, still a multinational today.[105] The state, as it asserted its power over territories and people, no longer allowed for private territorial sovereignty.

King Leopold of Belgium's claims to Congo, as discussed, were initially also reminiscent of earlier war capitalism, when private individuals ruled distant territories and peoples. His Association Internationale du Congo declared control over a vast territory and its diverse peoples in 1882; it was a private business undertaking (financed by Swiss banks, among others) that did the work of colonialization, including assuming sovereign rights. Contemporary legal experts struggled to come to terms with this seemingly old-fashioned arrangement. In 1884, grappling with the question of "whether the agent of an association which had not the political character of a State could, by a cession of the actual sovereign of the country, acquire and exercise the sovereignty of a territory situated outside of Europe," the United States Senate cited European settlers' claims to sovereignty in North America a few centuries earlier to support Leopold's power grab.[106] They were encouraged to do so by the testimony of English jurist Sir Travers Twiss and his Belgian counterpart, Egide Arntz, who affirmed that "a concession [can] be made to a private citizen."[107] "Why should it be forbidden to a native chief to cede his territory to an international European company," Twiss asked, "which, according to the law of nations, is perfectly capable of accepting and exercising such sovereignty?"[108] But King Leopold's resurrection of war capitalism collapsed in short order (though not before it killed or maimed millions of Congolese people), and by 1908, the Belgian state formally controlled the territory. Private claims to territory became increasingly illegitimate. Instead of sovereigns, corporations became nationals of states. In reconstructed capitalism, companies and states constituted each other, distinct but mutually dependent entities, each with its own sharply demarcated realm.[109]

In fact, it was the state that played the crucial role in enclosure, using an entirely new arsenal of powers that not even the mightiest states or companies a century earlier had possessed. There are many examples of this newfound presence and power: In Ceylon, the colonial administration built infrastructure to transport first coffee and then tea to the coast for export. In British Columbia, European settlers used the law and brute military force to drive Indigenous peoples off their lands and capture their labor power. The theft was brazen. As the British governor of the colony of Vancouver Island signed treaties with various groups of Indigenous peoples to cede their lands, the latter agreed, among other things, that "it is understood however that the land itself, with these small exceptions, becomes the entire property of the white people for Ever."[110] In La Réunion, the state-chartered Parisian bank Crédit Foncier Colonial provided long-term credit to planters, anticipating later Japanese efforts in Taiwan and Korea to energize and expand commercial agriculture. In the Punjab, the British built seventeen thousand miles of canals to bring in enough water for the growth of cotton and wheat, increasing irrigated land by a factor of about six between 1878 and 1918. Colonists also penetrated the newly captured territory with statistical science: To turn Punjabi peasants into tax-paying subjects, the British surveyed the land, ascertained its productivity in painstaking detail, determined the agricultural skills of various populations, and assessed the irrigation systems—all to set taxes that were payable only in currency and not, as before, in goods. In Fiji, the British colonial government focused on legitimizing and formalizing land claims. As early as the 1840s, settlers had begun claiming ownership of Fiji lands, at first small plots on islands just offshore that were used as trading entrepôts. During the cotton boom of the 1860s, British cotton-growing planters acquired coastal strips of land from Indigenous rulers who, in dire need of funds for weaponry to fight one another, often "sold" the lands of their enemies. Once Britain took formal control of Fiji in 1874, a land claims commission investigated these properties and made them permanent. In the 1890s, in southern Chile's Patagonia, sheep-raising capital owners, with the support of the Chilean state, enclosed the land, undermining the ability of the Indigenous Selk'nam and Haush to subsist by consuming the wild guanaco; when they resisted, the Sociedad Explotadora de Tierra del Fuego, a settler-funded ranching company, deemed them "uncivilized" and began killing them. In faraway Siam, British logging companies, aided by British diplomatic interventions, successfully claimed new rights to log teak trees in the forests around Chiang Mai, muscling out Chinese merchants and local princes. Between 1873 and 1876, they exported 5,600 cubic meters of teakwood exported through Bangkok; between 1905 and 1909 exports peaked at 122,000.[111] The boom put enormous pressure on the forests, which had already started showing signs of depletion by the 1890s.

The newly assertive and powerful colonial states did not just enclose people and land, but also animals. In the Punjab, in a decades-long and contentious process, determined state action removed animals from open pastures and streets to fenced lands, stables, and homes. Before these colonial enclosures, cattle had been communally owned, and property rights were fluid. When the British came to the Punjab in 1849, they initially adjusted to these traditions, but it was not long before they turned cattle into private property and policed that property through new laws. In 1862, the Indian Penal Code made cattle theft a property crime. By the 1870s, the colonial administration criminalized collective Indigenous claims to property. The Evidence Act of 1872 then formalized how cattle theft was to be investigated by the police and the courts.[112] And by the 1890s, colonial officials had branded millions of animals, aiming for "absolute notions of ownership."[113]

A seemingly small technical innovation had an outsize impact on this radical project of enclosure: barbed wire. In 1857, John Grinning, an iron foundry worker from Austin, Texas, was the first person to incorporate barbed wire into fencing by attaching sharp metal pieces to wire. Others improved on his design, patented it, and then spread it around the world, facilitating the inexpensive fencing of large pastures to keep cattle in and other animals out. By 1877, Washburn & Moen Manufacturing Company and other US manufacturers produced almost thirteen million pounds of barbed wire. The industry quickly went worldwide, with wire fences built in Rio de Janeiro in 1877 and throughout Australia in 1880.[114]

Barbed wire enabled the enclosure of vast stretches of land and livestock, undermining the livelihoods of pastoralists the world over. In the British-dominated hinterlands of the Cape Colony at the southern tip of Africa, this transformation involved separating cows from the land on which they grazed, turning both land and animals into separately tradable commodities. In the Pedi polity of the Eastern Transvaal, cattle had long been an important store of wealth, a symbol of prestige, and a political tool, but under colonial rule, the venerated cow was reduced to private property. This enclosure of cattle (and their grazing lands) had begun under Boer rule, when ownership of cows was newly tracked by certificates of sale, registrations by auctioneers, and rough marks carved into cows' hides. When Boers claimed dominion over Pedi grazing lands and extracted rents and harsh tenancies from existing Indigenous villages, they violently brought cattle under their jurisdiction. Public debt also worked to enclose grazing lands: In the 1860s and '70s, the Boers' South African Republic issued public debt backed by promises of land titles, putting pressure on land users to formalize their claims. Black Africans at the same time were legally barred from owning land, and the government introduced an anti-squatting law in 1870.[115]

At the end of the century, a combined economic, epidemiological, and military assault sounded the death knell for communal cattle holdings. A viral cow disease—the rinderpest—killed up to 90 percent of cattle in the Cape Colony, eliminating in one generation the collective capital of smallholders and forcing many villagers to abandon their communal holdings to look for waged work. Then, in 1899, the Boer republics declared war on the British Empire, setting off another round of expropriation. Boers and Black tenant farmers used the conflict to assert their differing conceptions of bovine property, raiding and claiming what few cattle remained in the Transvaal. Indigenous people systematically destroyed the beacons that marked property lines.[116]

The ultimate peace treaty left wealthy white farmers in a privileged position, as the British further formalized pastoral property. The Brands Ordinance of 1904, designed to make cattle thefts more traceable, established a registry of brands burned into animal flesh. The practice of seasonally shifting herds to grazing grounds, which had already begun to be replaced by more fixed cultivation systems before the war, was abandoned. To curtail more epidemics, the British established veterinary authority to track imports of cattle and separate herds. The British also subsidized rail rates for fencing materials and made snipping a wire fence punishable by six months of jail time. From 1905 to 1906, more than fifteen hundred miles of fencing went up, and Black Africans lost control of their lands and cattle. Dispossession was ongoing, but by 1910, the collapse of communal holdings was irreversible.[117]

In all these enclosures, the law played a crucial role: It defined new forms of property, supported the claims of some people over others, and mobilized resources for commercial activities of all kinds. Land law secured claims to property in Fiji; contract law allowed for the insertion of metropolitan capital into the cotton-growing Indian countryside; and new taxation regimes forced cultivators into market production everywhere.

That law, of course, was made and imposed by the colonizers as powerful colonial states marginalized Indigenous legal traditions and customs. With the conclusion of the Opium Wars, Britain imposed new legal mechanisms on Chinese commercial transactions, pushing the logic of capital, instead of the logic of statecraft, into the Chinese countryside.[118] When Britain remade Burma, once a subsistence economy, into a major rice exporter, one of its first moves was to impose a new legal order. Burma's prior, well-developed legal system was informed by customs and religious beliefs and included courts and professional lawyers. The British slowly dismantled and replaced this system using the laws they had developed in the process of colonializing India, laws focused on enforceable property rights and contracts. After 1891, the British legal system took over almost all conflict resolution in Burma, disempowering the village headman and traditional administrators of justice. It was a dramatic change: Under Burmese law, an owner who had to sell land could reacquire it as soon as they had the resources to do so, as the buyer could not resell that land to a third party without the original owner's consent. In traditional law, contracts had to be not only legally binding but also "just." The British changes had ill effects on rural cultivators, who were increasingly enmeshed in debt and thus vulnerable to foreclosure.[119] Law became a powerful tool of dispossession and disempowerment.

UNSURPRISINGLY, THESE MASS enclosures met massive resistance. After all, until the late nineteenth century, despite the awe-inspiring advances of the empire of capital and states, many of the world's people still lived beyond their reach. They had different ideas about property and lived within political structures of their own making. Conflicts between Indigenous people and settlers became common—in the American West and southern Africa, in British Columbia and Morocco, in Burma and Hokkaido.[120]

Their resistance reminds us that the global seepage of capitalism into the nooks and crannies of many societies was not the result of a "natural" expansion of self-propelling markets, as many contemporary myths hold. Instead, the state engineered multiple forms of enclosure, envelopment, and encasement that drove capitalism's spread, often pursuing policies with a pronounced anti-market twist. As alternative forms of organizing political and economic life proved no match for capitalism's proliferation, a once multipolar world rapidly became brutally hierarchical. Perhaps most consequentially, colonial enclosures diminished local state power in vast swaths of the world, further amplifying these hierarchies. State power did not just intensify; it concentrated.

These disparities allowed small parts of the world to further accumulate wealth, state power, and technologies, thus begetting still further inequalities. Economic hierarchies shaped by colonialism became sources of capital, allowing for the amassing of even more wealth in Europe, Japan, and the United States. As we saw earlier, Britain had long drawn significant wealth from its Indian holdings and continued to do so. It has been estimated that between 1871 and 1916 alone, 3.2 billion pounds were transferred from India to Britain. Economist Utsa Patnaik additionally estimated that this drain amounted to 9.2 trillion pounds between 1765 and 1938. France derived 5 percent of its GDP from foreign possessions between 1900 and 1914, and while this seems low, it equaled the contribution of all the industries of northern and eastern France. In early twentieth-century France, between one-fourth and one-fifth of property was owned abroad; in 1912, between a quarter and a third of Parisians' international investments were located in France's colonies. In the Netherlands, during the 1870s, one-third of state revenue derived from Java. Investments begot income: Between 1905 and 1939, British overseas investments contributed between 5 and 10 percent to the national income. British investments in Africa—at least in the short term—produced significant profits: The rate of return (in real terms) of some seven hundred British companies invested in Africa was slightly more than 10 percent in the 1870s and 15 percent in the 1880s, falling to about 6 percent in the 1890s. These were not the enormous profits that have been cited as the wages of colonialism, yet particular investments—the diamond fields of South Africa, the Suez Canal, copper mining—were substantially more profitable than most domestic investments. And African mining ventures were more profitable than mining ventures anywhere else.[121]

Returns small and big made global inequalities in wealth and state power more pronounced than ever before. As industrialized nations brought ever more territories under their control, they created a radically unbalanced distribution of state power across the world—the same state power that was now essential to maintaining a competitive productive economy. Imperialism devoured lesser centers of power; its destruction of states was as significant as its capturing of markets and resources. As late as the second half of the eighteenth century, the Global South had accounted for 70 percent of world manufacturing; by 1950, at the nadir of a long period of decline, it was just 10 percent. In

1820, China and India had still produced about half of the world's GDP, while Europe and the United States had contributed a quarter. By 1913, however, Europe and the United States produced about 57 percent of the world's output; India and China, just 16 percent.[122] For the Global South, the reconstruction of capitalism inaugurated an age of calamity. It was stuck exporting commodities as trade terms grew worse. When Algerian intellectual Frantz Fanon drew up an account of these devastations in *Les damnés de la terre*, published in 1961, he concluded that "Europe is literally the creation of the Third World" and European "riches" the result of an ongoing process of plunder.[123]

Colonial subjects critiquing colonialism focused on these massive dispossessions and sharpened hierarchies. Born and raised in Bombay, Dadabhai Naoroji—teacher, writer, sometime merchant, and eventual member of British Parliament—was among the earliest, formulating his "drain theory," which chronicled the mechanisms through which India's wealth was siphoned off to Britain. W. E. B. Du Bois, in many ways Naoroji's American counterpart, showed how the construction of racial hierarchies in the United States and abroad had enabled the transfer of resources and power on a spectacular scale. Du Bois and Naoroji were but two voices in an increasingly globalized politics that drew in activists and intellectuals from all continents, and both were outspoken critics of exploitation and racism, no matter where they occurred and who was affected. Naoroji interacted with, among many others, American activist Ida B. Wells and Trinidadian Henry Sylvester Williams. After Naoroji spoke at the 1906 Calcutta Congress, Du Bois printed Naoroji's speech in his magazine, *The Horizon*, in Washington, DC.[124] These politics and solidarities would eventually radically reshape global capitalism, but that process would take decades.

The states that enclosed many of the territories and peoples of the world were also crucial to capitalism's reconstruction in the industrial heartlands. Turn-of-the-century reconstructions of capital and of labor rested on states that had a taste for a much broader scope of action and developed the technologies to enable it. These states penetrated and then enclosed their chosen turfs in novel ways. Even in the United States, often described as having a feeble federal government, the state's alleged weakness was a myth.[125]

Colonial expansion often fed into increased state power. In the United States, capturing the vast Western territories increased state capacity—all that surveying, mapping, fighting, infrastructure building, legislating, and land enclosing in areas remote from the industrial heartlands created capabilities, resources, and templates that left a deep imprint on the machinery of the American state. While the precise mechanisms were different elsewhere, Britain, France, Germany, Italy, Belgium, and the Netherlands also drew state strength from colonial expansions. The feedback loop between the colonial integration of a hinterland and state development in the heartland existed in Japan as well: When Japan and China signed the Treaty of Shimonoseki after their war in 1895, Japan claimed an indemnity of 360 million yen, or 4.5 times its 1893 government budget.[126] This windfall allowed for, among many other things, significant investments in the infrastructures and textile factories that were crucial to Japan's industrial takeoff.

Historian Charles S. Maier called the modern nation-state "the most efficient engine of expansion and governance that the world had seen." Enabled by new technologies, especially the railroad and the telegraph, and by new bureaucratic and administrative capacities—policing, taxation, statistics, and education, to name just a few—an invigorated state infused all realms of late nineteenth-century heartland capitalism.[127]

A good index of the growth of the state and its role in the remaking of capitalism can be found in tax revenues. They increased in the United States by a factor of 19 between 1860 and 1910 (including both federal and state taxes); in Prussia-Germany, by a factor of 13; in the United Kingdom, by a factor of 3; and in France (1870–1910), by a factor of 1.8. Government spending also grew: By 1910, it amounted to 16 percent of national income in Germany, 15 percent in France, 12 percent in the United Kingdom, between 7 and 11 percent in Japan, and 8.2 percent in the United States.[128] State expenditures per capita at constant prices approximately doubled between 1860 and 1910 in France, Germany, and the United Kingdom; they quintupled in the United States. By 1910, all these states were also significant employers of labor. Even without counting its substantial military forces, the French government employed 2.14 percent of its citizens; the British state, 2.6 percent; Germany, 1.57 percent; and the United States, 1.68 percent. No other entity joined personnel and resources to an even remotely comparable degree; the late nineteenth century was a launching pad for a spectacular flourishing of capitalism's institution of institutions—the state, refreshed after the fires of the midcentury rebellions. At the same time, new groups—capital owners and representatives of the working class—entered political and administrative positions, serving shoulder to shoulder with older, more established power holders, especially the aristocracy.[129]

State power infused once-isolated corners of society, often taking the form of efforts to better understand increasingly complex societies. States mapped their territories, counted their people, and assessed the productive potential of their lands. Censuses, geographic surveys, and property registers allowed administrators to understand, then govern, their territory and residents; to mobilize resources; and to tax, police, and coordinate them.[130] State powers even altered the very notion of time: In 1884, the International Meridian Conference met in Washington, DC, under the auspices of President Chester A. Arthur to determine the location of a zero meridian (it ended up in Greenwich, England), allowing for the standardization of time zones throughout the world.[131] Millions of people began measuring time not by the movement of the sun but by the fiat of their home state—a symbol of its awesome power.

Japan is a good example of this reconstructed nation-state and its new relationship to capital. Before 1868, the island country had a largely tributary society with powerful lords who controlled individual domains and were loosely federated under the Tokugawa shogun. Despite tentative forays into industrial development and a longer history of proto-industrialization and commercialization, Japan was still a society in which capitalism had not spread much beyond its island fortresses.

With the Meiji Restoration, essentially a revolution, the Japanese state was rebuilt from the ground up. The new rulers centralized power in ways far different from the feudal fiefs that had governed the archipelago of capital. They developed new postal and police systems; launched investments in economic development; and developed infrastructure across Japan, including railroads. They jump-started a novel banking system with the National Banking Act of 1872 and opened new banks, including the government-controlled Bank of Japan and the Industrial Bank of Japan, to channel economic development. Significant investments in industry followed, amounting to between 30 and 40 percent of all capital investments. In particular, the government targeted telegraphs, steel production (notably symbolized by the 1901 opening of the state-owned Yawata Iron and Steelworks), and the shipping and cotton industries. This reorientation of the state toward the interests of capitalist elites was extended by the forging of alliances between new business leaders and older aristocratic groups, giving capital owners access to political power. It was hardly surprising that economic nationalists like German Friedrich List became guiding stars to Japanese policymakers. And their models worked: Japan's GDP grew by a factor of 2.8 between 1885 and 1920.[132]

As state power in Japan and other places intensified, it also became more nationalist, focused on integrating its respective national territory and creating national markets. Infrastructure was crucial to this project, especially railroads, which knit together economic and political spaces and diffused state power across the national territory. In the United States, to cite an extreme example, land grants to railroads equaled the size of the states of Texas and California combined, but the US was not alone—everywhere, these nation-building infrastructures rested on state support.[133]

Great infrastructure projects did not just open a national territory to the empire of capital; they also enclosed that territory with fortified demarcations—firmly defining economic and political spaces. Other forms of boundary codification included tariffs, national regulations of business enterprises, and the delineations of entirely new forms of property. This nationalization of economic space was also visible when it came to gathering information: Economic statistics both described and constructed the idea of a "national" economy, encouraging economists, as well as latter-day economic historians reliant on this data, to conceive of the economy and of capitalism in nationalist terms.[134] Our present-day view of capitalism was shaped by the very processes described in this chapter.

The law played an ever more prominent role as capitalism became a legally constituted social order. As English theorist John Robert Seeley explained in 1883, "[P]roperty can exist only under the guardianship of the state." And under the guardianship of the state, new forms of corporate law produced new forms of property, providing the legal basis for the reconstruction of capital. In the antebellum American South, new crop lien laws gave merchants novel control over the products of farmers, especially their cotton, in return for advances—a mechanism that greatly expanded market production. At the same time, new stock laws limited traditional grazing rights for livestock outside fenced fields—another mechanism that made life outside the market more difficult. New limits on hunting and fishing rights, such as Georgia's new game laws of 1872, restricted access to unenclosed lands.[135]

The law did important work in national, not just colonial, enclosures: When New York's Phelps, Dodge & Co. invested in Southern pinelands and Western mining areas in the late nineteenth century, it encountered different property rights, including yeoman farmers claiming common rights to the land and independent miners in the West claiming rights to minerals. In response, Phelps, Dodge & Co. successfully pushed for legal enclosures. In the South, Dodge's Georgia Land & Lumber Company undermined yeoman farmers' privileged access to subsistence and a system in which "household property was often determined by local knowledge," and it expended enormous efforts to claim land with uncertain title.[136] The federal government enabled Native American dispossessions in the West to make mineral claims accessible to settlers, and mining laws passed in 1872 favored the property claims of capital-intensive miners over those of small artisanal producers.[137] Fencing in land, defining boundaries, and providing clear ownership titles—all elements of the enclosure process—rendered common land less accessible and made it harder to avoid the expanding empire of capital. Then, as now, the framing of these enclosures was couched in a discourse of improvement, rationality, and civilization. In his voluminous writings, Italian economist Achille Loria theorized this relationship between enclosures and capitalism, concluding that "[w]hen free land exists, when every man can so soon as he wishes, occupy a terrain and commit his own labor for his own account, capitalist property is impossible."[138] The reconstructed state in capitalism's heartland played a key role in making such escape progressively harder.

Collectively, these legal changes simplified property rights. Around the globe, systems involving multiple uses of property and multiple claims to the same piece of property were aggressively retired. In May 1872, Germany produced its Grundbuchordnung, which regulated the acquisition of real estate property and formalized the registration of all real properties with the state. This gave lenders an enforceable security, which made it easier to mortgage land. In France, the Livre Foncier did the same work, bringing the state into all real estate transactions. Land, there and elsewhere, became real estate, and since it was territorial, it could be firmly attached to the nation-state, unlike commercial capital.[139]

Heartland capitalism's enclosures were not only about physical space; they were also about social space. As states created a new relationship to capital, they encased their workers within the nation, making special claims on their labor, loyalty, and willingness to serve in the military while also giving them access to an expanding universe of rights, powers, and claims to material support. The state enclosed labor in two key ways: First, by facilitating the proletarianization of workers, it helped turn labor into a commodity, just as it had done for land. These enclosures of people as proletarians separated capital owners from workers.[140] Second, a bundle of reforms linked workers directly to the state through education, labor law, welfare policies, and the regulation of domestic life.

In a sharp departure from the direct domination of workers by their enslavers, which had constituted the core of war capitalism, the state began inserting itself into the relationship between workers and employers in new ways. Increasingly, labor market regulation became a state-driven national project. Somewhat unexpectedly, the labor movement, despite its often internationalist rhetoric, helped further this national enclosure by organizing workers in national organizations. Along with employers and the state, national labor movements created a "national" working class: Labor's collective action became national.[141]

While proponents of welfare policies engaged in global conversations, the emerging welfare state had the net effect of attaching workers more tightly to the nation. In the United States, usually considered a laggard in these matters, a vast system of social benefits arose in the late nineteenth century, initially focused on impoverished mothers and Civil War veterans. Perhaps unsurprisingly, the particular American political and state structures produced a particular welfare state. The welfare state was different in Europe; public health insurance, for example, came to Germany in 1883 and Britain in 1911—half a century before a patchwork American counterpart emerged. Old-age insurance followed in Germany in 1889, New Zealand in 1898, and Britain and Australia in 1908.[142] It arrived in the US three decades later in the wake of the seismic earthquake that was the Great Depression. European welfare provisioning was also more centralized than in the US. The different systems, however, had one thing in common: Social provisioning was always national, reinforcing the labor movement's focus on national strategies for security and emancipation.

Another consequential development accompanied the enclosures of land, labor, capital, and state power—the enclosure of ideas about economic life. By the late nineteenth century, a new way of thinking about economic life began to emerge in Europe and the United States. Its basic tenets would become axiomatic to the academic discipline we know as "economics." The hegemony of these ideas continues to this day, resting on a revolutionary set of writings as important to modern capitalism as those of Adam Smith and Karl Marx and their disciples. These ideas not only reflected on the capitalist revolution but also participated in it.[143]

The core of this emerging view of economic life was the determination to enclose a sphere of social life—soon to be called "economics"—by making it a discrete object of analysis. This was a truly radical step: Prior economic theorizing, starting with the Greek philosopher Aristotle, had been deeply embedded in moral philosophy, theology, history, and politics. For all their disagreements, the economic thinkers of Renaissance Italy, the French physiocrats, the English political economists, and the nineteenth-century Marxists agreed that analysis of economic life had to be rooted in a broader set of historical, sociological, political, and moral considerations. There were huge differences between Antonio Serra's 1613 *Breve trattato* and François Quesnay's 1758 *Tableau économique*, between David Ricardo and Pierre-Joseph Proudhon, between Smith and Marx, but they shared an intellectual universe that was strikingly different from the one being defined in the late nineteenth century. These changes involved the naturalization of the capitalist economy, its dehistoricization, and what might be called its microfication—that is, its intense focus on individuals and their preferences, what economist Joseph Schumpeter called "methodological individualism."[144]

So radical were these shifts that they are considered a revolution—the "marginalist revolution." Making undiluted markets in which rational actors maximized their utility the linchpin of their modeling, these thinkers laid the groundwork for what they came to call "micro-economics" and "neoclassical economics." Their moves opened new ways of thinking about economic life under capitalism, but at the cost of flattening the rich diversity of economic life into a homogenous, ahistorical desert. And the flattening allowed for yet another consequential move—quantification and mathematification—that let economists cloak their work in the authority of its allegedly scientific method.

This new orientation emerged in different parts of the world almost simultaneously: Its beginnings can be traced most usefully to England and William Stanley Jevons's 1871 *Theory of Political Economy*, to Austria and Menger's 1871 *Principles of Economics*, and to France and Léon Walras's 1874 *Elements of Pure Economics*. American John Bates Clark followed suit in 1886 with his *Philosophy of Wealth: Economic Principles Newly Formulated*, trailed by Alfred Marshall's 1890 *Principles of Economics*, which emphasized demand and supply, and then Irving Fisher and his 1892 Yale doctoral dissertation, *Mathematical Investigations in the Theory of Value and Prices*.

Marginalism responded to two distinct sets of changes that threatened existing theories. First, a theoretical crisis was brewing in the field of political economy. The Ricardian–Malthusian "natural wage" doctrine, which held that wages are naturally pushed to the subsistence level through demographic pressures, had been proved false by the developments of the late century. Populations increased, but so did wages. Moreover, a "historical school" of political economists had emerged that aimed to analyze the differences between economic systems across time—quite different from Smith and Ricardo's more axiomatic approach. The German Historical School, in particular, spawned an institutionalist, comparative, and historical analysis of capitalism that included luminaries such as Max Weber and Gustav von Schmoller. The early marginalists, in contrast, were vehemently opposed to what they saw as the imprecise methodology of the German Historical School, insisting on the necessity of modeling economics on the natural sciences.[145]

Second, the economic crisis of the early 1870s had escalated social conflict while leading to an increase in state spending, the regularization of unions, and an expansion of the franchise. Marginalism provided tools to assess specific state spending and regulatory policies without having to resolve questions of class interest. Its more rigid, quantified, and ahistorical approach was an attempt to insulate economic policy from contestable political interests and values.[146]

The resulting "marginalist revolution" occurred in two stages.[147] During the first, running roughly from 1865 to 1885, some economists explicitly challenged the classical orthodoxy. Jevons, Walras, and Menger articulated subjectivist notions of economic value—a break with the dominant labor theory of value embraced by Smith, Ricardo, and Marx. Unlike classical political economy, which held a commodity's value to be an objective fact determined by the difficulty of production or the time required to produce it, the marginalists posited that commodities derived their value from their subjective usefulness to consumers. According to Jevons, the most important factor determining the price of a product was how much extra pleasure, or "marginal utility," a consumer obtained from using an extra unit of the commodity (hence the name). Individual purchasers, he argued, signaled this marginal utility to sellers through the price they were willing to pay.[148] Goods, they assumed, have diminishing marginal utility (i.e., every additional unit consumed would provide slightly less satisfaction than the previous one, meaning that as the quantity increased, the price consumers would pay per unit decreased).

The marginalists argued they could quantify the pleasure that goods provided for consumers and therefore study utility in a universally valid and ahistorical manner. They shifted the primary question of economics from the classical Smithian problem—the problem of how a system of accumulation with a division of labor could continue expanding—to the problem of how scarce resources should be allocated; they changed the unit of analysis from classes operating in society as a whole to individual economic agents such as firms or consumers. Italian economist Piero Sraffa accurately described marginalism as an economic theory that moved from the problem of production to that of consumption. Its core theoretical innovation was to see the consumer's view of the utility of a good—rather than labor input—as determinative of price.[149]

At first, these ideas were met with skepticism. "Utility," as the marginalists had suggested, was impossible to measure, according to the *Encyclopedia Britannica*'s 1885 edition, and such "researches . . . will never be anything more than academic playthings."[150] The second stage of the marginalist revolution, however, achieved the institutionalization of this previously heterodox theory, with the establishment of a neoclassical orthodoxy in the final years of the nineteenth century. The key figure in this sea change was Alfred Marshall at the University of Cambridge. Marshall reconciled the subjectivist approach of the early marginalists with some tenets of classical political economy by developing what is now called "microeconomics." His concept of "partial equilibrium" showed how the supply of a commodity balanced with its marginal utility to consumers.[151] He achieved this by dividing the economy into independent "industries," within which firms produced similar goods and therefore competed with one another. For any and every industry, supply-and-demand curves could chart the price that consumers would pay for different quantities of the commodity and the readiness of a hypothetical "representative firm" to supply the commodity at various prices.[152] Setting the price at the level where the two lines of the graph intersected maximized the additional utility for both consumers and producers: There would be a "consumer surplus" of utility, as consumers would be buying the commodity at a lower price than the maximum they would hypothetically be willing to pay, alongside a "producer surplus," as producers would be providing the commodity at a higher price than their professed minimum.[153] While classical political economy had focused on the dynamism of accumulation in the economy as a whole, Marshall's segmentation of the economy allowed him to posit an equilibrium point within particular industries that optimized producer and consumer satisfaction.

Marshall's reinterpretation of the classical political economists made marginalism palatable to a larger group of classically schooled economists. Its influence grew even further under the influence of Ir-

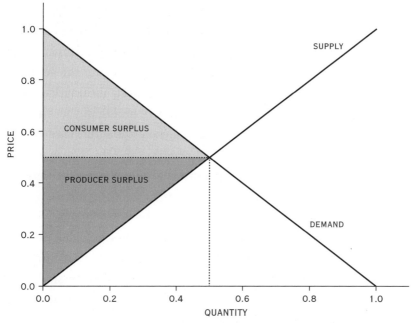

*Marshall's consumer and producer surplus, showing how utility
is maximized at an equilibrium price within a single industry.*

ving Fisher, a young American economist who suggested that utility
could be measured by price—that price, in effect, expressed marginal
utility. This meant that economic life could be modeled by mathematics.[154] While political economists had focused on social relations,
Fisher imagined individuals as "fully individual, autonomous, atom-
ized, and preexisting beings with a certain set of wants and desires that
should simply be taken as a natural given."[155]

The marginalist revolution divorced economics from other social
science disciplines; at universities, "economics" increasingly became a
separate academic field. At the University of California, Berkeley, political economy, which had been part of the political science department, became its own department in 1903, following Harvard
University's precocious move to establish an economics department in
1897. Marshall helped create an institutional complex that propagated
the new orthodoxy: In 1890, he cofounded the British Economics Association and its influential publication, *The Economic Journal.* Then,

in 1903, he created the Faculty of Economics, with its own professorial chairs, at the University of Cambridge, divorcing himself and his field from the "Moral Sciences" program that had taught political economy up to that point.[156] That the study of "economics" became an academic field in its own right and largely succeeded in establishing itself as a science closer to, say, physics than to history or philosophy was a testament to the processes it purportedly analyzed: the infusion of the reconstructed empire of capital into all realms of society. The erasure of history, society, class, and power from thinking about economic life was not an oversight; it was part of the design.

Marginalism removed economics not only from notions of social conflict of the sort that Marx and Weber had seen as crucial but from the very notion of economic life as a political project. It did so by naturalizing and atomizing economics—that is, by building its analysis upon the discovery of "laws" that operated independently of political, social, or cultural circumstances and that could be quantitatively measured. Marginalists focused on the granular and individual level. In this way, they mirrored a broader trend in other scientific disciplines, as contemporary biologists were beginning to understand organisms from the cellular level up, and chemists increasingly analyzed matter on a molecular level.[157]

In some ways, marginalism's insistence on ignoring history, power, culture, and even ethics was hard to fathom, as the world in which the movement emerged was characterized by increasingly powerful categorical inequalities, huge imbalances in power, and massive coercion that could hardly be explained by individual preferences. It seems counterintuitive that at the very moment the state became so much more important in economic life, the state and its politics were declared external to the economy's inner working. At the same time, the move was not surprising, because the recasting of economics was, in fact, a political project itself intended to naturalize the economic order and remove economic questions from consideration by increasingly democratic polities in capitalism's heartlands (though by emphasizing the importance of consumer demand, it also gave credence to policies that encouraged such demand).

The radical reduction in scope and contextualization of economic thought had many consequences, not least the impoverishment of our understanding of capitalism. It also left space for rival theories to explain persistent inequalities and categorical hierarchies, with social Darwinism and what came to be called "scientific racism" prominent among them. As utility-maximizing individuals and firms moved to the center of thinking about economic life, categorical inequalities dropped from sight. While marginalism as such was neither racist nor imperialist—indeed, its axiomatic point of departure was the absolute equality of all individuals—its inability to explain the massive inequalities that emerged within and between nations encouraged a recourse to what one scholar has called "the big idea" of the late nineteenth century: race.[158] A strikingly wide assortment of people and institutions propagated a corrupted Darwinism to preach ideas of "scientific racism," eugenics, the "Anglo-Saxon race," and the "survival of the fittest" to explain the age's stunning lack of equality. Harvard University zoologist Louis Agassiz and his disciples even questioned the common humanity of the world's people. The ideological prominence of an entirely fictive category—race—powered an all-too-real racism that legitimized, among other things, the abrogation of otherwise sacrosanct property rights; endorsed massive, coercive state interventions; and corrupted the rule of law by subjecting different groups of people to very different legal regimes.[159] As categorical inequalities continued to power capitalism's expansion, ideas of "race" enabled reconstructed capitalism to rest itself on a massive contradiction: hierarchies there, abstract utility-maximizing individuals and a politics of civic equality here.

────

The explosive qualities of this reconstructed capitalism became starkly obvious in 1914. The bourgeois civilization that had so often emphasized the peace-inducing qualities of its empire of capital based on trade, not war, descended into the conflagrations later known as World War I. To the surprise of many, the reconstructions of capitalism during the previous four decades had laid the groundwork not just for the flourishing of industry, technology, and trade but for one of the deadliest military conflicts in human history. The war radicalized the project of enclosures by drawing on virtually all the productive capacities of reconstructed capital, labor, and the state. Newly organized industries churned out unprecedented amounts of military hardware for use on the battlefield, strengthening the bond between capital owners and the state. The survival of many new forms of capital seemed to rest on a nation-state that could guarantee access to raw materials, agricultural commodities, labor, and markets. At the same time, the survival of the nation-state seemed to rest on the ability of national capital, especially industrial capital, to flourish. And because the new warfare, unlike earlier modes of warfare, called upon the mobilization of entire societies, it further integrated the vastly expanded industrial proletariat, providing new social and political rights that widened the rapidly growing gap between the material well-being and rights of workers in the industrial heartlands of the Global North and those of workers in the Global South. The capitalist civilization that had posed as a utopian project beyond productivity enhancements and capital accumulation as early as the French Revolution (1789–1799) and the short-lived upheavals of 1848 descended into a dystopian orgy of violence. A generation of European and American, as well as African and Asian, young men lost their lives in the industrialized conflict. Governments sent them to the front lines by steamship and train, their movements coordinated by telegraphs; they attacked one another with newly powerful steel weaponry, amplified by the poisonous products of newfangled chemical industries, with automobiles and airplanes transforming the speed and angle at which the savagery was assessed.[160]

No industry exemplified the possibilities and the abyss of this reconstructed capitalism better than the iron and steel industry, that quintessential branch of the Second Industrial Revolution that both powered modern warfare and provided some of the impetus behind imperial ventures. The Röchlings were deeply involved in warfare, territorial reordering, and state strengthening. They enthusiastically embraced the militant nationalism that laid the groundwork for the mass

Reconstructed capitalism comes home to roost:
Röchling steel helmets, World War I.

mobilizations that powered World War I, and just as enthusiastically produced the grenades, machine-gun parts, plane armor, steel for helmets (they produced more than 80 percent), cannon, and various other armaments that fed trench warfare. Röchling workers labored at the furnaces and in the rolling mills to produce that war material, but they also served on the front, where 461 of them died.[161]

For the Röchlings, however, the war was not only, not even primarily, about selling war materials or sending their workers to fight. Their greatest focus was on securing Germany's territorial expansion—in particular, iron-ore and coal deposits in neighboring countries. Along with their better-known counterparts in the Ruhr (the Krupps, for example), they embraced what can be considered, in business historian Alfred D. Chandler Jr.'s parlance, the horizontal and vertical integration of their businesses through military means. They hoped war would give Germany access to the raw materials, agricultural commodities, labor, and markets that would let it dominate the global economy—to confront, in essence, the "American danger." While their involvement in war was deeper than most, the general idea was common—after all, US commodity chains had been integrated through relentless war with the continent's Indigenous peoples, while British, French, Belgian,

The horrors of industrial warfare: Shock Troops Advance Under Gas
(Sturmtruppe geht unter Gas vor), *Otto Dix, 1924.*

Italian, and Japanese troops had conquered colonial lands for similar reasons.

In 1914, the Röchlings had set their sights on the French parts of nearby Lorraine, which was the core of a region that produced 45 percent of the entire European iron-ore output.[162] They had learned from the Franco-Prussian War (1870–1871) that territorial expansion benefited their company, and they aimed to capture a territory whose existing political divisions made it difficult to create integrated production processes.

Passionate nationalist that he was, the company's rising patriarch, forty-two-year-old Hermann Röchling, participated in battles on the Western Front. On August 31, 1914, less than a month after Germany declared war on France, he camped with his regiment outside the French spa town of Lunéville. Contemplating the heady possibilities of the conflict, he wrote to the German administrator of Alsace-Lorraine, Johann von Dallwitz, to offer his ideas about restructuring the Lorrainian iron and steel industry after the war. He suggested that the border between France and Germany be redrawn, integrating French iron-ore areas into the German Reich.[163] Around the same time, he shared his fantasies in a letter to the ministry of the interior in Berlin, confiding his ideas about the need for a "shift of the border north of Metz," suggesting precisely where the new border between Germany and France should be drawn, based on his goal of bringing more French iron-ore deposits into German territory.[164]

The first months of the war left German steel industrialists giddy with anticipation over the loot coming their way: In February 1915, Röchling, along with the German administrator of Lorraine and steel industrialist August Thyssen, again wrote to the ministry of the interior in Berlin about the necessity of claiming French iron-ore deposits. At the same time, Thyssen celebrated the "greatness of our army" and enthusiastically shared his "views about the future order of Europe" with political authorities in Berlin, including his expectation that large parts of France and Belgium, the Caucasus, the Belgian Congo, and Morocco would be integrated into the postwar German Reich. He imagined this new Germany as part of a gigantic customs union with formally independent states in much of the rest of Europe, something that could be created, he admitted, only by "coercion."[165] AEG's Walther Rathenau suggested that a customs union be forced on France; chemical manufacturer Carl Duisberg claimed Belgian coal deposits. Steel and coal industrialist Hugo Stinnes eyed vast areas of Europe, Morocco, the Belgian Congo, and territories bordering the existing German colony of Togo. Another strand of German expansionist thought advocated expansion into the Balkans and the Ottoman Empire, hoping, among other things, that cotton could be produced in Mesopotamia and Egypt, envisioned as part of a new German empire. Japanese observers looked at these efforts to nationalize commodity chains and concluded that national autarky of inputs and markets was the precondition for winning a modern war.[166] War provided a free hand for enclosure, encompassment, and encasement.

More pragmatic and immediate actions accompanied these dreams. Louis Röchling, Hermann's brother, became part of the national iron council that coordinated war production throughout the German Reich and its occupied territories—a politically powerful position in

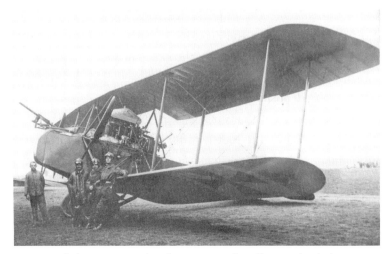

*Industry meets nationalism meets warfare: German electrical
conglomerate AEG produces bomber planes.*

which capital and state power almost completely merged. He also drew
on forced labor, with six hundred Russian prisoners of war arriving in
Völklingen in 1916 alone, bringing the coercions of the Global South
into the heartland of industrial capitalism. Members of the Röchling
family ensured that they managed the captured iron and steel mills in
eastern France, personally supervising the dismantling of various
French mills and transporting their machinery, in a brazen act of theft,
to Völklingen. Stolen French machinery was used to produce armaments used against French troops.[167]

While the Röchlings were perhaps uniquely aggressive in reenvi-
sioning their commodity chains, links between industrial capital and
the reconstructed state characterized this moment in the history of
capitalism more broadly. The underlying logic of this new political
economy was self-evident. As early as 1898, Röchling had written to
his American friend James W. Miller in Pittsburgh with evident
sympathies for American colonial expansion: "Now you have your war
with Spain. . . . [I]t will affect your prosperity very much . . . that
means for the possession of the Cuban ore and sugar fields."[168] In December 1913, about six months before the war began, Röchling exchanged information with French metal manufacturer and engineer

Paul Girod about producing munitions for the navy. Both saw the military as a major customer, even though a few months later, their weapons would be directed at each other.[169]

But the Röchlings' dreams came to naught. Not only would there be no newly captured territory, but Germany's loss of the lands it had occupied in 1871 would also cost the Röchlings a number of factories and mines. Moreover, in 1918, the French brought the Röchling family to trial, sentencing Robert and Hermann Röchling to ten years in prison and a huge fine for the theft of steelmaking equipment from French factories. While Robert served his time, Hermann fled. Only in 1942 did Philippe Pétain's Vichy regime reverse that judgment—under pressure from another contingent of German occupiers in France.[170]

———

I n 1918, the world looked in horror at the devastation wrought by war. Many wondered whether the enormous human creativity that had produced massive mills, interconnected railroad networks, and chemical wonders had also released a deadly genie impossible to put back into its shiny steel bottle. German anarchist Erich Mühsam, fated to be

Machines and men: Renault FT tank with Girod turret.

murdered in a Nazi concentration camp, expressed that widely shared sentiment in a poem he called "Barbarians."

> They quarrel who amongst them is a Barbarian,
> and to prove that it is invariably only the others
> who earn such reputation for all of posterity
> they devastate with horrific machines
> Galipoli, Galicia, Serbia, Flanders,
> Wolhynia and the land of the Bedouins.[171]

The basic tensions powering the conflict had emerged from reconstructed capitalism, and they persisted. Three were crucial: first, the "national question" of the sharpening international conflicts generated by territorialized capital and heavily capitalized states; second, the "social question" of radical inequality caused by a castelike congealing of social divisions within the increasingly dominant structures of capitalist societies; and third, the "colonial question" of almost unfathomably deep and divisive global hierarchies, backed by an increasingly orthodox pseudoscience of racial rankings. Stirred up by the inferno of world war, these questions continued tormenting humanity in the coming decades, a period that Italian philosopher Antonio Gramsci grimly called a "time of monsters."[172]

In November 1918, surviving soldiers left the trenches high in the French Vosges and departed from the fields of Belgium, whose beautiful bright-red poppies came to symbolize the war throughout the former British Empire. They returned to the factories and fields of Europe, America, Asia, and Africa, where they immediately faced the trifecta of persistent nationalism, sharp inequality, and colonial domination that strained the empire of capital as never before. These tensions exploded into the open even before the war had formally ended. One of the places they did so was along the railroad tracks stretching between Dakar and Saint-Louis in West Africa.

14.

A TIME OF MONSTERS:
INDUSTRIAL CAPITALISM,
1918–1945

*New dystopias: Fiat aims to make transportation
for the "Terra Mare Cielo" (Earth, Sea, Sky),
marrying fantasies of mass production to
nationalism. Fiat, Turin, Italy.*

On April 8, 1919, Gabriel Louis Angoulvant, the newly appointed French governor of Senegal, received most unwelcome news. A telegram arrived from a group of workers who labored on that jewel of French West African colonialism, the 164-miles-long Dakar–Saint-Louis Railway constructed in the early 1880s; in their dispatch, they demanded a wage hike and more

Modern industry—and modern social conflict—come to West Africa:
the railway station of Saint-Louis in 1905.

generous benefits.[1] The telegram gave Angoulvant five days to meet their requests or else face a strike at midnight on April 12.[2]

The shocking rise in prices after World War I precipitated these Senegalese workers' call for cost-of-living adjustments, a more generous vacation schedule, sick pay, and a general wage increase. Workers were also emboldened by the relaxation of wartime suspensions of civil liberties and the upcoming rainy season. Timely transportation of peanut seeds was a priority for French business interests, making this threat to shut down the colony's only railroad more effective. Workers who had just returned from the battlefields of the Great War showed particular assertiveness.[3]

For several years, French employees, who occupied skilled positions, had already been agitating for higher wages and benefits equal to those enjoyed in France, such as a pension scheme. African-born workers, who made up about 95 percent of the workforce, were given the backbreaking tasks of loading and unloading freight, maintaining the tracks, and lifting machinery in the repair shop. Over time, they had gained access to certain skilled positions as well, such as foreman of the locomotive engineers and track work gangs, and such skilled workers played a disproportionate role in organizing the potential strike.

Even among their unskilled counterparts, many a worker had made the transition from seasonal migrant (from elsewhere in Senegal) to permanent settler in one of the urban locations along the railroad. Together, they had become a proletariat with much greater stability and much greater willingness to engage in collective action.[4]

Faced with the threat of a strike, the railroad company and colonial authorities responded harshly at first.[5] The inspector general of public works, M. Léopold Mouneyres, declared that if the demands had been presented in the "usual manner," most of them could have been met without a strike. In fact, workers had demanded such benefits as early as 1914—to no avail.[6] Making no move to address the workers' concerns, the railroad's management and the colony's government readied and signed a decree on April 10 to place the tracks under military command.[7] On April 12, on the eve of the announced strike deadline, the governor convened a "crisis council." Unable to identify the leaders of the rebellion, Angoulvant placed the railroad under "a regime of total requisition":[8] The laws governing the army were now applicable to railway staff, who would be subject to military discipline.

Such threats did not stop the workers from walking out. The next day, 585 workers went on strike, including fitter Souleye N'Dour from the road's iron workshop; Doudou Diagne, an apprentice in the road's depot; and Mamadou Diop, a mechanic. A French colonial administrator telegraphed "that regular train this day did not leave Saint-Louis (stop) despite written order of the military authority."[9] The impact was felt almost immediately. As Giraud, president of the Rufisque Chamber of Commerce, remarked: "Trade very affected by strike . . . suspending economic life and causing delay in grain shipments." He begged the governor "to arbitrate . . . to give it prompt solution in the interests of all."[10] Pressure built along the railroad's path into the peanut-growing hinterland. Giraud urged giving "immediate satisfaction to the native staff" to get the trains running again. Representatives of the three Senegalese chambers of commerce, their commercial interests threatened, also demanded a swift settlement. But that was easier said than done. Governor Angoulvant expressed his frustration that he was unable to even locate a representative of the workers, since all their correspondence had been anonymous.[11]

The railroad and the colonial administration ramped up the military discipline: When some of the strikers lingered in the vicinity of Dakar's station on April 13, authorities arrested three of them. In Saint-Louis, they detained four mechanics who refused to start a train.[12] Pressured by the governor, the *chefs de service* of the road in Dakar eventually got a short train running, and it proceeded a few miles to the colony's major peanut port, Rufisque. There, workers again stopped it, and officials arrested two African mechanics for "abandoning their post."[13]

As trains remained frozen, the railroad's European workers boldly marched to Dakar's station the following day. Their Senegalese colleagues, understandably fearful of arrest, stayed away, prompting charges that they had "defected." The lieutenant colonel, now in charge of the railway under military requisition, immediately took advantage of the workers' presence and ordered one of the workers to ready a train. The worker refused, even after the code of military justice was read to him, and was arrested. Railroad agents tried with a second worker and this time succeeded. Soon most French-born workers agreed to return to work. What the lieutenant colonel did not realize, however, was that while the French workers could assemble the train in the station, only the African-born engineers could start it. It was only with the help of two "defectors," along with the chief operating officer serving as mechanic, that a train eventually proceeded toward Saint-Louis via Rufisque. Difficulties soon arose, however, as no African-born mechanics or drivers could be coerced into breaking the strike, despite "one or two arrests." The train turned back to Dakar in the evening, driven by the same crew.[14] The military requisition had subdued the French-born workers but proved ineffective against their African-born colleagues, most critically the locomotive engineers.[15]

That same day, the senior commanding general came to Dakar's station to arrange for a negotiation between the French workers and the governor on the condition that they return to work immediately.

The French staff hesitated and asked to contact their comrades in Rufisque to coordinate the conditions for resuming work. Ultimately, they agreed that a delegation of both French and Senegalese representatives would go to the governor's office at 3:00 p.m. the next day.[16]

At that meeting with Angoulvant, the workers learned, perhaps to their surprise, that their protests had been effective. Many of their demands were met, especially those of the Senegalese workers, who had proved their centrality to the road's technical operations. The governor offered a higher minimum wage, increased wages, and better vacations. The lowest daily wage tripled. Workers and railroad officials agreed to a new contract on April 15, and strikers agreed to resume work on April 16. The strike was a resounding success, not least because colonial officials feared it could undermine "social peace," as the governor put it in a telegram to Paris on April 15.[17] The railroad's board of directors in Paris initially deemed the concessions excessive and dispatched a telegram to the road's director, stating their intention to limit them. Convinced of the power of worker mobilization, and given the difficulties it had encountered in trying to identify strike leaders, the colonial government permitted the railroad workers to form *associations amicales*—legal entities distinct from unions but at least capable of voicing workers' concerns. The strike of 1919 also demonstrated just how dependent French workers had become on the support of their Senegalese colleagues. The African workers, in turn, realized their power and had already initiated a second strike by late April, calling on French workers to join their action. And in June 1920, 320 Senegalese workers walked out again, resulting in yet another 30 percent wage hike. This began a powerful and militant workers' movement that would continue until Senegal's independence in 1960. Individual desertions, which had been the first response to proletarianization in West Africa and elsewhere, gradually transitioned into workers' collective action. Ultimately, the strike settlement revealed the colonial administration's move toward accommodation of African workers' rights and recognition of their economic power. The signal victories of Senegal's railroad workers inspired future movements, many of which went on to play important roles in later anticolonial rebellions.[18]

———

By the end of World War I, waves of connected rebellions shook the empire of capital. As in Dakar, social conflict burst onto the scene with unprecedented ferocity, accelerated by the war itself. Workers struck around the world; they also protested, organized, occupied factories, set up paramilitary forces, and even staged revolutions, aspiring to improve their social situations and grasping for—and sometimes capturing—state power.

In scale and impact, this wave of rebellions was markedly different from those of a century earlier. Workers now wielded greater institutional power; they had created resourceful, complex, stable, and very large organizations—unions, and political parties, counting millions of supporters. Laboring people embraced powerful ideologies that gave purpose to their activities. Their collective action was no longer defending a precapitalist world of autonomy, subsistence production, and dependencies; it increasingly aspired to achieve capitalism's reform, or even its overcoming.

The breadth of the upheaval was remarkable. In October 1919, in New York, approximately 150,000 longshoremen, teamsters, sailors, and warehouse workers went on strike for higher wages and recognition of their union. Their uprising brought activity in the port to a standstill. It took the combined might of strikebreakers and the US Army, as well as pleas from the American Federation of Labor and the International Longshoremen's Association, to reopen the port. In Rio de Janeiro in 1918, seventeen men were arrested on suspicion of anarchist activity as part of a general crackdown on labor insurgency. In Hokkaido, when both coal prices and demand for labor fell at the end of the war, Japanese and Korean miners responded by founding the

Islands of postcapitalism: Turin general strike, 1920.

island's first union in 1919: the Yubari Federation of the National Union of Miners. Labor turmoil became common in Völklingen as well: When a local leader of the Communist Party spoke in 1921, 800 workers attended, a stunning number considering the previous weakness of socialist activity in that city.[19] That summer, Völklingen workers also went on strike to protest wage cuts, followed by escalating conflicts in the years thereafter.[20]

The social upheavals in these storied capitalist entrepôts were just the tip of the iceberg. In 1919, a strike wave crisscrossed the United States, with more than four million workers participating, culminating in a general strike in Seattle. The "air is . . . rather thundery," observed a British colonial bureaucrat in India in 1920.[21] In January of that year, two hundred thousand textile workers struck at more than eighty mills in Bombay; from there, unrest spread to other industries, with demands for a 50 percent wage increase and a ten-hour workday. By February, confrontations in Bombay became violent, and on the nineteenth of that month, troops killed six strikers. In Ahmedabad that same month, fifteen thousand weavers from local textile mills went on strike. By March, reports of "wide-spread economic unrest" flooded

into the colonial administration, and that same month, the first Labour Conference, held in Madras (now Chennai), attracted three thousand workers. Calcutta railway workers, as well as jute, flour, and oil
mill workers, joined in too. A young Mahatma Gandhi—soon to in-
spire one of the twentieth century's most powerful social movements—
stood in solidarity with these workers by fasting until their demands
were met. Colonial authorities in Calcutta reported on the "overt sign
of the rise of the spirit of rebellion and discontent" among postal workers.[22] Workers on trams, at gasworks, and in locomotive workshops
also rebelled, their protests often intersecting with nationalist organizing and agitating.[23]

In Europe, by the early 1920s, more than twenty million women and
men voted for socialist, social democratic, or newly founded communist
parties—almost three times as many as before the war—all of them committed to significant reform or the overthrow of capitalism. And in many
regions of Africa, workers organized and walked off their jobs in unprecedented numbers. Masons in Rufisque struck in 1918. In South Africa,
activists created the Industrial and Commercial Workers' Union under
the leadership of Clements Kadalie in January 1919. Dockworkers in
Conakry struck in 1919, railroad workers in Sierra Leone in 1919 and
1920, and public employees on the Gold Coast in 1919 and 1921, while
strikes also took place in Gambia in 1921. Efforts even emerged to organize workers on a global level: The International Federation of Textile
Workers' Associations organized unions in thirteen countries, with a total of almost one and a half million members in 1928.[24]

Some conflicts approached the scale of military confrontations:
Informed by the lessons they had learned in the trenches of World
War I, South African white mine workers formed heavily armed com-
mandos during the Rand Rebellion of 1922. Government troops
shelled the workers' barricades to end the conflict—an action that generally would have been unthinkable before the war. In the German
Ruhr, workers formed Arbeiter- und Soldatenräte, advocating the nationalization of coal mining and other industries. In 1920, the so-
called Ruhrkampf brought armed workers into the streets of the steel

South African union leader Clements Kadalie.

and mining heartland of German industrialization. In early 1919, more than ten thousand troops, equipped with heavy armaments from the recent war, suppressed a mass strike in Glasgow. In Turin, and throughout Italy's industrialized northern regions, the years of 1919 and 1920 are remembered as the *biennio rosso*, or "two red years," with workers militantly demanding improvements and power, occupying factories, and staging massive and even armed uprisings. In 1919, the Turinese working class mobilized in eighty-three strikes with 84,000 participants; a year later, Turin's 140,000 workers went on seventy-two distinct strikes with 130,635 participants. In Italy as a whole, more than a million workers walked out in both 1919 and 1920—more than ever before.[25]

The epicenter of this global rebellion, however, was not in the centers of modern industry, such as the Ruhr, Turin, or Pittsburgh, but in war-exhausted and still mostly agrarian Russia. There, a broad uprising of working-class women and men, along with soldiers, swept away a centuries-old monarchy. It began in February 1917 in Petrograd (today's Saint Petersburg), where thousands of women textile workers and homemakers marched to protest the shortage of bread. Women, while often marginalized among the leadership of workers' organizations throughout the empire of capital, were crucial actors in fomenting and sustaining working-class rebellion. From there, the uprising spread to other groups of workers and to soldiers. With the abdication of the tsar in March, a coalition of industrial-agrarian interests on one side and the Petrograd Soviet on the other briefly attempted to govern. Facing rising conflict, the Bolsheviks, under the leadership of Vladimir Lenin,

The social question explodes: working-class activists from the Rote Ruhrarmee (Red Ruhr Army) setting up a machine gun in the streets of Dortmund, Germany, 1920.

seized control of key institutions. On October 25, 1917, Lenin declared in Petrograd that "in Russia we must now set about building a proletarian socialist state."[26] As they violently consolidated their rule over the next few years, they declared themselves a socialist society, the first to be defined by its explicit rejection of capitalism—no longer oriented toward a precapitalist past but toward an irrevocably postcapitalist future.[27]

The revolution transformed Russian society and altered the trajectory of global capitalism.[28] The Russian Revolution was to industrial capitalism what the Haitian Revolution had been to war capitalism: Plantation elites had obsessed about Toussaint Louverture for almost a century, and now a fear of the Russian Revolution and of all forms of socialism would become the polestar of politics in capitalist societies all the way up to 1991. For a long time, the expansion of capitalism had generated a panoply of countermovements, some more consequential than others, but now for the first time, this way of structuring economic life encountered a self-declared opponent dedicated to the destruction of capitalism—and it was not just any state, but one of Europe's "great powers."

World War I military strategies inform South Africa's responses to militant workers during the Rand Rebellion of 1922.

The "social question" powered hundreds, even thousands, of rebellions in the 1910s and 1920s. Activists also launched withering attacks against another pillar of the prewar empire of capital: colonialism. In so doing, they often intersected with working-class and peasant movements, as when Gandhi had supported the textile workers of Ahmedabad. In Barbados in 1919, Bajan veterans returning from the Great War (in which they fought for Britain) formed the island's first chapter of Marcus Garvey's Universal Negro Improvement Association to address the racist policies of the British colonial administration, not least anti-vagrancy laws specifically targeting returning veterans. In Bengal, a notoriously radical protest movement had already motivated the British to pass the 1915 Defence of India Act, authorizing the government to suspend habeas corpus and imprison suspected "seditionists." By 1918, over eight hundred Bengali political activists had been imprisoned—a testament to the groundswell of anticolonial sentiment. In 1916, Irish nationalists had staged an uprising against British rule; three years later, the anticolonial Egyptian Revolution broke out. In July of that same year, returning Black servicemen in British Honduras (today's Belize) rebelled against their ill-treatment back home, only to be subdued by the army. In April 1919, when thousands congregated in the Punjabi city of Amritsar to demand the release of a number of Indian anticolonial activists, the British Army opened fire and killed hundreds. The Amritsar bloodshed, known as the Jallianwala Bagh Massacre, became a touchstone in mobilizing against British rule. In late 1919, mass strikes broke out in Trinidad to protest rising living costs, articulating a critique of colonialism along the way. In the summer of 1920, protests turned into an armed uprising in the British mandate of Mesopotamia (present-day Iraq). Everywhere, anticolonial activists took inspiration from the anti-imperial rhetoric of the newly constituted Soviet Union as much as they did from the vague pledges of self-determination for all peoples made by Woodrow Wilson, president of the other surging continental power.[29]

These movements combined demands for the right to self-determination with demands for access to resources.[30] And while some of this resistance remained directed against the fresh imposition of capitalist institutions, it also targeted, to an unprecedented extent, reconstructed industrial capitalism itself. It seemed that in the aftermath of the Great War, industrial capitalism had lost its legitimacy to a re-

Working-class politics meets anticolonialism: Sixth Congress of the Second International, Amsterdam, 1904, with Rosa Luxemburg and Dadabhai Naoroji among the delegates.

markable degree, its domestic inequalities and global hierarchies sparking mass resistance.

———

Capitalism, as a way of organizing economic life, has always been unstable and contested. It is hard to overstate that instability: It was part of capitalism's innermost dynamic, the taproot of its surprising radicalism. But rarely was that instability more evident than in the two and a half decades after World War I. In 1918 and 1919, just two generations after industrial capitalism's flamboyant rise, it met its first existential threat—massive social movements propelled by the hopes and needs of the very masses mobilized and concentrated by capitalism itself. These movements sought to erode several of capitalism's pillars, including the new patterns of inequality it had generated, its colonial infatuations, and even private property as such. War capitalism, to be sure, had seen its own trials and systemic instabilities, but it had taken centuries for it to be challenged on a system-wide basis. Industrial capitalism, uniquely capable as it was of mass transformation, was different.

Indeed, in the entire five-hundred-year-long history of capitalism, the twenty-seven years between 1918 and 1945 were perhaps the most tumultuous. Capitalism, as we have seen over and over, was a state of constant revolution; stable capitalism was a contradiction in terms. The economic and political upheavals of these decades, however, produced some of history's greatest catastrophes, what historian Arno J. Mayer termed a "second Thirty Years' War," or, in Antonio Gramsci's chilling phrase, a "time of monsters."[31] It was a moment when observers of all political persuasions prophesied capitalism's imminent collapse—a prediction that seems plausible even in retrospect. Reconstructed capitalism's very pillars—proletarianization, commodity frontier expansion, intensification of global connections, sharpened nationalism, and colonial domination—now seemed to undermine the empire of capital itself. That capitalism survived testifies not just to its enormous flexibility but to the power of two innovations that characterized these decades as well: a much expanded and recast state and a burst of extraordinary creativity that reinvented industrial production itself. Combined, they would enable a sustained and substantial improvement in living standards in the world's industrial heartlands, striking at the heart of the rebellions of the 1920s and 1930s that challenged capitalism's legitimacy.

Three changes stand out: First, a new state—the United States—emerged as an ever more hegemonic actor in the global economy. Second, the 1930s saw a vast expansion in the scale and scope of the state—accelerating trends that had powered the reconstruction of capitalism since the 1870s. And third, capital-rich entrepreneurs, workers, intellectuals, and peasants in the Global South developed a sharpened awareness of the importance of a state and jockeyed for a say in its constitution. In that remaking of the state, a wide variety of post-liberal (in the nineteenth-century sense), even illiberal, regimes came to manage that new industrial capitalism—from the US New Deal program to German fascism. By 1945, even capital owners were advocating for government-directed planning and the nationalization of key industries—an astounding development explained only by the depth of the abyss they had faced.

Novel state formations combined with fast-evolving business enterprises and astonishingly productive industrial processes to power a new social settlement in select areas of the world. They envisioned and partly constituted a new capitalist utopia—a mass-consumption-driven, fossil-fuel-powered civilization rooted in unprecedented productivity advances. European and North American contemporaries were in awe of the promise of capitalist modernity, or what Robert Musil called "the reconstruction of man on the basis of an Americanized world-labor plan, by means of mechanized energy."[32] In 1928, German economist Werner Sombart perceptively remarked that the world was on the verge of "a new economic epoch . . . which will distinguish itself in essential ways from the one that we lived through in the nineteenth century."[33] For the socialist left, the end of capitalism was near, while the authoritarian and often fascist far right believed that capitalism could be preserved only in a radical anti-liberal mode. After 1929, that swelling chorus was also joined by many in the political center, who doubted that capitalism would have much of a future. How it survived and eventually thrived was a wild ride, ever at risk of taking down the entire political, economic, and social edifice.

A small but growing cohort of capital owners embarked upon their own pioneering projects in the years after World War I, stoking utopian fantasies that would shape twentieth-century capitalism no less than the new worlds dreamed up by working-class radicals and anticolonial militants in cities such as Saint Petersburg, Berlin, Calcutta, Cairo, and Dakar.

Giovanni Agnelli was one of them. A quintessential Turinese bourgeois with a military background in Italy's still-aristocratic cavalry, Agnelli turned the northern Italian city of Turin into a center of innovation based on the mass production of a durable consumer good: the automobile.[34] A "notorious person little known," according to one historian, the family patriarch was perceived as cold, harsh, and single-mindedly dedicated to his work—but also daring and imaginative.[35] To Antonio Gramsci—Italian philosopher, activist, and Agnelli nemesis—he was the "lonely hero of modern capitalism," and the company he created was a "small absolutist state" that would come to play a key role in the emergence of Italian industrial capitalism.[36]

Once a center of Italian nationalism, and even the first capital of the young nation, Turin had a rich history of trade, banking, and manufacturing. By the turn of the century, almost fifteen thousand metalworkers labored in the city. By the 1920s, its principal claim to fame, however, was not its flamboyant thinkers, nationalist politicians, artisanal workshops, or fashionable cafés but a huge factory on its outskirts—Lingotto. For a while the largest automobile factory in Europe, the massive edifice measured half a kilometer in length and eighty meters in width and was five floors high—providing about four million square feet of space. Raw materials and parts entered the factory on its ground floor, transferred directly from the railroad cars that pulled up next to it. Conveyor belts moved the unfinished cars along the factory floor and up the building, with workers assembling them along the way. Finished cars emerged on the top floor—onto a racetrack that had been built on the roof of the factory, where they were test-driven before their delivery to dealers. The gigantic factory had a capacity to produce fifty thousand cars a year—a sizable number for a country that had only one hundred thousand automobiles on its roads in 1922.[37]

Today, Lingotto has been turned into a Renzo Piano–designed shopping mall and conference center, symbolizing yet another age of capitalism, but during the 1920s, it was the physical embodiment of the entirely new world of mass production. Though it accounted for only a small percentage of global manufacturing, Lingotto played an outsize role in defining the future. Enabling a quantum leap in human productivity by

making a complex mechanical product into one of the world's most common consumption goods, Lingotto, along with its counterparts in other parts of the globe, altered not just the production process but also business structures, forms of labor control, working-class collective action, and politics. Here, Agnelli and his engineers laid some of the founda-

Europe's largest factory: Fiat, Turin, early 1920s.

Proud skilled manufacturing workers,
Fiat, early twentieth century.

tions of the new twentieth-century capitalism.

Lingotto was the crown jewel of an upstart company in a new industry, the Fabbrica Italiana Automobili Torino, or Fiat. Founded in 1899 by Agnelli and others, Fiat produced just 24 cars in its first year, a number that would increase to a still-modest 1,780 by 1910. Like all early automobile factories, Fiat assembled this expensive consumer good with the labor of highly skilled craftworkers for a small market of wealthy customers. In its first factory on Via Dante in Turin, Fiat employed just 150 such workers, expanding to about 4,000 workers by 1914, most of them highly skilled, and privileged, artisans who forged one vehicle after another, each an almost unique and precious symbol of the expanding accomplishments of the mechanical arts.[38]

Though the company built relatively few cars, it sold them all over the world, and by 1910, it also licensed production in the US city of Poughkeepsie, New York. An American-built Fiat cost between $4,500 and $5,500 in US dollars (the equivalent of between $143,000 and $175,000 in 2024), a true luxury item.[39] Fiat's advertising featured the wealthy and powerful owners of its vehicles: the queen of Holland, the nizam of Hyderabad, the Prince of Wales, and so on.

Catering to this profitable but limited market, Fiat became a successful manufacturer, outcompeting other Italian carmakers. By 1910, Agnelli and his coconspirators, however, began to reimagine all aspects of their business. Their inspiration came from the American city of Detroit. Agnelli had visited that fledgling industrial center, with its handful of car manufacturers, for the first time in 1906. He was so

Before mass production: Fiat advertises its automobiles to US customers.

enthused by what he saw that he returned at regular intervals, including in 1909, 1911, and 1912, when he visited the newly opened Highland Park factory and met for the first time with auto impresario Henry Ford, whose work fascinated Agnelli above anyone else's.[40] He became so attached to Ford that he kept a photo of one of their later meetings on his desk.

What Agnelli saw was indeed stunning. Inspired by the meatpacking plants of Chicago and Cincinnati, Ford had embarked upon the continuous assembly of automobiles, or what he called the "orderly progression of the commodity through the shop."[41] By 1908, Ford had begun to move goods, not workers, on the factory floor. Then, in 1913, he took the revolutionary next step of attaching the vehicle itself to a conveyor belt. To succeed, Ford made sure that all parts used in production were identical—and thus interchangeable—and that each step in the production deployed its own purpose-built and single-use machines. Going beyond Taylor's scientific management, Ford focused on the factory process and the machine, which optimized the movements of workers. As the "[f]actory had become one huge, integrated machine," productivity skyrocketed: It had taken Ford workers about twelve and a half hours to assemble an automobile before the introduction of the moving assembly line; afterward, the same tasks could be accomplished with just ninety-three minutes of human labor time.[42] Of course, continuous-flow production had already been implemented in other industries—in

Revolutionaries in suits: Giovanni Agnelli (right) with Henry Ford, 1934.

not just meatpacking but also cigarette production and the iron and steel industry. Ford's inspired leap was to apply the technique to one of the most complicated pieces of engineering ever invented. And it was spectacularly successful: Ford, the "automobileer" whom John Dos Passos called "nuts about machinery," churned out 250,000 Model Ts in 1914 and produced a total of 15 million cars before 1927—at rapidly falling prices.[43] It was a world-historic revolution.[44]

Inspired by these sights—especially Highland Park—Agnelli began to conceive of a radically different kind of factory and of a radically new way to organize the production of his Fiats. Starting the Lingotto project in 1916, Agnelli and his engineers imagined "a new American-style factory."[45] His investment was driven not only by the latest possibilities exemplified by Ford but also by fresh opportunities. During the war, Fiat had become a major supplier to the Italian armed forces and, as a result, had grown at astounding speed: By war's end, about fourteen thousand women and men worked for the company. It had become clear that huge opportunities would come with a more efficient organization of production.[46]

Agnelli's search for novel ways to position his firm in Italian and European markets found a champion in one of Fiat's chief engineers—Bernadino Maraini. In 1918, he traveled to the United States to develop a better understanding of "American manufacturing." The report he wrote upon his return emphasized the great cost advantages that Americans derived from their "grand production in series."[47] While Maraini proudly asserted that "our vehicles are of superior quality to those of Americans," thanks to the "genius" of the construction and the "great quality of our workers," he understood that the new ways of production pioneered in Detroit enabled Americans to sell cars more cheaply, and therefore in much greater quantity.[48] Celebrating the "magnificence of the American auto industry," he was impressed by the American search for "maximum efficiency," made possible by the limited number of models produced and the standardization of parts, even of chassis.[49] Americans, he concluded, produced a "highly marketable good": The US car industry was a "splendor of perfections."[50]

Consequently, Maraini advised Agnelli to produce in "large series," catering to a "large base."[51] Imagining a radically different future of manufacturing in Italy while imitating Ford, he detailed American construction techniques and emphasized the large volume of Ford's production, the standardization of his products, his extremely specialized machinery, and his ability to churn out an ever cheaper product—in short, his "colossal production."[52] The secret of his success, according to Maraini, was "the movement of materials" by "the automatic conveying system." Materials, he observed, "arrive at the factory in a continuous flow; in assembly work, the worker or several workers must carry out the operation within the time frame during which the material travels its area." It was for that reason that "in our new Lingotto workshops it will be necessary to adequately develop material conveying systems, both in relation to transport and in relation to assembly, especially since the new buildings . . . are well suited to such applications."[53] In later visits to Ford, Fiat engineers continued to marvel at the availability of precisely engineered and completely uniform materials; they saw a "radiant splendor of activity that manifests itself in the penetration that invades all countries."[54] Fiat needed to take on these challenges, the engineers concluded. "[T]ime is running out, the struggle is bitter, but faith is great: we must succeed."[55]

Inspired and alarmed in equal parts, Agnelli and his team embarked on a radical reorganization of production. Building on specialized machines, the conveyor belt, and production in series, Lingotto opened in March 1923—a temple dedicated to the "rational organization of the work process that avoids unnecessary movements of the materials."[56] At the same time, a greatly increased supervision of labor enabled "the control of the processing times and the regularity of the final assembly, making the accumulations and the shortcomings of components immediately visible."[57] The factory had become a complex mechanism in which specialized workers operated specialized machines to assemble a good that was in a state of constant motion.[58]

As a result of such innovations, Fiat produced vastly more cars at much lower prices: The number of cars on Italian roads quadrupled between 1922 and 1932, largely thanks to Fiat's production. Its Italian market share exceeded 80 percent during the 1920s and 1930s. While just one car per 5,554 people had navigated Italy's roads in 1907, there was one car per 335 inhabitants by 1925. And then there was the export market: As one of the first European firms to use Fordist production techniques, Fiat exported more than 70 percent of its output. When it introduced a new model in 1926, the 509, built at Lingotto, the car became a stunning success, not least because of yet another innovation: allowing for installment purchases.[59]

Lurking behind all the technical marvels was one basic truth: The core of the enhanced productivity at Lingotto was the reorganization of labor. Partly, that goal was politically motivated: During the "red years" after World War I, Fiat had largely lost control over its rapidly expanding workforce, even over its own factories, as Fiat workers had become the vanguard of the Italian labor movement. In response to the strikes, Fiat fired thousands of them, especially activists. Agnelli also assumed a leading role in organizing Italian industrialists, forming L'AMMA—the Aziende Meccaniche Meccatroniche Associate—in 1919 to regain the political initiative.[60]

With the threat of revolution contained, Fiat redoubled its efforts to control workers' labor power. Craftworkers, so important to earlier production, became much less central. Instead, "specialized workers," or machine attendants, who could operate one particular machine or navigate one particular work process, replaced the famously independent-minded craftsmen.[61] They were mostly young, male, and unencumbered by family ties.[62] According to the daily *La Stampa*, "The worker is a kind of cell assigned to a given place. Many times he does not have more than one or two square meters of space to move around. He does not need to move; he must not. Every useless movement would represent a loss or destruction of energy."[63]

The importance of reorganizing work was one of the key lessons that Fiat engineers like Maraini took from the United States.[64] At Ford, workers always had all needed materials at their disposal, which allowed the operator "to devote all of his physical and intellectual energy to the work assigned to him."[65] Best of all, expensive "[i]ndividual manual skills are limited, and the large mass of workers is mostly made up of the middle category, with few craftworkers and few manuals."[66] In his 1919 report, Maraini observed "the intensity of individual work" in American factories, work that was "ferocious and develops almost in a feverish speed," work that left workers "tormented by the anxiety of increasing" output.[67] Such control of workers was necessary, he argued, "to route our production in such a way that it too functions continuously and consistently as a mechanism in which everyone is obliged to do a certain work in a given time and in a given way."[68] For him, the beauty of the system was that "the inept, incapable worker, the sluggish and slow worker cannot remain there, he is automatically thrown out of the mechanism."[69]

Maraini hoped for a factory in which "[t]he product of the work so organized and uniform is equal to itself, independent of the greater or lesser ability of the workers. The worker, even though he is the intelligent part of the mechanism, has no personal or individual importance, but a collective one, he can be replaced with the same ease with which one can replace a cog in a machine."[70] To get there, argued Mariani, workers needed to be reeducated. Taylorist ideas about coordination, time management, and the shift of skills from workers to management were crucial to Fiat's production regime as well. Yet piecework—so vital to Taylorism—was done away with; workers became appendages of the machines and lost control of the pace of work.[71]

Unsurprisingly, such strategies greatly worried Fiat workers. They feared unemployment, harsh demands for speed, and loss of control over their work. Fiat's workers knew that Ford's basic idea had been to rush operators to keep up with the preset speed of their machines, and that as a result, their Detroit counterparts had reported coming down with a condition called "Forditis." Ford's workers had voted with their feet: By 1913, turnover among Ford's fourteen thousand workers was at a stunning 370 percent, forcing Ford to hire massive numbers of new workers on a daily basis, 71 percent of whom were recent immigrants streaming out of the European countryside. Every day, one in ten of his employees did not show up—a huge problem for Ford's management. To address this problem, Ford promised higher wages (the famous "five-dollar day") and became deeply involved in his workers' daily lives, with a "Sociological Department" involving itself in workers' family dynamics and behaviors, such as drinking.[72] An alarmed Antonio Gramsci warned that the Ford project was nothing short of an effort to forge "a new type of man suited to the new type of work and productive process."[73] He stressed that "the new methods of work are inseparable from a specific mode of living and of thinking and feeling life."[74]

Such a reorganization of labor brought about a remaking of the working class in Turin as well. Facing high turnover, Fiat tapped new sources of labor, primarily refugees from the deeply depressed Italian countryside, peasants who were unable to compete with the wheat belts of the American Midwest or the cattle ranches of the Argentinean pampas. Where once they would have immigrated to Brazil, Argentina, or the United States, now these peasants turned to Fiat, which promised them the chance to become semiskilled factory operatives— with about half of Fiat's workers categorized as "machine attendants."[75] Gramsci's "new type of man" had emerged en masse, a new working class. This emergent labor force could also be disciplined in new ways—including by the machines themselves—a form of discipline that spoke to Agnelli's own military background.[76]

For machines to reliably dominate workers, the work process itself needed to be administered with a new kind of bureaucratic intensity that mirrored the contemporaneous growth of state bureaucracies. Fiat

Managing mass production:
clerical workers at Fiat's Lingotto factory, 1923.

introduced elaborate accounting mechanisms that allowed the company to see the costs of each production process. Such bureaucratiza-
tion led, in turn, to the emergence of a new group of clerical workers,
remaking the working class in yet another way, opening up new opportunities for women to fill these jobs. By December 1923, Fiat employed
a total of 890 such workers, most of them female. Managing workers
became a big task of the bureaucracy, including an effort to statistically
and informationally understand the company's workforce and calculate
labor costs. Clerical work itself was newly rationalized, with new machines and technologies entering the office: calculators, Dictaphones,
telephones, cash registers, pneumatic mail, and classification systems
for document storage.[77]

But managing such a vastly expanded working class was not left to
the logic of machine production alone. Fiat aimed to integrate and stabilize the new working class in other ways too. Like Ford, Fiat paid its
factory workers unusually well. In the 1920s, moreover, the company
institutionalized a whole range of new social goods and services: health
care for workers, a school for apprentices, sports groups, and more. Fiat

built a company welfare state that would eventually stretch from cradle to grave, comprising even such things as a ski resort in the nearby Alps.[78] Turin thus became a kind of company town in which Fiat dominated everything, including its newspapers, stores, soccer club, and insurance companies.

For all their energy and creativity, Agnelli and his engineers, like all twentieth-century revolutionaries, depended in critical ways on the support and public coffers of the state. The Italian state provided some of the capital that private banks would not supply. In Fiat's early years, the state also gave the company very broad tax concessions, placed military procurement orders that kept the factories humming, and set the institutional framework for the "regulation of conflicts through the centralization of labor bargaining."[79] Import restrictions and tariffs limited competition in the domestic market. And, last but not least, the state provided the basic infrastructures for the automobile, roads and gas stations, and, in 1926, Azienda Generale Italiana Petroli (Agip) to facilitate gasoline production and distribution in Italy.[80]

Fiat and its counterparts elsewhere (such as the French carmaker Citroën, which started assembly-line production in 1919) reorganized not just industrial capitalism but also society, as commented on by philosophers, journalists, and artists such as Gramsci, Piero Gobetti, and the futurists. For them, Lingotto was a symbol of the new kind of rationality, order, and scale that emerged from the Great War and a response to the social turmoil in its aftermath.[81] Fiat, they agreed, represented a novel way of organizing industrial society—one that, for better or worse, pointed toward the future.

No one theorized that new society more effectively than Henry Ford. His 1922 ghostwritten memoir, *My Life and Work*, was translated into sixteen languages and found readers all over the world. In twenty-nine short chapters, Ford aimed to solve a puzzle that had stymied most observers of industrial capitalism: how to reconcile inequality and permanent proletarianization with reconstructed capital. Ford believed that consumption drove the economy. In 1930, he proclaimed that high wages and shorter working hours were essential to encourage consumption and thus create markets for industry. Embracing the virtues of productive capital within a broader producerist vision, he included a sharp critique of finance in particular and liberal capitalism in general, often shading into antisemitism. In this way, Fordism—as Gramsci coined it—was a populist revolt against investor capitalism and, indeed, Ford financed his expansion not via Wall Street but via retained earnings, reinvesting the profits he collected.[82]

Ford asserted that demand was crucial for mass-production industries. Other entrepreneurs began to accept the doctrine of marrying mass production to mass consumption as well. In 1924, Boston department store owner Edward Filene argued that the goal of business was to produce "prosperous customers as well as saleable goods," the one enabling the other.[83] Nazi ideologues also appreciated Ford's producerist vision: integration of production, the cutting out of middlemen, low prices, and mass consumption. They understood the productivity gains that such a system could enable and sought to appropriate it.[84] Soviet economic planners were just as drawn to Ford and brought significant numbers of Ford engineers and workers to the So-

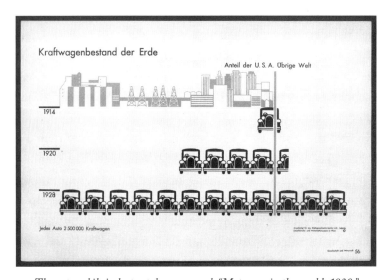

The automobile industry takes command: "Motorcars in the world, 1930."

viet Union. Leftists, in general, were of two minds when it came to Fordism, some celebrating Ford's system as a crucial step toward human emancipation and others denouncing the dehumanization of workers who became adjuncts of their machines. Angelo Tasca, founding member of the Partito Comunista Italiano (PCI), admired, like many socialists of his generation, the "amazing technical perfection" of the Lingotto, but at the same time, he stressed that "the working and peasant class" needed to exercise "energetic control" and gain "firm economic power" to harvest the emancipatory potential of such a new form of production.[85]

No matter whether one thinks of Lingotto and similar sites as capitalist utopias or dystopias (or as one of socialism's stepping stones, as they were thought of by Joseph Stalin, perhaps the world's most ruthless advocate of industrialization), they certainly testified to capitalism's vitality, its capacity to fuel economic growth, and its stunning technical innovation. Labor productivity grew rapidly. And it was not just automobiles that began to fill streets and spaces. A cornucopia of household appliances, electrical products, chemical compounds, and various newfangled devices entered homes in significant, though still limited, areas of the world. While Fiat was an innovator in a sea of traditional production, it was not alone. Writers and artists remarked on the modernity of their age, showcasing a machine civilization in which new technologies, both wondrous and destructive, had revolutionized the lives of ordinary people. Charlie Chaplin's 1936 film, *Modern Times*, depicted workers at the mercy of machines. Mexican muralist Diego Rivera admired both the technical wonders of the age and the resistance against them in an elaborate 1932/33 series of murals for the Detroit Institute of Arts (frescoes largely paid for by auto heir Edsel Ford). British writer Virginia Woolf evoked the disjointed and fractured nature of modern existence and revealed that for all its promises, modernity had done little to alter the conventional gender expectations of the age. American novelist John Dos Passos's *U.S.A.* trilogy portrayed a world in which the capitalist logic had seeped into almost all realms of life, leaving his characters alienated and adrift. Italian futurist poets and painters such as Filippo Tommaso Marinetti, Umberto Boccioni, and Giacomo Balla celebrated speed and technology—but also the violence of the new order.[86]

Whatever hopes these grand experiments fostered for the liberatory potential of these modern technologies, they foundered on these grave social, colonial, and national tensions left unresolved by World War I. This was partly the result of the very insularity of the Fordist revolution. It was concentrated in just a few areas of the world's industrial heartlands. Even in the United States, much of economic life remained outside the Fordist paradigm. Only an estimated 29 percent of Americans could purchase most of the new consumer goods. Southerners, African Americans, and Native Americans, among others, were left outside the new consumer utopia. The United States, in particular, was characterized by poorly integrated labor markets with stark regional differences. In some parts of the country, Fordist factories paid good wages to the producers of mass-consumption goods, while in others, debt peonage, chain gangs, and convict leasing marked the economic order. Indeed, labor mobilizations in the American South were not so different from those in much of colonial Africa.[87] As the secretary of the International Federation of Textile Workers' Associations argued at the organization's twelfth international congress in Ghent in 1928:

> Perhaps one of the most peculiar international developments is that of the United States, where factories have been built in the cotton belt itself, where workers can be induced to work for long hours and where wages are miserably low in comparison with those of the New England States. A comparison of the hours of labour and the wages between one part of the United States and the other is almost like a comparison between Europe and some of the Far Eastern countries.[88]

Sharp social inequality continued to mark the 1920s,
one of the conditions for the Great Depression:
Zeitungsträger, *Georg Scholz, 1924.*

Such staggering inequality sharpened in the 1920s and fed into the instability of an increasingly consumption-driven industrial heartland—in the United States, about half of all income went to the top 10 percent of earners, and 22 percent to the top 1 percent alone. Wealth inequality accelerated to yet starker levels. While the wealthiest 1 percent of all Americans had owned 35 percent of the nation's assets in 1923, they owned 52 percent by 1928. Eighty-four percent of wealth was now concentrated in the hands of the richest 10 percent of all Americans. In Britain, just 2 percent of all households gained almost half of all income in 1929.[89]

Other tensions compromised the industrial heartland's Roaring Twenties as well. In agriculture, which still occupied the vast majority of humanity, high rates of indebtedness by cultivators and falling commodity prices made life increasingly difficult. As agriculture industrialized and became more productive in some areas of the world, cultivators in less-developed regions could not compete and fled the countryside in droves. European peasants, in particular, suffered from competition with the expanding agrarian output of Canada, Australia,

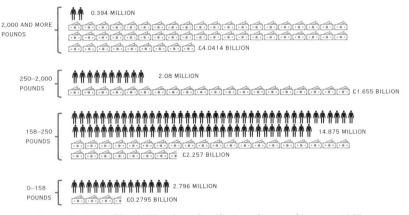

Inequality in the United Kingdom: distribution of personal incomes, 1929.

Argentina, Russia, and the United States. As agrarian productivity increased, ever fewer rural cultivators were able to feed an ever larger number of urbanites.

Moreover, the world economy itself showed its fragility in the early 1920s: Drastic inflation in much of the eastern and central parts of Europe, most prominently in Germany, wreaked economic havoc and wiped out the life savings of much of the middle class. And while prices stabilized after 1924 and economic growth was rapid until 1929, the world economy stood on wobbly legs—especially because it remained reliant on ongoing US capital infusions.[90] Most prominently, American capital underwrote the Great War reparations payments that Germany made to France and the United Kingdom.

Despite these deep structural imbalances, no country took on the task of stabilizing the rickety scaffolding that held the global economy together. Already by the 1870s, as we have seen, the cutting edge of the reconstruction of capital had moved to the United States, and economic growth had been decisively faster there as well. By 1916, US industries produced more than those of the entire British Empire. During World War I, the US economy boomed, while Britain was increasingly dependent on US capital infusions, leading British bankers to liquidate many of their US holdings, often at bargain prices. Such diminishing economic fortunes limited Britain's ability to manage the global economy. While the Bank of England had once played a crucial role in regulating global economic activities by stabilizing the gold standard system and serving as a lender of last resort, Britain had lost this ability by 1918.[91] What followed was what one historian has called the "Big Brexit," or the retreat of Britan as the global hegemon willing and able to regulate the global economy.[92]

Though the rise of the United States in the global economy was, according to a 1926 assessment by *New York Times* financial editor Alexander D. Noyes, "perhaps the most dramatic transformation of economic history," the United States did not fill the leadership gap vacated by Britain.[93] As British economist and liberal politician Hubert Henderson wrote in the summer of 1932: "It is of the essence of the present world difficulties that London has failed in the discharge of that vital function [to maintain global solvency], and that no other centre has been willing and able to discharge it."[94] One key failure of US economic "leadership" in the 1920s, besides demanding repayment of war debts, was increasing tariffs in 1921, 1922, and, most radically, in 1930, making it impossible for borrowers to earn income by exporting to wealthy US consumers, which would have enabled them to serve their debts in the United States. Protectionism played a key role in prolonging the Depression.

———

I n the fall of 1929, the shaky edifice of global capitalism came crashing down. Almost all people alive in the late 1920s and early 1930s remembered these years as a discrete event, often with drastic implications for their own biographies—evidence of capitalism's deepening seepage into global society. This depression's economic, social, and political consequences were dire, constituting the most severe crisis of capitalism to date. The Great Depression, as it came to be known, was a truly global event, affecting the entire empire of capital. The heartbeat of capitalism—for better or worse—had been synchronized worldwide, making the downturn much more consequential. We can see this clearly if we return to some of the places we visited before. In Barbados, as the price of sugar, still the island country's principal product, collapsed, a series of revolts unfolded. In Lower Silesia around the town of Jelenia Góra, the Depression brought a wave of business failures for its artisans, small shopkeepers, and farmers. In the early 1930s, many of them began to support the National Socialist German Workers' Party, which promised to reverse their fortunes. In Bordeaux, in the absence of demand for fine red wines, growers mixed their grapes to create cheaper blends. They even ripped up sections of their vineyards occupied by coveted Languedoc grapes to plant white grapes for vinification, which they hoped might sell more and cheaper bottles. In Haiti, formerly Saint-Domingue, on December 6, 1929, approximately fifteen hundred customs officials, students, and farmers in the seaport of Les Cayes peacefully demonstrated against US occupation of the island and poor economic conditions caused by the contraction of the coffee market. US Marines opened fire upon them, killing twelve and wounding another twenty-three. In New York, thousands of homeless people slept on the city's streets, while countless more took their meals at soup kitchens. In Bengal, owners of jute mills dismissed between one-fifth and one-third of the workforce. In the Saarland, with the local coal and steel industry in crisis, the German Communist Party (KPD) won 23.2 percent of the vote in 1932, making it the region's second-strongest party. In La Réunion in 1936/37, a wave of strikes spread along the railroads, docks, fields, and sugar refineries; it was met with police repression. In Hokkaido, during the early years of the Depression, the Japanese government established public works programs to keep growing numbers of unemployed residents off the streets. In Senegal, the Depression's devastating effects on the countryside sent tens of thousands of rural people into the city of Dakar in search of work, the number of urban inhabitants more than doubling to 92,600 in the eight years before 1936. In Java, sugar workers went on hunger marches and, in the vain hope of driving sugar prices up, set sugar warehouses ablaze to prevent sugar from entering a glutted global market. Meanwhile, in 1934, after putting pen to paper against Dutch occupation and the hardships of the Depression, prominent Indonesian nationalists Mohammad Hatta and Sutan Sjahrir were arrested and detained by the colonial government, then eventually exiled to the remote island of Banda Neira in the winter of 1936, the very site of the seventeenth-century genocide that we encountered earlier. In 1934, a wave of strikes in the transportation, communication, and banking industries rocked Rio de Janeiro, with twenty-two thousand workers striking the Leopoldina Railway between Rio de Janeiro and Minas Gerais alone. And in Turin, the Italian car market collapsed as sales dropped by almost half.[95]

The waves engulfing these disparate locations emanated like a global tsunami from the collapse of the industrial core. Between 1929 and 1932, global production decreased by 37.3 percent. Economic output declined everywhere by double digits, in some places even by as much as one-third. It was a global crisis—in fact, a collapse of the entire global capitalist economy—but it was also an assortment of multiple national crises. In the United States, industrial production fell by 26 percent between August 1929 and October 1930. Unemployment there stood at 16 percent in 1931 and at 25 percent in 1933. Half of all New England textile workers had lost their jobs by late 1930. The size of the Ford Motor Company's workforce shrank by almost 70 percent. In Germany, unemployment in 1931 stood at 34 percent; by late 1932, it might have reached as high as 44 percent. In post-crash Japan, as agricultural commodity prices fell by about 50 percent (including those in the crucial cotton, silk, and rice sectors), unemployment shot up; it has been calculated at between 15 and 20 percent at the nadir of the crisis. In South Africa, the nominal value of output fell by 19 percent between 1929/30 and 1932/33, with the social impact disproportionately hitting Black workers. Egyptian per capita income fell by 9 percent between 1929 and 1937. As France's industrial output plummeted by 26 percent, its GDP took a hit, falling by almost 15 percent between 1929 and 1932. In Britain, GDP fell by 11 percent.[96]

International trade collapsed as well: Chilean exports declined by over 80 percent; Chinese, by about 75 percent; Bolivian and Cuban, by between 70 and 75 percent; and Argentinean, Indian, and Spanish, by between 65 and 70 percent. French and British exports collapsed, and by 1932, they were valued at only 40 percent of what they had been just three years earlier. All in all, according to the International Monetary Fund, by 1932, world trade had plunged to just 35 percent of its 1929 value. It had gone from making up 10.84 percent of the global GDP in 1920 to just 5.01 percent in 1935. As trade collapsed, many countries could not afford to serve their debts, and they defaulted. In 1931, every Latin American country except Argentina defaulted. In 1932, southern and eastern Europe followed suit. And then, in 1933, Germany defaulted as well.[97]

Such declining trade and production destabilized national financial systems. Stock markets went into a tailspin, and currencies went through wild swings in value. Banking systems began to collapse in May 1931, first in eastern Europe, then in central and western parts of the continent before spreading to the United States, Mexico, Turkey, and other places. In the United States alone, around nine thousand banks failed.[98] As these banks teetered on the brink, people tried to withdraw their money, which destabilized the system even further. In July 1931, the government closed German banks for a few days. In March 1933, a federal decree closed all US banks for a week.

Policy responses accelerated and deepened the Depression's impact. As the crisis spread to Europe, US capital dried up. Since European recovery had depended almost entirely on these infusions, governments desperately tried to stem the outflow of capital and to encourage further investment. To do so, they raised interest rates, balanced budgets, increased tariffs, and imposed austerity to save their foreign exchange reserves—strategies they had inherited from the nineteenth century. Even free-trade Britain, for the first time in a century, put tariffs in place and, in 1932, erected a system of imperial preferences.[99]

The need to stabilize their currencies in relation to gold further constrained governments' policy options. But despite all their efforts,

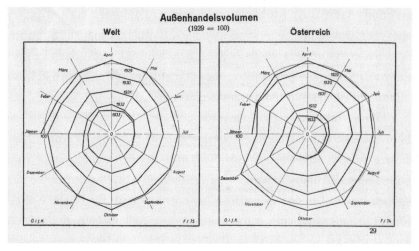

During the Great Depression, Oskar Morgenstern depicted declining trade (here for the world and for Austria) in what became famous as his "spiral."

they still failed to defend the gold standard. As country after country experienced a balance-of-payments crisis, it was forced to devalue its currency to make exports cheaper and imports pricier, encouraging others to leave the gold standard. Germany and Japan abandoned gold in 1931. Britain, the standard-bearer of this particular way of integrating the global economy, suspended convertibility of the pound to gold in September 1931. The United States followed in April 1933. That same year, even South Africa, the world's most important gold producer, left the gold standard. Gold had been the old economic mainstay, but nineteenth-century economic ideas clearly no longer worked to regulate the economy that had emerged.[100] Inadvertently, all efforts to safeguard national economies only further deepened the calamity.

Since the nineteenth century, many economic crises had spread around the world. But the depth of this contagion in the late 1920s and early 1930s was unprecedented and demonstrated once again that capitalism was a truly global process. Intense competition for agricultural commodities on global markets had destabilized the countryside everywhere, laying the groundwork for the Depression. Financial flows resulting from World War I weakened European economies, especially Germany, while the gold standard severely limited policy options for everyone. Combined with escalating inequality in the industrial heartland and the absence of sufficiently large markets for ever more efficient mass production, these factors created the seismic wave of economic catastrophies around the world.

The social effects that accompanied the crisis were dire. When Hans Fallada chronicled the rapid descent of a fictional Johannes Pinneberg from a respected salesperson in a Berlin clothing store to a poverty-stricken jobless worker being shuffled along by police, he described him as "one of six million," a "nothing at all."[101] In the United States, people who had lost their housing camped out in parks in what came to be known as Hoovervilles (after the president who presided over the disaster), went hungry, and traveled the country in search of work. In 1931, the hospitals of New York reported one hundred cases of starvation.[102] When George Orwell toured the northern industrial districts of England in 1936, he saw a "frightful extent of unemployment." He wrote that "getting a job seems about as probable as owning an aeroplane." Such misery, he observed, had a "deadening, debilitating effect" on workers. On his journey, Orwell encountered a world of "beastly" homes, of "underfed" workers who did "not act" but were "acted upon," and of life in "squalid" conditions—beds without bedcovers, rags for clothes, stunted physical growth. Families, he observed, gained their subsistence calories from eating around eight pounds of sugar per week (a testament to the continued importance of the coercive system of sugar production in the Global South), indeed so much so that "in industrial districts a person over thirty with any of his or her own teeth is coming to be an abnormality." In the midst of the Depression it seemed entirely possible that the future of the working class was, in Orwell's words, "a lifetime of unemployment mitigated by endless cups of tea."[103]

The crisis was particularly stark in the commodity-producing countryside, in areas already depleted during the 1920s, as prices had dropped while indebted farmers were bound to serve their loans. And because commodity frontiers had expanded considerably after World War I, their collapse in the 1930s was all the more dramatic. To stabilize prices, Brazilian coffee planters burned and discarded seventy-seven million sacks of coffee between 1931 and 1943. In Colombia, coffee acreage had increased by almost 60 percent between 1910 and 1925, as ever more railroads pushed into the countryside, bringing about more dispossessions and expanded labor mobilizations. When the world market price of coffee collapsed after 1929, many coffee growers and merchants went bankrupt. The Burmese rice industry experienced a drastic price collapse as well, with a 50 percent decline between 1926 and 1934. Rubber fell even more: from twenty-one cents per pound in the summer of 1929 to just three cents in early 1932. Copper dropped from sixteen to five cents per pound; cotton (the world's most widely traded agricultural commodity), from eighteen to six cents; coffee, from twenty-three to eight cents per pound; corn, from ninety-two to nineteen cents; and wheat, from a dollar and fifty cents per bushel to forty-nine cents.[104]

The Depression could have been—and often seemed like—a terminal crisis for capitalism. For University of Chicago historian Frederick L. Schuman, the Depression appeared, from his vantage point in 1938, to be "no mere dip in the business cycle; it is a manifestation of the general crisis and collapse of capitalism."[105] Conservative German journalist and later member of the Nazi Party Ferdinand Zimmermann published a book in 1931 with the programmatic title *Das Ende des Kapitalismus* (*The End of Capitalism*), in which he argued that since the Depression, "the system has lost its way, within it, there is no way out."[106] In France, observers saw the Depression as the sure result of the final "maturation" of capitalism.[107] American fascist ideologue Lawrence Dennis concurred in his 1932 book, *Is Capitalism Doomed?*, explaining that "the private enterprise system must sooner or later be replaced by some system of economic dictatorship, which will eliminate the intolerable condition, known only under modern industrial capitalism, namely, unemployment and want in the midst of unlimited productive capacity."[108] In 1941, the American political philosopher James Burnham predicted that capitalism would soon disappear and be replaced by the management of businesses by administrators.[109] Leon Trotsky, under different political auspices, signaled the same sentiment with his 1938 title *The Death Agony of Capitalism*, arguing that "[t]he objective prerequisites for the proletarian revolution have not only 'ripened'; they have begun to get somewhat rotten."[110]

Such readings were not relegated to the edges of political discourse; they were found in the center as well. Representative Oliver Harlan Cross, a New Deal Democrat from Texas, believed "that if we continue in this helpless condition, in substance, it will get in time where it means the end of capitalism."[111] Montana politician Thomas S. Hogan similarly asserted that "[c]apitalism as a system of industry and government is a demonstrated failure in the face of national crisis and has been destroyed by the practice of its adherents."[112] In a significantly more sophisticated analysis, the Austrian economist Joseph Schumpeter, living in exile in the United States, believed capitalism's demise to be inevitable. In his 1942 *Capitalism, Socialism and Democracy*, he predicted that "[f]aced by the increasing hostility of the environment and by the legislative, administrative and judicial practice born of that hostility, entrepreneurs and capitalists . . . will eventually cease to function."[113] As US philosopher John Katz asked in 1938: "[A]re we not witnessing the failure of capitalism or at least the exhaustion of its creative impulse?[114]

The Depression deeply shook confidence in capitalism. Doubts about its future proliferated. That pessimism is hard to fathom a century later, when capitalism's domination of economic life seems to many the natural order of things. But during the mid-1930s, the crisis sparked an almost ubiquitous search for possible escapes, for new departures, both within and beyond capitalism."[115] It was a moment of experimentation, focused on hedging in markets, empowering states, embracing economic planning, restraining global economic integration, and developing new ways of thinking about the connection between political and economic spaces. Building upon, but also radicalizing, some of the crucial features of capitalism as it had emerged since the 1870s, this moment was also a decisively post-liberal one— the final stab, the coup de grâce, into the near-lifeless corpse of mid-nineteenth-century liberalism.

Political, economic, social, cultural, and ideological responses to the Depression took starkly different forms in different countries, but they all arose out of common and transnational conversation— Americans, Italians, Germans, Brazilians, and Japanese, among others, observing, meeting, and reacting to one another in a series of networked experiments and improvisations. During the 1940s, Karl Polanyi, the great contemporary analyst of capitalism, glimpsed what he came to call the "Great Transformation"—the moment when liberal capitalism had encountered its "natural" limits and its protagonists, confronted with its collapse, chose to "re-embed" markets into society to save it. The Depression had undermined the belief that the solution to economic crisis could be found in the self-directed workings of the world market alone.[116] Massive social movements of workers and peasants—some highly organized, some spontaneous—demanded state-driven relief; capital owners called for investments, regulations, and coordination by the state; economists began to rethink the very foundations of their discipline; and bureaucrats and politicians endeavored to stabilize the foundations of their governments. The Depression had translated into a broad and fundamental rethinking of capitalist economies, often harking back, implicitly if not explicitly, to such state-centric thinkers as Alexander Hamilton, Friedrich List, and the policymakers of Meiji Japan.

Beneath the surface, the diverse political forms that emerged from that crisis-driven rethinking had common foundations, especially in their universal emphasis on the government as a prime regulator of economic life. Market-as-God worship had always been an ideological illusion, not a reflection of the workings of actually existing capitalism. Still, by the end of the 1930s, the points of reference shifted. It was now almost universally acknowledged that markets could not be trusted to generate the best possible economic, social, and political outcomes and that different forms of regulating economic life had to be considered. At a time of existential threat, a huge variety of actors acknowledged capitalism's foundations in the state and employed that insight by vastly expanding the scale and scope of this institution of institutions. The state employed more people, deployed more resources, and entered new realms of economic life, from social provisioning to planning to import-substitution industrialization. The lesson of the Depression seemed clear: Without a much larger and more powerful state, capitalism undermined the very foundations of society, and, in the end, its own.

This new insight and its very urgency derived not only from the severity of the downturn and its global scope, as important as these factors were; it also derived from the very success of the capitalist revolution itself. The connection between the much-enlarged working class and the countryside had weakened, just as the possibilities of subsistence production had been severely curtailed by wave after wave of enclosures, dispossessions, and commodity frontier expansions, pushing commercial agriculture (often monoculture) into much-extended territories. No matter how these processes unfolded, the result was a vastly increased number of people who had become almost entirely dependent on markets for their own and their families' survival. As a result, long-lasting and severe disturbances in labor or commodity markets, such as the Depression, undermined in a deep and sudden way the livelihoods of many, making political responses unavoidable.

Within this common universe, however, politics varied greatly and produced a wide variety of outcomes. Some governments embraced a form of developmentalism.[117] Others expanded the welfare state. Some were guided by corporatist ideas, while others focused on territorial reordering. Some embraced democratic forms of governance, while others did away with most of the legacies of the American, French,

Haitian, and 1848 Revolutions, creating a new and extraordinarily powerful political formation—fascism. At its most extreme edge, in its German variant, this development combined with a vicious racism to create a murderous regime of domestic repression, warfare, and ultimately genocide. But no matter the differences, political changes throughout the empire of capital had a common flavor and were all driven by the crisis of the world economy.

The new economic concepts and strategies and new forms of political mobilization rested on a much-sharpened economic nationalism. World economic integration, in this telling, had created economic contractions, unemployment, new inequalities, balance-of-payment crises, and widespread misery. In response, capital owners, intellectuals, politicians, workers, and peasants searched for new perspectives to politically reengineer domestic economies and decouple them, to the greatest extent possible, from the larger world. Even British economist John Maynard Keynes was forceful on that issue: In a 1933 article titled "National Self-Sufficiency," which appeared in *The Yale Review*, he acknowledged that it was difficult to "shuffle out of the mental habits of the prewar nineteenth-century world," that "bundle of obsolete habiliments [of] one's mind."[118] These ideas had been well intentioned, but Keynes, animated by a wish to secure peace and prosperity, now "sympathize[d] . . . with those who would minimize . . . economic entanglement among nations."[119] He advocated bringing "the product and the consumer within the ambit of the same national, economic, and financial organization," proposing a new way of thinking: "We wish . . . to be our own masters, and to be as free as we can make ourselves from the interferences of the outside world."[120] While Keynes saw risks to such economic nationalism—it could be too doctrinaire, too hateful, and too unwilling to learn from its critics—he articulated what had essentially become common wisdom in the early 1930s.[121]

In terms of practical policies, protectionism through tariffs, trade barriers, and currency devaluations were the tools of choice.[122] Yet decoupling was just one of the policy responses. Efforts to forge ever more national—even autarkic—economic spaces and to double down on imperial commodity chains were its corollary. If economic special-ization had been one of the reasons for the depth of the crisis, policy-makers and others reasoned, forging a new correspondence between economic and political spaces, both national and imperial, was the log-ical response.

In Italy, the fascist government of Benito Mussolini aimed to de-couple the nation from the world economy, engaging in what Indian sociologist Benoy Kumar Sarkar called "Italian *swadeshi*," naming it after the Indian effort to replace British-made products with domesti-cally manufactured ones.[123] Mussolini had come to power a decade earlier, during yet another, much shorter economic crisis, but his poli-cies now came to serve as a source of inspiration. Food self-sufficiency was one such goal, to be accomplished through land reclamation proj-ects and financial incentives for grain production. Mussolini also fo-cused on a much-extended role of the state in heavy industry, building steel mills, chemical plants, and shipbuilding facilities. As a result, by the late 1930s, a state holding company controlled half of the nation's share of capital, making it enormously influential in many of the na-tion's core industries and its banking sector.[124]

Germany's fascist government embraced economic nationalism as well. Hjalmar Schacht, appointed in 1933 as Hitler's president of the Reichsbank, advocated Germany's decoupling from the world market; economic subjugation of eastern Europe by making it into a producer of primary products and customers for German industry; massive pub-lic works programs; and expanded state spending enabled by taking on debt. Under his auspices, government spending increased from 16 per-cent of the GNP in 1929 to 23 percent in 1934. Given the emphasis on autarky, much of that spending went toward military hardware, which was meant to enable, in turn, the economic integration of eastern and central Europe into the German economy. The Nazis also built hun-dreds of state-owned firms. By 1936, they had further institutional-ized their Four-Year Plan, with the explicit goal of self-sufficiency in food production and manufacturing.[125]

Japan, a developmental state that had always been deeply engaged in economic planning, was another example of such policies. When the Depression first hit this island country, policy responses had been broadly in line with those elsewhere—retrenchment, austerity, an effort to keep budgets balanced, a defense of the gold standard—and explicitly attacked what was called the "frivolity and self-indulgence" of the Japanese people as the alleged root cause of the downturn.[126] By 1931, however, the thinking had changed. A new finance minister, Takahashi Korekiyo, suspended the gold standard, encouraged deficit spending, and pushed for government interventions to encourage demand. For him, luxury and prosperity went hand in hand just as much as austerity and poverty. As in Germany, deficit spending focused on military expansion and investments in Manchuria, which in turn generated domestic demand, encouraged further investment, and then increased production.[127]

Economic nationalism, in Japan and other places, continued to rest on imperial expansion. For Japan, as we saw earlier, imperial enclosures had started in Hokkaido in the 1870s and then been further elaborated in Korea, Taiwan, and parts of China. They radically accelerated in response to the Depression, when the Japanese state and Japanese capital focused their energies on imperial expansion into northeast Asia in general and Manchuria in particular before embarking upon an exaggeratedly ambitious project to remake Asian economic space more broadly.[128]

Japan's military planners had had an eye on Manchuria since the 1880s and had acquired, in 1905, the South Manchurian Railway Zone. When poet Yosano Akiko turned to her diary in 1928 to wax lyrical about the vistas she had seen from a train traversing the Chinese countryside, she "imagined that in the future northern Manchuria would probably become enormously valuable economically."[129] With the enthusiastic support of private capital, Japan erected a puppet state in Manchuria—Manchukuo—in 1932. Once Japan had conquered Manchuria, the government worked hard on integrating it economically. The South Manchurian Railway had first been used as a corridor to transport soy, and it stimulated the reorganization of local

Japan's Keynes: Takahashi Korekiyo, finance minister, 1931–1936.

agriculture. Manchukuo, however, was to become more than a provider of cheap agricultural commodities; it was to not only be industrialized but also provide homes for Japanese settlers. Technocrats from Japan arrived to restructure its economy and society, planning development and experimenting with new forms of economic organization that they believed might become relevant to Japan itself. Such imperial expansion, then and earlier, was a project of state strengthening—not least to gain access to resources that could sustain the nation during a major war.[130]

But it was also a project that brought Japanese businesses into the field. Formed in 1933, the Japan–Manchuria Business Council supported enterprises that came to be deeply devoted to the Manchurian economy. Between 1932 and 1941, these businesses invested almost six billion yen in Manchukuo, making it the most important capital outlet of the Japanese Empire—there they built steel mills, oil refineries, chemical factories, and even automobile manufacturing plants. Nissan even moved its headquarters to Manchuria and became newly known as Manchuria Heavy Industries. But the direct capital of *zaibatsu*—large conglomerates—made up only 10 percent of total Japanese investments, as most private investments took the form of bond purchases with guaranteed returns, leaving the risk to the government. By the 1930s, businesspeople enthusiastically embraced such visions: "[W]e have developed Taiwan and we have developed Korea and we have developed Hokkaidō," argued one of them. "In the same way we will shock the world by transforming the continent within the space of ten or twenty years . . . with Japanese capital, Japanese efforts, and Japanese technology."[131] Later that same decade, the Japanese economic journal *Ekonomisuto* celebrated the "acceleration of the East Asian bloc."[132] By 1940, Manchuria provided the market for more than a third of all Japanese exports, the result of both the collapse of the world market and the realization of autarky.[133]

Business and government cooperated in colonial policymaking, but there were disagreements among them. Some capital owners saw the export potential of colonial holdings; others were concerned about losing access to noncolonial markets, especially the textile industry. Some companies also had internally divided interests, such as the huge, integrated zaibatsu Mitsui and Mitsubishi. All in all, however, Japanese businesses were, from the get-go, greatly excited about new export possibilities secured by imperial holdings. They published many reports on the potential of newly captured areas, reinforcing the interests of a government that focused on issues of "economic security," "economic expansion," and social stability at home. As business and governing elites worked toward the integration of imperial holdings into the Japanese economy, a kind of "imperial corporatism" emerged. At its core was the creation of a large, politically unified economic bloc—the Yen bloc—that would enable Japanese autarky and secure its standing in the world. Rōyama Masamichi hoped that Japan would "liberate and overcome the spatial and regional limitations of the Japanese economy."[134]

To be detached from the world economy meant, in reality, to be in control of territories of sufficient size and diversity to enable that separation. In Europe, such territorial reordering harked back to the pre-Depression years. Throughout the 1920s, Africa had remained the focus of European aims, part answer to the "American danger," part global trend to segment the world economy into "blocs."[135] While national ambitions for individual African colonies had persisted, during the interwar years, a new idea had risen to prominence: the integration of Africa as a Pan-European, rather than competitive, project. One of the most important contributors to this debate was Austrian aristocrat Richard N. Coudenhove-Kalergi, whose 1923 *Pan-Europa* was translated into nearly every European language.[136] He advocated for the creation of a gigantic European free-trade zone, modeled after the American Union and motivated by fears of the US as a "leading power": "Today, the United States is the wealthiest, most powerful, and most progressive empire in the world," Coudenhove-Kalergi wrote in his bestseller, "a country in the process of dividing up . . . the peoples and raw materials of the world."[137] America's great advantage was its "tremendous economic territory," which had raw materials in abundance and allowed for cheaper production, thanks to a more rational division of labor.[138]

Coudenhove-Kalergi was clear on what needed to happen: Europe had to integrate its own market and "expand that market by opening up Africa." Central to his thinking was what he called Eurafrica, a geographic unit that stretched from the North Cape to Congo.[139] "Africa could offer Europe raw materials for its industry, food for its

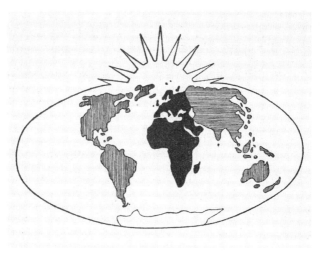

*Eurafrica: the dream of integrating Africa
into the European economy.*

people, land for its surplus population, job opportunities for its unemployed, [and] markets for its sales."[140] Coudenhove-Kalergi saw Africa as "the tropical garden of Europe" and "Europe's plantation."[141] "One day," he explained, "our descendants will live in world cities on the shores of the Congo River."[142] Pan-Europe would turn Africa into "the future granary and raw material source of Europe."[143] In his view, Europe was "the head of Eurafrica, and Africa its body."[144]

Coudenhove-Kalergi was not alone in suggesting joint European exploitation and domination of Africa. The most ambitious and quixotic project along these lines came from a German engineer, Herman Sörgel. The Atlantropa movement he inspired was a loose association of people who believed that Europe and Africa should be forged into a single economic space. The organization developed painstakingly detailed plans, going so far as to suggest that the Mediterranean be partly drained to bridge—quite literally—the divide between Europe and Africa. Visions of huge dams and transcontinental railway lines, including a nine-thousand-mile railroad stretching from Berlin to Cape Town, were crucial to this pie-in-the-sky project. The irrigation of the Sahara would, in turn, create vast new agricultural lands that would give Europe more "living space" to produce grains and cotton, potatoes and sugar.[145]

In response to the Depression, such European projects of territorial reordering radicalized and veered in sharply nationalist directions. In Italy, Eurafrica advocates celebrated Mussolini's aggressive policies toward that continent, especially his colonizing of Ethiopia: In the spring of 1938, a congress of Africa experts at the Reale Accademia d'Italia in Rome concluded that "Africa is the future of Europe." "Africa," argued Francesco Orestano, philosopher and president of the proceedings, "belongs to Europe"—indeed, Ethiopia was "our Far West."[146] In the eyes of fascist ideologue J. Mazzei, the twentieth century was the moment when the "problem of economic space was born," and Eurafrica was its solution.[147] The only issue was speed: Europe had to act soon, before the United States became so powerful that such expansions were rendered impossible.

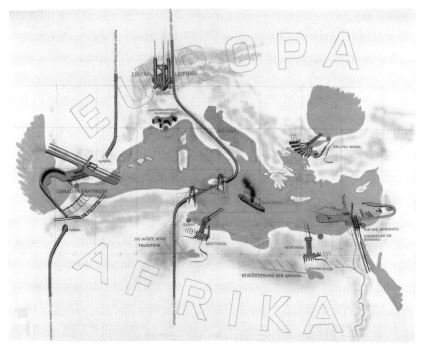

Merging Europe with Africa: Herman Sörgel's Atlantropa plans, 1932.

When the Nazis took power in January 1933, ideas of "economic space," especially the creation of a contiguous territorial empire, took on new urgency.[148] That month, Schacht allegedly promised Coudenhove-Kalergi: "You will see! Hitler will create Pan-Europa."[149] The Führer and his supporters wholeheartedly embraced this project, but projected rival dreams of colonial empire in Europe's East rather than to the south.[150] When journalist Ferdinand Zimmermann, now an SS member, gave a lecture at the University of (German-occupied) Prague in 1941 (the same writer who had authored *The End of Capitalism* in 1931 had moved on to *The Rise of the Jews*), he praised the United States for having grasped the importance of a "greater independent economic space and the concept of greater space as a modern form of national economic thought"—an almost perfect example for Germany itself.[151] Hitler was just as focused on the US, writing in 1928 that the significant expansion of German territory was the only way to confront the "American danger."[152] For him, the United States posed a threat because of its access to a plenitude of raw materials and a large market, as well as its "vast open space."[153] Hitler compared German expansion to the conquest of the American West, calling the Volga Germany's Mississippi, and equated Russians to Native Americans.[154] He declared:

> The struggle for hegemony in the world is decided for Europe by the possession of Russian territory; it makes Europe the place in the world most secure from blockade. . . . The Slavic peoples . . . are not destined for their own life. . . . We will supply the Ukrainians with headscarves, glass chains as jewelry, and whatever else colonial peoples like.[155]

Though seemingly contradictory, imperial expansion and autarkic retrenchment went hand in hand.

And in Germany, just like in Japan, this odd pair found significant support among capital owners. Unlike some more export-oriented industries—leather, for example—the iron and steel industry, unsurprisingly, latched on to Nazi plans. Few people illustrated that affinity better than Hermann Röchling, whose history of efforts to forge a vertically integrated firm independent of many markets suggested radical moves toward autarky. This tightly held conviction grew even stronger in response to Röchling's personal experience after World War I. Following the war, the Saarland came under French administration, and French companies came to be involved with Saar businesses, while Röchling lost control of his investments in France. This created new uncertainties for his supplies of iron ore and coal—things that he now had to buy "for dear money," rather than produce within his own company.[156] Before the war, the Saar's steelworks as a whole had control of iron-ore supplies expected to last for the next 125 years, but all of that was now lost, as ores had to be imported from France.[157]

Röchling turned to politics to resolve this dilemma, even creating a lobbying office in Berlin to push for the reintegration of the Saar into Germany. Throughout the interwar years, he continued to emphasize to Berlin his urgent need to secure access to inputs. Fearful that the

French government would blockade iron-ore exports from the territories it had recaptured in World War I, Röchling gunned for yet another round of territorial reordering. His dogged fight for the return of the Saar to Germany became almost a full-time job—a politics that also brought him into close contact with Adolf Hitler. When Röchling met the Führer for the first time on March 31, 1933, they talked about the Saar. Six weeks later, at another meeting, they focused on the mobilization of nationalist forces in the Saar.[158] In 1934, Röchling published the book *Saarkampf*, documenting the struggle to recover the Saar. His consistent support of Hitler and German territorial expansion eventually brought him to the forefront of yet another effort to reorder Europe's economic spaces more broadly.

Other countries followed similar autarkic and imperial politics. Portugal endeavored to make itself independent of the world market for cotton by violently developing cotton agriculture in its African colonies, especially in Mozambique; it had stunning success, eventually securing 90 percent of the needs of its textile industry in those territories. Even in the United States (which was largely free of world market dependency, thanks to the size and diversity of its territory and people), autarkic ideas gained prominence. During the 1920s, Herbert Hoover, then secretary of commerce, ventured to secure rubber supplies for the United States' vital automobile industry by supporting Harvey Samuel Firestone's vast concession in Liberia, even as Henry Ford was building massive rubber plantations deep in the Brazilian rainforest.[159]

Heim ins Reich:
Hermann Röchling
goes into politics.

E conomic nationalism embraced not just protectionism, territorial reordering, and the construction of imperial commodity chains but also the intensification of industrial production in the homeland itself. At the most aspirational end, former breadbaskets and mineral exporters aimed to build a new global division of labor, ditching the previous subservience to the industrial core in favor of domestic industrialization.[160]

Where possible, the agricultural exporters hardest hit by the Depression followed a policy of import-substitution industrialization. Faced with falling prices, worsening trade terms, and drastically declining demand for traditional agricultural and mineral exports, they embarked upon the creation of a more protected industrial economic space. As Egyptian entrepreneurs moved capital into manufacturing, a substantial textile industry took shape, expanding sevenfold during the 1930s alone. Brazilian manufacturing doubled in size between 1920 and 1938. China launched protectionist policies too, aiming to develop its domestic industry. And industry in British India doubled in size during this period. Such growth was in part the result of political realignments: Commodity exporters had been politically weakened, bringing to power new elites with interests in domestic industrialization.[161]

Turkey exemplified this trend. The new nation, born in 1923 from the ashes of the Ottoman Empire, depended on the export of agricultural commodities—tobacco, for example—and the import of manufactured goods. Once the Depression hit, these links spiraled into a rapid decline, further accelerated by Turkey's dependency on foreign loans that were ever more difficult to secure. In response, the young nation builders around leader Mustafa Kemal Atatürk undertook a massive effort to achieve domestic industrialization, embracing an economic nationalism that envisioned a new integration of Turkey into the global economy. Its principal propelling force was the much more pronounced involvement of the state, as economic planning, infrastructure development, and nationalizations pushed what is known as Kemalism into its "classical phase," lasting from 1933 to 1940. The First Five-Year Plan, the Birinci Beş Yıllık Sanayi Plan, was implemented in 1933. In it, Atatürk enthusiastically espoused the idea of autarky, building upon decades-old traditions of economic nationalism tracing all the way back to Ahmet Mithat's 1880 *Ekonomi politik* and Istanbul finance professor Munis Tekinalp's 1916 dissecting of Germany's rapid economic development, which saw Friedrich List's ideas as its foundations. Such economic nationalism sharpened after 1929 and won new sway, partly because of the declining influence of elites who had gained power from their world market connections and partly because of the drastic worsening of Turkey's trade terms during the years from 1929 to 1933. The share of imports in the nation's GDP fell from 13 percent in 1928/29 to 7 percent in 1938/39, as tariffs and quotas on manufactured goods boosted Turkish industrial production.[162]

Mexico took up similar policies and also saw significant industrialization during the 1930s. Its First Six-Year Plan—the Plano Sexenal—was implemented in 1933 (at that point, the country's GNP had fallen by 30.9 percent since 1926). And then, in 1934, Lázaro Cárdenas became president, deeply committed to a policy of economic nationalism, including the nationalization of the country's critical oil sector. Farther south, Argentina, the poster child of development based on the export of agricultural commodities, responded to the crisis in similar ways. It was there that a young economist, Raúl Prebisch, ditched his deeply anchored beliefs in free trade and comparative advantage and embraced economic nationalism, leading him to rethink the shape of the global economy. By the second half of the 1940s, Prebisch was articulating the fundamentally different possibilities of what he called the "center" and the "periphery" in systems of unequal exchange.[163]

In the industrialized world, capital owners and governments also collaborated on efforts principally aimed at better competing with the United States in the most cutting-edge industries. They were drawn to the new manufacturing order that had emerged out of Detroit, promising greater productivity, higher profits, better living standards, heightened military power, and improved social stability. Technological leaps and productivity enhancements would enable a weaning from the world market under the auspices of the state and, importantly, a vastly expanded stimulus through the production of military hardware. Testifying to the importance of the United States, European visitors continued to flock to Detroit during the 1930s, admiring the gargantuan River Rouge factory that Ford had opened in 1928. By then the biggest factory in the world, it employed 102,811 workers who transformed iron ore, coal, and wood—delivered from Ford's own mines and timber lands—into gleaming automobiles. German, Soviet, Italian, and Japanese delegations walked its extensive grounds, determined to replicate Ford's productivity miracle in their own countries. German automobile specialist William Werner was so enamored by what he saw in 1937 that he celebrated the River Rouge as one of "the most brilliant technical achievements in the history of the world."[164] Ford shared many of the underlying technologies with his visitors. In 1932, the giant Gorky factory opened in Nizhny Novgorod; Toyota inaugurated its Koromo-cho plant near Nagoya in 1938; Volkswagen got its Wolfsburg factory off the ground in 1939; and that same year, Fiat began operating its Mirafiori factory near Turin (a much-enlarged version of the Lingotto)—all thanks to Ford's help. All drew on significant state support, and all would become central to military production during the coming war. American production technologies particularly attracted the attention of the world's most authoritarian rulers: Hitler demanded "territory and Fordism."[165] His Italian counterpart, Benito Mussolini, embraced his notion of a "people's car," advocated "fordismo," and demanded that Fiat build a truly popular car.[166] The Topolino—Little Mouse—came onto the market in 1936 at a retail cost of just 8,900 lira (about $700 in US dollars).[167] Despite anti-American rhetoric, America was the example to follow.[168]

All these efforts at industrialization relied on unprecedented government interventions. Of course, capitalism had always depended on the state and expanded alongside it, but the 1930s saw a significant jump in the state's scale and scope. Driven by the perceived success of the Soviet economy, which did not seem to suffer under the Depression, governments all around the world passed three-, four-, five-, or six-year plans. Even in the United States, planning became politically palatable. In 1933, the country embarked on its most comprehensive regional planning effort ever when the Tennessee Valley Authority set out to develop millions of acres in the impoverished South. Economic development had become too important to be left to the market alone. State planning was seen as superior to the investment decisions of private entrepreneurs. In the United States, the National Recovery Administration brought the government, business leaders, and labor together to limit competition and set prices.[169] For its director, Hugh S. Johnson, such New Deal policies amounted to nothing less than a substitute "to the murderous doctrine of savage and wolfish competition and rugged individualism."[170]

As a result, states as instituitions grew in size: In the United States, a huge bureaucracy emerged to manage the crisis response. While there had been 604,000 civilian federal employees in 1933, that number had expanded to 867,000 by 1936. Federal government spending almost doubled between 1933 and 1939, as it did in France, Germany, and Italy as well. There, government spending as a share of the GNP rose to about 20 to 25 percent, twice as much as in 1913. So all-encompassing had the state's machinery become that it now drew on the most modern technologies to administer its realm, with computers such as IBM's Hollerith system processing the vast amounts of data involved in both US Social Security payments and the Nazis' project to deport Germany's Jews.[171]

Economic nationalism, including moves toward autarky, was the most prominent policy response to the Depression, leaving a profound imprint on twentieth-century capitalism. It deepened the link between national capital and national states that had been strengthening since the 1870s, responding as much to the particular needs of particular forms of capital (namely, its industrial variety) as to the new dependence of states on exactly these same forms of capital. By 1930, however, economic nationalism was also motivated by efforts to overcome the grave social dislocations of the Depression, making it a form of social policy as well. Limiting trade promised urgently needed domestic employment. Making concerted efforts to build and expand national industries promised stability. And even territorial reordering, enabling the transfer of resources into capitalism's industrial heartlands, could be (and was) seen as a form of social policy.[172]

The social question had become of utmost urgency. As we have seen, labor upheaval, unionization, rebellions, and revolutions—not to speak of the rapid rise of socialist politics, beginning with and promoted by the Soviet Union—had brought social tensions into new focus. Millions of highly organized and mobilized workers clamored for a share of the wealth produced by newly productive industries—and questioned the legitimacy of a small group of capital owners controlling these crucial resources. When the Depression hit, that urgency sharpened considerably. Stark poverty and debilitating insecurity in the midst of plenty delegitimized the existing economic order.

Yet the reason for the new prominence of the social question was also structural. Social dislocations, as policymakers and economists increasingly understood, undermined economic recovery, as they limited demand. This was particularly clear in light of the new importance of mass-production industries in the consumer sector, which depended on the ability of people, including people of modest means, to purchase the goods coming out of these ever more efficient factories. And it was structural for other reasons as well—namely, the depth of the capitalist revolution itself. Tens of millions of people in the centers of commodity production had become proletarians. They had lost access to the land and thus had no choice but to try to make a living in urban areas and in industry. In that sense, reproduction of society, so it seemed, could not be left to the market alone. When the cotton mills of Alsace had gone through a deep crisis in the 1860s, many of the mill workers could return to the countryside and survive there. But when Japan's industry shed millions of workers in the 1930s, they had nowhere to go.[173] As one textile worker, a young Japanese woman, remarked in 1930: "Even if we go back to the country, our parents and our brothers do not have enough to eat. Knowing this, how can we possibly go back?"[174]

Such factors combined with a widespread fear among capital owners, state bureaucrats, and politicians of rebellions. After all, the Depression went hand in hand with another spike in social upheaval. In the United States, to cite just one example, the crisis provoked significant political mobilization among workers, employed and unemployed. Poor people took food from markets, tens of thousands of unemployed assembled in American cities, and World War I veterans congregated in Washington in the summer of 1932 to demand "bonus payments" for their war service, only to be chased off the grounds by US Army tanks commanded by General Douglas MacArthur. Rent riots in American cities frequently turned into massive and even violent gatherings, and a "relief insurgency" mobilized people to demand welfare payments.[175] Those still employed also became increasingly restless, and as companies in distress reduced wages, workers took to the streets. "[T]he spirit of revolt is widespread," reported O. Max Gardner, North Carolina's governor, in the summer of 1932.[176] By 1933, with the passage of the National Industrial Recovery Act (NIRA)—especially its pro-union section, 7(a)—strikes started to spread as well. In 1932, there had been just 841 strikes in the United States; in 1933, that number increased to 1,695, and in 1934, it swelled to 1,856, with 1.5 million workers participating. Toledo, Minneapolis, and San Francisco saw massive and often violent labor conflicts. By 1935, the Congress of Industrial Organizations (CIO) had formed, a union dedicated to the organization of workers in the new mass-production industries. In early 1936, rubber workers in Akron, Ohio, engaged in the first sit-down strike against wage cuts, a tactic that spread to the automobile industry—for example, to Cleveland and, later that year, to the workers at GM's Fisher Body factory in Flint, Michigan. Almost 5 million workers went on strike in 1937 alone. By 1945, the US counted 14.8 million union members, 1 in every 3 a nonagricultural worker.[177]

Such rebellions took place throughout the industrialized world. In Germany, sailors and port workers mobilized soon after the crash, as a staggering 63.5 percent of the shipbuilding workforce experienced unemployment. In 1931, as employers cut wages, workers staged strikes in Stettin, Hamburg, and Bremerhaven. Transport workers struck in Berlin in 1932, as communist unions mobilized against right-wing forces around Hitler. In Japan, workers, both those still employed and those already unemployed, mobilized widely. One study assessed a metal district on the outskirts of Tokyo and found that between 1930 and 1932, 15 percent of all its factories, and 38 percent of its larger factories, faced at least one labor dispute.[178] While the conditions for successful collective action were as bad as they could possibly be, the unemployed still engaged in a constant struggle to improve their fate. And in Bombay, textile workers continued to engage in collective action, only to be met by a repressive government and "the menacing presence of an army of starving unemployed."[179]

Fear and necessity drove the state to take on a new role in providing social supports and safeguards. It employed, ordered, healed, fed, supplied, housed, and schooled millions of proletarians in ways unimaginable just a few decades earlier. In 1945, when historian Edward Hallett Carr published his extended critique of nationalism, *Nationalism and After*, he observed that the state had entered a new phase in which the "socialization of the nation" had taken place. With mass politics emerging, "[t]he primary aim of national policy was no longer merely to maintain order and conduct what was narrowly defined as public business, but to minister to the welfare of members of the nation and to enable them to earn their living," bringing "the economic claims of the masses into the forefront of the picture."[180]

Governments, and at times also companies, dramatically expanded the welfare state. Some of these expansions were temporary, others permanent, but altogether they prefigured a radically recast state throughout the heartlands of industrial capitalism and, increasingly, beyond. In Japan, the Depression at first ushered in only a modest expansion of public works that never employed more than 4 percent of those out of work. In 1936, however, partly in response to the sustained collective mobilizations of Japanese workers, the National Diet passed the Retirement and Severance Pay Law, which required many employers to pay their workers when they were fired or when they retired. The new law would cover about 62 percent of all factory workers. Then, after the Second Sino-Japanese War began in 1937, social policy expanded once more, turning the war years into a period of blossoming for the Japanese welfare state. In 1938, as war mobilization weakened political opposition from business interests, Japan created a new cabinet-level welfare ministry, which immediately designed and implemented the National Health Insurance Law, providing almost universal coverage. Pension schemes soon followed with the 1942 passage of a workers' pension law. Public welfare was improved as well, and by 1941, the Public Housing Corporation had started constructing workers' homes.[181]

In the United States, the welfare state also saw significant expansion, both in response to the immediate crisis and in more permanent ways. To address the problem of massive unemployment, hundreds of thousands of youths were recruited into the Civilian Conservation Corps. Public works provided employment to millions more, as massive state investments, amounting to 6 percent of the nation's GDP in 1933, were injected into a construction spree. Half a million miles of roads, forty thousand schools, and one thousand airfields were added to the American-built environment. Public housing construction also expanded. Then, in 1935, the Social Security Act provided Americans with a modicum of security in old age for the first time. Labor gained new institutional legitimacy through the 1935 Wagner Act, which put the authority and power of the state behind labor's collective bargaining. The unionization rate jumped from 5 percent in 1933 to 16 percent in 1940 to 22 percent in 1945.[182]

Even outside the heartlands of industrial capitalism, governments built new welfare states, however incomplete they might have been. By mid-1933, in response to worker mobilizations, massive public works programs sustained about 8 percent of white South African workers.

Their principal aim was to aid poor whites and to shelter white workers from competition with their Black counterparts. During the 1930s, these welfare measures were vastly expanded. South Africa's old-age pension system, inaugurated in 1928, grew rapidly—expenditures for pensions almost doubled between 1936 and 1939. And disability pension schemes came about in 1937, the same year that the Department of Labour and Social Welfare was created. Unemployment insurance followed. In 1944, the pension system was extended to cover Black men and women, though its payments to them remained distinctly lower. By 1948, about one in seventeen South Africans received transfer payments from the state.[183]

On a much smaller scale, British India also saw the emergence of an incipient welfare state. The Workmen's Compensation Act, which covered workers in case of industrial accidents in certain industries (principally textiles, steel, and railroads), had already been passed in 1923, partly in response to the high degree of mobilization among India's industrial workers and the desire of some employers to stabilize their workforces. Those measures expanded during the 1930s, and by 1945, the act covered six million workers. By the late 1930s, the Congress was pressing for further expansions of the welfare state. Pushed by the Bombay Provincial Trade Union Congress, it demanded a comprehensive system of social insurance for "the industrial population," including provisions for old age, sickness, and unemployment. It also suggested implementing, as a temporary measure, a scheme of mandatory sick pay for industrial workers.[184]

Everywhere, the role of the state in society expanded—sometimes tentatively, as in India, and sometimes on a larger scale, as in the United States. So profound was this rethinking that it even affected legal theorizing, which became more oriented toward producing desirable social outcomes. Throughout the world, legal scholars and judges—American justice Louis Brandeis prominently among them—became more aware of the social crises produced by proletarianization, urbanization, and industrialization. They sought new legal answers that gave greater emphasis to the social question—including protective labor legislation, the regulation of financial systems, social protections, and corporatist arrangements.[185] During the Depression, this rethinking accelerated universally. As it turned out, the spreading and deepening of the capitalist revolution demanded ever more—not less—of the state. Securing citizens' ability to raise families, educate their children, access health care, and subsist during unemployment and old age—their social reproduction, in the language of scholars—was now recognized as the bedrock of the capitalist revolution, a foundation that required an expanded state apparatus.

This rethinking of the role of the state within capitalist society went hand in hand with a rethinking of the discipline of economics. No one was more important to that project than British economist John Maynard Keynes, who had nourished a dislike of mainstream economics since before the Depression, accusing the field of making "[t]he whole conduct of life . . . into a sort of parody of an accountant's nightmare."[186] For him, mainstream economic ideas—those coming out of the marginalist revolution—amounted to "bogus calculations" informed by "false analogies from an irrelevant accountancy."[187] For Keynes, it seemed absurd that "[w]e have to remain poor because it does not 'pay' to be rich. We have to live in hovels, not because we cannot build palaces, but because we cannot 'afford' them."[188] In 1932, in the depths of the Depression, he declared that "[t]he voices which . . . tell us that the path of escape is to be found in strict economy and in refraining, wherever possible, from utilizing the world's potential production are the voices of fools and madmen."[189]

In casting these voices as "fools and madmen," Keynes questioned the shibboleths of many of his colleagues: their embrace of austerity in times of crisis and their seemingly unshakable belief in the self-regulating properties of markets. Instead, he demanded "direct government intervention to promote and subsidize new investment."[190] Already in the mid-1920s, he was lecturing in Oxford and Berlin on

"The End of Laissez-Faire," suggesting that society needed to be rethought in light of the Russian Revolution, labor upheavals, and anti-colonial movements.[191] He doubted that economic self-interest alone would be sufficient to regulate society or even produce the best economic outcomes.

In the wake of the Depression, his ideas sharpened. In 1930, he presented his *Treatise on Money*, an attempt to solve a major conundrum in classical economics: why the economy experienced booms and busts. According to Keynes, classical economics assumes that the key levers of the economy—saving and investment—are self-regulating.[192] Saving money in banks, stocks, or bonds is an investment that generates income. If that investment stagnates, the economy does not expand, income is not created, and a recession follows. Because private investment is at times not forthcoming, Keynes argued that in such cases investment should be induced by government policy—an early intimation of the idea that came to be known as "Keynesian stimulus."[193] Without it, saving, investment, and consumption—the mutually dependent processes that propelled capitalist economies—could become stuck.

But Keynes's theory was incomplete. As economist Robert Heilbroner noted, it could not possibly explain how the economy could stay in a state of "prolonged depression."[194] A more complete account was required. In 1936, Keynes completed his magnum opus—*The General Theory of Employment, Interest, and Money*—to address the problem. Keynes's *General Theory* was as much a set of solutions to the crisis as it was a book of theory. The first chapter explained that *The General Theory* was meant to clarify and expand "the postulates of classical economics."[195] Classical theories of production and value, he argued, operated with a given volume of employed resources and a determined set of conditions. He sought to instead develop a theory of what determines the employment of resources. Keynes's revision shattered the classical orthodoxy of an economy that fixes itself. *The General Theory* proposed that in a slump, the opposite would happen: Savings would be so restricted that there could not possibly be enough investment to create income. His theory of employment explained that the level of employment was determined by the amount of investment and by a nation's "propensity to consume."[196] With these two variables, each determined by policy and economic decisions, he transformed ideas about the level of employment—it went from being seen as something that was automatically determined by the operation of markets to something that could be achieved with the right policies. The core solution Keynes proposed was deficit spending in times of cyclical downturns— state investment would rekindle the cycles of private saving and investment crucial to the expansion of a capitalist economy. He argued that the state had to intervene to tame "the fluctuations of the private economy and restore it to full employment," that the government might "best deal with economic depression by raising the level of aggregate demand for goods."[197] Countercyclical demand management, Keynes understood, could keep the economy "on a knife-edge between full employment and inflation."[198] If private investment was not forthcoming, the government had to secure a certain stability of consumption. Arguing that state policy could help a depressed economy become unstuck, Keynes effectively reduced the existential problem of crisis to a technocratic issue that could be overcome with the right policies. Having been deeply immersed in managing Britain's colonial empire since the 1910s (his first job was as economic policy adviser to the Royal Commission on Indian Currency and Finance of 1913–1914), Keynes took inspiration from the interventionism that had characterized colonial policies all along.[199]

Once put to paper, Keynes's theoretical tools infiltrated the halls of power in places such as the United Kingdom and the United States and played a key role in guiding further policy responses to the Depression. He was hardly a revolutionary; he proposed what he thought was necessary, jettisoning neither classical economics nor capitalism. As many historians and economists have shown, his thinking advanced policies that would generate an unprecedented decrease in inequality and boost the developed world's standards of living. His work, among other things, helped to steer the developed world from an "Age of Catastrophe" toward its "Golden Age."[200]

———

These responses to crisis produced and were enabled by strikingly different political outcomes, again demonstrating that capitalism can inhabit a great variety of political forms. Scholars have spent decades debating which political form best corresponds to capitalism, with answers ranging from liberal democracy to fascism. What we can see when we look at the global 1930s, however, is something different— namely, that capitalism can flourish within a wide range of forms of political rule. As with diverse labor and territorial regimes, capitalism is undogmatic in regard to political systems as well.

In some senses, this is a pessimistic assessment, particularly if compared with the once popular modernization theory that drew a more or less straight line from the capitalist organization of economic life to the emergence of liberal, even democratic, regimes.[201] But the 1930s responses to depression showed that such Whiggish views were unwarranted, as it became clear that various forms of authoritarian rule—even fascism—were perfectly compatible with capitalism. As capitalism entered its most severe crisis, as social upheaval proliferated and economic nationalism took wing, post-liberal regimes multiplied with their promises of national regeneration, territorial reordering, economic prosperity, security, and an end to unrest.

Yet to insist on the undogmatic nature of capitalism's relationship to political regimes is a more optimistic reading than that suggested by some strains of Marxism (such as that spouted by communist parties in the 1920s and early 1930s) that see authoritarianism as an almost necessary outcome of capitalist crisis and thus of capitalism. The Depression, after all, showed that even the most severe economic crisis could be addressed by democratic regimes. Strengthened by vastly expanding the welfare state, reigniting economic growth, and unleashing human creativity within a liberal framework, democracies succeeded in rele-gitimizing capitalist regimes beyond the wildest expectations of most observers during the 1930s, and in effect launched another crucial component of what would later be seen as the golden years.

In Sweden, for example, the governing Social Democratic Party, the SAP, alleviated the effects of the Depression through a wide vari-ety of social supports, beginning to build what became the legendary Scandinavian welfare state. Many of the basic ideas that propelled this response had already been hashed out in the 1920s, but now, during the 1930s, Social Democrats deepened their coalition with agrarian interests to implement a complex program of social and economic re-forms. Promising farmers protection against foreign competition, they received the farmers' support for their working-class-friendly policies. The resulting 1933 agreement, the so-called Cow Deal, provided agri-cultural loans to farmers and government spending for public works, as demand management and the expansion of the welfare state forged a historic compromise between the Social Democrats and the Agrarian Party. Deficit spending to pay for relief measures and expanded social security followed. Steeply progressive tax rates instituted in the 1930s and 1940s funded these measures. The Social Democratic welfare state severely limited the powers of private capital but protected the princi-ple of private ownership and control.[202]

In the United States, too, capitalism and liberal democracy recon-ciled under social democratic auspices. Forging an alliance between urban Northern workers and white Southerners, the Democratic Party, under the leadership of President Roosevelt, pushed through a series of radical reforms that came to recast core aspects of American capital-ism. As government came to play a much larger role in US life, the state provided urgently needed relief, regulated businesses in new ways (especially in the financial sector), provided supports for agriculture, vastly improved the social security of many American citizens (though many African Americans, such as domestic and agricultural workers, remained excluded), and embraced corporatist forms of coordination within the economy (for example, reducing production of commodities in order to maintain price levels). This agenda, like in Sweden, found the support of some capital owners who came to appreciate the state's ability to stabilize the economy. Largely deploying similar strategies, democratic liberal regimes also persisted elsewhere, including in France and the UK. These social democracies also began to coordinate their economic policies across borders and to lighten up on protectionism—sketching the outlines of the postwar order.[203]

Still, in the wake of the Depression, many democratic regimes floundered. It has been estimated that at the height of this wave, up to half of the world's people lived under authoritarian rule. Already in the early 1920s, Italy, along with Spain, Hungary, and Albania, had turned authoritarian, even fascist. By the mid-1920s, Portugal, Poland, and Lithuania had followed. And then came Yugoslavia in 1929; Romania in 1930; Germany in 1933; Austria, Latvia, Estonia, and Bulgaria in 1934; and Greece in 1936. All these regimes embraced authoritarian measures in response to the Depression, which made them, despite some policy similarities, radically different from their social democratic counterparts.[204]

There were, of course, significant differences among these regimes. What they all had in common was their embrace of corporatism. Corporatism—systems in which organized and cooperating business, state, and labor interests steered all or parts of the economy through formal or informal agreements—became a dominant characteristic of authoritarian countries, such as Brazil, Portugal, and Argentina. Even though corporatism came along in nationalist guises, the yearning for a more organized order was a truly transnational development.

These corporatist regimes shared certain features. For one, they articulated a critique of liberalism, individualism, and markets. Since 1933, Portugal's Estado Novo had described its own project as overcoming the "unjust nature of social organization [that] helped to spread the idea of class inequality and warfare."[205] Guided by the "beacon light of nationalism," it espoused the idea of "corporate government" to enable "the proper adjustment of individual and collective interests."[206] Seeing itself as a crucial part of a global movement against "individualism," it had "abandoned the absurd tendency of considering individuals as abstract beings, geometrically equal."[207] Brazil's authoritarian Estado Novo searched for similar alternatives to liberalism.[208] Its leading ideologue, the sociologist and jurist Francisco José de Oliveira Viana, believed that a corporatist organization of Brazilian society could tamp down social conflict and induce economic growth. For him, corporatism was "an alternative to liberalism and socialism by organizing society into state-directed collective groups, differentiated and ranked according to economic profession and social role."[209] As Viana argued, "[I]ndividual[s] and their economic liberty will only be saved by the State, intervening as an equilibrium force between the individual and the large organisms created by industrial capitalism."[210] And that state was also crucial in the effort to "correct chronic backwardness."[211]

Corporatist regimes everywhere gave a central role to the state when it came to economic matters. In Brazil, the state regulated wages and prices, created labor tribunals, and favored unelected technical expert councils as the best way to solve policy issues. Argentina followed suit: When the military came to power in June 1943, Secretary of Labor Juan Domingo Perón became an important advocate of corporatism, creating a new system of labor courts to settle conflicts between employers and workers under state supervision.[212]

Ideologically, corporatists aimed to reconstitute what they considered a more organic society in which civil society groups came to govern in an almost guildlike fashion. Portugal's Estado Novo was to be based on "corporative organizations and families," which would thus "improve . . . on private capitalism."[213] The goal was a new, organized harmony in which the state would create "the coordination and higher regulation of social life," protect the nation against "enterprises of a parasitical nature," and outlaw "class warfare," including strikes.[214] Trade-specific labor organizations and trade-specific employer organizations were to steer industry and to represent it vis-à-vis the state. Brazilian authoritarian president Getúlio Vargas, too, was guided by the idea that distinct sectors of the economy should be self-governed by councils bringing together industry and labor.[215] Argentinean corporatists also departed from liberal principles and favored economic policies conducive to domestic industrialization.[216] While Perón was to build a "new Argentina," Vargas advocated for a "new Brazil," and Portuguese dictator António de Oliveira Salazar believed in the advent of a "new Portugal."

Fascist regimes also embraced corporatist policies but broke more decisively from the politics of the nineteenth century that had emerged in fits and starts alongside industrial capitalism. Their radicalism was rooted in their complete negation of liberal conceptions of statehood, their extreme hostility toward all traces of democratic governance, their fixation on a charismatic leader, their determined destruction of the labor movement, their aggressive militarism, and their complete disregard for any of the rights—the rule of law, freedom of expression, and the division of powers, for example—that had been articulated in the revolutions of 1776, 1789, 1791, 1848, and 1917. They styled themselves as, and indeed were, a total break from previous liberal regimes, even as these regimes partly embraced similar policies in response to the Depression. In many ways, this break was surprising, since it undermined the proclaimed universal values of the capitalist revolution as they had been articulated in the nineteenth century and earlier.

Despite its radicalism, however, fascism never broke with a fundamentally capitalist organization of economic life. Capitalism's basic building blocks—the commodification of inputs, outputs, and labor; private property; entrepreneurship; and the accumulation and productive reinvestment of capital—all remained firmly in place. But fascism offered a radical answer to the social, national, and colonial questions that had come out of World War I and sharpened during the Depression. It suppressed the social question in the name of nationalism. By leaping beyond previous boundaries, it gained both a highly mobilized mass following and elite support, including from many capital owners.

In this way, fascism featured the spectacle of a bourgeoisie mobilizing against bourgeois society. Giovanni Agnelli was appointed as a senator for the National Fascist Party in 1923 (a largely honorary position he retained until 1944). Ten years later, he welcomed Mussolini to Turin wearing the black shirt of the party, and in the 1930s, he drew on Mussolini's support for the construction of the massive new Mirafiori assembly plant. He was drawn to the regime for its harsh treatment of labor, its protectionist policies (keeping American cars largely out of the Italian market), and its corporatist solutions. When the Turin daily *La Stampa* printed articles critical of Mussolini in 1924, the regime forced its sale to Fiat; Agnelli was considered to be a more reliable toer of the fascist line. His son, Edoardo, was so drawn to Mussolini that in 1934, he wanted to join the fascist Chamber of Deputies, only stopped by his father, who preferred him to focus on company affairs.[217]

Agnelli's disenchantment with liberalism and democracy was widely shared. The destruction of capitalism's liberal basis, according to historian Jürgen Kocka, was "significantly promoted by capitalist leadership groups and parts of the bourgeoisie."[218] Even a fundamental erosion of property rights elicited little opposition among capital owners.[219] In Germany, most prominently, plenty of gentile capital owners participated in, and supported, the violent expropriations from Europe's Jews—showing once again that property rights in actually existing capitalism have hardly ever been secure. In fact, the capitalist revolution's twin—noneconomic hierarchies—enabled extreme exploitation, dispossession, and genocide, not only in its agrarian hinterlands but also in the industrial heartland itself.

Fascism's most extreme variant unfolded in Germany. This powerhouse of the Second Industrial Revolution emerged from the Depression firmly in the grasp of an aggressive authoritarianism. Its fascist turn was contingent on many factors and garnered widespread popular support, but capital owners played a significant role in mobilizing against democracy and the Weimar constitutional order. Of course, not all capital owners embraced the fascist turn, and some would resist it at great personal cost—Oskar Schindler in Kraków, for example—but those who did were primarily attracted by fascism's repression of

The bourgeoisie mobilizes against bourgeois society:
Hermann Röchling gives a Hitler salute, 1935.

the labor movement, its aim for territorial reorganization, and its commitment to order.[220] Autarky, military prowess, and corporatist structures also found sway among German capital owners.

Unsurprisingly, Hermann Röchling was one of them. Building upon his decades-old extreme nationalism, he admired the Führer.[221] He was deeply entangled with the Nazi elite, welcoming high-ranking Nazi visitors to his factory, including, in 1935, the Reich's minister of propaganda, Joseph Goebbels. The Nazis reciprocated. In 1938, Hermann Göring named Röchling a *Wehrwirtschaftsführer*—an honorific title meant to bind industrialists to the regime.[222] Hitler personally invited him to that year's Reich Party Congress in Nuremberg.[223] Ideologically, Röchling saw eye to eye with some of the most extreme Nazi projects and published articles on the "Jewified British aristocracy," attacking "Bolshevism" and condemning what he called the "Jewish influence" on Roosevelt.[224]

What drew Röchling to the Nazis was not just their nationalism and antisemitism. As a lifelong enemy of organized labor, he shared the Nazis' wholesale hostility toward Germany's powerful trade unions and left-wing parties.[225] Röchling feared communism and "Bolshevism" to such a degree that he even appealed to entrepreneurs in occupied France to cooperate with the German invaders against their common enemies on the left, hoping that class solidarity would trump French nationalism.[226] He believed that "no democracy in the world" could successfully resist "Bolshevism" and argued in his company's newspaper, *Der Völklinger Hüttenmann*, for abolishing all parliaments. (The article was headlined FOR THE FÜHRER!)[227] Less publicly, in 1935, he authored a memo for Hitler himself that bore the prophetic title "About the Preparation for War and Its Conduct," in which he advocated for war against the Soviet Union and supported measures against what he called "world Jewry."[228]

While his fascist sympathies were fed by deeply held beliefs, Röchling, like many German industrialists, also benefited handsomely from the Nazis' rise to power. He rightly believed that Hitler's policies would create growing markets for iron and steel. Not least thanks to the Nazis' rearmament programs, steel production had already increased by almost 15 percent in 1933, the year Hitler seized power. As one chronicler of the Röchlings dryly remarked, "[H]e put the company in the service of the national-socialist armament policy."[229] These economic interests also led Röchling to support a politics of autarky—anticipating that his long-held dream of nationalizing commodity chains would finally come to fruition. In 1937, he prepared an article to be published in the journal *Der Vierjahresplan* (*The Four-Year Plan*); his piece dealt with the sourcing of iron ore and his belief that it should and could be secured domestically.[230] As a longtime enemy of markets, he saw state coordination as a way to "avoid unlimited competition."[231]

Röchling was just one of many German industrialists, bankers, and traders who enthusiastically folded himself into the Nazi camp. And such fascist proclivities were not uniquely German—Italian, French, and Norwegian capital owners, among many others, embraced fascism just as enthusiastically in response to economic tumult. Even in the United States, auto mogul Henry Ford dabbled in fascist ideas, proudly sported the medals bestowed upon him by the Nazi regime, and spread antisemitic conspiracy theories through his newspaper, *The Dearborn Independent*.[232]

Fascism also propelled the most extreme response on the most radical edge of economic nationalism: war. For some states, territorial reordering became a response to the long-lasting national, social, and colonial questions that industrial capitalism had posed with increasing urgency since its emergence.[233] War was a likely outcome of quickening economic nationalism—and when such economic nationalism mixed with authoritarian and fascist rule, war was almost always the result.

For Japanese policymakers, colonial expansion in North Asia during the 1930s led to the idea of what came to be called the Greater East Asia Co-Prosperity Sphere in 1940—the plan to create, by military force, an economic and political bloc stretching from Sakhalin in the North to the Dutch East Indies in the South. Military expansion was the only way to create the "living space" deemed necessary for the Japanese people. A top-secret Japanese government plan of July 9, 1940, envisioned the integration of much of Asia, Australia, and New Zealand into a Japanese-dominated economic sphere.[234] However impossible this might now appear, Japanese policymakers saw it as no different from comparable American, British, or Russian expansionism, and, of course, much of the plan succeeded, at least temporarily. By the summer of 1941, "regional autarky" had become policymakers' central goal, as they believed that they needed the regions' resources, exploited by a "managed economy," to solidify the Japanese industrial heartland.[235] Italy followed suit. It invaded Ethiopia in 1935 and then occupied Albania in 1939 and parts of Greece in 1940.[236]

Germany sought territorial reordering as well. Since the 1920s, Hitler and his supporters had envisioned a German-dominated, continentally integrated European economy stretching from the Atlantic to the Urals, from the North Cape to the Mediterranean. In 1939, as Germany invaded its European neighbors, the plan seemed to have come to fruition. Such a continental economy was painstakingly planned: Some newly captured territories were to be annexed, while others were to be organized

Fiat tanks in Ethiopia, 1936.

as satellites to the German industrial heartland, supplying raw materials, agricultural commodities, and labor. Since 1940, the ever evolving "Generalplan Ost" provided detailed blueprints for ethnic cleansing and colonization of much of central and Eastern Europe. Based on the territorial integration of Europe, according to Hitler's nightmarish vision, Germany would become the new "land of unlimited opportunity," in effect, a new America.[237]

While that territorial reordering was a project of the Nazi state, driven by deeply held racist beliefs, it was also driven by an extreme variant of economic nationalism that often found support among economic elites. Along with many like him, Hermann Röchling threw himself enthusiastically into the project, a goal he had tirelessly promoted for at least three decades. After war with Poland in late 1939, he became administrator of a Katovice steel mill and was also put in charge of a munitions factory in occupied Poland. The following year, with France under German occupation, Röchling began to administer French-owned companies as well, reconstituting some of his long-wished-for pre–World War I commodity chains. By June of that year, Hermann Göring had appointed Röchling as the general commissioner for iron and steel in the Meurthe-et-Moselle region and then as Reich commissioner for iron and steel in the occupied territories. Inspired, Röchling inundated Hitler with plans for the territorial reordering of Europe—guided by his business concerns about access to raw materials and securing sufficient numbers of workers. In 1942, under Röchling's leadership, an association of the German iron and steel industry was formed—the Reichsvereinigung Eisen (Imperial Iron Association)—that coordinated iron and steel production throughout the German Empire and distributed forcibly conscripted workers to its member firms. That same year, Röchling moved into the highest coordinating office for German war production: the Rüstungsrat (Armaments Council). As an armaments producer himself—Röchling produced grenades, artillery, and antiaircraft guns, as well as parts for machine guns—he seemed well qualified for such a position. But he also fit the ideological mold, truly believing that economic space had to be reimagined on a continental scale: "The unified control of the economy, especially that of iron, is necessary beyond the borders of Germany."[238] He closely coordinated his activities with the highest levels of government and met with Hitler several times to discuss war production. Enabling all these far-flung goings-on in the newly imagined German economic space, Röchling and his son flew one million kilometers during the war in the plane he owned (a rarity at the time).[239]

Thanks to such efforts, and defined by their utter absence of concern for human life, the war allowed for a return of slavery to the heartland of industrial capitalism. Japan's heavy industry—companies such as Mitsubishi Shipbuilding—resorted to forced labor. Prisoners of war, along with Chinese and Korean forced workers, entered the Japanese industrial heartland. It has been estimated that, in total, up to 1.3 million forced workers from Korea labored in Japan during the war, especially in mining and construction.[240]

In Nazi Europe, forced labor became the principal modus operandi. In 1944, an estimated 43.4 percent of workers in the Nazi empire toiled under duress—a stunning number historically only outdone by the plantation colonies of the Caribbean. Workers, especially in Eastern Europe, were hunted down and deported to Germany to work in factories, on farms, or in households. There was a strict hierarchy among such workers, with Soviets on the lowest rung. Röchling played a key role in this mobilization for the iron and steel industry, so much so that these deportations of workers came to be known as "Röchling Transporte."[241] Visionary that he was, Röchling also developed big plans for moving populations throughout Europe. He believed that 1.2 million people could be "registered and correctly sorted" in Belgium and the Netherlands alone.[242]

Almost all industries drew on such forced labor. Unsurprisingly, this was also the case at the Röchling iron- and steelworks. By the early summer of 1940, a group of forced workers had arrived in Völklingen. By 1943, about 40 percent of all workers at the Völklinger Hütte worked under duress, most of them French, Belgian, and—especially—Soviet. So many forced workers labored at the Röchling complex that by the summer of 1942, the company operated twenty-eight distinct camps to house them. In total, Röchling exploited the labor of about 12,000 forced workers. He enjoyed enormous power over them, including the right to corporally punish them and put them in company-owned prisons. Tatjana Jarosch, born in 1926 in Sosnovka, in the Soviet Union, was deported in the summer of 1941 to Völklingen, where, as she recalled in a later interview, "Röchling stole my life."[243] A special *Werkschutz*—the factory's own security forces, with more than one hundred members—guarded her and her fellow forced workers. Minor "crimes" were penalized, including gathering wood in the forest, spreading or listening to "enemy propaganda," and leaving one's place of work.[244] Some workers were also sent to concentration camps: Cermil Agrisowitch, from Yugoslavia, was sent to the Natzweiler concentration camp because of his refusal to work. Frenchman Dominique Crispini was sent to an unspecified concentration camp because of "slow work." Röchling's regime was so brutal that a total of 290 foreign workers died in Völklingen during the war.[245]

Slave labor, then as before, provided access to workers when time and place made other forms of labor unavailable. It shattered fundamental accomplishments of the capitalist revolution, such as the freedom of contract. It was an act of barbarity, but barbarity itself now infused many businesses. Kühne & Nagel, a German logistics company based in Bremen, transported the furniture of Parisian Jews, deported to camps, into the Reich. IG Farben, the chemical colossus, employed Auschwitz prisoners at its factories. In 1942, prisoners from concentration camps began working for car manufacturer BMW, a company that also activated two satellite camps at its Allach and Dürrerhof plants. By 1944, over 50 percent of BMW's workforce consisted

*Modern slavery in the industrial heartland: Soviet forced
worker at the Röchlings' iron- and steelworks
between 1942 and 1944.*

of forced laborers—a total of twenty-nine thousand women and men. "Without this massive deployment of forced labourers, mass production would not have been possible," a report commissioned by the company stated.[246] Mercedes-Benz was also critically implicated in the Third Reich. The company had deep cultural ties to the Nazis—after all, it produced Hitler's favorite car. Just like at BMW, forced laborers made up nearly half of its workforce—a total of nearly twenty-seven thousand workers by the end of 1944. According to a historical study commissioned by the company, they were subject to "arbitrary brutality at shop-floor level and constant exposure to SS terror, intense hunger, cold and illness, and long hours of hard physical labour."[247] Other car manufacturers that deployed forced labor include Audi, Porsche, and Volkswagen. IG Farben—the chemical and pharmaceutical manufacturer that had emerged in 1925 as the world's largest (bringing together Bayer, BASF, Hoechst, and others)—was seized by the United States at war's end, and many of its executives were put on trial for their involvement in war crimes and crimes against humanity. One of its subsidiaries produced Zyklon B, the gas used to murder millions of European Jews. Dozens of lawsuits were later filed against such companies for their use of forced labor and their complicity in the

Slavery returns to the industrial heartland: concentration camp inmates laboring at a BMW factory in the 1940s.

atrocities of the Third Reich. According to historian Anita Ramasastry, companies that have been sued include Agfa-Gevaert, Audi, BASF, Beiersdorf, BMW, Bosch, Continental, Daimler-Benz, Heidelberger Zement, Hochtief, Hoechst, Hugo Boss, Krupp, Leica Camera, Lufthansa, MAN, Mannesmann, Messerschmitt-Bölkow-Blohm, Miele, Pfaff, Philipp Holzmann, Rheinmetall, Rodenstock, Siemens, Thyssen, VARTA, Volkswagen, WMF, and Zeppelin—a who's who of German industry.[248]

When the war ended, the United States government investigated many German firms for war crimes, including such giants as Deutsche Bank and Dresdner Bank. IG Farben directors were convicted for their participation in exploiting the last remaining labor power of the deportees in death camps such as Auschwitz.[249] As Primo Levi—a Jewish Italian chemist and Auschwitz survivor who later wrote from Fiat's hometown of Turin—warned when the catastrophe was over: "It happened, therefore it can happen again: this is the core of what we have to say."[250] The bourgeois civilization that had emerged in some parts of the empire of capital, such barbarity showed, was vulnerable, as it continues to be.

Yet by 1945, Soviet resilience and US production capacities enabled liberal capitalism to outlive its fascist variant. As one symbol of this defeat among many, Hermann Röchling was arrested by US troops and handed over to the French, who jailed him, first in Saarbrücken and then in Rastatt, ironically one of the centers of the German (Democratic) Revolution of 1848–1849. On January 25, 1949, he was sentenced as a "war criminal" to ten years in prison for "economic plunder" in German-occupied territories and for his role in organizing and exploiting forced labor.[251]

The aftereffects of the "global thirties" were many, and not just in the industrial heartlands but everywhere. As less-developed regions found themselves sucked into the wars of Europe and Asia, it became painfully obvious that most people in the world, including many capital owners, lacked a state responsive to their interests. People living under colonial regimes saw that they were beholden to the interests of distant peoples, and watched as their resources and skills were transferred for the benefit of these distant peoples at war. World War II made them increasingly aware of the hierarchy of rights that distinguished the colonizers from the colonized.

An unintended consequence of the war, then, was that colonial subjects began to reenvision the global economic order and to mobilize mass movements that might make change possible. It was, in fact, the beginning of the end of the "Great Divergence," as it brought to the fore the importance of economic sovereignty. In many narratives of the global thirties, these developments have been little noticed. Yet world war, depression, and then another world war weakened imperial powers and provoked new waves of resistance against their dream of colonial empire. Europeans were also newly dependent on soldiers and resources from their colonies, forcing them into compromises with local elites who helped provide these resources, while the newly powerful United States lacked enthusiasm for a defense of the European colonial order. At the same time, elites in the colonial world began to accumulate

knowledge, capacity, capital, and—during the Second World War—
even prosperity, encouraging them to think about the benefits of
controlling a newly constituted national state to enable national
development.

Such sentiments and politics would change the twentieth-century
global economic order, perhaps more than any other single development. Already in 1928, the German economist Werner Sombart had
foretold that "the new capitalism will be a 'colored' capitalism. It will
govern Asia and Africa."[252] This "young capitalism," he augured, "was
to influence our economic life."[253] Lost in all of Europe's self-regard
and navel-gazing, this was a prescient insight.

Insurgents

*Unleashing postcolonial industry: Indian
capitalists imagine a future after British rule.*

For more than a century, no office anywhere in the world could function without a typewriter. This ubiquitous machine helped to produce the endless letters, compilations, and reports that characterized the capitalist civilization. Invented for the demands of business, the device became critical to state-building as well. As governments grew in size and bureaucratic complexity, the typewriter morphed into an essential tool of modern statehood.[1]

Commercialized in the United States during the 1880s, the

typewriter spread rapidly around the world, leapfrogging from one node of state power and capital to the next. In India, colonial offices and businesses began using typewriters by the 1890s. Like most sophisticated machines, they were imported, at first from Britain, then, by 1910, from the United States in general and the Remington company in particular.[2]

When India gained its independence in 1947, the demand for typewriters skyrocketed, especially for models that could accommodate the Indian scripts and languages now required by government offices. Naval Godrej, scion of a storied Bombay manufacturing family deeply dedicated to *swadeshi*—the movement to replace imported goods with domestically produced ones—had anticipated as much and had begun to engineer just such a typewriter in 1942. In 1948, encouraged by the new government's promises to purchase such machines, he accelerated his plans. "[G]overnment themselves having sponsored our project," his company noted in a 1952 memorandum, "we ourselves would never have thought of manufacturing them had not the government of India themselves taken the initiative and encouraged us to work on this project."[3] Godrej believed that for India to advance, "it had to itself produce what it needed."[4] After a careful study of typewriter manufacturing elsewhere, he offered the first Indian-manufactured typewriter in 1953, the aptly named All Indian. Godrej elevated India into the rarefied ranks of countries capable of producing typewriters—a complex product that consisted of 1,800 distinct pieces, including a staggering 150 types of precision-manufactured screws.[5] "We had to begin here from the scratch," the company noted with justified pride in its technical know-how and highly skilled workers.[6] When the governing Congress Party met at the Madras city of Avadi in 1955, Prime Minister Pandit Jawaharlal Nehru was personally introduced to the device and reportedly called Godrej's typewriter a "symbol of independent and industrialised India."[7]

This very public marriage between the postcolonial state and postcolonial private capital intensified as the government of India became a crucial customer of Godrej's. Burgeoning bureaucracies craved type-

Postcolonial state-building: Prime Minister Pandit Jawaharlal Nehru at a Godrej typewriter during a 1955 meeting of the Indian National Congress in Avadi, Madras (now Chennai).

writers, as did courts and political parties. The state placed orders regularly, and production was "earmarked for supply against government orders." In 1960, the company noted prospective sales to state-owned Indian Airlines; in 1967, the state-owned Life Insurance Corporation of India was under orders to purchase 30 percent of its typewriters from Godrej.[8]

Enabled by such supports and accelerated by a newly created sales network, Godrej expanded production. He sold 9,000 typewriters between 1955 and 1959, and even though he complained incessantly about the lack of energy among his sales agents, he sold 12,000 improved machines between 1959 and 1964. By 1967, Godrej partnerd with the East German VEB Büromaschinenwerk to enable further technological innovation. Between 1965 and 1970, he sold 23,984 typewriters; between 1971 and 1979, 158,433 units.[9]

Typewriters transformed Indian society, helping to facilitate the assembly and flow of information in businesses and bureaucracies. A new profession—the typist—emerged, with skilled workers receiving specialized training in vocational schools. Part and parcel of a massive expansion of white-collar employment, this was, of course, a global development: By 1930 in the United States, there were already 811,000 typists and stenographers, who, unlike their Indian counterparts, were almost all women. In India, typists also offered their services as microscale entrepreneurs to illiterate peasants and workers in their

Test typists trying out the Godrej M-12, circa 1960s.

dealings with the state, their places of business located on the streets out in front of government offices. While the advent of computers led Godrej to end typewriter production in 2011, India's move into the market for advanced machinery was a harbinger of a shifting center of gravity in capitalism's history—one where India would send rockets into space, China would ultimately become the workshop of the world, and Brazil would become a top aviation manufacturer.[10]

Colonialism had been one of the pillars of industrial capitalism since the 1870s, producing a particular integration of the industrial heartland with ever expanding agricultural-, mineral-, and labor-extracting hinterlands. By 1945, that pillar was about to come crashing down. In that year, one-third of the earth's land was still administered by colonial powers, and one-third of its population lived under colonial rule. Thirty years later, the mostly European rulers held less than 1 percent of the world's land as colonial dependencies. In that vast space, dozens of independent states sprouted. In early 1945, there had been just 69 fully autonomous independent nations worldwide, a number that more than doubled to 151 by the end of 1975. Syria, Lebanon, Pakistan, India, Burma, Indonesia, and the Philippines, among others, gained independence in the second half of the 1940s; Ghana, Laos, Morocco, Tunisia, and Malaya, in the 1950s. They were followed by a burst of newly constituted nations in the early 1960s, among them Nigeria, Mali, Cameroon, Congo, Kuwait, Tanzania, Jamaica, Algeria, and Zambia, with the Portuguese colonies of Mozambique, Cape Verde, Guinea-Bissau, and Angola finishing the wave of successful anticolonial rebellions by the 1970s. By 1980, no large colonies remained anywhere in the world.[11] The process by which most of the world's people saw their status shift from that of colonial subjects to that of citizens of their own nation brought forth a new term: decolonization.

Decolonization was the beginning of the end of the most Eurocentric moment in capitalism's history. During the colonial age, as we saw earlier, capitalist development had focused on the North Atlantic region. In 1950, Europe and its "Western offshoots" generated about 70 percent of the world's GDP and about 90 percent of world manufacturing output (compared with just 30 percent in the second half of the eighteenth century). By 1975, their share of the world's GDP had shrunk to 62.5 percent, further withering to 50.7 percent in 2000 and just 39.1 percent in 2023.[12] No single twentieth-century development recast global capitalism in more consequential ways than decolonization.

For centuries, colonialism had produced extreme global inequalities and transferred wealth through contract, dispossession, and enslavement from one part of the world to another. It had deeply impacted economic relationships within societies and between them. But perhaps the most momentous effect of colonialism had been more insidious: It weakened, even destroyed, local sources of state power. In much of the world, after all, policymaking, including economic policymaking, was primarily oriented not toward the interests of local peasants, workers, or local elites (including capital owners) but toward the interests of people in distant metropoles. This was particularly pivotal because, as we have seen, the state had been decisive to capitalism's development, especially to its industrial variety as it had spread after 1870 during capitalism's reconstruction. The lack of a government oriented toward local interests dealt a devastating blow to any chance of domestic development. It not only condemned subjects to often extraordinarily violent dispossessions of their labor and resources but also fixed local capital owners in a subordinate position.

Unsurprisingly, such dramatic inequalities inspired challenges. Some were led by intellectuals trained in those very imperial metropoles. Others emerged from peasants and industrial workers whose local battles led to ever sharper critiques of the entire imperial edifice. Local insurgent capital owners sparked still others, concluding that toppling the old regime—colonialism—was the only way forward, just as their European counterparts had reluctantly embraced the toppling of old-regime capitalism a century earlier. Despite frequently being at odds with one another, these very different groups, in a great variety of configurations, challenged the colonial order.[13] In the process, they reordered the world of capitalism. They insisted, successfully, on the right of all the world's people to national self-determination and the formal equality of states. And they agreed across continents, countries, and classes on the need for economic development, on a reversal of the staggering global inequalities that the capitalist revolution had produced. Their most radical movements even challenged capitalism itself.

Nearly all anticolonial revolutionaries aspired to remake postcolonial economic life, but in ways distinct from the developmental trajectory of the world's industrial heartland one or even two centuries earlier. They focused on economic nationalism, protectionism, and centrally planned import-substitution industrialization. Such anticolonial policies were deeply rooted in the Depression years, which had generated a flourishing of institutional creativity that not only motivated anticolonialism but also generated blueprints for economic development across the world. No matter what precise road a newly formed country took, economic development and nation-building became deeply enmeshed with each other in all of them—indeed, they became almost one and the same.

While this recentering and realigning of postcolonial capital was never complete or entirely free of entanglements with former colonial centers, the many fresh nexuses of state power nonetheless constituted a distinctly novel riverbed for the flows of capital. Decolonization created new channels, new nodes of power, and new islands of capital capable of reaching new hinterlands, creating new industries, and driving new forms of agriculture. Bombay, Calcutta, Shanghai, and other such cities had been centers of modern business enterprises since the early twentieth century—but now they pushed outward.[14] And even though the break with colonial capitalism was unequivocal, the postcolonial project unfolded in a world that had been profoundly shaped by colonialism and its inequalities, a world in which capital, technology, and skills remained concentrated in just a few areas. When Britain industrialized in the eighteenth century, it was alone. When India embarked upon domestic industrialization, it encountered an already industrialized world.

Moreover, India and its postcolonial counterparts remained strongly connected to the imperial trajectory of capitalism itself—in fact, they often radicalized it. Economic life in extended parts of the world came to follow a capitalist logic, and new spaces of human life were subjected to that logic. Anticolonialism, in effect, produced new forms of internal colonialism: further transformations of the countryside, massive industrializations, gorging of fossil fuels, and a social transformation that came to be world history's most significant wave of proletarianization.

Over several decades, these new forms of state power would alter the enormous global hierarchies of the empire of capital. Largely unrecognized by contemporaries, decolonialization would shift inequalities of wealth and power, reverse some of the effects of the Great Divergence, allow for the emergence of new businesses and new forms of business organization, shift power within commodity chains, and radically alter the world's competitive environment. Werner Sombart's prediction some decades earlier that the capitalist revolution would accelerate under "colored" auspices would seem to come true by the

1950s—and, eventually, despite all its many setbacks and tragedies, come to challenge the very industrial heartland and social settlement that emerged there after World War II.[15] Twenty-first-century capitalism would be carried and shaped by the mighty and multitudinous streams of decolonization.

Ardeshir Godrej was a man with a mission. An "ardent nationalist," as a Bombay newspaper editor described him in 1927, like his nephew Navak, he believed in India's ability to produce the things it needed. While he eventually became one of India's leading industrialists, his venture into manufacturing was somewhat of a surprise: Born into a well-off Parsi family, Godrej was trained as a lawyer, and his move into industry came largely as a result of his political commitments, not from experience in business or in engineering. He wanted to demonstrate to the world that Indians could manufacture the things they had previously imported and produce them to high-quality standards, a central tenet of the nationalist movement. Starting in 1897 with the production of locks, he moved on to safes in 1902 and then on to soaps in 1918.[16]

As Godrej engaged in import-substitution manufacturing on a modest scale, he became ever more sensitive to the ill effects of colonial rule and gravitated ever more toward anticolonial thinkers and activists. "A true nationalist Indian to his core," Godrej embraced swadeshi so enthusiastically that the journalists at India's *National Herald* gushed that

Insurgent entrepreneur: Ardeshir Burjorji Sorabji Godrej (1868–1936).

"our friend's heart has been burning . . . furiously" for national economic self-sufficiency.[17] A student of early anticolonial thinkers, especially of fellow Parsi Dadabhai Naoroji, Godrej believed that the British had plundered India, drained its wealth, and destroyed an older Indian manufacturing tradition.[18] As he put it, "Mother India has been bled white by foreign exploiters who have made us slaves of their tastes and goods."[19]

A political activist as much as a businessman, Godrej contributed generously to the Indian freedom struggle. He befriended early nationalists such as Bal Gangadhar Tilak (later serving as a pallbearer at his funeral) and Gopal Krishna Gokhale, the founder of the Servants of India Society; he was particularly drawn to their advocacy of "State Protection" for industry. According to a 1927 newspaper account, Godrej also "lent a great support to Mahatma Gandhi by organizing spinning and weaving in Bombay on a large scale and contributed the amount of three lakhs of rupees" to the Tilak Swaraj Fund, a fundraising operation for the anticolonial movement.[20] Such generosity, reported Gandhi, "provoked a secret circular from the [British colonial] Government to the effect that no Godrej safe should be ordered for any of its departments."[21] In 1906, reciprocating Godrej's support of its political project, the Indian National Congress "administered the Swadeshi vow in respect of soap"—that is, pledged to buy Godrej's soap. In 1936, freedom fighter Nehru visited Godrej's plant.[22] When Godrej died a year later, *The Bombay Chronicle* described him as

> an intense lover of Swadeshi. . . . Besides being a highly successful manufacturer and industrialist, the late Mr. Godrej was intensely nationalist in his views and outlook. His one anxiety was how India could be made independent in regard to the articles of daily necessity. . . . The late Mr. Godrej's sympathy towards the Congress and its activities in the field of Swadeshi is too well-known to need any special mention.[23]

Ardeshir Godrej and his family were nation-builders—they believed that the Indian nation depended on economic development to prosper just as much as private entrepreneurs depended on a state receptive to their interests. But they were also talented entrepreneurs capable of building one of India's prime industrial enterprises. Long before independence, Godrej saw his company-building as indivisible from his nation-building project.

Other members of Godrej's family followed suit. Ardeshir's brother Pirojsha spoke of the tight link between industrialization and nation-building. His nephew (and later chairman of the Godrej Group) Sohrab, "brought up in the Gandhian philosophy," became the treasurer of the Swadeshi League in 1952.[24] Naval, Pirojsha's son, "believed deeply in the country developing its own technology."[25] And Naval's mother-in-law, Gulbai Dastoor, became an activist in the freedom movement as well.[26] The rebellion of capital owners against European imperialism, though far from universal, stretched back a long time.

For all members of the family, the Indian political project merged with their business interests, fueling their insurgency. Indeed, they fabricated an ever greater panoply of goods, building the kind of family-dominated business groups that would come to characterize not just the Indian economy but economies throughout the Global South. After 1918, they produced washing powder, household chemicals, and

The business of nation-building: Godrej advertisement in The Statesman, *August 15, 1947.*

personal hygiene products in ever greater variety. In 1923, they added steel cupboards; in 1942, machine tools.[27] As they complemented their product lines, the Godrejes decided to build new factories outside Bombay, driven by the belief that "India would soon be free and freedom would open up undreamt-of opportunities and create unforeseen demands for growth."[28] Beginning in 1943, they created "an industrial garden township" at Vikhroli, an almost utopian community dedicated to an amalgam of national improvement and profit.[29]

Vikhroli's new factories began operating in the early 1950s, in the wake of independence. They enabled the Godrejes to add more product lines: During India's first election in 1951/52, they produced almost 1.3 million steel ballot boxes. Typewriters were added in 1953. They continued making various kinds of soaps, too, launching Cinthol, a germicidal soap, on Independence Day in 1952. In 1956, they added steel doors, windows, and other steel home goods to their offerings. Refrigerators followed in 1958, in cooperation with the US firm General Electric. In 1961, they began producing forklifts and even added baked goods to their product repertoire. In 1965, they created a steel foundry. Hospital equipment came next. So significant was this expansion that by 1954, the Godrej family's factories used about one-third of the nation's steel output. In the process, the Godrej brand embedded itself deep into Indian culture: A 1991 marketing study found that the Godrej steel cupboard was a favored possession of Indians, commonly gifted to newlyweds.[30]

As the Godrejes innovated in product lines, they professionalized their management. In 1968, they employed, for the first time, a group of aspiring managers trained at the Indian Institute of Management in Ahmedabad. They also found new ways of financing corporate expansion: When British banks refused them financing, they received loans from India's Central Bank. The Godrejes also worked to strengthen the institutional basis of Indian businesses. A senior manager at Godrej Soaps, K. R. Gokulam, joined the Bombay Management Association, the Bombay Productivity Council, the Indian Chemical Manufacturers Association, and the Indian Soap & Toiletries Makers' Association.

Concerned with the social stability of the society they helped forge, they also created a company-focused form of welfare capitalism, providing paid holidays, meals, medical care, housing, and even family planning services to many of their workers.[31]

Throughout these years, the Godrejes stayed close to the new government of India, not least because their business was deeply enmeshed with the state that they had contributed to building. India's mixed economy combined a very large public sector with private enterprise. Most industries, and the Godrejes' in particular, depended on access to government-controlled resources such as steel, electric power, banking, and transport. Like capital owners elsewhere, they also had to navigate myriad government regulations and controls.[32]

In the 1950s, symbolizing the merging of political projects with business interests, the Godrej company advertised its contribution to the Indian economy with the slogan "Freedom Wears a Smile."[33] By 1985, it had become part of India's space program. The political project of state-building and the economic project of industrialization had merged, despite significant setbacks, creating a new node of capital accumulation and state power. Tellingly, another large Indian conglomerate, Tata, bought Kirkman Finlay's tea business in 1977. When another Indian industrialist, Anand Mahindra, purchased the East India Company in 2005 (by then just an

State-building and industrialization: Godrej ballot boxes.

empty corporate shell), decolonized capitalism had come full circle. Mahindra said he was pleased at "turning history upside down."[34]

⸻

Anand Mahindra, Tata, the Godrejes, and many others built on a rich intellectual and political tradition of anticolonial economic nationalism that had sprouted in Asia and Africa, expanding on earlier American precedents. Chinese entrepreneur and political activist Zhang Jian had advocated for import-substitution industrialization since the turn of the century. "People," he had argued, "all say that foreign nations maintain themselves through commerce. This is a superficial view. They do not know that the basis of foreign nations' riches and strength is industry. . . . Therefore we must concentrate with single purpose [to promote industry]. . . . Factories should be set up to produce items of foreign goods which have the greatest sale in China."[35] Naval officer Yan Fu's "On the Origin of Strength" sought to understand the sources of North Atlantic economic development by drawing on Charles Darwin and Herbert Spencer, while Chinese statesman Sun Yat-sen outlined a strategy for national economic development in his 1920 book, *The International Development of China*, which proposed a massive infrastructure and industrialization program, steered by both the state and private investors. A few years later, in 1927, Lamine Senghor, his Senegalese counterpart, published *La violation d'un pays*, at once a forceful condemnation of colonialism's ill effects and a blueprint for the country's liberation.[36] When Senghor spoke that same year in Brussels at the National Conference of the League Against Imperialism on "The Negro's Fight for Freedom," he concluded that "[t]he imperialist oppression which we call colonization at home and which here you term imperialism is one and the same thing. It all stems from capitalism. It is capitalism which breeds imperialism in the peoples of the leading countries. Therefore those who suffer under colonial oppression must join hands and stand side by side with those who suffer under the imperialism of the leading countries."[37] West

African–born lawyer Kojo Tovalou Houénou agreed, articulating a devastating critique of colonialism's disdain for African property rights:

> The native possesses nothing. Thanks to the regime of despoiling concessions, he has been expressly forbidden to own property. The land, conceded to him for the cultivation of corn, manioc and other crops, is taken away as soon as the European disembarks. We wish to have the property of the native assured to him. It is necessary that he should have the right to exploit the land and its resources. Do not forget that the land is his own; that the blood of black men has conquered distant possessions for France; and that the sweat of Negroes has cleared, ploughed, sowed and fertilized them as it had fertilized that of ungrateful America.[38]

In Egypt, at the same time, economic nationalist Tal'at Harb agitated against foreign control of Egyptian companies and called for the infusion of Egyptian capital into such ventures. In his book *'Alāj Miṣr al-Iqtiṣādī*, Tal'at Harb argued that an Egyptian-owned bank was an urgent necessity to liberate the country from "financial slavery."[39] Economist Winifred Tete-Ansá agreed with his premise and founded the first African-owned bank in Nigeria.[40]

The roots of postcolonial capitalism lay in the ideas, politics, businesses, and economic structures of the colonial era. India was perhaps the most prominent example of such links, not least because it looked back on a distinguished history of entrepreneurship and a once conspicuous position in global trade and manufacturing. Some Indian entrepreneurs had managed to hold on in the colonial econ-

Anticolonial insurgent: Lamine Senghor (second from the left in the first row) and other delegates at the International Congress Against Colonial Oppression, Brussels, Belgium, February 1927.

*Postcolonial industrialization: industrialist and banker Tal'at
Harb Pasha (second from left) with Prince Mohamed Ali Tewfik
at Misr Press, Cairo, early 1920s.*

omy, while others had taken advantage of new opportunities and
accumulated wealth, first in finance and trade, then in modest manufacturing activities—interests that brought many of them to a critique
of the colonial state, and a vision of the postcolonial future.

For centuries, Indian merchants had connected hinterland producers of agricultural commodities (such as cotton) and manufactured
wares (such as textiles) to Asian, African, and European traders and
markets—just think back to the vibrant community of Cambay in the
fourteenth century. Some families had accumulated capital over centuries, such as the Labhais, whose business in Ahmedabad went back at
least twelve generations. By the 1870s, this once prominent role in
overseas trade had been largely usurped by European traders. But Indian capital maintained its position in domestic trade circuits and even
in some intercontinental trade (for example, by connecting India to
East Africa). As early as 1873, the former governor of Bombay, Sir
Bartle Frere, had commented on that relationship, observing that
"throughout the Zanzibar coast-line . . . all banking and mortgage
business passes through Indian hands. Hardly a loan can be negotiated,

a mortgage effected, or a bill cashed without Indian agency. . . . The European or American, the Arab or Swahili may trade and profit but only as an occasional link in the chain between producer and consumer, of which the Indian trader is the one invariable and most important link of all."[41] Some decades later, the French consul in Mozambique grumbled about the "growing malaise" of Indians becoming middlemen between local growers and European merchants.[42] Building on these networks, several Indian-owned banks, such as the Bank of Baroda and the Indian Overseas Bank, were able to set up operations abroad by the 1930s. The postcolonial history of capitalism can indeed only be understood in light of the long history of economic life, as chronicled in this book.[43]

In INDIA ITSELF, mercantile capital in cities such as Ahmedabad, Calcutta, and Bombay increasingly also had found outlets in manufacturing, especially in the country's burgeoning cotton industry. The Bombay Spinning and Weaving Company had opened as early as 1854; by 1861, there were 12 spinning mills in India. By 1897, Indian capital owners operated 102 mills in the Bombay Presidency (a province of British India) alone. The number of spindles increased six times from 1879 to 1929. Jamsetji Nusserwanji Tata had started in the cotton and opium trade to China, but when that had become difficult, he moved into cotton manufacturing. In 1869, he opened the Alexandra Mill in Bombay; in 1874, the Empress Mill in Nagpur; and in 1886, the aptly named Swadeshi Mill in Bombay. The wealth that these investments produced in turn went into other sectors: the Tata Iron and Steel Company, for example, and hydroelectric power projects. As overseas trade became an ever more challenging terrain for Indian merchants, Indian capital focused ever more inward on the domestic market, further encouraged by a strengthening nationalist movement and the idea of swadeshi.[44] "The time has come, or rather past, when it is necessary for each and every Indian to observe a vow to buy and use only pure Indian goods to the exclusion of all others," argued Walchand Hirachand, president of the Federation of Indian Chambers of Commerce and Industry (FICCI), in 1933.[45]

Such investments, however, brought Indian capital owners into conflict with the colonial state. The British government gave preferential treatment to Lancashire textiles imported into India (for example, by charging excise taxes on domestic production), resulting in almost constant bickering between the colonial state and Indian textile entrepreneurs. Such frictions fueled a broader economic critique of colonialism, which activists such as Dadabhai Naoroji, as mentioned, had already begun to articulate in the 1860s. British rule, Naoroji said, drained the wealth of India and sapped its "vitality and vigour."[46] Economic and political nationalism were deeply intertwined in such thinking; eventually, he and others concluded that only political independence could secure national economic development.[47] As early as 1890, MIT-trained Indian engineer Keshav Malhar Bhat saw the need for domestic industrialization but also understood the greatest hurdle: "There is very little hope of getting any material help from England."[48] Founded in 1885, the Indian National Congress, known simply as the Congress, gave voice to such ideas.

As with the Godrejes, a vanguard of Indian capital owners began to collaborate with the freedom struggle. One of the Congress's founding members, Dinshaw Edulji Wacha, was associated with the Morarji Gokuldas cotton mills in Bombay and was also a member of the Bombay Millowners' Association. Jamnalal Bajaj, who in the 1920s founded the progenitors of one of India's major industrial conglomerates, was so close to the struggle that Gandhi described him as his "fifth son."[49] Though not without its own tensions, the Congress articulated many demands made by the business community, including protectionism and calls for both fiscal and monetary autonomy. Capital owners agreed with the 1945 assessment of senior government official Akbar Hydari, who stressed that "in no case goods competitive to those manufactured at present in the country should be allowed to be imported."[50] Some businessmen were so close to Gandhi that they supported him financially, including not only the Godrejes but also industrialists

Jamnalal Bajaj and G. D. Birla. When Delhi cotton manufacturer Lala Shri Ram spoke at the FICCI's annual meeting in 1931, he affirmed his support for Gandhi: "The Indian Commercial community has stood by the just cause which you, Sir, so earnestly espoused."[51] Of course, these sentiments were hardly unequivocal, and Indian capital owners still built connections to the British, some of whom greeted the arrival of nationalist forces with hostility.[52]

World War I, in particular, had broadened the economic and political vision of Indian capital owners. Their new assertiveness derived not least from the profitability of the war itself. Military production had been a huge boon to the Tatas, among others. In 1918, *The Bombay Chronicle* ran a piece titled "Our Prosperous Mill Industry" that spoke of the "colossal profits" generated by the European carnage.[53] Such profits enabled Indian capital owners to expand their investments in industry, as well as their share in both internal and external trade— and to limit their dependence on foreign inputs and capital.[54] The most perceptive observers saw a new level of political energy emerging. For Gopal Krishna Gokhale, moderate nationalist and founder of the Servants of India Society, the subordination of the East by the West was increasingly contested:

> The victories of Japan over Russia, the entry of Turkey among constitutionally-governed countries, the awakening of China, the spread of the national movement in India, Persia and Egypt, all point to the necessity of the West revising her conception of the East—revising also the standards by which she has sought in the past to regulate her relations with the East.[55]

The greater assertiveness expressed itself in organization. Most prominently, textile industrialists G. D. Birla and Purshottamdas Thakurdas created the FICCI in 1927, building on earlier, more local forms of the organization of Indian capital.[56] They understood that their economic interests demanded political mobilization. Birla spoke of the need for "every action of the Government to breathe a national policy, which might be summed up as 'India first and India last.'"[57]

The Great Depression and World War II further strengthened Indian capital owners and augmented their nationalist orientation. The Depression forced the Tatas to focus on the domestic market, which, in turn, encouraged them to decisively concentrate on the development of Indian capacities more broadly. By the mid-1930s, even Indian entrepreneurs who had remained ambivalent about nationalist mobilizations entered into a rapprochement with the Indian National Congress. As they fixated on domestic markets, they saw the benefits of a protectionist developmental state promised by the Congress. They made heavy philanthropic investments in education, building the Tata Institute of Social Sciences in Bombay and the Tata Institute of Fundamental Research, institutions that came to play an important role in the development of Indian capitalism after 1947.[58] And then, during the war, as British power weakened and demand skyrocketed, entrepreneurs made enormous profits, which allowed them to broaden their investments yet again.

Indian entrepreneurs and others almost universally acknowledged that to enable economic development, a strong state dedicated to the interests of Indian capital was essential. The history of European capitalism suggested as much: In the 1920s, Indian sociologist (and Mussolini admirer) Benoy Kumar Sarkar supported such a stance by investigating the economic histories and institutions of a potpourri of countries ranging from Germany to Turkey. He was driven by his belief that "[w]hatever has happened in the economic sphere in Eur-America during the last half century is bound also to happen more or less on similar and even identical lines in Asia and of course in India during the next generation or so."[59] What did it take, he asked, to develop? Looking at French educational institutions, the Turkish banking system, and Italian industrial modernization, he understood the differences between Europe and India:[60] "But while these pioneers were getting industrialized there was not much competition from outside in the shape of more powerfully established industries. And what small or great competition there was, the state was nationalistic, free and powerful enough to withstand and crush it by using economic as well as political means"—a scenario that was not the case in contemporary India.[61] Colonialism, in fact, meant that "a fully industrialized and economically vigorous India cannot make its appearance on earth as quickly as the history of the last three generations should induce one to suspect."[62]

YET THE MATERIAL conditions for envisioning a postcolonial society under the auspices of Indian capital were good. There was an economic base from which to develop. By independence, Indian manufacturers controlled 75 percent of the domestic market for industrial products. Indian capital had also made important advances in the financial sector. By 1947, Indian-owned banks controlled 83 percent of all deposits. One of the sources of strength of this Indian capitalist class was its control of sufficient capital resources for investments. There was a growing group of Indian managers as well. And new linkages had emerged between local industry, local agriculture, and a domestic market. Indian capital owners advocated for the development of a domestic economic space, and because of their size and diversification, they were also able to withstand imperial pressures.[63]

Yet as the struggle for independence accelerated, Indian capital owners found themselves on treacherous terrain. On the one hand, they accommodated themselves to a relatively moderate Indian National Congress and embraced its nationalist agenda. They also used the colonial government's alarm about more radical tactics to win concessions. On the other hand, as anticolonial civil disobedience spread, and as the Congress's leaders moved to the left, capital owners feared the movement's larger implications. In March 1936, after Nehru called on India to embrace socialism, economic elites protested. When the British jailed all of the top Congress leaders in August 1942 in response to Gandhi's Quit India campaign, Tata workers struck in solidarity, demonstrating the risks that such mobilizations entailed. Faced with mobilized peasants and workers increasingly aware of their collective power, capital owners became anxious about what policies the Congress would embrace should India become independent.[64]

To succeed, however, anticolonial rebellions had to be cross-class mobilizations, and capital owners had to accommodate themselves to the political realities of the moment. To build a national state that gave room for national capital to develop, they had to build coalitions with political forces that they also worried about. In a world devoid of such political dilemmas, they would have perhaps forgone an emphasis on planning and other left-wing policy strands in the Congress, but this was not the world they inhabited.[65]

In India, as elsewhere, labor played an important role in this struggle, not least because the Indian industrial proletariat had expanded dramatically to perhaps as many as seven million workers by World War II. Working-class and anticolonial mobilization increasingly intersected. The Great Indian Peninsula Railway strike of 1930 used the nationalist *satyagraha*—nonviolent civil disobedience—as a tactic, while the 1932 dockworkers' strike drew on the Congress's logistical support. During the war, there were also explicitly anticolonial strikes. In Bombay, two one-day strikes in 1939 and 1940 mobilized against the impositions of the war and the reintroduction of bureaucratic rule. In 1942, strikes in several provinces protested the arrest of Gandhi. The postal strike of 1946 gained widespread public sympathy, inaugurating an intense two-year period of working-class collective action. And unions embedded themselves within the very structures of the Congress.[66] When a Bombay union official wrote to the general secretary of the All-India Trade Union Congress (AITUC) in 1926, he argued that it was necessary to "strengthen its policy of United Front with the Indian National Congress in the anti-imperialist struggle and in the struggle of the Working class for its rights."[67] The Lal Bavta Press Kamgar Union in Bombay indeed believed that "[t]he development of the Anti-Imperialist struggle is the first and foremost task of the Indian Working class."[68]

Inevitably, as the Congress danced with both capital owners and workers, tensions arose, especially after it had gained significant political clout after 1937. A 1937 jute workers' strike was initially supported by the Congress, as jute was a largely British-dominated industry, but when the Congress came to play an active role in Bengali governance, it vacillated. In Bombay, the Congress Ministry initially supported unrest in the textile mills, but in 1938, it introduced the Bombay Trade Disputes Bill, which introduced a mandatory arbitration mechanism and attempted to outlaw strikes. In response, unions organized a general strike, with over two hundred thousand workers protesting against the "Black Act." Yet all in all, the Congress managed to navigate the tensions.[69] This dance, in India and elsewhere, produced one of the differentiating traits of postcolonial capitalism: The state that local capital so urgently needed could only be built by drawing on the collective mobilizations of workers and peasants who demanded that their interests be represented in the new nation as well, even to local capital's detriment. That dance was the starting point for postcolonial capitalism everywhere.

INDIA WAS SOMEWHAT of an outlier because of the material and political strength of its capital owners, but elsewhere in the colonized world, local capital owners also found spaces of accumulation within the colonial edifice and at times began to formulate a critique of colonialism, even envisioning a postcolonial future. In Nigeria, a small but powerful elite of local rulers, merchants, professionals, and officers, whose deep roots stretched back to the nineteenth century, had slowly improved their position within the colonial economy during World War II and began interacting with a broader anticolonial movement. In this struggle, economic concerns were paramount. There was, for example, the Dantata firm in Kano that traced back to the nineteenth-century kola trade, its owner, Alhassan Dantata, becoming one of the richest men in West Africa by the 1950s. There were cocoa exporters like the Ibadan trader I. B. Ogun. Nigerians controlled 5 percent of imports in 1949, but 20 percent in 1963. Some of the most prominent Nigerian entrepreneurs made their fortunes: Ayo Otaru manufactured "Lion" bread; the Odutola brothers transitioned from trade to manufacturing; transport company owner and merchant Sir Louis Odumegwu Ojukwu became Nigeria's first billionaire; Mobolaji Bank Anthony invested in the contraction, transport, and media industries; Chief Bisoye Tejuoso was a merchant and real estate speculator; and Alhaji S. L. Edu supplied to the government sector. Nigerians T. A. Doherty, Dr. A. Maja, and H. A. Subair founded the first successful West African–owned bank, the National Bank of Nigeria, in 1933.[70]

From this position of growing economic influence, Nigerian capital owners began articulating a critique of a colonial economy that had enabled British firms to extract profits and resources.[71] In 1947, Nnamdi Azikiwe—entrepreneur, newspaper editor, and later president of Nigeria—complained that "[t]here exists in colonial territories a regime of monopoly which has a stranglehold on the country's economy."[72] A year later, he "felt that other things being equal, it was morally wrong for Europeans to establish banks in Nigeria and then make it difficult for Nigerians to use them to the mutual advantage of both parties. Then it dawned on me that political freedom was not enough; economic freedom must be won also."[73] In 1949, he announced that "[i]t is our opinion that factors of capitalism and imperialism have stultified the normal growth of Nigeria in the community of nations. We are confident that only by the crystallization of democracy in all aspects of our national life and thought—political, economic and social—can we develop *pari passu* with the other progressive nations of the peace-loving world."[74]

These local capital owners, most of whom had accumulated their wealth either in trade or in agriculture, pressured the British colonial administration for what they called the "indigenization" of the private sector. Merchants such as T. A. Odutola of Ijebu-Ode, S. O. Gbadamosi of Ikorodu, and J. O. Fadahunsi of Ilesha joined the nationalist Nigerian Youth Movement in the 1930s, resisting the monopolistic marketing of cocoa formalized in the so-called cocoa pool of 1937/38. In the western region of Nigeria, business owner Gbadamosi played a crucial role in the anticolonial Action Group. In the early 1940s, the Nigerian Association of African Importers and Exporters pushed for more access to foreign trade, state support for local businesses (loans, for example), and protection from foreign competition. Nigerian newspapers such as the *West African Pilot* and the *Daily Service* published a barrage of articles on these subjects.[75]

After World War II, these Nigerian capital owners, buoyed by new economic opportunities, became increasingly outspoken in their support of independence. They were ready to finance, and politically support, movements that had their (nationalist) interests in mind. Claiming their own state, they saw independence as the only viable path for continued local capital accumulation. They built coalitions with peasants, wageworkers, and small traders to get there. Festus Okotie-Eboh, one of Nigeria's wealthiest entrepreneurs, became deeply involved in politics. Born in 1912 to a minor Itsekiri ruler, he became a player in the timber and rubber trade. In the 1950s, he embarked on a stellar political career that brought him to the Western Region House of Representatives, then the Federal Parliament in Lagos. By 1955 he was minister of labor, and became minister of finance in 1957. Industrialist and real estate tycoon Igwe Mathias Nwafor Ugochukwu also became a political activist. Businesspeople such as Ugochukwu and Okotie-Eboh moved beyond opposing foreign capital to opposing the colonial state as such, exemplified by the 1947 boycott of imported goods in Ibadan. Kingsley O. Mbadiwe, businessman and federal minister of commerce and industry, appealed to the British government to "set up various agencies to provide Nigerian businessmen with necessary capital, technical knowhow, and management skills for an effective indigenization programme."[76] And in 1956, Nigerian capitalists from the North created the Northern Amalgamated Merchants' Union to represent their interests.[77]

In Nigeria, as elsewhere in the colonized world, business and politics became linked, with independence seen as the condition for continued accumulation among growing numbers of local capital owners. In 1946, giving voice to such politics, the *Eastern Nigeria Guardian* editorialized that "Nigerians should be given a hand in directing the destinies of the millions in the country and that the time should be hastened for the eventual handing over of the government."[78]

Such pressures did have an impact: In 1946, a new British creation, the Nigerian Local Development Board, was created to support Nigerian businessmen. In the late 1950s, moreover, an advisory committee was set up to consider how local capitalists could be supported—a committee that included Nigerian businesspeople among its members.[79]

BY THE 1950S, such nodes of local capital—some new, some rooted in precolonial times—had emerged elsewhere in the colonized world as well and began to lay claims to political power. In Tanganyika, a small local business elite put pressure on the colonial state. Already in the 1930s, Kleist Sykes, a Dar es Salaam entrepreneur, had combined trade with political activism, cofounding the African Association in 1929. He was probably the first African member of the Dar es Salaam Chamber of Commerce. Another small-scale entrepreneur, Erica Fiah, engaged in retail trade, property investments, and moneylending and became a founding member of the African Commercial Association (ACA), mobilizing "the African trader through co-operation against prejudicial Government legislation and against the near-monopoly of Asians in . . . retail

trade."[80] He was critical of the lack of government support for Africans' entrepreneurial activities, which was, he said, "UnEnglish, unfair and unchristian."[81] Later, Fiah published a small newspaper and ran a commercial farm.[82] And even though he never explicitly called for an end to colonialism, the ever

Entrepreneur and political activist Kleist Sykes with his three sons in Dar es Salaam, 1942.

paranoid British government complained of him that "[u]nderneath there is really a sort of demand for local self-government."[83]

One of the most important nodes of Indigenous capital accumulation in Africa was to be found on the northern edge of the continent, in Egypt.[84] Egypt, as we have seen, was one of the world's earliest centers of significant merchant power and wealth. Almost a millennium later, the country had become marginal to global capitalism, its two principal contributions the export of long-staple cotton to European factories and the operation of that essential passage to Asia—the Suez Canal.

Yet local capital owners had ambitious ideas about the future of Egyptian capitalism. World War I had created new openings for them, too, especially in manufacturing. Then, in the aftermath of the 1919 anti-British uprising, nationalists—capital owners among them—pushed for not only further state-supported industrialization but also a modernization of the countryside and the development of a specifically domestic economy.[85]

Merchant capital, often accumulated in agriculture, thus pushed outward into industry. Three family groups took on a particularly prominent role in this process: One formed around Tal'at Harb, the other around the Yahya family, and a third around Muhammad Ahmad 'Abbud. All three had gained their wealth from agrarian investments. But now these families moved into manufacturing and banking: Tal'at Harb created Banque Misr as a kind of holding company in 1920 and then, most famously, established the massive Misr Spinning and Weaving Company in al-Mahalla al-Kubra in 1927. He and other local capitalists sought to build an alliance with the state. The scope of these families' ambitions became clear when they founded the Egyptian Federation of Industries in 1922. Local Egyptian capital extended its importance. In 1900, just 9 percent of the share capital of companies active in the country had been controlled by Egyptians; by 1948, that number had shot up to 39 percent. Textiles remained at the heart of the Egyptian business elite's activities: In 1947, 43 percent of the value added in manufacturing was produced in that sector, followed by beverages, tobacco, and food processing.[86]

This rise of Egyptian capital owners went hand in glove with their connections to the postcolonial state. When Egypt gained tariff autonomy in 1930, new import duties protected their fledgling manufacturing enterprises from foreign competition. Yet despite their ties to the nationalist project, and their connections to the newly powerful state, they continued to cooperate with foreign capital: British and French, of course, but increasingly North American. Tellingly, as British cloth manufacturers lost markets in Egypt, British textile machine manufacturers stepped up to supply these local factories. Until 1952, Egyptian capitalists expanded their sphere of activities by combining their access to the national state with their access to foreign capital. Unlike their Indian counterparts, they lacked the continental mass to dream seriously of building an autonomous Egyptian capitalism.[87]

In this multifaceted struggle against colonial domination, one set of independent countries outside the developed core served as an example: Turkey, Brazil, Mexico, and Colombia among them. Their ascent suggested that given the right policies, and given a capable and resourceful state, development was possible. There, capital owners and states had focused on import-substitution industrialization, often against the resistance of both rural elites and peasants who had benefited from dynamic export markets and cheap imports. They now inspired postcolonial capitalists and states everywhere.[88]

This import-substitution reorientation in South America, Turkey, and elsewhere, as we have seen, had accelerated during the Great Depression, the moment when markets for agricultural and mineral commodities had suddenly collapsed by more than half of their precrisis value and drastically worsened the terms of trade.[89] Disempowering agricultural elites, this crisis had opened up opportunities for the construction of new political economies. They were often formulated with strong doses of nationalism and at times had an anti-imperialist flavor. As an Argentinean writer remarked in 1946, "The desire for dominance, which is born as a spontaneous consequence of financial power, has come to be concretized in supercapitalist organizations that constantly tend to expand the orbit of their actions, an instrument of slavery for the producers of the land; of political subjugation in the countries that treasure their natural resources or constitute consumer markets, and of storms between the nations that dispute the hegemony of the same."[90] Something had to be done to leave this world behind. And it was.

Turkey was among the first to seize the promise of the moment. In response to the Depression, as we have seen, it had embarked upon a state-directed industrialization project. Supported by its substantial domestic market, the Turkish state planned the country's industrial transformation. By the 1960s, the state controlled between 40 and 50 percent of the entire economy under the auspices of its powerful State Planning Organization.[91]

In Latin America, such state-driven import-substitution industrialization had also become a self-conscious project built on both previous nuclei of industry and a political alliance between national capital and labor. Relevant policies had been worked out in the wake of the Depression and accelerated during World War II, with governments encouraging industrialization by developing infrastructures and policies that favored domestic manufacturing enterprises. In Brazil, the state came to operate, among other things, steel mills, refineries, heavy machinery producers, and banks. Consequential infrastructure projects followed, such as in 1958, when Brazil started building the "Road of the Jaguars" into Amazonia. Under the government of Lázaro Cárdenas, Mexico had nationalized the country's important oil industry in 1937, and by 1960, the state was Mexico's largest employer. The country had become a mixed economy, spending lavishly on infrastructure and public works projects, intervening regularly to guide and encourage certain industries and to expand the scope of state welfare programs. Nationalizing many sectors of the economy, from railroads to phone service, Mexico self-consciously followed the example of nineteenth-century German and American developmentalism, focusing on protecting its economies through import prohibitions, licensing controls, provisions of credit, state subsidies, and investments in infrastructure. Tariffs, at the heart of these strategies, increased dramatically: In the 1960s, in Brazil, they averaged 260 percent on consumer nondurables and 328 percent on consumer durables; in Colombia, those respective numbers were 247 and 108 percent; and in Mexico, 114 and 147 percent.[92]

Such state-directed industrial expansion continued to lead to rapid economic growth. Between 1945 and 1973, Mexico's industrial output increased by a factor of four and Brazil's by a factor of eight. Turkey's growth rates between 1945 and 1973 averaged about 5.5 percent annually—higher than in the developed world—and they compared favorably with an estimated growth of less than 1 percent per year in the century after 1850. Turkey's per capita income in fact doubled between 1950 and 1980.[93]

Not only did these economies expand rapidly, but their structures also changed. The share of industrial activity in economic output rose. During the war years, industrial production had increased annually by 3.6 percent in Argentina, 5.3 percent in Brazil, 9.3 percent in Chile, 5.1 percent in Colombia, and 9.4 percent in Mexico—trends that continued into the postwar decades. By 1975, manufacturing made up 29 percent of the Colombian economy. The size of industry in Argentina more than doubled between 1929 and 1957; it quadrupled in Mexico and Brazil and increased eightfold in Colombia. Exports became rapidly less important to these economies; by 1950, they equaled just 2 percent of Argentina's output and 4 percent of Brazil's, remarkably low for countries that had for centuries focused on exporting agricultural commodities to world markets. Economic growth in Latin America as a whole has been estimated at an annual 5.3 percent in the 1950s and 5.4 percent in the 1960s—astounding numbers that advertised such strategies to the decolonizing world.[94]

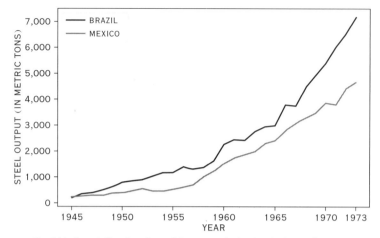

Rapid industrialization through import-substitution industrialization:
steel output in Brazil and Mexico, 1945–1973.

As economic nationalism spread, new forms of business enterprises emerged as well. Business groups—especially family-dominated ones with heavily diversified undertakings—became major players. They were long-lasting because they internalized markets and integrated vertically.[95]

In Colombia, families were crucial to the country's business world, and family-controlled diversified business groups quickly became dominant. German, Latvian, Lebanese, and Jewish immigrants played an important role in the founding of these groups. As state-supported industrialization began in the 1930s, wealthy cattle ranchers, coffee barons, and merchants moved some of their capital into new sectors. They first focused on beverages, food, and textiles, then later added construction materials and basic chemicals to their investments. And by the 1970s, they had added financial services to the mix as well. The decoupling from the world market allowed them to grow and diversify their enterprises. Each group controlled a range of companies, some in related businesses, some not. By the 1960s, such groups were common, and by 2018, they made up forty-seven of the largest one hundred Colombian companies, with 66.4 percent of total sales. Of twenty-five such groups that existed in 2018, a study found that four had consolidated before 1950, seven in the 1950s, nine in the 1960s, and five in the 1970s. During the 1970s, these twenty-five business groups controlled a total of 428 companies. Well adapted to the project of import-substitution industrialization, family groups such as Grupo Santo Domingo, Organización Sarmiento Angulo, Organización Ardila Lülle, and Empresarial Antioqueño became legendary.[96]

In Mexico, such family groups became crucial as well. Because the capital-intensive sector was occupied by state and foreign companies (mining and iron and steel were basically in US hands), Mexican family groups, like their Colombian counterparts, focused on consumption goods, especially foodstuffs and beverages. The 1960s, in particular, were bountiful for them—close to the governing Partido Revolucionario Institucional, they benefited from growing markets and state protections.[97] As in Colombia, Mexican economic nationalism helped shelter these family groups, enabling rapid ascents in the world of business. Perhaps most spectacularly, Carlos Slim, son of Lebanese immigrants, built Grupo Carso, a diversified conglomerate, and eventually turned himself into one of the richest (and at times the richest) person in the world.

Elsewhere, the family-dominated business group also became the chief form of organizing firms, well adjusted as it was to the structure of local markets and the particular intersections with the state. In Brazil, it was the Gerdau Group, which focused on steel production under the direction of German immigrant Curt Johannpeter. Integrating vertically and expanding first to other regions of Brazil and Latin America, then beyond, it was to become one of Brazil's biggest multinationals by the second decade of the twenty-first century. In Turkey, diversified business groups, among them the large holding companies of the Koç and Sabançi families, came to dominate the privately held sectors of the economy: food processing, textiles, consumer durables, automobiles, and tourism. As in Latin America, they benefited from the protection of the domestic market. In India, too, as we have seen, diversified family business groups—centered on the Tata, Mahindra,

Godrej, and Birla families—came to play crucial roles in the national economy, while in Pakistan, just twenty-two families came to control two-thirds of its industry and four-fifths of its insurance funds as well as its bank assets.[98] As they began to challenge global inequalities, spectacular domestic inequalities emerged.

⸻

As capital owners in the Global South—along with professionals, peasants, intellectuals, and workers—challenged colonial rule, this unstable but powerful coalition began to undermine not only colonialism's legitimacy but also the willingness and ability of imperial powers to defend it. As a result, colonialism unraveled at astounding speed. In just three decades after 1945, almost all colonies gained their independence. What had one day seemed, to many Europeans, to be the nearly natural order, essential to the upkeep of the world economy, even to civilization as such, became irrelevant the next.

As economic life in the newly emancipated regions of the world changed, it was the very condition of their emergence that decisively shaped their present and future. Perhaps most important here is that the founding of many of these new nations was the result of broad-based and popular rebellions. In some ways, this trajectory of struggle against an old order was not that different from the struggle of the European bourgeoisie against the old order, a struggle that unfolded in the nineteenth century in general and in 1848 in particular. Yet capital owners in the Global South, unlike their European counterparts more than a century earlier, participated in nation-building in a world where they retained a deeply subordinate position within the global economy, confronted the continued power of foreign capital, and navigated the often spectacular limitations of the local economies they sought to dominate. When the Rhineland bourgeoisie had struggled against the old regime in 1848, they had inhabited one of the most developed economic spaces in the world, not least because of the infusions of wealth made possible by Europe's expansion into the rest of the world—an expansion driven by war capitalism. A century later, their Indian, Nigerian, and Tanganyikan counterparts aimed to accumulate capital and state power in some of the poorest, least developed, and least powerful nations.

Still, these were heady days in the decolonizing world, propelled by a sense of possibility, even talk of the "advantages of backwardness."[99] For Kenyan writer Ngũgĩ wa Thiong'o, "the impossible seemed possible."[100] Decolonization seemed to open up bright vistas of development; the two seemed to become, in effect, the same thing.[101] A huge project beckoned on the horizon: "What other countries have taken three hundred years or more to achieve," argued Ghana's first president, Kwame Nkrumah, "a once dependent territory must try to accomplish in a generation if it is to survive."[102] Guinean writer and politician Fodéba Keïta concurred: "Our main task is to free our economy, our culture, and all our life."[103] To get there, everyone agreed, one needed "development," and that included, first and foremost, modern industry—steel and tractors but also dams, clinics, and improvements in life expectancy, education, health, food output, and other statistics.[104]

Whatever the specific trajectory, across the world a consensus had formed that the to-be-built economic order was to be strongly statist.[105] For Nkrumah, "The domestic economy must be planned to promote the interests of its own nationals. . . . Otherwise the newly-independent country may fall victim to the highly dangerous forces of economic imperialism, and find that it has merely substituted one kind of colonialism for another."[106] Modibo Keita, Mali's first president, joined the chorus: To develop was "to make the state the instrument of the reorganization of our economy, and to operate in such a way that our economy is balanced, no longer as a complementary economy of the French economy, but as an independent one, based on the sole interest of our country and of the working people."[107]

For Swedish sociologist Gunnar Myrdal, these efforts equaled nothing less than what he called the "Great Awakening."[108] What "underdeveloped countries" needed, he argued in 1957, was "a national economic development policy"—a focus on not only industry, investments in infrastructure, and improvements to agricultural productivity but also health, education, and training.[109] Taking a bird's-eye view of what he called the "global New Deal," he stressed the need for a "political process toward social democracy in the world at large."[110] And Myrdal was no outlier: Such developmentalism had become widely important, reaching its zenith during the 1960s.[111]

The shaping of postcolonial capitalism, this "global New Deal," took particular forms. The most prominent was the one in which the state played a crucial role in economic development—a trend that was fueled not just by the evident economic successes of the Soviet Union, which stood as a model for the powers of planning, but by the example of states in South America and parts of Asia (such as Turkey) that had been decolonized for longer, and by the statist reorientation of economies in the world's capitalist heartlands, including the United States.[112] As industrialization and vaguely defined "modernization" were crucial to all anticolonial state builders, they sought models that would enable such development—both to create new opportunities for accumulation and to stabilize their newly formed states.

But what, precisely, would economic life look like under national auspices? The Indian example, again, is instructive. Long before independence, anticolonial forces converged on a consensus that postcolonial economic life needed to unfold under the management of a powerful state and be driven by long-term planning. As early as 1934, engineer and administrator M. Visvesvaraya had published *Planned Economy for India*, in which he argued for the adoption of a ten-year plan that would coordinate investment, production, and infrastructural development, embedded in protectionist laws and coordinated by corporatist organizations steered by government officials, economists, and businesspeople. Inspired by the spread of planning throughout the world, he remarked that "[t]he people of India without the support of political power have been unable to put their house in order," and thus control of government needed to be transferred "to Indian hands."[113] That same year, insurance entrepreneur and Bengali political activist Nalini Ranjan Sarkar argued that "the remedy is . . . a planned economy. . . . [T]he importance of planning for both defensive and developmental perspective can hardly be exaggerated."[114] As the FICCI, the peak organization of Indian capital, stated categorically, "The days of undiluted laissez-faire are gone forever."[115] In 1938, then president of the Indian National Congress Subhas Chandra Bose crafted a National Planning Committee, chaired by Jawaharlal Nehru, to provide a perspective on the Indian economy and Indian economic policymaking. In all these deliberations, economic nationalism was key. In 1946, just before independence, the Indian Merchants' Chamber in Bombay insisted that India needed to rapidly expand its textile industry and produce its own machines: "The textile industry is the most important industry of the country and the precarious dependence on external sources for its requirements of machinery and equipment should be ended as early as possible."[116] Nehru warned that "though we may be politically free [i]t is not over in the economic sense."[117]

Capital owners, not least pushed by the political exigency of the moment, were among the most forceful proponents of such a political economy: In December 1942, a small group of prominent Indian businesspeople—G. D. Birla, Ardeshir Dalal, Kasturbhai Lalbhai, John Matthai, J. R. D. Tata, Purshottamdas Thakurdas, Ardeshir Darabshaw Shroff, and Lala Shri Ram among them—had started deliberations on the possible shape of the postindependence economy. Meeting at the headquarters of the Tata company, they called themselves the "Committee on Post-War Economic Development." Two years later, they published their *Memorandum Outlining a Plan of Economic Development for India*, which came to be known as the Bombay Plan.[118] Laying out a blueprint for the postcolonial order, the memorandum presented "the general lines on which development should proceed and the demands which planning is likely to make on the country's resources."[119] Recognizing "that the existing economic organization, based on private enterprise and ownership, has failed to bring about a satisfactory distribution of the national income," the document suggested the need for a national economic planning committee.[120] The goal was to map out a plan for rapid industrialization and modernization of agriculture that would double per capita income in fifteen years. Remarkably, industrial output itself was prefigured to increase by a factor of five. The emphasis would be on heavy industry, especially the generation of electric power and the development of basic industries, such as steelmaking. Yet the elite members of the committee also wanted to support consumer-goods industries, build roads, expand health care, and develop educational opportunities. Explicitly inspired by Soviet economic performance but also desirous of keeping their own privileged position, they imagined a mixed economy. "The principle of *laissez faire*, which is regarded as the dominant note of capitalism, has during the last hundred years been so largely modified in the direction of State intervention in various spheres of economic activity that in many of its characteristic aspects capitalism has been transformed almost beyond recognition," they stated.[121] They and other Indian entrepreneurs endorsed a powerful state, in hopes that it would not only increase output and secure a potentially very large home market but also control labor and forces within the Congress who proposed even more radical measures.[122] Strikingly, this group of capital owners argued that "the distinction between capitalism and socialism has lost much of its significance from a practical standpoint."[123] *The Economist*, reviewing the plan in London, was hardly convinced by such unorthodox demands from entrepreneurs and deemed their proposal "not a very impressive document when examined in detail."[124] But soon it would be of no consequence what the former British overlords thought about such matters.

Upon the Tatas' wishes, the Bombay Plan was popularized by freedom fighter Minoo Masani in a handsomely illustrated book with the programmatic title *Our India*. The book displays in striking ways some of the optimism and sense of possibility that infused this moment. Masani outlined the rich natural and human resources of the Indian continent and set out a perspective for a prosperous, self-sufficient India embarking upon an industrialization effort led by mining, electric power, steel, chemicals, and a newly envisioned machinery industry—all built on and feeding into a rationalized and partly collectivized agricultural system.[125] "The State or Government," the book went on to explain, "is the machine or instrument which does . . . what you and I and all those who live in a country want to be done. . . . When we have a government of our own, let us hope one of the first things it will do is to start on a Plan which will . . . get the most out of our country and our people for their own benefit."[126] For sure, there would also be a place for private capital, especially for J. R. D. Tata himself, "a very wise Indian," who had already constructed, among other things, the British Empire's largest steelworks.[127] Yet "big factories and plants should have no owners. . . . Key Industries . . . ought to be made the common property of the nation and to be run for its benefit."[128] While not explicitly advocating socialism, Masani urged more planning: "In addition to the control of key industries and public utilities the State would also, during the period of the Plan, have to exercise a more general control over economic processes. Such a control would include that of prices, of priorities in the distribution of raw materials and manufactured goods, of the flow of investment of capital, and of foreign trade and exchange."[129] The American Tennessee Valley Authority (TVA)—a New Deal project of comprehensive regional planning—was held up as a model.[130] In retrospect, industrialist Shroff, one the architects of the plan, saw its radical nature quite clearly:

> [I]t may seem curious that a set of eight businessmen who are so largely interested as capitalists should put forth proposals which would involve Government regulation and Governmental interference with which they intimately connected every day of their lives, but we are convinced that no planned development can take place in the conditions in which we live in our own country unless the State assumes a positive role in regulating the economic life of the country.[131]

Tata himself was just as supportive. In a 1944 speech, "A Fifteen-Year Plan of Economic Development for India," delivered at the Rotary Club of Bombay, he embraced the need for economic planning: "[O]ur economic destiny," Tata said, "need no longer be left to the mercy of chance and the chaotic interplay of uncontrolled forces."[132] Japan was one of his models for successful industrialization.[133] Hoping for "long-term economic development," he paid "warm tribute" to Nehru and argued that India needed to "construct," not "reconstruct," to "build up our economic structure from the foundations."[134] He understood that India faced a very different situation than countries that had industrialized 150 years earlier. Because of "the political subjection and economic degradation" of India's people under colonialism, laissez-faire "will lead her to famine, chaos, and despair." Therefore, India needed a National Planning Committee that would steer the country toward industrialization, with a focus on basic industries, a doubling of living standards in the fifteen years to come, and modernizations in agriculture, education, health, and infrastructure. In the process, according to Tata, "every aspect of our economic life should be rigorously controlled by the State"—a state no longer governed by a distant colonial power but "a Government founded on the will of the people."[135] Not all businesspeople agreed, but at the Tata Staff College, students learned to tell apart a "fully socialist economy" from a "mixed economy," which, they were taught, had "arisen out of the Gandhian thinking."[136]

WHEN INDIA GAINED independence in 1947, such ideas were put into practice, guided by the lodestar of swadeshi: Though swadeshi—by other names—had come to influence many countries' political economies and flourished globally in the 1930s and 1940s, in India it was a substantial break with two centuries of colonial domination. It set up an entirely novel political economy.[137] The state, so declared the FICCI's policy statement in 1946, was "to pursue national economic policies in the interests of India" only.[138]

As elsewhere, the newly independent government faced tremendous challenges: India was poor and still a very rural society. In 1951, of its roughly 340 million people, 82.3 percent lived in the countryside, and 70 percent (in 1941) worked in agriculture—more than at the turn of the century. Sixty-five percent of rural people lived in absolute poverty. Only 3,061 of India's 558,089 villages had access to electricity. And India produced only 3 percent of the global GDP, even though it accounted for 15 percent of the world's people.[139]

But India also had certain structural advantages, especially a strong national capitalist class, even substantial capitalists. For Nehru, the country's first prime minister, rapid economic development was the precondition for securing India's independence:[140]

> I have seen . . . the throbbing agony of India's masses, the call of their eyes for relief from the terrible burdens they carry. That is our problem; all others are secondary and merely lead up to it. To solve that problem, we shall have to end the imperialist control and exploitation of India. But what is this Imperialism of today? It is not merely the physical possession of one country by another; its roots lie deeper. Modern imperialism is an outgrowth of capitalism and cannot be separated from it.[141]

Though Nehru championed a "mixed economy," he hoped for not just government-directed planning but the initiative of Indian capital owners, an elite that had been "hamstrung by its British overlords."[142] Nehru believed in a socialist future for India, but he saw it as a long-term process with an outcome that was distinctly different from the Soviet or Chinese examples, especially because his vision relied on the ongoing role of, and cooperation with, private capital. The three pillars of his economic policy were "rapid industrial and agricultural growth, a public sector to develop strategic industries and a mixed economy."[143] Nehru set up a hugely powerful National Planning Commission in March 1950 and appointed physicist Prasanta Chandra Mahalanobis as its head.[144]

In 1951, this new government launched its First Five-Year Plan, which, just like the second one that followed, focused on heavy capital goods (such as steel), import substitution, agricultural modernization, and domestic investment. As steel mills, hydropower plants, and fertilizer plants sprouted on the subcontinent, they came to symbolize the new nation. That same year, the Development and Regulation Act stipulated an intricate system for the licensing of industries. In Nehru's fifteen years of governing, he launched three such five-year plans, some more successful than others. To manage the plan, a massive infrastructure of data acquisition and analysis was built, housed in the Central Statistical Organization and the National Sample Survey, creating a remarkable new state capacity.[145]

Capital owners benefited from greatly accelerated economic growth and a wave of industrialization. From 1947/48 to 1952/53, industrial production increased by 20 percent. Between 1951 and 1965, India's economy grew by about 4 percent a year—quite high by historical standards. Industry grew by 7.1 percent on average during these years. During the same time, Indian agriculture expanded by about 3 percent annually, which was good but insufficient to feed a rapidly growing population. Some industries, such as machine tools, succeeded in limiting import dependence, reducing it from 89.8 percent in 1950 to 43 percent in 1960 and to just 9 percent in 1974. In 1970, India produced five million tons of steel, five times more than at independence. While there was significant private investment, public companies rose to the commanding heights of the Indian economy. Public capital as a share of total corporate capital had been 3.4 percent in 1951, but it rose to 30 percent in 1961 and to 50 percent by the early 1970s. Lots of government funds also went into science and technology, research, and higher education, producing the structural basis for what became the enormously dynamic economic development of India after the turn of the millennium. Economic growth accelerated to theretofore unseen levels.[146]

The postcolonial state provided significant benefits to capital owners too: High tariff barriers and other protectionist measures sheltered domestic businesses. As Shanti Prasad Jain, then president of the FICCI, observed in a 1952 meeting with the minister of commerce and industry: "Government should not permit competitive imports of these items and thus safeguard the interests of the consumers as well as indigenous manufacturers."[147] They also benefited from policies aimed at keeping foreign capital out, a concern that was, for example, close to the heart of the Godrej family. In 1949/50, 94 percent of the railways, 85 percent of the jute industry, 56 percent of the electric companies, and 53 percent of the coal mines were still under foreign control.[148] That was unacceptable to Indian capital owners. As the FICCI stated, "[T]he general feeling in the country is opposed to any such participation by private foreign capital."[149] For a letter writer to *The Times of India*, D. D. Anklesaria, foreign capital investments were indeed a remnant of "the mighty edifice of Empire, both financial and political, . . . built on the blood, tears, toil and sweat of crores [tens of millions] of our countrymen."[150]

Capital owners managed to keep widespread nationalizations at bay and recruited state support for the containment of labor. Airlines were nationalized in 1953 (including Tata Airlines), but most assets remained in private hands. And the state played a crucial role in taming working-class politics and, indeed, repressing it. The two-year strike wave of 1946 to 1948, which saw millions of workers in almost four thousand distinct strikes demand higher wages, was forcefully, even violently, repressed by the new postcolonial government. New labor regulations that were passed in response gave the state an inordinately central role in what amounted to a corporatist labor relations regime. Years later, in 1958, one of the biggest and most violent strikes at the Tata steel plant came to a grim end when police fired on groups of workers, and the army was brought to Jamshedpur. Such labor unrest, in turn, brought the Tatas and other capitalists closer to the state.[151]

As a result, some industrialists enjoyed exceptionally tight-knit connections to the government, perhaps no one more so than steel industrialist G. D. Birla, who was fully committed to a project that focused on domestic industrialization, the home market, and a deliberate, planned construction of a modern economy.[152] He and Nehru met often and corresponded intensely. Economic policies, such as "the question of planning," were a frequent topic of their discussions.[153] Birla also provided Nehru with significant funds to be used for relief efforts.[154]

Yet the nationalist economic project was soon riven by conflicts as well. The postcolonial Indian government had to walk a fine line between the push and pull of various actors. This became clear in 1948, when the new government got deeply drawn into a labor conflict involving the country's textile industry, India's leading industrial sector. When workers' representatives, textile industrialists, and government bureaucrats met in Delhi early that year, they negotiated wage rates, minimum wages, social standards, and other such issues in an industry that had been beset by labor woes since the nineteenth century. Despite a shared nationalist agenda, interests clashed: S. C. Roy of the Bengal Millowners' Association in Calcutta saw a need for "rationalization" of production to increase output.[155] By contrast, and reflective of their newfound power, union representatives aggressively argued for improved conditions and threatened that if no solution was found, they would demand nationalization. They suggested that the profit payout to owners should be limited to "what a Bank would pay to its clients as there was hardly any risk in the investment."[156] P. B. Vaidya, adviser to the All-India Trade Union Congress, contended that if the industry would not provide living wages to its workers, it had no "right to survive," and he suggested that in such a case, the state needed to be prepared to take it over.[157] For P. Ramamurti, with the same Congress, it was clear that "the textile industry had not been built by the Capitalists but by the working class."[158]

Representatives of the state, meanwhile, focused on output, arguing that there was an urgent need for more textiles—and that required pacifying labor. While they forced employers to pay higher wages, they also said that workers needed to tend more machines, embracing the "rationalization" of production that employers had demanded. They suggested adding a new night shift to textile mills and pushed for an agreement so that strikes could be averted.[159] India's labor minister, Jagjivan Ram, reminded participants that the "cotton industry is our premier industry" and emphasized "the extreme importance of increasing production to raise the standard of living of the common man."[160] Labor leader N. M. Joshi agreed with the need for much higher production. But to him it was important that labor not shoulder this effort alone. Capitalists needed to be taxed higher: Though he recognized "the need for industrial peace for increased production," the wealth of private capitalists had to be mobilized to make national development possible.[161]

There were indeed substantial fissures in the nationalist alliance. Nehru and Tata, for one, did not get along; Tata stayed at arm's length from the new government. In the 1950s, the FICCI also became even more nervous about Nehru's socialist proclivities, especially once the government nationalized the life insurance industry.[162] In 1956, the FICCI's president, Shantilal Mangaldas, concluded a speech in which he had addressed his audience of businesspeople as "my comrades and fellow workers in the business field," probably the only time in history that a businessperson used the socialist honorific *comrades* to address peers. He pleaded "that we be given a reasonable opportunity and a fair deal."[163] That same year, the head of the Employers' Association of Calcutta, Shanti Prasad Jain, implored India to "lay emphasis on the philosophy of initiative and enterprise," while Ramanbhai R. Amin of the Federation of Gujarat Mills & Industries, Baroda, called for nationalizations to remain a "temporary measure."[164] On the other side of the great social divide, labor activist Joshi also expressed disappointment with the nationalist project, bemoaning the continued poverty of India, the woefully inadequate food, housing, and clothing:

> After the war when Congress came into power . . . people expected a change in policy in dealing with the difficulties of the workers. The British rulers had made no plans to change war-time

production into peace-time production. Neither did the national government show any interest in this essential task, with the result that a large number of industrial workers and public servants became unemployed.[165]

Despite these tensions, capital owners and labor agreed on planning, partial nationalizations, and a significant public sector. They retained their attachment to anti-imperialism and democracy, and they never moved toward authoritarian models, as was the case elsewhere in the postcolonial world. US economist John Kenneth Galbraith once quipped that "[e]ven the most intransigent Indian capitalist may observe on occasion that he is really a socialist at heart."[166] As national capital became central to independent India and an independent state central to national capital, their interests moved into alignment, despite all the tensions.[167]

EVERYWHERE IN THE decolonizing world, such new nodes of state power and capital emerged. Everywhere, the new state mediated between capital owners, peasants, and workers while pursuing a project of development. The outcomes, however, diverged greatly. Egypt's postcolonial configurations were probably closest in flavor to those of India. In the wake of World War II, powerful nationalist forces put an end to Egypt's halfway house between colonialism and freedom, in which a powerful group of national capital owners, despite having gained formal independence in 1922, continued to confront deep foreign meddling. In 1952, a young army lieutenant colonel, Gamal Abdel Nasser, rose to power, and with him emerged a new developmental vision for the country. Building on the ideas that had come to restructure the global political economy since the 1930s, he embraced nationalizations, planning, price controls, and wealth redistributions.[168] He attacked the all-powerful business groups. His new regime was committed to anti-monopoly policies, its populist agenda directed against the institutionalized settlement of 1922.

Under the advisement of left-wing economists such as Rashid al-Barrawi, the public sector expanded tremendously. The Revolutionary Command Council (RCC) that had orchestrated Nasser's rise embarked upon a development project heavily focused on industrialization, especially in fertilizers, construction, petroleum, and heavy industry. Set on breaking up the continued dominance of British and French investments in the Egyptian economy, the state became deeply involved in industrial projects such as steelmaking, with half of the massive 1954 investment in the Iron and Steel Company at Helwan drawn from the state. Most importantly, the 364-foot-tall Aswan High Dam, for which planning began in the 1950s, was envisioned by the nationalist regime as the cornerstone for jump-starting Egypt's industry and expanding its agriculture. Completed in 1970, it became one of the world's largest hydraulic projects. (Like all such dams, it would have drastic environmental consequences, removing the naturally fertilizing silt from the river and making Egyptian agriculture dependent on huge amounts of artificial fertilizer.) Partly in response to conflicts over the financing of that dam, Nasser nationalized the Suez Canal in 1956, provoking a failed British, French, and Israeli military response. Then, in 1957, the government stipulated that all banks and insurance companies were to have exclusively Egyptian shareholders and directors. That same year, the al-Mu'assasa al-Iqtisadiya (Egyptian Economic Organization) was created, which took control of formerly British- and French-owned firms. As in India, a national planning commission was set up. By 1960, the National Bank of Egypt and Banque Misr were nationalized. Shipping came under the control of a state agency, as did cotton pressing. Land reforms weakened agrarian elites. The emphasis on state-directed development increased; the importance of state investments in capital formation tripled in the 1950s. Symbolizing this sea change, the powerful Abbud business group was partly nationalized in 1955/56, and then, in October 1961, the state took ownership of Abbud's family property and that of 167 other "reactionary capitalists." By 1961, the Egyptian state had ascended to a towering position within most economic sectors.

Five-year plans, like elsewhere, steered the direction of the national economy, partly enabled by Soviet development aid.[169]

While Nasser and the RCC followed state-centric policies, their relationship to labor remained ambivalent: As in India, working-class activists and institutions had played an important role in the struggle against the foreign presence. Indeed, elite nationalists and working-class activists had been aligned since after World War II. Trade unions had also supported the nationalization of the Suez Canal. As labor saw an opportunity in the emergence of a regime sympathetic to its concerns, strikes skyrocketed. Between 1952 and 1958, labor conflicts tripled, as compared with the preceding seven years. Also as in India, the nation's largest industry—textiles—became the epicenter of such conflicts. And workers celebrated some successes: The government passed new labor laws, giving workers new rights. Workers' standard of living improved. And, rhetorically, the government lionized industrial workers, making them central actors in the creation of Egyptian modernity. Yet at the same time, the new regime repressed the labor movement. When textile workers in Alexandria went on strike in 1952, the new government immediately sent the army to arrest 545 workers. Labor activism was eventually even constrained by law, as the government declared strikes to be illegal.[170]

Promises of domestic industrialization, Egypt: "Yesterday we used to depend on agriculture alone. Today we build our industrial glory with iron and steel."

PostColonial Nigeria differed from both Egypt and India. After independence, the new government built what has been called "nurture-capitalism."[171] Pressured by local capital owners who pushed their interests in the political realm, the state supported local entrepreneurship with what became known as "indigenization."[172] The Nigerian newspaper *Pilot* had urged such a policy:

> Charity, they say, begins at home. The Government should act swiftly now, to protect young industries and ensure their survival. It is clear that soap, textile, or cement, for example, manufactured in Nigeria cannot compete on equal footing with similar products by experienced foreign manufacturers. In a situation like this, what should the Government do? It should legislate to protect our industries. Where a local manufacturer can serve the need, tariff on a similar foreign manufacture should be sufficiently high as to ensure that the local industry is not threatened with extinction.[173]

In the 1960s, there was even more pressure on foreign capital. The 1962 National Development Plan put an emphasis on developing national capital to "Nigerianize" the economy. The 1968 Companies Decree put additional pressure on foreign firms, and by the early 1970s, nationalizations were on the table. In 1972, the Indigenization Decree (formally known as the Nigerian Enterprises Promotion Decree) restricted the presence of foreign firms and capital and required such foreign firms to have Nigerian partners.[174]

Despite the high hopes that had been articulated during the 1950s and 1960s, and that had brought Nigerian capital owners into the anticolonial camp, however, the success of such policies was limited: Notwithstanding independence, and notwithstanding the emergence of new trading opportunities outside the ambit of the British Empire, the share of national capital in Nigerian industries hovered around the minuscule 10 percent mark during the 1960s, with two-thirds of capital still foreign and the rest provided by the state. In almost all sectors, the share of paid-in capital deriving from the state was higher than that from private Nigerian capitalists, with almost 28 percent of the textile, leather, and apparel industries, as well as 53 percent of the mining sector (excluding oil and coal), in state hands.[175]

Foreign capital remained dominant in Nigeria's private sector. Its power limited domestic industrialization, and when political pressures led to more industrial investments, foreign firms came to dominate that sector as well. One problem was that commercial banking remained under foreign control, hampering the ability of Nigerian entrepreneurs to access loans. Nigerian capitalists continued to press against this neocolonial order, becoming more organized (for example, in the Small Businessmen's Committee of the Lagos Chamber of Commerce, which later became the Indigenous Businessmen's Group), but to little avail. University of Ibadan political economist Ola Oni found government policy totally wanting, calling for a "frontal attack" and "indigenization by drastic measures." He advised replacing a "neocolonial development policy" with a "drastic development policy." This included, first and foremost, "strengthening the state."[176] Yet by the late 1970s, some observers considered the indigenization policies of Nigeria a failure, not least because they benefited only a small elite.[177]

EVEN MORE THAN in Nigeria, in the former French colony of Senegal, local capital remained weak, foreign influence great, and the state fragile. There, the capitalist revolution floundered on the shoals of a social stalemate between power holders in the countryside (the marabouts, who made up a kind of rural aristocracy), a powerful ongoing French presence, and the subordinate role of local capital owners vis-à-vis their French counterparts. The postcolonial state engineered such a settlement because it drew privileges from foreign capital for its own elites. As a result, Senegal developed into what came to be called a "neocolonial economy."[178]

This outcome was not for lack of trying. Import-substitution industrialization was a crucial element of economic policy after independence. And it succeeded: Supported by government subsidies and policies that isolated the local market from international competition, a textile industry emerged in the 1950s and flourished in the 1960s. Dakar, the country's capital, became a hub of industry. By 1975, a full 46 percent of textiles bought in Senegal were manufactured domestically. The share of manufacturing as a percentage of Senegal's GDP almost doubled to 18 percent during the 1960s. That was a stunning accomplishment. Yet in sharp contrast to India, Egypt, or even Nigeria, this industrialization did not result in the emergence of a class of Senegalese industrialists. Instead, factories were usually owned by French textile multinationals. Not only was Senegal's industrialization entirely dependent on foreign capital, but the degree to which profits were repatriated made the nation a net exporter of capital. Highly profitable for only its French owners and a small elite of Senegalese associated with them, the seemingly strong industry was weak in developmental terms.[179]

Indeed, in Senegal's postindependence economy, as in other postcolonial countries, merchant capital—not industry—remained key. Building on a long tradition of mercantile dominance—capital owners exporting peanuts and importing consumption items—postindependence development remained largely within its earlier confines.[180] And the state inserted itself into that mix in ways that hardened such a trajectory.

Most basically, and unlike in India, the local elites came to build their power on the control of the state, not the ownership of capital, their fundamental interests thus focused on retaining access to state resources. When consolidating power conflicted with economic development, these new elites focused on shoring up their political position. They cooperated with the marabouts, who were deeply vested in retaining a social structure in the countryside that had been built during the late colonial era to facilitate the extraction of resources from peasant producers. In turn, with the marabouts at the helm, the regime gained access to rural resources by monopolizing the export trade in peanuts, which amounted to a staggering 70 percent of all Senegalese exports.

Revenues from that trade then funded the state, allowing it to employ thirty-five thousand people by 1965—another power source for political elites. Peanut production did increase, and peanut agriculture was extended to new areas, but in the face of worsening trade terms and government demands to keep up revenue, producers felt enormous pressures descend upon them. At the same time, possibilities for private accumulation rested on closeness to these state elites and the access and privileges they could bestow. For sure, there were substantial Senegalese capital owners—about 250 in 1968—but their activities, like those of their colonial forebears, were limited to commerce and to jealously guarding their position.[181]

A s Senegal exemplified, independence and the construction of a national state did not suffice to launch national economic development and to overcome the effects of decades, even centuries, of colonial rule. Most basically, decolonization itself at times undermined development as Europeans withdrew their assets. As often as not, they transferred them to offshore tax havens.[182]

Many newly emerging countries, moreover, lacked the expertise, infrastructure, and state capacity to embark upon a decisive departure from the extreme poverty and powerlessness that they had inherited. There was not much of a national bourgeoisie independent of positions within these newly forged states, and there was little ability to shift the economic integration of a nation away from the supply of raw materials to the industrial heartland. Trade terms worsened. And foreign capital still reigned supreme. Local elites at times benefited, thanks to their attachment to the new state and foreign capital, but their precarious position favored their own ability to accumulate riches over the enrichment of the countries they governed.

An extreme example of the utter inability to use independence as a platform for accelerated economic development is Burkina Faso, formerly Upper Volta. This landlocked onetime French colony, within borders set somewhat arbitrarily by its colonizers, gained its formal independence in 1960, a year in which small-scale subsistence-oriented agriculture along with household manufacturing remained its principal economic activity, employing more than 90 percent of its people. Even wage labor was almost unknown—in 1960, perhaps as few as twenty-five thousand Burkinabe, out of a population of almost five million, received wages. Burkina Faso's economic links to the outside world were marginal, its economy by and large not monetized. Raw cotton emerged as its most significant export, yet infrastructure, education, capital formation, and industrial undertakings were almost entirely absent. Industrially manufactured goods were almost all imported.[183]

As elsewhere, the postcolonial state aimed to change this situation. The economy was to grow through planned development: The first plans were drawn up and carried out in 1962 and 1963, without much success. Burkina Faso's rulers elaborated and implemented further five-year plans from 1967 to 1982.[184] There was also some direct investment by the state: In the 1980s, the Burkinabe state owned approximately thirty companies. There was some economic growth: GDP increased between 3 and 3.5 percent annually in the decade after independence. But a rapidly growing population meant that, per capita, the people of Burkina Faso were left almost as poor as before. In 1985, the country counted just seventy registered industrial enterprises, of which fifteen were defunct. Capitalists were rare: Oumarou Kanazoé had started out in business by opening a restaurant in his hometown of Yako in 1950; he had gone on to create one of the most influential construction enterprises in the 1970s and 1980s, building roads and dams, among other things, linking, in telling fashion, private initiative and access to state funds.[185] But even Kanazoé's rise could not distract from the fact that Burkina Faso remained made up of mostly illiterate subsistence farmers in a country bereft of sufficient infrastructures, medical care, and education.

Even twenty years after independence, in 1980, the capacity of the state was almost nonexistent, with one observer stating flatly that "most citizens had only the most sporadic contact with any state agent, even a tax collector."[186] The state's policy space was also severely circumscribed by its continued dependence on foreign aid, and by the fact that its currency remained linked to the French franc; monetary policy was made in Paris, not in Ouagadougou. The trivial resources that the state could provide, often accessed through international aid, largely ended up in the pockets of the rulers of the day, and the only group of people who accumulated significant resources were elites linked to the state.[187]

———

For all the disappointments, shortcomings, and failures that would surface (especially after 1970), decolonization ignited significant economic growth of 2 or 3 percent per year throughout much of Asia and Africa after many decades, or even centuries, of no growth at all.[188] Most notably, industry expanded, including, as we have seen, in Senegal, Nigeria, Egypt, and India. While it often did not translate into sustained per capita improvements, given a simultaneous and very rapid population explosion after midcentury, it did undermine the stark hierarchies that had emerged in the nineteenth century between geographically small industrial heartlands and a vast hinterland that churned out raw materials and agricultural commodities with the support of new state capacities. It was these shifts that made decolonization so tectonic to global capitalism.

And in some parts of the world, the end of colonialism produced truly spectacular economic growth. Taiwan and Korea were outliers, to be sure, favored by very particular political and economic circumstances, but they were pioneers in creating new nodes of capital built upon new nodes of state power that would in meaningful ways anticipate the shifting geographies of capitalism in the twenty-first century. By the end of World War II, both Korea and Taiwan had been dirt poor, ravaged by Japanese colonialism and the effects of the war. Taiwan's per capita GDP had fallen by 41 percent between 1937 and 1945; Korea's by 58 percent.[189] The 1940s and 1950s were just as difficult for both of them. Korea was torn apart by a vicious civil war and massive foreign interventions, while Taiwan faced its much larger communist neighbor.

Their difficult political position, however, had its advantages too. As frontline states in the newly emerging Cold War between the Soviet Union (and, after 1949, China) and the United States (and their respective allies), both Korea and Taiwan received generous support from the United States, so much so that it has been estimated that Taiwan's 1964 GDP would have been 40 percent lower without the $1.5 billion in US aid that reached the island from 1950 to 1965. In South Korea, many earlier sugar-producing companies transformed into industrial behemoths after the 1960s. Granted exclusive access to American raw sugar by the South Korean government, these companies reaped a windfall during a time when demand for sugar in the country

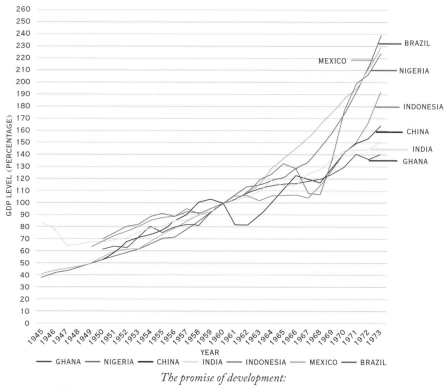

The promise of development:
GDP growth in seven countries of the Global South, 1945–1973 (1960=100).

was rapidly rising. From these sugar processors and dealers, many of the modern chaebols—industrial conglomerates often associated with specific families—emerged. One of the notable examples was Samsung, whose founder, Lee Byung-chul, built South Korea's first sugar refinery in 1953.[190]

At the same time, these authoritarian regimes understood that their material and political survival rested on economic development. Accordingly, both embarked upon state-led development projects that focused not just on import-substitution but also and especially on export-oriented industrialization. Bolstered by politically enabled access to the vast US market, they helped local capital owners build industries that catered to foreign markets, first and especially textiles, then, by the 1970s, electronics.[191] They also invested heavily in primary and secondary education.

As a result, both Korea and Taiwan experienced a most extraordinary boom during the 1960s and beyond. They did so by creating conditions, including direct investment subsidies, that increased returns on private capital in certain sectors of the economy and thus encouraged further investment. In 1960, Taiwan launched the Nineteen-Point Reform Program, which included massive tax cuts for businesses, especially exporters. South Korea was even more heavy-handed: When President Park took power in a military coup in 1961, he defined priorities for economic development. Arresting many of the country's most prominent entrepreneurs and charging them with "illicit wealth accumulation," he forced them to engage in certain investments prioritized by the state as a condition of their release. But Korea combined the stick with the carrot: After nationalization of the country's banks in 1961, the newly government-controlled financial institutions provided below-market-rate loans to expanding government-prioritized businesses in industries such as steel, electronics, and shipbuilding; indeed, they provided credit at negative interest. Because they especially favored the large conglomerates, the chaebols, economic activity rapidly concentrated: In 1966, 58 percent of value added to the Korean economy came from companies employing more than two hundred workers; just 5 years later, that share had increased to 72 percent. The government also directly assumed the risk of investments in sectors that it deemed important.[192]

Both countries also reformed their agrarian sectors, which created more dynamic domestic markets and allowed labor to move into industry. They also made sure that wage growth remained subdued by repressing workers' collective action and forgoing government regulation of wages. As a result, they increased capital profitability and world market competitiveness. Taiwan's savings-to-income ratio was a staggering 30 percent in the early 1970s.[193]

The economic results of these repressive development policies were impressive: Per capita economic output in Taiwan increased more than 3.6 times between 1950 and 1975; in South Korea, it increased 4.1 times. Though both countries had been bastions of extreme poverty, they respectively ranked as the thirty-ninth- and thirty-third-richest countries by 1975—and became, by the twenty-first century, two of the wealthiest places on the planet.[194]

———

Decolonization as a whole, in all its varieties, represented a major caesura in the world history of capitalism. Yet looked at from a slightly different perspective, it also connected to some aspects of the colonial project itself, even widening, deepening, and radicalizing them. After all, planning—and state-centric development projects more broadly—had deep roots within colonialism itself.[195]

Most importantly, postcolonial societies, without exception, continued to push core features of the colonial project. When it came to transforming the countryside, for example, postcolonial governments matched or even outdid their colonial forerunners. In Taiwan, the sugarcane transformation of the countryside continued after independence. The large-scale sugar holdings created during the Japanese colonial

period remained under state control post-liberation, despite land reforms. A new state-run Taiwan Sugar Corporation was created that
retained the lands taken by the Japanese for the purpose of sugar production. As a result, in 1952, more than two-thirds of Taiwan's agricultural export income still derived from sugar. Indeed, sugar
production became the core of the state-led capital accumulation project that would eventually power Taiwan's industrialization in the 1960s
and beyond. In similar ways, the Indian Merchants' Chamber in Bombay was just as concerned with cotton quality as its former imperial
overlords had been, and it advocated for a further transformation of the
cotton-growing countryside. Tata pushed for new crop varieties, such
as Egyptian cotton, in ways not fundamentally different from the
Manchester Cotton Supply Association a century earlier. The company also used colonial-era land laws to gain control over property on
which it located its steelworks in Jamshedpur. The FICCI pressed for
the better "exploitation of the mineral wealth."[196] And the Senegalese
state pushed for the intensification and extension of cotton agriculture
and the development of new crop varieties.[197] Indeed, the postcolonial
state produced what geographer Salma Abouelhossein has called "anticolonial hinterlands," feeding into national development projects.[198]

Furthermore, if a defining element of the capitalist revolution was
the commodification of labor power, the postcolonial governments and
capital owners advanced that agenda radically. Indeed, they propelled
the transition of massive numbers of African, Latin American, and
Asian rural cultivators into wage work. Until the 1950s, most people in
the Global South still worked in agriculture with very few ties to the
world market. Only during the 1960s did this begin to change in significant ways. In Egypt, the Misr Spinning and Weaving Company at
al-Mahalla al-Kubra and other such undertakings led to significant
proletarianization. In less than a decade, from 1952 to 1960, the number of Egyptian wage earners in industrial enterprises with more than
10 workers grew by 23.5 percent. In India during that same decade, the
number of workers in industry doubled, from around 9 million to 18
million. In Brazil, from 1960 to 1970, workers in manufacturing in-

Postcolonial transformations of agriculture: a cotton field near Tambacounda, Senegal, 1968.

creased by 61.6 percent. In Indonesia, from 1961 to 1971, the number of industrial workers increased by 44.5 percent, from 1.86 million to 2.68 million. In this context of rapid industrialization, cities in the Global South began to see meteoric population increases as well: Greater Bombay had 2.84 million inhabitants in 1951 and 6 million twenty years later. Jakarta had a population of roughly 3 million in 1961 and 4.5 million a decade later, while São Paulo had a population of 2.2 million in 1960 and 6 million in 1970. As late as 1900, only 16 percent of the global population lived in what could remotely be considered cities, but as urbanization took off after World War II, that all changed, and by 2020, roughly 55 percent of humanity lived in cities. And while many new arrivals entered wage work, the majority pushed into the informal economy, giving the latest chapter of the capitalist revolution a distinct flavor. Across Latin America and the Caribbean, 53 percent of adults worked in the informal sector by 2016.[199]

If decolonization was a moment of nation-building, it was also a moment when a panoply of new ideas about economic life in general and capitalism in particular came to the fore, forms of economic theorizing greatly influential among policymakers, intellectuals, and social movements in the developing world—though not in Western economics departments.

Perhaps most influential was the argument by scholars ranging from Walter Rodney to Samir Amin and Raúl Prebisch that capitalism was a deeply hierarchical, historical, and global economic order. Emphasizing the long-term impact of colonialism and slavery, these thinkers saw the wealth of one part of the world as related to the poverty of another. They also claimed that the very structure of the global economy made development difficult, if not impossible. Their emphasis on political economy went back to a time before the marginalist reorientation of economics; their centering of global perspectives and noneconomic hierarchies went beyond many approaches inspired by Smith, Marx, and Keynes.

Colonialism, this diverse group of African, Asian, and Latin American thinkers argued, had systematically skewed the possibility of development by moving resources out of the colony and by undermining institutional capacity in the Global South. They understood these relations of power as a crucial component of global capitalism. Prominently, Guyanese historian Walter Rodney not only wrote an important book on the making of the Guyanese working class under conditions of colonialism and enslavement but also launched a withering critique in *How Europe Underdeveloped Africa*.[200] Slavery played an important role in many of these accounts, both for its material effects in the past and for its racist legacies that continued to hinder development in the present.[201] More generally, the Egyptian economist Samir Amin argued that "unequal development" persisted under the conditions of postcolonialism.[202] In his 1970 *Accumulation on a World Scale*, among other works, he observed that "the center of gravity of the exploitation of labor by capital . . . has been displaced from the center of the system to its periphery."[203] According to Amin, peripheral spaces were crucial to capitalism's dynamic, and while their specific integration changed over time, they always remained in a subordinate position, with "the local ruling classes in capitalism's peripheral lands" having only "subaltern status," making them what he called a "comprador class."[204] The only way out of this condition—what Amin called "emergence"—was to limit connections to the global economy. Without such decoupling, only a neocolonial developmental trajectory was possible.

Inspired by such a reading of the history of capitalism and in response to the declining trade terms that newly decolonized countries encountered, new ideas moved to the fore. Economists provided the theoretical scaffolding for emerging strategies (often with recourse to the Hamiltonian United States, the Listian German states, and Meiji Japan), arguing that the international division of labor injured those nations that focused on the export of agrarian products. The resulting unequal exchange made necessary policies that would encourage domestic development. For influential Saint Lucian and later Nobel Prize–winning economist W. Arthur Lewis, development necessitated not only decolonization but also fighting off the many-headed hydra of racism.[205] Attributing much of the Caribbean's poverty—which he regarded as a "legacy of West Indian slavery"—to the low profitability of sugar and banana exports, the only long-term solution for the region was a radical redistribution of wealth.[206]

Argentinean economist Raúl Prebisch, who led the United Nations Economic Commission for Latin America and the Caribbean (known by its Spanish acronym, CEPAL, and headquartered in Santiago, Chile), similarly declared that the unequal integration of countries in the global economy necessitated the embrace of state-driven development strategies. In 1963, he coined the term "New International Economic Order," pushing against the existing arrangements that, according to him, systematically disadvantaged what he called "the periphery."[207] He claimed that peripheral countries—such as his native Argentina—benefited from the global division of labor less than those at the forefront of technical development for the simple reason that manufactured goods were more price-elastic than primary products. Consequentially, to redistribute the benefits of global trade toward the periphery, less developed countries had to focus all their energies on industrialization.[208] Eventually, he reasoned that to allow for such development in the Global South, an entire New International Economic Order (NIEO) had to be institutionalized on a global level.

Mexican intellectuals, economists, and politicians agreed: They envisioned a mixed economy, both domestically and globally. Their impetus came from a particular reading of property rights in Mexico itself—namely, that the state's interest trumped individual property rights.[209] In 1940, according to Mexican economist Ramón Beteta,

> Mexico questioned the sacredness of a profit-making system based on an absolute right of private property, in her Agrarian Reform and in her Labor Laws—to mention but two of her fundamental reforms—she could not accept without reserve the so-called "principles of international law" which often were but means to protect that very system and absolute right which foreigners might not have at home, but which they expected to enjoy in the small countries where they had made their investments, as much as in the colonies belonging to their powerful fatherlands.[210]

Economic ideas, as they had throughout capitalism's history, fed directly into the anticolonial revolutions and saw them, in turn, as possible avenues for a radical reconstruction of the global economy. They also intersected with the ideas of the first generation of postcolonial statesmen, such as Ghana's first president, Kwame Nkrumah, who spoke of the "unequal integration" produced by global capitalism and the predations of those he called "neocolonialist masters."[211] Nehru, who believed that capitalism's tendency was to create an ever widening gap between rich and poor, envisioned a world economy in which that gap narrowed. Jamaican politician Michael Manley wanted a "fair share" of the wealth that his island had produced.[212] At an international conference in Bandung in 1955, this worldview found yet another voice.[213] The conference began on the morning of April 18 with an opening address by President Sukarno of Indonesia: "Let a New Asia and a New Africa Be Born."[214] "Our nations and countries are colonies no more," Sukarno thundered, but "[c]olonialism is not dead, so long as vast areas of Asia and Africa are unfree."[215] The Bandung Conference led to the Afro-Asian Peoples' Solidarity Conference in

1957 and in 1961 to the Belgrade Conference, which was the first of many Non-Aligned Movement (NAM) meetings, organized under the leadership of representatives from Yugoslavia, Egypt, India, Ghana, and Indonesia.[216] After colonialism, a different global economic order seemed possible, one not straightjacketed by the simple binary division of the Cold War. As Mexican president Luis Echeverría declared: "Our people are aware that their misery produces wealth for others."[217]

All these thinkers and politicians believed that creating capable states in the formerly colonized world was crucial to unleashing the possibilities of development. Yet their theorizing about global capitalism, though deeply nationalist, always embraced a fundamentally global perspective as well. Their focus on forging powerful national states intersected with cosmopolitan ways of envisioning the future, or what political scientist Adom Getachew has called "worldmaking."[218] Such claims to worldmaking partly originated from the very internationalism of anticolonialism itself. Already in 1920, many intellectuals from various colonies had assembled in Paris and other places and developed ever more sophisticated critiques of colonialism. Among them were Ho Chi Minh, Léopold Sédar Senghor, Zhou Enlai, and Messali Hadj, all of whom became important spokespeople and political advocates for independence and economic liberation. In 1921, Ho Chi Minh founded the Intercolonial Union, which drew together activists from throughout the colonized world. Out of this organization emerged the League for the Defense of the Negro Race, the Algerian nationalist movement Étoile Nord-Africaine, and Nguyễn Thế Truyền's Vietnamese Independence Party.[219] Such solidarities also emerged in London, which became an important node of Pan-Africanism, Pan-Arabism, Pan-Caribbeanism, and Afro-Asian solidarities. Their way of thinking about the global economy was yet another countermovement within global capitalism, and it was recognized as such by an emergent cohort of neoliberal intellectuals who would perceive the politics of anticolonialism as a threat to global capitalism.[220]

Postcolonial economic development, however halting and disappointing to its protagonists, would come to challenge the global capitalist centers that had been forged by an earlier war capitalism, then spectacularly reshaped by a reconstructed industrial capitalism. Industrialization in the Global South would lay the groundwork for a radical recentering of the global economy.

And then, of course, there was the most radical edge of postcolonial worldmaking: the effort to entirely opt out of the capitalist world order and to find a different way of organizing economic life. In the aftermath of World War II, new islands of postcapitalism emerged, usually with decisive support from the Soviet Union. Prominently among them were North Vietnam in 1945, China in 1949, Cuba after 1959, and Mozambique in 1975. In these years there also emerged the People's Democratic Republic of Algeria, the United Republic of Tanzania, the People's Republic of Angola, the People's Republic of Benin, the People's Republic of Congo, the People's Republic of Kampuchea (in 1979), the Lao People's Democratic Republic, and the Democratic People's Republic of Korea. By 1975, 1.4 billion people lived in countries that had embraced postcapitalist forms of organizing economic life—more than one-third of the global population.[221]

No country was more prominent and, in the long term, more influential than China. China turned communist in 1949 and embarked upon a strongly state-centric model of development, largely following the Soviet example. It nationalized most companies and engaged in centralized planning. The roots of its vast planning and management apparatus extended from its "industrial bureaucracy," set up by Mao during the Second Sino-Japanese War (1937–1945) and then expanded during the second phase of the Chinese Civil War (1945–1949).[222] After the revolution, these bureaucrats and technical experts moved into China's ministries and industries to coordinate, plan, and manage the country's economy.[223]

As planning became omnipresent, output and productivity increased significantly, a remarkable feat considering that China could not build upon a century of industrial capitalism and had to create the infrastructures for industrialization almost from scratch. Levels of consumption by Chinese workers grew. During the First Five-Year Plan, from 1953 to 1957, national income in constant prices rose by 8.9 percent annually, with industrial production expanding by a remarkable 18.7 percent a year. Growth was especially focused on the steel, machinery, and chemical industries. The Second Five-Year Plan doubled down on some of these goals, but employing different policies, envisioning a "great leap forward," but growth rates fell back to just 3.2 percent annually, and the effort to radically recast agriculture and to produce industrial products at the village level resulted in terrible food shortages and the twentieth century's most terrifying famine.[224] Yet the very radicalism of the Chinese socialist revolution would, a few years later, lay the groundwork for the world's most intense industrialization ever—not least because China was also able to draw on a network of "national capitalists" who had spent the Mao years subdued but in relative privilege in cities such as Shanghai as well as Chinese capital owners who had remained outside the influence of the People's Republic—in Hong Kong, Macau, and Taiwan.[225] Together, this entrepreneurial energy and capital, along with the restructuring of China's economy and society under the People's Republic, would eventually unleash the fastest economic growth the world had ever seen.

For all the upheaval and conflict that the spread of socialism in the Global South produced, it was the longer process of decolonization that would most fundamentally reshape global capitalism. An unstable coalition of peasants, industrial workers, and capital owners (many at the helm of family-centric business groups) had created new nodes of capital and state power. In doing so, they had altered the Eurocentric industrial capitalism that had been forged out of the rebellions of the mid-nineteenth century. They had laid the groundwork for a radical acceleration of the capitalist revolution. Less visibly, but just as importantly, they had also begun to subtly undermine central tenets of the golden age of European and North American capitalism.

In the 1950s and 1960s, this future could not be known. People's aspirations for national independence brought about great hope and great anxiety. Almost unnoticed at the time yet of deep future consequence, these aspirations also brought to the fore a group of European and North American intellectuals who formulated critiques of the postcolonial order very different from the analysis presented in this chapter. Fearful that decolonization was empowering large numbers of propertyless people in now self-governing nations, they strongly believed that an international order had to be constructed to constrain the policy options of newly independent nations, thereby protecting capital and its global mobility. Neoliberals believed that the rights of capital trumped national sovereignty. Frightened by democratic decision-making and more concerned about decolonization than even the Cold War, they wanted to see the creation of mechanisms that bound states to certain rules when it came to capital, rules that were outside the purview of national, and potentially democratic, policy-making.[226] At the height of the anticolonial fervor of the 1950s and 1960s, their ideas and politics were marginal. But by the 1970s, they would play a central role in once again recasting global capitalism by constructing what eventually came to be known as the "neoliberal order."

16.

Taming Industrial Capitalism, 1945–1973

*Stabilizing industrial capitalism,
one washing machine at a time:
Nixon and Khrushchev's famous "kitchen debate."*

I n the late 1970s, French economist Jean Fourastié sat down to chronicle the drastic changes he had witnessed in France since World War II. This was an extraordinary period, he observed, a break with centuries of French history, a moment when living standards skyrocketed, inequality declined, productivity soared, and the texture of French life changed beyond recognition. So drastic was this "invisible revolution" that it deserved to be known, according to Fourastié, as a distinct moment in French history—*les trente glorieuses*.[1]

In texture and feeling, the capitalism of the "thirty glorious years" stood out across the industrial heartlands, particularly in retrospect. In Germany, they came to be known as the *Wirtschaftswunderjahre*—the "years of economic miracle"; in the United States, the "golden years"; in

Japan, the *kōdo keizai seichō*—the "high-speed growth era"; and in Sweden, the *rekordåren*—the "record years." Already in 1959, Richard Nixon, then US vice president, was advertising this new age, albeit in an unlikely location: standing in front of what his delegation described as a typical American kitchen re-created in a Moscow exhibition space at Sokolniki Park. Nixon explained to the slightly irritated Soviet leadership, including Premier Nikita Khrushchev, that this was what life was like in the United States: labor-saving gizmos galore—dishwashers, washing machines, toasters, and an electric range, designed and manufactured by a who's who of US industry (General Electric, RCA Whirlpool, and General Mills).[2] Emphasizing domestic comforts as the mainspring of capitalism, Nixon celebrated American consumerism—the novel marriage between mass production and mass consumption. "In America, we like to make life easier for women," he bragged, indirectly celebrating women's role as homemakers. Khrushchev retorted that "[y]our capitalistic attitude toward women does not occur under Communism."[3] Nixon's explanation of capitalism leaned heavily on market freedom, as he highlighted "[d]iversity, the right to choose, the fact that we have one thousand builders building one thousand different houses." Again, Khrushchev was unimpressed: "Don't you have a machine that puts food in the mouth and pushes it down? Many things you've shown us are interesting, but they are not needed in life. They have no useful purpose. They are merely gadgets."[4] When *Izvestiia*, a leading Soviet newspaper, reported on this battle of ideological tropes, it was equally unimpressed by American displays: "What is this, a national exhibit of a great country, or a branch department store?"[5]

Scholars usually read the so-called kitchen debate as putting considerable pressure on Soviet leaders to deliver consumer goods to their citizens, which it did. Less noted is the telling fact that the leader of the capitalist world focused his account of American economic power on its ability to deliver consumer goods to ordinary people. Technical change and continued access to cheap raw materials from the Global South had made it possible; powerful labor movements, the needs of mass-production industries for markets, and an expanding communist

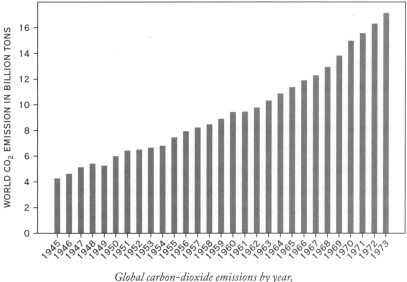

Global carbon-dioxide emissions by year,
1945–1973.

world had made it imperative. After the devastations of the Great Depression, capitalism was relegitimized—and consumer choice was at the core of this globe-spanning project. It succeeded spectacularly, not least because living standards in capitalism's European, North American, and Japanese industrial heartlands rose dramatically during these thirty glorious years. And never had carbon-dioxide emissions exploded so drastically either.

The thirty years after the war were an exceptional age in capitalism's long history. They not only carved new vistas for the former colonies; they reordered capitalist civilization in what Pakistani engineer and politician Muhammad Hashim Gazdar called the "overdeveloped" world.[6] These years witnessed rapid economic growth and diminished inequality with state-centric development and liberal democracy. In 1993, when historian Giuliano Muzzioli published *Modena,* his account of an Italian city, he found that "transformation accelerated at the speed of lightning. People now came to enjoy a standard of living previously confined to a tiny elite." He called the postwar decades a "great leap forward."[7]

For the United States, the golden age was in some ways a continuation of the 1920s—though even then, the promises of a Fordist mass-productive and mass-consumptive society were now much broader. In Europe, by contrast, it was only in the 1960s that what came to be known as the "affluent society" became widespread. As the world's industrial heartlands generalized the lessons of the Fordist revolution and combined them with a sharply more powerful interventionist state and a secure flow of cheap commodities from the decolonizing world, their economic potential soared. And it had staying power. The postwar boom created what historian Charles S. Maier called a "particular equilibrium among states, capital, and the realm of governance."[8] Former luxuries became common. Unemployment ceased to be a widespread concern. Life expectancy rose significantly. Formerly agricultural countries like Spain and Finland industrialized.[9] Even a British socialist conceded in 1957 that "[c]apitalism has been reformed out of all recognition."[10]

In India, Ghana, or Jamaica—indeed, in most of the world—the golden years seemed impossibly remote. But in those areas of the world where they took root, the good times seemed destined to last forever. Capitalism appeared to have escaped the boom-and-bust cycles that had caused so much hardship. Gone, too (for the most part), were the "satanic mills," child labor, and dire poverty of early industrial capitalism; instead, a widespread (though not universal) middle-class-inflected life floated on a truly unbelievable assembly of consumer goods. Keynesian economic ideas had triumphed: "We stand at the gates of an age of plenty, key in hand," argued political scientist and policy adviser Charles Edward Merriam during the war, expressing US policymakers' unbounded optimism for the bright future that lay just beyond those gates.[11] The "golden age," many people believed at the time, was the natural, even necessary, culmination of capitalism's history. In the 1950s, US economist Simon Kuznets developed a theory of economic development he called the "bell curve." It demonstrated the alleged correlation between income inequality and eco-

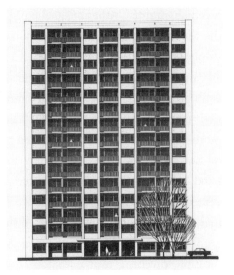

A bright future in the industrial heartland: the architecture of the trente glorieuses as envisioned by architect Guillaume Gillet.

nomic growth, explaining a historical shift in Western economies from an early industrialized stage characterized by a high level of disparity to one in which these inequalities were much reduced, thanks to the many opportunities created by economic growth, stimulated by demographic expansion and new technologies.[12] His theory foretold the dawn of a "golden age" and naturalized the progression of capitalism's history toward greater equality—an inspiring argument that, alas, turned out to be overly optimistic.[13]

While this narrative rang true for a few decades after the war in those islands of prosperity that had arisen out of the capitalist revolution, surprises lay ahead. When many pillars of golden-age capitalism collapsed after 1973, their historical specificity was exposed. For one, the Great Depression and the war had challenged liberal capitalism as never before—and the golden age was the response to that challenge. A vibrant labor movement was also crucial to postwar stability, as was the seemingly endless flow of cheap inputs from the Global South. And with about a third of humanity living by choice or force outside the bounds of capitalism, there was constant pressure on capitalist societies to legitimize themselves—to win kitchen debates.

━━━

By the 1970s, workers in the heartlands of industrial capitalism lived in ways that would have been unimaginable only one or two generations earlier. Take, for example, a working-class family in the

Swedish city of Gothenburg. An old trading port and former home of the Swedish East India Company, and an emerging industrial hub of shipbuilding and heavy industry, Gothenburg was the second-largest city in a country that, in many ways, most clearly symbolized capitalism's golden age. This imaginary family, if typical, consisted of a married couple with two children. As the children were young, the mother—let's call her Ulla—worked part-time at a local hospital, relying on her mother and mother-in-law for help with childcare. Ulla's husband, whom we'll call Stig, worked on an assembly line at Torslandaverken, one of thirteen thousand workers producing supplies for the car manufacturer Volvo, headquartered in Gothenburg.[14]

The family likely lived in a rented terraced house or a multiple-dwelling unit with four rooms, the children sharing a bedroom. The housing might have been built with government subsidies (in the shape of loans), or the family might have received a rental allowance from the government. They had access to decent housing, food, and clothing. They consumed things that would have been undreamed of by previous generations of workers, with access to household appliances of the sort that Nixon had touted in Moscow, including a radio, a television, and even a car. They could live this way partly because wages had risen. Though they were markedly better off than most Swedes had ever been, theirs was still a modest prosperity. When Hans Rosling, who became one of Sweden's leading public health experts, looked back on his working-class childhood, he recalled that his parents carefully repaired things that broke, including clothing in need of mending, and that his family drew on food they grew in their garden to supplement their grocery purchases.[15] Ulla and Stig would have done the same.

Long-established patriarchal relations structured the family's division of labor—another cornerstone of the golden age. Men's wages were significantly higher than women's: In 1960, 84 percent of Swedish industrial workers were men and the few women who labored in industrial employment earned only around 70 percent of what their male counterparts made.[16] Plus, Stig had access to extra shifts beyond the legally required minimum. Ulla probably would have sympathized with a woman who remembered that during these years, she "was completely alone with the kids all the time."[17] Day-care centers had emerged, yet according to a government report, "[m]any mothers harbor . . . feelings of guilt" over leaving their children there—and, in any case, there were not enough of these childcare centers.[18]

Like almost all working-class Swedes, Ulla and Stig had attended school only until age twelve or thirteen. But they could take advantage of adult education programs instituted in the 1960s. Stig's strenuous work took a heavy toll on his body, because of both its intense pace and the heavy lifting it required. Moreover, factories were dangerous, and workers risked serious accidents. Stig's total hours, however, had diminished: In 1960, the workweek was reduced to forty-five hours, and in 1970, to forty. Health care had also drastically improved: Stig and Ulla's family enjoyed access to universal health insurance through the Riksförsäkringsverket, the government agency tasked with administering social insurance, which was funded by a combination of governmental payments and employer contributions.[19]

Ulla and Stig's children went to public school for at least nine years, thanks to the Education Act of 1962. If they qualified (which was becoming more common for working-class kids in the 1960s), they could attend publicly financed universities and receive a government stipend to cover their living expenses. Since 1964, the Swedish Board of Student Finance had provided a combination of student grants and student loans. Rosling, who we have encountered before, assumed his right to a state-paid medical education to be so secure that he took a six-month break from his studies to travel in Asia. His parents' bewilderment illustrated how rapidly the expanding welfare state had changed the sense of possibility. As Rosling recalled in his memoir, his parents believed that the possibility of higher education "was just a dream" and spoke about their sense that their son had "educated [himself] away from us."[20] Ulla and Stig, for their part, could look forward to state-secured pensions based on the number of years they had worked and the amount of their incomes. Because Ulla worked fewer hours at lower pay than her husband, her pension would be much lower. And if Stig lost his job, he could draw on unemployment insurance, which would provide him with about 80 percent of his prior income for ten months.[21]

With a shorter workweek and ever more vacations, leisure time had also expanded, as had the spaces in which it unfolded. Ulla and Stig could take their modest car, a Volvo (of course), on weekend outings—for example, to the small beach town of Varberg, forty-seven miles south of Gothenburg. In the summers, they would go on two- or even three-week vacations, either in Sweden or perhaps to neighboring Denmark or Norway.

The world had radically improved for Swedish working-class families—and so rapidly that the old ways lingered within Ulla and Stig's living memories. It was thus not surprising that they, like most workers, were union members, and that they, like almost all members of the working class, cast their votes year after year for the Social Democratic Party, the Sveriges Socialdemokratiska Arbetareparti (SAP).

Ulla and Stig are statistical fictions, exemplars of the particularly pronounced gains made by Sweden's common people during the golden age. In part, this was the result of the Swedish government successfully combining a Keynesian full-employment strategy with an expansion of the welfare state. Such largesse, however, would have been impossible without the era's unprecedented rate of economic growth: From 1945 to 1974, the Swedish economy grew by an average of 3.5 percent a year, with annual

"On Saturdays, Dad belongs to me":
Unions struggle to decommodify time
and reduce work hours. German
trade union campaign, 1956.

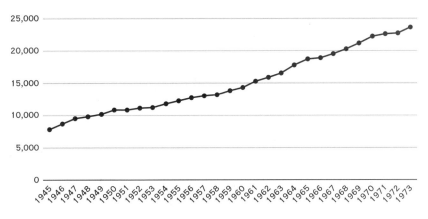

*The Energizer Bunny economy: Sweden's GDP from 1945 to 1973 in
Swedish crowns in constant prices (1910–1912 price level).*

growth rarely falling below 3 percent. As a result, Sweden's per capita
GDP almost tripled. By the mid-1970s, Swedes had become among
the wealthiest people in the world.[22]

The Swedish economy not only grew but also underwent structural transformation: As elsewhere, agricultural pursuits waned (from
about 20 percent to just 7 percent of the entire workforce) between
1951 and 1975. As women entered employment—especially in the
(low-paid) service sector—unpaid housework as a full-time occupation
declined during the same years (from 32.5 percent to 25.2 percent of
the workforce). On the other hand, industrial employment exploded—
indeed, industrial workers represented the highest share of the active
Swedish labor force ever in 1960, at 47.1 percent. There was also a
significant rise in the number of white-collar workers: In 1940, they
represented 18 percent of the active labor force; by 1970, they represented 40 percent, many of them state employees, whose numbers (out
of a population of about 8 million) grew from 353,001 in 1954 to
481,691 in 1970. Manufactured goods replaced raw materials in the
rapidly growing export sector, especially the "machinery and means of
transport" industries, which by the early 1970s made up more than 40
percent of all Swedish exports.[23] These industries responded most to
the rapid productivity advances made by postwar factories. From 1950

to 1975, productivity rose by 5.6 percent annually. Increases in the energy intensity of production followed suit, in heavy industry by more than 6 percent annually per hour worked between 1954 and 1973.[24] Such intense use of fossil fuels and the attendant productivity gains landed, at least partially, in workers' pockets, helping to further stabilize the "record years."

Working-class living standards improved in two ways: First, real wages skyrocketed. In 1945, an industrial worker had an average monthly wage of 364 crowns; in 1960, 1,066 crowns; and in 1970, 2,182 crowns. For twenty-five years, from 1945 to 1970, real wages negotiated between employers and unions increased at a rate of 3.4 percent annually.[25] The second factor was the unprecedented growth of the welfare state. In the post–World War II years, Sweden built a cradle-to-grave welfare state, more developed and universal than anywhere in the industrial heartland, yet broadly representative of wider trends. That welfare state has taken on almost mythic proportions in the collective memories of many Swedes (and others). While the earliest welfare policies focused on the very poorest, after World War II, the policies became more universal. The Swedish state increasingly saw its central role as provisioning its citizens and mitigating the inequalities generated by market outcomes to create what politicians of the time called a "people's home."[26]

This welfare state expansion accelerated immediately after the war. In 1946, the Swedish Riksdag (Parliament) advised local authorities to launch so-called public housing companies that would expand rental housing and improve the quality of that housing. The goal was to provide homes at the highest possible standard to all citizens, especially families with children. Put differently, the housing market was socialized. State subsidies to renters and loans to local governments guaranteed that rental costs amounted to no more than 20 percent of average industrial wages. In the early 1960s, the Swedish government launched the Million Dwellings Program (Miljonprogrammet), constructing over one million new dwellings between 1965 and 1975. All in all, between 1946 and 1985, more than 90 percent of Swedish housing was funded, to some extent, by the state, as access to housing became a government-guaranteed right.[27]

Other social rights quickly emerged. In 1948, all workers gained the right to two weeks of paid holidays. That same year, family supports improved: The child allowance, in place since 1937, was made universal. By 1948, the direct cash payment for each child amounted to 260 Swedish crowns annually, or 6 percent of the average annual household income at that time. In 1955, a universal maternal allowance was established, building on a 1938 law that had supported only poor mothers. (In 1974, fathers were also granted this allowance.) As we saw with Ulla and Stig, beginning in 1962, nine years of schooling became compulsory. In 1953, paid vacation time was extended to three weeks, increasing to four weeks in 1963 and five weeks in 1975. National health insurance followed in 1955. Starting in the 1950s, preschools and schools began providing free meals as well as health care to all children.[28]

Crucially, by 1960, Sweden had also vastly expanded its public pension system. Before the reforms, there was a modest flat-rate universal pension, the *folkpension*. Those with more resources signed on for additional private insurance. In 1959, the Riksdag added the *allmän tillägspension*, or ATP, which were payments based on previous work incomes. These reforms significantly increased economic security for seniors and drew white-collar workers and the middle class more firmly into the welfare state. And more was to come: In 1969, universal rental subsidies for families became law, and in 1970, a medical care compensation reform provided employees with the right to 80 percent of their salaries if they were sick for longer than thirty days. In 1971, the forty-hour workweek was legislated, further decommodifying the lives of Swedish workers. In 1973, the preschool law required Sweden's municipalities to offer children a free spot at a preschool.[29]

Entitlements thus became universal throughout Swedish society. During the 1960s and 1970s, so-called "transfer payments" were the fastest-growing sector of public expenditures—they went from 25 percent (1963) to 50 percent (1980) of total public expenditures. Most of

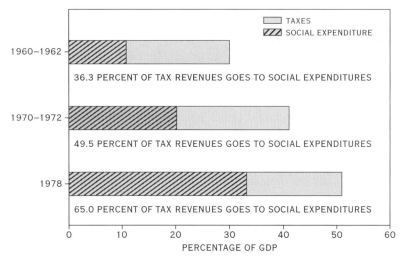

Swedish welfare state at work: social expenditures and total taxes, 1960–1978.

them went into the burgeoning social security system that protected the unemployed, families, and the elderly. Taxation rates increased correspondingly.[30]

This extensive welfare state radically improved the lives of Swedes. There was a drastic drop in infant mortality. More people lived to retirement, and once retired, they lived longer than any previous generation. Around the turn of the last century, life expectancy (at birth) in Sweden was about fifty-two years; by the mid-1950s, it had grown to seventy-two years, and by 1973, to seventy-five years. Swedes also grew: In 1945, the mean height of twenty-year-old male conscripts was 5 feet 7 inches; in 1970, it was 5 feet 8 inches. The well-developed welfare state also boosted intergenerational social mobility, which eclipsed that of the world's prior symbol of such mobility, the United States.[31] Since the 1930s, the SAP had called social policy "a productive investment," meaning that society was made more efficient when citizens could rely on social security provisions.[32] And the SAP was right.

The expansion of the welfare state in Sweden, as elsewhere during golden-age capitalism, was profoundly shaped by the country's political

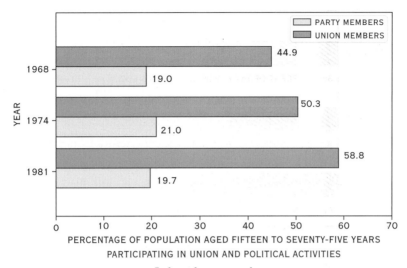

Labor takes command.

context. Governed by the Social Democratic SAP throughout the "record years," Sweden maintained high unionization rates that dovetailed with membership in the SAP. To cite just three numbers: By 1970, 81 percent of industrial workers were trade union members; by 1974, 50.3 percent of the entire population between the ages of fifteen and seventy-five belonged to a union.[33] In 1974, 21 percent of the adult population carried an SAP membership card. Given that distribution of power, the SAP delivered extraordinary benefits back to Swedish workers.

As workers won gains, the policies they favored altered Sweden's class structure, at first subtly, then rapidly, facilitating the "middle-classification" of the working class itself.[34] Well aware that such trends might undermine the social basis of the SAP, the party took steps to universalize social provisioning, a political tactic that ensured relevance across class lines.[35] As ever more Swedes benefited from the welfare state, more supported its continued expansion politically. During the "record years," it gained further strength from the support of powerful Swedish capital owners. Prominent Swedish business families like the Wallenbergs, who by 1969 controlled 23 percent of Sweden's

entire industrial sector—including Asea (electrical generators), Erics-
son (telephone equipment), and Saab (automobiles and defense, including aerospace)—had close ties to the SAP, the unions, and the state.[36]
Such links were vital for the family's companies. After all, much of the
demand for telecommunication and electricity-generation equipment,
as well as for military hardware (military expenditures in the 1960s
hovered between 3 and 4 percent of the GNP), came from the state.[37]
Company patriarch Marcus Wallenberg appreciated what social democracy and trade unions had done for the people and the country. In
1969, when Arne Geijer, chairman of the Swedish Confederation of
Trade Unions—the LO—congratulated Wallenberg on his seventieth
birthday, Wallenberg responded by telegram: "May I return your kind
words with a tribute to your endeavor to keep the balance between
desired social progress and an efficient and productive Swedish industry."[38] The close relationship between Swedish big business and the
SAP continued until the early 1970s.

Swedes expected these trends to last: In 1964, the minister of
health and social affairs, Sven Aspling, said that the Swedish people
(and the Swedish state) stood "not at the end of a reform era, but rather
on the threshold of new tasks, new needs and emerging, urgent demands."[39] Expressing the view that welfare politics, combined with
Sweden's economic and industrial boom, would create a strong and
prosperous people, Swedish prime minister Olof Palme confidently
proclaimed in the late 1960s that "economic growth and social policy
must not be viewed as enemies. Instead, I believe that social policy
stimulates growth. At the same time, growth is a prerequisite for the
solidarity that supports socio-political efforts. Security and growth go
hand-in-hand."[40] The unions agreed. In 1961, the LO remarked that
"we accept the continued strong growth of the public sector's role in
our economy. Such growth is much more justifiable, as those needs
that would be satisfied many times over are much more important for
society than are large segments of private consumption."[41] As the economy grew and productivity rose, the competitiveness of Swedish firms
on the international market solidified. Living standards exploded, in-

equality diminished, and Swedes looked with almost unbridled optimism at the society they had created. In a song released at the tail end of that era, the globally popular Swedish band ABBA proclaimed, "Shining like the sun. Smiling, having fun. Feeling like a number one."[42]

———

Welfare states expanded throughout capitalism's industrial heartland in Western Europe, the United States, Japan, and sometimes beyond. Few were as extensive or universal as the Swedish one, but the general tendency was the same. Between 1960 and 1973, social expenditures as a share of the GDP increased by about 19 percent in Germany, 37 percent in France, 46 percent in Italy, and 60 percent in the United States. In 1973, the Netherlands spent the highest percentage of its GDP on social expenditures (20.6 percent) and Japan spent the lowest (5.7 percent) among member countries of the Organization for Economic Co-Operation and Development, or OECD, whose membership represents the world's most developed capitalist economies. Even relatively feeble welfare states, such as the United States (which spent 10 percent of its GDP on social provisioning), provided old-age insurance and health care and income supports for the poor.[43]

This enormous expansion rested on rapid economic growth, which made the distributional consequences of welfare state expansion more palatable to everyone. To cite some numbers: The OECD reported that in its heavily industrialized member countries, annual growth averaged 4 percent in the 1950s and 5 percent in the 1960s. As a result, output per person doubled in just sixteen years (between 1948 and 1964), a significant acceleration; the previous doubling of per capita output in western Europe had taken fifty-nine years (between 1870 and 1929). In the heartland of industrial capitalism, private consumption rose annually by 4.2 percent and production by 4.5 percent between 1952 and 1970. In the two decades after 1950, world manufacturing increased four times, when the developed capitalist countries

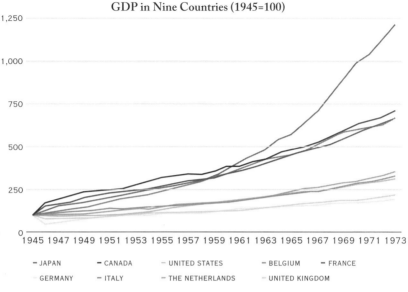

GDP in Nine Countries (1945=100)

Rapid economic growth in capitalism's industrial heartland,
1945–1973 (indexed to 1945).

produced about three-quarters of all goods and services worldwide—a level of economic development and global inequality unprecedented in the history of capitalism.[44]

While economic growth was general, its speed varied by country. Japan grew the fastest. Its GDP more than doubled in the 1950s, then increased by another 144 percent in the 1960s. Heavily damaged during World War II, with about one-quarter of its wealth destroyed, the country had seen rural living standards decline to 65 percent of their prewar level and urban living standards to about 35 percent. That changed after the war: Up to 1973, the Japanese economy averaged growth of about 10 percent annually, accelerating at first on account of the demand unleashed by the Korean War. After that, growth was driven by plant and equipment investment, as the capital stock grew by an astounding 12 percent per year in the early 1960s. The steel, auto-mobile, petrochemical, and gas and electric industries were leaders in this type of investment, increasing labor productivity and becoming more competitive internationally. Nikon and Canon became the world's leading camera producers; Toyota and Nissan moved to the cutting edge of car-manufacturing efficiency; and Sony became a world market leader in consumer electronics.[45]

West Germany's economy followed suit, almost doubling in size in the 1950s and growing another 44 percent in the 1960s. Such eye-popping growth rates were, as in Japan, partly the result of catch-ups related to war devastation. But other economies grew rapidly too: French output increased by 46 percent in the 1950s and by another 63 percent in the 1960s; the Dutch economy expanded by 45 percent in the 1950s and by 55 percent in the 1960s; and the Italian economy did even better, expanding by 71 percent in the 1950s and 72 percent in the 1960s. Fiat, to give an example of what this growth looked like at the company level, had employed 61,000 workers in Italy in 1950; twenty years later, that number had skyrocketed to 153,000. Farther south, growth accelerated as well: Greece lived through an economic miracle—from 1950 to 1973, its economy expanded by an average of 5.88 percent a year. Even the world's largest economy, the United States', continued to grow rapidly—37 percent in the 1950s and 50 percent in the 1960s. Such dramatic changes were embedded in, and partly enabled by, the reconstruction of international connections that had been damaged by the Depression and the subsequent war, as world trade in manufactured goods grew by a factor of eight.[46]

Not only was there rapid growth, but the business cycles that structured economic life under capitalism also became less volatile: Economic swings were shallower and their social effects (unemployment) much more muted.[47] Capitalism—to the surprise of many— seemed almost tame.

As in Sweden, growth throughout the industrial heartland went along with rapid productivity advances. Between 1950 and 1973, real GDP per working hour increased annually by 2.6 percent in the United States, 3.1 percent in the United Kingdom, 5.1 percent in France, 5.8 percent in Italy, 6 percent in Germany, and 8 percent in Japan. These productivity gains were fueled by rapidly growing investments, which were encouraged by predictable, expanding demand and high profits.

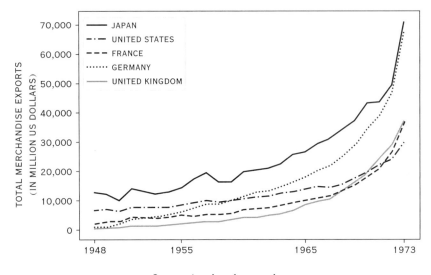

International trade expands.

As wages increased during the 1950s, Japanese workers were able to purchase durable consumer goods such as televisions, refrigerators, and washing machines, collectively known as the "three sacred treasures."[48] By the 1960s, these "treasures" were replaced by the "three Cs" (color TVs, coolers [air conditioners], and cars).[49] In 1955, very few Japanese people owned refrigerators or washing machines; by 1975, almost every household did, and half owned a car. In similar ways, as real wages rose in postwar Australia, consumption expanded: In 1945, there was one motor vehicle for every 8.7 people; by 1968, there was one for every 2.8.[50]

Productivity advanced because of investment in a restructuring of production. In agriculture, mechanization cut labor requirements; tractors and other machinery revolutionized peasant life. In Western Europe, the number of tractors per one hundred cultivators increased tenfold, to over fifty, between 1950 and 1972. The use of fertilizers per hectare of land more than tripled between 1950 and 1972. Mass use of newly developed herbicides and insecticides further increased output. In 1964, US farmers sprayed their crops with 320 million pounds of pesticides. Thanks to better feed and the use of antibiotics, a cow in Germany produced

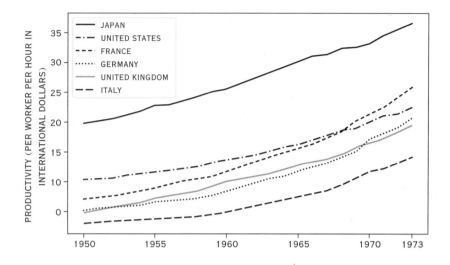

Productivity advances in the industrial heartland.

3,800 liters of milk per year in 1970, compared with just 2,500 liters in 1950, and hens laid 216 instead of 120 eggs annually.[51]

In industry, the shop-floor transformations that had begun at companies like Fiat during the 1910s and 1920s continued to spread. The core industries of the golden age remained remarkably similar to those that had emerged during the reconstruction of capitalism in the 1870s: coal, steel, chemicals, electrical machinery, and metal goods. All required massive investments in immovable assets. Unlike before the war, they now generally organized along Fordist principles, with assembly-line production for consumer mass markets. New goods and industries emerged as well, notably plastics, consumer electronics, and pharmaceuticals.[52]

From a bird's-eye view, the golden age's productive order can be seen as the diffusion of production techniques that had already become dominant in the United States a generation earlier. Countries and firms sent so-called productivity missions to the US to see how things were done. Germany's Volkswagen focused so single-mindedly on ever greater efficiencies in producing the Beetle that some considered the company "more Fordist than Ford."[53] Both Peugeot and Renault, once high-end artisanal manufacturers of luxury vehicles, followed suit, moving into the lower end of a vastly expanded market. Volvo, which had been a truck manufacturer, entered the passenger-car market after the war to capture more gains from mass production. The Fordist organization of production was so prevalent that an entire school of cultural critics—the Frankfurt School—gained traction for its unrelenting critique of the order's alleged homogenizing and depoliticizing tendencies.[54] "Most men are born into a prison," Max Horkheimer wrote darkly. "Precisely for this reason the present form of society, so-called individualism, is in truth a society of sameness and mass culture."[55]

Within these new, usually Fordized industries, scientific research became ever more important. As research labs grew and research expenses exploded, engineers and university-trained scientists entered firms. By 1946, 45,941 scientists and engineers worked in 2,300 industrial research laboratories located within US firms alone. Tens of thousands of other engineers and managers worked in production, the heroes of a new age. As US writer Kurt Vonnegut notes in his novel *Player Piano*, which observes the dystopian possibility of a civilization run by machines and is set in the postwar years, "[T]his elite business, this assurance of superiority, this sense of rightness about the hierarchy topped by management and engineers—this was installed in all college graduates and there were no bones about it." The pharmaceutical company Pfizer invested heavily in chemical research after 1945, hiring organic chemists and consulting with leading academic scientists to move into the development of new drugs by molecular manipulation. At Kodak, research laboratories played an increasingly significant role. There was similar growth in Japan, where the number of industrial researchers increased from 57,126 to 143,364 in the decade after 1965. The production of Seiko watches at Hattori & Co. offers a good example of how scientific research informed manufacturing: Before the war, the company had hired only one engineering graduate, as skilled craftsmen oversaw assembly. That changed in 1945, when the company hired many university-trained engineers. Matsumoto Dai—a

graduate of the University of Tokyo's prewar Department of Arms
Production—oversaw these changes, drawing up designs with sharply
defined tolerance standards for interchangeable parts, turning Hattori
into one of the world's leading watch manufacturers.[56]

One effect of these developments was the tremendous growth of
higher education. The percentage of Americans aged eighteen to twenty-
four enrolled in institutions of higher learning—not least thanks to the
GI Bill, which provided access to and financial support for university
education to veterans—almost tripled from the fall of 1946, when it
stood at 12.5 percent, to the fall of 1973, when it had increased to 36.5
percent. The total number of students almost quintupled, to more than
9.5 million. In Europe, this jump was just as impressive—from 4 or 5
percent of an age cohort just after World War II to between 10 and 20
percent twenty-five years later. In Japan in 1944, there were eighty-four
thousand students in attendance across 48 universities; in 1971, there
were 1.5 million young people (or one-quarter of the total in their age
cohort) in attendance across 389 universities.[57]

As a result of this growth and the distributional policies that came
to characterize the trente glorieuses, inequality diminished. In early

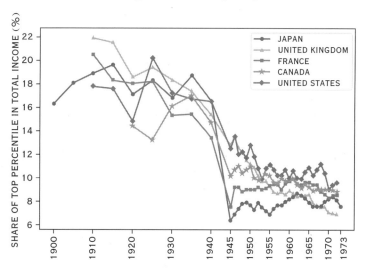

The Great Compression: declining inequality.

twentieth-century western Europe, the richest 10 percent of people had controlled 90 percent of all private property; by the 1980s, their share fell to somewhere between 50 and 55 percent. In the United States, the decline was less dramatic but still significant—from 80 percent to about 65 percent. When it came to income, the richest 10 percent of western Europeans controlled half of all income in the early twentieth century but only around 30 percent in the postwar decades, while in the United States, their share fell from somewhere between 40 and 45 percent to 35 percent.[58]

ONE CRITICAL SIDE effect of this great acceleration was the draining and pollution of the natural environment. Just as with other periods in capitalism's history, the golden age rested on extraction: Iron ore, coal, copper, and sugar, among other commodities, were produced and consumed in unprecedented quantities.[59] As commodity frontiers expanded into ever more territories and social spaces, industrial processes impinged on the natural world in novel ways—polluting air, rivers, lakes, seas, and soils. John Maynard Keynes put it simply but memorably: "We destroy the beauty of the countryside because the unappropriated splendours of nature have no economic value."[60] Man-made chemicals, some carcinogenic, accumulated in plants and animals and, eventually, human bodies. Already in the 1950s, methyl mercury produced by waste discharged from Japan's Chisso Corporation had caused what was called a "strange disease of unknown causes."[61] A highway running through the Keihin Industrial Zone was popularly known as the "Pollution Observation Route," the air so polluted that at a rest stop, drivers could purchase thirty seconds of pure oxygen for a few yen.[62] The American state of Louisiana had its "Cancer Alley," as did New Jersey. In the 1960s, in the Ruhr area, the center of Germany's heavy industry, more than five kilograms of dust landed on every one hundred square meters of ground every month.[63] So many pollutants were poured into the Rhine River that by the mid-1970s its "biological life" was almost extinct.[64] The Rhine was, in a word, dead.

Selling oxygen at a rest stop in Japan: fifty yen for thirty seconds, 1968.

酸素自動販売器

As early as the 1960s, alarms sounded over this unwelcome but inevitable effect of the golden years. Among the first was Rachel Carson's 1962 *Silent Spring*. A US biologist, she depicted a world fallen silent because the widespread use of chemicals in agricultural production had destroyed fauna and flora. Focusing on the accelerating use of chemicals, she chronicled "the contamination of air, earth, rivers, and sea with dangerous and even lethal materials," observing the unprecedented speed with which "the tide of chemicals born of the Industrial Age has arisen to engulf our environment."[65] Carson hung her story on DDT, but her concerns were much broader, and her protest resonated with many who grasped that humans had arrogantly and dangerously meddled in the "web of life."[66] Exactly a decade later, the Club of Rome, financed by the Volkswagen Foundation, commissioned a group of experts led by MIT's environmental scientist Donella H. Meadows to chart the state of the world, resulting in the publication of the deeply impactful *The Limits to Growth: A Report for the Club of Rome's Project on the Predicament of Mankind*.[67] The scientists developed a computerized model of resource flows that extrapolated from historical data to chart the resource use of industrial civilization. They concluded that there were objective and insurmountable "limits to growth" that capitalism would confront in the course of the next century.[68] Indeed, "earthly limitations" would affect growth of "nearly all of mankind's current activities."[69] What was needed, they said, was a new "global equilibrium" that limited the use of nonrenewable resources and the pollution of ecosystems.[70] In Japan in 1968, economist Shigeto Tsuru published

Gendai shihon shugi to kōgai (*Modern capitalism and pollution*), making similar arguments.[71] Less prominently, but with cumulative impact, journalists started reporting on environmental disasters, civil society organizations began to push for protections, and state institutions made policy changes in the early 1970s to protect the natural environment. The first "Earth Day" was observed in the United States on April 22, 1970. In 1972, a UN conference on the environment met in Stockholm, symbolizing that environmental concerns were global. Increasingly, governments began to regulate against practices that harmed the environment (for example, through a much improved Clean Air Act, passed in the United States in 1970).

The exponential growth in fossil-fuel use exemplifies the severe environmental impact of the golden age. As business historian Alfred D. Chandler Jr. noted, the key innovations of the Second Industrial Revolution had all been based on the acceleration of throughput, that is, the movement of materials through the factory, which relied on heat and velocity produced by nonhuman sources of energy. As late as 2018, 80 percent of such energy was fossil-fuel-based. The very availability of cheap fuels, particularly oil, had enabled the huge productivity advances that had also pacified the global working class. During the golden age, there was a brief moment when supplies of oil seemed inexhaustible and inexpensive—indeed, from 1950 to 1973, the average cost of Saudi oil was less than two dollars a barrel.[72] As most oil drilling took place in authoritarian regimes, especially in the Middle East, the golden years produced the spectacle of a flourishing of liberal regimes, all providing new opportunities for their citizens, that were powered, quite literally, by their illiberal opposite. Such connected diversity, of course, was nothing new in capitalism's history.

Fossil-fuel-powered economic growth and productivity gains revolutionized daily life in the industrial heartland. They encouraged a politics of energy-intensive decentralized development.[73] As car ownership became ever more common, millions of people moved out of cities and into suburbs, where they dispersed over very large areas and took up residence in single-family dwellings surrounded by greenery, thus becoming dependent on fossil fuels to access work and places of consumption, as well as recreational and educational facilities.

While the United States is correctly considered the quintessential suburban society (by the 1950s, it consumed 60 percent of worldwide oil production), the most radical model unfolded in Australia, another vast resource-producing and -consuming settler society.[74] In his 1964 book, *The Lucky Country*, Australian public intellectual and social critic Donald Horne described his native country as the "first suburban nation."[75] For him, the suburban home became the site of "the Australian way of life," a phrase that was popularly deployed in the golden years to describe a shared set of supposedly white Australian national values and morals (independence, freedom, self-determination, democracy), along with material prosperity and the celebration of the nuclear family.[76]

In Australia's largest city, Sydney, suburbanization took off right after the war. As political elites became committed Keynesians, Labor prime ministers John Curtin (1941–1945) and Ben Chifley (1945–1949) put housing at the center of postwar planning. As early as 1943, the Australian Commonwealth Housing Commission concluded that "a dwelling of good standard and equipment is not only the need but the right of every citizen"—a condition not met for hundreds of thousands of city dwellers.[77] In 1945, in response, the Australian Commonwealth entered into an

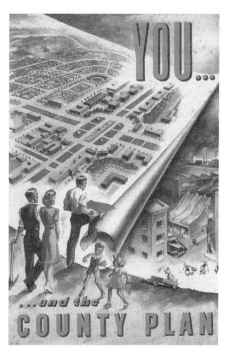

A fossil-fuel civilization finds its way out of social conflict: cover of the Cumberland County Council's You . . . and the County Plan *brochure.*

agreement with state governments: It would fund a public-housing program that the states would administer. In 1951, the Cumberland Plan expanded Sydney's suburbs, connecting the city's new suburbs by corridors of expressways through a "green belt" of forests and bush. In the process, the state encouraged developers to also clear what had been deemed "slum" areas.[78] To support this radical spatial rearrangement, the government rezoned land, constructed highways and other infrastructures, and subsidized private home construction. In Sydney, homeownership increased from 40 percent in 1947 to 70 percent in 1966, paralleling national trends. By the 1960s, a higher percentage of people owned homes in Australia than in the United States, the United Kingdom, or Canada.[79]

This expansion was made possible in part by a new material that made it easier to build inexpensive housing. The so-called fibro house was built from fibrous asbestos cement; Fibrolite, as the trademarked version of the material was called by its largest supplier, James Hardie, enabled a three-bedroom house to be built for 2,480 pounds (about 100,000 2024 US dollars), or about half as much as a traditional brick-veneer home, not least because the building material could be used by owners who wanted to build their own houses, as about 50 percent opted to do. Architect Robin Boyd called suburbanization "the fibro frontier" in his 1960 book, *The Australian Ugliness*. Such suburbanization also reinforced reigning gender ideologies. Traditional gender roles were reflected in the pages of *The Australian Women's Weekly*, where wives and mothers submitted recipes and photos for baking, cooking, and homemaking contests. Sydney women's role as homemakers came to be ever more defined by consumption than by domestic production.[80]

Similar drastic changes to the basic structures of daily life unfolded throughout the industrial heartland. When French economist Jean Fourastié compared two fictional villages, one representing France in 1945, the other representing France in 1975, he found that the village had gone from a state of "underdevelopment" to "development."[81] The "trente glorieuses," he claimed, "have solved the tragic and millennial problems of humanity."[82] The changes Fourastié observed were multi-dimensional, touching on almost every aspect of life. Consider the massive numbers moving out of agriculture: While 36 percent of French workers cultivated the land in 1936, just 10 percent did so in 1975. In effect, more than 4 million Frenchwomen and -men had left rural labor behind. At the same time, agricultural productivity sky-rocketed: In 1946, the output of one person in agriculture fed 55 people; in 1975, one person's output fed 260. While the industrial sector grew from 6 to 8 million workers, the service sector expanded even more dramatically, from 6.2 to 10.8 million. Within the industrial sector, employment patterns changed. The number of jobs fell by 44.7 percent in mining and by 17 percent in the textile industry, while it increased by 37.3 percent in auto production. Because much higher qualifications were now needed for these jobs, the educational sector made a remarkable jump, propelling the society to what Fourastié called "scolarisation."[83] In 1958, only 17 percent of French eighteen-year-olds studied in educational institutions; by 1975/76, that number had more than tripled to 54 percent. The French state's outlays for education increased by a factor of almost ten during these years.[84]

France also built massive new infrastructure: In the seven years prior to 1945, 450,000 new homes had been constructed; in the seven years before 1975, that number increased to 4 million, not least to house the millions of migrants from the French (and North African) countryside. In 1946, there had been 12.7 million housing units in France; in 1975, there were 21.1 million. Telephones went from five to twenty-five per every hundred inhabitants, refrigerators from three to ninety-one, televisions from none to eighty-six, and automobiles from one to fifteen and a half. Purchasing power went up astronomically, too, more than ever before in French history. Total consumption increased by a factor of 2.23 between 1959 and 1974. By 1973, France was a "society of consumption."[85]

People consumed much more but worked less: In France, average annual labor time decreased from 2,100 hours in the 1940s to 1,875 hours in 1975. People worked fewer weeks each year, fewer days each week, and fewer hours each day. Given all that free time, the 1970s saw "signs of a real explosion in leisure budgets."[86] Movie theaters were built, and sales of TVs, music-recording equipment, and sports equipment skyrocketed. In France, expenditures per person for "culture and leisure" increased fivefold between 1946 and 1975.[87] Many more people went on vacations; by 1975, 48.8 percent of all French manual workers took at least one annual vacation. One in five farmers took a yearly vacation, while among the French middle class, the rate was around 90 percent, or essentially everyone. Life expectancy rose as well (from 69.9 years in 1960 to 72.4 years in 1973); the country now had many more very old people. This was in part the result of improved medical care. The number of doctors in France increased from twenty-nine thousand in 1946 to eighty-one thousand in 1975. In 1946, the average person in France spent about an hour and a half with a doctor yearly; by 1975, that metric had tripled.[88] France, Fourastié observed, palpably frustrated by his compatriots' ingratitude, "registered in 30 years, and often in 20 or 15 years, more changes than it had since the beginning of the industrial revolution in 1830 or 1850."[89]

———

The golden age was not just a period of rapid economic growth, productivity advances, and concomitant escalation of dependence on fossil fuels (and other resources). It also marked a novel institutional settlement founded on a particular distribution of political power between and within countries. Capitalism, of course, had always been deeply embedded in institutions, some private, some public, and these institutions had changed dramatically over time. In the postwar golden age, this order changed again, and a new political economy emerged. In the United States, it has been dubbed the "New Deal order" for its origin in the 1930s. It exhibited strong similarities across the industrial heartland, albeit with specifics unique to each country.[90]

The particulars of this new order took shape from the World War II mobilizations that had eclipsed peacetime responses to the Great Depression. In the 1930s and early 1940s, these transformations had been tightly linked to the exigencies of the moment and had been widely understood to be temporary half measures. Instead, during the golden age, these strategies stabilized and then flourished.[91]

After World War II, powerful forces in industrial capitalism's heartland promoted a deep reform of capitalism. Labor and its organizations were at the forefront. But support came from other quarters too: When the German CDU, a conservative Christian party, wrote its party program in 1947, it stated flatly that "[t]he capitalist economic system has not done justice to the vital state and social interests of the German people. . . . The content and goal of this social and economic reorganization can no longer be the capitalist pursuit of profit and power, but only the well-being of our people."[92] The German Constitution, written under US oversight, to this day stipulates that property must be deployed to further the well-being of the community as a whole.[93] France's Catholics, meanwhile, demanded a "revolution" of the economy under the auspices of a government "liberated from the power of those who possess wealth." The Mouvement Républicain Populaire, the Centre Catholique des Intellectuels Français, and intellectuals such as Emmanuel Mounier and Dominican priest and economist Louis-Joseph Lebret argued that economic development should focus on a "broad increase in well-being," not economic growth for its own sake.[94] In the United Kingdom, the war was still on when John Maynard Keynes, Lionel Robbins, and Clement Attlee expressed their support for William Beveridge's plan to expand the welfare state, which was, according to a contemporary observer,

> essentially concerned with assuring freedom from want, in so far as want is due to interruptions of income or to the occurrence of

costs unrelated to income to which all or the vast majority of the population are at some time or other liable . . . unemployment, disability, loss of livelihood by a person not dependent on paid employment, retirement through age, marriage needs of a woman, funeral expenses, childhood and physical disease or incapacity.[95]

The Beveridge Plan resulted in a vast limitation on the powers of private capital, especially in the huge health-care sector. Universal and free health care became a right of British citizens. Eventually, even the conservative Winston Churchill came to support it. In Italy, centrist forces joined this resurgent left to support drastic reforms as well.[96]

This outcome, which arose out of novel configurations of social and political power, meant that certain institutional features of the golden age were common to all the states in the industrial heartland. As powerful trade unions and leftist parties grew strong from the crucial role they had played in liberating Europe from fascism, and as many business leaders lost legitimacy for their collaboration with the Nazi regime, a political compromise emerged: The new economic order would be a "mixed economy" that preserved private enterprise—and capitalism with it—but was balanced by strong regulations, state power of expanded scope and scale, and, in Europe, government ownership of many businesses.[97]

Everywhere, the state's administrative capacity and impact expanded. It did so in seemingly obscure policy domains, as when Germany regulated the milk market in excruciating detail, stipulating production quotas for individual farmers and prices under the Milk and Fat Law of 1951. The big picture, however, was this: Among member countries of the OECD, the percentage of the GNP spent by the state rose from 28 percent in the mid-1950s to 41 percent two decades later. Consequently, taxes captured more and more of people's incomes: Even in the United States, the wartime marginal tax rate of 91 percent on the highest incomes was reaffirmed by Republican president Dwight D. Eisenhower. During the golden years, the top marginal income tax rate averaged 89 percent in the United Kingdom, 60 percent in France, and 58 percent in Germany.[98]

Most of these increasing revenues went to fund the welfare state, with two key consequences: reduced market-based inequalities and more consistent consumer demand. This, in turn, stabilized mass-production industries. Everywhere, the welfare state grew tremendously. Public pensions, public health care, and public unemployment insurance became common.[99]

These policies were animated by a commitment to Keynesian economic policy.[100] Keynesianism was not a doctrinaire set of policies. It was a set of tools that could be combined and recombined in a variety of ways, which is why, broadly speaking, Keynesian political economies could still be quite distinct from one another. But the policies shared the belief that economic life should be regulated on a national scale, as one organism, requiring state guidance and planning.[101] As Vittorio Valletta, Fiat's general manager, argued in 1951: "The fabric of contemporary social life is sufficiently complex that in every economic sector and every country state intervention in production has become inevitable."[102] In Australia, H. C. "Nugget" Coombs, the director general of the Commonwealth's Department of Post-War Reconstruction from 1943 to 1949, was so inspired by Keynes's *General Theory* that in his memoir, *Trial Balance*, he recalled that upon reading it, he "had become convinced that in the Keynesian analysis lay the key to comprehension of the economic system."[103] For Coombs and his peers, *General Theory*'s publication was "the most seminal intellectual event of our time."[104]

Keynes's ideas created the intellectual struts for deficit spending and welfare state expansion. The goal was to tame the business cycle, ensure full employment, and create social stability at a moment when societies had more radically proletarianized and working-class political power, unions, and socialist ideas were more powerful than at any other time in the history of capitalism. After World War II, even capital owners understood that social peace was founded on providing well-paying and secure jobs, a necessary corollary to mass production.[105] Deficit spending became an important tool in the post-war policy arsenal, and even though Keynes had not explicitly endorsed it, he had assumed that fiscal policy would be used "through preventative means, not reactionary, ex post interventions in the economy."[106]

One form of such interventions focused on military expenditures, creating what scholars have called "military Keynesianism," or a "permanent war economy."[107] Significant defense spending driven by the heating up of the Cold War was common (though it tended to fall as a share of the GDP during the golden age), hovering between roughly 5 and 14 percent between 1945 and 1973. In the United States, in particular, military spending was constitutive of the New Deal order, with massive defense outlays politically more palatable than social spending. US defense spending was also important to Japanese economic growth. Yet everywhere, social spending exceeded military outlays, and by 1973, social spending was 6.83 times as high as defense spending in Japan, 4.9 times as high in France, 5.79 times as high in Germany, 7.09 times as high in Italy, and 2.61 times as high in Britain. Even in the United States, the world leader in defense spending, social spending was almost double that of military outlays.[108]

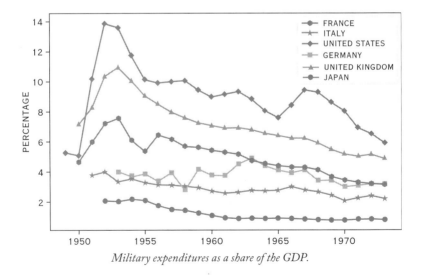

Military expenditures as a share of the GDP.

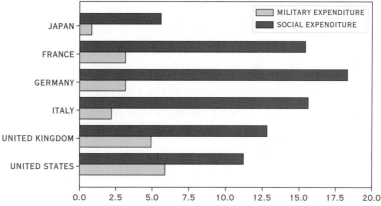

Social expenditures and military expenditures as a percentage of the GDP in 1973.

Crucial to the golden age, furthermore, was governments' engagement in economic planning, a policy that found support in surprising places: In 1946, Truman's secretary of commerce, the banker and industrialist W. Averell Harriman, argued that "[p]eople in this country are no longer scared of such words as 'planning.' . . . [P]eople have accepted the fact the government has got to plan."[109] Across the Atlantic, Charles de Gaulle created a French planning agency—the Commissariat Général du Plan—in 1946. Headed by Jean Monnet, it brought ministers, administrators, workers' unions, employers' representatives, and experts together with three primary aims:

> first, to increase production in metropolitan France and the overseas territories and their trade with the world, particularly in those areas where their position is most favorable; second, to ensure full employment of the workforce; third, to raise the standard of living of the population and to improve housing conditions and community life.[110]

In 1949, building on earlier efforts, Japan created the Ministry for International Trade and Industry (MITI) to provide "administrative guidance" to businesses—including "to issue directives (*shiji*), requests (*yōbō*), warnings (*keikoku*), suggestions (*kankoku*), and encouragements (*kanshō*)." It also gained responsibility to "nurture" (*ikusei*) new industries. In 1953, the government decided upon a five-year plan to build up the synthetic fibers industry; it provided capital, research support, and tax breaks. The industry experienced stellar growth. Similar measures were applied four years later to the electronics industry, again with stunning success.[111] As Norman Macrae of *The Economist* put it at the time, Japan had built "the most intelligently *dirigiste* system in the world."[112] After 1955, the government agreed to twelve economic plans, a mixture of "prediction and guidelines," the most important being the Income Doubling Plan of 1960, which planned for average annual growth rates of 7.8 percent during the following decade but then outperformed its goals with a 10 percent growth rate.[113] Ikeda Hayato, Japan's finance minister (and later premier), a key character in the planification of the Japanese economy, was derided by French president Charles de Gaulle as a "transistor radio salesman" for his unrelenting efforts to help Japanese businesses ascend in the world.[114] Aside from de Gaulle's racism, Hayato's efforts illustrate a truism too: Capitalism continued to be as much a project of states as of capital owners.

The leading edge of the new order was the nationalization of key industries, a long-term demand of the labor movement made more powerful by the urgent necessity to resurrect production and prosperity in the wake of the war. In France, to bring order to the chaotic postwar months, the state took control of four of the country's largest banks, along with Air France, coal mines, dozens of insurance companies, the aircraft engine producer Gnome et Rhône, the car manufacturer Renault, and energy companies such as Électricité de France (EDF) and Gaz de France. In energy, banking, and insurance, state-owned businesses dominated their sectors—a striking 35 percent of industrial production came under state control. In Germany, along with the postal and telecommunications sectors, the government owned and managed Lufthansa Airlines, steelworks such as Salzgitter AG, mines such as Saarbergwerke AG, car manufacturers such as Volkswagen, conglomerates such as VIAG and VEBA, and a host of regional banks.

The United Kingdom nationalized, in addition to its health sector, also its railroads in 1948.[115] Tellingly, when the dyed-in-the-wool liberal (in the nineteenth-century sense) British journal *The Economist* considered widespread Italian nationalizations (in insurance, transport, and heavy industry), it observed that "the real question is not to nationalise but what to do with the nationalised undertakings."[116]

Organized labor, as we saw in Sweden, was an important player in this new world. Everywhere in the industrial heartland, the postwar years witnessed union growth. Union density in Sweden, Denmark, Norway, Ireland, Britain, Belgium, Austria, West Germany, and the Netherlands increased by around 10 percent. To be sure, there remained large national differences: In 1960, only 19 percent of the French workforce was organized, but 69 percent of the Swedish. Yet overall, labor became, according to US economist John Kenneth Galbraith, a "countervailing" force to concentrated capital. These were times of social turmoil and political strife, with strong labor and left-wing political parties having a major say in structuring the political economy of the industrial heartland. In Japan, for example, the institutional settlement between capital and labor in the postwar years had arrived in the 1950s only after an extensive battle on the factory floors and in the streets.[117]

Labor power extended into politics: Throughout the golden age, the Australian, British, and Swedish labor parties controlled about half the seats in their respective parliaments; in Belgium and Germany, the socialist and communist parties together controlled a little less than half; in France, around half (with a strong Communist Party presence); and in Italy, a little less than half, but again with a strong Communist Party.[118]

Labor was integrated into the new order in part because it benefited (sometimes contractually) from rapid productivity growth. Wages were increasingly set by collective bargaining, and workers gained significant wage increases and improved working conditions, often under the watchful eyes of state regulators. In the United States, labor

	1961–1970	1971–1980
AUSTRALIA	45.6	46.2
BELGIUM	40.6	50.8
FRANCE	20.1	21.0
GERMANY	32.9	34.1
ITALY	28.0	46.9
JAPAN	34.1	32.5
SWEDEN	66.4	73.4
UNITED KINGDOM	40.9	47.6
UNITED STATES	26.9	22.9

Net union density, averages (in percentage) by decade.

unions became a powerful presence in the country's dynamic industrial sector. In 1950, the United Auto Workers struck a deal with General Motors that guaranteed a 20 percent wage hike, annual cost-of-living adjustments to wages, and generous health and retirement benefits in return for a five-year contract; the agreement, which came to be known as Reuther's Treaty of Detroit, set labor-relations patterns for other industries as well. Workers also gained more institutional representation, particularly in Germany, where in the 1950s "co-determination" gave workers' representatives seats on boards of German companies in certain industries—beginning in coal and steel.[119] These accomplishments amounted to much less than many labor leaders and workers hoped for, but in the long history of capitalism, they constituted a sea change.

The global political situation amplified labor's crucial role in shaping the institutional order of the golden years, which compelled governments and business leaders in the industrial heartland to lessen the overt social conflicts that had accompanied capitalism's emergence and spread. The stabilization and expansion of socialism—capitalism's outside—in the Soviet Union, Eastern Europe, China, and, increasingly, the Global South gave workers in the West new power and influence; so much so that it could be argued that the greatest beneficiaries of global communism were not Russian but Western European and American workers. Labor politics might have seemed local, but they played out on a global stage, just like capitalism more broadly. Capital was politically weakened by communism's removal of people and terri-

The wages of prosperity: average nominal wage in manufacturing,
1948–1973 (1955=100).

tories from the capitalist world, and by the bargain it made with an increasingly powerful state and mobilized working class.

As a new "outside" to capitalism emerged, even some conservative Western policymakers supported social democratic policies and unions—if only to weaken their communist competitors. In the United States, the Republican Party moved away from its once dominant attachment to fiscal conservativism. The party came to accept, even expand, the New Deal order; in fact, it was under Eisenhower's Republican presidency that the order stabilized in the United States. Republicans were motivated not least by the geopolitical realities of the Cold War and their fear of the Soviet Union. It was Eisenhower who supported Reuther's Treaty of Detroit, who continued very high marginal tax rates, and who oversaw the massive public works program that built the nation's Interstate Highway System. This coalition was the mold that formed the unprecedented political economy of the golden age.[120]

These changes were not just political but also ideological. Some intellectuals in the industrial heartland began to propagate the idea that they lived in a middle-class society—indeed, that all human history had trended toward a "middle-classification," as Galbraith's *Affluent Society*, Michael Biddiss's *Age of the Masses*, Salvador Giner's *Mass Society*, and Gunnar Myrdal's *Beyond the Welfare State* all argued.[121] For American sociologist Daniel Bell, welfare states foreshadowed the end of class ideologies, while Ralf Dahrendorf, his German British counterpart, argued in 1959 that class was no longer the relevant axis of social divisions in an "industrial society."[122] Similarly, US sociologist Harold Wilensky thought that the welfare state made ideology based on class identity obsolete, and Swedish economist Myrdal identified a "post-class world order" propelled by the "convergence of attitudes and ideologies" in rich nations.[123]

However flawed these arguments were, a vaguely defined but robust vast middle class really did emerge, which—along with the new ideological framing of capitalism, economic growth, wage increases, and the Cold War—relegitimized business leaders and capitalism itself. During the Depression, capitalism's legitimacy had diminished so precipitously that in 1942, Harvard economist Joseph Schumpeter had predicted it would not survive. He was wrong. Even though some

Defeating socialism by motorizing the working class: After millennia of walking, workers take to the car. Fiat advertisement, 1957.

workers in the industrial heartland continued to be drawn to forging a postcapitalist world, capitalism's hold strengthened—ideologically, for its promise of individual freedom and as a counterpoint to the communist world; materially, for its uncanny ability to provide prosperity to so many.[124]

In some countries, business leaders again turned into heroes. Yet these heroes were not the rugged entrepreneurs of the nineteenth century (or of the early twenty-first century) but technical and managerial wizards in command of large and complex organizations.[125] Peter Drucker, a US management consultant who was considered a "managerial prophet" by *The Manchester Guardian*, observed in 1975 that "[o]nly seventy years ago, organizations and managers were quite insignificant. In this century, the United States, and indeed every other developed country, has become a society of organizations, each requiring a great many managers and a high degree of management."[126] *The New York Times* listed among the manager's "immense" tasks the responsibility "to pick the right worker for the job, to set up work teams, to create identification with the product and the plant. Managerial function becomes universal."[127] This manager was tailor-made for the newly tamed capitalism of the golden age. In the heat of Cold War competition for hearts and minds, and also because of it, capitalism had been civilized, or at least so it seemed from the privileged precincts of the industrial heartland.

For all of the golden age's accomplishments, prosperity, and flattening of the class structure, noneconomic hierarchies persisted and even hardened—most prominently, gender hierarchies. Let us return to Sweden, the poster child of the golden age's full gleam. Swedish postwar policies discouraged women's labor-market participation, privileging the male-centered breadwinner family. During its height in the 1950s, the number of women working full time in the home, so-called housewives, peaked at 1.5 million. Prohibitions on women working at night remained on the books until 1962, keeping women out of many labor markets. Equal pay was not legally stipulated until 1965. Indeed, the call for women to remain at home—what sociologist Maria Mies called "housewifization"—had been one of the central demands of the labor movement since its founding. Intersecting with century-old bourgeois reform efforts, such housewifization became, as Mies brilliantly argued, "the Colony of the Little White Men."[128] "I would like to point out," she said, "that housewifization means the externalization, or ex-territorialization of costs which otherwise would have to be covered by the capitalists."[129] Arguably, the improved working conditions of Swedish industrial workers depended, in part, on keeping women out of the labor market, which both lessened competition for men and addressed household reproduction through women's unpaid labor. Intellectuals at the time—such as sociologist and Social Democratic political activist Alva Myrdal—favored such "protections" for women and, more generally, a hierarchy that put men's wage labor above women's. Before a woman married and became a mother, Myrdal believed, she should get an education and gain work experience. Afterward, she should stay home until all of her children were old enough to go to school, at which point she could go back to work. Indeed, Myrdal and others saw women's ability to stay home as a credit to the power of the labor movement; when men earned enough to support a family, women could follow their "natural" calling. Myrdal expressed this in her influential *Women's Two Roles* (*Kvinnans två roller*), written with Austrian sociologist Viola Klein and published in the mid-1950s.[130] Many labor activists and Social Democrats shared her view: Until well into the 1960s, the SAP and its LO allies supported the nuclear family as an institution and had reservations about women participating in the labor market to the same extent as men. Day-care centers were not a priority and were not seriously expanded until well into the 1970s. Pension reforms (the income-based ATP) guaranteed that women remained economically dependent on their husbands even in old age.

Racial hierarchies were just as constitutive of the golden age. In

Japan, even longtime Korean residents could not access Japanese citizenship and were excluded from large swaths of the job market. In 1974, Pak Chŏng-sŏk brought a lawsuit against Hitachi, where he had applied for work four years earlier under his Japanese name. After offering Pak a job, Hitachi had later revoked the offer when the firm discovered that he was Korean (born in Japan but with Korean ancestry and nationality). Pak's subsequent lawsuit was successful, and he was employed by Hitachi as a software systems developer in September 1974. Yet racial hierarchies remained powerful. In the United States, many African Americans not only remained disenfranchised until 1965 but also got slotted into the lowest ranks of the labor market. The median family income of African Americans in 1968 was only slightly more than half of that of their white counterparts. When Portugal sent so-called guest workers to Germany in the mid-1960s, it explicitly excluded workers of "African or Indian skin colour."[131] In 1965, the UK's Campaign Against Racial Discrimination (CARD) reported that in the West London community of Southall, 85 percent of South Asian migrants who had come to the UK on work vouchers given to them on the grounds of their skills and qualifications found themselves in semi-skilled or even unskilled work instead.[132] At the same time that Sydney's growing white middle-class suburbs became the nation's pride, Indigenous peoples had their children removed from their families without due legal process, were subject to racially discriminatory laws, and endured vast expropriations of their lands.

Racism was everywhere, but no country was more extreme than South Africa. Building a flourishing welfare state for its white working class, it excluded Black Africans from its benefits, legitimating such a divide by appealing to racial hierarchy.[133] Such a system of domestic apartheid was at least subject to political challenges that ultimately had some success. But the industrial heartland's place within global capitalism, the golden age itself, also rested on the heartland's position within a world structured by severely unequal exchanges between South and North, as well as on heavily fortified labor markets that were inaccessible to almost all of the world's people—a kind of global apartheid.

―――――

If the domestic order of the golden age was anchored within gendered and racial hierarchies, that process also unfolded in a particular set of international economic institutions. The central facet of these arrangements was the dominance of the United States. The golden age was, in the words of Henry Luce, the "American Century": If London had been the central node of global capitalism throughout the nineteenth century, New York and Washington, DC, took that role after 1945.

War had strengthened the US economy while shattering most of its peers. In 1948, the GDP of the United States was roughly twice that of France, Germany, Italy, Belgium, and the Netherlands combined. After the war, the US produced two-thirds of global industrial output, a position no country had ever attained. US companies were by far the most productive in the world, essentially without competition.[134] As Leon Fraser, president of New York's First National Bank, said somewhat presciently in 1940, "As America goes, so goes the world."[135]

Not only did the United States produce more goods and services than any other country, it set and enforced the rules that governed the global economy. The Depression and the ensuing war had solidified elite experts' belief that the international economy had to be put on a new footing. In hindsight, it was clear that escalating economic nationalism and an utter lack of global coordination had worsened the Depression. As American secretary of state Dean Acheson put it: "We cannot go through another ten years like the ten years at the end of the Twenties and the beginning of the Thirties without having the most far-reaching consequences upon our economic and social system."[136] Cold War competition with the Soviet Union added urgency to US policymakers' efforts to forge prosperity in Europe, Japan, and beyond.[137]

As a result, the United States took the lead in hammering out a set of global, rule-based relationships and institutions—the United Nations, the World Bank, and the International Monetary Fund (IMF) prominently among them—that promoted market opening, capital mobility, and democracy. For diplomat George F. Kennan, the motives were clear: "[W]e have about 50 percent of the world's wealth but only 6.3 percent of its population. This disparity is particularly great as between ourselves and the peoples of Asia. In this situation, we cannot fail to be the object of envy and resentment. Our real task in the coming period is to devise a pattern of relationships which will permit us to maintain this position of disparity."[138]

Crucially, the new economic order included a new monetary order. Designed in 1944 at Bretton Woods—a resort in New Hampshire—under the leadership of the United States, the system consisted of defined but flexible exchange rates secured by international capital controls. The gold-backed US dollar became the world's leading currency, with all other currencies defined in relationship to the dollar. The system was overseen by the IMF, which also provided countries with loans to stabilize the global capitalist economy. Bretton Woods steadied the value of currencies but also allowed for some flexibility should circumstances change. It restricted the international flows of capital by putting a brake on short-term and speculative investments while allowing for long-term investments, thus creating breathing space for Keynesian economic policies.[139]

THE TRADE ORDER changed too. American policymakers began to think of freer trade as advantageous to the United States, a departure from many decades of protectionism. Already during the war, the US had used the lend-lease program to force the British to accept liberalized trade. When the General Agreement on Tariffs and Trade (GATT) was signed under US auspices in 1947, it committed American policymakers to global trade liberalization (including other countries' access to its markets), an interest that maintained the US's unchallenged position in the world economy. Yet the United States advocated not just its own narrow interests but also the stability of the capitalist world as a whole, which it saw as crucial to its national aims. Trade liberalization, while important, was muted and slow so as not to undermine the social stability of other countries.[140] European agriculture, with America's blessing, remained highly protected.

At the same time, American and British policymakers created the World Bank as a lender for large-scale infrastructure projects crucial for global development. The United States also invested heavily in rebuilding war-torn Europe. Launched in 1948, the Marshall Plan provided $13.5 billion for the reconstruction of Europe—equivalent to 5 percent of the United States' GNP at the time. When the Korean War hit in 1950, massive US investments in armaments further helped European and Japanese industry. These American interventions had a notable impact on European economic growth, enabling, for example, a European export boom—exports doubled between 1946 and 1948 and then more than tripled by 1951.[141]

Taken together, this new framework produced an innovative international economic order. Effectively, Bretton Woods allowed two seemingly contradictory things to happen simultaneously. On the one hand, it forged a liberalized world economy with freer trade facilitated by semifixed exchange rates. On the other hand, it protected nations' ability to maintain their domestic welfare states.[142] In 1982, John Ruggie called this new order "embedded liberalism," enabled by what others have called "Keynes at home and Smith abroad."[143]

Overseen by the United States, the order, as we have seen, generated spectacular growth.[144] And it also helped forge peace within the industrial heartland itself (but not in the Global South): After decades of competition and warfare in capitalism's industrial heartland, the assumption of system-wide responsibilities by the United States, undoubtedly encouraged by escalating confrontations with Soviet communism, brought a moment of relative unity. The Russian Revolution, in a roundabout way, thus brought far-reaching peace, not just to capitalist societies domestically but to their international relations as well. It domesticated capitalism at the exact moment that the system faced its greatest challenges.

This reordering of global capitalism was furthered by the slow but ultimately far-reaching economic unification of the European continent—again, with US support. The idea, and to some degree the political impetus for this change, had a long history: Despite all the nationalist disasters of the age of catastrophe, statesmen and capitalists had toyed with the idea of integrating the European economy since the 1870s.[145] After two world wars and an aggressive Nazi effort to create hierarchically ordered European economic space had revealed the tremendous costs of nationalism, the project of a territorially reorganized European capitalism (albeit on more liberal terms) was eventually realized: in the creation of the Organization for European Economic Co-Operation in 1948; the Schuman Plan of 1950, which coordinated the French and German steel and coal industries; the European Coal and Steel Community of 1951; the 1957 Treaty of Rome, which created the European Economic Community; the inauguration of the European Monetary System in 1979; and finally, in 1993, the founding of the European Union. This integration provided increasingly freer and extended trade opportunities (with significant economic effects), monetary coordination and joint agricultural policies, as well as important initiatives in the continent-wide development of infrastructure and scientific projects. A continent-spanning market and, later, an (almost) continent-spanning currency were radical departures from earlier European traditions. The economic effects were intoxicating: Trade within the European Economic Community increased by a factor of nine between 1958 and 1972.[146] That project had the explicit support of the United States and was directed against a new "danger": the Soviet Union. It represented a sea change—not just for Europe but for global capitalism, distant from the poisonous politics that had embroiled the likes of the Röchling family in the Saar during the first half of the century.

———

The many consequential social, economic, and institutional departures of the golden age also accelerated the basic impetus of the capitalist revolution as capital owners pushed the logic of commodification into new areas of the world and new nooks and crannies of society. Among almost endless examples of such commodity frontiers, three were emblematic: the spread of wage labor, tourism, and commercial food preparation.

First, as manufacturing intensified throughout the industrial heartlands and as the service sector expanded rapidly, enormous new labor needs emerged. This, combined with the persistence of categorical inequalities and the peculiar social settlement of the golden years, made it increasingly difficult for entrepreneurs to recruit low-wage unskilled workers locally, so states and employers organized labor migrations funneling millions of workers into the industrial heartlands.[147]

Several principal frontiers of labor mobilization emerged: southern Europe, western Asia, North Africa, the Japanese countryside, and the internal and external peripheries of the United States, including its southern regions and Mexico. During the 1950s and 1960s, several European countries signed labor recruitment treaties—called "guest worker agreements"—with governments on Europe's southern periphery (largely Italy and Turkey) to facilitate the recruitment of workers.[148] Additional migrants arrived from Spain, Yugoslavia, Greece, and former colonial dependencies. Businesses supported these programs, assuming they would provide a reliable influx of inexpensive workers to fill the lowest-skilled, often manual positions. By 1975, a quarter of French, Swiss, and Belgian industrial workers were immigrants; in Britian and Germany, they made up almost 15 percent of that workforce.[149] By boosting the supply of unskilled labor, migrants supported the general reduction in working hours that characterized the golden age—a prime strategy of native working-class integration. Tellingly, when the international edition of *Time* magazine covered these massive migrations in 1973, it headlined its issue MIGRANT WORKERS: EUROPE'S OTHER ENERGY SOURCE.[150]

Italy signed several labor-recruiting treaties between 1946 and 1956, exchanging Italian workers for raw materials and energy from northwestern Europe. Before 1970, almost 6 million Italian migrants arrived in Germany, France, and Switzerland alone, following in the footsteps of earlier mass Italian migrations to South America and the United States. Starting in 1961, Turkey signed similar treaties as well. As a result, about 1 million Turks migrated to northwestern Europe between 1961 and 1975. This was alongside 2 million Greeks, 2 million Spaniards, and at least 650,000 Yugoslavs. Male migrants often performed manual labor at manufacturing enterprises, mines, and construction sites, but they also worked as semiskilled machine operators in the automobile industry, while women worked not only in light manufacturing, such as textiles, but also in the service sector. The sending countries joined these agreements to address issues of under- or unemployment and to gain access to remittances that could fund their own development. Indeed, by 1975, Turks were annually sending the equivalent of over $1.3 billion in US dollars back home, often to invest in housing and land and to open small businesses.[151]

In the United States, employers recruited—in addition to millions of African Americans fleeing the poverty, racism, and disenfranchisement of the American South—millions of Mexicans. Between 1942 and 1964, the so-called Bracero Program brought 4.8 million Mexicans into the United States on temporary work assignments, especially in agro-industry, with millions more entering and staying illegally. Millions arrived thereafter to power US industry. At the same time, hundreds of thousands of North Africans, especially from Algeria, arrived in France to fill unskilled jobs in France's construction industry, domestic service, and automobile manufacturing plants. In 1946, only about 22,000 Algerians lived in France; by 1975, that number had skyrocketed to more than 710,000. In Britain, increasing numbers of workers arrived from former colonies, including what would come to be known as the Windrush generation of West Indians, named for the boat that some of them arrived on. They came to work in transport, health care, car manufacturing, and the hospitality industry. Caribbean-born immigrants to England and Wales numbered 15,301 in 1951 and 304,070 in 1971.[152]

Japan was something of an outlier, as it sourced its labor from its own rural periphery. The exodus from small towns and villages was extremely rapid: In just six years, from 1960 to 1966, almost four million rural cultivators joined the industrial and service workforces as massive industrialization took over sprawling cities from Kitakyushu to Tokyo. While 62.7 percent of Japanese people lived in rural towns and villages in 1950, that percentage dropped to just 24.1 by 1974. Even so, workers from the countryside were still not sufficient, and Japan also hosted a substantial number of illegal Korean immigrants, who mostly joined the proletariat of the heavily industrialized Kansai region.[153]

JUST AS VAST investments in fixed assets created new labor needs and pushed labor frontiers into new spaces, the logic of capitalism also spread along other rapidly expanding commodity frontiers. One of the most significant—indeed, the late twentieth century's most significant—was tourism.

A novel feature of golden-age capitalism, the tourism commodity frontier spread at astounding speed. People have traveled for many centuries, but leisure travel is a relatively recent phenomenon. It gained traction in the nineteenth century, when the emerging bourgeoisie took to the road to visit spas, mountains, the seaside, and the sites of power of previous ruling classes, such as the ruins of ancient Rome and Athens. Until the middle of the twentieth century, they remained largely among themselves on such trips. Few other people traveled, except perhaps in Britain, where, by 1938, 40 percent of adults annually journeyed away from home for at least a week, though mostly going just a few dozen miles to proletarian seaside destinations, such as Blackpool and Morecambe. The Nazi propaganda machine highlighted mass tourism for working-class gentiles as one of its accomplishments, but even at its height, in 1939, only 15 percent of all eligible Germans took a trip of more than five days.[154]

By the 1950s, however, middle-class and eventually working-class tourists became a noticeable feature of the golden years. As incomes in some parts of the world rose and paid vacations became more common, people began to leave their homes in predictable rhythms to go to the seaside or the mountains. By 1970, two weeks of paid leave was a standard legal requirement across Europe. In Norway, Sweden, Denmark, and France, workers had three weeks. In Finland, workers had a minimum of four weeks, and these state-mandated vacations were often further extended by company- or industry-wide collective bargaining agreements. By the 2010s, as vacation time was extended, only six countries in the world still lacked mandated paid leave: Gambia, India, Kiribati, Pakistan, Sri Lanka—and the USA.[155] Yet even there, most employers granted some time off to workers.

At first, travel was particularly popular among white-collar workers with substantial and growing disposable incomes. By 1956, about 45 percent of all German white-collar workers vacationed for at least five days each year.[156] At the same time, a stunning 83 percent of German survey respondents believed that vacations were "a legitimate consumer good," anticipating the travel boom among this and other countries' working class.[157] By the 1960s, vacations became not just a rite of passage but a social right.

Increased vacation travel was a result of rising incomes (and technological innovations, including the railroad, the automobile, and the airplane), but it was also the one moment in the year for workers to regain some power to structure their lives and control the rhythms of their day, free from the alienation that accompanied highly regimented regimes.

As a result, the industry exploded. Worldwide, tourism grew from 25 million arrivals (overnight visitors) in 1950 to over 200 million by 1975 and to 1.4 billion in 2018, a growth of fifty-six times in not quite seventy years. The vast majority of these tourists vacationed in Europe, with the Caribbean a distant second choice. Much of this growth was the result of travel becoming more affordable. The price-adjusted cost of a typical Mediterranean vacation for the average British tourist plummeted by more than 20 percent between 1966 and 1972, becoming equal to about 76 percent of the average British male wage earner's monthly salary.[158] The impressive growth of this industry popularized the belief that tourism could serve as a "panacea" for countries across the globe. In 1966, the United Nations Conference on Trade and Development (UNCTAD) released a recommendation that member countries promote tourism. Finally, the UN declared 1967 the "International Tourism Year" (eight years before declaring the first "International Women's Year").[159]

The state became deeply involved, as it did with all twentieth-century commodity frontiers. Airports needed to be built, rural cultivators removed from their land, and energy systems shaped. The administrators of the Marshall Plan even got involved, eyeing the possibility that tourism could create entirely new markets in Europe's rural peripheries, allowing middle-class American consumers to par-

	1950	1960	1975
AFRICA	0.5 MILLION	0.8 MILLION	4.7 MILLION
AMERICAS	7.5 MILLION	16.7 MILLION	50 MILLION
ASIA & PACIFIC	0.2 MILLION	0.9 MILLION	10.2 MILLION
EUROPE	16.8 MILLION	50.4 MILLION	153.9 MILLION
MIDDLE EAST	0.2 MILLION	0.6 MILLION	3.5 MILLION

International tourist arrivals per year by region.

ticipate in the reconstruction of European economies through their vacation dollars.[160]

Private-capital investment in tourism grew as well. Some of today's major tourism conglomerates entered the field in the postwar era, including the US's Marriott International in 1957, Germany's TUI in 1968, and a predecessor to France's Accor in 1967. Both TUI and Marriott shifted from other industries (Ruhr Valley coal mining and root beer, respectively) once tourism's growth prospects became apparent. Such large companies could also recast the very mechanisms of travel: Package tours emerged as one of the prime ways that people vacationed. Touropa, founded in Munich in 1951, allowed customers to choose their destination, then organized every aspect of the journey, in the process inserting larger companies into a business that had been largely dominated by small operators—hotels, restaurants, and so on. The popularity of package tours grew substantially during the 1950s and 1960s, not least because they came at a relatively low price. Touropa offered an all-inclusive nine-day trip to Germany for 141 marks in 1956 (at the time, about 70 percent of an average monthly salary).[161]

As a result of these large-scale state and business investments, tourism increasingly came to resemble the world of Fordist production that its customers sought to escape: massive cookie-cutter

New commodity frontiers: tourism in the spring of 1959.

hotels; "*spiagge organizzate*" (organized beaches), as the Italians still call them; and large groups of visitors herded efficiently through the key sights of (mostly European) civilization. While nineteenth-century travelers could be compared to artisans, the late twentieth-century traveler was more like an assembly-line worker.

Unlike other industries, the postwar tourism industry was highly seasonal, concentrated around vacation times like Christmas and summer break, the latter of which became, in many countries, a season almost as deeply rooted as a religious holiday. The French tellingly characterize the end of their summer holiday season as "the return." Tourism centered around the warm, sunny coastal regions of destination countries. Just like its sugar, cotton, and copper antecedents, it drew heavily on local ecological resources, such as water, energy, and land. Energy consumption and traffic would reach new peaks during the high season, then plummet for the rest of the year. Local infrastructure had to meet the needs of the peak population, even if that level of demand was only present for a few months of the year. In much of the world, tourist season began to resemble harvest season in agriculture—intense but short. As fishing villages turned into megaresorts and cities became open-air museums almost uninhabitable for the people living there, the tourism commodity frontier proved to be as transformative as its predecessors.

Spain was one of the countries that experienced this most dramatically. Prior to World War II, tourism was nearly nonexistent there, but by 1973, the country had become one of the world's foremost travel destinations. Its relative lack of previous tourism was a blessing in disguise: On its Mediterranean coast, Spain offered balmy weather, beaches, and entertainment but none of the canonical sites of old elite tourism. It was thus open to a complete reinvention by public relations experts.[162]

Take the Balearic Islands, famed for their beaches and resorts. While the number of tourists grew to over 4.3 million by 1973, the local population stood at about 550,000. As it built resorts, the construction sector destroyed much of the islands' agricultural economy, replacing it with shopping districts, hotels, and airport runways. Peasants became construction workers and hotel staff. As historic landscapes gave way to the enormous infrastructural demands of the industry, tourism took a devastating toll on the environment, extracting often scarce resources, such as water, and polluting the land and air.[163]

Even more drastic was the development on the Yucatán coast of southeastern Mexico. In the 1970s, Mexican tourism planners identified a spit of sand that stretched into the Caribbean Sea, uninhabited except for a small Mayan village, as the ideal site for a major resort catering to US tourists. While private companies were initially reluctant to invest in the distant, jungle-covered Yucatán, the governing Institutional Revolutionary Party (PRI) viewed the project as a national priority, seeing the development of beach leisure tourism as too great an economic opportunity to pass up. In 1965, Secretary of Tourism Antonio Enríquez Savignac had conducted a major study of global tourism, traveling to Florida, the Caribbean, and other beach destinations that had become popular in the prior decade. Savignac then traveled Mexico's six thousand miles of coastline, gathering statistics on climate, rainfall, hurricane and tidal patterns, socioeconomic development, and even possible supply routes and pests.[164] He was looking for the perfect location to build a resort. As *The New York Times* reported, "In one place, sharks meant an immediate negative vote; in another, cannibal ants moving down from the mountains and devouring everything in their path sent the investigators scurrying."[165] The data pointed to Cancún.

It was quite a feat to turn a stretch of almost uninhabited jungle into one of the world's mega tourist destinations. The state paved the way. At first there was a significant public investment of 142 million Mexican pesos drawn from the 1969 budget; this was accompanied by a private-sector investment of 192.5 million Mexican pesos. As on the sugar and cotton commodity frontiers of previous centuries, one of the keys to success was the mobilization of cheap labor. Initial investments spurred construction, creating primarily low-skilled jobs. But few workers could be recruited locally. A census in 1969 had counted merely 117 local Mayan inhabitants in all the nearby villages. Developers thus recruited workers from neighboring states, initiating migration waves of campesinos turned construction workers who attempted to live in the surrounding forests and in nearby Puerto Juárez.[166] Ongoing processes of migration and proletarianization had once again merged with the dynamics of a new commodity frontier.

The tourism frontier spread ever farther: The descendants of Europe's aristocracy began to open their castles and châteaus to paying guests. In Barbados, in the wake of the abolition of slavery, many freedpeople had been forced to continue working on the plantations or otherwise face eviction. The only available plots of land that were not cultivated as part of plantations were on the parts of the island that were least valuable to the sugar planters—the coastal areas. Almost two centuries later, when beachfront properties turned into the only real assets of value on the island, the descendants of former slaves were pushed off their land once again, with harsh property tax assessments making it almost impossible for them to hold on to their properties. In the Dominican Republic, beaches that had previously been almost worthless rapidly became commodified. The bodies of the descendants of local peasants became commodified, too, as sex work that catered to tourists became one of the most promising options for impoverished young women and men. And tourism kept capturing ever new spaces: By the 1980s, the Dominican Republic had completely reshaped its economy, shifting from the production of agricultural commodities such as sugar, coffee, bananas, and tobacco to tourism. Cheap fossil fuels and the income gains of the golden age meant that Europeans and North Americans could travel long distances to vacation in faraway locales. As stretches of coastal territory transformed into hotels, beach clubs, golf courses, and airports, usually constructed with international capital, former plantation lands were supplanted by mega tourist enclaves. In these places, almost everything was for sale, but because the most profitable parts of the business were controlled by foreign companies, profit opportunities for locals often remained limited. Resorts, like special economic zones, remained insulated from the host society. As elsewhere, this went along with a massive shift away from agricultural work. While 60 percent of Dominicans pursued agricultural labor in 1960, just 18 percent did in 2000.[167]

DURING CAPITALISM'S GOLDEN age, commodification spread to other realms of life as well. Even something as basic as preparing food—a human activity since time immemorial and one that was deeply embedded within household and community structures—increasingly moved into the market. The task of preparing food shifted increasingly into factories and specialized facilities—restaurants. For centuries, of course, wealthy people had looked to others to prepare their food. They had hired or enslaved cooks and servants, and those segments of the nineteenth-century bourgeoisie who could not afford to hire staff for their homes frequented restaurants. Establishments for consuming food outside the home were commonplace long before the twentieth century, and even "restaurants" (albeit mostly just serving soup) had already emerged in late eighteenth-century France.[168] Yet almost all people in all regions of the world—even once they began acquiring food in markets instead of growing it themselves—relied on household labor, usually women's, for the preparation of meals.

After World War II, this began changing in select regions of the world. The United States was pathbreaking: In 1949, Albert and Meyer Bernstein founded Frozen Dinners, Inc., in Pittsburgh, providing frozen dinners on aluminum trays. Using cheap, heat-conductive containers made out of lightweight metal that had previously been used in weapons manufacturing, the Bernstein brothers cooked up something new: ready-made meals that could be quickly heated and served. In their first year, they sold more than 400,000 frozen dinners; five years later, more than 2.5 million. In 1953, Swanson began marketing prepackaged meals, also advertised as "TV dinners." These meals could remain frozen for weeks, then be heated in minutes and eaten in front of the TV with far less effort than preparing meals from

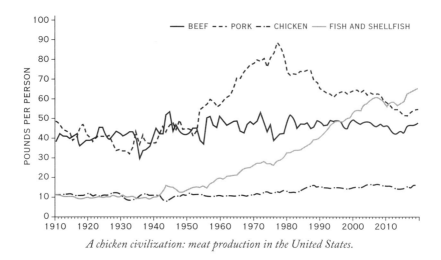

A chicken civilization: meat production in the United States.

scratch. In a society obsessed with convenience and leisure time, and in an economy where women's workplace participation was growing (and thus their time spent homemaking gradually decreasing), Swanson sold some 25 million TV dinners in 1954 alone.[169] Canned and frozen foods also became more popular as they enabled home cooks to economize on meal preparation.

At the same time, people increasingly ate meals outside the home. This was partly related to the rise of the automobile as drivers sought familiar foods along roads far from home. "America the beautiful, let me sing of thee," *New York Times* writer Ada Louise Huxtable bitingly commented in 1971, "Burger King and Dairy Queen from sea to shining sea."[170] One fast-food restaurant's affordability caught the attention of consumers like no other: McDonald's. Its "All-American Meal" (burger, fries, and a milkshake) cost forty-five cents in 1960, the equivalent of about forty minutes of paid labor for the average American worker. It all started in 1948, when Dick and Maurice McDonald transformed their restaurant into a hamburger stand with a small menu of standard-fare foods and a rationalized system of service efficiency they dubbed the "Speedee Service System." They streamlined the menu, removed waiters, and resorted to single-use paper tableware.[171]

Frontier capitalist Richard "Dick" McDonald eating the fifty billionth McDonald's hamburger, 1984.

Under the leadership of Ray Kroc, McDonald's focused on making its products efficiently and reliably. As Kroc said, "We put the hamburger on the assembly line."[172] Setting an influential precedent, McDonald's franchised its restaurants and trained staff at an institution it called Hamburger University.[173] There were 7 McDonald's restaurants in 1955 but 1,500 fifteen years later.[174] By 1973, they were joined by 30,000 pizza franchises, 104,000 franchised restaurants selling hot dogs and roast beef (including burgers), and 14,000 selling Mexican food.[175] These inexpensive chain restaurants applied Fordist reengineering to meal preparation and spread globally during the golden age: Dairy Queen opened its first location in Canada in 1953, followed by KFC in 1959. KFC opened in Britain in 1964, in Germany and Australia in 1968, and in Japan in 1970. McDonald's set up a formal International Division in 1969 and opened its first establishment in Moscow in 1990—the final nail in the coffin of the Soviet Union and international communism.[176]

By 1983, fast-food restaurants made up 40 percent of restaurants in the United States, and Americans spent 40 percent of their food budget eating out three to four times a week on average.[177] Dining at restaurants was a symbol of the economic and social opportunities of the postwar order. For working-class Americans (the dominant market for these restaurants), eating out represented an end to previous decades

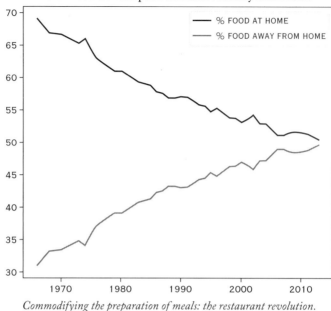

U.S. Food Consumption at Home vs. Away from Home

— % FOOD AT HOME
— % FOOD AWAY FROM HOME

Commodifying the preparation of meals: the restaurant revolution.

of scarcity and rationing and an ability to demonstrate one's wealth by consuming meat.

While this change may have been motivated in part by the increasing participation of women in the workforce, food advertising still targeted women as the "chef" of the household. The KFC ad slogan, for example, told consumers that "Colonel Sanders is a woman's best friend. . . . [He] fixes Sunday dinner seven days a week. For weary wives. For working women. All you do is pick it up."[178]

At the height of the golden years, observers in Europe and North America had no cause to think they could end. As late as 1972, the United Nations reported that "there is no special reason to doubt that the underlying trends of growth in the early and middle 1970s will continue much as in the 1960s."[179]

They did not. Tensions emerged as early as the mid-1960s and

Wife-savers

Colonel Sanders is a woman's best friend. The Colonel's the man who fixes Sunday dinner seven days a week. For weary wives. For working women. All you do is pick it up. Boxes, buckets and barrels full of finger lickin' good chicken and all the trimmings. It's ready to go in minutes at over 1700 locations. Colonel Sanders' Kentucky Fried Chicken . . . mother's little helper. "It's finger lickin' good."

COLONEL SANDERS' RECIPE
Kentucky Fried Chicken.

Commodification as emancipation.

bubbled to the surface by the 1970s. That decade brought crisis, not triumph, to the capitalist heartland and to the peculiar political economy that had characterized it since 1945. Not only did the golden years end, but so did the whole order of industrial capitalism that had risen since the 1870s. The 1970s were no mere blip—they were an epochal break in capitalism's history.[180]

The signs of the coming crisis were at first scattered and ambiguous. Contemporaries read them mostly as hiccups, short disruptions of a fundamentally ongoing pattern. Perhaps it was the number and wide dispersal of signs that proved telling in retrospect. Economic growth decelerated. Productivity advances slackened. Profitability decreased. Basic inputs became much pricier as an emboldened Global South sought its share of the fabulous expansion of human productivity, testifying in a roundabout way to how crucial the Global South's cheap inputs had been to the golden years in the first place. Economic downturns became deeper and more persistent for the first time since the 1930s. The United States economy, the world's largest, shrank in real terms by 2 percent in 1974 and by close to 3 percent in 1975. Companies there and elsewhere started to shut down or shrink their workforces. The core industries of the entire edifice of industrial capital—steel, mining, and automobiles—declined dramatically in the industrial heartland. Unemployment rose. Global economic hierarchies destabilized as many US companies lost their once towering position, and the United States recorded trade deficits every year from 1976 on. There and elsewhere, profits declined.

Influential economist Herbert Giersch diagnosed "a compression of profits and weakness in investments" as the root causes of the crisis. International competition squeezed profits even more—Hong Kong textile workers, for example, worked for drastically lower wages than their European and US counterparts. Economists have found that in the United States, the share of profits in national output declined by about one-third.[181] Still, despite these signs that the golden years had tarnished, many contemporaries believed that some minor adjustments could hold things together.

It is easier to see the depth of the multifaceted global crisis in retrospect. One factor was the weakening of the golden age's institutional scaffolding. The Bretton Woods system had limited cross-border capital flows through what has been called "cooperative decentralization," allowing nations to defend their independent monetary systems against destabilizing inflows or outflows of capital. Beginning in 1958, unregulated and rapidly expanding markets for dollar-denominated financial assets traded in Europe, so-called Eurodollar markets, undermining the stability of that system. They emerged in London, fed first by Soviet oil dollars and then by Middle Eastern oil profits. As these markets grew by a factor of almost ninety from 1959 to 1973, they pressured the system that stabilized the global economy—the cooperative control of capital flows and the semifixed exchange rates agreed upon at Bretton Woods in 1944.[182]

The lofty position of the US dollar was further felled by the Vietnam War, which created enormous inflationary pressures, especially after US president Johnson financed a decisive escalation of the war in 1965/66 with deficits. Expansive US monetary and fiscal policies had created a global dollar glut, dollars that were increasingly not backed by adequate US gold reserves, which led to a weakening of the dollar as both individuals and governments speculated against it. The US balance of payments deteriorated at the same time, leading to significant gold outflows. As Western Europe, especially Germany, and Japan produced growing trade surpluses, it was no longer a certainty that their dollar balances could be converted to gold at the official rate, or at all. France converted much of its dollar reserves into gold, further weakening the system. After 1969, Germany floated the mark freely. As the United States failed to cut its spending or raise interest rates, Germany and Japan, both of which exercised greater monetary and fiscal constraints, offered more attractive returns for their mark and yen bonds. The dollar came under even more pressure.[183]

By the late 1960s and early 1970s, Bretton Woods was becoming unsustainable. Economists and policymakers, who had previously largely opposed flexible exchange rates, now advocated for them. Large US banks also demanded the liberalization of capital markets, seeing the crisis as an opportunity. They became particularly influential once Richard Nixon assumed the US presidency in 1969.[184]

It was in this snowballing crisis that the United States moved away from some of the institutional foundations of the golden age. On August 15, 1971, President Richard Nixon suspended the dollar's convertibility into gold, a move that toppled a core pillar of Bretton Woods and inaugurated a new global regime of flexible exchange rates. And because the fixed-exchange-rate regime had been based on limiting international capital flows, the end of fixed exchange rates meant that the cooperative control of capital flows under Bretton Woods also began to wither away. International financial markets grew spectacularly in size, bringing greater volatility in currency markets and new pressures on monetary stability in many countries. The end of Bretton Woods in effect set the scene for what came to be known as the neoliberal project of a deregulated global market economy.[185]

Longer established than Bretton Woods, the New Deal order now came under immense stress as well, thanks to a supply crisis in the industrial world's most important input—oil. Cheap oil had been one of the foundations of its stability after World War II. When the price of oil suddenly shot up in October 1973, it reverberated across the world. There were two stages to what came to be called the oil crisis. When during the Yom Kippur War of 1973 Western powers supported Israel, the Organization of Arab Petroleum Exporting Countries (OAPEC) reduced oil production and cut off oil deliveries to the United States (and later also to the Netherlands and Portugal). Price hikes by the Organization of Petroleum Exporting Countries (OPEC) followed. Cumulatively, oil prices quadrupled in less than three months. The promise of indefinite economic growth in the industrial heartland, driven by cheap fossil fuels and the marginalization of raw material producers, suddenly rang hollow.[186]

The oil crisis, also remembered as the "oil revolution" in the Global South for its promise to redistribute some of the world's wealth, was a turning point, the first time that a group of countries from the Global South used their control over an essential raw material to shift the global economy's basic structure. OPEC had been founded in 1960, initially bringing together Venezuela, Iran, Iraq, Saudi Arabia, and Kuwait, which were soon joined by the United Arab Emirates, Qatar, Ecuador, Indonesia, Nigeria, Algeria, and Libya. By building new solidarities, the resource-rich countries of the Global South attained a more powerful voice not just in their own affairs but also in the affairs of the world economy at large. Two centuries earlier, the war capitalist order, as we have seen, was challenged from the periphery, from places like Saint-Domingue. The periphery was now destabilizing the industrial capitalist order, with its energy intensity becoming its Achilles' heel. Even though some European powers, particularly France, turned to nuclear energy, price hikes accelerated inflationary pressures. The 1973 oil price increase alone resulted in the flow of $70 billion in US dollars from oil-consuming to oil-producing countries.[187]

For the Global South, it seemed for the first time that the national development projects of the 1950s and 1960s might lead to a meaningful recasting of global economic hierarchies. Oil-exporting countries made a fortune, though they recycled much of their new revenues into purchasing military hardware.[188] Elsewhere in the Global South, however, the oil crisis ultimately had a devastating impact: The increase in the price of energy set oil-importing countries on a trajectory toward ever higher debt. Already in mid-1974, the US State Department noted the coming "Impact of the Energy Crisis on LDC [Less Developed Countries'] Balance of Payment" and predicted severe shocks. In Senegal, "[t]he petroleum bill is expected to rise from approximately $23 million to $76 million, an increase equal to one quarter of the national budget."[189]

Oil-exporting countries, in turn, increasingly sought outlets for their massive wealth in global financial markets. After the end of the embargo, this wealth flowed into the centers of US finance, a trend that accelerated as the United States began massively importing Saudi oil for the first time, while the Saudis agreed to channel their revenues into the US finance sector. Rich in Saudi petrodollars, New York banks funded escalating loans to oil-importing countries in the Global South. The oil crisis set the stage for the global debt crisis of the 1980s, when the IMF forced austerity policies upon debtor countries to rebalance their budgets—diminishing, if not ending, hopes for a realization of the New International Economic Order. And the petrodollars sloshing through the global economy helped fuel what came to be known as "financialization"—the increasing centrality of the finance sector and the intermediation of financial instruments to economic life.[190]

Capital owners also shifted their business strategies to escape some constraints of the golden age and, in the process, further undermined it. They organized themselves in ways that enabled them to dodge the regulatory reach and taxing power of a particular nation-state. Just as the governments became more powerful and more interventionist, new economic spaces emerged that circumvented the golden-age order.

Capitalism had always been global, but now production became increasingly transnational, with a significant impact on the social settlement in the industrial heartland. Throughout the golden years, a small but growing number of companies had begun to loosen their attachments to nation-states. Direct foreign investment in manufacturing grew tenfold. Most notably, American foreign investments exploded. Some of these investments had a long history; IBM's precursor had a presence in Australia as early as 1914 and in China since

1928. Ford had opened plants in Britain in 1911, in Argentina in 1913, in Germany in 1925, and in South Africa in 1923. But such investments became much larger and more common after the war. In 1957, forty-five American companies (including IBM and Newmont Mining) each invested more than $100 million abroad, while twenty-eight hundred other US firms had made more modest but collectively significant foreign investments.[191] As the empires they were once part of crumbled, colonial companies—the British Australian mining company Rio Tinto, the British HSBC (Hong Kong and Shanghai Banking Corporation), and the textile mills of Mulhouse in France—now reinvented themselves as multinationals.

Japanese multinationals were comparatively fewer and moved more slowly in the immediate postwar years, but they, too, embarked on global investments. By 1974, thirty-six of the five hundred largest industrial firms in Japan could be considered multinationals, among them Toray, Teijin, Toyobo, Kanebo, Hitachi, Toshiba, Sanyo, Ajinomoto, Mitsubishi, Matsushita Electric, Nippon Steel, and Nissan Motor. By the early 1970s, Japanese firms were hiring workers to mine copper in Congo, drill for oil in Saudi Arabia, spin cotton in Thailand, assemble televisions in the United States, construct cars in Mexico, and build ships in Brazil. Companies in other countries embraced similar strategies: One of the world's most global companies, shoemaker Bata, had started out in the small Czech town of Zlín in 1894. Bata had production and sales outlets all over the world by the 1920s, and by the 1980s, now headquartered in Canada, it produced and sold shoes in ninety countries and employed a staggering eighty-eight thousand workers. In similar fashion, by the 1970s, the German car manufacturer Volkswagen had production facilities in Brazil, Mexico, South Africa, Australia, Indonesia, and Nigeria—and by 1975, 37 percent of its cars came from such non-German assembly lines.[192]

In the 1970s, that trend accelerated. In a prescient 1977 analysis, three German social scientists—Folker Fröbel, Jürgen Heinrichs, and Otto Kreye—chronicled what they called the "new international division of labor." Their exhaustive analysis of the German textile and clothing industry showed how an ever increasing number of firms during the preceding decade had moved their production to low-wage locations in the Global South. Enabled by the addition of massive numbers of potential workers from the global countryside, new transport and communication technologies, and an ability to break production processes into ever smaller and potentially geographically dispersed constituent parts, entrepreneurs had fled high-wage, highly regulated regions. Competitive pressures accelerated, at first tentatively, then everywhere. Manufacturers abandoned the industrial heartland for the Global South, where they hired young women (90 percent of the workforce was female), a move so significant that the authors considered it an entirely new phase in the history of capitalism. Wages were lower, workdays were longer, a seemingly endless number of potential workers were available, and employment was insecure. The government of Malaysia, in an effort to attract international capital, emphasized the "manual dexterity" of the "oriental female": Her stamina and her speed, they boasted, made her an efficient worker for "bench-assembly production."[193] Such export-oriented manufacturing increasingly replaced raw material exports in the Global South and generated a worldwide reorganization of production. The one-hundred-year honeymoon between the nation-state and national capital ended in a (conditional) divorce during the 1970s. Not that the state no longer mattered—it did—but capital moved into the enviable position of being able to pick "its" state from an ever increasing number of locations competing to host it. There was now a world market as much for production locations as for labor power.[194]

Such relocations challenged the production model that had been foundational to the postwar order: Fordism. The mass-production, mass-consumption nexus of high wages, stable employment, and generous benefits was undermined from the outside and weakened from the inside.[195] As the system unraveled, scholars tried to understand why and how this sea change had occurred: For a group of French scholars who called themselves the "regulation school," Fordism as a particular mode of regulation within capitalism had come into a crisis so deep that it could not replicate itself.[196] Others claimed that a "Kondratiev wave" (a particular long economic cycle driven by a particular set of technologies) had come to an end and was waiting to be replaced by a new paradigm.[197] Prominent US sociologist Daniel Bell argued that capitalism had entered a radically new moment, its "postindustrial" phase.[198] (This assessment was spectacularly wrong, considering that the world was on the verge of the most intense wave of industrialization ever.) Scholars sought ways out of the crisis, with American social scientists Michael J. Piore and Charles Sabel celebrating what they called "flexible specialization," exemplified by the small, high-quality, high-skilled, high-pay firms that dotted the countryside of Tuscany, among other places.[199] Others saw the future in a rebirth of Joseph Schumpeter's heroic entrepreneurs (his writings became fashionable again), while still others saw a vaguely defined "Toyotism"—a more flexible form of mass production—as the future.[200] But no matter what reforms and futures were imagined, the old Fordist order was done.

It was not just production that relocated but capital itself. It moved to where its further production (i.e., its accumulation) was cheaper (fewer taxes) and less regulated (more options). One of the distinguishing characteristics of the twentieth century was, as we have seen, for governments to restrict capital—by taxing it, regulating its forms, and limiting its mobility. The multiplication of jurisdictions following decolonialization offered an escape from these costs and regulations. Jurisdictions known as tax havens had emerged after World War I, just as some countries introduced income taxes (for example, in Switzerland). As historian Vanessa Ogle has shown, these jurisdictions multiplied after World War II, when tax havens including the Cayman Islands, the Bahamas, the British Virgin Islands, Hong Kong, Singapore, and Malta emerged, often set up to facilitate the removal of investments from decolonizing parts of the world without subjecting future returns to the high-taxation regimes that had emerged in the industrial heartlands. Kleinwort Benson, the London investment bank, created Bahamian discretionary trusts as a vehicle to avoid tax liabilities. With this institutional structure and expertise in place, experts managed a rapid increase in offshoring during the 1970s and beyond. The massive amounts of capital that accumulated in these places allowed for further financialization, as the money circulating was not bound to any specific physical assets—it chased the highest return wherever and in whatever industry seemed most promising. By 2014, about $7.6 trillion in US dollars, or 8 percent of total global financial assets, were legally domiciled in tax havens. Once more, it was not ever greater homogeneity but ever greater difference that propelled global capitalism.[201]

Tax havens, the exhaustion of Fordism, and the new international division of labor all contributed to economic malaise in the industrial heartland—undermining government's tax base by furthering tax competition and undermining the high-wage economies by facilitating cheaper imports from low-wage countries. The islands of the golden age, after all, remained connected to the sea. And then came unemployment. In France, unemployment rose from 2.23 percent in 1970 to 5.16 percent in 1979; in Germany, it was less than 1 percent in 1970 but almost 5 percent in 1975. In the United States, in early 1970, it

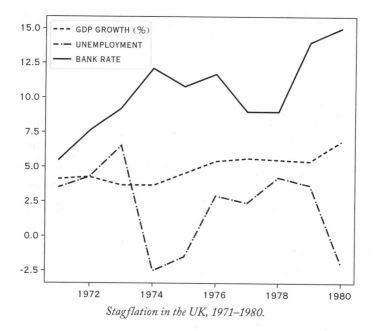

Stagflation in the UK, 1971–1980.

hovered around 4 percent; by 1975, it had reached 9 percent. At the same time, and against reigning economic orthodoxy, inflation rose as well. In 1970, the inflation rates in France, Germany, the US, and Italy were 5.6, 3.0, 6.2, and 4.3 percent, respectively. In 1975, they had risen to 14.5 percent in France, 6 percent in Germany, 11.8 percent in the United States, and 24.1 percent in Italy. In Japan, inflation increased from 6.1 percent in 1971 to 11.8 percent in 1975.[202]

The significant rise of inflation and unemployment surprised many economists. They dubbed this unexpected amalgam "stagflation." A portmanteau of *stagnation* and *inflation*, the word *stagflation* describes a world in which there is high unemployment, high inflation, and slow economic growth. It was probably the British Conservative MP Iain Macleod who coined the term as early as in November 1965.[203] In September 1970, *Time* magazine published an article giving a US perspective on "Britain's struggle with stagflation." The journalist reported that Britain was once again falling into one of its "periodic economic crises that made the country the chronic invalid of Europe." In the first quarter of 1970, the country's real output had decreased by 1 percent, while between January and September 1970, retail prices had increased by 7.7 percent. To add to this, from January to July, basic wage rates had risen by 9.9 percent.[204]

In September 1970, it was possible to see stagflation as a British problem. As the 1970s unfolded, however, it became clear that stagflation was a Western problem. Inflation had started to accelerate in the United States in the late 1960s, when debt-financed expenditures for the Vietnam War and social expenditures increased at the same time. The term began to be deployed more widely by economists, policy-makers, politicians, and journalists, with use of the word in English-language books peaking in the early 1980s. It challenged mainstream economic thinking, as the Keynesian-endorsed Phillips curve suggested that when unemployment increased, inflation would decrease. In the 1970s, it did not. When economists tried to understand stagflation's causes, they listed the oil price shock and a decrease in productivity advances among its potential causes.[205]

Throughout the industrial heartlands, inflation had different impacts on different groups of people, provoking powerful political responses—not least because inflation was particularly bad for investors who owned financial assets, as their value declined. Workers, by contrast, were less affected if their powerful unions negotiated appropriate wage increases (as they often had), while working-class and middle-class homeowners directly benefited from inflation, as the share of their income going to their mortgages declined.[206] This differentiated impact of inflation testified again to the power of organized labor in the context of the golden years. Politically conservative investment banker George Gilder went so far as to argue that inflation was a "war against wealth."[207] Arthur Burns, chairman of the Federal Reserve, concurred wholeheartedly and called for "difficult adjustments."[208]

The emerging crisis soon spread to the Global South. As oil-importing countries faced rapidly rising energy bills, they took on escalating amounts of debt to supply their people and businesses with fossil fuels. The first hit were exporters of metals that required energy-intensive refining. Jamaica's bauxite industry, for example, suffered as American and European demand for aluminum fell, putting pressure on Prime Minister Michael Manley's social improvement programs. The country received a loan from the IMF under stringent conditions in 1977, but it also turned to commodity trading firms for relief. The Swiss metals trader Marc Rich arranged for an emergency shipment of three hundred thousand barrels of oil for the Caribbean nation. He also loaned the Jamaican government money to buy out the ailing Alcoa bauxite plant in 1985, obtaining in return exclusive rights to the plant's aluminum for just 9.25 percent of the price it fetched in London, a deal negotiated directly with the Jamaican government. Zaire faced a similar crisis after global demand for copper slumped amid the oil crisis. It turned to the IMF for dollars and was forced to reprivatize its nationalized mining companies, lay off workers, and increase taxes on its farmers.[209] The age of nationalizations had come to a sordid end in fire sales.

Dollars could be had, but when interest rates rose astronomically in the wake of Federal Reserve chairman Paul Volcker's decision to increase interest rates to fight inflation (what came to be known as the Volcker Shock), the house of cards that had sustained these desperate efforts fell apart. By 1982, at least forty countries were in arrears on their debt payments, and US banks became reluctant to roll over the debt. Costa Rica, Nicaragua, Honduras, Argentina, Brazil, and El Salvador all faced default. Over the course of IMF-led restructuring, the GDP across South America fell by 9 percent per capita, and inequality skyrocketed. The crisis was most severe in Mexico, which suspended debt payments and entered negotiations with the IMF and a consortium of banks in 1982. Oil-exporting Mexico suffered from both the drastic drop in the price of oil following the Volcker measures and the new tight monetary conditions. By 1986, Mexico's GNP still remained at 1982 levels. In exchange for a bailout in 1985, it was forced to lay off twenty thousand civil servants.[210] Even though colonialism had largely ended by the 1980s (and in Mexico, it had ended almost two centuries earlier), the disparities of global capitalism still weakened many states to such a degree that they had almost no room to maneuver.

I n addition to these strident tensions within the golden-age order, there were also multiple rebellions against its core tenets. As we saw when we looked at the emergence of industrial capitalism more than a century before, the shape-shifting of global capitalism was always conditioned, and even propelled, by popular and elite rebellions. So, too, with the trente glorieuses.

Some of these rebellions came from capital owners. Deeply dissatisfied with the institutional constraints that embedded liberalism had created—labor's powerful position, a vastly expanded scale and scope of the state, and the constraints of the international order, with its assertive decolonizing states and expanding sphere of communist influence—they quit the social compact of the postwar years. In the early 1970s, increasingly squeezed by rising wages, sharpening competition (and thus the inability to increase prices), heavy investments in ill-performing but spatially fixed assets, and inflation (which cut the value of their funds), they rebelled. The crucial indicator, perhaps, was profits: As wages grew faster than productivity, profits fell. In the period between 1969 and 1973, wages in the United States rose twice as fast as productivity, not least thanks to the power of organized labor. In Europe, productivity expanded by 4.2 percent and wages rose by 5 percent; in Japan, by 7.8 and 10.6 percent, respectively.[211]

In this situation, and despite being a group whose mentalities and inclinations had been schooled in competing with one another, businesspeople showed an impressive ability to act collectively. Of course, there were entrepreneurs who had always rejected the institutional order that emerged in the industrial heartland after 1945, but they had been a distinct minority, pushed to the margins by powerful social and political forces. In the US, among the business community, early opposition to the New Deal order and to the Keynesian political economy had come from the National Association of Manufacturers, the Foundation for Economic Education, and the American Enterprise Institute, but these voices had been drowned out by the supporters of the institutional framework of the postwar years.[212] In the United Kingdom, the Institute of Economic Affairs, established in 1955, had kept anti-Keynesianism alive, while in France, the Association de la Libre Enterprise (ALE) had sprung into action in 1947 with the support of the Centre National du Patronat Français (CNPF), "defending and . . . recommending freedom of enterprise."[213]

These business groups had connected to (and financed) a group of equally marginal intellectuals, most of them economists, whose long-term project was undermining the institutional arrangements of the golden age. They had organized into a rather obscure but global group: the Mont Pèlerin Society, named after a Swiss mountain range in whose shadow they met in 1947 on the initiative of an Austrian-born utopian economist by the name of Friedrich Hayek. Throughout the 1950s and 1960s, they agitated against the "Road to Serfdom"—the welfare state, the accommodation of labor, the economic nationalism of the decolonized countries, and the international regulatory institutions agreed upon at Bretton Woods.[214]

These marginal but well-funded voices went from being ideologically pure but politically inconsequential to providing the ideological underpinnings of the rebellion of capital owners that began unfolding in the industrial heartland in the 1970s. They railed against the critical pillars of the golden age. Currencies should float freely. The welfare state should be cut back. Unions had to be weakened, returns on capital increased, wages and inflation reduced. Perhaps most important, the economy had to be insulated from what these thinkers considered political meddling, and the economic nationalism of the New International Economic Order variety had to be ended. The Mont Pèlerinites understood that theirs was a radical project that would generate political pushback, but they were ready to engage in battle. For *Business Week*, the direction in which to move was clear in 1974: "[I]t will be a hard pill for many Americans to swallow—the idea of doing with less so that big business can have more."[215]

To get traction for their project, capital owners and neoliberal intellectuals engaged in concerted collective action, both nationally and across borders. In the United States, in 1972, they created the Business Roundtable, organizing significant sectors of the US business community to agitate against the New Deal order. Corporate political action committees (PACs) became yet further vehicles of business political mobilization. The founding of think tanks followed suit: among many others, the Heritage Foundation in 1973, the Cato Institute in 1977, and the Manhattan Institute in 1978. While they focused on slightly different themes and embraced different political strategies, they all agreed on the need to recast the American (and global) political economy. And they were all funded by wealthy capital owners. In Britain, a similar development took place. In 1974, with the support of businesspeople, activists created the Centre for Policy Studies; in 1967, a group of businessmen supportive of "free enterprise" came together to form the Industrial Policy Group; and then, in 1977, they established the Adam Smith Institute."[216]

Less often remarked upon but nonetheless crucial, capital owners in the Global South also increasingly bridled at their subordinate position in their own countries, which, while initially useful in gaining the ability to emancipate themselves from European colonialism, now palpably limited their ambitions. In 1956, to cite a very early example, Indian capital owners' discontent with government economic policies resulted in entrepreneur Ardeshir Darabshaw Shroff founding the Forum of Free Enterprise.[217] It campaigned to "educate the public about the mistaken policy of the ruling party and to satisfy the country that the attempt to establish a Socialist State is not calculated to serve the best interests of the hundreds of millions inhabiting this country."[218] A few years later, a number of Parsi and Gujarati businessmen, most prominently the Tatas, chose to challenge the Indian National Congress from the outside, helping to launch and support the Swatantra Party, which focused on opposing the "socialistic pattern undertaken by the Congress since the mid-1950s."[219] "The business of the State is not business but Government," its manifesto read.[220] J. R. D. Tata expressed these attitudes forcefully in August 1968:

> In fact, the only fearsome concentration of economic power that exists today, lies in the hands of our Ministers, Planners and Government officials. It is that concentration of economic power which is the real threat to our democracy. It is the economic power wielded by those gentlemen and not by industrialists which causes the agonising delays, the misconceived policies and the mismanagement from which our economy has suffered for so long.[221]

Such sentiments, while far from being universal among businesspeople, spread through the Global South to eventually create a politically powerful group of capital-owning activists who sought new ways to shape their worlds. In Chile, for example, segments of that country's business community increasingly came to oppose the national developmental state, especially the left-wing tilt of Chilean politics in the 1960s and early 1970s. Intellectuals and capital owners such as Álvaro Saieh and Agustín Edwards built an institutional infrastructure to oppose the reigning economic nationalism, such as the Center for Social and Economic Studies (CESEC) in 1963 and the Naval Brotherhood of the South Pacific in 1968. They agitated within the business community and moved into broader political activism after Salvador Allende's election as president. Eventually, the so-called Monday Club became a nucleus from which Chilean economic elites sought to overthrow Allende.[222] Even in socialist Tanzania, business owners began raising their voices against the old order. When businesspeople met in the capital of Dar es Salaam on October 8, 1977 (their first meeting since 1967), they complained about difficulties in accessing foreign exchange, political meddling in managerial decision-making, and the "overprotection" of workers.[223] The rebellion of capital owners had become global.

Such rebellions unfolded in national frameworks but had a transnational thrust that unlocked powerful new solidarities. Historically, as we have seen, capital owners had oscillated between nationalism and transnational class solidarities; the history of the French and German iron and steel industrialists dramatically illustrates this tension. The anti-Keynesian mobilization clearly appealed to global class solidarities—their fundamental impetus was to push back the nation-state. Expressing this cosmopolitan spirit, they increasingly forged their rebellions within a global network of institutions. Regular meetings (since 1971) of the World Economic Forum at Davos became opportunities to elaborate global positions and politics. Neoliberal think tanks closely cooperated across the world. Business schools began to have global reach, and their alumni networks fostered global solidarities. At the same time, older organizations that had tried to elaborate global class positions since the 1920s, such as the International Chamber of Commerce, a "world parliament of business," gained a new lease on life. Focused on free trade and the rights of multinational corporations, it agitated against the New International Economic Order espoused by many leaders in the Global South. Connecting businessmen with an intelligentsia, this coalition eventually launched a frontal attack against golden-age capitalism.[224]

As FORCEFUL AS these elite insurgencies were, they probably would have failed if they had not intersected with other, more popular rebellions. These rebellions focused on three of the central pillars of the golden age: the gendered division of labor, national and global racial hierarchies, and industrial capitalism's environmental impact. Together, they further undermined the golden-age order, even though their visions for the future were not in sync with those of rebellious business elites; indeed, they were radically different.

Let us look at these rebellions in turn. First, gender. As we saw when we looked at Sweden, the golden age was built on a rigid gendered division of labor. But even as this order solidified, it proved brittle. In Sweden, as the number of "housewives" (as they were then called) reached a historic peak, intellectuals and activists pushed against these constraints. In 1961, twenty-nine-year-old Eva Moberg published an essay titled "Kvinnans villkorliga frigivning" ("The conditional liberation of women"). Drawing inspiration from Simone de Beauvoir's *Le deuxième sexe* (*The Second Sex*), published in 1949 to global acclaim, Moberg asserted that men and women had an equal moral obligation to their children. Although the demand for female workers could be seen as an opportunity for emancipation, Moberg cautioned her readers that this emancipation forced women to take on double responsibilities. Women could become breadwinners, but they were still raising the children and keeping the house. The current situation had to end, Moberg contended, as "the most generous offer society has to give women is to be slaves in their homes and tricked into believing that they are doing their natural duty."[225] Instead, according to Moberg, everyone needed to abandon the notion that women should have two roles and realize that "both men and women have only one role: being human." "The *human role* includes," she wrote, "as a necessity and a moral duty but also as a rich asset, a delightful experience and much more, taking good care of the offspring."[226] Those who failed to recognize this fact, she argued, should know they were part of the reason why women would never be fully emancipated but, rather, only ever "on parole."[227]

Moberg proposed that marriage as an institution of provisioning should be abolished.[228]

Moberg's polemic struck a nerve in Sweden. Newspaper editors accused her of attacking not the patriarchy but housewives and other women by supposedly denying them their right to choose a homemaking life. Moberg's critics argued that women, because of their nature, would rather care for their families than work outside the home.[229]

But the debate did not go away. Just the opposite.[230] It moved into the political realm. Toward the end of the 1960s, the Swedish Social Democratic party, the SAP, adopted Moberg's idea of two parents having equal family responsibilities and provided a collective solution: a further expansion of the public sector, opening more day-care centers, which in turn meant more jobs for women.

Moberg's writings were on the very early edge of so-called second-wave feminism—the first wave being the suffrage mobilizations at the turn of the century. With new fervor, women challenged traditional gender divisions of labor. In economist Giandomenica Becchio's summary, the full spectrum of second-wave feminists shared two critiques of golden-age capitalism: "men's dominance" in the "cultural, economic, and political sphere" and the idea that "sexual differences had generated strict gender social roles within both private and public life."[231] They challenged sex discrimination, called attention to the unpaid work done by women in the home, and problematized welfare-state policies that privileged the male-breadwinner family structure. A segment of the movement, radical feminism, rejected bureaucrat-led state structures and emphasized the importance of nonhierarchical democratic bodies for consciousness raising and bringing about change. Some second-wave activists were liberal; others favored socialism because they saw gendered hierarchies as integral to capitalism.[232]

Inspired by these ideas, feminists took to the political stage as well. The National Organization for Women (NOW), founded in the United States in 1966, called for breaking down barriers for women's full participation in national life. In 1970, it organized a Women's Equality Strike, demanding "free abortion on demand, free 24-hour child-care centers and equal opportunity in jobs and education."[233] As many as fifty thousand people marched through New York City in support of its cause. In Iceland, a national "day off" was declared by feminists in October 1975, with 90 percent of women participating, compelling the country's parliament to pass equal-rights legislation less than twelve months later. British women founded the London Women's Liberation Workshop in 1969, the same year that their Italian counterparts created the highly influential Rivolta Femminile, followed by a campaign for wages for housework by Lotta Femminista in 1972. French women created the Mouvement de Libération des Femmes (MLF) in 1970. Many of these activists also moved into publishing, with a Florence-based collective of women creating the feminist magazine *Rosa* in 1973 and West German activist Alice Schwarzer founding *EMMA*, a feminist journal, in 1977.[234] Britain saw the founding of Virago Press in 1973 and the Women's Press in 1977.

Such political mobilizations also encouraged theoretical reflection among a group of feminist scholars thinking about economic life more broadly and golden-age capitalism in particular. Not all of them were economists—indeed, Keynesian and neoliberal economists had backed themselves into an analytical corner that made it difficult for them to see the role of the nonmarket in economic life, so they excluded such considerations, and such related scholarship, from their deliberations. When economist Cecilia Conrad searched the comprehensive EconLit database for the terms *gender, women, female,* and *sex,* she could locate only 22 articles (out of 15,970) for the 1950s, 48 articles (out of 26,698) for the 1960s, and 476 (out of 62,525) for the 1970s. Even by that last-mentioned decade, only 0.7 percent of all economics articles even mentioned gender.[235] Moreover, the voices of feminist economists were often marginalized within the profession—just as the voices of Caribbean scholars had been sidelined in the debates on early capitalism. Yet their contributions to understanding economic life, even if unrecognized by the discipline itself, were among the most important in twentieth-century economic thought.

With the shortcomings of mainstream understandings so evident and their real-life implications so clear, feminist economics found traction in the context of second-wave feminism, emerging partly from a critique of an earlier field of "household economics" and partly from a new field, women's studies. Feminist scholars challenged neoclassical economics. Their critique began with the economics of the household and labor markets. Mainstream models were unable to explain the persistence of wage discrimination and the power dynamics within the household. Soon the critique spread to macroeconomics, international trade, development, and the feminization of poverty—namely, that women everywhere faced a much greater likelihood than men of living in poverty. Ultimately, feminist economics extended to all traditions of economic analysis.[236]

Second-wave feminism made possible the rise of feminist economics by drawing attention to and stimulating interest in the gender pay gap and the small number of women economists who were studying such gendered phenomena. Scholars such as Barbara Bergmann (and her 1986 book, *The Economic Emergence of Women*), Nancy Folbre, Claudia Goldin, and Paula England—to name just a few US scholars—became central actors in the field.[237]

Among these scholars' most important contributions was the recognition of the household as an important economic sphere, a notion that went straight back to ancient Greek conceptions of *oikonomos*—the management of the household. As these feminist economists asked new questions, they delivered a devastating blow to some of the fundamental concepts underlying mainstream economics. Most basically, as we have seen, since the 1930s, efforts to statistically capture economic activity (through the construction of the GNP) had focused exclusively on economic activities that surfaced in markets. Feminist scholars demonstrated, however, that much economic activity, even in the world's most developed countries, took place outside the market—principally in households. For sociologist Maria Mies, "the role of domestic labour

```
Fac-Similé de la 4ème couverture des Cahiers du GRIF
         n° 2 1974 - Transédition Bruxelles


                    P R I X   D '  U N E   F E M M E


Femme de ménage    :   60 heures par mois à 65 FB .........    3.900 FB
Cuisinière         :   60 heures par mois à 100 FB ........    6.000 FB
Serveuse           :   40 heures par mois à 42,50 FB ......    1.700 FB
Bonne d'enfants    :   182 heures par mois à 48,50 FB .....    8.827 FB
Répétitrice        :   40 heures à 200 FB .................    8.000 FB
Blanchisseuse      :   26 kg de linge par mois ............      676 FB
Repasseuse         :   .................................       1.315 FB
Couturière         :   12 heures à 57 FB .................      684 FB
Infirmière         :   4 heures à 61 FB ..................      244 FB

                                                          -----------

                 .... et j'en passe !....   Au total   31.346 FB

Si on ajoute       :   plaisir sexuel : 1/4 d'heure par jour
                       en moyenne, à 500 FB (prix moyen d'une
                       prostituée) ........................  15.000 FB
                                                          -----------

Soit au total, en gros, par mois .....................    46.346 FB


              Calculé par le M.L.F. (Paris)
```

"Why value domestic work?" within the capitalist family and society was decisive for my understanding of capitalism," and indeed, she titled one of her essays "Women: The Last Colony."[238] Other feminist scholars showed that as late as 1981, a minimum of one-third of French economic activity took place in households, much of it undertaken by women outside the market—a staggering number. Women's unpaid work was hugely important to economic life, but it was omitted from the fundamental statistical tools developed by male economists and thus made invisible.[239]

Rebellions spread to other sectors of society as well, further undermining the golden-age order. Importantly, resistance against racial hierarchies sharpened. In the United States, the civil rights movement demanded economic justice and the inclusion of African Americans within the golden-age order.[240] It brought an end to segregation in the southern states and to Black disenfranchisement. African American demands for economic justice and growing calls for government action exposed deep fissures within the New Deal order, challenging the privileges of white Americans not just in the South but also from Boston to Los Angeles (and within the ranks of organized labor). Immigrants in Europe mobilized for inclusion at the same time. In the small country of Belgium alone, migrants formed the Association des Travailleurs Marocains en Belgique (ATMB), the Fédération des Associations de Solidarité avec les Travailleurs Immigrés (FASTI), and many others.

Inspired in no small part by the courageous mobilizations of civil rights activists, the student movement of the 1960s congealed into what has been called the "New Left." They formulated still another radical critique of golden-age capitalism. When American student radicals assembled at Port Huron in Michigan in 1962, they railed against what they considered the complacency produced by prosperity, a society that had left them with "unfulfilled capacities for reason, freedom, and love."[241] Attacking the giant bureaucratic machine of the university, Berkeley students pronounced that "I will not be folded, spindled, or mutilated," a play on the DO NOT FOLD, SPINDLE, OR MU-TILATE punch cards that fed data into computers at the time.[242] In December 1964, Mario Savio, one of the key figures of the Berkeley Free Speech Movement, spoke the memorable lines: "There is a time when the operation of the machine becomes so odious, makes you so sick at heart that you can't take part! You can't even passively take part! And you've got to put your bodies upon the gears and upon the wheels . . . upon the levers, upon all the apparatus, and you've got to make it stop! And you've got to indicate to the people who run it, to the people who own it, that unless you're free, the machine will be prevented from working at all!"[243] In Britain, students at the University of Essex formed the Socialist Society and published a pamphlet that drew upon Savio's speech, asserting that "we don't want to be trained to be new parts in an old machine."[244] They claimed that government, university administrators, and businessmen "merely want a flow of ready-made technologists, managers and teachers with which to perpetuate our capitalist system."[245] And in May 1968, massive student rallies and mass strikes in France grew into an insurrection unparalleled in the postwar "overdeveloped world."[246] After students occupied the Sorbonne, strikes flared through the country, with around three to six million participants, combining a critique of imperialism with a critique of the very society that the golden age had produced: "Beneath the pavement, the beach," they wrote.[247] Some such critiques emerging from student protests would later be picked up by capital owners who attacked the new golden-age order in terms of human freedom as well.

Last but not least, the earlier discussed critiques of the environmental impact of the golden age increasingly translated into political mobilizations. In the US, middle-class women and men campaigned for environmental protections against pollution (air, water, and now, in the nuclear era, radioactive), pesticide use, and urban sprawl. Soon an environmental justice movement emerged calling attention to the disparate impact of pollutants on poor and nonwhite communities and demanding stricter environmental regulations. Further, in Japan and throughout Western Europe, environmental groups started to mobilize in the mid-1960s to combat rapidly rising levels of environmental degradation—in the process offering a grim critique of the resource-hungry golden age as such.[248]

By 1977, the sense that an old world was collapsing had become pronounced. Even in Sweden, growth and redistribution ran out of steam as inflationary pressures continued, and workers began to oppose the constant flexibility (in terms of changing jobs) that this model asked of them. They began engaging in wildcat strikes. To keep workers engaged, both the unions and the SAP radicalized their programs, with the Riksdag passing a series of laws that enhanced the power of workers' voices in nonwage workplace issues. In 1975, the unions adopted the economist Rudolf Meidner's proposal to gradually expand workers' collective ownership of businesses through "wage-earner funds," a proposal that alarmed the business community.[249] As Swedish industry faced these pressures in the context of a more challenging international environment, employers began to push back. Export industrialists led the charge against higher wages, first by taking a harder stance nationally, then by coaxing smaller unions away from the national bargaining table. At this point, even the Swedish industrialist

Wallenberg family, whose members had accommodated themselves and profited handsomely from the golden age, moved away from the SAP and their cautious embrace of an expanding welfare state. In 1983, the Association of Engineering Employers signed a deal with the Metalworkers' Union outside the national wage compact. By the early 1990s, national bargaining had been abandoned in almost all sectors. Social policies increasingly started to be depicted as expenses that must be avoided.[250]

As Fourastié convincingly argued, the previous thirty years had seen some of the most significant economic changes in human history. But in Sweden and elsewhere, it was clear by the late 1970s that the glorious golden age had ended. Despite all the intellectuals and politicians of the 1950s and 1960s claiming that capitalism had entered a permanent new phase, that extraordinary moment, like all the others in capitalism's long history, passed. And as the trente glorieuses ended, capitalism's institutional order was once again up for grabs.[251]

Part IV

The Future of Capitalism?

Larry Gonick, cover art for the book Hypercapitalism
by Larry Gonick and Tim Kasser.

17.

Riding the Tiger:
A Neoliberal Age,
1973–2008

Freedom restored with an iron fist:
Augusto Pinochet (seated).

In the fall of 1974, a staff member of the US embassy in Santiago de Chile sat down to read a report on the current state of Chilean economic policy, most probably written by his colleague Samuel F. Hart. Just fifteen months prior, a bloody military coup had brought a junta to power and unleashed a wave of terror on members of the previous government, labor activists, and intellectuals. Global condemnations rained down on the new regime for the blatantly undemocratic seizure of government and the severe human-rights violations that went with it. While the report mentioned myriad criticisms of the regime's neoliberal economic policy—that it favored the rich, impoverished the working class, and made things hard for Chile's middle class—the writer discounted these criticisms, insisting that the policies "have been aimed in the right direction." The only problem, as he saw it, was that they should have come sooner, and that the government might "abandon or relax austerity needlessly." Yet largely thanks to the "many local economists trained in a pragmatic stream of economics (many in US universities)," he remained hopeful that the junta's "basically correct" approach would be maintained.[1]

His anonymous embassy reader was not convinced. With a sense of the risks of this novel form of political economy that the junta had begun building—fears rooted in the sensibilities of the golden age—he attached a note to the report: "One wonders if so much of the austerity medicine might not kill the patient." He added, "I find the report a sophisticated rationalization for all-out US economic support for the Junta, and damn the (political, social) consequences. I don't want to live in Sam's economist paradise."[2]

Yet large swaths of the world came to live "in Sam's economist paradise." The coup in Chile was but an early overthrow of golden-age capitalism, a rehearsal for a reconstruction of gargantuan scope and dazzling speed in which both the import-substitution development policies of the Global South and the labor-centric Keynesianism of stabilization and redistribution of the industrial heartland came under sustained attack. The changes eventually leapt into the industrial heartland as well, accelerated by the rapid decline of the islands of postcapitalism that had emerged in places like Russia and Eastern Europe in the previous half century. By the 1980s, the once exotic neoliberal project had become mainstream; by the 1990s, it dominated most of the world's political economies. Chile was in the vanguard of this latest shape-shifting of global capitalism. That it arrived under authoritarian auspices was no accident: As the US embassy staffer had noted, most of the world's people, given a choice, preferred not to live under such a regime.[3]

Chile's military junta took power on September 11, 1973, with a spectacle of tanks, battalions, and even aerial bombardment of the presidential palace. It ousted the democratically elected president, Salvador Allende, a Social Democrat who governed in a coalition with forces to his left. The previous years had been full of political and economic turmoil. Important sectors of the economy had been nationalized, labor-friendly legislation had improved the conditions of urban workers and the poor, and agrarian reforms had been launched. But these accomplishments had gone hand in hand with spiraling inflation and a foreign-exchange crisis worsened by US "financial pressures" intended to cut Chile off from global credit flows. The "basic policy objective," argued US diplomats, was "to prevent the consolidation of the Allende regime"—a project that succeeded.[4]

The Allende government that so concerned the United States had radicalized many economic policies of previous decades, but it had not invented them out of whole cloth. Like Chile's Latin American counterparts and much of the Global South, the country had embraced economic nationalism since the 1930s, motivated by a desire for domestic industrialization, a program that the US had supported at various moments and in various places. The most important sector of the Chilean economy, then and now, was copper, much of it mined by US companies, especially the Anaconda Copper Mining Company of New York. By the 1960s, the mines produced 80 percent of the value of Chile's exports and were entrenched in the world economy as one of the most important sources for a crucial raw material of the Second Industrial Revolution. Intense labor conflict characterized the industry, and calls to nationalize the mines had emerged as early as the 1950s. By 1965, Christian Democratic president Eduardo Frei had toyed with the idea of nationalizing them in hopes of pacifying labor relations and giving Chile greater control of its copper. Even Anaconda had resigned itself to nationalization with compensation. Allende won the election in September 1970, and in 1971, with the enthusiastic support of the company's twelve thousand workers, the Chilean state took over the mines.[5]

It was the radicalization of this long history of economic nationalism during the Allende years that brought opposing forces to the fore, not just in the military but among businesspeople and intellectuals as well. Among their leaders was Agustín Edwards Eastman, the owner of Chile's most important opposition newspaper—*El Mercurio*—whose relentless anti-Allende propaganda, though homegrown in inspiration, received its financing from the CIA. They also included Hernán Cubillos, a former naval officer who went into business before becoming one of the organizers of the coup against Allende. This amalgam of opposition forces made plans for a recast political economy that broke not just with Allende but with Chile's long history of economic nationalism, or what the US embassy in Santiago called "45 years of pervasive government control" under right-wing, Christian Democratic, and Social Democratic governments.[6]

The US embassy in Santiago floated the idea of a possible "successor government" just days before the coup, but plans for the recasting of the Chilean political economy had already been formulated in amazing detail. One embassy memo aimed at reassuring American leaders noted that

> [s]everal groups of non-Marxist Chileans are presently studying the type of economic measures they believe would be necessary to start rehabilitating the Chilean economy, if and when political conditions should change. The economists, principally from the University of Chile and the Catholic University, have been giving advice to the National Party, the PDC and (we are reliably told) to certain members of the Chilean military. Their proposals follow generally orthodox lines with some modifications for the Chilean context. . . . In brief, they are thinking in terms of an orthodox stabilization plan, in which market forces would reduce consumption, increase investment, stimulate production and exports, and discourage imports.[7]

The plan that the US embassy referred to was known as *El ladrillo*—the Brick—a voluminous study that detailed a neoliberal reform agenda for Chile. The document had emerged from discussions between economists and business leaders over many years, even decades, and it was an almost fantastic, certainly utopian, blueprint for an improbable Chilean future. Even before it moved to the center of Chilean policymaking in September 1973, the US embassy was aware of its risks—namely, the potential social turmoil that these radical reforms would generate. "Any successor government," the embassy told its superiors in Washington, "would probably be forced in one way or another to reduce consumption. Since the lower income groups have benefited relatively most under the UP [Allende's Unidad Popular] and they make up such a large proportion of the population, that would be the logical place for much of the belt-tightening to occur." But "how could it be done? Would the bottom of Chile's economic pyramid accept such measures without a brutal fight? If the market were allowed once again to allocate resources, this would tend to redistribute income along the traditional patterns in Chile and away from UP supporters. . . . How can a successor government remedy this while at the same time reducing real wages?" The answer was as forceful as it was surprising: "Considering the constraints confronting any future government, an orthodox economic stabilization program could only be put into effect by a very strong government." Such a "strong government," the embassy continued, "might imply a military regime." As a result, "[t]he trade-off might become democracy against sound economic measures."[8]

"Sound economic measures" won out: When the junta took power in September 1973, it swiftly launched the country into a radically new kind of political economy. Years later, Chile, that "long petal of sea and wine and snow," as poet Pablo Neruda longingly called it, would be recognized as a crucial launching pad for a global neoliberal revolution.[9] Augusto Pinochet, a sunglasses-wearing strongman who had little love for even the most basic human-rights protections, became its unexpected prophet—the Lenin of neoliberalism.

THE FIRST STEP the new military government took was to move decisively and brutally against one of the crucial pillars of the golden age—Chile's entrenched labor movement. The junta's "caravan of death" traveled the country to imprison, torture, disappear, and execute real or perceived enemies on the left. When the labor attaché of the US embassy in Santiago visited the three largest copper mines in May 1974 to meet with managers and workers, his chronicle made for depressing reading: "There are widespread reports," he said, speaking of just one mine, "of executions of twenty-seven employees (most of whom reportedly were workers)." Strikes were declared illegal. Even the cultural icons of the labor movement found themselves in the crosshairs of the junta, which arrested, intimidated, and even murdered cultural figures such as Neruda and folk singer Víctor Jara.[10]

With its leading enemies silenced, the Chilean neoliberal revolution unfolded in stages. In its first, "gradualist phase," which lasted until 1975, there was still a division between reformers who wanted to go slow and a group of neoliberal economists who wanted to move fast. But the groups agreed on privatizing nationalized businesses, phasing out price controls, drastically reducing public expenditures, lengthening the workweek, liberalizing foreign investments, and lowering tariffs. Already by 1974, unskilled workers' real income had been halved. The government returned one hundred and fifty nationalized businesses to their owners, including nineteen US-owned companies. Compensation payments were agreed upon with US copper mine owners. The new government also promised to honor its debt obligations. "[B]loated workforces are being trimmed," reported the US embassy.[11] The "[c]ivilian economists" at the helm of policymaking—people such as Fernando Léniz, minister of the economy, Jorge Cauas, finance minister, and Raúl Sáez, minister of economic coordination ("world-renowned economists," according to the junta's meeting minutes)— held austerity as their North Star.[12] But they kept some safeguards in place: Wage policy continued to be adjusted to the exceedingly high inflation, and Allende-era price controls and even subsidies remained on a small but critical range of twenty-three commodities, as the junta feared that removing them would spark social unrest.[13]

Despite the persistence of this handful of Allende-era measures, the US embassy saw the Chileans' policy—rightly—as "pathbreaking." They noted that "no previous government has had the political will or power to put [such policies] into effect."[14] The junta had effectively ended the post-Depression-era import-substitution development strategy. US trade with Chile sharply expanded, and foreign loans again flowed into Chile. According to the US embassy, in just the last three months of 1973, $157.5 million in US dollars were provided by, among others, Bank of America, Manufacturers Hanover Trust, and Fidelity.[15] These funds were amplified by moneys from the IMF, the Export-Import Bank of the US, and USAID.[16] On October 5, 1973, just a few weeks after the coup, Ambassador Nathaniel Davis sent this hopeful memorandum to Washington:

> A group of orthodox economists, mostly trained at the University of Chicago, are trying to convince Chile's military government to adopt a package of measures designed to accelerate the country's economic growth through use of free market forces, rational monetary and fiscal policies, economic decentralization, and the promotion of domestic and foreign investment. The plan was drawn up before September 11 and has the advantage of being the only comprehensive set of policies recently before the military. Most of these young Technocrats are now in influential advisory posts.[17]

Perhaps prematurely, Davis celebrated that "civilian economic advisors to the Junta believe that their short-term and medium-term proposals have been completely adopted."[18]

Economists had been influential in Chilean policymaking since the 1930s—an outcome of the Keynesian reorientation that promoted the state's management of the economy, with economic experts playing a leading role. The early years of the junta were an extreme example of this tendency. But now, instead of Keynesians, it was a new brand of self-described "neoliberals" who called the shots. In Chile, they came to be known as the Chicagos, or the Chicago Boys, because they had studied in the United States under the auspices of the US State

Department with funding from the Ford and Rockefeller Foundations.[19] In the Windy City on Lake Michigan, Milton Friedman and his colleagues had fed the Chileans a diet of calls for privatization, tight fiscal policies, deregulation, and a limited state. And even though US policymaking in 1973 was certainly not Friedmanite, Samuel F. Hart of the US embassy, likely the "Sam" behind the prophetic memo cited earlier, recalled years later that he felt at home with this new breed of economists: "I spent endless, endless days with these people. We developed a symbiotic relationship."[20] Their "yearn[ing] for an economic revolution" enjoyed widespread support among not just this small group of economists but also Chilean business elites and fractions of the military.[21]

While it is true that the Chicago Boys were strongly influenced by foreign ideas, it would be wrong to see Chilean neoliberalism as an entirely foreign import. All key actors were Chilean, and their policies reflected decades-old, sometimes highly local frustrations with the dominant Latin American struggles to find a foothold in the global economy. Starting in the 1960s, a neoliberal right had begun emerging in the region, with a network of intellectuals, foundations, and research centers, among them the Centro de Productividad in Montevideo, the Instituto de Pesquisas e Estudos Sociais in Brazil, the Centro de Documentación Económico-Social in Peru, and the Adolfo Ibáñez Foundation in Chile. These homegrown tendencies intersected with international developments, as important links had been forged and payments made: The German Hanns Seidel and Ludwig Erhard Foundations supported some of the Chilean initiatives, as did the United States by granting moneys to scholars at the Universidad Católica de Chile.[22]

As the junta stabilized and the push from neoliberal networks intensified, economic policies became ever more radical. By 1975, opponents of "shock policies," disproportionally represented by the military, lost control of most economic policymaking to the Chicago Boys, while the government was driven to radicalization by seemingly intractable inflation that plagued its initial gradualist program. "Applied neoliberalism" became a reality. In April 1975 (with inflation still at 70 percent), Finance Minister Cauas announced the National Recovery Plan, which cut government expenditures by 15 to 25 percent, increased openness to international competition, and privatized another five hundred or so businesses. Technocrats such as Cauas feared traditional Chilean conservatives who favored highly protected domestic industries almost as much as they feared the left, and they were determined to outmaneuver any moves toward a restoration of the pre-Allende status quo.[23]

Their position was further consolidated at the end of 1976 and early 1977, when economist Sergio de Castro was appointed as economy and finance minister and Chile withdrew from the Andean Pact, allowing it to reduce import tariffs even further and end the import-substitution policies of the previous four decades. Heavily protected industries like textiles fell apart under import pressures (almost half of all textile factories were bankrupt by the early 1980s), while industries in the export sector, especially agriculture, expanded. Inflation fell but still remained stubbornly high. Further structural changes followed: Social security schemes were privatized, and the education system was reformed, allowing for private investments and giving parents vouchers to send their children to schools of their choice, a key neoliberal policy initiative that would later spread to other parts of the world as well. Even earlier, in 1979, the Plan Laboral had banned storied Chilean unions and empowered employers. At the same time, the Indigenous Mapuche were encouraged to privatize their collective lands, in the hope that this would undo ancient communitarian organizations of economic life that seemed counter to the new order.[24]

These neoliberal policies had devastating social effects on large segments of Chilean society. As prices rose and real wages fell, huge new inequalities and mass poverty took hold—an allegedly necessary price to pay to fight inflation. Unemployment reached close to 20 percent in 1975. Many Chileans faced a drastic drop in their standard of living.[25] In March 1974, a confidential US diplomatic memorandum admitted that "[c]ertainly the *poblaciónes* are in a period of genuine suffering economically, and unquestionably they are seething with bitter frustration."[26] Also that month, US Ambassador to Chile David H. Popper predicted "a very difficult winter ahead. Some of the Conservatives to whom I am talking recognize that things must be difficult in the *poblaciónes*, but I wouldn't call them models of compassion. There is still a great deal of rancor—'They turned the screws on us, and now by God we'll show them.'"[27] But, he noticed with relief, "[s]ince [the] principal labor confederation has been abolished, and collective bargaining and [the] right to strike suspended, major means which those who might oppose those incomes policies can use to protest have been eliminated."[28] About the opposition among Chileans, the embassy observed that "[b]eing able to rule by decree is a big help in this respect."[29]

While most suffered, some individuals and groups benefited from the widening class divisions within Chilean society. José Piñera helped privatize the Chilean pension system and became wealthy as a consultant on related matters. More broadly, the Chilean economic elite made very real gains: As the US embassy noted, "The return of local trade to established patterns will benefit upper and middle income groups. . . . Poorer people can presently only gaze at the high-priced wares displayed in downtown Santiago and hope for a better day—but this is what austerity is all about."[30] As Hart reminisced decades later:

> The middle class and the upper class suddenly found themselves in heaven. For example, the house I rented, and I could have bought for probably $35,000 during the Allende time, overnight was worth half a million dollars. Overnight. Right after the coup. People who had things that they had collected before and during the Allende time, and who had become poor as the Allende policies hit hard on the middle class, suddenly found themselves at least partially restored. They were able to buy from the Chilean government, at bargain-basement prices, businesses that had been taken over by Allende. There were tremendous economic opportunities again for the wealthy people.[31]

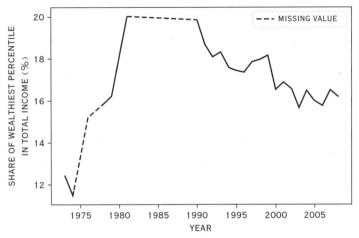

Redistributing income to the wealthiest 1 percent: the effects of the Pinochet regime on Chilean inequality, 1973–2007.

These policies were adjusted over time, but they represented an early and fundamental break with the political economy of the golden age.[32]

As Chile's economic situation improved and inflation declined, the country became a poster child for the possibilities of neoliberal reforms, despite the fact that workers generally did not benefit from the boom. However politically isolated the Pinochet regime was in significant quarters of the world, and however atrocious its human-rights record, it found admirers in a global network of neoliberals who saw in Chile the future they ardently desired.[33] As the world's most influential neoliberal, Friedrich Hayek, put it in 1981: "I personally prefer a liberal dictator to a democratic government lacking liberalism."[34] In 1983, Francisco Orrego, the Chilean ambassador to Britain, observed that Thatcherites and British neoconservatives showed "to some extent political-doctrinaire identification . . . with the Chilean experiment."[35]

From the beginning of the Pinochet regime, neoliberal intellectuals made pilgrimages to Chile to be feted by the junta. Milton Friedman came twice: first in March 1975, when he personally advised Pinochet to reduce "the rate of growth of the money supply" and cut government expenditures, then again in 1981 for a meeting of the Mont Pèlerin Society, where he confirmed that "Chile's government knew how to handle economic and monetary policy according to the soundest economic principles."[36] In 1977, his Chicago colleague Arnold C. Harberger visited Chile to lecture—and to confirm the soundness of the country's postcoup economic policies—with the US embassy emphasizing in its report "the esteem in which Harberger and his University are held in Chile."[37] Hayek came in 1981 and met briefly with the dictator. Chile's Constitution, the "Constitution of Liberty," mirrored the title of Hayek's most influential book, *Constitution of Liberty*, which he had published in 1960.[38]

Lesser luminaries admired the new order as well: When the Chilean government contacted the US-based J. Walter Thompson advertising agency about hiring it to improve Chile's image abroad, Jack Webster of the Buenos Aires office expressed admiration for the junta: "On the economic side—if they manage to carry it out—it will be particularly interesting as we don't think any of us have ever lived in a country where the government didn't meddle with the economy. (Including the U.S.)"[39] He added: "I want Chile to win. It will be a worldwide example of one system against another."[40]

I n 1974, when Webster spoke these words, he could not have imagined that Chile would indeed be in the vanguard of a global political and economic recasting—a reconfiguration that began almost unnoticed in the 1970s, spread throughout the 1980s, and flourished during the 1990s, marking a significant break in the long history of capitalism. The 1970s were a fin de siècle. They stamped the end of the century-long moment that had emerged in the global reconstructions of the 1870s.[41]

But the 1970s were also a beginning: Out of the shell of the old, a new global political economy arose. Some scholars have labeled it a "neoliberal order," others have put it through the lens of "globalization," and still others have seen it as "financialization."[42] Despite the different emphases, they agree that by the 2000s, global capitalism had metamorphosed in ways that would have been unrecognizable to a mid-twentieth-century observer.

Once again, what seemed "solid" had "melt[ed] into air."[43] If the previous century of capitalism's history was marked by massive industrialization in relatively few parts of the world, the decades after the 1970s saw a rapid shift of industry into the Global South in general and Asia in particular. If the century before had been characterized by investments in spatially fixed assets such as steel mills and railroads and the resultant deep link between national capital and national states, the new capitalism still drew on the state but not necessarily on a particular one, as the link between (footloose) capital and nation weakened. And if the century before had been characterized by the dominance of industrial capital, commercial capital, deeply enmeshed with finance, now returned with a vengeance. Not only did capitalism's territorial order shift, but the dominant economic ideas went from golden-age "Keynesian" to "neoliberal"—perhaps best demonstrated by the fact that people were now primarily seen not as citizens but as consumers and investors.[44]

This shape-shifting of capitalism, as before, looked very different in different places and was created by interests and conflicts that were often intensely local. Rebellions of capital owners, workers, and peasants and a wide variety of social movements had destabilized the existing order—locally, regionally, or nationally—in many ways. Yet these conflicts' outcomes, the horizon of their possibilities, and the newly emergent form of capitalism were also determined by the global connections in which they were embedded. As it had been for five centuries, the shape-shifting of the empire of capital was global, with developments in remote corners of the world rippling outward and causing drastic transformations elsewhere. Capitalism may have changed faces, but its dynamic was still propelled by its connected diversity. Despite libraries full of books that bemoaned the homogenization of everything (another feature of the neoliberal era), capital continued to power differentiating forces as well.

The shifting of the world's political economy between 1973 and 2008 was enabled by, and in turn furthered, radical changes to economic life everywhere. From a long-term perspective, this might be the most lasting legacy of those years: the most dramatic wave of industrialization the world had ever seen. Areas remote from the new machine production that had captured the collective imagination as early as 1800 suddenly sprouted massive textile factories, steel mills, auto assembly plants, electronics factories, call centers, and other projects in former rice fields. Millions of peasants entered factories: In 1991, 60 percent of the Chinese workforce labored in agriculture; by 2021, that percentage had fallen to just 24 percent—reflecting a mass exodus into cities, industry, and the service sector, and a massive new wave of rapid proletarianization.[45]

As many more people engaged in production for markets, and as their productivity skyrocketed, industrial output saw unheard-of peaks. In 1973, the world manufactured more than thirty-nine million motor vehicles, but more than seventy-seven million in 2010. In 1986, the worldwide market for semiconductors was around twenty-six billion in US dollars; twenty-four years later, it amounted to almost three hundred billion. In 1973, the world's first cell phone was assembled; in 2010, nearly three hundred million were sold. In 1970, there were but a few hundred bulky, heavy, and costly computers in the world's central nodes of capital and power; in 2010, billions of people owned these technical marvels, many of which were now pocket-size. Medical research made quantum leaps, as did food production. It is likely that humans produced more "stuff" during the lifetimes of many of this book's readers than during all past human generations put together. The exponential increase in human productivity is one of the most notable hallmarks of the age.[46]

CAPITALISM DOMINATED IN entirely new ways. Though it had been centuries since capital left its ancient islands and moved into the hinterlands—into agriculture, manufacturing, and services—a very significant share of the human population had remained largely untouched as late as the 1950s. There were even a growing number of putatively postcapitalist countries, covering about a quarter of the world's landmass and 33 percent of its population.[47] And then there were the hundreds of millions living in subsistence-oriented economies (growing the food they needed and manufacturing much of what they consumed), people whose intersection with anything that could remotely be considered "capitalism" was quite marginal.

By 2008, this world was largely gone—as were almost all postcapitalist countries. At the same time, the logic of endless accumulation infused novel spheres of life with new intensity: Childcare, love, information, and even human organs became subject to an intensified capitalist logic. The state-agnostic forces of financial capital moved into the space so recently vacated by formal colonialism and colonized ever more spheres of human life. In the years after the mid-1970s, perhaps the most significant change was that for the first time ever, capitalism truly dominated economic life on Earth. Not coincidentally and at the same time, the capitalist revolution ever more rapidly undermined the natural conditions for life on Earth.

———

Chile's transformation was ahead of its time, but everywhere, political, ideological, cultural, and, most importantly, economic cracks spread. The golden age had long rested on a settlement between a particular form of capital, a particular kind of working class, and a particular balance of power among capital, labor, and the state. All these arrangements weakened in the 1970s; by the subsequent decade, they were beyond repair. The emerging new face of global capitalism was not just a creation of "neoliberal" ideologues and politicians but a formidable recomposition of capital itself.

Among the most extraordinary changes was the formation of new nodes of capital: Local capital owners and international investors forged new agglomerations of capital in what came to be called the Global South. Building upon the novel nodes of state power that had emerged in the wake of decolonialization, these superclusters of capital powered the world's most significant industrialization ever.[48] In the process, the world's working class expanded at lightning speed.

The Global South, as we have seen throughout this book, had a rich history of commerce, manufacturing, and capital accumulation. Its manufacturing base had expanded after the Great Depression of the 1930s thanks to import-substitution industrialization policies amplified by the economic nationalism of newly decolonized states. During the 1970s and beyond, these departures accelerated in some countries at gravity-defying speed and changed direction: away from import substitution and toward producing for export. At first, the so-called Four Tigers—Korea, Taiwan, Hong Kong, and Singapore—were in the vanguard, but other countries swiftly industrialized as well, including Indonesia, Malaysia, Thailand, Mexico, and Brazil. No part of the world, however, industrialized as quickly and as radically as China. The value of the world's manufacturing output increased almost five times in the years between 1973 and 2008, most of it coming from the Global South, with China contributing a stunning 31.5 percent by 2008. That year, Chinese manufacturing added more value than the whole world had produced in 1973, a time when scholars in the North Atlantic area were convinced that Europe's marked manufacturing prowess gave it an enduring global advantage. In retrospect, the theories they developed then to explain such a divergence seem like dated artifacts, better relegated to the status of a window on Western self-fashioning than to social science analysis.[49]

It is difficult to exaggerate the importance of this shift. While the decades from 1970 to 2008 are often described in the North Atlantic region as an age of "deindustrialization," from a global perspective, this

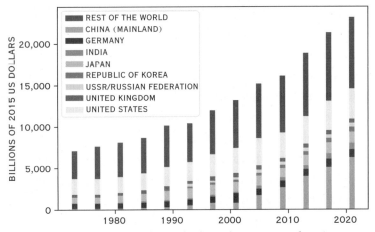

World history's most significant wave of industrialization: manufacturing output by country (in billions of constant 2015 US dollars), 1970–2022.

period marked the most rapid industrialization in history. In the wake of the Industrial Revolution of the 1800s and the new hierarchies it helped produce, Global South exports had been largely limited to raw materials and agricultural commodities—as late as the 1970s, manufactured goods made up less than one-fifth of the Global South's outbound trade. By 2000, these goods made up a stunning 70 percent of exports.[50] While the percentage of the world's population engaged in manufacturing remained stable—about 14 percent—the geographic patterns of where these people worked changed dramatically. In 1973, about 20 percent of the world's manufacturing workers labored in Chinese factories; by 2008, that figure had doubled to more than 40 percent. In parallel, North America and Europe's combined share decreased from about 40 to about 20 percent.[51]

If cities such as Manchester and Detroit had symbolized North Atlantic industrialization, the city of Shenzhen, located in the Pearl River Delta, symbolized Chinese ascendancy. With 314,100 inhabitants in 1979, Shenzhen was adjacent to the British colony of Hong Kong, which, since the 1950s, had been a cheap-labor manufacturing base for textiles, toys, and plastics. There, a novel but also very old economic space was created by the Chinese government: the special economic zone (SEZ). As labor costs in Hong Kong rose, China offered a new institutional framework for international investments, and Hong Kong capital owners (many of whom had emigrated from China after the revolution) found the cheap manufacturing labor they craved across the border. These entrepreneurs built an export-oriented manufacturing industry, first in textiles, then in other sectors. In these companies, more than thirty thousand of which were eventually sanctioned, Hong Kong (and Taiwanese) capital combined with Chinese rural labor to mount an unprecedented challenge to the manufacturing supremacy of the North Atlantic region.[52]

Indeed, the area became the workshop of the world. By 2008, Shenzhen had 9,542,800 inhabitants, or 30.4 times as many residents as nineteen years earlier, making it the fastest-growing city in world history. (By 2021, its population had almost doubled again.) The expansion of the city's economy was equally unprecedented: According to official Chinese figures, the total volume of the city's imports and exports grew 78 times between 1979 and 1985. Between 1980 and 2008, Shenzhen's GDP growth rate averaged 26.9 percent annually, with manufacturing expanding annually by 37.8 percent. By 2008, the city of Shenzhen alone produced goods and services valued at $110 billion in US dollars, roughly equivalent to the GDP of a country like Peru or Slovakia.[53]

In the Pearl River Delta, where Shenzhen is located, industrial output climbed by 21.23 percent annually between 1980 and 1990, while the value of exports increased by 29.28 percent. The success of the labor-intensive textile industry prompted other industries to move there, and the city became a high-tech manufacturing hub as well. In 2003, Samsung relocated its PC manufacturing from South Korea to China, employing a workforce of forty-two thousand. The Taiwanese electronics manufacturer Foxconn moved to Shenzhen in 1988, building a factory that would hire the largest number of workers in world history:[54] Its Longhua Science and Technology Park was dubbed "Foxconn City." Hundreds of thousands of workers (the precise number is not publicly known) labored in the factory. This extraordinary industrialization not only changed the face of China but also made global the horizon of possibilities for capital, as it allowed entrepreneurs to bypass the social settlement that had characterized the golden age in North America, Japan, and Europe; to develop new production strategies embedded within globe-spanning commodity chains; and to give financial capital new powers. In short, it enabled a new form of capitalism—not just in China but worldwide.

While China's rapid industrialization led the world, manufacturing spread to other regions as well—no longer oriented toward import substitution (along the lines of the United States during the 1840s and India during the 1950s) but instead focused on exports. Before China, Indonesia had already catapulted itself into a manufacturing powerhouse: Its industrial output between 1965 and 1996 doubled, on average, every six years, as clothing brands like Nike began contracting work out to Indonesian sweatshops, and investments from Japan, South Korea, and Hong Kong poured in. The manufacturing share of Indonesian exports climbed from 7.4 percent in 1980 to 55.1 percent in 2000; textiles and garments accounted for 15.3 percent of exports in 2000, up from just 0.3 percent in 1980.[55]

Thailand followed suit: Currency devaluation, deregulation of foreign investment, and repression of labor activism, among other policies, allowed it to expand production that relied on low-cost labor. Its exports skyrocketed by 24 percent annually in the second half of the 1980s. By 1995, five million people worked in Thai manufacturing, twice as many as a decade earlier. Beginning in the 1990s, the country moved on to more complex manufacturing processes, especially as a subcontractor for South Korean and Japanese manufacturers. So many Japanese factories moved in that an observer estimated the rate to be one every three days in the early 1990s. The world's chief manufacturer of miniature ball bearings, Minebea (now MinebeaMitsumi), bought out plants in California and New Hampshire in the late 1960s. It then followed its competitors to Singapore in 1972, but rising labor costs there pushed its managers to Thailand, where it opened its first plant in Ayutthaya Province in 1980. "[T]he two greatest selling points," explained one manager to a journalist, "were the generous tax privileges offered by the Board of Investment, and the availability of cheap labor twenty-four hours a day." The expensive machines that the company deployed "should be run twenty-four hours a day. In other countries we couldn't do that."[56] By 1989, 90 percent of Minebea's ball bearings were made in Singapore and Thailand; the manufacturer was Thailand's largest single employer, with fourteen thousand uniformed women working on its assembly lines. And just as more complex manufacturers moved into Thailand, less complex labor-intensive industry shifted to border regions, where undocumented Burmese and Cambodian migrants found precarious employment in garment factories. It was estimated that in 1997, around 10 percent of Thailand's total labor force consisted of undocumented migrants from neighboring countries.[57]

Other countries swung into line: Mexico saw a vast expansion of its maquiladoras, which grew to more than thirty-five hundred plants with almost 1.3 million workers by 2000.[58] US car manufacturers, among others, relocated some of their production south of the border. And there were newly sprung nodes of capital based on newly lucrative exports of raw materials, especially oil. Vast wealth streamed into the Middle East, Nigeria, and a few other countries after the oil price hikes of the 1970s, making them globally significant centers in the empire of capital. Their newfound wealth flowed back into global investments and local development—especially into cities and infrastructure. That rapid development required labor in construction and services and new raw material imports, especially food crops. Cities developed into what Janet Abu-Lughod called "giant vacuum cleaners."[59] Gulf governments built linkages to agricultural regions in places such as Egypt and Sudan, which became known as the "Arab breadbasket."[60] They mobilized labor in Pakistan and India, turning these regions, too, into their hinterlands. Women's reproductive labor in the poorer parts of Asia became crucial to the supply of laborers for these economies—another sign that capitalist expansion's age-old dependence on spheres of life outside its orbit was also accelerating.

As nodes of concentrated capital multiplied, the most remarkable divergence from the Western-dominated "golden age" was the emergence of companies from the Global South as global power brokers. After the 1970s, strengthened by the postcolonial national development policies of the postwar decades, they struck out into the wider world as they encountered limits to further expansion within their national borders. The Gerdau Group, a Brazilian steelmaker that we encountered earlier, became one of Brazil's largest multinationals. The company, which had started out with one plant in Porto Alegre, had expanded in the 1960s within Brazil. It had also benefited greatly from the National Development Plan of the 1970s, doubling in size. By the 1980s, it enjoyed a dominant position in the Brazilian market. Its first international investment was in Uruguay in 1980, followed by efforts to enter the North American market by purchasing a steel mill in Canada in 1989. It acquired production facilities in Chile in 1992, Argentina in 1997, the United States in 1999, Colombia in 2005, Spain and Peru in 2006, Venezuela and the Dominican Republic in 2007, and Mexico and India in 2008. As it internationalized between 1980 and 2014, its steel production increased by a factor of fourteen.[61] By 2010, it was the world's tenth-biggest steel manufacturer.

In a very different industry, a trio of Brazilian businessmen took over Rio de Janeiro's century-old beer-brewing company Brahma in 1989; a decade later, they merged with their main rival, Antarctica from São Paolo, to create Ambev. The firm not only oversaw beer factories but also managed PepsiCo's South American sales. By 2004, when it was Latin America's dominant beverage producer, it merged with Belgian Interbrew to form InBev, the world's largest brewer. In 2008, it purchased the American giant Anheuser-Busch. Other multinationals emerged in the Global South as well: Aramco, the Saudi state-owned oil company, invested in the SsangYong Oil Refining Company (now known as S-Oil) in South Korea and, in 1996, formed its first European joint venture to enable control over the oil commodity chain from oil well to gas pump. In 2000, Tata bought Tetley, the storied British tea group, and also built auto assembly plants in South

Africa and Senegal. Indian pharmaceutical hulk Dr. Reddy's Laboratories purchased its counterparts in Britain in 2002 and acquired a US biotech company in 2004. Alibaba had set up offices in thirteen countries by 2000, with joint ventures in Japan, South Korea, and Taiwan.[62]

Not surprisingly, such rapid industrialization set in motion a proportional wave of proletarianization. By 2008, China's workforce counted almost eight hundred million women and men, 27 percent of whom worked in industry. As they had throughout the history of capitalism, these workers mostly came from the countryside—in 2007, 64.4 percent of those in industry and 33 percent of those in service work had poured in from rural areas.[63]

This rapid mobilization of rural labor for industry was enabled by the loosening of tight restrictions that had previously forced people to remain in the countryside. The Chinese state created a two-tier urban workforce: Those who were officially registered as city residents had access to a broad array of social services. The rest were considered a "temporary population" and excluded from such benefits. In the Pearl River Delta alone, their numbers climbed from 184,000 in 1982 to almost 3 million in 1990. These rural migrants offered factories a cheap pool of precarious labor—in the late 1990s, a worker was paid $.30 (in US currency) an hour in a Chinese textile factory, $2.75 in a Mexican or South Korean one, $5 in Hong Kong and Taiwan, and more than $10 in the United States.[64] As before, the reproductive labor of farmers in general and rural women in particular fueled modern industry as much as did massive agglomerations of capital and modern machinery.

As women had operated spinning machinery in the first wave of industrialization in Lancashire and Lowell, Massachusetts, women were the backbone of early Chinese industrialization too: About 60 percent of migrants were young unmarried women. In 2004, in Shenzhen's light manufacturing sector, about 90 percent of workers were women under the age of twenty-five. They were often referred to as *wailai mei*, "the girls from outside." Sociologist Pun Ngai has cited the example of China Wonder Garments. Here, in 1989, a director from Hong Kong oversaw six hundred workers, most of them women, just as his 1840 counterparts had done in New England. The company provided dormitories located near the factory, with twelve to sixteen workers per room. They were controlled by brassbound regulations: A rule book outlined acceptable behaviors in painful detail, and they were expected to labor fourteen hours a day, sometimes even longer if urgent orders came in.[65]

The ability to escape the confines of village life could be liberating for women, yet conditions in factories were harsh: Work hours were long, pay was low, and working conditions were often dangerous— while supervisors' power over workers remained largely unchecked. Of the 120 million migrant workers from the countryside who labored in Chinese cities in 2004, only 12.5 percent had signed employment contracts. The Chinese state tried to contain the resulting conflicts by extending the law into employment relations, as had happened elsewhere a century earlier, passing the National Labor Law (1994), the Trade Union Law (1992 and 2002), the Labor Contract Law (2007), and the Arbitration Law (2007), but it remained committed to exploiting China's competitive advantage of the moment—extremely low labor costs.[66] And workers, pitted against a seemingly unending supply of eager new recruits into the world of industry, had little power.

Yet the mammoth proletarianizations in the Global South brought an equally massive expansion of labor conflict. As we have seen, violent repression devastated the Chilean labor movement in the early 1970s. In South Africa, workers confronted employers and the apartheid regime with growing vigor but also faced severe government repression. That nation's 1987 Labour Relations Act had limited workers' ability to strike and had even made unions liable for damages due to strikes. In protest, COSATU, the country's largest union federation, called for a general strike, to which 2.5 million workers responded. That strike quickly challenged the general legitimacy of the apartheid regime. Though state retaliation was heavy (Minister for Law and Order Adriaan Vlok had

Striking mine workers holding a meeting in South Africa, 1987.

COSATU's headquarters in Johannesburg bombed by the secret police) and the strike defeated, it still marked the beginning of the end of apartheid.[67]

In South Korea, a massively enlarged working class also faced off against a repressive state bent on attracting foreign capital. The country was among the first to create so-called export-processing zones (EPZs) intended to attract garment manufacturers employing cheap female labor; between 1963 and 1979, the number of women in the industry increased sevenfold, to 1.2 million. Attempting to control this growing industrial workforce became a priority for the Park Chung-hee regime (1961–1979). In January 1970, the government enacted the Provisional Exceptional Law Concerning Labor Unions and the Settlement of Labor Disputes in Foreign-Invested Firms, which severely restricted the activities of unions in EPZs. In November of that year, garment worker Jeon Tae-il protested the dire labor conditions by immolating himself in downtown Seoul. Jeon's suicide initiated a wave of labor unrest. The following year, four hundred technicians occupied the headquarters of Korean Air. The state doubled down on repression: In December, Park seized "permanent" power, declared a national emergency, and implemented the Special Law Regarding National Security, which restricted unions' collective bargaining even further. Unions were tasked with promoting patriotism and labor productivity, not protecting workers. As a result, South Koreans had some of the longest working hours in the world: Ten- to twelve-hour workdays were normal in Korean industry in the 1970s and 1980s.

As these stories reveal, many attempts at labor organizing were quashed by state violence.[68] Nevertheless, they continued: "[T]here was nothing that could scare me," recounted Han Myŏnghŭi, a South Korean union activist, of her time organizing.[69] The late 1980s saw an upswing of labor unrest that turned against the regime, and 1987 is remembered as the year of the "Great Workers' Struggle." From July to September, an average of forty-four labor disputes occurred daily.[70] Here, too, the strikes set in motion the regime's shift to democratization and are thus remembered as a political victory. The long-term economic demands, however, were roundly defeated.

This defeat can be seen most clearly in the deindustrializing pangs of the Busan shoe industry. In the 1980s, shoe manufacturing comprised South Korea's third-most-important export industry after electronics and textiles. At its peak in 1988, Busan's workshops assembled 573 million pairs of shoes for companies like Nike and Reebok. That year, it employed 155,000 workers. Five years later, just over 30,000 jobs remained.[71] In the meantime, companies squeezed their workers for every last hour they could get to counter international competition. One company, Taebong, started a "Work Thirty More Minutes" campaign, demanding half an hour of overtime from its employees. At Taebong,

[a] big wall poster with a slogan of "Let's Die Together, If We Fail to Reach the Production Target" was hung prominently in the shop to add psychological pressure on workers. [Twenty-two-year-old union activist Kwŏn Migyŏng] and several other women workers had to forgo dinner one day because their supervisor kept them on the floor, all the while insulting them with abusive language. Suffering pangs of hunger, they tried to eat bread and tangerines while working, but they were subjected to insults from a supervisor who yelled at them.[72]

In protesting these conditions, Kwŏn died by suicide on company premises. She carried a message with her addressed to "My beloved siblings," movingly pleading that they "do not bury" her "in the icy land of repression but . . . in your bosoms." She "wanted to live like a human being" and demanded: "Do not repress us anymore."[73] Other activists kept up the struggle: A woman worker-activist, Pak Sunhŭi, declared that "[w]e frequented police stations as if they were our houses."[74]

As low-cost manufacturing moved on to the next low-wage frontier under the pressures of trade liberalization, Korean women were increasingly forced into irregular service jobs. The East Asian financial crisis of 1997 initiated another round of assault on labor—and another major moment of resistance, motivated not least by the government's passing of new laws that granted employers more powers to fire workers and hire strikebreaking temps.[75] Three million workers struck for three weeks, forcing the government to amend the laws. Like their counterparts in the Global North, businesspeople in the Global South faced sometimes insurmountable hurdles to gain access to and control the enormous numbers of workers they needed to deploy their capital profitably.

Seen from our end of the long history of capitalism, this new arrangement of the spatial order of the empire of capital, however unstable, was the most significant development of the late twentieth and early twenty-first centuries. As these novel nodes of capital built new connections to other nodes within a vastly extended global hinterland, capital owners in the Global South began to wrest the vital center of capitalism away from the North Atlantic region.

In the process, these new nodes of capital indeed put tremendous pressure on the former industrial heartland, in effect hollowing out the golden age from the outside in. This was the second crucial change in the structure of capital after 1973. If workers in Hong Kong could spin and weave cottons for a fraction of the cost of workers in the Alsatian city of Mulhouse, would capital remain invested in the Alsatian textile industry? If Taiwanese workers could assemble a television for a small percentage of the wages received by workers in Celle, how could Telefunken survive? If millions of displaced rural workers could assemble electronics cheaply in China, would anyone invest in a factory in California? The resulting dislocations were an unwelcome reminder that the core of capitalism was neither a durable national ensemble of businesses, labor, and the state nor a particular set of businesses. It was something completely fungible and now increasingly mobile: capital. And its owners' impetus to multiply it made capital behave almost like a sentient force.

In response, capital owners in the industrial heartland began eroding the social contract that had structured the golden years. Dissatisfied with the burdensome fixed investments that locked them into places where the balance of power was not always in their favor, they looked for greater flexibility. "Flexible accumulation" and "nimble" became fashionable terms in the social sciences to describe this trend.[76] Access to "flexible" labor and "flexible" locations became crucial. With much cheaper transport and telecommunications, manufacturers created ever more extensive networks of production, sourcing parts from multiple locations for final assembly in yet another location—a transformation that has been called the "global value chain revolution."[77] Even some of the most complicated goods of the age were subject to this production reengineering: Toyota reduced its investments in its Japanese home base and began coordinating vast networks of Asian component manufacturers. There was thus a "synergy" (another fashionable word of the age) between Japanese and North Atlantic capital owners' efforts to escape the golden age and the strategies of their counterparts in the Global South to acquire new nodes of accumulation.[78]

This spatial reorganization of manufacturing had drastic implications for the North Atlantic heartland. While the world experienced its most massive wave of industrialization ever, and while manufacturing output everywhere—including in the North Atlantic region—kept increasing in value, large swaths of the industrial heartland saw a decline in many of its storied manufacturing industries and a significant decline in employment in manufacturing.[79]

In some regions, that decline in employment amounted to full-fledged deindustrialization. Even though the IMF announced in 1997 that "deindustrialization is not a negative phenomenon, but a natural consequence of further growth in advanced economies," its social and distributional consequences caused upheaval, undermining the material basis of the golden age in the industrial heartland.[80] In the twenty-three most advanced economies, manufacturing employment decreased from 28 percent of the workforce to 18 percent between 1970 and 1994. In the United States, 28 percent of jobs in 1965 had been in manufacturing; this dropped to just 11.8 percent in 2008. In Japan, manufacturing jobs declined from 27 percent in 1973 to 18.4 percent in 1994; in the European Union (including Norway), from 30 percent in 1970 to 18.3 percent in 2007. Of course, there was some variation: Among OECD member countries, the UK experienced the greatest absolute decline in manufacturing employment, while Germany's fall was quite modest.[81] Yet the trend everywhere was the same.

The American city of Detroit became an example of such deindustrialization. No other place had symbolized the possibilities of mass production and consumption better than the city on Lake Erie, the world's leading site for automobile production since the early twentieth century. A third of all Detroit jobs in 1970 were in manufacturing, dominated by Ford, Chrysler, and GM. Thirty years later, that percentage had fallen to just 18.1 percent, as more than half of all manufacturing jobs had vanished. In the greater Metro Detroit area, almost two hundred thousand manufacturing jobs disappeared between 1970 and 2000. With employers threatening further layoffs without workers' acceptance of wage concessions, the jobs that remained often came with lower pay.[82] The city's decline was so rapid and extreme that it became the favorite site of what has been dubbed "ruin porn"—films depicting the devastations of industrial decline, including *Requiem for Detroit?*, *Detroit Disassembled*, and *Detroit: Ruin of a City*. Eminem, one of the era's most influential musicians, paid homage to "the city that made me" and that like no other seemed to speak to how so many Americans experienced this moment of disillusionment, precarity, and violence:[83] "[Detroit]—I can't never leave this bitch, / Sick of bein' treated like me and shit."[84]

There, as elsewhere, the social consequences of industrial decline were dire: Many Detroit houses stood empty or not at all, demolished by municipal order. Motor City increasingly resembled a bombed-out World War II landscape. Detroit had counted 1.5 million inhabitants in 1970; only 713,000 remained by 2010. As white workers left the city for its suburbs or other parts of the United States, Black workers with fewer opportunities stayed behind, deepening social tensions. Detroit's residents were left with the carcass of a city: Already by 1980, one in two adult men, most of them African Americans, were unemployed. With government assistance inadequate, survival increasingly depended on informal entrepreneurship, much of it illicit, leading to frequent confrontations with the state and the mass incarceration of a de-proletarianized Black working class. Between 1975 and 1997, the prison population in Michigan increased by a factor of four and a half, with most new inmates coming from Detroit. More Black men were in prison than in college. As many as one in five Black men in Detroit were under some form of criminal supervision. By 2013, the city was bankrupt, subject to a "plan of adjustment" that in striking ways echoed the "structural adjustment" plans the IMF and World Bank forced upon many countries in the Global South at the same time.[85]

Manufacturing also changed on the shop floor. New "post-Fordist" production systems increased productivity and lessened the need for workers, with microprocessor-controlled robots taking on much of the labor. Even the assembly line—that great symbol of capitalist modernity throughout the twentieth century—was sometimes abandoned. As early as 1974, Volvo had started replacing some of its assembly lines with stationary assembly to improve working conditions—a seemingly necessary step, as turnover at its Torslandaverken had reached 50 percent annually. Some workers favored such work settings, and by giving car assembly a higher status, this strategy attracted new, more highly qualified, workers. Japanese companies followed suit, then innovated even further: Toyota, for example, perfected what came to be called the "Just-In-Time System," in which inputs arrived at the factory just when they were needed, reducing warehousing costs. This was a production

Postindustrial devastation: Detroit, October 2009.

organizing mode enabled by another new technology—the computer, which would rapidly spread around the world, making production more efficient but also much more vulnerable to supply chain disruptions.[86]

As the spatial organization of capitalism shifted once more, new groups of entrepreneurs came to the fore. While industrial capitalism since the 1870s had been driven by industrialists investing huge amounts of capital into spatially immobile production facilities (steel mills, coal mines), the neoliberal age witnessed the reemergence of merchant capital in general and finance in particular. Entrepreneurs revived their age-old preference for keeping their capital liquid, and not too tightly attached to any one particular physical asset. The entrepreneurial hero of the era was not a steel baron or an automobile magnate but a portfolio investor (epitomized by American Warren Buffett) or a modern-day merchant (typified by Alibaba's Chinese founder, Jack Ma) and Walmart's Walton family.

This fluid capital roamed the globe as insurgent capital owners searched for profitable investment opportunities. Their ambitions, unlike those of, say, steel manufacturing or coal mining firms, were better able to escape the regulatory reach of the much-strengthened state.

According to former US Treasury secretary Lawrence Summers, "[F]inancial markets don't just oil the wheels of economic growth—they are the wheels."[87] Of course, the financialization of assets had a long history; the French Crédit Mobilier of the 1850s had been structured as a kind of investment fund "born from" what it called "an intimate solidarity" of capital.[88] Yet by the 1990s, finance capital was so prevalent that scholars began to speak of the entire period as characterized by "financialization." Financial assets gained a major boost from the new restrictive monetary policy of the late 1970s and early 1980s, also known as the "Volcker Shock," which drove down inflation and drove up asset value. People controlling these assets made money not by manufacturing or by trading physical objects but by buying and selling financial instruments that related to some underlying asset (stocks, bonds, mortgages, raw materials) or to expectations about the future (interest rates, stock market indexes, grain harvests). Technical experts who produced and traded these instruments proliferated, as did companies specializing in their production and sale. In some parts of the world, financial services themselves became an important part of the economy; in the United Kingdom in 2007, these services produced 11 percent of the national GDP, accounted for 20 percent of total profits (quadrupling since the 1960s), and employed roughly 1.2 million people. Investing in financial assets became common not only for countries (such as Norway with its huge sovereign wealth fund) but also for women and men of modest means (such as Americans stashing their retirement savings away in so-called individual retirement accounts, or IRAs).[89]

Entirely new industries emerged as well, none more important than those related to the semiconductor. Based on government-enabled inventions largely related to preparation for war (both semiconductors and the internet were initially designed for military applications), computing became crucial to the neoliberal age—as a source of capital accumulation, as a technology that enabled the global reorganization of production, and as a tool that would allow for the further commodification of life. Companies that focused on computing hardware and software emerged and grew, including IBM, Microsoft, and Apple. IBM introduced the personal computer (PC) in 1981, Microsoft created the MS-DOS operating system in 1983, and Apple released the first Macintosh in 1984. In the mid-1980s, as the US Department of Defense's ARPANET (created in 1969) opened up to civilian users, the internet as we know it was born. At first a communications hub, it evolved into a commercial entity after 1990, when Tim Berners-Lee of CERN in Geneva introduced the URL, HTTP protocols, and HTML formatting and surfing via web browsers—the foundational technology of the World Wide Web. So-called dot-com companies such as Yahoo!, Amazon, and eBay arrived on the scene in the mid-1990s. Internet use exploded rapidly: In 1990, fewer than 2 percent of all Americans used this new technology; by 2004, almost two-thirds did. In 2008, there were an estimated 1.5 billion internet users worldwide; in 2024, 5.5 billion.[90]

As the composition of capital changed, the relationship between capital, territory, and states shifted once more. In the decades after 1870, capital had attached itself to nation-states (or empires) in almost symbiotic ways, and nation-states had tried to enclose capital within their borders to the best of their ability. A century later, capital took flight. Consider the textile industry: Once, huge spinning and weaving concerns had operated in places like Mulhouse, Manchester, and Lowell, Massachusetts. Now, brand-creating merchants like Nike and H&M sourced materials, labor, and production facilities in all corners of the globe to assemble a final product that was also sold all around the world. Should costs rise in China, production could be moved at almost a moment's notice to, say, Vietnam. Manufacturers became subordinates in these production networks, at the mercy of multinationals that were only tenuously rooted anywhere. Hermann Röchling's steel mill was a bulky behemoth that was forever tied to its location in Völklingen, but Adidas could easily redirect its production from contract manufacturers in one part of the world to contract manufacturers in another, while any given contract manufacturer could cart her machinery, modest as it was, on a caravan of trucks from Vietnam to Cambodia. And by legally domiciling intellectual property

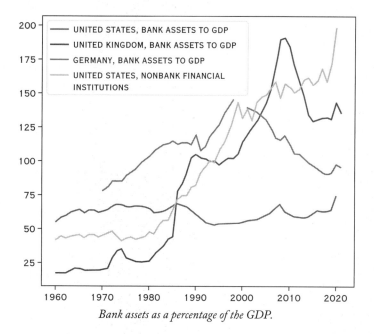

Bank assets as a percentage of the GDP.

rights in low-tax countries, they could shift much of their profits to yet another location. Yes, H&M was a Swedish company, just as Nike was American, but their dependence on their "home" countries was minimal—except, perhaps, as part of their brand identities.

Switzerland was in many ways the vanguard of this kind of capitalism, demonstrating its most far-reaching possibilities. Domiciled in a small, mountainous country with almost no natural resources, Swiss entrepreneurs never had privileged access to significant territory, raw materials, labor, or markets. Despite these seemingly fatal limits, Switzerland became one of the richest enclaves in the empire of capital, not least because Swiss capital owners found creative ways to conduct business largely independently of the national territory itself by exporting services—trade, finance, and mediation. Most telling here were the activities of Swiss commodity merchants—the Volkarts in cotton and the Andrés in grains, among others—who engaged in transit trade, bringing together remote sellers and buyers without the goods ever touching Swiss territory. While many of these Swiss companies went under after the end of the Cold War, they were replaced by a new generation of commodity traders who adopted Switzerland as their congenial home base. Glencore, for example, was founded by American Marc Rich in Zug in 1974. Their trade grew radically: Between 1998 and 2010, the income from trade in raw materials exploded by a factor of fifteen. By 2000, Switzerland was the world's most significant hub for commodity trade, and the commodity trade produced (in 2021) about 8 percent of the country's GDP, more than its entire construction sector. By the 2020s, about 40 percent of the world's oil and wheat, 55 percent of its coffee, and 60 percent of its metals were traded from Switzerland. The companies involved produced more profits than all the Swiss banks combined (another source of wealth for the country) and became Switzerland's single most important service exporter.[91]

Swiss capital owners were exceptional, yet capital's escape from the nation-state became common and took other forms, including special economic zones. By 2019, the world was dotted with 5,400 of these SEZs in 147 countries, spaces of production and trade that had essentially evaded the territorial order of the nation-state. Sixty million people labored in them. These "zones," of course, had a very long history, including many a trading post in sixteenth-century Asia and Africa, though they were then called factories." Their modern incarnation can be traced to Puerto Rico in 1947. Throughout the golden years, they spread across the world, representing an alternative way to organize labor and production. Wages in these zones were low (often below the costs of housing, clothing, and food), and workers, usually women, depended on family or village resources, or what one scholar called "involuntary indirect subsidies from local populations."[92] For good reason, workers laboring in such zones in Mauritius turned their official name—*zone franche* (free zone)—into *zone sufrance* (suffering zone).[93] In similar fashion, while "bigness" was considered an asset for national economies for much of the nineteenth and twentieth centuries, in the neoliberal age, very small states rose to prominence within the empire of capital, something last seen in the Middle Ages. It was not just

Switzerland and the Caribbean tax havens but also Singapore and Hong Kong—places feted by neoliberal theorists for embracing freedom of trade and competing to attract mobile capital.[94]

As capital de-territorialized and commodity chains globalized, international trade skyrocketed. In 1973, goods valued at $586 billion in US dollars were traded globally across national borders; in 2008, that number stood at $16,010 billion—almost thirty times more. The value of oceanborne US commerce exploded from $45 billion in 1970 to $520 billion by 1995.[95] Logistics itself became a major business, with companies such as DHL and FedEx whirling packages across the globe and Amazon delivering goods to households almost everywhere, thanks to an army of low-paid delivery workers.

This trade binge was crucially accelerated by the adoption of shipping containers. Malcolm McLean, owner of McLean Trucking in Hoboken, New Jersey, developed the first container in 1956, replacing irregularly packaged goods moved by armies of longshoremen. Though workers initially resisted containers, the early 1980s saw a fiery growth in their use, and by 1990, almost all cargo in developed countries moved by container. As a result, employment in ports decreased drastically. There had been twenty thousand longshoremen at the giant Port Newark–Elizabeth Marine Terminal on Newark Bay in the 1960s, but their number had dwindled to only two thousand by 1998.[96]

This intensification of trade and the new nonterritorial organization of production came to be known as "globalization"—perhaps *the* buzzword of the neoliberal age. Books with titles such as *Globalizing Capital, Modernity at Large: Cultural Dimensions of Globalization, Globalization and Its Discontents, One World Now: The Ethics of Globalization, Why Globalization Works, Understanding Globalization,* and *The Globalization Paradox* flooded the market.[97] Kofi Annan, the secretary-general of the United Nations, spoke in 1999 of globalization as "a fact of life." Anne O. Krueger of the IMF boldly asserted that "[s]upporting globalization is one of the best investments we can make to

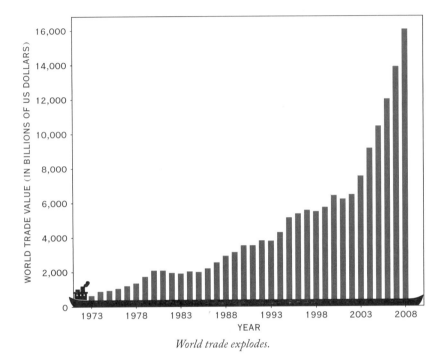

World trade explodes.

improve today's security environment," while Pascal Lamy of the World Trade Organization (WTO) saw it as "a historical stage."[98]

As readers of this book know, there was nothing new about capitalism's global reach. What was new was how capital, states, and territory related to one another and how this dissolved the golden-age era of welfare states, strong labor unions, and Global South import-substitution industrialization. When German economist Herbert Giersch envisioned a new geography of neoliberal economic space, he clearly saw its potential for empowering capital owners: The "[m]edicine of imported competition from less developed countries with their vast supply of low-wage labor that can be trained to produce the same goods and services for which producers in developed countries still seem to have a monopoly" would not only intensify trade but also weaken the welfare state, disempower labor unions, and diminish calls for a New International Economic Order in the Global South.[99] To Giersch, national borders were "traffic obstructions" to be overcome; he empha-

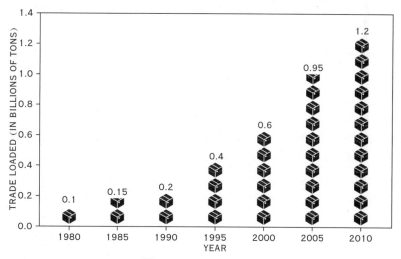

The container revolution.

sized the benefits of competition between nations, or what he called "Standortwettbewerb"—locational competition.[100] An aficionado of Hayek, Giersch was opposed to "nationalist thought," wanting nothing less than the emergence of the (entrepreneurial) "age of Schumpeter" after the previous (statist) "age of Keynes," which would be brought about, he hoped, by regions all around the world competing for mobile capital.[101] Not everyone shared his enthusiasm: French sociologist Pierre Bourdieu warned of a "utopia of unlimited exploitation."[102] And for Egyptian economist Samir Amin, neoliberalism ended the project of "emergence" in the Global South, bringing about what he called its "re-compradorization," by which he meant that local elites once again became just intermediaries for foreign capital.[103]

This new order of capitalism was thus not just the outcome of changing structures of capital; it was also the result of political interventions and of the vast, but selective, assertions of states. States liberalized trade, deregulated financial markets, privatized state functions, abetted tax "optimization," facilitated capital mobility, and enabled "lean government." States weakened labor power, privatized state-owned enterprises, cut back on welfare, and lowered tariffs.

There were, of course, national differences in this reorientation: There were "aggressive" variants (in Chile, the US, and the UK) and "moderate forms" (in Germany, France, Italy, New Zealand, and the Netherlands). But everywhere, the institutional regulation of capitalism changed.[104]

The political space for the new policies emerged in part because two of the core pillars of the golden-age order wobbled: Labor weakened, and the Soviet Union and its sphere of influence disintegrated. These changes, which came to pass in the 1990s, undermined the need for capital owners and the state to accommodate labor, as they had been forced to do during the golden age.[105]

Even neoliberalism's former opponents now embraced its central elements: Much as conservative forces in Europe and the United States had embraced central tenets of the Keynesian golden age in the 1940s, 1950s, and 1960s, social democratic forces embraced central tenets of neoliberalism. Remarkably, the height of the neoliberal moment was the 1990s, when Democratic president Bill Clinton, Labour prime minister Tony Blair, and Social Democratic chancellor Gerhard Schröder steered some of the world's largest economies into neoliberal waters. In the United States, crucial neoliberal accomplishments such as the North American Free Trade Agreement (NAFTA, signed in 1992), the deregulation of the telecoms (1996), the deregulation of electricity markets (1992), and the reworking of the Glass–Steagall Act (1999) occurred during Clinton's presidency.[106] When Clinton addressed the American nation in January 2000, he conveyed an almost messianic optimism about the world he had helped usher in, telling his audience that "[w]e are fortunate to be alive at this moment in history" because "[n]ever before has our Nation enjoyed, at once, so much prosperity . . . and so few external threats." He bragged that "[w]e have built a new economy" and that "welfare as we knew it" had ended. When he described globalization as "the central reality of our time," it was an almost Kantian celebration of a free-trade-based liberal utopia, boosted by the heady mood of the end of the Cold War.[107]

As the world economy fundamentally shifted, the project of re-thinking the global political economy gained traction. The project of overcoming the institutional structure of the golden age was driven, as we have seen, by the immediate interests of various actors, especially capital owners who hoped for more space in which to maneuver, new profit opportunities, lower taxation, lower labor costs, and the preservation of the value of their assets. As they embarked upon yet another reconstruction of capitalism, however, their interests intersected with new ways of making sense of the world, a set of ideas that cast the forging of a new political economy as something beyond the narrow interests of a small group of people (thus making it politically viable), and connected to an intellectual edifice with universalist visions and virtues as well.

Intellectuals such as Friedrich Hayek, Milton Friedman, and Ludwig von Mises rose to prominence. Despite their differences, they were all utopian thinkers with an almost religious belief in markets—in both their liberatory potential and their ability to produce wealth. With characteristic passion, Hayek called for "a deed of courage" to create "a liberal Utopia."[108]

The foundation of neoliberalism was the deeply liberal idea of what has been called the "articulation of the universalism of particularisms."[109] Private actors following their own interests would create a better world for everyone. Because the economy was unknowable, efficiency depended on the institutional protection of the workings of the price mechanism, a crowdsourced means of regulating consumption, production, and, really, all economic activities.[110] In what came to be known as the "socialist calculation debate," one of the progenitors of the neoliberal edifice, Austrian economist von Mises, had argued as early as the 1920s that the economy could not be calculated and that planning of the Keynesian or socialist varieties was thus a logical impossibility.[111] When Friedman published his *Capitalism and Freedom* in

1962, he categorically stated that the "invisible hand" of the market was superior to any other institution regulating economic life.[112] Markets were always the best mechanism for allocating resources. At its most radical edge, their theorizing had a truly imperial reach, in that they believed that all goods and services—indeed, all human interactions—were essentially the same, could be reduced to their cost, and should be regulated by the market. When put into practice, this theory had far-reaching implications for not just economic life but life more broadly.

Like Hayek, but opposite most Keynesians, neoliberals saw capitalism from an intrinsically global perspective. Von Mises conceptualized "the earth as a vast territory of varying natural endowments that needed to be exploited as thoroughly as possible through the mobility of capital, labor, and commerce."[113] The world economy was one entity and should be managed as such.[114] Neoliberals criticized nation-states' ability to rein in markets (for example, through protectionism) and believed that "nations must remain embedded in an international institutional order that safeguarded capital and protected its rights to move throughout the world."[115]

Theirs was an intellectually coherent and even brilliant edifice. Yet it was constantly under threat. Their fundamentalist belief in the superiority of the price mechanism to allocate resources led neoliberals to fear the people and democracy. After all, many among the first generation of these intellectuals had observed firsthand how the labor movement, fascism, socialism, golden-age Keynesian states, and anticolonial movements—all driven by mass politics—had hobbled the functioning of markets with a vast panoply of political measures (tariffs, minimum wages, environmental regulations, even state ownership of firms). Both the Keynesian order and the economic nationalism of postcolonial states threatened what they believed was the proper functioning of markets. Acknowledging that market outcomes—and even capitalism itself—were unpopular among a very large number of people, neoliberals like Hayek feared popular sovereignty, calls for a New International Economic Order, and the resource nationalism of the Global South.[116]

To insulate markets from political threats, strategies had to be devised to secure the workings of the price mechanism—which called for a state-organized and -enforced order. From its beginnings, neoliberal capitalism was thus yet another state-centric political economy, albeit one fundamentally at odds with that of golden-age capitalism. Neoliberalism was always more than a mere celebration of the superiority of markets in allocating resources; it saw itself as a particular form of a statist order in which the state's job was to create a self-enforcing institutional framework that entrenched and safeguarded the functioning of markets. Neoliberals sought to construct a political order that removed markets from popular politics and protected them within a fortress of laws and institutions. Just as nineteenth-century liberalism had drawn on state interventions to create the rules, habits, and mentalities it deemed "natural," neoliberals called on the state to create the laws, supranational organizations, and treaties (like the WTO) that would constrain an increasingly empowered and mobilized people and an ever larger number of recently decolonized states.[117] Neoliberalism worked to protect the rights of capital (rather than people or societies), though adherents believed that this focus was also in the best interest of individuals.

Because of the absolute primacy of securing the workings of the price mechanism, neoliberalism was also strikingly undogmatic about the political forms it favored. In Chile and much of Latin America, early neoliberalism and authoritarianism went hand in hand. Neoliberals at times even expressed admiration for fascism, with von Mises arguing in 1927 that fascists were "full of the best intentions" and had "for the moment, saved European civilization." While fascism's "merit . . . will live on eternally in history," von Mises continued, "it is not of the kind which could promise continued success. Fascism was an emergency makeshift. To view it as something more would be a fatal error."[118] But versions of neoliberalism also thrived in liberal democratic Britain and theocratic Saudi Arabia. If "property rights, freedom of contract, and protections from government interference in commercial affairs" were secured, no matter what the majority of a people thought about such matters, the political form in which these protections were embedded was of little consequence. Neoliberalism also had a striking ability to accommodate older customs, especially religious traditions, as long as they did not interfere with the protections to be granted to capital.[119]

Many of the foundational ideas of neoliberalism had emerged as early as the 1920s, stemming especially from a private seminar run by von Mises and attended by Hayek in Vienna. The intellectual tenor of the movement would be forever shaped by that experience. The term *neoliberalism*, however, was first programmatically deployed a few years later, during a 1938 meeting in Paris at what was known as the Walter Lippmann Colloquium. It was there that it was defined as

> the use of the price mechanism as the best way to obtain the maximal satisfaction of human expectations; the responsibility of the state for instituting a juridical framework adjusted to the order defined by the market; the possibility for the state to follow goals other than short-term expedients and to further them by levying taxes; the acceptance of state intervention if it does not favor any particular group and seeks to act upon the causes of the economic difficulties.[120]

After the war, this concept and the ideas associated with it were further developed by the Mont Pèlerin Society, whose founding moment we encountered previously. Early members included von Mises, Friedman, German economist Wilhelm Röpke, British economist Lionel Robbins, and US economist George Stigler. Its original statement of aims warned that "[t]he central values of civilization are in danger. Members feared the "decline of belief in private property and the competitive market" because without "these institutions it is difficult to imagine a society in which freedom may be effectively preserved."[121] This loose association of intellectuals became important to the propagation of neoliberal ideas; they became, according to one scholar, the "organic intellectuals of global capitalism."[122] For Hayek, the moving spirit behind the venture, the strategy was as clear as the objectives: to create "a truly liberal radicalism which does not spare the susceptibilities of the mighty . . . , which is not too severely practical, and which does not confine itself to what appears today as politically possible."[123]

Despite their intellectual confidence and the emergence of a group of schools that adhered to their ideas, neoliberals had remained marginal during the golden years.[124] Indian economist Bellikoth Raghunath Shenoy, who was close to Hayek and eventually became a member of the Mont Pèlerin Society, admitted as much in 1959 when he concluded that "[s]upporters of the free market economy, even in the universities, are an insignificant minority."[125] What these neoliberals had from the beginning, however, was stamina, a belief that it was worthwhile to agitate from the margins, and enough strategic insight to know that organization was important.

The power of their movement was rooted not just in the force of their ideas but in the institutional infrastructure they created—and, ultimately, in their connection to powerful capital groups that saw their own interests align with the policy recommendations coming from the "neoliberal thought collective."[126] They hoped for a "liberal Reconquista."[127] Their institutions kept growing, and by the turn of the millennium, the Mont Pèlerin Society included about one thousand intellectuals from every region of the world. Even though it often focused on obscure technical topics, its members always had explicit political ambitions: They wanted to change the world.[128]

Mont Pèlerinites, as we have seen, also played an important role in creating a novel set of further institutions—think tanks—to spread their ideas. The 1980s were a decade of rapid growth for these increasingly sophisticated and well-endowed institutions, not least because capital owners upped investing in these activities. Businessman William E. Simon, Nixon's treasury secretary, had demanded as much in his 1978 memoir, *A Time for Truth*, which encouraged "a massive and unprecedented mobilization of the moral, intellectual and financial

resources" of business "to come to the aid of the intellectuals and writers who are fighting on my side."[129] Neoliberal intellectuals also systematically pursued and ingratiated themselves with powerful political
forces, such as the Thatcher and Reagan administrations, and increasingly focused on providing policy advice on nearly any policy issue.
Their ideas moved ever closer to the center of political life in capitalism's heartland.[130]

Inexorably, such institutions emerged in other regions as well.
Neoliberalism found fertile ground in the Global South, not least because of its refreshingly global frame of reference—a cosmopolitan
spirit it shared with both classical liberalism and Marxism, but also,
more importantly, it appealed to the shifting inclinations and interests
of capital owners in the Global South. And in 1981, US industrialist
Antony Fisher, with the encouragement of Hayek, founded the Atlas
Economic Research Foundation in Fairfax, Virginia, to spread neoliberalism across the globe. By 2020, it boasted five hundred member in-
stitutes. Like so many faiths, neoliberalism spread not only through a
series of diverse local adaptions and traditions but also through the
pressures exerted by increasingly neoliberal governments and institutions in the industrial heartlands, rewriting elements of its script as
needed.[131]

We have already chronicled neoliberalism's early flourishing in
Chile. Other countries in Latin America followed suit. Brazilian intellectuals and entrepreneurs, sometimes with the support of US think
tanks, founded the Instituto Liberal in 1983 and the Instituto de Estudos Empresariais in 1984, followed by the Instituto Millenium in 2005
and the Mises Institute in 2008.[132] At the same time, a school of thought
dubbed "ultraliberalism" found Brazilian adherents, especially among
younger adults, forming a kind of countercultural right.[133] Similar ideas
spread in Turkey: Inspired by Thatcher and Reagan, and influenced by
pressure from institutions like the IMF and the World Bank and their
"structural adjustment programs," the Association for Liberal Thinking
(ALT) was founded in Ankara in 1992 as a neoliberal think tank.[134]

As neoliberalism itself globalized, its font of ideas became global as well: Japanese neoliberals such as Kiuchi Nobutane and Nishiyama Chiaki insisted on the need to provide a moral order to neoliberalism and saw national culture as the glue for a society governed by market principles. Indian neoliberalism, which emerged in the 1950s as a critique of the Nehruvian developmental state, eventually took that idea to heart as well, fusing market radicalism with Hindu nationalism. In Turkey, where neoliberal ideas had taken hold as a critique of the Kemalist project of economic nationalism, intellectuals and politicians inserted identity politics into the policy mix, giving unprecedented political prominence to Islam and emphasizing the fact that the Prophet Muhammad himself had been a merchant. Given these thinkers' close cooperation with the Islamicist Justice and Development Party, Islam came to flavor the neoliberal project in Turkey just as much as Hinduism in India and Christianity in the United States.[135]

South African neoliberals, in turn, were at the forefront of conceptualizing new ways of reconciling neoliberalism with maintaining racial hierarchies. Allowing for a less overtly racist regime and diminishing the overwhelmingly statist order that South Africa had become under apartheid, they sought to give urban Black South Africans freedoms that would allow for the formation of a Black middle class, which would then, they hoped, become a bulwark against popular mobilizations against the apartheid regime. At the same time, they relegitimized extreme racial hierarchies by emphasizing the importance of "culture" in a "free market." Arguing that people needed an education to participate rationally in markets, South African economist Jan A. Lombard advocated that people be readied "to read the signs of the market, to make the necessary calculations and to act upon their findings."[136] Since Black Africans were not "market rational," they had to be excluded until such time as they were "educated."[137] Liberal universalism and racist particularism could be reconciled in response to local conditions.

Within the limits of its most general assumptions, neoliberalism thus allowed for a diversity of approaches and a diversity of ideas. It was alive. Its four major schools—the ordoliberals of Freiburg, Austrian economics, the Virginia School of Political Economy (which focused on public choice theory and brought economic analysis to the understanding of politics), and the Chicago School—converged on certain core insights despite their differences when it came to questions about the role of mathematics in economics or the role of racial hierarchies in economic life. This flexibility in adjusting to local circumstances and this willingness to allow for a modicum of debate help explain how neoliberal ways of thinking about the world became globally dominant and, by the 1990s, almost a form of "common sense." So powerful were these ideas that they migrated to other realms of life.[138]

As such ideas blossomed, the "neoliberal thought collective" provided a conceptual map that legitimized particular economic, social, and political choices and imbued what became a radical recasting of the world's political economy with a sheen of universalizing values—an apparent organizing ethic that was, in fact, a radical abdication of ethics to the human-created but external logic of capital.

In mines, factories, offices, parliaments, and government departments, this recasting of global capitalism had a much rawer flavor than in seminar rooms and the halls of deep-pocketed think tanks, often involving dramatic political contestations, street battles, and various forms of coercion. Chile was notable for the violence of its conflict, but across the empire of capital, there were struggles over neoliberals' efforts to redefine the world's political economy. As in earlier moments, capitalism's shape-shifting was again embedded within a globe-spanning social conflict.

By the early 1970s, in various parts of the world, as we have seen, business leaders, associated organizations, and sympathetic politicians had begun battling the golden-age order, both in the industrial heartland and in the recently decolonized world. As the "[s]ocial responsibility of business is to increase its profits," in Friedman's words, they had to enter the political realm, and when they did, they fueled what has been called a "revolt of capital against the postwar mixed economy."[139] A core element of this revolt was businesses' efforts against labor. This was hardly surprising, considering that unions had been a foundational pillar of the golden age. In 2019, a report by the UN's International Labour Organization, looking back a few decades, found legal restrictions on strikes, right-to-work legislation, deindustrialization and relocation of supply chains, automation's disproportionate effect on heavily unionized industries, and the growth of employment in informal and flexible sectors had severely weakened unions. While massive strike waves such as the Great Railroad Strike of 1877 in the United States, the "two red years" (1919 and 1920) in northern Italy, and the 1926 General Strike in Britain had once reinforced the claims of labor and served as stepping stones to a new place for it in industrial capitalism's heartlands (though not elsewhere), by the neoliberal age, such confrontations symbolized the dismantling of labor's former power. The playing field was far from level: Capital played a global game, while workers were, by definition, local, and their organizations were at best national in scope. Moreover, these global assaults against labor were emboldened by the deep structural changes of capital that had enervated the centers of labor's power in the industrial heartland. Capital owners built upon old divisions in the world's working class and created new ones, their power backed by neoliberal-inflected governments.[140] It suddenly became easy to discard workers in some part of the world in favor of cheaper, more pliant laborers somewhere else.

Just as British workers had been at the forefront of developing new institutional forms and strategies during the emergence of industrial capitalism in the early nineteenth century, they were now among the first to suffer a series of devastating defeats. The quintessential conflict of Britain's neoliberal age was with the country's miners—a strike that began at South Yorkshire's coal mines in March 1984 after the head of the National Coal Board, Ian MacGregor, announced that twenty coalpits would close. The conflict quickly spread to other mines, as well as to power plants and steelworks, and resulted in pitched battles between workers and police. At the Orgreave coking plant, six thousand police officers fought their way through five thousand picketers in June 1984, producing images that garnered worldwide attention. A union paper reported that one of the mining towns, Blidworth, "resembled not a mining village in the heart of Notts, but the bloodied, oppressive and fearful streets of Belfast."[141] It was clear to all participants that what was at stake in this conflict was nothing less than the future of the British union movement. As Margaret Valling, a member of the Women's Action Committee that provided food to the families of strikers, explained: "It's not charity; charity is what rich people give to poor people as a token. This is what working-class people are doing to help other working-class people, because they realize that if the National Union of Mineworkers are crushed, then the rest of the trade union movement will capitulate, and that this is the last stand. This is it."[142]

Margaret Thatcher's Conservative government agreed. It had extensively prepared for the conflict, setting up a Civil Contingencies Unit to ensure the continued delivery of supplies by the army and gradually building up advance coal stocks in power stations.[143] In 1984, moreover, it implemented a new Trade Union Act that restricted industrial action and was later used to declare the miners' strike "illegal."[144] When the Trades Union Congress (TUC), the peak association of British unions, hosted an international conference on "Trade Union Rights in Multinational Companies" in January the following year, the International Labour, Trade & Aid Project circulated a fact sheet on the law, claiming that "[a]t present world labour is enduring a level of repression unprecedented in post-war years."[145]

Despite massive mobilizations and global solidarity, the miners were unable to shut down British electricity generation. Eventually, dwindling strike benefits and, for some families, literal hunger forced many back to work. In 1985, the unraveling of this strike dealt the British labor movement its hardest blow. Miners who for two centuries had literally fueled industrial capitalism found themselves superfluous, stuck in

*Toy-gun class war in the industrial heartland: "Miner's wife Gail
Downes (left) was one of the many miners and their families
who protested the closures of the mines across the country.
She is pictured here outside Harworth Colliery," 1984.*

decaying mining towns. Already by 1986, 48,000 of the 139,000 miners
at work two years earlier had been declared redundant.[146]

Such class warfare from above also occurred in the United States,
where the quintessential conflict involved air traffic controllers employed by the federal government. Unionized since 1970, 13,000 (of
17,000) controllers walked out in August 1981, demanding better retirement benefits, higher wages, and a shorter workweek. The same
day, President Reagan ordered the workers to return within two days
or be terminated. On August 5, 1981, after 1,650 strikers had returned,
Reagan fired the remaining 11,350 workers and banned them from
ever being rehired by the Federal Aviation Administration (FAA). To
maintain air travel, the FAA coordinated a scab force of 2,000
non-striking workers, 3,000 supervisors, and 900 military controllers.
The administration fined the Professional Air Traffic Controllers Organization (PATCO) $34 million for breaking the law that prohibited
federal workers from going on strike and, in a first in US history, de-
certified the union. As James M. Pierce, head of the National Federation of Federal Employees, observed: "If Reagan can destroy PATCO,
he can destroy us too."[147] The intervention had its desired effect—there

was a massive decline in the number of work stoppages. In the 1960s and '70s, an average of 285 private-sector work stoppages had occurred annually; by 2009, that number had plummeted to only 5.[148] And wages stagnated.

These confrontations at the beginning of the neoliberal age almost never ended well for labor. Union density fell everywhere, and unions found themselves on the defensive. Forty-four percent of all workers in the European Union had been members of trade unions in 1978; by 2008, that figure had fallen to just 23 percent. In New Zealand, union density collapsed by 20 percent between 1980 and 1992; in Britain, by 15 percent; and in the United States, where numbers had always been lower, by 10 percent. In the industrial heartland, unions lost a total of 14 million members between 2000 and 2008 alone. The International Trade Union Confederation's member unions counted 168 million members in 2008—an impressive number but still only between 5 and 10 percent of the world's wage earners.[149] The wind had been snatched from labor's sails.

The political parties representing labor's interests, built with enormous effort and sacrifice since the late nineteenth century, also declined. Partly, this was because they had to cobble up new coalitions with a wide range of social forces outside the traditional, now shrinking, blue-collar working class. While that strategy sometimes succeeded, with Tony Blair, Gerhard Schröder, and Bill Clinton governing in the midst of the neoliberal revolution, the price of victory was relinquishing their traditional emphasis on workers' interests. And political marginalization deepened nonetheless: In Germany, the world's most powerful social democratic party, the SPD, saw its share of votes fall from more than 40 percent to the 30 percent range, then down to the 20 percent range. In Italy and France, once powerful communist parties became empty shells of their former selves, accelerated not least by the collapse of the communist world beginning in the late 1980s. In the mid-1970s, the Italian Communist Party, the strongest in the capitalist world, commanded more than 30 percent of the national vote; in

1991, it dissolved itself. In the long term, the collapse of the entire edifice of working-class institutions was perhaps even more important. After publishing for more than a century, the SPD's storied newspaper, *Vorwärts*, had become a ghost of its former self by the 1980s. In 1990, amid financial difficulties and scandals, the German Trade Union Confederation's Neue Heimat sold its 320,000 apartments, which had provided affordable working-class housing.[150] Singing clubs, gymnastics associations, hiking clubs, youth organizations, and working-class soccer clubs either shrank and disappeared or lost their former political orientation.

As labor became weaker, businesspeople gained new power and political energies. They mobilized against the network of regulations that had structured the golden-age economy, and for the privatization of assets under state control. A wave of privatizations soon swept across the industrial heartland. In France, the first wave of denationalization took off when Jacques Chirac became prime minister for a second time in 1986, privatizing eleven large companies, including diversified manufacturer Saint-Gobain, banks Paribas and Société Générale, and the TV station TF1. In 1993, a second wave of privatizations commenced, claiming such stalwarts of the French economy as BNP, Rhône-Poulenc, Elf Aquitaine, and Renault. In Italy, the wave of privatizations began after 1992 and included Telecom Italia (1997, sold to the public); the toll company Autostrade (2000, to the Benetton family); and Aeroporti di Roma (2000, to the Gemina family). In the banking sector, Credito Italiano and Banca Commerciale Italiana were privatized in 1993 and 1994, respectively. Privatizations had started even earlier in Britain as a condition for an urgently needed IMF loan during the 1970s, but they accelerated under Thatcher, including BP and British Aerospace, followed later by "British Telecom and Jaguar (1984), British Airways (1986), Rolls-Royce (1987), British Steel (1998), and British Coal (1990)."[151] The Thatcher government also sold off one million so-called council houses to tenants, not least because it assumed that the new homeowners would then support the neoliberal project politically. The "mixed economy" of the golden age weakened, and private capital found new and profitable outlets in huge sectors that had previously been off-limits—telecommunications, postal services, rail transport, even highways, prisons, and security services.[152] There had often been good reasons for such privatizations—these companies had frequently been inefficient and uncompetitive in global markets—yet from a long-term perspective, what mattered was that the spheres of economic life outside the control of private capital shrank dramatically.

Regulations were in the crosshairs of powerful capital interests as well. In the United States, the airline, trucking, and telecommunications industries were deregulated. The Airline Deregulation Act of 1978, to cite just one example, removed airlines from the oversight of the Civil Aeronautics Board (terminated in 1984) and granted private airlines oversight of fares and flights, resulting in losses of air service at many smaller airports and giving some airlines near-monopoly positions in local markets. Mexico, too, deregulated its finance sector and privatized many state services in the 1980s. In Argentina, deregulation came later, when Carlos Menem took presidential power in 1992 and deregulated the financial sector to encourage foreign direct investment, a policy that South Korea, Egypt, and South Africa also embraced.[153]

Neoliberal ideologues and their business elite allies fought just as passionately against the welfare state, another key feature of the golden age. To them, welfare and the attendant redistributions undermined the functioning of labor markets and disincentivized work. The proper source of support in times of need was, they believed, the family. In the United Kingdom, the Institute of Directors (IOD), a neoliberal business organization, demanded that public spending as a percentage of the GDP be reduced by half, an obviously arbitrary figure that served only as a form of puffery. In 1984, the institute announced that "[c]hild benefits should be reduced; it weakens the family by replacing parental provision with state provision."[154] British lawyer and economist Arthur Shenfield, future director of the Industrial Policy Group (IPG), whose members represented big business, announced:

The Welfare State rests on humbug. . . . The method of the welfare state is to require that everyone must pay for and be free to take state-provided services in order that those that cannot provide them for themselves shall have them. . . . It undermines both the personal responsibilities which are the warp and woof of freedom and the family responsibilities on which the wholesomeness of society rests. It teaches the electorate to vote for things that most of them do not intend to pay for. Above all, by providing services for all it fails to provide fully effective services for those that are really in need.[155]

Members of the Selsdon Group, named for the hotel where they had their first meeting, pushed the Conservative Party to embrace this agenda and announced in 1973 that "[w]e believe that individual enterprise is the source of all progress in economics, the sciences and the arts, and that the task of politics is to create a framework within which the individual can flourish. . . . We oppose the view that the State should have a monopoly in health, housing, education and welfare."[156] The risk of failure was to be privatized, with the family conceived as a support of last resort.[157]

Such rhetoric had put the welfare state in Thatcher's iron sights when she came to power in 1979. Her government sharply cut welfare services, with the nation's education expenditures dropping from 6.5 percent of the GDP in 1975 to 4.25 percent in 1989; health expenditures fell from about 5 percent in the late 1970s to 4.25 percent in 1989. Thatcher cut back on unemployment benefits, made welfare more conditional, and cut taxes on the highest earners.[158]

While many of these rollbacks were limited and short-term, what mattered more than the cuts themselves were the changes to how the welfare state worked. It became more punitive, more market-driven, and more oriented toward the needs of employers. *Marketization* became a watchword of British reforms, not only under the Conservative Party but also under Tony Blair's Labour Party, which continued to stress "personal responsibility."[159] Pressure on the unemployed increased considerably—they had to show up for regular interviews at job centers and could be forced into lower-paying jobs. At the same time, if the unemployed ventured into entrepreneurship, their benefits rose, enabled by the so-called Enterprise Allowance Scheme.[160] The vision was clear and focused on returning spheres of economic life that had been "decommodified" to the logic of the market.

The famously comprehensive Swedish welfare state also faced cuts. It had experienced a last flowering during the 1970s, as the Social Democratic Party, the SAP, aimed to safeguard its model even during slower productivity growth, a slowing world economy, and a radicalized working class. In 1991, the Social Democrats gained less than 40 percent of the vote for the first time since 1928, a rebuttal that brought critiques of the welfare state to the fore. In 1993, a nonsocialist government appointed the so-called Lindbeck Commission (Lindbeckkommissionen), chaired by Assar Lindbeck, economics professor and head of the Ministry of Finance. The commission traced back to the 1970s what it considered to be the problematic state of the Swedish economy of the 1990s, the expansion of the public sector, and the increase in public spending. It described the labor market of the time as overheated, with demands for raises that did not consider "reality." Furthermore, it stated that workers' rights and job security had been prioritized over the need for industrial companies to be flexible and adaptive to a changing economy. The commission also criticized the Swedish wage negotiation system: Developed during a period when industrial productivity experienced rapid growth, it had not changed along with a slowdown in productivity growth, and labor costs now threatened the competitiveness of Swedish industry. By the 1990s, even the SAP accepted a market-driven "third way" ideology, including a marketization of the welfare state, marking a radical break with its long history.[161]

In the United States, the pattern was similar. President Reagan cut back some welfare programs, including, in 1981, Aid to Families with Dependent Children. But radical reforms awaited Bill Clinton's presidency. The 1996 Personal Responsibility and Work Opportunity Reconciliation Act terminated Aid to Families with Dependent Children.

These policies forced people into the labor market and rescinded an open-ended federal commitment to minimal welfare payments. Families, according to neoliberal theorist Gary Becker, were an integral component of capitalism and the prime vehicle to cushion market risk—a doubling down on the importance of the nonmarket to the very formation of contractual markets. Such notions allowed neoliberals to build alliances with social conservatives, who had all along emphasized the family as the desirable building block of society. At the same time, health-care reforms pushed people into forms of managed care that limited, among other things, the duration of stays in hospitals and offloaded care work onto families. And as the state retreated from financing tertiary education, there was a massive expansion of student debt, especially in the United States, reinscribing the role of the family in mobilizing resources for education. Total student debt for undergraduates, graduates, and parents of undergraduates in the United States rose from approximately $7.6 billion in 1970/71 to approximately $102.5 billion in 2008/9, both calculated in 2012 US dollars. Neoliberalism replaced, in the apt words of sociologist Melinda Cooper, "public with private deficit spending."[162]

YET DESPITE ALL these attacks on the welfare state, its storied accomplishments had surprising staying power. In a world of overwhelming proletarianization and one that depended on mass consumption for economic prosperity, the welfare state was so important that it survived even the most committed, ideological, and powerful countervailing forces. They could weaken its decommodifying tendencies, but they could not dislodge it. In the United Kingdom, health care and education both remained overwhelmingly under public control. Cash transfers to working-age adults and children even tripled in the three decades after 1979. Total public spending in Britain as a percentage of national income reached 25 percent in the mid-1970s and stayed level until the mid-1990s. And the share of social spending as a percentage of total public spending (which declined) increased from slightly over

50 percent in 1978/79 to 60 percent in 1996/97. Between 1974 and 1995, spending on housing fell from 4 percent to 2 percent of the GDP, but spending on the National Health Service (NHS) increased from 3.8 percent to 5.7 percent, and spending on social security (mostly state pensions) increased from 8.2 percent to 11.4 percent. Despite all that radical rhetoric, the welfare state—not just in the UK but everywhere—remained astoundingly resilient; it was recast but neither abolished nor significantly reduced.[163]

Yet the social compact weakened in many societies, and many of the material underpinnings of the golden age collapsed. Enormous tensions came to the fore as a result, and governments relied ever more on coercion to control these dislocations. In the mid-1980s, America's neoliberal Manhattan Institute recast the "social question" as a question of crime and urban violence, suggesting that what was needed was for the state to have fewer welfare payments and more effective repressive capacities. These beliefs were acted on, and money once spent on welfare now flowed to prisons. The United States, more than anywhere in the industrial heartland, expanded its prison complex, increasingly opting to solve social problems by imprisoning poor people, especially minorities. In 1973, about 200,000 Americans were in prison. By the waning of the neoliberal era in 2008, that number had increased to 1.55 million, slightly more than 1 in 200 Americans. Indeed, a nationwide onslaught against America's Black population unfolded, with an increasingly militarized police force working to secure the boundaries of exclusion from the liberal order. Its often traumatized victims became a prominent presence on the streets of urban America, at times massing into short-lived rebellions and uprisings. This underlying violence of the neoliberal order was often hidden, but it attracted the attention of careful observers, such as science-fiction writer J. G. Ballard, whose dystopian novel *Super-Cannes* portrayed the sordid underbelly of a well-manicured gated community.[164] At the same time, racializing the sharpening economic hierarchies that were, to neoliberal proponents, a necessary and desired outcome of the neoliberal order helped make the neoliberal project more politically palatable to many white Americans, as racialized economic inequality led to "segmented work, divided workers" (as two sociologists put it in the 1980s).[165] A global working class at war with itself—both domestically and globally—faced highly mobilized liquid capital that could shape-shift and propel itself at the speed of light from one corner of the world to another. Workers, with their definite bodies in definite places, could not match this newfound power and were left dependent on radically weakened collective institutions, such as trade unions and an increasingly unwilling state.

Just as the social settlement and institutional structures of the golden age eroded in capitalism's industrial heartlands, the economic order of the postcolonial Global South was under pressure too. As we have seen, postcolonial countries had engaged in manifold efforts to develop their national economies in the 1960s and 1970s. Various forms of economic nationalism had resulted in the expropriation of foreign-owned companies, such as mines in Zambia and oil fields in Iraq. Import-substitution industrialization had limited market access for North Atlantic businesses, and calls for a New International Economic Order along with resource nationalism had promised further limits on the privileges and rights of American and European capital. There was a possibility, however remote, that the postcolonial world might successfully challenge the ability of a few wealthy countries to set the rules for the world economy as a whole. Undermining this possibility became a prime concern for governments and capital owners in the industrial heartland in general and for neoliberal ideologues in particular.[166]

An opportunity to limit the political space available to governments in the Global South came in the wake of the oil price shock and the attendant slowdown of the global economy. Paying their oil bills and maintaining domestic industries landed many governments in debt, so much so that by the 1980s, they needed supports from international lending organizations. US bank loans to developing countries amounted to $150 billion in 1979—over four times more than six years earlier.[167] This need became even more urgent as the Volcker Shock made that debt increasingly unaffordable.

This indebtedness was a perfect solvent for the assertiveness of the postcolonial world. The World Bank and the IMF pushed for so-called structural adjustment programs (SAPs) that included forcing countries to privatize state-owned assets, embrace austerity, and cut back on welfare payments. These institutions became especially interventionist after the Mexican debt crisis of 1982, when the IMF became a sort of "global financial police."[168] When former US defense secretary Robert McNamara became president of the World Bank, he began a program of "structural adjustment lending" (SAL) that made loans contingent on policy changes in the recipient countries.[169] As he argued in 1979, "[I]n order to benefit fully from an improved trade environment, developing countries will need to carry out structural adjustments favoring their export sectors." He "urge[d] the international community [to] consider sympathetically the possibility of additional assistance to developing countries that undertake the needed structural adjustments for export promotion in line with their long-term comparative advantage."[170] Between 1980 and 2000, the World Bank made 537 such structural adjustment loans worth nearly $100 billion in US dollars; in 2012, such loans accounted for nearly a quarter of its overall lending. This was a policy driven by the desire for what, in a different context, came to be known as "regime change." As US Treasury official James Conrow argued in a 1982 report, the bank should "encourage adherence to free and open markets, emphasis on the private sector as a vehicle for growth, minimal government involvement, and assistance to the needy who are willing to help themselves."[171] The "Washington Consensus," as it was dubbed by economist John Williamson, encouraged, even required, a set of policies for loan recipients, including financial deregulation, lowered trade barriers, the easing of rules governing foreign investment, and the fighting of inflation; when these policies were embraced, would-be borrowers curried favor with international lending organizations.[172]

Other initiatives also fundamentally undermined the power of countries in the Global South to determine their own economic policies. The negotiation of international investment codes was but one. By the 1990s, two thousand such bilateral treaties had been signed, all giving far-reaching rights to foreign investors. (Some of these were negotiated by Hermann Josef Abs, head of Deutsche Bank; he was once involved in the Nazi plunder of Jewish-owned assets, and now he negotiated agreements that sought to secure property rights in distant countries.) "Rankings" such as the Economic Freedom of the World index, which became popular during the 1990s, further pressured countries to create environments that favored the interests of international investors over the kinds of developmental policies dominant since the 1930s. Pressured by the IMF and the World Bank, the Dominican Republic embraced structural adjustment to balance its budget, resulting in severe cuts to public services, including education and health care. Ghana embraced structural adjustment in 1983 under President Jerry Rawlings. A few years later, neoliberal policies began to put their stamp on Colombia too.[173]

Like in Chile, attacks against the postcolonial order came from capital owners in the Global South; indeed, by the 1970s, the core principles of anticolonial politics, including its import-substitution industrialization strategy, came under domestic attack not just from abroad, but from domestic sources too.[174] Nowhere was the shift as radical as in India, where entrepreneurs were increasingly dissatisfied with Indian economic policy. Shaken by a wave of strikes, Pirojsha Godrej—a committed supporter of postcolonial governance—gave a depressing account of the state of India in his Diwali speech in 1969. "[T]he law and order situation is very bad," he said, and "[u]nscrupulous politics . . . aggravate the situation." For him, the "real reason for the general discontent is that there is hardly any improvement in the real per capita income after independence." Planning had failed: "Take, for example, the case of steel production in this country, which affects this Company very badly. The big steelworks, especially ones in the public sector, do not or cannot work to capacity because of labour trouble or other causes." In conclusion, he said, "[t]he country is groaning under false economic policies."[175] J. R. D. Tata became an outspoken critic of the Planning Commission's Nehruvian mixed economy too. As the Indian economy became unstable in the late 1960s, with spiking inflation, foreign-exchange shortages, slowing growth, food crises, and severe inefficiencies, opposition became even more widespread. Labor relations went south, and the Godrej company faced strikes and worker mobilizations in 1972 and again in 1977. By the late 1960s, Indian enthusiasm for planning diminished, as the Third Five-Year Plan (1961–1966) largely failed.[176]

These forces set the stage for neoliberalism's arrival in India in the 1990s. A balance-of-payments crisis in 1990/91 diminished Indian foreign-exchange reserves, and both the IMF and the World Bank pressured the country to enact policy reforms as a condition for their backing. Such outside pressure found support within the government, informed by a small subset of businesspeople's, intellectuals', and policymakers' longer-term engagement with neoliberalism—and by the rebellion of some capital owners against the postcolonial Indian political economy.[177]

Turkey went through a similar set of internal pressures and changes. Kemalism's state-directed import-substitution regime had been prominent since the 1930s, but by the 1970s, this model was under attack from a variety of domestic forces. Business leaders who wanted less state interference, for example, organized against the existing economic order through the formation of the Turkish Industry and Business Association in 1971. While they understood that the state had played a crucial role in national economic development, they now sought more space for private enterprise. At the same time, because of tumultuous changes of government during the 1970s, the public sector increasingly lost its ability to engage in long-term strategic planning, undermining its strength. The earlier Turkish model had depended on high rates of growth, and as those diminished, it became more politically difficult to sustain. Meanwhile, new capitalist elites gained political influence as they gathered wealth, eventually becoming key players in recasting the Turkish political economy. The Union of Industrialists of Istanbul demanded both liberalization and "respect" from society, which, it said, often thought of businessmen as "thieves with a necktie."[178] These domestic concerns were fueled by outside pressures, and they eventually led to a transition away from state-directed import-substitution industrialization toward private-capital-fueled production for export and for the domestic consumer market. With the military coup of 1980, neoliberal policies surged to the fore.[179]

Other countries faced similar domestic rebellions and international pressures. When oil prices faltered in the first half of the 1980s, Nigeria's national debt almost tripled. Continuing the economic nationalism of the postcolonial moment, the Nigerian government at first moved to implement a set of protective policies, including high tariffs, import licenses, and prohibitions to increase its revenue. However, in 1985, when a military coup ended the regime amid a deepening economic crisis, plans for structural adjustment moved to the center of policymaking. In 1986, the national government pursued a shift from a public-controlled exchange rate to a market-determined one. Privatization programs followed suit after 1989, with banks, hotels, oil marketing companies, cement companies, media outlets, insurance firms, auto assembly plants, and large chunks of other industries being sold, often favoring a small elite with the resources to purchase such assets. The World Bank and the IMF further pushed this agenda by making loans contingent on such policy shifts, and in 1986, Nigeria adopted a World Bank–stipulated structural adjustment program.[180]

Looking back from the vantage point of the late 1980s, it was clear that the 1981 North-South summit (which had brought together a small group of rich and poor countries in Cancún, Mexico) had been at once the zenith of the Global South's efforts to move discussions about a New International Economic Order onto the international agenda and its death knell. United States president Ronald Reagan had made that very clear on the occasion: What the world needed, he said, was not a New International Economic Order but trade liberalization and a commitment to "economic freedom."[181]

The neoliberal project to recast the world's political economy had picked up speed in the late 1980s but got its most momentous boost when the communist world collapsed. This single most important postcapitalist project—the North Star of global politics, either as friend or foe, for many decades—suddenly unraveled with astounding celerity in the late 1980s and early 1990s. Overnight, the political calculus in the capitalist world changed. Even more consequentially, capitalism gained new breathing room by expanding into vast new areas of the globe—into the homes, workplaces, and public spaces of billions of Russian, Chinese, and Eastern European people.

In 1980, about one-third of the world's people lived under communist rule in economies governed by a variety of noncapitalist mechanisms. Some of these systems simply imploded, opening them up to what came to be known as "shock therapy"—a way of bringing (almost overnight) capitalist social relations into economies that had functioned according to very different logics for up to seventy years. The Soviet Union and much of Eastern Europe experienced chaotic transitions as privatizations, decontrol of prices, and the opening of markets for goods and investments created societal turmoil.[182]

Often these policies were informed by neoliberal ideas, and neoliberal activists played a leading role in their implementation. Former communist elites acquired immense resources on the cheap (or for free), while workers found themselves out of jobs, without accustomed social safeguards and with rapidly declining living standards. In Poland, former communist functionaries created private enterprises that drew on the assets of the state-owned companies they had previously directed. As an elite few captured many—even most—resources, so-called oligarchs gained power, forging what has been described as "crony capitalism."[183] High inflation, drops in output, and very slow economic growth followed. Never did life expectancy, a very good gauge for social well-being, collapse as rapidly and as radically in peacetime as it did in the former Soviet Union: In the USSR's last year, life expectancy for men was 63.7 years; five years post-fall, men died, on average, over six years younger than that. The Soviet Union and its descendant states' share of the world's GDP almost halved between 1990 and 2017; living standards in 2015 Russia were lower for 99 percent of the country's people than they had been before the end of communism in 1991.[184]

For the capitalist industrial heartland, however, the collapse of the Soviet Union and its allies heralded new opportunities: Large new markets opened up, and cheaper labor became accessible (Hungary, for example, turned into the extended workbench of German industry, with Audi employing 12,000 workers and Bosch 18,300 locally by the early 2020s)—all while the threats of labor mobilizations, labor politics, and anti-imperialism that had so decisively shaped capitalism for more than a century receded, giving entrepreneurs new economic and political space in which to maneuver. To cite just one case, core sectors of the Polish economy, such as finance, came to be controlled by foreign investors, and its manufacturing sector simply became integrated into Western European production networks. As a result, Poland became one of the world's most significant manufacturers of household appliances, with firms such as Siemens, Merloni, Bosch, Electrolux, and Whirlpool taking advantage of much lower labor costs.[185]

Farther east, these transitions were equally consequential but followed a very different trajectory. By far the most important transformation occurred in China. As we have seen, China had a very long tradition of vibrant trade, mercantile communities, and commercialized agriculture and industry, as well as a storied capacity for technical innovation. It was most likely the world's leading economy well into the early modern period. In the nineteenth and twentieth centuries, however, it became drastically less important; by the 1947 revolution, it was one of the poorest countries on earth. And even though per capita economic growth picked up under Mao (estimates put that growth between 2.33 and 2.7 percent annually) and significant industrial expansion, especially in heavy industry, took place (mostly by moving resources out of the countryside and into cities), China remained very poor.[186] Maoist policies, moreover, created drastic dislocations and almost unfathomable economic problems, including a devastating famine between 1959 and 1961 that killed millions.

After Mao's death in 1976, Deng Xiaoping's ascendancy to the presidency in 1978 reflected the desire of Chinese elites to escape the quagmire of Maoist economics. A narrow political space opened up to rethink the Chinese economy, especially the relationship between planning and markets. Seeking inspiration elsewhere—and looking to postwar American, British, German, and Japanese price decontrols after World War II—intellectuals and policymakers debated how markets and planning could be reconciled.[187] As Deng said in 1984:

> It is wrong to maintain that a market economy exists only in capitalist society and that there is only [a] "capitalist" market economy. Why can't we develop a market economy under socialism? Developing a market economy does not mean practicing capitalism. While maintaining a planned economy as the mainstay of our economic system, we are also introducing a market economy. But it is a socialist market economy.[188]

In the debate on how to get there, two positions emerged: Some advocated for a "big bang"; others focused on more gradual reforms. The gradualists won out, but it was an epic struggle. "Shock therapy" almost happened twice, in 1986 and in 1988, but China ultimately embraced a "gradual and state-guided marketization" instead. At its core was the maintenance of a dual-track price system, with prices in some industries still regulated by the state, achieving a degree of stability as markets slowly came to play a more important role in economic life.[189]

Such strategies had deep roots in Chinese economic thought, or what was traditionally called "the study of making the country rich."[190] Even before communism, that tradition had given a prominent role to the state; both the market and prices were often set by the bureaucracy. For centuries, the state had stabilized grain prices, for example, and had created depots to store grain for times of famine. In China, there was indeed little tradition of thinking about the market as autonomous. The *Guanzi* (an ancient body of economic writings) had already distinguished between dispensable "light" and critical "heavy" commodities—a way of thinking about the economy that presupposed a significant intervention of the state to secure the production and availability of "heavy" commodities. But just as the role of the state in market regulation had long historical roots in China, so, too, did experience with markets: Even during the revolution itself, Chinese revolutionaries had used market strategies to further economic warfare against the nationalists and obtain resources for the revolution.[191]

As reformers gained breathing space after Mao's death, these rich traditions informed debates. Unlike in the increasingly doctrinaire market approaches fashionable elsewhere, there was a sense of experimentation baked into Chinese strategies that epitomized an old proverb about how it is best "to make the path while walking."[192] All reforms were driven by a wish to give markets a greater role, but how and how much remained controversial. There was a deeply held belief that no one theoretical model could inform the entire project. In contrast to neoliberalism, Chinese economic thinking remained ideologically and theoretically flexible and paid attention to older traditions, such as the distinction between "heavy" and "light."[193] While "light" goods could "be exposed to the market," "heavy" ones could not.[194] By insisting on this distinction, Chinese reformers discarded the advice that they had received from, for example, Eastern European émigré economists who counseled China to change its system entirely.[195]

Slowly, these reformers tiptoed their way into an unknowable future. The first wave of reforms focused on the countryside. During the 1980s, they turned a collectivized and state-controlled agricultural sector into a market system, albeit one in which the state continued to play a crucial role. Led by a cohort of young economists who, under Mao, had been forced to live for a decade in the countryside and thus knew it well, they created the so-called household responsibility system that gave rural cultivators control over production, while land and some inputs remained under state control. Grain had to be sold in certain quantities and at fixed prices. When market prices were high, this served as a tax on peasants. But when prices were low, this system supported peasants' revenues, moderating income fluctuations. It was a slow liberalization, not a sudden shock, and the state retained control over the prices of major commodities.[196]

By 1984, such a model extended to industry: Prices for "light" commodities were deregulated.[197] A school of economists, including Lou Jiwei and Guo Shuqing, pushed for more radical measures, or what they called "package reform," going up against economists such as Li Yining, who defended a slow approach.[198] The conflict came to a head in 1986, and the less radical path was chosen.[199] As China focused on what it considered the development of "the forces of production" to engineer what its policy elites saw as the preconditions for communism, policymakers developed coastal enclaves as low-wage manufacturing regions, taking the Four Tigers—Hong Kong, Singapore, South Korea, and Taiwan—as a model.[200]

The result was nothing short of spectacular: The Chinese economy grew by 10 percent per year in the first two decades of reform—the fastest economic growth ever recorded. Creating what came to be designated a "socialist market economy with Chinese characteristics," the Chinese path was more successful than the "shock therapy" implemented in post-Soviet Russia and other parts of Eastern Europe.[201] It resulted in a vast expansion of the market logic into new areas of the world—an astounding compression of the capitalist revolution that this book has chronicled. And though observers disagreed about whether this was a way station on the path to communism or a form of capitalism or perhaps both, it was clear that China's was a political economy radically at odds with the neoliberal experiment unfolding

Warning against the "big bang,"
engineering the most rapid economic
development in world history: economists
Li Yining and (a young) Chen Yun.

elsewhere (while having enabled it in the first place by allowing for the global reorganization of production and consumption).

By 1991, the postwar order was no more, and the golden age had ended. Labor's influence had been rolled back, welfare states recast, many enterprises privatized, entire sectors of the economy deregulated, the economic nationalism of the postcolonial world effectively dismantled, and the world of postcapitalism radically reduced, even dissolved. It was a new world—not solely of neoliberals' making but to their liking, notwithstanding the glaring contradiction of China, whose very different and highly statist political economy sealed the victory of the neoliberal revolution. When historian Niall Ferguson and economist Moritz Schularick spoke of "Chimerica," the economic mergence between China and America, they captured exactly the nature of that symbiotic relationship.[202] Capitalism's new diversity powered, as always, its further expansion.

As they unfolded across the world, these reconstructions of global capitalism took a wide variety of forms and policy approaches. Despite their diversity, they mutually shaped one another. As low-wage manufacturing became a core feature of economies in the Global South, it put pressure on manufacturing employment in the industrial heartlands of the North Atlantic. In turn, as the pressure on labor and the welfare state increased in the industrial heartland, the deeper integration of Global South economies into commodity chains allowed for the relocation of the production of many consumer goods to low-wage locations. Cheaper products allowed working-class consumers in the Global North to maintain high levels of consumption despite stagnant incomes.[203]

The effects of this recasting can be seen in many ways. They inscribed themselves into the great edifices of economic life and into the most intimate nooks of societies. Almost everywhere, life under neoliberalism was shockingly different. Perhaps most obviously, patterns of inequality changed. Within all societies, income and wealth inequalities sharpened. These changes became so noteworthy that in 2013, when French economist Thomas Piketty published a book on their historical patterns with the succinct but unsexy title *Capital in the Twenty-First Century*, it became one of the great bestsellers of its age and its author a celebrity. The work of Piketty and his colleagues demonstrated, for example, that in Chile, one of the earliest examples of neoliberal reengineering, the top 1 percent of taxpayers had received 9.8 percent of all income in 1974; seven years later, their share had almost doubled to 17 percent. The most far-reaching changes they chronicled, however, occurred in the United States and the United Kingdom, the two countries in the world's historic industrial heartland that had most aggressively embraced neoliberalism. In the US, less than 35 percent of total income had gone to the top 10 percent of taxpayers in the 1970s; by the 2000s, that share had gone up to around 50 percent. In the UK, the top 10 percent's share rose from less than 30 percent to more than 40 percent. Even more remarkable was the share received by the top 1 percent, which increased in the United States from around 8 percent in 1973 to around 18 percent in 2008, and in the UK from 7 percent to 15 percent—more than double. Similar trends could be observed in continental European countries and Japan, although they were less pronounced.[204]

When it came to wealth, inequality was even starker: By 2010, the "one-percenters," as they came to be known in the United States, owned almost 40 percent of all assets. Wherever we look, a small minority of citizens owned dramatically greater shares of wealth. In 2010, the top 10 percent owned 60 percent of all assets in France and 70 percent in Britain and the United States. Worldwide, the richest one-tenth of 1 percent, or 0.1 percent, controlled 20 percent of all assets on Earth; the richest 1 percent, 50 percent; and the richest 10 percent, somewhere between 80 and 90 percent. Looked at from a different perspective, it is striking that capitalist societies generated such wealth but at the same time remained societies in which most people owned almost nothing.[205] Despite the fantastic claims of many neoliberal intellectuals, capitalism thus never even came close to producing an "ownership society" and in fact, under their stewardship, moved sharply away from that ideal.

Unsurprisingly, these redistributions track with labor's waning power. In the United States, the decline of the wage share in the nation's GDP paralleled the fall of the union movement almost exactly.

Politics mattered greatly in this redistribution. Not only was the fading of labor's power related to political choices, but other policies

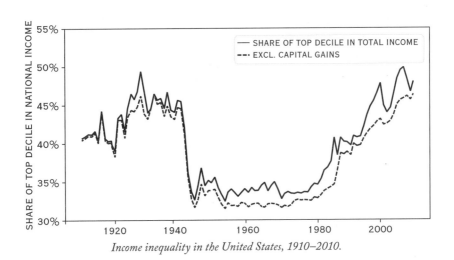

Income inequality in the United States, 1910–2010.

also increased inequality. California's Proposition 13, amending the California Constitution to limit property tax increases, unleashed a torrent of regressive tax policies across the United States. Tax cuts on capital gains and much lower marginal income tax rates accelerated inequality. Estate taxes came under attack as well, with US Republican activist Jim Martin labeling them the "death tax" in the early 1990s. Under pressure from business organizations such as the Chamber of Commerce, the United States temporarily repealed and then lowered them in the early 2000s. As a result, inherited wealth became much more important, making up, according to Piketty, between 60 and 70 percent of the world's largest fortunes in the early 2010s.[206] Such manifestly unfair advantages threw into sharp and painful question capitalism's legitimizing myths of equal opportunity.

The effects of such redistributions of wealth and income were plainly visible on the streets of the industrial heartland. In 1980, the number of homeless people in the United States was estimated to be 250,000; in January 2008, the Department of Housing and Urban Development re-

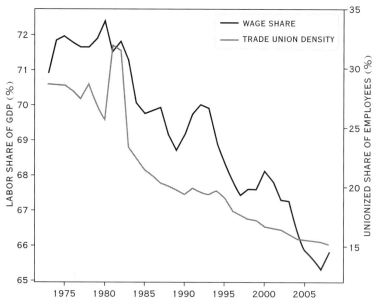

Wage share and trade union density for Austria, Belgium, France, Germany, Italy, Portugal, Spain, the Netherlands, and the United States.

ported a dismally higher figure—664,000. The number of shelter beds in the US tripled between 1984 and 1988. The tent cities that were common in Gilded Age America and during the Great Depression had all but disappeared after the rise of New Deal programs, yet by the early 1980s, they had returned in force to American cities.[207]

These sharpened inequalities even etched themselves into people's very biology. Life expectancy diverged: At the end of the aughts, the average at-birth life expectancy in the UK was 78.2 years for men and 82.3 years for women. It was highest in the wealthy London neighborhoods of Kensington and Chelsea, where life expectancy at birth was 85.1 years for men and 89.8 years for women. It was lowest in Glasgow, where life expectancy at birth was 71.6 years for men and 78.0 years for women. In other words, a man born in Kensington lived almost fourteen years longer than one born in Glasgow, where, during the 1990s, 30 percent of inhabitants lived below the official poverty line. In the United States, low-skilled white American workers without a college degree, increasingly shunted aside by structural economic changes, also faced rapidly rising mortality, experiencing what economists Anne Case and Angus Deaton have called "deaths of despair"—that is, suicide, accidental overdose, and liver disease. Between 1995 and 2015, the likelihood of dying tripled among middle-aged men (between forty-five and fifty-four years old) without a BA. Early in the twenty-first century, the richest 1 percent of male income earners in the United States had a life expectancy of 87.3 years at age forty to seventy-six, while the bottom 1 percent lived almost fifteen years shorter, on average, with a life expectancy of 72.7 years. On average, rich women lived exactly 10.1 years longer than their poor counterparts.[208]

While the shifts in the patterns of inequality amounted to radical changes in some of society's macrostructures, neoliberalism's effects reshaped some of life's most intimate aspects as well, particularly gender relations. As wages stopped rising, it became increasingly difficult to sustain a family on one income. To maintain levels of consumption, families worked longer hours and more jobs, and sent more members of the household into the paid labor force, opening new opportunities for women. At the same time, dependence on reproductive work for pay—cooking, cleaning, child-rearing, and elder care, among others—increased, and the family itself became infused with new market relations. A new "gender order" emerged. Capitalism had always reinvented labor regimes, political arrangements, and territorial regimes, but now it was inventing and reinventing the family too. Ironically, neoliberalism's economic impetus undermined existing family structures more effectively than social movements such as feminism ever did. In a show of staggering hypocrisy, neoliberals at the same time endowed the family with new ideological and economic importance, holding it out as a kind of welfare state in miniature that was to cushion market blows. As Margaret Thatcher had argued at the very beginning of these shifts: "There is no such thing [as society]. . . . There are individual men and women and there are families."[209] As often as not, these women and men now worked double shifts to pay their day-care bills.

Just as the neoliberal order altered the greatest macrostructures of society in tandem with life's most intimate aspects, it also created a rapid spread of the logic of capital into new spaces and spheres. The expansive nature of capital and its tendency to grow, flow, and permeate all areas of activity was age-old, an essential, irreducible quality of capitalism. So, too, was its restless, always surprisingly unfinished and unsettled nature—time and again finding new levels and further frontiers, touching and transforming fresh lands, fresh labor, and fresh realms of human life. But after the 1970s, its expansion reached a new intensity, both in its speed and in its social and geographic scope.

Markets spread across space and society through a new wave of enclosures, as more land, food, information, ideas, and stretches of nature were fenced off and turned into marketable private properties, whether through old-fashioned land grabs or the framing of novel property rights to biological life and information. Spheres of production and social life that had historically been outside the capitalist logic were now pressed into its service, creating linked opportunities for both accumulation and dispossession.[210] These enclosures were stunningly diverse in scale and character—some as small as a soccer field, some as extensive as the plains of Ethiopia or the vast forests on the Indonesian island of Kalimantan. They were rural and urban, material assets and immaterial ones.

Cities, for example, saw new enclosures, as formerly public spaces were privatized. The Lebanese capital of Beirut illustrates such privatization: Spaces once accessible to, and used by, the public were turned over to the control of private interests that made these spaces either inaccessible or limited to those who could pay for them. Public access to Beirut's seafront became more difficult as private developers encroached. The Dalieh shoreline, a vibrant open-air space that, even though privately owned, had always been used by the public for picnicking, bathing, practicing yoga, and meeting with friends, was purchased by three politically connected development companies in 1995. In 2004, they started negotiations with the few resident fishermen-squatters to get them to leave the area, then fenced it in and began building a luxury hotel and marina. A long Lebanese tradition of *sirān*—family outings into nature—became more constricted as nature was increasingly demarcated, closed off, and policed. Youth-controlled informal soccer fields in the city were also paved over into parking lots or built up. A careful study found that by 2013, 85 percent of informal soccer fields that had existed in 2003 had been turned into pay-to-park lots. Perhaps even more dramatically, the Solidere real estate development resulted in the government handing over large stretches of downtown Beirut to a Gulf-funded private real estate company for redevelopment, thus putting full state power behind a massive reimagining of one of the most important Lebanese urban spaces. This kind of urban restructuring became a hallmark of neoliberalism—and an important frontier of enclosure the world over.[211]

The world's countryside also experienced a new wave of enclosures. In Africa, what came to be called "land grabbing" was an overwhelming sign of the neoliberal moment, as investors focused on the continent's ample mining, agricultural, and water resources or appropriated land for real estate speculation and oil exploitation. Investors came from Europe and the United States, as well as from China, India, South Korea, the Gulf States, and African countries such as Kenya and Nigeria. Chinese firms such as Sinopec, Huawei, the Chinese National Petroleum Corporation, and the China Minmetals Corporation invested in Africa, as did British-Australian multinational Rio Tinto, Brazilian corporation Vale, and American mining giant Newmont. Soy projects in Mozambique expanded under Brazilian technical assistance during the late 2000s, pushing rural cultivators off their land and out of their traditional rural economy. Saudi companies invested in vast swaths of Sudan and Ethiopia, disrupting—dislodging, really—existing local economies. Saudi-owned Hadco acquired nine thousand hectares of land in Sudan; Saudi Star purchased three hundred thousand hectares in Ethiopia. Unlike in the nineteenth century, capital from the Global South now played major roles in these enclosures. In Nigeria, political and economic elites used their power and wealth to acquire large commercial farms: Abdullahi Adamu, the former governor of Nasarawa, built Africa's largest dairy farm, with thirty-seven thousand cows. Ota Farms, owned by former president Olusegun Obasanjo, employs seven thousand workers. Murtala Nyako, the former governor of Adamawa State, operates one of the country's largest cattle farms, along with mango plantations. Other members of the elite manage palm oil and cassava plantations.[212]

From 1973 to 2008, capital owners pushed commodity frontiers into the global countryside at a speed that would have been inconceivable to even the most boosterish actors on the Caribbean sugar frontier three hundred years earlier. Despite all the neoliberal rhetoric, the state continued to play a central role in advancing these frontiers—indeed so important that massive US-launched military campaigns in the Middle East secured inexpensive supplies of fossil fuels. As former Fed chairman Alan Greenspan wrote, "I am saddened that it is politically inconvenient to acknowledge what everyone knows: the Iraq war is largely about oil."[213]

Also consider something as mundane as palm oil, extracted from the oil palm plant and used in the production of not only processed food products but also agrofuels such as ethanol. Oil palm was a relatively minor crop until the 1970s, when its production expanded at breakneck speed. By 2016, 10 percent of all oil-crop producing lands worldwide were dedicated to oil palm production—a total of twenty-one million hectares, almost equal to the surface area of the United Kingdom. Oil palm had become the fastest-growing monoculture in the world.[214]

No country was as important to the industry as Indonesia, a nation that controlled more than half of global oil palm production by the 2010s. The growth of its plantations was astonishing: Between 2000 and 2010, they quadrupled in size. By the 2010s more than one-third of all Indonesian agricultural land was under oil palm cultivation, a change enabled by state land concessions, deforestation, the dispossession and expulsion of Indigeneous people, an eager World Bank, and international investments.[215]

It was the new postcolonial Indonesian government, not the Dutch Empire, that provided the framework for this new commodity frontier. In the 1970s, Indonesia greatly benefited from fossil fuels—that is, the oil boom. As this subsided and the strategy of import-substitution industrialization receded, the country looked for new revenue streams. Oil palm was one possibility. By the mid-1980s, as Indonesia embraced neoliberal policy strategies—privatization, deregulation, reduced trade barriers, export-driven industrialization, and agrarian world market production—it provided ever more concessions to oil palm plantations. To provide the labor that they required, the state moved people out of densely inhabited Java to islands slotted for oil palm production, and to open space for growers, it pushed people off their lands. In southern Jambi on Sumatra, for example, the Batin Sembilan's land was turned into oil palm plantations in the 1980s. As the government provided the framework for investments, large multinational corporations pressed into the market and got access to land concessions; just fifty conglomerates came to control 75 percent of global oil palm production, while just fifteen companies came to control more than 75 percent of global processing. Small peasant producers of oil palm became subcontractors to these conglomerates. Most investors came from Singapore and Malaysia, while some were from Indonesia itself, the huge multinational Salim Group among them. At the same time, the actual market for palm oil, the plant's "liquid gold," was dominated by a small number of powerful multinationals, including Unilever, Nestlé, and Procter & Gamble.[216]

A focus on new forms of commodification emerged in the formerly socialist world too. There, almost all firms had been under state ownership. After 1990, they were privatized. The Hungarian State Property Agency, which took control of the privatization process in that country, sold almost one-third of its assets by late 1993, with about half going to foreign investors. Before the end of socialism, foreign direct investment in Hungary had been almost nonexistent. By 1995, it amounted to US $12 billion; by 2001, to US $23.5 billion. Germany and the Netherlands were the most important investors (accounting for more than half), followed by Austria and the United States. After acquiring large swaths of the Hungarian postal, telecommunications, and transportation sectors, German investors built manufacturing plants that drew on cheap Hungarian labor to produce parts for the booming German export sector.[217]

SUCH EXPANSION HELPED maintain a high level of consumption in the industrial heartland despite the redistribution of wealth toward the rich. It also enabled an immense expansion of consumption for an ascendant middle class in the Global South. But these came at the cost of drastic environmental consequences. As the ecological effects of production were by and large not priced, capital drew generously on these free inputs; indeed, it devoured them, flattening vast rainforests, poisoning the atmosphere and oceans, and killing off a significant share of the world's beautifully diverse forms of life that had evolved over millions of years. Most dramatic, and symbolic of the age, was the almost doubling of carbon-dioxide emissions between 1973 and 2008, largely the result of an unprecedented expansion of industry in China and India, where carbon-dioxide emissions soared approximately sevenfold (from a very low base, since these countries had previously contributed very little). With energy- and pollution-intensive production moving into the Global South, that region carried the environmental burdens of ever accelerating production, creating what British geographer Laurie Parsons has called "carbon colonialism"—that is, the spewing of carbon dioxide in the Global South producing things consumed in the Global North.[218]

The escalating environmental footprint of capitalism existed on a scale inconceivable to the early merchant capitalists of Aden and Florence (who seem quaint in retrospect), the planters of Barbados, and even the lords of the loom in Manchester. No wonder geologists began debating if Earth had entered a new geological age, one some scholars called "Capitalocene."[219]

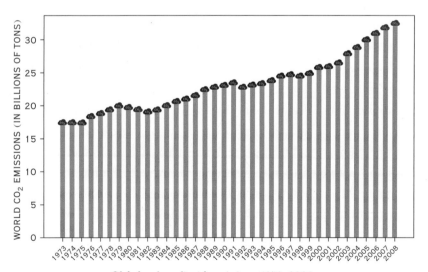

Global carbon-dioxide emissions, 1973–2008.

F rontiers of commodification spread more deeply in society as well. More relations were thought of and structured in terms of markets, what political scientist Wendy Brown called the emergence of "*Homo oeconomicus.*"[220] Older schools of economic thinking had made allowances for spheres of life outside economic logic—religion, family, community. Under neoliberalism, individuals became the embodiment of what was now considered "human capital."[221] People came to be seen—and to see themselves—as objects to be "invested" in; they jockeyed to improve their position on the market. Even branding the self became a trope, with books such as *How to Brand Yourself* and *Find a Husband After 35: Using What I Learned at Harvard Business School* hitting the shelves. In contradistinction to the notion held by all the world's religious and philosophical traditions that humans had a value in and of themselves, radical ideologues primarily valued people for their position in the market. Even the very notion of "freedom" moved from political to economic life.[222] Karl Polanyi, characteristically, had already seen the truly radical notion of this change in the 1940s, when he suggested that the dominance of market patterns "means no less than the running of society as an adjunct to the market," for him a project to be resisted.[223]

Even the state became increasingly conceived of, and subject to, the logic of markets, not just in terms of its military prowess but in terms of its ability to attract mobile capital. In the 1990s, Germany was drawn into a debate about whether it was still an attractive *Standort* (location) for global investors and, if not, how it could be made into one. Subnational spaces—regions—also engaged in such competitions and marketed themselves to capital owners, aiming to draw investors to Massachusetts or to France's Grand Est. India engaged in such locational politics with its "India Shining" campaign, which celebrated the country's newfound wealth and newly created middle class, propagating an "investor-citizenship shaped around the language and logic of loss and profits"—and sold itself to global capital owners as an attractive location for investment and extraction.[224]

If the nation could be turned into a branded commodity and the individual could be reduced to human capital, almost nothing escaped commodification. Even human reproduction—eggs, sperm, wombs— could be had for a price; "buying babies" was now possible.[225] Dating could be commoditized by large firms as well, with new websites and apps like Match.com inserting commercial transactions into how people met one another. Love could be had, but it would cost you. Even the long-sought possibility of conquering death turned into a business. As ever more realms of life turned into commodities, the logic of commodities dominate life, including when it came to love and sex. "Romantic forms," in fact, had always mirrored certain moments in the history of capitalism, with the latest stage focused on flexibility and fluidity—what came to be known as "hookup culture," a perfect supplement to the neoliberal age. At the same time, care work, both of children and of the elderly, was increasingly commodified, as was education.[226]

Looking back from the vantage point of 2019, a former lead economist at the World Bank, Branko Milanovic, could publish a book with the provocative and slightly exaggerated title *Capitalism, Alone,* in which he argued that "the entire globe now operates to the same economic principles." It was, as he rightly observed, a world

The neoliberal utopia: the Bharatiya Janata Party's "India Shining" campaign, 2003.

"without historical precedent." "The domination of capitalism . . . seems absolute."[227]

========

Yet the newly established global order came with a multitude of insurgencies, as had been the case throughout capitalism's history. To contemporaries, these resistances often seemed intensely local, marked by failure, even quixotism. They had a kind of David-versus-Goliath feel—more spectacle than historically meaningful. Yet in the end, they brought the neoliberal order to its knees, if not yet to its deathbed.

Insurgencies unfolded in many different parts of the world and assumed a wide variety of forms. In Beirut, as urban spaces were enclosed, youths looked for access to alternative venues and even mobilized to protect the spaces they had previously used, attacking cars in the parking lots that had once been their soccer fields. In South Africa, landless workers mobilized against land enclosures, while anti-privatization movements tried to secure continued access to electricity. China was riven by labor unrest. In 2005, official reports listed eighty-seven thousand "mass incidents," many of them labor-related. There were strikes among Hebei miners in 1999 and among Nanjing chemical workers in 2001. Sugar workers demanded back pay that same year, and up to fifty thousand workers protested in the Daqing Oil Field in 2002. In the mid-1990s, in the southern Mexican state of Chiapas, a movement of Indigenous people who styled themselves as the Ejército Zapatista de Liberación Nacional rebelled against neoliberal reforms and demanded "land and democracy."[228] Africans resisted land grabbing—for example, fighting against the expropriation of Ejeme land in the delta region of Nigeria. Between 1987 and 1989, student activists shook Nigeria when they led urban riots against structural adjustments and removal of state subsidies.[229] A strike wave in France in the winter of 1995 successfully agitated against planned reforms of the French welfare state. Peak events of the neoliberal revolution, such as meetings of the World Trade Organization in Seattle and Genoa or gatherings of the World Economic Forum in Davos, regularly attracted dissent. Opponents of the new order met regularly at what came to be called the World Social Forum, first in Porto Alegre, then in Mumbai and Nairobi, among other cities. In 2011, the United States was rocked by social upheaval when a movement known as Occupy Wall Street took over a park in the financial heart of New York.

Challenges came from the right as well. In many parts of the world, ethnonationalist and populist movements emerged, articulating a fundamental critique of the neoliberal order. As Polish agriculture was thrown into turmoil by its integration into European markets, and as farmers suffered from freer trade, higher interest rates, competition with producers elsewhere, and lack of political representation, they launched the Samoobrona movement, which, beginning in 1991, demanded state support for highly indebted peasants and militantly agitated against political and economic elites. Just like elsewhere, Polish anti-neoliberal movements fed their energies into right-wing populist

Rebellions against neoliberalism (clockwise from top left): London (2008); Dakar, Senegal (2011); La Garrucha, Mexico (2007); and Orléans, France (2009).

forces. The backlash led to the emergence of newly powerful forces on the right in many parts of the world, among them the Tea Party in the United States, the National Front in France, the Freedom Party in Austria, the AfD in Germany, and the Lega Nord in Italy. These movements had many disturbing features (such as the National Front's origin among former members of the Waffen-SS and the AfD's embrace of *völkische* ideologues last seen during the Nazi regime), but one oddity was that their critique of neoliberalism was an acute one and certainly far more perceptive than that of an identitarian left. Not all these political forces broke with neoliberalism entirely—indeed, some just repackaged it by bringing to the fore the culturally conservative, racist, and ethnonationalist strands that had been embedded within the neoliberal movement all along. But deep dissatisfaction with the actually existing neoliberal order as it had been constructed in the previous three decades mobilized most of these new movements, with their yearning for an exclusionary nationalism.[230]

And then came 2008, the year the world financial system almost melted down. The worst economic crisis since the Great Depression started with the collapse of the US housing market. For years, financial institutions had speculated in this booming market; as prices rose rapidly (they almost doubled between 1996 and 2006), they financed mortgages for millions of Americans who were ill-equipped to shoulder their costs. As prices surged, Americans who had very little (or no) capital opted to invest in the housing market, taking advantage of low interest rates, including so-called teaser rates, believing that the rise in value of the underlying assets would eventually allow them to refinance their mortgages. In 2003 alone, US institutions issued mortgages adding up to $3.8 trillion. They made much of that capital available through a new tool they had invented, mortgage-backed securities, which allowed them to securitize mortgages and then sell them on in tranches across the world—a pensioner in Germany, for example, might purchase slices of what came to be called the subprime housing market. For many of the underlying mortgages there was no realistic chance that they would ever be paid back. By 2007, $1.3 trillion worth of such securities had been issued. The expansion of this shaky business was, according to the foremost chronicler of the crisis, Adam Tooze, "spectacular, not to say grotesque."[231] As a writer for Bloomberg observed in retrospect: These were "Ponzi-like conditions."[232] By 2005, two-thirds of the mortgages wrapped into mortgage-backed securities issued by the storied US investment bank Lehman Brothers were such subprime mortgages.[233]

Financial institutions sucked up these securities because capital searched for presumably secure investment opportunities. Yet when US home prices began to decline in 2006, the entire house of cards came tumbling down. Banks had retained on their books hundreds of billions of dollars in such mortgage-backed securities. Sometimes they had financed the acquisition of such mortgages with so-called repo (repurchasing) agreements in which they sold the securities for a period of time, agreeing to repurchase them at a specified price in the future. With the accelerating decline of the value of the underlying assets—houses in the United States—this scheme collapsed, and banks found themselves facing huge losses. Rapidly, the entire US mortgage market crumpled, and with it the finances of millions of individual households. Major financial institutions failed, as did a wide variety of companies dependent on credit and, eventually, entire countries. As one banker remembered: "It was something none of us had experienced. It was as if your entire life you had turned the spigot and water came out. And now there was no water."[234] Nine million Americans lost their homes and eight million their jobs.[235]

The effects swiftly spread around the world, testifying to the density of links that had been established by the financialized capitalism of the neoliberal order. US real estate made up about 20 percent of global assets, so the sector's downward spiral had global consequences. As the credit markets crumbled, firms and households went bankrupt. German exports fell by 18 percent in 2008/9, making it the most severe economic crisis since the founding of the Federal Republic of

Germany. For the president of Japanese car manufacturer Toyota, "the change in the world economy is of a magnitude that comes once every hundred years. . . . We are facing an unprecedented emergency."[236] In Chile—the country that had played such a pioneering role in the neoliberal revolution—the crisis struck just as suddenly and just as hard. As the global economy decelerated, demand for Chile's crucial export—copper—fell, and its price declined precipitously. Effects rippled across its economy: Investments wilted along with exports and imports, and unemployment skyrocketed. In 2009, about one-quarter of Chile's workers, 1,516,325 women and men, received termination letters. By the end of the decade, half of all Chilean workers in regular employment drew a wage that was lower than the poverty line for families. When union activist Lilian Gallardo in Santiago de Chile was interviewed by a journalist during a protest march of twelve thousand workers through Santiago, she shared a widely held sentiment: She was "fed up with abuses by businessmen who are sheltering behind the crisis and making huge layoffs."[237]

Throughout the world, governments, fearful of a redux of the Great Depression of the 1930s, did their best to pump huge sums of taxpayer money into failing businesses. According to one estimate, China, Japan, Germany, and the US spent a total of $1.45 trillion to support their respective economies, confirming once more that the very condition for capitalism's survival was an ever escalating involvement of the state.[238] Despite all the noise made by neoliberal ideologues, capitalism remained a most thoroughly statist economic order. And the trillions of dollars in state funds eventually succeeded in stabilizing that order once more. But the Great Recession, as it came to be known, severely eroded capitalism's, and especially neoliberalism's, legitimacy in the eyes of many millions.

Epilogue:

The Possibilities of an Island and the Future of Capitalism

Capital secedes: Brecqhou in the Channel Islands.

It is early morning on the dimly lit streets at the outskirts of the Cambodian capital of Phnom Penh. Tuk-tuks zip along dusty roads carrying women dressed in the colorful uniforms required by their factories; makeshift trailers full of people towed by motorcycles pull up next to trucks carrying dozens upon dozens of workers, tightly squeezed together. The women pick up cheap lunches from sidewalk vendors—fried vegetables, banana and beans in steamed sticky rice, or grilled coconut cakes—before hurrying past the factory's guarded gates to spend the day bent over sewing machines, stitching the avalanche of clothing that inundates the richer parts of the world. At 7:00 a.m. sharp, the factory gates close. Latecomers are fined.[1]

*The commute: Cambodian garment workers on the way
to their shift, Phnom Penh, February 2023.*

Cambodia is a small country with about seventeen million inhabitants, its horrifying history evinced by the eerie absence of older people (in the early 2020s, only 3.8 percent of its population was older than sixty), its memorials to the killing fields, and the nightmares of many of its people. By the time the Khmer Rouge's terrifying rule came to an end in 1979, the regime had killed about one-fifth of the country's citizens. Though still one of the world's poorest countries, Cambodia changed at a dizzying pace as the capitalist revolution arrived on its shores. One million of its citizens began working in the garment industry, including one in five women, producing a volume of clothing that grew eleven times in twenty years. A who's who of global brands depends on Cambodia's cheap labor, Adidas, Nike, and H&M among them.[2] This extraordinary growth was driven by a wave of proletarianization that unfolded at breakneck speed: Less than a generation ago, the women stitching clothing lived with their extended families in rural areas, grew rice, harvested mangos, and raised chickens.

Srey Mau was one of them. Thirty-eight years old in 2023, she lives in a small village about three hours southeast of Phnom Penh, near the border with Vietnam. Sustaining rural life had become almost impossible for her family when the old barter economy that had still structured rural life in her parents' lifetime collapsed. They, like most others in their village, had taken up wage work in addition to growing and selling rice and vegetables. Suddenly their lives were connected to the far corners of the world. Srey's older sister migrated to Korea, and at age twenty-five, Srey left the rice fields, too, when a friend recruited her to work in a garment factory in Phnom Penh. After a short stint, she moved to neighboring Thailand to clean supermarkets, spending much of her earnings to pay back the employment agency that had funded her journey abroad. Homesick, she returned to her village. By then a factory had been built nearby, a nondescript and unmarked concrete building that ran billboard ads to draw in workers. In a reverse mobilization, the factory had come to the countryside rather than the other way around. Srey was paid a monthly wage of $175 for working eight hours a day (six, often seven, days a week) to stitch together clothing for her Chinese employer. A brand-new Chinese-constructed road connected her once remote rice-growing region to the capital and, more importantly, to Vietnam, and from there on to China. Depending on the factory's orders, she sometimes had to work overtime; at other times she was laid off. Sometimes, she reports, wages were not paid at all. It is "too easy to be thrown away as garbage," Srey says, summarizing her experience of a life that just a generation earlier would have been extraordinary, even unimaginable, to people in her village but is now so common as to have become a cliché.[3]

As in much of the history of capitalism, a crisis in rural life had propelled people to make a little extra income to send back to the villages where their families still lived or to permanently move to the sprawling slums of the capital. Wage labor also became critical to the economic security of families who stayed on the land. As they changed their farming practices to produce for long-distance markets, they required fertilizers, pesticides, new seeds, and mechanical harvesting. These things all cost money, and the interest on the loans taken out to acquire them had to be paid too.[4] Without cash contributions from family members, their tenuous hold on their land could loosen and give way at any moment.

Again, as in the past, factory conditions are often harsh, with supervisors and employers abusing workers and withholding salaries for errors. Women can be fired for pregnancy. But the workers' income is unmatched elsewhere: In 2023, the Cambodian legal minimum wage was the equivalent of $200 a month. Workers try to keep expenses to a minimum, often sharing windowless rooms, with three to eight people to a room. Rent per person comes to somewhere between $30 and $50 a month.[5] Because they cannot take care of their children, parents usually leave them behind in the countryside with their grandparents, seeing them only on holidays.

Workers make attempts to collectively improve their conditions: A strike wave in 2013 shook the industry but achieved little in the face of confident employer and state resistance. The Cambodian government understands its competitive advantage in providing cheap labor for the world market. According to a local American observer of the labor scene, the country practices a form of "authoritarian capitalism," with opposition parties outlawed and the free press squashed.[6]

In the aughts, Cambodia was one of the newest hot spots of the capitalist revolution, a capitalist wonderland. Capitalism came to Cambodia late. Until well into the nineteenth century, Cambodians had relied almost exclusively on barter, with the capitalist logic merely on the margins of economic life.[7] Only in the twenty-first century did that logic arrive with full force on the shores of the Mekong, and when it did, it came with such a bang that transformations that had taken centuries elsewhere unfolded in a fraction of the time. Capitalism had gained so much energy that industrial complexes and cities mushroomed in years, not decades; infrastructures that typically took decades to build sprouted up almost overnight, and lives were turned upside down over just one generation. Any doubts about the vitality of capitalism, for better or worse, vanish after a visit to its present-day frontiers, places like Cambodia.

The city of Kampong Saom, also known as Sihanoukville, in the country's South, is a showcase for this madcap transformation, full of high-rises, glittering shopping malls, casinos, and brand-new boulevards. Before the turn of the millennium, the Lonely Planet travel guide *Southeast Asia on a Shoestring* had little to say about it, other than that "near town, there are superb beaches."[8] Perhaps sixteen thousand people lived in wooden houses along the palm-fringed coastline. Some worked at the port. Most fished. Others, farther inland, grew some rice. Savmit Chea, who moved to the city in 1994 as a teacher—after an odyssey as a soldier in a children's unit of Pol Pot's army, a stint in an orphanage, and studies abroad—remembers the town as "calm," with unpaved streets and dense forests between homes, its pleasant beaches simply places of work, mostly fishing, and sometimes sunbathing spots for a few backpacking refugees from the capitalist revolution in the industrial heartlands.[9]

Not even a generation later, one hundred thousand Cambodians and an estimated two hundred thousand Chinese live in a city with no shortage of Rolls-Royces and Bentleys, a city where an air-conditioned Starbucks inside a luxury residential high-rise sells coffee and where shopping malls carry coveted Western brands. It has become an island of Chinese capital in a foreign land. Its vastly expanded and modernized container-based port transports Cambodian-made goods and raw materials to far-flung parts of the world. Special economic zones surround the city. But the beating heart of Kampong Saom is its gambling industry, the prime location for Cambodia's casinos, which are more numerous than in Las Vegas and Macau combined.[10]

The swiftness of this transformation was truly astounding. New construction started in around 2000, but it was after the subprime crisis of 2008 that international investors rushed to buy up land. When gambling arrived in 2015, construction exploded. Individual investors and private equity funds, supported by Hun Sen's authoritarian government, grabbed properties as quickly as they could. Beachfronts sold fast, and entire islands were brought to market. Russian investor Alexander Trofimov bought Koh Puos, an island, to build a resort, still unfinished. But most of the massive influx of money came from China. Land prices in Kampong Saom increased tenfold between 2014 and 2019, to about $3,000 per square meter.[11]

Development was anarchic. Investors bypassed residents, bribing local officials for access to land and construction permits. They turned beaches into private property, even though Cambodian law stipulated that all beaches are public. Fishermen were forcefully relocated into forested areas away from the coast. A beachside settlement of 229 families was razed in 2006, with the police evicting residents and bulldozers immediately rolling in to make room for a hotel.[12] Investors had mango, breadfruit, papaya, jackfruit, and coconut trees systematically uprooted, robbing residents of the resources that had nurtured them. As an eyewitness to this transformation, Savmit recalls that the "rich and powerful people took land from poor people" who could neither produce land titles nor afford to pay bribes. "Developers destroyed existing dwellings, took the land, supported by the police and the army. Poor people never win in court."[13] Savmit saw entire families just walk away from their land with all they owned on their backs—an echo of a process that had propelled the capitalist revolution since the expulsion of European peasants from their fields and the dispossessions of Indigenous peoples in the Americas centuries before.

But Kampong Saom's boom ended as quickly as it had begun. In 2019, online gambling for Chinese citizens, one of the city's most lucrative businesses, was outlawed. Then came COVID-19, which kept Chinese gambling tourists away. The city became a hub for organized crime, contraband trading, money laundering, and human and wildlife trafficking. Online scamming became another stream of business, with thousands of

The beach frontier, July 2018: children living near a garbage dump in Kampong Saom (Sihanoukville), Cambodia, after their families were expelled from their beachside properties.

underpaid (or unpaid) workers. According to Cambodian government official Sok Phal, in 2023, eighty thousand to one hundred thousand workers labored under duress in the digital industry, some quite literally imprisoned. Trade in illegal ivory and timber exports to feed China's furniture industry was another new outlet. But despite this diversification, a stunning one thousand unfinished buildings blight the city today—at least until new ventures swoop in.[14] When they do, China will take the lead. Already in 2023, new master plans were drawn up in Shenzhen to reorient Kampong Saom's development around Chinese investment in its special economic zones "to enhance the integration of a diversified Cambodia–China production capacity."[15]

GAMBLING, BEACHFRONT TOURISM, and apparel manufacturing were not the only commodity frontiers draining the energy of Cambodia's workers and gobbling up their land. In 2008, reporters at *The Guardian* filed a story on the country that ran with the headline COUNTRY FOR SALE and detailed how "almost half of Cambodia has been sold to foreign speculators in the past 18 months."[16] By 2020, one-fifth of all people in the countryside had lost access to the land.[17] Global capital's capture of Cambodia was the economic equivalent of a blitzkrieg.

The contours of this new frontier are visible everywhere: Drivers on the brand-new highway between Phnom Penh and Kampong Saom pass mile upon mile of densely planted rubber, mango, and oil palm crops. In the southwestern province of Koh Kong, business mogul Ly Yong Phat partnered with a Taiwanese company accused of land grabs and human-rights abuses to build sugar plantations. Pepper plantations spread in Kampot and elsewhere. The Thai-owned multinational Charoen Pokphand Foods Company Limited (CPF) arrived in Cambodia in 1996, seeing an opportunity in the chicken and pork industries to sell feed to local peasants and engage in contract farming. It moved into the food business in 2000 and into retail in 2020. With twenty-three hundred employees in 2023, the company has grown annually by 15 percent the past few years. Tourism—from southern beaches to the ruins of Angkor Wat—is another pulsating commodity frontier.[18]

Other commodity frontiers are far more sinister, including the sexual exploitation and export of Cambodian citizens. Tens of thousands of Cambodian women and children, some as young as nine, are brought to Thailand and other places to work off their debt in the sex industry. Poor and vulnerable rural families encourage their daughters to sign up with labor recruiters just to secure the funds necessary to raise their other children. But when their daughters return, many are traumatized, isolated, infected with HIV, and ostracized at home.[19]

Other families sell their daughters into marriage: Chinese men pay up to $10,000 for a Cambodian wife, much of it to an agency, with just $500 typically going to her family. Cambodian women are also used as surrogate mothers. The industry was criminalized in 2016, but women still agree to surrogacy to service their debts.[20]

As ever, women on the front lines of the empire of capital are particularly at risk, but Cambodian men are also sold into forced labor. Brokers organize an illegal funnel of workers, mostly to Thailand, to supply its construction, manufacturing, fishing, sex, and domestic service industries. Some are paid, some not. Yi Lim, today a tuk-tuk driver in Kampong Saom, spent three years in Thailand as a forced worker. Smuggled across the border by a labor agent who walked with him through the jungle, he ended up in the construction industry in Bangkok, laboring on constantly shifting worksites, living in a dormitory with six to eight other men, and earning $200 a month. As he had no passport or other papers, he lived in constant fear of the police.[21]

And then there is the trade in money itself. Cambodia leads the world in microfinance. Heralded as a miracle cure for underdevelopment—even yielding a Nobel Prize for one of its chief advocates, Bangladeshi economist Muhammad Yunus—microfinance loans promised to harness the entrepreneurial energies of marginalized groups. Instead, by the 2020s, they had turned Cambodians into the most highly indebted people in the world as a percentage of their income (allegedly $5,000 per capita on average), forcing them into ever deepening engagement with the market. By 2022, half of all Cambodians had taken out one of these loans. An author researching Cambodia's brick industry found that many of its workers are "debt-bonded." Farmers are also heavily indebted, with many losing their land as a result.[22] But the Phnom Penh president of the Global Real Estate Association, Vichet Lor, thinks that "private debt has positive aspects as well. Private debt will push the economic activities and growth of Cambodia because borrowers need to earn more or work more to get extra income to finance their increasing debt."[23] This sentence could have been uttered by a Belgian colonial official in Congo in 1900 or by a British imperial bureaucrat in India in 1830.

As the labor patterns in Cambodia replicate past capitalist expansions, so, too, does the rapacious consumption of nature. The ample rainforests that covered much of Cambodia as late as 1990 have been cut down not only to feed global markets but also, more prosaically, to power industry, which to this day burns wood to save on electricity costs. As a result, Cambodia's rate of deforestation is the world's fastest.[24]

To be sure, Cambodia's capitalist revolution has also produced tremendous wealth, however wildly concentrated and unequally distributed. In the twenty-first century, its GNP quadrupled—to $1,550 per person in 2023. A very small group of Cambodians became exceedingly rich, a rising new oligarchy closely tied to the governing elite.[25] Elite wealth is visible in Phnom Penh, where high-end high-rises shadow the city, swanky cars cruise well-maintained streets, and fancy cafés and restaurants entertain the rich.

This Cambodian elite originated from an unlikely group: warlords who discovered their entrepreneurial streak when they went into smuggling after the downfall of the Khmer Rouge. Next, they linked themselves to international aid funders who streamed into the country after its civil wars ended. Some moved from abject poverty to ostentatious wealth in just a few years. They make up an elite whose total size is tiny, about five hundred families, and violence has played such an important role in their rise that one observer calls the society they created "predator capitalism."[26] Cambodian author Sokunthea Hang has written about "the contradictions of Phnom Penh" as an "urban witness," reporting that when "friends come to visit from Europe, I have to bear with their amazement at the inequalities of the city"—inequalities that, to her, have become part of the normal fabric of daily life.[27] These elites, reports an American observer, "live in a [well-guarded] bubble."[28]

In a remarkable change that would have been unimaginable to most observers as late as the 1990s, the exterior pole to which Cambodia's transformation is attached is not the United States or the once powerful European centers of the capitalist revolution but China—a country that itself was chasing garment investments only two decades earlier. China's investments have "skyrocketed," driving two-thirds of Cambodia's garment production. By 2017, half of Cambodia's land concessions were held by Chinese companies, and in February of 2023, high-level meetings in Beijing confirmed the "impregnable ironclad friendship" between the two countries.[29]

—————

By the twenty-first century, the capitalist revolution had arrived almost everywhere and impacted virtually all spheres of life. Expansive and radical, it remains the most consequential revolution in world history. And it was global in a thoroughgoing way that no other revolution has ever been, even those that made internationalism a hallmark of their agenda. Workers may have sung "The Internationale," but capital owners practiced it. Capitalism is now so astoundingly and intrinsically global that we can finally grasp the inadequacy of the stories told about it for the past two centuries. If its present is so global, its past cannot possibly be understood solely from national or North Atlantic perspectives.

Despite its overwhelming reach and ubiquitous presence, capitalism continues to be difficult to see. Its totality (and capitalism has always been one totality) cannot be experienced from any one location, because its agents, conditions, and events can seem radically disconnected from other global sites. On the shores of Lake Zurich or in the haunts of the rich in the Hamptons, Singapore, or Mumbai, the worlds of Srey Mau and Yi Lim seem unfathomably far away. Visitors to downtown Shanghai find themselves in a bustling and prosperous mega-metropolis with no palpable connection to the abject poverty of Flint, Michigan. The fresh air of the Black Forest makes preposterous the very idea of the toxic haze settling over Delhi on a December morning. In the seemingly unending and violence-riddled favelas of Rio de Janeiro, it is hard to picture the wealth exuding from the youthful precincts of Palo Alto, or, for that matter, the rich districts of Rio itself. It is clichéd to wonder if such extremes can coexist on a single planet.

But, as has been the case throughout capitalism's history, each node in the global capitalist network either feeds or consumes others, and the connected diversity forged in ever changing combinations of people and places produces the enormous dynamism of capitalist economic development. The wealthy (and the not so wealthy) in a few parts of the world benefit from the ill-paid labor of people elsewhere— and often from the literal destruction of the places in which those people were born. If you are reading this book in Europe, China, or the United States, the physical and mental energies of Srey Mau hang quite literally in your closet; the destruction of the Brazilian rainforest literally props up your retirement portfolio (and mine too), should you be lucky enough to have one.

Capitalism's dynamic is enduring, but to understand its varied expressions requires a careful excavation of its history. Moreover, its history marks our present as the capitalist revolution leverages the wealth, institutions, capacities, and resultant inequalities of past centuries in each new era. Capitalism is thus historical not just in the sense that it stretches back in time but, importantly, in the way it redeploys the past against the challenges of the present and future. A small set of

Europeans and Americans accumulated the obscene riches generated by the slave-powered sugar revolution, not the millions of Africans and their descendants who were forced to tend the crop—a reality that still shapes inequalities today, three centuries later.[30] Closer to home, Harvard University, like other wealthy institutions, is rich in no small part because of the unpaid labor of enslaved people, and its storied leaders transformed that wealth into institutional capacity and cachet that made globe-spanning projects like this book possible. In much of the world, the colonialism-generated destruction of state power is still generating pernicious aftereffects. Opportunities for both individuals and entire nations remain deeply unequal, an inequality shaped by five hundred years of divergences between places and classes. The wealth and power from previous depredations and dispossessions have accumulated in certain regions of the world and among certain groups of people. When we turn to the present, we see that the remnants of this history are now camouflaged in infrastructures and institutions housed in modern structures of marble, steel, and glass.

Such inequalities power our world even in the age of planetary interconnectedness. Some of these inequalities are next door. Others are remote. Where you are born and to whom largely determines where you find yourself within the empire of capital. A child born today in Massachusetts is likely to live nearly ten years longer than a newborn in Mississippi. The opportunities available to a United States citizen are incomparably greater than those available to a person born in Cambodia. Despite unbelievable increases in global wealth over the past five centuries, almost everyone in the world starts life without inheriting any resources transferred from the previous generation—indeed, starting from nothing—with about half of humanity living a life of barest subsistence.

In 2016, a writer at the American magazine *Salon* made a radical argument: Capitalism had reached a point at which "its complete penetration into every realm of being" had become a distinct possibility.

Soon, if not already, everything would be for sale. While systemic limits might, as we have seen, render it impossible to make all human life submit to a capitalist logic, Anis Shivani is right that the logic of capital has spread—and spreads—tentacularly. As this book has demonstrated, no imperial or totalitarian project has ever come close to capitalism's success at nestling into the nooks and crannies of human life. No religion, no ideology, no philosophy, has ever been as all-encompassing as the economic logic of capitalism. Professor of theology Harvey Cox put it succinctly in *The Market as God* when he said that the "religion of the Market" has become omnipresent.[31]

In the twenty-first century, that energy and imperial thrust continue to propel economic life. There are the almost quaint frontiers of the old-fashioned kind, the geographic and physical expansions of the sugar, soy, tea, coffee, and oil palm frontiers. At their cutting edge are deep-sea mining and mining on celestial bodies, bringing private property rights into the world's oceans and outer space.[32]

Commodification—the turning of things into products that can be bought and sold on markets—pushes into yet more surprising spaces as well. Sports, for example, has been radically commodified, with soccer becoming a multibillion-euro industry where everything is for sale—players, images, clubs. Our very attention has become a commodity, too, with social media companies working to lure and hook our preferences in order to sell them. Knowledge about our personal demographics, about what we like and dislike, and about how we see the world is netted and sold on markets. "Capitalism," says Cameroonian philosopher Achille Mbembe, "is the only religion without taboos."[33] Even recordings of our brain waves are on the cusp of being commodified, as companies hope to make our thoughts and emotions visible and salable.[34]

Already in the seventeenth century, William Petty had begun to understand how land and labor could be seen as capital—that is, as profit-producing assets. But he could not have known that many other realms of life would eventually be subjected to this same logic as well. Everything is for sale: You need a new kidney? Estimates suggest that ten thousand kidneys are sold on the black market yearly; in

Afghanistan, where the business flourishes, it is usually debt that drives people to make such a bargain. The illicit trade in human organs rakes in an estimated $1 billion in US dollars annually. You have an underutilized capital asset in your driveway? Start driving for Uber. An empty space in your home? Rent it on Airbnb. Craving some human contact? In Japan, a company called Family Romance rents spouses, colleagues, parents, and even children to keep you company or allow you to display "your" social networks to friends and coworkers. Entirely fake weddings with fake brides, fake bridegrooms, fake parents, and fake guests can be arranged.[35]

Rosa Luxemburg was only half right when she insisted on the importance of the continued spatial expansion of capitalism. Capitalism draws its energy not just by widening in space but by drilling ever deeper into our bodies, our minds, and our most intimate social relations—our very humanity. In 2015, Pope Francis warned of a world where we would become avatars of a logic that had been of our own making, but that had also emancipated itself from us—capitalism as a kind of artificial intelligence that had escaped from the lab and come to govern us, even subdue us.[36]

The constant interaction on markets and the need to sell and consume increasingly define us. Even the time we spend sleeping is diminishing. In Switzerland, the average time that people spent sleeping decreased by a full forty minutes between 1983 and 2011. Time itself is colonized by market logic, as speed dictates the circulation and accumulation of capital. The more churn, the more profit. Efficiency becomes crucial as market-oriented labor colonizes all of life. An "efficient" life is valorized because it serves the market. And as our lives accelerate, we face the market in new ways: According to *The New York Times*, 94 percent of jobs created in the US between 2008 and 2018 were "freelance or contract based," making self-marketing crucial.[37] Gig economy workers must constantly promote themselves, leaving them "paranoid, jittery, self-critical and judgmental."[38] *Homo economicus* strides to the fore and reduces our very humanity to the embodiment of an economic logic—an economic logic that, as this book has shown, is neither natural nor outside history but a revolutionary departure in human affairs.[39]

―――――

This departure has also been defined by historically unique rates of economic growth, especially since the dawn of the industrial age in the early nineteenth century. That growth continued into the new millennium. In 2023, the world produced goods and services valued at about $166 trillion in US dollars, reflecting an additional output of $60 trillion compared with 2008—with that sum more than the world's total output in 1990.[40] As always, this stunning growth resulted from multiple factors: a growing population, larger takings from nature, and extraction from the commons—earth, air, water—into that part of the economy that is statistically counted.

But it is especially the result of greater productivity. Millions of people continued to leave the countryside to enter economic sectors that produced greater value per person. At the same time, a seemingly unending stream of technical innovations made human labor ever more productive, allowing any individual to create greater value per hour worked than ever before. Still more elaborate machinery, often controlled by microchips, made it possible to eliminate much human labor from the process of making things. At the most radical edge were so-called dark factories that did not need to be lit, since the robots doing the work required no light to operate.[41] Klaus Schwab, former head of the World Economic Forum, host of the famous yearly meetings at Davos, sees the mixing of technologies "across the physical, digital and biological domains" as "unlike anything humankind has experienced before."[42] And yet technological changes have been constant throughout capitalism. They testify to enormous human creativity and make possible the imagining of a world in which human needs are more fully met and in which we liberate ourselves from the drudgery of the past as we open up new horizons of possibility for human life.

We are very far from harvesting these possibilities—so far that most of us cannot even begin to picture them. The greatest paradox is this: Though we can produce ever more with ever less labor, the fruits of our efforts and our creativity continue to be distributed in astoundingly unequal ways, leaving many on Earth with absolutely nothing. In 2022, the world's five hundred richest individuals collectively owned as much wealth as the combined poorest half of humanity, or four billion people. Credit Suisse calculated, in 2022, that 1.1 percent of the world's people controlled 45.8 percent of its wealth, almost as much as the other 98.9 percent of the human population taken together. In this "winner-take-all economy," a tiny group of oligarchs have diverted resource flows into their pockets and then used their wealth to shape public opinion and politics in ways that further those flows. As the return on capital exceeds the rate of economic growth, inequality sharpens.[43] Inequalities are further amplified by what economist Branko Milanovic has called "assortative mating," a common strategy throughout five centuries of capitalism's history, with the rich marrying one another and "creating a kind of new aristocracy."[44] This concentration of humanity's wealth in a small stratum of society has largely undone the gains in ameliorating inequality that came out of the postcolonial moment and capitalism's "golden years," which this book has chronicled. The richest 1 percent in India now control more of India's income than the richest 1 percent (Indian and British) had under British colonial rule, 22.6.[45]

As wealth concentrates in a narrower segment of society, economic power concentrates in a smaller number of firms. Capitalism tends toward monopoly, which is bad not just for society and politics but also for markets. When looking at early modern Europe, Fernand Braudel once defined capitalism as the "anti-market," and while at first glance this will strike most readers as intuitively wrong (as it once did me), perhaps it seems less so as we come to the end of this book. Where there were once vast numbers of retailers—small stores that sold fruit, or shoes, or clothing—there are now massive, often global megachains and hyperonline retailers, such as Jeff Bezos's Amazon and Jack Ma's

Alibaba, which have colonized and almost monopolized a global virtual retail space. The world's grain trade is almost completely controlled by just five firms: ADM, Bunge, COFCO, Cargill, and the Louis Dreyfus Company. Half of all seeds traded are today produced by just four firms: Syngenta, Bayer, BASF, and Corteva. Gigantic investment firms such as Vanguard, Fidelity, and BlackRock bundle significant investments in firms that operate in the same markets, creating anticompetitive incentives. Almost all industries see this high level of concentration. In 2020, the market cap of the world's fifty largest corporations equaled 27.6 percent of the global GDP; in 1990, it had been just 4.7 percent. In 2023, for the first time, Apple's valuation exceeded $3 trillion in US dollars, or more than the GDP of any of the world's countries except China, Japan, Germany, India, the United Kingdom, and the United States.[46] Capitalism has moved so far away from its Smithian conceptual underpinnings that Adam Smith himself would find it almost unrecognizable. Markets may allocate resources efficiently, but the capitalist revolution has undermined them to a mind-boggling degree.

As resources have concentrated in the grip of the world's yachting oligarchy and a small collection of dominant firms, workers, farmers, and even some professionals have come under tremendous pressure. In the former industrial heartlands, lives that the working and middle classes had long been accustomed to, thanks to a century of social and political mobilizations, became ever harder to maintain. Social mobility had become severely limited. "Median wages for US workers have stagnated for nearly fifty years," a team of US economists reported in 2019.[47] Families have had to spend ever more hours working, often at multiple jobs, just to maintain their standard of living.[48] And the welfare states that protected citizens from the worst dislocations came into the crosshairs of cost-cutting oligarchs who saw labor's weakened power as a perfect opportunity to undo labor's wins of the past century and a half.

One reason for this increasing inequality was the dramatic assault on the world's working class undertaken in the neoliberal era and beyond. Globally, unions, cooperatives, and labor parties—the three pillars of the labor movement, as it had been built since the global reconstructions of capitalism in the 1870s—weakened. In a review of the state of labor, two Dutch sociologists matter-of-factly declared that the "time of social emancipation" had ended.[49] Moreover, most of the global economy's new workers never organized in the first place: It has been estimated that in 2014, out of a total workforce of 2.9 billion people, only about 200 million workers were members of trade unions. Union density was, at best, a minuscule 7 percent.[50]

The factors that explain this downfall are varied. Most basically, the world's working class expanded, increasing competition and inhibiting solidarity. In 1991, 44 percent of the global labor force worked for wages; in 2019, that number reached 53 percent. The most significant expansion of wage labor occurred in China, where it has been estimated that 400 million rural cultivators joined the working class between 1992 and 2020 alone.[51]

Then there was the continued pressure of automation. "Humans have priced themselves out of the market," one journalist reported.[52] In 2016, the World Bank estimated that two-thirds of all jobs in low- and medium-income countries could be lost before long. In 2019, one author predicted that in the short run, about one-third of all human work will be taken over by robots, and in the

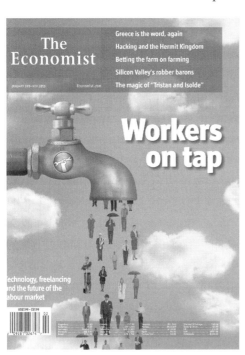

A capitalist dream realized: proletarian labor everywhere.

long term, about half. Artificial intelligence will make many workers in the service sector superfluous—just think of all those call centers, law clerks, and software engineers.[53]

Ever more densely connected by intensifying trade and migration and thus brought into competition with one another, members of the world's working class had few effective means of resistance. Unlike capital, the labor movement clung to the late nineteenth-century structures that had powered its ascent in the former industrial heartlands, becoming increasingly ill-equipped for a changed and changing world. With a low degree of organization and intense competition, workers in the industrial heartlands (outside a few islands, like Detroit's auto industry and the metal industry of the German state of Baden-Württemberg) struggled to maintain the hard-won victories of the golden years. The "standard employment relationship"—including a stable, predictable full-time job with one employer and a guaranteed income sufficient to raise a family, plus benefits and a set of rights—became less common, even in the few areas of the world where it once dominated. Outsourcing, subcontracting, and self-employment replaced wage work, which forced workers to become "flexible"—undermining the stability and security that had characterized labor during the golden age. As access to social benefits diminished, working-class lives gradually became more precarious. The living standards of the more privileged segments of the world's working class became ever more dependent on the hyperexploitation of workers in the Global South, as cheap production there allowed workers in the industrial heartland to continue consuming despite wage stagnation.[54] Debt again became a prime mechanism for extracting labor, with educational and medical debt entrapping large segments of the working and middle classes in a vicious, almost inescapable cycle.

Of course, much of the working class in the Global South never experienced anything remotely like the standard employment relationship that had characterized the industrial heartlands for a few decades. If they did, it came under assault as well: In Chile's mining industry, wageworkers were turned into subcontractors—by 2012, there were more than seven hundred thousand such contract workers. Throughout the Global South, work was mostly insecure, flexible, and contingent, constituting a vast informal sector—a form of labor that eventually traveled to the industrial heartlands as well. Such development was the exact opposite of what optimistic accounts informed by modernization theory had predicted in the 1950s and 1960s, when it was said that the future of the "rest" could be imagined by looking at the "West."[55] But it does show something I have noted throughout: The story of capitalism is often made from its margins, not its centers.

SHARPENED INEQUALITY WITHIN societies and accelerating proletarianization characterize contemporary capitalism. As this spatial and social expansion rolls across the world, it draws further energy from vast dispossessions. "[L]arge-scale land acquisitions in the developing world have intensified over the past ten years," a 2019 report by the Oakland Institute stated flatly. "In most instances they have involved forced evictions, widespread human rights violations, environmental degradation, increased food insecurity, and the destruction of livelihoods."[56] In Egypt, small-scale rice farmers have been forced to give up their crops to preserve scarce water resources. Meanwhile, the country's elites live in new cities that feature water-intensive green areas and are fed by capital-intensive farms in the desert, which draw on the nonrenewable water resources of aquifers. In Tanzania, Maasai herders have seen their lost lands turned into hunting grounds for wealthy tourists. In the wake of the 2008–2009 financial crisis, my employer, Harvard University, and the fund that controls my retirement assets, TIAA, invested in the Brazilian Cerrado to profit from the monocultural production of soybeans, eucalyptus, and cattle, which causes significant deforestation and forces Indigenous communities off their homelands. These newly created hinterlands are then increasingly divided by barbed wire, surveilled by cameras, and patrolled by private and public police forces. Dispossession occurs in the industrial heartlands as well: Small shop owners lose their stores because of competition from chains and online retailers, colossal agglomerations of capital. Small farmers lose their land. One group that has been particularly affected in the United States is African Americans, who have now lost an estimated 90 percent of the farmland they controlled in 1900.[57]

Beachfront properties are frequent targets too: On Georgia's Sapelo Island, increases in property taxes, propelled by the tourism frontier, made it impossible for Black landowners to hold on to their properties. And, perhaps surprisingly, many more dispossessions may yet occur. The World Bank has estimated that up to "65 percent of the world's land is still" managed by "communities under customary systems" and thus potentially available to the bank's project of "formalizing private property rights" so that land can be turned into a commodified asset—buyable, salable, and usable as loan collateral.[58]

Dispossessions need not be of land; intellectual property rights can be enclosed and plundered too. Agribusinesses patent the seeds of plants that Indigenous peoples have grown and harvested for centuries, and the pharma industry does the same with long-used medicinal components. This expropriation of Indigenous peoples' intellectual property has been called "biopiracy." One example is Japanese pharmaceutical giant Sankyo, which took out a series of patents on the derivative extracts of the *plao-noi* plant, found in Thailand, where it has been used for generations by Indigenous communities to treat stomachaches.[59]

The data we produce as we go about our daily lives is also taken without compensation by many-tentacled social media firms—a largely unremarked-upon and normalized theft. Scholarly knowledge also becomes enclosed and commodified: Giant publishing companies such as Elsevier and Springer charge libraries small fortunes to subscribe to their publications. In 2023, Elsevier (which describes itself as "the world's largest publisher of academic journals") made a gross profit of $1.44 billion in US dollars, with a profit margin of 37.1 percent, while between 1986 and 2014, US university library budgets for "ongoing resource expenditures (including journals)" rose by 521 percent.[60]

ENCLOSURE—SOMETIMES MEDIATED BY markets, sometimes not—still defines capitalism's relationship to nature, as takings from the natural world continue to accelerate and outstrip the carrying capacity of our planet. During the half century after 1970, the mining of raw materials tripled, and by the mid-2010s, people in the Global North devoured 26.71 tons of raw materials per capita per year, or about four times what ecologists have calculated as Earth's maximum carrying capacity. Trade in mining and construction machinery quadrupled. The weight of all human-made things is now essentially equal to the weight of all biological matter.[61]

These extractions, along with the dumping of often toxic human-made substances, threaten the basic conditions for human life.[62] The threats are everywhere, and they multiply and interact with one another. "The world's insects are hurtling down the path of extinction," according to scientists, who note that the mass of insects, an essential part of the ecology of plants, falls by 2.5 percent annually.[63] The chemicals used in products like Teflon nonstick pans, food packaging, and clothing are called "forever" because that's how long they last, and they are seeping into all parts of the ecosystem. In fact, they are now found in the blood of virtually all Americans. The production of plastic has increased 225 times since 1950, and the result is that plastic, an exclusively human-made substance, is inundating our ecosystems. Soon more plastic than fish will float in the seas. While the green revolution has drastically increased agricultural productivity, it has done so through massive use of fossil fuels, fertilizers, and pesticides. Viruses find new opportunities to spread in human populations: As humans press against the habitats of animals, new diseases emerge, and old ones spread. It is likely that COVID-19 is one such zoonotic disease. The World Health Organization found that the occurrence of dengue, a mosquito-borne disease, increased thirty times in the past half century, as warmer weather and new rainfall patterns provided ideal breeding conditions for mosquitoes, and hit the world's most vulnerable people the hardest. "The earth, our home, is beginning to look more and more like an immense pile of filth," observed Pope Francis. "Never have we so hurt and mistreated our common home as we have in the last two hundred years."[64]

No environmental catastrophe gained more attention in the twenty-first century than carbon-dioxide-induced climate change. This attention makes sense, not only because global warming threatens a plethora of ecosystems, but also because these emissions index economic growth since the nineteenth century. As we have seen, since 1800, the capitalist revolution has become ever more dependent on fossil fuels, yet the real acceleration is very recent—more than half of all carbon dioxide in the atmosphere was emitted after 1990. At present, the world's greatest carbon-dioxide emitter is China, but because carbon dioxide lingers in the atmosphere for so long, today's climate change is the result of all the emissions since the beginning of the fossil-fuel age. The United States produced 25 percent of these, twice as much as the second-greatest emitter, China.[65]

The hypothetical cost of sucking all that carbon dioxide from the atmosphere, which would require a technology that does not exist, has been estimated at $250 trillion US dollars, of which the United States would be responsible for a staggering one-quarter. The burden is ongoing and cumulative: The IMF has estimated that fossil-fuel emissions produce environmental damage amounting to $5 trillion annually, or 5 percent of the world's economic output, yet the costs of restoration will be borne not by contemporary producers or consumers but by future generations.[66] Capitalism thus does not just draw nutrients from our past but also consumes our future.

Today these costs are borne by the portion of humanity least involved in producing them. The benefits and damages reaped by the takings from nature have been radically unequally distributed. Some people got to conquer the natural environment and create lives of relative security (in their mad moments, they even aim to defeat death itself), but the vast majority became newly vulnerable to floods, heat waves, and the destruction of crops. These climate refugees now flee uninhabitable parts of the world in ever higher numbers, with poor nations hosting millions of them, as wealthier countries push them away. And although European nations, Japan, and the United States have cut carbon emissions, they increasingly externalize them by importing goods and services from the Global South. In the 2020s, about 25 percent of global emissions were embedded within products traded from South to North—that is, their production in the Global South puts carbon-dioxide emissions on that balance sheet, even though the products are consumed in the Global North. In 2022, a group of social scientists estimated that "in 2015, the North net appropriated from the South 12 billion tons of embodied raw material equivalents, 822 million hectares of embodied land, 21 exajoules of embodied energy and 188 million person-years of embodied labour," representing "a significant windfall for the Global North equivalent to a quarter of Northern GDP."[67]

It is no longer controversial to say that the takings from nature and the dumping of refuse into the environment have reached unsustainable levels. A 2019 study by the Institute for Public Policy Research warned that amid ongoing environmental breakdown, a confluence of developments has created a "new domain of risk" that could lead to "systemic collapse."[68] Günther Thalinger, board member of the world's largest insurance company, Allianz, has warned that accelerating climate change might mean that "capitalism as we know it ceases to be viable." Domino effects are possible, as is a sudden "state shift" in the ecological conditions of Earth, whereby multiple ecosystems would suddenly fall apart simultaneously. "Is Earth f*cked?" scientist Brad Werner asked in 2012 at the American Geophysical Union's meeting—a meeting not generally given to overheated rhetoric. He answered that "the mismatch between short-timescale market and political forces driving resource extraction/use and longer-timescale accommodations of the Earth system to these changes" could produce breakdown. Earth was, in fact, well and truly f*cked.[69] Of course, the enormous creativity lodged within the capitalist revolution suggests that a decoupling of economic growth from fossil-fuel consumption is possible. But can capitalism, characterized by its dependence on ever more accumulation and commodification, coexist with a natural world that will always be finite?[70] The jury is out.

———

Beyond rising inequality, the reshuffling of the social contract, and the appropriation of material and social resources, Asia's rise to prominence within global capitalism is perhaps what future historians will see most clearly when they study the early twenty-first century. Capitalism's dynamic core has clearly shifted as new actors spin new webs of capital, labor, and state power. On all indicators, Asia in general and China in particular stand out: Asia's share of global manufacturing was 25 percent in 1990; by 2022, it was 51 percent and rising continuously. By 2024, China was well on its way to becoming the world's largest economy. Measured by purchasing power parity, it already was. China's share of the global GDP rose to 18.4 percent in 2022; as recently as 2000, it had been just 7.3 percent. It became the workshop of the world and the world leader in many advanced technologies. If readers in the former industrial heartlands of Europe, Japan, and the United States perceive contemporary capitalism as stagnant, they could not be more wrong, showing again how a local perspective is woefully inadequate to understand the totality of capitalism. It is indeed stunning how much progress—not just economic but also social—has left capitalism's former heartlands and reemerged in Asia: China had no high-speed rail lines as of 2000 but now has 25,149 miles, more than ten times as many as Japan. The number of university students more than tripled in Asia in the first two decades of the new millennium; in China, it increased almost ninefold. In 2022, almost every second patent filed anywhere in the world was filed in China, including at the cutting edge of innovation. That year, China filed 29,583 AI-related patents, compared with 16,805 in the US, 8,870 in Japan, and 7,899 in Korea.[71] The EU did not even make the top four.

On account of Asia's reemergence as a world-historical force, the stark inequalities between the "West and the rest" continue to diminish. Vast but vaguely defined middle classes have emerged in China and India, as have fabulously wealthy oligarchs. In 2000, statisticians counted a minuscule 3.1 percent of China's people "middle class"; by 2018, that share had risen to about 50 percent. India's middle class today makes up about a third of its population. Their rise has reduced what has been termed "extreme poverty" (with a threshold income of $2.15 a day), which included 37.9 percent of the world's people in 1990 but just 9 percent in 2022, a reduction largely fueled by successful anti-poverty measures in China. Despite these improvements, almost half of the world's people—46.4 percent, or a total of 3.6 billion—still live on $6.85 or less a day.[72]

This reemergence of Asia was a rebuke not just to generations of racist analysis that had posited a transhistorical superiority of Western civilization but also to some neo-Marxist theorizing of the 1960s and 1970s, which had seen the world economy as structured in ways that would not allow for the emergence of prosperity outside the Western industrial heartlands. As it turned out, the opposite was true. Not only are the speed and depth of China's development without historical example, but it is also reshaping global capitalism more generally. China's Belt and Road Initiative makes massive investments in global infrastructure and has become a major force in Asia, Africa, and Latin America. By building roads, railways, and ports, and by investing in mines, agriculture, and construction, China has remade large areas of the Global South. Exports from Latin America to China increased almost tenfold in the decade after 2003. Chilean metal exports to China, mostly copper, increased twenty-four times between 2001 and 2011 alone.[73] Brazil's soy feeds Chinese consumers.

Such a world was unimaginable in 1850, when Britain was the center of the global economy. It was just as unimaginable in 1960, when the United States accounted for 40 percent of global GDP. It is nothing short of a marvel—and a powerful refutation of many of the West's cherished ideologies—that the world's most dynamic development unfolded in an economy that, despite many openings for private capital, took a path deeply marked by state-directed planning, nationalized industries, and, most surprising of all, Communist Party leadership. It was by *not* following the wisdom of American economics professors that China flourished. Between 2019 and 2023 alone, China's economy grew by 20 percent, while that of the United States expanded by 9.4 percent and that of Europe by 4.5 percent.[74] Achille Mbembe might have summed it up best: "Europe is no longer the center of gravity of the world. This is the significant event, the fundamental experience, of our era."[75] Indeed, as difficult as this may be for some readers to see, we now live "after the Western phase of capitalism."[76] As Singaporean diplomat and writer Kishore Mahbubani remarked, "All assumptions, all certainties, that the West has are completely fallen out of their time."[77]

As THE GEOGRAPHY of capital shifted, so did its composition. Industrial capital continued its decline from its exposed perch. Core firms divested from the factory, indeed from production itself, replaced by ones that had more in common with the capital owners of the early modern moment in capitalism's history—the merchants, financiers, and chartered companies that many centuries ago pushed the logic of capital out of its islands and into rural hinterlands and industry.[78]

If we think of the world's clothing brands, few directly employ workers who engage in much, or any, sewing. They design products, provide work orders to subcontractors (such as the ones we saw in Cambodia), and then retail the clothing around the world. In 2023, Nike employed 15,932 people in the United States, while its subcontracted workers numbered 632,923, most of them in Vietnam, China, and Indonesia. Even famous manufacturing brands engage in these strategies. Volkswagen Brazil, for instance, has 4,500 workers laboring in its factory in Resende, but almost none of them are employed by VW. Instead, they work for subcontractors who organize production.[79] Workers, lots of them, still power production, but along with physical assets, they increasingly labor outside the legal boundaries of core firms. Instead of making things, giants like Apple focus, according to the apt summary of one scholar, on "intellectual property rights . . . to extract monopoly rents from other firms and consumers."[80] Apple engages in no actual production. By 2005, 80 percent of assets held by S&P 500 firms in the United States were intangible, up from less than 20 percent in the 1960s.[81] Akin to the merchants who developed global trade from islands of capital like Aden but did not invest in the actual production of the goods they traded, modern companies organize production networks and trade. Unlike Aden merchants, however, they engage in massive research and design efforts. In 1800, as we have seen, the most important property right was in land and, in some parts of the world, in people. In the 1950s, it was in industrial hardware. Today it is in ideas.

Whether this moment should be seen as a return of a modified form of merchant capital or the emergence of something entirely new, knowledge capitalism, it is a wrenching reversal, and it is most radical in its financialized form. Rapidly increasing funds of capital circle the globe in search of new speculative investments, their growth totally out of sync with the development of the productive economy itself.[82] Giant investment firms insert capital into every industry in every part of the world, chasing higher returns—the next big thing, the ever elusive unicorn—without committing to any one industry or location. Their investments appear as quickly as they disappear, the purest form of the capitalist logic, in which nothing but the ongoing accumulation of capital drives entrepreneurial decisions. Even manufacturers, these once dominant actors, are as subordinate to the flows of capital that dominate them as workers once were to industrialists. Recalling the diversity of firms we have encountered in these pages—the Noells in Barbados, the Röchlings in Völklingen, the Godrejes in Bombay—we can picture the great distance that this newest version of capitalism has traveled.

But there is continuity too: As it has throughout history, the state remains central to the success of these firms. It creates and then protects the property rights they depend on, such as patents. Moreover, much of the technology behind the new firms' products was developed or nurtured by governments—the transistor, the computer, the microchip, and the internet prominently among them; Silicon Valley owed its dynamic to massive state investment. Governments fund developments such as the COVID-19 vaccine, but companies (in this case, Big Pharma) reap the profits. Even the companies controlled by 2020s entrepreneur par excellence Elon Musk saw billions of dollars of government support flow into their coffers. By 2015, Tesla, SolarCity, and SpaceX had already been the lucky recipients of $4.9 billion in government investment. In addition, Tesla received grants of almost 200 million pounds from the British government. And the money keeps flowing.[83] It was thus hardly surprising that Musk entered the sphere of politics in 2025, in many ways returning to some of the foundational mechanisms of early modern capitalism.

But attachment to the state does not mean that economic elites are attached to any one state. Like earlier merchants, they need the state but no state in particular, and they thrive when they attach themselves to a galaxy of states, each of which provides specific benefits. The United States provides strong intellectual property protections, China has a disciplined and inexpensive workforce, Peru permits the extraction of vital minerals, and Ireland grants low taxation on the profits generated from intellectual property rights. In the wings sits a whole set of other states eager to provide the same supports should any among the first set of states change their policies.[84]

At the same time, some companies take on statelike functions, much as their predecessors did centuries ago. Businesses have claimed sovereignty throughout the history of capitalism, but as we have seen, this telltale trait of war capitalism was on the wane during the reconstructions of capitalism in the late nineteenth century. Now a resurgence has begun: Today, mining companies become territorial rulers, investors control infrastructures, and private military contractors provide security. In 2017, it was reported that Erik Prince, founder of the American private security company Blackwater, had proposed a scheme to the US government in which he would take charge of parts of the war in Afghanistan in return for the right to mine rare earth minerals there—a project that Prince himself likened to the "East India Company approach." Mining companies are even beginning to claim first-mover property rights in extraterrestrial bodies—just as their ancestors did during the first wave of European colonialism five centuries ago.[85]

States also provide the essential backstop to the functioning of global capitalism. When the financial system was on the brink of collapse during the 2008–2009 crisis, states stepped in, and trillions of dollars flowed into the financial sector. Banks were deemed "too big to fail" and institutions crucial to the system protected.[86] Multilateral bodies like the WTO, IMF, and World Bank, made up of nation-states, underpin the operation of markets and monetary systems within the capitalist world order. Centuries ago, capitalists hitched their wagons to states, and 2008–2009 showed that the argument made throughout this book—that capitalism is as much a project of states as of capital owners—still holds. Whether by supporting it in its day-to-day operations or during its most severe crises, states have propelled and backstopped the capitalist revolution throughout its history.

When neoliberalism was hegemonic," wrote historian Gary Gerstle, "the virtues of free trade and globalization were unassailable" in mainstream circles in North America and Europe.[87] After 2008, this changed. Policymakers on the left and the right, as well as social movements and intellectuals, pushed against the neoliberal order. Something that had seemed irrefutable, even natural, became historical and, perhaps, fleeting—one of many peculiar politico-economic orders that we have seen rise and fall over capitalism's five hundred years of history. The neoliberal order had always had its critics, but in the wake of the financial crisis, it came under attack from all sides.

Consider the discipline of economics, a bellwether of shifting paradigms. Despite unlimited confidence in their models and a pronounced tendency to naturalize the neoliberal order, the 2008–2009 crisis shook the discipline and led to what has been called an "intellectual catastrophe" for the theology of modern capitalism. Most basically, the crisis undermined the idea that the system is stable and self-monitoring, as predicted by general equilibrium theory, an almost banal insight that comes as no surprise to readers of this book. When history falsified this theory, the response was swift: In July 2009, the cover of *The Economist* depicted a dissolving economics textbook with the headline WHERE IT WENT WRONG.[88] Meanwhile, in Britain, public criticism reached such heights that a group of leading economists wrote to Her Majesty to explain their failure to accurately predict the timing and severity of the meltdown, a repudiation of almost Galilean scope.[89]

The critique quickly broadened, as when students rebelled against their professors: In November 2011, Harvard students walked out of an introductory economics lecture, protesting the "bias inherent" in the course that they claimed espoused "a specific—and limited—view of economics that we believe perpetuates problematic and inefficient systems of economic inequality in our society today."[90] From the Political Economy Society of Istanbul's Boğaziçi University to Copenhagen's Kritiske Politter (Critical Students of Economics) group to the global Rethinking Economics movement, students demanded a more pluralistic view of economics and a more pluralistic approach to teaching the history of economic thought.[91]

Soon more established circles embraced that critique: Economists Suresh Naidu, Dani Rodrik, and Gabriel Zucman demanded economics thinking "beyond neoliberalism," which they called a "primitive, simplistic perversion."[92] Nobel Prize–winning economist Joseph Stiglitz agreed, saying that the neoliberal experiment had "in every aspect failed."[93] At a congress to "rethink economics," the chief economist of Deutsche Bank compared his disciplinary colleagues to dentists working with great precision and competence on a tiny part of the human body but ignoring the organism as a whole. If mathematical modeling did not allow prognosis or even an understanding of the present, other economists argued, perhaps a look to history would help. Hermann Ramsperger, a former member of the board of the Bundesbank, called for attention to economic history and the history of economic ideas. In 2012, the German weekly *Frankfurter Allgemeine Sonntagszeitung*, under the headline WHY IS ECONOMIC HISTORY SUDDENLY SEXY?, observed that economic life can be understood from a historical perspective only, a perspective this book shares.[94]

Challenges to the neoliberal order went beyond economics. Social movements on six continents—from peasant protests across India to the Occupy Wall Street movement in the United States, from Chico Mendes's struggle to stop ecological degradation in Brazil to Bangladeshi women's fight for fair wages in the garment industry—pushed against a regime that had increased inequality and environmental destruction. The poor in postapartheid South Africa protested unemployment, privatizations, and evictions from homes and land, pinning the blame on neoliberal reforms. So significant was that wave of global dissatisfaction that in 2023, the *Financial Times* headlined CIVIL UNREST OVERTAKES TERRORISM IN INSURANCE CLAIMS.[95] Indian writer Arundhati Roy spoke for many when she bemoaned the social dislocations, radical sharpening of inequalities, massive expropriations of the poor, and environmental devastations that had accompanied India's, and the world's, neoliberal turn.[96]

Yet the most serious challenge to the neoliberal order came not from the left but from the right, as ethnonationalism and right-wing populist parties rose to power globally—symbolized by figures such as Viktor Orbán, Jair Bolsonaro, Recep Erdoğan, and Donald Trump. They emerged from a grassroots critique of neoliberalism and a political reorientation among elites sidestepped by the heyday of neoliberal globalization, such as executives and investors in the the United States' ailing steel industry. In the United States, activists such as Wilbur Ross, Peter Navarro, and Robert Lighthizer attacked one of the shibboleths of the neoliberal era: free trade.[97] The rebellion then spread beyond such particular sectoral interests. United States investor Peter Thiel signed on to a statement that argued that "the free market cannot be absolute. Economic policy must serve the general welfare of the nation."[98] For investor Mario Gabelli, Trump's election in 2016 "meant a rebirth of capitalism," a hyperbolic phrase seen frequently at moments of capitalism's shape-shifting.[99]

And, indeed, there are signs that capitalism may have reached a new moment of reinvention in which tariffs, nationalized commodity chains, immigration restrictions, and statist industrial policies were re-emerging as important policy tools, as belief in an omniscient, infallible market declined in the face of massive protests, financial meltdown, global competition, and then the COVID-19 crisis. The growth of world trade slowed drastically. For Moritz Schularick, president of the Kiel Institute for the World Economy, questions of geo-economic strategy had become important again, with a field called geo-economics reemerging to bring together the study of economics and the study of state power in the international arena, or what American security strategist Edward Luttwak has called "the logic of war in the grammar of commerce."[100] New forms of economic nationalism now went along with anti-immigration activism. Even neoliberals themselves tried to jump onto this bandwagon, injecting ethnonationalism into their policy stance in what had come to be called the "redneck strategy."[101] On a global scale, these changes went along with a massive wave of militarization, as commodity chains were seen as so fragile that they needed enhanced military guard. As readers of this book will recognize, the practice of nationalizing commodity chains, and enclosing capital in nation-states, had its heyday in the early decades of the twentieth century. It did not end well.

Not all, but many neoliberals had at least provided lip service to liberal democracy while propelling a full-fledged crisis of that democracy, furthered by a rising wave of right-wing populism. At the leading edge of this populism, distinctly authoritarian voices emerged to question the link between capitalism and liberal democracy in general, suggesting the possibility, even the promise, of an authoritarian and illiberal capitalist alternative. "Can democracy survive global capitalism?" asked US economist Robert Kuttner in 2018. The answer was unclear.[102]

Economic elites in the homelands of liberal democracy increasingly questioned the connection between capitalism and democracy, with some seeing democracy as a mortal threat to market freedoms.[103] Capitalism's shape-shifting, as we have seen, allows it to accommodate different political forms, as it has throughout a half millennium of history, suggesting that confidence in a timeless marriage between capitalism and liberal democracy, once so prominent, is misplaced. In the twenty-first century, some of the most dynamic capitalist economies were neither liberal nor democratic. As we have seen, capitalism is undogmatic in this regard too.

———

Capitalism—the book—ends as it began: with islands. Some real, some metaphorical.

Metaphorical: the fenced-in ensemble of factories built in the Phnom Penh Special Economic Zone and the coastal city of Kampong Saom. Similarly fortified production sites dot the globe, pushing the logic of capitalism, of commodification, into the last areas of the world unchurned by the capitalist revolution.

Real: the islands that interest capital owners—for example, the tiny island of Brecqhou. In 1993, British businessmen David and Frederick Barclay, whose investments in real estate, shipping, energy, and newspapers had made them rich, paid 2.3 million British pounds for this nearly eighty-acre island, which was located off the coast of one of the Channel Islands, Sark, and enjoyed its own tax autonomy, resulting in the absence of any income, capital-gains or inheritance taxes. They replaced the existing manor with a Norman-style castle—a massive home larger than any built in the UK during the past two centuries. Like capital owners of the early modern period, they hoped to combine this display of ostentatious wealth with political control by taking over nearby Sark, to which Brecqhou politically belonged. By 2012, they controlled about a quarter of that island's arable land, two-thirds of its hotels, and many of its stores. They also employed a quarter of the island's workers.[104]

Their real goal, however, was not control over a rather barren island but political power over the territory and its 575 long-term residents. Sark, and Brecqhou with it, is a Bailiwick of Guernsey and a Crown dependency of the United Kingdom; until recent reforms it was the last remnant of feudal rule in Europe, with power inherited by landowners and the chief seigneur, who is entitled to a thirteenth of any property transactions. The Barclays tried to undermine the existing order and gain political power using all legal means at their disposal. When they failed, they attempted to buy the seigneur's title (reportedly offering two million pounds) and failed again.[105]

The Barclays' travails on Sark were a farce: a failed bourgeois revolution beaten back by the island's feisty inhabitants. Yet it was just one instantiation of a much larger move. As inequalities intensified to staggering proportions, secessionist impulses spread among capital owners. Even before their maneuverings on Brecqhou, the Barclays had built a complex network of offshore companies that safeguarded their profits from taxation, including establishing their own tax residency in Monaco. For them and many other members of the 1 percent, assets were to be moved wherever they could escape the state's grasp: In Geneva's landlocked "free port," highly protected warehouses stored what was probably the world's greatest art collection—1.2 million pieces, including 1,000 Picassos—and allowed owners to trade or mortgage their art without triggering any estate or sales taxes. Hiding wealth offshore became common, with tax havens in the mid-2010s harboring assets equal to almost 10 percent of the global GDP. It has been estimated that in some countries, including Britain, Spain, and France, the wealthiest 0.01 percent hold as much as 30 to 40 percent of their liquid assets in these havens. Tiny Monaco (in which every second inhabitant is a millionaire) is so crowded with tax cheats that it is expanding in the only way it can—into the sea. Apartments there are said to cost one hundred thousand euros per square meter.[106]

Not satisfied with squirreling assets away from the powerful nation-states that had been so crucial to the rise of capitalism (and to their own wealth), some capital owners sought even more hermetic enclaves, building new jurisdictions with all the trappings of sovereignty, states run as businesses in which relations between residents were entirely contractual and democratic politics could be done away with. Historian Quinn Slobodian has called these capitalist redoubts "zones," of which there existed fifty-four hundred worldwide in the early 2020s—including tax havens such as the Cayman Islands, special economic zones such as Shenzhen in China, and "private city-states" such as New Songdo City in South Korea and Neom in Saudia Arabia.[107]

Even more fantastic plans were launched: Investor Peter Thiel saw a future in "seasteads" and helped plan a libertarian colony off the coast of San Francisco, one that would have no welfare provisions, no minimum wage, and few restrictions on the carrying of guns, housing at first 270 people, with the ultimate plan to bring many of these floating islands together. He cofounded the Seasteading Institute with Patri Friedman, Milton Friedman's grandson, to build, in their own words, "startup communities that float on the ocean with any measure of political autonomy."[108] Inspired by economist Paul Romer, a group of utopian investors made plans to create Próspera, a privately run city-state within the territory, but outside the jurisdiction, of Honduras.[109] Others sought settlements even farther afield, such as on Mars.[110] While these projects were (mostly) fantasies, they spoke to the secessionist impulses of capital owners, their desire to return to the fortified islands that their forebears had been so eager to leave behind a few centuries earlier.

These moves also suggest that some capital owners lost faith in the stability of the civilization and political order they have played such a critical role in creating. When the rich retreat into former silos for intercontinental ballistic missiles and convert them into luxury bunkers with air-cleaning systems, access to groundwater, swimming pools, and well-stocked survival pantries to weather whatever doomsday event they fear most, it is either a triumph of real-estate marketing or a sign that capitalist civilization has lost its belief in a shared future. Thiel acquired both land and citizenship in New Zealand, and he has a plane and pilot ready to whisk him away if life in the United States becomes ecologically or politically unsustainable.[111]

While islands have played a crucial role in capitalism's history, and while islands of concentrated capital were the launching pads of the capitalist revolution, the difference is that capital owners pushed outward for much of that five-hundred-year history. In the twenty-first century, these islands remain deeply embedded in constantly shifting webs of capital and state power, yet some capital owners again pulled up the drawbridges and fell back into fortresses. In a far cry from their mid-nineteenth-century optimism and universalist inclinations, capital owners in the 2020s seemed to fear that the world they made might devour them. "These immensely powerful people," argued philosopher Jean-Pierre Dupuy, "in their heart of hearts, no longer believe in the future."[112]

The story this book tells does not have an end. Capitalism is an ongoing process; we live within it. We do not have the privilege of hindsight to trace a bygone economic order and dissect its weaknesses and strengths.[113] And because capitalism is not cyclical, we cannot directly extrapolate its future from its past.

What we can say with some confidence is that the insights gained from analyzing capitalism's long history can help us think about the present and the future in new ways. We can anticipate that capitalism will remain a global totality, even if the nature of that totality continues to change, perhaps in radical and surprising ways. We can expect capitalism's enormous creativity to persist, along with its amazing adaptability—including its to-date undeniable record of generating technical, ecological, political, and social fixes for the multiple crises it has itself engendered. We can reasonably foresee that marginalized groups' social and political mobilizations will continue to spur capitalism to innovate, confirming that it will remain undogmatic and generate ever new combinations of capital, labor, technology, state power, territorial order, and forms of political rule. Resistances continue to emerge everywhere, from unionizaton efforts among Starbucks workers in the United States to demonstrations in Buenos Aires against austerity politics. As we have seen, change in capitalism is neither continual nor cyclical but episodic; its intensity clusters around certain key moments, and some of its most momentous changes have been driven by the world's most marginalized people. This will continue. Since we are living through one of those episodic transformations today, we can look to past moments of upheaval to help us understand the concatenation of forces that drive the most likely outcomes. As this book has shown, it is on the terrain of history, not natural sciences, that capitalism has unfolded and will continue to unfold.

Eventually, however, there will be a moment when capitalism ends. Regardless of whether we fear or hope for that end, capitalism, like everything in human history, is finite, even if it is impossible to say when or how it will end or what will replace it. Certainly, there is no shortage of predictions. Bookstores are filled with titles discussing capitalism's demise. Egyptian economist Samir Amin saw "the dominant system's implosion" on the horizon; Nancy Fraser believes we are living in a "general crisis of this social order"; and Wolfgang Streeck thinks the crisis of capitalism is becoming so chronic that its end is imminent.[114] Jason Moore predicts the "end of the *Capitalocene*" as capital runs out of "cheap natures" and "cheap labor." For Paul Mason, the "long-term prospects for capitalism are bleak," as the world is riven by a panoply of economic, social, and political crises that will soon lead to a slow transition out of capitalism.[115] If capitalism is best compared to a supernova, then it may be "a star exploding brilliantly on the eve of its death."[116] The severity of the ecological and social crises, clearly visible in the early twenty-first century, certainly suggests such a possibility.

Yet what should give us pause is that smart people have made similar predictions throughout capitalism's history. Capitalism boasts a distinguished lineage of obituaries going back almost two hundred years and penned from across the political spectrum—from Karl Marx to Joseph Schumpeter.

If we take the emergence of capitalism as our yardstick, we could envision that whatever comes after capitalism would take a long time to emerge and would, for a long time, be interwoven within capitalism itself, just as capitalism was itself embedded in noncapitalist societies for centuries. Within that old order, as we have seen in this book, capitalism began to emerge on islands, some real, like Barbados, some metaphorical. Over time, the islands spread into the hinterland, then connected with other islands and their hinterlands and ultimately with state power. But it took hundreds of years. Centuries stretched between the emergence of these islands and the formation of "capitalist society" in the 1850s. Islands of capital owners existed deep within the tributary era, just as marginal remnants of the tributary order remain today.

Perhaps capitalism will end in ways that parallel its emergence. New noncapitalist islands will arise and eventually connect to each other and expand to form a different kind of society. Some such islands are already here: Noncommodified spaces—from public housing to public education to libraries—exist, after all. The welfare state has created a sphere outside the logic of markets. Experiments with providing a guaranteed basic income suggest the possibility of decoupling subsistence from market participation. On a much smaller scale, spaces beyond capitalism, from communes to alternative forms of living, are built everywhere. A movement in Japan aims to construct what it calls "Satoyama capitalism." Its most prominent advocate, Kosuke Motani, published a book of the same name, promoting new forms of economic life by escaping large companies, restarting artisanal agriculture, producing and exchanging in smaller networks, and living with a greatly reduced ecological footprint. His book sold four hundred thousand copies.[117] In the small Italian town of Rima, high up in the Lombardian

Alps, forms of communal property have been rejuvenated, connected to what in times past was "a concept of property open to collective social needs."[118] In the 2010s, so-called blue zones, noted for the remarkable longevity of their residents, captured the imaginations of many. One of them, the Greek island of Ikaria, distinguished itself by preserving nature, prioritizing local production, and facilitating dense social connections among its people, who live extraordinarily long lives, keeping the capitalist logic of commodification and marketization at bay.

Social movements or individuals can create further spaces outside capitalism, but sometimes governments do so, too, because such spaces become the precondition for capitalism's continued vitality. We saw this with the responses to the Great Depression in the 1930s. Capitalism itself might create pressures to build or expand spaces beyond its logic—just as the tributary order became increasingly dependent on the capitalist logic to postpone its own crisis of reproduction. Today's ecological crisis might, in similar fashion, require a response outside capitalism—that is, saving the economic logic of capitalism might require following a different logic in very substantive ways. Sociologist Erik Olin Wright indeed believes that capitalism will be eroded through the emergence of alternative logics within it that slowly, wearingly expand from the inside out.[119] If that is in fact what happens, it would directly parallel the emergence of capitalism half a millennium ago. Yet in sharp contrast to the world then, such long-term scenarios might be entirely moot in the face of the ecological and social crises unfolding right now and right here. Despite my insistence throughout the book on capitalism's flexibility as the foundation for its enormous dynamic, capitalism is dogmatic in one sense: It rests on the ever expanding accumulation of capital. It is expansionary not by choice but by necessity.

IN THE DISTANT future, if we manage to get there, historians not yet born will look back at our civilization in all the ways we now look at civilizations gone by before us. They will find it difficult to understand our ways of thinking, and our ways of being. They might celebrate us for our accomplishments or blame us for the long aftereffects of the world we created. They may struggle to grasp why we made sacrifices to a human-created god that threatened our species' very existence. They might ask how we could have allowed an infinitesimal minority of the world's people to control so much of our resources. They might have difficulty understanding how we allowed for deprivation in the midst of unprecedented abundance.

If they are truly good historians, however, they will try to grasp us on our own terms. They will bring their readers into the bowels of a truly puzzling past civilization, one ordered around a logic that will no doubt seem strange to these visitors from a far-future world. In finding us puzzling, they will come to better know us and, perhaps, themselves.

Acknowledgments

This book, much like capitalism, draws on the labor, resources, and creativity of people and institutions on every continent. Without their help, an outlandish idea—to write the global history of capitalism, all of it—would have remained a dream.

Historical research suggests lonely days in dusty archives, but it is also so much more: I spent hours wandering through the sugar fields of Ingham, Australia, under the expert guidance of a cane cutter's daughter, Bianka Vidonja Balanzategui; I learned much about Barbados's history from William Ward, who drove me to the far ends of his island; and Glasgow's past came alive on a rainy walk under the expert guidance of Stephen Mullen. In Mumbai, I had the great fortune of Vrunda Pathare guiding my work at the Godrej Archives before enjoying a fabulous dinner conversation with the Godrej family; in Kampong Saom, I benefited from the eagle-eyed observations of a local teacher; and in Völklingen, I walked the grounds of the hulking steel mill built by the family that came to play such an important role in my telling of the history of the Second Industrial Revolution.

Historian Marc Bloch once wrote that carefully observing the world was just as important to understanding history as time spent in archives and libraries. I agree. Standing before sunrise in front of the factory gates just outside of Phnom Penh suggested the scale of contemporary (and historical) proletarianization in a way that no amount of reading could have conveyed; walking the grounds of the Drax plantation in Barbados, still surrounded by cane fields, brought back the ghosts of slavery; gazing at the faded Beaux Arts buildings of downtown Rio de Janeiro provided me with a window into the celebrated world of its Francophile nineteenth-century bourgeoisie; sitting on the shores of the Senegal River helped me imagine an early mercantile colonialism in which African and French traders exchanged goods procured from a vast hinterland for the products of European and Indian proto-industrialization; walking the test track on the roof of Turin's Lingotto factory gave me an appreciation for the scale of modern industry; and the warehouses, mansions, churches, and mosques of Bukhara, Samarkand, Florence, Venice, Genoa, Cairo, and Amsterdam provided insights into medieval and early modern mercantile wealth and power that could not be gleaned from the holdings of even the world's best libraries. It was only when Klaus Weber took me to Jelenia Góra that I could imagine the daily procession of impoverished weavers on the city's market square; when I discovered a cotton mill built in the 1830s in the back alleys of the Yucatecan city of Valladolid, I sensed the enormous powers of the new manufacturing techniques and their rapid capture of the nineteenth-century world.

I am glad to finally be able to properly thank the many people, and institutions, who made this book possible. I must first mention the librarians and archivists who preserved and made accessible the materials on which this book is based. In India, they include the staff of the National Archives and the Nehru Memorial Library in New Delhi and those at the Maharashtra State Archives and the Godrej Archives in Mumbai. In Australia, I had the good fortune to use materials held by the New South Wales State Archives and the State Library of New South Wales in Sydney, as well as the historical archives at James Cook University in Townsville. In Barbados, I spent a fruitful week at the Barbadian National Archives. I researched at the National Archives of the United States and the National Archives of the United Kingdom; I perused the holdings of the University of Glasgow Archives and the Glasgow City Archives; in Völklingen, I visited the Stadtarchiv under the expert guidance of Michael Röhrig and also the historical collection of the Saarstahl AG, steered by Antje Fuchs; then I went on to the

Landesarchiv Saarland in Saarbrücken. In Berlin, I consulted the holdings of the Bundesarchiv and the Archiv des Auswärtigen Amts; in Aix-en-Provence, I spent a productive research stay at the Centre des Archives d'Outre Mer; and in Turin, I was hosted by Fiat's historical archives. In Newport, Rhode Island, I was able to consult merchants' records in the Newport Historical Society's archives; and in Solingen, I had the good fortune to consult the holdings of the Stadtarchiv, where I benefited from the expert council of its director, Ralf Rogge; Janine Aures helped me to navigate the Stadtarchiv Frankfurt. In Rio de Janeiro, I was able to consult the holdings of the National Archives of Brazil, the Biblioteca Nacional, and the Instituto Histórico e Geográfico Brasileiro. I found important documents in Sevilla at the Archivo de Indias; and in Dakar, I had an opportunity to consult some of the extraordinary holdings of the Archives Nationales du Senegal. I also drew on the digital records of many archives and libraries, including the Biblioteca del Congreso Nacional de Chile in Santiago and the Archivo Histórico Nacional in Madrid.

Historical research on the scale necessary for this book is expensive, and I was fortunate to have access to a variety of resources. Thank you to Harvard University for providing me with a grant from the Dean's Competitive Fund for Promising Scholarship, later supplemented by a research grant from the Weatherhead Center for International Affairs. The Ford Foundation generously supported the project during its second half, and I want to thank its president, Darren Walker, for his enthusiasm, as well as Juliet Mureriwa for making this an all-around fantastic experience. Early on, the Henkel Foundation provided some much-needed travel funds as well.

For a writer, the most precious resource is time. I was privileged to receive funding from many institutions that provided me with time to focus on research and writing. It all began with a fellowship from Re-work at the Humboldt University in Berlin, an exceptionally vibrant international research center focused on the long history of labor. Its directors, Andreas Eckert and Jürgen Kocka, created a community in which I had time to think while interacting with a group of scholars from all corners of the world interested in the history of capitalism and dedicated to getting it right. Later on, I spent a semester at the Netherlands Institute for Advanced Studies in Amsterdam (NIAS), where I benefited from discussing the global history of capitalism with a group of like-minded colleagues and friends—Ulbe Bosma, Eric Vanhaute, and Mindi Schneider—and then a semester at the Freiburg Institute for Advanced Studies (FRIAS) as a European Union–funded Marie Curie Fellow. FRIAS also generously hosted me during the bulk of the COVID years and every summer thereafter, becoming the place where much of this book was written. Its directors—first Bernd Kortmann, and then Ralf von den Hoff—have created a setting that is exceptionally conducive to academic work. Without FRIAS, this book would not have seen the light of day. Finally, with the support of a sabbatical grant by Harvard's Weatherhead Center for International Affairs, I spent a year at another superlative European institution—the European University Institute in the beautiful city of Florence, where I had the good luck to enter an academic scene in which both faculty and students were engaged with understanding the global history of capitalism. Their influence can be found on many pages of this book. Thank you, Regina Grafe, Giorgio Riello, Glenda Sluga, Corinna Unger, and Fabrizio Borchi, for your hospitality.

A book of this scale and size cannot be written without the support of others, and I had the good fortune of working with a talented group of research assistants, many of whom are now published authors. I want to especially thank five students who have been associated with this project for many years and have done extraordinary work helping me figure out important parts of the history of capitalism. Alexandra Leonzini was there at the beginning, and for many years thereafter she helped me research a huge variety of places and moments in the history of capitalism. She died tragically last year when engaged in her dissertation research in South Korea. Her good work infuses this book in so many places. Marten Dondorp, first in Amsterdam and later in Cambridge, who is writing an important dissertation on the expansion of capitalism in Asia, was there almost from the beginning as well, and helped me take the first steps to disentangle Dutch history and so much more. Angela Yan joined the team at midpoint, and since then has done an extraordinary job figuring out complex debates and gathering minute details, while single-handedly designing every graph in this book. She is about to embark upon PhD studies at the University of Toronto. At the very end, David Fetzer in Freiburg, fresh off his PhD research on the comparative history of popular nationalism, came on board and has done extraordinary work—answering what must have been hundreds of queries at very short notice and then heroically securing permissions for the almost three hundred illustrations that grace the book. And also a special thank-you to Franco Paz, whose research for this project was always meticulous, and whose own important and beautifully written work on capitalism, coercion, and unfreedom is about to be published.

Many more students helped me figure out problems small and big during the past eight years. At Harvard, they included Abraham Atwood, Natalie Behrends, Aaron Bekemeyer, Anne Brandes, Chambi Chachage, Raghav Chopra, Christine Corcoran, Mathew DeShaw, Shruti Gautam, Matteo Giardano, Jordan Howell, Allison Jones, Stephanie Leitzel, Ifeosa Anwulika Nkem-Onyekpe, Samantha Payne, Sanjay Paul, Elena Shadrina, Rachel Steely, Jesus Solis, and Elmo Tumbokon. I also benefited from the help and insights of Breno Tommasi in Rio de Janeiro; David Avilés Espinoza in Santiago de Chile; Michael Thornton in New Haven; Jacob Pomerantz in Barbados; Marie Bergmann in Newport; Giovanni Santoro in Turin; Yifan Liao in Cambridge; Verena Muth in Vienna; Israel Garcia Solares in Mexico City; Luisa Fernanda Rojas Monroy in Bogotá; Peter Aiken in Glasgow; Shay Prasad in London; Salma Abouelhossein in Cairo; Jibran Anand in Mumbai; Nila Krishnamurthy in Cambridge; Roland Muntschick and Paulina Malys in Freiburg; James Watson in Sydney; Rebecca Orr and Lucile Boucher in Florence; Luke Robert and Alex de Jong in Amsterdam; Julio Decker, Felix Dietzsch, Felix Fugh, Felicitas Hentschke, Lorena López Jáuregui, and Anne Zetsche in Berlin; Joanna Szczepankowska in Warsaw; Francisco Amor in Sevilla; and David Sourdillon in Paris.

Many people helped me understand the history of global capitalism and write this book. I could not have done it without their insights and their support. First, I want to acknowledge the generations of scholars who have analyzed important parts of the history of capitalism, and without whose work I could not have written this book. A long time ago, two historians at Harvard Business School, Alfred D. Chandler Jr. and Thomas K. McCraw, exposed me to the possibility of thinking of my work as part of an undertaking they called the "history of capitalism." This book is the long-delayed result of their encouragement. More recently, Martha Schulman carefully edited every one of the book's chapters with exceptional patience, making the book much better in matters as small as a comma and as large as an idea. On Barbados, Christen Cwik helped me launch my research and introduced me to William Ward, whose deep knowledge of the island taught me many lessons, and to Philip Whitehead, who gave me a tour of Drax Hall plantation. Anka Steffen, now in Vienna, generously shared her important work on the Silesian linen industry and patiently put up with my all too many questions. Tanja Seelbach guided me in the world of publishing. Sven Hansen and Yuko Shimazaki helped me navigate Cambodia and introduced me to the many people who generously shared their time and their insights into that country's current history but prefer to remain unnamed. Roxani Margariti's research was invaluable to navigating medieval trade in the Arab world; she helped me understand its history over a wonderful lunch in Athens. Guanmian Xu generously shared his unpublished work on Taiwanese sugar. I also had the good fortune of drawing on the insights and support of a group of colleagues and friends in Senegal, especially Babacar Fall, Lamine Faye, Omar Gueye, and Mamoudou Sy, who went out of their way to help me access sources and understand the history of that part of the world. In Brazil, Rafael Marquese, Tamis Paron, and Marcelo Ferraro were always available to answer questions about Latin America and share their brilliant insights into the history of capitalism. In India, I had the good luck of learning from its extraordinarily rich tradition of historical scholarship and enjoying the hospitality and friendship of Aditya and Mridula Mukherjee, Prabhu Mohapatra, and Chitra Joshi. In Dar es Salaam, Mohamed Said shared an image from his private collection and gave me permission to use it in this book. Historian Hongzhe Sun, first in Cambridge, then in Beijing, was extraordinarily helpful, aiding me in my use of Chinese language sources and then helping to secure the rights to use Chinese images. Koen Stapelbroek introduced me to the history and archives of Townsville in Queensland, Australia, while Bettina and Moritz von Bethmann provided me access to the archives of their distant ancestor Jean-Jacques Bethmann. A special thank-you also to the historical archives at BMW and Saarstahl, whose openness to publishing historical documents that showed their respective companies' involvement in some of the worst crimes in history was a refreshing contrast to the Catholic church of Cádiz's reluctance to share images that seemed to reflect poorly on its history. Wolfgang Ludwig, Doris Wolf, and Johannes Zuber kept me going on what was a challenging, and sometimes taxing, project. A big thank-you also to Matthias Kilian-Jacobsohn for last-minute help, and for your friendship all along. I also want to thank the editors of the *American Historical Review* for granting me permission to reprint some parts of an article that they originally published in 2017. And a special thank-you to Simmon Yu and his team for their hospitality through the years.

Closer to home, at Harvard University, I had the great privilege of being surrounded by supportive colleagues and a dedicated staff. No one has been more influential on my way of "doing history" than my friend and long-term coteacher Charles Maier. Charlie taught me how to think about large processes on a global scale—and that every day there is something new to be learned. We have also jointly launched a scholarly venture that is dear to my heart—the Weatherhead Initiative on Global History—that became a venue to discuss many of the questions that animate this book with a group of postdoctoral fellows from all continents. William Kirby has done more than anyone else to allow me to have an academic career that I could not have imagined was possible and has generously helped me navigate the modern university that he himself writes about with such deep insights. Dean Laura Fisher also deserves a special mention; I am deeply appreciative for all she has done for me. Teaching for many years with Christine Desan of Harvard Law School has made me grasp the importance of the state to every moment of capitalism's history; Cemal Kafadar has helped me traverse the pitfalls of Ottoman history; Sugata Bose has always been ready to answer any question I might have about Indian history (and I have many); Lorenzo Bondioli shared his always illuminating insights into the biggest questions about capitalism as well as the most minute details of medieval history; and Alexander Keyssar has been there from the very beginning, starting all too many years ago, when we cotaught our very first seminar on American capitalism, to last summer, when he provided another round of feedback on the finished manuscript. Thank you to all of you! And thank you also to Suma Baidya, Michelle Cicerano, Kimberly O'Hagan, Cory Paulsen, and Robin Yun for making sure that grant reports were written, bills paid, and contracts signed.

My editors have been extraordinarily patient during the past few years, but once they received the manuscript, they did their magic in ways rarely seen in the world of modern publishing. I want to thank Scott Moyers and Mia Council at Penguin Press in New York and Simon Winder in Penguin's London office for their thoughtful, thorough, and always encouraging engagement with the manuscript. The team they recruited was just as extraordinary—first and foremost, copy editor Lauren Morgan Whitticom, who caught even very obscure inconsistencies in what I am sure was a challenging editing process, and the production and design team of Randee Marullo, Tess Espinoza, Aly D'Amato, Amanda Dewey, Ryan Benitez, and Gloria Arminio. And, of course, the whole process started with agent extraordinaire Don Fehr at Trident. I appreciate all your hard work on what I am told is one of the longest books ever produced by Penguin Press.

Writing is often a lonely undertaking, but the result, this book, is also the outcome of countless discussions and an unending stream of comments and feedback. No one was more important than Charles

Forcey, whose historical imagination and ability to put very complex arguments into accessible prose is unmatched. We discussed every chapter, every page, and sometimes every word in this book over many years, ending with a weeklong conversation in Florence. Thank you, Charlie, for always being there!

I also want to thank the many people who read all or parts of the manuscript and gave me valuable feedback, including Debjani Bhattacharyya, Elizabeth Blackmar, Ulbe Bosma, Moritz von Brescius, Franz-Josef Brüggemeier, Eli Cook, Bettina Engels, Johanna Gautier-Morin, Lea Haller, Arno Herzig, David Howe, Marcel van der Linden, Noam Maggor, Julia McClure, Dinyar Patel, Dieter Plehwe, Michael Ralph, Sophus Reinhart, Seth Rockman, Eric Vanhaute, and Cyrus Veeser.

During the past few years, I was also privileged to draw upon the feedback of audiences around the world. Scholars in Belfast, Amsterdam, Berlin, Freiburg, Beijing, Florence, Tokyo, Mumbai, Cambridge, Bloomington, Providence, Saint-Louis (Senegal), Jerusalem, Townsville, and Boston engaged in lively discussions and helped me refine my ideas. I have particularly fond memories of a seminar organized by Sophus Reinert's *Holmgang* at Harvard Business School, and a one-week discussion on global capitalism with students and colleagues at the University of Sydney, facilitated by Hannah Forsyth and Sophie Loy-Wilson. The most intense discussions of the manuscript, however, took place at Harvard University with the amazingly gifted students in my seminars on Global History and Global Capitalism in 2024.

At home, everyone but the dog and cat participated in making this book possible. Lisa McGirr has been there throughout, reading and then rereading (and perhaps re-rereading) every chapter; her sharp observations and fine-tuned edits made the book so much better and her love made it possible to achieve. Our children, Noah and Pascal, have engaged with this project since its inception, contributing ideas small and enormous as it unfolded. For better or for worse, they will live in the world whose emergence this book chronicles. I dedicate it to them in admiration and love.

Notes

Abbreviations

AGI: Archivo General de Indias, Seville, Spain

AHN: Archivo Histórico Nacional, Madrid, Spain

AHR: American Historical Review

ANOM: Archives Nationales d'Outre-Mer, Aix-en-Provence, France

ANS: Archives Nationales du Sénégal, Dakar, Senegal

BA Berlin: Bundesarchiv Berlin

BNA: Barbados National Archives, St. Michael, Barbados

BNRio: Biblioteca Nacional, Rio de Janeiro, Brazil

CSF: Centro Storico Fiat, Turin, Italy

CUP: Cambridge University Press

GAM: Godrej Archives, Mumbai, India

EHN: Economic History Network

EHR: Economic History Review

EIC: East India Company

GCA: Glasgow City Archives, Mitchell Library, Glasgow, UK

HMMCR: Hunt's Merchants' Magazine and Commercial Review

HUP: Harvard University Press

IOR: India Office Record, British Library, London, UK

JAH: Journal of American History

JEH: Journal of Economic History

JGH: Journal of Global History

LAS: Landesarchiv Saarbrücken, Saarbrücken, Germany

MSA: Maharashtra State Archives, Mumbai, India

NAB: National Archives of Brazil, Rio de Janeiro, Brazil

NAI: National Archives of India, New Delhi, India

NARA CP: National Archives of the United States, College Park, Maryland

NMML: Teen Murti, Nehru Memorial Museum and Library, New Delhi, India

NYHS: New York Historical Society

NYT: New York Times

OUP: Oxford University Press

PUP: Princeton University Press

SAS: Stadtarchiv Solingen, Solingen, Germany

SAV: Stadtarchiv Völklingen, Völklingen, Germany

UGA: University of Glasgow Archives & Special Collections, Glasgow, Scotland

UP: University Press

VH: Archiv der Saarstahl AG, Völklingen, Germany

WEHC: World Economic History Conference

Preface

1. Timothy Morton, *Hyperobjects: Philosophy and Ecology After the End of the World* (University of Minnesota Press, 2013).

2. As cited in Isabella M. Weber, *How China Escaped Shock Therapy: The Market Reform Debate* (Routledge, 2021), 36.

Introduction

1. The quotes are from James Kendall Hosmer, ed., *Winthrop's Journal: "History of New England," 1630–1649*, vol. 1 (Charles Scribner's Sons, 1908), 315–18. On this case, see Bernard Bailyn, ed., "The Apologia of Robert Keayne: Last Will and Testament," in *Transactions of the Colonial Society of Massachusetts*, vol. 42, *1952–1956*, ed. Walter Muir Whitehill (Colonial Society of Massachusetts, 1964), 243–341; Bernard Bailyn, *The New England Merchants in the Seventeenth Century* (HUP, 1955), 35–44; Bernard Bailyn, "The Apologia of Robert Keayne," *William and Mary Quarterly* 7, no. 4 (October 1950): 568–87; Stephen Innes, *Creating the Commonwealth: The Economic Culture of Puritan New England* (W. W. Norton, 1995), 163–91; and Mark Valeri, *Heavenly Merchandize: How Religion Shaped Commerce in Puritan America* (PUP, 2010), 11–73. On the conviction, see Nathaniel B. Shurtleff, ed., *Records of the Governor and Company of the Massachu-setts Bay in New England*, vol. 1 (Boston: Press of William White, 1853), 281. On the value of £200 in 1639, see "Currency Converter: 1270–2017," National Archives, UK, accessed January 15, 2024, https://www.nationalarchives.gov.uk/currency-converter/#currency-result. The only year for which such data was available was 1640.

2. This is Winthrop's recollection of a speech by John Cotton on the case. See Hosmer, *Winthrop's Journal*, 1:317–18.

3. Bailyn, "The Apologia of Robert Keayne: Last Will and Testament," 294, 299, 310.

4. Branko Milanovic, *Capitalism, Alone: The Future of the System That Rules the World* (HUP, 2019).

5. See Karl Polanyi, *The Great Transformation: The Political and Economic Origins of Our Time* (Farrar & Rinehart, 1944; repr., Beacon Press, 2001), 60. Citations refer to the Beacon Press edition. See also Eren Duzgun, "Capitalism, Jacobinism and International Relations: Re-Interpreting the Ottoman Path to Modernity," *Review of International Studies* 44, no. 2 (2018): 259.

6. "Die Zukunft des Kapitalismus," a series of articles published in the *Frankfurter Allgemeine Zeitung* throughout 2009; and Paul Polman, "Business, Society, and the Future of Capitalism," *McKinsey Quarterly*, no. 3, 2014, 170. On the Davos meeting, see, for example, Tim Weber, "Davos 2012: Has Capitalism Got a Future?," BBC News, January 24, 2012.

7. Jennifer Schuessler, "Cheeseburgers, Oil and Minimum Wage: Building a Museum of Capitalism," *NYT*, November 13, 2019; Ben Dooley and Hisako Ueno, "Can Shrinking Be Good for Japan? A Marxist Best Seller Makes the Case," *NYT*, August 23, 2023; Sven Astheimer, "Deutsche zweifeln am Kapitalismus," *Frankfurter Allgemeine Zeitung*, January 21, 2020. For similar numbers on the UK, see "Trust Barometer 2020: Capitalism in the Dock," Edelman, accessed September 29, 2023, https://www.edelman.co.uk/research/trust-barometer-2020-capitalism-dock. See also Lydia Saad, "Socialism as Popular as Capitalism Among Young Adults in U.S.," Gallup, November 25, 2019, https://news.gallup.com/poll/268766/socialism-popular-capitalism-among-young-adults.aspx; Max Ehrenfreund, "A Majority of Millennials Now Reject Capitalism, Poll Shows," *Washington Post*, April 25, 2016; Paul Mason, *Postcapitalism: A Guide to Our Future* (Farrar, Straus and Giroux, 2016); Immanuel Wallerstein, ed., *Does Capitalism Have a Future?* (OUP, 2013); Wolfgang Streeck, "How Will Capitalism End?," *New Left Review*, no. 87 (May/June 2014): 35–64; Ulrike Hermann, *Das Ende des Kapitalismus* (Kiepenheuer & Witsch, 2022); and Fabian Scheidler, *The End of the Megamachine: A Brief History of a Failing Civilization* (Zero Books, 2020).

8. As cited in Will Daniel, "'We May Be Looking at the End of Capitalism': One of the World's Oldest and Largest Investment Banks Warns 'Greedflation' Has Gone Too Far," *Fortune*, April 5, 2023, https://fortune.com/2023/04/05/end-of-capitalism-inflation-greedflation-societe-generale-corporate-profits/.

9. Such a reading can, for example, be found in Steven Pinker, *Enlightenment Now: The Case for Reason, Science, Humanism, and Progress* (Allen Lane, 2018). For an overview of different interpretations of capitalism and accompanying debates, see Sven Beckert and Seth Rockman, eds., *Slavery's Capitalism: A New History of American Economic Development* (University of Pennsylvania Press, 2016).

10. Jürgen Kocka, "Durch die Brille der Kritik: Wie Man Kapitalismusgeschichte auch schreiben kann," *Journal of Modern European History / Zeitschrift für moderne europäische Geschichte / Revue d'histoire européenne contemporaine* 15, no. 4 (2017): 480–88; Michael Mauke, *Die Klassentheorie von Marx und Engels* (Europäische Verlagsanstalt, 1970), 53–55, 112; Albert O. Hirschman, *Rival Views of Market Society and Other Recent Essays* (Viking, 1986), 105–41; Jerry Z. Muller, "Justus Möser and the Conservative Critique of Early Modern Capitalism," *Central European History* 23, no. 2/3 (1990): 153–78; Isabella M. Weber, "Neoliberal Economic Thinking and the Quest for Rational Socialism in China: Ludwig von Mises and the Market Reform Debate," *Journal of the History of Ideas* 83, no. 2 (2022), 333–56; and Yan Sun, *The Chinese Reassessment of Socialism, 1976–1992* (PUP, 1995), 95–152, 206–8.

11. Marcel van der Linden, "Final Thoughts," in *Capitalism: The Reemergence of a Historical Concept*, ed. Jürgen Kocka and Marcel van der Linden (Bloomsbury Academic, 2016), 251. The importance of qualitative change is also emphasized in the insightful Andrew Liu, "Notes Toward a More Global History of Capitalism," *Spectre*, July 6, 2020, https://spectrejournal.com/notes-toward-a-more-global-history-of-capitalism/.

12. Joyce Appleby, *The Relentless Revolution: A History of Capitalism* (W. W. Norton, 2010).

13. Jason W. Moore, ed., *Anthropocene or Capitalocene? Nature, History, and the Crisis of Capitalism* (PM Press, 2016). For the relevance of the Neolithic Revolution to the understanding of the history of capitalism, see also Jim Henle, "Capitalism in the Light of the Neolithic Revolution," unpublished paper (in author's possession), 2021; and Eric Vanhaute, *Peasants in World History* (Routledge, 2021), 12–13.

14. Pierre Bourdieu, *On the State* (Polity Books, 2014), 115.

15. Fernand Braudel, *Civilization and Capitalism, 15th–18th Century*, trans. Siân Reynolds, vol. 2, *The Wheels of Commerce* (University of California Press, 1992), 455. On the twentieth century, see also Walter Benjamin, "Kapitalismus als Religion [Fragment]," in *Gesammelte Schriften*, ed. Rolf Tiedemann and Hermann Schweppenhäuser, vol. 6 (Suhrkamp, 1991), 100–102.

16. Thomas Piketty, *Capital and Ideology*, trans. Arthur Goldhammer (HUP, 2020), 16. In 1830, an average French worker spent more than a quarter of their wages on bread; by the 1970s, that number had fallen to just 3 percent. See Jean Fourastié, *Les Trente Glorieuses, ou La révolution invisible de 1946 à 1975* (Fayard, 1979), 154. To make this calculation, I assumed a sixty-hour workweek in 1830 and a forty-hour workweek in 1970.

17. Jürgen Kocka, "Capitalism: The History of a Concept," in *International Encyclopedia of the Social & Behavioral Sciences*, ed. James D. Wright, 2nd ed., vol. 3 (Elsevier, 2015), 108. The story of Mikhail Pokrovsky is told in Jairus Banaji, "Merchant Capitalism, Peasant Households and Industrial Accumulation: Integration of a Model," *Journal of Agrarian Change* 16, no. 3 (July 2016): 426–27. See also Mikhail Pokrovsky, *History of Russia from the Earliest Times to the Rise of Commercial Capitalism*, trans. D. S. Mirsky (International Publishers, 1931); Haig Bosmajian, *Burning Books* (McFarland & Co., 2006), 165–68, 170–75, 179; Joseph Malherek, *Free-Market Socialists: European Émigrés Who Made Capitalist Culture in America, 1918–1968* (Central European UP, 2022), 113–14; Manuel Felipe Burgos-Gallego, "A la sombra del Plan Cóndor: Funcionamiento y aplicación del Estatuto de Seguridad Nacional en Colombia (1978–1982)," *Anuario de Historia Regional y de las Fronteras* 28, no. 1 (2023): 243–48, 259–67; Catalina Jiménez, "Aplicación e instrumentalización de la Doctrina de Seguridad Nacional en Colombia (1978–1982): Efectos sobre la temática de derechos humanos," *Reflexión Política* 11, no. 22 (2009): 167–69; and *Schauprozesse unter Stalin, 1932–1952*, trans. Hilde Ettinger et al. (Dietz, 1990), esp. 21.

18. Michel-Rolph Trouillot, *Global Transformations, Anthropology and the Modern World* (Palgrave Macmillan, 2003), 34.

19. Jawaharlal Nehru, "A New Perspective of History," in *Jawaharlal Nehru's Speeches, 1957–1963*, vol. 4

(Publications Division, Ministry of Information and Broadcasting, Government of India, 1961), 178.

20. Caio Prado Jr., *História Econômica do Brasil* (Brasiliense, 1945; repr., 1985), 280. The citation refers to the reprint. For a very similar observation, see Aaron Jakes and Ahmad Shokr, "Capitalism in Egypt, Not Egyptian Capitalism," in *A Critical Political Economy of the Middle East and North Africa*, ed. Joel Beinin, Bassam Haddad, and Sherene Seikaly (Stanford UP, 2021), 123, 142. Rudolf Hilferding had already observed in 1910 that "[c]apitalist development did not take place independently in each individual country." See Rudolf Hilferding, *Finance Capital: A Study of the Latest Phase of Capitalist Development*, ed. Tom Bottomore (Routledge & Kegan Paul, 1981), 322–23. Note that the original German edition was published in Vienna in 1910.

21. Such Eurocentricity has a long and distinguished history. Despite Karl Marx's very best efforts, his accounts are infused with Eurocentric thought—for example, that the world's people can see their future by looking at European history. Another prominent Marxist chronicler of capitalism, Maurice Dobb, does not even note that his story of capitalism focuses exclusively on Europe. See, for example, Maurice Dobb, *Studies in the Development of Capitalism* (International Publisher, 1947), 19. For a non-Marxist Eurocentric perspective, see Appleby, *Relentless Revolution*. The importance of moving our account of capitalism beyond Eurocentric notions has also been emphasized by Dilip Menon and Kaveh Yazdani. See Centre for Indian Studies in Africa and Johannesburg Institute for Advanced Study, "Revisiting the History of Capitalism," proceedings of a workshop held at the University of the Witwatersrand, June 14–15, 2016, 2, 3; and Kaveh Yazdani and Dilip M. Menon, *Capitalisms: Towards a Global History* (OUP, 2021). In general, see Henry Heller, "The Birth of Capitalism in Global Perspective," in Yazdani and Menon, *Capitalisms*, 201–24. See also Chambi Chachage, introduction to "A Capitalizing City: Dar es Salaam and the Emergence of an African Entrepreneurial Elite (c. 1862–2015)" (PhD diss., Harvard University, 2018). For an example of a Eurocentric perspective, see Joel Mokyr, *The Gifts of Athena: Historical Origins of the Knowledge Economy* (PUP, 2002). For a short summary of

the approach of failures and successes, see Francesco Boldizzoni and Pat Hudson, "Global Economic History: Towards an Interpretative Turn," in *Routledge Handbook of Global Economic History*, ed. Francesco Boldizzoni and Pat Hudson (Routledge, 2015), 3–4. For a critique, see also William J. Ashworth, "The Ghost of Rostow: Science, Culture and the British Industrial Revolution," *Historical Science* 46, no. 3 (2008): 255, 258; and Jack Goody, *The Theft of History* (CUP, 2006), 6.

22. For this argument, see also David Washbrook in Centre for Indian Studies in Africa and Johannesburg Institute for Advanced Study, "Revisiting the History of Capitalism," 10.

23. See, for example, Alexander Anievas and Kerem Nişancıoğlu, *How the West Came to Rule: The Geopolitical Origins of Capitalism* (Pluto Press, 2015), 10.

24. For the quote, see Jason W. Moore, "Nature and the Transition from Feudalism to Capitalism," *Review* (Fernand Braudel Center) 26, no. 2 (2003): 99. On the importance of ecological change to our view of capitalism, see, for example, Timothy Mitchell, "Ten Propositions on Oil," in *A Critical Political Economy of the Middle East and North Africa*, ed. Joel Beinin, Bassam Haddad, and Sherene Seikaly (Stanford UP, 2021), 83. See also Charles Fletcher et al., "Earth at Risk: An Urgent Call to End the Age of Destruction and Forge a Just and Sustainable Future," *PNAS Nexus* 3, no. 4 (April 2024): 106; Christopher H. Trisos, Cory Merow, and Alex L. Pigot, "The Projected Timing of Abrupt Ecological Disruption from Climate Change," *Nature* 580, no. 7804 (2020): 496–501; and Alex L. Pigot, Cory Merow, Adam Wilson, and Christopher H. Trisos, "Abrupt Expansion of Climate Change Risks for Species Globally," *Nature Ecology & Evolution* 7, no. 7 (July 2023): 1060–71. For a more detailed exposition of consumed but not priced ecological resources and a discussion of the relevant literature, see Sven Beckert, Ulbe Bosma, Mindi Schneider, and Eric Vanhaute, "Commodity Frontiers and the Transformation of the Global Countryside: A Research Agenda," *JGH* 16, no. 3 (November 2021): 435–50.

25. Pokrovsky, *History of Russia*. The book thus disagrees with an important strand of Marxist writing on capitalism, as embraced by Dobb, *Studies in the Development of Capitalism*; and Robert Brenner, "Agrarian

Class Structure and Economic Development in Pre-Industrial Europe," *Past & Present* 70, no. 1 (February 1976): 30–75. See also Ellen Meiksins-Wood, "The Agrarian Origins of Capitalism," *Monthly Review* 50, no. 3 (1949): 14–31; R. H. Tawney, "A History of Capitalism," *EHR* 2, no. 3 (1950): 310–11. Some of these arguments are also crucial to Jairus Banaji's work, for example, Jairus Banaji, *A Brief History of Commercial Capitalism* (Haymarket, 2020).

26. The book follows Janet Abu-Lughod's wise counsel that we need "to analyze concrete moments in history in concrete places." See Janet L. Abu-Lughod, *Before European Hegemony: The World System A.D. 1250–1350* (OUP, 1989), 11. For a very similar argument, see also Piketty, *Capital and Ideology*, 9. As the Polish historian Witold Kula once said in his analysis of Polish feudalism: "[T]he validity of most essential economic propositions is limited in time and place—limits set, for the most part, by a particular socio-economic system." See Witold Kula, *An Economic Theory of the Feudal System: Towards a Model of the Polish Economy, 1500–1800* (Humanities Press, 1976), 13. See also Neil Smith, *Uneven Development: Nature, Capital, and the Production of Space* (University of Georgia Press, 2008). This is also argued by Eve Darian-Smith and Philip McCarty, "Beyond Interdisciplinarity: Developing a Global Transdisciplinary Framework," *Transience: A Journal of Global Studies* 7, no. 2 (2016): 15.

27. For a persuasive critique of some strands of global history, see Stefanie Gänger, "Circulation: Reflections in Circularity, Entity, and Liquidity in the Language of Global History," *JGH* 12, no. 3 (2017): 303–18. See also Henri Lefebvre, *La production de l'espace* (Anthropos, 1974); and David Harvey, *Spaces of Global Capitalism: A Theory of Uneven Geographical Development* (Version, 2006).

28. Kenneth Lipartito, "Reassembling the Economic: New Departures in Historical Materialism," *AHR* 121, no. 1 (February 2016): 127.

29. Braudel also stressed the "flexibility" and "eclecticism" of capitalism. See Fernand Braudel, *Civilization and Capitalism, 15th–18th Century*, vol. 1, *The Structure of Everyday Life* (Harper & Row, 1982), 433. See also Ernst Langthaler and Elke Schüßler, "Commodity Studies with Polanyi: Disembedding and Re-Embedding

Labour and Land in Contemporary Capitalism," *Österreichische Zeitschrift für Soziologie* 44, no. 2 (June 2019): 213. The importance of spatial analysis is also emphasized by Bob Jessop, Neil Brenner, and Martin Jones, "Theorizing Sociospatial Relations," *Environment and Planning D: Society and Space* 26 (2008): 389–401. See, too, Fernand Braudel, *Afterthoughts on Material Civilization and Capitalism*, trans. Patricia M. Ranum (Johns Hopkins UP, 1977), 93; Rafael de Bivar Marquese, *Asymmetrical Dependencies in the Making of a Global Commodity: Coffee in the Longue Durée*, ed. Abdelkader Al Ghouz, Jeannine Bischoff, and Sarah Dusend, Jospeh C. Miller Memorial Lecture Series, vol. 15 (EB-Verlag, 2023), 50–51; Leonardo Marques and Rafael de Bivar Marquese, "Gold, Coffee, and Slaves: Brazil and 'the So-Called Primitive Accumulation,'" *Critical Historical Studies* 10, no. 2 (Fall 2023): 215; and Karl Marx and Friedrich Engels, *Gesamtausgabe (MEGA) [Collected Works]*, sec. 2, *Das Kapital und Vorarbeiten* [*Capital* and Preliminary Works], vol. 3, *Zur Kritik der Politischen Ökonomie (Manuskript 1861–1863)* [*A Contribution to the Critique of Political Economy (Manuscript 1861–1863)*], part 6 (Dietz, 1982), 1972. The notion of capitalisms is, for example, crucial to the excellent work of Kaveh and Menon, *Capitalisms*. Ernst Bloch, "Nonsynchronism and the Obligation to Its Dialectics," *New German Critique* 11 (Spring 1977; originally 1932): 22–38.

30. "Power, politics, violence and economics," according to historian Peer Vries, were "inseparable and almost undistinguishable" in the origins of capitalism. See Peer Vries, *State, Economy and the Great Divergence: Great Britain and China, 1680s–1850s* (Bloomsbury Academic, 2015), 35.

31. Nancy Fraser, "Behind Marx's Hidden Abode," *New Left Review*, no. 86 (March/April 2014): 66; Polanyi, *Great Transformation*, 55; Joseph A. Schumpeter, *Capitalism, Socialism and Democracy* (Harper & Brothers, 1942; repr., George Allen & Unwin, 1976), 162. Citations refer to the George Allen & Unwin edition.

32. A parallel argument is made by Prasannan Parthasarathi, *Why Europe Grew Rich and Asia Did Not: Global Economic Divergence, 1600–1850* (CUP, 2011), 269. For an emphasis on actors, see also Martin. J. Sklar, *The Corporate Reconstruction of American Capitalism, 1890–1916*

(CUP, 1988), 2; Thomas Welskopp, "Zukunft Bewirtschaften," *Mittelweg* 36, no. 1 (2017): 84; Braudel, *Afterthoughts on Material Civilization*, 47; and Fahad Ahmad Bishara, *A Sea of Debt: Law and Economic Life in the Western Indian Ocean, 1780–1950* (CUP, 2017), 8–9.

33. See also Jürgen Kocka, "Karl Marx and the History of Capitalism," *Bulletin of the German Historical Institute* 63 (Fall 2018): 17. As historian Bernd Weisbrod has argued persuasively, violence is "constitutive" of capitalism. See Bernd Weisbrod, "Kapitalismus & Gewalt," unpublished paper (in author's possession), Humboldt University colloquium by Michael Wildt, October 16, 2015, 2.

34. Herbert Butterfield, *The Whig Interpretation of History* (Scribner, 1951), 16.

35. For capitalism as a process, see Jonathan Levy, *Ages of American Capitalism: A History of the United States* (Random House, 2021), xiv.

36. Adam Smith, *The Wealth of Nations* (London: W. Strahan and T. Cadeli, 1776; repr., Vintage Classics, 2020), book 1, chapter 2, 12; Karl Marx, *Capital: A Critique of Political Economy*, trans. Ben Fowkes, vol. 1 (Penguin Classics, 1990), chapter 24, 725–61; Max Weber, *The Protestant Ethic and the Spirit of Capitalism*, trans. Talcott Parsons (Scribner, 1930); and Larry Neal and Jeffrey G. Williamson, eds., *The Cambridge History of Capitalism*, vols. 1 and 2 (CUP, 2014). Or is it, as historian Werner Plumpe observes, best seen as technology-driven "capital intensive commodity production"? See Werner Plumpe, "Der Kapitalismus als Problem der Geschichtsschreibung," *Journal of Modern European History / Zeitschrift für moderne europäische Geschichte / Revue d'histoire européenne contemporaine* 15, no. 4 (2017): 457. On Weber, see also Kocka, "Capitalism: The History of a Concept," 107.

37. See also Kocka, "Capitalism: The History of a Concept," 105–6; and Anievas and Nişancıoğlu, *How the West Came to Rule*, 8.

38. Marc Bloch, *Feudal Society*, vol. 1 (University of Chicago Press, 1961), xix.

39. Karl Marx, *Das Kapital: Kritik der politischen Oekonomie*, vol. 1, *Der Produktionsprocess des Kapitals* (Hamburg: Otto Meisner, 1883), 781. The "power of generation" is a translation of the German word *Zeugungskraft*.

40. Schumpeter, *Capitalism, Socialism and Democracy*, 82–83.

41. Piero Sraffa, *Production of Commodities by Means of Commodities:*

Prelude to a Critique of Economic Theory (CUP, 1960). For a similar definition, see Polanyi, *The Great Transformation*, 71–72. See also Marcel van der Linden, "The Future of Labor History in a World Perspective," unpublished paper (in author's possession), University of Pittsburgh, May 2014, 12.

42. For the importance of wage labor to capitalism, see Milanovic, *Capitalism, Alone*, 12; Robert S. DuPlessis, *Transitions to Capitalism in Early Modern Europe* (CUP, 2019), 5; Anievas and Nişancıoğlu, *How the West Came to Rule*, 8; and Marcel van der Linden, *Workers of the World: Essays Toward a Global Labor History* (Brill, 2008). For the commodification of labor power to take on different forms, including slavery, see the important contributions of, among others, van der Linden, "The Future of Labor History in a World Perspective," 12.

43. See, among many others, Nancy Fraser and Rahel Jaeggi, *Capitalism: A Conversation in Critical Theory* (Polity Press, 2018), 52; Melinda Cooper, *Family Values: Between Neoliberalism and the New Social Conservatism* (Zone Books, 2017); Maria Mies, *Patriarchy and Accumulation on a World Stage: Women in the International Division of Labour* (Zed Books, 1985; Anievas and Nişancıoğlu, *How the West Came to Rule*, 9; Braudel, *Afterthoughts on Material Civilization*, 112; Fraser, "Behind Marx's Hidden Abode," 55–72; and Giandomenica Becchio, *A History of Feminist and Gender Economics* (Routledge, 2020). For the general point, see also Pepijn Brandon, "Elements of Original Accumulation: Dispossession, War, and Slavery in the History of Capitalism," inaugural lecture, Vrije Universiteit Amsterdam, May 26, 2023, publisher's PDF, 23, https://research .vu.nl/ws/portalfiles/portal/2282 34131/Inaugural_lecture_Brandon _Elements_of_original_accumula tion_ENG.pdf.

44. R. H. Tawney, *Religion and the Rise of Capitalism: A Historical Study* (Penguin, 1937), vii–viii.

45. Bloch, *Feudal Society*, 1:xx.

46. A vast literature has been aggregated under this moniker. See, for example, Seth Rockman, *Scraping By: Wage Labor, Slavery, and Survival in Early Baltimore* (Johns Hopkins UP, 2009); Bethany Moreton, *To Serve God and Wal-Mart* (HUP, 2010); Julia Ott, *When Wall Street Met Main Street: The Quest for an Investors' Democracy* (HUP, 2014); and Levy, *Ages of American Capitalism*. One important source of this devel-

opment was the Harvard Business School, especially Alfred D. Chandler Jr. and Thomas K. McCraw, who both wrote and taught on various aspects of what they called "the history of capitalism." For an excellent review, see Richard R. John, "Prophet of Perspective: Thomas K. McCraw," *Business History Review* 89, no. 1 (Spring 2015): 129–53. See also Kenneth Lipartito, "Reassembling the Economic," 135; and Seth Rockman, "What Makes the History of Capitalism Newsworthy?," review of *Capitalism Takes Command: The Social Transformation of Nineteenth-Century America*, by Michael Zakim and Gary J. Kornblith, *Journal of the Early Republic* 34, no. 3 (Fall 2014): 450.

47. There I am specifically referring to Roxani Eleni Margariti, *Aden & the Indian Ocean Trade: 150 Years in the Life of a Medieval Arabian Port* (University of North Carolina Press, 2007); and Philip Mirowski and Dieter Plehwe, eds., *The Road from Mont Pèlerin: The Making of the Neoliberal Thought Collective* (HUP, 2009). Many other works are cited throughout the book.

48. This literature is vast. For a general overview, see Jürgen Osterhammel, *Geschichtswissenschaft Jenseits des Nationalstaates* (Vandenhoeck & Ruprecht, 2001); Sven Beckert and Dominic Sachsenmaier, eds., *Global History, Globally* (Bloomsbury, 2018). For critical debates, see Jeremy Adelman, "What Is Global History Now?," *Aeon*, March 2, 2017. See also the response of Richard Drayton and David Motadel, "Discussion: The Futures of Global History," *JGH* 13, no. 1 (March 2018): 1–21; Darian-Smith and McCarty, "Beyond Interdisciplinarity," 13; and Ulrike von Hirschhausen, "A New Imperial History? Programm, Potenzial, Perspektiven," *Geschichte und Gesellschaft* 41 (2015): 718–57. For an earlier example of a connected history that gives voice to marginalized groups, see Eric R. Wolf, *Europe and the People Without History* (University of California Press, 1982).

49. Chang Ha-Joon, *Kicking Away the Ladder: Development Strategy in Historical Perspective* (Anthem Press, 2002), 5–6; and Marshall Hodgson, *The Venture of Islam*, vol. 3, *The Gunpowder Empires and Modern Times* (University of Chicago Press, 1974); Welskopp, "Zukunft Bewirtschaften," 83, 91. *Neal and Williamson's Cambridge History of Capitalism*, a massive two-volume edition, has a tendency to naturalize capitalism by stretching its history into Babylonian times. This is

very effectively criticized in Peter Temin, "The Cambridge History of Capitalism,'" Working Paper No. 20638 (National Bureau of Economic Research, November 2014). See also Antara Haldar, "The Future of Capitalism? The Time-Space Continuum of History and Development in the Story of Capitalism," unpublished paper presented at the Workshop on the History of Capitalism, Harvard University, November 2019, 3. Counterintuitively, even some strands of economic history, informed by such theories, dehistoricized economic life by seeking to apply universal laws to disentangling problems of the deep past. On some of these tensions, see, for example, Francesco Boldizzoni and Pat Hudson, "Culture, Power and Contestation: Multiple Roads from the Past to the Future," in *Routledge Handbook of Global Economic History*, ed. Francesco Boldizzoni and Pat Hudson (Routledge, 2015); Philip Mirowski, *More Heat Than Light: Economics as Social Physics, Physics as Nature's Economics* (CUP, 1991); on economists writing history, see Piketty, *Capital and Ideology*; Jeffery D. Sachs, *The Ages of Globalization* (CUP, 2020); and Denis Cogneau, *Un empire bon marché: Histoire et économie politique de la colonisation française, XIXe–XXIe siècle* (Seuil, 2023); Isabella M. Weber, *How China Escaped Shock Therapy: The Market Reform Debate* (Routledge, 2021).

50. Joseph A. Schumpeter, *History of Economic Analysis*, ed. Elizabeth Boody Schumpeter (OUP, 1954), 12–13.

51. Braudel, like me, emphasized the importance of commerce and merchants to capitalism's history, the open-endedness of historical process, and the need to think about capitalism from a global perspective. See all three volumes of Braudel, *Civilization and Capitalism*; and Braudel, *Afterthoughts on Material Civilization*. Additionally, a significant strand of the literature has focused, in historian Seth Rockman's words, on "dismantl[ing] the black box that obscures the substantial work involved in transforming aspects of the material world into exchangeable units," a project important to this book as well. For example, see Brenner, "Agrarian Class Structure and Economic Development in Pre-Industrial Europe," 30–75; and Meiskins-Wood, "Agrarian Origins of Capitalism," 14–31. Janet Abu-Lughod has encouraged me to go back in time. A whole slew of scholars—from Douglas North to Christine Desan, from

Oscar Gelderblom to Niall Ferguson—have helpfully emphasized the importance of institutions, while Charles Tilly, John Brewer, and John Ashworth have given the state the central role it deserves.

52. On the notion of "regimes," see Harriet Friedmann, "From Colonialism to Green Capitalism: Social Movements and the Emergence of Food Regimes," in *New Directions in the Sociology of Global Development*, ed. Frederick H. Buttel and Philip D. McMichael (Emerald Group Publishing Limited, 2005), 227–26.

53. For the original Italian, see Italo Calvino, *Le città invisibili* (Einaudi, 1972), 18–19. For the English translation, see Italo Calvino, *Invisible Cities*, trans. William Weaver (Harcourt Brace Jovanovich, 1974), 11.

Chapter 1: Islands of Capital

1. Nancy Fraser, *Cannibal Capitalism: How Our System Is Devouring Democracy, Care, and the Planet—and What We Can Do About It* (Verso, 2022); and Branko Milanovic, *Capitalism, Alone: The Future of the System That Rules the World* (HUP, 2019).

2. Roxani Eleni Margariti, *Aden & the Indian Ocean Trade: 150 Years in the Life of a Medieval Arabian Port* (University of North Carolina Press, 2007), 2.

3. S. D. Goitein and Mordechai A. Friedman, *India Traders of the Middle Ages: Documents from the Cairo Geniza* (Brill, 2008), 7; Georges Lefebvre, *The French Revolution*, trans. Elizabeth Moss Evanson, vol. 1 (Routledge Classics, 2001), 25–27; and Ibn Battuta, *The Travels of Ibn Battuta, A.D. 1325–1354*, vol. 2, ed. and trans. H. A. R. Gibb, orig. ed. C. Defrémery and B. R. Sanguinetti (CUP for Hakluyt Society, 1962), 372.

4. Ibn Battuta, *Travels of Ibn Battuta*, 2:372.

5. Goitein and Friedman, *India Traders of the Middle Ages*, 7; and Ibn al-Mujāwir, *A Traveller in Thirteenth-Century Arabia: Ibn al-Mujāwir's Tārikh al-Mustabsir*, ed. and trans. G. Rex Smith (Routledge, 2022), 129.

6. Chau Ju-ka, *Chau Ju-kua: His Work on the Chinese and Arab Trade in the Twelfth and Thirteenth Centuries, Entitled Chu-fan-chï*, ed. and trans. Friedrich Hirth and W. W. Rockhill (Imperial Academy of Sciences, 1911), 25.

7. Al-Muqaddasī, *The Best Divisions for Knowledge of the Regions: Ahsan al-Taqāsīm fī Maʿrifat al-Aqālīm*, trans. Basil Collins, rev. Mohammad Hamid Altaʾi (Garnet Publishing,

1994), 82–83. See also K. N. Chaudhuri, *Trade and Civilisation in the Indian Ocean: An Economic History from the Rise of Islam to 1750* (CUP, 1985), 49, 93, 101–8; André Wink, *Al-Hind and the Making of the Indo-Islamic World: The Slave Kings and the Islamic Conquest, 11th–13th Centuries*, vol. 2 (Brill, 2002), 1. Much of what we know about this trade is based on decades-long investigation of a trove of records found in storerooms (*geniza*) of the Ben Ezra Synagogue in Fustat. These records are known as the Cairo Geniza, and they have been expertly analyzed by Shelomo Dov Goitein, Mordechai A. Friedman, Marina Rustow, Eve Krakowski, Jessica Goldberg, and (especially important for the history of Aden) Roxani Margariti, among others. There is also a trove of Muslim merchant records that have been analyzed in Li Guo, *Commerce, Culture, and Community in a Red Sea Port in the Thirteenth Century: The Arabic Documents from Quseir* (Brill, 2004). See also the critique of this project by Mordechai A. Friedman, "Qusayr and Geniza Documents on the Indian Ocean Trade," *Journal of the American Oriental Society* 126 (July 2006): 401–9. For the possibilities and limits of the extant sources, see also Maya Shatzmiller, "A Misconstrued Link: Europe and the Economic History of Islamic Trade," in *Relazioni economiche tra Europa e mondo islamico, secc. XIII–XVIII*, ed. F. Datini (Le Monnier, 2007), 387–418; and al-Muqaddasī, *The Best Divisions for Knowledge of the Regions*, 82–83.

8. The document is cited in Margariti, *Aden & the Indian Ocean Trade*, 153–54.

9. Cited in Goitein and Friedman, *India Traders of the Middle Ages*, 159; and al-Mujāwir, *A Traveller in Thirteenth-Century Arabia*, 147.

10. On al-Mujāwir, see also Nayef Abdullah Shamrookh, "The Commerce and Trade of the Rasulids in the Yemen: 630–858 / 1231–1454" (PhD diss., University of Manchester, 1993), 24; James Beresford, "The Sailing Season of the Indian Ocean," in *The Ancient Sailing Season* (Brill, 2013), 215–16. The Cairo Geniza letters of merchants active in Aden, some of them edited by S. D. Goitein, reveal such activities in their daily lives. See S. D. Goitein, *Letters of Medieval Jewish Traders* (PUP, 2015), 175–229; and Goitein and Friedman, *India Traders of the Middle Ages*. On Aden as a link between "two great trade areas," see Goitein, *Letters of Medieval Jewish Traders*, 25.

For a portrait of Aden as a commercial entrepôt, see the foundational work on the medieval city by Margariti, *Aden & the Indian Ocean Trade*. The centrality of Aden to various trade circuits is also emphasized by Chaudhuri, *Trade and Civilisation*, 101–8; and Şevket Pamuk, "Wirtschaft und Institutionen im Nahen Osten seit dem Mittelalter," in *Die Ursrpünge der modernen Welt: Geschichte im wissenschaftlichen Vergleich*, ed. James A. Robinson and Klaus Wiegandt (S. Fischer Verlag, 2008), 552.

11. Margariti, *Aden & the Indian Ocean Trade*, 87, 102, 146, 154; on dhows, see George Fadlo Hourani, *Arab Seafaring in the Indian Ocean in Ancient and Early Medieval Times* (PUP, 1995), 89–100.

12. Al-Mujāwir, *A Traveller in Thirteenth-Century Arabia*, 155.

13. On the number of ships, see al-Mujāwir, *A Traveller in Thirteenth-Century Arabia*, 161. For the identification of him as a businessperson, see al-Mujāwir, *A Traveller in Thirteenth-Century Arabia*, 2. The disembarkation and inspection process is described in al-Mujāwir, 155.

14. On the number of ships, see al-Mujāwir, *A Traveller in Thirteenth-Century Arabia*, 161. The disembarkation and inspection process is described in al-Mujāwir, 155.

15. Margariti, *Aden & the Indian Ocean Trade*, 52, 59, 64, 96, 98, 195; al-Mujāwir, *A Traveller in Thirteenth-Century Arabia*, 147; Mark Horton and John Middleton, *The Swahili: The Social Landscape of a Mercantile Society* (Blackwell Publishers, 2000), 76.

16. Margariti, *Aden & the Indian Ocean Trade*, 135–36.

17. S. D. Goitein, "From Aden to India: Specimens of the Correspondence of India Traders of the Twelfth Century," *Journal of the Economic and Social History of the Orient* 23, no. 1/2 (April 1980): 45; and Goitein and Friedman, *India Traders of the Middle Ages*, 38.

18. Ranabir Chakravarti, "Nakhudas and Nauvittakas: Ship-Owning Merchants in the West Coast of India (c. AD 1000–1500)," *Journal of the Economic and Social History of the Orient* 43, no. 1 (2000): 44; and Margariti, *Aden & the Indian Ocean Trade*, 163.

19. Margariti, *Aden & the Indian Ocean Trade*, 19, 145–49, 158, 163. For the scale and diversity of merchants who plied the Indian Ocean trade, and whose names survive in the records of the Cairo Geniza, see Goitein and Friedman, *India Traders of the Middle Ages*, 12–14; S. D. Goi-

tein, "From Aden to India," 45–46, 57, 62–63; and Margariti, *Aden & the Indian Ocean Trade*, 79–81, 144–48. Boats from East Africa were observed in the port of Aden around 1232 by Ibn al-Mujāwir. See Horton and Middleton, *Swahili*, 80. See also Chaudhuri, *Trade and Civilisation*, 49, 101; and al-Mujāwir, *A Traveller in Thirteenth-Century Arabia*, 145. On Lebdi's journey to India, see Goitein and Friedman, *India Traders of the Middle Ages*, 28. On the lac trade, see Goitein and Friedman, *India Traders of the Middle Ages*, 30, 39; and Chakravarti, "Nakhudas and Nauvittakas," 44.

20. Éric Vallet, "L'horizon indien et la politique océanique des Rasūlides," in *L'arabie marchande: État et commerce sous les sultans rasūlides du Yémen (626–858 / 1229–1454)* (Éditions de la Sorbonne, 2010), 541–623; Eric Vallet, "Yemeni 'Oceanic Policy' at the End of the Thirteenth Century," *Proceedings of the Seminar for Arabian Studies* 36 (2006): 289–96. On the importance of gold as payment for wares coming from the East, see, for example, two fragments from a letter that Madmūn b. Hasan wrote to Abraham ben Yijū in Aden, circa 1134 (No. 11, 25, ENA 3616, f. 19, and No. II, 26, ULC Or. 1081 J 3), as quoted in Goitein and Friedman, *India Traders of the Middle Ages*, 352–55; Margariti, *Aden & the Indian Ocean Trade*, 121; and Horton and Middleton, *Swahili*, 80–81. A Portuguese traveler by the name of Barbosa witnessed these boats in the early sixteenth century. See Janet L. Abu-Lughod, *Before European Hegemony: The World System A.D. 1250–1350* (OUP, 1989), 272. See also Madmūn b. Hasan b. Bundār to Abraham b. Perahyā Ben Yijū, Aden, 1146/47 (exact date unknown), as quoted in Goitein, "From Aden to India," 58–63; and Margariti, *Aden & the Indian Ocean Trade*, 151–52. On glassmaking, see Margariti, *Aden & the Indian Ocean Trade*, 61. On boatbuilding, see Margariti, *Aden & the Indian Ocean Trade*, 159–60. For one example, see "Deed of Partnership in the Late Abu 'l-Barakat II's Sugar Factory," Fustat, September 1239, as translated in Goitein and Friedman, *India Traders of the Middle Ages*, 277; and Tsugitaka Sato, "The Ups and Downs of the Sugar Merchants," in *Sugar in the Social Life of Medieval Islam* (Brill, 2015), 74–90.

21. Madmun ben Hasan ben Bundar to Abraham b. Perahyā Ben Yijū, Aden, September 11, 1149, as quoted in Goitein, "From Aden to India," 52.

22. On the location of these residences, see Margariti, *Aden & the Indian Ocean Trade*, 192. See also Margariti, *Aden & the Indian Ocean Trade*, 101–3, 156, 159, 181; Abraham L. Udovitch, *Partnership and Profit in Medieval Islam* (PUP, 1970); Jessica L. Goldberg, *Trade and Institutions in the Medieval Mediterranean: The Geniza Merchants and Their Business World* (CUP, 2012), 178; John H. Pryor, "The Origins of the Commenda Contract," in *Commerce, Shipping and Naval Warfare in the Medieval Mediterranean* (Variorum Reprints, 1987), 5–37; and Ron Harris, "The Commenda," in *Going the Distance: Eurasian Trade and the Rise of the Business Corporation, 1400–1700* (PUP, 2020), 130–70.

23. See also Goldberg, *Trade and Institutions*, 178–79; and Margariti, *Aden & the Indian Ocean Trade*, 6, 158, 178.

24. Goldberg, *Trade and Institutions*, 145. A rich sampling of such correspondence can be found in Goitein and Friedman, *India Traders of the Middle Ages*; Goitein, *Letters of Medieval Jewish Traders*; Goitein and Friedman, *India Traders of the Middle Ages*, 12; Jessica L. Goldberg, "The Courts, the Qadi, and the 'People': Resolving Mercantile Disputes in the Medieval Islamic Mediterranean," in *Conflict Management in the Mediterranean and the Atlantic, 1000–1800: Actors, Institutions and Strategies of Dispute Settlement*, ed. Louis Sicking and Alain Wijffels (Brill/Nijhoff, 2020), 19–42; S. D. Goitein, *A Mediterranean Society: The Jewish Communities of the Arab World as Portrayed in the Documents of the Cairo Geniza*, vol. 1, *Economic Foundations* (University of California Press, 1999), 186–92; Margariti, *Aden & the Indian Ocean Trade*, 178; and Goldberg, *Trade and Institutions*, 65, 111–14, 138–39, 180. On Madmun ben Hasan ben Bundar specifically, see Goitein and Friedman, *India Traders of the Middle Ages*, 37.

25. On the state, see S. D. Goitein, *A Mediterranean Society: The Jewish Communities of the Arab World as Portrayed in the Documents of the Cairo Geniza*, vol. 2, *The Community* (University of California Press, 2018), 404; and Marina Rustow, "Fatimid State Documents," *Jewish History* 32 (2019): 221–77. There were significant variations—some goods were not taxed at all, while others garnered 30 percent in duty payments. See Norman A. Stillman, "The Eleventh-Century Merchant House of Ibn 'Awkal (a Geniza Study)," *Journal of the Economic and Social His-*

tory of the Orient 16, no. 1 (January 1973): 15; and Margariti, *Aden & the Indian Ocean Trade*, 113–14, 133–34.

26. Abu-Lughod, *Before European Hegemony*, 353.

27. See Margariti, *Aden & the Indian Ocean Trade*, 177. For the size of container ships in the 2020s, see Alexander Arnfinn Olson, "Container Ships," in *Merchant Ship Types* (Taylor & Francis, 2023).

28. N. S. B. Gras, *Business and Capitalism: An Introduction to Business History* (F. S. Crafts, 1939), 67. For a similar argument, see Maurice Dobb, *Studies in the Development of Capitalism* (International Publisher, 1947), 26. This argument comes as a surprise, since Dobb generally argues against the importance of merchants to the emergence of capitalism.

29. Fernand Braudel emphasizes the importance of economic growth to the expansion of merchant capital. Fernand Braudel, *Civilization and Capitalism, 15th–18th Century*, trans. Siân Reynolds, vol. 2, *The Wheels of Commerce* (University of California Press, 1992), 382.

30. Charles Tilly, *Coercion, Capital, and European States, AD 900–1900* (Basil Blackwell, 1990), 17; Fernand Braudel, *Afterthoughts on Material Civilization and Capitalism*, trans. Patricia M. Ranum (Johns Hopkins UP, 1977), 39, 47, 63.

31. Giovanni Botero, *Le relazioni universali*, ed. Blythe Alice Raviola, vol. 1 (Nino Aragno Editore, 2015), 441.

32. Abu-Lughod, *Before European Hegemony*, 14.

33. Braudel, *Afterthoughts on Material Civilization*, 85–89. In regard to India, see George W. Spencer, *The Politics of Expansion: The Chola Conquest of Sri Lanka and Sri Vijaya* (New Era, 1983), 74. For the notion of archipelagos, see Richard Haepke, as cited in Fernand Braudel, *Civilization and Capitalism, 15th–18th Century*, trans. Siân Reynolds, vol. 2, *The Wheels of Commerce* (University of California Press, 1992), 3, 30, 382. For the "capitalist archipelago," see Giovanni Arrighi, *The Long Twentieth Century: Money, Power, and the Origins of Our Time* (Verso, 1994), 23. For one of the most influential statements on this issue, see Douglass C. North and Barry R. Weingast, "Constitutions and Commitment: The Evolution of Institutions Governing Public Choice in Seventeenth-Century England," *JEH* 49, no. 4 (December 1989): 803–32; Karl Polanyi, *The Great Transformation: The Political and Eco-*

nomic Origins of Our Time (Beacon Press, 2001), 40. These institutions were not just the enablers of capitalism's dynamics; they were a consequence of their emergence. See, for example, Daron Acemoglu and James A. Robinson, "The Rise and Decline of General Laws of Capitalism," *Journal of Economic Perspectives* 29, no. 1 (2015): 3–28; Thomas Ferguson, *Golden Rule: The Investment Theory of Party Competition and the Logic of Money-Driven Political Systems* (University of Chicago Press, 1995); and Douglass C. North, *Institutions, Institutional Change and Economic Performance* (CUP, 1990). The importance of looking at the history of these institutions and the processes behind their emergence is also noted by Stanley L. Engerman and Kenneth L. Sokoloff, "Factor Endowments, Inequality, and Paths of Development Among New World Economies," NBER Working Paper No. 9259 (October 2002), 1–5.

34. The notion of "sprouts of capitalism" was developed in the literature on Chinese capitalism. See, for example, Zhengzhong Guo, "Capitalist Buds in the Production in the Salt Industry of Sichuan During the Song Dynasty," *Social Science Research* no. 11 (1981): 43–48. See also Chris Wickham, "How Did the Feudal Economy Work? The Economic Logic of Medieval Societies," *Past & Present* 251, no. 1 (May 2020): 3–40.

35. Chris Wickham, *The Donkey and the Boat: Reinterpreting the Mediterranean Economy, 950–1180* (OUP, 2023), esp. 621–62; Richard Smith, "Trade and Commerce Across Afro-Eurasia," in *The Cambridge World History*, vol. 5, *Expanding Webs of Exchange and Conflict, 500 CE–1500 CE*, ed. Benjamin Z. Kedar and Merry E. Wiesner-Hanks (CUP, 2015), 233–56. For overviews of the medieval commercial revolution across Afro-Eurasia, see Peter Turchin, "Modeling Periodic Waves of Integration in the Afro-Eurasian World-System," in *Globalization as Evolutionary Process: Modeling Global Change*, ed. George Modelski, Tessaleno Devezas, and William R. Thompson (Routledge, 2007), 161–89; Lorenzo Bondioli, "Towards a Longer History of Commercial Capital," *Storica: Rivista Quadrimestrale* 83/84 (2022): 177–94; Smith, "Trade and Commerce," 233–56; Colleen C. Ho, "Overland Trade in the Mongol World," in *The Mongol World* (Routledge, 2022), 484–504; Philippe Beaujard, *The Worlds of the Indian Ocean: A Global History*, vol. 1, *From*

the Fourth Millennium BCE to the Sixth Century CE (CUP, 2019); Kenneth R. Hall, "Eleventh-Century Commercial Developments in Angkor and Champa," in Maritime Trade and State Development in Early Southeast Asia (University of Hawaii Press, 1985), 169–93; Roberto S. Lopez, The Commercial Revolution of the Middle Ages, 950–1350 (CUP, 1976); and Wickham, "How Did the Feudal Economy Work?," 6.

36. Angus Maddison, Contours of the World Economy, 1–2030 AD: Essays in Macro-Economic History (OUP, 2007); Peregrine Horden and Nicholas Purcell, The Corrupting Sea: A Study of Mediterranean History (Blackwell Publishers, 2000); Hyun Jin Kim, Samuel N. C. Lieu, and Raoul McLaughlin, Rome and China: Points of Contact (Routledge, 2021); and Sitta von Reden, ed., Handbook of Ancient Afro-Eurasian Economies, vol. 3, Frontier-Zone Processes and Transimperial Exchange (De Gruyter Oldenbourg, 2023).

37. Maya Shatzmiller, "Transcontinental Trade and Economic Growth in the Early Islamic Empire: The Red Sea Corridor in the 8th–10th Centuries," in Connected Hinterlands: Proceedings of the Red Sea Project IV, ed. Lucy Blue, John Cooper, Ross Thomas, and Julian Whitewright (Archaeopress, 2009), 119–30, here 120–21.

38. Chau, Chau Ju-kua, 102; Chaudhuri, Trade and Civilisation, 45, 47–48, 98.

39. For the quote, see Ḥudūd al-'Ālam, "The Regions of the World": A Persian Geography, 372 A.H.–982 A.D, trans. V. V. Minorsky (Messrs. Luzac & Co., 1937), 137–38. On much earlier instances, see, for example, Maurice Sartre, Le bateau de Palmyre: Quand les mondes anciens se rencontraient (Tallandier, 2021); and Michael McCormick, "New Light on the 'Dark Ages': How the Slave Trade Fuelled the Carolingian Economy," Past & Present 177, no. 1 (November 2002): 40, 53. See, generally, Michael McCormick, Origins of the European Economy: Communications and Commerce AD 300–900 (CUP, 2001); Abu-Lughod, Before European Hegemony, 189–90; John Chaffee, The Muslim Merchants of Premodern China: The History of a Maritime Asian Trade Diaspora, 750–1400 (CUP, 2018), 40, 50–41; Chaudhuri, Trade and Civilisation, 44, 50–51; Hall, Maritime Trade and State Development, 183; and Shatzmiller, "Transcontinental Trade and Economic Growth," 119–30, here 119, 121.

40. For overviews, see Bondioli, "Towards a Longer History," 177–94; and Wickham, Donkey and the Boat. On the Indian Ocean, see Abu-Lughod, Before European Hegemony, 268. For environmental changes in this period, see Ellen F. Arnold, "An Introduction to Medieval Environmental History," History Compass 6, no. 3 (2008): 898–916. For expansion of trade, see Philippe Beaujard, "Gujarat and Long-Distance Trade in the Indian Ocean Region Before the Sixteenth Century," in Transregional Trade and Traders: Situating Gujarat in the Indian Ocean from Early Times to 1900, ed. Edward A. Alpers and Chhaya Goswami (OUP, 2019), 80. For changes in the countryside, see especially Eric Vanhaute, Peasants in World History (Routledge, 2021), esp. 49, 53; and Jason W. Moore, "Nature and the Transition from Feudalism to Capitalism," Review (Fernand Braudel Center) 26, no. 2 (2003): 105. The importance of a tradable surplus is also emphasized by Chaudhuri, Trade and Civilisation, 184.

41. See Wickham, Donkey and the Boat; Goldberg, Trade and Institutions; Lisa Blaydes and Christopher Paik, "Muslim Trade and City Growth Before the Nineteenth Century: Comparative Urbanization in Europe, the Middle East and Central Asia," British Journal of Political Science 51, no. 2 (2021): 848; and Étienne de la Vaissière, "Trans-Asian Trade, or the Silk Road Deconstructed (Antiquity, Middle Ages)," in The Cambridge History of Capitalism, vol. 1, The Rise of Capitalism: From Ancient Origins to 1848, ed. Larry Neal and Jeffrey G. Williamson (CUP, 2014), 101–24.

42. Chaudhuri, Trade and Civilisation, 11, 36; Jairus Banaji, "Islam, the Mediterranean and the Rise of Capitalism," Historical Materialism 15, no. 1 (2007): 59; Ira M. Lapidus, Muslim Cities in the Later Middle Ages (CUP, 1984); Andrew Petersen, The Towns of Palestine Under Muslim Rule: AD 600–1600 (Archaeopress, 2005); Julio Navarro and Pedro Jiménez, "Evolution of the Andalusi Urban Landscape: From the Dispersed to the Saturated Medina," in Revisiting al-Andalus: Perspectives on the Material Culture of Islamic Iberia and Beyond, ed. Glaire D. Anderson and Mariam Rosser-Owen (Brill, 2007), 113–42; Sa'ad al-Rashid, Al-Rabadhah: A Portrait of Early Islamic Civilization in Saudi Arabia (King Saud University, 1986); and Bethany J. Walker, Jordan in the Late Middle

Ages: Transformation of the Mamluk Frontier (Middle East Documentation Center, 2011).

43. Chaudhuri, Trade and Civilisation, 207.

44. Banaji, "Islam, the Mediterranean and the Rise of Capitalism," 58.

45. Banaji, "Islam, the Mediterranean and the Rise of Capitalism," 60; Goitein, Mediterranean Society, 1:59. Trade in the Indian Ocean area was a "capitalistic activity," reports Chaudhuri, Trade and Civilisation, 228. See also Paul Balog, The Coinage of the Ayyūbids (Royal Numismatic Society, 1980); Andrew M. Watson, "Back to Gold—and Silver," EHR 20, no. 1 (1967): 1–34; Robert S. Lopez and Irving W. Raymond, trans., Medieval Trade in the Late Medieval Mediterranean World: Illustrative Documents (CUP, 2001), 201; Chaudhuri, Trade and Civilisation, 36, 213; Banaji, "Islam, the Mediterranean and the Rise of Capitalism," 60; Shatzmiller, "A Misconstrued Link," 387–415; Udovitch, Partnership and Profit; Goitein, Mediterranean Society, 1:61; and Margariti, Aden & the Indian Ocean Trade, 114, 134.

46. Banaji, "Islam, the Mediterranean and the Rise of Capitalism," 57–62; Chaudhuri, Trade and Civilisation, 2, 39, 207–9. See also "The Rise of Islam and the Pattern of Pre-Emporia Trade in Early Asia," in Chaudhuri, Trade and Civilisation, 34–62. On the thirteenth-century world economy, see Abu-Lughod, Before European Hegemony, 8–20; Valeria Fiorani Piacentini, L'emporio ed il regno di Hormoz (VIII–fine XV sec. d. Cr.): Vicende storiche, problem ed aspetti di una civiltà costiera del Golfo Persico (Istituto Lombardo di Scienze e Lettere, 1975), 49–51; Allen Fromherz, "Towards a World History of the Medieval Gulf: Distinctive Cosmopolitanism and Trade," Journal of Medieval Worlds 2, no. 1/2 (2020): 1–10; and Chaudhuri, Trade and Civilisation, 48. Chaudhuri's evidence is dated circa 851. See also Bertold Spuler, "Trade in the Eastern Islamic Countries in the Early Centuries," in Islam and the Trade of Asia: A Colloquium, ed. D. S. Richards (University of Pennsylvania Press, 1970), 11–20, esp. 14–15; The Cambridge Economic History of India, vol. 1, c. 1200–c. 1750, ed. Tapan Raychaudhuri and Irfan Habib (CUP, 1982), 144; Piacentini, L'emporio ed il regno di Hormoz; Valeria Piacentini, "Merchant Families in the Gulf: A Mercantile and Cosmopolitan Dimension: The Written Evidence (11–13th Centuries AD),"

ARAM Periodical 11, no. 1 (1999): 145–59.

47. Chaudhuri, *Trade and Civilisation*, 4, 163, 204, 208; Roxani Eleni Margariti, "Mercantile Networks, Port Cities, and 'Pirate' States: Conflict and Competition in the Indian Ocean World of Trade Before the Sixteenth Century," *Journal of the Economic and Social History of the Orient* 51, no. 4 (2008): 543–77; John E. G. Sutton, "Kilwa: A History of the Ancient Swahili Town with a Guide to the Monuments of Kilwa Kisiwani and Adjacent Islands," *Azania: Archaeological Research in Africa* 33, no. 1 (1998): 113–69; Henry T. Wright, "Early Islam, Oceanic Trade and Town Development on Nzwani: The Comorian Archipelago in the XIth–XVth Centuries AD," *Azania: Archaeological Research in Africa* 27, no. 1 (1992): 81–128; and Abu-Lughod, *Before European Hegemony*, 137.

48. For more on the geography of trade routes, see Zayde Antrim, *Routes and Realms: The Power of Place in the Early Islamic World* (OUP, 2012), 185; Abu-Lughod, *Before European Hegemony*, 203, 205; Bruce Masters, "Aleppo: The Ottoman Empire's Caravan City," in *The Ottoman City Between East and West: Aleppo, Izmir, and Istanbul*, ed. Edhem Eldem, Daniel Goffman, and Bruce Masters (CUP, 1999), 1; and Jean Sauvaget, *Alep: Essai sur le développement d'une grande ville syrienne des origines au milieu du XIXe siècle* (Paul Geuthner, 1941).

49. Sven Hedin, *The Silk Road: Ten Thousand Miles Through Central Asia* (Tauris Parke Paperbacks, 2009), 228.

50. Abu-Lughod, *Before European Hegemony*, 141, 146, 154, 167; Anievas and Kerem Nişancioğlu, 67; Otgonsaikhan Nyamdaa, "Silk Road and Trade of the Mongol Empire," *Mongolian Diaspora: Journal of Mongolian History and Culture* 3, no. 1 (2023): 69–79; Valerie Hansen, *The Silk Road: A New History* (OUP, 2012), 6; and Iftikhar H. Malik, *The Silk Road and Beyond: Narratives of a Muslim Historian* (OUP, 2020), 114. On the Islamic Renaissance, see Malik, *Silk Road and Beyond*, 57, 59, 75. On the scale of these cities and their relationship to trade, see also Blaydes and Paik, "Muslim Trade and City Growth," 848; and Ronald E. Latham, trans., *The Travels of Marco Polo* (Penguin Books, 1958), 35.

51. Ruy González de Clavijo, *Narrative of the Embassy of Ruy González de Clavijo to the Court of Timour, at Samarcand, A.D. 1403–6* (London: Hakluyt Society, 1859), 165, 169, 175.

52. Abu-Lughod, *Before European Hegemony*, 157, 179; Malik, *Silk Road and Beyond*, 11–13, 26, 125; Clavijo, *Narrative of the Embassy*, 171; Hansen, *Silk Road*, 3.

53. Abu-Lughod, *Before European Hegemony*, 147, 213, 229. On the Karimi merchants, see Francisco Javier Apellániz Ruiz de Galarreta, *Pouvoir et finance en Méditerranée pré-moderne: Le deuxième État mamelouk et le commerce des épices (1382–1517)* (CSIC, 2009), 47–83.

54. As cited in Banaji, "Islam, the Mediterranean and the Rise of Capitalism," 61; see also Ibn Battuta, *The Travels of Ibn Battuta, A.D. 1325–1354*, vol. 1, ed. and trans. H. A. R. Gibb, orig. ed. C. Defrémery and B. R. Sanguinetti (CUP for Hakluyt Society, 1958), 41. On Cairo, see also Susan Jane Staffa, *Conquest and Fusion: The Social Evolution of Cairo A.D. 642–1850* (E. J. Brill, 1977); Stillman, "Eleventh-Century Merchant House," 15; Abu-Lughod, *Before European Hegemony*, 148, 225.

55. As cited in Chaudhuri, *Trade and Civilisation*, 58.

56. Abu-Lughod, *Before European Hegemony*, 212; Goitein and Friedman, *India Traders of the Middle Ages*, 10; Tertius Chandler and Gerald Fox, *3000 Years of Urban Growth* (Academic Press, 1974), 196–97; Goldberg, *Trade and Institutions*, 336; and Chaudhuri, *Trade and Civilisation*, 59, 109, 213. See also Stillman, "Eleventh-Century Merchant House," 24, 58–74. Goitein and Friedman's *India Traders of the Middle Ages* focuses heavily on the Lebdi family, providing editions and translations of correspondence related to the Indian Ocean trade. For more details, see Goitein's India book and letter editions, as well as Claude Cahen, "Le commerce d'Amalfi dans le Proche-Orient musulman avant et après la Croisade" in *Comptes rendus des séances de l'Académie des Inscriptions et Belles-Lettres* 121, no. 2 (1977): 291–301. See also S. Labib, "Egyptian Commercial Policy in the Middle Ages," in *Studies in the Economic History of the Middle East: From the Rise of Islam to the Present Day*, ed. M. A. Cook (OUP, 1970), 77.

57. Stillman, "Eleventh-Century Merchant House," 27, 30–58.

58. Stillman, "Eleventh-Century Merchant House," 15, 16–17, 19, 23, 24, 28, 29 78, 83, 87; Norman Arthur Stillman, "East-West Relations in the Islamic Mediterranean in the Early Eleventh Century—A Study in the Geniza Correspondence of the

House of Ibn 'Awkal" (PhD diss. University of Pennsylvania, 1970), 45; Goldberg, *Trade and Institutions*, 309–10.

59. Banaji, "Islam, the Mediterranean and the Rise of Capitalism," 62; Lorenzo M. Bondioli, "Peasants, Merchants, and Caliphs: Capital and Empire in Fatimid Egypt" (PhD diss., Princeton University, 2021), 103–15; Shatzmiller, "Transcontinental Trade and Economic Growth," 123–25; Shatzmiller, "A Misconstrued Link," 392; and Abu-Lughod, *Before European Hegemony*, 232. See also the terrific Maya Shatzmiller, *Labour in the Medieval Islamic World* (Brill, 1994), esp. 200–203; and Ibn Khaldûn, *The Muqaddimah: An Introduction to History*, abr. ed. (PUP, 2015), 298.

60. Chaudhuri, *Trade and Civilisation*, 185; Abu-Lughod, *Before European Hegemony*, 271, 291; Kenneth R. Hall, "Ports-of-Trade, Maritime Diasporas, and Networks of Trade and Cultural Integration in the Bay of Bengal Region of the Indian Ocean: C. 1300–1500," *Journal of the Economic and Social History of the Orient* 53, no. 1/2 (2009): 109–45; Margariti, "Mercantile Networks, Port Cities, and 'Pirate' States," 543–77; and Simon Digby, "The Maritime Trade of India," in Raychaudhuri and Habib, *Cambridge Economic History of India*, 1:139, 140, 142, 144. On these trade goods, see also Beaujard, "Gujarat and Long-Distance Trade," 80. See too Sven Beckert, *Empire of Cotton: A Global History* (Alfred A. Knopf, 2014).

61. Chaudhuri, *Trade and Civilisation*, 100. Such sparse surviving documentation is typical for merchant communities around the world. See also Beaujard, "Gujarat and Long-Distance Trade," 80; Chakravarti, "Nakhudas and Nauvittakas," 38, 51, 105; and Nicolò Conti, "The Travels of Nicolò Conti in the East in the Early Part of the Fifteenth Century," in *India in the Fifteenth Century: Being a Collection of Narratives of Voyages to India in the Century Preceding the Portuguese Discovery of the Cape of Good Hope, from Latin, Persian, Russian, and Italian Sources*, ed. Richard Henry Major (CUP, 2010), 21, 51–90. This narrative was translated by J. Winter Jones from the original Latin in Poggio Bracciolini, *De varietate fortunae*, book 4 (Paris: Gaston Van Ravelingen, 1723).

62. Digby, "Maritime Trade of India," 1:158.

63. As cited in Beaujard, "Gujarat and Long-Distance Trade," 85.

64. Beaujard, "Gujarat and Long-Distance Trade," 84; Chaudhuri, *Trade and Civilisation*, 112, 114; A. Das Gupta, "Indian Merchants and the Trade in the Indian Ocean, c. 1500–1750," in Raychaudhuri and Habib, *Cambridge Economic History of India*, 1:409; Abu-Lughod, *Before European Hegemony*, 298–305; and Digby, "Maritime Trade of India," 1:143–44.

65. Ibn Battuta, *The Travels of Ibn Battuta*, 797.

66. David Hardiman, "Penetration of Merchant Capital in Pre-Colonial Gujarat," in *Capitalist Development: Critical Essays*, ed. Ghanshyam Shah (Sangam Books, 1992), 30, 39; and Chaudhuri, *Trade and Civilisation*, 105, 108. Ashin Das Gupta, "Indian Merchants and the Trade in the Indian Ocean c. 1500–1750," in Ashin Das Gupta, *Merchants of Maritime India, 1500–1800* (Routledge, 2024), 30–35.

67. Ibn Battuta, *The Travels of Ibn Battuta*, 733.

68. Chakravarti, "Nakhudas and Nauvittakas," 34; Beaujard, "Gujarat and Long-Distance Trade," 80–81; and Ashin Das Gupta, "Indian Merchants and the Trade in the Indian Ocean, c. 1500–1750," in *The World of the Indian Ocean Merchant, 1500–1800: Collected Essays of Ashin Das Gupta*, comp. Uma Das Gupta (OUP, 2001), 65.

69. Beaujard, "Gujarat and Long-Distance Trade," 82, 91; Sebastian R. Prange, *Monsoon Islam: Trade and Faith in the Medieval Malabar Coast* (CUP, 2018), 261–62; Goitein, "From Aden to India," 43, 45. On the workers, see "Accounts of Abraham Ben Yijū's Workshop for Bronze Vessels India," 1132–39, 1145–49 (ULC Or. 1080 J 95), as reprinted in Goitein and Friedman, *India Traders of the Middle Ages*, 644–46; and Goitein and Friedman, *India Traders of the Middle Ages*, 6, 43, 52, 55, 57–58.

70. Such pottery has been excavated in East Africa. See Horton and Middleton, *Swahili*, 78, 80, 82.

71. Ibn Battuta, *Travels of Ibn Battuta*, 2:379.

72. On Mombasa, see Chandra Richard De Silva, "Indian Ocean but Not African Sea: The Erasure of East African Commerce from History," *Journal of Black Studies* 29, no. 5 (1999): 686. On Mogadishu, see Ibn Battuta, *Travels of Ibn Battuta*, 2:379. See also Chaudhuri, *Trade and Civilisation*, 56.

73. Cited in M. N. Pearson, *The World of the Indian Ocean, 1500–1800: Studies in Economic, Social and Cultural History* (Ashgate, 2005), 230.

74. Horton and Middleton, *Swahili*, 10; and Tor Sellström, *Africa in the Indian Ocean: Islands in Ebb and Flow* (Brill, 2015), 149. See also G. S. P. Freeman-Grenville, *The East African Coast: Select Documents from the First to the Earlier Nineteenth Century* (Collings, 1975), 19–31, 125, 132; and Horton and Middleton, *Swahili*, 82.

75. Horton and Middleton, *Swahili*, 1, 9; and Freeman-Grenville, *East African Coast*, 19–20. See also Karim Kassam Janmohamed, "A History of Mombasa, c. 1895–1939: Some Aspects of Economic and Social Life in an East African Port Town During Colonial Rule" (PhD diss., Northwestern University, 1978), 33; and Abdul Sheriff, *Dhow Cultures of the Indian Ocean: Cosmopolitanism, Commerce and Islam* (CUP, 2010), 182.

76. Horton and Middleton, *Swahili*, 9, 12–13, 18, 22, 31, 37–38, 51, 72, 79–90; Pedro Machado, *Ocean of Trade: South Asian Merchants, Africa and the Indian Ocean, c. 1750–1850* (CUP, 2014), 36, 171.

77. William Atwell, "Ming China and the Emerging World Economy, c. 1470–1650," in *The Cambridge History of China*, vol. 8, *The Ming Dynasty, 1368–1644*, part 2, ed. Denis Twitchett and Frederick W. Mote (CUP, 1998), 376; Jonathan Porter, *Imperial China, 1350–1900* (Rowman & Littlefield, 2016), 194; and Angela Schottenhammer, "The 'China Seas' in World History: A General Outline of the Role of Chinese and East Asian Maritime Space from Its Origins to c. 1800," *Journal of Marine and Island Cultures* 1, no. 2 (2012): 76.

78. Adam Smith, *The Wealth of Nations Books I–III* (Penguin Books, 1982), 174.

79. Atwell, "Ming China," 378; and Abu-Lughod, *Before European Hegemony*, 316. Other scholars agree, for example, Chaffee, *Muslim Merchants of Premodern China*; Yoshinobu Shiba, *Commerce and Society in Sung China* (University of Michigan Center for Chinese Studies, 1970); Joseph P. McDermott and Yoshinobu Shiba, "Economic Change in China, 960–1279," in *The Cambridge History of China*, vol. 5, part 2, *Sung China, 960–1279*, ed. John W. Chaffee and Denis Twitchett (CUP, 2015), 321–436; Robert Hartwell, "Markets, Technology, and the Structure of Enterprise in the Development of the Eleventh-Century Chinese Iron and Steel Industry," *JEH* 26, no. 1 (1966): 29–58; Tim Wright, "An Economic Cycle in Imperial China? Revisiting Robert Hartwell on Iron and Coal," *Journal of the Economic and Social History of the Orient* 50, no. 4 (2007): 398–423; Donald B. Wagner, "The Administration of the Iron Industry in Eleventh-Century China," *Journal of the Economic and Social History of the Orient* 44, no. 2 (2001): 175–97; Paul Jakov Smith, "Eurasian Transformations of the Tenth to Thirteenth Centuries: The View from Song China, 960–1279," in *Eurasian Transformations, Tenth to Thirteenth Centuries* (Brill, 2004), 279–308; Richard von Glahn, "Imagining Pre-Modern China," in *The Song-Yuan-Ming Transition in Chinese History*, ed. Paul Jakov Smith and Richard von Glahn (Harvard University Asia Center, 2003), 35–70; Abu-Lughod, *Before European Hegemony*, 317, 319, 320; Billy K. L. So, *Prosperity, Region, and Institutions in Maritime China: The South Fukien Pattern, 946–1368* (Harvard University Asia Center, 2000), 27–28, 30; William T. Rowe, *China's Last Empire: The Great Qing* (HUP, 2009), 123; and Schottenhammer, "'China Seas' in World History," 76. See, for example, *The Cambridge History of China*, vol. 2, *The Six Dynasties, 220–589*, ed. Albert E. Dien and Keith N. Knapp (CUP, 2019), 378.

80. Wang Gungwu, *The Nanhai Trade: The Early History of Chinese Trade in the South China Sea* (Times Academic Press, 1998), 96; Raychaudhuri and Habib, *Cambridge Economic History of India*, 1:133; Shiba, *Commerce and Society*; McDermott and Shiba, "Economic Change in China," 321–436; Hartwell, "Markets, Technology, and the Structure of Enterprise," 29–58; Timothy Brook, "Communications and Commerce," in Twitchett and Mote, *Cambridge History of China*, 8:580; Porter, *Imperial China*, 200; Timothy Brook, "The Merchant Network in 16th Century China: A Discussion and Translation of Zhang Han's 'On Merchants,'" *Journal of the Economic and Social History of the Orient* 24, no. 2 (1981): 165–214; Schottenhammer, "'China Seas' in World History," 74–76; Raychaudhuri and Habib, *Cambridge Economic History of India*, 1:131; Derek Heng, "Shipping, Customs Procedures, and the Foreign Community: The 'Pingzhou ketan' on Aspects of Guangzhou's Maritime Economy in the Late Eleventh Century," *Journal of Song-Yuan Studies* 38, no. 1 (2008): 15; Banaji, "Islam, the Mediterranean and the Rise of Capitalism," 62. This is the price of wheat

in Syria in the eleventh century; naturally, prices went up and down and differed depending on location. See E. Ashtor, "The Development of Prices in the Medieval Near East," in Bernard Lewis, *Wirtschaftsgeschichte des Vorderen Orients in islamischer Zeit* (Brill, 1977), 101; Chaudhuri, *Trade and Civilisation*, 59, 206; Heng, "Shipping, Customs Procedures, and the Foreign Community," 1–4; Laurence J. C. Ma, *Commercial Development and Urban Change in Sung China (960–1279)* (University of Michigan Department of Geography, 1971); Angela Schottenhammer, *Early Global Interconnectivity Across the Indian Ocean World*, vol. 1, *Commercial Structures and Exchanges* (Springer International Publishing, 2019); Gang Deng, *Chinese Maritime Activities and Socioeconomic Development, c. 2100 B.C.–1900 A.D.* (Greenwood, 1997); So, *Prosperity, Region, and Institutions in Maritime China*; Rowe, *China's Last Empire*, 123; Philip C. Huang, *The Peasant Family and Rural Development in the Yangzi Delta, 1350–1988* (Stanford UP, 1990); Brook, "Communications and Commerce," 583–84; Angus Maddison, *Chinese Economic Performance in the Long Run* (Development Centre of the Organisation Co-operation and Development, 1998); E. L. Jones, "The Real Question About China: Why Was the Song Economic Achievement Not Repeated?," in *Growth Recurring: Economic Change in World History* (University of Michigan Press, 2000); Mark Elvin, *The Pattern of the Chinese Past: A Social and Economic Interpretation* (Stanford UP, 1973); and Timothy Brook, *The Confusions of Pleasure: Commerce and Culture in Ming China* (University of California Press, 1998), xix. For the cities, see Ray Huang, "The Grand Canal During the Ming Dynasty, 1368–1644" (PhD diss., University of Michigan, 1964), 308.

81. Ruy González de Clavijo, *Embassy to Tamerlane, 1403–1406*, trans. Guy Le Strange (Harper, 1928), 288–89.

82. Ibn Battuta, *Travels of Ibn Battuta*, 4:891.

83. 莫旦,《弘治吳江志·舊事》, 刊行于弘治元年, 中国史学丛书三编: 第四辑. 台北: 学生书局, 1987 (Mo Dan, *The Local History of Wujiang: Things in the Past*, first published in the first year of the Hongzhi reign [1488], republished in the third edition of Chinese History Series: vol. 4 [Taipei: Student Book, 1987]).

84. Abu-Lughod, *Before European Hegemony*, 335; Chaffee, *Muslim Merchants of Premodern China*, 2.

85. Chaffee, *Muslim Merchants of Premodern China*, 1, 3, 21; Raychaudhuri and Habib, *Cambridge Economic History of India*, 1:126–42; Abu-Lughod, *Before European Hegemony*, 311–32; Heng, "Shipping, Customs Procedures, and the Foreign Community," 15; and Chau, *Chau Ju-kua*, 37, 93–99.

86. 蕃 坊,海外, 蕃 長, as quoted in Chau, *Chau Ju-kau*, 17, 35.

87. Angela Schottenhammer, "China's Gate to the Indian Ocean: Iranian and Arab Long-Distance Traders," *Harvard Journal of Asiatic Studies* 76, no. 1/2 (2016): 135, 137; Chau, *Chau Ju-kua*, 14, 16; Hourani, *Arab Seafaring in the Indian Ocean*; Sulaymân al-Tajir and Abû Zayd Hasan ibn Yazîd, *Voyage du marchand arabe Sulaymân en Inde et en Chine, rédigé en 851, suivi de remarques par Abû Zayd Hasan (vers 916)*, ed. and trans. Gabriel Ferrand (Éditions Bossard, 1922), 38–39; Raychaudhuri and Habib, *Cambridge Economic History of India*, 1:127–29. See also Angela Schottenhammer, *Das Songzeitliche Quanzhou im Spannungsfeld Zwischen Zentralregierung und Maritimem Handel: Unerwartete Konsequenzen des Zentralstaatlichen Zugriffs auf den Reichtum einer Küstenregion* (F. Steiner, 2002), 57; Chaffee, *Muslim Merchants of Premodern China*, 2, 41–42; Gu Yanwu, as cited in John W. Chaffee, *Muslim Merchant Communities on the Coast of China, 700–1400* (CUP, 2018), 101.

88. See 郭正忠:《宋代包买商人的考察》,《江淮论坛》1985年第2期: 18–25 (Guo Zhengzhong, "A Survey of Putting-Out Merchants in the Song Dynasty," Jianghuai Forum, no. 2 [1985]: 18–25); 郭正忠:《宋代四川盐业生产中的资本主义萌芽》,《社会科学研究》, 1981年第11期: 第43–48页 (Guo Zhengzhong, "Budding Capitalism in the Song Dynasty Sichuan Salt Industry," *Social Science Research*, no. 11 [1981]: 43–48); and 李晓:《论宋代茶叶生产中的资本主义萌芽》,《山东大学学报 (哲学社会科学版)》, 1989年第4期: 第45–50 (Li Xiao, "On Budding Capitalism in the Song Dynasty Tea Production," *Shandong University Journal* [Philosophy and Social Science Edition], no. 4 [1989]: 45–50). See also 陶德臣:《宋代茶业生产经营中的包买商—兼与姚治中先生商榷》,《农业考古》2008年第5: 第268–73页 (Tao Dechen, "Putting-Out Merchants in the Production and Management of the Song Dynasty Tea Industry—with a Discussion by Mr. Yao Zhizhong," *Agricultural Archaeology*, no. 5 [2008]: 268–73); and 重立章:《略论

中国资本主义萌芽于宋》,《华南师范大学学报 (社会科学版)》, 2001年第3期:第66–74 (Dong Lizhang, "A Preliminary Discussion on How Chinese Capitalism Budded in the Song Dynasty," *Journal of South China Normal University* [Social Science Edition], no. 3 [2001]: 66–74).

89. E. L. Jones, *The European Miracle: Environments, Economies, and Geopolitics in the History of Europe and Asia* (CUP, 1981), 202; Robert Hartwell, "A Cycle of Economic Change in Imperial China: Coal and Iron in Northwest China, 750–1350," *Journal of the Economic and Social History of the Orient* 10, no. 1 (1967): 102–59; and Wagner, "Administration of the Iron Industry," 175–97. For a recent reevaluation of Hartwell's estimates, see Abu-Lughod, *Before European Hegemony*, 323; and Raychaudhuri and Habib, *Cambridge Economic History of India*, 1:128. On the size of European ships, see Arthur Davies, "The Loss of the *Santa Maria* Christmas Day, 1492," *AHR* 58, no. 4 (July 1953): 861; and Lars Berggren, Nils Hybel, and Annette Landen, eds., *Cogs, Cargoes and Commerce: Maritime Bulk Trade in Northern Europe, 1150–1400* (Pontifical Institute of Mediaeval Studies, 2002), 102. This discussion is part of the good overview on Indian Ocean / South China Sea shipping in Raychaudhuri and Habib, *Cambridge Economic History of India*, 1:130–32; Chaffee, *Muslim Merchants of Premodern China*, 7; and Schottenhammer, "'China Seas' in World History," 76.

90. Quoted from Richard von Glahn, "Monies of Account and Monetary Transition in China, Twelfth to Fourteenth Centuries," *Journal of the Economic and Social History of the Orient* 53, no. 3 (June 2010): 501.

91. Hansen, *Silk Road*, 15; von Glahn, "Monies of Account," 465; and Braudel, *Civilization and Capitalism*, 2:113. See also von Glahn, "Monies of Account," 482, 484; and Richard von Glahn, "Paper Money in Song-Yuan China," in *Money, Currency and Crisis: In Search of Trust, 2000 BC to AD 2000*, ed. R. J. van der Spek and Bas van Leeuwen (Routledge, 2018), 260. For the quote, see Ibn Battuta, *Travels of Ibn Battuta*, 4:890.

92. Abu-Lughod, *Before European Hegemony*, 13, 15, 46, 47, 67, 125; Goldberg, *Trade and Institutions*, 306; Goitein, *Mediterranean Society*, 1:43, 45–46; Eliyahu Ashtor, *Levant Trade in the Middle Ages* (PUP, 2014), 23; Herman van der Wee, "Structural Changes in European Long-Distance

Trade, and Particularly on the Re-Export Trade from South to North, 1350–1750," in *The Rise of Merchant Empires: Long-Distance Trade in the Early Modern World, 1350–1750*, ed. James D. Tracy (CUP, 1993), 14–15; and Sylvia L. Thrupp, *Society and History: Essays* (University of Michigan Press, 1977), 74.

93. Banaji, "Islam, the Mediterranean and the Rise of Capitalism," 62; Abu-Lughod, *Before European Hegemony*, 47.

94. For the most recent account of this process, see Wickham, *Donkey and the Boat*. See also Chaudhuri, *Trade and Civilisation*, 58; Abu-Lughod, *Before European Hegemony*, 107, 110; and Jeffrey Miner and Stefan Stantchev, "The Genoese Economy," in *A Companion to Medieval Genoa*, ed. Carrie E. Beneš (Brill, 2018), 401. On this historiographical turn to consider the importance of the Crusades to Genoese economic development, see Quentin van Doosselaere, *Commercial Agreements and Social Dynamics in Medieval Genoa* (CUP, 2009); Miner and Stantchev, "Genoese Economy," 401; and Abu-Lughod, *Before European Hegemony*, 108, 110.

95. Van der Wee, "Structural Changes in European Long-Distance Trade," 14, 16, 23; Abu-Lughod, *Before European Hegemony*, 68; and Ashtor, *Levant Trade*, 6, 25, 81, 121.

96. Anonymous author, "Collaudatio quedam urbis Genuensis," 1430 [Bibl. Civica Berio di Genova, ms. mr. 1.3.14, cc. 1v-12r], as transcribed in Giovanna Petti Balbi, *Genova medievale vista dai contemporanei* (Sagep, 1978), 95–96. The English rendition of the quote is the author's translation.

97. Steven A. Epstein, *Speaking of Slavery: Color, Ethnicity, and Human Bondage in Italy* (Cornell UP, 2001); Thomas Allison Kirk, *Genoa and the Sea: Policy and Power in an Early Modern Maritime Republic, 1559–1684* (Johns Hopkins UP, 2005), 10; Steven A. Epstein, *Genoa & the Genoese, 958–1528* (University of North Carolina Press, 1996), 14. On the source in Arabic, see Benjamin Z. Kedar, "Una nuova fonte per l'incursione musulmana del 934–935 e le sue implicazioni per la storia genovese," in *From Genoa to Jerusalem and Beyond: Studies in Medieval and World History* (Libreriauniversitaria.it, 2019), 19–30. See also Denise Bezzina, "Social Landscapes," in *A Companion to Medieval Genoa*, Carrie E. Beneš (Brill, 2018), 167; and Epstein, *Genoa & the Genoese*, 29. In a footnote on p. 332, Epstein

states that "the estimates of the Genoese population in these centuries remain (more or less) educated guesses." See, too, Luisa Piccinno, "Genoa, a City with a Port or a Port City?," in *The Routledge Handbook of Maritime Trade Around Europe 1300–1600: Commercial Networks and Urban Autonomy*, ed. Wim Blockmans, Mikhail Krom, and Justyna Wubs-Mrozewicz (Routledge, 2017), 162–63; Miner and Stantchev, "Genoese Economy," 400, 402; Halil İnalcık and Donald Quataert, eds., *An Economic and Social History of the Ottoman Empire*, vol 1., *1300–1914* (CUP, 1994), 285; Ashtor, *Levant Trade*, 11; Robert S. Lopez, *The Commercial Revolution of the Middle Ages, 950–1350* (CUP, 1976), 94; Sandra Origone, "Colonies and Colonization," in *A Companion to Medieval Genoa*, ed. Carrie E. Beneš (Brill, 2018), 500, 504; Dino Puncuh, ed., *Storia di Genova: Mediterraneo, Europa, Atlantico* (Società Ligure di Storia Patria, 2003), 222; Miner and Stantchev, "Genoese Economy," 405; B. Z. Kedar, *Segurano-Sakrān Salvaygo: Un mercante genovese al servizio dei sultani mamelucchi* (Liberiauniversitaria.it, 2019); Miner and Stantchev, "Genoese Economy," 402; Carlo Taviani, "The Genoese Casa di San Giorgio as a Micro-Economic and Territorial Nodal System," in Blockmans, Krom, and Wubs-Mrozewicz, *Routledge Handbook of Maritime Trade*, 182. On the Genoese colonies and the Black Sea, see Evgeny Khvalkov, *The Colonies of Genoa in the Black Sea Region: Evolution and Transformation* (Routledge, 2018); Piccinno, "Genoa," 163; and Eliyahu Ashtor, *Studies on the Levantine Trade in the Middle Ages* (Variorum Reprints, 1978), 590.

98. McCormick, "New Light on the 'Dark Ages,'" 17–54; McCormick, *Origins of the European Economy*, 344, 356–67, 523–31, 731–77; Alice Rio, "Slave Raiding and Slave Trading," in *Slavery After Rome, 500–1100* (Oxford Studies in Medieval European History, 2017), 19–41; Willem van de Lare, *Regula transporti*, Plantin-Moretus Museum Archive, arch. 318, as quoted in Donald J. Harreld, "Merchants and International Trade Networks in the Sixteenth Century," presented at Session 110 of the XIV International Economic History Congress, Helsinki, August 2006; Lorenz Meder, *Das Meder'sche Handelsbuch und die Welser'schen Nachträge*, ed. Hermann Kellenbenz (Franz Steiner, 1974); Lucas Rem, *Tagebuch des Lucas Rem*

aus den Jahren 1494–1541: Ein Beitrag zur Handelgeschichte der Stadt Augsburg, ed. von B. Greiff (J. N. Hartmann, 1861); Maria Pia Pendani, "Venice," in *Encyclopedia of the Ottoman Empire*, ed. Gábor Ágoston and Bruce Alan Masters (Facts on File, 2009), 581–82; Paola Lanaro, "At the Centre of the Old World, Reinterpreting Venetian Economic History," in *At the Centre of the Old World: Trade and Manufacturing in Venice and on the Venetian Mainland, 1400–1800*, ed. Paola Lanaro (Centre for Reformation and Renaissance Studies, 2006), 19; Fredrick C. Lane, *Andrea Barbarigo, Merchant of Venice, 1418–1449* (Johns Hopkins UP, 1944), 59; and Ashtor, *Levant Trade*, 24–25.

99. Edgcumbe Staley, *The Guilds of Florence* (Methuen & Co., 1906); Francesca Trivellato, "Renaissance Florence and the Origins of Capitalism: A Business History Perspective," *Business History Review* 94, no. 1 (2020): 229–51; Marvin B. Becker, *Florence in Transition*, vol. 1, *The Decline of the Commune* (Johns Hopkins UP, 1967), 89–96; Richard Lachmann, *Capitalists in Spite of Themselves: Elite Conflict and Economic Transitions in Early Modern Europe* (OUP, 2002), 78; Anna Maria Pult Quaglia, *Per provvedere ai popoli: Il sistema annonario nella Toscana dei Medici* (Leo S. Olschki, 1990), 120–21; and Richard A. Goldthwaite, *The Economy of Renaissance Florence* (Johns Hopkins UP, 2008), 47.

100. Ferdinand Schevill, *Medieval and Renaissance Florence* (Harper & Row, 1963), 30. For the original quote about the smallness of the city, see Enrico Faini, *Firenze nell'età romanica (1000–1211): L'espansione urbana, lo sviluppo istituzionale, il rapporto con il territorio* (Leo S. Olschki, 2010), 37. See also Brian Jeffrey Maxson, "Introduction: The Birth of Florence, Origins to 1250," in *A Short History of Florence and the Florentine Republic* (I. B. Tauris & Company, 2023), 5.

101. The first quote comes from Antonio Pucci, "The Mercato Vecchio, Florence," in *The Towns of Italy in the Later Middle Ages*, trans. and ed. Trevor Dean (Manchester UP, 2013), 122–24. For the original quote, see the Italian source text: Antonio Pucci, "Proprietà di Mercato Vecchio," in *Poeti minori del Trecento*, ed. Natalino Sapegno (Ricciardini, 1952), 403–7. The second quote comes from Giovanni Villani, "Description of Florence (Book XI, Chap. XCIV)," in *Medieval Trade in the Mediterranean World: Il-*

lustrative Documents, ed. Robert S. Lopez and Irving W. Raymond (W. W. Norton, 2001), 71–74. For the original quote, see the Italian source text: Giovanni Villani, *Cronica di Giovanni Villani*, vol. 6 (Florence: Magheri, 1823), 183–87.

102. Jean Boutier and Yves Sintomer, "The Republic of Florence (from the Twelfth to the Sixteenth Centuries): Historical and Political Issues," *Revue Française de Science Politique* 64, no. 6 (2014): 1062; W. R. Day, "The Population of Florence Before the Black Death: Survey and Synthesis," *Journal of Medieval History* 28, no. 2 (2002): 94, 120. Samarkand had 150,000 inhabitants during the 1390s. On Pisa, see Giuseppe Petralia, "The Late Middle Ages and the Florentine Conquest," in *A Companion to Medieval Pisa*, ed. Karen Rose Mathews, Silvia Orvietani Busch, and Stefano Bruni (Brill, 2022), 163–83, here 163.

103. Herman van der Wee, *The Growth of the Antwerp Market and the European Economy (Fourteenth to Sixteenth Centuries)* (Martinus Nijhoff, 1963).

104. Alma Poloni, "Una società fluida: L'economia di Firenze nel tardo Medioevo," *Storica* 61–62 (2015): 186; Eliyahu Ashtor, "The Wool Guild in Medieval Florence," *Journal of European Economic History* 12, no. 1 (1983): 198. See also Hidetoshi Hoshino, *L'arte della lana in Firenze nel basso Medioevo: Il commercio della lana e il mercato dei panni fiorentini nei secoli XIII–XV* (Leo S. Olschki, 1980); Fabrizio Ricciardelli, *A Short History of Florence* (Edizione Polistampa, 2019), 35; Abu-Lughod, *Before European Hegemony*, 56, 71; Braudel, *Civilization and Capitalism*, 3: 111; Robert-Henri Bautier, "The Fairs of Champagne," in *Essays in French Economic History*, ed. Rondo E. Cameron (R. D. Irwin for the American Economic Association, 1970), 42–63; Wim Blockmans, "Transactions at the Fairs of Champagne and Flanders 1249–1291," in *Fiere e mercati nella integrazione delle economie europee secc. XIII–XVIII, Serie II*—Atti delle "Settimane di Studi" e altri Convegni, ed. Simonetta Cavaciocchi (Le Monnier, 2001), 993–1000; Oscar Gelderblom, "The Decline of Fairs and Merchant Guilds in the Low Countries, 1250–1650," *Jaarboek voor Middeleeuwse Geschiedenis* 7 (2004): 199–238; James M. Murray, *Bruges, Cradle of Capitalism, 1280–1390* (CUP, 2005); Oscar Gelderblom, *Cities of Commerce: The Institutional Foundations of International Trade in the Low Countries, 1250–1650* (PUP, 2013); Sophus A. Reinert and Robert Fredona, "Merchants and the Origins of Capitalism," Harvard Business School Working Paper No. 18-021 (September 2017), 27; Van der Wee, *Growth of the Antwerp Market*; Goldthwaite, *Economy of Renaissance Florence*; Poloni, "Una società fluida," 165–90; and David Abulafia, "Southern Italy and the Florentine Economy, 1265–1370," *EHR* 34, no. 3 (1981): 377–88.

105. Poloni, "Una società fluida," 170; Banaji, "Islam, the Mediterranean and the Rise of Capitalism," 55; Elisa Gagliardi Mangilli, "Florence and Islamic Fabrics," in *Islamic Art and Florence from the Medici to the 20th Century*, ed. Giovanni Curatola (Giunto Editore, 2018), 112; and İnalcik and Quataert, *Economic History of the Ottoman Empire*, 232. This was shown in a fabulous 2018 exhibit, as documented in Curatola, *Islamic Art and Florence from the Medici to the 20th Century*, 10. See also Hans Belting, *Florence and Baghdad: Renaissance Art and Arab Science*, trans. Deborah Lucas Schneider (Belknap Press of HUP, 2011).

106. George Holmes, "How the Medici Became the Pope's Bankers," in *Florentine Studies: Politics and Society in Renaissance Florence*, ed. Nicolai Rubinstein (Northwestern UP, 1968), 357–80; and Luciano Pezzolo, "Government Debts and Credit Markets in Renaissance Italy," in *Government Debts and Financial Markets in Europe*, ed. Fausto Piola Caselli (Pickering & Chatto, 2008), 17–32.

107. Goldthwaite, *Economy of Renaissance Florence*, 210–30; John H. Munro, "The Medieval Origins of the Financial Revolution: Usury, Rentes, and Negotiability," *International History Review* 25, no. 3 (September 2003): 505–62; Bernardino Barbadoro, *Le finanze della Repubblica fiorentina: Imposta diretta e debito pubblico fino all'istituzione del Monte* (Leo S. Olschki, 1929), 629–87; Anthony Molho, *Florentine Public Finance in the Early Renaissance, 1400–1430* (HUP, 1971), 63–74; Lawrin D. Armstrong, "The Politics of Usury in Trecento Florence: The Questio de Monte of Francesco da Empoli," *Mediaeval Studies* 61 (1999): 1–44; Lawrin D. Armstrong, *Usury and Public Debt in Early Renaissance Florence: Lorenzo Ridolfi on the Monte Comune* (Pontifical Institute of Mediaeval Studies, 2003), 63–65; Giovanni Ceccarelli, *Risky Markets: Marine Insurance in Renaissance Florence*, vol. 8 (Brill, 2020);

John F. Padgett and Paul D. McLean, "Economic Credit in Renaissance Florence," *Journal of Modern History* 83, no. 1 (2011): 1–47; Bautier, "Fairs of Champagne," 42–63; M. M. Postan, *Medieval Trade and Finance* (CUP, 1973); Cavaciocchi, *Fiere e mercati nella integrazione delle economie europee*; Abu-Lughod, *Before European Hegemony*, 69, 91; Reinhold C. Mueller, *The Venetian Money Market: Banks, Panics, and the Public Debt, 1200–1500* (Johns Hopkins UP, 2019); Lopez, *Commercial Revolution*; David Abulafia, "The Impact of Italian Banking in the Late Middle Ages and the Renaissance, 1300–1500," in *Banking, Trade, and Industry: Europe, America, and Asia from the Thirteenth to the Twentieth Century*, ed. Alice Teichova, Ginette Kurgan–Van Hentenryk, and Dieter Ziegler (CUP, 1997), 17–34. See also Edwin S. Hunt, *The Medieval Super-Companies: A Study of the Peruzzi Company of Florence* (CUP, 1994); William J. Magnuson, *For Profit: A History of Corporations* (Basic Books, 2022); and Raymond de Roover, *The Rise and Decline of the Medici Bank, 1397–1494* (HUP, 1963).

108. Stanley R. H. Jones, "Transaction Costs, Institutional Change, and the Emergence of a Market Economy in Later Anglo-Saxon England," *EHR* 46, no. 4 (November 1993): 658–78; Marianne Hem Eriksen et al., eds., *Viking Worlds: Things, Spaces and Movement* (Oxbow Books, 2015), 144–59; Barrie Cook and Gareth Williams, eds., *Coinage and History in the North Sea World, c. AD 500–1200: Essays in Honour of Marian Archibald*, vol. 19 (Brill, 2006); Nils Hybel, "The Grain Trade in Northern Europe Before 1350," *EHR* 55, no. 2 (May 2002): 219–47; R. H. Britnell, *The Commercialization of English Society, 1000–1500* (CUP, 1993); W. G. Hoskins, *The Age of Plunder: King Henry's England, 1500–1547* (Longman, 1976), 14; James Anthony Froude, *History of England from the Fall of Wolsey to the Defeat of the Spanish Armada* (London: Longmans, Green & Co., 1893); James E. Thorold Rogers, *Six Centuries of Work and Wages: The History of English Labour* (London: W. S. Sonnenschein & Co., 1884), 151; James E. Thorold Rogers, *A History of Agriculture and Prices in England, from the Year After the Oxford Parliament (1259) to the Commencement of the Continental War (1793)*, vol. 1 (Clarendon Press, 1902), 142–44; Henry de Beltgens Gibbins, *Industry in England: Historical Outlines*

(London: Methuen & Co., 1897), 137; and Dobb, *Studies in the Development of Capitalism*, 109.

109. Abu-Lughod, *Before European Hegemony*, 131, 137, 189; Goitein, *Mediterranean Society*, 1:40, 45; Goldberg, *Trade and Institutions*, 335–36; Chaudhuri, *Trade and Civilisation*, 63, 100.

110. As cited in David Robinson and Douglas Smith, *Sources of the African Past: Case Studies of Five Nineteenth-Century African Societies* (Africana Publishing Co., 1979), 125.

111. Lamine Faye, "Guerre et art de la guerre dans l'Ouest-africain au temps de grand empires: Des dynamique contrastées" (PhD thesis, Cheikh Anta Diop University, Dakar, Senegal, 2020); Kathleen Bickford Berzock, "Caravans of Gold, Fragments of Time: An Introduction," in *Caravans of Gold, Fragments of Time: Art, Culture, and Exchange Across Medieval Saharan Africa*, ed. Kathleen Bickford Berzock (PUP, 2019), 28; Roman Loimeier, *Muslim Societies in Africa: A Historical Anthropology* (Indiana UP, 2013), 81, 91. On ivory, see Mamadi Dembélé, "Urbanization and Trade Networks in the Inland Niger Delta," in Berzock, *Caravans of Gold, Fragments of Time*, 153, 156; see also Detlef Gronenborn, "Polities and Trade in Medieval Northern Nigeria," in Berzock, *Caravans of Gold, Fragments of Time*, 169; and Sarah M. Guérin, "Gold, Ivory, and Copper: Materials and Arts of Trans-Saharan Trade," in Berzock, *Caravans of Gold, Fragments of Time*, 184, 192. On copper, see Guérin, "Gold, Ivory, and Copper," 185. See also Loimeier, *Muslim Societies in Africa*, 81; Detlef Gronenborn, "State and Trade in Central Sahel," in *The Oxford Handbook of African Archaeology*, ed. Peter Mitchell and Paul Lane (OUP, 2013), 853; and Berzock, *Caravans of Gold, Fragments of Time*, 28–29.

112. Sam Nixon, "Essouk-Tadmekka: A Southern Saharan Center of the Early Islamic Camel Caravan Trade," in Berzock, *Caravans of Gold, Fragments of Time*, 123, 129.

113. Nixon, "Essouk-Tadmekka," 138–39. On Gao, see Mamadou Cissé, "Gao, a Middle Niger City in Medieval Trade," in Berzock, *Caravans of Gold, Fragments of Time*, 141. See also Nixon, "Essouk-Tadmekka," 123, 129; Gianluca Pastorelli, Marc Walton, and Sam Nixon, "Gold Processing at the Early Islamic Market Town of Tadmekka, Mali: Preliminary Results from Experimental Replication," in Berzock, *Caravans of Gold, Fragments of Time*, 213; Rob-

ert Launay, "Views from Afar: Reading Medieval Trans-Saharan Trade Through Arabic Accounts," in Berzock, *Caravans of Gold, Fragments of Time*, 56; Dembélé, "Urbanization and Trade Networks," 158; and A. G. Hopkins, *An Economic History of West Africa* (CUP, 1973), 19.

114. The numbers are cited in Ralph A. Austen, "The Sources of Gold: Narratives, Technology, and Visual Culture from the Mande and Akan Worlds," in Berzock, *Caravans of Gold, Fragments of Time*, 68.

115. Austen, "Sources of Gold," 63, 68–69; Gronenborn, "Polities and Trade," 169; and Howard W. French, *Born in Blackness: Africa, Africans, and the Making of the Modern World, 1471 to the Second World War* (Liveright Publishing, 2021), 68.

116. Barbara Krasner, *Mana Musa: The Most Famous African Traveler to Mecca* (Rosen Publishing, 2016), 50, 52.

117. As cited in Launay, "Views from Afar," 50.

118. As quoted in J. F. P. Hopkins and Nehemia Levtzion, eds. and trans., *Corpus of Early Arabic Sources for West African History* (Markus Wiener Publishers, 2000), 43, 47.

119. Ronald A. Messier and Abdallah Fili, "Sijilmasa's Role in the Africana Gold Trade," in Berzock, *Caravans of Gold, Fragments of Time*, 115; and Launay, "Views from Afar," 52.

120. Messier and Fili, "Sijilmasa's Role," 115.

121. Messier and Fili, "Sijilmasa's Role," 107, 115; Launay, "Views from Afar," 52; and Guérin, "Gold, Ivory, and Copper," 184.

122. Ibn Battuta, *Travels of Ibn Battuta*, 4:952.

123. Ibn Battuta, *Travels of Ibn Battuta*, 4:965. See also Toby Green, *A Fistful of Shells: West Africa from the Rise of the Slave Trade to the Age of Revolution* (University of Chicago Press, 2021). On commercial paper, see Paul E. Lovejoy, "Interregional Monetary Flows in the Precolonial Trade of Nigeria," *Journal of African History* 15, no. 4 (1974): 582.

124. French, *Born in Blackness*, 28–33; Jean-Louis Roy, *Mansa Musa I: Kankan Moussa, from Niani to Mecca: A Historical Narrative* (Mosaic Press, 2019); Michael A. Gomez, *African Dominion: A New History of Empire in Early and Medieval West Africa* (PUP, 2018), 106–7.

125. Hall, *Maritime Trade and State Development*, 173, 176.

126. Hall, *Maritime Trade and State Development*, 173, 176, 226–27; Martine Julia van Ittersum, "Debating Natural Law in the Banda Is-

lands: A Case Study in Anglo-Dutch Imperial Competition in the East Indies, 1609–1621," *History of European Ideas* 42, no. 4 (2016): 460; and Das Gupta, 410.

127. Hall, *Maritime Trade and State Development*, 173, 176, 226–27; Van Ittersum, "Debating Natural Law in the Banda Islands," 460; Das Gupta, "Indian Merchants and the Trade," 410; and Michael Jacq-Hergoualc'h, *The Malay Peninsula: Crossroads of the Maritime Silk Road (100 BC–1300 AD)* (Brill, 2018), 391.

128. Michael E. Smith, *The Aztecs* (Wiley-Blackwell, 2011), 315; Chester S. Chard, "Pre-Columbian Trade Between North and South America," *Kroeber Anthropological Society Papers* 1 (1950): 6; Kenneth Pomeranz and Steven Topik, *The World That Trade Created: Society, Culture, and the World Economy, 1400 to the Present* (M. E. Sharpe, 2006), 21.

129. Bernal Díaz del Castillo, *The Conquest of New Spain* (Penguin Books, 1963), 232.

130. Marcel van der Linden, "Final Thoughts," in *Capitalism: The Re-Emergence of a Historical Concept*, ed. Jürgen Kocka and Marcel van der Linden (Bloomsbury Academic, 2016), 252; Pomeranz and Topik, *The World That Trade Created*, 22; and del Castillo, *Conquest of New Spain*, 232–34.

131. Anthony Pagden, ed. and trans., *Hernán Cortés: Letters from Mexico* (Yale UP, 1986), 103–5.

132. Fray Diego Durán, *Book of the Gods and Rites and the Ancient Calendar* (University of Oklahoma Press, 1971), 138.

133. Pomeranz and Topik, *The World That Trade Created*, 22. For other eyewitness accounts of the Tlatelolco market, see del Castillo, *Conquest of New Spain*, 232–34; Bernardino de Sahagun, *Florentine Codex*, vol. 8, *Kings and Lords* (School of American Research, 1954), 67–69; Fray Juan de Torquemada, *Monarquía Indiana*, vol. 4 (Universidad Nacional Autónoma de México, 1977), 348–52; and David M. Carballo, "Trade Routes in the Americas Before Columbus," in *The Great Trade Routes: A History of Cargo and Commerce Over Land and Sea*, ed. Philip Parker (Conway Publishing, 2012), 169. For discussions of social and economic conditions pertinent to Mesoamerican transport systems, see Robert D. Drennan, "Long-Distance Movement of Goods in the Mesoamerican Formative and Classic," *American Antiquity* 49, no. 1 (January 1984): 27–43; Andrew Sluyter, "Long-Distance Staple Transport in West-

ern Mesoamerica: Insights Through Quantitative Modeling," *Ancient Mesoamerica* 4, no. 2 (1993): 193–99; Fernando Winfield Capitaine, "Otatitlán y Yacatecuhtli," *La palabra y el hombre* 32 (1979): 25; and Durán, *Book of the Gods and Rites and the Ancient Calendar*, 29.

134. See, for this argument, Braudel, *Afterthoughts on Material Civilization*, 50–51.

Chapter 2: Capitalists Without Capitalism

1. Simon Digby, "The Broach Coin-Hoard as Evidence of the Import of Valuta Across the Arabian Sea During the 13th and 14th Centuries," *Journal of the Royal Asiatic Society* 112, no. 2 (1980): 129–38.

2. Janet L. Abu-Lughod, *Before European Hegemony: The World System A.D. 1250–1350* (OUP, 1989), 15–16; and George Von-der-Muhl, "Janet L. Abu-Lughod. Before European Hegemony: The World System A.D. 1250–1350," *Comparative Civilizations Review* 29, no. 29 (Fall 1993): 6. See also K. N. Chaudhuri, *Trade and Civilisation in the Indian Ocean: An Economic History from the Rise of Islam to 1750* (CUP, 1985), 99; and Patrick O'Brien, "Was the First Industrial Revolution a Conjuncture in the History of the World Economy?," Economic History Working Paper No. 259/2017 (London School of Economics and Political Science, March 2017), 24.

3. On this point, see also J. M. Blaut, "Fourteen Ninety-Two," *Political Geography* 11, no. 4 (July 1992): 355–85.

4. Wellington K. K. Chan, "Chinese Business Networking and the Pacific Rim: The Family Firm's Roles Past and Present," *Journal of American-East Asian Relations* 1, no. 2 (1992): 171–90; Kwang-Ching Liu, "Chinese Merchant Guilds: An Historical Inquiry," *Pacific Historical Review* 57, no. 1 (1988): 1–23; David Rudner, "Banker's Trust and the Culture of Banking Among the Nattukottai Chettiars of Colonial South India," *Modern Asian Studies* 23, no. 3 (1989): 417–58; Himanshu Prabha Ray, "Early Historic Gujarat and the Trading World of the Western Indian Ocean," in *Transregional Trade and Traders: Situating Gujarat in the Indian Ocean from Early Times to 1900*, ed. Edward A. Alpers and Chhaya Goswami (OUP, 2019), 100–122; Pedro Machado, *Ocean of Trade: South Asian Merchants, Africa and the Indian Ocean, c. 1750–1850* (CUP, 2014), 45; Andreas W. Massing, "The Wangara, an Old Soninke Di-

aspora in West Africa?," *Cahiers d'études africaines* 40, no. 158 (2000): 281–308; Andreas W. Massing, "Baghayogho: A Soninke Muslim Diaspora in the Mande World," *Cahiers d'études africaines* 44, no. 176 (2004): 887–922; Paul E. Lovejoy, "The Role of the Wangara in the Economic Transformation of the Central Sudan in the Fifteenth and Sixteenth Centuries," *Journal of African History* 19, no. 2 (1978): 173–93; Russell Ives Court, "The Brignole: Family and Relationships, Networks and the Conservation of Trust in el *Siglo de los Genovéses*, 1514–1640" (PhD diss., University of California, 2002), 2; Jessica Goldberg, *Trade and Institutions in the Medieval Mediterranean: The Geniza Merchants and Their Business World* (CUP, 2012), 50, 56–92, 187–210, 295; and Philippe Minard, "Colbertism Continued? The Inspectorate of Manufactures and Strategies of Exchange in Eighteenth-Century France," *French Historical Studies* 23, no.3 (2000): 490.

5. Francesca Trivellato, *The Familiarity of Strangers: The Sephardic Diaspora, Livorno, and Cross-Cultural Trade in the Early Modern Period* (Yale UP, 2009), 12–13, 16; Ian Forrest and Anne Haour, "Trust in Long-Distance Relationships, 1000–1600 CE," *Past & Present* 238, no. 13 (November 2018): 190–213; Goldberg, *Trade and Institutions*, 33–36; S. D. Goitein, *A Mediterranean Society: The Jewish Communities of the Arab World as Portrayed in the Documents of the Cairo Geniza*, vol. 2 (University of California Press, 1967–1993), 295; Sheilagh Ogilvie and A. W. Carus, "Institutions and Economic Growth in Historical Perspective," *Handbook of Economic Growth* 2 (2014): 403–513; and Jeremy Edwards and Sheilagh Ogilvie, "Contract Enforcement, Institutions and Social Capital: The Maghribi Traders Reappraised," *EHR* 65, no. 2 (2012): 421–44. See also Greif's response: Avner Greif, "The Maghribi Traders: A Reappraisal?," *EHR* 65, no. 2 (2012): 445–69; and Goldberg's critique of Greif: Jessica L. Goldberg, "Choosing and Enforcing Business Relationships in the Eleventh-Century Mediterranean: Reassessing the 'Maghribi Traders,'" *Past & Present* 216, no. 1 (August 2012): 3–40.

6. Roberto S. Lopez, *The Commercial Revolution of the Middle Ages, 950–1350* (Prentice Hall, 1971); Patricia Skinner, *Medieval Amalfi and Its Diaspora, 800–1250* (OUP, 2013), 212–33; Michele Fuiano, "Amalfi tra i

secoli XI e XII," *Studi storici meridionali* 5 (1985): 45–67; Bruno Figliuolo, "Amalfi e il Levante nel medioevo," in *I Comuni italiani nel regno crociato di Gerusalemme: Atti del colloquio*, ed. Gabriella Airaldi and B. Z. Kedar (Università di Genova, 1986), 571–664; G. Sangermano, "La diaspora degli Amalfitani," in *Genoa e genovesi a Palermo* (Palermo, 21–23 March 1980) (Sagep, 1982), 35–51; Irmgard Fees, "Ein venezianischer Kaufmann des 12. Jahrhunderts: Romano Mairano," in *Il mito di Venezia: Una città tra realtà e rappresentazione*, ed. Peter Schreiner (Storia e Letteratura, 2006), 25–59; Gino Luzzatto, *Studi di storia economica veneziana* (CEDAM, 1954), 108–16; Gerhard Rösch, "Lo sviluppo mercantile," in *Storia di Venezia*, vol. 2, *L'età del comune*, ed. Giorgio Cracco and Gherardo Ortalli (Treccani, 1995), 146–50; Silvano Borsari, *Venezia e Bisanzio nel XII secolo: I rapporti economici* (Deputazione Editrice, 1988), 116–28; Raymond de Roover, "The Organization of Trade," in *The Cambridge Economic History of Europe*, vol. 3, *Economic Organisation and Policies in the Middle Ages*, ed. M. M. Postan, E. E. Rich, and Edward Miller (CUP, 1963), 88; and Quentin van Doosselaere, *Commercial Agreements and Social Dynamics in Medieval Genoa* (CUP, 2009).

7. Iris Origo, *The Merchant of Prato: Daily Life in a Medieval Italian City* (Penguin, 1992); Margherita Datini, *Letters to Francesco Datini*, trans. Carolyn James and Antonio Pagliaro, *The Other Voice in Early Modern Europe: The Toronto Series*, 16 (Iter Press and the Centre for Reformation and Renaissance Studies Press, 2012); Richard K. Marshall, *The Local Merchants of Prato: Small Entrepreneurs in the Late Economy* (Johns Hopkins UP, 1999); Martha C. Howell, *The Marriage Exchange: Property, Social Place, and Gender in Cities of the Low Countries, 1300–1550* (University of Chicago Press, 1998); Sabine von Heusinger, "Mutter, Kind: Die Zunftfamilie als Wirtschaftseinheit," in *Craftsmen and Guilds in the Medieval and Early Modern Periods*, ed. Eva Jullien and Michael Pauly (Franz Steiner Verlag, 2016), 156–73; Fernanda Sorelli, "Capacità giuridiche e disponibilità economiche delle donne a Venezia. Dai testamenti femminili medievali," in *Margini di libertà: Testamenti femminili nel Medioevo* (Cierre Edizioni, 2010), 155–75; Silvia Carraro, *La laguna delle donne: Il monachesimo femminile a Venezia tra IX e

XIV secolo (Pisa UP, 2015); and Olivia Remie Constable, *Trade and Traders in Muslim Spain: The Commercial Realignment of the Iberian Peninsula, 900–1500* (CUP, 1996), 103–5.

8. Xabier Lamikiz, *Trade and Trust in the Eighteenth-Century Atlantic World: Spanish Merchants and Their Overseas Networks* (Boydell Press, 2010), 145; Court, "The Brignole," 53; Daviken Studnicki-Gizbert, "Interdependence and the Collective Pursuit of Profits: Portuguese Commercial Networks in the Early Modern Atlantic," in *Commercial Networks in the Early Modern Period*, ed. Diogo Ramada Curto and Anthony Molho (European University Institute, 2002), 112; and Richard T. Chu, *Chinese and Chinese Mestizos of Manila: Family, Identity, and Culture, 1860s–1930s* (Brill, 2010), 207.

9. Richard von Glahn, *The Economic History of China: From Antiquity to the Nineteenth Century* (CUP, 2016). On lineage and its institutionalization, see also William Rowe, *China's Last Empire: The Great Qing* (HUP, 2009), 127–29; Yongtao Du, *The Order of Places: Translocal Practices of the Huizhou Merchants in Late Imperial China*, Sinica Leidensia 119 (Brill, 2015); Joseph P. McDermott, "Ming Markets and Huizhou Merchants," in *The Making of a New Rural Order in South China*, vol. 2, *Merchants, Markets, and Lineages, 1500–1700* (CUP, 2020), 7–59; and Jean-Laurent Rosenthal and R. Bin Wong, *Before and Beyond Divergence: The Politics of Economic Change in China and Europe* (HUP, 2011), 71.

10. Jean S. K. Lee & Hong Li, *Wealth Doesn't Last 3 Generations: How Family Businesses Can Maintain Prosperity* (World Scientific, 2009), 216; Jonathan Porter, *Imperial China, 1350–1900* (Rowman & Littlefield, 2016), 198; and Justyna Wubs-Mrozewicz, "The Late Medieval and Early Modern Hanse as an Institution of Conflict Management," *Continuity and Change* 32, no. 1 (2017): 60. See also Eva Marie Distler, *Städtebünde im deutschen Spätmittelalter. Eine rechtshistorische Untersuchung zu Begriff, Verfassung und Funktion* (Vittorio Klostermann, 2006); and Horst Carl, *Der Schwäbische Bund, 1488–1534: Landfrieden und Genossenschaft im Übergang vom Spätmittelalter zur Reformation* (DRW-Verlag Weinbrenner, 2000); Court, "The Brignole," 50–53; Wubs-Mrozewicz, "The Late Medieval and Early Modern Hanse," 59; Justyna Wubs-Mrozewicz, "The Hanse in Medieval and Early Modern Europe: An In-

troduction," in *The Hanse in Medieval and Early Modern Europe*, ed. Justyna Wubs-Mrozewicz and Stuart Jenks (Brill, 2013), 1–35; Rolf Hammel-Kiesow, *Die Hanse* (Beck, 2000); Stephan Selzer, *Die mittelalterliche Hanse* (WBG, 2010); Carsten Jahnke, *Die Hanse* (Reclam, 2014); Ella Natalie Rothman, *Brokering Empire: Trans-Imperial Subjects Between Venice and Istanbul* (Cornell UP, 2012), 38; Paola Lanaro, *I mercati nella Repubblica veneta: Economie cittadine e stato territoriale (secoli XV–XVIII)* (Marsilio, 1999), 86; Kanakalatha Mukund, *The Trading World of the Tamil Merchant: Evolution of Capitalism in the Coromandel* (Orient Longman, 1999), 39; Richard A. Goldthwaite, *The Economy of Renaissance Florence* (Johns Hopkins UP, 2008), 109–11; and Halil İnalcik and Donald Quataert, eds., *An Economic and Social History of the Ottoman Empire*, vol. 2, *1600–1914*, ed. Suraiya Faroqhi, Bruce McGowan, Donald Quataert, and Şevket Pamuk (CUP, 1994), 592. For the "voice" in the case of China, see Abu-Lughod, *Before European Hegemony*, 331.

11. Margrit Schulte Beerbühl, "Networks of the Hanseatic League," *European History Online* 13, no. 1 (2012); Monique O'Connell, "Venice: City of Merchants or City for Merchandise?," in *The Routledge Handbook of Maritime Trade Around Europe 1300–1600*, ed. Wim Blockmans, Mikhail Krom, and Justyna Wubs-Mrozewicz (Routledge, 2017), 114; Benjamin Ravid, "The Venetian Government and the Jews," in *The Jews of Early Modern Venice*, ed. Robert C. Davis and Benjamin Ravid (Johns Hopkins UP, 2001), 18–19; Rothman, *Brokering Empire*, 189–210; Maria Pia Pedani, *Venezia porta d'Oriente* (Società Editrice il Mulino, 2010), 211–22; Ennio Concina, *Fondaci: architettura, arte, e mercatura tra Levante, Venezia, e Alemagna* (Marsilio, 1997), 219–46; Regina Grafe and Oscar Gelderblom, "The Rise and Fall of the Merchant Guilds: Re-Thinking the Comparative Study of Commercial Institutions in Pre-Modern Europe," *Journal of Interdisciplinary History* 40, no. 4 (Spring 2010): 485; Olivia Remie Constable, *Housing the Stranger in the Mediterranean World: Lodging, Trade, and Travel in Late Antiquity and the Middle Ages* (CUP, 2003); Deborah Howard, *Venice and the East: The Impact of the Islamic World on Venetian Architecture 1100–1500* (Yale UP, 2000), 32; David Jacoby, "Les Italiens en Égypte aux XIIe et

XIIIe siècles: Du comptoir à la colonie?," in *Coloniser au Moyen Âge*, ed. Michel Balard and Alain Ducellier (Armand Colin, 1995), 76–107; David Jacoby, "Le consulat vénitien d'Alexandrie d'après un document inédit de 1284," in *Chemins d'outremer: Études d'histoire sur la Méditerranée médiévale offertes à Michel Balard* (Éditions de la Sorbonne, 2015), 461–74; Abu-Lughod, *Before European Hegemony*, 221; Irfan Habib, "Merchant Communities in Precolonial India," in *Rise of Merchant Empires: Long-Distance Trade in the Early Modern World, 1350–1750*, ed. James D. Tracy (CUP, 1990), 379; Abū al-Fazl ibn Mubārak, *Ā'in-i Akbari*, trans. H. Blochmann, vol. 2, Bibliotheca Indica (Calcutta: Asiatic Society of Bengal: 1873), 57; Nancy Um, *The Merchant Houses of Mocha: Trade and Architecture in an Indian Ocean Port* (University of Washington Press, 2011), 164; Douglas E. Haynes, *Rhetoric and Ritual in Colonial India: The Shaping of a Public Culture in Surat City, 1852–1928* (University of California Press, 1991), 37; Prasannan Parthasarathi, *Why Europe Grew Rich and Asia Did Not: Global Economic Divergence, 1600–1850* (CUP, 2011), 6; and Machado, *Ocean of Trade* (CUP), 10. There is some controversy about how to tackle the question of "trust." See Philip D. Curtin, *Cross-Cultural Trade in World History* (CUP, 1984); and Sebouh David Aslanian, *From the Indian Ocean to the Mediterranean: The Global Trade Networks of Armenian Merchants from New Julfa* (University of California Press, 2011). For critics of this concept, see, for example, Chaudhuri, *Trade and Civilisation*, 224–26; and Francesca Trivellato, Leor Halevi, and Cátia Antunes, eds., *Religion and Trade: Cross-Cultural Exchanges in World History, 1000–1900* (OUP, 2014), 15–16. There is a rich literature on merchant networks, including Avner Greif, "Reputation and Coalitions in Medieval Trade: Evidence on the Maghribi Traders," *JEH* 49, no. 4 (1989): 857–82; Francesca Trivellato, "Sephardic Merchants in the Early Modern Atlantic and Beyond: Toward a Comparative Historical Approach to Business Cooperation," in *Atlantic Diasporas: Jews, Conversos, and Crypto-Jews in the Age of Mercantilism, 1500–1800*, ed. Richard L. Kagan and Philip D. Morgan (Johns Hopkins UP, 2009), 99–123; and Francesca Trivellato, *Familiarity of Strangers*. See also Michael Pearson, "Islamic Trade, Shipping, Port-States and Merchant

Communities in the Indian Ocean, Seventh to Sixteenth Centuries," in *The New Cambridge History of Islam*, vol. 3, *The Eastern Islamic World, Eleventh to Eighteenth Centuries*, ed. David O. Morgan and Anthony Reid (CUP, 2010), 326.

12. As quoted in G. S. P. Freeman-Grenville, *The East African Coast: Select Documents from the First to the Earlier Nineteenth Century* (Collings, 1975), 133–34; and "General Prologue to *The Canterbury Tales*," in *The Riverside Chaucer*, ed. Larry D. Benson (OUP, 2008), 23–36. See also Laura F. Hodges, *Chaucer and Clothing: Clerical and Academic Costume in the General Prologue to the Canterbury Tales* (D. S. Brewer, 2005), 75–77; and Kellie Robertson, "Medieval Things: Materiality, Historicism, and the Premodern Object," *Literature Compass* 5, no. 6 (2008): 1060–80.

13. Jennifer Ball, *Byzantine Dress: Representations of Secular Dress* (Palgrave Macmillan, 2005), 79–104; Catherine Kovesi Killerby, *Sumptuary Law in Italy 1200–1500* (OUP, 2002), 2; and Joseph P. McDermott, "The 'Way of the Merchant' in Late Imperial China," in *Merchant Cultures: A Global Approach to Spaces, Representations and Worlds of Trade, 1500–1800*, ed. Cátia Antunes and Francisco Bethencourt (Brill, 2022).

14. From Douglass North to James Robinson, there is a distinguished tradition of emphasizing the importance of institutions to the development of capitalism. This literature makes an important point—namely, that institutions matter. What it largely fails to do, however, is account for the history of these institutions themselves and not see them as part of an assemblage of factors that cannot be insulated from one another. This literature privileges certain institutions (rule of law, for example) over others (slavery), arbitrarily ascribing Western economic ascendancy to so-called good institutions in isolation from less pleasant ones. The emphasis on the importance of a vast range of institutions to economics has a long and distinguished history, and by the 1970s, it reemerged within the discipline of economics after a long hiatus. Important works here include Douglass C. North, *Institutions, Institutional Change and Economic Performance* (CUP, 1990); Dan Rodrik, Arvind Subramanian, and Francesco Trebbi, "Institutions Rule: The Primacy of Institutions over Geography and Integration to Economic Development," *Journal of Economic Growth* 9,

no. 12 (2004): 131–65; and Daron Acemoglu and James Robinson, *Why Nations Fail: The Origins of Power, Prosperity, and Poverty* (Crown, 2012). For a historical overview, see also Niall Ferguson, *Civilization: The West and the Rest* (Allen Lane, 2011), which identifies six institutions as crucial for explaining the Great Divergence between the West and the rest. For a very effective critique of some of the underlying assumptions of this work, see Peter Spiegler and William Milberg, "The Taming of Institutions in Economics: The Rise and Methodology of the 'New Economic Institutionalism,'" *Journal of Institutional Economics* 5, no. 3 (2009): 289–313.

15. Ethan Isaac Segal, *Coins, Trade, and the State: Economic Growth in Early Medieval Japan* (HUP, 2011), 169–79, esp. 169; David Hardiman, "Penetration of Merchant Capital in Pre-Colonial Gujarat," in *Capitalist Development: Critical Essays*, ed. Ghanshyam Shah (Sangam Books, 1992), 36; Muzaffar Alam and Sanjay Subrahmanyam, eds., *The Mughal State, 1526–1750* (OUP, 1998), 403; and Rahul Chandrashekhar Oka, "Resilience and Adaptation of Trade Networks in East African and South Asian Port Polities, 1500–1800 C.E." (PhD diss., University of Illinois at Chicago, 2008). On hundis, see also Irfan Habib, "Usury in Medieval India," *Comparative Studies in Society and History* 6, no. 4 (1964): 393–419; Ranabir Chakravarti, *Trade and Early Indian Society* (Routledge, 2021), 288–300; Ranabir Chakravarti, "Indic Mercantile Networks and the Indian Ocean World: A Millennial Overview (c. 500–1500 CE)," in *Early Global Interconnectivity Across the Indian Ocean World*, vol. 1, *Commercial Structures and Exchanges*, ed. Angela Schottenhammer (Springer International Publishing, 2019): 191–224; Roxani Eleni Margariti, "Mercantile Networks, Port Cities, and 'Pirate' States: Conflict and Competition in the Indian Ocean World of Trade Before the Sixteenth Century," *Journal of the Economic and Social History of the Orient* 51, no. 4 (2008): 543–77; Paul E. Lovejoy, "Interregional Monetary Flows in the Precolonial Trade of Nigeria," *Journal of African History* 15, no. 4 (1974): 582; Abraham L. Udovitch, *Partnership and Profit in Medieval Islam* (PUP, 1970), 80; Philippe Beaujard, "Gujarat and Long-Distance Trade in the Indian Ocean Region Before the Sixteenth Century," in *Transregional Trade and Traders: Situating Gujarat in the In-*

dian Ocean from Early Times to 1900, ed. Edward A. Alpers and Chhaya Goswami (OUP, 2019), 75–76; and Abu-Lughod, *Before European Hegemony*, 223.

16. Marshall G. S. Hodgson, "The Role of Islam in World History," in *International Journal of Middle East Studies* 1, no. 2 (1970): 99–123; Fernand Braudel, *Civilization and Capitalism, 15th–18th Century*, trans. Siân Reynolds, vol. 2, *The Wheels of Commerce* (University of California Press, 1992), 390. Islamic financial and business institutions proved important to the emergence of such institutions in Europe. See also Şevket Pamuk, "Wirtschaft und Institutionen im Nahen Osten seit dem Mittelalter," in *Die Ursprünge der modernen Welt: Geschichte im wissenschaftlichen Vergleich*, ed. James A. Robinson and Klaus Wiegandt (Fischer Taschenbuch Verlag, 2008), 541; and Abu-Lughod, *Before European Hegemony*, 93.

17. R. Bin Wong, "China Before Capitalism," in *The Cambridge History of Capitalism*, vol. 1, *The Rise of Capitalism: From Ancient Origins to 1848*, ed. Larry Neal and Jeffrey G. Williamson (CUP, 2014), 125–64; Sebastian R. Prange, *Monsoon Islam: Trade and Faith on the Medieval Malabar Coast* (CUP, 2018), 252–54; Vardit Rispler-Chaim, "Insurance and Semi-Insurance Transactions in Islamic History Until the 19th Century," *Journal of the Economic and Social History of the Orient* 34, no. 2 (1991): 144–45; Edwin Hunt and James Murra, *1200–1550* (CUP, 1999), 155, 159; Tirthankar Roy, "When Gujarat's Kachchhi Traders Had the World in Their Palms," *Wire*, July 4, 2016; Machado, *Ocean of Trade*, 28, 65–67, 101, 210, 245, 270; Irfan Habib, "Merchant Communities in Precolonial India," in *The Rise of Merchant Empires: Long-Distance Trade in the Early Modern World, 1350–1750*, ed. James D. Tracy (CUP, 1990), 395; Chhaya Goswami, *Globalization Before Its Time: The Gujarati Merchants from Kachchh* (Portfolio, 2016), 44–46; Aryeh Shmuelevitz, *The Jews of the Ottoman Empire in the Late 15th and 16th Centuries: Administrative, Economic, Legal, and Social Relations as Reflected in the Responsa* (Brill, 1984), 151–53; Takau Yoneyama, "Japan: The Role of Insurance in the Rapid Modernization of Japan," in *World Insurance: The Evolution of a Global Risk Network*, ed. Peter Borscheid and Niels Viggo Haueter (OUP, 2012), 495; Patricia A. Risso, *Merchants and Faith: Muslim Commerce*

and Culture in the Indian Ocean (Routledge, 2018), 71–75; and Shmuelevitz, *Jews of the Ottoman Empire*, 151–53. On caravan trade, see R. J. Barendse, *The Arabian Seas: The Indian Ocean World of the Seventeenth Century* (M. E. Sharpe, 2002), 160; Habib, "Merchant Communities in Precolonial India," 395; and Goswami, *Globalization Before Its Time*, 44–45.

18. See Arthur Coke Burnell, ed., *The Voyage of John Huyghen van Linschoten to the East Indies: From the Old English Translation of 1598*, vol. 1 (London: Burt Franklin, 1885), 252–53. I have modified the English translation according to corrections suggested by the editor. The earliest extant Indian account is from the late eighteenth century. See also Michael E. Scorgie and Somendra Chandra Nandy, "Emerging Evidence of Early Indian Accounting," *Abacus* 28, no. 1 (1992): 88; Moshe Gil, "The Jewish Merchants in the Light of Eleventh-Century Geniza Documents," *Journal of the Economic and Social History of the Orient* 46, no. 3 (2003): 273–319, esp. 284–87; Abu-Lughod, *Before European Hegemony*, 224; Chaudhuri, *Trade and Civilisation*, 204; Ashin Das Gupta, "Trade and Politics in 18th Century India," in *The East India Company: 1600–1858*, vol. 4, *Trade, Finance and Power*, ed. Patrick Tuck (Routledge, 1998), 47–48; Habib, "Merchant Communities in Precolonial India," 383; and Hardiman, "Penetration of Merchant Capital," 36.

19. Raymond de Roover, "The Development of Accounting Prior to Luca Pacioli According to the Account Books of Medieval Merchants," in *Business, Banking, and Economic Thought in Late Medieval and Early Modern Europe: Selected Studies of Raymond De Roover*, ed. Julius Kirshner (University of Chicago Press, 1974), 59, 125, 132, 141; Joel Kaye, *A History of Balance, 1250–1375: The Emergence of a New Model of Equilibrium and Its Impact on Medieval Thought* (CUP, 2014), 26; Bruce G. Carruthers and Wendy Nelson Espeland, "Accounting for Rationality: Double-Entry Bookkeeping and the Rhetoric of Economic Rationality," *American Journal of Sociology* 97, no. 1 (1991): 31–69; and Alan Sangster, "The Genesis of Double-Entry Bookkeeping," *Accounting Review* 91, no. 1 (2016): 299–315. For some of the foundations, see Alfred W. Crosby, *The Measure of Reality: Quantification in Western Europe, 1250–1600* (CUP, 1997); Sophus A. Reinert and Robert Fredona, "Mer-

chants and the Origins of Capitalism," Harvard Business School Working Paper No. 18-021 (September 2017), 14; and Luca Pacioli, *Summa de arithmetica, geometria, proportioni et proportionalita* (orig. pub. 1523). On the Armenians, see Levon Khachikyan, "The Ledger of the Merchant Hovhannes Joughayetsi," *Journal of the Asiatic Society* 8, no. 3 (1966): 153–86. On China, see Maxwell Aiken and Wei Lu, "The Evolution of Bookkeeping in China: Integrating Historical Trends with Western Influences," *Abacus* 34, no. 1 (1998): 147.

20. Udovitch, *Partnership and Profit*, 3, 16, 23, 40, 170–71, 260; Pamuk, "Wirtschaft und Institutionen im Nahen Osten," 572–87; Abu-Lughod, *Before European Hegemony*, 218; Jairus Banaji, "Islam, the Mediterranean and the Rise of Capitalism," *Historical Materialism: Research in Critical Marxist Theory* 15, no. 1 (2007), 47–74, here 57; Abraham L. Udovitch, "Commercial Techniques in Early Medieval Islamic Trade," in *Islam and the Trade of Asia: A Colloquium*, ed. D. S. Richards (University of Pennsylvania Press, 2016), 37–39; and Jeffrey Miner and Stefan Stantchev, "The Genoese Economy," in *A Companion to Medieval Genoa*, ed. Carrie E. Beneš (Brill, 2018), 397–426, here 403.

21. John H. Pryor, "The Origins of the Commenda Contract," *Speculum* 52, no. 1 (1977): 5–37. See also Van Doosselaere, *Commercial Agreements and Social Dynamics*, 63–65; Jon Harris, "The Commenda," in *Going the Distance: Eurasian Trade and the Rise of the Business Corporation, 1400–1700* (PUP, 2020), 130–70; Robert S. Lopez and Irving W. Raymond, eds., *Medieval Trade in the Mediterranean World: Illustrative Documents* (W. W. Norton, 2001), 176–77; Emmanouil M. L. Economou and Nicholas C. Kyriazis, "The First Globalized Economy: Privateers, Joint-Stock Companies, Commerce and the Rise of the United Provinces," *International Journal of Social Science Research* 3, no. 2 (2015): 92; Oscar Gelderblom, "The Golden Age of the Dutch Republic," in *The Invention of Enterprise: Entrepreneurship from Ancient Mesopotamia to Modern Times*, ed. David S. Landes, Joel Mokyr, and William J. Baumol (PUP, 2012), 164–66; Abu-Lughod, *Before European Hegemony*, 121; and Van Doosselaere, *Commercial Agreements and Social Dynamics*.

22. Murat Çizakça, *A Comparative Evolution of Business Partnerships: The Islamic World and Europe, with*

Specific Reference to the Ottoman Archives (Brill, 1996), 18–19.

23. Banaji, "Islam, the Mediterranean and the Rise of Capitalism," 55–57; Braudel, *Civilization and Capitalism*, 2:436, 438; John F. Padgett and Paul D. McLean, "Organizational Invention and Elite Transformation: The Birth of Partnership Systems in Renaissance Florence," *American Journal of Sociology* 111, no. 5 (2006): 1474; and Richard A. Goldthwaite, "The Medici Bank and the World of Florentine Capitalism," *Past & Present*, no. 114 (February 1987): 14.

24. Udovitch, *Partnership and Profit*, 77–78; Angela Ning-Jy Sun Hsi, "Social and Economic Status of the Merchant Class of the Ming Dynasty, 1368–1644" (PhD diss., University of Illinois at Urbana–Champaign, 1972), 64; Porter, *Imperial China*, 204–5; Zhaojin Ji, *A History of Modern Shanghai Banking: The Rise and Decline of China's Finance Capitalism* (M. E. Sharpe, 2003), 4; Braudel, *Civilization and Capitalism*, 2:393; and Carlo Taviani, "Companies, Commerce, and Credit," in *A Companion to Medieval Genoa*, ed. Carrie E. Beneš (Brill, 2018), 438, 441. On the Casa di San Giorgio, see Carlo Taviani, *The Making of the Modern Corporation: The Casa di San Giorgio and Its Legacy (1446–1720)* (Routledge, 2022).

25. Yi Xu, Bas van Leeuwen, and Jan Luiten van Zanden, "Urbanization in China, ca. 1100–1900," *Frontiers of Economics in China* 13, no. 3 (2018): 322–68, here 345; Şevket Pamuk, "The Black Death and the Origins of the 'Great Divergence' Across Europe, 1300–1600," *European Review of Economic History* 11, no. 3 (2007): 305; Remi Jedwab, Noel D. Johnson, and Mark Koyama, "Medieval Cities Through the Lens of Urban Economics," *Regional Science and Urban Economics* 94 (2022): 1–11; and Lisa Blaydes and Christopher Paik, "Muslim Trade and City Growth Before the Nineteenth Century: Comparative Urbanization in Europe, the Middle East and Central Asia," *British Journal of Political Science* 51, no. 2 (2021): 845–68, here 854. The 6 and 8.5 percent estimates come from Maarten Bosker, Eltjo Buringh, and Jan Luiten van Zanden, "From Baghdad to London: Unraveling Urban Development in Europe, the Middle East, and North Africa, 800–1800," *Review of Economics and Statistics* 95, no. 4 (2013): 1418–37, here 1424; M. M. Postan, *The Medieval Economy and Society: An Economic History of Britain in the*

Middle Ages (Weidenfeld & Nicolson, 1972), 212; and André Wink, *Al-Hind and the Making of the Indo-Islamic World*, vol. 2, *The Slave Kings and the Islamic Conquest, 11th–13th Centuries* (Brill, 1991), 1.

26. The quotations are from Marcel van der Linden, "Final Thoughts," in *Capitalism: The Reemergence of a Historical Concept*, ed. Jürgen Kocka and Marcel van der Linden (Bloomsburg, 2017), 252; and Fernand Braudel, *Afterthoughts on Material Civilization and Capitalism*, trans. Patricia M. Ranum (Johns Hopkins UP, 1977), 19, 40. See also Karl Polanyi, *The Great Transformation: The Political and Economic Origins of Our Time* (Beacon Press, 2001), 63; and Abu-Lughod, *Before European Hegemony*, 253.

27. Aristotle, *The Politics*, trans. B. Jowett, vol. 1, book 1, part 10 (Clarendon Press, 1885), 19. The translation here uses *retail trade* in place of *commerce*, which I take to be a mistranslation. In other languages, the phrase is translated as "commerce" or "commercial activity." For the quote on commerce as a hazard to well-being, see Jerry Z. Muller, *The Mind and the Market: Capitalism in Modern European Thought* (Alfred A. Knopf, 2002); 5. See also Peregrine Horden and Nicholas Purcell, *The Corrupting Sea: A Study of Mediterranean History* (Blackwell Publishers, 1999); Brent D. Shaw, "Challenging Braudel: A New Vision of the Mediterranean," *Journal of Roman Archaeology* 14 (2001): 419–53; and Polanyi, *Great Transformation*, 55.

28. The quotation is from Ahrar Ahmad, "Analysing Pre-Colonial South Asia: Mode of Production and Proto-Industrialisation?," *Journal of Contemporary Asia* 27, no. 3 (1997): 323. See also Hardiman, "Penetration of Merchant Capital," 30–32.

29. The quotations are from Polanyi, *Great Transformation*, 45, 48, 57; and Marc Bloch, *French Rural Society: An Essay on Its Basic Characteristics* (Routledge & Kegan Paul, 1966), 71. See also Norbert Götz, "'Moral Economy': Its Conceptual History and Analytical Prospects," *Journal of Global Ethics* 11, no. 2 (2015): 148.

30. Robert S. DuPlessis, *Transitions to Capitalism in Early Modern Europe* (CUP, 1997), 28. On Tamerlane, see Iftikhar H. Malik, *The Silk Road and Beyond: Narratives of a Muslim Historian* (OUP, 2020), 124.

31. Witold Kula, *An Economic Theory of the Feudal System: Towards a Model of the Polish Economy, 1500–1800* (NLB, 1976), 36; John S. Cohen and Martin L. Weitzman, "A Marxian

Model of Enclosures," *Journal of Development Economics* 1, no. 4 (1975): 293; and Samir Amin, *L'eurocentrisme: Critique d'une idéologie* (Anthropos, 1988), 13. This argument is also made by Chris Wickham, "How Did the Feudal Economy Work? The Economic Logic of Medieval Societies," *Past & Present* 251, no. 1 (2021): 10. On European feudalism being a variant of tributary regimes, see John Haldon, *The State and the Tributary Mode of Production* (Verso, 1993), 64–65. See also Eric Hobsbawm, "From Feudalism to Capitalism," in Paul Sweezy et al., *The Transition from Feudalism to Capitalism: A Symposium* (NLB, 1976), 159.

32. Witold Kula, *Teoria ekonomiczna ustroju feudalnego* (Twarda, 1983), 36–37; Kula, *Economic Theory of the Feudal System*, 10, 15–16, 26, 46; Polanyi, *Great Transformation*, 72; Wickham, "How Did the Feudal Economy Work?," 3, 9–10, 32, 37; DuPlessis, *Transitions to Capitalism*, 15, 23; and John Merrington, "Town and Country in the Transition to Capitalism," in Sweezy et al., *Transition from Feudalism to Capitalism*, 170–95. For an overview of some of the more notable debates on the nature and existence of European feudalism, see Richard Abels, "The Historiography of a Construct: 'Feudalism' and the Medieval Historian," *History Compass* 7, no. 3 (2009): 1008–31.

33. DuPlessis, *Transitions to Capitalism*, 34–35, 78; S. R. Epstein, "Craft Guilds, Apprenticeship, and Technological Change in Preindustrial Europe," *JEH* 58, no. 3 (1998): 684–713; Steven A. Epstein, *Wage Labor and Guilds in Medieval Europe* (University of North Carolina Press, 1991); and Sheilagh Ogilvie, "'Whatever Is, Is Right'? Economic Institutions in Pre-Industrial Europe," *EHR* 60, no. 4 (2007): 649–84.

34. Ravi Palat, *The Making of an Indian Ocean World-Economy, 1250–1650: Princes, Paddy Fields, and Bazaars* (Palgrave Macmillan, 2015); Judith Herrin, *Byzantium: The Surprising Life of a Medieval Empire* (Allen Lane, 2007), 150, 158; and Chris Wickham, *The Donkey and the Boat: Reinterpreting the Mediterranean Economy, 950–1180* (OUP, 2023): 269–364.

35. As cited in John W. Chaffee, *The Muslim Merchants of Premodern China: The History of a Maritime Asian Trade Diaspora, 750–1400* (CUP, 2018), 89. See also Merrington, "Town and Country," 77;

Chaudhuri, *Trade and Civilisation*, 16; Abu-Lughod, *Before European Hegemony*, 149, 213; Lorenzo M. Bondioli, "Peasants, Merchants, and Caliphs: Capital and Empire in Fatimid Egypt" (PhD diss., Princeton University, 2021); Lorenzo M. Bondioli, "Islam, Merchants, and Capitalism: Fifty-Five Years in the Socio-Economic History of Medieval Islam," *Capitalism: A Journal of History and Economics* 4, no. 2 (2023): 258–307; Paul Wheatley, "Geographical Notes on Some Commodities Involved in Sung Maritime Trade," *Journal of the Malayan Branch of the Royal Asiatic Society* 32, no. 2 (186) (1959): 24; and R. Bin Wong, "Dimensions of State Expansion and Contraction in Imperial China," *Journal of the Economic and Social History of the Orient* 37, no. 1 (1994): 54–66. Gaozong's reign was disrupted by rebellion for a few months in 1127.

36. Ibn Battuta, *The Travels of Ibn Battuta, AD 1325–1354*, vol. 4, ed. H. A. R. Gibb and C. F. Beckingham, trans. H. A. R. Gibb, orig. ed. C. Defrémery and B. R. Sanguinetti (CUP for Hakluyt Society, 1994), 893.

37. Bosworth, Heffening, and Shatzmiller, "Tidjara"; Timothy Brook, "Communications and Commerce," in *The Cambridge History of China*, vol. 8, *The Ming Dynasty, 1368–1644*, part 2, ed. Denis Twitchett and Frederick W. Mote (CUP, 1998), 580; Abu-Lughod, *Before European Hegemony*, 321; David Robinson, *Muslim Societies in African History* (CUP, 2004), 141; Yusufu Bala Usman, *The Transformation of Katsina, 1400–1883: The Emergence and Overthrow of the Sarauta System and the Establishment of the Emirate* (Ahmadu Bello UP, 1981), 32; Rasheed Olaniyi, "Kano: The Development of a Trading City in Central Sudan," in *Precolonial Nigeria: Essays in Honor of Toyin Falola*, ed. Akinwumi Ogundiran (Africa World Press, 2005), 304–5; and Merrington, "Town and Country," 77–78.

38. "Table 8b. Rate of Growth of World Per Capita GDP, 20 Countries and Regional Averages, 1–2001 AD (annual average compound growth rates)," in Angus Maddison, *The World Economy: Historical Statistics* (OECD, 2003), 263; and DuPlessis, *Transitions to Capitalism*.

39. These resistances are also emphasized by Hobsbawm, "From Feudalism to Capitalism," 163.

40. James Davis, *Medieval Market Morality: Life, Law and Ethics in the English Marketplace, 1200–1500*

(CUP, 2011); James Davis, "Selling Food and Drink in the Aftermath of the Black Death," in *Town and Countryside in the Age of the Black Death: Essays in Honour of John Hatcher*, ed. Mark Bailey and Stephen Rigby (Brepols, 2012), 351–406; Alison Brown, "The Revolution of 1494 in Florence and Its Aftermath: A Reassessment," in *Italy in Crisis, 1494*, ed. Jane E. Everson and Diego Zancani (European Humanities Research Centre, 2000), 13–40; Guidubaldo Guidi, *Lotte, pensiero e istituzioni politiche nella Repubblica fiorentina dal 1494 al 1512*, 1–3 (Leo S. Olschki, 1992); Lawrin D. Armstrong, *Usury and Public Debt in Early Renaissance Florence: Lorenzo Ridolfi on the Monte Comune* (Pontifical Institute of Mediaeval Studies, 2003); Dennis Romano, *Markets and Marketplaces in Medieval Italy c. 1100–1440* (Yale UP, 2015); Segal, *Coins, Trade, and the State*, 77; Kozo Yamamura, "The Growth of Commerce in Medieval Japan," in *The Cambridge History of Japan*, vol. 3, *Medieval Japan*, ed. Kozo Yamamura (CUP, 1990), 344–95; Hugh R. Clark, *Community, Trade and Networks: Southern Fujian Province from the Third to the Thirteenth Century* (CUP, 1991); and Denis Twitchett, "The T'ang Market System," *Asia Major* 12, no. 2 (1966): 202–48.

41. For India, for example, see Chaudhuri, *Trade and Civilisation*, 201.

42. Samuel Kline Cohn Jr., *Lust for Liberty: The Politics of Social Revolt in Medieval Europe, 1200–1425: Italy, France, and Flanders* (HUP, 2006); Rodney Hilton, *Bond Men Made Free: Medieval Peasant Movements and the English Rising of 1381* (Temple Smith, 1973); Rodney Hilton and T. H. Aston, eds., *The English Rising of 1381* (CUP, 1984); William H. TeBrake, *A Plague of Insurrection: Popular Politics and Peasant Revolt in Flanders, 1323–1328* (University of Pennsylvania Press, 1993); John Bell Henneman, *Royal Taxation in Fourteenth-Century France: The Captivity and Ransom of John II, 1356–1370* (American Philosophical Society, 1976); and John Hatcher and Mark Bailey, *Modelling the Middle Ages: The History and Theory of England's Economic Development* (OUP, 2001).

43. See, for example, Immanuel Wallerstein, *The Modern World-System*, vol. 2, *Mercantilism and the Consolidation of the European World-Economy, 1600–1750* (University of California Press, 2011).

44. Chaffee, *Muslim Merchants of Premodern China*, 163; Simon Digby,

"The Maritime Trade of India," in *The Cambridge Economic History of India*, vol. 1, *c. 1200–c. 1750*, ed. Tapan Raychaudhuri and Irfan Habib (CUP, 1982), 138–39; Eliyahu Ashtor, *Levant Trade in the Middle Ages* (PUP, 2014), 17–22; William Wayne Farris, *Japan's Medieval Population: Famine, Fertility, and Warfare in a Transformative Age* (University of Hawaii Press, 2006), 44–47; and Ethan Isaac Segal, "Virtue, Vice, and the Kamakura Bakufu," in Segal, *Coins, Trade, and the State*, 108–47.

45. Abu-Lughod, *Before European Hegemony*, 81, 85; Fabrizio Ricciardelli, *A Short History of Florence* (Mauro Pagliai Editore, 2019), 45; Samuel Kline Cohn Jr., *The Laboring Classes in Renaissance Florence* (Academic Press, 1980), 136, 153; Jason W. Moore, "Nature and the Transition from Feudalism to Capitalism," *Review* (Fernand Braudel Center) 26, no. 2 (2003): 118. For a survey of these rebellions, see Steven A. Epstein, *Genoa & the Genoese, 958–1528* (University of North Carolina Press, 1996), 90, 325–27.

46. Karl Jordan, "Zur päpstlichen Finanzgeschichte im 11. und 12. Jahrhundert," *Quellen und Forschungen aus italienischen Archiven und Bibliotheken* 25 (1933): 61–104; Chris Wickham, "The City Politics, 1050–1150," in *Europa e Italia: Studi in onore di Giorgio Chittolini* (Firenze UP, 2011), 15, 437–53; Glen Olsen, "Italian Merchants and the Performance of Papal Banking Functions in the Early Thirteenth Century," *Explorations in Economic History* 7, no. 1 (1969): 43–63; Volkert Pfaff, "Aufgaben und Probleme der päpstlichen Finanzverwaltung am Ende des 12. Jahrhunderts," *Institut für Österreichische Geschichtsforschung* 64, no. 1–2 (1956): 1–24; Peter Partner, "The Papacy and the Papal States," in *The Rise of the Fiscal State in Europe, c. 1200–1815* (OUP, 1999); Jean Favier, *Les Finances pontificales à l'époque du grand schisme d'Occident, 1378–1409* (E. de Boccard, 1966); Ignazio Del Punta, "Tuscan Merchant-Bankers and Moneyers and Their Relations with the Roman Curia in the XIIIth and Early XIVth Centuries," *Rivista di storia della Chiesa in Italia* 64, no. 1 (2010): 39–53; Melissa M. Bullard, "Farming Spiritual Revenues: Innocent VIII's Appalto of 1486," in *Renaissance Studies in Honor of Craig Hugh Smyth*, ed. Andrew Morrogh, Fiorella Superbi Gioffredi, Piero Morselli, and Eve Borsook (Giunti Barbèra, 1985), 229–42.

47. The quotations are from Kenneth R. Hall, *Maritime Trade and State Development in Early Southeast Asia* (University of Hawaii Press, 1985), 187. See also Chaudhuri, *Trade and Civilisation*, 16, 214; Mary G. Hodge, "Archaeological Views of Aztec Culture," *Journal of Archaeological Research* 6, no. 3 (1998): 220; and Michael E. Smith, *At Home with the Aztecs: An Archaeologist Uncovers Their Daily Life* (Routledge, 2016), 114.

48. The quotations are, in order, from Hellmut Ritter, "Ein arabisches Handbuch der Handelswissenschaft," *Der Islam* 7, no. 1 (1916): 3–4; Shaikh Mohammad Ghazanfar and Abdul Azim Islahi, *Economic Thought of al-Ghazali (450–505 A.H. / 1058–1111 C.E.)*, 2nd ed. (King Abdulaziz UP, 2011), 12–13, 32, 40; ʿAbd-Elṣamad ʿAbd-Elḥamīd Elschazlī, ed., *Das Kriterium des Handelns* (Wissenschaftliche Buchgesellschaft, 2006), 212–21, here 214. See also Abbas J. Ali, Abdulrahman al-Aali, and Abdullah al-Owaihan, "Islamic Perspectives on Profit Maximization," *Journal of Business Ethics* 117, no. 3 (October 2013): 467–75; S. M. Ghazanfar and A. Azim Islahi, "Economic Thought of an Arab Scholastic: Abu Hamid al-Ghazali (A.H. 450–505 / A.D. 1058–1111)," *History of Political Economy* 22, no. 2 (1990): 381–403; Abraham L. Udovitch, "Bankers Without Banks," in *The Dawn of Modern Banking*, ed. Center for Medieval and Renaissance Studies, UCLA (Yale UP, 1979), 256; and Irfan Habib, "Usury in Medieval India," *Comparative Studies in Society and History* 6, no. 4 (1964): 396.

49. The quotations are, in order, from Timothy Brook, *The Confusions of Pleasure: Commerce and Culture in Ming China* (University of California Press, 1998), 127; and Porter, *Imperial China*, 192, 194. See also Timothy Brook, "The Merchant Network in 16th Century China: A Discussion and Translation of Zhang Han's 'On Merchants,'" *Journal of the Economic and Social History of the Orient*, 24, no. 2 (1981); Abu-Lughod, *Before European Hegemony*, 332; Timothy Brook, "Profit and Righteousness in Chinese Economic Culture," in *Culture and Economy: The Shaping of Capitalism in Eastern Asia*, ed. Timothy Brook and Hy V. Luong (University of Michigan Press, 1999), 28, 33, 40; and Ye Sheng, *Shuidong Riji* [Diary from East of the River], comp. 1465–72 (Siku Quanshu; repr., Zhonghua Shuju, 1999). Scholars have gone back and forth, sometimes seeing

Confucianism as the fundamental source of China's economic backwardness (especially during the 1950s and 1960s) and other times seeing it as the source of China's success. Max Weber started that tradition in *Die Wirtschaftsethik der Weltreligionen: Konfuzianismus und Taoismus: Schriften 1915–1920*, ed. Helwig Schmidt-Glintzer and Petra Kolonko (Mohr, 1991). Weber argued that Confucianism held China back. Culturalism, according to Zurndorfer, does not explain Chinese economic development, a viewpoint that stands in opposition to culturalist arguments made by Joel Mokyr and others. For a summary of this debate, see Harriet Zurndorfer, "Confusing Capitalism with Confucianism: Culture as Impediment and/or Stimulus to Chinese Economic Development," 《《中国史学》》 [Studies in Chinese History] 27 (2017): 1–20.

50. The quotations are, in order, from Ezekiel 18:13; and Matthew 19:24. See also Lester K. Little, *Religious Poverty and the Profit Economy in Medieval Europe* (Cornell UP, 1978), 35, 38.

51. The quotations are, in order, from Little, *Religious Poverty*, 38; and John T. Noonan, trans., *The Scholastic Analysis of Usury* (HUP, 1957), 42. See also Christoph Fleischmann, "Wem gehört die Zeit?: Der Mensch im Takt des Kapitalismus," *Blätter für deutsche und internationale Politik* 59, no.1 (2014): 111.

52. The quotations are, in order, from 1 Timothy 6:10 (King James Version); Bernhard Groethuysen, *The Bourgeois: Catholicism vs. Capitalism in Eighteenth-Century France* (Barrie & Rockliff Press, 1968), 203; Giovanni Boccaccio, *The Decameron*, trans. J. M. Rigg (Henry F. Bumpus, 1906; orig. pub. 1353), 25. See also Muller, *Mind and the Market*, 5; and Little, *Religious Poverty*, 39. Scenes like in Reims are found elsewhere as well.

53. Tim Parks, *Medici Money: Banking, Metaphysics, and Art in Fifteenth-Century Florence* (Profile Books, 2006), 9–11.

54. Braudel, *Civilization and Capitalism*, 2:400.

55. Wickham, "How Did the Feudal Economy Work?," 30, 37–40. On the expansion, and also the retreat, of market economies, see Bas van Bavel, *The Invisible Hand? How Market Economies Have Emerged and Declined Since AD 500* (OUP, 2016).

56. Robert Kurz, *Weltkrise und Ignoranz: Kapitalismus im Niedergang, Ausgewählte Schriften 1992–2012* (Edition Tiamat, 2013), 99.

Chapter 3: The Great Connecting, 1450–1650

1. Fernand Braudel, *Civilization and Capitalism, 15th–18th Century*, trans. Siân Reynolds, vol. 3, *The Perspective of the World* (Collins, 1984), 511. It had two hundred thousand inhabitants by 1700. See also Irfan Habib, "Potentialities of Capitalistic Development in the Economy of Mughal India," *JEH* 29, no. 1 (March 1969): 61.

2. Johan Albrecht von Mandelslo, *Des HochEdelgebornen Johan Albrechts von Mandelslo Morgenländische Reyse-Beschreibung: Worinnen Zugleich die Gelegenheit vnd Heutiger Zustand Etlicher Fürnehmen Indianischen Länder, Provincien, Städte vnd Insulen, Sampt Derer Einwohner Leben, Sitten, Glauben vnd Handthierung; wie Auch die Beschaffenheit der Seefahrt Über das Oceanische Meer* (Hamburg: Guth, 1658), 45, 46, 47, 48.

3. Edward Terry, *A Voyage to East-India: Wherein Some Things Are Taken Notice of, in Our Passage Thither, but Many More in Our Abode There, Within That Rich and Most Spacious Empire of the Great Mogul: Mixt with Some Parallel Observations and Inferences upon the Story, to Profit as Well as Delight the Reader* (Salisbury: Cater, S. Hayes, J. Wilkie, and E. Easton, 1777), 80.

4. C. G. Brouwer, "Non-Western Shipping Movements in the Red Sea and Gulf of Aden During the 2nd and 3rd Decades of the 17th Century, According to the Records of the Dutch East India Company (Part 2)," *Die Welt des Islams* 32, no. 1 (1992): 17; Ashin Das Gupta, "Gujarati Merchants and the Red Sea Trade, 1700–1725," in *The World of the Indian Ocean Merchant, 1500–1800: Collected Essays of Ashin Das Gupta*, comp. Uma Das Gupta (OUP, 2004), 4f, 369–70; Surendra Gopal, *Commerce and Crafts in Gujarat: 16th and 17th Centuries* (People's Publishing House, 1975), 43; R. J. Barendse, *The Arabian Sea: The Indian Ocean World of the Seventeenth Century* (M. E. Sharpe, 2002), 5; Sanjay Subrahmanyam, "A Note on the Rise of Surat in the Sixteenth Century," *Journal of the Economic and Social History of the Orient* 43, no. 1 (2000): 31. For other contemporary descriptions of Surat, see "Voyages de Mr Thevenot, contenant la relation de l'Indostan, des nouveaux Mogols, & des autres Peuples & Pays des Indes," as quoted in *Indian Travels of Thevenot and Careri*, ed. Surendranath Sen (National Archives of India, 1949), 25, first published in 1684.

5. Kaveh Yazdani, *India, Modernity and the Great Divergence: Mysore and Gujarat (17th to 19th C.)* (Brill, 2017), 408.

6. M. N. Pearson, *The World of the Indian Ocean, 1500–1800: Studies in Economic, Social and Cultural History* (Ashgate, 2005), 460; Rusheed R. Wadia, "Bombay Paris Merchants in the Eighteenth and Nineteenth Centuries," in *Parsis in India and the Diaspora*, ed. John R. Hinnells and Allan Williams (Routledge, 2007), 122. As late as the eighteenth century, European trade represented just one-eighth of the city's maritime commerce. See B. G. Gokhale, *Surat in the Seventeenth Century* (Curzon Press, 1979), 125; Ashin Das Gupta, "Indian Merchants in the Age of Partnership, c. 1500–1800," in *Das Gupta, World of the Indian Ocean Merchant*, 123; and Om Prakash, "English Private Trade in the Western Indian Ocean, 1720–1740," *Journal of the Economic and Social History of the Orient* 50, no. 2/3 (2007): 216.

7. Sen, *Indian Travels of Thevenot and Careri*, 22; and Yazdani, *India, Modernity and the Great Divergence*, 422.

8. Pedro Machado, *Ocean of Trade: South Asian Merchants, Africa and the Indian Ocean, c. 1750–1850* (CUP, 2014), 70, 87; Yazdani, *India, Modernity and the Great Divergence*, 378; Braudel, *Civilization and Capitalism*, 3:519; Giancarlo Casale, *The Ottoman Age of Exploration* (OUP, 2010), 5, 56; Edward A. Alpers, *The Indian Ocean in World History* (OUP, 2014), 56. See also George Hourani, *Arab Seafaring in the Indian Ocean in Ancient and Early Medieval Times* (PUP, 1995); Patricia Risso, *Merchants and Faith: Muslim Commerce and Culture in the Indian Ocean* (Westview Press, 1995); Sagufta Parveen, "Surat: As a Major Port-Town of Gujarat and Its Trade History," *IOSR Journal of Humanities and Social Science* 19, no. 5 (2014): 70; Mohd Afzal Khan, "The Chalebi Merchants at Surat 16th–18th Centuries," *Proceedings of the Indian History Congress* 40 (1979): 408, 410; David Hardiman, "Penetration of Merchant Capital in Pre-Colonial Gujarat," in *Capitalist Development: Critical Essays*, ed. Ghanshyam Shah (Sangam Books, 1992), 35; Ruquia Hussain, "Turkish Merchants at Surat in Mughal Times," *Studies in History* 30, no. 1 (2014): 48, 52; and Ruquia Hussain, "Armenian, Iranian and Turkish Merchants in India 1550–1800" (PhD diss., Aligarh Muslim University, 2005), 294.

9. The notion of "islands" is also used by Marcel van der Linden in his

discussion of the seventeenth-century Netherlands in Marcel van der Linden, "Marx and Engels, Dutch Marxism and the 'Model Capitalist Nation" of the Seventeenth Century," *Science & Society* 61, no. 2 (1997): 161–83. For "top layer," see Fernand Braudel, *Civilization and Capitalism, 15th–18th Century*, trans. Siân Reynolds, vol. 2, *The Wheels of Commerce* (University of California Press, 1992), 378, 381, 404, 408, 428.

10. Richard Hakluyt, *Principal Navigations, Voyages, and Discoveries of the English Nation* (London: G. Bishop, R. Newberie, and R. Barker, 1589), 353; Leonhart Rauwolf, *A Collection of Curious Travels and Voyages: Containing Dr. Leonhart Rauwolf's Journey into the Eastern Countries*, trans. Nicolas Staphorst (London: Olive Payne, Thomas Woodman, and William Shropshire, 1738), 145.

11. Rauwolf, *Collection of Curious Travels and Voyages*, 145–46. See also Pedro Teixeira, *The Travels of Pedro Teixeira: With His "Kings of Harmuz" and Extracts from His "Kings of Persia,"* trans. William F. Sinclair (Hakluyt Society, 1902), 66–67.

12. Jean-Baptiste Tavernier, *The Six Voyages of Jean-Baptiste Tavernier, a Noble Man of France Now Living, Through Turky into Persia and the East Indies*, trans. John Phillips (London: R. L. and M. P., 1678), book 2, chap. 8, 89.

13. Nelly Hanna, *Making Big Money in 1600: The Life and Times of Ismaʿil Abu Taqiyya Egyptian Merchant* (Syracuse UP, 1998), 82; Ronald Findlay and Kevin H. O'Rourke, *Power and Plenty: Trade, War, and the World Economy in the Second Millennium* (PUP, 2007), 222; Levon Khachikyan, "The Ledger of the Merchant Hovhannes Joughayetsi," *Journal of the Asiatic Society* 8, no. 3 (1966): 153–86; Şevket Pamuk, "Wirtschaft und Institutionen im Nahen Osten seit dem Mittelalter," in *Die Ursprünge der modernen Welt: Geschichte im wissenschaftlichen Vergleich*, ed. James A. Robinson and Klaus Wiegandt (Fischer Taschenbuch Verlag, 2008), 552; Abdul-Karim Rafeq, "The Socioeconomic and Political Implications of the Introduction of Coffee into Syria, 16th–18th Centuries," in *Le commerce du café avant l'ère des plantations coloniales*, ed. Michel Tuchscherer (Institut Français d'Archéologie Orientale, 2001), 127–42; Abdul-Karim Rafeq, "Damascus and the Pilgrim Caravan," in *Modernity and Culture: From the Mediterranean to the Indian Ocean*, ed. Leila Tarazi Fawaz and C. A.

Bayly (CUP, 2002), 130–31. Regarding caravans, see Francesca Trivellato, *The Familiarity of Strangers: The Sephardic Diaspora, Livorno, and Cross-Cultural Trade in the Early Modern Period* (Yale UP, 2009), 6. See also Bruce Masters, "Aleppo: The Ottoman Empire's Caravan City," in *The Ottoman City Between East and West: Aleppo, Izmir, and Istanbul*, ed. Edhem Eldem, Daniel Goffman, and Bruce Alan Masters (CUP, 1999), 2; Bruce Masters, *The Arabs of the Ottoman Empire, 1516–1918: A Social and Cultural History* (CUP, 2013), 75, 76; and letter of João de Meira to King D. Manuel in Ronald Bishop Smith, *The First Age of Portuguese Embassies: Navigations and Peregrinations in Persia (1507–1524)* (Decatur Press, 1970), 60.

14. Jürgen Osterhammel, *Unfabling the East: The Enlightenment's Encounter with Asia*, trans. Robert Savage (PUP, 2018), 53.

15. Prasannan Parthasarathi, *Why Europe Grew Rich and Asia Did Not: Global Economic Divergence, 1600–1850* (CUP, 2011), 4–5, 21, 23, 61, 185; Hardiman, "Penetration of Merchant Capital," 34. See also Fahad Ahmad Bishara, *A Sea of Debt: Law and Economic Life in the Western Indian Ocean, 1780–1950* (CUP, 2017); Meghnad Desai, Dharma Kumar, Irfan Habib, and Tapan Raychaudhuri, *The Cambridge Economic History of India*, vol. 1, *c. 1200–c. 1750* (CUP, 1982), 155–56; and Michael Pearson, *The Indian Ocean* (Routledge, 2003), 3.

16. As quoted in Richard von Glahn, *The Economic History of China: From Antiquity to the Nineteenth Century* (CUP, 2016), 304.

17. R. Bin Wong, "The Role of the Chinese State in Long-Distance Commerce," Working Paper No. 05/04 EHN Conference, Bankside, London (September 17–20, 2003); 5; Jonathan Porter, *Imperial China, 1350–1900* (Rowman & Littlefield, 2016), 194–96; Timothy Brook, "The Merchant Network in 16th Century China: A Discussion and Translation of Zhang Han's 'On Merchants,'" *Journal of the Economic and Social History of the Orient* 24, no. 2 (1981): 165, 168f; and Ping-Ti Ho, "The Salt Merchants of Yang-Chou: A Study of Commercial Capitalism in Eighteenth-Century China," *Harvard Journal of Asiatic Studies* 17, no. 1/2 (1954): 130, 141, 152, 156. On the amount of silver, the consensus is that one tael of unminted silver weighed around thirty-seven grams in the eighteenth century. See, for

example, Robert C. Allen et al., "Wages, Prices, and Living Standards in China, 1738–1925: In Comparison with Europe, Japan, and India," *EHR* 64, no. 1 (February 2011): 9; Robert Gardella, *Harvesting Mountains: Fujian and the China Tea Trade, 1757 to 1937* (University of California Press, 1997), 29, 31; and William Rowe, *China's Last Empire: The Great Qing* (HUP, 2009), 122–28, 135–37.

18. Dennis O. Flynn and Arturo Giraldez, "Born with a 'Silver Spoon': The Origin of World Trade in 1571," *Journal of World History* 6, no. 2 (1995): 212–13; Charles David Sheldon, *The Rise of the Merchant Class in Tokugawa Japan, 1600–1868: An Introductory Survey* (J. J. Augustin Incorporated, 1958), 4, 69; Kikuchi Hitomi, *Edo Ishō Zukan* (Tokyodō Shuppan, 2011), 96; *The Cambridge History of Japan*, vol. 4, *Early Modern Japan*, ed. John Whitney Hall and James L. McClain (CUP, 1991), 559, 562.

19. Jody Benjamin, "Global Textiles and the Centripetal Pull of the Western African Savannah, 1740–1780," unpublished paper, Towards a Global History Conference, Delhi, December 3–5, 2017, 3.

20. As cited in Freeman-Grenville, *The East African Coast*, 125–26.

21. The contemporary price of silver is for November 18, 2023. Fernand Braudel also emphasizes the importance of cities and merchant communities in the early history of capitalism, for example in Braudel, *Civilization and Capitalism*, 2:29–47, 90–120. See also Findlay and O'Rourke, *Power and Plenty*, 204; John E. Wills Jr., "Relations with Maritime Europeans, 1514–1662," in *The Cambridge History of China*, vol. 8, *The Ming Dynasty, 1368–1644*, part 2, ed. Denis Twitchett and Frederick W. Mote (CUP, 1998), 374; Wang Gungwu, "The Hokkien Sojourning Communities," in *The Rise of Merchant Empires: Long-Distance Trade in the Early Modern World, 1350–1750*, ed. James D. Tracy (CUP, 1990), 405f; Xing Hang, "Bridging the Bipolar: Zheng Jing's Decade on Taiwan, 1663–1673," in *Sea Rovers, Silver, and Samurai: Maritime East Asia in Global History, 1550–1700*, ed. Tonio Andrade and Xing Hang (University of Hawaii Press, 2016), 240; Findlay and O'Rourke, *Power and Plenty*, 286–87; Xing Hang, *Conflict and Commerce in Maritime East Asia: The Zheng Family and the Shaping of the Modern World, c. 1620–1720* (CUP,

2016), 1; and Huei-Ying Kuo, *Networks Beyond Empires: Chinese Business and Nationalism in the Hong Kong–Singapore Corridor, 1914–1941* (Brill, 2014), 3.

22. Findlay and O'Rourke, *Power and Plenty*, 18, 22, 212; Halil İnalcik, "The Ottoman State: Economy and Society, 1300–1600," in *An Economic and Social History of the Ottoman Empire*, vol. 1, *1300–1600*, ed. Halil İnalcik and Donald Quataert (CUP, 1997), 345–47; Raffaello de' Medici to Filippo da Empoli and Antonio Bartoli in Pera, 24 April 1521, MS 553, Letter XX, as cited in Gertrude R. B. Richards, *Florentine Merchants in the Age of Medici: Letters and Documents from the Selfridge Collection of Medici Manuscripts* (HUP, 1932), 226; M. Rozen, "Strangers in a Strange Land: The Extraterritorial Status of Jews in Italy and the Ottoman Empire in the Sixteenth to Eighteenth Centuries," in *Ottoman and Turkish Jewry: Community and Leadership*, ed. Aron Rodigue (Indiana UP, 1992), 126–36; Chhaya Goswami and Jaithirth Rao, *Globalization Before Its Time: The Gujarati Merchants from Kachchh* (Portfolio, 2016), xv, xviii, 212; Pearson, *World of the Indian Ocean*, 92–93, 96–112, 227; Machado, *Ocean of Trade*, 183; Moses E. Ochonu, "The Wangara Factor in West African Business History," in *Entrepreneurship in Africa: A Historical Approach*, ed. Moses E. Ochonu (Indiana UP, 2018), 53, 61; Ivor Wilks, "Wangara, Akan, and Portuguese in the Fifteenth and Sixteenth Centuries: 1. The Matter of Bitu," *Journal of African History* 23, no. 3 (1982): 333–49; Pacheco Pereira, *Esmeraldo de Situ Orbis*, trans. G. H. Kimble (Hakluyt Society, 1937), 87; and Rasheed Olaniyi, "Hausa-Yoruba Relations, 1500–1800: A Historical Perspective," in *Inter-Group Relations in Nigeria: The Historian's Perspectives: Essays in Honour of Professor Obaro Ikime at 70*, ed. A. E. Ekoko and S. O. Aghalino (Department of History, University of Ibadan, 2006), 303.

23. Benjamin Arbel, *Trading Nations: Jews and Venetians in the Early Modern Eastern Mediterranean* (Brill, 1995); James Olson, *Historical Dictionary of the British Empire: K–Z* (Greenwood Publishing Group, 1996), 769; Hugh Thomas, *The Slave Trade: The Story of the Atlantic Slave Trade: 1440–1870* (Simon & Schuster, 2013), 177; P. E. H. Hair and Robin Law, "The English in Western Africa to 1700," in *The Oxford History of the British Empire*, vol. 1,

The Origins of Empire: British Overseas Enterprise to the Close of the Seventeenth Century, ed. Nicholas Canny and Alaine Low (OUP, 1998), 253; Merrick Posnansky, "Aspects of Early West African Trade," *World Archaeology* 5, no. 2 (October 1973): 149–62; J. D. Fage, "Ancient Ghana: A Review of the Evidence," *Transactions of the Historical Society of Ghana* 3, no. 2 (1957): 3–24; David Henige, "John Kabes of Komenda: An Early African Entrepreneur and State Builder," *Journal of African History* 18, no. 1 (1977): 1–19; Kwame Yeboa Daaku, *Trade and Politics on the Gold Coast* (OUP, 1970); Ballong-Wen-Mewuda, "A instalação de fortalezas na costa africana. Os casos de Arguim e da Mina. Comércio e contactos culturais," in *Portugal no mundo*, vol. 2, *As zonas de influência do Ocidente. Origem e desenvolvimento da colonização*, ed. Luís de Albuquerque (Alfa, 1989), 137–49; and Filipa Ribeiro da Silva, *Dutch and Portuguese in Western Africa: Empires, Merchants and the Atlantic System, 1580–1674* (Brill, 2011), 195.

24. Wills, "Relations with Maritime Europeans," 374. See also Machado, *Ocean of Trade*, 275.

25. Tiago Nasser Appel, "Why Was There No Capitalism in Early Modern China?," *Brazilian Journal of Political Economy* 37, no. 1 (2017): 171.

26. For the notion of "false starts," reverses, backsliding," see also John Merrington, "Town and Country in the Transition to Capitalism," in *The Transition from Feudalism to Capitalism*, ed. Rodney Hilton (Humanities Press, 1976), 173.

27. Jason W. Moore, "Nature and the Transition from Feudalism to Capitalism," *Review* (Fernand Braudel Center) 26, no. 2 (2003): 102; and Franz Mehring, *Absolutism and Revolution in Germany, 1525–1848* (New Park Publications, 1975), 1, as cited in Jairus Banaji, *A Brief History of Commercial Capitalism* (Haymarket Books, 2020), 120.

28. This is also observed by K. N. Chaudhuri, *Trade and Civilisation in the Indian Ocean: An Economic History from the Rise of Islam to 1750* (CUP, 1985), 15; and Tonio Andrade, *How Taiwan Became Chinese: Dutch, Spanish, and Han Colonization in the Seventeenth Century* (CUP, 2008).

29. Moore, "Nature and the Transition from Feudalism to Capitalism," 42; James D. Tracy, ed., introduction to *The Rise of Merchant Empires: Long-Distance Trade in the Early Modern World 1350–1750*, vol. 1 (CUP, 1993), 2.

30. Abu-Lughod, *Before European Hegemony*, 189; Carlo Taviani, "In the Shadow of Other Empires: Genoese Merchant Networks and Their Conflicts Across the Atlantic Ocean, ca. 1450–1530," in *Conflict Management in the Mediterranean and the Atlantic, 1000–1800*, ed. Louis Sickling and Alain Wijffels (Brill/Nijhoff, 2020), 217–36.

31. Howard French, *Born in Blackness: Africa, Africans, and the Making of the Modern World, 1471 to the Second World War* (Liveright Publishing, 2021), 8, 36–38, 66–68, 171, 186–87.

32. Trevor Hall, *The Role of Cape Verde Islanders in Organizing and Operating Maritime Trade Between West Africa and Iberian Territories, 1441–1616* (Johns Hopkins UP, 1992), 96, 136, 215–16, 218–19, 304–5, 472–73, 676–77. On the importance of slaves as collateral, see the brilliant article by Joseph C. Miller, "The Sixteenth Century: Specie, Sugar, and Slaves," in *The Princeton Companion to Atlantic History*, ed. Joseph C. Miller (PUP, 2015), 14. See also Richard Lobban, *Historical Dictionary of the Republics of Guinea-Bissau and Cape Verde* (Scarecrow Press, 1979), 6–7; Hall, *Role of Cape Verde Islanders*, 195; Tomich, "Original Accumulation," 13, 14; and French, *Born in Blackness*, 114–17, 121–22.

33. Thomas Allison Kirk, *Genoa and the Sea: Policy and Power in an Early Modern Maritime Republic, 1559–1684* (Johns Hopkins UP, 2013), 15–16, 22–28, 51–84; Steven A. Epstein, *Genoa & the Genoese, 958–1528* (University of North Carolina Press, 1996), 73–107; Dale Tomich, "Original Accumulation: The Genoese Cycle of Accumulation, Atlantic Slavery, and the Formation of the World-Market," unpublished paper, Towards a Global History of Primitive Accumulation Conference, IISH, Amsterdam, May 2019, 9, 22; Banaji, "Islam, the Mediterranean and the Rise of Capitalism," 48; and French, *Born in Blackness*, 37, 62–70, 77. For the translated quotation ("più memorabili che da molti secoli in quà siano accadute nel mondo"), see Vitorino Magalhães Godinho, *L'économie de l'Empire portug ais aux XVe et XVIe siècles* (S.E.V.P.E.N., 1969), 730.

34. For the quote, see "Manuel Nunes Dias, "O capitalismo monárquico português, 1415–1549: Contribuição para o estudo das origens do capitalismo moderno" (PhD diss., Universidade de Coimbra, 1963), 37, as cited in Banaji, "Islam, the Mediterranean and the Rise of Capitalism,"

49. See also Alberto da Veiga-Simoes, *La Flandre, le Portugal, et les débuts du capitalisme moderne* (Brussels, n.p., 1933).

35. French, *Born in Blackness*, 113–17, 200, 216; John Tutino, *The Mexican Heartland: How Communities Shaped Capitalism, a Nation, and World History, 1500–2000* (PUP, 2017), 9; and Leonardo Marques and Rafael Marquese, "Gold, Coffee, and Slaves: Brazil and World Accumulation," unpublished paper, Towards a Global History of Primitive Accumulation Conference, IISH, Amsterdam, 2019, 14.

36. On imperial expansion, see Gurminder K. Bhambra and Julia McClure, "Introduction: Imperial Inequalities," in *Imperial Inequalities: The Politics of Economic Governance Across European Empires*, ed. Gurminder Bhambra and Julia McClure (Manchester UP, 2022), 138–56. On Adam Smith, see Adam Smith, *The Wealth of Nations*, vol. 1, book 1, (Penguin, 1986), 276–77; and Adam Smith, *The Wealth of Nations*, vol. 2, book 4 (Penguin, 1986), 90–91. On modern scholarship, much of which debunks the notion that Atlantic trade impoverished the Iberian kingdoms, see C. Jago, "Habsburg Absolutism and the Cortes of Castile," *AHR* 86, no. 2 (April 1981), 307–26; and J. B. Owens, *"By My Absolute Royal Authority": Justice and the Castilian Commonwealth at the Beginning of the First Global Age* (Rochester UP, 2005); Regina Grafe, "Economic and Social Trends," in *The Oxford Handbook of Early Modern European History, 1350–1750*, vol. 1, *Peoples and Place*, ed. Hamish Scott (OUP, 2015); French, *Born in Blackness*, 237; Pepijn Brandon, "Marxism and the 'Dutch Miracle': The Dutch Republic and the Transition-Debate," *Historical Materialism* 19 (2011): 117–20, 123–28. On manufacturing, see Marcel van der Linden, "Marx and Engels, Dutch Marxism and the 'Model Capitalist Nation of the Seventeenth Century,'" *Science & Society* 61, no. 2 (Summer 1997): 167, 171 (the Marx quote is on 161). See also Jan de Vries, *European Urbanization, 1500–1800* (Methuen, 1984), 39; and William Sewell, "On the Emergence of Capitalism: Marx, Brenner and the Troublesome Case of the Dutch," in *Critical Historical Studies* 11 (Spring 2024), 1–46, esp. 5, 10.

37. See Alfred C. Wood, *A History of the Levant Company* (OUP, 1935); Arthur Williamson, "An Empire to End Empire: The Dynamic of Early Modern British Expansion," *Huntington Library Quarterly* 68, no. 1/2

(March 2005): 227–56; Andrew D. Nicholls, *A Fleeting Empire: Early Stuart Britain and the Merchant Adventurers to Canada* (McGill-Queen's UP, 2010); Rupali Mishra, *A Business of State: Commerce, Politics, and the Birth of the East India Company* (HUP, 2018); Robert Brenner, *Merchants and Revolution: Commercial Change, Political Conflict, and London's Overseas Traders, 1550–1653* (PUP, 1993); Michael G. Moran, *Inventing Virginia: Sir Walter Raleigh and the Rhetoric of Colonization, 1584–1590* (Peter Lang, 2006); Karen Ordahl Kupperman, *The Jamestown Project* (Belknap Press of HUP, 2007); Peter C. Mancall, *Hakluyt's Promise: An Elizabethan's Obsession for an English America* (Yale UP, 2007); Alison Games, *Migration and the Origins of the English Atlantic World* (HUP, 1999); and David Hackett Fischer and James C. Kelly, *Bound Away: Virginia and the Westward Movement* (University of Virginia Press, 2000).

38. Sidney W. Mintz, *Sweetness and Power: The Place of Sugar in Modern History* (Penguin Books, 1986), 32; Maria Luiza Marcílio, "The Population of Colonial Brazil," in *The Cambridge History of Latin America*, vol. 2, *Colonial Latin America*, ed. Leslie Bethell (CUP, 1984), 60; Kenneth G. Kelly, "Entrepots," in *The Historical Encyclopedia of World Slavery*, ed. Junius P. Rodriguez, vol. 1 (ABC-CLIO, 1997), 57; and Anthony Todman, "Goree Island," in Rodriguez, *Historical Encyclopedia of World Slavery*, 1:308.

39. Adam Smith, *An Inquiry into the Nature and Causes of the Wealth of Nations*, vol. 2 (William Allason, J. Maynard, and W. Blair, 1819), 488.

40. Appel, "Why Was There No Capitalism in Early Modern China?," 169.

41. Alexander Anievas and Kerem Nisancioğlu, *How the West Came to Rule: The Geopolitical Origins of Capitalism* (Pluto Press, 2015), 94.

42. Anievas and Nisancioğlu, *How the West Came to Rule*, 115, 117; Eric R. Wolf, *Europe and the People Without History* (University of California Press, 1982), 125; Luisa Piccinno, "Genoa: A City with a Port or a Port City?," in *The Routledge Handbook of Maritime Trade Around Europe, 1300–1600*, ed. Wim Blockmans, Mikhail Krom, and Justyna Wubs-Mrozewics (Routledge, 2017), 162, 165; Kirk, *Genoa and the Sea*, 29; and Moore, "Nature and the Transition from Feudalism to Capitalism," 119.

43. The crisis of feudalism as an impetus for aristocratic elites in the Iberian Peninsula to expand globally is also emphasized by Jerzy Topolski, "Causes of Dualism in the Economic Development of Modern Europe," *Studia Historiae Oeconomicae* 3 (1968): 9; Maurice Dobb, *Studies in the Development of Capitalism* (International Publisher, 1947), 46, 48–49, 60–61, 71; and Anievas and Nisancioğlu, *How the West Came to Rule*, 77, 81. On the effect of the plague pandemic on European populations, see Şevket Pamuk, "The Black Death and the Origins of the 'Great Divergence' Across Europe, 1300–1600," *European Review of Economic History* 11, no. 3 (December 2007): 292, 294, 312; Tomich, "Original Accumulation," 7, 8; and Dobb, *Studies in the Development of Capitalism*, 71. On the crisis of feudalism, see also Immanuel Maurice Wallerstein, *The Modern World-System*, vol. 1, *Capitalist Agriculture and the Origins of the European World-Economy in the Sixteenth Century* (University of California Press, 2011), 21–51. The importance of cities in the early history of capitalism is also emphasized by Fernand Braudel, *Afterthoughts on Material Civilization and Capitalism*, trans. Patricia M. Ranum (Johns Hopkins UP, 1977), 95.

44. Moore, "Nature and the Transition from Feudalism to Capitalism," 109, 116; Jason W. Moore, "Class, Climate & the Great Frontier," unpublished paper, Commodity Frontier Network, June 2021, 9; Wallerstein, *Modern World-System*, 1:33–35; and Dobb, *Studies in the Development of Capitalism*, 70–71.

45. Smith, *Wealth of Nations*, 1:147.

46. Patrick Greenfield, "Story of Cities #6: How Silver Turned Potosí into 'The First City of Capitalism,'" *Guardian*, March 21, 2016; and Lewis Hanke, *The Imperial City of Potosí: An Unwritten Chapter in the History of Spanish America* (Martinus Nijhoff, 1956), 1. By 1650, Potosí had 160,000 inhabitants, making it the largest city in South America. See Brooke Larson, "Andean Communities, Cultures and Markets: The Changing Contours of Ethnicity, Markets and Migration in the Andes," in *Ethnicity, Markets and Migration in the Andes: At the Crossroads of History and Anthropology*, ed. Brooke Larson and Olivia Harris (Duke UP, 1995), 10; Jack Weatherford, *Indian Givers: How the Indians of the Americas Transformed the World* (Crown, 1988), 12–15; Gwendolen Cobb, "Supply and Transportation for the Potosí Mines, 1545–1640," *Hispanic American Historical Review*

29 (1949): 25; P. J. Bakewell, *Silver and Entrepreneurship in Seventeenth-Century Potosí: The Life and Times of Antonio López de Quiroga* (University of New Mexico Press, 1988), 191; Tutino, *Mexican Heartland*, 30–35; Eduardo Galeano, *The Open Veins of Latin America* (Monthly Review Press, 1973), 22; Kenneth Pomeranz and Steven Topik, *The World That Trade Created: Society, Culture and the World Economy, 1400 to the Present* (M. E. Sharpe, 2006), 152; and Moore, "Nature and the Transition from Feudalism to Capitalism," 137. On the theater, see Susana Salgado, *The Teatro Solís: 150 Years of Opera, Concert, and Ballet in Montevideo* (Wesleyan UP, 2003), 4. The quotation comes from the motto in Potosí's coat of arms, granted by Holy Roman Emperor Charles V. See Kris Lane, *Potosí: The Silver City That Changed the World* (University of California Press, 2019), vi.

47. Hanke, *Imperial City of Potosí*, 19; Flynn and Giraldez, "Born with a 'Silver Spoon,'" 201–9; and J. Bohorquez, "Rio de Janeiro and the Silver Mining Economy of Potosi: Trans-Imperial, Global, and Contractual Approaches to South Atlantic Markets (18th Century)," *Almanack* 24 (2020): 17. The conversion rate of silver into US dollars is from November 18, 2023. For these numbers, see Ward Barrett, "World Bullion Flows, 1450–1800," in *The Rise of Merchant Empires: Long-Distance Trade in the Early Modern World, 1350–1750*, ed. J. Tracy (CUP, 1990), 224–25. See also Charles Mann, *1493: Uncovering the New World Columbus Created* (Alfred A. Knopf, 2011), 148, 154.

48. Moore, "Nature and the Transition from Feudalism to Capitalism," 138–39; Peter Bakewell, *Miners of the Red Mountain: Indian Labor in Potosí* (University of New Mexico Press, 1984), 18, 59; Carlos Sempat Assadourian, "The Colonial Economy: The Transfer of the European System of Production to New Spain and Peru," *Journal of Latin American Studies* 24 (1992): 56, 58–59. Mita labor was combined with a form of wage labor known as minga labor. For an excellent discussion of the labor systems in the Potosí mines, see Rossana Barrangán Romano, "Extractive Economy and Institutions? Technology, Labour and Land at Potosí," in *Colonialism, Institutional Change and Shifts in Global Labour Relations*, ed. Karin Hofmeester and Pim de Zwart (Amsterdam UP, 2018), 207–38. See also Mann, *1493*, 142; Kris Lane, *Pillaging the Empire:*

Piracy in the Americas, 1500–1750 (M. E. Sharpe, 1998), 114–16; Nicholas A. Robins, *Mercury, Mining, and Empire: The Human and Ecological Cost of Colonial Silver Mining in the Andes* (Indiana UP, 2011), 59–63; and Tutino, *Mexican Heartland*, 25–40. The estimates of how many people died as a result of the Potosí silver mining complex vary greatly, with some putting the number in the millions. My numbers here reflect the lower estimates. Additionally, a league is assumed to be 4,180 meters in length.

49. Maria M. Ferraz Torrão, "Traite négrière entre les Îles du Cap-vert et l'Amérique espagnole: Formation et développement d'une route commerciale atlantique au seizième siècle," *African Economic History* 39, no. 1 (2011): 7, 14–16, 21, 25; Hall, *Role of Cape Verde Islanders*, 115, 221–22, 238–46, 267–68, 369, 403; Rafael Pérez and Manuel Fernández, "Sevilla y la trata negrera atlántica: Envíos de esclavos desde Cabo Verde a la América española, 1569–1579," in *Estudios de historia moderna en homenaje al Profesor Antonio García-Barquero* (Universidad de Sevilla, 2009), 602–3; Andrés Reséndez, *The Other Slavery: The Uncovered Story of Indian Enslavement in America* (Houghton Mifflin Harcourt, 2016), 78; Germano Almeida, *Cabo Verde: Viagem pela história das ilhas* (Editorial Caminho, 2004), 171–92; Hall, *Role of Cape Verde Islanders*, 235–37; Maria João Soares, "The British Presence on the Cape Verdean Archipelago (Sixteenth to Eighteenth Centuries)," *African Economic History* 39, no. 1 (2011): 130–31, 142; and Alberto Vieira, "Las islas: Navegación y economía en el Atlántico en los siglos XV y XVI," in *Islas y sistemas de navegación durante las Edades Media y Moderna*, ed. Adela Fábregas (La Nao, 2010), 193.

50. Joseph C. Miller, "Captives, Collateral, Credit, and Currencies: Slaves and the Debt Financing of the Atlantic World," unpublished paper, McGill University, Montreal, May 2009, 20. See also Hall, *Role of Cape Verde Islanders*, 632–33.

51. Tutino, *Mexican Heartland*; F. P. Braudel and F. Spooner, "Prices in Europe from 1450 to 1750," in *The Cambridge Economic History of Europe*, vol. 4, *The Economy of Expanding Europe in the Sixteenth and Seventeenth Centuries*, ed. E. E. Rich and C. H. Wilson (University of Cambridge Press, 1967), 448, 449; Flynn and Giraldez, "Born with a 'Silver Spoon,'" 207; Braudel, *Civilization and Capitalism*, 2:393; Ulrich

Ufer, *Welthandelszentrum Amsterdam: Globale Dynamik und modernes Leben im 17. Jahrhundert* (Boehlau Verlag, 2008), 51; Z. P. Pach, "The East-Central European Aspect of the Overseas Discoveries and Colonialization," *Vierteljahreshefte für Sozial- und Wirtschaftsgeschichte, Beihefte* 89 (1990): 184; and Frank Uekötter, *Im Strudel: Eine Umweltgeschichte der modernen Welt* (Campus, 2020), 29.

52. Guillaume Thomas Raynal, *Histoire philosophique et politique des établissements et du commerce des Européens dans les deux Indes*, ed. Anthony Strugnell et al., vol. 5 (CIE XVIII, 2010), ch. 33, §10. The translation is from Elizabeth Helen Cross, "The French East India Company and the Politics of Commerce in the Revolutionary Era" (PhD diss., Harvard University, 2017), 47.

53. Findlay and O'Rourke, *Power and Plenty*, 214; Jan de Vries, "Connecting Europe and Asia: A Quantitative Analysis of the Cape-Route Trade, 1497–1795," in *Global Connections and Monetary History, 1470–1800*, ed. Dennis O. Flynn, Arturo Giraldez, and Richard van Glahn (Ashgate, 2003), 82; Mann, *1493*, 148, 154; Dennis Owen Flynn and Arthuro Giraldez, "Cycles of Silver: Global Economic Unity Through the Mid-Eighteenth Century," *Journal of World History* 13, no. 2 (September 2002): 399, 400.

54. Findlay and O'Rourke, *Power and Plenty*, 216, 221, 224–25; Machado, *Ocean of Trade*, 3, 28; Flynn and Giraldez, "Born with a 'Silver Spoon,'" 202, 203; John Tutino, *Making a New World: Founding Capitalism in the Bajío and Spanish North America* (Duke UP, 2011), 19. There was also American gold, especially from Brazil. By the 1730s, two-thirds of global gold production came from Brazil. Gold was especially important to English economic development, as it stabilized the Bank of England and eventually formed the basis for the gold standard. See Marques and Marquese, "Gold, Coffee, and Slaves," 6–7, 12, 14, 15; and John J. TePaske, *A New World of Gold and Silver* (Brill, 2010), 49.

55. The quote is translated from German, as cited in Kurt Schottmueller, "Reiseeindrücke aus Danzig, Lübeck, Hamburg und Holland, 1636," *Zeitschrift des Westpreussischen Geschichtsverein* 52 (1910): 259. On the number of inhabitants, see Richard Paping, "General Dutch Population Development, 1400–1850: Cities and Countryside," paper presented at the first ESHD conference, Alghero,

Italy, 2014, 13. See also Hubert Nusteling, "La population d'Amsterdam de la fin du XVIe siècle au début du XIXe siècle. Une méthode de reconstitution," *Population* 6 (1986): 961–77; and A. M. van der Woude, "Population Developments in the Northern Netherlands (1500–1800) and the Validity of the 'Urban Graveyard' Effect," *Annales de démographie historique* (1982): 55–75.

56. The quotes are translated from German and come from Schottmueller, "Reiseeindrücke aus Danzig, Lübeck, Hamburg und Holland," 259–60.

57. The first quote is translated from German and comes from Schottmueller, "Reiseeindrücke aus Danzig, Lübeck, Hamburg und Holland," 261. The second is translated from Dutch and cited in Sven Veldhuijzen, *Spiegel van Mijn Leven, een Haags Dagboek uit 1624* (Hilversum, 1993), 280.

58. Oscar Gelderblom, *Cities of Commerce: The Institutional Foundations of International Trade in the Low Countries, 1250–1650* (PUP, 2013), 15.

59. Jonathan Israel, *Dutch Primacy in World Trade, 1585–1740* (Clarendon Press, 1989), 6, 12; Ufer, *Welthandelszentrum Amsterdam*, 23. See also Findlay and O'Rourke, *Power and Plenty*, 176; and Gelderblom, *Cities of Commerce*, 37.

60. Ufer, *Welthandelszentrum Amsterdam*, 68, 156, 281; Peter Burke, *Venice and Amsterdam: A Study of Seventeenth-Century Elites* (Temple Smith, 1974), 40–55; Paul Spies et al., *Het Grachtenboek* (SDU, 1992), 277; and Israel, *Dutch Primacy in World Trade*, 60–67.

61. Gelderblom, *Cities of Commerce*, 200; Ufer, *Welthandelszentrum Amsterdam*, 111, 142, 149, 113, 232–36; and Brandon, "Marxism and the 'Dutch Miracle,'" 107.

62. Translated from Dutch, the quote comes from Adriaan Koerbagh, introduction to *Een Bloemhof van allerley Lieflijkheyd sonder verdriet* (Amsterdam, 1668), 5v.

63. Max Weber, *Wirtschaftsgeschichte* (Duncker & Humblot, 1923), 256. The same argument is also made by Anievas and Nisancioğlu, *How the West Came to Rule*, 169. See also Daron Acemoglu, Simon Johnson, and James Robinson, "The Rise of Europe: Atlantic Trade, Institutional Change, and Economic Growth," *American Economic Review* 95, no. 3 (June 2005): 550.

64. Acemoglu, Johnson, and Robinson, "Rise of Europe," 546, 548. This is also argued by Jeffrey D. Sachs. "From the start," he says,

"trade, warfare, and colonialization were inextricably linked." See Jeffrey D. Sachs, *The Ages of Globalization: Geography, Technology, and Institutions* (CUP, 2019), 107, 110.

65. As Stanziani also emphasizes, institutions are not just the result of purely economic responses but also of "power and values." See Alessandro Stanziani, *Labor on the Fringes of Empire: Voice, Exit and the Law* (Palgrave Macmillan, 2018), 34. See also Marie-Laure Djelic, "When Limited Liability Was (Still) an Issue: Mobilizaton and Politics of Signification in 19th-Century England," *Organization Studies* 34, no. 5/6 (2013): 3.

66. Braudel, *Civilization and Capitalism*, 2:439, 453; Ann M. Carlos and Stephen Nicholas, "Theory and History: Seventeenth-Century Joint-Stock Chartered Trading Companies," *JEH* 56, no. 4 (1996): 917; Nicholas Kyriazis and Theodore Metaxas, "Path Dependence, Change and the Emergence of the First Joint-Stock Companies," *Business History* 53, no. 3 (2011): 364; Huw Bowen, "Making Money, Making Empires: The Case of the East India Company," in *An Introduction to the History of Capitalism, 600–1900 AD*, ed. Benedikt Koehler et al., (Legatum Institute, 2014), 32.

67. Edmund Burke, *Burke's Speech at the Impeachment of Warren Hastings*, vol. 1 ("Bangabasi" Press, 1909), 21. On EIC trade, see William Dalrymple, *The Anarchy: The Relentless Rise of the East India Company* (Bloomsbury, 2019), 3.

68. Thomas Cochran, "The Business Revolution," *AHR* 79, no. 1 (1977): 449–50; Alfred D. Chandler Jr., *The Visible Hand* (Harvard Belknap, 1977), 240–50; K. N. Chaudhuri, "The English East India Company in the 17th and 18th Centuries: A Premodern Multinational Organization," in *Companies and Trade: Essays on Overseas Trading Companies During the Ancien Régime*, ed. P. H. Boulle, L. Blussé, and F. Gaastra (Leiden UP, 1981), 29–46; Ann M. Carlos and Stephen Nicholas, "'Giants of an Earlier Capitalism': The Chartered Trading Companies as Modern Multinationals," *Business Historical Review* 62, no. 3 (Autumn 1988): 398–419; Kyriazis and Metaxas, "Path Dependence, Change and the Emergence of the First Joint-Stock Companies," 365; Findlay and O'Rourke, *Power and Plenty*, 272; Chris Nierstrasz, *Rivalry for Trade in Tea and Textiles: The English and Dutch East India Companies, 1700–1800* (Palgrave Macmillan, 2015), 6, 8; and Braudel,

Civilization and Capitalism, 2:448; Peter J. Cain and Anthony Gerald Hopkins, *British Imperialism, 1688–2000*, 2nd ed. (Longman, 2002), 88.

69. Henk den Heijer, *The VOC and the Exchange* (Euronext, 2002); Oscar Gelderblom and Joost Jonker, "Completing a Financial Revolution: The Finance of the Dutch East India Trade and the Rise of the Amsterdam Capital Market, 1595–1612," *JEH* 64, no. 3 (September 2004): 641–72; N. Steensgaard, "The Dutch East India Company as an Institutional Innovation," in *Dutch Capitalism and World Capitalism*, ed. M. Aymard (CUP, 1982), 235–57; and Kyriazis and Metaxas, "Path Dependence, Change and the Emergence of the First Joint-Stock Companies," 369. These figures represent not annual payments but payments made over time. See Lodewijk Petram, *The World's First Stock Exchange* (Columbia Business School Press, 2014), 49, 112. See also Ufer, *Welthandelszentrum Amsterdam*, 53, 87–88; and Findlay and O'Rourke, *Power and Plenty*, 182.

70. Petram, *World's First Stock Exchange*, 13, 31, 240; John Bruce, *Annals of the Honorable East-India Company, from Their Establishment by the Charter of Queen Elizabeth, 1600, to the Union of the London and English East-India Companies, 1707–8* (London: Black, Parry, and Kingsbury, 1810), 28; Oscar Gelderblom, Abe de Jong, and Joost Jonker, "The Formative Years of the Modern Corporation: The Dutch East India Company VOC, 1602–1623," *JEH* 73, no. 4 (2013): 1054, 1056, fig. 1.

71. Petram, *World's First Stock Exchange*, 57, 238, 241; Ranald Michie, *The London Stock Exchange: A History* (OUP, 2001), 2–3, 16, 18.

72. Gelderblom, *Cities of Commerce*, 207.

73. On the centrality of family, see also Eva Illouz, *The End of Love: A Sociology of Negative Relations* (OUP, 2019), 60; David Herlihy, "The Family," in *Women, Family, and Society in Medieval Europe: Historical Essays 1978–1991*, ed. Anthony Molho (Berghahn Books, 1995), 113–34; David Herlihy, *Medieval Households* (HUP, 1985); Ralph A. Houlbrooke, *The English Family, 1450–1700* (Longman, 1984), 52; Jack Goody, *The Development of the Family and Marriage in Europe* (CUP, 1983), 136–37; Charles Donahue Jr., "The Canon Law on the Formation of Marriage and Social Practice in the Later Middle Ages," *Journal of Family History* 8, no. 2 (1983): 144–58; James A. Brundage, *Law, Sex, and*

Christian Society in Medieval Europe (University of Chicago Press, 2009), 606–7; Sara McDougall, *Royal Bastards: The Birth of Illegitimacy, 800–1230* (OUP, 2017); Conor McCarthy, *Marriage in Medieval England: Law, Literature, and Practice* (Boydell Press, 2004), 126–39; Linda E. Mitchell, *Family Life in the Middle Ages* (Greenwood, 2007); and Angeliki Laiou, "Family Structure and the Transmission of Property," in *The Social History of Byzantium*, ed. John Haldon (Wiley-Blackwell, 2009), 51–75.

74. Marjolein van den Boogaard, *Maria Jacoba Daemen, 1658–1733: Koopvrouw te Amsterdam* (Universiteit van Amsterdam, 1979), 1, 5, 9. For the quotation, see Julia Adams, *The Familial State: Ruling Families and Merchant Capitalism in Early Modern Europe* (Cornell UP, 2005), 91.

75. Torquato Tasso, *Discorso della virtù feminile e donnesca*, ed. Maria Luisa Doglio (Sellerio, 1997), 56–57.

76. An excellent example of institutional change designed to privilege a small group of traders is the Republic of Venice. See Diego Puga and Daniel Trefler, "International Trade and Institutional Change: Medieval Venice's Response to Globalization," *Quarterly Journal of Economics* 129, no. 2 (May 2014): 753–821; Douglass North, *Institutions, Institutional Change, and Economic Performance* (CUP, 1990), 73–78; and Wallerstein, *Modern World-System*, 1:123–28. For the case of Venice, see also Roberto Lopez, *The Commercial Revolution of the Middle Ages, 950–1350* (CUP, 1976), 100–110; Frederic Lane, *Venice: A Maritime Republic* (Johns Hopkins UP, 1973), 135–45; and Gino Luzzatto, *An Economic History of Italy: From the Fall of the Roman Empire to the Beginning of the Sixteenth Century* (Barnes & Noble, 1961), 220–25.

77. Adam Smith, *An Inquiry into the Nature and Causes of the Wealth of Nations*, vol. 2, book 3 (MetaLibri Digital Library, 2007), 441.

78. Peer Vries, "Does Wealth Entirely Depend on Inclusive Institutions and Pluralist Politics?," *Tijdschrift voor sociale en economische geschiedis* 9, no. 2 (2012): 76, 91; Smith, *Wealth of Nations*, 2:441; Sophus A. Reinert and Robert Fredona, "Merchants and the Origins of Capitalism," Harvard Business School Working Paper No. 18-021 (September 2017), 21.

79. This argument is made forcefully by Philipp R. Rössner, "New Inroads into Well-Known Territory? On the Virtues of Re-Discovering Pre-Classical Political Economy," in

Economic Growth and the Origins of Modern Political Economy, ed. Philipp R. Rössner (Routledge, 2016), 4; Jan de Vries and Ad van der Woude, *The First Modern Economy: Success, Failure, and Perseverance of the Dutch Economy, 1500–1815* (CUP, 1997), 90–105; and Wallerstein, *Modern World-System*, 1:125–30.

80. Thomas Munn, *A Discourse of Trade, from England unto the East-Indies, 1621*, as cited in Sophus A. Reinert, *Translating Empire: Emulation and the Origins of Political Economy* (HUP, 2011), 17.

81. Braudel, *Afterthoughts on Material Civilization*, 64. Essentially the same argument can be found in Karl Polanyi, *The Great Transformation: The Political and Economic Origins of Our Time* (Beacon Press, 2001), 39, 71.

82. Sachs, *Ages of Globalization*, 115; Gelderblom, *Cities of Commerce*, 9, 78, 139; Petram, *World's First Stock Exchange*, 107; Aryeh Shmuelevitz, *The Jews of the Ottoman Empire in the Late 15th and 16th Centuries* (Brill, 1984), 148–55; Halil İnalcık and Donald Quataert, *An Economic and Social History of the Ottoman Empire*, vol. 1, *1300–1914* (CUP, 1997), 267; Helen Julia Paul, "Suppliers to the Royal African Company and the Royal Navy in the Early Eighteenth Century," in *War, Entrepreneurs, and the State in Europe and the Mediterranean, 1300–1800*, ed. Jeff Flynn-Paul (Brill, 2014), 131; Braudel, *Civilization and Capitalism*, 2:443; and Abraham L. Udovitch, *Partnership and Profit in Medieval Islam* (PUP, 1970), 86–96.

83. There is a lively scholarly debate on this issue. Acemoglu and Robinson argue strongly for the importance of institutions, as does Niall Ferguson. See Acemoglu and Robinson, *Why Nations Fail* (Crown, 2012), 429–30; Ferguson, *Civilization* (Allen Lane, 2011), 13. Various critiques come from, among others, Jeffery G. Williamson, *Trade and Poverty: When the Third World Fell Behind* (Massachusetts Institute of Technology Press, 2011), 191; Vries, "Does Wealth Entirely Depend on Inclusive Institutions and Pluralist Politics?"; Patrick O'Brien, "Was the First Industrial Revolution a Conjuncture in the History of the World Economy?," Economic History Working Paper No. 259/2017 (London School of Economics and Political Science, March 2017), 24; and David Graeber and David Wengrow, *The Dawn of Everything: A New History of Humanity* (Farrar, Straus and Giroux, 2021), 374–85; 479–500.

84. Ironically, historians of India have charted a long history of secure and well-defined property rights on the subcontinent. See Parthasarathi, *Why Europe Grew Rich and Asia Did Not*, 5, 65; and Julian Hoppit, "Compulsion, Compensation and Property Rights in Britain, 1688–1833," *Past & Present* 210, no. 1 (February 2011): 93, 99–100, 102, 108.

85. Timothy Brook, "Communications and Commerce," in *The Cambridge History of China*, vol. 8, *The Ming Dynasty, 1368–1644*, part 2, ed. Denis Twitchett and Frederick W. Mote (CUP, 1998), 582; Ruby Maloni, "Europeans in Seventeenth Century Gujarat," *Social Scientist* 36, no. 3/4 (2008): 66, 580; Prasannan Parthasarathi, "State Formation and Economic Growth in South Asia, 1600–1800," in Rössner, *Economic Growth*, 189–203; Sheldon, *Rise of the Merchant Class*, 23–24; Gelderblom, *Cities of Commerce*, 71; Stephen Quinn and William Roberds, "The Big Problem of Large Bills: The Bank of Amsterdam and the Origins of Central Banking," Federal Reserve Bank of Atlanta Working Paper 2005–16 (August 2005), 1–36. See also De Vries and van der Woude, *First Modern Economy*; Charles Goodhart, *The Evolution of Central Banks* (Massachusetts Institute of Technology Press, 1988); and Larry Neal, "How It All Began: The Monetary and Financial Architecture of Europe During the First Global Capital Markets, 1648–1815," *Financial History Review* 7 (October 2000): 121.

86. As cited in Arthur Weststeijn, "The VOC as a Company-State: Debating Seventeenth-Century Dutch Colonial Expansion," *Itinerario* 38, no. 1 (2014): 15. On the desire for monopoly, see also Om Prakash, "Restrictive Trading Regimes: VOC and the Asian Spice Trade in the Seventeenth Century," in *Spices in the Indian Ocean World*, ed. M. N. Pearson (Variorum, 1996), 319.

87. Dobb, *Studies in the Development of Capitalism*, 89; Braudel, *Civilization and Capitalism*, 2:374; Ochonu, "Wangara Factor in West African Business History," 54–55; von Glahn, *The Economic History of China*, 755–56; Wong, "Role of the Chinese State," 6; P. J. A. Guinote, "Ascensão e declínio da carreira da Índia," in *Vasco da Gama e a Índia*, vol. 2 (Fundação Calouste Gulbenkian, 1999), 7–39; M. D. Newitt, *A History of Portuguese Overseas Expansion, 1400–1668* (Routledge, 2005), 70; Israel, *Dutch Primacy in World Trade*, 16–17; Eduardo Lemaitre, *A Brief History of Cartagena* (Compania

Litografica Nacional S.A., 1994), 30; Rodolfo Segovia, *The Fortifications of Cartagena de Indias* (Ancora Editores, 2009), 130; and Susannah Ferreira, *The Crown, the Court and the Casa da Índia: Political Centralization in Portugal 1479–1521* (Brill, 2015), 169. For the general history of *consulados*, see R. S. Smith, *The Spanish Guild Merchant: A History of the Consulado, 1250–1700* (Octagon Books, 1972), 95.

88. O'Brien, "Was the First Industrial Revolution a Conjuncture in the History of the World Economy?," 8, 23; Findlay and O'Rourke, *Power and Plenty*, 247.

89. Thomas Hobbes, *Leviathan*, ed. Richard Tuck (CUP, 1996), 7.

90. Gaetano Filangieri, *Science of Legislation*, as cited in Reinert, *Translating Empire*, 28.

91. David Hume, *Of Civil Liberty*, as cited in Knud Haakonssen, *Hume: Political Essays* (CUP, 1994), 52, 94.

92. On political economy, see the brilliant Reinert, *Translating Empire*, 4. On wealth and the nation-state, this argument is made forcefully by Rössner, "New Inroads into Well-Known Territory?," 13; and Philip J. Stern and Carl Wennerlind, eds., introduction to *Mercantilism Reimagined: Political Economy in Early Modern Britain and Its Empire* (OUP, 2014), 7.

93. Hall and McClain, *Cambridge History of Japan*, 59–60; Sheldon, *Rise of the Merchant Class*, 10; Edmund Morgan, *American Slavery, American Freedom* (W. W. Norton, 1975), 189, 193; Parthasarathi, *Why Europe Grew Rich*, 185; Charles Tilly, *Coercion, Capital, and European States, AD 990–1990* (B. Blackwell, 1990); and Braudel, *Civilization and Capitalism*, 2:444.

94. Ochonu, "Wangara Factor in West African Business History," 59; and Cornelia Giesing and Valentin Vydrine, eds., *Ta:rikh Mandinka de Bijini (Guinée-Bissau): La mémoire des Mandinka et des Sòoninkee du Kaabu* (Brill, 2007).

95. Sheldon, *Rise of the Merchant Class*, 134.

96. A related argument is made by Harman, "From Feudalism to Capitalism," 44–46. See also Sheldon, *Rise of the Merchant Class*, 75; Yazdani, *India, Modernity and the Great Divergence*, 409, 527–35; Chhaya Goswami, *Globalization Before Its Time: The Gujarati Merchants from Kachchh* (London, 2016); Sanjay Subrahmanyam and C. A. Bayly, "Portfolio Capitalists and the Political Economy of Early Modern India," in *Merchants, Markets and the State in Early Modern India*, ed. Sanjay Subrahmanyam (OUP, 1990), 242; Machado, *Ocean of Trade*, 271; and Pepijn Brandon, *War, Capital, and the Dutch State (1558–1795)* (Brill, 2015), 30, 31.

97. Parthasarathi, *Why Europe Grew Rich*, 55–56. On the centralized monarchy, see "Douglass C. North, "Institutions and Economic Growth: An Historical Introduction," *World Development* 17, no. 9 (1989): 1328. For recent writings on the Spanish state, see the terrific article by Alejandra Irigoin and Regina Grafe, "Bargaining for Absolutism: A Spanish Path to Nation-State and Empire Building," *Hispanic American Historical Review* 88, no. 2 (2008): 173–209. The quote is on p. 176. See also Julia McClure, "Rethinking the Historic Models of the Role of Constitutions in Shaping Patterns of Inequality," in *Markets, Constitutions, and Inequality*, ed. A. Chadwick, E. Lozano-Rodriguez, A. Palacios-Lleras, and J. Solana (Routledge, 2023), 142–55; Julia McClure, *Empire of Poverty: The Moral-Political Economy of the Spanish Empire* (OUP, 2024); and H. V. Bowen, et al., "Forum: The Contractor State, c. 1650 to 1815," *International Journal of Maritime History* 25, no. 1 (June 2013): 260.

98. The quote, translated from French, comes from Ferdinand Verbiest, "Dédicace à Louis XIV," as cited in Antonella Romano, *Impressions de Chine: L'Europe et l'englobement du monde* (Fayard, 2016), 289.

99. Wong, "Role of the Chinese State in Long-Distance Commerce," 14–15.

100. Chaudhuri, *Trade and Civilisation*, 208; Appel, "Why Was There No Capitalism in Early Modern China?," 167, 172; R. Bin Wong, *China Transformed: Historical Change and the Limits of European Experience* (Cornell UP, 1997), 146–47; Wong, "Role of the Chinese State in Long-Distance Commerce," 17; Peer Vries, *State, Economy and the Great Divergence: Great Britain and China, 1680s–1850s* (Bloomsbury Academic Press, 2015), 234.

101. "Europe's true superiority," argues historian Jürgen Osterhammel, "was shown in the dynamism of its expansion." See Jürgen Osterhammel, *Unfabling the East: The Enlightenment's Encounter with Asia* (PUP, 2018), 59. See also Peer Vries, "Economic Reasons of State in Qing China," in *Economic Growth and the Origins of Modern Political Economy*, ed. Philipp R. Rössner (Routledge, 2016), 204–19. On the developed character of the Chinese bureaucracy, see, for example, R. Bin Wong, "Review Article," *JGH* 11 (2016): 145; Appel, "Why Was There No Capitalism in Early Modern China?," 176, 178, 183, 184; and Andrade, *How Taiwan Became Chinese*, 105–15, 265–90.

102. "窃臣直觅利商海，卖货浙福，与人同利，为国捐business，绝无勾引党贼侵扰事情，此天地神人所共知者。" 采为德《倭变事略·附录》，广文书局，1967，第113页, as cited in 张丽." 从王直和德瑞克的个人命运看16世纪中英两国在对外贸易政策和官商关系上的不同". 海洋史研究 2 (2015): 48–66. Thanks to Dr. Yang Yang for the translation.

103. Wang Gungwu, "Merchants Without Empire: The Hokkien Sojourning Communities," in *The Rise of Merchant Empires: Long Distance Trade in the Early Modern World, 1350–1750*, ed. James D. Tracy (CUP, 1990), 400.

104. Sudev Sheth, *Bankrolling Empire: Family Fortunes and Political Transformation in Mughal India* (CUP, 2024), 21, 25. For the statistic, see Jadunath Sarkar, *Studies in Aurangzeb's Reign* (M. C. Sakar & Sons, 1933), 273; and Andrade, *How Taiwan Became Chinese*, 115–59. For state income and Gujarat, see discussion in Philippe Beaujard, "Gujarat and Long-Distance Trade in the Indian Ocean Region Before the Sixteenth Century," in *Transregional Trade and Traders* (OUP, 2019), 26, 92; Chaudhuri, *Trade and Civilisation*, 210.

105. The importance of that relationship is also emphasized by Banaji, *Brief History of Commercial Capitalism*, 132–33; Jessica Goldberg, *Trade and Institutions in the Medieval Mediterranean: The Geniza Merchants and Their Business World* (CUP, 2012), 12–13, 85–115; Ravi Palat, *The Making of an Indian Ocean World-Economy, 1250–1650* (Palgrave Macmillan, 2015), 9; Pamuk, "Wirtschaft und Institutionen im Nahen Osten seit dem Mittelalter," 560; and Anievas and Nisancioğlu, *How the West Came to Rule*, 105.

106. Anievas and Nisancioğlu, *How the West Came to Rule*, 94–95, 104.

107. Fürstendarlehen, W 1/9: IV, Nos. 61, 54, 56, 62, 63, 53, 59, Bethmann-Archiv, Stadtarchiv Frankfurt, Germany.

108. Andrea Komlosy, "Entanglements of Catching-Up: Rethinking 'Industrial Revolution' from a Global Perspective," *Journal of Globalization Studies* 12, no. 1 (2021): 17; Banaji, *Brief History of Commercial Capitalism*, 120; Robert Kurz, *Weltkrise und Ignoranz: Kapitalismus im Niedergang*

(Tiamat, 2013), 92, 95; Geoffrey Parker, *The Military Revolution: Early Modern Europe and the Rise of the West, 1500–1800* (CUP, 1990), 20; Thomas Piketty, *Capital and Ideology* (HUP, 2020), 370; and Brandon, *War, Capital, and the Dutch State*, 4.

109. Piketty, *Capital and Ideology*, 364; John Brewer, *Sinews of Power: War, Money and the English State, 1688–1783* (CUP, 1989), 40; Findlay and O'Rourke, *Power and Plenty*, 256; O'Brien, "Was the First Industrial Revolution a Conjuncture in the History of the World Economy?," 27; Jeff Fynn-Paul, Marjolein 't Hart, and Griet Vermeesch, "Introduction," in *War, Entrepreneurs, and the State in Europe and the Mediterranean, 1300–1800*, 2; and Bhambra and McClure, *Imperial Inequalities*.

110. Kurz, *Weltkrise und Ignoranz*, 97; Brewer, *Sinews of Power*; William J. Ashworth, "The Ghost of Rostow: Science, Culture and the British Industrial Revolution," *Historical Science* 46, no. 3 (2008): 263. On the Dutch, see Pepijn Brandon, "Accounting for Power: Bookkeeping and the Rationalization of Dutch Naval Administration," in Fynn-Paul, *War, Entrepreneurs, and the State*, 152.

111. The connection between debts and attachment to the state is also observed by Abu-Lughod, *Before European Hegemony*, 114; Christine Desan, *Making Money: Coin, Currency, and the Coming of Capitalism* (OUP, 2014), 295–329; Toby Green, *Fistful of Shells: West Africa from the Rise of the Slave Trade to the Age of Revolution* (University of Chicago Press, 2021); and Christine Desan, "The Constitutional Approach to Money: Monetary Design and the Production of the Modern World," in *Money Talks*, ed. Nina Bandelj, Frederick F. Wherry, and Vivianna A. Zelizer (PUP, 2017), 113, 116. For a quick overview of various perspectives on the history of money, see Andrew David Edwards, "The American Revolution and Christine Desan's New History of Money," *Law & Social Inquiry* 42, no. 1 (Winter 2017): 252–78. On the Caribbean dimensions of that story, see Katherine Smoak, "The Weight of Necessity: Counterfeit Coins in the British Atlantic World, Circa 1760–1800," *William and Mary Quarterly* 74, no. 3 (July 2017): 470. See also Dobb, *Studies in the Development of Capitalism*, 190.

112. Eliyahu Ashtor, *Levant Trade in the Middle Ages* (PUP, 2014), 10; Max Weber, *Economy and Society: An Outline of Interpretive Sociology* (University of California Press, 1978), 353–54; Chaudhuri, *Trade and Civilisation*, 247–49; Reinert and Fredona, "Merchants and the Origins of Capitalism," 12; and Brandon, *War, Capital, and the Dutch State*, 33. The weakness of the early modern European state is also emphasized by Stern and Wennerlind, *Mercantilism Reimagined*, 5. See also Acemoglu, Johnson, and Robinson, "Rise of Europe," 46–79; Giovanni Arrighi, *The Long Twentieth Century: Money, Power, and the Origins of Our Time* (Verso, 2010), 11; Tilly, *Coercion, Capital, and European States*, 58–61; and Vanhaute, "Making Sense of the Great Divergence," 12.

113. Acemoglu, Johnson, and Robinson, "Rise of Europe," 550; Moore, "Nature and the Transition from Feudalism to Capitalism," 155; Gopal, *Commerce and Crafts in Gujarat*, 55; and Tomich, "The Atlantic Slave-Sugar Complex," 22.

114. Gelderblom, *Cities of Commerce*, 142. For quotation, see "Chronicle of Occurrences" in "Naval Affairs," in *The Grand Magazine of Magazines, or Universal Register for the Months of January, February, March, April, May, June 1759*, vol. 2 (London, 1759), 366.

115. Thomas Paine, *Rights of Man: Being an Answer to Mr. Burke's Attack on the French Revolution*, part 2 (CUP, 2011), 89–91.

116. Charles de Secondat Montesquieu, *The Spirit of Laws: Including d'Alembert's Analysis of the Work*, trans. Thomas Nugent (New York: Colonial Press, 1899), 316. See also, more generally, Albert Hirschman, "Rival Views of Market Society," in *The Essential Hirschman*, ed. Jeremy Adelman (PUP, 2013), 214–47.

117. As quoted in H. T. Colenbrander, *Jan Pieterszoon Coen* (Nijhoff Uitgeverij, 1934), 64.

118. NA, VOC, 478, f. 1v, 2v, as quoted in Martine Julia van Ittersum, "Debating Natural Law in the Banda Islands: A Case Study in Anglo-Dutch Imperial Competition in the East Indies, 1609–1621," *History of European Ideas* 42, no. 4 (2016): 465.

119. Israel, *Dutch Primacy in World Trade*, 142; and Petram, *World's First Stock Exchange*, 68.

120. Richard Ehrenberg, *Das Zeitalter der Fugger. Geldkapital und Creditverkehr im 16. Jahrhundert*, vol. 1, *Die Geldmächte des 16. Jahrhunderts* (Gustav Fischer, 1922); Richard Ehrenberg, *Das Zeitalter der Fugger. Geldkapital und Creditverkehr im 16. Jahrhundert*, vol. 2, *Die Weltbörsen und Finanzkrisen des 16. Jahrhunderts* (Gustav Fischer, 1896); and Mark Häberlein, *Die Fugger: Geschichte einer Augsburger Familie (1367–1650)* (W. Kohlhammer, 2006), 96. See also Greg Steinmetz, *The Richest Man Who Ever Lived: The Life and Times of Jacob Fugger* (Simon & Schuster, 2015).

121. Häberlein, *Die Fugger*, 17–20, 54–56; Hartmut Schiele, "Betriebswirtschaftliche Aufschlüsse aus den Fugger-Veröffentlichungen von Götz Freiherrn von Pölnitz," in *Betriebswirtschaftliche Aufschlüsse aus der Fuggerzeit*, ed. Hartmut Schiele and Manfred Ricker (Duncker & Humblot, 1967), 9–13, 16, 18–19; Jacob Streider, ed., *Die Inventur der Firma Fugger aus dem Jahre 1527* (Verlag der Lauppschen Buchhandlung, 1905), 35; Regina Dauser, "Handelsgesellschaften (15. bis 17. Jahrhundert)," *Historisches Lexikon Bayerns*, July 11, 2017, https://www.historisches-lexikon-bayerns.de/Lexikon/Handelsgesellschaften_(15._bis_17._Jahrhundert); Michael North, "Von der Atlantischen Handelexpansion bis zu den Agrarreformen (1450–1815)," in *Deutsche Wirtschaftsgeschichte. Ein Jahrtausend im Überblick*, ed. Michael North (C. H. Beck, 2005), 162; Rolf Walter, "Einleitung: Oberdeutsche Kaufleute und Genuesen in Sevilla und Cadiz (1525–1560)," in *Oberdeutsche Kaufleute in Sevilla und Cadiz (1525–1560): Eine Edition von Notariatsakten aus den dortigen Archiven*, ed. Hermann Kellenbenz and Rolf Walter (Franz Steiner, 2001), 14. Ehrenberg, *Das Zeitalter der Fugger*, 1:149; Peter Geffcken, "Jakob Fugger der Reiche (1459–1525): 'Königsmacher, Stratege und Organisator," *Damals: Das Magazin für Geschichte* 36, no. 7 (2004): 14–24; Götz von Pölnitz, *Jakob Fugger: Kaiser, Kirche und Kapital in der Oberdeutschen Renaissance*, vol. 1 (J. C. B. Mohr [Paul Siebeck], 1949); Hermann Kellenbenz, "Jakob Fugger der Reiche (1459–1525)," in *Lebensbilder aus dem Bayerischen Schwaben*, vol. 10, ed. Wolfgang Zorn (Konrad, 1973), 35–76; Johannes Burkhardt, ed., *Anton Fugger 1493–1560: Das fünfhundertjährige Jubiläum. Vorträge und Dokumentation* (Anton H. Konrad, 1994); Hermann Kellenbenz, "Anton Fugger (1493–1560)," in *Lebensbilder aus dem Bayerischen Schwaben*, ed. Adolf Layer, vol. 11 (Konrad, 1976), 46–124; and Götz von Pölnitz and Hermann Kellenbenz, *Anton Fugger: Persönlichkeit und Werk* (J. C. B. Mohr [Paul Siebeck], 1958). Fugger's wealth translates into more than half a billion contemporary

(2023) US dollars. Hermann Kellenbenz has suggested an acceptable method for translation by taking the gold content of 1 Rhenish guilder as a basis. There were 2.527 grams of gold per Rhenish guilder in 1495 and 2.504 in 1557. If we take an approximate value of 2.5 grams of gold, five million guilders would have been approximately 12,500 kilograms of gold. The current gold price (December 2024) is about $84,000 per kilogram, which makes a sum of approximately $1.05 billion US dollars.
122. Geffcken, "Jakob Fugger der Reiche," 35; and Häberlein, *Die Fugger*, 26–27, 49.
123. Reinhard Hildebrandt, *Die 'Georg Fuggerischen Erben': Kaufmännische Tätigkeit und sozialer Status 1555–1600* (Duncker & Humblot, 1966), 84–85; North, "Von der Atlantischen Handelexpansion," 34–45; Häberlein, *Die Fugger*, 46–56, 112; Hermann Kellenbenz, *Die Fugger in Spanien und Portugal bis 1560: Ein Großunternehmen des 16. Jahrhunderts* (Ernst Vögel, 1990), 158, 166, 394–95; and Wolfgang Reinhard, *Parasit oder Partner? Europäische Wirtschaft und Neue Welt 1500–1800* (LIT, 1997), 27. A list of modern production sites referenced can be found at E. Schremmer, "Handel und Gewerbe bis zum Beginn des Merkantilismus," in *Handbuch der Bayerischen Geschichte*, ed. Andreas Kraus, vol. 2, *Geschichte Schwabens bis zum Ausgang des 18. Jahrhunderts* (C. H. Beck, 2001), 550; and Mark A. Denzel, "Eine Handelspraktik aus dem Hause Fugger (erste Hälfte des 16. Jahrhunderts). Ein Werkstattbericht," in *Kaufmannsbücher und Handelspraktiken vom Spätmittelalter bis zum beginnenden 20. Jahrhundert / Merchant's Books and Mercantile Pratice from the Late Middle Ages to the Beginning of the 20th Century*, ed. Markus A. Denzel, Jean-Claude Hocquet, and Harald Witthöft (Franz Steiner, 2002), 132 (map 1). See also Regina Dauser, *Informationskultur und Beziehungswissen: Das Korrespondenznetz Hans Fuggers (1531–1598)* (Max Niemeyer, 2008); Beatrix Bastl, *Das Tagebuch des Philipp Eduard Fugger (1560–1569) als Quelle zur Fuggergeschichte* (J. C. B. Mohr [Paul Siebeck], 1987), 252–55; and Franz Karg, "Hans Fugger wird 'Regierer' der Fuggerschen Firma," in *Die Welt des Hans Fugger (1531–1598)*, ed. Johannes Burkhardt and Franz Karg (Wißner, 2007), 133.
124. Katarina Sieh-Burens, *Oligar-

chie, Konfession und Politik im 16. Jahrhundert. Zur Sozialen Verflechtung der Augsburger Bürgermeister und Stadtpfleger 1518–1618* (Vögel, 1986), 94; Stephanie Haberer, *Ott Heinrich Fugger (1592–1644): Biographische Analyse typologischer Handlungsfelder in der Epoche des Dreißigjährigen Krieges* (Wißner, 2004), 5, 18, 104–7; Kellenbenz, *Die Fugger in Spanien und Portugal*, 12; Martha Schad, *Die Frauen des Hauses Fugger von der Lilie (15.–17. Jahrhundert): Augsburg–Ortenburg–Trient* (J. C. B. Mohr [Paul Siebeck], 1989), esp. chap. 2 (provides detailed insight into the matrimonial policy of the Fuggers); Hildebrandt, *Die Georg Fuggerischen Erben*, 102–21; Carlos Álvarez Nogal, "Banqueros alemanes de Felipe IV: Los Fugger jóvenes y Julio César Scazuola (1618–1641)," *Studia Historica: Historia Moderna* 39, no. 1 (2017): 265–99; Häberlein, *Die Fugger*, 26, 48–52, 65, 89, 188; and Götz von Pölnitz, *Fugger und Medici: Deutsche kaufleute und handwerker in Italien* (Koehler & Amelang, 1942). For a general approach to this topic, see especially Peter Rauscher, Andrea Serles, and Thomas Winkelbauer, eds., *Das 'Blut des Staatskörpers': Forschungen zur Finanzgeschichte der Frühen Neuzeit* (Oldenbourg, 2012); Edelmayer, Lanzinner, and Rauscher, *Finanzen und Herrschaft*; Peter Rauscher, *Zwischen Ständen und Gläubigern: Die kaiserlichen Finanzen unter Ferdinand I. und Maximilian II. (1556–1576)* (Oldenbourg, 2004); North, "Von der Atlantischen Handelexpansion," 164; Schiele, "Betriebswirtschaftliche Aufschlüsse," 12, 23. See also Haberer, *Ott Heinrich Fugger*, 103; Mark Häberlein, "Handelshäuser," Europäische Geschichte Online (EGO), November 14, 2016, https://ieg-ego.eu/de/threads/europaeische-netzwerke/wirtschaftliche-netzwerke/mark-haeberlein-handelshaeuser; Peter Rauscher, "La Casa de Austria y sus anqueros lemanes," in *Carlos V: Europeismo y universalidad: Congreso internacional, Granada, mayo de 2000*, vol. 3, *Los escenarios del imperio*, coord. Juan Luis Castellano Castellano and Francisco Sánchez-Montes González (Sociedad Estatal para la Conmemoración de los Centenarios de Felipe II y Carlos V, 2001), 413–14; and Mark Häberlein, *Aufbruch ins Globale Zeitalter: Die Handelswelt der Fugger und Welser* (Theiss, 2016), 134. For a general approach to the relation between Charles V and his financiers, see Ramón Carande,

Carlos V y sus banqueros (Crítica, 2004). Anton Fugger's role as court factor or finance minister is discussed in Johannes Burkhardt, "Jubiläumsvortrag Anton Fugger," in *Anton Fugger 1493–1560: Das fünfhundertjährige Jubiläum. Vorträge und Dokumentation*, ed. Johannes Burkhardt, Studien zur Fuggergeschichte 36 (Anton H. Konrad, 1994), 137–50; Alfred Kohler, *Karl V: 1500–1558: Eine Biographie*, 3rd rev. ed. (C. H. Beck, 2005), 148; and Nogal, "Banqueros alemanes de Felipe IV," 265–99.
125. Peter Bakewell with Jacqueline Holler, *A History of Latin America to 1825* (Wiley-Blackwell, 2010), 228; Dennis O. Flynn, "Silver in a Global Context, 1400–1800," in *Cambridge World History*, vol. 6, *The Construction of a Global World, 1400–1800 CE*, ed. Jerry H. Bentley, Sanjay Subrahmanyam, and Merry E. Wiesner-Hanks (CUP, 2015), 226; Stanley J. Stein and Barbara H. Stein, *Silver, Trade, and War: Spain and America in the Making of Early Modern Europe* (Johns Hopkins UP, 2000), 28; Götz von Pölnitz, *Anton Fugger*, vol. 3, *1548–1554* (J. C. B. Mohr (Paul Siebeck) 1971), 292, 295, 326; Häberlein, *Aufbruch ins Globale Zeitalter*, 137; and Kellenbenz, *Die Fugger in Spanien und Portugal*, 387.
126. Michael Diefenbacher and Bertold Haller von Hallerstein, "Welser von Neunhof, Patrizierfamilie," in *Stadtlexikon Nürnberg*, ed. Michael Diefenbacher and Rudolf Endres (W. Tümmels, 2000). The "Upper-German" merchant families were "the most financially sound investors" at the turn of the fifteenth century: See Maximilian Kalus, *Pfeffer–Kupfer–Nachrichten: Kaufmannsnetzwerke und Handelsstrukturen im europäisch-asiatischen Handel am Ende des 16. Jahrhunderts* (Wissner-Verlag, 2010), 11. The merchants "co-shaped the trails and intertwining relations of the world economy and continued along them at the same time": See Rolf Walter, "Was bedeutete Proto-Globalisierung? Auf den Spuren Oberdeutscher Fernhändler in der Frühen Neuzeit," in *Zwischen Stadt, Staat und Nation: Bürgertum in Deutschland*, ed. Stefan Gerber, Werner Greiling, Tobias Kaiser, and Klaus Ries (Vandenhoeck & Ruprecht, 2014), 63. A collective trade between "Bartelme dem Waellser und Hannsen dem Prunen seinem swager" appears in written sources in 1414 and a "Bartlome

Wellsers und seiner gesellschafft aller unser ingesessen burger aigen guot" in 1422. See Peter Geffcken, "Die Welser und ihr Handel 1246–1496," in *Die Welser: Neue Forschungen zur Geschichte und Kultur eines oberdeutschen Handelshauses*, ed. Mark Häberlein and Johannes Burkhardt (Akademie-Verlag: 2002), 68–70. See also Walter, "Was könnte Proto-Globalisierung bedeuten?," 65–67; Magnus Ulrich Ferber, "Welser, Familie," Historisches Lexikon Bayerns, September 5, 2016, https://www.historisches-lexikon-bayerns.de/Lexikon/Welser,_Familie; Häberlein, *Aufbruch ins globale Zeitalter*, 109–11; and Walter, "Einleitung," 30, 54, 59. Walter emphasizes the role of the Welsers along with the Fuggers in regard to their banking business in Seville. Their loan was about 143,000 florins. See E. Schremmer, "Handel und Gewerbe bis zum Beginn des Merkantilismus," in *Handbuch der bayerischen Geschichte*, vol. 2, *Geschichte Schwabens bis zum Ausgang des 18. Jahrhunderts*, ed. Andreas Kraus (C. H. Beck, 2001), 559, 561. At that time, the Welsers were already participating in the saffron trade in Zaragoza and were part of a "purchasing cartel," with the Tuchers, Imhoffs, and Zollikofens of St. Gallen. See Walter, "Einleitung," 29–30, inclusive of note 107. See Jörg Denzer, "Die Welser in Venezuela – Das Scheitern ihrer wirtschaftlichen Ziele," in Häberlein and Burkhardt, *Die Welser*, 290, 292; and Jörg Denzer, *Die Konquista der Augsburger Welser-Gesellschaft in Südamerika (1528–1556): Historische Rekonstruktion, Historiografie und lokale Erinnerungskultur in Kolumbien und Venezuela* (C. H. Beck, 2005), 49–50, 53.

127. Elizabeth Cross, *Company Politics: Commerce, Scandal, and French Visions of Indian Empire in the Revolutionary Era* (OUP, 2023), esp. 101–23; Kellenbenz, *Die Fugger in Spanien und Portugal*, 160–62, 394; Häberlein, *Die Fugger*, 80; Häberlein, *Aufbruch ins Globale Zeitalter*, 130–31; Reinhard, *Parasit oder Partner?*, 27–28; and Denzer, *Die Konquista der Augsburger*, 55–57; Findlay and O'Rourke, *Power and Plenty*, 275; Paul, "Suppliers to the Royal African Company and the Royal Navy in the Early Eighteenth Century," 131–32, 134. See also Brandon, *War, Capital, and the Dutch State*, 2. For the quote, see Meeting 6th and 7th September 1692, 239–40, in Council Minutes, 1689–1696, BNA.

128. Brewer, *Sinews of Power*, 251.

129. James A. Williamson, *Builders of the Empire* (Clarendon Press, 1925), 60.

130. Letter from the King, 15 December 1682, as entered into the Council Minutes, 1684–1689, 177, BNA.

131. Dunn, "Barbados Census of 1680," 6; Lettre de Mr. Duchilleau et Mr. de Marbois au Chambre d'agriculture du Cap, Port-au-Prince, 20 January 1789, in Correspondence Envoyee au Minstre, Counceil Superior de Port-au-Prince, 6 DPPC/4, ANOM.

132. Fynn-Paul, t'Hart, and Vermeesch, "Introduction," 9. See also H. V. Bowen et al., "Forum: The Contractor State, C. 1650 to 1815," *International Journal of Maritime History* 25, no. 1 (June 2013): 239–74; Brandon, *War, Capital, and the Dutch State*, 310–13 (and throughout, showing how brokerage structures remained central to the Dutch state well into the eighteenth century); Charles Ralph Boxer, *The Dutch Seaborne Empire 1600–1800* (Hutchinson, 1960), 69; Tristan Mostert, "Chain of Command: The Military System of the Dutch East India Company, 1655–1663" (MA thesis, Leiden University, 2007), 19; and Stern and Wennerlind, *Mercantilism Reimagined*, 15; and Marcus Rediker, *Villains of all Nations: Atlantic Pirates in the Golden Age* (Verso, 2004).

133. EIC to Fort St. George [hereinafter FSG], 29 February 1683/4, IOR E/3/90 f. 154; EIC to Surat, 7 April 1684, E/3/90 f. 165; EIC to Bengal, 5 March 1683/4, IOR E/3/90 f. 159; EIC to Bengal, 20 June 1683, EIC to Saint Helena, 1 August 1683, and EIC to Saint Helena, 5 August 1684, IOR E/3/90 f. 83, 95, 175–77, as quoted in Philip J. Stern, "Politics and Ideology in the Early East India Company-State: The Case of St Helena, 1673–1709," *Journal of Imperial and Commonwealth History* 35, no. 1 (2007): 4–5; John McAleer, "Looking East: St. Helena, the South Atlantic and Britain's Indian Ocean World," *Atlantic Studies* 13, no. 1 (2016): 78–98; and Opinions of Edward Northey and John Hungerford, 2 and 3 December 1715, IOR H/23 ff. 127–28, as quoted in Stern, "Politics and Ideology," 5. See also Virginia Bever Platt, "The East India Company and the Madagascar Slave Trade," *William and Mary Quarterly* 26, no. 4 (December 1969): 555–56; and Stephen Royle, *The Company's Island: St.*

Helena, Company Colonies and the Colonial Endeavor (I. B. Tauris, 2007), 84–89, 177.

134. Copy of the First Commission of the Government After the Retaking of the Island from the Dutch, 19 December 1673, G/32/1, 3, as quoted in Stern, "Politics and Ideology," 7.

135. "Laws and Ordinances of St. Helena," IOR G/32/1 f. 1, as quoted in Stern, "Politics and Ideology," 8.

136. Stern, "Politics and Ideology," 2.

137. M. Craton, "Property and Propriety: Land Tenure and Slave Property in the Creation of a British West Indian Plantocracy, 1612–1740," in *Early Modern Conceptions of Property*, ed. J. Brewer and S. Staves (Routledge, 1996), 499. See also B. H. McPherson, "Revisiting the Manor of East Greenwich," *American Journal of Legal History* 42, no. 1 (January 1998): 35–56; and the excellent Andrew Phillips and J. C. Sharman, *Outsourcing Empire: How Company-States Made the Modern World* (PUP, 2022).

138. Jane Ohlmeyer, "Eastward Enterprises: Colonial Ireland, Colonial India," in *Past & Present* 240, no. 1 (August 2018): 87; Carl Wennerlind, *Casualties of Credit: The English Financial Revolution, 1620–1720* (HUP, 2011); and Adam Smith, *An Inquiry into the Nature and Causes of the Wealth of Nations*, vol. II, book IV, ed. Edwin Cannan (University of Chicago Press, 1976), 75; Paul Cheney, "Aufklärung und die politische Ökonomie des Kolonialismus," in *Der moderne Staat und "le doux commerce": Politik, Ökonomie und internationale Beziehungen im politischen Denken der Aufklärung*, ed. Olaf Asbach (Nomos, 2014), 207.

139. Nuno Palma and Jaime Reis, "From Convergence to Divergence: Portuguese Economic Growth, 1527–1850," *JEH* 79, no. 2 (June 2019): 477, 478, 499; on the resource flow from the rest of world into parts of Europe, see also Sewell, "On the Emergence of Capitalism," 44.

140. Francesca Trivellato, *The Promise and Peril of Credit: What a Forgotten Legend About Jews and Finance Tells Us About the Making of European Commercial Society* (PUP, 2021), 29, 49–65.

141. Jerry Z. Muller, *The Mind and the Market: Capitalism in Modern European Thought* (Alfred A. Knopf, 2002), 7–8.

142. Juliann Vitullo and Diane Wolfthal, "Trading Values: Negotiating Masculinity in Late Medieval and Early Modern Europe," in

Money, Morality and Culture in Late Medieval and Early Modern Europe, ed. Juliann Vitullo and Diane Wolfthal (Ashgate, 2010), 156f. On the "fruitful and sterile" debate in France, see Bernhard Groethuysen, *The Bourgeois: Catholicism vs. Capitalism in Eighteenth-Century France* (Barrie & Rockliff Press, 1968), 205–14; Odd Langholm, *Economics in the Medieval Schools, Wealth, Exchange, Value, Money and Usury According to the Paris Theologian Tradition 1200–1350* (Brill, 1992); Giacomo Todeschini, "Franciscan Economics and Jews in the Middle Ages: From a Theological to an Economic Lexicon," in *The Friars and Jews in the Middle Ages and Renaissance* (Brill, 2004), 99–117; Julia McClure, "The Globalization of Franciscan Poverty," *Journal of World History* 30, no. 3 (2019): 1–28; and Mark Häberlein, *The Fuggers of Augsburg: Pursuing Wealth and Honor in Renaissance Germany* (University of Virginia Press, 2006), 176, 180f.

143. Matthew 16:19; and Brodie Waddell, *God, Duty and Community in English Economic Life, 1660–1720* (Boydell Press, 2012), 78.

144. Sheldon, *Rise of the Merchant Class*, 133; Donald H. Shively, "Sumptuary Regulation and Status in Early Tokugawa Japan," *Harvard Journal of Asiatic Studies* 25 (1964–65): 125.

145. Abu-Lughod, *Before European Hegemony*, 361; and Arrighi, *Long Twentieth Century*.

146. Acemoglu and Robinson, *Why Nations Fail*.

147. For the quote, see Bernal Diaz del Castillo, *The Conquest of New Spain* (Penguin Books, 1963), 232–34. On Aztec merchants more generally, see David M. Carballo, "Trade Routes in the Americas Before Columbus," in *The Great Trade Routes: A History of Cargo and Commerce over Land and Sea*, ed. Philip Parker (Conway Publishing, 2012), 169; Robert D. Drennan, "Long-Distance Movement of Goods in the Mesoamerican Formative and Classic," *American Antiquity* 49, no. 1 (January 1994): 27–43; Andrew Sluyter, "Long-Distance Staple Transport in Western Mesoamerica: Insights Through Quantitative Modeling," *Ancient Mesoamerica* 4 (1993): 193–99; Fray Diego Durán, *Book of the Gods and Rites and the Ancient Calendar* (University of Oklahoma Press, 1971), 138; and Pomeranz and Topik, *World That Trade Created*, 21.

148. Bas van Bavel, "Land, Lease and Agriculture: The Transition of the Rural Economy in the Dutch River Area from the Fourteenth to the Sixteenth Century," *Past & Present* 172 (August 2001): 3; Yazdani, *India, Modernity and the Great Divergence*, 335; Machado, *Ocean of Trade*, 11; and Tracy, *Rise of Merchant Empires*, 9.

149. Gopal, *Commerce and Crafts in Gujarat*, 59, 61–62; NA, VOC, 1064, f.24–25, Resolution of 6 March 1617, as cited in Van Ittersum, "Debating Natural Law in the Banda Islands," 476; Hardiman, "Penetration of Merchant Capital," 38; and Yazdani, *India, Modernity and the Great Divergence*, 453.

150. Freeman-Grenville, *East African*, 190.

151. Robert O. Collins and James M. Burns, *A History of Sub-Saharan Africa* (CUP, 2007), 189; B. S. Hoyle, *Seaports and Development: The Experience of Kenya and Tanzania* (Routledge, 1983), 63; Mark Horton and John Middleton, *The Swahili: The Social Landscape of a Mercantile Society* (Blackwell, 2000), 24; and Machado, *Ocean of Trade*, 13.

152. Shaykh Zainuddin Makhdum, *Tuhfat al-Mujahidin: A Historical Epic of the Sixteenth Century*, trans. S. Muhammad Husayn Naimar (Other Books, 2006), 5.

153. Makhdum, *Tuhfat al-Mujahidin*, 81.

154. Makhdum, *Tuhfat al-Mujahidin*, 81.

155. Tracy, *Rise of Merchant Empires*, 6; Masters, *Arabs of the Ottoman Empire*, 74; Lisa Blaydes and Christopher Paik, "Muslim Trade and City Growth Before the Nineteenth Century: Comparative Urbanization in Europe, the Middle East and Central Asia," *British Journal of Political Science* 51, no. 2 (2021): 845–68; Abu-Lughod, *Before European Hegemony*, 242–43; and J. Meloy, *Imperial Power and Maritime Trade: Mecca and Cairo in the Late Middle Ages* (Middle East Documentation Center, 2015), 219.

156. Smith, *An Inquiry*, 2:601.

157. As quoted in Chaudhuri, *Trade and Civilisation*, 113.

158. Hardiman, "Penetration of Merchant Capital," 35. For this argument, see also Banaji, *Brief History of Commercial Capitalism*, 41; Abu-Lughod, *Before European Hegemony*, 20, 243, 272, 275–76, 361; Ashin Das Gupta, *Indian Merchants and the Decline of Surat, c. 1700–1750* (Franz Steiner Verlag, 1967), 7–9; and Chaudhuri, *Trade and Civilisation*, 113.

159. Abu-Lughod, *Before European Hegemony*, 18; Barendse, *Arabian Sea*, 8.

160. K. H. O'Rourke and J. G. Williamson, "After Columbus: Explaining the Global Trade Boom, 1500–1800," NBER Working Paper No. 8186 (March 2001), 3, 32–33; and Braudel, *Civilization and Capitalism*, 2:601. John Tutino makes essentially the same argument. See Tutino, *Making a New World*, 2. See also Polanyi, *Great Transformation*, 45; Bartolomé Yun, *Marte contra Minerva: El Precio del Imperio Español, c. 1450–1600* (Crítica, 2004), 150; and Findlay and O'Rourke, *Power and Plenty*, 226.

161. Lia Markey, *Imagining the Americas in Medici Florence* (University of Chicago Press, 2016); Machado, *Ocean of Trade*, 61, 64; Robert Brenner, *The Economics of Global Turbulence: A Special Report on the World Economy, 1950–1998* (Verso, 2006); and Wallerstein, *Modern World-System*, vol 1. Dutch capital played a significant role in international production and industrialization, including in Java, the West Indies, and the UK. See Häberlein, *Die Fugger*, 77; Douglas Catterall, "Metropolitan Locales, Global Commerce, and East Indies Capital and Credit in the Eighteenth Century," *JGH* 12, no. 1 (2017): 95, 114.

162. Felicia Gottman, "Do Merchants Have No Country?," unpublished paper (in author's possession), Harvard Business School, October 21, 2019; Felicia Gottman, "Prussia All at Sea? The Emden-Based East India Companies and the Challenges of Transnational Enterprise in the Eighteenth Century," *Journal of World History* 31, no. 2 (2020), 539–66; Sewell, "On the Emergence of Capitalism," 10.

163. Fernand Braudel, "European Expansion and Capitalism, 1450–1650," in *Chapters in Western Civilization*, ed. Contemporary Civilization Staff of Columbia College, Columbia University (CUP, 1961), 260; B. W. Higman, "The Sugar Revolution," *EHR* 53, no. 2 (2000): 231; Richard White, *The Middle Ground: Indians, Empires, and Republics in the Great Lakes Region, 1650–1815* (CUP, 2010); Tutino, *Making a New World*, 33; Freg J. Stokes, "The Hummingbird's Atlas: Mapping Guaraní Resistance in the Atlantic Rainforest During the Emergence of Capitalism, 1500–1760" (PhD diss., University of Melbourne, 2022).

164. Braudel, *Afterthoughts on Material Civilization*, 40. For a related argument, see Tomich, "Original Accumulation," 22. The notion of "breaking through" can also be

found in Eric Hobsbawm, "From Feudalism to Capitalism," in *The Transition from Feudalism to Capitalism*, ed. Rodney Hilton (New Left Books, 1976), 161.

165. Findlay and O'Rourke, *Power and Plenty*, 231; Eric Vanhaute, "Global and Regional Comparisons: The Great Divergence Debate and Europe," in *The Practice of Global History: European Perspectives*, ed. Matthias Middell (Bloomsbury, 2019), 195. For a related argument, see also Kenneth R. Andrews, *Trade, Plunder, and Settlement: Maritime Enterprise and the Genesis of the British Empire, 1480–1630* (CUP, 1984), 356. Peer Vries insists on institutions being a problem of "global political economy." See Vries, "Does Wealth Entirely Depend on Inclusive Institutions and Pluralist Politics?," 14.

166. There is a long tradition of arguing that merchant capital is fundamentally conservative and almost outside capitalism and its history. As will become clearer in the following chapters, I disagree with that notion. For a very stimulating discussion of this issue, see Jairus Banaji, "Merchant Capitalism, Peasant Households and Industrial Accumulation: Integration of a Model," *Journal of Agrarian Change* 16, no. 3 (July 2016): 410–31, esp. 427.

Chapter 4: Transforming the Countryside, 1550–1750

1. Guillaume Thomas François Raynal, *Historie philosophique et politique: Des établissements & du commerce des Européens dans les deux Indes*, book 1 (Geneva: Librairies Associes, 1775), 1–2.
2. Russell R. Menard, *Sweet Negotiations: Sugar, Slavery, and Plantation Agriculture in Early Barbados* (University of Virginia Press, 2006), 54.
3. Russell R. Menard, "Law, Credit, the Supply of Labour, and the Organization of Sugar Production in the Colonial Greater Caribbean: A Comparison of Brazil and Barbados in the Seventeenth Century," in *The Early Modern Atlantic Economy*, ed. John J. McCusker and Kenneth Morgan (CUP, 2000), 156; William E. Dodd, "The Emergence of the First Social Order in the United States," *AHR* 40, no. 2 (January 1935): 217–31; Abigail Leslie Swingen, *Competing Visions of Empire: Labor, Slavery, and the Origins of the British Atlantic Empire* (Yale UP, 2015), 18, 20.
4. Thomas Noell, Recopied Deeds Books, 195, 222, 264, 523. Generally, land was sold along with labor.

See, for example, Recopied Deeds Books, RB 3/3, entry of 10 June 1657, BNA.
5. Menard, *Sweet Negotiations*, 54; Thomas Noell, Recopied Deeds Books, RB 3/3, 1648–1667, 109–10, BNA; and Menard, "Law, Credit, the Supply of Labour," 156.
6. Michel-Rolph Trouillot, "North Atlantic Universals: Analytical Fictions, 1492–1945," *South Atlantic Quarterly* 101, no. 4 (2002): 842.
7. Marion Menzin, "The Sugar Revolution in New England: Barbados, Massachusetts Bay, and the Atlantic Sugar Economy, 1600–1700" (PhD diss., Harvard University, 2019). Later in his life, Thomas Noell moved to the North American colonies, and by 1701, he had become mayor of New York. He died in 1702 on his New Jersey farm, located in an area that came to be known as New Barbadoes. See Graham Russell Hodges, *Slavery, Freedom & Culture Among Early American Workers* (Routledge, 2015), 33.
8. As cited in Hilary McD. Beckles, *A History of Barbados: From Amerindian Settlement to Caribbean Single Market* (CUP, 2006), 9.
9. Richard Ligon, *A True and Exact History of the Island of Barbados*, ed. Karen Ordahl Kupperman (Hackett Publishing Co., 2011), 85. Originally published in 1673.
10. Ligon, *True and Exact History*, 86.
11. John L. McCusker and Russell R. Menard, "The Sugar Industry in the Seventeenth Century," in *Tropical Babylons: Sugar and the Making of the Atlantic World, 1450–1680*, ed. Stuart B. Schwartz (University of North Carolina Press, 2004), 290–91; For a review of the literature on the "sugar revolution," see Barry W. Higman, "The Sugar Revolution," *EHR* 53, no. 2 (2000): 213–36; Carl and Roberta Bridenbaugh, *No Peace Beyond the Line: The English in the Caribbean, 1624–1690* (OUP, 1972), 79; and Beckles, *History of Barbados*, 28–29. These figures represent exports between 1650 and 1679.
12. J. H. Galloway, *The Sugar Cane Industry: An Historical Geography from Its Origins to 1914* (CUP, 1989), 81; Beckles, *A History of Barbados*, 28–29.
13. Trevor G. Burnard and John Garrigus, *The Plantation Machine: Atlantic Capitalism in French Saint-Domingue and British Jamaica* (University of Pennsylvania Press, 2016), 1; and J. R. Ward, "The Profitability of Sugar Planting in the British West Indies, 1650–1834," *EHR* 31, no. 2 (May 1978): 208.

14. Thomas Piketty, *Capital and Ideology* (The Belknap Press of HUP, 2020), 260.
15. Fernand Braudel, *Civilization and Capitalism, 15th–18th Century*, trans. Siân Reynolds, vol. 2, *The Wheels of Commerce* (University of California Press, 1992), 272. The central importance of Barbados to the history of capitalism is also emphasized by Marcel van der Linden, "The Future of Labor History in a World Perspective," unpublished paper (in author's possession), University of Pittsburgh, May 2014. Immanuel Wallerstein also emphasized the capitalist nature of slavery. See, for example, Immanuel Wallerstein, *The Modern World-System*, vol. 1, *Capitalist Agriculture and the Origins of the European World-Economy in the Sixteenth Century* (University of California Press, 2011), 87–88. For the feudal resistances to the transformation of the countryside in Europe, see Dale Tomich, "The Atlantic Slave-Sugar Complex in the Genoese Cycle of Accumulation: Origins of the Capitalist World Economy," unpublished paper, presented at the Global History Workshop, Harvard University, October 8, 2019, 16. On the various land acquisitions that assembled the Drax plantation, see RB3.1.725–26, deeds of conveyance to James Drax, November 1639 and June 1640, BNA; and RB3.2.53–57, deeds of conveyance, 1647, BNA.
16. Robert S. DuPlessis, *Transitions to Capitalism in Early Modern Europe* (CUP, 1997), 16. For Braudel, capitalism originates in urban contexts and spreads out from there. See Fernand Braudel, *Civilization and Capitalism, 15th–18th Century*, trans. Siân Reynolds, vol. 3, *The Perspective of the World* (Collins, 1984), 27; and Braudel, *Civilization and Capitalism*, 2:265.
17. On the importance of agriculture to the history of capitalism, and its reevaluation by many scholars, see also Marcel van der Linden, "Globalization's Agricultural Roots: Some Final Considerations," in *Embedding Agricultural Commodities: Using Historical Evidence, 1840s to 1940s*, ed. Willem van Schendel (Routledge, 2017), 149.
18. Jairus Banaji, "Globalising the History of Capital: Ways Forward," in *Historical Materialism* 26 (2018), 11, 13; Franz Mehring, *Absolutism and Revolution in Germany, 1525–1848* (New Park Publications, 1975), 1–7; Jairus Banaji, "Islam, the Mediterranean and the Rise of Capitalism,"

Historical Materialism 15 (2007), 47–74, here 66; George Lefebvre, "Some Observations," in Paul Sweezy et al., *The Transition from Feudalism to Capitalism: A Symposium* (NLB, 1976), 125–26, Celso Furtado, *Accumulation and Development: The Logic of Industrial Civilization* (Robertson, 1983); Robert Brenner, "The Origins of Capitalist Development: A Critique of Neo-Smithian Marxism," in *New Left Review* 104 (July–August 1977).

19. John Tutino, *The Mexican Heartland: How Communities Shaped Capitalism, a Nation, and World History, 1500–2000* (PUP, 2017); Braudel, *Civilization and Capitalism*, 2:281.

20. Braudel, *Civilization and Capitalism*, 2:249, 251, 265.

21. Montesquieu, *The Spirit of Laws*, trans. and ed. Anne M. Cohler, Basia Caroyln Miller, and Harold Samuel Stone (CUP, 1989), 341.

22. Braudel, *Civilization and Capitalism*, 2:256.

23. Samuel K. Cohn, *Creating the Florentine State: Peasants and Rebellion, 1348–1434* (CUP, 1999), 103; Braudel, *Civilization and Capitalism*, 2:291; and Rebecca Jean Emigh, *The Undevelopment of Capitalism: Sectors and Markets in Fifteenth-Century Tuscany* (Temple UP, 2009), 96.

24. Denis Cosgrove, "Los Angeles and the Italian 'Citta Diffusa': Landscapes of the Cultural Space and Economy," in *Landscapes of a New Cultural Economy of Space*, ed. Theano S. Terkenli and Anne Marie d'Hautesserre (Springer, 2006), 80; Braudel, *Civilization and Capitalism*, 2:284, 286–87; Salvatore Ciriacono, *Building on Water: Venice, Holland and the Construction of the European Landscape in Early Modern Times*, trans. Jeremy Scott (Berghahn Books, 2006), 66; and Marian Małowist, "Commercial Capitalism and Agriculture," in *Western Europe, Eastern Europe and World Development, 13th to 18th Centuries: Collection of Essays of Marian Małowist*, ed. Jean Batou and Henryk Szlajfer (Brill, 2010), 67.

25. Tutino, *The Mexican Heartland*, 7, 8, 12, 33, 44, 78.

26. Pedro Machado, *Ocean of Trade: South Asian Merchants, Africa and the Indian Ocean, c. 1750–1850* (CUP, 2014), 65; Peter Langer Koffsky, "History of Takaungu, East Africa 1830–1896" (PhD diss., University of Wisconsin–Madison, 1977), 23; Raul Chandrashekhar Oka, "Resilience and Adaptation of Trade Networks in East African and South Asian Port Polities, 1500–1800 C.E." (PhD diss., University of Illi-

nois at Chicago, 2008), 299; Abdul Sheriff, *Slaves, Spices, & Ivory in Zanzibar: Integration of an East African Commercial Empire into the World Economy, 1770–1873* (James Currey, 1987), 70; Charles David Sheldon, *The Rise of the Merchant Class in Tokugawa Japan, 1600–1868: An Introductory Survey* (J. J. Augustin Incorporated Publisher, 1958), 82–83; Fu Yiling, *Merchants and Commercial Capital in the Ming and Qing Dynasties* (People's Press, 1956), 36–37 [傅衣凌著:《明清时代商人及商业资本》(北京: 人民出版社, 1956年),第36–7页]; Fang Xing, "The Rural Usury Capital in the Early Qing Dynasty," *Qing History Research* 3 (1994): 11–26 [方行:《清代前期农村的高利贷资本》,《清史研究》第三辑 (1994年): 第11–26页]; Richard von Glahn, *The Economic History of China: From Antiquity to the Nineteenth Century* (CUP, 2016), 741; and Robert Gardella, *Harvesting Mountains: Fujian and the China Tea Trade, 1757 to 1937* (University of California Press, 1994), 32; 郭正忠:《宋代包买商人的考察》,《江淮论坛》1985年第2期, 18–25 (Guo Zhengzhong, "Songdai Baomai Shangren de Kaocha," *Jianghuai Luntan*, no. 2 [1985], 18–25); Ji Xianlin, *A History of Sugar* (New Star Press, 2013), 80; Xu Guanmian, "A Sugar Triangle: The Expansion of Commodity Frontiers on the Early Modern China Coast, 1600s to 1800s," unpublished paper, 2018 (in author's possession), 1; William Rowe, *China's Last Empire: The Great Qing* (HUP, 2009), 125, 126; Kwangmin Kim, *Borderland Capitalism: Turkestan Produce, Qing Silver, and the Birth of an Eastern Market* (Stanford UP, 2016).

27. David Howell, "Proto-Industrial Origins of Japanese Capitalism," *Journal of Asiatic Studies* 51, no. 2 (1992): 271; David Hardiman, "Penetration of Merchant Capital in Pre-Colonial Gujarat," in *Capitalist Development: Critical Essays*, ed. Ghanshyam Shah (Sangam Books, 1992), 32, 34, 36, 41. For the general argument about the importance of how commercial capital entered the countryside, see Małowist, "Commercial Capitalism and Agriculture," 17; Nelly Hanna, *Making Big Money in 1600: The Life and Times of Isma'il Abu Taqiyya Egyptian Merchant* (Syracuse UP, 1998), 82, 84–86; Bruce Masters, *The Arabs of the Ottoman Empire, 1516–1918: A Social and Cultural History* (CUP, 2013), 75; Ahrar Ahmad, "Analysing Pre-colonial South Asia: Mode of Production or Proto-Industrialisation,'" *Journal of*

Contemporary India 27, no. 3 (1997): 324; Sheldon, *Rise of the Merchant Class*, 81–82; Liu Chen 刘宸, "On the Development of Cotton in Henan in the Ming and Qing Dynasties" [《论明清时期河南棉花的商品化发展》] (master's thesis, Southwest University, 2014), 18; David Howell, "Proto-Industrial Origins of Japanese Capitalism," *Journal of Asiatic Studies* 51, no. 2 (1992): 271.

28. Charles Loyseau, *Traité du déguerpissement et délaissement par hypothèque* (Chez Abel L'Angelier, 1610).

29. Philip Benedict, "More Than Market and Manufactory: The Cities of Early Modern France," *French Historical Studies* 20, no. 3 (1997): 514. See also Braudel, *Civilization and Capitalism*, 2:283; and Emmanuel Le Roy Ladurie, *The French Peasantry, 1450–1660*, trans. Alan Sheridan (University of California Press, 1987), 336.

30. Hilton L. Root, *Peasants and King in Burgundy: Agrarian Foundations of French Absolutism* (University of California Press, 1992), 40.

31. Claude Rossignol, *Le Bailliage de Dijon après la Bataille de Rocroy (1643): Procès-verbaux de la visite des feux* (Dijon: M. Rossignol, 1857), 53–56; Pierre de Saint-Jacob, "Mutations économiques et sociales dans les campagnes bourguignonnes à la fin du XVIe siècle," no. 1 (1961): 34–49; Henri Drouot, "Vin, vignes et vignerons de la côte dijonnaise pendant la Ligue," *Revue de Bourgogne* 1 (1911): 343–61; Jean Richard, "Dijon au début des temps modernes (1515–1659)," in *Histoire de Dijon*, ed. Pierre Gras (Toulouse, 1980): 109–42; Benedict, "More Than Market and Manufactory," 514; Mark Potter and Jean-Laurent Rosenthal, "The Development of Intermediation in French Credit Markets: Evidence from the Estates of Burgundy," *JEH* 62, no. 4 (2002): 1024–25, 1032; Pierre de Saint Jacob, *Les paysans de la Bourgogne du nord au dernier siècle de l'ancien régime* (Publications de l'Université de Dijon, 1960), 377; and Jeffrey Houghtby, "Les Biens Communaux: Common Lands, Property Rights, and Agrarian Modernization in Early Modern Burgundy, 1550–1789" (PhD diss., Emory University, 2006), 27–28.

32. Houghtby, "Les Biens Communaux," 22–23, 32, 314–23. For other examples, see register of 20 May 1679, 152, in Houghtby, "Les Biens Communaux," 44; and transcript of 17 March 1666, in Houghtby, "Les

Biens Communaux," 313. For a full legal history on the law regarding use of forests, see Guy Antonetti, "Le partage des forêts usagères ou communales entre les seigneurs et les communautés d'habitants," *Revue historique du droit français et étranger* 41, no. 2 (1963): 238–86, 418–42, 592–634; and Henry Kamen, *Early Modern European Society* (Routledge, 2000), 101. See also James R. Farr, "Consumers, Commerce, and the Craftsmen of Dijon: The Changing Social and Economic Structure of Provincial Capital, 1450–1750," in *Cities and Social Change in Early Modern France*, ed. Philip Benedict (Routledge, 1989), 138–39; Gaston Roupnel, *La ville et la campagne au XVIIe siècle: Étude sur les populations du pays dijonnais* (Éditions Ernest Leroux, 1922), 188–228; and Norman J. G. Pounds, *An Historical Geography of Europe* (CUP, 1990), 275.
33. Van Bavel, "Land, Lease and Agriculture," 23, 26, 43; Jan de Vries, *The Dutch Rural Economy in the Golden Age, 1500–1700* (Yale UP, 1974), 192; and see the very detailed study by Han van Zwet, *Lofwaerdighe dijckagies en miserabele polders: Een financiële analyse van landaanwinningsprojecten in Hollands Noorderkwartier, 1597–1643* (Verloren, 2009). On the connection between changes in agriculture and urban merchants, see Pepijn Brandon, *War, Capital, and the Dutch State (1558–1795)* (Brill, 2015), 29; William Sewell, "On the Emergence of Capitalism: Marx, Brenner, and the Troublesome Case of the Dutch," in *Critical Historical Studies* 11 (Spring 2024): 26.
34. Van Bavel, "Land, Lease and Agriculture," 27, 31–32; Edouard Gruter, *La Naissance d'un grand vignoble: Les seigneuries de Pizay et Tana en Beaujolais au XVIe et au XXIIe siècles* (Lyon, 1977), 83–91; Julie Marfany, *Land, Proto-Industry and Population in Catalonia, c. 1680–1829: An Alternative Transition to Capitalism?* (Ashgate, 2013), 25–53; De Vries, *Dutch Rural Economy*, 192; Pepijn Brandon, "Marxism and the 'Dutch Miracle': The Dutch Republic and the Transition Debate," *Historical Materialism* 19, no. 3 (2011): 118; Bruno Blondé and Ilja vam Damme, "Early Modern Europe, 1500–1800," in *Oxford Handbook of Cities in World History* (2013), 245.
35. De Vries, *Dutch Rural Economy*, 193, 200, 213; J. L. Price, *Dutch Society 1588–1713* (Longman, 2000), 68; Bas van Bavel, "The Transition in the Low Countries: Wage Labour as an Indicator of the Rise of Capital-

ism in the Countryside, 1300–1700," *Rodney Hilton's Middle Ages: An Exploration of Historical Themes*, ed. Christopher Dyer, Peter Cross, and Chris Wickham, supplement, *Past & Present* 195, no. S2 (2007): S165, S292; and Maarten Duijvendak, "Balance Between City and Countryside in the Netherlands," *Bijdragen en mededelingen betreffende de geschiedenis der Nederlanden* 127, no. 3 (2012): 39. To convert guilders into contemporary US dollars I followed appendix 6 of Leon Voet, *The Golden Compasses: The History of the House of Plantin-Moretus* (Vangendt, 1969), 443, who takes one 1590 guilder to be the equivalent of 500 Belgian francs in 1969. This was equivalent to approximately 10 US dollars in 1969, the equivalent of 85.72 US dollars in 2024. For this last conversion, I used the Federal Reserve Bank of Minneapolis's Inflation Calculator.
36. Karl Marx's insistence on depicting commercial capital as removed from production failed to capture this involvement in the global countryside. Banaji, "Globalising the History of Capital,'" 9; Immanuel Wallerstein, *The Modern World-System*, vol. 2, *Mercantilism and the Consolidation of the European World-Economy, 1600–1750* (University of California Press, 2011), 36–73; "Dutch Hegemony in the Seventeenth Century World Economy," in *Dutch Capitalism and World Capitalism*, ed. Maurice Aymard (CUP, 1982), 93–146; and Robert P. Brenner, "The Low Countries in the Transition to Capitalism," *Journal of Agrarian Change* 1, no. 2 (2001): 169–241. Brenner is of course right in emphasizing the importance of the transformation of the English countryside and its impact on class structures. Yet we need to see that the transformation of the English countryside was just one part of a much larger process of transformation of the countryside. And the nature of class conflict in these transformations varied greatly—it was, for example, fundamentally different in Barbados. Regarding Karl Marx's depiction of commercial capital, this is one of the many excellent points made by Jairus Banaji, "Merchant Capitalism, Peasant Households and Industrial Accumulation: Integration of a Model," *Journal of Agrarian Change* 16, no. 3 (July 2016): 414, 425. See also Karl Marx, *Capital*, vol. 3 (Penguin, 1981), 381. Of course, in his historical analysis, Marx did allow for that connection.

37. Maurice Dobb, *Studies in the Development of Capitalism* (International Publisher, 1947), 124 181, 187.
38. On this process, see especially Brenner, "The Origins of Capitalist Development"; Henry French and Richard Hoyle, *The Character of English Rural Society: Earls Colne, 1550–1750* (Manchester UP, 2007); Bruce M. S. Campbell, "Agricultural Progress in Medieval England: Some Evidence from Norfolk," *EHR* 36, no. 1 (1983): 26–46; and Robert C. Allen, *Enclosure and the Yeoman: The Agricultural Development of the South Midlands, 1450–1850* (Clarendon Press, 1992). Ellen Meiksin Wood, *The Origins of Capital: A Longer View* (Verso, 2017); J. M. Blaut, "Robert Brenner in the Tunnel of Time," *Antipode* 26, no. 4 (1994): 351–74; Dobb, *Studies in the Development of Capitalism*, 124 181, 187; Brenner, "Agrarian Class Structures," 41–49; Braudel, *Civilization and Capitalism*, 2: 281; and Shami Ghosh, "Rural Economies and Transitions to Capitalism: Germany and England Compared (c. 1200–c. 1800)," *Journal of Agrarian Change* 16, no. 2 (April 2016): 255. For a critique of Brenner's take on the origins of capitalism, see, among many others, Patricia Croot and David Parker, "Agrarian Class Structure and the Development of Capitalism: France and England Compared," in *The Brenner Debate: Agrarian Class Structure and Economic Development in Pre-Industrial Europe*, ed. T. H. Aston and C. H. E. Philpin (CUP, 1985), 79–90; Heide Wunder, "Peasant Organization and Class Conflict in Eastern and Western Germany," in Aston and Philpin, *The Brenner Debate*, 91–100; Jaime Torras, "Class Struggle in Catalonia: A Note on Brenner," *Review* (Fernand Braudel Center) 4, no. 2 (1980): 253–65; and James Simpson, "European Farmers and the British 'Agricultural Revolution,'" in *Exceptionalism and Industrialisation: Britain and Its European Rivals, 1688–1815*, ed. Leandro Prados de la Escosura (CUP, 2004), 69–85. On the so-called political Marxists in general, see also Alexander Anievas and Kerem Nisancioğlu, *How the West Came to Rule: The Geopolitical Origins of Capitalism* (Pluto Press, 2015), 28.
39. Paul Glennie, "Town and Country in England, 1570–1750," in *Town and Country in Europe, 1300–1800*, ed. S. R. Epstein (CUP, 2001), 138; Dobb, *Studies in the Development of Capitalism*, 124–25, 186, 187. For the increasing capital intensity of agriculture, see Allen, *Enclosure and the*

Yeoman, 4, 186; on the "enclosure lobby," see J. M. Neeson, *Commoners: Common Right, Enclosure and Social Change in England, 1700–1820* (CUP, 1993), 44–45; E. P. Thompson, *The Making of the English Working Class* (Gollancz, 1963), 218; E. L. Jones, *Agriculture and the Industrial Revolution* (Halsted Press, 1974), 105. On the investment of urban capital in the countryside, see also DuPlessis, *Transitions to Capitalism*, 16.

40. Dobb, *Studies in the Development of Capitalism*, 181.

41. L. A. Parker, "The Agrarian Revolution in Cotesbach, 1501–1612," in *Studies in Leicestershire Agrarian History*, ed. W. G. Hoskins (Leicestershire Archaeological Society, 1949), 41–76; William Burton, *History of Leicestershire* (1771), 72, as quoted in Parker, "Agrarian Revolution in Cotesbach," 41; and John S. Cohen and Martin L. Weitzman, "A Marxian Model of Enclosures," in *Journal of Development Economics* 1 (1975): 296.

42. Machado, *Ocean of Trade*, 15, 64–65, 168; Fahad Ahmad Bishara, *A Sea of Debt: Law and Economic Life in the Western Indian Ocean, 1780–1950* (CUP, 2017), 25.

43. August Meitzen, *Der Boden und die landwirtschaftlichen Verhältnisse des Preussischen Staates* (Wiegandt & Hemel, 1901), 167–69; Kasimir Rakowski, *Entstehung des Grossgrundbesitzes im XV. und XVI. Jahrhundert in Polen* (M. Biedermann, 1899), 23; Walter Maas, "The 'Dutch' Villages in Poland," *Geography* 36, no. 4 (1951): 266; Norman Davies, *God's Playground: A History of Poland*, vol. 1, *The Origins to 1795* (OUP, 2005), 199; and Antoni Mączak, "Zusammenhänge zwischen Fernhandel und ungleichmässiger entwicklung polnischer Wirtschaftsgebiete im 16. und 17. Jahrhundert," *Jahrbuch für Wirtschaftsgeschichte* (1971): 219–28. For the importance of the Netherlands to Baltic trade, see also Henryk Samsonowicz, *Późne średniowiecze miast nadbałtyckich: Studia nad dziejami Hanzy nad Bałtykiem w XIV–XV w* (Państwowe Wydawnictwo Naukowe, 1968), 113. On the importance of wood, see Samsonowicz, *Późne średniowiecze miast nadbałtyckich*, 138; Jan de Vries, "The Role of the Rural Sector in the Development of the Dutch Economy: 1500–1700," *JEH* 31, no. 1 (1971): 266–68; Dariusz Adamczyk, *Zur Stellung Polens im modernen Weltsystem der frühen Neuzeit* (Verlag Dr. Kovač, 2001), 175; Samsonowicz, *Późne średniowiecze miast nadbałtyckich*, 121; Mar-

ian Małowist, *Wschód a Zachód Europy w XIII–XVI wieku: Konfrontacja struktur społeczno-gospodarczych* (Wydawnictwo Naukowe PWN, 2006), 85, 97; William Sewell, "On the Emergence of Capitalism: Marx, Brenner, and the Troublesome Case of the Dutch," in *Critical Historical Studies* 11 (Spring 2024): 29–30; Jan de Vries and A. M. van der Woude, *The First Modern Economy: Success, Failure, and Perseverance of the Dutch Economy, 1500–1815* (CUP, 1977), 423; and Jason W. Moore, "'Amsterdam Is Standing on Norway' Part II: The Global North Atlantic in the Ecological Revolution of the Long Seventeenth Century," *Journal of Agrarian Change* 10 no. 2 (April 2010): 188–227.

44. As cited in Kurt Schottmueller, "Reiseeindrücke aus Danzig, Lübeck, Hamburg und Holland, 1636," *Zeitschrift des Westpreussischen Geschichtsverein* 52 (1910): 212.

45. Davies, *God's Playground*, 1:200. For the quote, see Hans-Heinrich Nolte, "Zur Stellung Osteuropas im internationalen System der frühen Neuzeit. Außenhandel und Sozialgeschichte bei der Bestimmung der Regionen," *Jahrbücher für Geschichte Osteuropas* 28, no. 2 (1980): 197. On the importance of Danzig, see Marian Małowist, *Wschód a Zachód Europy*, 277.

46. M. van Tielhof, *De Hollandse graanhandel, 1450–1570: Korean op de Amsterdamse molen* (Stichting Hollandse Historische Reeks, 1995), 177–80; Maria Bogucka, "Dutch Merchants' Activities in Gdansk in the First Half of the 17th Century," in *Baltic Affairs: Relations Between the Netherlands and North-Eastern Europe, 1500–1800*, ed. J. Ph. S. Lemmink and J. S. A. M. van Koningsbrugge (Institute for Northern and Eastern European Studies, 1990), 24–25; Tonko Ufkes, "Vlielanders, Friezen en andere Nederlanders te Danzig. Zeventiendeen achttiende eeuwse gegevens uit het burgerboek en de geloofsbrieven," *Jaarboek van het Centraal Bureau voor Genealogie en het Iconografisch Bureau* 45 (1991): 166; M. van Tielhof, *The "Mother of All Trades": The Baltic Grain Trade in Amsterdam from the Late 16th to the Early 19th Century* (Brill, 2002), 38, 167. On the centrality of the Dutch in that trade, see also Adamczyk, *Zur Stellung Polens im modernen Weltsystem*, 130; and Marian Małowist, *Wschód a Zachód Europy*, 280.

47. Maria Bogucka, "Veranderingen in de Baltische handel in de zeventiende eeuw. Transacties tussen Hol-

landse kooplieden en de Poolse adel," *Jaarboek Amstelodamum* 87 (1995): 254–56; Małowist, *Wschód a Zachód Europy*, 142; Marian Małowist, "A Certain Trade Technique in the Baltic Countries in the XVth to the XVIIth Century," in *Poland at the XIth International Congress of Historical Sciences*, ed. International Congress of Historical Sciences (Wydawnictwo Naukowe PWN, 1960), 103–16; Maria Bogucka, "Danzigs Bedeutung für die Wirtschaft des Ostseeraumes in der frühen Neuzeit," *Studia Historiae Oeconomicae* 9 (1974): 105; Ronald Findlay and Kevin H. O'Rourke, *Power and Plenty: Trade, War, and the World Economy in the Second Millennium* (PUP, 2007), 104, 106, 212; and Edmund Cieślak and C. Biernat, *History of Gdańsk*, trans. Bożenna Blaim and George M. Hyde (Wydawnictwo Morskie, 1988), 120; Kristof Glamann, "The Changing Patterns of Trade," in *The Cambridge Economic History of Europe*, vol. 5, *The Economic Organization of Early Modern Europe*, ed. E. E. Rich and C. H. Wilson (CUP, 1977), 271.

48. Rudolf Häpke, ed., *Niederländischen akten und urkunden zur geschichte der Hanse und zur deutschen Seegeschichte: 1558–1669*, vol. 1 (Duncker & Humblot, 1913), 200; D. G. Kirby, *Northern Europe in the Early Modern Period: The Baltic World, 1492–1722* (Longman, 1990), 9.

49. Henryk Samsonowicz, *Nieznane dzieje Polski: W Europie czy na jej skraju?* (Wydawnictwo Bellona, 2012), 127–28; Marian Małowist, "East and West Europe in the 13th–16th Centuries: Confrontation of Social and Economic Structures," in Batou and Szlajfer, *Western Europe, Eastern Europe and World Development*, 227. On the grain trade, see Z. P. Pach, "The East-Central European Aspect of the Overseas Discoveries and Colonialization," *Vierteljahreshefte für Sozial- und Wirtschaftsgeschichte, Beihefte* 89 (1990): 181. On the idea of a "colonial relationship," see Bogucka, "Danzigs Bedeutung," 96. See also Witold Kula, *Economic Theory of the Feudal System: Towards a Model of the Polish Economy, 1500–1800* (Humanities Press, 1976), 40; Davies, *God's Playground*, 1:215; Bogucka, "Danzigs Bedeutung," 100; Braudel, *Civilization and Capitalism*, 2:271.

50. For this argument, see also Findlay and O'Rourke, *Power and Plenty*, 143.

51. Carlo Taviani and Steven Teasdale, "Genoese Merchant Networks from the Black Sea to West Africa and the Americas (15th to 16th Centuries),"

unpublished paper presented at the ENIUGH Congress, Budapest, 2017; Jalil Sued Badillo, *Cristóbal Colon y la Esclavitud del Indio en las Antillas* (Fundación Arqueológica, Antropológica, Histórica de Puerto Rico, 1983); Felipe Fernández-Armesto, *Amerigo: The Man Who Gave His Name to America* (Weidenfeld & Nicolson, 2006), 52, 55, 89, 182.

52. Jason W. Moore, "Madeira, Sugar & the Conquest of Nature on the 'First' Sixteenth Century, Part 1: From 'Island of Timber' to Sugar Revolution, 1420–1506," *Review* 32, no. 4 (2010): 345–90; Tomich, "The Atlantic Slave-Sugar Complex," 23, 24, 25; Howard French, *Born in Blackness: Africa, Africans, and the Making of the Modern World, 1471 to the Second World War* (Liveright Publishing, 2021), 122.

53. Beckles, Hilary McD., "The 'Hub of Empire': The Caribbean and Britain in the Seventeenth Century," in Nicholas Canny and William Roger Louis (eds.), *The Oxford History of the British Empire: Volume I: The Origins of Empire: British Overseas Enterprise to the Close of the Seventeenth Century*, Oxford History of the British Empire (Oxford, 1998): 225, 235; Richard S. Dunn, "The Barbados Census of 1680: Profile of the Richest Colony in English America," *William and Mary Quarterly* 26, no. 1 (1969): 7, 235; McCusker and Menard, "Sugar Industry in the Seventeenth Century," 152, 295–97, 299, 303; Richard S. Dunn, *Sugar and Slaves: The Rise of the Planter Class in the English West Indies, 1624–1713* (University of North Carolina Press, 1972), 66, 112–13; Ryan Dennis McGuinness, "'They Can Now Digest Strong Meats': Two Decades of Expansion, Adaption, Innovation, and Maturation on Barbados, 1680–1700" (PhD diss., University of Edinburgh, 2017), 119; Beckles, *History of Barbados*, 29–31; Jason W. Moore, "Nature and the Transition from Feudalism to Capitalism," *Review* (Fernand Braudel Center) 26, no. 2 (2003): 150; Marcel van der Linden, "Re-Constructing the Origins of Modern Labor Management," *Labor History* 51, no. 4 (November 2010): 511.

54. Johannes Petrus van de Voort, "De Westindische plantages van 1720 tot 1796: Financiën en handel" (PhD diss., Nijmegen, 1973), 101; McCusker and Menard, "Sugar Industry in the Seventeenth Century," 296, 301, 319, 324; and William A. Green, "Supply Versus Demand in the Barbadian Sugar Revolution," *Journal of Interdisciplinary History* 18, no. 3 (Winter

1988): 415–17. For the role of Dutch slave traders in providing workers to Barbados, see also P. C. Emmer, *The Dutch Slave Trade, 1500–1850* (Berghahn Books, 2006), 25–27; Moore, "Nature and the Transition from Feudalism to Capitalism," 149; Barbara L. Solow, "Capitalism and Slavery in the Exceedingly Long Run," *Journal of Interdisciplinary History* 17, no. 4 (Spring 1987): 727; Higman, "Sugar Revolution," 223; Menard, *Sweet Negotiations*, 49; Michael D. Bennett, "Merchant Capital and the Origins of the Barbados Sugar Boom, 1627–1672," (unpublished PhD thesis, University of Sheffield, 2020), 4, 13–15, 119; Dale Tomich, "Rethinking the Plantation: Concepts and Histories," *Review* (Fernand Braudel Center) 34, no. 1/2 (2011): 32.

55. The total revenue for the English government between 1604 and 1625 was 12,544,000 pounds. The total revenue between 1626 and 1640 was 11,996,000 pounds. Between 1649 and 1659, it was 18,919,000 pounds. The average annual revenue between 1649 and 1659 was 1,719,910 pounds. Between 1661 and 1685, total government revenue was 41,066,000 pounds. Revenue was composed of Crown income, direct taxation, indirect taxation, sales of assets, and mint profits. See Michael Braddick, *The Nerves of State: Taxation and the Financing of the English State, 1558–1714* (Manchester UP, 1996), 10; and Beckles, "Hub of Empire,'" 224–25. See also Dunn, "Barbados Census of 1680," 4.

56. David Eltis, "New Estimates of Exports from Barbados and Jamaica, 1665–1701," *William and Mary Quarterly* 52, no. 4 (October 1995): 638, 644. Of these exports, in 1683–1691, 43 percent went to the Americas, especially North America, and 57 percent to England. See also Nuala Zahedieh, "Trade, Plunder, and Economic Development in Early English Jamaica, 1655–1689," *EHR* 39, no. 2 (May 1986): 206; Solow, "Capitalism and Slavery in the Exceedingly Long Run," 730; and Dunn, "Barbados Census of 1680," 4.

57. Eltis, "New Estimates of Exports," 646.

58. Dunn, "Barbados Census of 1680," 4; Ligon, *True and Exact History*, 96.

59. Robert William Fogel, *Without Consent or Contract: The Rise and Fall of American Slavery* (W. W. Norton, 1991), 21–22.

60. Ligon, *True and Exact History*, 96, 109.

61. Bridenbaugh, *No Peace Beyond the Line*, 69.

62. This crucial difference between Europe and the Americas is also emphasized by Fernando A. Novais, *Aproximações: Estudos de história e historiografia* (Cosac Naify, 2005), 41.

63. Fogel, *Without Consent or Contract*, 24; Dunn, *Sugar and Slaves*, 84, 91, 114; David Eltis, "The Total Product of Barbados, 1664–1701," *JEH* 55, no. 2 (1995): 334–37. On the Danish West Indies, see Niklas Thode Jensen and Gunvor Simonsen, "The Historiography of Slavery in the Danish-Norwegian West Indies, c. 1950–2016," *Scandinavian Journal of History* 41, no. 4–5 (2016): 475–94. For plantation as first modern industry, see Sidney W. Mintz, *Sweetness and Power: The Place of Sugar in Modern History* (Penguin Books, 1986), 51, 55.

64. The very global nature of the sugar commodity chain is also emphasized by Pedro Antonio Vieira, "'Brazil' in the Capitalist World Economy from 1550 to c. 1800: An Empirical Demonstration Through the Sugar Commodity," *Review* (Fernand Braudel Center) 37, no. 1 (2014): 1–34; and Beckles, "'Hub of Empire,'" 221.

65. Christian Schnakenbourg, "Note sur les origines de l'industrie sucrière en Guadeloupe au XVIIe siècle, 1640–1670," *Revue française d'histoire d'outre-mer* 55, no. 3 (1968): 267–315; Higman, "Sugar Revolution," 214; Dunn, *Sugar and Slaves*, 19–20; and Stewart L. Mims, *Colbert's West India Policy* (Yale UP, 1977), 33. On the plantation revolution as a "project," see the brilliant Karsten Voss, *Sklaven als Ware und Kapital: Die Plantagenökonomie von Saint-Domingue als Entwicklungsprojekt, 1697–1715* (C. H. Beck Verlag, 2016), 9; Extrait des recensements des différentes colonies en ce qui concerne les esclaves pour l'année 1787 etc., Martinique, Recensements, 1664–1799, No. 1–40, G/1/499, ANOM; Burnard and Garrigus, *Plantation Machine*, 31, 35, 37–38; and Bennett, "Merchant Capital and the Origins of the Barbados Sugar Boom, 1627–1672," 3, 283.

66. Adam Smith, *An Inquiry into the Nature and Causes of the Wealth of Nations*, ed. Edwin Cannan (Modern Library, 1937), 366.

67. See Recensement Général de l'Isle St. Domingue de l'année 1715, Recensement Général de la côte St. Domingue de l'année 1721, Recensement Général de l'Isle St. Domingue de l'année 1739, Recensement Général de l'Isle St. Domingue de l'année 1771, and Recensement Général de l'Isle St. Domingue de l'année 1786, all in G/1/509,

ANOM. Production numbers regarding sugar plantations refer to 1740; the number of plantations is from the year 1739. See also Alex Dupuy, "French Merchant Capital and Slavery in Saint-Domingue," *Latin American Perspectives* 12, no. 3 (1985): 77, 91; Burnard and Garrigus, *Plantation Machine*, 34, 36, 43; and Karsten Voss and Klaus Weber, "War, Crisis and the Development of the Slave-Plantation Economy of Saint-Domingue (1697–1715)," unpublished manuscript (in author's possession), 2017, 5. See also the detailed analysis of this process in Voss, *Sklaven als Ware und Kapital*, 24, 39.

68. Burnard and Garrigus, *Plantation Machine*, 35, 253; Moreau de Saint-Méry, *Description topographique, physique, civile, politique et historique de la partie française de l'isle Saint-Domingue* (Société de l'Histoire des Colonies Françaises, 1958), 28, 111; Albane Forestier, "A 'Considerable Credit' in the Late Eighteenth-Century French West India Trade: The Chaurands of Nantes," *French History* 25, no. 1 (2011), 54; and Kenneth Pomeranz and Steven Topik, *The World That Trade Created: Society, Culture and the World Economy, 1400 to the Present* (M. E. Sharpe, 2006), 89. In this case, *1780s* refers to the time between 1784 and 1790.

69. Voss, *Sklaven als Ware und Kapital*, 17, 44; Burnard and Garrigus, *Plantation Machine*, 35, 253; de Saint-Méry, *Description topographique*, 28, 111; Forestier, "Chaurands of Nantes," 54; and Pomeranz and Topik, *World That Trade Created*, 89. In this case, *1780s* refers to the time between 1784 and 1790.

70. Charles C. Perkins, "Narrative of the Insurrection in St. Domingo, and of a Voyage from Port au Prince to Boston in 1793, by Samuel G. Perkins, Communicated, with Notes," *Proceedings of the Massachusetts Historical Society*, vol. 2, Second Series 1885–1886 (Massachusetts Historical Society, 1886), 307.

71. Burnard and Garrigus, *Plantation Machine*, 43.

72. Forestier, "Chaurands of Nantes," 49, 50–51, 55–57, 59, 61, 63; Jean Tarrade, *Le commerce colonial de la France à la fin de l'ancien régime: L'évolution du régime de l'exclusif de 1763 à 1789* (Presses Universitaires de France, 1972); J. R. Ward, "The Profitability of Sugar Planting in the British West Indies, 1650–1834," *EHR* 31, no. 2 (May 1978): 197–213, as cited in Forestier, "Chaurands of Nantes," 59. For the Chaurands, about 10 percent of their capital invested in the Caribbean trade came from Paris.

73. Forestier, "Chaurands of Nantes," 65; Burnard and Garrigus, *Plantation Machine*, 165, 224; and Allan Potofsky, "Paris-on-the-Atlantic from the Old Regime to the Revolution," *French History* 25, no. 1 (2011): 99.

74. Ministère des Finances, *État détaillé des liquidations opérées à l'époque du 1er Janvier 1828, par la commission chargée de répartir l'indemnité attribuée aux anciens colons de Saint-Domingue* (Paris: Imprimerie Royale, 1828), vi.

75. Forestier, "Chaurands of Nantes," 48; Ministère des Finances, *État détaillé des liquidations*, vi.

76. Moore, "Nature and the Transition from Feudalism to Capitalism," 131; Burnard and Garrigus, *Plantation Machine*, 2; and Higman, "Sugar Revolution," 232.

77. As cited in Burnard and Garrigus, *Plantation Machine*, 95.

78. Raynal, *Historie philosophique et politique*, 1–2; Smith, *An Inquiry into the Nature and Causes of the Wealth of Nations*, 366.

79. Tamira Combrink, "Who Profited from an Eighteenth-Century Cup of Coffee? Added Value in a Slave-Based Commodity Chain," unpublished paper (in author's possession), WEHC, 2015, 6.

80. Jordan Goodman, *Tobacco in History: The Cultures of Dependence* (Routledge, 1993), 37, 131, 135; and Edmund Morgan, *American Slavery, American Freedom: The Ordeal of Colonial Virginia* (W. W. Norton, 1975), 72, 110, 185.

81. Jacob Price, "Glasgow in the Chesapeake Tobacco Trade, 1707–1775," in *Tobacco in Atlantic Trade: The Chesapeake, London and Glasgow, 1675–1775* (Variorum, 1995), 190, 197.

82. Burnard and Garrigus, *Plantation Machine*, 3.

83. Henry Drax, "Instructions for the Management of Drax-Hall, and the Irish-Hope Plantations: to Archibald Johnson," as reprinted, William Belgrove, *A Treatise upon Husbandry or Planting* (Boston: D. Fowle, 1755), 56, 73.

84. Solow, "Capitalism and Slavery in the Exceedingly Long Run," 737; Burnard and Garrigus, *Plantation Machine*, 8; "Compte que tend à M. le Macquis de Paroy Avalle, chargé de l'administration de ses biens situés à St. Domingue de la recette et dépense générale des ses habitations & établissements en sucrerie la ditte cette & dépense depuis le 1er janvier au 31 décembre 1780," in Le Gentil de Paroy, 164APOM/1, Fond Privés, Archives Privées, ANOM; Barry Supple, "The Nature of Enterprise," in Rich and Wilson, *Cambridge Economic History of Europe*, 5:430; and Reed G. Geiger, *The Anzin Coal Company, 1800–1833: Big Business in the Early Stages of the French Industrial Revolution* (University of Delaware Press, 1974), 17. For the small size of most European undertakings, see Michael W. Flinn, *The History of the British Coal Industry*, vol. 2, 1700–1830: The Industrial Revolution (Clarendon Press, 1984), 361–62.

85. Solow, "Capitalism and Slavery in the Exceedingly Long Run," 715. On slaves as collateral, see the brilliant Joseph Miller, "Captives, Collateral, Credit, and Currencies: Slaves and the Debt Financing of the Atlantic World," unpublished paper (in the author's possession), McGill University, Montreal, May 2009, 2, 5, 12, 39, see also Geoffrey M. Hodgson, *The Wealth of a Nation: Institutional Foundations of English Capitalism* (PUP, 2023), 149.

86. Ellen Meiksins Wood, *The Origins of Capitalism: A Longer View* (Verso, 2017), 94; and Stuart B. Schwartz, "Looking for a New Brazil: Crisis and Rebirth in the Atlantic World After the Fall of Pernambuco," in *The Legacy of Dutch Brazil*, ed. Michiel van Groesen (CUP, 2014).

87. Ulrich Ufer, *Welthandelszentrum Amsterdam: Globale Dynamik und modernes Leben im 17. Jahrhundert* (Böhlau Verlag, 2008), 331.

88. Meiksins Wood, *The Origins of Capitalism*, 94; Stuart B. Schwartz, "Looking for a New Brazil: Crisis and Rebirth in the Atlantic World After the Fall of Pernambuco," in *The Legacy of Dutch Brazil*, ed. Michiel van Groesen (CUP, 2014): 41–58; Ufer, *Welthandelszentrum Amsterdam*, 331; S. D. Smith, "Gedney Clarke of Salem and Barbados: Transatlantic Super-Merchant," in *New England Quarterly* 76 (2003): 314.

89. Pomeranz and Topik, *World That Trade Created*, 41. See also Moore, "Nature and the Transition from Feudalism to Capitalism," 133. For the French islands, see Yvan Debbasch, "Au coeur du 'gouvernement des esclaves': la souveraineté domestique aux Antilles françaises (XVIIe–XVIIe siècles)," *Revue française d'histoire d'outre-mer* 72, no. 1 (1985): 31–54; see also Miller, "Captives, Collateral, Credit, and Currencies," 35; and Barbara L. Solow, *The Economic Consequences of the Slave Trade* (Lexington Books, 2014), 107. See also Burnard and Garrigus, *The Plantation Machine*, 3.

90. Karl Marx, *Capital: A Critique of Political Economy*, vol. 1, *The Process of Capitalist Production* (Charles H. Kerr & Company, 1932), 832. See, for example, the work of Eugene Genovese, such as Eugene Genovese, *The Political Economy of Slavery: Studies in the Economy & Society of the Slave South* (Pantheon, 1962).

91. C. L. R. James, *The Black Jacobins: Toussaint L'Ouverture and the San Domingo Revolution* (Random House, 1989); Eric Williams, *Capitalism and Slavery* (University of North Carolina Press, 1944); John Tutino, *Making a New World: Founding Capitalism in the Bajío and Spanish North America* (Duke UP, 2011), 43; Mintz, *Sweetness and Power*, 55.

92. M. C. Ricklefs, *A History of Modern Indonesia Since c. 1300* (Macmillan, 1993), 25, 27; John Villiers, "Trade and Society in the Banda Islands in the Sixteenth Century," *Modern Asian Studies* 15, no. 4 (1981): 729, 749; and Adam Clulow, "The Art of Claiming: Possession and Resistance in Early Modern Asia," *AHR* 121, no. 1 (2016): 30.

93. Ricklefs, *History of Modern Indonesia*, 24, 27; Villiers, "Trade and Society in the Banda Islands," 749; Amitav Gosh, *The Nutmeg's Curse: Parables for a Planet in Crisis* (University of Chicago Press, 2021), 9; Martine Julia van Ittersum, "Debating Natural Law in the Banda Islands: A Case Study in Anglo-Dutch Imperial Competition in the East Indies, 1609–1621," *History of European Ideas* 42, no. 4 (2016): 469; Samuel Purchas, *Hakluytus Posthumus or Purchas His Pilgrimes: Contayning a History of the World in Sea Voyages and Lande Travells by Englishmen and Others*, vol. 2 (James MacLehose and Sons, 1905), 530–53, as quoted in Van Ittersum, "Debating Natural Law in the Banda Islands," 459, 465–66. For the quote, see J. E. Heeres and F. W. Stapel, eds., *Corpus diplomaticum Neerlando-Indicum: Verzameling van politieke contracten en verdere verdragen door de Nederlanders in het Oosten gesloten, van privilegebrieven aan hen verleend, enz*, vol. 1 (Martinus Nijhoff, 1907), 122–24, as cited in Van Ittersum, "Debating Natural Law in the Banda Islands," 470.

94. J. A. van der Chijs, *De Vestiging van het Nederlandsche Gezag over da Banda-Eilandem (159901621)* (Albrecht & Co., 1886), 147; van Ittersum, "Debating Natural Law in the Banda Islands," 461, 463; Findlay and O'Rourke, *Power and Plenty*, 180; Van Goor, *Jan Pieterszoon Coen 1587–1629: Koopmankoning in Azïen*

(Boom, 2015), 433–66; Philip Winn, "Slavery and Cultural Creativity in the Banda Islands," *Journal of Southeast Asian Studies* 41, no. 3 (2010): 365–89; Vincent C. Loth, "Pioneers and Perkeniers: The Banda Islands in the 17th Century," *Cakalele* 6 (1995): 13–36. They all quote Williard A. Hanna, *Indonesian Banda: Colonialism and Its Aftermath in the Nutmeg Islands* (Institute for the Study of Human Issues, 1978), 55. See also D. G. E. Hall, *A History of South-East Asia* (Macmillan, 1968), 307–9; Anthony Reid, "Trade and State Power in Sixteenth and Seventeenth Century Southeast Asia," in *Proceedings of the Seventh IAHA Conference* (Chulalongkorn UP, 1977), 400–401; B. H. M. Vlekke, *Nusantara: A History of Indonesia* (HUP, 1943), 124–41; Jacob Cornelis van Leur, *Indonesian Trade and Society: Essays in Asian Social and Economic History*, trans. James S. Holmes and A. van Marle (W. Van Hoeve, 1955), 182–84; S. Arasaratnam, "Monopoly and Free Trade in Dutch-Asian Commercial Policy: Debate and Controversy Within the VOC," *Journal of Southeast Asian Studies* 4, no. 1 (March 1973): 1–15; Vincent C. Loth, "Armed Incidents and Unpaid Bills," *Modern Asian Studies* 29, no. 4 (1995): 724–27; Jan Pietersz Coen, "Discoers aen de E. Heeren Bewinthebberen touscherende den Nederlandche Indischeinstaet, 1 Januari 1614," in Colenbrander, *Jan Pietersz Coen, Levensbeschrijving*, 470–72, as quoted in Arasaratnam, "Monopoly and Free Trade," 3; Ralph Shlomowitz, "Slave Trade: Asia and Oceania," in *A Historical Guide to World Slavery*, ed. Seymour Drescher and Stanley L. Engerman (OUP, 1998), 362, as quoted in Winn, "Slavery and Cultural Creativity in the Banda Islands," 366; and W. G. Miller, "An Account of Trade Patterns in the Banda Sea in 1707, from an Unpublished Manuscript in the India Office Library," *Indonesia Circle* 8, no. 23 (1980): 42, 44. On genocide, see Bart Luttikhuis and A. Dirk Moses, "Mass Violence and the End of the Dutch Colonial Empire in Indonesia," *Journal of Genocide Research* 14 (2012).

95. For the Caribbean cuckoo, see Vincent C. Loth, "Pioneers and Perkeniers: The Banda Islands in the 17th Century," *Cakalele* 6 (1995): 9.

96. For the numbers of slaves, see Matthias van Rossum, "'Vervloekte goudzugt,' De VOC, slavenhandel en slavernij in Azië," *Tijdschrift voor sociale en economische geschiedenis* 12,

no. 4 (2015): 42. On the difference between the role of slavery in Asia and the Americas, see also the insightful comments in Pepijn Brandon, "Dutch Capitalism and Slavery in the Longer Run: A Reorientation" (Fernand Braudel Center Colloquium, 2018), 16. For a general discussion of the slave trade in the Indian Ocean (and its relatively limited importance in seventeenth- and seventeenth-century expansion), see Machado, *Ocean of Trade*, 209–19. For the important Dutch role in expanding slavery in Asia, see Matthias van Rossum, "Global Trade, Local Markets—Prices and Slave Trade in Dutch Asia, 1600–1800," unpublished paper (in author's possession), WEHC, 2015. For that history, see the important work of Richard B. Allen, *European Slave Trading in the Indian Ocean, 1500–1850* (Ohio UP, 2014), esp. 19, 22; and Solow, "Capitalism and Slavery in the Exceedingly Long Run," 724.

97. Forestier, "Chaurands of Nantes," 48, 67. Moore, like Harvey, emphasizes the need for "spatial fixes" of capitalism—the integration of new natural resources. See Moore, "Nature and the Transition from Feudalism to Capitalism," 100. For capitalism as "frontier-making," see Jason W. Moore, "Sugar and the Expansion of the Early Modern World-Economy: Commodity Frontiers, Ecological Transformations, and Industrialization," *Review* (Fernand Braudel Center) 23, no. 3 (2000): 409–33; Eric Vanhaute, "Making Sense of the Great Divergence. The Limits and Challenges of World History," *Comparativ* 3 (2016): 112.

98. Karl Marx, "Part IV, Conversion of Commodity-Capital and Money-Capital into Commercial Capital and Money-Dealing Capital," in *Capital*, vol. III (Foreign Languages Publishing House, 1959): 262–331; Karl Marx, *The Poverty of Philosophy, Being a Translation of the Misere de La Philosophie (a Reply to "La Philosophie de La Misere" of m. Proudhon)* (C. H. Kerr & Company, 1910), 119.

99. Dobb, *Studies in the Development of Capitalism*, 121–23.

100. Brenner, "Low Countries in the Transition to Capitalism," 171.

101. Brandon, "Marxism and the Dutch Miracle," 123; Chris Harman, "From Feudalism to Capitalism," *International Socialism* 2, no. 45 (Winter 1989): 35–87.

102. Smith, *An Inquiry into the Nature and Causes of the Wealth of Nations*, 259–60.

103. W. G. Hoskins, *The Age of Plunder: King Henry's England, 1500–1547* (Longman, 1976), xii, 121–22, 124, 132, 136. This expropriation is also analyzed with fascinating imperial detail in Leander Heldring, James A. Robinson, and Sebastian Vollmer, "Monks, Gents and Industrialists: The Long-Run Impact of the Dissolution of the English Monasteries," NBER Working Paper No. 21450 (August 2015), 9.

104. De Vries, *Dutch Rural Economy*, 210, 213; Van Bavel, "Land, Lease and Agriculture," 13; dispossessions sharpened again during the French Revolution, as discussed in Potofsky, "Paris-on-the-Atlantic from the Old Regime to the Revolution," 102.

105. Karl Polanyi, *The Great Transformation: The Political and Economic Origins of Our Time* (Beacon Press, 2001), 37.

106. James Walvin, *Sugar: The World Corrupted, from Slavery to Obesity* (Robinson, 2017), 54.

107. Bartolomé de las Casas, *Historia de las Indias*, vol. V (Miguel Ginesta, 1876), 32.

108. John S. Cohen and Martin L. Weitzman, "A Marxian Model of Enclosures," *Journal of Development Economics* 1, no. 4 (1975): 299; Polanyi, *Great Transformation*, 37; James Simpson, "European Farmers and the British 'Agricultural Revolution,'" in *Exceptionalism and Industrialisation: Britain and Its European Rivals, 1688–1815*, ed. Leandro Prados de la Escosura (CUP, 2004), 81; William J. Smyth, *Map-Making, Landscapes and Memory: A Geography of Colonial and Early Modern Ireland, c. 1530–1750* (Cork UP, 2006); Kevon McKenny, "The Restoration Land Settlement in Ireland: A Statistical Interpretation," in *Restoration Ireland: Always Selling and Never Settled*, ed. Coleman A. Denneby (Ashgate, 2008), 35–52.

109. Ian D. Whyte, *Scotland Before the Industrial Revolution: An Economic and Social History, c. 1050–c. 1750* (Longman, 1995), 145.

110. Whyte, *Scotland Before the Industrial Revolution*, 136–44; Charles Jedrej and Mark Nuttall, *White Settlers: The Impact of Rural Repopulation in Scotland* (Harwood Academic Publishers, 1996), 31; Robert Maxwell, ed., *Select Transactions of the Honourable the Society of Improvers in the Knowledge of Agriculture in Scotland, Directing the Husbandry of the Different Soils for the Most Profitable Purposes, and Containing Other Directions, Receipts and Descriptions: Together with an Account of the Society's Endeavors to Promote Our Manufactures* (Edinburgh: Sands, Brymer, Murray and Cochran, 1743); Brian Bonnyman, "Agrarian Patriotism and the Landed Interest: The Scottish 'Society of Improvers in the Knowledge of Agriculture,' 1723–1746," in *The Rise of Economic Societies in the Eighteenth Century*, ed. Koen Stapelbroek and Jani Marjanen (Palgrave Macmillan, 2012), 26.

111. Patrick O'Brien, "Was the First Industrial Revolution a Conjuncture in the History of the World Economy?," Economic History Working Paper No. 259/2017 (London School of Economics and Political Science, March 2017), 10, 11; Allen, *Enclosure and the Yeoman*, 1, 15, 17, 19; Cohen and Weitzman, "A Marxian Model of Enclosures," 304, 316, 318–19, 326; Robert C. Allen, "Tracking the Agricultural Revolution in England," *EHR* 52 (1999): 215.

112. Andrés Reséndez, *The Other Slavery: The Uncovered Story of Indian Enslavement in America* (Houghton Mifflin Harcourt, 2016), 14, see also 3–4, 24–25.

113. As cited in Reséndez, *The Other Slavery*, 28.

114. Bartolomé de las Casas, *Brevísima relación de la destrucción de las Indias*, ed. and ann. José Miguel Martínez Torrejón (Universidad de Antioquía, 2011), 16, 17. The book was first published in 1552.

115. Beckles, *A History of Barbados*, 21–22; Menard, *Sweet Negotiations*, 45, 93; McCusker and Menard, "Sugar Industry in the Seventeenth Century," 298; John J. McCusker, *The Economy of British America, 1607–1789* (University of North Carolina Press, 1985), 149. This point is made in a powerful way by Solow, *Economic Consequences of the Slave Trade*, 97–110.

116. Abigail Swingen, "Labor: Employment, Colonial Servitude, and Slavery in the Seventeenth-Century Atlantic," in *Mercantilism Reimagined: Political Economy in Early Modern Britain and Its Empire*, ed. Philip J. Stern and Carl Wennerlind (OUP, 2014), 61.

117. Solow, *Economic Consequences of the Slave Trade*, 107; McCusker and Menard, "Sugar Industry in the Seventeenth Century," 292, 297; Eltis, "New Estimates of Exports," 648; Beckles, "'Hub of Empire,'" citing Richard B. Sheridan, *Sugar and Slavery: An Economic History of the British West Indies, 1623–1775* (Johns Hopkins UP, 1974), 234–60; Dunn, *Sugar and Slaves*, 224–63; McCusker, *Economy of British America*, 151; and Jan de Vries, *The Industrious Revolution: Consumer Behavior and the Household Economy, 1650 to the Present* (CUP, 2008). In the 1710s, precisely 38,076 slaves arrived. See "List of Such Vessels That Have Imported Negroes to the Island of Barbados with the Number of Negros Transported by Which Vessel in the Naval Office Off the Said Island, 1708 to 1726," in RB 9/1/1, BNA; and Menard, *Sweet Negotiations*, 48. For the critique of "industriousness," see Voss and Weber, "War, Crisis and the Development of the Slave-Plantation Economy," 52. On the total forced migration of Africans between 1500 and 1760, see David Eltis, *The Rise of African Slavery in the Americas* (CUP, 2000), 9; See also Pomeranz and Topik, *World That Trade Created*, 41; Moore, "Nature and the Transition from Feudalism to Capitalism," 133, and, for the French islands, Debbasch, "Au coeur du 'gouvernement des esclaves'"; and Miller, "Captives, Collateral, Credit, and Currencies," 35.

118. Voss, *Sklaven als Ware und Kapital*, 122. I came to this total for the enslaved population by adding population aggregates by region. I drew the aggregates from a number of books, listed here by region. For British North America, see Ira Berlin, *Many Thousands Gone: The First Two Centuries of Slavery in North America* (HUP, 1998), 370. For Brazil, the French Caribbean, and the British Caribbean, see Robin Blackburn, *The Making of New World Slavery: From the Baroque to the Modern, 1492–1800* (Verso Press, 1997), 404, 486, 501. For the Danish and Dutch West Indies, see Orlando Patterson, *Slavery and Social Death: A Comparative Study* (HUP, 1982), 471, 482. For the Spanish colonies, see Herbert S. Klein, *African Slavery in Latin America and the Caribbean* (OUP, 1986), 295; Julie Jefferies, "The UK Population: Past, Present and Future," in *Focus on People and Migration* (Palgrave Macmillan UK, 2005), 3; and D. B. Grigg, *Population Growth and Agrarian Change: An Historical Perspective* (CUP, 1980), 191. The UK population is from Jefferies, the French from Grigg. For the 1800 population figure, see Blackburn, *Making of New World Slavery*, 581. To estimate the size of the workforce, I used the estimates from N. L. Tranter, "The Labour Supply, 1780–1860," in *The Economic History of Britain Since 1700*, vol. 1, *1700–1860*, ed. Roderick Floud and Donald McCloskey (CUP, 1981), 206, who estimates it at 45.7 percent for 1801.

119. Trevor Hall, *The Role of Cape Verde Islanders in Organizing and Operating Maritime Trade Between West Africa and Iberian Territories, 1441–1616* (Johns Hopkins UP, 1992), ii–iii, 90, 92–93, 159–60, 307; Maria Manuel Ferraz Torrão, "Traite négrière entre les îles du Cap-vert et l'Amérique espagnole: Formation et développement d'une route commerciale atlantique au seizième siècle" *African Economic History* 39, no. 1, (2011), 2–3; Inés Amorim, "Las islas de Cabo Verde en la ruta de la sal. La construcción de un complejo económico de época moderna" in A. Fábregas, ed., *Islas y sistemas de navegación durante las Edades Media y Moderna* (La Nao, 2010), 367–69; Richard Lobban, *Historical Dictionary of the Republics of Guinea-Bissau and Cape Verde* (Scarecrow Press, 1979), 69.

120. Hall, *The Role of Cape Verde Islanders*, 130–35, 342–48; Bentley Duncan, *Atlantic Islands: Madeira, the Azores, and the Cape Verdes in Seventeenth Century Commerce and Navigation* (CUP, 1972), 215.

121. Beckles, *History of Barbados*, 37; Beckles, "'Hub of Empire,'" 233; McCusker and Menard, "Sugar Industry in the Seventeenth Century," 300; and Van der Linden, "Re-Constructing the Origins," 512. On the various land acquisitions that assembled the plantation, see RB3.1.725–726, deeds of conveyance to James Drax, November 1639 and June 1640, and RB3.2.53–57, deeds of conveyance, 1647, both in BNA. See also "Drax Hall," in Hughes/Queree Papers, BNA.

122. Ligon, *True and Exact History*, 97.

123. Beckles, "'Hub of Empire,'" 226, and McCusker and Menard, "Sugar Industry in the Seventeenth Century," 293. There was also a shortfall of imports of indentured servants. See "Supply Versus Demand in the Barbadian Sugar Revolution," 404, 414; Ira Berlin and P. Morgan, *Cultivation and Culture: Labor and the Shaping of Slave Life in the Americas* (University of Virginia Press, 1993), 7.

124. James E. McClellan, *Colonialism and Science: Saint Domingue in the Old Regime* (Johns Hopkins UP, 1992), 188–89.

125. "Habitation Paroy, État des negres, negresses, negrillons, negrittes au 1 Mars 1783," and "Inventaire del meuble qui son sur l'habitation de Paroy, folder 3, inventories de habitations," both in Le Gentil de Paroy Papers, folder 1, 164APOM/1, Archives Privées, ANOM; see also

Paroy to Donnemarie [?], Messidor, an 10, D.P.P.C., 8 SUPSDOM/305, ANOM. See also Ministère des Finances, *État détaille des liquidations opérées à l'époque du 1er janvier 1828* (Paris: Imprimerie Royale, 1828), 33. On the costs of Alsatian spinning mills, see Colin Heywood, *The Development of the French Economy, 1750–1914* (Macmillan Press, 1992), 35.

126. Van der Linden, "Re-Constructing the Origins of Modern Labor Management," *Labor History* 51, no. 4 (November 2010): 511, 513, 514; and Burnard and Garrigus, *Plantation Machine*, 4, 17, 41. For the earliest mention of this idea, see Godinho Magalhaes, "Industrie et commerce antillais: Sur le sucre de Antilles," *Annales: Historie, Sciences Sociales* 3, no. 4 (1948): 541–45; and Robert William Fogel, *Without Consent or Contract: The Rise and Fall of American Slavery* (W. W. Norton, 1989), 23–26.

127. Ligon, *True and Exact History*, 55.

128. See "A List of Negroes on the Drax Hall Plantation," September 22, 1804, Z9/11/5, BNA.

129. Journal d'exploitation de l'habitation Bellevue Paroy 1784 in Le Gentil de Paroy, 164APOM/1, Fond Prives, Archives Privées, Centre d'archives d'outre mer, Aix-en-Provence, France.

130. "Règlement pour les Nègres dans mes habitations," Le Gentil de Paroy Papers, 164APOM/1, Archives Privées, ANOM.

131. As cited in Stuart B. Schwartz, *Early Brazil: A Documentary Collection to 1700* (CUP, 2010), 245.

132. Moore, "Sugar and the Expansion of the Early Modern World-Economy," 409–33; Dale Tomich, "Original Accumulation: The Genoese Cycle of Accumulation, Atlantic Slavery, and the Formation of the World-Market," unpublished paper presented at the Towards a Global History of Primitive Accumulation Conference, IISH, Amsterdam, May 2019, 16, 32–33.

133. Dunn, "Barbados Census of 1680," 26.

134. Burnard and Garrigus, *Plantation Machine*, 42; G. W. Roberts, "A Life Table for a West Indian Slave Population," *Population Studies* 5, no. 3 (March 1952): 24; Philip D. Morgan, "Slavery in the British Caribbean," in *The Cambridge World History of Slavery*, vol. 3, *AD 1420–AD 1840*, ed. David Eltis and Stanley L. Engerman (CUP, 2011), 382; Kenneth Morgan, "The Struggle for Survival: Slave Infant Mortality in the British Caribbean in the Late

Eighteenth and Nineteenth Centuries," in *Children in Slavery Through the Ages*, ed. Gwyn Campbell, Suzanne Miers, and Joseph C. Miller (Ohio UP, 2009); and Beckles, "'Hub of Empire,'" 223, 226.

135. William Fox, *Address to the People of Great Britain on the Propriety of Refraining from West India Sugar and Rum*, 10th ed. (Daniel Lawrence, 1792), 5.

136. Institutiones colonial indios, vol. 6, 1e parte, 1504/315 Archivo National Mexico, as cited in Julia McClure, *Empire of Poverty: The Moral-Political Economy of the Spanish Empire* (OUP, 2024), 150.

137. David Hume, "Of National Characters," in *Essays Moral, Political and Literary*, ed. David Hume and Eugene F. Miller (Liberty Fund, 1987); Voltaire, *An Essay on Universal History, the Manners, and Spirit of Nations, from the Reign of Charlemaign to the Age of Lewis XIV*, vol. 3, trans. Mr. Nugent (London: J. Nourse, 1759), 215–16; and Immanuel Kant, *Observations on the Feeling of the Beautiful and the Sublime*, trans. John T. Goldthwait (University of California Press, 1965).

138. For a good overview of the research landscape, see Adamczyk, *Zur Stellung Polens im modernen Weltsystem*. On Dutch landlords, see Johannes Nichtweiss and Gwyn Seward, "The Second Serfdom and the So-Called 'Prussian Way': The Development of Capitalism in Eastern German Agricultural Institutions," *Review* (Fernand Braudel Center) 3, no. 1 (1979): 115, 117. On landlords' control of workers, see Nichtweiss and Seward, "Second Serfdom," 102, 140; and Amiya Kumar Bagchi, *Perilous Passage: Mankind and the Global Ascendancy of Capital* (Rowman & Littlefield, 2005), 91. On the spread of serfdom, see Immanuel Wallerstein, "The West, Capitalism, and the Modern World-System," *Review* (Fernand Braudel Center) 15, no. 4 (1992): 561–619.

139. Nichtweiss and Seward, "Second Serfdom," 112.

140. Braudel, *Civilization and Capitalism*, 2:265; Vladimir Ilyich Lenin, *The Development of Capitalism in Russia: The Process of the Formation of a Home Market for Large-Scale Industry* (Foreign Languages Publishing House, 1956), 192.

141. Alice Velkova, "The Role of the Manor in Property Transfers of Serf Holdings in Bohemia in the Period of the 'Second Serfdom,'" *Social History* 37, no. 4 (2012): 508; Braudel, *Civilization and Capitalism*, 3:447;

Braudel, *Civilization and Capitalism,* 2:267, 271; Robert Bideleux and Ian Jeffries, *A History of Eastern Europe: Crisis and Change* (Routledge, 2007), 145, 186; and Mikolaj Malinowski, "Serfs and the City: Market Conditions, Surplus Extraction Institutions, and Urban Growth in Early Modern Poland," *European Review of Economic History* 20, no. 2 (2016): 124. The transition to serfdom was a slow process. See also Marian Małowist, *Wschód a Zachód Europy,* 113; and Sheilagh Ogilvie and A. W. Carus, "Institutions and Economic Growth in Historical Perspective," in *Handbook of Economic Growth,* vol. 2, ed. Philippe Aghion and Steven Durlauf (Elsevier, 2014), 420. See also Hartmut Harnisch, "Der preußische Absolutismus und die Bauern. Sozialkonservative Gesellschaftspolitik und Vorleistung zur Modernisierung," *Jahrbuch für Wirtschaftsgeschichte* 35, no. 3 (1994); Markus Cerman, *Villages and Lords in Eastern Europe, 1300–1800* (Palgrave Macmillan, 2012); Sheilagh Ogilvie, "Serfdom and the Institutional System in Early Modern Germany," in *Schiavitu e servaggio nell'economia europea. Secc. XI–XVIII,* ed. Simonetta Cavaciocchi (Florence UP, 2013); Alexander Klein and Sheilagh Ogilvie, "Occupational Structure in the Czech Lands Under the Second Serfdom," *EHR* 69, no. 2 (2016): 494; and Adamczyk, *Zur Stellung Polens im modernen Weltsystem,* 180. The intensification of that labor is chronicled in Andrzej Wyczánski, *Studia nad gospodarką starostwa korczyńskiego, 1500–1660* (Państwowe Wydawn Nauk, 1964); Adamczyk, *Zur Stellung Polens im modernen Weltsystem,* 195–99; and Braudel, *Civilization and Capitalism,* 2:267. On the limits of exploitation, see Witold Kula, *Teoria ekonomiczna ustroju feudalnego: próba modelu* (Państwowe Wydawn Nauk, 1983), 59–60.
142. Montesquieu, *Spirit of Laws,* 20, 23.
143. Davies, *God's Playground,* 201, 216–18, 284.
144. A brilliant analysis of this process is to be found in Jerzy Topolski, "Causes of Dualism in the Economic Development of Modern Europe," *Studia Historiae Oeconomicae* 3 (1968): 1–12; Malinowski, "Serfs and the City," 123–46; and Mikolaj Malinowski and Jan Luiten van Zanden, "Income and Its Distribution in Preindustrial Poland," *Cliometrica* 11, no. 3 (2017): 376.
145. Gaston de Montesquieu, *Pensées et fragments inédits de Montesquieu,*

vol. 2 (Gounoulihou, 1899), 292 (Pensée 777).
146. Nancy Fraser, "Behind Marx's Hidden Abode: For an Expanded Conception of Capitalism," *New Left Review* 86 (March–April 2014): 57.
147. Karl Marx, *Wage-Labor and Capital* (New York Labor News Co., 1946), 41.
148. Reséndez, *Other Slavery,* 71, 106.
149. Tutino, *Making a New World,* 40, 44, 103–6; and Reséndez, *Other Slavery,* 109–12.
150. Reséndez, *Other Slavery,* 113; and Tutino, *Mexican Heartland,* 94–96.
151. Steven A. Epstein, *Wage Labor and Guilds in Medieval Europe* (University of North Carolina Press, 1991), 258; Mark Bailey, *The Decline of Serfdom in Late Medieval England: From Bondage to Freedom* (Boydell Press, 2014), 6; Colin Platt, *King Death: The Black Death and Its Aftermath in Late Medieval England* (UCL Press, 1996); Norman F. Cantor, *In the Wake of the Plague: The Black Death and the World It Made* (Free Press, 2001), esp. 63–100; John Hatcher, *Plague, Population, and the English Economy 1348–1530* (Macmillan, 1977); Leonard W. Cowie, *The Black Death and Peasants' Revolt* (Wayland Publishers, 1988); David Green, *Edward the Black Prince: Power in Medieval Europe* (Longman, 2007), 51–73; A. Musson, "New Labour Laws, New Remedies? Legal Reaction to the Black Death Crisis," in *Fourteenth Century England,* vol. 1, ed. Nigel Saul (Boydell Press, 2000), 73–88; and Samuel K. Cohn, "After the Black Death: Labour Legislation and Attitudes Toward Labour in Late-Medieval Western Europe," *EHR* 60, no. 3 (2007): 457–85. In 1349, the Ordinance of Labourers came into existence, which is seen as the beginning of the long history of English labor law. See Catharina Lis and Hugo Soly, "Labor Laws in Western Europe, 13th–16th Centuries: Patterns of Political and Socio-Economic Rationality," in *Working on Labor: Essays in Honor of Jan Lucassen,* ed. Marcel van der Linden and Leo Lucassen (Brill, 2012), 299–322, esp. 307. See also Gerald Liu, "Agricultural Wage Labour in Fifteenth-Century England" (PhD diss., Durham University, 2012), 135; Dobb, *Studies in the Development of Capitalism,* 20–21; Brenner, "The Origins of Capitalist Development"; Shami Gosh, "Rural Economies and Transitions to Capitalism: Germany and England Compared (c. 1200–c. 1800)," *Journal of*

Agrarian Change 16, no. 2 (April 2016): 255; and Nicholas Abercrombie, Stephen Hill, and Bryan S. Turner, *Sovereign Individuals of Capitalism* (Routledge, 2015), 103. See also Robert Braid, "Behind the Ordinance of Labourers: Economic Regulation and Market Control in London Before the Black Death," *Journal of Legal History* 34, no. 1 (2013): 3–30; Christopher Dyer, *Making a Living in the Middle Ages: The People of Britain, 850–1520* (Yale UP, 2009), 279.
152. Halil İnalcık, "Rice-Cultivation and the Çeltükçi-re'âyâ System in the Ottoman Empire," *Turcica* 14 (1982): 69–141; Van Bavel, "Transition in the Low Countries," 289, 295, 298, 301; Bas van Bavel, "Rural Wage Labour in the Sixteenth-Century Low Countries: An Assessment of the Importance and Nature of Wage Labour in the Countryside of Holland, Guelders and Flanders," *Continuity and Change* 21, no. 1 (2006): 38; and Brandon, "Marxism and the 'Dutch Miracle,'" 120.
153. Braudel, *Civilization and Capitalism,* 2:288.
154. Braudel, *Civilization and Capitalism,* 2:293, 294; Eric Hobsbawm, "The General Crisis of the European Economy in the 17th Century," *Past & Present* 5 (May 1954): 33–53.
155. John Donoghue, "Resisting the 'Enslaving Design': Conscription and Its Discontents in England's Atlantic Empire, ca. 1649–1660," *Labor: Studies in Working-Class Histories of the Americas* 13, no. 3 / 4 (December 2016): 3–30; and Peter Way, "Strike a Terror: Military Justice the Guerilla Warfare of Class Struggle," unpublished paper (in author's possession), University of Pittsburgh, 2014.
156. Henry Heller, *The Birth of Capitalism: A Twenty-First-Century Perspective* (Pluto Press, 2011), 6. Vanhaute, "Making Sense of the Great Divergence," 12.
157. Hardiman, "Penetration of Merchant Capital in Pre-Colonial Gujarat," 34, 36, 38–40; Kaveh Yazdani, *India, Modernity and the Great Divergence: Mysore and Gujarat (17th to 19th C.)* (Brill, 2017), 383.
158. De Vries, *Dutch Rural Economy,* 210.
159. Aleksandar Shopov, "Between the Pen and the Fields: Books on Farming, Changing Land Regimes, and Urban Agriculture in the Ottoman Eastern Mediterranean ca. 1500–1700" (PhD diss., Harvard University, 2016), 27–28, 30, 33–34, 42–45, 100, 115, 183–85, esp. 459.

See also Aleksandar Shopov, "Rice Agriculture, Commercial Farming and Environmental Change in the Early Modern Balkans," unpublished paper (in author's possession), 2018, 3; Çağlar Keyder, "Introduction: Large-Scale Commercial Agriculture in the Ottoman Empire?," in *Landholding and Commercial Agriculture in the Middle East*, ed. Çağlar Keyder and Faruk Tabak (State University of New York Press, 1991), 2–3; Gilles Veinstein, "On the Çiftlik Debate," in Keyder and Tabak, *Landholding and Commercial Agriculture in the Middle East*, 35–56; Halil İnalcık, "The Emergence of Big Farms, Çiftliks, State, Landlords and Tenants," in *Contributions à l'histoire économique et sociale de l'Empire ottoman*, ed. Jean-Louis Bacqué-Grammont and Paul Dumont (Peeters, 1983), 111–14; Bruce McGowan, "The Age of the Ayans, 1699–1812," in *An Economic and Social History of the Ottoman Empire*, vol. 1, *1300–1914*, ed. Halil İnalcik and Donald Quataert (CUP, 1994), 637–758; Huri İslamoğlu and Çağlar Keyder, "Agenda for the Ottoman History," in *The Ottoman Empire and the World Economy*, ed. Huri İslamoğlu-İnan (CUP, 1987), 59; Daniel Goffman, "Izmir: From Village to Colonial Port City, the Ottoman City Between East and West," in *The Ottoman City Between East and West: Aleppo, Izmir and Istanbul*, ed. Edhem Eldem, Daniel Goffman, and Bruce Masters (CUP, 1999), 79–134; Necmi Ülker, *The Rise of İzmir 1688–1740* (University of Michigan Press, 1975); Yūzō Nagata, "The Role of Ayans in Regional Development During the Pre-Tanzimat Period in Turkey: A Case Study of the Karaosmanoğlu Family," in *Studies on the Social and Economic History of the Ottoman Empire* (Akademi Kitabevi, 1995), 125; Abdel-Karim Rafeq, "City and Countryside in a Traditional Setting: The Case of Damascus in the First Quarter of the Eighteenth Century," in *The Syrian Land in the 18th and 19th Century: The Common and the Specific in the Historical Experience*, ed. Thomas Philipp (F. Steiner, 1992), 295–329; Sofia Bistra Cvetkova, "Le rôle du capital commercial-usuraire dans les terres balkaniques à l'époque ottomane aux XVI–XVIII s." in *Türk Tarih Kongresi*, vol. 7 (Türk Tarih Kurumu Basimevi, 1970): 483–92. Avdo Sućeska, "O nastanka čifluka u našim zemjama," *Godisnjak Drustva istoričara Bosne i Hercegovine* 16 (1965): 39–40. This was corroborated in the context of Edirne by Ömer Lütfi Barkan in his "Edirne ve Civarında Bazı Imaret Tesislerinin Muhasebe Bilançoları," *Belgeler* 1, no. 2 (1964): 235–377; and Ömer Lütfi Barkan, "Edirne Askeri Kassam'ına Ait Ter eke Defterleri (1545–1659)," *Belgeler* 3, no. 5–6 (1966): 47–58. Moreover, Mustafa Akdağ showed that farm estates specializing in livestock decreased the availability of grain from the mid-sixteenth century onward. See "Osmanlı İmperatorluğunun Kuruluş ve İnkişafi Devrinde Türkiye'nin İktisadi Vaziyeti," *Belleten* 13, no. 51 (1949): 390–95.

160. Smith, "Gedney Clarke of Salem and Barbados," 516–19.

161. Beckles, "'Hub of Empire,'" 231–32; Dunn, "The Barbados Census of 1680," 23; On the Royal African Company's sales in Barbados, see also Meetings of 6 and 7 September 1692, 241, in Minutes of Council Meetings, 1689–1696, BNA.

162. De Vries, *Dutch Rural Economy*, 197; Alan Mikhail, *Nature and Empire in Ottoman Egypt: An Environmental History* (CUP, 2011); Dina Khoury, "The Ottoman Centre Versus Provincial Power-Holders: An Analysis of the Historiography," in *The Cambridge History of Turkey*, vol. 3, ed. Suraiya N. Faroqhi (CUP, 2006), 133–56; Suraiya N. Faroqhi, "Rural Life," in Faroqhi, *Cambridge History of Turkey*, 3:376–90, here 380; and Shopov, "Rice Agriculture, Commercial Farming and Environmental Change," 5.

163. For the process, see Dépôt des papier publics de colonies, Affaires relatives aux concessions de terrains, 6DPPC/184, ANOM; Beckles, *History of Barbados*, 9, 10; and Dunn, *Sugar and Slaves*, 15.

164. Voss, *Sklaven als Ware und Kapital*, 197; Burnard and Garrigus, *Plantation Machine*, 11; Niall Ferguson, *Civilization: The West and the Rest* (Penguin Press, 2011), 38.

165. See also the stimulating paper by Iris Dannemann, "Agricultural Capitalism in South Carolina: John Locke's Colonial Philosophy of Labour, Property and Slavery," unpublished paper (in author's possession), presented at Re:Work Annual Conference, July 2017.

166. John Locke, *Two Treatises of Government*, ed. Peter Laslett (CUP, 1988), 389.

167. Paul Cheney, "Aufklärung und die politische Ökonomie des Kolonialismus," in Olaf Asbach, ed., *Der Moderne Staat und 'le doux commerce:' Politik, Ökonomie und internationale Beziehungen im politischen Denken der Aufklärung* (Baden Baden, 2014), 211, 213; Regina Grafe and Alejandra Irigoin, "A Stakeholder Empire: The Political Economy of Spanish Imperial Rule in America," *EHR* 65 (2012): 635.

168. Morgan, *American Slavery, American Freedom*, 189, 193.

169. Guanmian Xu, "From the Atlantic to the Manchu: Taiwan Sugar and the Early Modern World, 1630s–1720s," *Journal of World History* 33, no. 2 (2022): 268–77. Sucheta Mazumdar suggests that sugar was being cultivated on Taiwan before the Dutch arrival. See Sucheta Mazumdar, *Sugar and Society in China: Peasants, Technology, and the World Market* (HUP, 1998), 71, 86, 206; Tonio Andrade, *How Taiwan Became Chinese: Dutch, Spanish, and Han Colonization in the Seventeenth Century* (CUP, 2008), 1, 56–60; Lian Heng, *Taiwan tongshi*, in *Taiwan shiji congshu*, vol. 26 (Yushi wenshua shiye gongsi, 1977), 503; Jack F. Williams, "Sugar: The Sweetener in Taiwan's Development," in *China's Island Frontier: Studies in the Historical Geography of Taiwan*, ed. Ronald G. Knapp (University of Hawai'i Press, 1980), 217; Hung Chien-Chao, *A History of Taiwan* (Il Cerichio, 2000), 78.

170. Xu, "From the Atlantic to the Manchu," 277–96; Guanmian Xu, "Sweetness and Chaozhou: Construction of Tropical Commodity Chains on the Early Modern China Coast, 1560s–1860s" (unpublished MPhil thesis, Chinese University of Hong Kong, 2017), 51–59; Williams, "Sugar: The Sweetener in Taiwan's Development," 218–19. The multiplier is a rough estimate, since we do not know precisely how much sugar was produced in Taiwan in 1636. Andrade, *How Taiwan Became Chinese*, 1, 256–308. See also Mazumdar, *Sugar and Society in China*, 86; Deng Kongzhao, *Studies on Zheng Chenggong and the History of Taiwan During the Ming-Zheng Era* [(Beijing: Taihai Publisher, 2000), 邓孔昭著：《郑成功与明郑台湾史研究》(北京：台海出版社，2000年)], 76–9; Pomeranz and Topik, *The World That Trade Created*, 126–28. The number of sugar mills in early eighteenth-century Taiwan was underreported by the local government. Their real scale was revealed only during land reform in the 1720s. See Guanmian Xu, "Buffalo Regimes: Animal Labour on Asia's Sugar Frontiers, 1630–1800" (paper presented at the Commodities and Environments in Early Modern Global Asia 1400–1800 Workshop, European University Institute, Florence, November 13–15, 2024).

171. Braudel, *Civilization and Capitalism*, 2:253.

172. Peter Linebaugh and Marcus Rediker, *The Many-Headed Hydra: Sailors, Slaves, Commoners, and the Hidden Story of the Revolutionary Atlantic* (Beacon Press, 2013).

173. Braudel, *Civilization and Capitalism*, 2:252.

174. Rafeq, "City and Countryside in a Traditional Setting," 295–329; and Shopov, "Between the Pen and the Fields," 43–45, 185.

175. See Robert Crowley, "An Informacion and Peticion," in *The Select Works of Robert Crowley*, ed. J. M. Cowper (Kraus Reprint Co., 1975), 161–64.

176. British Library, MS Harley 304, fols. 75r–78v.

177. *The Diggers of Warwickshire to All Other Diggers*, 1607, British Library, MS Harley 787, no. 11.

178. John Martin, "The Midland Revolt of 1607," in *An Atlas of Rural Protest in Britain 1548–1900*, ed. Andrew Charlesworth (Routledge, 2018), 33.

179. Alexander Areskine to Atholl, 20 October 1707, Blair Atholl Castle, Atholl MSS, box 43 (7), 189, as quoted in Christopher A. Whatley, *Scottish Society, 1707–1830: Beyond Jacobitism, Towards Industrialisation* (Manchester UP, 2000), 155.

180. Whyte, *Scotland Before the Industrial Revolution*, 145.

181. *Caledonian Mercury*, April 21, 1724.

182. W. A. J. Prevost, "Letters Reporting the Rising of the Levellers in 1724," *Transactions of Dumfriesshire and Galloway Natural History and Antiquarian Society* 44 (1967): 196, quoting Wodrow, MSS Folio XL, No. 80; and "Commonty Property," as quoted in Ian L. Donnachie and Innes F. MacLeod, *Old Galloway* (David & Charles, 1974), 55.

183. Prevost, "Letters Reporting the Rising of the Levellers in 1724," 200, 203.

184. *News from Galloway, or the Poor Man's Plea Against His Landlord in a Letter to a Friend Is Published*, June 1724, B.c.4.8/10, New College Library Special Collections Repository, Edinburgh University, Scotland.

185. Beckles, "'Hub of Empire,'" 234.

186. Velasco to the Viceroy, 22 March 1601, as quoted in *Don Juan de Oñate, Colonizer of New Mexico, 1595–1628*, vol. 2, trans. George P. Hammond and Agapito Rev (University of New Mexico Press, 1953), 609.

187. Beckles, *History of Barbados*, 22; Reséndez, *Other Slavery*, 9; Joe S.

Sando, *Pueblo Nations: Eight Centuries of Pueblo Indian History* (Clear Light Publishers, 1992), 63; Joe S. Sando, *Pueblo Profiles: Cultural Identity Through Centuries of Change* (Clear Light Publishers, 1998); Angelico Chavez, "Pohè-Yemo's Representative and the Pueblo Revolt of 1680," *New Mexico Historical Review* 42, no. 2 (April 1967), 85–126; Matthew Liebmann, T. J. Ferguson, and Robert W. Preucel, "Pueblo Settlement, Architecture, and Social Change in the Pueblo Revolt Era, A.D. 1680 to 1696," *Journal of Field Archaeology* 30, no. 1 (Spring 2005): 45–60; Andrew L. Knaut, *The Pueblo Revolt of 1680: Conquest and Resistance in Seventeenth-Century New Mexico* (University of Oklahoma Press, 1995), 168–69; Ramon A. Gutierrez, *When Jesus Came, the Corn Mothers Went Away: Marriage, Sexuality, and Power in New Mexico, 1500–1846* (Stanford UP, 1991), 133–35; and Sergio Villalobos, "Tres Siglos y Media de Vida Fronteriza," in *Relaciones fronterizas en la Araucanía* (Ediciones Universidad Católica de Chile, 1982), 43.

188. Jerome S. Handler, "Slave Revolts and Conspiracies in Seventeenth-Century Barbados," *New West Indian Guide* 56, no. 1–2 (1982): 7, 9; Ligon, *True and Exact History*, 29, 45–46, 70; Andrew White, "A Briefe Relation of the Voyage unto Maryland, by Father Andrew White, 1634," in *Narratives of Early Maryland, 1633–1684*, ed. Clayton Colman Hall (Charles Scribner's Sons, 1910), 37; and Meeting of 16 March 1685, 160, in Minutes of Council Meetings, 1684–1689, BNA.

189. Morgan, *American Slavery, American Freedom*, 230, 270, 292, 336.

190. On slave resistance in Saint-Domingue, see Voss, *Sklaven als Ware und Kapital*, 198–236; Ligon, *True and Exact History*, 51; Vincent Brown, *Tacky's Revolt: The Story of an Atlantic Slave War* (HUP, 2022).

191. "Dispositif de l'arrêt du Conseil des Dépêches rendu en faveur de Monsieur le Marquis de Paroi le 27 Novembre 1779 dans l'affaire du Nègre Antoine, Procédure relative à l'affaire du nègre Antoine," Le Gentil de Paroy Papers, 164APOM/1, Archives Privées, ANOM.

192. Handler, "Slave Revolts and Conspiracies," 5–42.

193. Ligon, *True and Exact History*, 46.

194. Dorman Newman, *The Present State of New-England with Respect to*

the Indian War (London: Dorman Newman, 1675), 66.

195. Handler, "Slave Revolts and Conspiracies," 9, 17–18, 24.

196. Meeting of 16 March 1685, 160–61, in Minutes of Council Meetings, 1684–1689, BNA. See also the notes on the meeting of 16 February 1685, 157, BNA.

197. Meeting of 25 October 1692, 248, and Meeting of 8 December 1692, 268–69, in Minutes of Council Meetings, 1689–1696, BNA.

198. Meeting of 16 February 1685, 158, in Minutes of Council Meetings, 1684–1689, BNA.

199. *Great News from Barbados, or, A True and Faithful Account of the Grand Conspiracy of the Negroes Against the English* (London: 1676), 11–2; and Beckles, *History of Barbados*, 49.

200. Extract of Letter from Barbados, 18 December 1683, CO 1/53, 264–66, PRO, as cited in Handler, "Slave Revolts and Conspiracies," 20.

201. Beckles, *History of Barbados*, 46. See Meeting of 11 October 1692, 246–47, in Minutes of Council Meetings, 1689–1696, BNA. The council ordered payments for such gibbets to a Latimer Richards. For payments to the executioner, see Meeting of 21 February 1692, 283, in Minutes of Council Meetings, 1689–1696, BNA.

202. See, for example, Meeting of 17 June 1685, 77, in Minutes of Council Meetings, 1684–1689, BNA. See also Meetings 12 May 1686, 186; 23 November 1686, 218; 27 January 1686, 248–49. That year, almost every council meeting reported on such executions, often of larger groups of slaves.

203. Address by the Council and Assembly to his Majesty William, 29 October 1692, in Meeting of 27 October 1692, 256–58, in Minutes of Council Meetings, 1689–1696, BNA.

204. Council Minutes, 17 April 1694, 375, Minutes of Council Meetings, 1689–1696, BNA.

205. Handler, "Slave Revolts and Conspiracies," 9.

206. Barbados Council, as cited in Handler, "Slave Revolts and Conspiracies," 9.

207. Burnard and Garrigus, *Plantation Machine*, 39.

208. David Buisseret, *Jamaica 1687: The Taylor Manuscript at the National Library of Jamaica* (UP of the West Indies, 2006), 276, as cited in Burnard and Garrigus, *Plantation Machine*, 39.

209. Manuel Barcia, *The Great African Slave Revolt of 1825* (Louisiana

State UP, 2012), 43; Potofsky, "Paris-on-the-Atlantic from the Old Regime to the Revolution," 104. See also Rapport au Directoire Éxécutif, Marine Bureau des Colonies, Paris, 7 Praivial 1799; Déplacement de la Marine et des colonies, 5e Trimestre 1807; Refugies, 1798, Consulate Savannah, all in G/1/512, ANOM; Burnard and Garrigus, *Plantation Machine*, 39, 130–31.

210. Braudel, *Civilization and Capitalism*, 2:258, 262; Polanyi, *Great Transformation*, 44.

211. Fraser, "Behind Marx's Hidden Abode," 57.

212. O'Brien, "Was the First Industrial Revolution a Conjuncture in the History of the World Economy?," 19; Peter Bakewell, *Miners of the Red Mountain: Indian Labor in Potosí* (University of New Mexico Press, 1984), 14–15, 17; Fraser, "Behind Marx's Hidden Abode," 63; Moore, "Nature and the Transition from Feudalism to Capitalism," 132; Moore, "Sugar and the Expansion of the Early Modern World-Economy," 420; Gosh, *Nutmeg's Curse*, 55.

213. Goodman, *Tobacco in History*, 37; Bakewell, *Miners of the Red Mountain*, 14–15, 17.

214. See Maria Mies, *Patriarchy and Accumulation on a World Stage: Women in the International Division of Labour* (Zed Books, 1985), xvi; Fraser, "Behind Marx's Hidden Abode," 59; and Tutino, *The Mexican Heartland*.

215. Fraser, "Behind Marx's Hidden Abode," 59, 62, 70–71. A point made by generations of feminists, including Maud Anne Bracke, "Between the Transnational and the Local: Mapping the Trajectories and Contexts of the Wages for Housework Campaign in 1970s Italian Feminism," *Women's History Review* 22, no. 4 (2013): 628; Mariarosa Dalla Costa and Selma James, *The Power of Women and the Subversion of the Community* (Falling Wall Press, 1972); Noah D. Zatz and Eileen Boris, "Seeing Work, Envisioning Citizenship," *Employee Rights and Employment Public Policy Journal* 18, no. 1 (2014): 96, 98–99; and Nancy Fraser and Rahel Jaeggi, *Capitalism: A Conversation in Critical Theory* (Polity Press, 2018), 24, 167.

216. This is cited by John Merrington, "Town and Country in the Transition to Capitalism," in *The Transition from Feudalism to Capitalism*, ed. Rodney Hilton (Verso, 1976), 181.

217. Immanuel Maurice Wallerstein, *The Capitalist World-Economy: Essays* (CUP, 1979), 214–55; G. E. Aylmer, *The State's Servants: The Civil Service*

of the English Republic 1649–1660 (Routledge & Kegan Paul, 1973), 251; and Sheridan, *Sugar and Slavery*, 94–99. See also Fernand Braudel, *Afterthoughts on Material Civilization and Capitalism*, trans. Patricia M. Ranum (Johns Hopkins UP, 1977), 93. He calls that diversity of "great significance."

218. Abbé Raynal, *Histoire Philosophique et Politique des Établissemens et du Commerce des Européens Dans les Deux Indes* (Amable Costes, 1820), 542–43.

Chapter 5: Intensifying Industry, 1600–1750

1. John Quincy Adams to Thomas Boylston Adams, 1800, in John Quincy Adams, *Letters on Silesia, Written During a Tour Through That Country in the Years 1800, 1801* (J. Rudd, 1804), 157–58.

2. Siegfried Kühn, *Der Hirschberger Leinwand- und Schleierhandel von 1648 bis 1806* (Verlag Priebatsch Buchhandel Breslau, 1938), 9, 11, 14; Marcel Boldorf, "Institutional Barriers to Economic Development: The Silesian Linen Proto-Industry (17th to 19th Century)," *Discussion Papers / Institut für Volkswirtschaftslehre und Statistik* 566 (1999): 10; and Alfred Zimmermann, *Bluethe und Verfall des Leinengewerbes in Schlesien. Gewerbe- und Handelspolitik dreier Jahrhunderte* (W. G. Korn, 1885), 57. For a contemporary report on Hirschberg, see Adams, *Letters on Silesia*, 50–58. For the bleaching factories, see Boldorf, "Institutional Barriers to Economic Development," 3, 10. For trade, see Marian Małowist, *Wschód a Zachód Europy w XIII-XVI wieku: Konfrontacja struktur społeczno-gospodarczych* (Wydawnictwo Naukowe PWN, 2006), 171.

3. Zimmermann, *Blüthe und Verfall des Leinengewerbes in Schlesien*, 48–51. On the poverty, see the discussion on nutritional standards in Anka Steffen et al., "Spinning and Weaving for the Slave Trade: Proto-Industry in Eighteenth-Century Silesia," in *Slavery Hinterland*, vol. 7 (Boydell & Brewer, 2016), 97; Hermann Rubin, "Die Wirtschaft," in *Geschichte Schlesiens Vol. 2: Die Habsburger Zeit 1526–1740*, ed. Ludwig Petry and Josef Joachim Menzel (Jan Thorbecke Verlag, 2000), 108f; Boldorf, "Institutional Barriers to Economic Development," 3; Anka Steffen, "Schlesische Leinwand als Handelsgut im atlantischen Sklavenhandel der frühen Neuzeit. Das Beispiel der Hirschberger Kaufmanns-Societät," *Themenportal Europäische Geschichte*

(2017): 4; and Marcel Boldorf, *Europäische Leinenregionen im Wandel: Institutionelle Weichenstellungen in Schlesien und Irland (1750–1850)* (Böhlau Verlag, 2006), 34. The prevalence of flax is also remarked upon by Adams, *Letters on Silesia*, 27–28; Arno Herzig, "Der Üebergang von der Proto-Industrie zum Industriellen Zeitalter in Niederschlesien," *Schlesische Geschichtsblaetter* 46 (2019): 77; Lujo Brentano, "Ueber den grundherrlichen Charakter des hausindustriellen Leinengewerbes in Schlesien," *Zeitschrift für Social- und Wirthschaftsgeschichte* 1, no. 2/3 (1893): 328; Rubin, "Die Wirtschaft," 127f; and Boldorf, *Europäische Leinenregionen im Wandel*, 33–35.

4. Ursula Lewald, "Die Entwicklung der ländlichen Textilindustrie im Rheinland und in Schlesien. Ein Vergleich," *Zeitschrift für Ostforschung* 10 (1961): 628.

5. Zespół 3, akta miasta Jeleniej Góry, Bestand 3, Akten der Stadt Jelenia Góra (jedn. 2272, Geschäftsbriefe der Firma Ketzler 1756–1791, Archiwum Państwowe we Wrocławiu, oddział w Jeleniej Górze. See also Peter Kriedte, Hans Medick, and Jürgen Schlumbohm, *Industrialisierung vor der Industrialisierung* (Vandenhoeck & Ruprecht, 1978), 86; Adams, *Letters on Silesia*, 133.

6. Zimmermann, *Blüthe und Verfall des Leinengewerbes in Schlesien*, 1–12; Brentano, "Ueber den grundherrlichen Charakter," 327; Konrad Fuchs, *Beiträge zur Wirtschafts- und Sozialgeschichte Schlesiens* (Forschungsstelle Ostmitteleuropa, 1985), 21; and Anka Steffen, "A Cloth That Binds: New Perspectives on the Eighteenth-Century Prussian Economy," *Slavery & Abolition* 42, no. 1 (2021): 110.

7. Rubin, "Die Wirtschaft," 127f; Konrad Fuchs, *Beiträge zur Wirtschafts- und Sozialgeschichte Schlesiens*, 22f; Steffen, "Schlesische Leinwand als Handelsgut im atlantischen Sklavenhandel der frühen Neuzeit," 12–13; Boldorf, "Institutional Barriers to Economic Development," 4–5; Anka Steffen, "Silesia, Serfdom, and Slavery: A Relationship History from the Late Seventeenth to the Early Twentieth Century," in *Journal of Global Slavery* 8, no. 2–3 (October 2023): 245; Kühn, *Der Hirschberger Leinwand*, 48–49; and Rubin, "Die Wirtschaft," 127f. By 1750, there were 129 merchants in Hirschberg dedicated to the linen trade. Anka Steffen, "Johann Friedrich Ketzler, "Insonders hochgeehrter

Herr!"—Ein Beitrag zur Einbindung der Gewerbelandschaft Schlesien in den kolonialen Transatlantikhandel im 18. Jahrhundert am Beispiel der Geschäftskorrespondenz" (master's thesis, Europa-Universität Viadrina, Frankfurt/Oder, 2013), 31. To get the 2018 value of this amount, I assumed that the thalers in consideration were so-called speciesthaler, which equaled one-ninth of a Cologne mark, each of which contained 233.856 grams of silver. Assuming a silver price of $0.47 per gram, the total value of these thalers is $17,705,370 in US dollars. See Steffen, "Cloth That Binds," 105–29, table 4. See also C. Grünhagen, "Ueber den angeblich grundherrlichen Charakter des hausindustriellen Leinengewerbes in Schlesien und die Webernöthe," Zeitschrift für Social- und Wirthschaftsgeschichte 2, no. 2 (1894): 253. Indeed, as late as 1828, linen constituted one-quarter of all German exports. See Bondi Gerhard, Deutschlands Außenhandel, 1815–1870 (Akademie Verlag, 1958), 55.
8. Rubin, "Die Wirtschaft," 127–28; and Milan Myška, "Proto-Industrialisierung in Böhmen, Mähren und Schlesien," in Protoindustrialisierung in Europa. Industrielle Produktion vor dem Fabrikzeitalter, ed. Markus Cerman and Sheilagh C. Ogilvie (Verlag für Gesellschaftskritik, 1994), 185.
9. Grünhagen, "Ueber den angeblich grundherrlichen Charakter," 246; Rubin, "Die Wirtschaft," 125; Steffen et al., "Spinning and Weaving for the Slave Trade," 94; Boldorf, Europäische Leinenregionen im Wandel, 34f; Brentano, "Ueber den grundherrlichen Charakter," 327; Herzig, "Der Übergang von der Proto-Industrie zum Industriellen Zeitalter in Niederschlesien," 78. Steffen, "Cloth That Binds," 105–29; and Boldorf, "Institutional Barriers to Economic Development," 10.
10. Steffen et al., "Spinning and Weaving for the Slave Trade," 87–107, here 104–5.
11. Gerhart Hauptmann, The Weavers, trans. Mary Morison (W. B. Huebsch, 1916), 89. The play, originally published in 1892 as Die Weber, was first performed by the Freie Bühne in 1893.
12. Hauptmann, Weavers, 117.
13. Hauptmann, Weavers, 85.
14. Adams, Letters on Silesia, 157.
15. Unterstützungs und Wohltätigkeitsverein, 1844–1854, Spinner und Weber, W 1/9: III, No. 45, Bethmann-Archiv, Stadtarchiv

Frankfurt, Germany. See also "Aufruf an edle Menschenfreunde zur Unterstützung der nothleidenden Spinner und Weber in der Kreisen Landshut und Bolkenhain," Frankfurter Journal, March 23, 1844.
16. Fernand Braudel, Civilization and Capitalism, 15th–18th Century, trans. Siân Reynolds, vol. 2, The Wheels of Commerce (University of California Press, 1992), 298.
17. Braudel, Civilization and Capitalism, 2:372; and Karl Polanyi, The Great Transformation: The Political and Economic Origins of Our Time (Beacon Press, 2001), 77.
18. Peter Kriedte, Hans Medick, and Jürgen Schlumbohm, Industrialization Before Industrialization: Rural Industry in the Genesis of Capitalism, trans. Beate Schempp (CUP, 1981), 6. On the expansion of manufacturing, see also H. M. Scott, "Manufacturing," in The Oxford Handbook of Early Modern European History, 1350–1750, vol. 1, Peoples and Places (OUP, 2015), 510; Karl-Heinrich Kaufhold, "Gewerbelandschaften in der frühen Neuzeit (1650–1800)," in Gewerbe- und Industrielandschaften vom Spätmittelalter bis ins 20. Jahrhundert, ed. Hans Pohl (F. Steiner Verlag Wiesbaden, 1986), 112–202, here 112–16; Jan de Vries, The Industrious Revolution: Consumer Behavior and the Household Economy, 1650 to the Present (CUP, 2008), 7–9; Robert Allen, "Agriculture During the Industrial Revolution," in The Economic History of Britain Since 1700, ed. Roderick Flood and D. N. McCloskey, vol. 1, 1700–1860 (CUP, 1994), 120; Braudel, Civilization and Capitalism, 2:309, 372; Polanyi, Great Transformation, 77; Charles Verlinden, Les origines de la civilisation atlantique: De la Renaissance a l'Age des Lumières (Editions de la Baconniere, 1966), 140; Violet Barbour, Capitalism in Amsterdam in the Seventeeth Century (Johns Hopkins UP, 1950), 67; and Jairus Banaji, "Globalising the History of Capital: Ways Forward," Historical Materialism 26, no. 3 (September 2018): 143–66. On this process, see also Bruno Blondé and Ilja Van Damme, "Early Modern Europe: 1500–1800," in Oxford Handbook of Cities in World History (OUP, 2013), 249; and Boldorf, "Institutional Barriers to Economic Development," 4–5.
19. Sophus Reinert, "Medici Industrial Entrepreneurs and the Origins of Political Economy," unpublished paper, 2018, 6–7, 713, 724.
20. Maria Bogucka, "Danzigs Bedeutung für die Wirtschaft des Ost-

seeraumes in der Frühen Neuzeit," in Studia Historiae Oeconomicae 9 (1974): 100; and Maria Bogucka, Gdasnkie rzemioslo tekstylne od XVI do polowy XVII wieku (Zakland Imiebia Ossolinskich, 1956), 294, 295, 297, 298, 301.
21. Suraiya Faroqhi, The Ottoman Empire and the World Around It (I. B. Tauris, 2004), 70–71. The connection between intensifying trade and manufacturing is also made by Nelly Hanna, Artisan Entrepreneurs in Cairo and Early Modern Capitalism (1600–1800) (Syracuse UP, 2011), 2–3, 37–38, 42, 44–45, 52, 194.
22. Lucette Valensi, "Islam et capitalisme: Production et commerce des chéchias en Tunisie et en France aux XVIIIe et XIXe siècles," Revue d'histoire moderne et contemporaine 16 (July–September 1969): 376–400; Beshara Doumani, Rediscovering Palestine: Merchants and Peasants in Jabal Nablus, 1700–1900 (University of California Press, 1995): 187–94; Donald Quataert, "The Ottoman Empire, 1650–1922," in The Ashgate Companion to the History of Textile Workers, 1650–2000, ed. Lex Heerma van Voss, Els Hiemstra-Kuperus, and Elise van Nederveen Meerkerk (Ashgate Publishing, 2010), 477–96; and Şevket Pamuk, "Wirtschaft und Institutionen im Nahen Osten seit dem Mittelalter," in Die Ursprünge der modernen Welt: Geschichte im wissenschaftlichen Vergleich, ed. James A. Robinson and Klaus Wiegandt (Fischer Taschenbuch Verlag, 2008), 541–90. A more general and very useful discussion on the thinking on Ottoman economic history can be found in Cemal Kafadar, "The Question of Ottoman Decline," Harvard Middle Eastern and Islamic Review 4, no. 1–2 (1997–1998): 30–75, esp. 47–52.
23. Timothy Brook, "The Merchant Network in 16th Century China: A Discussion and Translation of Zhang Han's 'On Merchants,'" Journal of the Economic and Social History of the Orient 24, no. 2 (May 1981): 167; Michael Dillon, "Transport and Marketing in the Development of the Jingdezhen Porcelain Industry During the Ming and Qing Dynasties," Journal of the Economic and Social History of the Orient 35, no. 3 (1992): 278, 286; Susan Naquin and Evelyn S. Rawski, Chinese Society in the Eighteenth Century (Yale UP, 1987), 164; Porcelain Research Institute of Jiangxi Province Light InDustry Department (Jiangxisheng qinggongyeting taociyanjiusuo), ed.,

History of Jingdezhen Porcelain (Jingdezhen taoci shigao) (Sanlian Shudian, 1959), 107–11; and Stanislas Julien, *Histoire et fabrication de la porcelaine chinoise ouvrage traduit du chinois* (Paris: Mallet-Bachelier, 1856). On the importance of merchants to the organizing of this intensified industry, see Xu Dixin and Wu Chengming, eds., *History of Capitalism in China*, vol. 1, *The Capitalist Buds in China* (Zhongguo zibenzhuyi fazhanshi: Diyijuan zhongguo zibenzhuyi de mengya), 582. On porcelain "brokers" becoming wealthy, see Maris Boyd Gillette, *China's Porcelain Capital* (Bloomsbury, 2016), 27. On Surat, see T. Volker, *Porcelain and the Dutch East India Company: As Recorded in the Dagh-Registers of Batavia Castle, Those of Hirado and Deshima, and Other Contemporary Papers, 1602–1682* (Brill, 1954), 181. On Aleppo, see John Carswell, "More About the Mongols: Chinese Porcelain from Asia to Europe," *Asian Affairs* 36, no. 11 (2005): 158–67, esp. 161–62, 164.
24. Luisa Piccinno, "Genoa: A City with a Port or a Port City?," in *The Routledge Handbook of Maritime Trade Around Europe 1300–1600*, ed. Wim Blockmans, Mikhail Krom, and Justyna Wubs-Mrozewicz (Routledge, 2017), 163; and J. Heers, *Genova nel quattrocento: Città mediterranea, grande capitalism e capitalism populare* (Jaca Book, 1984), 201–2.
25. Braudel, *Civilization and Capitalism*, 2:314–15; Hanna, *Artisan Entrepreneurs in Cairo*, 70; Abdul-Karim Rafeq, "Craft Organization, Work Ethics, and the Strains of Change in Ottoman Syria," *Journal of the American Oriental Society* 111, no. 3 (1991): 495, 497–98, 508–9. For the Ottoman Empire, see Abdul-Karim Rafeq, "A Different Balance of Power: Europe and the Middle East in the Eighteenth and Nineteenth Centuries," in *A Companion to the History of the Middle East*, ed. Youssef M. Choueiri (Blackwell, 2005), 238.
26. Peter Kriedte, "Die Stadt im Prozeß der europäischen Proto-Industrialisierung," *Die Alte Stadt* 9 (1982), 27f; Kriedte, Medick, and Schlumbohm, *Industrialization Before Industrialization*, 22; and Pierre Deyon, *Amiens capitale provinciale: Étude sur la société urbaine au 17e siècle* (Mouton, 1967), 209f.
27. Maarten Prak, *Early Modern Capitalism: Economic and Social Change in Europe, 1400–1800* (Routledge, 2001), 13; Kriedte, "Die Stadt im Prozeß der europäischen

Proto-Industrialisierung," 21; and "Mémoire des fabriquants d'étoffes de Soie de la ville de Nîmes," 1756, and "Mémoire des syndics des marchands faisant fabriquer des étoffes de soie de la ville de Nîmes," 1777, as quoted in Edward A. Allen, "The Genesis of Revolution in the Gard: The Convocation of the Estates General of 1789 in the Sénéchaussée de Nîmes" (PhD diss., Tulane University, 1982). See also Léon Dutil, *L'État économique du Languedoc à la fin de l'ancien régime (1750–1789)* (Librairie Hachette et Cie, 1911), 460–61; Simon-Charles-Sébastien Bernard Ballainvilliers, *Mémoires sur le Languedoc; suivis du Traité sur le commerce en Languedoc de l'intendant Ballainvilliers (1788)* (L'Entente Bibliophile, 1989), 359–60; Stephen J. Miller, "The Economy of France in the Eighteenth and Nineteenth Centuries: Market Opportunity and Labour Productivity in Languedoc," *Rural History* 20 (2009): 13–14; Braudel, *Civilization and Capitalism*, 2:317; and Emmanuel Le Roy Ladurie, *The French Peasantry, 1450–1660*, trans. Alan Sheridan (University of California Press, 1987), 316. See E. V. Tarle, *L'industrie dans les campagnes en France à la fin de l'ancien régime* (E. Cornely et Cie, 1910). See also "Unsigned letter to Redacteur, 10 août 1787," *Journal de Nismes* 33 (August 16, 1787): 261, as quoted in Allen, "Genesis of Revolution in the Gard," 220.
28. Braudel, *Civilization and Capitalism*, 2:318; and Maurice Dobb, *Studies in the Development of Capitalism* (International Publisher, 1947), 124; and Blondé and Van Damme, "Early Modern Europe," 249.
29. Prak, *Early Modern Capitalism*, 13. For the general argument, see also Jairus Banaji, "Islam, the Mediterranean and the Rise of Capitalism," *Historical Materialism* 15, no. 1 (March 2007): 47–74; Douglas E. Haynes, *Rhetoric and Ritual in Colonial India: The Shaping of a Public Culture in Surat City, 1852–1928* (University of California Press, 1991), 38f; K. N. Chaudhuri, *Asia Before Europe: Economy and Civilisation of the Indian Ocean from the Rise of Islam to 1750* (CUP, 1990), 304; and Sheilagh C. Ogilvie and Markus Cerman, "The Theories of Proto-Industrialization," in *European Proto-Industrialization: An Introductory Handbook*, ed. Sheilagh Ogilvie and Markus Cerman (CUP, 1996), 1.
30. R. Bin Wong, *China Transformed: Historical Change and the

Limits of European Experience* (Cornell UP, 1997), 37; David Howell, "Proto-Industrial Origins of Japanese Capitalism," *Journal of Asiatic Studies* 51, no. 2 (1992): 275; and Sheilagh C. Ogilvie, "Proto-Industrialization in Europe," *Continuity and Change* 8, no. 2 (1993): 159. The concept of proto-industrialization comes from the important work of Franklin F. Mendels, "Proto-Industrialization: The First Phase of the Industrialization Process," *JEH* 32, no. 1 (1972): 241–61.
31. Karl Marx, "The British Rule in India," *New-York Daily Tribune*, June 25, 1853; Jürgen Osterhammel, *Unfabling the East: The Enlightenment's Encounter with Asia* (PUP, 2018), 68; and R. J. Barendse, *The Arabian Seas: The Indian Ocean World of the Seventeenth Century* (Routledge, 2002), 180.
32. Chaudhuri, *Asia Before Europe*, 297.
33. Markus Cerman, "Rural Economy and Society," in Peter H. Wilson, *A Companion to Eighteenth-Century Europe* (Wiley-Blackwell, 2008), 61. On woolens in England, see John S. Lee, *The Medieval Clothier* (Boydell Press, 2018); Guillaume Daudin, *Commerce et prospérité: La France au XVIIIe siècle* (Presse de l'Université Paris-Sorbonne, 2005), 30; M. Jha, "Ganga Global: Implications of the Ganges River's Integration with the Global Maritime Economy During the Early Modern Period, 1600–1800," unpublished paper, 2018, 19; Braudel, *Civilization and Capitalism*, 2:312; Bruce E. Stanley, "Herat," in *Cities of the Middle East and North Africa: A Historical Encyclopedia*, ed. Michael R. T. Dumper and Bruce E. Stanley (ABC-Clio, 2007), 170; Prasannan Parthasarathi, *Why Europe Grew Rich and Asia Did Not: Global Economic Divergence, 1600–1850* (CUP, 2011), 46; Giorgio Riello, "The Indian Apprenticeship: The Trade of Indian Textiles and the Making of European Cottons," in *How India Clothed the World: The World of South Asian Textiles, 1500–1850*, ed. Giorgio Riello and Tirthankar Roy (Brill, 2013), 304–40.
34. Ruby Maloni, "Europeans in Seventeenth Century Gujarat," *Social Scientist* 36, no. 3/4 (2008): 71f; Ashin Das Gupta, "The Merchants of Surat, c. 1700–1750," in M. N. Pearson, *The World of the Indian Ocean Merchant 1500–1800* (OUP, 2004), 332; and Pedro Machado, *Ocean of Trade: South Asian Merchants, Africa and the Indian Ocean, c. 1750–1850* (CUP, 2014), 6.

35. This story, and the translation, are from Mark Elvin, *The Pattern of the Chinese Past: A Social and Economic Interpretation* (Stanford UP, 1973), 275.

36. Li Bozhong, *Agricultural Development in Jiangnan, 1620–1850* (Macmillan, 1998), 55; Fu Yiling, *Mingdai Jiangnan shimin jingji shitan* (Renmin Chubanshe, 1957) [傅衣凌：《明代江南市民经济试探》（上海：上海人民出版社，1957年）]; Wong, *China Transformed*, 37, 40f; Brook, "Merchant Network in 16th Century China," 168; Elvin, *Pattern of the Chinese Past*, 274; Li Bozhong, *The Early Industrialization of Jiangnan (1550–1850)* (Social Science Documentation Publishing House, 2000), 38–43, 40–41; and Kenneth Pomeranz, *The Great Divergence: China, Europe, and the Making of the Modern World Economy* (PUP, 2000), 86.

37. For the dating on Japanese proto-industrial expansion, see David Howell, *Capitalism from Within: Economy, Society, and the State in a Japanese Fishery* (University of California Press, 1995), 10–12, 26, 44, 49, 77, 179; Janet Hunter, "Modern Business and the Rise of the Japanese Middle Classes," in *The Global Bourgeoisie: The Rise of the Middle Classes in the Age of Empire*, ed. Christof Dejung, David Motadel, and Jürgen Osterhammel (PUP, 2019), 166; Howell, "Proto-Industrial Origins of Japanese Capitalism," 248–49; Shinbo Hiroshi and Hasegawa Akira, "Shōhin Seisan Ryūtsū no Dainamikku," in *Keizaishakai no seiritsu, 17–18 seiki*, ed. Hayami Akira and Miyamoto Mataji (Iwanami Shoten, 1988): 239–40; Kenneth Pomeranz, "Scale, Scope, and Scholarship: Regional Practices and Economic History," in *Global History, Globally: Research and Practice Around the World*, ed. Sven Beckert and Dominic Sachsenmaier (Bloomsbury Academic, 2018), 176; and Kären Wigen, *The Making of a Japanese Periphery, 1750–1920* (University of California Press, 1995), 8, 10, 80, 93, 95, 120, 127, 128.

38. Suraiya Faroqhi, "Trade: Regional, Inter-Regional, and International," in *Economic and Social History of the Ottoman Empire, 1300–1914*, ed. Halil İnalcık and Donald Quataert (CUP, 1994), 474–531; Quataert, "Ottoman Empire," 477–96; Hanna, *Artisan Entrepreneurs in Cairo*, 69, 71, 91; Bruce McGowan, "Merchants and Craftsmen," in İnalcık and Quataert, *Economic and Social History of the Ottoman Empire, 1300–1914*, 695–709, here 698.

39. Cerman, "Rural Economy and Society," 61f. On London Merchants, see David Ormrod, *Rise of Commercial Empires: England and the Netherlands in the Age of Mercantilism, 1650–1770* (CUP, 2003), 16; Braudel, *Civilization and Capitalism*, 2:312; Wolfgang Mager, "Proto-Industrialization and Proto-Industry: The Uses and Drawbacks of Two Concepts," *Continuity and Change* 8, no. 2 (1993): 192; Myška, "Proto-Industrialisierung in Böhmen, Mähren und Schlesien," 178–79; Reinert, "Medici Industrial Entrepreneurs," 7; Dobb, *Studies in the Development of Capitalism*; Julie Marfany, *Land, Proto-Industry and Population in Catalonia, c. 1680–1829: An Alternative Transition to Capitalism?* (Ashgate, 2013), 21, 55, 59, 68; and Sven Beckert, *Empire of Cotton: A Global History* (Alfred A. Knopf, 2014), chap. 4.

40. Claude Boucard, "Relation de Bambouc, 1729," as reprinted in *Bulletin de l'institut fondamental d'Afrique Noire (Series B: Sciences humaines)* 36 (1974): 246–75, here 257.

41. Toby Green, *Fistful of Shells: West Africa from the Rise of the Slave Trade to the Age of Revolution* (University of Chicago Press, 2021), 472; Philip J. Shea, "Big Is Sometimes Best: The Sokoto Caliphate and Economic Advantages of Size in the Textile Industry," *African Economic History* 34 (2006): 5–21; Jody Benjamin, "Global Textiles and the Centripetal Pull of the Western African Savannah, 1740–1780," unpublished paper, presented at Towards a Global History Conference, Delhi, December 3–5, 2017, 14; John Thornton, *Africa and Africans in the Making of the Atlantic World, 1400–1800* (CUP, 1998), 49; Rasheed Olaniyi, "Kano: The Development of a Trading City in Central Sudan," in *Precolonial Nigeria: Essays in Honor of Toyin Falola*, ed. Akinwumi Ogundiran (Africa World Press, 2005), 301–2; and Moses E. Ochonu, "The Wangara Factor in West African Business History," in *Entrepreneurship in Africa: A Historical Approach*, ed. Moses E. Ochonu (Indiana UP, 2018), 68.

42. As quoted in Basil Davidson, *The Lost Cities of Africa* (Little, Brown, 1959), 96–97.

43. Irfan Habib, "Potentialities of Capitalistic Development in the Economy of Mughal India," *JEH* 29, no. 2 (1969): 67–68; Yazdani, *India, Modernity and the Great Divergence*, 136, 140; Chaudhuri, *Asia Before Europe*, 320–21, 366–68; Pomeranz, *Great Divergence*, 99f; Machado, *Ocean of Trade*, 44; Prasannan Parthasarathi, *The Transition to a Colonial Economy: Weavers, Merchants and Kings in South India, 1720–1800* (CUP, 2001); Habib, "Potentialities of Capitalistic Development," 77; Chaudhuri, *Asia Before Europe*, 303; and Ahrar Ahmad, "Analysing Pre-Colonial South Asia: Mode of Production or Proto-Industrialisation?," *Journal of Contemporary India* 27, no. 3 (1997): 315.

44. As cited in James C. Shih, *Chinese Rural Society in Transition: A Case Study of the Lake Tai Area, 1368–1800* (Institute of East Asian Studies, University of California, 1992), 120–21.

45. Wong, *China Transformed*, 40f; Daudin, *Commerce et prospérité*, 50–52; Jean-Laurent Rosenthal and Roy Bin Wong, *Before and Beyond Divergence: The Politics of Economic Change in China and Europe* (HUP, 2011), 71; Michael Dillon, "The Merchants of Huizhou: Commerce and Confucianism," *History Today* 39, no. 2 (1989): 28; and Richard von Glahn, *The Economic History of China: From Antiquity to the Nineteenth Century* (CUP, 2016), 298. See also Philip Huang, *The Peasant Family and Rural Development in the Yangzi Delta, 1350–1988* (Stanford UP, 1990), 51f; Craig Dietrich: "Cotton Culture and Manufacture in Early Ch'ing China," in *Economic Organization in Chinese Society*, ed. W. E. Willmott (Stanford UP, 1972), 128; and von Glahn, *Economic History of China*, 298; and Li, *Early Industrialization of Jiangnan*, 80–83. For a summary of that debate, see von Glahn, *Economic History of China*, 298f.

46. Charles David Sheldon, *The Rise of the Merchant Class in Tokugawa Japan, 1600–1868: An Introductory Survey* (J. J. Augustin Incorporated Publisher, 1958), 83, 144; Masayuki Tanimoto, "The Role of Tradition in Japan's Industrialization: Another Path to Industrialization," in *The Role of Tradition in Japan's Industrialization: Another Path to Industrialization*, ed. Masayuki Tanimoto (OUP, 2006), 14; Nakamura Tetsu, "Edokōki ni okeru nōsonkōgyō no hatatsu: nihon keizai kindaika no rekishitekikizentei toshiteno," *Keizai Ronsō* 140, no. 3 and 4 (1987): 108–110.

47. Gupta, "Merchants of Surat," 332–33. See also Yazdani, *India, Modernity and the Great Divergence*, 459; Barendse, *Arabian Seas*, 180; Habib, "Potentialities of Capitalistic Development," 37.

48. Rab Houston and K. D. M. Snell, "Proto-Industrialization? Cottage Industry, Social Change,

and Industrial Revolution," *Historical Journal* 27, no. 2 (1984): 473; Prak, *Early Modern Capitalism*, 13–14; Ulrich Pfister, "Proto-industrielles Wachstum: Ein theoretisches Modell," *Jahrbuch für Wirtschaftsgeschichte* 39, no. 2 (1998): 24; and Kriedte, "Die Stadt im Prozeß der europäischen Proto-Industrialisierung," 28. For Lyon, this is argued in Carlo Poni, "Proto-Industrialization, Rural and Urban," *Review* (Fernand Braudel Center) 9, no. 2 (Fall 1985): 313f.

49. Chaudhuri, *Asia Before Europe*, 299; Braudel, *Civilization and Capitalism*, 2:304; Marfany, *Land, Proto-Industry and Population in Catalonia*, 23; and Houston and Snell, "Proto-Industrialization? Cottage Industry, Social Change, and Industrial Revolution," 473.

50. Barendse, *Arabian Seas*, 243f.

51. Li, *Early Industrialization of Jiangnan*, 46–50, 54–57; Parthasarathi, *Why Europe Grew Rich*, 187, 191, 195, 201, 203, 214; and Beckert, *Empire of Cotton*, 65.

52. Parthasarathi, *Why Europe Grew Rich*, 222; and Ravi Palat, *The Making of an Indian Ocean World-Economy, 1250–1650* (Palgrave Macmillan, 2015), 130, 134. For China, see Christopher Mills, *State, Peasant, and Merchants in Qing Manchuria, 1644–1862* (Stanford UP, 2007), 220; and Elvin, *Pattern of the Chinese Past*, 276f.

53. See Jan de Vries, "Between Purchasing Power and the World of Goods: Understanding the Household Economy in Early Modern Europe," in *Consumption and the World of Goods*, ed. J. Brewer and R. Porter (Routledge, 1993), 85–132; De Vries, *Industrious Revolution*; and Palat, *Making of an Indian Ocean World-Economy*, 130, 141. I am, however, using the term more in the sense in which it has been used by historians of Japan such as Kaoru Sugihara, "The East Asian Path of Economic Development and the Quality of Labor and Life: An Historical Perspective (Impact of Social Policy on the Economic Development: Differences and Similarities in East Asia)," *Journal of Social Policy and Labor Studies* 19 (2007). I am not arguing here that the intensification of labor that De Vries accurately describes is primarily the result of the desire to consume more. For that critique, see also Marfany, *Land, Proto-Industry and Population in Catalonia*, 15.

54. Braudel, *Civilization and Capitalism*, 2:300.

55. Daudin, *Commerce et prospérité*, 38–39. For the general point, see the important work by Peer Vries such as Peer Vries, *State, Economy and the Great Divergence: Great Britain and China, 1680s–1850s* (Bloomsbury, 2015).

56. Louis Chaumeil, "Abrégé d'histoire de Lorient de la fondation (1666) à nos jours (1939)," *Annales de Bretagne et des Pays de l'Oest* 46, no. 1 (1939): 67, 68.

57. Chaumeil, "Abrégé d'histoire de Lorient de la fondation," 68–69, 71; Frederic C. Lane, "The Mediterranean Spice Trade: Further Evidence of Its Revival in the Sixteenth Century," in *Crisis and Change in the Venetian Economy in the Sixteenth and Seventeenth Centuries*, ed. Brian Pullan (Routledge, 2006), 78; and Sophus A. Reinert and Robert Fredona, "Merchants and the Origins of Capitalism," Harvard Business School Working Paper 18-021 (2017), 23.

58. That is what Li Bozhong calculated. See Li, *Early Industrialization of Jiangnan*, 194–99.

59. Li, *Early Industrialization of Jiangnan*, 174–84, 186–87, 204–10.

60. Daudin, *Commerce et prospérité*, 38.

61. Vipul Singh, *The Artisans in 18th Century Eastern India: A History of Survival* (Concept Publishing Company, 2005), 58. For more information, see Irfan Habib, "Potentialities of Capitalistic Development," 44–45, 68–69.

62. Jonathan Israel, *Dutch Primacy in World Trade, 1585–1740* (Clarendon Press, 1989), 415; and Ogilvie, "Proto-Industrialization in Europe," 172; Hanna, *Artisan Entrepreneurs in Cairo*, 53. See also "Rum Still, c. 18th Century," exhibited in Museum of Newport History, Newport, Rhode Island, United States.

63. Daudin, *Commerce et prospérité*, 38; Joseph-Antoine Roy, *Histoire de la famille Scheider et du Creusot* (Marcel Rivière et Cie, 1962), 13; Maria Ågren, "Introduction: Swedish and Russian Iron-Making as Forms of Early Industry," in *Iron-Making Societies: Early Industrial Development in Sweden and Russia, 1600–1900*, ed. Maria Ågren (Berghahn Books, 1998), 6–7; Roger Portal, *L'Oural au XVIIIe siècle: Étude d'histoire économique et sociale* (Institut d'Études Slaves, 1950), 101f; A. A. Preobrazhenskii *Istoriia Urala s drevneishikh vremën do 1861 g.* (Nauka Hayка, 1989), 270, 274; John Bezís-Selfa, *Forging America: Ironworkers, Adventurers, and the Industrious Revolution* (Cornell UP, 2004), 19; and Arthur Cecil Bining, *British Regulations of the Colonial Iron Industry* (University of Pennsylvania Press, 1933), 3–4, 24–

31, 122, 134. The number of workers is from the year 1785.

64. Braudel, *Civilization and Capitalism*, 2:330.

65. Li, *Early Industrialization of Jiangnan*, 78–80; Kaufhold, "Gewerbelandschaften in der Frühen Neuzeit," 181; and Braudel, *Civilization and Capitalism*, 2:332. The dating is somewhat unclear here, and the number includes even very small enterprises.

66. As cited in Reinhard Hildebrandt, *Die "Georg Fuggerischen Erben": Kaufmännische Tätigkeit und sozialer Status 1555–1600*, Schriften zur Wirtschafts- und Sozialgeschichte 6 (Duncker & Humblot, 1966), 56."

67. Braudel, *Civilization and Capitalism*, 2:322, 325; Małowist, *Wschód a Zachód Europy*, 146, 163; Ochonu, "Wangara Factor in West African Business History," 61; and Daudin, *Commerce et prospérité*, 38. The importance of mercantile investments in mining is also emphasized by Jakob Strieder, *Studien zur Geschichte kapitalischer Organisationsformen* (Duncker & Humblot, 1914). See also Dobb, *Studies in the Development of Capitalism*, 139.

68. P. W. Klein, *De Trippen in de 17e Eeuw* (Van Gorcum & Comp., 1965), 43.

69. Klein, *De Trippen*, 26, 30, 161, 162, 105, 220, 243.

70. Chris Evans and Göran Rydén, *Baltic Iron in the Atlantic World in the Eighteenth Century* (Brill, 2007), 31–32; and Klein, *De Trippen*, 247.

71. E. W. Dahlgren, ed., *Louis de Geers brev och affärshandlingar, 1614–1652* (P. A. Norstedt & Söner, 1934), 104–6.

72. Michiel de Jong, *"Staat van oorlog": Wapenbedrijf en militaire hervorming in de Republiek der Verenigde Nederlanden, 1585–1621* (Uitgeverij Verloren, 2005), 213–17; Klein, *De Trippen*, 253, 255, 276–77, 447; and D. G. Nijman, "Louis de Geer (1587–1652), vader van de Zweedse industrie?," *Tijdschrift voor Geschiedenis* 104 (1991): 230.

73. Hanna, *Artisan Entrepreneurs in Cairo*, 62–64; and John Tutino, *The Mexican Heartland: How Communities Shaped Capitalism, a Nation, and World History, 1500–2000* (PUP, 2017), 46–47.

74. Braudel, *Civilization and Capitalism*, 2:307; and Myška, "Proto-Industrialisierung in Böhmen, Mähren und Schlesien," 182.

75. Hanna, *Artisan Entrepreneurs in Cairo*, 64; John Tutino, *Making a New World: Founding Capitalism in the Bajío and Spanish North America*

(Duke UP, 2011), 112; and Suraiya Faroqhi, "Making a Living: Economic Crisis and Partial Recovery," in *An Economic and Social History of the Ottoman Empire*, vol. 2, *1600–1914, ed.* Suraiya Faroqhi, Bruce McGowan, Donald Quataert, and Şevket Pamuk (CUP, 1994), 433–73.

76. Yazdani, *India, Modernity and the Great Divergence*, 366–68; and Ahmad, "Analysing Pre-Colonial South Asia," 325.

77. Hanna, *Artisan Entrepreneurs in Cairo*, 63, 64; Pepijn Brandon, "Wage Labor, Forced Labor and Industrialization: Naval Shipyards as Laboratories of Capitalism," unpublished paper, Global History Seminar, Harvard University, January 29, 2018, 4, 9; and Pepijn Brandon, *War, Capital, and the Dutch State (1558–1795)* (Brill, 2015), esp. chap. 3, "Production, Supply, and Labour Relations at the Naval Shipyards," 139–209.

78. Gustav Schmoller, "Studien über die wirthschaftliche Politik Friedrichs des Großen und Preußens überhaupt von 1680–1786," *Jahrbuch für Gesetzgebung* 8 (1884), 1–61, here 42.

79. Ogilvie, "Proto-Industrialization in Europe," 171.

80. R. Bin Wong, "The Political Economy of Chinese Rural Industry and Commerce in Historical Perspective," *Études rurales* 161/162 (2002): 154; Olaniyi, "Kano," 301; and Ogilvie, "Proto-Industrialization in Europe," 172. For India, see Michael O'Sullivan and Giorgio Riello, "Where Is Asia in Global Histories of Early Modern Capitalism?," HEC Working Paper No. 2023/03 (European University Institute, 2023), 14.

81. Ha-Joon Chang, *Kicking Away the Ladder: Development Strategy in Historical Perspective* (Anthem Press, 2002), 20.

82. Parthasarathi, *Why Europe Grew Rich*, 152, 168, 170, 173; Ha-Joon Chang, *Kicking Away the Ladder*, 21–22; and Braudel, *Civilization and Capitalism*, 2:322, 324. On the state and coal, see especially J. U. Nef, *The Rise of the British Coal Industry*, vol. 2 (George Routledge and Sons, 1932), 201–32, esp. 203, 219–20, 259–62.

83. Brentano, "Ueber den grundherrlichen Charakter," 332; Boldorf, "Institutional Barriers to Economic Development," 5–6, 8; Daudin, *Commerce et prospérité*, 53–57; and Chang, *Kicking Away the Ladder*, 21–22. On Colbert, see Salvatore Ciriacono, "Silk Manufacturing in France and Italy in the XVIIth Century: Two Models Compared," *Journal of European Economic History* 10, no. 1 (1981): 176–77.

84. William J. Ashworth, *The Industrial Revolution: The State, Knowledge and Global Trade* (Bloomsbury, 2017), 1–14; William J. Ashworth, "The Ghost of Rostow: Science, Culture and the British Industrial Revolution," *Historical Science* 46 (2008): 249–74; Chang, *Kicking Away the Ladder*, 9.

85. Adam Smith, *An Inquiry into the Nature and Causes of the Wealth of Nations*, ed. Edwin Cannan (Modern Library, 1937), 95.

86. Braudel, *Civilization and Capitalism*, 2:338; Patrick O'Brien, "Was the First Industrial Revolution a Conjuncture in the History of the World Economy?," Economic History Working Paper No. 259/2017 (London School of Economics and Political Science, March 2017), 31; and Ogilvie, "Proto-Industrialization in Europe," 172.

87. Cerman, "Rural Economy and Society," 61; Kriedte, Medick, and Schlumbohm, *Industrialization Before Industrialization*, 15; Boldorf, *Europäische Leinenregionen im Wandel*, 16.

88. Boldorf, *Europäische Leinenregionen im Wandel*, 158–202.

89. Barendse, *Arabian Seas*, 243f; Habib, "Potentialities of Capitalistic Development," 70.

90. Pomeranz, "Scale, Scope, and Scholarship," 177. See also Wong, *China Transformed*, 38. It is for this reason that Chinese economic historians have found the concept of proto-industrialization problematic, especially because it is seen as not directly leading to industrialization. See Li, *Early Industrialization of Jiangnan*, 11–12.

91. Parthasarathi, *Why Europe Grew Rich*, 10.

92. Karl Marx, *Das Kapital: Kritik der Politischen Oekonomie*, vol. 3, part 1, book 3, *Der Gesamtprozess der kapitalistischen Produktion, Kapitel I bis XXVIII* (Hamburg: Otto Meisner, 1894), 311–12.

Chapter 6: The Perfect Storm

1. There is disagreement among historians about the exact date of that journey, and whether it even started in Amsterdam, but late 1740 is the most likely time and Amsterdam the most likely departure city. See Allgemeines Verwaltungsarchiv Vienna, Reichsadelsakten Bethmann, f. 8r, Vienna, Austria. For that discussion, see also Wolfgang Henninger, *Johann Jakob von Bethmann, 1717–1792: Kaufmann, Reeder und Kaiserlicher Konsul in Bourdeaux*, vol. 1 (Universitätsverlag Dr. N. Brockmeyer, 1993), 83–89, 91–95, 104.

2. "Mémoire pour les Sieurs Bethman et Compagnie (Liquidation des Maisons de Commerce Bethman et Fils, Bethmann et Fils et Compagnie) Contre Les Sieurs Weltner et Compagnie, et en Présence du Sieur Gramont (Liquidation de la Maison Feger, Gramont et Compagnie)," Bordeaux, 1812, 3, W1-9, VII, 15, Bethmann-Archiv, Stadtarchiv Frankfurt, Germany; Michel-René Ca Hilliard d'Auberteuil, *Considérations sur l'état présent de la colonie française de Saint Domingue* (Paris: Chez Grangé, 1776), 148.

3. Henninger, *Johann Jakob von Bethmann*, 17, 62; Butel, *Les négociants*, 8; Thésée, "Négociants bordelaise et colons de Saint-Domingue," 9; Weber, "Deutsche Kaufleute im Atlantikhandel," 370–81, drawing on data from Saugera, *Bordeaux port négrier*, 351–62.

4. Inventaire General des Biena (?) délaissé par feu Pierre Desclaux, Bordeaux, December 28, 1765, in Wq-9, VII, No. 1m Bethmann Papers, Stadtarchiv Frankfurt, Germany.

5. Contrat de mariage de M. Jean Jaques Bethmann avec Mademoiselle Élisabeth Desclaux, 13 August 1745, in W 1-9, VII, No. 1, Bethmann-Archiv, Stadtarchiv Frankfurt, Germany; and Henninger, *Johann Jakob von Bethmann*, 466–74.

6. Henninger, *Johann Jakob von Bethmann*, 105, 112–13, 287–95, 318, 344–45.

7. Silvia Marzagalli, "The Atlantic World Between Markets and State in 18th-Century France: The Sephardim Firm Gradis in Bordeaux," Working Paper No. 16019 (Economic History Society, 2016), 20; and Henninger, *Johann Jakob von Bethmann*, 346.

8. Henninger, *Johann Jakob von Bethmann*, 352–56; and Saugera, *Bordeaux port négrier*, 201–2, 239, 272–74. It is estimated that almost 80 percent of all Bordeaux journeys ended in Saint-Domingue. See Saugera, *Bordeaux port négrier*, 218. See also Weber, *Deutsche Kaufleute im Atlantikhandel*, 198.

9. Henninger, *Johann Jakob von Bethmann*, 258, 262, 264–66; Mark Häberlein, "Migration and Business Ventures: German-Speaking Migrants and Commercial Networks in the Eighteenth-Century British Atlantic World," in *Transnational Networks: German Migrants in the British Empire, 1670–1914*, ed. John R. Davis, Stefan Manz, and Margrit Schulte Beerbühr (Brill, 2012), 36. On that investment, and the conflicts that arose from it, see W 1-9, VII, Nr. 15–16, Bethmann-Archiv,

Stadtarchiv Frankfurt, Germany. On that firm, see Thésée, "Négociants bordelais et colons de Saint-Domingue," 86, 93, 106. The number of 2.2 million livres is from Henninger, *Johann Jakob von Bethmann*, 26f.

10. Thésée, "Négociants bordelais et colons de Saint-Domingue," 10, 21, 24, 27; Häberlein, "Migration and Business Ventures," 36; and Henninger, *Johann Jakob von Bethmann*, 259–62.

11. Thésée, "Négociants bordelais et colons de Saint-Domingue," 27.

12. "Consultation délibérée par MM. Martignac Père, Moutardier, Denucé et Emérigon, avocats, pour les Sieurs Bethmann et Compagnie; contre les Sieurs Weltner et Compagnie," Bordeaux, 20 January 1814, W1-9, VII, 15, Bethmann-Archiv, Stadtarchiv Frankfurt, Germany.

13. Henninger, *Johann Jakob von Bethmann*, 260f, 261, 355; Weber, "Deutsche Kaufleute im Atlantikhandel," 369; I am drawing on data from Saugera, *Bordeaux port négrier*, 351–62; Thésée, "Négociants bordelais et colons de Saint-Domingue," 25, 3, 46, 140; Häberlein, "Migration and Business Ventures," 36; and "Mémoire pour les Sieurs Bethman et Compagnie (Liquidation des Maisons de Commerce Bethman et Fils, Bethman et Fils et Compagnie) Contre Les Sieurs Weltner et Compagnie, et en Présence du Sieur Gramont (Liquidation de la Maison Feger, Gramont et Compagnie)," Bordeaux 1812, 3, 4, W1-9, VII, 15, Bethmann-Archiv, Stadtarchiv Frankfurt, Germany. On Bordeaux's slave-trading boom during these years, see Saugera, *Bordeaux port négrier*, 87–124.

14. Bapst to Capitaine Guilleau, Bordeaux, 2 April 1789, Archive Departementale de la Gironde, 7 B 2001, as cited in Thésée, "Négociants bordelais et colons de Saint-Domingue," 50.

15. Letter from Cramer to P. H. von Bethmann, January 16, 1792, as reprinted in Henninger, *Johann Jakob von Bethmann*, 310–11; and David Garrioch, Christophe Jaquet, and Daniel Roche, *La Fabrique du Paris Révolutionnaire* (La Découverte, 2015), 58–59. For the conversion, see "Historical Currency Converter," Historicalstatistics.org, accessed August 7, 2024, http://www.historicalstatistics.org/Currencyconverter .html. For wage data, see, for example, D. G., 5L22, District of Bazas, "Tableau du coût de la vie et des salaires dans le District de Bazas," 28 *Ventôse* Year III, as quoted in Alan

Forrest, "The Condition of the Poor in Revolutionary Bordeaux," *Past & Present* 59, no. 1 (1973): 174.

16. Friedrich Zellfelder, *Das Kundennetz des Bankhauses Gebrüder Bethmann, Frankfurt am Main, im Spiegel der Hauptbücher (1738–1816)* (F. Steiner, 1994), 140–41.

17. The importance of this feedback loop is also emphasized by Charles Verlinden, *Les origines de la civilisation atlantique: De la Renaissance à l'Âge des Lumières* (Editions de la Baconniere, 1966), 140. For the rest of the paragraph, see Jean-Baptiste Le Mascrier, *Description de l'Egypte, contenant plusieurs remarques curieuses sur la géographie ancienne et moderne de ce païs . . . composée sur les Mémoires de M. de Maillet, ancien consul de France au Caire* (Paris, chez L. Genneau et J. Rollin, 1735), 199; Salvatore Ciriacono, "Silk Manufacturing in France and Italy in the XVIIth Century: Two Models Compared," *Journal of European Economic History* 10, no. 1 (1981): 174–75; M. Jha, "Ganga Global: Implications of the Ganges River's Integration with the Global Maritime Economy During the Early Modern Period, 1600–1800," unpublished paper, 2018, 19, 38; and Pedro Machado, *Ocean of Trade: South Asian Merchants, Africa and the Indian Ocean, c. 1750–1850* (CUP, 2014), 7, 121, 126, 142, 143.

18. Irfan Habib, "Potentialities of Capitalistic Development in the Economy of Mughal India," *Journal of Economic History* 29, no. 2 (1969): 66; Gilbert Rozman, "East Asian Urbanization in the Nineteenth Century," in *Urbanization in History: A Process of Dynamic Interactions*, ed. Ad van der Woude, Jan de Vries, and Akira Hayami (Clarendon Press, 1990), 63; Andre Gunder Frank, *Re-ORIENT: Global Economy in the Asian Age* (University of California Press, 1998), 108–17, esp. 116. The numbers are imprecise, and estimates vary, but there is consensus in the literature that Japan became more urban. See, among others, Osamu Saito and Masanori Takashima, "Population, Urbanisation, and Farm Output in Early Modern Japan, 1600–1874: A Review of Data and Benchmark Estimates," RCESR Discussion Paper Series DP15-3 (Research Center for Economic and Social Risks, Institute of Economic Research, Hitotsubashi University, May 2015), 7; Peer Vries, *Ursprünge des modernen Wirtschaftswachstums: England, China und die Welt in der Frühen Neuzeit* (Vandenhoeck & Ruprecht, 2013), 203; and Jean-Pascal Bassino et al., "Japan and

the Great Divergence, 730–1874," CEI Working Paper Series 2018-13 (Center for Economic Institutions, Institute of Economic Research, Hitotsubashi University, 2018), https://ideas.repec.org/p/hit/hitcei/2018 -13.html.

19. Peter Clark, "Small Towns in England 1550–1850: National and Regional Population Trends," in *Small Towns in Early Modern Europe* (CUP, 1995), 99. See also the data and general discussion in Jan de Vries, *European Urbanization, 1500–1800* (Methuen, 1984), 40; Christopher Chalklin, *The Rise of the English Town, 1650–1850* (CUP, 2001), 8; P. M. G. Harris, *The History of Human Populations*, vol. 2, *Migration, Urbanization, and Structural Change* (Praeger, 2003), 273; Klaus Weber, "Mitteleuropa und der transatlantische Sklavenhandel: Eine lange Geschicte," *Werkstatt Geschicte* 66/67 (2014): 25; and Robert C. Allen, "Britain's Economic Ascendancy in a European Context," in *Exceptionalism and Industrialisation: Britain and Its European Rivals, 1688–1815*, ed. Leandro Prados de la Escosura (CUP, 2004), 16, 134. Robert C. Allen provides a brilliant analysis of the divergence of a few early modern economies, especially the Dutch and British. He argues against the "agricultural revolution thesis." What really counted, he says, was change in proto-industrialization and trade in cities.

20. Kenneth Pomeranz, *The Great Divergence: China, Europe, and the Making of the Modern World Economy* (PUP, 2000), 3–28.

21. Ronald Findlay and Kevin H. O'Rourke, *Power and Plenty: Trade, War, and the World Economy in the Second Millennium* (PUP, 2007), 26; Guillaume Daudin, *Commerce et prospérité: La France au XVIIIe siècle* (Presse de l'Université Paris-Sorbonne, 2005), 206; Ralph Davis, "English Foreign Trade, 1660–1700," in *The Growth of English Overseas Trade in the Seventeenth and Eighteenth Centuries*, ed. Walter E. Minchinton (Methuen, 1969), 78–120; Patrick O'Brien, "Was the First Industrial Revolution a Conjuncture in the History of the World Economy?," Economic History Working Paper No. 259/2017 (London School of Economics and Political Science, March 2017), 21, 22; Barbara L. Solow, *The Economic Consequences of the Slave Trade* (Lexington Books, 2014), 107; and Daron Acemoglu, Simon Johnson, and James Robinson, "The Rise of Europe: Atlantic Trade, Institutional Change, and Economic

Growth," *American Economic Review* 95, no. 3 (June 2005): 572; and Weimin Zhong, "The Roles of Tea and Opium in Early Economic Globalization: A Perspective on China's Crisis in the 19th Century," *Frontiers of History in China* 5, no. 1 (March 2010): 96; O'Brien, "Was the First Industrial Revolution a Conjuncture in the History of the World Economy?," 21; Javier Cuenca Esteban, "Comparative Patterns of Colonial Trade: Britain and Its Rivals," in Prados de la Escosura, *Exceptionalism and Industrialisation*, 38, 40, 60; Barbara L. Solow, "Capitalism and Slavery in the Exceedingly Long Run," *Journal of Interdisciplinary History* 17, no. 4 (Spring 1987): 733, citing Nicholas F. R. Crafts, "British Economic Growth," *EHR* 36 (1983): 177–99. In the context of this paragraph, the 1720s and the 1780s refer to 1722–1724 and 1784–1786.
22. Daudin, *Commerce et prospérité*, 25, 199, 201, 210, 340–41, 405, 406.
23. Maxine Berg, *Luxury and Pleasure in Eighteenth-Century Britain* (OUP, 2005), 82. For delftware-imitating Chinese porcelain, see C. J. A. Jörg, *Interactions in Ceramics: Oriental Porcelain and Delftware* (Urban Council, 1984), 19; and Nancy F. Koehn, "Josiah Wedgwood and the First Industrial Revolution," in *Creating Modern Capitalism: How Entrepreneurs, Companies, and Countries Triumphed in Three Industrial Revolutions*, ed. Thomas K. McGraw (HUP, 1999), 35.
24. As cited in Koehn, "Josiah Wedgwood and the First Industrial Revolution," 40–41.
25. Saugera, *Bordeaux port négrier*, 54; and Thésée, "Négociants bordelais et colons de Saint-Domingue," 164.
26. "Inventaire des meubles qui sont sur l'habitation de Paroy," folder 3, Inventaires des Habitations, Le Gentil de Paroy, folder 1, 164 APOM 1, Fonds Le Gentil de Paroy, Archives Privées, ANOM.
27. Peter Kriedte, Hans Medick, and Jürgen Schlumbohm, *Industrialization Before Industrialization: Rural Industry in the Genesis of Capitalism*, trans. Beate Schempp (CUP, 1981), 33.
28. Anka Steffen, "A Cloth That Binds: New Perspectives on the Eighteenth-Century Prussian Economy," *Slavery & Abolition* 42, no. 1 (2021): 105–29; Siegfried Kühn, *Der Hirschberger Leinwand- und Schleierhandel von 1648 bis 1806* (Verlag Priebatschs Buchhandel Breslau, 1938), 43, 99; Hermann Fechner,

"Der Zustand des schlesischen Handels vor der Besitzergreifung des Landes durch Friedrich den Grossen," *Jahrbücher für Nationalökonomie und Statistik* 10 (1885): 214; Anka Steffen, "'Insonders hochgeehrter Herr!'—Ein Beitrag zur Einbindung der Gewerbelandschaft Schlesien in den kolonialen Transatlantikhandel im 18. Jahrhundert am Beispiel der Geschäftskorrespondenz des Johann Friedrich Ketzler" (master's thesis, European University Viadrina in Frankfurt [Oder], 2013), 23; Marion Johnson, *Anglo-African Trade in the Eighteenth Century: English Statistics on African Trade 1699–1808* (Center for the History of European Expansion, 1990), 52–60; Saugera, *Bordeaux port négrier*, 247; and Anka Steffen, "Schlesische Leinwand als Handelsgut im atlantischen Sklavenhandel der frühen Neuzeit. Das Beispiel der Hirschberger Kaufmanns-Societät," *Themenportal Europäische Geschichte* (2017): 3f. Between 1748 and 1790, three-quarters of Silesian linens were exported, and of those, three-quarters went to the New World. See Weber, "Mitteleuropa und der transatlantische Sklavenhandel," 18. Regarding export of German linens, see Weber, "Mitteleuropa und der transatlantische Sklavenhandel," 26, 29. For France, see Karsten Voss and Klaus Weber, "War, Crisis and the Development of the Slave-Plantation Economy of Saint-Domingue (1697–1715)," unpublished paper, 2017, 9.
29. Findlay and O'Rourke, *Power and Plenty*, 260, 261; and Gerard van Gurp, "Proto-Industrialization and World Trade of Textiles in Dutch Brabant, 1620–1820," *Jahrbuch für Wirtschaftsgeschichte* 49, no. 1 (2008): 308. For ironworks, see Göran Rydén and Chris Evans, "Stocktaking at Christiansborg: Metals and Slaves in the Danish Atlantic Trade in the Mid-Eighteenth Century," in *Locating the Global: Spaces, Networks and Interactions from the Seventeenth to the Twentieth Century*, ed. Holger Weiss (De Gruyter Oldenbourg, 2020), 71. For copper, see Robert S. DuPlessis, *The Material Atlantic: Clothing, Commerce, and Colonization in the Atlantic World* (CUP, 2016). For copper, see Nuala Zahedieh, "Colonies, Copper, and the Market for Inventive Activity in England and Wales, 1680–1730," *EHR* 66, no. 3 (August 2013): 805–25.
30. Robert Allen, "Agriculture During the Industrial Revolution," in *The Economic History of Britain since 1700*, ed. Roderick Flood and

D. N. McCloskey, vol. 1, *1700–1860* (CUP, 1994), 119.
31. Weber, "Mitteleuropa und der transatlantische Sklavenhandel," 7; Zahedieh, "Colonies, Copper, and the Market," 807.
32. Regarding new demand for copper, I am citing evidence from one plantation in Saint Kitts in 1732. See Zahedieh, "Colonies, Copper, and the Market," 810, 812.
33. Zahedieh, "Colonies, Copper, and the Market," 818, 821, 822–23.
34. Zahedieh, "Colonies, Copper, and the Market," 784–87, 804. It was not just English manufacturers who benefited from these new markets. Holstein copper manufacturer Rudolph Amsinck created a copper mill on the outskirts of Hamburg in the early seventeenth century for similar reasons, producing brass wires, copper sheets for roofs and shipbuilding, and copper kettles for sugar mills. See Axel Lohr, "Kupfermühlen in Stormarn und Umgebung," *Jahrbuch für den Kreis Stormarn 34* (2016): 33.
35. Dieudonné Rinchon, *Les armements négriers au XVIIIe siècle, d'après la correspondance et la comptabilité des armateurs et des capitaines nantais* (Royal Sciences Colon, 1955), 31.
36. Sidney W. Mintz, *Sweetness and Power: The Place of Sugar in Modern History* (Penguin Books, 1986), 77, 116–17, 146; James Walvin, *Sugar: The World Corrupted, from Slavery to Obesity* (Robinson, 2017), 98–99; Robin Blackburn, *The Making of New World Slavery: From the Baroque to the Modern, 1492–1800* (Verso, 1997), 403; Seymour Drescher, *Econocide* (University of Pittsburgh Press, 1977), 78; and "Sugars, Granulated," Natural Nutrient Database, United States Department of Agriculture. Sidney Mintz estimates that the total caloric intake of a working-class individual in England was about 2,000 calories a day in the early 1800s (2,000 calories/day times 365 days/year = 730,000 calories/year). From Seymour Drescher, we know that total sugar production in the New World in 1805 was 297,400 tons. From the USDA, we know that there are 3,549,854 calories in one ton of sugar (297,400 tons times 3,549,854 calories = 1,055,726,000,000 calories of sugar produced in 1805). From there, I divided total calories of sugar produced by the number of calories an English worker consumed per year. This gives you the amount of sugar produced in 1805 in terms of the caloric intake of English workers (1,055,726,000,000 calories of sugar produced in 1805 / 730,000

calories per year = 1,446,200 consumers).

37. "J. S. Fry's Chocolate Tin," Smithsonian National Museum of American History, accessed August 12, 2024, https://www.si.edu/object/j-s-fry-sons-chocolate-tin%3Anmah_8 69968; Peter Jackson, "How Did Quakers Conquer the British Sweet Shop?," BBC News, January 20, 2010; and Roman Rossfeld, *Schweizer Schokolade: Industrielle Produktion und Kulturelle Konstruktion eines Nationalen Symbols 1860–1920* (Hier & Jetzt, 2007), 49.

38. Javier Cuenca Esteban, "Comparative Patterns of Colonial Trade: Britain and Its Rivals," in *Exceptionalism and Industrialisation: Britain and Its European Rivals, 1688–1815*, ed. Leandro Prados de la Escosura (CUP, 2004), 54.

39. Allen, "Britain's Economic Ascendancy in a European Context," 20.

40. See also Fernand Braudel, *Civilization and Capitalism, 15th–18th Century*, trans. Siân Reynolds, vol. 2, *The Wheels of Commerce* (University of California Press, 1992), 277, 279, 280.

41. See, for example, Allan Potofsky, "Paris-on-the-Atlantic from the Old Regime to the Revolution," *French History* 25, no. 1 (March 2011): 90; and Walter Johnson, *River of Dark Dreams: Slavery and Empire in the Cotton Kingdom* (HUP, 2013). See Eric Williams, *Capitalism and Slavery* (University of North Carolina Press, 1944), 210; Walter Rodney, *How Europe Underdeveloped Africa* (Howard UP, 1982), 174; C. L. R. James, *The Black Jacobins: Toussaint L'Ouverture and the Haitian Revolution* (Vintage Books, 1989), 48; and W. E. B. Du Bois, *Black Reconstruction in America* (Atheneum, 1969), 5. Aimé Césaire, *Toussaint Louverture: La Révolution française et le problème colonial* (Présence Africaine, 1962), 21; Anton de Kom, *Wij Slaven van Suriname* (Uitgevers-Maatschappij Contact, 1934), 60. For similar arguments, see also George Blackford, *Persistent Poverty: Underdevelopment in Plantation Economies of the Third World* (OUP, 1972); Lloyd Best, "The Mechanism of Plantation-type Economies: Outlines of a Pure Plantation Economy," in *Social and Economic Studies* 17 (1968), 283–326.

42. For France, see Potofsky, "Paris-on-the-Atlantic from the Old Regime to the Revolution," 90.

43. As cited in Williams, *Capitalism and Slavery*, 51.

44. John Cary, *An Essay on the State of England, in Relation to Its Trade, Its Poor, and Its Taxes for Carrying on the Present War Against France* (London: W. Bonny, 1695), https://www.gutenberg.org/cache/epub/61964/pg 61964-images.html.

45. C. L. F. Hüpeden, "Vom Linnenhandel in Hessen," *Staatsanzeigen* 41 (1787): 3–12.

46. Hüpeden, "Vom Linnenhandel in Hessen," 3–12.

47. As reprinted in J. G. van Dillen, "Memorie betreffende de kolonie de Suriname," *Economisch-historisch jaarboek* 24 (1950): 162–67.

48. Alex Dupuy, "French Merchant Capital and Slavery in Saint-Domingue," *Latin American Perspectives* 12, no. 3 (1985): 83; Potofsky, "Paris-on-the-Atlantic from the Old Regime to the Revolution," 89, 90, 92, 99, 101, 105; Daudin, *Commerce et prospérité*, 221–333; James, *Black Jacobins*, 50; Dieudonné Rinchon, *Pierre-Ignace-Liévin van Alstein, capitaine négrier: Gand 1733–Nantes 1793* (Institut Français d'Afrique Noire, 1964), 126–27; and Darrell Meadows, "Engineering Exile: Social Networks and the French Atlantic Community, 1789–1809," *French Historical Studies* 23, no. 1 (Winter 2000): 67–102. They were more profitable not least because the capital intensity of foreign trade along with the need to access networks of trust limited the number of participants, lessening competition. See Daudin, *Commerce et prospérité*, 332; and Albane Forestier, "A 'Considerable Credit' in the Late Eighteenth-Century French West Indian Trade: The Chaurands of Nantes," *French History* 25, no. 1 (2011): 63. See also Trevor Burnard and John Garrigus, *The Plantation Machine: Atlantic Capitalism in French Saint-Domingue and British Jamaica* (University of Pennsylvania Press, 2016), 21.

49. For the first site, see Karwan Fatah-Black and Matthias van Rossum, "Slavery in a 'Slave Free Enclave'? Historical Links Between the Dutch Republic, Empire and Slavery, 1580s–1860s," *Werkstatt Geschichte* 66/67 (2014): 55. There is a rich literature on this history, including Jan de Vries and Ad van der Woude, *The First Modern Economy: Success, Failure, and Perseverance of the Dutch Economy, 1500–1815* (CUP, 1997); P. C. Emmer, *Geschiedenis vamn de Nefderlandse slavenhandel* (Nieuw Amsterdam, 2019); and, most recently, Pepijn Brandon and Ulbe Bosma, "De betekenis van de Atlantische slavernij voor de Nederlandse economie in de tweede helft van de achttiende eeuw," *Low Countries Journal of Social and Economic History* 16, no. 2 (June 2019): 5–46. For Holland's fisheries and agriculture, see app., table 3.

50. This sentence is from Sven Beckert, "Making Europe's Economy," in David Motadel, ed., *Globalizing Europe* (CUP, 2025), 42–55, based on Martin Seiwert and Stefan Reccius, "So abhängig ist Deutschland von der Autoindustrie," *Wirtschafts-Woche*, July 27, 2017; and Matthew C. Klein, "The US Tech Sector Is Really Small," *Financial Times*, January 8, 2016.

51. Fatah-Black and Van Rossum, "Slavery in a 'Slave Free Enclave'?" 59, 60; Matthias van Rossum and Karwan Fatah-Black, "Wat is winst? De economische impact van de Nederlandse trans-Atlantische slavenhandel," *Tijdschrift voor sociale en economische geschiedenis* 9, no. 4 (2012): 23; Brandon and Bosma, "De Betekenis," 6; Tamira Combrink, "Rhine Trade in Slave-Based Commodities in the Eighteenth Century," *Low Countries Journal of Social and Economic History* 19, no. 2 (2022): 112; Tamira Combrink, "From French Harbors to German Rivers: European Distribution of Sugar by the Dutch in the Eighteenth Century," in *La diffusion des produits ultramarins en Europe*, ed. Marguerite Martin and Maud Villeret (Presse Universitaire de Rennes, 2017), 40, 50; and Matthias van Rossum and Karwan Fatah-Black, "Een marginale bijdrage?," *Tijdschrift voor sociale en economische geschiedenis* 9, no. 4 (2012): 72. It has been estimated that the Dutch shipped 608,849 slaves from 1595 to 1829. See Van Rossum and Fatah-Black, "Wat is winst?," 14. On slavery profits, see Fatah-Black and Van Rossum, "Slavery in a 'Slave Free Enclave'?," 69. In 1780, slave trade gross margins were between 600,000 and 1.4 million guilders, but the total overseas trade of the republic that year amounted to 300 million guilders. See Van Rossum and Fatah-Black, "Een marginale bijdrage?," 73. Piet Emmer disagreed with that analysis, but more recent research has largely disproved his arguments. See Piet Emmer, "Winst in de Marge?," *Tijdschrift voor sociale en economische geschiedenis* 9, no. 4 (2012): 64–70. See also the reply in Van Rossum and Fatah-Black, "Een marginale bijdrage?," 71–78; and Van Rossum and Fatah-Black, "Wat is winst?," 9.

52. Weber, "Mitteleuropa und der transatlantische Sklavenhandel," 7, 13–14.

53. Weber, "Mitteleuropa und der transatlantische Sklavenhandel," 8, 16, 19–20.

54. Richard Drayton, "Race, Culture and Class: European Hegemony and Global Class Formation, c. 1800–1950," in *The Global Bourgeoisie: The Rise of the Middle Classes in the Age of Empire*, ed. Christof Dejung, David Motadel, and Jürgen Osterhammel (PUP, 2019), 351.

55. Weber, "Mitteleuropa und der transatlantische Sklavenhandel," 22; K. J. Kuhn and B. Ziegler, "Die Schweiz und die Sklaverei: Zum Spannungsfeld zwischen Geschichtspolitik und Wissenschaft," *Traverse* 16, no. 1 (2009): 116–30; Niklaus Stettler, Peter Haenger, and Robert Labhardt, *Baumwolle, Sklaven und Kredite: Die Basler Welthandelsfirma Christoph Burckhardt & Cie. in revolutionärer Zeit (1789–1815)* (Merian, 2004), 10; and "Liste der im Sklavenhandel involvierten Schweizer," Stiftung Cooperaxion, 2018, accessed February 12, 2019, https://cooperaxion.org/datenbank. On population, see Anne-Lise Head-König, "Bevölkerung," *Historisches Lexikon der Schweiz*, March 30, 2012. For an important study of the Basel economic elite in the Atlantic economy, see Susanna Burghartz, "Localizing Globality in Early Capitalist Basel," in *Journal of Early Modern History* 25 (2023), 83–107.

56. Felipe Ribeiro da Silva, "The Profits of the Portuguese-Brazilian Transatlantic Slave Trade: Challenges and Possibilities," *Slavery & Abolition* 4, no. 1 (2021): 96; and Leonardo Marques and Rafael Marquese, "Gold, Coffee, and Slaves: Brazil and World Accumulation," unpublished paper, presented at Towards a Global History of Primitive Accumulation Conference, IISH, Amsterdam, 2019, 212–32.

57. Esteban, "Comparative Patterns of Colonial Trade," 732, 735; Klas Rönnbäck, "The Economic Importance of the Slave Plantation Complex to the British Economy in the Eighteenth Century: A Value-Added Approach," *JGH* 13, no. 3 (2018): 327.

58. Manesty to John Banister, Liverpool, April 8, 1747, in John Banister Papers, Letter Book, 238, Newport Historical Society, Newport, Rhode Island, USA.

59. Solow, "Capitalism and Slavery in the Exceedingly Long Run," 717; J. R. Ward, "The Profitability of Sugar Planting in the British West Indies, 1650–1834," *EHR* 31, no. 2 (May 1978): 209; Blackburn, *Making*

of New World Slavery, 541; Burnard and Garrigus, *Plantation Machine*, 98. Regarding the slavery complex in Britain, see the important paper by Stephan Heblich, Stephen J. Redding, and Hans-Joachim Voth, "Slavery and the British Industrial Revolution," IDEAS Working Paper No. 30451 (National Bureau of Economic Research, 2022). The slave trade significantly contributed to the British economy; the author estimates that the total of "net inflows from the slave trade" to Britain was 344,000 pounds annually in 1786–1790. See Esteban, "Comparative Patterns of Colonial Trade," 45. Regarding annual rate of return on invested capital, these numbers are cited in Maxine Berg and Pat Hudson, *Slavery, Capitalism and the Industrial Revolution* (Polity Press, 2023), 43.

60. Catherine Hall, "John Samuel Wanley Sawbridge Erle-Drax," Centre for the Study of the Legacies of British Slavery Database, University College London, accessed November 2, 2018, https://www.ucl.ac.uk/lbs/person/view/2246.

61. Catherine Hall, "Barbados 3784 (Drax Hall)," Centre for the Study of the Legacies of British Slavery Database, University College London, accessed May 2, 2019, https://www.ucl.ac.uk/lbs/claim/view/2182; Laura Kitching and Catherine Bolado, "Election 2010: Sweeping Victory for Tory Richard Drax," *Dorset Echo*, May 7, 2010; "Drax Hall," in Hughes/Queree Papers, BNA; John L. McCusker and Russell R. Menard, "The Sugar Industry in the Seventeenth Century," in *Tropical Babylons*, ed. Stuart B. Schwartz (University of North Carolina Press, 2004), 300; "John Samuel Wanley Sawbridge Erle-Drax," Centre for the Study of the Legacies of British Slavery Database; and Piketty, *Capital and Ideology*, 298.

62. Nick Draper, "'Possessing Slaves': Ownership, Compensation and Metropolitan Society in Britain at the Time of Emancipation 1834–40," *History Workshop Journal* 64, no. 1 (October 2007): 76–78, 89; Heblich, Redding, and Voth, "Slavery and the British Industrial Revolution," 3; and Kris Manjapra, "When Will Britain Face Up to Its Crimes Against Humanity?," *Guardian*, March 29, 2018.

63. The crucial importance of the Atlantic is also emphasized by, among many others, Jairus Banaji, "Globalising the History of Capital: Ways Forward," *Historical Material-*

ism 26, no. 3 (September 2018): 7; and Pilar Nogues-Marco, "Measuring Colonial Extraction: The East India Company's Rule and the Drain of Wealth, 1757–1858," *Capitalism: A Journal of History and Economics* 2, no. 1 (January 2021): 186–87.

64. Prasannan Parthasarathi, *Why Europe Grew Rich and Asia Did Not: Global Economic Divergence, 1600–1850* (CUP, 2011), 187, 191, 195, 201, 203; William T. Rowe, "Political, Social and Economic Factors Affecting the Transmission of Technical Knowledge in Early Modern China," in *Cultures of Knowledge: Technology in Chinese History*, ed. Dagmar Schäfer (Brill, 2012), 25–44; Francesca Bray, *Technology, Gender and History in Imperial China* (Routledge, 2013); R. Bin Wong, *China Transformed: Historical China and the Limits of European Experience* (Cornell UP, 1997); Jack A. Goldstone, "Cultural Orthodoxy, Risk, and Innovation: The Divergence of East and West in the Early Modern World," *Sociological Theory* 5, no. 2 (Autumn 1987): 119–35; and Cemal Kafadar, "The Question of Ottoman Decline," *Harvard Middle Eastern and Islamic Review* 4, no 1–2 (1997–1998): 30–75.

65. Esteban, "Comparative Patterns of Colonial Trade," 58; Sven Beckert, *Empire of Cotton: A Global History* (Knopf, 2014), 65; and Niall Ferguson, *Civilization: The West and the Rest* (Allen Lane, 2011), 305.

66. Joel Mokyr, *The Gifts of Athena: Historical Origins of the Knowledge Economy* (PUP, 2002), 35.

67. Mokyr, *Gifts of Athena*, 29. For the (persuasive) argument that much of the new industrial processes had little to do with "pure science," see Steven Shapin, *The Scientific Revolution* (Chicago UP, 1996), 140–41.

68. Parthasarathi, *Why Europe Grew Rich*, 13, 222; and Jean-Laurent Rosenthal and Roy Bin Wong, *Before and Beyond Divergence: The Politics of Economic Change in China and Europe* (HUP, 2011).

69. Marcel van der Linden, "Re-Constructing the Origins of Modern Labor Management," *Labor History* 51, no. 4 (November 2010): 514; and Richard Rottenburg, "Social and Public Experiments and New Figurations of Science and Politics in Postcolonial Africa," *Postcolonial Studies* 12, no. 4 (2009): 434.

70. Rafael de Bivar Marquese, "Asymmetrical Dependencies in the Making of a Global Commodity: Coffee in the Longue Durée," *Joseph C. Miller Memorial Lecture Series*, vol.

15, eds. Abdelkader Al Ghouz et al. (EB Verlag, 2023), 17. More generally, see Ulbe Bosma, "Enlightenment in the Global Periphery: Tropical Agricultural Innovation in the Age of Transition, 1750s to 1860s," unpublished paper (in author's possession), presented at Colonial Agricultural Modernities Conference, Wissenschaftskolleg zu Berlin, 2018, 9, 11, 14.

71. Parthasarathi, *Why Europe Grew Rich*, and Michael Kwass, *Contraband: Louis Mandrin and the Making of a Global Underground* (HUP, 2014), 8, 43.

72. Banaji, "Globalising the History of Capital"; Robert Kurz, *Weltkrise und Ignoranz: Kapitalismus im Niedergang* (Tiamat, 2013), 88, 89.

73. This paragraph is drawn from Beckert, *Empire of Cotton*, 38. See also Carl Wennerlind, *Casualties of Credit: The English Financial Revolution, 1620–1720* (HUP, 2011); Adam Smith, *An Inquiry into the Nature and Causes of the Wealth of Nations*, vol. II, book IV, ed. Edwin Cannan (University of Chicago Press, 1976), 75.

74. Banaji, "Globalising the History of Capital," 11.

75. Parthasarathi, *Why Europe Grew Rich*, 13; and Ashin Das Gupta, *Indian Merchants and the Decline of Surat, c. 1700–1750* (Franz Steiner Verlag, 1967), 19.

76. As cited in Alan Heimert and Andrew Delbanco, eds., *The Puritans in America: A Narrative Anthology* (HUP, 1985), 7.

77. McCusker and Menard, "Sugar Industry in the Seventeenth Century," 145.

78. Copy of letter from John Banister to Joseph Harrison, March 10, 1745, in John Banister Papers, Letter Book, 238, Newport Historical Society, Newport, Rhode Island, USA.

79. Richard Vines to John Winthrop, Barbados, 19 July 1647, in "Papers of the Winthrop Family," vol. 5, ed. Stewart Mitchell, Allyn Bailey Forbes, and Malcolm Freiberg (Massachusetts Historical Society, 1929–1992), 172.

80. Richard Ligon, *A True and Exact History of the Island of Barbados* (London: Peter Parker, 1673), 21, 40, 41, 53, 120. The shortage of supplies is a topic throughout the book.

81. Richard S. Dunn, "The Barbados Census of 1680: Profile of the Richest Colony in English America," *William and Mary Quarterly* 26, no. 1 (1969): 30.

82. Ligon, *True and Exact History*, 42.

83. Larry Dale Gragg, "An Am-

biguous Response to the Market: The Early New England–Barbados Trade," *Historical Journal of Massachusetts* 17, no. 2 (Summer 1989): 178; and Wendy Warren, *New England Bound: Slavery and Colonization in Early America* (Liveright Publishing, 2016), 11, 52.

84. Henry Winthrop to Emmanuel Downing, August 22, 1627, and Henry Winthrop to John Winthrop, October 15, 1627, both in "Papers of the Winthrop Family," vol. 1 (Massachusetts Historical Society), 180–81; see also George Downing to John Winthrop Jr., in "Papers of the Winthrop Family," 5:43–44; and Warren, *New England Bound*, 67.

85. Richard Dunn, James Savage, and Laetitia Yeandle, eds., *The Journal of John Winthrop* (HUP, 1996), 692.

86. S. D. Smith, "Gedney Clarke of Salem and Barbados: Transatlantic Super-Merchant," *New England Quarterly* 76, no. 4: 506, 509, 512–14.

87. "Captain Bredon's Relations of the State of Affaires in New England at His Coming from Thence in 1660," Massachusetts Historical Society, carton 36, folder 41, Endicott Family Papers, as cited in Warren, *New England Bound*, 58.

88. "Mémoire de la chambre d'agricultre du Cap sur les nouvelle prohibitions contre la liberté de l'introduction des américaines du continent dans les port de St. Domingue 1784," in Le Gentil de Paroy, 164APOM/1, Archives Privées, ANOM; and Findlay and O'Rourke, *Power and Plenty*, 248.

89. William Weeden, "Early African Slave-Trade in New England," *Proceedings from the American Antiquarian Society* (Worcester, Massachusetts: American Antiquarian Society, 1887), 116; Burnard and Garrigus, *Plantation Machine*, 21.

90. Weeden, "Early African Slave-Trade in New England," 110, 111, 112, 120.

91. Warren, *New England Bound*, 10.

92. Warren, *New England Bound*, 79; Sven Beckert and Katherine Stevens, *Harvard and Slavery: Seeking a Forgotten History* (Harvard University, 2011), 10–12; Rachel Tamar Van, "Free Trade & Family Values: Kinship Networks and the Culture of Early American Capitalism" (PhD diss., Columbia University, 2011).

93. Solow, "Capitalism and Slavery in the Exceedingly Long Run," 731; Solow, *Economic Consequences of the Slave Trade*, 106.

94. Beckert, *Empire of Cotton*, 3–28; Parthasarathi, *Why Europe Grew Rich*, 89.

95. Julie Marfany, *Land, Proto-Industry and Population in Catalonia, c. 1680–1829: An Alternative Transition to Capitalism?* (Ashgate, 2013), 77; Herbert Kisch, *From Domestic Manufacture to Industrial Revolution: The Case of the Rhineland Textile Districts* (OUP, 1989), 131.

96. J. H. Campe, *Reise von Braunschweig nach Paris im Heumonat 1789* (Schulbuchhandlung, 1790), 80–81, as cited in Kisch, *From Domestic Manufacture to Industrial Revolution*, 138.

97. Parthasarathi, *Why Europe Grew Rich*, 134; and Esteban, "Comparative Patterns of Colonial Trade," 134.

98. For a discussion of this process, see Maxine Berg, "Useful Knowledge, 'Industrial Enlightenment,' and the Place of India," *JGH* 8, no. 1 (March 2013): 117–41. See also Parthasarathi, *Why Europe Grew Rich*, 10, 106; and Esteban, "Comparative Patterns of Colonial Trade," 46.

99. Letter to Mr. Augur, Versailles, 9 January 1698, Table Registre, Concernant les Isles de l'amerique, 1698, Secrétariat d'État à la Marine, Correspondance au départ avec les colonies, FM/B//21, ANOM.

100. Seymour Shapiro, *Capital and the Cotton Industry in the Industrial Revolution* (Cornell UP, 1967), 8, 204.

101. Parthasarathi, *Why Europe Grew Rich*, 116–17, 127; "Rekest van de linnenkooplieden om op landsniveau de import van katoen door de VOC te doen staken; met ingebonden bijlage, c. 1676," folder 3863, Stadsbestuur van Haarlem (Stadsarchief van Haarlem), Noord-Hollands Archief, Haarlem, Netherlands. (Thank you to Dineke Stam for bringing this document to my attention.) See also Céline Cousquer, *Nantes: une capitale des indiennes au XVIIIe siècle* (Coiffard, 2002), 12, 23, 43; and *Arrêt du Conseil d'État du roi, 10 juillet 1785* (Paris: Imprimerie Royale, 1785); and Kwass, *Contraband*, 9, 56, 57.

102. N. F. R. Crafts, *British Economic Growth During the Industrial Revolution* (Clarendon Press, 1985), 62–63.

Chapter 7: The Rise of Industrial Capitalism, 1760–1850

1. Thomas Ellison, *The Cotton Trade of Great Britain* (Frank Cass and Company, 1968), 27.

2. Fernand Braudel, *Afterthoughts on Material Civilization and Capitalism* (Johns Hopkins UP, 1977), 105.

3. T. M. Devine, ed., *Recovering Scotland's Slavery Past: The Caribbean Connection* (Edinburgh UP, 2015), 3, 227, 228, 230, 234.

4. Devine, *Recovering Scotland's Slavery Past*, 3, 227, 228, 230, 231, 234; Stephen Mullen, *The Glasgow Sugar Aristocracy, 1775–1838* (University of London Press, 2022). See also Ministers of the Respective Parishes, Under the Superintendence of a Committee of the Society for the Benefit of the Sons and Daughters of the Clergy, *The New Statistical Account of Scotland* (William Blackwood and Sons, 1845); "Transcript from Extract Registered Deposition by Robert Dunmore to the Company of Proprietors of the Forth and Clyte Navigation," 31 October 1789, Document No. 13502, Fr/Bar, UGA; Nathaniel Jones, *Jones' Directory: Or, Useful Pocket Companies for the Year 1787 with an Introduction and Notes of Old Glasgow* (Glasgow: John Mennons, 1787), 40; and Seymour Shapiro, *Capital and the Cotton Industry in the Industrial Revolution* (Cornell UP, 1967), 174. For his plantation ownership, see "Robert Dunmore of Ballindalloch," Centre for the Study of the Legacies of British Slavery Database, University College London, accessed September 10, 2021, https://www.ucl.ac.uk/lbs/person/view/2146649299.

5. Anthony Cooke, *The Rise and Fall of the Scottish Cotton Industry, 1778–1914* (Manchester UP, 2010), 2, 20, 30, 39, 42, 43, 56, 194; Ballindalloch Mill, GB 248 UGD 091/1/5/1, 1809, Finlay Papers, UGA; typescript notes on origins of Deanston Works, undated but after 1881, GB 248 UGD 091/1/5/3/14/1, Finlay Papers, UGA; Matthew Blair, *The Paisley Thread Industry and the Men Who Created and Developed It* (Alexander Gardner, 1907), 44, 45; I. G. C. Hutchison, *Industry, Reform and Empire: Scotland, 1790–1880* (Edinburgh UP, 2020), 37, 53; Maxine Berg and Pat Hudson, *Slavery, Capitalism and the Industrial Revolution* (Polity Press, 2023), 109.

6. Cooke, *Rise and Fall*, 51; Hutchison, *Industry, Reform and Empire*, 38. From 11,784 British pounds in 1789 to 161,285 pounds 1800. See also James Finlay & Co., balance book, GB 248 UGD 091/1/4/1/3/1, 1789–1800, Ledger "C," typescript notes on origins of Deanston Works, UGA.

7. Cooke, *Rise and Fall*, 17, 30–32.

8. Alexander Niven, *New Statistical Account for Balfron* (Stirlingshire: Balfron, 1841), 4–5.

9. Cooke, *Rise and Fall*, 23, 34–35, 39, 100–129; "Contracts between George Houston of Johnstone, Robert Corse, merchant at Wallneuk, Paisley, and the trustees of James Milliken of Milliken, in connection with the cotton mill at Newmill, alias Easter Cochrane," TD263/193, GCA. On landowners, see Cooke, *Rise and Fall*, 178. See also Devine, *Recovering Scotland's Slavery Past*, 236. The Scottish cotton manufacturers frequently appealed to the state for support. See, for example, "Report of the Committee Appointed by the Chamber of Commerce and Manufactures of Glasgow Regarding Cotton Manufacture," February 29, 1788, TD1670/4/49, GCA; "Petition of the Linen and Cotton Manufacturers of Perth to the House of Commons," November 17, 1796, TD1670/4/83, GCA; and "Two Printed Resolutions of the Cotton Manufacturers of Glasgow and Environs," GCA February 29, 1788, TD1670/4/49. See also Committee of Management of the Board of the Cotton Trade, "Observations on the Cotton Trade of Great Britain," February 2, 1803, in Greggory Claeys, *Selected Works of Robert Owen* (Routledge, 1993). In 1801 and 1802, a little less than half of all cotton arriving in Glasgow came from the United States, with the rest from the Caribbean and Brazil. See lists of cotton imports to various Scottish ports, 1801–1802, TD1670/4/96, GCA. See also Cooke, *Rise and Fall*, 46; T. M. Devine, "An Eighteenth-Century Business Elite: Glasgow–West India Merchants, c. 1750–1815," *Scottish Historical Review* 57 (April 1978): 40; and Devine, *Recovering Scotland's Slavery Past*, 231.

10. Cooke, *Rise and Fall*, 175.

11. Cooke, *Rise and Fall*, 184–85.

12. Cooke, *Rise and Fall*, 3, 12, 16, 19, 20, 175, 178; Shapiro, *Capital and the Cotton Industry*, 176; Blair, *Paisley Thread Industry*, 34, 35, 37; Cooke, *Rise and Fall*, 19, 20, 178; Devine, "Eighteenth-Century Business Elite," 46; Finlay Papers, UGA.

13. Mullen, *Glasgow Sugar Aristocracy*, chapter 3; Shapiro, *Capital and the Cotton Industry*, 173; Cooke, *Rise and Fall*, 20, 176; Devine, *Recovering Scotland's Slavery Past*, 227, 228, 229, 236–37; T. M. Devine, "The Colonial Trades and Industrial Investment in Scotland, c. 1700–1815," *EHR* 29 (1976): 3, 4, 10; Devine, "Eighteenth-Century Business Elite," 41–45, 49; Berg and Hudson, *Slavery, Capitalism and the Industrial Revolution*, 156, 157; Shapiro, *Capital and the Cotton Industry*, 13, 16, 147–81. Not only did Glaswegian merchants ship slavery's products into European markets, but they also supplied plantations with a huge variety of consumer goods such as textiles and provisions, and provided credit to planters. See Devine, *Recovering Scotland's Slavery Past*, 229. It was Scottish credit that funded the transformation of the Chesapeake. See Devine, *Recovering Scotland's Slavery Past*, 229.

14. This included also linens. See Devine, *Recovering Scotland's Slavery Past*, 235.

15. As cited in Cooke, *Rise and Fall*, 142.

16. T. M. Devine, *The Transformation of Rural Scotland: Social Change and the Agrarian Economy, 1660–1815* (Edinburgh UP, 1994), 43, 45, 46, 47; and Cooke, *Rise and Fall*, 137–38.

17. As cited in Lionell Gossman, *Thomas Annan of Glasgow: Pioneer of the Documentary Photograph* (Open Book, 2015), 90.

18. Jelinger Symmons, as cited in Gossman, *Thomas Annan of Glasgow*, 90–91.

19. For a contemporary argument along these lines, see undated cotton and linen laws and petition, TD1670/4/266, GCA; and Cooke, *Rise and Fall*, 2, 5, 67. See also Hutchison, *Industry, Reform and Empire*, 38; Anthony Slaven and Sydney Checkland, eds., *Dictionary of Scottish Business Biography, 1860–1960*, vol. 1, *The Staple Industries* (Aberdeen UP, 1986), 297; and Gossman, *Thomas Annan of Glasgow*, 89. The extent of inequality is detailed in J. R. Kellett, "Property Speculators and the Building of Glasgow, 1780–1830," *Scottish Journal of Political Economy* 8 (1961): 211, 214–17; and Gossman, *Thomas Annan of Glasgow*, 91.

20. As cited in Gossman, *Thomas Annan of Glasgow*, 92.

21. Fernand Braudel, "European Expansion and Capitalism, 1450–1650," in *Chapters in Western Civilization*, ed. Contemporary Civilization Staff of Columbia College, Columbia University (CUP, 1961), 260.

22. Charles Tilly, "Did the Cake of Custom Break?," in *Consciousness and Class Experience in Nineteenth Century Europe*, ed. John M. Merriman (Holmes & Meier, 1979), 25. The difference in living standards in the eastern Mediterranean and in Europe before the Industrial Revolution was slim, argues Şevket Pamuk, "Wirtschaft und Institutionen im Nahen Osten seit dem Mittelalter,"

in *Die Ursprünge der Modernen Welt: Geschichte im wissenschaftlichen Vergleich*, ed. James A. Robinson and Klaus Wiegandt (Fischer, 2008), 543. See also Kenneth Pomeranz, *The Great Divergence: China, Europe, and the Making of the Modern World Economy* (PUP, 2000).

23. For a review, see Joseph E. Inikori, *Africans and the Industrial Revolution in England: A Study in International Trade and Economic Development* (CUP, 2002), esp. 110, 141.

24. Despite all this study, historians continue to fundamentally disagree about what the Industrial Revolution was and what caused it. See the wonderful overview in Inikori, *Africans and the Industrial Revolution*, 91. See also Arnold Toynbee, *Lectures on the Industrial Revolution of the Eighteenth Century in England: Popular Addresses, Notes, and Other Fragments* (London: Longmans, 1884); and Robert Allen, *The Industrial Revolution in Global Perspective* (CUP, 2009). Braudel observed that the debate between internal and external explanations of the Industrial Revolution is pointless; both are needed. See Braudel, *Afterthoughts on Material Civilization*, 110. See also Eric Vanhaute, "Global and Regional Comparisons: The Great Divergence Debate and Europe," in *The Practice of Global History* (Bloomsbury, 2019), 186; and Karl Polanyi, *The Great Transformation: The Political and Economic Origins of Our Time* (Beacon Press, 2001; orig. pub. 1944), 42.

25. For this argument, see also Andrea Komlosy, "Entanglements of Catching Up: Rethinking 'Industrial Revolution' from a Global Perspective," *Journal of Globalization Studies* 12, no. 1 (May 2021): 79, 80.

26. Pepijn Brandon, "Marxism and the 'Dutch Miracle': The Dutch Republic and the Transition Debate," *Historical Materialism* 19, no. 3 (2011): 108; Leandro Prados de la Escosura, "Was British Industrialisation Exceptional?," in *Exceptionalism and Industrialisation: Britain and Its European Rivals, 1688–1815*, ed. Leandro Prados de la Escosura (CUP, 2004), 3; and M. Hodgson, *Rethinking World History: Essays on Europe Islam and World History* (CUP, 2002), 68.

27. William J. Ashworth, "The Ghost of Rostow: Science, Culture and the British Industrial Revolution," *Historical Science* 46, no. 3 (2008): 267; and John Styles, "The Rise and Fall of the Spinning Jenny: Domestic Mechanisation in Eighteenth-Century Cotton Spin-

ning," *Textile History* 51, no. 2 (2020): 217, 220, 222.

28. James A. Mann, *The Cotton Trade of Great Britain* (London: Marshall & Co., 1860), 22. For cotton's share in the British economy, see Sven Beckert, *Empire of Cotton: A Global History* (Knopf, 2014), 150–53.

29. Ellison, *Cotton Trade of Great Britain*, 47. For the data on British cotton factories, see Beckert, *Empire of Cotton*, 56–82, esp. 67, 72; Ellison, *Cotton Trade of Great Britain*, 72.

30. For this argument on increases in productive capacities only making sense if requisite demand existed, see also Polanyi, *Great Transformation*, 43. Demand's importance is also emphasized by Ronald Findlay and Kevin H. O'Rourke, *Power and Plenty: Trade, War, and the World Economy in the Second Millennium* (PUP, 2007), 345. See also the excellent Inikori, *Africans and the Industrial Revolution*, 434–35; N. F. R. Crafts and C. Knick Harley, "Precocious British Industrialisation: A General Equilibrium Perspective," in Prados de la Escosura, *Exceptionalism and Industrialisation*, 96.

31. Speech in support of a motion "to enquire into the nature of the distresses of the Cotton Weavers," n.d., no author, T-PM/117/3/49, GCA.

32. Ellison, *Cotton Trade of Great Britain*, v. For the general point, see Andrea Komlosy, "Entanglements of Catching-Up: Rethinking 'Industrial Revolution' from a Global Perspective," *Journal of Globalization Studies* 12, no. 1 (May 2021): 79–100, here p. 84.

33. Mann, *Cotton Trade of Great Britain*, 43; Stephen Mosely, *The Chimney of the World: A History of Smoke Pollution in Victorian and Edwardian Manchester* (Routledge, 2001), 3, 4; and Ellison, *Cotton Trade of Great Britain*, 50, 55.

34. Mann, *Cotton Trade of Great Britain*, 6.

35. See, for example, Rondo Cameron, *A Concise Economic History of the World: From Paleolithic Times to the Present* (OUP 1989), 163–65; and Michael Fores, "The Myth of a British Industrial Revolution," *History* 66, no. 217 (1981): 181–98.

36. As quoted in Cooke, *Rise and Fall*, 75.

37. Kirkman Finlay, Glasgow, to Alexander S. Finlay, Bombay, Glasgow, 14 September 1837, in correspondence book (press copies) between Kirkman Finlay at Castle Toward and Glasgow to London, and to Alexander S. Finlay, Bombay, GB 248

UGD 091/1/3/3/1, Nov 1835–Nov 1837, Finlay Papers, UGA.

38. Cooke, *Rise and Fall*, 64; Kirkman Finlay, Glasgow, to Alexander S. Finlay, Bombay, Glasgow, 15 January 1836, in correspondence book (press copies) between Kirkman Finlay at Castle Toward and Glasgow to London, and to Alexander S. Finlay, Bombay, GB 248 UGD 091/1/3/3/1, Nov 1835–Nov 1837, Finlay Papers, UGA; and Cooke, *Rise and Fall*, 54, 83, 91.

39. Cooke, *Rise and Fall*, 75, 191, 204; and Hutchison, *Industry, Reform and Empire*, 39.

40. As cited in Mosely, *Chimney of the World*, 17. See also Cooke, *Rise and Fall*, 205.

41. Kirkman Finlay, Glasgow, to Alexander S. Finlay, Bombay, Glasgow, 19 December 1835, in correspondence book (press copies) between Kirkman Finlay at Castle Toward and Glasgow to London, and to Alexander S. Finlay, Bombay, GB 248 UGD 091/1/3/3/1, Nov 1835–Nov 1837, Finlay Papers, UGA.

42. Kirkman Finlay, Glasgow, to Alexander S. Finlay, Bombay, Glasgow, 27 January 1836, in correspondence book (press copies) between Kirkman Finlay at Castle Toward and Glasgow to London, and to Alexander S. Finlay, Bombay, GB 248 UGD 091/1/3/3/1, Nov 1835–Nov 1837, Finlay Papers, UGA.

43. See correspondence book (press copies) between Kirkman Finlay at Castle Toward and Glasgow to London, and to Alexander S. Finlay, Bombay, GB 248 UGD 091/1/3/3/1, Nov 1835–Nov 1837, Finlay Papers, UGA; and Private Journal No. 2, GB 248 UGD 091/1/4/3/1/1, 1825–1852, Finlay Papers, UGA.

44. Kirkman Finlay, Glasgow, to Alexander S. Finlay, Bombay, Glasgow, July 11, 1836, in correspondence book (press copies) between Kirkman Finlay at Castle Toward and Glasgow to London, and to Alexander S. Finlay, Bombay, GB 248 UGD 091/1/3/3/1, Nov 1835–Nov 1837, Finlay Papers, UGA.

45. For the debate on the importance of coal, see Gregory Clark and David Jacks, "Coal and the European Industrial Revolution," *European Review of Economic History* 2 (2007): 39–40; and E. A. Wrigley, *Energy and the English Industrial Revolution* (CUP, 2010), 193.

46. Franz-Joseph Brüggemeier, *Grubengold: Das Zeitalter der Kohle von 1750 bis Heute* (C. H. Beck, 2018), 15, 33. These numbers on coal output are rough and taken from Wrigley, *Energy and the English*

Industrial Revolution, 37. On ecological limits, see Pomeranz, *Great Divergence*, 61. On the importance of urban demand, see Clark and Jacks, "Coal and the European Industrial Revolution," 63. On the importance of London, see Robert C. Allen, *The British Industrial Revolution in Global Perspective* (CUP, 2014), 84. See also 82; Robert C. Allen, "The Transportation Revolution and the English Coal Industry, 1695–1842: A Geographical Approach," *JEH* 83, no. 4 (December 2023): 1175; E. A. Wrigley, "Energy and the English Industrial Revolution," *Philosophical Transactions of the Royal Society* 371, no. 1986 (2013): 1–10 ; Alan Fernihough and Kevin Hjortshøj O'Rourke, "Coal and the European Industrial Revolution," National Bureau of Economic Research Working Paper No. 19802 (January 2014, revised September 2014), 13; Joel Mokyr, "An Age of Progress," in *The Cambridge Economic History of Modern Britain*, vol. 1, ed. Roderick Floud, Jane Humphries, and Paul Johnson (CUP, 2014), 284; and Wrigley, *Energy and the English Industrial Revolution*, 46. The steam engine and its ability to pump water allowed miners to dig much deeper shafts.

47. William Fordyce, *A History of Coal, Coke, Coal Fields, Progress of Coal Mining, the Winning and Working of Collieries, Household, Steam, Gas, Coking, and Other Coals, Duration of the Great Northern Coal Field, Mine Surveying and Government Inspection. Iron, Its Ores, and Processes of Manufacture, More Particularly with Reference to the Recently-Discovered Iron Ores of the Cleveland District and of the Blast Furnaces Erected in the North of England. Including Estimates of the Capital Required to Embark in the Coal, Coke, or Iron Trades; the Probable Amount of Profit to Be Realized; Amount of Capital Invested in Collieries and Iron Works; Mode of Valuing Mineral Property, &c. A Brief History of the Coal and Iron Trades, Brought Down to the Present Time. Illustrated with Sketch Geological Map and Numerous Highly Finished Engravings* (London: Sampson Low, Son, and Co., 1860), 5.

48. Brüggemeier, *Grubengold*, 37, 159; Thomas Southcliffe Ashton and Joseph Sykes, *The Coal Industry of the Eighteenth Century* (Manchester UP, 1929), 2; Franz-Joseph Brüggemeier, Michael Farrenkopf, and Heinrich Theodor Grütter, eds., *Das Zeitalter der Kohle: Eine Europäische Geschichte*

(Klartext, 2018), 159, 160; and Fordyce, *History of Coal*, 44.

49. Leigh Shaw-Taylor and Xuesheng You, "The Development of the Railway Network in Britain 1825–1911," in *The Online Historical Atlas of Transport, Urbanization and Economic Development in England and Wales c. 1680–1911*, ed. L. Shaw-Taylor, D. Bogart, and M. Satchell (2018), accessed January 15, 2024, 1, 4, 5, 9–10, 11; Shaw-Taylor and You, "Development of the Railway Network in Britain 1825–1911," 11, 14, 20; Sean McCartney, "Managerial Failure in Early Victorian Britain: Network and Capital Expansion During the Railway Mania," *Business History* (August 15, 2022): 3; and Mark Casson, *The World's First Railway System: Enterprise, Competition, and Regulation on the Railway Network in Victorian Britain* (OUP, 2009), 285.

50. As cited in Charlotte Mathieson, *Mobility in the Victorian Novel: Placing the Nation* (Palgrave Macmillan, 2015), 6.

51. R. Davis, "English Foreign Trade, 1700–1774," *EHR* 15 (March, 1962): 285–303; Inikori, *Africans and the Industrial Revolution*, 456; Nuala Zahedieh, "Eric Williams and William Forbes: Copper, Colonial Markets and Commercial Capitalism," *EHR* 74 (2021): 789; and Berg and Hudson, *Slavery, Capitalism and the Industrial Revolution*, 139. For a summary of the literature on iron's relationship to capital accumulation, see Berg and Hudson, *Slavery, Capitalism and the Industrial Revolution*, 119–20. For details, see D. J. Hamilton, *Scotland, the Caribbean, and the Atlantic World, 1750–1820* (Manchester UP, 2005), 193–97; Ashworth, "Ghost of Rostow," 265; Hutchison, *Industry, Reform and Empire*, 41, 42; and Chris Evans and Göran Rydén, "The Industrial Revolution in Iron: An Introduction," in *The Industrial Revolution in Iron: The Impact of British Coal Technology in Nineteenth-Century Europe*, ed. Chris Evans and Göran Rydén (Routledge, 2005), 2.

52. Priya Satia, *Empire of Guns: The Violent Making of the Industrial Revolution* (Penguin Press, 2018), 19, 20.

53. Satia, *Empire of Guns*, 10.

54. Satia, *Empire of Guns*, 101.

55. Satia, *Empire of Guns*, 6, 8, 21, 141, 148, 153, 156, 157, 164; Eric Hobsbawm, *The Age of Revolution, 1789–1848* (Vintage, 1996), 46.

56. Robert B. Stuart, *A Descriptive History of the Steam Engine* (London: S. and R. Bentley, 1824), v–vi. See

also David Landes, *The Unbound Prometheus: Technological Change and Industrial Development in Western Europe from 1750 to the Present* (CUP, 2003), 104.

57. The spin-off effects of coal are also emphasized by Allen, *British Industrial Revolution in Global Perspective*, 83; and Nicholas F. R. Crafts, "British Industrialization in an International Context," *Journal of Interdisciplinary History* 19, no. 3 (1989): 417.

58. Patrick Colquhoun, *A Treatise on the Wealth, Power and Resources of the British Empire* (London: Joseph Mawman, 1814), 68.

59. Colquhoun, *Treatise on the Wealth, Power and Resources of the British*, 68.

60. William Chambers and Robert Chambers, *Chambers's Information for the People*, vol. 2 (Edinburgh: W. and R. Chambers, 1849), 213.

61. Patrick O'Brien, "Was the First Industrial Revolution a Conjuncture in the History of the World Economy?," Economic History Working Paper No. 259/2017 (London School of Economics and Political Science, March 2017), 7; Richard H. Tilly and Michael Kopsidis, *From Old Regime to Industrial State: A History of German Industrialization from the Eighteenth Century to World War I* (University of Chicago Press, 2020), 49.

62. Arthur L. Dunham, "The Development of the Cotton Industry in France and the Anglo-French Treaty of Commerce of 1860," *EHR* 1, no. 2 (January, 1928): 282; Gerhard Adelmann, *Die Baumwollgewebe Nordwestdeutschlands und der westlichen Nachbarländer beim Übergang von der vorindustriellen zur frühindustriellen Zeit, 1750–1815* (Franz Steiner Verlag, 2001), 76; Richard Dehn, *The German Cotton Industry* (Manchester UP, 1913), 3; J. K. J. Thomson, *A Distinctive Industrialization: Cotton in Barcelona, 1728–1832* (CUP, 1992), 248; Jan Dhondt, "The Cotton Industry at Ghent During the French Regime," in *Essays in European Economic History, 1789–1914*, ed. F. Crouzet, W. H. Chaloner, and W. M. Stern (Edward Arnold, 1969), 18; Georg Meerwein, "Die Entwicklung der Chemnitzer bezw. sächsischen Baumwollspinnerei von 1789–1879" (PhD diss., University of Heidelberg, 1914), 19; Rudolf Forberger, *Die industrielle Revolution in Sachsen 1800–1861*, vol. 1, *Zweiter Halbband: Die Revolution der Produktionskräfte in Sachsen 1800–1830. Übersichten zur Fabrikentwicklung*

(Akademie-Verlag, 1982), 14; Albert Tanner, "The Cotton Industry of Eastern Switzerland, 1750–1914: From Proto-Industry to Factory and Cottage Industry," *Textile History* 23, no. 2 (1992): 139; Wolfgang Müller, "Die Textilindustrie des Raumes Puebla (Mexiko) im 19. Jahrhundert" (PhD diss., University of Bonn, 1977), 144; E. R. J. Owen, *Cotton and the Egyptian Economy, 1820–1914: A Study in Trade and Development* (Clarendon Press, 1969), 23–24; Tilly and Kopsidis, *From Old Regime to Industrial State*, 36; Allen, *Industrial Revolution in Global Perspective*, 211; and Günter Kirchhain, "Das Wachstum der deutschen Baumwollindustrie im 19. Jahrhundert: Eine historische Modellstudie zur empirischen Wachstumsforschung" (PhD diss., University of Münster, 1973), 30, 41. See also Francisco Mariano Nipho, *Estafeta de Londres* (Madrid: n.p., 1770), 44, as quoted in Pierre Vilar, *La Catalogne dans l'Espagne moderne: Recherches sur les fondements économiques des structures nationales*, vol. 2, (S.E.V.P.E.N., 1962), 10; Howard F. Cline, "Spirit of Enterprise in Yucatán," in *History of Late*, ed. Lewis Hanke (Methuen, 1969), 133; Adelmann, *Die Baumwollgewerbe Nordwestdeutschlands*, 153; Dunham, "Development of the Cotton Industry," 288; B. M. Biucchi, "Switzerland 1700–1914," in *The Fontana Economic History of Europe*, vol. 4, ed. Carlo M. Cipolla (Collins, 1977), 634; Robert Lévy, *Histoire économique de l'industrie cotonnière en Alsace* (Felix Alcan, 1912), 87, 89; US Census Bureau, *Manufactures of the United States in 1860: Compiled from the Original Returns of the Eighth Census Under the Direction of the Secretary of the Interior* (US Government Printing Office, 1865), xvii; and Ronald Bailey, "The Slave(ry) Trade and the Development of Capitalism in the United States: The Textile Industry in New England," in *The Atlantic Slave Trade: Effects on Economies, Societies, and Peoples in Africa, the Americas, and Europe*, ed. Joseph E. Inikori and Stanley L. Engerman (Duke UP, 1992), 221.

63. Peter N. Stearns, *The Industrial Revolution in World History* (Westview Press, 2007), 56; W. O. Henderson, *Britain and Industrial Europe, 1750–1870: Studies in British Influence on the Industrial Revolution in Western Europe* (Liverpool UP, 1954), 4, 7, 102, 267; Kristine Bruland, *British Technology and European Industrialization: The Norwegian*

Textile Industry in the Mid-Nineteenth Century (CUP, 1989), 3, 14; David J. Jeremy, *Damming the Flood: British Government Efforts to Check the Outflow of Technicians and Machinery, 1780–1843* (Harvard Business School, 1977), 32–33; Jan Dhont and Marinette Bruwier, "The Low Countries, 1700–1914," in Cipolla, *Fontana Economic History of Europe*, 348; Adelmann, *Die Baumwollgewerbe Nordwestdeutschlands*, 77, 127; David J. Jeremy, *Transatlantic Industrial Revolution: The Diffusion of Textile Technology Between Britain and America, 1790–1830* (Massachusetts Institute of Technology Press, 1981), 17; Landes, *Unbound Prometheus*, 148; Rondo Cameron, "The Diffusion of Technology as a Problem in Economic History," *Economic Geography* 51, no. 3 (July 1975): 221; and John Macgregor, *The Commercial and Financial Legislation of Europe and North America* (Henry Hooper, 1841), 290.

64. Walter Bodmer, *Die Entwicklung der schweizerischen Textilwirtschaft im Rahmen der übrigen Industrien und Wirtschaftszweige* (Verlag Berichthaus, 1960), 279, 339; Alison K. Smith, "A Microhistory of the Global Empire of Cotton: Ivanovo, the 'Russian Manchester,'" *Past & Present* 244 (August 2019): 163; *Commonwealth of Massachusetts: In the year of our Lord one thousand eight hundred and thirteen; An act, to incorporate Francis C. Lowell, and others, by the name of the Massachusetts Manufacturing Company*, Boston, 1813.

65. For this argument on institutional frameworks, see also Beckert, *Empire of Cotton*, 173–74.

66. David Landes's classic history, for example, barely mentions the state. Seeing industrialization as driven by technological change, Landes instead attributed the revolution to a culture of independent rationalism unique to the Western European Enlightenment. See Landes, *Unbound Prometheus*, 15–18. For a Weberian reformulation of Landes, see also Margaret C. Jacob, "French Education in Science and the Puzzle of Retardation, 1790–1840," *História e Economia* 8 (2011), 13–38. See also Ashworth, "Ghost of Rostow," 259, 261; and William J. Ashworth, *The Industrial Revolution: The State, Knowledge and Global Trade* (Bloomsburg, 2017), 4. See also Prasannan Parthasarathi, *Why Europe Grew Rich and Asia Did Not: Global Economic Divergence, 1600–1850* (CUP, 2011), 143; Sophus A. Reinert, *Translating Empire: Emulation and*

the Origins of Political Economy (HUP, 2011), 275; Beckert, *Empire of Cotton*, 174; Inikori, *Africans and the Industrial Revolution*; and Ashworth, *The Industrial Revolution*.

67. Reinert, *Translating Empire*, 276.

68. As cited in Jeff Horn, *The Path Not Taken: French Industrialization in the Age of Revolution, 1750–1830* (Massachusetts Institute of Technology Press, 2006), 222.

69. Joel Mokyr, *Industrialization in the Low Countries* (Yale UP, 1976), 39; Adelmann, *Die Baumwollgewerbe Nordwestdeutschlands*, 89–90; Meerwein, "Die Entwicklung der Chemnitzer," 21, 23, 28, 37, 68; Lars K. Christensen, "Denmark: The Textile Industry and the Forming of Modern Industrial," in *The Ashgate Companion to the History of Textile Workers*, ed. Lex Heerma van Voss, Els Hiemstra-Kuperus, and Elise van Nederveen Meerkerk (Ashgate, 2009), 144; Alexander Hamilton, "Report on the Subject of Manufactures, December 5, 1971," in *Writings* (Library of America, 2001), 647–734; Samuel Rezneck, "The Rise and Early Development of Industrial Consciousness in the United States, 1760–1830," *Journal of Economic and Business History* 4 (1932): 784–811; Horn, *Path Not Taken*, 223; Joshua L. Rosenbloom, "The Economic History of North America, 1700–1870," in *The Cambridge Economic History of the Modern World*, ed. Stephen Broadberry and Kyoji Fukao, vol. 1 (CUP, 2021); and Marcel Boldorf, *Europäische Leinenregionen im Wandel: Institutionelle Weichenstellungen in Schlesien und Irland (1750–1850)* (Böhlau Verlag, 2006), 160.

70. As cited in Jan Dhondt, "The Cotton Industry at Ghent During the French Regime," in *Essays in European Economic History, 1789–1914*, ed. F. Crouzet, W. H. Chaloner, and W. M. Stern (Saint Martin's Press, 1969), 24.

71. Friedrich List, *National System of Political Economy* (Longmans, Green, and Co., 1904), 169. See also Paul Leuilliot, "L'essor économique du XIXe siècle et les transformations de la cité," in *Histoire de Mulhouse*, ed. Georges Livet and Raymond Oberlé (Éditions des Dernières Nouvelles d'Alsace: Diffusion, S.A.E.D., 1977), 190; Richard Dietsche, "Die industrielle Entwicklung des Wiesentales bis zum Jahre 1870: Wirtschaftsgeschichtliche Studien" (PhD diss., Uehlin, 1937), 56–57; and Meerwein, "Die Entwicklung der Chemnitzer," 47,

51–52. For the importance of tariffs, see also Dehn, *The German Cotton Industry*, 4; Kirchhain, "Das Wachstum der deutschen Baumwollindustrie," 185; and Angel Smith, Carles Enrech, Carme Molinero, and Pere Ysàs, "Spain," in Van Voss, Hiemstra-Kuperus, and Van Nederveen Meerkerk, *Ashgate Companion to the History of Textile Workers*, 455. There were many other states that charged high import duties; for a survey, see United States Department of State, *Report in the Commercial Relations of the United States with Foreign Nations: Comparative Tariffs; Tabular Statements of the Domestic Exports of the United States; Duties on Importation of the Staple or Principal Production of the United States into Foreign Countries* (Washington, D.C.: Gales and Seaton, 1842), 534–35.

72. Friedrich List, *Das nationale System der politischen Ökonomie* (G. Fischer, 1922), 476.

73. For the citation, see Henry Charles Carey, *Harmony of Interests, Agricultural, Manufacturing, and Commercial* (Philadelphia: J. S. Skinner, 1851), 72.

74. Beckert, *Empire of Cotton*, 158; Carey, *Harmony of Interests*, 67; Mary Jo Maynes, "Gender, Labor, and Globalization in Historical Perspective: European Spinsters in the International Textile Industry, 1750–1900," *Journal of Women's History* 15, no. 4 (Winter 2004): 48.

75. Dionysius Larder, *Railway Economy: A Treatise on the New Art of Transport, Its Management, Prospects and Relations* (London: Taylor, Walton, and Maberly, 1850), 55; Ian J. Kerr, *Engines of Change: The Railroads That Made India* (Praeger, 2007); Colleen A. Dunlavy, *Politics and Industrialization: Early Railroads in the United States and Prussia* (PUP, 1994), 29; Jesús Sanz Fernández, "Los ferrocarriles iberoamericanos en perspectiva histórica," in *Historia de los ferrocarriles de Iberoamérica (1837–1995)*, ed. Jesús Sanz Fernández (Ministerio de Fomento, 1998), 20; Tilly and Kopsidis, *From Old Regime to Industrial State*, 126; Kimon Apostolus Doukas, *The French Railroads and the State* (CUP, 1945), 17, 24; William G. Thomas, *The Iron Way: Railroads, the Civil War, and the Making of Modern America* (Yale UP, 2011); US Census Bureau, *Historical Statistics of the United States, Colonial Times to 1957* (US Government Printing Office, 1959), 357, 360; and Brian R. Mitchell, *International Historical Statistics: Europe, 1750–1988* (Stockton Press, 1992), 416–17. The German states produced 900,000 metric tons of brown and hard coals in 1815. This number grew to 4.4 million in 1850. See US Census Bureau, *Historical Statistics of the United States*, 366; and Mitchell, *International Historical Statistics*, 441, 446–48.

76. The importance of state capacity to industrialization is a theme that has been emphasized for a long time in the literature, and no one has done so more systematically than Alexander Gerschenkron, *Economic Backwardness in Historical Perspective: A Book of Essays* (Belknap Press, 1962), 25. The exception here is Landes, *Unbound Prometheus*, 137. See also W. R. Lee, "The Paradigm of German Industrialisation: Some Recent Issues and Debates in the Modern Historiography of German Industrial Development," in *German Industry and German Industrialisation: Essays in German Economic and Business History in the Nineteenth and Twentieth Centuries*, ed. W. R. Lee (Routledge, 1991); David Blackbourn and Geoffrey Eley, *The Peculiarities of German History, Bourgeois Society and Politics in Nineteenth-Century Germany* (OUP, 1984), 144; Jürgen Kocka, "Entrepreneurship in a Late-Comer Country: The German Case," in *Social Order and Entrepreneurship*, ed. K. Nakagawa (University of Tokyo Press, 1979), 174; Werner Sombart, *Krieg und Kapitalismus* (Duncker & Humblot, 1913); André Louat and Jean-Marc Servat, *Histoire de l'industrie française jusqu'en 1945: Une industrialisation sans révolutions* (Bréal, 1995), 42–43, 72 (author's translation); Allen, *Industrial Revolution in Global Perspective*, 232–33; and Carl von Clausewitz, *On War* (PUP, 1989), 149.

77. Stearns, *Industrial Revolution in World History*, 56.

78. Allen, *Industrial Revolution in Global Perspective*, 229–30; Stearns, *Industrial Revolution in World History*, 55; Paul van Vlissingen, *De Industrie van Groot-Britannië, een voorbeeld voor Nederland* (Amsterdam: C.A. Spin, 1838); J. L. van Zanden, *De industrialisatie in Amsterdam, 1825–1914* (Octavo, 1987), 25; Stearns, *Industrial Revolution in World History*, 92; Allen, *Industrial Revolution in Global Perspective*, 232–33; and Horn, *Path Not Taken*, 247.

79. Thomas L. Friedman, "How Elon Musk and Taylor Swift Can Resolve U.S.-China Relations," in *NYT*, December 17, 2024.

80. Friedmann Maurer, *Treibende Kräfte: Vom Leben und Arbeiten auf dem Hohen Wald* (Thorbecke, 2013),

188. See also the dissertation in progress by Johannes Staudt at the University of Freiburg (2024).

81. Rudolf Boch, "The Rise and Decline of 'Flexible Production': The German Cutlery Industry of Solingen Since the Eighteenth Century, 1760–1960," in *Arbeiter, Wirtschaftsbürger, Staat: Abhandlungen zur Industriellen Welt* (De Gruyter, 2017), 153; Heinrich Kelleter, *Geschichte der Familie J. A. Henckels* (J. A. Henckels, 1924), vii, 58, 63, 114; Jochen Putsch, *Vom Handwerk zur Fabrik* (Stadtarchiv Solingen, 1985), 26; Boch, "Rise and Decline of 'Flexible Production,'" 153; Putsch, *Vom Handwerk zur Fabrik*, 26; Wolfgang Eduard Peres, "Daniel Peres, 1776–1845," in *Bergisch-Märkische Unternehmer der Frühindustrialiserung*, ed. Ralf Stremmel and Jürgen Weise (Aschendorf, 2004), 281.

82. Kelleter, *Geschichte der Familie*, 119, 121, 124; Ralf Rogge, "Der Zucker und die Solinger Kaufleute Schimmelbusch und Joest, 1780–1840," *Zeitschrift des Bergischen Geschichtsvereins* 102 (2008–2009): 33; Karl-Gerhard Weck, "Die Bedeutung der Solinger Industrie als Anstoßfaktor für die Industrielle Entwicklung" (PhD diss., University of Cologne, 1937), 23; Rogge, "Der Zucker und die Solinger Kaufleute," 31.

83. Trade networks are perfectly visible in Wareneingangsbuch, Wareneingang von Lieferanten und Heimarbeitern, 1832–1833, Fi20-1, J. A. Schmidt & Söhne, Stahlwarenfabrik, Schlagbaum, 1820–1876, 172 AE, SAS. For Rau, see the entries under "Carl Rau" in Wareneingangsbuch, SAS; Hartmut Roher, "Die [sic] Archiv der Firma J. A. Schmidt & Söhne, Solingen," in Ralf Rogge und Horst Sassin, *Die Heimat: Beiträge zur Geschichte Solingens und des bergischen Landes* (Bergischer Geschichtsverein, 2008), 47. By 1852, he transacted with 126 outworkers and employed two workers. See Roher, "Die [sic] Archiv der Firma J. A. Schmidt & Söhne, Solingen," 47. On the history of the firms, see Roher, "Die [sic] Archiv der Firma J. A. Schmidt & Söhne, Solingen," 45–52. On calculating the value of the thaler, see Ronald A. Fullerton, *The Foundations of Marketing Practice: A History of Book Marketing in Germany* (Routledge, 2016), 5. He states that "[a] Thaler was set in value at 3 Marks in 1871. A Mark had a value of 25 US cents." So 1 thaler = 3 marks; 1 mark = 25 US cents (1871); 1 thaler = 75 US cents (1871); 75 US cents (1871) ≈ 19 US dollars (2024);

133,000 thaler = 133,000 * 19 = 2,527,000 US dollars (2024).
84. Georg Franz von Hauer, *Statistische Darstellung des Kreises Solingen im Regierungsbezirk Düsseldorf* (Köln: DuMont-Schauberg, 1832), 88.
85. Rogge, "Der Zucker und die Solinger Kaufleute," 33; Boch, "Rise and Decline of 'Flexible Production,'" 163; Ralf Rogge, "Peter Knecht, 1798–1852," in Ralf Stremmel and Jürgen Weise, *Bergisch-Märkische Unternehmer der Frühindustrialiserung* (Aschendorf, 2004), 436. See also Putsch, *Vom Handwerk zur Fabrik,* 46, 61, 80; Aus dem Jahresbericht der Solinger Handelskammer für das Jahr 1847, 16 February 1848, as cited in Putsch, *Vom Handwerk zur Fabrik,* 89; J. W. Spiritus, *Versuch einer medicinischen Topographie des Kreises Solingen,* 1823, as reprinted in *Alltag im Kreis Solingen,* ed. Ralf Stremmel (Stadt Solingen, 1991), 157, 162, 165, 169; and von Hauer, *Statistische Darstellung des Kreises Solingen,* 30, 38.
86. Bericht des Bürgermeisters von Höhscheid, as quoted in Putsch, *Vom Handwerk zur Fabrik,* 78; Boch, "Rise and Decline of 'Flexible Production,'" 164; Weck, "Die Bedeutung der Solinger Industrie," 23; and von Hauer, *Statistische Darstellung des Kreises Solingen,* 70, 89.
87. von Hauer, *Statistische Darstellung des Kreises Solingen,* 75–76; and Rogge, "Der Zucker und die Solinger Kaufleute," 33.
88. von Hauer, *Statistische Darstellung des Kreises Solingen,* 75, 83; Horst Sassin, "August Schnitzler, 1794–1861," in Stremmel and Weise, *Bergisch-Märkische Unternehmer,* 371; Rogge, "Der Zucker und die Solinger Kaufleute," 37, 39, 102; Carl Schimmelbusch to his parents, Pernambuco, 15 August 1828, KI 123, SAS; Albert Weyersberg, "Solinger Schwertschmiede-Familien," *Zeitschrift für historische Waffenkunde* 1 (1897–1899): 20–21; and Spiritus, *Versuch einer medicinischen Topographie,* 160, 163.
89. Rogge, "Peter Knecht," 432–33, 436, 438–39. See also Putsch, *Vom Handwerk zur Fabrik,* 46, 80. Daniel Peres, for example, built a factory in 1803, but it folded in 1815. See Peres, "Daniel Peres," 295; Ralf Rogge, "Fabrikzerstörungen und Tarifverträge," in *Petitionen und Barrikaden: Rheinische Revolutionen, 1848/49,* ed. Ottfried Dascher and Everhard Kleinertz (Aschendorff, 1998), 185, 440.
90. Kelleter, *Geschichte der Familie,* 159, 160–61, 166.

91. The numbers on comparative industry sizes refer to the period between 1835 and 1845. See Allen, *Industrial Revolution in Global Perspective,* 211. For more details about the assumptions that went into making the calculations on stationary steam engines, see Allen, *Industrial Revolution in Global Perspective,* 179.
92. See William Gervase Clarence-Smith, "The Industrialization of the Developing World 1840s to 1940s," in *Colonialism, Institutional Change and Shifts in Global Labour Relations,* ed. Karin Hofmeester and Pim de Zwart (Amsterdam UP, 2019), 47; Ulbe Bosma and Jonathan Curry-Machado, "Two Islands, One Commodity: Cuba, Java, and the Global Sugar Trade (1790–1930)," *New West Indian Guide* 86, no. 3–4 (2012): 237–62, 241; Stearns, *Industrial Revolution in World History,* 98; Manuel Moreno Fraginals, *The Sugar Mill: The Socio-Economic Complex of Sugar in Cuba 1760–1860* (Monthly Review Press, 1976), 83; and Fernández, "Los ferrocarriles iberoamericanos," 20.
93. Robert L. Tignor, *Egyptian Textiles and British Capital, 1930–1956* (American University in Cairo Press, 1989), 9; Afaf Lutfi Al-Sayyid Marsot, *A History of Egypt* (CUP, 2007), 166, 171; Owen, *Cotton and the Egyptian Economy,* 23–24, 44; Jean Batou, "Muhammad-Ali's Egypt, 1805–1848: A Command Economy in the 19th Century?," in *Between Development and Underdevelopment: The Precocious Attempts at Industrialization of the Periphery, 1800–1870,* ed. Jean Batou (Librairie Droz, 1991), 181, 185, 187, 199. By 1838, as many as thirty thousand workers might have labored in Egypt's cotton-spinning mills. See Colonel Campbell, Her Britannic Majesty's Agent and Consul-General in Egypt, to John Bowring, Cairo, 18 January 1838, as reprinted in John Bowring, *Report in Egypt and Candia* (London: Her Majesty's Stationery Office, 1840), 186; *Ausland* (1831), 1016; Campbell to Bowring, as reprinted in Bowring, *Report in Egypt,* 35; *Asiatic Journal and Monthly Register for British and Foreign India, China, and Australia* 4 (March, 1831): 133; *Asiatic Journal and Monthly Register for British and Foreign India, China, and Australia* 5 (May–August, 1831): 62; and *Asiatic Journal and Monthly Register for British and Foreign India, China, and Australia* 4 (April, 1831): 179, quoting an article from *The India Gazette,* October 5, 1830.
94. On silver capitalism, see John

Tutino, *Making a New World: Founding Capitalism in the Bajío and Spanish North America* (Duke UP, 2011).
95. Şevket Pamuk, "The Ottoman Empire, 1700–1870," in *The Cambridge Economic History of the Modern World,* ed. Stephen Broadberry and Kyoji Fukao, vol. 1 (CUP, 2021). On Puebla, see Colin M. Lewis, "Cotton Textiles and Industry in Latin America: From 'De-Industrialisation' to 'Re-Industrialisation,' c. 1800–1939," unpublished conference paper, GEHN Conference 5 (Cotton Textiles), Osaka, December 2004, accessed February 16, 2024, https://www.lse.ac.uk/Economic-History/Research3/GEHN/GEHN-Conferences/GEHN-Conference-5, 28–29. On Valladolid, see Beckert, *Empire of Cotton,* 136; Rafael Dobado González, Aurora Gómez Galvarriato, and Jeffrey G. Williamson, "Mexican Exceptionalism: Globalization and De-Industrialization, 1750–1877," *JEH* 68, no. 3 (2008): 772.
96. Crafts and Harley, "Precocious British Industrialisation," 86; Nicholas Crafts and Kevin H. O'Rourke, "Twentieth Century Growth," in *Handbook of Economic Growth,* ed. Steven N. Durlauf and Philippe Aghion, vol. 2 (North-Holland, 2014), 266, table 6.2 (c).
97. Patrick O'Brien, "The Mechanization of English Cotton Textile Production from Kay (1733) to Roberts (1822)," unpublished paper, November 2018, 3. On insistence upon using the term "Industrial Revolution," see also Thomas S. Ashton, *The Industrial Revolution, 1760–1830* (OUP, 1969), 4. See also O'Brien, "The Mechanization of English Cotton Textile Production," 3; O'Brien, "Was the First Industrial Revolution a Conjuncture in the History of the World Economy?," 5; Inikori, *Africans and the Industrial Revolution,* 93; Michael Andrew Žmolek, *Rethinking the Industrial Revolution: Five Centuries of Transition from Agrarian to Industrial Capitalism in England* (Brill, 2013), 1.
98. See Doug Hayes, "Wage Labor," in *Oxford Handbook of Global Labor History,* ed. Sven Beckert and Marcel van der Linden (OUP, 2026).
99. There were 50,000 handloom weavers and 331,000 textile factory workers in the UK in 1850, according to John Rule, *The Labouring Classes in Early Industrial England, 1750–1850* (Longman, 1986), 10. In Germany, 93,000 people were employed in cotton processing in 1861, according to Dietrich Ebeling et al., "The German Wool and Cotton

Industry from the Sixteenth to the Twentieth Century," in Van Voss, Hiemstra-Kuperus, and Van Nederveen Meerkerk, *Ashgate Companion to the History of Textile Workers*, 208. In Belgium, there were 14,318 industrial textile workers in 1846, according to *Statistique de la Belgique: Industrie* (Brussels: T. Lesigne, 1851), x. In France, there were 275,000 cotton workers in 1856, according to M. A. Moreau de Jonnès, *Statistique de l'industrie de la France* (Paris: Guillaume et Cie., 1856). In Twente, an eastern region of the Netherlands, there were about 10,000 cotton workers in 1850, according to E. J. Fischer, *Fabriquers en Fabrikanten* (Matrijs, 1983), 8. In the UK in 1841–1850, there were 178,000 coal miners, according to Roy Church, *The History of the British Coal Industry*, vol. 3 (Clarendon Press, 1986), 227. In Germany in 1850, there were 12,741 coal miners in the Ruhr, according to Klaus Tenfelde, *Sozialgeschichte der Bergarbeiterschaft an der Ruhr im 19. Jahrhundert* (Verlag Neue Gesellschaft, 1977), 603. In Belgium, there were 46,186 coal miners in 1846, according to *Statistique de la Belgique*, x.
100. Labour indenture between Claud Alexander & Co. and young people under twenty-one years of age, 1791–1792, GB 248 UGD 091/1/5/3/7/1, 1825, Finlay Papers, UGA.
101. Cooke, *Rise and Fall*, 137.
102. As cited in Cooke, *Rise and Fall*, 142.
103. Typescript notes on origins of Deanston Works, UGA.
104. Factories Inquiry Commission, *Royal Commission on Employment of Children in Factories. First Report, Minutes of Evidence* (London: 1833), 64–66; Paul Kaplowitz, "Pubertal Development in Girls: Secular Trends," *Current Opinion in Obstetrics and Gynecology* 18, no. 5 (2006): 487–91; Cooke, *Rise and Fall*, 147; "List of People Employed at Catrine Works, 1st January 1813, with a Description of the Present Employment and Residence of Those Now Alive and the Number of Who Have Died Since That Time Within the Parish," List of Workers at Catrine 1813–1833, GB 248 UGD 091/1/5/3/7/2, 1813–1920, Finlay Papers, UGA.
105. Cooke, *Rise and Fall*, 136, 137.
106. The fourth Duke of Atholl, as quoted in Cooke, *Rise and Fall*, 139.
107. As cited in Cooke, *Rise and Fall*, 139–40.
108. Devine, *The Transformation of Rural Scotland*, 161; Cooke, *Rise and*

Fall, 139; "List of People Employed at Catrine Works," UGA; and William H. Sewell Jr., *Capitalism and the Emergence of Civic Equality in Eighteenth-Century France* (Chicago UP, 2020), 56.
109. As cited in R. S. Fitton, *The Arkwrights: Spinners of Fortune* (Manchester UP, 1989), 205.
110. Cooke, *Rise and Fall*, 138.
111. As cited in Cooke, *Rise and Fall*, 138.
112. Cooke, *Rise and Fall*, 138.
113. Devine, *Transformation of Rural Scotland*, 2–4, 8–9, 40–47.
114. Devine, *Recovering Scotland's Slavery Past*, 79, 238; and Devine, *Transformation of Rural Scotland*, 79.
115. Cooke, *Rise and Fall*, 142; Tilly, "Did the Cake of Custom Break?," 17–39.
116. Berg and Hudson, *Slavery, Capitalism and the Industrial Revolution*, 162; Jane Humphries, "The Lure of Aggregates and the Pitfalls of the Patriarchal Perspective: A Critique of the High Wage Economy Interpretation of the British Industrial Revolution," *EHR* 66 (2013): 693–714; Allen, *Industrial Revolution in Global Perspective*; and O'Brien, "Mechanization of English Cotton Textile Production," 10. See also Parthasarathi, *Why Europe Grew Rich*, 39; and Ashworth, *Industrial Revolution*, 3.
117. For the data on child workers, see Cooke, *Rise and Fall*, 145; and Factories Inquiry Commission, ProQuest UK Parliamentary Papers, 69–70. For the price of bread, see Great Britain Board of Trade, *Wholesale and Retail Prices. Return to an Order of the Honourable the House of Commons, Dated 6th August, 1903:—for "Report on Wholesale and Retail Prices in the United Kingdom in 1902, with Comparative Statistical Tables for a Series of Years"* (Darling & Son, 1903), 221, 224.
118. Cooke, *Rise and Fall*, 150.
119. Printed report from the inquiry by the Factories Inquiry Commission into the employment of children at Catrine Cotton Works, GB 248 UGD 091/1/5/2/6/2/1, c1830, Finlay Papers, UGA.
120. Printed report from the inquiry, UGA.
121. Printed report from the inquiry, UGA.
122. Sederunt book of cotton spinners, other manufacturers, and proprietors of public works, meeting to consider a motion made in Parliament for inquiring into the necessity for restricting hours of labour of young persons and introducing a sys-

tem of education at the expense of the proprietors, April 1816, T-MJ/100, GCA.
123. Brüggemeier, *Grubengold*, 74; and sederunt book of cotton spinners, GCA.
124. Labour indenture between Claud Alexander & Co., UGA.
125. Labour indenture between Claud Alexander & Co., UGA; James Barrowman, "Slavery in the Coal-Mines of Scotland," *Mining Engineer: Journal of the Institution of Mining Engineers* 14 (1898): 267–79; and Brüggemeier, *Grubengold*, 34, 78.
126. Deanston Works, UGA; Cooke, *Rise and Fall*, 36.
127. Sidney Pollard, *The Genesis of Modern Management: A Study of the Industrial Revolution in Great Britain* (Edward Arnold, 1965), 207; and N. S. B. Gras, *Industrial Evolution* (HUP, 1930), 10–11.
128. Audrey Eccles, *Vagrancy in Law and Practice Under the Old Poor Law* (Routledge, 2016), 5–7.
129. Paul Lawrence, "The Vagrancy Act (1824) and the Persistence of Pre-Emptive Policing in England Since 1750," *British Journal of Criminology* 57 (2017): 516–17.
130. Pepijn Brandon, "Wage Labor, Forced Labor and Industrialization: Naval Shipyards as Laborites for Capitalism," unpublished paper, Global History Seminar, Harvard University, January 29, 2018, 2, 19; and Robert J. Steinfeld, *Coercion, Contract, and Free Labor in the Nineteenth Century* (CUP, 2001), 47, 74–75, 317.
131. For a brilliant history of this, see Steinfeld, *Coercion, Contract and Free Labor*. For the numbers, see pages 74–76. See also "Gesetzessammlung für die Königlichen Preussischen Staaten, 1845," as cited in Steinfeld, *Coercion, Contract and Free Labor*, 245.
132. David Peres, "Rede an die Arbeiter," as cited in Putsch, *Vom Handwerk zur Fabrik*, 57. Translated by the author.
133. See "The Humble Memorial of the Subscribers and Proprietors of Cotton Works in Glasgow and Its Vicinity, 1825," TD1670/4/115, GCA.
134. See "Minute Book of an Association of Master Cotton Spinners of Glasgow and District, Formed to Oppose a Combination of Operatives," 12 Oct 1810–15 Jan 1811, T-MJ/99, GCA; Cooke, *Rise and Fall*, 160.
135. Bill Robbins, "Governor Macquarie's Job Descriptions and the

Bureaucratic Control of the Convict Labour Process," *Labour History* 96 (May 2009): 3. See "The Humble Memorial of the Subscribers and Proprietors"; and O'Brien, "Was the First Industrial Revolution a Conjuncture in the History of the World Economy?," 33; Żmolek, *Rethinking the Industrial Revolution*, 827.

136. Marcel van der Linden, "Reconstructing the Origins of Modern Labor Management," *Labor History* 51, no. 4 (November 2010): 515–16; Robbins, "Governor Macquarie's Job Descriptions," 1–18; Government Regulation and Order, 20 October 1810, in Commonwealth of Australia, *Historical Records of Australia*, series 1, vol. 7, *Governors' Despatches to and from England* (Library Committee of the Commonwealth Parliament, 1916), 413–15, State Library of New South Wales, Sydney, Australia; and Macquarie to Liverpool, 18 October 1811, Enclosure No. 9: Police Regulations, Section 6, in Commonwealth of Australia, *Historical Records of Australia*, 7:410. For further evidence, see Macquarie to Bathurst, 28 June 1813, in Commonwealth of Australia, *Historical Records of Australia*, 7:715–17; and Governor Macquarie, instructions for George Thomas Palmer, Esquire, Superintendent of Government Stock, 28 June 1813, in Commonwealth of Australia, *Historical Records of Australia*, 7:745–47.

137. Rafael Marquese, "The Global History of Labor, 1750–1850," in *Global Labor Handbook*, eds. Sven Beckert and Marcel van der Linden (OUP, forthcoming).

138. Andreas Malm, *Fossil Capital: The Rise of Steam Power and the Roots of Global Warming* (Verso, 2016), 11; Wrigley, *Energy and the English Industrial Revolution*, 39.

139. Malm, *Fossil Capital*, 16, 25, 54, 55–56.

140. Malm, *Fossil Capital*, 56, 57, 61, 121, 150, 151.

141. Wrigley, *Energy and the English Industrial Revolution*, 39; Patrick O'Brien, "Was the British Industrial Revolution a Conjuncture in Global Economic History?," *JGH* 17, no. 1 (2022): 135. The calculation of the land required for the embodied energy of coal is based on the data in and arguments of Wrigley, *Energy and the English Industrial Revolution*, 39, 206; and Malm, *Fossil Capital*, 253.

142. Prasannan Parthasarathi presents a similar picture of an escalating timber shortage to make the argument that the British Industrial Revolution relied on state interven-

tion to guarantee fuel supplies. See Parthasarathi, *Why Europe Grew Rich*. There are, however, some voices that doubt the severity of wood shortages, among them Peter Warde, "Early Modern 'Resource Crisis': The Wood Shortage Debates in Europe," in *Crises in Economic and Social History: A Comparative Perspective*, ed. A. T. Brown, A. Burn, and R. Doherty (Boydell Press, 2015), 137–60; William M. Cavert, *The Smoke of London: Energy and Environment in the Early Modern City* (CUP, 2016); B. W. Clapp, *An Environmental History of Britain Since the Industrial Revolution* (Routledge, 2013), 14; Masahiko Akatsu, "The Air Pollution Problem in the British Industrial Revolution: The Enactment of the Smoke Nuisance Abatement Act of 1821," *Socio-Economic History* 69, no. 4 (2003); and W. Walker Hanlon, "Coal Smoke, City Growth, and the Costs of the Industrial Revolution," *Economic Journal* 130 (2020): 462–88.

143. Crafts and O'Rourke, "Twentieth Century Growth," 263–346, here table 6.2 (a) and (b), 266. See also Şevket Pamuk and Jan-Luiten van Zanden, "Standards of Living," in *Cambridge Economic History of Modern Europe*, vol. 1, *1700–1870*, ed. Stephen Broadberry and Kevin H. O'Rourke (CUP, 2010): 220.

144. Jan de Vries, *The Industrious Revolution: Consumer Behavior and the Household Economy, 1650 to the Present* (CUP, 2008), chaps. 1–4; Nicholas Crafts and C. K. Harley, "Output Growth and the British Industrial Revolution: A Restatement of the Crafts-Harley View," *EHR* 45, no. 4 (November 1992): 703–30; Pol Antràs and Hans-Joachim Voth, "Factor Prices and Productivity Growth During the British Industrial Revolution," *Explorations in Economic History* 40 (2003): 52–77. Escosura, "Was British Industrialisation Exceptional?," 3; Nicholas Crafts, "Steam as a General Purpose Technology: A Growth Accounting Perspective," *Economic Journal* 114 (2004): 338–51; and Allen, *Industrial Revolution in Global Perspective*, 194, 220.

145. Thomas Jefferson, *Notes on the State of Virginia* (Richmond, Virginia: J. W. Randolph, 1853), 176.

146. Thomas Bazley, *A Lecture upon Cotton as an Element of Industry* (Longman, Brown and Co., 1852), 57.

147. Cooke, *Rise and Fall*, 160. The motto is cited in "Minute Book of an Association of Master Cotton Spinners," GCA.

148. Cooke, *Rise and Fall*, 76, 159, 164; and Devine, *Transformation of Rural Scotland*, 1.

149. On some of the similarities between China and parts of Europe, as well as some differences, see Pomeranz, *Great Divergence*; and R. Bin Wong, *China Transformed: Historical Change and the Limits of the Human Experience* (Cornell UP, 2018). Some of the limits are discussed in Robert C. Allen, "Agricultural Productivity and Rural Incomes in England and the Yangtze Delta, c. 1620–c. 1820," *EHR* 62 (2009): 525–50; Stephen Broadberry and Bishnupriya Gupta, "The Early Modern Great Divergence: Wages, Prices and Economic Development in Europe and Asia, 1500–1800," *EHR* 59 (2006): 2–31; and Parthasarathi, *Why Europe Grew Rich*, 1. On China in particular, see the excellent discussion in Peer Vries, *State, Economy and the Great Divergence: Great Britain and China, 1680s–1850s* (Bloomsbury, 2015), 243; Parthasarathi, *Why Europe Grew Rich*, 224–59, esp. 231, 257, 259.

150. Tilly, "Did the Cake of Custom Break?," 36; Cormac Ó Gráda, *The Great Irish Famine* (CUP, 2000), 28, 277–78, 293; and Kevin Kenny, *The American Irish: A History* (Pearson Education, 2000), 30. Ó Gráda disagrees on the impact of the Act of Union, commenting that most industries only went into decline decades after the Union. See Cormac Ó Gráda, *Ireland: A New Economic History* (Clarendon Press, 1993), 307, 308; Kenny, *American Irish*, 52; Abdul-Karim Rafeq, "Craft Organization, Work Ethics, and the Strains of Change in Ottoman Syria," *Journal of the American Oriental Society* 111 (1991): 509; Abdul-Karim Rafeq, "The Impact of Europe on a Traditional Economy: The Case of Damascus, 1840–1870," in *Économie et Sociétés dans l'Empire Ottoman*, ed. Jean-Louis Bacqué-Grammont and Paul Dumont (CNRS, 1983), 420; Pamuk, "Ottoman Empire," 185; Rafeq, "Craft Organization, Work Ethics, and the Strains of Change in Ottoman Syria," 509, 510; and Rafeq, "Impact of Europe on a Traditional Economy," 426–27.

151. Polanyi, *Great Transformation*, 43, 60.

152. Charles S. Maier, *Once Within Borders: Territories of Power, Wealth, and Belonging Since 1500* (HUP, 2016), 185–232.

153. Tilly, "Did the Cake of Custom Break?," 28. See also Żmolek, *Rethinking the Industrial Revolution*, 41.

154. One dimension of the disjuncture brought on by the emergence of industrial capitalism is brilliantly illuminated by Pierre Gervais, "Capitalism and (or) Age of Commerce: The Peculiarities of Market Exchange in the Early Modern Era," *Revue de la Société d'études anglo-américaines des XVIIe et XVIIIe siècles* 77 (2020): 1–19; Pierre Gervais and Martin Quinn, "Costing in the Early Industrial Revolution: Gradual Change to Cost Calculations at US Cloth Mills in the 1820s," *Accounting History Review* 26, no. 3 (September 2016): 191–217; and Pierre Gervais, "From 'Pure Satisfaction and Curiosity' to the 'Particular Gain or Loss upon Each Article': Early Modern Philosophies of Accounting in English Accounting Textbooks," *Accounting History Review* 30, no. 3 (September 2020): 127. See also Alessandro Stanziani, *Rules of Exchange: French Capitalism in Comparative Perspective, Eighteenth to Early Twentieth Century* (CUP, 2012).

Chapter 8: Capturing the Hinterland, 1780–1860

1. Elizabeth Abbott, *Haiti: The Duvaliers and Their Legacy* (McGraw Hill, 1988), xiii.
2. Carolyn Fick, "Emancipation in Haiti: From Plantation Labour to Peasant Proprietorship," *Slavery & Abolition* 21, no. 2 (2000): 11–12; Trevor Burnard and John Garrigus, *The Plantation Machine: Atlantic Capitalism in French Saint-Domingue and British Jamaica* (University of Pennsylvania Press, 2016), 40, 245, 247–48; and Peter Boomgaard and Gert J. Oostindie, "Changing Sugar Technology and the Labour Nexus: The Caribbean, 1750–1900," *Nieuwe West-Indische Gids* 63, no. 1/2 (January 1989): 3–22.
3. Laurent Dubois, *Haiti: The Aftershocks of History* (Metropolitan Books, 2012), 25; Fick, "Emancipation in Haiti," 15.
4. Dubois, *Haiti*, 26; and Laurent Dubois, *Avengers of the New World: The Story of the Haitian Revolution* (Belknap Press, 2004), 92–93, 94.
5. Dubois, *Avengers of the New World*, 92.
6. "Mémoire pour les Sieurs Bethman et Compagnie (Liquidation des Maisons de Commerce Bethman et Fils, Bethman et Fils et Compagnie), contre les Sieurs Weltner et Compagnie, et en présence du Sieur Gramont (Liquidation de la Maison Feger, Gramont et Compagnie)," Bordeaux, 1812, 15, W1-9, VII, Nr. 15, Bethmann-Archiv, Stadtarchiv Frankfurt, Germany.

7. For more on this story, see also Gironde, Bordeaux, France, as quoted in Thésée, "Négociants bordelais et colons de Saint-Domingue," 150.
8. Thésée, "Négociants bordelais et colons de Saint-Domingue," 162.
9. Bapst to Jean Ozy & Fils, 26 Novembre 1791, 7 B 1999, Archives Départementales de la Gironde, Bordeaux, France, quoted in Thésée, "Négociants bordelais et colons de Saint-Domingue," 158.
10. Thésée, "Négociants bordelais et colons de Saint-Domingue," 183.
11. 7 Juin 1791, 7 B 2000, Archives Départementales de la Gironde, Bordeaux, France, as quoted in Thésée, "Négociants bordelais et colons de Saint-Domingue," 151.
12. Wolfgang Henninger, *Johann Jakob von Bethmann, 1717–1792: Kaufmann, Reeder und Kaiserlicher Konsul in Bourdeaux*, vol. 1 (Universitätsverlag Dr. N. Brockmeyer, 1993), 363. See also letter draft to Monsieur St. Martin à Paris, undated, W1-9, VII, Nr. 25, Bethmann-Archiv, Stadtarchiv Frankfurt, Germany.
13. Fick, "Emancipation in Haiti," 16.
14. Fick, "Emancipation in Haiti," 16, 22–23; and Carolyn E. Fick, *The Making of Haiti: The Saint Domingue Revolution from Below* (University of Tennessee Press, 1990), 210–36.
15. Sugar output revived somewhat after 1800. See J. H. Galloway, *The Sugar Cane Industry: An Historical Geography from Its Origins to 1914* (CUP, 1989), 212; Aurora Gómez-Galvarriato, "Premodern Manufacturing," in *Cambridge Economic History of Latin America*, vol. 1, ed. Victor Bulmer-Thomas, John Coatsworth, and Roberto Cortes-Conde (CUP, 2005), 368; Fick, "Emancipation in Haiti," 27–28; and Rafael Marquese, "Asymmetrical Dependencies and the Making of a Global Commodity: Coffee in the Longue Durée," in *Joseph C. Miller Lecture Series*, no. 15, ed. Abdelkader Al Ghouz, Jeannine Bischoff, and Sarah Dusend (Bonn Center for Dependency and Slavery Studies, 2023), 25.
16. Levi Marrero, "La rapida transformacion del paisaje viorgen de Guantanamo por lose immigrantes franceses (1802–1809)," in *Cuba, economía y sociedad: Azúcar, ilustración y conciencia, 1763–1868*, vol. 11 (Editorial Playor, 1983), 148; John Hebron Moore, *The Emergence of the Cotton Kingdom in the Old Southwest: Mississippi, 1770–1860* (Louisiana State UP, 1988), 4; Michael Edwards, *The Growth of the British Cotton Trade, 1780–1815* (Manchester UP, 1967), 92; Brian Schoen, *The Fragile Fabric of Union: Cotton, Federal Politics, and the Global Origins of the Civil War* (Johns Hopkins UP, 2009), 12; and Fick, "Emancipation in Haiti," 15.
17. Letter of Bethmann Desclaux to Pierre Henry Bethmann, 6 April 1793, W1-9, VII, Nr. 16, Bethmann-Archiv, Stadtarchiv Frankfurt, Germany. See also other letters in this file.
18. Henninger, *Johann Jakob von Bethmann*, 268. See also Thésée, "Négociants bordelais et colons de Saint-Domingue," 147–206, esp. 195–98, 200; Klaus Weber, "Deutschland, der atlantische Sklavenhandel und die Plantagenwirtschaft der Neuen Welt (15. bis 19. Jahrhundert)," *Journal of Modern European History* (Special Issue: "Europe, Slave Trade, and Colonial Forced Labour") 7, no. 1 (2009): 37–67; Klaus Weber, "Linen, Silver, Slaves, and Coffee: A Spatial Approach to Central Europe's Entanglements with the Atlantic Economy," *Culture & History Digital Journal* 4, no. 2 (2015): 7; Michael Zeuske, *Handbuch Geschichte der Sklaverei: Eine Globalgeschichte von den Anfängen bis zur Gegenwart* (De Gruyter, 2013), 512; Klaus Weber, *Deutsche Kaufleute im Atlantikhandel, 1680–1830: Unternehmen und Familien in Hamburg, Cádiz und Bordeaux* (C. H. Beck, 2004), 203; and Thésée, "Négociants bordelais et colons de Saint-Domingue," 197. Even though Johann Jakob Bethmann died in 1792, his descendants tried to gain compensation for the immense losses suffered during the Haitian Revolution. See Henninger, *Johann Jakob von Bethmann*, 361. For the calculation of the contemporary value, I used Markus A. Denzel, *Handbook of World Exchange Rates, 1590–1914* (Ashgate, 2010), 286; "Inflation Calculator," Bank of England, accessed August 19, 2024, https://www.bankofengland.co.uk/monetary-policy/inflation/inflation-calculator; and "GBP/USD Currency," Google Finance, accessed August 19, 2024.
19. Roderick Floud et al., *The Changing Body: Health, Nutrition and Human Development in the Western World Since 1700* (CUP, 2011), 160; and Dale Tomich, "Commodity Frontiers, Spatial Economy, and Technological Innovation in the Caribbean Sugar Industry, 1783–1878," in *The Caribbean and the Atlantic World Economy: Circuits of Trade, Money and Knowledge, 1650–1914*,

ed. A. B. Leonard and David Pretel (Palgrave Macmillan, 2015), 185.

20. Michael Kwass, *Contraband: Louis Mandrin and the Making of a Global Underground* (HUP, 2014), 20. On cotton, see Sven Beckert, *Empire of Cotton: A Global History* (Vintage Books, 2014), 86; Roman Sandgruber, "Österreich 1650–1850," in *Handbuch der europäischen Wirtschafts- und Sozialgeschichte*, vol. 4, ed. Wolfram Fischer et al. (Klett-Cotta, 1993), 670; J. K. J. Thomson, "Technology Transfer to the Catalan Cotton Industry," in *The Fibre That Changed the World: The Cotton Industry in International Perspective, 1600–1990s*, ed. Douglas A. Farnie and David J. Jeremy (OUP, 2004), 267; and B. R. Mitchell, *European Historical Statistics, 1750–1970* (Macmillan, 1975), 428.

21. Sven Beckert, Ulbe Bosma, Mindi Schneider, and Eric Vanhaute, "Commodity Frontiers and the Transformation of the Global Countryside: A Research Agenda," *JGH* 16, no. 3 (2021): 435–50; and Tâmis Parron, "The British Empire and the Suppression of the Slave Trade to Brazil: A Global History Analysis," *Journal of World History* 29, no. 1 (March 2018): 7–8.

22. Laird W. Bergad, "Slavery in Cuba and Puerto Rico, 1804 to Abolition," in *The Cambridge World History of Slavery*, vol. 4, *AD 1804–AD 2016*, ed. David Eltis et al. (CUP, 2017), 100, 111; João José Reis, "Slavery in Nineteenth Century Brazil," in Eltis et al., *Cambridge World History of Slavery*, 4:132; US Census Bureau, *Historical Statistics of the United States* (US Government Printing Office, 1975), 885, 899; Dale Tomich, "World Slavery and Caribbean Capitalism: The Cuban Sugar Industry, 1760–1868," *Theory and Society* (Special Issue on Slavery in the New World) 20, no. 3 (June 1991), 304; William Gervase Clarence-Smith and Steven Topik, *The Global Coffee Economy in Africa, Asia and Latin America, 1500–1989* (CUP, 2003), 31.

23. Anthony Webster, *The Richest East India Merchant: The Life and Business of John Palmer of Calcutta, 1767–1836* (Boydell Press, 2007), 16; Richard B. Allen, *European Slave Trading in the Indian Ocean, 1500–1850* (Ohio UP, 2014), 142; Peter Way, "Militarizing the Atlantic World: Army Discipline, Coerced Labor, and Britain's Commercial Empire," *Atlantic Studies* 13, no. 3 (2016): 345–69.

24. Javier Cuenca Esteban, "Comparative Patterns of Colonial Trade:

Britain and Its Rivals," in *Exceptionalism and Industrialisation: Britain and Its European Rivals, 1688–1815*, ed. Leandro Prados de la Escosura (CUP, 2004), 39.

25. US Census Bureau, "Hay, Cotton, Cottonseed, Shorn Wool, and Tobacco—Acreage, Production, and Price: 1790 to 1970," in *Historical Statistics of the United States, Colonial Times to 1970*, pt. 1 (US Government Printing Office, 1975), 518; Edward Baines, *History of the Cotton Manufacture in Great Britain* (London: H. Fisher, R. Fisher, and Jackson, 1835), 302; and Edwards, *Growth of the British Cotton Trade*, 89, 95; David Ramsay, *The History of South Carolina: From Its First Settlement in 1670, to the Year 1808* (Charleston, South Carolina: Published by David Longworth for the Author, 1809), 121. For Ottoman cotton production, see the excellent work of Kristen Alff, such as Kristen Alff, "Landed Property, Capital Accumulation, and Polymorphous Capitalism: Egypt and the Levant," in *A Critical Political Economy of the Middle East and North Africa*, ed. Joel Beinin et al. (Stanford UP, 2021), 25–45, esp. 35, 38.

26. Mann, *Cotton Trade of Great Britain*, 44.

27. Allan Kulikoff, "Uprooted Peoples: Black Migrants in the Age of the American Revolution 1790–1920," in *Slavery and Freedom in the Age of the American Revolution*, ed. Ira Berlin and Ronald Hoffman (UP of Virginia, 1983), 143–52; James McMillan, "The Final Victims: The Demography, Atlantic Origins, Merchants, and Nature of the Post-Revolutionary Foreign Slave Trade to North America, 1783–1810" (PhD diss., Duke University, 1999), 40–98; Walter Johnson, ed., "Introduction: The Future Store," in *The Chattel Principle: Internal Slave Trades in the Americas* (Yale UP, 2004), 6; Adam Rothman, "The Expansion of Slavery in the Deep South" (PhD diss., Columbia University, 2000), 59, 84, 314; James Scherer, *Cotton as a World Power: A Study in the Economic Interpretation of History* (Frederick A. Stokes Company, 1916), 151; Michael Tadman, *Speculators and Slaves: Masters, Traders, and Slaves in the Old South* (University of Wisconsin Press, 1989), 12; Beckert, *Empire of Cotton*, 290; and John Hebron Moore, "Two Cotton Kingdoms," *Agricultural History* 60, no. 4 (Fall 1986): 1–16. Numbers are from Gavin Wright, *The Political Economy of the Cotton South: Households, Markets, and Wealth in the*

Nineteenth Century (W. W. Norton, 1978), 27–28; Ronald Bailey, "The Other Side of Slavery: Black Labor, Cotton, and Textile Industrialization in Great Britain and the United States," *Agricultural History* 68, no. 2 (Spring 1994): 38; and Thomas Craemer, "Estimating Slavery Reparations: Present Value Comparisons of Historical Multigenerational Reparations Policies," *Social Science Quarterly* 96, no. 2 (2015): 639–55.

28. Frederick Law Olmsted, *The Cotton Kingdom: A Traveler's Observations on Cotton and Slavery in the American Slave States*, vol. 2 (New York: Mason Brothers, 1861), 202.

29. For a summary of the debate on productivity increases on American plantations, see Mark Stelzner and Enzo Cerrutti, "Workers and Technological Change in the United States," *Labor History* 59, no. 6 (2018): 161, see also 112–13; and Alan L. Olmstead and Paul W. Rhode, "Biological Innovation and Productivity Growth in the Antebellum Cotton Economy," *JEH* 68, no. 4 (2008): 1123–71.

30. Beckert, *Empire of Cotton*, 114.

31. Robert Lowry and William H. McCardle, *A History of Mississippi: From the Discovery of the Great River by Hernando DeSoto, Including the Earliest Settlement Made by the French Under Iberville, to the Death of Jefferson Davis* (Jackson, Mississippi: R. H. Henry & Co., 1891), 250; and Alfred John Brown, *History of Newton County, Mississippi: From 1834 to 1894* (Jackson, Mississippi: Clarion-Ledger Company, 1894), 6. On the removals, see the excellent Claudio Saunt, *Unworthy Republic: The Dispossession of Native Americans and the Road to Indian Territories* (W. W. Norton, 2020).

32. Daniel W. Jordan to Emily Jordan, Plymouth, 3 August 1833, Daniel W. Jordan Papers, Special Collections Department, Perkins Library, Duke University, Durham, North Carolina, as quoted in Beckert, *Empire of Cotton*, 118.

33. James L. Watkins, *King Cotton: A Historical and Statistical Review, 1790 to 1908* (Watkins & Sons, 1908), 160–87; and Beckert, *Empire of Cotton*, 104. See also William Chandler Bagley Jr., *Soil Exhaustion and the Civil War* (American Council on Public Affairs, 1942), 18–19; Stuart W. Bruchey, *Cotton and the Growth of the American Economy, 1790–1860: Sources and Readings* (Harcourt, Brace & World, 1967), 80–81.

34. Michael Chevalier, *Society, Manners and Politics in the United States:*

Being a Series of Letters on North America, trans. T. G. Bradford (Boston: Weeks, Jordan and Company, 1839), 309–10; Frederick Marryat, *A Diary in America, with Remarks on Its Institutions* (New York: William H. Colyer, 1839); and Thomas Cather, *Voyage to America: The Journals of Thomas Cather*, ed. Thomas Yoseloff (Thomas Yoseloff, 1961).

35. Representative John C. Calhoun, "An Argument for Internal Improvements (1817)," in *American History Told by Contemporaries*, ed. Albert Bushnell Hart and John Gould Curtis (Macmillan, 1901), 439.

36. James C. Cobb, *The Most Southern Place on Earth: The Mississippi Delta and the Roots of Regional Identity* (OUP, 1992), 7. For more on Choctaw and Chickasaw removal, see Arthur H. DeRosier Jr., *The Removal of the Choctaw Indians* (University of Tennessee Press, 1970); Mary Elizabeth Young, *Redskins, Ruffleshirts, and Rednecks: Indian Allotments in Alabama and Mississippi, 1830–1860* (University of Oklahoma Press, 1961); and Samuel J. Wells, "Federal Indian Policy: From Accommodation to Removal," in *The Choctaw Before Removal*, ed. Carolyn Keller Reeves (UP of Mississippi, 1985), 181–213.

37. Arrell M. Gibson, *The Chickasaws* (University of Oklahoma Press, 1971), 157.

38. Letter of Thomas Barker to Lewis Cass, 17 July 1834, quoted in Claudio Saunt, "Financing Dispossession: Stocks, Bonds, and the Deportation of Native Peoples in the Antebellum United States," *JAH* 106, no. 2 (September 2019): 318.

39. Malcolm Rohrbough, *The Land Office Business: The Settlement and Administration of American Public Lands, 1789–1837* (OUP, 1968), 226–32; Joshua D. Rothman, *Flush Times and Fever Dreams: A Story of Capitalism and Slavery in the Age of Jackson* (University of Georgia Press, 2012), 3; Don H. Doyle, "The Mississippi Frontier in Faulkner's Fiction and in Fact," *Southern Quarterly* 29, no. 4 (Summer 1991): 153; and Dennis East, "New York and Mississippi Land Company and the Panic of 1837," *Journal of Mississippi History* 33, no. 4 (1971): 303–4. For more on Joseph D. Beers, see Walter Barrett, *The Old Merchants of New York City*, vol. 3 (New York: Thomas R. Knox & Co., 1885), 108–9. On the process of how land transfers were financed, see also Saunt, *Unworthy Republic*, 19, 21, 173–201; East, "New York and Mississippi Land," 305–6; and

Saunt, "Financing Dispossession," 318, 324–6.

40. Saunt, *Unworthy Republic*, 62.

41. Cobb, *Most Southern Place on Earth*, 10; Saunt, "Financing Dispossession," 328; Rothman, *Flush Times and Fever Dreams*, 4, 7; Julius Marvin Bentley Jr., "Financial Institutions and Economic Development in Mississippi, 1809 to 1860" (PhD diss., Tulane University, 1969), 203; and Michael Zakim, "Capitalism and Slavery in the United States," in *The Routledge History of Nineteenth Century America*, ed. Jonathan Daniel Wells (Routledge, 2017), 154.

42. Joseph Holt Ingraham, *The South-West, by a Yankee*, vol. 2 (New York: Harper & Brothers, 1835), 91.

43. Rothman, *Flush Times and Fever Dreams*, 118; and Cobb, *Most Southern Place on Earth*, 8.

44. Calvin Schermerhorn, *The Business of Slavery and the Rise of American Capitalism, 1815–1860* (Yale UP, 2015), 97, 104, 105; Bray Hammond, *Banks and Politics in America from the Revolution to the Civil War* (PUP, 1957); Thomas Payne Govan, *Nicholas Biddle: Nationalist and Public Banker, 1786–1844* (University of Chicago Press, 1959); Stanley L. Engerman, "A Note on the Economic Consequences of the Second Bank of the United States," *Journal of Political Economy* 78, no. 4 (1970), 725–28; George Green, *Finance and American Development in the Old South: Louisiana Banking, 1804–1861* (Stanford UP, 1972), 112–13. For more on the CAPL, see Schermerhorn, *The Business of Slavery*, chapter 4.

45. Tomich, "Commodity Frontiers, Spatial Economy, and Technological," 187.

46. On the move to the Cuban countryside, see also Ada Ferrer, *Freedom's Mirror: Cuba and Haiti in the Age of Revolution* (CUP, 2014), 5; Reinaldo Funes Monzote, "Sugar Cane and Agricultural Transformations in Cuba," in *Oxford Research Encyclopedia of Latin American History* (OUP, 2016), 3; Manuel Moreno Fraginals, *El ingenio: Complejo económico social cubano del azúcar*, vol. 3 (Havana: Editorial de Ciencias Sociales, 1798), 3, 43–46; Reinaldo Funes Monzote, "El Azúcar, la era del vapor y los cambios ambientales en Sagua la Grande en el siglo XIX," in *La Reinvención Colonial de Cuba*, ed. Imilcy Balboa Navarro (Ediciones Idea, 2013), 34; and Ferrer, *Freedom's Mirror*, 10, 17.

47. Idelfonso Vivanco, "Excursión a la Vuelta de Arriba," in *La Siempre-*

viva, vol. 1, 3rd ed. (1838), 175–85, as quoted in Reinaldo Funes Monzote, "Paisajes de la nueva plantación esclavista azucarera en Cuba: La llanura de Colón, 1815–1880," in *Plantación, espacios agrarios y esclavitud en la Cuba colonial*, ed. José A. Piqueras (Universitat Jaume I, Casa de las Américas, 2017), 91–114.

48. Tomich, "Commodity Frontiers, Spatial Economy, and Technological," 189; and Fraginals, *El ingenio*, 35–36. On Cuban mills, see, for example, Funes Monzote, "Paisajes de la nueva plantación esclavista azucarera en Cuba," 91–114; Fraginals, *El ingenio*, 35–37; and Tomich, "Commodity Frontiers, Spatial Economy, and Technological," 212.

49. David Eltis, *Economic Growth and the Ending of the Transatlantic Slave Trade* (OUP, 1987), 245.

50. Oscar Zanetti, "The Last Sugar Frontier in Cuba: Expansion and Consequences," unpublished paper (in author's possession), presented at the Global Commodities Conference, London, 2015, 5. This equals exactly twenty-one thousand hectares. See Funes Monzote, "Paisajes de la nueva plantación esclavista azucarera en Cuba," 91–114. For a long discussion of these issues, see Reinaldo Funes Monzote, "Plantaciones esclavistas azucareras y transformación ecológica en Cuba," *Revista de Historia* no. 59–60 (2009): 40. Free trade and expansion into the American market in many ways duplicated earlier effects of sugar cultivation in the Caribbean. See Jason W. Moore, "Sugar and the Expansion of the Early Modern World-Economy: Commodity Frontiers, Ecological Transformations, and Industrialization," *Review* (Fernand Braudel Center) 23, no. 3 (May 2000): 409–33. For quote, see Ramón de La Sagra, *Historia economico-politica y estadística de la isla de Cuba ó sea de sus progresos en la poblacion, la agricultura, el comercio y las rentas* (Havana: Imprenta de las Viudas de Arazosa y Soler, 1831), 84–85.

51. Funes Monzote, "Sugar Cane and Agricultural Transformations in Cuba," 6.

52. Reinaldo Funes Monzote, "New Landscapes of Slavery Plantation Frontiers in 19th-Century Cuba: The Colon Plains, 1820–1880," paper (in author's possession) presented at the Global Commodity Frontiers in Comparative Historical Context, University of London, 2016); Esteban Pichardo, *Geografía de la isla de Cuba* (Havana: Establecimiento

Tipografico de D. M. Soler, 1854), xxxii.

53. "Ingenios de fabricar azúcar, rivalidad extranjera, excelencia de nuestro fruto y otras ventajas a favor de la isla de Cuba," *Memorias de la Sociedad Economica de La Habana* 10 (1840): 37, as quoted in Monzote, "Paisajes de la nueva plantación," 91–114.

54. Monzote, "Paisajes de la nueva plantación," 91–114; José Guadeloupe Ortega, "Machines, Modernity, and Sugar: The Greater Caribbean in a Global Context, 1812–50," *JGH* 9, no. 1 (2014): 1–25; and Funes Monzote, "El azúcar, la era del vapor y los cambios ambientales en Sagua la Grande en el siglo XIX," 33–75. A few were already there earlier, unsuccessfully, in 1797. See Funes Monzote, "New Landscapes of Slavery"; and Funes Monzote, "El azúcar, la era del vapor y los cambios ambientales en Sagua la Grande en el siglo XIX," 33–75.

55. "La isla de Cuba actual, agricultura, Articulo 2 cultivo de la cana y fabricación del azúcar," MSEAP (1848): 254, quoted in Funes Monzote, "Paisajes de la nueva plantación esclavista azucarera en Cuba," 91–114. For the original quote, see Justo G. Cantero, *Los ingenios: Colección de vistas de los principales ingenios de azúcar de la isla de Cuba* (Havana: Imp. Litográfica Luis Marquier, 1857), quoted in Cantero, *Los ingenios,* 213.

56. Tomich, "Commodity Frontiers, Spatial Economy, and Technological," 212; and Monzote, "Paisajes de la nueva plantación," 91–114.

57. Cantero, *Los ingenios,* 147.

58. Cantero, *Los ingenios,* 148.

59. Julian Zulueta al Gobernador Superior Civil, "Expediente a consecuencia de haber sido detenido varios esclavos de D. Julian Zulueta por carecer de documentación," Habana, 7 de Mayo 1866, legajo 968, no. 34242, Fondo Gobierno Superior Civil, Archivo Nacional de Cuba, La Habana, Cuba. The Alava plantation produced fourteen thousand boxes of sugar. If we assume that each box contained twenty-one arrobas and that each arroba weighed twenty-five pounds, we get this number.

60. Cantero, *Los ingenios,* 219, 281.

61. Cantero, *Los ingenios,* 219.

62. Cantero, *Los ingenios,* 213.

63. Cantero, *Los ingenios,* 244.

64. On Guyana, see the brilliant work by Walter Rodney, *A History of the Guyanese Working Class, 1881–1905* (Johns Hopkins UP, 1981). See also Tomich, "Commodity Frontiers,

Spatial Economy, and Technological," 199, 201, 203.

65. On sugar production, see Ulbe Bosma, *The World of Sugar: How the Sweet Stuff Transformed Our Politics, Health, and Environment over 2,000 Years* (HUP, 2023), 29. On trade, see Paul Bairoch and Bouda Etemad, *Structure par produits des exportations du Tiers Monde, 1830–1937* (Librarie Droz, 1985), 100.

66. Ulbe Bosma, "The Global Detour of Cane Sugar: From Plantation Land to Sugarlandia," in *Colonialism, Institutional Change, and Shifts in Global Labour Relations,* ed. Karin Hofmeester and Pim de Zwart (Amsterdam UP, 2018), 118; and Andrew Ratledge, "From Promise to Stagnation: East India Sugar 1792–1865" (PhD diss., Adelaide University, 2004), 107, 344.

67. Jan Luiten van Zanden and Arthur van Riel, *Nederland, 1780–1914: Staat, instituties en economische ontwikkeling* (Uitgeverij Balans, 2000), 122–29; and Ulbe Bosma, *The Sugar Plantation in India and Indonesia Industrial Production, 1770–2010* (CUP, 2013), 94.

68. Bosma, *Sugar Plantation in India and Indonesia,* 91–92.

69. D. C. Steijn Parvé, *Het koloniaal monopoliestelsel getoetst aan geschiedenis en staatshuishoudkunde* (Zaltbommel, Netherlands: Joh. Noman en Zoon, 1851), 274–93.

70. Parvé, *Het koloniaal monopoliestelsel,* 312.

71. Parvé, *Het koloniaal monopoliestelsel,* 316.

72. For Van den Bosch's system, see Ulbe Bosma, "The Cultivation System (1830–1870) and Its Private Entrepreneurs on Colonial Java," *Journal of Southeast Asian Studies* 38, no. 2 (2007): 275–91; and Van Zanden and Van Riel, *Nederland, 1780–1914,* 139.

73. Bosma, *Sugar Plantation in India and Indonesia,* 102; M. R. Fernando, "Coffee Cultivation in Java, 1830–1917," in *The Global Coffee Economy in Africa, Asia, and Latin America, 1500–1989,* eds. William Gervase Clarence-Smith and Steven Topik (CUP, 2003), 160; Bosma, *Sugar Plantation in India and Indonesia,* 29, 90–91; R. E. Elson, *Village Java Under the Cultivation System, 1830–1870* (Asian Studies Association of Australia in Association with Allen and Unwin, 1994), 304; and Elson, *Village Java Under the Cultivation System,* 129.

74. Bosma, *Sugar Plantation in India and Indonesia,* 29, 90–91; R. E. Elson, *Village Java Under the Cultivation System, 1830–1870* (Asian Studies Association of Australia in Association with Allen and Unwin, 1994), 304; and Elson, *Village Java Under the Cultivation System,* 129.

75. Van Zanden and Van Riel, *Nederland, 1780–1914,* 171, 172, 175–76.

76. Marquese, "Asymmetrical Dependencies," 11; and Steven Topik, "The Integration of the World Coffee Market," in Clarence-Smith and Topik, *Global Coffee Economy,* 36–38. On the coffee commodity chain, see also Dorothee Wierling, "German History as Global History: The Case of Coffee," *Bulletin of the German Historical Institute* 59 (Fall 2016): 9–26. For import numbers, see Mario Samper and Radin Fernando, "Appendix: Historical Statistics of Coffee Production and Trade from 1700 to 1960," in Clarence-Smith and Topik, *Global Coffee Economy,* 442; V. L. Baril, *L'empire du Brésil* (Paris: Ferdinand Sartorius, 1862), 190.

77. Marquese, "Asymmetrical Dependencies," 11, 17; Topik, "Integration of the World Coffee Market," 29; Rafael Marquese, "Capitalism, Slavery, and the Brazilian Coffee Economy in the Long Nineteenth Century," paper (in author's possession) presented at the New Perspectives on the Life and Work of Eric Williams Conference, Oxford University, 2011, 7; Tamira Combrink, "Slave-Based Coffee in the Eighteenth Century and the Role of the Dutch in Global Commodity Chains," *Slavery & Abolition* 42, no. 1 (2021): 15–42, esp. 26–27; and Rafael Marquese, "A Tale of Two Coffee Colonies: Environment and Slavery in Suriname and Saint-Domingue, ca. 1750–1790," *Comparative Studies in Society and History* 64, no. 3 (2022): 722–55.

78. Res Strehle, "Fernandos Wert," *Das Magazin,* May 2018, 26–27; Burnard and Garrigus, *Plantation Machine,* 167; Marquese, "Capitalism, Slavery, and the Brazilian Coffee Economy," 297; Rafael Marquese, "The Origins of Brazil and Java: Compulsory Labor and the Reconfiguration of the Coffee World Economy in the Age of Revolutions, c. 1760–1840," unpublished paper (in author's possession), 12; and Samper and Fernando, "Historical Statistics of Coffee Production," 436–37.

79. Rafael Marquese and Ricardo Salles, "A escravidão no Brasil oitocentista: Historia e historiografia," in *Escravidão e capitalismo histórico no século XIX: Cuba, Brasil e Estados Unidos,* ed. Rafael Marquese and Ricardo Salles (Civilização Brasileira, 2016), 137; Samper and Fernando, "Historical Statistics of Coffee Production," 412, 432; Topik, "Integration of the World Coffee Market," 31; Marquese, "Origins of Brazil and Java," 6–7; and Marquese and Salles,

"Escravidão no Brasil Oitocentista," 133.

80. Marquese, "Capitalism, Slavery, and the Brazilian Coffee Economy," 6; Marquese, "Origins of Brazil and Java," 11; C. F. van Delden Laërne, *Brazil and Java: Report on Coffee-Culture in America, Asia and Africa* (London: W. H. Allen & Co., 1885), 273; Topik, "Integration of the World Coffee Market," 31–32; *The Empire of Brazil at the Paris Universal Exhibition of 1867* (Rio de Janeiro: E. H. Laemmert, 1867), 73; and Topik, "Integration of the World Coffee Market," 35.

81. Laërne, *Brazil and Java*, 265.

82. Rodrigo Marins Marretto, "O opulento capitalista: O Barão de Nova Friburgo e as estratégias de formação e manutenção do patrimônio familiar no oitocentos" (PhD diss., Universidade Federal Fluminense, 2019), 31, 43. On the concentration of enslaved workers on larger plantations, see the analysis in Marretto, "O opulento capitalista," 82.

83. Ricardo Salles, "Passive Revolution and the Politics of Second Slavery in Brazil," in *The Politics of the Second Slavery*, ed. Dale Tomich (SUNY Press, 2016), 154; Marquese, "Capitalism, Slavery, and the Brazilian Coffee Economy," 13, 18; and Marquese, "Origins of Brazil and Java," 9. See also Immanuel Wallerstein, *The Modern World-System*, vol. 3, *The Second Era of Great Expansion of the Capitalist World-Economy, 1730–1840s* (University of California Press, 1974), 348.

84. Marquese, "Capitalism, Slavery, and the Brazilian Coffee Economy," 14.

85. For a discussion of how capital owners can use "social relations strategies" to increase productivity (including coercion), see Stelzner and Cerrutti, "Workers and Technological Change in the United States," 657–75.

86. For the quote, see "House of Commons," *Economist*, February 5, 1848, 150. See also "Foreign and Colonial," *Economist*, October 23, 1847, 1225.

87. "Can the Slave Trade Be Suppressed?," *Economist*, September 2, 1848.

88. For the general point, see Barbara Solow, "Caribbean Slavery and British Growth: The Eric Williams Hypothesis," *Journal of Development Economics* 17, no. 1/2 (1985): 109–13; on Manchester, see Martin Hewitt, *The Emergence of Stability in the Industrial City: Manchester, 1832–67* (Scolar Press, 1996), 42; on the Mississippi Delta, see Cleo Hearon,

"Mississippi and the Compromise of 1850" (PhD diss., University of Chicago, 1913), 10; and *The Seventh Census of the United States* (Robert Armstrong, 1853), 448–49. For the number of wage workers see chapter 7, endnote 99. To calculate the number of enslaved workers at midcentury I drew on the following sources: According to Breno Aparecido Servidone Morero, "Desbravando os sertões da Piedade: terra e trabalho no Vale do Paraíba cafeeiro (Banal, c.1800–1880)," PhD, Universidade de São Paulo, 2022, 266, in the mid-nineteenth-century Paraíba Valley, each worker produced about 1,000 kg of coffee. Taking the five-year average of coffee exports from Brazil we can assume that about 150,000 enslaved people grew coffee in Brazil in 1850. Sugar output was more varied, but it has been estimated that each enslaved worker on a sugar plantation produced about 1,500 kg per year. See for that estimate Bert Barickman, *A Bahian Counterpoint: Sugar, Tobacco, Cassava and Slavery in the Reconcavo, 1780–1860* (Stanford UP, 1998), 143. Considering that much sugar was also produced on smaller units, we can reasonably assume that average output across Brazil was closer to 1,000 kg. Average exports were 123,800 tons for the years 1851–1855, which would mean that about 124,000 enslaved people grew sugar in Brazil in 1853, the US Treasury estimated that 30 million pounds of cotton were grown, which would require 65,000 workers producing at the same productivity per worker as the US. See "Cotton and Its Prospects," *The American Cotton Planter*, vol. 1 (Montgomery, AL: 1853), 228. In the US in 1850, there were 1.8 million cotton-growing and 150,000 sugar-growing enslaved workers, according to Robert Cook, *Civil War in America: Making a Nation, 1803–1877* (Routledge, 2003), 15. In Cuba in 1850 there were between 170,000 and 200,000 enslaved workers laboring on sugar plantations, according to the data in Ulbe Bosma and Jonathan Curry-Machado, "Two Islands, One Commodity: Cuba, Java, and the Global Sugar Trade (1790–1930)"; *New West Indian Guide* 86:3–4 (2012), 237–62; and Alex van Stipriaan, *Surinaams contrast: Roofbouw en overleven in een Caraïbische plantagekolonie 1750–1863* (KITLV, 1993), 28, 138. In Surinam in 1854, there were 17,884 slaves on sugar plantations, 4,650 on cotton, and 6,039 on coffee, according to Alex van Stipriaan, *Surinaams contrast:*

Roofbouw en overleven in een Caraïbische plantagekolonie 1750–1863 (KITLV, 1993), 438–39. In Venezuela, there were 12,000 slaves at abolition, according to Joseph L. Arbena, "Book Review: John V. Lombardi. *The Decline and Abolition of Negro Slavery in Venezuela, 1820–1854*," *AHR* 77, no. 2 (April 1972): 605. In Martinique, there were 90,000 enslaved workers at abolition, according to Van Stipriaan, *Surinaams contrast*, 28. In Guadeloupe, there were 95,000 enslaved workers at abolition, according to Van Stipriaan, *Surinaams contrast*, 28. The total number thus amounts to about 3.5 million enslaved workers in these industries, a number that is imprecise but still gives a very good sense of the scale of that industry.

89. *Neue Münchner Zeitung (Abendblatt)*, February 28, 1856, as quoted in Patrick Gaul, *Ideale und Interessen: Die Mitteleuropäische Wirtschaft im Amerikanischen Bürgerkrieg* (Franz Steiner Verlag, 2021), 48.

90. Herman Merivale, *Lectures on Colonization and Colonies: Delivered Before the University of Oxford in 1839, 1840 & 1841* (OUP, 1928), 301–2, 304.

91. Laërne, *Brazil and Java*, 215.

92. Laërne, *Brazil and Java*, 215.

93. "Our Brazilian Trade and the Anti-Slavery Party," *Economist*, September 16, 1843, 33.

94. "Our Brazilian Trade and the Anti-Slavery Party," 34.

95. "House of Commons," *Economist*, August 1, 1846, 994.

96. There has long been debate on the question of slavery and American economic development. A very good summary of this debate is Zakim, "Capitalism and Slavery in the United States," 146–68. Robin Blackburn, in similar ways, distinguished three regimes of slavery, calling the last one, during the nineteenth century, the "new American slavery." See the brilliant Robin Blackburn, *The American Crucible: Slavery, Emancipation and Human Rights* (Verso, 2011). For a careful analysis of slavery as a very specific form of labor coercion, and the diversities within it, see Marcel van der Linden, "Dissecting Coerced Labour," in *On Coerced Labor: Work and Compulsion After Chattel Slavery*, vol. 25, ed. Marcel van der Linden and Magaly Rodríguez Garcia (Brill, 2016), 291–332. See also Marquese and Salles, "A Escravidão no Brasil oitocentista," 133; and Felipe Gonzales, Guillermo Marshall, and Suresh Naidu, "Start-Up Nation? Slave Wealth and Entrepreneurship

in Civil War Maryland," *JEH* 77, no. 2 (June 2017): 401.

97. For an even earlier, eighteenth-century episode, see Mary Terrall, "African Indigo in the French Atlantic: Michel Adanson's Encounter with Senegal," *Isis* 114, no. 1 (March 2023): 2–24.

98. Mamoudou Sy, *La vallée du fleuve Sénégal dans le jeu des échelles politiques: Le Dimar aux XVIIIe et XIXe siècles* (Éditions L'Harmattan, 2018), 129–31, 133.

99. Sy, *La vallée du fleuve Sénégal*, 136–37, 137–38.

100. Rapport de Mr. Huzard fils sur la Colonie du Sénégal, 13 April 1822, in Affaires Économiques, 1782–1919, Series Q, Q 16, Mise en Valeur du Sénégal, 1822–1830, ANS.

101. "Tableau synoptique de la culture d'indigo, 1828," in Séries R, Agriculture, 1R/00026: Culture de l'Indigo, 1823–1951, ANS; "Tableau des établissements de culture, existants au Sénégal au 1er Mai 1825," in Affaires Économiques, 1782–1919, séries Q, Q 16, Mise en Valeur du Sénégal, 1822–1830, ANS; "Tableaux qui indiqueraient sommairement l'étendue des plantations formées au Sénégal en 1822," in Affaires Économiques, 1782–1919, séries Q, Q 16, Mise en Valeur du Sénégal, 1822–1830, ANS; and "Établissement de Richard-Tol," in Affaires Économiques, 1782–1919, séries Q, Q 16, Mise en Valeur du Sénégal, 1822–1830, ANS.

102. "Rapport général sur les divers essais de culture particulièrement des indigotiers . . . Février 1827," in Séries R, agriculture, 1R/00026: Culture de l'Indigo, 1823–1951, ANS; "Sénégal et dépendances, Règlement pour le service administratif des établissements de culture du gouvernement 1824; Rapports sur la culture de l'indigo et la situation des indigonaise adressés aux gouverneurs du Sénégal à Saint Louis, 1826/29," in Séries R, Agriculture, 1R/00026: Culture de l'Indigo, 1823–1951, ANS; "Notes sur la culture et la fabrication d'indigo au Bengal, 1824; Note sur l'indigo par M. Cheraux, capitaine de vaisseau, administration de Karaikal; "Mémoire sur la culture et la fabrication de l'indigo par le Capitaine Darrac, 1824," in Séries R, Agriculture, 1R/00026: Culture de l'Indigo, 1823–1951, ANS; and "Tableau Synoptique de la culture d'indigo," ANS. For reduced cotton and indigo harvests, see the various reports and compilations in Affaires Économiques, 1782–1919, Series Q,

Q 16, Mise en Valeur du Sénégal, 1822–1830, ANS.

103. See, for example, copy of letter to M. Berton, 10 Octobre 1827, copy of letter to M. Dégoutin, 22 Octobre 1827, and copy of letter to M. Brunet, Novembre 20, 1827, in Registre de Correspondance relatif aux Cultures de la Colonie, Juin 1826 à Décembre 1828, Correspondance Générale, 3B/42, ANS. See copy of letter to M. Brunet, 9 Avril 1828, in Registre de Correspondance relatif aux Cultures de la Colonie, 1828, Séries R, Agriculture, 1R/00026: Culture de l'Indigo, 1823–1951, ANS.

104. See copy of letter to M. Brunet, 9 Avril 1828, ANS.

105. For the situation in Senegal, see also Jenna Nigro, "Colonial Logics: Agricultural, Commercial & Moral Experiments in the Making of French Senegal, 1763–1870" (PhD diss., University of Illinois, 2014), 134. For wage labor rates, see notes from M. Degoutin to Givernor Jubelin, 15 Mars 1828, as quoted in Nigro, "Colonial Logics," 158.

106. Copy of letter from François Roger, 19 Mars 1820, SEN XIII 19a., ANOM.

107. See copy of letter to M. Perrottet, 5 Mai 1827, in Registre de Correspondance relatif aux Cultures de la Colonie, Juin 1826 à Décembre 1828, Correspondance Générale, 3B/42, ANS.

108. On planter complaints, see copy of letter to M. Richard, 5 Mai 1827, in Registre de Correspondance relatif aux Cultures de la Colonie, Juin 1826 à Décembre 1828, Correspondance Générale, 3B/42, ANS; copy of letter to M. Berton, 25 Avril 1828, and copy of letter to M. Berton, 30 Mai 1828, both in Registre de Correspondance relatif aux Cultures de la Colonie, Juin 1826 à Décembre 1828, Correspondance Générale, 3B/42, ANS; and "Culture du coton au Sénégal, 1900/1924," 13, in Séries R, Agriculture, 1R/00035: Culture du Coton, 1889–1943, ANS.

109. "Answers to the Questions before the Lieutenant Colonel Maxell, Lieutenant Governor of Senegal and Goree, by his Majesty's Commission to Investigate the Forts and Settlements in Africa," in States of West Coast Settlements, 92–93, item 22, Co 267/29, TNA, Kew Gardens.

110. Nigro, "Colonial Logics," 214–15, 255–57.

111. Beckert, *Empire of Cotton*, 126.

112. This paragraph draws from Beckert, *Empire of Cotton*, 126. For the relevant sources, see "Cotton

Cultivation Under the Superintendence of the American Cotton Planters in N.W. Provinces, Bombay and Madras," 17 January 1842, No. 13–17, Revenue Department, Home Department, NAI; John MacFarquhar to East India Company, New Orleans, 13 January 11842, MSS EUR C157, Oriental and India Office Collection, British Library, London, UK; two letters dated 13 January and 10 June to the Directors of the East India Company, in Oriental and India Office Collection, British Library, London, UK; and W. W. Wood to East India Company, New Orleans, 10 June 1842, MSS EUR C157, Oriental and India Office Collection, British Library, London, UK. On the plans to do so, see Home Department, Revenue Branch, August 1839, No. 1/4, Oriental and India Office Collection, British Library, London, UK, NAI. See also resolution dated 21 September 1841, by the Revenue Branch of the Government of India, Revenue Department, Revenue Branch, 21 September 1840, No. 1/3, NAI; letter by [illegible] to T. H. Maddok, Territorial Department Revenue, Bombay, 10 February 1842, in Revenue and Agriculture Department, Revenue Branch, 28 February 1842, Nos. 2–5, NAI; J. G. Medlicott, *Cotton Hand-Book for Bengal* (Calcutta: Savielle & Cranenburgh, 1862), 305; and *Asiatic Journal and Monthly Register*, n.s., 36 (September–December 1841): 343.

113. This paragraph draws from Beckert, *Empire of Cotton*, 131; Arthur W. Silver, *Manchester Man and Indian Cotton, 1847–1872* (Manchester UP, 1966), 37–39; *Asiatic Journal and Monthly Register*, n.s., 35 (May–August 1841): 502; copy of letter from C. W. Martin, Superintendent Cotton Farm in Gujerat, Broach, November 1830, to William Stubbs, Esq., Principal Collector, Surat, in Compilations Vol. 22/350, 1831, Revenue Department, MSA; Gibbs, Broach, to Thomas Williamson, Esq., Secretary of Government, 5 October 1831, in Compilation Vol. 22/350, 1831, in Revenue Department, MSA; *Asiatic Journal and Monthly Register*, n.s., 39 (1842): 106; letter by [illegible] to T. H. Maddok, Territorial Department Revenue, Bombay, 10 February 1842, in Revenue and Agriculture Department, Revenue Branch, 28 February 1842, Nos. 2–5, NAI; and *Report of the Bombay Chamber of Commerce for the Year 1846–47* (Bombay: American Mission Press, 1847), 5.

114. This paragraph is drawn from Beckert, *Empire of Cotton*, 127; Medlicott, *Cotton Hand-Book*, 320, 322, 323, 331, 340, 352, 366.

115. This paragraph is based on Beckert, *Empire of Cotton*, 131. Peely, Acting Commercial Resident, Northern Factories, to Charles Norris, Esq., Civil Secretary to Government, Bombay, 21 July 1831, Compilations Vol. 22/350, 1831, Revenue Department, MSA; Committee of Commerce and Agriculture of the Royal Asiatic Society, *On the Cultivation of Cotton in India* (Harrison, 1840), 13; letter by H. A. Harrison, 1st Assistant Collector, Ootacamund, to L. R. Reid, Esq., Secretary to Government, Bombay, 14 October 1832, in Compilations Vol. 7/412, 1832, MSA; "Cotton Farms, Proceedings Respecting the Formation of in the Vicinity of Jails," Compilation No. 118, MSA; and copy of letter of T. H. Balier (?), Collector, Dharwar, to William Chaplin, Esq., Commissioner, Poona, 19 August 1825, in Compilations Vol. 26, 1835, "Consultation Cotton Investment," in Commercial Department, MSA. Long discussions on slavery in India can be found in *Asiatic Journal and Monthly Register*, n.s., 15 (September–December 1834): 81–90. See also Factory Records, Dacca, G 15, 21 (1779), Oriental and India Office Collections, British Library, London.

116. Michael McGrath, ed., *Cinnlae Amhlaoibh Ui Shúileabháin: The Diary of Humphrey O'Sullivan II: From 1st September, 1828, to the end of December, 1830*, vol. 2 (Simpkin & Marshall, 1936), 25.

117. On violent backlash in Ireland, see, for example, Terrence M. Dunne, "Letters of Blood and Fire: Primitive Accumulation, Peasant Resistance, and the Making of Agency in Early Nineteenth-Century Ireland," *Critical Historical Studies* 5, no. 1 (Spring 2018): 45–74; Marquese, "Asymmetrical Dependencies," 33; John Tutino, *The Mexican Heartland: How Communities Shaped Capitalism, a Nation, and World History, 1500–2000* (PUP, 2017), 239.

118. For this story, see Tutino, *Mexican Heartland*, 241–42.

119. As cited in Tutino, *Mexican Heartland*, 242.

120. Jairus Banaji, "Merchant Capitalism, Peasant Households and Industrial Accumulation: Integration of a Model," *Journal of Agrarian Change* 16, no. 3 (July 2016): 412; and Henry Bernstein, "Notes on

Capital and Peasantry," *Review of African Political Economy* 4, no. 10 (1977): 68.

121. Robert Gardella, *Harvesting Mountains: Fujian and the China Tea Trade, 1757 to 1937* (University of California Press, 1997), 6, 35–36.

122. Gardella, *Harvesting Mountains*, 6–7, 34, 37, and 38; Weimin Zhong, "The Roles of Tea and Opium in Early Economic Globalization: A Perspective on China's Crisis in the 19th Century," *Frontiers of History in China* 5, no. 1 (2010): 86, 89; Andrew B. Liu, "Incense and Industry: Labour and Capital in the Tea Districts of Huizhou, China," *Past & Present* 230 (February 2016): 164; and Marc Levinson, *The Great A&P and the Struggle for Small Business in America* (Hill and Wang, 2012), 16.

123. Gardella, *Harvesting Mountains*, 33; Zhong, "Roles of Tea and Opium," 88; and Parron, "British Empire and the Suppression of the Slave Trade to Brazil," 7.

124. William Rowe, "Approaches to Modern Chinese History," in *Reliving the Past: The Worlds of Social History*, ed. Olivier Zunz (University of North Carolina Press, 1985), 274–75; and Gardella, *Harvesting Mountains*, 40, 42–44.

125. Gardella, *Harvesting Mountains*, 43, 49. For that story, see the excellent article by Liu, "Incense and Industry," 161–95, esp. 169, 178, 181, 190.

126. Members of the Tea Committee to W. H. Macnaghten, Esq., Secretary to the Government in the Revenue Department, 24 December 1834, in *The Measures Adopted for Introducing the Cultivation of the Tea Plant* (British Parliamentary Papers, 1839), 32–33.

127. Tithi Bhattacharya, "Sacred Thirst: Producing Tea, Producing People in Colonial Bengal" (unpublished paper (in author's possession), Harvard University, 2019.

128. Sugata Bose, *Peasant Labour and Colonial Capital: Rural Bengal Since 1770* (CUP, 1993), 44; Marcel van der Linden, "Globalization's Agricultural Roots: Some Final Considerations," in *Embedding Agricultural Commodities: Using Historical Evidence, 1840s to 1940s*, ed. Willem van Schendel (Routledge, 2017), 151–52.

129. Willem van Schendel, "Staying Embedded: The Rocky Existence of an Indigo Maker in Bengal," in *Van Schendel, Embedding Commodities*, 12; Pierre-Paul Darrac and Willem van Schendel, *Global*

Blue: Indigo and Espionage in Colonial Bengal (The University Press Limited, 2006), 12; Asiaticus, "The Rise and Fall of the Indigo Industry in India," *Economic Journal* 22, no. 86 (1912): 239; and Van Schendel, "Staying Embedded," 13.

130. Sukanya Banerjee, "Drama, Ecology, and the Ground of Empire: The Play of Indigo," in *Ecological Form: System and Aesthetics in the Age of Empire*, ed. Nathan Hensley and Philip Steer (Fordham UP, 2018), 25; and Blair B. King, *The Blue Mutiny: The Indigo Disturbances in Bengal, 1859–1862* (University of Pennsylvania Press, 1966), 23, 27.

131. Extract from the Proceedings of 29 November 1829, Home Department, Public Branch, Proceedings January–February 1830, 360–64, NAI; Van der Linden, "Globalization's Agricultural Roots," 153; and W. H. Elliott, Esq., Officiating Commissioner of the Burdwan Division, to the Secretary to the Government of Bengal, 22 March 1855, in James Long, *Strike, but Hear! Evidence Explanatory of the Indigo System in Lower Bengal* (Calcutta: R. C. Lepage & Co., 1861), 15.

132. Bose, *Peasant Labour and Colonial Capital*, 5. See also Indrajit Ray, *Bengal Industries and the British Industrial Revolution (1757–1857)* (Routledge, 2011), 215.

133. Bose, *Peasant Labour and Colonial Capital*, 18; Dietmar Rothermund, "Land-Revenue and Land Records in British India," in *Our Laws, Their Lands: Land Laws and Land Use in Modern Colonial Societies*, ed. James de Moor and Dietmar Rothermund (LIT Verlag, 1994), 125; and Subhash Chandra Sen, *The Landed Middle Class and Their Politics in Hooghly: A Study in Horizontal Mobilisation, 1859–1914* (Progressive Publishers, 2003), 45.

134. Sen, *Landed Middle Class*, 59; Benoy Chowdhury, *Growth of Commercial Agriculture in Bengal (1757–1900)*, vol. 1 (Indian Studies Past & Present, 1964), 82; Asiaticus, "Rise and Fall of the Indigo Industry in India," 239; Ray, *Bengal Industries*, 223, 225; Hari Ranjan Ghosal, *Economic Transition in the Bengal Presidency, 1793–1833* (Firma K. L. Mukhopadhyay, 1966), 78–79; and Banerjee, "Drama, Ecology, and the Ground of Empire," 23.

135. Ray, *Bengal Industries*, 230; William Wilson Hunter, *Statistical Account of Bengal* (London: Trübner & Co., 1875), 98–103. On falsification of diplomatic documents, see the Afghan papers, report, and peti-

tion of the Newcastle Foreign Affairs Association, Effingham Wilson, London, 1860, 6, as quoted in Ray, *Bengal Industries*, 228.

136. East India Company (1836), letter from the Court of Directors to the Governor General in Council, Bengal, dated 11 April 1785, Collection No. 2, as quoted in Ray, *Bengal Industries*, 211.

137. Willem van Schendel, "Green Plants into Blue Cakes: Working for Wages in Colonial Bengal's Indigo Industry," in *Working on Labor: Essays in Honor of Jan Lucassen*, ed. Marcel van der Linden and Leo Lucassen (Brill, 2012), 50, 70; and Bose, *Peasant Labour and Colonial Capital*, 70, 75; and Van Schendel, "Green Plants into Blue Cakes," 49.

138. Rothermund, "Land-Revenue and Land Records in British India," 125.

139. John Dickinson, *Reply to the Indigo Planters' Pamphlet, Entitled "Brahmins & Pariahs"* (London: S. King, 1861), 14, 21.

140. G. G. Morris, Special Commissioner to the Secretary of the Government of Bengal, Camp Jessore, 8 July 1861, in "Report of the Results of the Proceedings of Mess.r [missing] . . . for Making Inquiries into the Alleged [missing] in the Nuddeas and Jessore Districts Against the Payment of Rent," Home Department, Judicial Branch, Consultation A, 1862, No. 11/16, 6 January 1862, NAI.

141. King, *Blue Mutiny*, 58.

142. Letter of Arthur Howell, Office Secretary to the Government of India, to the Secretary to the Government of Bengal, Fort William, 31 December 1868, in "Difficulties in connection with the cultivation of indigo in Chumparun and Tirhoot," Home Department Public Branch, 9 January 1869, No. 108/114, NAI.

143. Andrew Sartori, *Bengal in Global Concept History: Culturalism in the Age of Capital* (University of Chicago Press, 2009), 47.

144. As cited in Van der Linden, "Globalization's Agricultural Roots," 154.

145. Van Schendel, "Staying Embedded," 16, 20.

146. Dickinson, *Reply to the Indigo Planters' Pamphlet*, 3, 6. See also Amiya Rao and B. G. Rao, *The Blue Devil: Indigo and Colonial Bengal* (OUP, 1992), 37–38; and Grote, Esq., Commissioner of the Nuddes Division, to the Secretary to the Government of Bengal, 19 August 1856, as quoted in Long, *Strike, but Hear!*, 38.

147. As cited in Van der Linden, "Globalization's Agricultural Roots," 154; and Home Department, Revenue Branch, Proceedings, 2 December 1834 to 22 April 1835, NAI. See, for example, Fort William, 23 January 1835, and Fort William, 5 March 1835, in Home Department, Revenue Branch, Proceedings, 2 December 1834 to 22 April 1835, NAI; Dispatch of the Government of India Revenue Department, No 10. of 1841, to the Honorable the Court of Directors of the East India Company, 12 April 1841, in Home Department, Revenue Branch, Letters to the Court of Directors of the East India Company, 1841–1844, NAI.

148. François Crouzet, "The Historiography of French Economic Growth in the Nineteenth Century," *EHR* 56, no. 2 (2003): 215–42; Mark Overton, *Agricultural Revolution in England: The Transformation of the Agrarian Economy, 1500–1850* (CUP, 1996), 4; and Mitchell, *European Historical Statistics*, 199–277.

149. Eric L. Jones, "The Environment and the Economy," in *The New Cambridge Modern History*, vol. 13, ed. Peter Burke (CUP, 1979), 35; Wallerstein, *Modern World-System*, 3:13–14, 73–75, 113; Overton, *Agricultural Revolution in England*, 4; C. Knick Harley, "Transportation, the World Wheat Trade, and the Kuznets Cycle, 1850–1913," *Explorations in Economic History* 17, no. 3 (1980): 218; and William H. Newell, "The Agricultural Revolution in Nineteenth-Century France," *JEH* 33, no. 4 (1973): 697–731.

150. As cited in Roger Bartlett, *Human Capital: The Settlement of Foreigners in Russia 1762–1804* (CUP, 1976), 32.

151. As cited in Bartlett, *Human Capital*, 125.

152. Artur Attman, "The Russian Market in World Trade, 1500–1860," *Scandinavian Economic History Review* 29, no. 3 (1981): 177–202, esp. 196; Bartlett, *Human Capital*, 48, 236; Leonard Friesen, *Rural Revolutions in Southern Ukraine: Peasants, Nobles, and Colonists, 1774–1905* (HUP, 2008), 28–31, 51; Orest Subtelny, *Ukraine: A History* (University of Toronto Press, 2009), 187; Peter I. Lyashchenko, *History of the National Economy of Russia* (Macmillan, 1949), 318; Scott Reynolds Nelson, *Oceans of Grain: How American Wheat Remade the World* (Basic Books, 2022), 49, 86; Aleksander Kornilov, *Modern Russian History: Being an Authoritative and Detailed History from the Age of Catherine the*

Great to the End of the Nineteenth Century (Knopf, 1948), 247; and Ioanna Pepelasis Minoglou, "The Greek Merchant House of the Russian Black Sea: A Nineteenth-Century Example of a Traders' Coalition," *International Journal of Maritime History* 10, no. 1 (1998): 80.

153. Friesen, *Rural Revolutions in Southern Ukraine*, 29, 30, 32, 33, 37; Nelson, *Oceans of Grain*, 42–43, 86; Bartlett, *Human Capital*, 126; and Lyashchenko, *History of the National Economy of Russia*, 313.

154. Jeremy Atack, Fred Bateman, and William N. Parker, "Northern Agriculture and Westward Movement," in *The Cambridge Economic History of the United States*, vol. 2, *The Long Nineteenth Century* (CUP, 2008), 292, 296.

155. Argues Emilie Connolly, "Money Trails: Indian Trust Funds and the Midwest Transportation Revolution," paper (in author's possession) presented at the Before the City / Beyond the City: Capitalism in the Countryside Conference, Harvard University, October 2017. See also Argues Emilie Connolly, "Fiduciary Colonialism: Annuities and Native Dispossession in the Early United States," *AHR* 127, no. 1 (March 2022): 227–28.

156. Atack, Bateman, and Parker, "Northern Agriculture and Westward Movement," 263, 312, 314–19.

157. Edwin Williams, *The Wheat Trade of the United States and Europe* (New York: Office of the National Magazine, 1846), 12; J. D. B. De Bow, *The Industrial Resources, Statistics, etc., of the United States*, vol. 1 (New Orleans: De Bow's Review, 1853), 388; "Tariff Bill," H.R., 27th Cong., 2nd Sess. (June 1842), appendix to *The Congressional Globe of the Second Session of the Twenty-Seventh Congress*, 1841–1842, 823; Alan L. Olmstead and Paul W. Rhode, "Wheat for Grain-Acreage, Production, and Price: 1839–1877," in *Historical Statistics of the United States, Millennial Edition Online*, ed. Susan B. Carter et al. (CUP, 2006), 4–105; Douglas A. Irwin, "Exports of Selected Commodities: 1790–1989," table Ee569–89, in Carter et al., *Historical Statistics of the United States*; Ray Douglas Hurt, *American Agriculture: A Brief History* (Purdue UP, 2002), 53; Jeremy Atack, Fred Bateman, and William N. Parker, "The Farm, the Farmer, and the Market," in *Cambridge Economic History of the United States*, 2:250; and Nelson, *Oceans of Grain*, 165.

158. Hendrik Snyders, "From Peru to Ichaboe: The Dynamics of a Shifting Guano Frontier, 1840–5," *African Historical Review* 48, no. 2 (2016): 4; John Bellamy Foster, Brett Clark, and Richard York, *The Ecological Rift: Capitalism's War on the Earth* (New York UP, 2011), 355; Edward D. Melillo, "The First Green Revolution: Debt Peonage and the Making of the Nitrogen Fertilizer Trade, 1840–1930," *AHR* 117, no. 4 (2012): 1038; and Snyders, "From Peru to Ichaboe," 5.

159. Snyders, "From Peru to Ichaboe," 7; W. W. Matthew, *The House of Gibbs and the Peruvian Guano Monopoly* (Royal Historical Society, 1981), 226; and Melillo, "First Green Revolution," 1042.

160. On Peruvian revenues, see John Bellamy Foster and Brett Clark, "The Expropriation of Nature," *Monthly Review* 69, no. 10 (1949): 19; Foster, Clark, and York, *Ecological Rift*, 357; Freeman Hunt, *Hunt's Merchants' Magazine and Commercial Review*, vol. 35 (New York: 142 Fulton-Street, 1856), 450; Cecilia G. Méndez, *Los trabajadores guaneros del Peru, 1840–1879* (Universidad Nacional Mayor de San Marcos, 1987), 50.

161. Christina Duffy Barnett, "The Edges of Empire and the Limits of Sovereignty: American Guano Islands," *American Quarterly* 57, no. 3 (2005): 788.

162. Snyders, "From Peru to Ichaboe," 8, 11; Barnett, "Edges of Empire and the Limits of Sovereignty," 783, 787; Melillo, "First Green Revolution," 1045; Jimmy M. Skaggs, *The Great Guano Rush: Entrepreneurs and American Overseas Expansion* (St. Martin's Press, 1994).

163. Méndez, *Los trabajadores guaneros del Peru*, 43, 53.

164. As cited in Méndez, *Los trabajadores guaneros del Peru*, 53.

165. Méndez, *Los trabajadores guaneros del Peru*, 52, 55; Evelyn Hu-DeHart, "Opium and Social Control: Coolies on the Plantations of Peru and Cuba," *Journal of Chinese Overseas* 1, no. 2 (2005): 171; and Melillo, "First Green Revolution," 1039.

166. As cited in Hu-DeHart, "Opium and Social Control," 173.

167. Melillo, "First Green Revolution," 1040.

168. Méndez, *Los trabajadores guaneros del Peru*, 56–57, 62–63, 65; Hu-DeHart, "Opium and Social Control," 177; and Foster, Clark, and York, *Ecological Rift*, 355.

169. Fahad Ahmad Bishara, *A Sea of Debt: Law and Economic Life in the Western Indian Ocean, 1780–1950* (CUP, 2017), 34–35, 46, 49; Jack A. Goldstone, *Why Europe? The Rise of the West in World History, 1500–1850* (McGraw Hill, 2009), 31. On rice production in China, see Stephen Broadberry, Hanhui Guan, and David Daokui Li, "China, Europe, and the Great Divergence: A Study in Historical National Accounting, 980–1850," *JEH* 78, no. 4 (December 2018): 955–1000. On Japan, see Jean-Pascal Bassino et al., "Japan and the Great Divergence 730–1874," CEI Working Paper Series 2018-13 (Center for Economic Institutions, Institute of Economic Research, Hitotsubashi University, 2018), https://ideas.repec.org/p/hit/hitcei/2018-13.html; Christopher Mills Isset, *State, Peasant, and Merchant in Qing Manchuria, 1644–1862* (Stanford UP, 2007), 231, 234; Catherine Coquery-Vidrovitch, "African Slavery in the Nineteenth Century: Inseparable Partner of the Atlantic Slave Trade," in *The Atlantic and Africa: The Second Slavery and Beyond*, ed. Dale W. Tomich and Paul E. Lovejoy, trans. Dale W. Tomich (State University of New York Press, 2021), 7–18, esp. 13; Catherine Coquery-Vidrovitch, "L'esclavage africain au XIXe siècle, partenaire indissociable de la traite atlantique," paper (in author's possession) presented at the Fernand Braudel Center, Binghamton University, March 2018, 1, 5; and Paul Lovejoy, *Transformations of Slavery: A History of Slavery in Africa* (CUP, 1983), 179.

170. See Karl Polanyi, *The Great Transformation: The Political and Economic Origins of Our Time* (Beacon Press, 2001), 75. See also Ernst Langenthaler and Elke Schüßler, "Commodity Studies with Polanyi: Disembedding and Re-Embedding Labour and Land in Contemporary Capitalism," in *Österreichische Zeitschrift für Sozialgeschichte* 44, no. 2 (2019): 212.

171. Kevin Kenny, *The American Irish: A History* (Pearson Education, 2000), 45, 90. The excess mortality refers to the years between 1845 and 1851. See Mervyn Busteed, *The Irish in Manchester, c. 1750–1921: Resistance, Adaptation and Identity* (Manchester UP, 2016), 42.

172. John Belchem, *Irish, Catholic, and Scouse: The History of the Liverpool Irish, 1800–1940* (Liverpool UP, 2007), 1.

173. Kenny, *American Irish*, 105–6.

174. Cormac Ó Gráda, *Ireland: A New Economic History, 1780–1939* (Clarendon Press, 1993), 75; Belchem, *Irish, Catholic, and Scouse*, 27; and E. P. Thompson, *The Making of the English Working Class* (Vintage Books, 1966), 431.

175. Belchem, *Irish, Catholic, and Scouse*, 8, 29, 38; Kenny, *American Irish*, 62, 110; and Thomas Dublin, *Women at Work: The Transformation of Work and Community in Lowell, Massachusetts, 1826–1860* (Columbia UP, 1993), 140, 203–4.

176. Kenny, *American Irish*, 63.

177. Peter Way, *Common Labour: Workers and the Digging of North American Canals, 1780–1860* (CUP, 1993), 100; Kenny, *American Irish*, 63–64; Matthew E. Mason, "'The Hands Here Are Disposed to Be Turbulent': Unrest Among the Irish Trackmen of the Baltimore and Ohio Railroad, 1829–1851," *Labor History* 39, no. 3 (1998): 254; Kenny, *American Irish*, 107.

178. As cited in George Cornewall Lewis, *On Local Disturbances in Ireland; and on the Irish Church Question* (B. Fellowes, 1836), 319.

179. Gráda, *Ireland*, 28; Tom Yager, "Mass Eviction in the Mullet Peninsula During and After the Great Famine," *Irish Economic and Social History* (1996): 27; Belchem, *Irish, Catholic, and Scouse*, 12; and Gráda, *Ireland*, 67.

180. Cormac Ó Gráda, *The Great Irish Famine* (CUP, 2000), 26; Gráda, *Ireland*, 85, 128–30.

181. Gráda, *Great Irish Famine*, 30; Gráda, *Ireland*, 122; Yager, "Mass Eviction in the Mullet Peninsula," 24, 26–27, 37.

182. McGrath, *Cinnlae Amhlaoibh Ui Shúileabháin*, 22–26.

183. For this discussion on the racialization of the Irish, see Kavita Philip, "Race, Class and the Imperial Politics of Ethnography in India, Ireland and London, 1850–1910," *Irish Studies Review* 10, no. 3 (2002): 295.

184. Philip, "Race, Class and the Imperial Politics of Ethnography," 295.

185. As cited in Philip, "Race, Class and the Imperial Politics of Ethnography," 290.

186. Marx to Pavel Vasilyevich Annekov, Brussels, 28 December 1846, as reprinted in Karl Marx and Frederick Engels, *Marx & Engels Collected Works*, vol. 38, *Letters 1844–51* (Lawrence & Wishart, 2010), 101.

187. Coquery-Vidrovitch, "L'esclavage africain au XIXe siècle," 3. All the numbers on slave trade can be found in "Trans-Atlantic Slave Trade—Estimates," Slave Voyages, accessed March 11, 2019, https://

www.slavevoyages.org/assessment /estimates.
188. On the Arab trade, see Pedro Machado, *Ocean of Trade: South Asian Merchants, Africa and the Indian Ocean, c. 1750–1850* (CUP, 2014), 213; "Trans-Atlantic Slave Trade—Estimates"; Éric Saugera, *Bordeaux port négrier: Chronologie, économie, idéologie, XVIIe-XIXe siècles* (Karthala, 1995), 361; José Capela, "Slave Trade Networks in Eighteenth-Century Mozambique," in *Networks and Trans-Cultural Exchange: Slave Trading in the South Atlantic, 1590–1867*, ed. Filipa Ribeiro da Silva and David Richardson (Brill, 2015), 184; Machado, *Ocean of Trade*, 217–18; and Allen, *European Slave Trading in the Indian Ocean*, 147.
189. Machado, *Ocean of Trade*, 209, 212.
190. Coquery-Vidrovitch, "L'esclavage africain au XIXe siècle," 1.
191. Coquery-Vidrovitch, "L'esclavage africain au XIXe siècle," 1.
192. Machado, *Ocean of Trade*, 209–10, 228, 245; M. D. D. Newitt, *A History of Mozambique* (University of Indiana Press, 1995), 237; Capela, "Slave Trade Networks in Eighteenth-Century Mozambique," 193; Bishara, *Sea of Debt*, 37; and Newitt, *History of Mozambique*, 252.
193. Capela, "Slave Trade Networks in Eighteenth-Century Mozambique," 193.
194. Machado, *Ocean of Trade*, 233–34, 237; and Allen, *European Slave Trading in the Indian Ocean*, 153.
195. For an excellent survey of their role in the functioning of their enterprises, see Marina Christina Chatziioannou, *On Merchants' Agency and Capitalism in the Eastern Mediterranean, 1774–1914* (Isis Press, 2017); Alff, "Landed Property, Capital Accumulation, and Polymorphous Capitalism," 35; Bruno Carvalho, *Porous City: A Cultural History of Rio de Janeiro* (Liverpool UP, 2012), 19; Joseph E. Sweigart, *Coffee Factorage and the Emergence of a Brazilian Capital Market, 1850–1888* (Garland Publishing, 1987), 21, 24–30, 48; Beckert, *Empire of Cotton*, 199–241; and Topik, "Integration of the World Coffee Market," 34.
196. Sweigart, *Coffee Factorage*, 73; Eugene Ridings, *Business Interest Groups in Nineteenth-Century Brazil* (CUP, 1994), 41; Thomas Jefferson, "Statement on Accounts as Minister Plenipotentiary in France, 8 March," in *The Papers of Thomas Jefferson*, vol. 29, *1 March 1796 to 31 December 1797*, ed. Barbara B. Oberg (PUP, 2002), 22; Pepijn Brandon, "Dutch Capitalism and Slavery in the Lon-

ger Run: A Reorientation," in *The Atlantic and Africa: The Second Slavery and Beyond*, ed. Dale W. Tomich and Paul E. Lovejoy (State University of New York Press, 2021), 265; and Webster, *Richest East India Merchant*, 10, 11, 14, 29, 31.
197. Webster, *Richest East India Merchant*, 83.
198. Prasannan Parthasarathi, *Why Europe Grew Rich and Asia Did Not: Global Economic Divergence, 1600–1850* (CUP, 2011), 262.
199. Daron Acemoglu and James A. Robinson, *Why Nations Fail: The Origins of Power, Prosperity, and Poverty* (Crown, 2012). As they have correctly observed, a diversity of institutions characterized the global economic landscape. And they also correctly observed that this institutional setup would have very significant long-term historical consequences. The problem is that their argument takes national units as the containers for their analysis; but we are dealing here with a world economy—a world economy that often contained very different sets of institutions within the same empire.

Chapter 9: A Capitalist Civilization, 1830–1880

1. "The New Museum Opened," *NYT*, March 31, 1880, 8. Elsewhere it was reported that thirty-five hundred invitations had been sent. See "Metropolitan Museum, the Opening of the Institution to Take Place To-Day," *NYT*, March 30, 1880, 10.
2. *NYT*, September 29, 1873, 8; "Art Museum to Open," *NYT*, March 18, 1880, 5; and "New Museum Opened," 8.
3. Circular, Trustees of the Metropolitan Museum of Art, New York, April 14, 1879, as reprinted in *NYT*, April 16, 1879, 5. See also *NYT*, December 7, 1871, 6.
4. Howard Hibbard, *The Metropolitan Museum of Art* (Harrison House, 1986), 7, 8; and *NYT*, January 19, 1870, 2.
5. James Jackson Jarves, *The Art-Idea: Sculpture, Painting, and Architecture in America* (Boston: Hurd and Houghton, 1865), 174.
6. *NYT*, March 17, 1880, 5; Roy Rosenzweig and Elizabeth Blackmar, *The Park and the People: A History of Central Park* (Cornell UP, 1992), 357; *NYT*, May 6, 1873, 4; Hibbard, *Metropolitan Museum of Art*, 8; and *NYT*, August 18, 1874, 8. On the early history of the museum, see also "The Fine Art Museum," *NYT*, April 30, 1880, 2; and "Metropolitan Museum of Art," *NYT*, April 16, 1879, 5.

7. *NYT*, March 17, 1880, 5; and *NYT*, March 18, 1880, 5.
8. *NYT*, March 30, 1880, 10.
9. Joseph H. Choate, "Metropolitan Museum of Art: Address Delivered at the Opening of the Metropolitan Museum Building, New York City, March 30, 1880," in *Arguments and Addresses of Joseph Hodges Choate*, ed. Frederick C. Hicks (West Publishing Company, 1926), 761–68.
10. As cited in Rosenzweig and Blackmar, *Park and the People*, 341, 358, 359–60.
11. Jacob Riis, *How the Other Half Lives: Studies Among the Tenements of New York* (New York: C. Scribner's Sons, 1890).
12. Sven Beckert, *The Monied Metropolis: New York City and the Consolidation of the American Bourgeoisie, 1850–1896* (CUP, 2001), 261–62; Paul DiMaggio, "Cultural Entrepreneurship in Nineteenth-Century Boston: The Creation of an Organizational Base for High Culture in America," *Media, Culture and Society* 4, no. 1 (1982): 35–50.
13. "Metropolitan Museum of Art," *New York Herald*, March 30, 1880; and Michael Zakim, *Ready-Made Democracy: A History of Men's Dress in the American Republic, 1760–1860* (University of Chicago Press, 2003).
14. Walt W. Rostow, *The World Economy: History and Prospect* (University of Texas Press, 1978), 70. The calculation is based on numbers for 1800 and 1901–5.
15. A search for "natural law(s)" yields 298 entries for *The Economist* from 1843 to 1900. See, for example, "Follow Our Principles," *Economist*, December 20, 1845, 1267; "The Last Debate on the Navigation Law," *Economist*, May 26, 1849, 572; and "The Building Strike," *Economist*, April 6, 1861, 689. Martin Hewitt, *The Emergence of Stability in the Industrial City: Manchester, 1832–67* (Scolar Press, 1996), 80, 85.
16. Karl Marx and Friedrich Engels, *The Communist Manifesto* (Monthly Review Press, 1968), 7.
17. Karl Marx, "The Future Results of British Rule in India," in *Dispatches for the New York Tribune: Selected Journalism of Karl Marx*, ed. James Ledbetter (Penguin, 2007), 225.
18. Wilhelm Emmanuel Freiherr von Ketteler, *Die Arbeiterfrage und das Christenthum* (Mainz: Verlag Franz von Kirchheim, 1864), 186, 194. On clothing, see Lothar Schneider, *Der Arbeiterhaushalt im 18. und 19. Jahrhundert: Dargestellt am Beispiel des Heim- und Fabrikarbeiters* (Duncker & Humblot, 1967), 136. On wageworkers, see

Henriette Davidis, *Die Hausfrau: Praktische Anleitung zur Selbstständigen und Sparsamen Führung des Haushaltes* (E. A. Seemann, 1865), 283–92.

19. In the United States, 25 percent lived in cities; in France, 28 percent. See Paul Bairoch and Gary Goertz, "Factors of Urbanisation in the Nineteenth Century Developed Countries: A Descriptive and Econometric Analysis," *Urban Studies* 23, (1986): 286, 288. Bairoch and Goertz includes in that number almost all countries in northern, central, and western Europe but also Russia, Bulgaria, Greece, and Spain. Twenty-four percent of Europeans lived in cities in 1880, compared with just 11 percent in 1800. See B. R. Mitchell, *International Historical Statistics: Europe 1750–2005* (Palgrave Macmillan, 2007), 76f; B. R. Mitchell, *International Historical Statistics: The Americas 1750–2005* (Palgrave Macmillan, 2007), 46–48; and Charles Tilly, "Did the Cake of Custom Break?," in *Consciousness and Class Experience in Nineteenth Century Europe*, ed. John M. Merriman (Holmes & Meier, 1979), 26.

20. Eugene Ridings, *Business Interest Groups in Nineteenth-Century Brazil* (CUP, 1994), 36, 161; Eugene Ridings, "Business Associationalism, the Legitimation of Enterprise, and the Emergence of a Business Elite in Nineteenth-Century Brazil," *Business History Review* 63, no 4. (1989): 778.

21. Rodrigo Marins Marretto, "O opulento capitalista: O Barão de Nova Friburgo e as estratégias de formação e manutenção do patrimônio familiar no oitocentos" (PhD diss., Universidade Federal Fluminense, 2019), 229; and Chitra Joshi, "Time, Work, and Wages: Regulating Labour on the Road," unpublished paper presented at Re:Work Berlin, March 2017, 10.

22. Peter Scholliers, "Grown-Ups, Boys and Girls in the Ghent Cotton Industry: The Voortman Mills, 1835–1914," *Social History* 20, no. 2 (May 1995): 201.

23. Act to Make Further Provisions for the Regulation of Cotton Mills and Factories and for the Better Preservation of the Health of Young Persons Employed Therein, 1825, 6 Geo. 4, c. 63; E. P. Thompson, *The Making of the English Working Class* (Vintage Books, 1966), 267, 291–306; and Gregory Clark, "Factory Discipline" *JEH* 54, no. 1 (1994): 128–63.

24. "Your Uncle Sam," N. W. Ayer Advertising Agency Records, box 28, folder 2, Archives Center, Smithsonian National Museum of American History, Washington, DC, as quoted in Augustine Sedgewick, *Coffeeland: One Man's Dark Empire and the Making of Our Favorite Drink* (Penguin Press, 2020), 189, 195.

25. E. P. Thompson, "Time, Work-Discipline and Industrial Capitalism," *Past & Present* 38 (December 1967): 90. On new understandings of time, see Vanessa Ogle, *The Global Transformation of Time, 1870–1950* (PUP, 2015).

26. T. S. Arthur put it in his *Advice to Young Men* (Philadelphia: G. G. Evans, 1860), 69, as cited in Michael Zakim, *Accounting for Capitalism: The World the Clerk Made* (Chicago UP, 2018), 47.

27. William Hazlitt, "On the Look of a Gentleman," Table-Talk, *London Magazine*, January–June 1821, 39.

28. David Blackbourn and Geoffrey Eley, *The Peculiarities of German History, Bourgeois Society, and Politics in Nineteenth-Century Germany* (OUP, 1984), 202–4; Zakim, *Accounting for Capitalism*, 50, 86.

29. Thomas Piketty, *Capital and Ideology* (HUP, 2020), 61.

30. See also Raymond Williams, *Keywords: A Vocabulary of Culture and Society* (Croom Helm, 1976), 61–62.

31. "Middle-Class Education," *Economist*, June 13, 1857, 641–42.

32. Leila Vilela Alegrio, *Os Clemente Pinto: Importantes cafeicultores do sertão do leste fluminense* (Letra Capital, 2015), 2, 38, 65, 71, 144, 153. On his role as a slave trader, see also Marretto, "O opulento capitalista," 14, 147, 162, 181, 186–89.

33. Jeffrey D. Needell, *A Tropical Belle Époque: Elite Culture and Society in Turn-of-the-Century Rio de Janeiro* (CUP, 1987), 238–39.

34. Needell, *Tropical Belle Époque*, 22, 117.

35. Ida Pfeiffer, *Eine Frauenfahrt um die Welt* (Vienna: Carl Gerold, 1850), 53."

36. Christa Wetzel, "A Short Biography of Heinrich Witt," in *The Diary of Heinrich Witt*, ed. Ulrich Mücke, vol. 1 (Brill, 2016), xv, xxi, xxxiv; entry of August 5, 1862, as quoted in Mücke, *Diary of Heinrich Witt*, 6:284; entry of April 13, 1864, as quoted in Mücke, *Diary of Heinrich Witt*, 6:489; entry of April 19, 1864, as quoted in Mücke, *Diary of Heinrich Witt*, 6:490; entry of October 24, 1847, as quoted in Mücke, *Diary of Heinrich Witt*, 6:128–29; and entry of September 4, 1864, as quoted in Mücke, *Diary of Heinrich Witt*, 6:513.

37. Entry of April 6, 1848, as quoted in Mücke, *Diary of Heinrich Witt*, 4:163.

38. Sabine Dabringhaus and Jürgen Osterhammel, "Chinese Middle Classes Between Empire and Revolution," in *The Global Bourgeoisie: The Rise of the Middle Classes in the Age of Empire*, ed. Christof Dejung, David Motadel, and Jürgen Osterhammel (PUP, 2019), 323; Christof Dejung, "Auf dem Weg zu Einer Globalen Sozialgeschichte? Neuere Studien zur Globalgeschichte des Bürgertums," *Neue Politische Literatur* 59, no. 2 (2014): 239; Janet Hunter, "Modern Business and the Rise of the Japanese Middle Classes," in Dejung et al., *Global Bourgeoisie*, 168–69; Simon Partner, *The Merchant's Tale: Yokohama and the Transformation of Japan* (Columbia UP, 2018); Kenneth Pomeranz and Steven Topik, *The World That Trade Created: Society, Culture and the World Economy, 1400 to the Present* (M. E. Sharpe, 2006), 38; Prashant Kidamdi, "Colonial Bombay, 1890–1940," in *The Making of the Middle Class: Toward a Transnational History*, ed. A. Ricardo López and Barbara Weinstein (Duke UP, 2012), 141–60; Sanjay Joshi, *The Middle Class in Colonial India* (OUP, 2010), xv–lvi; Claude Markovits, "What About the Merchants? A Mercantile Perspective on the Middle Class of Colonial India," in Joshi, *Middle Class in Colonial India*, 122–23; Sven Beckert, *Empire of Cotton: A Global History* (Knopf, 2014), 172.

39. Dejung et al., *Global Bourgeoisie*.

40. A. Ricardo López and Barbara Weinstein, "We Shall Be All: Toward a Transnational History of the Middle Class," in López and Weinstein, *Making of the Middle Class*, 5; and Christof Dejung, David Motadel, and Jürgen Osterhammel, "Worlds of the Bourgeoisie," in Dejung, Motadel, and Osterhammel, *Global Bourgeoisie*, 3–4.

41. Needell, *Tropical Belle Époque*, 116, 120, 131; Beckert, *Monied Metropolis*, 34, 39; Fernand Braudel, *Afterthoughts on Material Civilization and Capitalism* (Johns Hopkins UP, 1977), 70; Nancy F. Cott, *The Bonds of Womanhood: "Woman's Sphere" in New England, 1780–1835* (Yale UP, 1977); Maria Mies, *Patriarchy and Accumulation on a World Stage: Women in the International Division of Labour* (Zed Books, 1985), 104.

42. Needell, *Tropical Belle Époque*, 123.

43. Needell, *Tropical Belle Époque*, 120–21.

44. Needell, *Tropical Belle Époque*, 93; Sudipto Basu, "Spatial Imagination and Development in Colonial Calcutta, c. 1850–1900," *History and Sociology of South Asia* 10, no. 1, (2016): 48f; Luiz Felipe de Alencastro, "Vida privada e ordem privada no império," in Luiz Felipe de Alencastro, ed., *História da vida privada no Brasil*, vol. 2, *Império: A Corte e a modernidade nacional* (Companhia das Letras, 1997), 45; Jeffrey Needell, *the Party of Order: The Conservatives, the State, and Slavery in the Brazilian Monarchy, 1831–1871* (Stanford UP, 2006), 24; marriage trust of Thomas Mitchell, cotton spinner in Glasgow, and Ellen Maria Poyser, daughter of Samuel Poyser, The Elms, Derbyshire, 1853–1856, T-MJ/180, GCA; Hartmut Roehr, "Die [sic] Archiv der Firma J. A. Schmidt & Soehne, Solingen," in Ralf Rogge and Horst Sassin, *Die Heimat: Beiträge zur Geschichte Solingens und des bergischen Landes* (Bergischer Geschichtsverein, 2008), 45–52.

45. Needell, *Tropical Belle Époque*, 103, 152–53; Beckert, *Monied Metropolis*, 56–57; and lists of summer residents of Newport, RI, 1895, box 5849, Newport Historical Society, Newport, Rhode Island.

46. Needell, *Tropical Belle Époque*, 53–54; and Ronald Story, *The Forging of an Aristocracy: Harvard and the Boston Upper Class, 1800–1870* (Wesleyan UP, 1980), 30–32.

47. Beckert, *Monied Metropolis*, 58; Jean Merley, "Naissance et développement d'une métropole industrielle (1815–vers 1900): La vie politique et culturelle," in *Histoire de Saint-Étienne*, ed. John Merley (Éditions Privat, 1990), 202f; Jürgen Osterhammel, *Die Verwandlung der Welt: Eine Geschichte des 19. Jahrhunderts* (C. H. Beck, 2016), 431; Dabringhaus and Osterhammel, "Chinese Middle Classes Between Empire and Revolution," 326; Comitê de Figure de [illegible] para um concerto no casino fluminense, 109/1874, Manuscritos, BNRio; handwritten report, Rio, 24 May 1877, Banquete no General Osário, Casino Fluminense, in Coleção Gen. Osário, 243.22, Instituto Historio e Geográfica Brasileira, Rio de Janeiro, Brazil; Decretos do Executivo—Período, Decreto No. 5615, Aprova os estatutos da Sociedade Anomia Jockey Clube, 25 April 1874, BR Janeiro 22.0.0.3365, NAB. For other such clubs, see, for example, Decretos do Executivo, Período, Fundo 22/Codes/DEL, BR Janeiro 22.0.0.3394, Decreto Número 7122,

Aprova os estatutos do Club de Regatas Guarabirense, NAB; various documents, W1-9, III, No. 31–41, Bethmann-Archiv, Stadtarchiv Frankfurt, Germany; Ulrich Luckhardt, "Die Anfänge der Hamburgischen Kunstsammlungen und die Erste Kunsthalle," in Uwe M. Schneede und Helmut R. Leppien, *Die Hamburger Kunsthalle: Bauten und Bilder* (Seemann, 1997), 20–21; "Städtische Gemäldegalerie," January 1859, Verwaltung der Kunsthalle, 364–2/1 III 20, Staatsarchiv Hamburg; Birgit-Katharine Seemann, *Stadt, Bürgertum und Kultur: Kulturelle Entwicklung und Kulturpolitik in Hamburg von 1839 bis 1933 am Beispiel des Museumswesens* (Matthiesen Verlag, 1998); Sven Beckert, "Die Kultur des Kapitals: Bürgerliche Kultur in New York und Hamburg im Neunzehnten Jahrhundert," in *Mitteilungen aus dem Warburg Institut* 4 (2000), 139–73; Hewitt, *Emergence of Stability in the Industrial City*, 86; Blackbourn and Eley, *Peculiarities of German History*, 195; Rudi Batzell, "Reconstructing Global Capitalism: Class, Corporations, and the Rise of Welfare States, 1870–1930" (PhD diss., Harvard University, 2017), 219; Arno Mayer, *The Persistence of the Old Regime: Europe to the Great War* (Pantheon, 1981), 20; diaries of André Pinto Rebouças, June 13, 1886, June 15, 1886 June 16, 1886, June 17, 1886, June 18, 1886, and June 20, 1886, in DL 464.3, LATA 464, Manuscript 3, Instituto Historio e Geográfica Brasileira, Rio de Janeiro, Brazil.

48. Joaquim Maria Machado de Assis, *The Posthumous Memoirs of Brás Cubas* (OUP, 1997).

49. Machado de Assis, *Posthumous Memoirs of Brás Cubas*, 25, 28, 81, 105, 106, 137, 157, 160, 169, 201.

50. Maria Alice Resende de Carvalho, "Rio de Janeiro Crepúsculo de Ouvidor," in *Ciudades Sudamericanas como Arenas Culturales: Artes y Medios, Barrios de Élite y Villas Miseria, Intelectuales y Urbanistas: Cómo Cuidad y Cultura se Activan Mutuamente*, ed. Adrián Gorelik and Fernanda Áreas Peixoto (Siglo Veintiuno Argentina, 2016), 23, 31.

51. Needell, *Tropical Belle Époque*, 102.

52. E. de Carvalho, *Esplendor e decadência da sociedade brasileira* (Garnier Irmaos, 1911), 238–40, as cited in Needell, *Tropical Belle Époque*, 104.

53. Needell, *Tropical Belle Époque*, 28; and Alencastro, "Vida privada e ordem privada no império," 43.

54. Needell, *Tropical Belle Époque*, 33, 139, 144.

55. Needell, *Tropical Belle Époque*, 147.

56. *The Empire of Brazil at the Paris Universal Exhibition of 1867* (Rio de Janeiro: E. H. Laemmert, 1867), 72; *The Empire of Brazil at the Vienna Universal Exhibition of 1873* (Rio de Janeiro: E. & H. Laemmert, 1873), 42–57, 153–60; *The Empire of Brazil at the Universal Exhibition of 1876 in Philadelphia* (Rio de Janeiro: Imperial Instituto Artistico, 1876), v–vi. See also, and very similar, *Das Kaiserthum Brasilien im Jahre 1873* (Rio de Janeiro: Paul Hildebrandt, 1874).

57. *Journal das Senhoras*, January 11, 1854. See also Needell, *Tropical Belle Époque*, 124–25, 129. On bourgeois dress codes in nineteenth-century Brazil, see also Maria do Carmo Teixeira Rainho, *A cidade e a moda* (Editora Universidade de Brasilia, 2002).

58. See Francisco Lellis e André Boccato, *Os banquetes do imperador* (Senac, 2013); "Aprontos Genealógica sobre a família Warneck," BRJaneiro PYO.TXT.7, NAB. See also BRJaneiro, PY.O.TMT.TXT.15, NAB.

59. For "civilidade," see *Elementos de Civilidade* (n.p, n.d.), 7, 9, 23, 25, consulted in BNRio. For a very similar set of rules, see Guilhermina dê Neves, *Azambuja: Entretenimentos sobre os deveres de civilidade colecionadas para uso da puerícia brasileira de ambos os sexos* (Rio de Janeiro: Tipografia Cinode Marca, 1875), 98, 103, 114.

60. Beckert, *Monied Metropolis*, 39; "Inventory January 10, 1850, Furniture at House St. Vincent Street," GB 248 UGD 091/1/10/1/1/1; bundle of legal documents, 1835–1865, item no. 20, Finlay Papers, UGA.

61. Anthony Webster, *The Richest East India Merchant: The Life and Business of John Palmer of Calcutta, 1767–1836* (Boydell Press, 2007), 65.

62. Webster, *Richest East India Merchant*, 20–21, 66–67, 71, 78, 80; Anthony Webster, "An Early Global Business in a Colonial Context: The Strategies, Management, and Failure of John Palmer and Company of Calcutta, 1780–1830," *Enterprise and Society* 6, no. 1 (2005): 98–103; Utsa Ray, "Cosmopolitan Consumption: Domesticity, Cooking, and the Middle Class in Colonial India," in Dejung, Motadel, and Osterhammel, *Global Bourgeoisie*, 133; Tithi Bhattacharya, *The Sentinels of Culture: Class, Education, and the Colonial Intellectual in Bengal (1848–85)* (OUP, 2005); Brian A. Hatcher, "Indigent Brahmans, Industrious Pandits: Bourgeois Ideology and Sanskrit

Pandits in Colonial Calcutta," *Comparative Studies of South Asia, Africa and the Middle East* 16, no. 1 (1996): 17; and Ray, "Cosmopolitan Consumption," 138–40.

63. Dejung, "Auf dem Weg zu einer Globalen Sozialgeschichte?," 234; Bruce Masters, *The Arabs of the Ottoman Empire, 1516–1918: A Social and Cultural History* (CUP, 2013), 198, 203; Adam Mestyan, "The Muslim Bourgeoisie and Philanthropy in the Late Ottoman Empire," in Dejung, Motadel, and Osterhammel, *Global Bourgeoisie*, 174, 208, 212, 217–27.

64. Mona Abaza, *The Cotton Plantation Remembered: An Egyptian Family Story* (American University in Cairo Press, 2013), 66, 114.

65. Mücke, *Diary of Heinrich Witt*, 4:lxxii.

66. For background on Witt, see Ulrich Mücke, "Ein Rassist gibt Auskunft," *Die Zeit*, July 14, 2016, 17; Wetzel, "A Short Biography of Heinrich Witt," xix; entry of October 30, 1847, as quoted in Mücke, *Diary of Heinrich Witt*, 4:130; Wetzel, "A Short Biography of Heinrich Witt," viii; entry of December 5–11, 1847, as quoted in Mücke, *Diary of Heinrich Witt*, 4:138; entry of November 19, 1848, as quoted in Mücke, *Diary of Heinrich Witt*, 4:248; and entry of December 22, 1847, as quoted in Mücke, *Diary of Heinrich Witt*, 4:143.

67. Wetzel, "A Short Biography of Heinrich Witt," xxxv; entry of December 25, 1847, as quoted in Mücke, *Diary of Heinrich Witt*, 4:145; entry of November 21, 1847, as quoted in Mücke, *Diary of Heinrich Witt*, 4:136; Wetzel, "A Short Biography of Heinrich Witt," xxiv; entry of December 22, 1847, as quoted in Mücke, *Diary of Heinrich Witt*, 4:142. For the list of people present, see entry of October 6, 1848, as quoted in Mücke, *Diary of Heinrich Witt*, 4:230–32.

68. Entry of January 9, 1848, as quoted in Mücke, *Diary of Heinrich Witt*, 4:148.

69. Entry of May 24–27, 1848, as quoted in Mücke, *Diary of Heinrich Witt*, 4:176.

70. Entry of June 18, 1848, as quoted in Mücke, *Diary of Heinrich Witt*, 4:189; and entry of July 21, 1848, as quoted in Mücke, *Diary of Heinrich Witt*, 4:202.

71. Various documents, W1-9, III, No. 142, Bethmann-Archiv, Stadtarchiv Frankfurt, Germany

72. Needell, *Tropical Belle Époque*, 77. On Le Cap, see Robin Blackburn, *The Making of New World*

Slavery: From the Baroque to the Modern, 1492–1800* (Verso, 2010), 451; and Alegrio, *Os Clemente Pinto*, 193–94.

73. William Foster Apthorp, *The Opera Past and Present* (Charles Scribner's Sons, 1910), 26; Sebastiano De Filippi and Daniel Varacalli Costas, *The Other Toscanini: The Life and Works of Hector Panizza* (University of North Texas Press, 2019), 10; Eduard Andorfer, *Die Baugeschichte: In 50 Jahre Grazer Opernhaus, 1899–1949* (Graz, 1949), 21; David A. Hanser, *Architecture of France* (Greenwood Press, 2006), 172; Andrew Ayers, *The Architecture of Paris* (Edition Axel Menges, 2004), 188; Nicole Wild, *Dictionnaire des théâtres parisiens au XIXe siècle: Les théâtres et la musique* (Aux Amateurs de Livres, 1989), 76; Frederic Spotts, *Bayreuth: A History of the Wagner Festival* (Yale UP, 1994); Paul Busse, *Geschichte des Gärtnerplatztheaters in München* (Verlag A. Waldbauer, 1924), 13–15; Victor F. Denaro, "Houses in Kingsway and Old Bakery Street, Valletta," *Melita Historica: Journal of the Malta Historical Society* 2, no. 4 (1959): 202; N. C. Curtis, "New Orleans: The French Opera House 1859–1917," *Western Architect* 38, no. 1 (1929): 5–8; and Drew Reed, "Manaus's Opulent Amazon Theatre—A History of Cities in 50 Buildings, Day 15," *Guardian*, April 14, 2015.

74. See, for example, speech by John Ward, 1857, John Ward, Box 1, Ward Family Papers, NYHS.

75. *HMMCR* 35 (1856): 388; *HMMCR* 31 (1854): 263; *HMMCR* 34 (1856): 60; *HMMCR* 31 (1854): 59; *HMMCR* 41 (1859): 644; *HMMCR* 34 (1856): 59, as cited in Beckert, *Monied Metropolis*, 41.

76. For a comprehensive discussion of these different positions, see Martin J. Burke, *The Conundrum of Class: Public Discourse on the Social Order in America* (University of Chicago Press, 1995), 76–132.

77. *HMMCR* 37 (1857): 702.

78. *Fifteenth Annual Report of the New-York Association for Improving the Conditions of the Poor* (New York: John F. Trow, 1858), 32.

79. On the importance of this naturalization of the capitalist economy, see also Blackbourn and Eley, *Peculiarities of German History*, 190.

80. Manisha Sinha, *The Slave's Cause: A History of Abolition* (Yale UP, 2016), 253.

81. George Opdyke, *Treatise on Political Economy* (New York: G. P. Putnam, 1851), 327, 330, 331.

82. For the quotes, see Henry W. Bellows, *Historical Sketch of the Union*

League Club of New York* (New York, 1879), 132, as cited in Beckert, *Monied Metropolis*, 211; "The Recent Strike in the Iron Trade in the North of England," *Economist*, January 5, 1867, 4.

83. *Manufacturer and Builder* 8 (January 1875): 10.

84. "The Malay Peninsula," *Economist*, November 20, 1875, 1364.

85. Mücke, "Ein Rassist gibt Auskunft," 17.

86. For the quote, see Pfeiffer, *Eine Frauenfahrt um die Welt*, 32.

87. For the quote, see Webster, *Richest East India Merchant*, 84, 85.

88. Richard Drayton, "Race, Culture and Class: European Hegemony and Global Class Formation, c. 1800–1950," in Dejung, Motadel, and Osterhammel, *Global Bourgeoisie*, 351–52; Louis Menand, "Morton, Agassiz, and the Origins of Scientific Racism in the United States," *Journal of Blacks in Higher Education* 34 (Winter 2001–2002): 111.

89. Jürgen Osterhammel, *Unfabling the East: The Enlightenment's Encounter with Asia* (PUP, 2017); Drayton, "Race, Culture and Class," 352; Dejung, Motadel, and Osterhammel, "Worlds of the Bourgeoisie," 25; Menand, "Morton, Agassiz, and the Origins of Scientific Racism in the United States," 111.

90. *Twenty-Fourth Annual Report of the New York Association for the Improvement of the Conditions of the Poor for the Year 1867* (New York: Trow, 1867), 69, as cited in Beckert, *Monied Metropolis*, 179.

91. *NYT*, June 25, 1871, 4, as cited in Beckert, *Monied Metropolis*, 179.

92. Hewitt, *Emergence of Stability in the Industrial City*, 58.

93. Charles Dickens, "Oliver Twist; or, The Parish Boy's Progress," *Bentley's Miscellany*, vols. 1–5 (1837–1839); Charles Dickens, "Hard Times: For These Times," *Household Words*, vols. 8–13, part 2 (1854); and Charles Dickens, "Great Expectations," *All the Year Round* (1860–1861).

94. Hewitt, *Emergence of Stability in the Industrial City*, 87–89.

95. Hewitt, *Emergence of Stability in the Industrial City*, 90.

96. General Booth, *In Darkest England and the Way Out* (London: International Headquarters of the Salvation Army, 1890), 9.

97. Booth, *In Darkest England and the Way Out*, 14.

98. Booth, *In Darkest England and the Way Out*, 11–12.

99. Christof Dejung, "From Global Civilizing Missions to Racial War-

fare: Class Conflicts and the Representation of the Colonial World in European Middle Class Thought," in Dejung, Motadel, and Osterhammel, *Global Bourgeoisie*, 259.

100. Gustav von Bodelschwingh, *Friedrich von Bodelschwingh: Ein Lebensbild* (Pfenningverein Bethel, 1922), 273 as cited in and translated by Dejung, "From Global Civilizing Missions to Racial Warfare," 259.

101. Hewitt, *Emergence of Stability in the Industrial City*, 69, 81, 295.

102. Tilly, "Did the Cake of Custom Break?," 25; Mitchell, *International Historical Statistics*, 116, 153, 168. These numbers are imprecise and include and exclude various groups of workers, yet they demonstrate beyond doubt the huge and quite sudden increase in manufacturing employment.

103. *Morning Chronicle*, October 1849, as cited in *Angus Bethune Reach: Manchester and the Textile Districts in 1849*, ed. C. Aspin (Helmshore Local History Society, 1972), 20, 29; Andrew Davies, Steven Fielding, and Terry Wyke, introduction to *Workers' Worlds: Cultures and Communities in Manchester and Salford, 1880–1939*, ed. Andrew Davies and Steven Fielding (Manchester UP, 1992), 1.

104. Steven Marcus, *Engels, Manchester & the Working Class* (Vintage, 1975), 4; and Hewitt, *Emergence of Stability in the Industrial City*, 31. The numbers have been rounded. See also Hewitt, *Emergence of Stability in the Industrial City*, 33.

105. Benjamin Disraeli, *The Works of Benjamin Disraeli, Earl of Beaconsfield* (London: M. W. Dunne, n.d.), 203.

106. Asa Briggs, *Victorian Cities* (Penguin, 1963), 116.

107. G. J. Holyoake, ed., *The Reasoner*, vol. 5 (London: n.p., 1848), 92.

108. As cited in Stephen Mosely, *The Chimney of the World: A History of Smoke Pollution in Victorian and Edwardian Manchester* (Routledge, 2001), 20.

109. Both are cited in Mosely, *Chimney of the World*, 21; see also 13, 19, 20, 23.

110. Hewitt, *Emergence of Stability in the Industrial City*, 21.

111. Alexis de Tocqueville, *Journeys to England and Ireland*, ed. J. P. Mayer, trans. George Lawrence and K. P. Mayer (Yale UP, 1958), 104.

112. Tocqueville, *Journeys to England and Ireland*, 108.

113. A Salford Clergyman, MC (18 January 1834), as cited in Hewitt, *Emergence of Stability in the Industrial City*, 26.

114. Hewitt, *Emergence of Stability in the Industrial City*, 50.

115. Stuart Hylton, *A History of Manchester* (Phillimore, 2003), 169; "Work," Workhouse Life, The Workhouse: The Story of an Institution (website), last modified 2016, accessed July 12, 2024, https://www.workhouses.org.uk/life/work.shtml; and "Children in the Workhouse," Children & Education, The Workhouse: The Story of an Institution, last modified 2016, accessed July 12, 2024, https://www.workhouses.org.uk/education/.

116. Hewitt, *Emergence of Stability in the Industrial City*, 6, 50, 52. On real wages throughout Europe, see Şevket Pamuk and Jan-Luiten van Zanden, "Standards of Living," in *Cambridge Economic History of Modern Europe*, vol. 1, *1700–1870*, ed. Stephen Broadberry and Kevin H. O'Rourke (CUP, 2010), 224. An excellent survey of the "standard-of-living debate" can be found in Pamuk and Van Zanden, "Standards of Living," 217–34; John Komlos, "Shrinking in a Growing Economy? The Mystery of Physical Stature During the Industrial Revolution" *JEH* 58, no. 3 (1998): 779–802; M. E. Poole and C. G. Pooley, "Health, Society and Environment in Victorian Manchester," in *Urban Disease and Mortality in Nineteenth Century England*, ed. R. Woods and J. Woodward (St. Martin's Press, 1984), 148–77; Gustav Schmoller, *Zur Geschichte der deutschen Kleingewerbe im 19. Jahrhundert* (Halle, 1870), 692; Simon Szreter and Graham Mooney, "Urbanization, Mortality, and the Standard of Living Debate: New Estimates of the Expectation of Life at Birth in Nineteenth-Century British Cities," *EHR* 51, no. 1 (1998): 93; and Robert C. Allen, "Tracking the Agricultural Revolution in England," *EHR* 52 (1999), 217.

117. Patrick Joyce, *Visions of the People: Industrial England and the Question of Class 1848–1914* (CUP, 1991), 104.

118. *Morning Chronicle*, October 1849, 8.

119. Friedrich Engels, as cited in Mervyn Busteed, *The Irish in Manchester, c. 1750–1921: Resistance, Adaptation, and Identity* (Manchester UP, 2016), 49.

120. Busteed, *Irish in Manchester*, 50, 53; Friedrich Engels, *The Condition of the Working Class in England in 1844: With a Preface Written in 1892* (London: G. Allen & Unwin, 1892), 54.

121. *Morning Chronicle*, October 1849, 9. See also Hylton, *History of Manchester*, 144.

122. *Morning Chronicle*, October 1849, 18.

123. *Morning Chronicle*, October 1849, 25.

124. *Morning Chronicle*, October 1849, as cited in Aspin, *Angus Bethune Reach*, 58; Melanie Tebbutt, "Women's Talk? Gossip and 'Women's Words' in Working-Class Communities, 1880–1939," in Davies and Fielding, *Workers' Worlds*, 49.

125. Busteed, *Irish in Manchester*, 56; Tebbutt, "Women's Talk?," 49–50, 53–54, 59; and Hewitt, *Emergence of Stability in the Industrial City*, 165. On working-class literacy, see Gregory Vargo, "Questions from Workers Who Read: Education and Self-Formation in Chartist Print Culture and Elizabeth Gaskell's Mary Barton," *Victorian Literature and Culture* 44, no. 1 (March 2016): 137; John Dixon, "Reading/Literacy—For the Lower Orders?," *Changing English* 20, no. 2 (May 2013): 219; and Thomas W. Laqueur, "Literacy and Social Mobility in the Industrial Revolution in England," *Past & Present* 64 (August 1974): 99.

126. Hewitt, *The Emergence of Stability in the Industrial City*, 158, 177, 187; and Hylton, *History of Manchester*, 132. The heavy consumption of alcohol was typical for working-class communities the world over. See, for Russia, Franz-Joseph Brüggemeier, *Grubengold: Das Zeitalter der Kohle von 1750 bis Heute* (C. H. Beck, 2018), 169.

127. Hewitt, *Emergence of Stability in the Industrial City*, 174–75; Hylton, *History of Manchester*, 173.

128. Colin Smethurst, *Emile Zola, Germinal* (University of Glasgow French and German Publications, 1996); Andrew Gordon, *The Evolution of Labor Relations in Japan: Heavy Industry, 1853–1955* (HUP, 1985), 28; Ashita Saga, "Urban Lower-Class Society in Modern Osaka," *City, Culture and Society* 3, no. 1 (2012): 66; David F. Crew, *Town in the Ruhr: A Social History of Bochum, 1860–1914* (Columbia UP, 1979), 60, 152; and Lynn Abrams, *Workers' Culture in Imperial Germany: Leisure and Recreation in the Rhineland and Westphalia* (Routledge, 1992), 65, 67.

129. Crew, *Town in the Ruhr*, 60, 152; Abrams, *Workers' Culture in Imperial Germany*, 65, 67; Gordon, *Evolution of Labor Relations in Japan*, 28; Ashita Saga, "Urban Lower-Class Society in Modern Osaka," *City, Culture and Society* 3, no. 1 (2012): 66; Michael R. Haines, "Fertility and Marriage in a Nineteenth-Century Industrial City: Philadelphia 1850–1880," *JEH* 40, no. 1

(1980): 152; John F. Sutherland, "Housing the Poor," in Allen F. Davis and Mark H. Haller, *The Peoples of Philadelphia: A History of Ethnic Groups and Lower-Class Life, 1790–1940* (Temple UP, 1973), 179; Theodore Hershberg, Dale Light Jr., Harold E. Cox, and Richard R. Greenfield, "The 'Journey to Work,'" in *Philadelphia: Work, Space, Family, and Group Experience in the Nineteenth Century*, ed. Theodore Hershberg (OUP, 1981), 143; Brian E. Alnutt, "'The Negro Excursions': Recreational Outings Among Philadelphia African Americans, 1876–1926," *Pennsylvania Magazine of History and Biography* 129, no. 1 (2005): 81; Mark Edward Lender and James Kirby Martin, *Drinking in America: A History* (Free Press, 1982), 60; Claudia Goldin, "Family Strategies and the Family Economy in the Late Nineteenth Century: The Role of Secondary Workers," in Hershberg, *Philadelphia* 283.

130. Hewitt, *Emergence of Stability in the Industrial City*, 21, 28, 30.

131. Hewitt, *Emergence of Stability in the Industrial City*, 41, 44.

132. Busteed, *Irish in Manchester*, 43.

133. Steven Fielding, "A Separate Culture? Irish Catholics in Working-Class Manchester and Salford, c. 1890–1939," in Davies and Fielding, *Workers' Worlds*, 25, 28, 46; and Busteed, *Irish in Manchester*, 41–42, 45, 48.

134. As cited in Jacqueline Roberts, *Working Class Housing in Nineteenth Century Manchester: The Example of John Street, Irk Town, 1826–1936* (Neil Richardson, 1986), 13.

135. Roberts, *Working Class Housing in Nineteenth Century Manchester*, 15.

136. Busteed, *Irish in Manchester*, 76.

137. Unsigned editorial, "English and Irish Distress," *Manchester Courier*, November 3, 1847.

138. Royal Commission into the Condition of the Poorer Classes in Ireland, *Condition of the Poorer Classes in Ireland, Appendix G: State of the Irish Poor in Great Britain* (London: W. Cloves and Sons, 1835), 75.

139. Busteed, *Irish in Manchester*, 60–61, 122, 125.

140. Hewitt, *Emergence of Stability in the Industrial City*, 155, 156, 163, 178, 179; and Arno Herzig, *Unterschichtenprotest in Deutschland, 1790–1870* (VR, 1988), 41.

141. According to Hobsbawm, a working class and a working-class consciousness developed only in the 1880s—after that point, it was "everywhere." See Eric Hobsbawm, *Worlds of Labour: Further Studies in the History of Labour* (Weidenfeld and Nicolson, 1984), 190. According to Thompson, such class consciousness can be found much earlier, in the late eighteenth century. See Thompson, *Making of the English Working Class*, 725, 727. See also Hewitt, *Emergence of Stability in the Industrial City*, 195, 199.

142. "[I]ts th'competishun wi separate un opposing individual interests uts sappin un undermoinin, wi its selfishness, th'morals oth foak." Cited in Hewitt, *Emergence of Stability in the Industrial City*, 214.

143. "The Address of the Delegates of South Lancashire to Their Constituents, and the Chartists Throughout the United Kingdom" signed by James Cartledge and Wm. Grocott on behalf of the delegates," in *Northern Star*, December 24, 1841, 4.

144. Iorwerth Prothero, *Radical Artisans in England and France, 1830–1870* (CUP, 1997), 101.

145. Prothero, *Radical Artisans*, 104.

146. As cited in Ronald Aminzade, *Class, Politics, and Early Industrial Capitalism: A Study of Mid-Nineteenth-Century Toulouse, France* (State University of New York Press, 1981), 76.

147. "Bericht der Verhandlungen vor den Assisen zu Köln 1831 zum Aufruhr in Aachen," as cited in Beate Althammer, *Herrschaft, Fürsorge, Protest: Eliten und Unterschichten in den Textilgewerbestädten Aachen und Barcelona, 1830–1870* (Verlag J. H. W. Dietz Nachf., 2002), 199.

148. Cited in Eric Hobsbawm, *How to Change the World: Reflections on Marx and Marxism* (Yale UP, 2011), 27; Gareth Stedman Jones, "European Socialism from the 1790s to the 1890s," in *The Cambridge History of Modern European Thought*, ed. Warren Breckman and Peter E. Gordon (CUP, 2019), 207.

149. Hobsbawm, *How to Change the World*, 29; Jacques Rancière, "The Myth of the Artisan: Critical Reflections on a Category of Social History," *International Labor and Working-Class History* 24 (1983): 1–16.

150. Charles Fourier, *The Utopian Vision of Charles Fourier: Selected Texts on Work, Love, and Passionate Attraction*, trans. and ed. Jonathan Beecher and Richard Bienvenu (Beacon Press, 1971), 1.

151. David Harvey, *Paris: Capital of Modernity* (Routledge, 2004), 71; Jones, "European Socialism," 201.

152. Robert Sutton, introduction to Étienne Cabet, *Travels in Icaria* (Syracuse UP, 2003), xii–xv, xx.

153. Keith Taylor, *Political Ideas of the Utopian Socialists* (Frank Cass, 1982), 187.

154. Harvey, *Paris*, 61, 76.

155. Jones, "European Socialism from the 1790s to the 1890s," 214.

156. Peter Marshall, *Demanding the Impossible: A History of Anarchism* (Harper Perennial, 2008), 242, 244.

157. Taylor, *Political Ideas of the Utopian Socialists*, 189–90.

158. Working Men's Association, *The People's Charter* (London: H. Hetherington, 1838), 14.

159. Louis Blanc, *Organization of Labour* (London: H. G. Clarke & Co., 1848), 16, 25, 51.

160. Spencer M. Di Scala, "The Class Struggle: Socialism, Communism, and Social Democracy," in *European Political Thought, 1815–1989* (Routledge, 2018).

161. Jones, "European Socialism," 227.

162. For a very similar observation, see George Orwell, *The Road to Wigan Pier* (Penguin, 2001), 181.

163. Karl Marx and Frederick Engels, *Deutsche Ideologie: Zur Kritik der Philosophie*, ed. Gerald Hubmann and Ulrich Pagel (de Gruyter, 2018), esp. 8–36.

164. Karl Marx and Friedrich Engels, *Manifest der Kommunistischen Partei* (London: J. E. Burghard, 1848); and Gareth Stedman Jones, *Karl Marx: Greatness and Illusion* (Penguin, 2017), 201–4, 212–16, 219–22, 231–35.

165. Jones, "European Socialism," 218.

166. Karl Marx, *Das Kapital: Kritik der Politischen Oekonomie* (Hamburg: Otto Meisner, 1867); and Jones, "European Socialism," 221, 231.

167. For that speech, see Karl Marx, "Inaugural Address of the International Working Men's Association," as quoted in Marcello Musto, ed., *Workers Unite! The International 150 Years Later* (Bloomsbury Academic Press, 2014), 79.

168. Walt Whitman, "Years of the Modern," in *Leaves of Grass: Including Sands at Seventy, Good Bye My Fancy, Old Age Echoes, and a Backward Glance o'er Travel'd Roads* (Boston: Small, Maynard & Company, 1897), 374.

169. Kevin O'Rourke and Jeffrey Williamson, "When Did Globalization Begin?," NBER Working Paper No. 77632 (2000), http://www.nber.org/papers/w7632.

170. *Journal des Débats*, December 8, 1831, 1.

171. Jessica M. Lepler, *The Many Panics of 1837: People, Politics, and the*

Creation of a Transatlantic Financial Crisis (CUP, 2013), 42.

172. On an even earlier crisis, see Andrew H. Browning, *The Panic of 1819: The First Great Depression* (University of Missouri Press, 2019); and Lepler, *Many Panics*, 55, 100.

173. Lepler, *Many Panics*, 117; and "The Crisis Come—Great Commercial Calamity—Failure of the Messrs. Josephs," *Herald* (New York), March 18, 1837.

174. William H. Wills, "A Southern Traveler's Diary, 1840," in *Publications of the Southern History Association*, ed. Colyer Meriwether, vol. 8 (Southern History Association, 1904), 35.

175. J. R. Hutchinson, *Reminiscences, Sketches, and Addresses Selected from My Papers During a Ministry of Forty-Five Years in Mississippi, Louisiana, and Texas* (Houston: E. H. Cushing, 1874), 53.

176. Diary of George Templeton Strong, Allan Nevins and Milton Thomas, eds., vol 1, February 21, 1840.

177. *Times* (London), June 5, 1837.

178. Alain le Pichon, ed., *China Trade and Empire: Jardine, Matheson & Co. and the Origins of British Rule in Hong Kong, 1827–1843* (OUP, 2006), 314.

179. Charles Kindleberger, *Manias, Panics, and Crashes: A History of Financial Crises* (Macmillan, 1978), 126; Le Pichon, *China Trade and Empire*, 301–14; Angela Redish, "The Economic Crisis of 1837–1839 in Upper Canada: Case Study of a Temporary Suspension of Specie Payments," *Explorations in Economic History* 20, no. 4 (October 1983): 404; Clément Juglar, *Des crises commerciales et de leur retour périodique* (Paris: Guillaumin, 1862), 70; Kindleberger, *Manias, Panics, and Crashes*, 185; C. A. Bayly, *Rulers, Townsmen and Bazaars: North Indian Society in the Age of British Expansion, 1770–1870* (OUP, 1998), 225, 229; *Algemeen Handelsblad* (Amsterdam), November 13, 1839; and Lepler, *Many Panics*, 232.

180. Lepler, *Many Panics*, 190.

181. J. R. T. Hughes, "The Commercial Crisis of 1857," *Oxford Economic Papers* 8, no. 2 (June 1956): 194.

182. Hans Rosenberg, *Die Weltwirtschaftskrise 1857–1859* (Vandenhoeck & Ruprecht, 1974), 108–11, 114, 130; Hugh Rockoff, "Crisis of 1857," in *Business Cycles and Depressions: An Encyclopedia*, ed. David Glasner (Routledge, 2013), 128–29; and James L. Huston, *The Panic of 1857 and the Coming of the Civil War* (Louisiana State UP, 1987), 17–18.

183. *Aktionär*, October 18, 1857, as cited in Rosenberg, *Die Weltwirtschaftskrise*, 136.

184. Rosenberg, *Die Weltwirtschaftskrise*, 123, 126, 129, 134; Huston, *Panic of 1857*, 26.

185. "The Unemployed," *New-York Daily Tribune*, November 12, 1857, https://chroniclingamerica.loc.gov/lccn/sn83030213/1857-11-12/ed-1/seq-5/.

186. As cited in Hamerow, *Social Foundations of German Unification*, 8.

187. Marc Bloch, *Feudal Society*, vol. 1 (University of Chicago Press, 1961), xix.

188. Jürgen Kocka, *Capitalism: A Short History* (PUP, 2017), 2.

189. Instituut voor de Nederlandse Taal, "Kapitalisme," in *Woordenboek der Nederlandse Taal (WNT) Online* (2007); and Machado de Assis, *Posthumous Memoirs of Brás Cubas*, 201.

190. As cited in *Gazette de Lausanne* 9 (July 31, 1807): 72. See also *Gazette de Lausanne* 5 (July 15, 1806): 33; and *Gaceta del Gobierno de México*, June 4, 1810, 5. For the original quote, see Joseph-Henri Réveillé-Parise and Antonio Bachiller y Morales, *Fisiologia e higiene de los hombres dedicados a trabajos literarios, ó, Investigaciones sobre lo físico y moral costumbres, enfermedades, y régimen de los literatos, artístas, aabios, estadistas, jurisconsultos, &c.* (Havana: Oficina del Faro Industrial, 1843), 17; and *Astro da Lusitania*, June 17, 1822, 3.

191. Adam Smith, "Of the Nature of Virtue," in *The Works of Adam Smith*, ed. Dugald Stewart, vol. 1 (London: T. Cadell & W. Davies, 1812), 390.

192. Emma Rothschild, "Political Economy," in *The Cambridge History of Nineteenth-Century Political Thought*, ed. Gareth Stedman Jones and Gregory Claeys (CUP, 2011), 764. For the uses of that term, see Google Ngram Viewer, accessed August 21, 2019.

193. Quoted in Rothschild, "Political Economy," 777.

194. Quoted in Rothschild, 777.

195. On this use of the word *capitalism*, see, for example, Henry Marie Brackenridge, *Voyage to Buenos Ayres: Performed in the Years 1817 and 1818* (London: Printed for Sir Richard Phillips and Co., 1820), 107; and *Mercurio de España*, May 1818, 89. On a (perhaps) similar use of the word *capitalism*, see the Brazilian magazine *Filho da Terra* 13 (January 21, 1832): 6.

196. Marquis de Villeneuve, *L'agonie de la France* (Paris: Perisse, 1839), 139.

197. Jean-Baptiste Richard, *Enrichissement de la langue française, dictionnaire de mots nouveaux: système d'éducation, pensées politiques, philosophiques, morales et sociales* (Paris: Pilout/Troyes: Laloy, 1842), 88.

198. *Mémoires de l'Académie Royale des Sciences, Belles-Lettres et Arts de Lyon, Section de Lettres*, vol. 2 (Lyon: Boitel, 1846), 282.

199. As quoted in Jean Dubois, *Le vocabulaire politique et social en France de 1869 à 1872* (Librairie Larousse, 1962), 238.

200. As quoted in Edmond Silberner, "Le mot *capitalisme*," *Annales d'histoire sociale* 2, no. 2 (April 1940): 133–34. See also Louis Blanc's writing in 1851 in the *Journal de Genève*.

201. The first quote is from Pierre-Joseph Proudhon, *Idée générale de la révolution au dix-neuvième siècle* (Paris: Librairie de Garnier Frères, 1851), 223. The second is from Pierre-Joseph Proudhon, *De la justice dans la révolution et dans l'Église* (Paris: Librairie de Garnier Frères, 1858), 351.

202. Pierre Larousse, *Grand dictionnaire universel du XIXe siècle*, vol. 3 (Paris: Larousse et Cie, 1867), 320.

203. Jürgen Kocka and Marcel van der Linden, *Capitalism* (Bloomsbury, 2017), 1–3.

204. Rothschild, "Political Economy," 764; Edwin R. A. Seligman, "Social Aspects of Economic Law," *Publications of the American Economic Association* 5, no. 1 (February 1904): 69; and as cited in Chuhei Sugiyama, "The Development of Economic Thought in Meiji Japan," *Modern Asian Studies* 2, no. 4 (1968): 336.

205. Jürgen Kocka puts 1851 as the earliest known mention, while Hartwell and Engerman place it in 1854. See Kocka and van der Linden, *Capitalism*, 5; R. Hartwell and S. Engerman, "Capitalism," in *Oxford Encyclopedia of Economic History*, ed. J. Mokyr (Oxford, 2003), 319. See also Kocka, *Capitalism: A Short History*, 5; Thorstein Veblen, *The Instinct of Workmanship and the State of Industrial Art* (Macmillan, 1914), 282, 302; and Steven G. Marks, "The Word 'Capitalism': The Soviet Union's Gift to America," *Society* (2012): 156.

206. Cited in Marks, "The Word 'Capitalism,'" 155.

207. F. A. Stilch, *Demokratie und Sozialismus* (Schulz und Comp, 1848), 12, 15.

208. Kocka, *Capitalism: A Short History*, 4.

209. Rothschild, "Political Economy," 762–63.

210. Albert Schaeffle, *Struttura del corpo sociale. Introduzione di Gerolamo*

Boccardo l'animale e l'uomo (Unione Tipografico, 1881).

211. Achille Loria, *Le basi economiche della costituzione sociale* (Milan: Fratelli Bocca, 1886); and Salvatore Cognetti de Martiis, *Socialismo Antico* (Milan: Fratelli Bocca, 1889).

212. Jan Stoffel, *Het sociale vraagstuk opgelost (Maar niet door een huismiddel)* (Deventer: Hulscher, 1885), 15.

213. "De Arbeiders-Beweging in Nederland," De Vrije Gedachte (1874), 452; Abraham Kuyper, *Het sociale vraagstuk en de christelijk religie: Rede ter opening van het Sociaal Congres op 9 november 1891* (Amsterdam: J. A. Wormser, 1891), 18.

214. In "Eikoku Seifu to Morugan," *Asahi Shinbun*, November 23, 1902. The phrase used was "*shihonshugi no enkaku* 資本主義の沿革" (history of capitalism).

215. Nihon kokugo daijiten [日本国語大辞典], s.v. "しほん-しゅぎ [資本主義]," accessed February 18, 2025, https://japanknowledge-com.ezp-prod1.hul.harvard.edu/lib/display/?lid=200201f4ce144i59cXH.

216. 秀助 阿部. "宗教改革時代と資本主義." 三田学会雑誌 3, no. 6 (June 1910): 67–76.

217. 东方法学会编纂:《经济学要览》(*Guidebook on Economics*), 上海: 上海泰东图书局, 1914年, 第46页 The Eastern Law Society, ed., *Guidebook on Economics* (Shanghai Tai-Dong Press, 1914), 46.

218. Hagmann, "Bericht über die landwirtschaftlichen Verhältnisse der Gemeinde Neukirch, Bezirksamt Triberg," in *Erhebungen über die Lage der Landwirthschaft im Großherzogtum Baden*, vol. 3, ed. Großherzogliches Ministerium des Innern (Karlsruhe, 1883), part XXX, 65. See also, more generally, Braudel, *Afterthoughts on Material Civilization and Capitalism*, 16–17.

219. Hugh B. Urban, "The Marketplace and the Temple: Economic Metaphors and Religious Meanings in the Folk Songs of Colonial Bengal," *Journal of Asian Studies* 60 (November 2001): 1086.

220. Urban, "Marketplace and the Temple," 1093.

221. As cited in Urban, "Marketplace and the Temple," 1097.

Chapter 10: Rebellions: The Crisis of Old-Regime Capitalism, 1830–1870

1. Ernest Feydeau, *Mémoires d'un coulissier* (Paris: Calmann-Lévy, 1882), 186.

2. See also William H. Sewell Jr., *Capitalism and the Emergence of Civic Equality in Eighteenth-Century France* (Chicago UP, 2020), 17.

3. David Montgomery, *The Fall of the House of Labor: The Workplace, the State, and American Labor Activism, 1865–1925* (CUP, 1987), 9.

4. *Economist*, October 13, 1866, 1193; letter from G. G. Morris, Special Commissioner, to the Secretary to the Government of Bengal, 31 July 1861, in "Report of the Results of the Proceedings of Messr [missing] . . . for Making Inquiries into the Alleged [missing] in the Nuddea and Jessore Districts Against the Payment of Rent," in Home Department, Judicial Branch, Consultation A, No. 11/16, 6 January 1862, NAI; Peter Hinks and John McKivigan, eds., *Abolition and Antislavery: A Historical Encyclopedia of the American Mosaic* (ABC-CLIO, 2015), 155. See also "Levantamiento de los negros del cafetal 'Perserverancia' en Lagunillas y su sofocacion," 1842, ULTRAMAR, 4615, Exp. 3, National Archives of Spain, Madrid. The notion of a confluence of these rebellions (though without mentioning workers) can also be found in Giovanni Arrighi, *The Long Twentieth Century: Money, Power, and the Origins of Our Times* (Verso, 1994), 52; Hermann Schulze-Delitzsch, *Schriften und Reden*, vol. 2 (Guttentag, 1910), 214. For the quotes, see Victor Considérant, *Le socialisme devant le vieux monde ou Le vivant devant les morts* (Paris: Librairie Phalanstérienne, 1849), 13–14.

5. Charles S. Maier, *Leviathan 2.0: Inventing Modern Statehood* (HUP, 2012), 22. For similar arguments, see also Jürgen Osterhammel, *Die Verwandlung der Welt: Eine Geschichte des 19. Jahrhunderts* (Verlag C. H. Beck, 2009), 110, 777; and Charles S. Maier, "Consigning the Twentieth Century to History: Alternative Narratives for the Modern Era," *AHR* 105, no. 3 (2000): 815–16.

6. Andrea Giovene, *The Book of Giuliano Sansevero*, transl. Marguerite Waldman (Penguin Books, 1972), 51.

7. Von Wolfgang Büttner, "Der Weberaufstand," *Die Zeit*, June 3, 1994; and Christina von Hodenberg, *Aufstand der Weber: die Revolte von 1844 und ihr Aufstieg zum Mythos* (Dietz, 1997), 229.

8. As cited in Arno Herzig, *Unterschichtenprotest in Deutschland, 1790–1870* (Vandenhoeck & Ruprecht, 1988), 66.

9. As cited in Herzig, *Unterschichtenprotest in Deutschland*, 83. See also Karl Obermann, *Deutschland von 1815 bis 1849*, 3rd ed. (VEB Deutscher Verlag der Wissenschaften, 1967), 153.

10. *Vorwärts*, July 7, 1844, 1. The translation is from *The Poems of Heine: Complete, Translated into the Original Metres with a Sketch of His Life*, ed. Edgar Alfred Bowring, C.B. (George Bell and Sons, 1908), 395.

11. Gerhart Hauptmann, *Die Weber*, fifth act, first produced by the Freie Bühne on February 23, 1893.

12. Herzig, *Unterschichtenprotest in Deutschland*, 15–17; and Jonathan Sperber, *Rhineland Radicals: The Democratic Movement and the Revolution of 1848–1849* (PUP, 1991), 55–59.

13. For the quote, see Herzig, *Unterschichtenprotest in Deutschland*, 27, 64, 95. See also Rudi Batzell, "Reconstructing Global Capitalism: Class, Corporations, and the Future of Welfare States, 1870–1930" (PhD diss., Harvard University, 2017), 90.

14. Herzig, *Unterschichtenprotest in Deutschland*, 22–23, 26–27, 55, 64, 83–85.

15. *Pittsburgh Daily Gazette and Advertiser*, October 8, 1845; and Jason Martinek, "The Amazons of Allegheny: The Fire, the Riot, and the Textile Strike of 1845," *Western Pennsylvania History* 94 (Spring 2011), 38–48.

16. Peter Way, *Common Labour: Workers and the Digging of North American Canals, 1780–1860* (CUP, 1993), 291–94; Franz-Joseph Brüggemeier, *Grubengold: Das Zeitalter der Kohle von 1750 bis Heute* (Verlag C. H. Beck, 2018), 78; and Paul E. Johnson, *Sam Patch, the Famous Jumper* (Hill and Wang, 2003), 71. For these numbers, see Paul A. Gilje, "Riots in the United States," Ohio State University Criminal Justice Research Center, last modified October 2009, https://cjrc.osu.edu/research/interdisciplinary/hvd/united-states/riots. While the list is most likely incomplete, it is the most comprehensive compilation we have; it shows conclusively that rioting was a prominent form of working-class collective action. As we will see later, rioting declined dramatically as a form of protest in the twentieth century.

17. Herzig, *Unterschichtenprotest, Deutschland*, 63–64; Yavuz Selim Karakışla, "The Emergence of the Ottoman Industrial Working Class, 1839–1923," in *Workers and the Working Class in the Ottoman Empire and the Turkish Republic 1839–1950*, ed. Donald Quataert and Erik J. Zürcher (I. B. Tauris Publishers, 1995), 20, 30.

18. *Journal des Débats*, December 8, 1831, 1.

19. *Journal des Débats*, December 8, 1831, 1.

20. Brüggemeier, *Grubengold*, 81.

21. Edward Shorter and Charles Tilly, *Strikes in France, 1830–1968* (CUP, 1974), 1, 11, 16, 67, 176.

22. Robert Sykes, "Early Chartism and Trade-Unionism in Southeast Lancashire," in *The Chartist Experience: Studies in Working-Class Radicalism and Culture, 1830–60*, ed. James Epstein and Dorothy Thompson (Macmillan, 1982), 154; and *London Working Men's Association, The People's Charter: With the Address to the Radical Reformers of Great Britain and Ireland and a Brief Sketch of Its Origin* (London: C. H. Elt, Charles Fox, 1848), 14.

23. Brüggemeier, *Grubengold*, 81; Franz-Josef Brüggemeier, Michael Farrenkopf, and Henirich Theodor Grütter, *Das Zeitalter der Kohle: Eine europäische Geschichte* (Klartext Verlag, 2018), 169; Sean Wilentz, *Chants Democratic: New York City and the Rise of the American Working Class, 1788–1850* (OUP, 1984), 219–21; Theodore S. Hamerow, *The Social Foundations of German Unification, 1858–1871*, vol. 1, *Ideas and Institutions* (PUP, 2015), 75; and Karakışla, "Emergence of the Ottoman Industrial Working Class," 20–21, 30.

24. Letter from the Secretary to the Government of Bengal to the Secretary to the Government of India, Fort William, 20 January 1856, in Home Department, Public Branch, 4 February 1856, No. 20, NAI.

25. Letter from [illegible] to the Secretary to the Government of Bengal, 18 February 1856, in Home Department, Public Branch, 28 February 1856, No. 21, NAI.

26. A. Grote, Esq., Commissioner of the Nuddea Division, to the Secretary to the Government of Bengal, 19 August 1856, as cited in James Long, *Strike, but Hear! Evidence Explanatory of the Indigo System in Lower Bengal by the Rev. J. Long* (Calcutta: R. C. Lepage & Co., 1861), 22.

27. Letter from E. Grey to Officiating Secretary to the Government of Bengal, 18 March 1864, in "Report of the Occurrence of an Affray? Attending Loss of Life at the Bagadangah Indigo Facility Nuddea District," in Home Department, Judicial Branch, Proceedings 18 June 1864, Nos. 36–46, NAI. For such a contract, see letter from H. L. Oliphant, Joint Magistrate of Nuddea, to the Magistrate of Nuddea, 15 April 1864, in "Report of the Occurrence of an Affray?"

28. Letter from F. R. Cockerell to the Commissioner of the Nuddea Division, Fort William, 4 April 1864, in "Report of the Occurrence

of an Affray?" Blair B. King, *The Blue Mutiny: The Indigo Disturbances in Bengal, 1859–1862* (University of Pennsylvania Press, 1966), 36; and letter from E. Grey to Officiating Secretary to the Government of Bengal, 18 March 1864, NAI.

29. King, *Blue Mutiny*, 92.

30. King, *Blue Mutiny*, 93.

31. Terence R. Blackburn, *A Miscellany of Mutinies and Massacres in India* (Associated Publishing House, 2007), 166; and King, *Blue Mutiny*, 102.

32. Subhas Bhattacharya, "The Indigo Revolt of Bengal," *Social Scientist* 5, no. 12 (1977): 14; and King, *Blue Mutiny*, 67, 85, 91–94, 102. There was frequent resistance to such land surveys. See, for example, G. G. Morris, Special Commissioner, to the Secretary to the Government of Bengal, Camp Jessore, 8 July 1861, in "Report of the Results of the Proceedings." For another example, see "Petition from—of—in the District of Moorshedabad, to the Hon'ble the Lieutenant Governor of Bengal," 24 March 1860, in Long, *Strike, but Hear!*, 28–29.

33. King, *Blue Mutiny*, 66, 114, 125–26, 129, 130–31, 134, 148, 164.

34. Letter by C. F. Montresor, Esq., to W. S. Sexton-Karr, 8 May 1861, 4, 7, in "Report of the Results of the Proceedings."

35. Another British colonial official in Nadia found a "strong feeling against indigo." See letter from E. H. Lightington, Officiating Commissioner of the Nuddea Division, to Secretary to the Government of Bengal, 19 February 1861, in "Report of the Results of the Proceedings," and King, *Blue Mutiny*, 151.

36. Letter, Calcutta, 13 July 1860, by Mss. Thomas to Secretary of Government of India, "Communication from Messrs. R. Thomas and Co. Complaining That No Proper Protection Is Given to an Indigo Planter in the Pursuit of His Business," in Home Department, Judicial Branch, "A," 1861, No. 13/16, 17 July 1861, NAI.

37. Letter from Thomas Kenny to Mr. Robinson, Esq., Sulzurmoodhere (?), 6 July 1860, in Home Department, Judicial Branch, "A," 1861, No. 13/16, 17 July 1861, NAI.

38. Letter from Thomas Kenny to Mr. Robinson, Esq., Sulzurmoodhere (?), 6 July 1860. The citation is from letter of H. D. Tripp to "My Dear Kenny," Bamundi, 4 July 1861. Both are held by the NAI. See also "Communication from Messrs Thomas and Co.," NAI.

39. G. G. Morris, Special Commissioner, to the Secretary to the Government of Bengal, Camp Jessore, 8 July 1861, NAI.

40. T. R. Kenny to G. G. Morris, Salgamoodia, 21 June 1861, in Home Department, Judicial Branch, Consultation A, 1862, No. 11/16, 6 January 1862, NAI. See also letter from T. R. Knox to G. G. Morris, Salgamoodia, 21 June 1861, in "Report of the Results of the Proceedings."

41. T. R. Kenny to G. G. Morris.

42. T. R. Kenny to G. G. Morris.

43. Letter from C. F. Montresor, Special Commissioner in the Nuddea District, to the Secretary to the Government of Bengal, 10 June 1861, in "Report of the Results of the Proceedings"; and G. G. Morris Special Commissioner, to the Secretary to the Government of Bengal, Camp Jessore, 8 July 1861, NAI.

44. Letter from G. G. Morris, Special Commissioner, to the Secretary to the Government of Bengal, 31 July 1861, NAI.

45. As cited in King, *Blue Mutiny*, 169.

46. Letter from J. Beckwith, Secretary of the Landholders' and Commercial Association, to F. R. Cockerell, Officiating Secretary to the Government of Bengal, 3 May 1864, in "Report of the Occurrence of an Affray?"

47. King, *Blue Mutiny*, 173.

48. Letter from E. Grey, Magistrate of Nuddea to the Officiating Secretary, to the Government of Bengal, 1 March 1864, in "Report of the Occurrence of an Affray?."

49. Letter from E. Grey, NAI. In 1869, similar conflicts occurred in Bihar. See, for example, letter from Arthur Howell, Officiating. Secretary to the Government of India, to the Secretary to the Government of Bengal, Fort William, 31 December 1868, in "Difficulties in Connection with the Cultivation of Indigo in Chumparun and Tirhoot," in Home Department Public Branch, 9 January 1869, No. 108/114, NAI.

50. Letter from Capitán General of Caracas, Manuel de Guevara Vasconcelos, to the King, Caracas, 29 January 1802, No. 41, and copy of a letter from Capitán General of Caracas, Manuel de Guevara, to the State and War Ministers, Caracas, 31 January 1801, in AGI, Estado, 59, No. 14: Capitán General Caracas sobre los sucesos de Santo Domingo, 127 fols., AGI; Robert Paquette, "Revolutionary Saint-Domingue in the Making of Territorial Louisiana," in *A Turbulent Time: The French Revolution and the Greater Caribbean*, ed. David B. Gaspar and David Geggus

(Indiana UP, 1997), 204–25; Julius S. Scott III, *The Common Wind: Currents of Afro-American Communication in the Era of the Haitian Revolution* (PhD. diss., Duke University 1986), 169; David Geggus, "Slave Rebellion During the Age of Revolution," in *Curaçao in the Age of Revolutions, 1795–1800*, ed. Wim Klooster and Geert Oostindie (KITLV Press, 2011); Pedro A. Gil Rivas, Luis Dovale Prado, and Lidia Lusmila Bello, *La insurrección de los negros de la sierra coriana, 10 de mayo de 1795* (Dirección de Cultura, 1996); Ramón Aizpurua, "La insurrección de los negros de la Serrania de Coro de 1795: Una revision necesaria," *Boltein de la Academia Nacional de la Historia*, 1988; Frederico Brito Figueroa, *Las insurreciones de los esclavos negros en la sociedad colonial venezolana* (Editorial Cantaclaro, 1961); Gloria García Rodríguez, *Conspiraciones y revueltas: La actividad política de los negros en Cuba (1790–1845)* (Editorial Oriente, 2003), 23–25; Ada Ferrer, *Freedom's Mirror: Cuba and Haiti in the Age of Revolution* (CUP, 2014); Michael Craton, *Testing the Chains: Resistance to Slavery in the British West Indies* (Cornell UP, 1982); and Douglas Egerton, *Gabriel's Rebellion: The Virginia Slave Conspiracies of 1800 and 1802* (University of North Carolina Press, 1993), 115, 187. As late as the 1840s, the memory of the Haitian Revolution was everywhere. See, for example, letter from the Municipal Council of Santiago de Cuba to the Queen, Santiago de Cuba, 14 May 1841, in AHN, Ultramar, 91, Exp. 3: Sobre remplazar con blancos los colonos de color (1841–1862), AGI.
51. João José Reis and Flavio dos Santos Gomes, "Repercussions of the Haitian Revolution in Brazil, 1791–1850," in *The World of the Haitian Revolution*, ed. David Geggus and Norman Fiering (Indiana UP, 2009), 284–313; and Stuart B. Schwartz, *Sugar Plantations in the Formation of Brazilian Society: Bahia, 1550–1835* (CUP, 1985), 482. For the quote, see George Reid Andrews, *Afro-Latin America, 1800–2000* (OUP, 2004), 68.
52. *The Report from a Select Committee of the House of Assembly Appointed to Inquire into the Origin, Causes, and Progress of the Late Insurrection* (Barbados: W. Walker, Mercury and Gazette Office, 1818), 4; Craton, *Testing the Chains*, 264–66; and Michael Craton, "The Passion to Exist: Slave Rebellions in the British West Indies," *Journal of Caribbean History* 13 (1980), 12–13.

53. Minuta de comunicación al Embajador, Palace, 23 April 1817, in Estado, 17, No. 42, AGI.
54. Minuta de comunicación al Embajador, Palace, 23 April 1817, AGI.
55. David Geggus, "Slave Rebellion During the Age of Revolution," in Klooster and Oostindie, *Curaçao in the Age of Revolutions*, 13, 24, 43; Egerton, *Gabriel's Rebellion*, 188; Schwartz, *Sugar Plantations in the Formation of Brazilian Society*, 482; Adam Rothman, *Slave Country: American Expansion and the Origins of the Deep South* (HUP, 2005), 108–17; Tommy R. Young, "The United States Army and the Institution of Slavery in Louisiana, 1803–1815," *Louisiana Studies* 13, no. 3 (1974); Gaspar and Geggus, *Turbulent Time*, 19, 127–30; Figueroa, *Las insurreciones*; Matt D. Childs, *The 1812 Aponte Rebellion in Cuba and the Struggle Against Atlantic Slavery* (University of North Carolina Press, 2006); John Lofton, *Insurrection in South Carolina: The Turbulent World of Denmark Vesey* (Antioch Press, 1964); John O. Killens, introduction to *The Trial Record of Denmark Vesey* (Beacon Press, 1970), 141–46, 156; and Michael Johnson, "Denmark Vesey and His Co-Conspirators," *William and Mary Quarterly* 58, no. 4 (2001).
56. For the quote ("grave insurrection"), see "Indes occidentales anglaises, Faits commerciaux. No. 1," from the series "Documens [*sic*] sur le commerce extérieur," Ministry of Agriculture and Commerce, March and April 1848, 17, in "Réunion," "Réponses relatives à la liquidation de l'indemnité," Fonds ministériels, K // 5, ANOM. On Demerara, see also Emília Viotti da Costa, *Crowns of Glory, Tears of Blood: The Demerara Slave Rebellion of 1823* (OUP, 1994).
57. Manuel Barcia, *Seeds of Insurrection: Domination and Resistance on Western Cuban Plantations, 1808–1848* (Louisiana State UP, 2008), 67; Rodríguez, *Conspiraciones y revueltas*; Manuel Barcia, *The Great African Slave Revolt of 1825: Cuba and the Fight for Freedom in Matanzas* (Louisiana State UP, 2012), 3, 5–6, 12, 22, 97–98, 103, 105, 107, 108, 113–14, 117–18, 126, 137–38; John K. Thornton as quoted in Barcia, *Great African Slave Revolt of 1825*, 119; Paul Lovejoy, "Identifying Enslaved Africans in the African Diaspora," in *Identity in the Shadow of Slavery*, ed. Paul Lovejoy (Continuum International, 2000), 7; Geggus, "Slave Rebellion." 46.
58. Barcia, *Great African Slave Revolt*, 148.

59. As cited in Barcia, *Great African Slave Revolt*, 52.
60. Nota en la que se manifesta haber pasado al despacho de S. E. un ofico del Ministerio de Marina, 11 July 1833, Estado, 17, No. 113: Nota Sobre la Insurrección de los Negros de la Jamaica, AGI; Mary Reckord, "The Jamaica Slave Rebellion of 1831," *Past & Present* 40, no. 1 (July 1968), 108–25; Edward Rugemer, *The Problem of Emancipation: The Caribbean Roots of the American Civil War* (Louisiana State UP, 2008), 115; and Craton, *Testing the Chains*, 291–321; Craton, "The Passion to Exist," 14–20.
61. Letter No. 1161, Ministerio del España, Francisco Tacón, to Manuel González Salmón, Secretario, dando cuenta de la insurrección de mulatos en Santo Domingo de negros en la Antigua y Guadalupe, 28 April 1831, Estado, 95, No. 38, Insurrección de negros y mulatos, AGI.
62. João José Reis, *Slave Rebellion in Brazil: The Muslim Uprising of 1835 in Bahia* (Johns Hopkins UP, 1993); and Schwartz, *Sugar Plantations in the Formation of Brazilian Society*, 487–88.
63. Barcia, *Great African Slave Revolt*, 47, 64–67; Matthias Röhrig Assunção, "Elite Politics and Popular Rebellion in the Construction of Post-Colonial Order. The Case of Maranhão, Brazil (1820–41)," *Journal of Latin American Studies* 31, no. 1 (1999); Douglas R. Egerton, "Nat Turner in a Hemispheric Context," in *Nat Turner: A Slave Rebellion in History and Memory*, ed. Kenneth S. Greenberg (OUP, 2003), 134–47; Stephen B. Oates, *The Fires of Jubilee: Nat Turner's Fierce Rebellion* (Harper Perennial, 1990), 134–47; Eric Foner, ed., *Nat Turner* (Prentice Hall, 1971), 4–5; Letter No. 1161, AGI; Letter No. 1241, Ministerio de España, Francisco Tacón, to Manuel González Salmón, Secretario de Estado, dando cuenta de la revolución de los negros en la Isla de la Tortola, con decreto al dorso (s.f.), Philadelphia, 17 October 1831, Estado, 95, No. 64, Revolución en la Isla de la Tortola, AGI; Tâmis Parron, "A política de escravidão na era da liberdade: Estados Unidos, Brasil e Cuba, 1787–1846" (PhD diss., University of São Paulo, 2015), 313–17; and Markus Rediker, *The Amistad Rebellion: An Atlantic Odyssey of Slavery and Freedom* (Penguin Books, 2012), chap. 2.
64. El Tribunal de Comercio de La Habana (firman Jorge de Urtelegui, Nicolás Galcerán y Alejandro Morales) to la Regencia Provisional,

Havana, 30 March 1841, AHN, Ul-tramar, 91, Exp. 3, Sobre remplazar con blancos los colonos de color (1841–1862), AGI. See also Robert Paquette, *Sugar Is Made with Blood: The Conspiracy of La Escalera and the Conflict Between Empires over Slavery in Cuba* (Wesleyan UP, 1988); and Geggus, "Slave Rebellion," 47.

65. "Apoyando una sublevacion los esclavos incendian una hacienda," 1843, Ultramar, 5063, Exp. 40, AHN.

66. Aisha K. Finch, *Rethinking Slave Rebellion in Cuba: La Escalera and the Insurgencies of 1841–1844* (University of North Carolina Press, 2015), 82–83.

67. On this uprising, see "Expediente reservado sobre una sublevación de negros de varias fincas de Cuba," Ul-tramar, 8, Exp. 14, AHN.

68. Capitán General de la Isla de la Cuba to Madrid to [missing], Havana, 16 January 1844, in "Expediente reservado sobre una sublevación de negros de varias fincas de Cuba," Ultramar, 8, Exp. 14, AHN. On the connection between the uprising and the harvest, see Civil Governor of Havana to the Secretary of State in Madrid, Havana, 21 December 1843, in "Expediente reservado sobre una sublevación de negros de varias fincas de Cuba," Ultramar, 8, Exp. 14, AHN. See also Finch, *Re-thinking Slave Rebellion in Cuba*, 84–85, 87.

69. Letter from Civil Governor of Havana (Leopoldo O'Donnell) to the Secretary of State in Madrid, Havana, 8 November 1843, in "Ex-pediente reservado sobre una sub-levacion de negros de varias fincas de Cuba," Ultramar, 8, Exp. 14, AHN; and Finch, *Rethinking Slave Rebel-lion in Cuba*, 88–92, 100.

70. Finch, *Rethinking Slave Rebellion in Cuba*, 96–97, 102, 186.

71. Finch, *Rethinking Slave Rebellion in Cuba*, 146.

72. Finch, *Rethinking Slave Rebellion in Cuba*, 1, 3, 9, 55, 79, 115, 120, 135, 145, 147, 171, 176, 180, 183. The role of free Black Cubans is also observed in "Expediente reservado sobre una sublevación de negros de varias fincas de Cuba," Ultramar, 8, Exp. 14, AHN. See also Letter No. 99, Civil Governor of Havana (Leo-poldo O'Donnell) to the Secretary of State in Madrid, Havana, 5 April 1844, AHN.

73. Letter from Civil Governor of Havana (Leopoldo O'Donnell) to the Secretary of State in Madrid, Havana, 8 November 1843, AHN. On the number of insurgents, see Finch, *Rethinking Slave Rebellion in*

Cuba, 91–92, 146; letter from Capitán General de la Isla de la Cuba to Madrid, 16 January 1844, AHN. See also letter from Civil Governor of Havana (Leopoldo O'Donnell) to the Secretary of State in Madrid, Havana, 8 November 1843, AHN.

74. Letter from Capitán General de la Isla de la Cuba to Madrid, 16 Jan-uary 1844, AHN.

75. For the original quote, see Letter No. 99, Civil Governor of Havana (Leopoldo O'Donnell) to the Secre-tary of State in Madrid, Havana, 5 April 1844, AHN.

76. Letter No. 110, Civil Governor of Havana (Leopoldo O'Donnell) to the Secretary of State in Madrid, Havana, 30 April 1844, in "Expedi-ente reservado sobre una sublevación de negros de varias fincas de Cuba," Ultramar, 8, Exp. 14, AHN.

77. Finch, *Rethinking Slave Rebellion in Cuba*, 5, 9.

78. Letter No. 110, Civil Governor of Havana (Leopoldo O'Donnell) to the Secretary of State in Madrid, Havana, 30 April 1844, AHN.

79. Finch, *Rethinking Slave Rebellion in Cuba*, 2.

80. Letter from [unclear] to Capitán General de la Isla de Cuba, Madrid, 23 February 1844, in "Expediente reservado sobre una sublevación de negros de varias fincas de Cuba," Ul-tramar, 8, Exp. 14, AHN; and Finch, *Rethinking Slave Rebellion in Cuba*, 1.

81. Civil Governor of Havana (Leo-poldo O'Donnell) to the Secretary of State in Madrid, Havana, 31 De-cember 1843, "Expediente reservado sobre una sublevación de negros de varias fincas de Cuba," Ultramar, 8, Exp. 14, AHN; and Paquette, *Sugar Is Made with Blood*, 229.

82. W. E. B. Du Bois, *Black Recon-struction in America: An Essay Toward a History of the Part Which Black Folk Played in the Attempt to Reconstruct Democracy in America, 1860–1880* (Russell & Russell, 1935), 55–83; Stephanie McCurry, *Confederate Reckoning: Power and Politics in the Civil War* (HUP, 2010).

83. As cited in Samantha Payne, "The Last Atlantic Revolution: Re-construction and the Struggle for Democracy in the Americas, 1861–1912" (PhD diss., HUP, 2022), 57.

84. Paul Butel, *Histoire des Antilles françaises: XVIIe–XXe siècle* (Perrin, 2002), 291–94; Neville A. T. Hall, *Slave Society in the Danish West Indies: St. Thomas, St. John, and St. Croix* (Johns Hopkins UP, 1992), 208–11; Eugène-Edouard Boyer-Peyreleau, *Les Antilles françaises, particulière-ment la Guadeloupe, depuis leur décou-*

verte jusqu'au 1er Janvier, 1823, vol. 3 (Paris: 1823), 421; João José Reis, "The Revolution of the Ganhadores: Urban Labour, Ethnicity and the African Strike of 1857 in Bahia, Bra-zil," *Journal of Latin American Studies* 29, no. 2 (May 1997), 355–93; Isa-dora Mota, "On the Imminence of Emancipation: Black Geopolitical Literacy and Anglo-American Abo-litionism in Nineteenth-Century Brazil" (PhD diss., Brown Univer-sity, 2017); Clícea Maria Augusto de Miranda, "Repercussões da Guerra Civil americana no destino da es-cravidão no Brasil—1861–1888" (PhD diss., University of São Paulo, 2017); Martha Rebelatto, "Uma saída pelo mar: Rotas marítimas de fuga escrava em Santa Catarina no século XIX," *Revista de Ciências Hu-manas*, no. 40 (November 2006): 423–42; Walter F. Piazza, *A es-cravidão negra numa província per-ifèrica* (Garapuvu, 1999); and Payne, "Last Atlantic Revolution," chapter 1. On the number of casualties, see "Civil War Casualties. The Cost of War: Killed, Wounded, Captured, and Missing," last modified Septem-ber 15, 2023, https://www.battle fields.org/learn/articles/civil-war -casualties. See also Rugemer, *Prob-lem of Emancipation*, 291–93; and Payne, "Last Atlantic Revolution," 55–57. Mass slave insurrection and flight in Cuba begins with the Ten Years' War in October of 1868. See Rebecca Scott, *Slave Emancipation in Cuba: The Transition to Free Labor, 1860–1899* (University of Pittsburgh Press, 2000), 116–24; Rebecca Scott, *Degrees of Freedom: Louisiana and Cuba After Slavery* (Belknap, 2005), 106–9; Ada Ferrer, *Insurgent Cuba: Race, Nation, and Revolution, 1868–1898* (University of North Carolina Press, 1999), 76–89; Ramiro Guerra Sánchez, *Guerra de los Diez Años*, vol. 1, book 1 (Editorial de Ciencias So-ciales, 1950), 34–54; Arthur Cor-win, *Spain and the Abolition of Slavery in Cuba, 1817–1886* (University of Texas Press, 1967), 149; Emilia Vi-otti da Costa, *Da senzala à colônia* (Livraria Editora Ciências Hu-manas, 1982), 324–28; Robert Brent Toplin, *The Abolition of Slavery in Brazil* (Atheneum, 1975), 194–246; Robert Edgar Conrad, *The Destruc-tion of Brazilian Slavery, 1850–1888* (Krieger Publishing Company, 1993), 230–77; Sidney Chalhoub, "The Politics of Ambiguity: Condi-tional Manumission, Labor Con-tracts, and Slave Emancipation in Brazil (1850s–1888)," *International Review of Social History* 60, no. 2 (2015), 207–14; Maria Helena P. T.

Machado, *Crime e escravidão: Trabalho, luta e resistência nas lavouras paulistas, 1830–1888* (Editora Brasiliense, 1987), 14, 39–40, 49; Maria Helena P. T. Machado, *O plano e o pânico: Os movimentos sociais na década da abolição* (Rio de Janeiro: Editora UFRJ; São Paulo: EDUSP, 1994); Angela Alonso, *Flores, votos e balas: O movimento abolicionista brasileiro (1868–88)* (Companhia das Letras, 2015), 326–29, 335; Samantha Payne, "A General Insurrection in the Countries with Slaves: The US Civil War and the Origins of an Atlantic Revolution, 1861–1866," *Past & Present* 257 (November 2022): 248–79.

85. Sartono Kartodirdjo, "The Peasants' Revolt of Banten in 1888: Its Conditions, Course and Sequel" (PhD diss., University of Amsterdam, 1966), 1–2, 33–41, 43, 45–46, 104–6, 115, 118–19, 122, 127–28, 172–75.

86. Kartodirdjo, "Peasants' Revolt of Banten," 176, 198, 214–17, 221, 235, 239, 279.

87. On that confrontation, see *Gazeta Krakowska*, no. 44–45 (February 1846); and *Gazeta Krakowska*, no. 46 (March 1846). For a contemporary account of these events, see *Österreichischer Beobachter*, August 14, 1847, 914–16. For citational material, see Larry Wolff, *The Idea of Galicia: History and Fantasy in Habsburg Political Culture* (Stanford UP, 2010), 144; Bartosz Ogórek, "Galicia's Escape from the Malthusian Trap: A Long and Short-Term Analysis of the Demographic Response to Economic Conditions in the Population of Galicia 1819–1913," in *Roczniki Dziejów Społecznych i Gospodarczych* 75 (2015): 96; and Stanislaw Hoszowski, *Ceny we Lwowie w latach 1701–1914. Les prix a Lwów de 701 a 1914 z 19 diagramami* (Skład Główny, 1934). For a fictional description of that poverty, see Leopold Sacher-Masoch, *Graf Donski: Eine galizische Geschichte, 1846* (Schaffhausen, Switzerland: Verlag der Hurter'schen Buchhandlung, 1864), 192.

88. Wolff, *Idea of Galicia*, 142–43; Hans Henning Hahn, "The Polish Nation in the Revolution of 1846–49," in *Europe in 1848: Revolution and Reform*, ed. Dieter Dowe, Heinz-Gerhard Haupt, Dieter Langewiesche, and Jonathan Sperber, trans. David Higgins (Berghahn Books, 2001), 173; Michał Tymowski, Jan Kieniewicz, and Jerzy Holzer, *Historia Polski* (Inicjatywa Wydawnicza Aspekt, 1986), 234.

89. Sacher-Masoch, *Graf Donski*, 367, 419.

90. Bernard Michel, *Sacher-Masoch, 1836–1895* (Éditions Robert Laffont, 1989), 56, 63.

91. For the quote, see *Kemptner Zeitung*, July 2, 1847, 2.

92. Wolff, *Idea of Galicia*, 142, 148.

93. The *Österreichischer Beobachter* was translated in *Gazeta Krakowska* 50, no. 10 (March 1846), and then again translated and cited in Wolff, *Idea of Galicia*, 150.

94. Charles Maier, *Leviathan 2.0: Inventing Modern Statehood* (Belknap Press of HUP, 2012), 35, 47; Kumari Jayawardena, *Class, Patriarchy and Ethnicity on Sri Lankan Plantations: Two Centuries of Power and Protest*, ed. Kumari Jayawardena and Rachel Kurian (Orient Blackswan, 2015), 58–59; M. Şükrü Hanioğlu, *A Brief History of the Late Ottoman Empire* (PUP, 2008), 66; Khaled Fahmy, *All the Pasha's Men: Mehmed Ali, His Army, and the Making of Modern Egypt* (CUP, 1997), 265; Dominique Chevallier, "Aspects sociaux de la Question d'Orient: Aux origines des troubles agraires libanais en 1858," in *Annales: Histoire, Sciences Sociales* 14, no. 1 (March 1959), 35–64, esp. 52–54; Marwan Buheiry, "The Peasant Revolt of 1858 in Mount Lebanon: Rising Expectations, Economic Malaise and the Incentive to Arm," in *Land Tenure and Social Transformation in the Middle East*, ed. Tarif Khalidi (American University of Beirut, 1984), 291–301; Yehoshua Porath, "The Peasant Revolt of 1858–1861 in Kisrawan," *Asian and African Studies* 2 (1966): 77–157; and Kären Wigen, *The Making of a Japanese Periphery, 1750–1920* (University of California Press, 1995), 170. See also Andrew Phemister, "Natural Harmony and 'True Civilization': The Ideological Impact of the Irish Land League on Anglo-American Liberalism," in *Agrarian Reform and Resistance in an Age of Globalisation*, ed. Joe Regan and Cathal Smith (Routledge, 2019), 75–89; Cecilia G. Méndez, *Los trabajadores guaneros del Peru, 1840–1879* (Universidad Nacional Mayor de San Marcos, 1987), 62–65; and Hendrik Snyders, "From Peru to Ichaboe: The Dynamics of a Shifting Guano Frontier, 1840–5," *African Historical Review* 48, no. 2 (2016): 15.

95. Ranajit Guha, as cited in Dipesh Chakrabarty, *Provincializing Europe: Postcolonial Thought and Historical Difference* (PUP, 2000), 14.

96. Cited in Dinyar Patel, *Naoroji: Pioneer of Indian Nationalism* (HUP, 2020), 200. See also Oster-

hammel, *Die Verwandlung der Welt*, 790.

97. Rudrangshu Mukherjee, *Awadh in Revolt, 1857–1858: A Study of Popular Resistance* (Anthem Press, 2002), 62–63, 156, 158, 164–66, 168–69.

98. "Proclamation," as quoted in Mukherjee, *Awadh in Revolt*, 148.

99. Tithi Bhattacharya, "Sacred Thirst: Producing Tea, Producing People in Colonial Bengal," paper (in author's possession) presented at the Weatherhead Center for International Affairs Global History Seminar, Harvard University, 2020; James C. Scott, *Seeing Like a State: How Certain Schemes to Improve the Human Condition Have Failed* (Yale UP, 1998), 89, 93, 343, 348; John Tutino, *The Mexican Heartland: How Communities Shaped Capitalism, a Nation, and World History, 1500–2000* (PUP, 2017); and Herzig, *Unterschichtenprotest in Deutschland*, 27–29.

100. Karl Marx, *Eighteenth Brumaire of Louis Bonaparte*, trans. Eden Paul and Cedar Paul (International Publishers, 1926), 127–44.

101. Eugene Ridings, "Business Associationalism, the Legitimation of Enterprise, and the Emergence of a Business Elite in Nineteenth-Century Brazil," *Business History Review* 63, no 4. (1989): 794; Hamerow, *Social Foundations of German Unification*, 152–53.

102. *Die Verhandlungen des Vierten Congresses Deutscher Volkswirthe zu Stuttgart, am 9., 10., 11. und 12. September 1861* (Stuttgart: Congress Deutscher Volkswirthe, 1861), 36.

103. Hamerow, *Social Foundations of German Unification*, 54–55.

104. Georg Büchner and Friedrich Ludwig Weidig, *Der Hessische Landbote* (Offenbach am Main, Germany: 1834), as quoted in and translated by Christopher Clark, *Revolutionary Spring: Europe Aflame and the Fight for a New World, 1848–1849* (Crown, 2023), 198.

105. As cited in Hamerow, *Social Foundations of German Unification*, 135.

106. "Eingabe von Gewerken des westfälischen Oberbergamtsbezirks an das Finanzministerium vom 27.6.1848," as quoted in Clemens Wischermann, *Preußischer Staat und Westfälische Unternehmer zwischen Spätmerkantilismus und Liberalismus* (Böhlau, 1992), 236.

107. Carlo Cattaneo, *Civilization and Democracy: The Salvemini Anthology of Cattaneo's Writings*, ed. Carlo G. Lacaita and Filippo Sa-

betti, trans. David Gibbons (Toronto UP, 2006); 109.
108. Hamerow, *Social Foundations of German Unification*, 136–37. For bourgeois critiques of the old regime, see also the brilliant Sewell, *Capitalism and the Emergence of Civic Equality*, 12–13; Cattaneo, *Civilization and Democracy*, 103–5, 116.
109. Sperber, *Rhineland Radicals*, 53, 60, 62, 254–56, 264–65, 270–71.
110. Hamerow, *Social Foundations of German Unification*, 96–99.
111. As cited in Hamerow, *Social Foundations of German Unification*, 97, 106–7.
112. "Die Forderungen der entschiedenen Verfassungsfreunde am 12. September 1847," as reprinted in Franz Huber, *Der 47er Ruf aus Offenburg. Die Versammlung Entschiedener Verfassungsfreunde am 12. September 1847 in Offenburg* (Druck u. Verlag Graph. Werkstätte, 1931), 25–27.
113. Hamerow, *Social Foundations of German Unification*, 96, 98, 159, 161; Das Heppenheimer Programm der südwestdeutschen Liberalen, October 10, 1847, as reprinted in *Dokumente zur deutschen Verfassungsgeschichte: Deutsche Verfassungsdokumente 1803–1850*, ed. Ernst Rudolf Huber (W. Kohlhammer, 1978), 324–26. See also Christof Dejung, David Motadel, and Jürgen Osterhammel, "Worlds of the Bourgeoise," in *The Global Bourgeoisie: The Rise of the Middle Classes in the Age of Empire*, ed. Christof Dejung, David Motadel, and Jürgen Osterhammel, (PUP, 2019), 20.
114. James J. Sheehan, *Der Deutsche Liberalismus: Von den Anfängen im 18. Jahrhundert bis zum Ersten Weltkrieg, 1770–1914* (C. H. Beck, 1983), 21. On the Asian Enlightenment, see Sebastian Conrad, "Enlightenment in Global History: A Historiographical Critique," *AHR* 117, no. 4 (October 2012): 999–1027.
115. Ridings, "Business Associationalism," 780.
116. As cited in Samuel Hayat, "The Revolution of 1848 in the History of French Republicanism," *History of Political Thought* 36, no. 2 (2015): 349.
117. Jonathan Sperber, *The European Revolutions, 1848–1851* (CUP, 2005), 175; Sperber, *Rhineland Radicals*, 92–94; R. J. W. Evans, "Liberalism, Nationalism, and the Coming of the Revolution," in Robert Evans and Hartmut Pogge von Strandmann, *The Revolutions in Europe, 1848–1849* (OUP, 2000), 18–19; Sperber, *European Revolutions*, 72, 108, 127, 196, 198, 202–4; Wolfgang J. Mommsen, *1848, die ungewollte Revolution: Die revolutionären Bewegungen in Europa*

1830–1849 (S. Fischer, 1998), 17; Charles Tilly, *Contention and Democracy in Europe, 1650–2000* (CUP, 2004), 15–6, 121, 166.
118. The importance of nation-building to this process is also emphasized by A. G. Hopkins, *American Empire: A Global History* (PUP, 2018), 249. See also Sperber, *Rhineland Radicals*, 469; and Hamerow, *Social Foundations of German Unification*, 95, 144.
119. Ridings, "Business Associationalism," 773.
120. Cattaneo, *Civilization and Democracy*, 191.
121. Cattaneo, *Civilization and Democracy*, 202, 214.
122. Ridings, "Business Associationalism," 785–86. For a summary of these debates, see Hans-Ulrich Wehler, *Deutsche Gesellschaftsgeschichte, 1815–1848/9* (C. H. Beck, 1987), 742–45.
123. Confidential Circular, Union League Club, New York, 15 January 1863, as quoted in Henry W. Bellows, *Historical Sketch of the Union League Club of New York: Its Origin, Organization, and Work, 1863–1879* (New York: Club House, 1879), 21–22. See also Paul Migliore, "The Business of Union: The New York Business Community and the Civil War" (PhD. diss., Columbia University, 1975), 176; and "Entry of December 6, 1862," in *The Diary of George Templeton Strong*, ed. Allans Nevins and Milton Halsey Thomas, vol. 3 (Octagon Books, 1974), 224, 276.
124. For the quote, see Jürgen Osterhammel, *Die Verwandlung der Welt: Eine Geschichte des 19. Jahrhunderts* (C. H. Beck, 2009), 778. See also Hamerow, *Social Foundations of German Unification*, 65–66.
125. On the French Revolution, see Sewell, *Capitalism and the Emergence of Civic Equality*, 365–68.
126. As cited in Hayat, "Revolution of 1848 in the History of French Republicanism," 351; and Sigmund Neumann, "The Structure and Strategy of Revolution: 1848 and 1948," *Journal of Politics* 11, no. 3 (August 1949): 538.
127. Cattaneo, *Civilization and Democracy*, 214.
128. Kurt Weyland, "The Diffusion of Revolution: '1848' in Europe and Latin America," *International Organization* 63, no. 3 (2009): 391; Lawrence C. Jennings, *French Anti-Slavery: The Movement for the Abolition of Slavery in France, 1802–1848* (CUP, 2000), 282; Eric Hobsbawm, *The Age of Capital, 1848–1875* (Scribner, 1975), 10;

Sperber, *European Revolutions*, 148–50; Christopher Clark, *Iron Kingdom: The Rise and Downfall of Prussia, 1600–1947* (Belknap Press of HUP, 2006), 471; "Verfassung des Deutschen Reiches," *Reichs-Gesetz-Blatt*, no. 16 (April 1849), retrieved from "Westfälische Geschichte," accessed February 19, 2020, https://www.lwl.org/westfaelische-geschichte/portal/Internet/finde/langDatensatz.php?url ID=835&url_tabelle=tab_quelle; Thomas Maissen, "The 1848 Conflicts and Their Significance in Swiss Historiography," in *The Making of Modern Switzerland, 1848–1998*, ed. Michael Butler, Malcolm Pender, and Joy Charnley (St. Martin's Press, 2000), 13–14; Dominik Fugler, "The Swiss Economy: Facing the Future," in Butler et al., *Making of Modern Switzerland*, 124; Felix Bühlmann et al., "Elites in Switzerland: The Rise and Fall of a Model of Elite Coordination," *Tempo Social: Revista de Sociologia Da USP* 29, no. 3 (2017): 181; Jiří Kořalka, "Revolutionen in der Habsburgermonarchie," in *Europa 1848. Revolution und Reform*, ed. Dieter Dowe, Heinz-Gerhard Haupt, and Dieter Langewiesche (J. H. W. Dietz, 1998), 226; Gábór Gangó, "1848–1849 in Hungary," *Hungarian Studies*, 2001, 42.
129. Entry of July 2, 1848, as quoted in Ulrich Mücke, ed., *The Diary of Heinrich Witt*, vol. 4 (Brill, 2016), 191.
130. Few histories of the 1848 revolutions published in the past three decades refer explicitly to "bourgeois revolutions." Many have instead emphasized the "complexity of 1848," pointing to the variety of political ideologies, the diversity of the middle classes, and the salience of non-economic demands. This has been accompanied by a shift away from the bourgeoisies and industrial workers of Paris, Berlin, and Vienna—the traditional protagonists in the historiography of 1848—and toward artisans, rural workers, innkeepers, and landowners. See Hartmut Pogge von Strandmann, "1848–1849: A European Revolution?," in Evans and Pogge, *Revolutions in Europe*, 8; Sperber, *European Revolutions*, 271; Weyland, "Diffusion of Revolution," 392; Mike Rapport, *1848: Year of Revolution* (Basic Books, 2008), 32; Charles Pouthas, "Die Komplexität von 1848," in *Die Europäischen Revolutionen von 1848*, ed. Horst Stuke and Wilfried Forstmann (Verlagsgruppe Athenäum, Hain, Scriptor, Hanstein, 1979);

Heinz-Gerhard Haupt and Dieter Langewiesche, "Die Revolution in Europa 1848. Reform der Herrschafts- und Gesellschaftsordnung—Nationalrevolution—Wirkungen," in Dowe, Haupt, and Langewiesche, *Europa 1848*, 21; Neil Davidson, *How Revolutionary Were the Bourgeois Revolutions?* (Haymarket Books, 2012); Heide Gerstenberger, "'How Bourgeois Were the Bourgeois Revolutions?,' Remarks on Neil Davidson's Book," *Historical Materialism: Research in Critical Marxist Theory* 27, no. 3 (2019): 206; Gareth Stedman Jones, "Society and Politics at the Beginning of the World Economy," *Cambridge Journal of Economics* 1, no. 1 (1977): 88; and Charles Post, "How Capitalist Were the 'Bourgeois Revolutions'?," *Historical Materialism: Research in Critical Marxist Theory* 27, no. 3 (2019): 89. For a wonderful discussion of the criticism launched against Marxist interpretations of the French Revolution, see Sewell, *Capitalism and the Emergence of Civic Equality*, 53–70.
131. Sperber, *Rhineland Radicals*, 144, 151; Sheehan, *Der Deutsche Liberalismus*, 31, 69; Hans Fenske, *Quellen zur deutschen Revolution 1848–1849* (Wissenschaftliche Buchgesellschaft, 1996), 8; and Sewell, *Capitalism and the Emergence of Civic Equality*, 167. Regarding the composition of elected representatives, the precise figures are 9.4 percent and 35 percent, respectively.
132. John Sagers, "Shibusawa Eiichi, Dai Ichi Bank, and the Spirit of Japanese Capitalism, 1860–1930," in *Shashi: The Journal of Japanese Business and Company History* 3, no. 1 (2011): 3, 4
133. Sagers, "Shibusawa Eiichi, Dai Ichi Bank, and the Spirit of Japanese Capitalism," 4.
134. Some of these debates on the bourgeois nature of the Meiji Restauration are summarized in Germaine A. Hoston, "Conceptualizing Bourgeois Revolution: The Prewar Japanese Left and the Meiji Restoration," *Comparative Studies in Society and History* 33, no. 3 (1991): 539–81.
135. Maik Hendrik Sproite, "Zivilgesellschaft als staatliche Veranstaltung? Eine Spurensuche im Japan vor 1945," in *Bürger und Staat in Japan*, ed. Gesine Foljanty-Jost and Momoyo Hüstebeck (UV Halle-Wittenberg, 2013), 89–129; Hiroshi Mitani, "Die Formierung von Öffentlichkeit in Japan: Eine Bilanz in vergleichender Perspektive," in Foljanty-Jost and Hüstebeck *Bürger und Staat in Japan*, 43; Sagers,

"Shibusawa Eiichi, Dai Ichi Bank, and the Spirit of Japanese Capitalism," 4; Gesine Foljanty-Jost and Momoyo Hüstebeck, "Bürgerinnen und Staat in Japan: Eine Einfüehrung," in *Bürger und Staat in Japan*, 9; and Mitani, "Die Formierung von Öffentlichkeit in Japan," 45–46.
136. Hamerow, *Social Foundations of German Unification*, 96; and Marcello Mustè, *Rivoluzioni passive. Il mondo tra le due guerre nei Quaderni del carcere di Gramsci* (Viella, 2022).
137. Hamerow, *Social Foundations of German Unification*, 95; Osterhammel, *Die Verwandlung der Welt*, 780; and David Blackbourn and Geoffrey Eley, *The Peculiarities of German History, Bourgeois Society and Politics in Nineteenth-Century Germany* (OUP, 1984), 13.
138. Victor Böhmert, *Rückblicke und Ausblicke eines Siebzigers* (Böhmert, 1900), 14.
139. The most brilliant critique of the concept of "bourgeois revolution"—in Germany and beyond—is Blackbourn and Eley, *Peculiarities of German History*. See, for example, page 144 for an explicit argument about Germany's "successful bourgeois revolution." See also Hamerow, *Social Foundations of German Unification*, 95, 139, 309; Blackbourn and Eley, *Peculiarities of German History*, 164, 176, 178, 181–82, 191–92; and Duncan Kennedy, "Three Globalizations of Law and Legal Thought, 1850–2000," in *The New Law and Economic Development: A Critical Appraisal*, ed. David M. Trubek and Alvaro Santos (CUP, 2006), 19, 20, 22–23, 26, 29, 35.
140. Lydia Maria Child, *Letters from New York: Second Series* (New York: C. S. Francis & Co., 1846), 280.
141. See the fascinating study by Lukas Rieppel, *Assembling the Dinosaur: Fossil Hunters, Tycoons, and the Making of a Spectacle* (HUP, 2019), 73–109.
142. Patel, *Naoroji*, 69.
143. Patel, *Naoroji*, 55–57; Dadabhai Naoroji, "The Poverty of India," in *Papers Read Before the Bombay Branch of the East India Association* (Mumbai: Ranima Union Press, 1876), 1.
144. Patel, *Naoroji*, 47, 52–54, 59–61, 66, 100, 107, 126–28, 158.
145. As cited in Arthur Waley, *The Opium War Through Chinese Eyes* (Stanford UP, 1968), 33.
146. For the quote, see James Africanus Horton, *West African Countries and Peoples British and Natives, with the Requirements Necessary for Establishing That Self-Government Recommended by the Committee of the House of Commons, 1865; and a Vindication*

of the African Race (London: W. J. Johnson, 1868). On Horton, see A. A. Boahen, "New Trends and Processes in Africa in the Nineteenth Century," in *General History of Africa*, vol. 6, *Africa in the Nineteenth Century Until the 1880s*, ed. J. F. Ade Ajayi and the UNESCO International Scientific Committee for the Drafting of a General History of Africa (UNESCO, 1989), 53.
147. Boahen, "New Trends and Processes in Africa," 54–55.
148. Robert Gildea, "1848 in European Collective Memory," in Evans and Pogge, *Revolutions in Europe*, 232.
149. Jennings, *French Anti-Slavery*, 278.
150. Jennings, 282–83; David Brian Davis, *The Problem of Slavery in the Age of Revolution, 1770–1823* (Cornell UP, 1975).
151. See *Gazette officielle de la Guadeloupe*, February 1848, 1.
152. Karl Marx, *Capital: A Critical Analysis of Capitalist Production*, ed. Frederick Engels, trans. Samuel Moore and Edward Aveling (Swan Sonnenschien & Co., 1906), 287. For the anti-capitalist proclivities of some abolitionists, see also Manisha Sinha, "The Problem of Abolition in the Age of Capitalism: The Problem of Slavery in the Age of Revolution, 1770–1823, by David Brion Davis," *AHR* 124, no. 1 (February 2019): 159.
153. See the brilliant Tâmis Parron, "The British Empire and the Suppression of the Slave Trade to Brazil: A Global History Analysis," *Journal of World History* 29, no. 1 (2018): 21–26.
154. Sven Beckert, *The Monied Metropolis: New York City and the Consolidation of the American Bourgeoisie, 1850–1896* (CUP, 2001), 85–97; and Don Doyle, *The Cause of All Nations: An International History of the American Civil War* (Basic Books, 2015), 301.
155. King, *Blue Mutiny*, 85–86, 91, 108; Finch, *Rethinking Slave Rebellion in Cuba*, 5.
156. As cited in Thomas N. Brown, *Irish-American Nationalism, 1870–1879* (J. B. Lippincott, 1966), 108.
157. Mervyn Busteed, *The Irish in Manchester, c. 1750–1921: Resistance, Adaptation and Identity* (Manchester UP, 2016), 5, 224; and Patel, *Naoroji*, 84, 132, 136, 161–64.
158. Walter Bagehot, "Principles of Political Economy," in *The Works and Life of Walter Bagehot*, ed. Russell Barrington, vol. 8 (Longman, Green & Co., 1915), 218–19.

159. Geoffrey Ellis, "The Revolution of 1848–1849 in France," in Evans and Pogge, *Revolutions in Europe*, 42; and Sperber, *European Revolutions*, 213.

160. Entry of July 8, 1848, as quoted in Mücke, *Diary of Heinrich Witt*, 4:196.

161. Entry of June 1, 1848, as quoted in Mücke, *Diary of Heinrich Witt*, 4:177.

162. Entry of July 2, 1848, as quoted in Mücke, *Diary of Heinrich Witt*, 4:193.

163. Entry of June 1, 1848, as quoted in Mücke, *Diary of Heinrich Witt*, 4:177; and entry of April 6, 1848, as quoted in Mücke, 4:181.

164. Entry of September 10, 1849, as quoted in Mücke, *Diary of Heinrich Witt*, 4:345.

165. Entry of October 9 to October 13, 1849, as quoted in Mücke, *Diary of Heinrich Witt*, 4:353.

166. For evidence, see Ciarán O'Murchadha, *The Great Famine: Ireland's Agony 1845–1852* (Continuum 2011), 48. See also Brueggemeier, *Grubengold*, 81; Herzig, *Unterschichtenprotest in Deutschland*, 24; Way, *Common Labour*, 205; and Blackbourn and Eley, *Peculiarities of German History*, 174.

167. Blackbourn and Eley, *Peculiarities of German History*, 241.

168. Martin Breaugh, *The Plebeian Experience: A Discontinuous History of Political Freedom*, trans. Lazer Lederhendler (Columbia UP, 2013), 183.

169. Entry of April 29, 1871, as quoted in Mücke, *Diary of Heinrich Witt*, 4:206.

170. Entry of June 4, 1871, as quoted in Mücke, *Diary of Heinrich Witt*, 7:212.

171. Entry of June 16, 1871, as quoted in Mücke, *Diary of Heinrich Witt*, 7:214.

172. Edmond de Goncourt and Jules de Goncourt, *Journal des Goncourt*, vol. 4 (Paris: Bibliothèque Charpentier, 1890), 239.

173. Gemeente Amsterdam Stadsarchief, "Archief van de Familie Boissevain en Aanverwante Families," 394.107P, scans 15–16.

174. "The Republic and the Commune," *Harper's Weekly*, July 1, 1871, 594–95.

175. "To Those, and They Must Be Very Many, Who Were Bewildered with the Story of the International Association," *Times* (of London), October 28, 1871.

176. Allan Pinkerton, *Strikers, Communists, Tramps and Detectives* (G. W. Carleton & Co., 1878), 78.

177. Jeffrey Needell, *The Party of Order: The Conservatives, the State, and Slavery in the Brazilian Monarchy, 1831–1871* (Stanford UP, 2006), 75.

178. Sven Beckert, "Democracy and Its Discontents: Contesting Suffrage Rights in Gilded Age New York," *Past & Present* 174, no. 1 (February 2002); and Jürgen Kocka, "Kapitalismus und Demokratie," *Archiv für Sozialgeschichte* 56 (2016): 41.

179. Odd Arne Westad, *The Cold War: A Global History* (Basic Books, 2017), 17; Fahad Ahmad Bishara, *A Sea of Debt: Law and Economic Life in the Western Indian Ocean, 1780–1950* (CUP, 2017), 116–17.

180. David Glasner, "Crisis of 1873," *Business Cycles and Depressions: An Encyclopedia*, ed. David Glasner (Routledge, 2013), 132–33. On the crisis, see also Hannah C. Davies, *Transatlantic Speculations: Globalization and the Panics of 1873* (Columbia UP, 2018).

181. Quoted in Eric Hobsbawm, *The Age of Empire, 1875–1914* (Pantheon Books, 1987), 34.

182. Fred Moseley, "Depression of 1873–1879," in *Business Cycles and Depressions: An Encyclopedia*, ed. David Glasner (Routledge, 2013), 148; Hobsbawm, *Age of Empire*, 62; and Şevket Pamuk, "The Ottoman Empire in the 'Great Depression' of 1873–1896," *JEH* 44, no. 1 (1984): 114.

183. "Canada: Québec, 26 Juin, 1875," *Journal de St-Roch*, June 26, 1875, as quoted in Guillaume Durou, "Il y a des gens d'humeur vagabonde qui déménagent tous les ans: Stratégies et mobilité sociale de la classe ouvrière de Québec durant la Longue Dépression de 1873," *Histoire Sociale* 51, no. 104 (2018): 213.

184. Ricardo Falcón, *La Primera Internacional y los orígenes del movimiento obrero en Argentina (1857–1879)* (Centro de Estudios Historico-Sociales de América Latina, 1980), 25; Amiya Bagchi, "The Great Depression (1873–96) and the Third World," in *India and the World Economy, 1850–1950*, ed. G. Balachandran (OUP, 2003), 165; and Moseley, "Depression of 1873–1879," 148–49.

185. See Kim Richardson, "Quebra-Quilos and Peasant Resistance: Peasants, Religion, and Politics in Nineteenth-Century Brazil" (PhD diss., Texas Tech University, 2008), 46–70, in author's possession; Roderick J. Barman, "The Brazilian Peasantry Reexamined: The Implications of the Quebra-Quilo Revolt, 1874–1875," *Hispanic American Historical Review* 57, no. 3 (August 1977): 401–24; Armando Souto Maior, *Quebra-Quilos: Lutas sociais no outono do império* (Companhia Editora Nacional, 1978); Kim Richardson, *Quebra-Quilos and Peasant Resistance: Peasants, Religion, and Politics in Nineteenth-Century Brazil* (University Press of America, 2011); and Herbert Bix, *Peasant Protest in Japan, 1590–1884* (Yale UP, 1986), 211–14.

186. Walt Whitman, "Years of the Modern," in *Leaves of Grass: Including Sands at Seventy, Good Bye My Fancy, Old Age Echoes, and a Backward Glance o'er Travel'd Roads* (Small, Maynard & Company, 1897), 370.

Chapter 11: Reconstructing Capital, 1870–1914

1. Inge Plettenberg, "Die Familie Röchling," in *Die Röchlings und die Völklinger Hütte*, ed. Meinrad Maria Grewenig (Springpunkt Verlag, 2014), 22–23.

2. Plettenberg, "Die Familie Röchling," 22; Richard Nutzinger, Hans Boehmer, and Otto Johannsen, eds., *50 Jahre Röchling Völklingen: Die Entwicklung eines Rheinischen Industrie-Unternehmens* (Gebr. Hofer A. G., 1931), 8; and Gerhard Seibold, *Röchling: Kontinuität im Wandel* (Thorbecke, 2001), 75–79.

3. Nutzinger, Boehmer, and Johannsen, *50 Jahre Röchling Völklingen*, 9; Seibold, *Röchling*, 69, 71, 80–81; Hendrik Kersten, "Carl Ludwig Röchling—Carl der Kühne," in Plettenberg, *Die Röchlings und die Völklinger Hütte*, 36.

4. Seibold, *Röchling*, 69, 71–72, 83, 115–16; Nutzinger, Boehmer, and Johannsen, *50 Jahre Röchling Völklingen*, 9; Kersten, "Carl Ludwig Röchling," 35; and Hans Horch, *Der Wandel der Gesellschafts- und Herrschaftsstrukturen in der Saarregion während der Industrialisierung (1740–1914)* (W. J. Röhrig Verlag, 1985), 223. The Röchlings eventually became a majority stakeholder in the mill that they acquired in 1862.

5. Robert Musil, *Der Mann ohne Eigenschaften*, vol. 1, *Kapitel 1–75* (Jung & Jung, 2016), 306. The translation is from Robert Musil, *The Man Without Qualities*, vol. 1, *A Sort of Introduction the Like of It Now Happens*, trans. Eithne Wilkins and Ernst Kaiser (Secker & Warburg, 1966), 226.

6. Seibold, *Röchling*, 80.

7. Kersten, "Carl Ludwig Röchling," 39; Nutzinger, Boehmer, and Johannsen, *50 Jahre Röchling Völklingen*, 13; Seibold, *Röchling*, 88, 97; Ralf Banken, *Die Industrialisierung der Saarregion 1815–1914*, vol. 2, *Take-Off-Phase und Hochindustrialisierung 1850–1914* (Franz Steiner,

2003), 307; Hubert Kesternich, *Aufstieg und Wandel: 140 Jahre Völklinger Hütte*, vol. 1, *1873–1945* (Blattlaus Verlag, 2015), 52, 60, 93, 134; Harald Glaser, *Auf Schicht und Daheim: Hüttenarbeit und Alltagsleben in Völklingen von der Gründerzeit der Hütte bis in die Sechziger Jahre* (Initiative Völklinger Hütte e.V., 1996), 5–6; RESW GmbH Personalwesen: Bewerbungen und Verschiedenes, 1897 bis 1900, Mappe, 1 C/K/64, Alter Bestand, VH; and Röchling to James W. Miller (Pittsburg), letter, Völklingen, April 23, 1898, VH.

8. Seibold, *Röchling*, 97; Glaser, *Auf Schicht und Daheim*, 5; Kesternich, *Aufstieg und Wandel*, 1:94.

9. Brief von Hermann Röchling an die Geschäftsstelle der Südwestdeutschen Eisen-Berufsgenossenschaft Saarbrücken, Völklingen den 18. März 1910, RESW GmbH, Abstinenz Bestrebung: Schriftwecksel, 1907–1910 D/K-21/95, Alter Bestand, VH; Seibold, *Röchling*, 89; Nutzinger et al., *50 Jahre Röchling Völklingen*, 92.

10. Seibold, *Röchling*, 96, 101.

11. Letter from Theodor Röchling to Carl Röchling, August 1881, as reprinted in Nutzinger et al., *50 Jahre Röchling Völklingen*, 15. Nutzinger et al., *50 Jahre Röchling Völklingen*, 48, 74; Seibold, *Röchling*, 72–74, 119–20, 140, 145–47, 152; and Bescheid des Bezirksausschusses, Trier, den 29. Juli 1913, an den Bürgermeister von Völklingen, Saar, Veranlagung der Teilhaber der Röchling'schen Eisen und Stahlwerke zur Gemeindeeinkommenssteuer, A 2206, SAV.

12. Seibold, *Röchling*, 84–85, 141–42; Horch, *Wandel der Gesellschafts- und Herrschaftsstrukturen*, 438–39; and Franz-Josef Brüggemeier, Michael Farrenkopf, und Heinrich Theodor Grütter, eds., *Das Zeitalter der Kohle: Eine europäische Geschichte* (Klartext, 2018), 165.

13. Seibold, *Röchling*, 110, 113.

14. Seibold, *Röchling*, 106.

15. The quotes are, in order, from Martin. J. Sklar, *The Corporate Reconstruction of American Capitalism, 1890–1916* (CUP, 1988), 4; Fernand Braudel, *Afterthoughts on Material Civilization and Capitalism* (Johns Hopkins UP, 1977); Joseph Schumpeter, *Capitalism, Socialism, and Democracy* (Harper & Brothers, 1942), 82–83. Sklar, *Corporate Reconstruction*, 13; and Alessandro Stanziani, "Labor and Historical Periodization of Capitalism," *ISHA Newsletter* 7, no. 1 (December 2018): 2.

16. Dipesh Chakrabarty, "The Climate of History: Four Theses," *Critical Inquiry* 35, no. 2 (January 2009):

206; Jairus Banaji, "Islam, the Mediterranean and the Rise of Capitalism," *Historical Materialism* 15 (2007): 53; Alessandro Stanziani, *Capital terre: Une histoire longue du monde d'après (XIIe–XXIe siècle)* (Payot, 2021); Jürgen Osterhammel, *Die Verwandlung der Welt: Eine Geschichte des 19. Jahrhunderts* (C. H. Beck, 2009), 112; Thomas Piketty, *A Brief History of Equality*, trans. Steven Rendall (HUP, 2022), 50–64; A. G. Hopkins, *American Empire: A Global History* (PUP, 2018), 241–42, 247–48; Pierre Gervais, "Capitalism and (or) Age of Commerce? A Brief Theoretical Introduction," *XVII-XVIII Revue de la Société d'études anglo-américaines des XVIIe et XVIIIe siècles* 77 (2020): 1–19; Arno Mayer, *The Persistence of the Old Regime: Europe to the Great War* (Pantheon, 1981), 20–21; and Odd Arne Westad, *The Cold War: A Global History* (Basic Books, 2017), 5. For the concept of a second great divergence, see Sven Beckert, "American Danger: United States Empire, Eurafrica, and the Territorialization of Industrial Capitalism, 1870–1950," *AHR* 122, no. 4 (October 2017), 1137–70. For the end of British hegemony, see Giovanni Arrighi, *The Long Twentieth Century: Money, Power and the Origins of Our Times* (Verso, 1994), 58.

17. The quotes are, in order, from William Dean Howells, *A Hazard of New Fortunes* (New York: Harper & Bros., 1889), 96, https://hdl.handle.net/2027/chi.42116029; and Émile Alfred Zola, *Money: [L'argent]*, trans. Ernest Alfred Vizetelly (Chatto & Windus, 1902), 72–73, 156, https://hdl.handle.net/2027/uva.x000274718; See also Émile Alfred Zola, *Germinal* (Paris: Charpentier, 1885); Oscar Wilde, *The Soul of Man Under Socialism*, ed. Robert Ross (Humphreys, 1912), 7–8; and Piketty, *Capital and Ideology*, 265.

18. Ivo Andrić, *Die Brücke über die Drina: Eine Wischegrader Chronik*, trans. Ernst E. Jonas (Carl Hanser, 1960), 237. Originally published in 1945. See also Angus Maddison, *The World Economy: A Millennial Perspective* (Development Centre of the Organisation for Economic Co-Operation and Development, 2001), 173; Jürgen Osterhammel, *The Transformation of the World: A Global History of the Nineteenth Century* (PUP, 2014), 655; Charles Maier, *Leviathan 2.0: Inventing Modern Statehood* (HUP, 2012), 86; Sven Beckert, *Empire of Cotton: A Global History* (Knopf, 2014), 261 278–79;

Gema Aparicio and Vicente Pinilla, "International Trade in Wheat and Other Cereals and the Collapse of the First Wave of Globalization, 1900–38," *JGH* 14, no. 1 (March 2019), 45, 47, 49. In Germany as a whole, production increased from 240,575 tons to 8,521,000 tons. See Otto Pflanze, *Bismarck and the Development of Germany*, vol. 3, *The Period of Fortification, 1880–1898* (PUP, 2014), 5; Mario Samper and Radin Fernando, "Appendix: Historical Statistics of Coffee Production and Trade from 1700 to 1969," in *The Global Coffee Economy in Africa, Asia and Latin America, 1500–1989*, ed. William Gervase Clarence-Smith and Steven Topik (CUP, 2003), 417; Ulbe Bosma, *The Sugar Plantation in India and Indonesia: Industrial Production, 1770–2010* (CUP, 2013), 29. In the Saar, pig-iron production increased from 6,633 tons in 1850 to 1,370,980 tons. See Banken, *Die Industrialisierung der Saarregion*, 285; and Seibold, *Röchling*, 143. For the 1870 number of cotton spindles, see Thomas Ellison, *The Cotton Trade of Great Britain: Including a History of the Liverpool Cotton Market and of the Liverpool Cotton Brokers' Association* (London: E. Wilson, 1886), 104. For the 1913 number, see "World's Consumption of All Kinds of Cotton, 1000s Running Bales, Data Assembled by John A. Todd," in Papers of John A. Todd, MD 230/44, Statistics of World Consumption of Cotton, 1910–1931, Liverpool Record Office, Liverpool, UK. The numbers are probably not entirely comparable, but they give a sense of the scale of the increase. The increases of world iron and world steel production are derived from my own calculations using data in Brian Mitchell, *International Historical Statistics* (Palgrave Macmillan, 2013), 838, 841, 846, 2676–77, 2680, 4052, 4056, 4060, 4067–68.

19. This amounts to 358 percent by value in constant prices. See "Growth of Global Exports, 1870," Our World in Data, https://ourworldindata.org/grapher/world-trade-exports-constant-prices?time=1870..1913, accessed December 8, 2020; Françoise Berger, "Iron and Steel," in *The Palgrave Dictionary of Transnational History: From the Mid-19th Century to the Present Day*, ed. Iriye Akira and Pierre-Yves Saunier (Palgrave Macmillan, 2009), 597–98; A. J. J. Latham and Larry Neal, "The International Market in Rice and Wheat, 1868–1914," *EHR* 36, no. 2

(May 1983), 278; Osterhammel, *Transformation of the World*, 719; and Andrea Giuntini, "Submarine Telegraphy as a Global Emerging Technology in the Second Half of the Nineteenth Century (1851–1902), *Storia Economica* 16, no. 2 (2013), 260, 266.

20. Eric Hobsbawm, *Age of Empire, 1875–1914* (Weidenfeld & Nicolson, 1987), 43.

21. Hobsbawm, *Age of Empire*, 35; James Livingston, *Pragmatism and the Political Economy of Cultural Revolution, 1850–1940* (University of North Carolina Press, 1994), 41.

22. Karl Marx, *Capital: A Critique of Political Economy*, vol. 1, trans. Ben Fowkes (Penguin, 1976), 506–7. See also Karl Marx, *Das Kapital. Kritik der Politischen Oekonomie*, vol. 1, *Der Produktionsprocess des Kapitals*, 3rd rev. ed. (Hamburg: Otto Meisner, 1883), 388–89; Hobsbawm, *Age of Empire*, 36–37; and Pflanze, *Bismarck and the Development of Germany*, 3:5, 9–10.

23. The investment figures for the Röchlings reflect the totals from 1881 to 1906. The multiplier is an estimate based on historical inflation data and exchange rates. See also Phil Scranton, *Endless Novelty: Specialty Production and American Industrialization, 1865–1925* (PUP, 1997).

24. Chris Evans and Göran Rydén, *Baltic Iron in the Atlantic World in the Eighteenth Century* (Koninklijke Brill, 2007), 32; Alfred D. Chandler Jr., *The Visible Hand: The Managerial Revolution in American Business* (HUP, 1977), chap. 3–5.

25. *The Derrick's Handbook of Petroleum* (Oil City, Pennsylvania: Derrick, 1898), 24, as quoted in: *Petroleum Investigation: Hearing Before a Subcommittee of the Committee on Interstate and Foreign Commerce, House of Representatives, Seventy-Sixth Congress, Third Session, on H. Res. 290 and H.R. 7372, to Promote the Conservation of Petroleum, to Provide for Cooperation with the States in Preventing the Waste of Petroleum, to Create an Office of Petroleum Conservation; to Amend the Act of February 22, 1935, as Amended, and for Other Purposes*, vol. 4 (US Government Printing Office, 1940), 1469. Alison Fleig Frank, *Oil Empire: Visions of Prosperity in Austrian Galicia* (HUP, 2005), 20, 92–93.

26. Louis C. Hunter and Lynwood Bryant, *A History of Industrial Power in the United States, 1730–1930*, vol. 3, *The Transmission of Power* (MIT Press, 1991), 191; John W. Howell and Henry Shroeder, *History of the Incandescent Lamp* (Maqua Company, 1927), 66–67; Chaim M. Rosenberg, *America at the Fair: Chicago's 1893 World's Columbian Exposition* (Arcadia, 2008); Robert L. Bradley Jr., *Edison to Enron: Energy Markets and Political Strategies* (John Wiley and Scrivener, 2011), 39–59; Quentin R. Skrabec, *George Westinghouse: Gentle Genius* (Algora, 2007), 97, 135; *Commercial and Financial Chronicle*, June 25, 1892, 1051; and John N. Ingham, *Biographical Dictionary of American Business Leaders, A–G* (Greenwood, 1983), 175.

27. *Handbuch der deutschen Aktiengesellschaften* 13 (1908/1909); Martin Fiedler, "Die 100 Größten Unternehmen in Deutschland—nach der Zahl ihrer Beschäftigten—1907, 1938, 1973 und 1995," *Zeitschrift für Unternehmensgeschichte* 44, no. 1 (1999): 44; Jürgen Kocka, *Unternehmensverwaltung und Angestelltenschaft am Beispiel Siemens 1847–1914: Zum Verhältnis von Kapitalismus und Bürokratie in der deutschen Industrialisierung* (Ernst Klett, 1969), 57–60, 119; Wilfried Feldenkirchen, *Werner von Siemens: Erfinder und internationaler Unternehmer* (Siemens AG, 1992), 79, 88–89; Wilfried Feldenkirchen, *Siemens 1918–1945* (Piper, 1995), 678; and Anton A. Huurdeman, *The Worldwide History of Telecommunications* (John Wiley & Sons, 2003), 125–26.

28. "Farming with Dynamite: A Few Hints to Farmers," accessed August 22, 2024, http://www.fourmilab.ch /etexts/www/dupont/FarmingWith Dynamite/Limage01.html; and John A. Munroe, *History of Delaware*, 5th ed. (University of Delaware Press, 2006), 138.

29. Imperial Chemical Industries PLC, Archives of Brunner, Mond and Company LTD and its subsidiaries, Cheshire Archives and Local Studies, Cheshire Record Office, National Archives, UK, http://dis covery.nationalarchives.gov.uk /details/r/110e9ce8-710e-48a7-a46d -d8045328faa3#0.

30. Derek Lewis and Ulrike Zitzlsperger, "Bayer AG," in *Historical Dictionary of Contemporary Germany* (Rowman & Littlefield, 2016), 92; Harry Braverman, *Labor and Monopoly Capitalism: The Degradation of Work in the Twentieth Century* (Monthly Review, 1974), 162; Bayer Global, "History: The Early Years, 1863–1881," accessed August 23, 2024, https://www.bayer.com/en /history/1863-1881; Charles C.

Mann and Mark L. Plummer, *The Aspirin Wars: Money, Medicine, and 100 Years of Rampant Competition* (Knopf, 1991), 27; Werner Abelshauser, *German Industry and Global Enterprise: BASF: The History of a Company* (CUP, 2003), 165.

31. William Cronon, *Nature's Metropolis: Chicago and the Great West* (W. W. Norton, 1992), 230–35; Chandler, *Visible Hand*, 299–302; James Livingston, *Pragmatism and the Political Economy of Cultural Revolution, 1850–1940* (University of North Carolina Press, 1994), 25; Richard Tedlow, *New and Improved: The Story of Mass Marketing in America* (Basic Books, 1990).

32. Braverman, *Labor and Monopoly Capitalism*, 156–67, 163–64. Nutzinger, Boehmer, and Johannsen, *50 Jahre Röchling*, 98; and "The Experimental Station," DuPont, accessed July 24, 2024, https://www.dupont .com/locations/wilmington-delaware -the-experimental-station.html.

33. George Orwell, *The Road to Wigan Pier* (Penguin UK, 2020), 18. Originally published in 1937. See also Paolo Malanima, "World Energy Consumption: A Database 1820–2018 (2020 revision)," accessed July 22, 2024, https://histe con.fas.harvard.edu/energyhistory /DATABASE%20World%20En ergy%20Consumption.pdf; Osterhammel, *Die Verwandlung der Welt*, 110; Vaclav Smil, *Energy Transitions: Global and National Perspectives*, 2nd ed. (Praeger, 2016), as quoted in Hannah Ritchie and Pablo Rosado, "Fossil Fuels," last revised January 2024, accessed August 23, 2024, https://our worldindata.org/fossil-fuels; and Spencer Weart, *The Discovery of Global Warming* (HUP: 2003), 7.

34. So argues Chandler, *Visible Hand*, 287–89, 315–39.

35. The quotes are, in order, from Sklar, *Corporate Reconstruction*, 17; E. Maschke, "Geran Cartels from 1873 to 1914," in *Essays in European Economic History 1789–1914*, ed. F. Crouzet, W. H. Chaloner and W. M. Stern (Edward Arnold, 1969), 243. For the German original of the quote, see Carl Duisberg, *Abhandlungen, Vorträge und Reden aus den Jahren 1882–1921* (Verlag Chemie, 1923), 344; Allan Nevins, *John D. Rockefeller*, vol. 1 (Scribner, 1959), 622; and Ray S. Baker and William E. Dodd, eds., *The Public Papers of Woodrow Wilson*, authorized ed., vol. 1, *College and State: Educational, Literary and Political Papers (1875–1913)* (Harper & Brothers, 1925), 328. Wilson's article "The Making of the

Nation" was originally published in *Atlantic Monthly* 80 (July 1897), 1–14. See also Rudolf Hilferding, *Organisierter Kapitalismus: Referat und Diskussion; Sozialdemokratischer Parteitag 1927 in Kiel* (Kiel, 1927); Braverman, *Labor and Monopoly Capitalism*; and Chandler, *Visible Hand*. For a historian who emphasized the fluidity of capital concentration, see Hobsbawm, *Age of Empire*, 44.

36. Chandler, *Visible Hand*, 486.

37. Ballard C. Campbell, *The Paradox of Power* (UP of Kansas, 2021), 100.

38. César J. Ayala, *American Sugar Kingdom: The Plantation Economy of the Spanish Caribbean, 1898–1934* (University of North Carolina Press, 1999), 31–37, 57; Susan Becker, *Multinationalität hat verschiedene Gesichter: Formen internationaler Unternehmenstätigkeit der Société anonyme des mines et fonderies de zinc de la Vieille Montagne und der Metallgesellschaft vor 1914* (Franz Steiner, 2002), 178–290; Charles S. Aiken, *The Cotton Plantation South Since the Civil War* (Johns Hopkins UP, 2019), 60; Gerhard Bleifuß und Gerhard Hergenröder, *Die "Otto-Plantage Kilossa" (1907–1914): Aufbau und Ende eines kolonialen Unternehmens in Deutsch-Ostafrika* (Stadt Wendlingen am Neckar, 1993), 43, 59; and Jairus Banaji, "Merchant Capitalism, Peasant Households and Industrial Accumulation: Integration of a Model," *Journal of Agrarian Change* 16, no. 3 (July 2016): 423. On the continued importance of merchants, see Haller, *Transithandel: Geld- und Warenströme im globalen Kapitalismus* (Suhrkamp, 2019), 25–26, 59, on European merchants in India's countryside, see Sven Beckert, *Empire of Cotton: A Global History* (Knopf, 2014), 234.

39. Chandler, *Visible Hand*, 485; Colleen Dunlavy, "Why Did Some American Businesses Get So Big?," in *Major Problems in American Business History*, ed. Regina Blaszczyk and Philip Scranton, 257–63; Chandler, *Visible Hand*, 315–44.

40. Harold F. Williams and Arnold R. Daum, *The American Petroleum Industry: The Age of Illumination 1859–1899* (Northwestern UP, 1959), 420, 426–29.

41. The quotes are from, in order, Ron Chernow, *Titan: The Life of John D. Rockefeller, Sr.* (Vintage Books, 1999), 160; *US Congress, Senate Select Committee on Interstate Commerce, Forty-Ninth Congress, First Session, January 18, 1886* (Washington, DC: US Government Printing Office,

1886), 199; Sklar, *Corporate Reconstruction*, 15.

42. Brüggemeier, Farrenkopf, and Grütter, *Das Zeitalter der Kohle*, 163; Ralf Stremmel, "Friedrich Alfred Krupp: Handeln und Selbstverständnis eines Unternehmers," in *Friedrich Alfred Krupp: Ein Unternehmer im Kaiserreich*, ed. Michael Epkenhans und Ralf Stremmel (C. H. Beck, 2010), 29; Harold James, *Krupp: A History of the Legendary German Firm* (PUP, 2012), 99–101; Jürgen Kocka und Hannes Siegrist, "Die hundert größten deutschen Industrieunternehmen im späten 19. und frühen 20. Jahrhundert: Expansion, Diversifikation und Integration im internationalen Vergleich," in: *Recht und Entwicklung der Großunternehmen in 19. und frühen 20. Jahrhundert: Wirtschafts-, Sozial- und Rechtshistorische Untersuchungen zur Industrialisierung in Deutschland, Frankreich, England und den USA*, ed. Norbert Horn und Jürgen Kocka (Vandenhoeck & Ruprecht, 1979), 107; Fiedler, "Die 100 Größten Unternehmen," 44; James, *Krupp*, 102–3.

43. David Blackbourn, *The Long Nineteenth Century: A History of Germany, 1780–1918* (New York: OUP, 1997), 312; Chandler, *The Visible Hand*, 333.

44. Sklar, *Corporate Reconstruction*; and Adam Smith, *An Inquiry into the Nature and Causes of the Wealth of Nations*, vol. 3., 3rd rev. ed. (London: W. Strahan and T. Cadell, 1784), 124.

45. William G. Roy, *Socializing Capital: The Rise of the Large Industrial Corporation in America* (PUP, 1997), xiii, 4–5, 10; William C. Kirby, "China Unincorporated: Company Law and Business Enterprise in Twentieth-Century China," *Journal of Asian Studies* 54 (February 1995): 48; Naomi R. Lamoreaux, *The Great Merger Movement in American Business, 1895–1904* (CUP, 1985), 1–2; and state of New Jersey, *An Act Concerning Corporations in the State of New Jersey: Revision of 1896 . . .* (Corporation Trust Company of New Jersey, 1896).

46. The importance of this moment to the emergence of the private business corporation is also emphasized by Doreen Lustig, *Veiled Power: International Law and the Private Corporation, 1886–1981* (OUP, 2020), 4, 15; Marie-Laure Djelic, "When Limited Liability Was (Still) an Issue: Mobilization and Politics of Signification in 19th-Century England," *Organization Studies* 34, no. 5/6 (May 2013): 1–27, especially 5,

19; and David A. Moss, "The Deutsche Bank," in *Creating Modern Capitalism: How Entrepreneurs, Companies, and Countries Triumphed in Three Industrial Revolutions*, ed. Thomas K. McCraw, 3rd ed. (HUP, 2000), 235.

47. Kirby, "China Unincorporated," 43–45, 49, 51.

48. Marta Macedo, "Standard Cocoa: Transnational Networks and Technoscientific Regimes in West African Plantations," *Technology and Culture* 57, no. 3 (July 2016): 564; Harold Woodman, *King Cotton and His Retainers* (University of Kentucky Press, 1968), 288–89; Eric Panthou, "Les formes de résistance de travailleurs de plantations d'hévéas d'Indochine," in *Le travail colonial: Engagés et autres mainsd'œuvre migrantes dans les empires, 1850–1950*, ed. Éric Guerassimoff and Issiaka Mandé (Riveneuve, 2015), 467; Oscar Zanetti, "The Last Sugar Frontier in Cuba: Expansion and Consequences," paper presented at the Global Commodity Frontiers in Comparative Context International Workshop, December 9–10, 2016, University College London, 8–10; and P. Courtenay, *Plantation Agriculture* (Bell & Hyman, 1980), 59.

49. Noam Maggor, *Brahmin Capitalism: Frontiers of Wealth and Populism in America's First Gilded Age* (HUP, 2017), 7, 9, 50.

50. Luiz Felipe de Alencastro, "Vida privada e ordem privada no Império," in *História da Vida Privada No Brasil*, vol. 2, *Império: A Corte e a modernidade nacional*, ed. Luiz Felipe de Alencastro (Companhia das Letras, 1997), 24; Sven Beckert, *The Monied Metropolis: New York City and the Consolidation of the American Bourgeoisie, 1850–1896* (CUP, 2001), 239; Henry Hall, ed., *America's Successful Men of Affairs: An Encyclopedia of Contemporary Biography*, vol. 2 (New York: New York Tribune, 1895), 75–77; *The National Cyclopedia of American Biography*, vol. 1. (New York: J. T. White, 1898), 13; Allen Churchill, *The Upper Crust: An Informal History of New York's Highest Society* (Prentice Hall, 1970), 108, 147; David C. Hammack, *Power and Society: Greater New York at the Turn of the Century* (Russell Sage, 1982), 44, 46; Matthew Josephson, *The Robber Barons: The Great American Capitalists, 1861–1901* (Harcourt, 1934), 326, 328; Harvey O'Connor, *The Guggenheims: The Making of an American Dynasty* (Covici, Friede, 1937), 70; and Allan Nevins, *Study in Power: John D. Rockefeller, Industrialist and Philan-*

thropist, vol. 2 (Charles Scribner's Sons, 1953), 80–81.

51. Joseph Hodges Choate, as cited in Ronald Story, *The Forging of an Aristocracy: Harvard and the Boston Upper Class, 1800–1870* (Wesleyan UP, 1980), 179; E. Digby Baltzell, *Philadelphia Gentlemen: The Making of a National Upper Class* (The Free Press, 1958), 302, 305; Peter Dobkin Hall, *The Organization of American Culture, 1700–1900: Private Institutions, Elites, and the Origins of American Nationality* (New York UP, 1982), 262, 264; Ron Chernow, *The House of Morgan: An American Banking Dynasty and the Rise of Modern Finance* (Simon & Schuster, 1990), 62; Frederic Cole Jaher, *The Urban Establishment: Upper Strata in Boston, New York, Charleston, Chicago and Los Angeles* (University of Illinois Press, 1982), 266; and Edward Sanford Martin, *The Life of Joseph Hodges Choate*, vol. 1 (Charles Scribner's Sons, 1920), 359.

52. Rudi Batzell, "Reconstructing Global Capitalism: Class, Corporations and the Rise of Welfare States, 1870–1930" (PhD diss., Harvard University, 2017), 372; Chandler, *Visible Hand*, 484; and Sklar, *Corporate Reconstruction*, 23.

53. Eli Cook, *The Pricing of Progress: Economic Indicators and the Capitalization of American Life* (HUP, 2017), 15, 151.

54. Pierre Gervais and Martin Quinn, "Costing in the Early Industrial Revolution: Gradual Change to Cost Calculations at US Cloth Mills in the 1820s," *Accounting History Review* 26, no. 3 (2016): 191–217; and, more generally, Pierre Gervais, *Les origines de la révolution industrielle aux États-Unis: Entre économie marchande et capitalisme industriel, 1800–1850* (Éditions de EHESS, 2004), especially chap. 7. See also John Richard Edwards, Malcolm Anderson, and Roy A. Chandler, "Claiming a Jurisdiction for the 'Public Accountant' in England Prior to Organisational Fusion," *Accounting, Organizations and Society* 32, no. 1–2 (2007): 62; Claude Bocqueraz, "The Development of Professional Associations: The Experience of French Accountants from the 1880s to the 1940s," *Accounting, Business & Financial History* 11, no. 1 (2001): 21; Edwards et al., "Claiming a Jurisdiction," 61–100; Lisa Evans, "Shifting Strategies: The Pursuit of Closure and the 'Association of German Auditors,'" *European Accounting Review* 27, no. 4 (2018): 683–712, esp. 686; and Evans, "Shifting Strategies," 686.

55. Werner Sombart, "Die Wandlungen des Kapitalismus," *Weltwirtschaftliches Archiv* 28 (1928): 249. See also Sklar, *Corporate Reconstruction*, 15–16.

56. Hobsbawm, *Age of Empire*, 53; and Blackbourn, *Long Nineteenth Century*, 324.

57. Chandler, *Visible Hand*, 361, 492.

58. Moss, "Deutsche Bank," 239; Chandler, *Visible Hand*, 499; Otto Jeidels, *Das Verhältnis der Deutschen Großbanken zur Industrie mit Besonderer Berücksichtigung der Eisenindustrie* (Duncker & Humblot, 1905), 161; Blackbourn, *Long Nineteenth Century*, 313; Lothar Gall, "Die Deutsche Bank von ihrer Gründung bis zum Ersten Weltkrieg, 1870–1914," in *Die Deutsche Bank 1870–1995*, ed. Lothar Gall et al. (C. H. Beck, 1995), 32–40; and Moss, "Deutsche Bank," 240.

59. Thorsten Veblen, *The Theory of Business Enterprise* (Charles Scribner's Sons, 1915), 27–28.

60. Brian R. Mitchell, *European Historical Statistics, 1750–1950* (Macmillan, 1975), 394–401; *Historical Statistics of the United States: Earliest Times to the Present*, vol. 4, *Part D: Economic Sectors*, millennial ed., ed. Susan B. Carter et al. (CUP, 2006), Series Db74 and Dd399.

61. Musil, *Der Mann ohne Eigenschaften*, 1:306. The translation is from Musil, *The Man Without Qualities*, 1:226–27. For the importance of politics, see also Sklar, *Corporate Reconstruction*, 13.

62. Seibold, *Röchling*, 157, 167–68.

63. Seibold, *Röchling*, 159; and Stenographischer Bericht über die gestern Abend im Lokal "Zum Karlsberg" hierselbst stattgefundene öffentliche Hüttenarbeiter-Versammlung, einberufen von der christlichen Gewerkschaft, Völklingen, den 3. Mai 1912, A 1590, Gemeinnützige Vereine, SAV. See also A 2397: Beobachtung von Sozialdemokraten und Anarchisten. For further evidence, see the huge range of correspondence between Hermann Röchling and the administration of the city of Völklingen in Stadtarchiv Völklingen. See also Kesternich, *Aufstieg*, 119–25.

64. Versammlung in Wehrden, Report, Völklingen, 5 January 1912, 3, in LRA SB 1751, RTW 1912, LAS; Abschrift eines Artikels im "Sächsischen Tageblatt" vom 15. Juni 1906, LRA SB 1750, RTW 1912, LAS; and Brüggemeier, Farrenkopf, and Grütter, *Das Zeitalter der Kohle*, 166.

65. James Livingston, *Pragmatism and the Political Economy of Cultural Revolution, 1850–1940* (University of North Carolina Press, 1994), 24–42; Beckert, *Monied Metropolis*, chap. 4; and Livingston, *Pragmatism and the Political Economy*, 39.

66. Nutzinger, Boehmer, and Johannsen, *50 Jahre Röchling Völklingen*, 10.

67. Mansel G. Blackford, *The Rise of Modern Business: Great Britain, the United States, Germany, Japan, and China* (University of North Carolina Press, 2008), 133–35; Loren Brandt, Debin Ma, and Thomas G. Rawski, "Industrialization in China," in *The Spread of Modern Industry to the Periphery Since 1871*, ed. Kevin H. O'Rourke and Jeffrey G. Williamson (OUP, 2017), 205–6; Aurora Gómez-Galvarriato and Graciela Márquez Colín, "Industrialization and Growth in Peru and Mexico, 1870–2000: A Long-Term Assessment," in Brandt, Ma, and Rawski, *Spread of Modern Industry*, 291–92; Bishnupriya Gupta and Tirthankar Roy, "From Artisanal Production to Machine Tools: Industrialization in India over the Long Run," in Brandt, Ma, and Rawski, *Spread of Modern Industry*, 240; Xavier Duran, Aldo Musacchio, and Gerardo della Paolera, "Industrial Growth in South America: Argentina, Brazil, Chile, and Colombia, 1890–2010," in Brandt, Ma, and Rawski, *Spread of Modern Industry*, 321–22; Bouda Etemad and Jean Luciani, *World Energy Production, 1800–1985* (Librarie Droz, 1991), 186; Giuntini, "Submarine Telegraphy," 240. For an extended discussion of what they term the "great specialization," see the excellent Ronald Findlay and Kevin H. O'Rourke, *Power and Plenty: Trade, War, and the World Economy in the Second Millennium* (PUP, 2007), chap. 7.

68. Douglas E. Haynes, "Market Formation in Khandesh, 1820–1930," *Indian Economic and Social History Review* 36, no. 3 (1999): 294; *Asiatic Review* (October 1, 1914): 299–330; C. A. Bayly, *The Birth of the Modern World, 1780–1914* (Blackwell, 2004), 138; Dwijendra Tripathi, "An Echo Beyond the Horizon: The Effect of American Civil War on India," in *Journal of Indian History: Golden Jubilee Volume*, ed. T. K. Ravindran (University of Kerala, 1973), 660; Marika Vicziany, "Bombay Merchants and Structural Changes in the Export Community 1850 to 1880," in *Economy and Society: Essays in Indian Economic and Social History*, ed. K. N. Chaudhuri and

Clive Dewey (OUP, 1979), 163–96; Marika Vicziany, "The Cotton Trade and the Commercial Development of Bombay, 1855–75" (PhD diss., University of London, 1975), 170–71.

69. "Decolonizing the Mind: Response to Gurminder Bhambra, Annual Lecture for *The British Journal of Sociology*, 'Relations of Extraction, Relations of Redistribution: Empire, Nation, and the Construction of the British Welfare State,'" *British Journal of Sociology* 73, no. 1 (2022): 16–22.

70. The quotes are, in order, from Fritz Stern, *Gold and Iron: Bismarck, Bleichröder, and the Building of the German Empire* (Knopf, 1977), 189; Richard T. Ely, *An Introduction to Political Economy* (Chautauqua Press, 1889): 22; *Revue mensuelle de la science économique et de la statistique* 55 (July to September 1896): 202; Franz Xaver von Neumann-Spallart, *Übersichten der Weltwirtschaft* (Berlin: Verlag für Sprach- und Handelswissenschaft, 1885); Quinn Slobodian, "How to See the World Economy: Statistics, Maps, and Schumpeter's Camera in the First Age of Globalization," *JGH* 10 (July 2015): 310.

Chapter 12: Reconstructing Labor, 1870–1920

1. Firmin Lacpatia, *Les Indiens de La Réunion* (Surya Editions, 2009), 25. Alessandro Stanziani, "Travail, droits et immigration: Une comparaison entre l'île Maurice et l'île de La Réunion, années 1840–1880," *Le Mouvement Social* 241 (2012): 51. For the original quote, see Chef de Mission to La Réunion to Ministre des Colonies, Saint-Denis, letter, 25 March 1907, in Main d'oeuvre: Madagascar et La Réunion, Recrutement de travailleurs dans l'Inde, dans l'Indo-Chine, dans la Chine, dans le Japon, Rapport Geismar, FM/7AFFECO/19, Travail, La Réunion, Recrutements, Extérieur, 1866–1939, Ministre des Colonies, ANOM.

2. Auguste Vison, *De l'immigration indienne* (Saint-Denis: Typographie de Gabriel Lahuppe, Imprimeur du Gouvernement, 1860), 10. The book is in Main d'œuvre: La Réunion, Recrutement de travailleurs en Indo-Chine, Java, Mozambique, FM/7AFFECO/19, Travail, La Réunion, Recrutements, Extérieur, 1866–1939, Ministre des Colonies, ANOM. See also Richard B. Allen, *European Slave Trading in the Indian Ocean, 1500–1850* (Ohio UP, 2014), 197.

3. "Mémoire des propriétaires des colonies sur l'indémnité pour l'émancipation des esclaves," 4, La Réunion, "Réponses relatives à la liquidation de l'indemnité," Fonds ministériels, K // 5, ANOM.

4. Annotated draft message to "Citoyens Représentants," La Réunion, "Réponses relatives à la liquidation de l'indemnité," Fonds ministériels, K // 5, ANOM; "Rapport au Ministre," Directeur des Colonies [name illegible], 6 May 1856, in La Réunion, "Réponses relatives à la liquidation de l'indemnité," Fonds ministériels, K // 5, ANOM; annotated draft message to "Citoyens Représentants," La Réunion, "Réponses relatives à la liquidation de l'indemnité," Fonds ministériels, K // 5, ANOM. On the discussions about the amount of money provided to French enslavers, see Frédérique Beauvois, "Indemniser les planteurs pour abolir l'esclavage?" (PhD diss., Université de Lausanne, 2011), 261–67; "Rapport au Ministre, Directeur des Colonies [name illegible], 6 May 1856, in La Réunion, "Réponses relatives à la liquidation de l'indemnité," Fonds ministériels, K // 5, ANOM. See also Frédérique Beauvois, *Between Blood and Gold: The Debates over Compensation for Slavery in the Americas* (Berghahn Books, 2016), 206; "Mémoire des propriétaires des colonies sur l'indémnité pour l'émancipation des esclaves," 8, 16; La Réunion, "Réponses relatives à la liquidation de l'indemnité," Fonds ministériels, K // 5, ANOM; and Ho Hai Quang, *Histoire économique de l'île de La Réunion (1849–1881): Engagisme, croissance et crise* (L'Harmattan, 2004), 55.

5. "Note sur la reprise de l'immigration indienne présentée à Mr le Directeur Roume par le Syndicat des Producteurs de Île de La Réunion," undated, Comité Central Français pour l'Outre-Mer, La Réunion, 1894/1909, Fonds privés, 100APOM/, 529, ANOM.

6. "Note sur la reprise de l'immigration indienne présentée à Mr le Directeur Roume par le Syndicat des Producteurs de Île de La Réunion," undated, Comité Central Français pour l' Outre-Mer, La Réunion, 1894/1909, Fonds privés, 100APOM /, 529, ANOM.

7. Delabarre de Nanteuil, Législation de l'île de La Réunion (1861–1865), 311–12, as cited in Ho, *Histoire économique*, 141.

8. Ho, *Histoire économique*, 11–12, 21, 61, 96, 155. On the number of slave owners, see Lacpatia, *Les Indi-*

ens de La Réunion (Surya Editions, 2009), 26; Virginie Chaillou-Atrous, "La reprise de l'immigration africaine à La Réunion à la fin du XIXème siècle: De la traite déguisée à l'engagement de travail libre," *French Colonial History* 16 (Spring 2016): 28; and Ho, *Histoire économique*, 147–48.

9. "Rapport sur l'immigration indienne à La Réunion, présenté à Monsieur le Ministre des Colonies par l'Union Coloniale Française [1907]," in Main d'œuvre: La Réunion, Recrutement de travailleurs en Indo-Chine, Java, Mozambique, FM/7AFFECO/19, Travail, La Réunion, Recrutements, Extérieur, 1866–1939, Ministre des Colonies, ANOM.

10. "Chef de Mission à la Réunion au Ministre des Colonies, Saint-Denis," Saint-Denis, letter, March 25, 1907, in Main d'œuvre, Madagascar et La Réunion, Recrutement de travailleurs dans l'Inde, dans l'Indo-Chine, dans la Chine, dans le Japon / Rapport Geismar, FM/7AFFECO/19, Travail, La Réunion, Recrutements, Extérieur, 1866–1939, Ministre des Colonies, ANOM; and Vison, *De l'Immigration Indienne*, 4. On colonial officials' survey of emancipation impacts, see, for example, "Indes occidentales anglaises, Faits commerciaux. No. 1," from the series "Documens [sic] sur le commerce extérieur," Ministry of Agriculture and Commerce, March and April 1848, La Réunion, "Réponses relatives à la liquidation de l'indemnité," Fonds ministériels, K // 5; Ho, *Histoire économique* 31, 33, 47; and Stanziani, "Travail, droits et immigration," 54.

11. Planters demanded new legislation that would allow them to recruit African workers from the continent. See Virginie Chaillou-Atrous, "Les engagés indiens et les engagés africains à la Réunion au XIXe siècle: Une histoire commune?," in *Le travail colonial: Engagés et autres mains-d'œuvre migrantes dans les empires, 1850–1950*, ed. Éric Guerassimoff and Issiaka Mandé (Riveneuve, 2015), 197–229; Stanziani, "Travail, droits et immigration," 53; Ho, *Histoire économique*, 76–77, 83; Chaillou-Atrous, "La reprise de l'immigration africaine," 29; and Ho, *Histoire économique*, 89, 90, 104.

12. G. Imhans, letter, London, 4 July 1860, as reprinted in Lacpatia, *Les Indiens de La Réunion*, 47. See also Chaillou-Atrous, "La reprise de l'immigration africaine," 29; "Règlements mis en vigueur à Bourbon, de

1826 à 1844, sur les introductions de travailleurs libres venant d'Asie," annotated, *Revue coloniale*, 2 mars 1845, Fonds ministériels, REU/406/3827, ANOM; "Copie de l'engagement pris à l'égard du Gouvernement de Bourbon, par 15 parias partis pour cette ile à bord de la Goëlette[?] de S. M. La Turquoise," undated, most likely late 1820s, in Fonds ministériels, REU/406/3827, ANOM; report, [author illegible], 10 February 1829, letterhead of the Ministry of the Marine and of Colonies, "Compte rendu de l'envoi à Bourbon de 15 engagés parias, venant des Établissements français de l'Inde," in Fonds ministériels, REU/ 406/3827, ANOM; Allen, *European Slave Trading*, 197; and A. Fitau, "Ile Bourbon," *Glaneur*, April 6, 1833, 1–3.

13. "Règlements mis en vigueur à Bourbon, de 1826 à 1844, sur les introductions de travailleurs libres venant d'Asie," annotated, *Revue coloniale*, 2 mars 1845, 283, 287, in Fonds ministériels, REU/406/3827, ANOM; Stanziani, "Travail, droits et immigration," 52.

14. "Note sur l'immigration malgache à La Réunion," author unknown, undated (but probably 1920s), Main d'œuvre: Madagascar et La Réunion, Recrutement de travailleurs dans l'Inde, dans l'Indo-Chine, dans la Chine, dans le Japon / Rapport Geismar; FM/7AF-FECO/19, Travail, Reuinion, Recrutements, Extérieur, 1866–1939, Ministre des Colonies, ANOM.

15. For the first quote, see Ho, *Histoire économique*, 259. For the second quote, see report by M. Saurin, inspecteur adjoint des colonies, on "la reprise de l'immigration indienne à La Réunion," March 1907, Main d'œuvre: Madagascar et La Réunion, Recrutement de travailleurs dans l'Inde, dans l'Indo-Chine, dans la Chine, dans le Japon / Rapport Geismar, FM/7AFFECO/19, Travail, La Réunion, Recrutements, Extérieur, 1866–1939, Ministre des Colonies, ANOM. See also Stanziani, "Travail, droits et immigration," 57.

16. Rachel Sturman, "Indian Indentured Labor and the History of International Rights Regimes," *AHR* 119, no. 5 (December 2014): 1458; Ho Hai Quang, *Histoire économique*, 255–57; and Chaillou-Atrous, "La reprise de l'immigration africaine," 31.

17. Sturman, "Indian Indentured Labor," 1459, 1460. A summary of the many complaints of Indian indentured workers to British consular authorities can be found in Sudel

Fuma, *De l'Inde du sud à l'ile de La Réunion: Les Réunionnais d'origine indienne d'après le Rapport Mackenzie* (Centre de Documentation et de Recherche en Histoire Régionale, 1999), 143–48.

18. "Rapport sur la question de la main-d'œuvre et la reprise de l'immigration indienne présenté à la Chambre d'Agriculture au nom de sa commission," La Réunion, 1905, 5, 12, Main d'œuvre: Madagascar et La Réunion, Recrutement de travailleurs dans l'Inde, dans l'Indo-Chine, dans la Chine, dans le Japon / Rapport Geismar, FM/7AFFECO/19, Travail, La Réunion, Recrutements, Extérieur, 1866–1939, Ministre des Colonies, ANOM; A. Delahanty, "La questions des bras à Île de La Réunion," April 1894, Comité Central Français pour l' Outre-Mer, Réunion, 1894/1909, Fonds privés, 100APOM/, 529, ANOM. See also "Rapport sur l'immigration indienne à La Réunion," présenté à Monsieur le Ministre des Colonies par l'Union Coloniale Française (1907), in Main d'œuvre: La Réunion, Recrutement de travailleurs en Indo-Chine, Java, Mozambique, FM/7AFFECO/19, Travail, La Réunion, Recrutements, Extérieur, 1866–1939, Ministre des Colonies, ANOM.

19. For the first quote, see Arthur Girault, *Principes de coloinsation et de legislation coloniale* (Éditions L. Larose, 1904), 128, as cited in Chaillou-Atrous, "La reprise de l'immigration africaine," 36. For the second quote, see C. Chatelain, "De l'immigration dans les colonies françaises en vue d'obtenir l'abolition graduelle de l'esclavage sur la continent," *Bulletin de la société des sciences et des arts de l'ile de la Réunion* (1870), 24, as cited in Chaillou-Atrous, "La reprise de l'immigration africaine," 32. See also "Rapport sur l'immigration indienne à La Réunion," présenté à Monsieur le Ministre des Colonies par l'Union Coloniale Française [1907], in Main d'œuvre: La Réunion, Recrutement de travailleurs en Indo-Chine, Java, Mozambique, FM/7AFFECO/19, Travail, La Réunion, Recrutements, Extérieur, 1866–1939, Ministre des Colonies, ANOM; and Chaillou-Atrous, "La reprise de l'immigration africaine," 37.

20. For the quote, see Chatelain, "De l'immigration dans les colonies françaises," 7, as cited in Chaillou-Atrous, "La reprise de l'immigration africaine," 33. See also Chaillou-Atrous, "La reprise de l'immigration africaine," 30, 38.

21. Chaillou-Atrous, "La reprise de l'immigration africaine," 35. For the distributions, see Main-d'oeuvre Antandroy à La Réunion—"Number of *engagés malgaches* by proprietor," Main d'œuvre: Madagascar et La Réunion, Recrutement de travailleurs dans l'Inde, dans l'Indo-Chine, dans la Chine, dans le Japon / Rapport Geismar, FM/7AFFECO/19, Travail, La Réunion, Recrutements, Extérieur, 1866–1939, Ministre des Colonies, ANOM. See also "Main d'oeuvre Antandroy à la La Réunion: Rapport," Administrateur en Chef Bereni à Monsieur le Gouverneur Général de Madagascar et Dépendances, 20 December 1924, 6, in Main d'œuvre: Madagascar et La Réunion, Recrutement de travailleurs dans l'Inde, dans l'Indo-Chine, dans la Chine, dans le Japon / Rapport Geismar, FM/7AFFECO/19, Travail, Réunion, Recrutements, Extérieur, 1866–1939, Ministre des Colonies, ANOM.

22. "Main d'oeuvre Antandroy à la La Réunion: Rapport," Administrateur en Chef Bereni to Monsieur le Gouverneur Général de Madagascar et Dépendances, 20 December 1924, 6, in Main d'œuvre: Madagascar et La Réunion, Recrutement de travailleurs dans l'Inde, dans l'Indo-Chine, dans la Chine, dans le Japon / Rapport Geismar, FM/7AFFECO/19, Travail, La Réunion, Recrutements, Extérieur, 1866–1939, Ministre des Colonies, ANOM; "Main-d'oeuvre Antandroy à la La Réunion: État nominatif des décès," 1922–1924, Main d'œuvre: Madagascar et La Réunion, Recrutement de travailleurs dans l'Inde, dans l'Indo-Chine, dans la Chine, dans le Japon / Rapport Geismar, FM/7AFFECO/19, Travail, La Réunion, Recrutements, Extérieur, 1866–1939, Ministre des Colonies, ANOM.

23. "Notes de tournées," undated, author unknown, but early 1920s, 3–4, 10, 14–18, Main d'œuvre: Madagascar et La Réunion, Recrutement de travailleurs dans l'Inde, dans l'Indo-Chine, dans la Chine, dans le Japon / Rapport Geismar, FM/7AFFECO/19, Travail, La Réunion, Recrutements, Extérieur, 1866–1939, Ministre des Colonies, ANOM.

24. For the quote, see "Notes de tournées," undated, author unknown, but early 1920s, 28, Main d'œuvre: Madagascar et La Réunion, Recrutement de travailleurs dans l'Inde, dans l'Indo-Chine, dans la Chine, dans le Japon / Rapport Geismar, FM/7AFFECO/19, Travail, La

Réunion, Recrutements, Extérieur, 1866–1939, Ministre des Colonies, ANOM.

25. "Note sur l'immigration malgache à La Réunion," author unknown, undated (but probably 1920s), Main d'œuvre: Madagascar et La Réunion, Recrutement de travailleurs dans l'Inde, dans l'Indo-Chine, dans la Chine, dans le Japon / Rapport Geismar, FM/7AFFECO/19, Travail, La Réunion, Recrutements, Extérieur, 1866–1939, Ministre des Colonies, ANOM.

26. *Journal de la Guadeloupe*, February 7, 1849, 1.

27. On the numbers for labor shortages, see Allen, *European Slave Trading*, 195. See also "Rapport sur la question de la main-d'œuvre et la reprise de l'immigration indienne présenté à la Chambre d'Agriculture au nom de sa commission," La Réunion, 1905, 4, Main d'œuvre: Madagascar et La Réunion, Recrutement de travailleurs dans l'Inde, dans l'Indo-Chine, dans la Chine, dans le Japon / Rapport Geismar, FM/7AFFECO/19, Travail, La Réunion, Recrutements, Extérieur, 1866–1939, Ministre des Colonies, ANOM; "Rapport sur l'immigration indienne à La Réunion," présenté à Monsieur le Ministre des Colonies par l'Union Coloniale Française [1907], in Main d'œuvre: La Réunion, Recrutement de travailleurs en Indo-Chine, Java, Mozambique, FM/7AFFECO/19, Travail, La Réunion, Recrutements, Extérieur, 1866–1939, Ministre des Colonies, ANOM; "Chef de Mission à La Réunion au Ministre des Colonies," Saint-Denis, letter, March 25, 1907, in Main d'œuvre: Madagascar et La Réunion, Recrutement de travailleurs dans l'Inde, dans l'Indo-Chine, dans la Chine, dans le Japon / Rapport Geismar, FM/7AFFECO/19, Travail, La Réunion, Recrutements, Extérieur, 1866–1939, Ministre des Colonies, ANOM; Philidor Payet to Saurin, Inspecteur des Colonies, Deux Rives, letter, 2 February 1907, Main d'œuvre: Madagascar et La Réunion, Recrutement de travailleurs dans l'Inde, dans l'Indo-Chine, dans la Chine, dans le Japon / Rapport Geismar, FM/7AFFECO/19, Travail, La Réunion, Recrutements, Extérieur, 1866–1939, Ministre des Colonies, ANOM; and Ho, *Histoire économique*, 7.

28. Président du Syndicat Central Agricole to Monsieur Chailley Bert, Secrétaire Général de l'Union Coloniale Française, letter, 21 January 1896, Comité Central Français pour

l'Outre-Mer, Réunion, 1894/1909, Fonds privés, 100APOM/, 529, ANOM; "Rapport sur la question de la main-d'œuvre et la reprise de l'immigration indienne présenté à la Chambre d'Agriculture au nom de sa commission," La Réunion, 1905, 30; Main d'œuvre: Madagascar et La Réunion, Recrutement de travailleurs dans l'Inde, dans l'Indo-Chine, dans la Chine, dans le Japon / Rapport Geismar, FM/7AFFECO/19, Travail, La Réunion, Recrutements, Extérieur, 1866–1939, Ministre des Colonies, ANOM; "Rapport sur la question de la main-d'œuvre et la reprise de l'immigration indienne présenté à la Chambre d'Agriculture au nom de sa commission," La Réunion, 1905, 32–35, Main d'œuvre: Madagascar et La Réunion, Recrutement de travailleurs dans l'Inde, dans l'Indo-Chine, dans la Chine, dans le Japon / Rapport Geismar, FM/7AFFECO/19, Travail, La Réunion, Recrutements, Extérieur, 1866–1939, Ministre des Colonies, ANOM. For the quote "profonde détresse," see "Rapport sur l'immigration indienne à La Réunion," présenté à Monsieur le Ministre des Colonies par l'Union Coloniale Française [1907], in Main d'œuvre: La Réunion, Recrutement de travailleurs en Indo-Chine, Java, Mozambique, FM/7AFFECO/19, Travail, La Réunion, Recrutements, Extérieur, 1866–1939, Ministre des Colonies, ANOM; "Rapport sur l'immigration indienne à La Réunion," présenté à Monsieur le Ministre des Colonies par l'Union Coloniale Française [1907], in Main d'œuvre: La Réunion, Recrutement de travailleurs en Indo-Chine, Java, Mozambique, FM/7AFFECO/19, Travail, La Réunion, Recrutements, Extérieur, 1866–1939, Ministre des Colonies, ANOM. See also "La Réunion a reçu des offres d'Indochine," *La Presse Coloniale*, March 17, 1926. These voluminous records are found in Comité Central Français pour l'Outre-Mer, Réunion, 1894/1909, Fonds privés, 100APOM/, 529, ANOM. For a story of a ship taking workers from Java to Réunion as early as 1827, see Allen, *European Slave Trading*, 179. "Règlements mis en vigueur à Bourbon, de 1826 à 1844, sur les introductions de travailleurs libres venant d'Asie" annotated, *Revue Coloniale*, 2 mars 1845, at the top of the first page, 291, in Fonds ministériels, REU/406/3827, ANOM.

29. "Chef de Mission à La Réunion au Ministre des Colonies," Saint-Denis, letter, 25 March 1907,

in Main d'œuvre: Madagascar et La Réunion, Recrutement de travailleurs dans l'Inde, dans l'Indo-Chine, dans la Chine, dans le Japon / Rapport Geismar, FM/7AFFECO/19, Travail, La Réunion, Recrutements, Extérieur, 1866–1939, Ministre des Colonies, ANOM; Président du Syndicat Central Agricole à Monsieur Chailley Bert, Secrétaire Général de l'Union Coloniale Française, letter, 21 January 1896, Comité Central Français pour l' Outre-Mer, Réunion, 1894/1909, Fonds privés, 100APOM/, 529, ANOM; Minister of Foreign Affairs to Minister of Colonies, letter, 31 July 1921, in "Recrutement de main-d'œuvre en Égypte pour Madagascar," FM/7AFFECO/19, Travail, La Réunion, Recrutements, Extérieur, 1866–1939, Ministre des Colonies, ANOM; Lapalaud to "Colonies. Paris," telegram, 31 January 1924, in Main d'œuvre: Madagascar et La Réunion, Recrutement de travailleurs dans l'Inde, dans l'Indo-Chine, dans la Chine, dans le Japon / Rapport Geismar, FM/7AFFECO/19, Travail, La Réunion, Recrutements, Extérieur, 1866–1939, Ministre des Colonies, ANOM; J. Repiquet, Governor of La Réunion, to Governor General of Dutch East Indies, letter, 15 April 1926, and Governor of La Réunion to Minister of Colonies, letter, 30 March 1926, both in Main d'œuvre: La Réunion, Recrutement de travailleurs en Indo-Chine, Java, Mozambique, FM/7AFFECO/19, Travail, La Réunion, Recrutements, Extérieur, 1866–1939, Ministre des Colonies, ANOM; letter, Minister of Colonies to Minister of Foreign Affairs, February 18, 1927, in Main d'œuvre: Madagascar et La Réunion, Recrutement de travailleurs dans l'Inde, dans l'Indo-Chine, dans la Chine, dans le Japon / Rapport Geismar, FM/7AFFECO/19, Travail, La Réunion, Recrutements, Extérieur, 1866–1939, Ministre des Colonies, ANOM.

30. "La isla de Cuba," *La Tribuna*, April 18, 1883, 402.

31. See Généralités, 127/1105, December 15, 1873, ANOM.

32. *Times* (London), April 13, 1850, 5. See also "The Future of the West Indies," *Spectator*, February 12, 1848, 152.

33. For the discussion on how to secure labor post-abolition, see, for example, Herman Merivale, *Lectures on Colonization and Colonies, Delivered Before the University of Oxford in 1839, 1840 & 1841* (London: Longman, Green, Longman, and Roberts,

1861; repr., OUP, 1928); C. F. van Delden Laërne, *Brazil and Java: Report on Coffee-Culture in America, Asia and Africa* (London: Martinus Nijhoff, 1885), 215.

34. Van Delden Laërne, *Brazil and Java* (London: W. H. Allen, 1885), 372.

35. Thomas Holt, *The Problem of Freedom: Race, Labor, and Politics in Jamaica and Britain, 1832–1938* (Johns Hopkins UP, 1992), 49, 69, 144, 146, 156. See also Merivale, *Lectures on Colonization and Colonies*, 315.

36. Merivale, *Lectures on Colonization and Colonies*, 310.

37. Claudia Leal, *Landscapes of Freedom: Building a Postemancipation Society in the Rainforests of Western Colombia* (University of Arizona Press, 2018), 62.

38. "West India Mail," *Economist*, February 5, 1848.

39. Letter from M. de la Motte Saint-Pierre to the Governor-General of Madagascar Olivier, 6 mar 1926, Main d'œuvre: Madagascar et La Réunion, Recrutement de travailleurs dans l'Inde, dans l'Indo-Chine, dans la Chine, dans le Japon / Rapport Geismar, FM/7AFFECO/19, Travail, La Réunion, Recrutements, Extérieur, 1866–1939, Ministre des Colonies, ANOM.

40. "La Main-d'oeuvre à La Réunion," *Le Temps*, November 7, 1899.

41. Commission du Régime du Travail aux Colonies, Séance du 29 novembre 1873, Séance du 8 décembre 1873, Séance du 15 décembre 1873, Séance du 16 mars 1874, Séance du 19 mai 1874, Procès-Verbal, in Généralités 127/1105, ANOM.

42. Cited in Carolyn Fick, "Emancipation in Haiti: From Plantation Labour to Peasant Proprietorship," *Slavery and Abolition* 21, no. 2 (2000): 24–25.

43. Fick, "Emancipation in Haiti," 22, 32, 209; and Michel-Rolph Trouillot, *Haiti: State Against Nation* (Monthly Review Press, 1990), 72.

44. Among many others, see Ulbe Bosma, *The World of Sugar: How the Sweet Stuff Transformed Our Politics, Health, and Environment over 2,000 Years* (HUP, 2023); Corey Ross, *Ecology and Power in the Age of Empire: Europe and the Transformation of the Tropical World* (OUP, 2017); Tomás Bartoletti, "The Transimperial Emergence of Pest Control Research: Economic Entomology Between Europe and the Tropical World, c. 1890–1930," *Comparativ: Zeitschrift für Globalgeschichte und vergleichende Gesellschaftsforschung*

32: 6 (2023): 704–25; Sven Beckert, *Empire of Cotton: A Global History* (Knopf, 2014).

45. "Culture du coton au Sénégal, 1900/1924," 12, Series R, Agriculture, Culture du Coton, 1889–1943, 1R/00035, ANS; Kumari Jayawardena and Rachel Kurian, *Class, Patriarchy and Ethnicity on Sri Lankan Plantations: Two Centuries of Power and Protest* (Orient Blackswan, 2015), 2; and Roberto Saba, *American Mirror: The United States and Brazil in the Age of Emancipation* (PUP, 2021), 132.

46. Tithi Bhattacharya, "Sacred Thirst: Producing Tea, Producing People in Colonial Bengal," unpublished paper, Harvard University, 2019; Brian Mitchell, ed., *International Historical Statistics, 1750–2010* (Palgrave Macmillan, 2013), 482; Mitchell, *International Historical Statistics*, 510, 535, 538; *Statistisches Handbuch für das Deutsche Reich* (Carl Heymanns, 1907), 249; *Statistisches Handbuch für das Deutsche Reich*, vol. 32 (Puttkammer & Mühlbrecht, 1911), 234; Mitchell, *International Historical Statistics*, 456; and J. A. Mollett, *Capital in Hawaiian Sugar: Its Formation and Relation to Labor and Output, 1870–1957* (University of Hawaii, 1961), 13; Augustine Sedgewick, *Coffeeland: One Man's Dark Empire and the Making of Our Favorite Drink* (Penguin Press, 2020), 171.

47. For the original quote, see "Une politique d'immigration à Madagascar," *La Dépêche*, June 3, 1926. Along similar lines, see Governor-General of Madagascar to Minister of Colonies, letter, 13 March 1926, Main d'œuvre: Madagascar et La Réunion, Recrutement de travailleurs dans l'Inde, dans l'Indo-Chine, dans la Chine, dans le Japon / Rapport Geismar, FM/7AFFECO/19, Travail, La Réunion, Recrutements, Extérieur, 1866–1939, Ministre des Colonies, ANOM.

48. Governor of La Réunion to Minister of Colonies, letter, 12 May 1923, Main d'œuvre: Madagascar et La Réunion, Recrutement de travailleurs dans l'Inde, dans l'Indo-Chine, dans la Chine, dans le Japon / Rapport Geismar, FM/7AFFECO/19, Travail, La Réunion, Recrutements, Extérieur, 1866–1939, Ministre des Colonies, ANOM; Governor of La Réunion to Minister of Colonies, letter, 29 March 1925, Main d'œuvre: La Réunion, Recrutement de travailleurs en Indo-Chine, Java, Mozambique, FM/7AFFECO/19, Travail, La Réunion, Recrutements, Extérieur, 1866–1939, Ministre des

Colonies, ANOM; M. Pasquier, Governor-General of Indochine, to Minister of Colonies, 30 April 1927, Main d'œuvre: Madagascar et La Réunion, Recrutement de travailleurs dans l'Inde, dans l'Indo-Chine, dans la Chine, dans le Japon / Rapport Geismar, FM/7AFFECO/19, Travail, La Réunion, Recrutements, Extérieur, 1866–1939, Ministre des Colonies, ANOM; Chaillou-Atrous, "La reprise de l'immigration africaine," 35.

49. Eric Foner, *Reconstruction: America's Unfinished Revolution, 1863–1877* (Perennial Library, 1989). For slavery's reliance on state support, see also Barbara Jeanne Fields, "The Advent of Capitalist Agriculture: The New South in a Bourgeois World," in *Essays on the Postbellum Southern Economy*, vol. 18, ed. Thavolia Glymph, et al. (Texas A&M UP, 1985), 80. The importance of seeing the differences between various forms of unfree labor and slavery is also emphasized by Marcel van der Linden and Magaly Rodríguez García, eds., introduction to *On Coerced Labor: Work and Compulsion After Chattel Slavery* (Brill, 2016), 3.

50. Van der Linden and García, *On Coerced Labor*, 1. For a case study that emphasizes that diversity, see Pablo F. Luna, "Capitalisme et relations de travail dans les haciendas du monde andin," in *Études rurales*, no. 205 (2020): 116–39; and Carlos Aguirre, *Breve historia de la esclavitud en el Perú: Una herida que no deja de sangrar* (Fondo Editorial del Congreso de Perú, 2005), 179. On Manchuria, see Rachel Steely, "Invisible Giant: The Global Rise of Soy in the Twentieth Century" (PhD diss., Harvard University, 2022), chap. 3.

51. Local outcomes producing labor diversity is shown, for example, by Eric Guerassimoff et Issiaka Mandé, *L'histoire du travail colonial s'est développée vigoureusement dans le Sud depuis la fin du XXe siècle* (Riveneuve, 2016). On the Congolese side of Lake Kivu, see Sven Van Melkebeke, "Divergence in Rural Development: The Curious Case of Coffee Production in the Lake Kivu Region," *African Economic History* 46, no. 2 (2018): 117; Van Melkebeke, "Divergence in Rural Development," 122, 124; Van Melkebeke, 123.

52. Eric Foner, *Nothing but Freedom: Emancipation and Its Legacy* (Louisiana State UP, 2007); Note from the Ambassade d'Espagne à Paris, 994/Gen 117/474, Fonds ministériels, ANOM; and "Le coton soudanais,

production—outillage—colonisation, rapport," chap. 2, 58, Series R, Agriculture, Culture du Coton, 1889–1943, 1R/00035, ANS. See, for example, "Colonie du Niger, les irrigation du Niger et la culture cotonnière au Soudan," octobre 1921, in Series R, Agriculture, Culture du Coton, 1889–1943, 1R/00035, ANS; "Le Consul de France a Bombay à son Exc. Monsieur le Ministre des Affaires Étrangères," Paris, January 25, 1905, and the files in Culture Cotonnière dans les Colonies Allemandes, in "Grande Bretagne et des Colonies Affaires," Commerciales, série A, carton 14, direction des consulats, commerce, 1902–1906, in Centre des Archives diplomatiques de La Courneuve, Paris, France; Marta Macedo, "Standard Cocoa: Trans-Imperial Plantations and the Making of the Global World," unpublished paper presented at the Global History of Colonialism Conference, University of Delhi, 2016, 7.

53. Jayawardena and Kurian, Class, Patriarchy and Ethnicity on Sri Lankan Plantations, 36, 39. For violence against workers on German Samoa, see Holger Droessler, "Islands of Labor: Community, Conflict, and Resistance in Colonial Samoa, 1889–1919" (PhD diss., Harvard University, 2015), 104; Allen, European Slave Trading, 178, 180, 182; Alessandro Stanziani, "L'immigration indentured à l'île Maurice, 1840–1870: Conditions, abus et résistance," Afriques 6 (2015): 1. For an analysis of the public debate around indentured labor, see Jonathan Connolly, "Indentured Labour Migration and the Meaning of Emancipation: Free Trade, Race, and Labour in British Public Debate, 1838–1860," Past & Present, 238 (2018): 85–119; Allen, European Slave Trading, 194; Stanziani, "L'immigration indentured à l'île Maurice," 3; Sturman, "Indian Indentured Labor," 1441; Laird Bergad, Cuban Rural Society in the Nineteenth Century: The Social and Economic History of Monoculture in Matanzas (PUP, 1990), 249; Rebecca Scott, Slave Emancipation in Cuba: The Transition to Free Labour, 1860–1899 (University of Pittsburgh Press, 1985), 91; Droessler, "Islands of Labor," 6, 84. Ritesh Kumar Jaiswal, "Ephemeral Mobility: Critical Appraisals of the Facets of Indian Migration and the Maistry Mediations in Burma (c. 1880–1940)," Almanack 19 (August 2018): 43.

54. Sturman, "Indian Indentured Labor," 1439–465; Allen, European Slave Trading, 194; S. D. Chapman, Merchant Enterprise in Britain: From the Industrial Revolution to World War I (CUP, 1992); and W. Kloosterboer, Involuntary Labour Since the Abolition of Slavery: A Survey of Compulsory Labour Throughout the World (Brill, 1960), 33. The numbers for Java are for the years 1890–1929. See Kloosterboer, Involuntary Labour Since the Abolition of Slavery, 33.

55. Rachel Kurian, "Labor, Race, and Gender on the Coffee Plantations in Ceylon (Sri Lanka), 1834–1880," in The Global Coffee Economy in Africa, Asia, and Latin America, 1500–1989, ed. William Gervase Clarence-Smith and Steven Topik (CUP, 2003), 174; Jayawardena and Kurian, Class, Patriarchy and Ethnicity on Sri Lankan Plantations, 25.

56. See entry of February 7, 1897, directors' meeting minutes, GB 248 UGD 091/2/6/1, 5 Aug 1896–29 Jul 1902, Finlay Papers, UGA; Kurian, "Labor, Race, and Gender on the Coffee Plantations," 177; Jayawardena and Kurian, Class, Patriarchy and Ethnicity on Sri Lankan Plantations, 8.

57. Consolidated Tea & Lands Co. Ltd. reports and accounts, GB 248 UGD 091/8/3/1/1, 1896–1900; Directors' meeting minutes, GB 248 UGD 091/2/6/1, 5 August 1896–29 July 1902, Finlay Papers; and Jayawardena and Kurian, Class, Patriarchy and Ethnicity on Sri Lankan Plantations, 27. For a rich analysis of the Assam process, see Nitin Varma, Coolies of Capitalism: Assam Tea and the Making of Coolie Labour (De Gruyter Oldenbourg, 2017); Tithi Bhattacharya, "Sacred Thirst"; Jaiswal, "Ephemeral Mobility," here especially 45, 49, 51, 70; and Droessler, "Islands of Labor," 49–50.

58. Jaiswal, "Ephemeral Mobility," 63. For Assam, see also Varma, Coolies of Capitalism, 23.

59. As cited in Kloosterboer, Involuntary Labour Since the Abolition of Slavery, 36. See also Alessandro Stanziani, Labor on the Fringes of Empire: Voice, Exit and the Law (Palgrave Macmillan, 2018), 219.

60. Stanziani, "Travail, droits et immigration," 50; and Kloosterboer, Involuntary Labour Since the Abolition of Slavery, 34. The story of the indentured Indian worker seeking legal aid is related in Stanziani, Labor on the Fringes of Empire, 1; Varma, Coolies of Capitalism, 52, 109; Stanziani, Labor on the Fringes of Empire,

3; and Stanziani, "L'immigration indentured à l'île Maurice," 18.

61. Sturman, "Indian Indentured Labor," 1463.

62. Mahatma Gandhi, "Petition to Natal Legislative Assembly (Durban, Before May 5, 1895)," in The Collected Works of Mahatma Gandhi, vol. 1, 2nd ed. (Publications Division, Ministry of Information and Broadcasting, Government of India, 1969), 231.

63. Mahatma Gandhi, "Indian Opinion (January 18, 1913)," in The Collected Works of Mahatma Gandhi, vol. 11 (Publications Division, Ministry of Information and Broadcasting, Government of India, 1969), 438. For another Indian nationalist protesting indentured labor, see Gopal Krishna Gokhale and G. A. Natesan, eds., Speeches of Gopal Krishna Gokhale (G. A. Natesan, 1916), 511.

64. For the general argument, see Foner, Reconstruction.

65. Foner, Reconstruction; Steven Hahn, "Class and Society in Postemancipation Societies: Southern Planters in Comparative Perspective," AHR 95 (February 1990): 75–98; Rafael Marquese, "The Legacies of Slavery: The Cotton and Coffee Economies of the United States and Brazil During Reconstruction, 1865–1904," in United States Reconstruction Across the Americas, ed. William A. Link (UP of Florida, 2019), 28; Foner, Reconstruction; Fields, "Advent of Capitalist Agriculture," 87; Bergad, Cuban Rural Society in the Nineteenth Century, 249, 254, 257; Scott, Slave Emancipation in Cuba, 91, 139, 191; Gillian McGillivray, Blazing Cane: Sugar Communities, Class, and State Formation in Cuba, 1868–1959 (Duke UP, 2009), 2, 31; and Mark Cohen, "Reforming States, Agricultural Transformation, and Economic Development in Russia and Japan, 1853–1913," Comparative Studies in Society and History 60, no. 3 (2018): 25–34. On the eastern Mediterranean, see Kristen Alff, "The Business of Property: Levantine Joint-Stock Companies and Nineteenth-Century Global Capitalism," Enterprise & Society 21, no.4 (December 2020): 853–65.

66. See Eric Foner, Free Soil, Free Labor, Free Men: The Ideology of the Republican Party Before the Civil War (OUP, 1970). See also Sven Beckert, The Monied Metropolis: New York City and the Consolidation of the American Bourgeoisie, 1850–1896 (CUP, 2001).

67. For the Philippines, this argument is also made by Justin F. Jackson, "'A Military Necessity Which Must Be Pressed': The US Army and Forced Road Labor in the Early American Colonial Philippines," in Van Der Linden and García, *On Coerced Labor*, 137.

68. Kelly Stauter-Halsted, *The Nation in the Village: The Genesis of Peasant National Identity in Austrian Poland, 1848–1914* (Cornell UP, 2001), 21, 22.

69. Quoted in Everett Wilson, "Crisis of National Integration in El Salvador, 1919–1935" (PhD diss., Stanford University, 1969), 122.

70. Kloosterboer, *Involuntary Labour Since the Abolition of Slavery*, 24, 44; Sedgewick, *Coffeeland*, 43–44, 69, 70, 71, 141, 159, 160; Bureau of the American Republics, *Coffee in America*.

71. Rafael Marquese, "Capitalism, Slavery, and the Brazilian Coffee Economy in the Long Nineteenth Century," paper presented at the New Perspectives on the Life and Work of Eric Williams, Oxford University, 2011, 32.

72. Marquese, "Capitalism, Slavery, and the Brazilian Coffee Economy," 29.

73. Marquese, "Legacies of Slavery," 11–46; Kevin H. O'Rourke, "The European Grain Invasion, 1870–1913," *JEH* 57 (December 1997): 775–801; Marquese, "Capitalism, Slavery, and the Brazilian Coffee Economy," 30. For the argument on Brazilian coffee lords controlling the government, see Marquese, "Legacies of Slavery," 11–46; Warren Dean, *Rio Claro: A Brazilian Plantation System, 1820–1920* (Stanford UP, 1976), 157, 158.

74. Jan Breman, *Labour Migration and Rural Transformation in Colonial Asia* (Free UP, 1990), 69.

75. Drax Hall, rent ledgers, 1847–1850, Z9/4/1, BNA.

76. An agent of the Government of India, 1931, as cited in Jayawardena and Kurian, *Class, Patriarchy and Ethnicity on Sri Lankan Plantations*, 45.

77. Jayawardena and Kurian, *Class, Patriarchy and Ethnicity on Sri Lankan Plantations*, 43, 44, 48, 60; Stanziani, "L'immigration indentured à l'île Maurice," 6; and Kloosterboer, *Involuntary Labour Since the Abolition of Slavery*, 37. Scholars debate whether this was a new form of slavery or the emergence of free contractual labor. See Stanziani, "Travail, droits et immigration," 47–8; Jaiswal, "Ephemeral Mobility," 59.

78. Che Rawick and Jules Rawick, *The American Slave: A Composite Autobiography*, vol. 11, Arkansas and Missouri Narratives (Greenwood Press, 1972), 117.

79. Foner, *Reconstruction*.

80. *Progressive Farmer*, 1904, as cited in Aaron Carico, "Freedom as Accumulation," *History of the Present* 6, no. 1 (Spring 2016): 9.

81. Sarah Washbrook, "Agrarian Modernisation in Chiapas, Mexico: Reform, Resistance, and Revolution, 1876–1911," in *Agrarian Reform and Resistance in an Age of Globalisation: The Euro-American World and Beyond, 1780–1914*, ed. Joe Regan and Cathal Smith (Routledge, 2018), 52; Washbrook, "Agrarian Modernisation in Chiapas," 48.

82. On cocoa growers in Ghana, see the excellent Corey Ross, "The Plantation Paradigm: Colonial Agronomy, African Farmers, and the Global Cocoa Boom, 1870–1940s," *JGH* 9, no. 1 (2014): 49–71 esp. 59. The numbers on peanut farmers are all from Tariq Omar Ali, *A Local History of Global Capital: Jute & Peasant Life in the Bengal Delta* (PUP, 2018), 3–4; Beckert, *Empire of Cotton*; Basma Fahoum, "Tobacco Cultivation in Mandatory Palestine: Zionist Farmers, Palestinian Peasants and Global Capitalism," unpublished paper presented at the Capitalism in the Countryside Conference, Harvard University, 2017; Ali, *Local History of Global Capital*, 1, 2, 5, 6, 9, 11, 21, 22, 28 30.

83. The quote is from Claude Markovits, "The Political Economy of Opium Smuggling in Early Nineteenth Century India: Leakage or Resistance?," *Modern Asian Studies* 43, no. 1 (2009): 89–111, here 89.

84. For a condensed summary of a huge number of studies on commodity prices collapsing, see Fields, "Advent of Capitalist Agriculture," 83; and Ali, *Local History of Global Capital*, 31–32.

85. "Rapport sur le coton, Haut Sénégal, Niger, 1910," 15, in Series R, Agriculture, Culture du Coton, 1889–1943, 1R/00035, ANS. See, for example, "Colonie du Niger, les irrigation du Niger et la culture cotonnière au Soudan, octobre 1921," "Dossier pour le coton du Niger, 1903," and "Le coton soudanais, production—outillage—colonisation, rapport," in Series R, Agriculture, Culture du Coton, 1889–1943, 1R/00035, ANS. For that urgency, see also "Circulaire sur la production du coton en A.O.F, 1924" and "Circulaire sur les essais

de culture du coton, 1899/1904," both in Series R, Agriculture, Culture du Coton, 1889–1943, 1R/0035. See also "Rapport sur le coton, Haut Sénégal, Niger, 1910," 1, in Series R, Agriculture, Culture du Coton, 1889–1943, 1R/00035, ANS; Sven Beckert, "From Tuskegee to Togo: The Problem of Freedom in the Empire of Cotton," *JAH* 92, no. 2 (2005): 498–526; "Le coton soudanais, production—outillage—colonisation, rapport," 8–9, Series R, Agriculture, Culture du Coton, 1889–1943, 1R/00035, ANS; Affaires commerciales, Series A, box 14, direction des consulats, commerce, 1902–1906, in Centre des Archives Diplomatiques de La Courneuve, Paris, France. Among the files I consulted are Industrie du Coton, Voyage d'Étude en Algérie, Cotons, Grande Bretagne, and Colonies, Culture Cotonniere dans les Colonies Allemandes.

86. "Rapport sur le coton, Haut Sénégal, Niger, 1910," 3, 5, in Series R, Agriculture, Culture du Coton, 1889–1943, 1R/00035, ANS; "Culture du Coton au Sénégal, 1900/1924," 36, Series R, Agriculture, Culture du Coton, 1889–1943, 1R/00035, ANS.

87. "Rapport sur le coton, Haut Sénégal, Niger, 1910," 4, 8; Letter of the Gouverneur Général de l'Afrique Occidentale Française to Monsieur le Lieutenant-Gouverneur du Haut Sénégal & Niger, Dakar, 21 November 1905; Gouvernement Général de L'Afrique Occidentale Française, Haut Sénégal et Niger, Service de l'Agriculture, "Rapport sur les essais cotonniers faits en 1905 dans la colonie du Haut Sénégal et Niger"; "Culture du Coton au Sénégal, 1900/1924," 21; "Rapport sur le coton, Haut Sénégal, Niger, 1910," 4, 13; and "Le coton soudanais, production—outillage—colonisation, rapport," 10; "Culture du coton au Sénégal, 1900/1924," 22–23, in Series R, Agriculture, Culture du Coton, 1889–1943, 1R/00035, ANS.

88. "Colonie du Niger, les irrigations du Niger et la culture cotonnière au Soudan, octobre 1921," in Series R, Agriculture, Culture du Coton, 1889–1943, 1R/00035, ANS.

89. "Rapport sur le coton, Haut Sénégal, Niger, 1910," 15, in Series R, Agriculture, Culture du Coton, 1889–1943, 1R/00035, ANS.

90. "Rapport sur le coton, Haut Sénégal, Niger, 1910," 10, in Series R, Agriculture, Culture du Coton, 1889–1943, 1R/00035, ANS.

91. "Rapport sur le coton, Haut Sénégal, Niger, 1910," 14, in Series R, Agriculture, Culture du Coton, 1889–1943, 1R/00035, ANS.

92. "Le coton soudanais, production— outillage— colonisation, rapport," 11, in Series R, Agriculture, Culture du Coton, 1889–1943, 1R/00035, ANS.

93. "Rapport sur le coton, Haut Sénégal, Niger, 1910," 9, in Series R, Agriculture, Culture du Coton, 1889–1943, 1R/00035, ANS; and "Le coton soudanais, production— outillage—colonisation, rapport," 41, in Series R, Agriculture, Culture du Coton, 1889–1943, 1R/00035, ANS.

94. "Le coton soudanais, production— outillage—colonisation, rapport," 11, in Series R, Agriculture, Culture du Coton, 1889–1943, 1R/00035, ANS.

95. "Le coton soudanais, production— outillage—colonisation, rapport," 42, in Series R, Agriculture, Culture du Coton, 1889–1943, 1R/00035, ANS.

96. "Le coton soudanais, production— outillage—colonisation, rapport," 41, in Series R, Agriculture, Culture du Coton, 1889–1943, 1R/00035, ANS.

97. "Le coton soudanais, produc-tion—outillage—colonisation, rap-port," 20, in Series R, Agriculture, Culture du Coton, 1889–1943, 1R/00035, ANS; "Colonie du Niger, les irrigations, du Niger et la culture cotonnière au Soudan, octobre 1921," in Series R, Agriculture, Culture du Coton, 1889–1943, 1R/00035, ANS; Droessler, "Islands of Labor," 57; and Kloosterboer, Involuntary Labour Since the Abolition of Slavery, 24.

98. As cited in Kloosterboer, Involuntary Labour Since the Abolition of Slavery, 24.

99. "Le coton soudanais, production— outillage—colonisation, rapport," 43, in Series R, Agriculture, Culture du Coton, 1889–1943, 1R/00035, ANS.

100. "Le coton soudanais, production— outillage— colonisation, rapport," chap. 2, 42, in Series R, Agriculture, Culture du Coton, 1889–1943, 1R/00035, ANS.

101. For one of many examples of the extreme racialization of laborers, see Issiaka Mandé, "La déraison de la république impériale française en Afrique de l'ouest: Le travail forcé et les villages de colonisation Mossi en Côte d'Ivoire," in Le travail colonial: Engagés et autres mains-d'oeuvre migrantes dans les empires, 1850–1950,

ed. Eric Guerassimoff and Issiaka Mandé (Riveneuve, 2015), 121–40. See also Fernand Braudel, After-thoughts on Material Civilization and Capitalism (Johns Hopkins UP, 1977), 75; W. E. B DuBois, On So-ciology and the Black Community (University of Chicago Press, 1980), 16; Adom Getachew, Worldmaking After Empire: The Rise and Fall of Self-Determination (PUP, 2020), 2, 20; Frederick Cooper, "States, Em-pire, and Political Imagination," in Colonialism in Question: Theory, Knowledge, History (University of California Press, 2005), 172; Joel Beinin, introduction to A Critical Po-litical Economy of the Middle East and North Africa, ed. Joel Beinin, Bassam Haddad, and Sherene Seikaly (Stan-ford UP, 2021), 3; and Tâmis Parron, "Capital e raça: Os segredos por trás dos nomes" ["Capital and Race: The Secrets Behind the Names"], Revista Rosa 2, no. 3 (2020): https://revista rosa.com/2/capital-e-raca.

102. Richard Adams, Farm Manage-ment: A Text-Book for Student, Inves-tigator, and Investor (McGraw Hill, 1921), 519–22.

103. Adams, Farm Management, 542.

104. Adachi Kinnosuké, Manchuria: A Survey (Robert M. McBride & Co., 1925), 44.

105. "Colonie du Niger, les irriga-tions du Niger et la culture coton-nière au Soudan, octobre 1921," in Series R, Agriculture, Culture du Coton, 1889–1943, 1R/00035, ANS. See also Sturman, "Indian In-dentured Labor," 1448, 1449; Jona-than Connolly, "Indentured Labour Migration and the Meaning of Emancipation: Free Trade, Race, and Labour in British Public Debate, 1838–1860," Past & Present 238 (2018): 1021.

106. Economist, November 13, 1847, 1299.

107. For the quote, see Friedrich List, Das Nationale System der Politischen Oekonomie (Cotta'schen Verlag, 1841), 185.

108. For the numbers on leased con-victs, see Talitha L. LeFlouria, Chained in Silence: Black Women and Convict Labor in the New South (Uni-versity of North Carolina Press, 2015), 11. For convict labor in gen-eral, see Alexander C. Lichtenstein, Twice the Work of Free Labor: The Po-litical Economy of Convict Labor in the New South (Verso, 1996); Miyamoto Takashi, "Convict Labor and Its Commemoration: The Mitsui Miike Coal Mine Experience," Asia-Pacific Journal 15 (January 2017): 1–15; and Marion Eggert and Jörg Plassen,

Kleine Geschichte Koreas: Von den An-fängen bis zur Gegenwart, 2nd rev. ed. (C. H. Beck, 2018), 138.

109. Kloosterboer, Involuntary La-bour Since the Abolition of Slavery, 79, 99–104; and Jackson, "'A Military Necessity," 127, 133.

110. Kloosterboer, Involuntary La-bour Since the Abolition of Slavery, 107–10. See also "Death in the Dev-il's Paradise," Survival, accessed June 16, 2024, https://www.survivalin ternational.org/articles/3282-rubber -boom; Alexandre Quintanilha, in-troduction to Trabalhos do Centro de Investigação Científica Algodoeira, vol.1 (Centro de Investigação Cientí-fica Algodoeira, 1948), 3–10; and Allen F. Isaacman, Cotton Is the Mother of Poverty: Peasants, Work, and Rural Struggle in Colonial Mo-zambique, 1938–1961 (Heinemann, 1996).

111. On the history of forced labor in the Congo, see Julia Seibert, In die globale Wirtschaft gezwungen: Arbeit und kolonialer Kapitalismus im Kongo, 1885–1960 (Campus, 2016). See also Kloosterboer, Involuntary Labour Since the Abolition of Slavery, 119. For a discussion of the atrocities com-mitted in the Belgian Congo, which should be considered genocide, see Georgi Verbeeck, "Un génocide s'est-il déroulé dans l'État indépen-dant du Congo?," in Le Congo colo-niale: Une histoire en questions, ed. Idesbald Goddeeris, Amandine Lauro, and Guy Vanthemsche (Re-naissance du Livre, 2020), 45–61.

112. Kloosterboer, Involuntary La-bour Since the Abolition of Slavery, 120, 121, 123.

113. Kloosterboer, Involuntary La-bour Since the Abolition of Slavery, 111, 116, 126.

114. Kloosterboer, Involuntary La-bour Since the Abolition of Slavery, 127, 129.

115. Spectator, December 15, 1906, 970.

116. Kloosterboer, Involuntary La-bour Since the Abolition of Slavery, 124, 125, 130, 134. A full forty-six thousand workers labored in the mines in 1916. See Guy Vanthem-sche, Belgium and the Congo, 1885– 1980, trans. Alice Cameron and Stephen Windross (CUP, 2012), 24– 25.

117. Kloosterboer, Involuntary La-bour Since the Abolition of Slavery, 163–64, 170; Harrison Ola Aking-bade, "The Liberian Problem of Forced Labor 1926–1940," Africa: Rivista trimestrale di studi e documen-tazione dell'Istituto Italiano per l'Af-rica e l'Oriente 52, no. 2 (June 1997): 261–73; Doreen Lustig, Veiled Power:

International Law and the Private Corporation, 1886–1981 (OUP, 2020), 29; Enrique Martino, "Money, Indenture, and Neo-Slavery in the Spanish Gulf of Guinea, 1820s to 1890s," *Comparativ* 30 (2020): 560–80; Enrique Martino, "Dash-Peonage: The Contradictions of Debt Bondage in the Colonial Plantations of Fernando Pó," *Africa* 87, no. 1 (2017): 53–78; and Jairo Munive, "A Political Economic History of the Liberian State, Forced Labour and Armed Mobilization," *Journal of Agrarian Change* 11, no. 3 (2011): 360–63. See also Lustig, *Veiled Power*, 54.

118. Marta Macedo, "Standard Cocoa," 9, 12, 13. See also Kloosterboer, *Involuntary Labour Since the Abolition of Slavery*, 68.

119. Macedo, "Standard Cocoa," 16–17.

120. *Daily Telegraph* (Sydney), September 4, 1882; and Tracey Flanagan, Meredith Wilkie, and Susanna Iuliano, Australian Human Rights Commission, "Australian South Sea Islanders: A Century of Race Discrimination Under Australian Law," archived March 14, 2011, at https://web.archive.org/web/201103140 80249/http:/www.hreoc.gov.au/racial_discrimination/forum/Erace/south_sea.html. On the diversity of destinations, see New South Wales, *Report of the Royal Commission, Appointed to Inquire into Certain Alleged Cases of Kidnapping of Natives of the Loyalty Islands, & c.* (Sidney Thomas Richards, 1869), 11, in NRS-1405-1 [4/774] Correspondence, Royal Commission of Enquiry into Certain Cases of Alleged Kidnapping of Natives of the Loyalty Islands in the Years 1865–68 and into State and Probable Results of Polynesian Immigration, State Archives and Records, New South Wales, Sydney, Australia.

121. Cited in Edward Wybergh Docker, *The Blackbirders: A Brutal Story of the Kanaka Slave-Trade* (Angus and Robertson, 1971), 45. On Levin and the violence of his trade, see also Alfred Davidson to Arthur Hodgson, Brisbane, 12 March 1869, as reprinted in Legislative Assembly, Queensland, *Progress Report from the Select Committee of the Operations of the Polynesian Labourers Act of 1868* (Brisbane: James C. Beal, 1869), 17–19, at State Archives and Records, New South Wales, Sydney, Australia.

122. Entry of 1 October 1870, typed copy of lost original, W. G. Farquhar Diaries, 1870–1872, PMB 496, Pacific Manuscripts Bureau, Canberra. Viewed at the State Library of New South Wales, Sydney, Australia. On payments, see entries of 17 December 1870 (Saturday) and 1 January 1871.

123. Entry of 6 January 1871, typed copy of lost original, W. G. Farquhar Diaries, 1870–1872, PMB 496, Pacific Manuscripts Bureau, Canberra. Viewed at the State Library of New South Wales, Sydney, Australia.

124. "A Cruise in a Queensland Slaver: By a Medical Student, 1882," George Ernest Morrison Diary, Series 1, Part 4, item 3: MLMSS 312/4, State Library of New South Wales, Sydney, Australia. On violent conflict, see also F. W. Galloway (Immigration Agent, Brisbane) to Henry Norman (Brisbane), letter, 14 July 1892, in *Queensland: Further Correspondence Relating to Polynesian Labour in the Colony of Queensland* (London: Majesty's Stationery Office, 1892), 7, State Library of New South Wales, Sydney, Australia.

125. On securing workers for cotton, see "South Sea Islanders (Queensland), Copy of Extracts of All Correspondence Relating to the Importation of South Sea Islanders into Queensland," Colonial Office, 6 July 1868, NRS-1405-1 [4/774] Correspondence, Royal Commission of Enquiry into Certain Cases of Alleged Kidnapping of Natives of the Loyalty Islands in the Years 1865–68 and into State and Probable Results of Polynesian Immigration, State Archives and Records, New South Wales, Sydney, Australia; for Robert Towns, see "Copy of Extracts of All Correspondence Relating to the Importation of South Sea Islanders into Queensland." Many of these skirmishes are documented in newspaper cuttings pertaining to the New Hebrides, archived at Q988.6/N, State Library of New South Wales, Sydney, Australia. See *North Australian*, January 28, 1865; "Report upon Muster and Inspection of South Sea Islanders per 'King Oscar,'" 19 November 1867, *Queensland Votes and Proceedings*, 1867, II, 135–37; *Brisbane Courier*, January 12 and 13, 1869; "Progress Report of the Select Committee on the Operation of the Polynesian Labourers Act of 1868," in *Queensland Votes and Proceedings*, 1869, II, 38, 44–45, 49–51; Robert Short, *Slave Trade in the Pacific: A Statement on the Introduction of Polynesian Labour into Queensland, and the Operation of the Polynesian Labourers Act, 1868* (London: 1870), 19–27; Docker, *Blackbirders*, 46–47; and Kay Saunders, *Workers in Bondage: The Origins and Bases of Unfree Labour in Queensland, 1824–1916* (University of Queensland Press, 1982), 20. On the mechanisms of securing labor—sometimes violently, sometimes by mutual agreement—see the evidence and testimonies contained in New South Wales, *Report of the Royal Commission*, 4. For an overview on blackbirding, see Doug Munro, "The Pacific Islands Labour Trade: Approaches, Methodologies, Debates," *Slavery and Abolition* 14, no. 2 (1993): 87–108; and Clive Moore, "Revising the Revisionists: The Historiography of Immigrant Melanesians in Australia," *Pacific Studies* 15, no. 2 (1992): 61–86.

126. *Brisbane Courier*, August 16, 1892, as reprinted in House of Commons (Queensland), *Further Correspondence Relating to Foreign Labour in the Colony of Queensland* (London: Majesty's Stationery Office, 1893), 16, State Library of New South Wales, Sydney, Australia.

127. New South Wales, *Report of the Royal Commission*, 4.

128. Statement by the New Hebrides Mission, 7 September 1867, in "Copy of Extracts of All Correspondence Relating to the Importation of South Sea Islanders into Queensland."

129. John Connell, "Blackbird Labor Trade," *Encyclopedia of Western Colonialism Since 1450*, vol. 1, ed. Thomas Benjamin (Macmillan Reference USA, 2007), 137. See also Hugh Tinker, *A New System of Slavery: The Export of Indian Labour Overseas, 1830–1920* (OUP for the Institute of Race Relations, 1974); Richard B. Allen, "European Slave Trading, Abolitionism, and 'New Systems of Slavery' in the Indian Ocean," *POR-TAL Journal of Multidisciplinary International Studies* 9, no. 1 (2012), http://epress.lib.uts.edu.au/journals/index.php/portal/article/view/2624; "Final Report of the Committee on Immigration (Indian and British) into New South Wales," 25 August 1837, vol. 19, *British Parliamentary Papers: Emigration* (Irish UP, 1968), 433–36, cited by Janet Doust in "Setting Up Boundaries in Colonial Eastern Australia: Race and Empire," *Australian Historical Studies* 35, no. 123 (2004): 161. On the demographic aspects, see also entry of 7/8 January 1871, typed copy of lost original, W. G. Farquhar Diaries, 1870–1872, PMB 496, Pacific Manuscripts Bureau, Canberra. Viewed at State Library of New South Wales, Sydney, Australia. See also report to "His Excellency William Stevenson, Esquire, Governor and Commander in Chief of Mauritius

and Dependencies," in NRS-906-1 4/754.1 Consuls—Appointment of all papers on alleged kidnapping of South Sea Islanders by Captain Joseph Wilson of the English Braque *Sutton*, 1858. For the Australian government's role, see, for example, many of the documents reprinted in House of Commons (Queensland), *Further Correspondence Relating to Foreign Labour in the Colony of Queensland*. On state involvement, see also Colonial Secretary's Office to the Secretary of the Government of New South Wales, 6 April 1858, NRS-906-1 4/754.1 Consuls—Appointment of all papers on alleged kidnapping of South Sea Islanders by Captain Joseph Wilson of the English Braque *Sutton* 1858, State Archives and Records, New South Wales, Sydney, Australia. See also "Act to Regulate and Control the Introduction of Polynesian Labourers (in the 31st year of Queen Victoria's Government)," in NRS-1405-1 [4/774] Correspondence, Royal Commission of Enquiry into Certain Cases of Alleged Kidnapping of Natives of the Loyalty Islands in the Years 1865–68 and into State and Probable Results of Polynesian Immigration, State Archives and Records, New South Wales, Sydney, Australia. For some of the regulations, see the documents in "Copy of Extracts of All Correspondence Relating to the Importation of South Sea Islanders into Queensland," 2–5. See also Queensland State Archives, "South Sea Islanders and the Kanaka Trade," Queensland State Archive, 7. In July 2021, the mayor of the town of Bundaberg was the first Australian government official to formally apologize for that practice. See https://www.sbs.com.au/nitv/article/2021/07/30/south-sea-islander-community-receive-first-formal-apology-slavery.

130. Christian Dippel, Avner Greif, and Dan Trefler, "Outside Options, Coercion, and Wages: Removing the Sugar Coating," *Economic Journal* 130, no. 630 (August 2020): 1703. For a very similar argument, see Herman Merivale, *Lectures on Colonization and Colonies*, 313.

131. Kloosterboer, *Involuntary Labour Since the Abolition of Slavery*, 4. For conclusive proof of the point on extra-economic coercion in the context of the plantation economy of the Carribean, see Dippel, Greif, and Trefler, "Outside Options, Coercion, and Wages," 1678–714. The same basic argument, however, was already made in 1960 by Kloosterboer, *Involuntary Labour Since the Abolition*

of Slavery, 6. See also Dippel, Greif, and Trefler, "Outside Options, Coercion, and Wages," 1678; and Carico, "Freedom as Accumulation," 2.

132. Fields, "Advent of Capitalist Agriculture," 77; and Rosa Luxemburg, *The Accumulation of Capital* (Routledge, 2003), 351.

133. Contemporaries were quite aware of the importance of the state. See "La Main-d'oeuvre à La Réunion," *Le Temps*, November 7, 1899; Ho, *Histoire économique*, 10; and Note sur l'immigration malgache à La Réunion," author unknown, undated (but probably 1920s), Main d'œuvre: Madagascar et La Réunion, Recrutement de travailleurs dans l'Inde, dans l'Indo-Chine, dans la Chine, dans le Japon / Rapport Geismar, FM/7AFFECO/19, Travail, La Réunion, Recrutements, Extérieur, 1866–1939, Ministre des Colonies, ANOM. See also the long list of rules and regulations listed in J. W. Muir-Mackenzie, "Rapport sur la condition et le traitement des immigrés indiens dans la colonie française de l'isle de La Réunion," Calcutta, 1891, as cited in Fuma, *De l'Inde du sud à l'île de La Réunion*, 181–222; Chaillou-Atrous, "La reprise de l'immigration africaine," 31, 43.

134. Stauter-Halsted, *The Nation in the Village*, 31; and Kloosterboer, *Involuntary Labour Since the Abolition of Slavery*, 10, 50, 67. The story of Deeken and Tsung is related in much greater detail in Droessler, "Islands of Labor," 78–80, 108; Jayawardena and Kurian, *Class, Patriarchy and Ethnicity on Sri Lankan Plantations*, 30; Jaiswal, "Ephemeral Mobility," 65.

135. Lieutenant Governor of Dahomey to Governor General of French West Africa, letter, 2 November 1918, in "Régime du travail: [illegible] . . . sur l'emploi de l'oeuvre indigène, 1905–1927," Esclavage et Travail, 1807–1920, Series K, K 35, 399/132, ANS.

136. Kloosterboer, *Involuntary Labour Since the Abolition of Slavery*, 9, 11, 26; Sedgewick, *Coffeeland*, 69, 162; Sturman, "Indian Indentured Labor," 1412, 1440, 1445, 1465.

137. Kloosterboer, *Involuntary Labour Since the Abolition of Slavery*, 15.

138. Kloosterboer, 6, 191; "Main d'oeuvre Antandroy à La Réunion: Rapport," Administrateur en Chef Bereni to Monsieur le Gouverneur Général de Madagascar et Dépendances, 20 December 1924, 40–41, in Main d'œuvre: Madagascar et La Réunion, Recrutement de travailleurs dans l'Inde, dans l'Indo-Chine, dans la Chine, dans le Japon / Rap-

port Geismar, FM/7AFFECO/19, Travail, La Réunion, Recrutements, Extérieur, 1866–1939, Ministre des Colonies, ANOM; Administrateur en Chef Bereni to Monsieur le Gouverneur Général de Madagascar et Dépendance, 27, 34, 42, in Main d'œuvre: Madagascar et La Réunion, Recrutement de travailleurs dans l'Inde, dans l'Indo-Chine, dans la Chine, dans le Japon / Rapport Geismar, FM/7AFFECO/19, Travail, La Réunion, Recrutements, Extérieur, 1866–1939, Ministre des Colonies, ANOM.

139. Inspector General of the Colonies Norès, Chef de la Mission de Madagascar, to the Minister of Colonies, letter, 7 April 1920, 6, 8, in Main d'œuvre: Madagascar et La Réunion, Recrutement de travailleurs dans l'Inde, dans l'Indo-Chine, dans la Chine, dans le Japon / Rapport Geismar, FM/7AFFECO/19, Travail, La Réunion, Recrutements, Exterieur, 1866–1939, Ministre des Colonies, ANOM.

140. Letter, Inspector General of the Colonies Norès, Chef de la Mission de Madagascar, to the Minister of Colonies, 7 April 1920, 9, in Main d'œuvre: Madagascar et La Réunion, Recrutement de travailleurs dans l'Inde, dans l'Indo-Chine, dans la Chine, dans le Japon / Rapport Geismar; FM/7AFFECO/19, Travail, La Réunion, Recrutements, Extérieur, 1866–1939, Ministre des Colonies, ANOM.

141. The argument on diversity of labor regimes is also made by Stanziani, "Travail, droits et immigration," 49.

142. On cultivators pushing against reconstruction, see, for example, Guerassimoff and Mandé, *Le travail colonial*, 17; and James Scott, *Weapons of the Weak: Everyday Forms of Peasant Resistance* (Yale UP, 1985).

143. Main d'oeuvre Antandoy a La Réunion, "Relevé des condamnations prononcées pour infraction de droit au décret de 1877," Main d'œuvre: Madagascar et La Réunion, Recrutement de travailleurs dans l'Inde, dans l'Indo-Chine, dans la Chine, dans le Japon / Rapport Geismar, FM/7AFFECO/19, Travail, La Réunion, Recrutements, Extérieur, 1866–1939, Ministre des Colonies, ANOM.

144. Main d'oeuvre Antandoy a La Réunion, "Relevé des condamnations prononcées pour infraction de droit au décret de 1887," in Main d'œuvre: Madagascar et La Réunion, Recrutement de travailleurs dans l'Inde, dans l'Indo-Chine, dans la Chine, dans le Japon / Rapport Geis-

mar, FM/7AFFECO/19, Travail, La Réunion, Recrutements, Extérieur, 1866–1939, Ministre des Colonies, ANOM; and Main d'oeuvre Antandoy a La Réunion, "Releve des condemnation pronounces pur infraction de droit de commun," Main d'œuvre: Madagascar et La Réunion, Recrutement de travailleurs dans l'Inde, dans l'Indo-Chine, dans la Chine, dans le Japon / Rapport Geismar, FM/7AFFECO/19, Travail, Reuinion, Recuritments, Exterieur, 1866–1939, Ministre des Colonies, ANOM.

145. Inspector General of the Colonies Norès, Chef de la Mission de Madagascar, to the Minister of Colonies, letter, 7 April 1920, in Main d'œuvre: Madagascar et La Réunion, Recrutement de travailleurs dans l'Inde, dans l'Indo-Chine, dans la Chine, dans le Japon / Rapport Geismar, FM/7AFFECO/19, Travail, La Réunion, Recrutements, Extérieur, 1866–1939, Ministre des Colonies, ANOM.

146. Eric Panthou, "Les formes de résistance de travailleurs de plantations d'hévéas d'Indochine," in Guerassimoff and Mandé, Le travail colonial, 467, 469, 471, 484; Jayawardena and Kurian, Class, Patriarchy and Ethnicity on Sri Lankan Plantations, 15; Varma, Coolies of Capitalism, 47, 141, 196–202; Macedo, "Standard Cocoa," 14; Stanziani, "L'immigration indentured à l'île Maurice," 10; and Stanziani, Labor on the Fringes of Empire, 41–43. For running away as a form of exit, see the argument by Stanziani, Labor on the Fringes of Empire, 41.

147. Sedgewick, Coffeeland, 286.

148. Beckert, Empire of Cotton, 338; Irina Marin, "Rural Social Combustibility in Eastern Europe (1880–1914): A Cross-Border Perspective," Rural History 28 (2017): 96; Marin, "Rural Social Combustibility in Eastern Europe," 96; Charles Postel, The Populist Vision (OUP, 2007); Steven Hahn, The Roots of Southern Populism: Yeoman Farmers and the Transformation of the Georgia Upcountry, 1850–1890 (OUP, 1985); William K. Meyers, "Seasons of Rebellion: Nature, Organisation of Cotton Production and the Dynamics of Revolution in La Laguna, Mexico, 1910–1816," Journal of Latin American Studies 30, no. 1 (February 1998): 36; and Timothy Mitchell, Rule of Experts: Egypt, Techno-Politics, Modernity (University of California Press, 2002), 63–64. On the riots, see Neil Charlesworth, "The Myth of the Deccan Riots of 1875," Modern Asian Studies 6, no. 4 (1972):

401–21; Deccan Riots Commission, Papers Relating to the Indebtedness of the Agricultural Classes in Bombay and Other Parts of India (Bombay: Deccan Riots Commission, 1876); Report of the Committee on the Riots in Poona and Ahmednagar, 1875 (Bombay: Government Central Press, 1876); Roderick J. Barman, "The Brazilian Peasantry Reexamined: The Implications of the Quebra-Quilo Revolt, 1874–1875," Hispanic AHR 57, no. 3 (1977): 401–24; and Armando Souto Maior, Quebra-Quilos: Lutas sociais no outono do império (Companhia Editora Nacional, 1978). The pressure of raising taxes was also felt by Egyptian peasants, who lost most of the profits that they had accumulated during the Civil War. See E. R. J. Owen, Cotton and the Egyptian Economy, 1820–1914: A Study in Trade and Development (Clarendon Press, 1969), 144; W. H. Wyllie, Agent of the Governor General in Central India, to the Revenue and Agriculture Department, 9 September 1899, in Proceedings, Part B, nos. 14–54, November 1899, Famine Branch, Department of Revenue and Agriculture, NAI; Wady E. Medawar, Études sur la question cotonnière et l'organisation agricole en Égypte (A. Gherson, 1900), 16, 20–21; Meyers, "Seasons of Rebellion," 63; William K. Meyers, Forge of Progress, Crucible of Revolt: Origins of the Mexican Revolution in La Comarca Lagunera, 1880–1911 (University of New Mexico Press, 1994), 132–34.

149. David Montgomery, The Fall of the House of Labor (CUP, 1987), 50, 51. The numbers on employment by industry are rounded and come from Montgomery, Fall of the House of Labor, 50, 54; Mitchell, International Historical Statistics, 153, 154, 159, 168; Franz-Josef Brüggemeier, Michael Farrenkopf, and Heinrich Theodor Grütter, eds., Das Zeitalter der Kohle: Eine Europäische Geschichte (Klartext, 2018), 169; Donald Sassoon, One Hundred Years of Socialism: The Western European Left in the Twentieth Century (I. B. Tauris, 2010), 10; P. Bairoch and J.-M. Limbor, "Changes in the Industrial Distribution of the World Labour Force by Region, 1880–1960," International Labour Review 98, no. 4 (October 1968): 317.

150. Peter Backes, "Die Wohlfahrtseinrichtungen der Röchling'schen Eisen-und Stahlwerke," in Die Röchlings und die Völklinger Hütte, ed. Meinrad Maria Grewenig (Springpunkt Verlag, 2014), 48; Fabian Trinkaus, Arbeiterexistenzen und Ar-

beiterbewegung in den Hüttenstädten Neunkirchen/Saar und Düdelingen/Luxemburg, 1880–1935/40 (Kommission für Saarländische Landesgeschichte, 2014), 51, 122–27; Gerhard Seibold, Röchling: Kontinuität im Wandel (Thorbecke Verlag, 2001), 156; Trinkaus, Arbeiterexistenzen und Arbeiterbewegung, 48; Ralf Banken, Die Industrialisierung der Saarregion 1815–1914, vol. 2, Take-Off-Phase und Hochindustrialisierung 1850–1914 (Franz Steiner Verlag, 2003), 307; Seibold, Röchling, 157; and Trinkaus, Arbeiterexistenzen und Arbeiterbewegung, 134; Banken, Die Industrialisierung der Saarregion, 2:421.

151. Trinkhaus, Arbeiterexistenzen und Arbeiterbewegung, 16–22, 105, 194; Marcel van der Linden, "At the End of a Very Long Cycle: Why the Global Labor Movement Is in Crisis," unpublished paper presented at the Global History Globally Workshop, Cambridge, MA, February 2021, 7. See also letter of the Zentralverband Deutscher Arbeiter und Schrebergärten, Berlin, 10 November 1909, A 1590, SAV; B/K-175: RESW GmbH (Röchling'sche Eisen und Stahlwerke GmbH), "Statistik über Viehhaltung, sowie Haus- und Grundbesitz der eigenen Belegschaft nach dem Stand von 31.12.1913," Alter Bestand, VH; Paul Edward Pheffer, "Railroads and Aspects of Social Change in Senegal, 1878–1933" (PhD diss., University of Pennsylvania, 1975), 311.

152. Harry Braverman, Labor and Monopoly Capitalism: The Degradation of Work in the Twentieth Century (Monthly Review Press, 1974), 63; and Montgomery, Fall of the House of Labor, 11.

153. Braverman, Labor and Monopoly Capitalism, 75.

154. Peter F. Drucker, The Practice of Management (Harper & Row, 1954), 280; Braverman, Labor and Monopoly Capitalism, 85.

155. Frederick W. Taylor, Principles of Scientific Management (Harper & Brothers, 1915), 36.

156. Taylor, Principles of Scientific Management, 98.

157. Braverman, Labor and Monopoly Capitalism, 87, 90, 107–9, 118, 126, 131; and Montgomery, Fall of the House of Labor, 5.

158. Walter Bagehot, "Principles of Political Economy," in The Works and Life of Walter Bagehot, ed. Russell Barrington, vol. 8 (Longmans, Green & Co., 1915), 231.

159. Braverman, Labor and Monopoly Capitalism, 92. See also The Taylor and Other Systems of Shop Management:

Hearings Before Special Committee of the House of Representatives to Investigate the Taylor and Other Systems of Shop Management under Authority of H. Res. 90, vol. 3 (US Government Printing Office, 1912), 1413.

160. Montgomery, *Fall of the House of Labor*, 28, 29, 36, 43.

161. Cited in Fritz Hellwig, *C. F. Stumm-Halberg, 1836–1901* (Heidelberg, 1936), 295.

162. Donald Quataert, "Machine Breaking and the Changing Carpet Industry of Western Anatolia, 1860–1908," *Journal of Social History* 19 (1986): 473–89; and Mircea Raianu, *Tata: The Global Corporation That Built Indian Capitalism* (HUP, 2021), 64. For "Work Regulations," see Hubert Kesternich, *Aufstieg und Wandel: 140 Jahre Völklinger Hütte* (Blattlausverlag, 2015), 1:42, 186. Kesternich, *Aufstieg und Wandel*; Hans Horch, *Der Wandel der Gesellschafts- und Herrschaftsstrukturen in der Saarregion während der Industrialisierung (1740–1914)* (W. J. Röhrig Verlag, 1985), 262; Banken, *Industrialisierung der Saarregion*, 2:423. The open resistence of the workers ("der offene Widerstand der Schweisser und Walzer") is an incident cited in Kesternich, *Aufstieg und Wandel*, 1:115.

163. "Arbeits-Ordnung für die Eisengiesserei und Maschinenfabrik von Eduard Laeis & Cie, Trier," n.d. but must be before 1910, in A/K 21/195: "Material ueber die Werkspensionskassen, 1908–1910 etc. etc.," Alter Bestand, VH.

164. Kesternich, *Aufstieg und Wandel*, 1:82.

165. On this process in general, see Horch, *Der Wandel der Gesellschafts- und Herrschaftsstrukturen*, 260; and Kesternich, *Aufstieg und Wandel*, 1:82–83. On the Röchling's teenage workers, see the court case referenced in Kesternich, *Aufstieg und Wandel*, 1:64, 89–91.

166. Kesternich, *Aufstieg und Wandel*, 1:1–2, 73, 95, 138; Peter Turned, "Über das Fortschreiten und das Zurückweichen des Puddelprozesses," in *Österreichische Zeitschrift für Berg- und Hüttenwesen*, 1886, 495. On the lack of workplace safety standards at the Röchling mill, see "Anzeige einer Verunglückung," and the compilation in Unglücksfaelle, 1853–1893, A 1531, SAV. See also the lists in Bewegung unter den Arbeitern, 1889, LRA, SB, 1837, LAS; and Trinkaus, *Arbeiterexistenzen und Arbeiterbewegung*, 218.

167. Gesuch des Hüttenarbeiters Johann Alles aus Völklingen, Völklin-

gen, 27 Februar 1923, D-K10/42: RESW GmbH, Wohnungswesen, Anträge auf Zuweisung einer Wohnung 1921, Mappe 1, Alter Bestand, VH; Note, D-K10/42: RESW GmbH, Wohnungswesen, Antraege auf Zuweisung einer Wohnung 1921, Mappe 1, Alter Bestand, VH; Antrag auf Zuweisung einer Zimmerwohnung gestellt am 14. Mai 1922, D-K10/42: RESW GmbH, Wohnungswesen, Anträge auf Zuweisung einer Wohnung 1921, Mappe 1, Alter Bestand, VH; Heuspeicher, Bürgermeister Völklingen an Röchling'schen Werke, Völklingen, April 1922, D-K10/42: RESW GmbH, Wohnungswesen, Antraege auf Zuweisung einer Wohnung 1921, Mappe 1, Alter Bestand, VH; and Trinkaus, Arbeiterexistenzen und Arbeiterbewegung, 271.

168. "Untersuchungen zu Misshandlungsfällen etc. 1847," A 119; Bürgermeisterei Völklingen, Acta Generalia, betreffend Jugendliche Verbrecher, 1826–1892, A 228, SAV. See the various letters between Röchling'schen Eisen- und Stahlwerke, die Völklingen city administration, and various other administrative agencies, 1908–1928, in Obstdiebstahl, Umherschweifen im Walde, A 634, SAV. Brief an die Direktion des Edelstahlwerkes, Völklingen, 19 Juli 1923 von Jakob Bennoit, Oberwalzer, D-K10/42: RESW GmbH, Wohnungswesen, Antraege auf Zuweisung einer Wohnung 1921, Mappe 1, Alter Bestand, VH.

169. For the quote, see Richard Nutzinger, Hans Böhmer, and Otto Johannsen, eds., *50 Jahre Röchling Völklingen: Die Entwicklung eines Rheinischen Industrie-Unternehmens* (Gebr. Hofer A. G., 1931), 17.

170. Trinkaus, *Arbeiterexistenzen und Arbeiterbewegung*, 320.

171. Trinkaus, *Arbeiterexistenzen und Arbeiterbewegung*, 325.

172. "Vorschlag des Kreisausschusses betreffend Unterstützung von Wohnungsbauten der minderbemittelten Bevölkerung," Saarbrücken, 5. März 1902, Gemeinnützige Vereine per procurationem Gemeinnütziger Bauverein, SAV. See also Hubert Kesternich, *Aufstieg und Wandel*, 66.

173. Seibold, *Röchling*, 160–61; Nutzinger, Böhmer, and Johannsen, *50 Jahre Röchling*, 26; Gewerkschaft Karl Alexander, Wertschätzung der Colonie II, 21 Gruppen Arbeiterhäuser, 1918/01/10, A/K 8/ 99, Alter Bestand, VH; Trinkaus, *Arbeiterexistenzen und Arbeiterbewegung*, 374.

For very similar welfare policies, see Fr. Karcher & Cie. in Beckingen a. d. Saar, in A/K 21/ 195: Material ueber die Werkspensionskassen, 1908–1910 etc., etc., Alter Bestand, VH.

174. Seibold, *Röchling*, 160–61. See also Huettenarbeiter Verein Völklingen, Schriftwechsel, 1912–1922, Mappe 1, D-K 26/115, Alter Bestand, VH; Hüttenarbeiterverein e.V. Geislautern, 1908–1912, A 1260, SAV; Kesternich, *Aufstieg und Wandel*, 98, 153; "Zur Morgenspeising hungriger Schulkinder, Kreisschulinspektoren, Saarlouis, 10. Mai 1909, A 1590, SAV; Gemeinnützige Vereine per procurationem Gemeinnütziger Bauverein, A 1590, SAV.

175. Kesternich, *Aufstieg und Wandel*, 44, 99; Bürgermeisterei Völklingen, Acta Generalia, Mässigkeitsvereine, 1899–1926, A 860, SAV; and Kesternich, *Aufstieg und Wandel*, 99. See also letter of the Völklinger Eisenhütte, Völklingen, 1 Juni 1878, Bürgermeisterei Völklingen, Acta Specialia, Bildung von Mässigkeitsvereinen, A 1101, SAV.

176. RESW GmbH, Abstinenz Bestrebung: Schriftwechsel, 1907–1910 D/K-21/94, Alter Bestand, VH.

177. Brief von Hermann Röchling an die Geschäftsstelle des Südwestdeutschen Eisen-Berufsgenossenschaft Saarbrücken, Völklingen, 18 Maerz 1910, RESW GmbH, Abstinenz Bestrebung: Schriftweckesl, 1907–1910 D/K-21/95, Alter Bestand, VH.

178. Jeffrey G. Williamson, "The Evolution of Global Labor Markets Since 1830: Background Evidence and Hypotheses," *Explorations in Economic History* 32 (April 1995): 148, 164–65. See also George Boyer, "The Convergence of Living Standards in the Atlantic Economy, 1870–1930," in *The New Comparative Economic History: Essays in Honor of Jeffrey G. Williamson* (MIT Press, 2007), 317–42. For slightly different numbers, see Peter Scholliers and Vera Zamagni, *Labour's Reward: Real Wages and Economic Change in 19th- and 20th-Century Europe* (Edward Elgar Publishing, 1995), xiii; Boyer, "Convergence of Living Standards," 320–21; Peter H. Lindert, *Growing Public: Social Spending and Economic Growth Since the Eighteenth Century*, vol. 1 (CUP, 2004), 171; and Éric Hobsbawm, *The Age of Empire* (Pantheon, 1987), 49.

179. For the argument on working-class racism, see Rudi Batzell, "Race, Ethnicity, and Global Labor History," in Sven Beckert and Marcel van der Linden, eds., *The Oxford*

Handbook on Global Labor History (OUP).

180. Clements Kadalie, General Secretary, Industrial and Commercial Workers' Union of Africa, to N. M. Joshi, Bombay, Johannesburg, 16 January 1928, in All-India Trade Union Congress Papers, List 18, File No. 17, 1925–1938, Papers and All Correspondence Relating to Trade Union Movement in Africa, NMML.

181. The wage and food cost numbers are rough (especially the expenditures), but they provide insight into the materially constrained living conditions of steelworkers in the 1880s. See Kesternich, *Aufstieg und Wandel*, 1:61.

182. Hatice Yildiz, "The Politics of Time in Colonial Bombay: Labor Patterns and Protest in Cotton Mills," *Journal of Social History* 54, no. 1 (2020): 8; Raianu, *Tata*, 69; and Patricia Tsurumi, *Factory Girls: Women in the Thread Mills of Meiji Japan* (PUP, 1990), 67.

183. Robert J. Steinfeld, *Coercion, Contract and Free Labor in the Nineteenth Century* (CUP, 2001), 10; Steinfeld, *Coercion, Contract and Free Labor*, 24–25.

184. As historian Rudi Batzell has so insightfully observed, "When centralized, bureaucratic trade unions developed in this period, they would increasingly disavow and work to suppress these [older] tactics of contention." See Rudi Batzell, "Reconstructing Global Capitalism: Class, Corporations, and the Rise of Welfare States, 1870–1930" (PhD diss., Harvard University, 2017), 140. On Torrents's life, see Judith Keene, "In Search of Acracia: The Antipodean Odyssey of Salvador Torrents," *Mediterranean Studies* 2 (1990): 87. See also Salvador Torrents, Diary of Salvador Torrents, "Mi Anarchism," 1917, 17, and Salvador Torrents, Diary of Salvador Torrents, "My Philosophies," 1949, 28, both in the Salvador Torrents Papers, James Cook University Library Special Collections, Townsville, Australia.

185. Hobsbawm, *Age of Empire*, 46; Edward Shorter and Charles Tilly, *Strikes in France, 1830–1968* (CUP, 1974), 22; Bernard A. Cook, *Belgium: A History* (Peter Lang, 2004), 87; Gita Deneckere, *Les turbulences de la Belle Époque, 1878–1905: Nouvelle histoire de Belgique* (Le Cri Éd., 2010), 53; Robert Magraw, *A History of the French Working Class*, vol. 1, *The Age of Artisan Revolution, 1815–1871* (Blackwell, 1992), 202, 247; Brüggemeier, Farrenkopf, and Grütter, *Das Zeitalter der Kohle*, 170–71;

Shorter and Tilly, *Strikes in France*, 49, 361–62; Franz-Josef Brüggemeier, *Grubengold: Das Zeitalter der Kohle von 1750 bis Heute* (Verlag C. H. Beck, 2018), 169; Brüggemeier, Farrenkopf, and Grütter, *Das Zeitalter der Kohle*, 169, 174; Peter Flora, Franz Kraus, and Winfried Pfenning, *State, Economy, and Society in Western Europe, 1815–1975*, vol. 2 (Campus Verlag, 1987), 718; Klaus Tenfelde and Heinrich Volkmann, *Streik: Zur Geschichte des Arbeitskampfes in Deutschland während der Industrialisierung* (Verlag C. H. Beck, 1981), 296; and Brüggemeier, Farrenkopf, and Grütter, *Das Zeitalter der Kohle*, 170, 171. For additional data, see Friedhelm Boll, "Changing Forms of Labor Conflict: Secular Development or Strike Waves?," in *Strikes, Wars, and Revolutions in an International Perspective*, ed. Leopold Haimson and Charles Tilly (CUP, 1989), 62; James E. Cronin, "Strikes and Power in Britain, 1870–1920," in Haimson and Tilly, *Strikes, Wars and Revolutions*, 81; Brüggemeier, *Grubengold*, 170; Tilly and Shorter, *Strikes in France*, 165ff.

186. Cronin, "Strikes and Power in Britain," 81.

187. Brüggemeier, *Grubengold*, 79; Cronin, "Strikes and Power in Britain," 81; Jason Kaufman, "Rise and Fall of a Nation of Joiners: The Knights of Labor Revisited," *Journal of Interdisciplinary History* 31, no. 4 (2001): 553–79; Howard Kimeldorf, "Worker Replacement Costs and Unionization: Origins of the U.S. Labor Movement," *American Sociological Review* 78, no. 6 (December 2013): 103; Leo Michielsen, *Geschiedenis van de Europese Arbeidersbeweging*, deel 1, tot 1914 (Frans Masereelfonds, 1976), 93, 138; David Blackbourn, *The Long Nineteenth Century: A History of Germany, 1780–1918* (OUP, 1997), 337; Boll, "Changing Forms of Labor Conflict," 71; Jaak Brepoels, *Wat zoudt gij zonder 't werkvolk zijn? Anderhalve eeuw arbeiderstrijd in België*, deel 1, *1830–1966* (Kritak, 1978), 44; Magnus Bergli Rasmussen and Jonas Pontusson, "Working-Class Strength by Institutional Design? Unionization, Partisan Politics, and Unemployment Insurance Systems, 1870 to 2010," *Comparative Political Studies* 51, no. 6 (2018): 796; Ralf Rogge, "Fabrikzerstörungen und Tarifverträge," in *Petitionen und Barrikaden: Rheinische Revolutionen, 1848/49*, ed. Ottfried Dascher and Everhard Kleinertz (Aschendorff, 1998), 188; Jochen Putsch, *Vom*

Handwerk zur Fabrik (Stadtarchiv Solingen, 1985), 68; Rudolf Boch, *Handwerker-Sozialisten gegen Fabrikgesellschaft: Lokale Fachvereine, Massengewerkschaft und industrielle Rationalisierung in Solingen 1870 bis 1914* (Vandenhoeck & Ruprecht, 1985), 35–43.

188. The quote is cited in Arno Herzig, *Unterschichtenprotest in Deutschland, 1790–1870* (VR, 1988), 113.

189. Herzig, *Unterschichtenprotest in Deutschland*, 112–13; Marcel van der Linden, *Workers of the World: Essays Toward a Global Labor History* (Brill, 2008), 10; and Herzig, *Unterschichtenprotest in Deutschland*, 108, 112–13.

190. Yildiz, "Politics of Time in Colonial Bombay," 4, 12. Yildiz's brilliant article is well worth a read. See also Can Nacar, *Labor and Power in the Late Ottoman Empire: Tobacco Workers, Managers, and the State, 1872–1912* (Palgrave Macmillan, 2019), 6, 12. For a detailed analysis of that strike, see Can Nacar, "The Régie Monopoly and Tobacco Workers in Late Ottoman Istanbul," *Comparative Studies of South Asia, Africa and the Middle East* 34 (2014): 206–18; and Yavuz Selim Karakışla, "The Emergence of the Ottoman Industrial Working Class, 1839–1923," in *Workers and the Working Class in the Ottoman Empire and the Turkish Republic, 1839–1950*, ed. Donald Quataert and Erik J. Zürcher (I. B. Tauris, 1995), 26.

191. Royal Commission on Strikes, Report, No. 25 in NRS-905-28-[5/6029] item 91/7122 Col Sec Corro, Royal Commission on Strikes, State Archives and Records, New South Wales, Sydney, Australia.

192. Julio Godio, *Historia del movimiento obrero de argentino, 1870–2000* (Ediciones Corregidor, 2000), 70; Ricardo Falcón, *La Primera Internacional y los origins del movimiento obrero en Argentina (1857–1879)* (Centro de Estudios Histórico-Sociales de América Latina, 1980), 16; Godio, *Historia del movimiento obrero de argentino*, 85; Ruth Thompson, "Argentine Syndicalism: Reformism Before Revolution," in *Revolutionary Syndicalism: An International Perspective*, ed. Marcel van der Linden and Wayne Thorpe (Scolar Press, 1990), 171; and Thompson, "Argentine Syndicalism," 169, 174.

193. Thompson, "Argentine Syndicalism, 168, 175; Godio, *Historia del movimiento obrero de argentino*, 78, 138, 148, 152, 170, 177.

194. Joseph Melling, *Rent Strikes: Peoples' Struggle for Housing in West Scotland, 1890–1916* (Polygon Books, 1983), 62; Godio, *Historia del movimiento obrero de argentino*, 173. Details on the "March of the Broomsticks," Buenos Aires, 1907, are from Inés Yujnovsky, "Vida cotidiana y participación política: 'La Marcha de las Escobas' en la huelga de inquilinos, Buenos Aires, 1907," *Feminismo/s* 3 (June 2004), 121, 129.

195. The dates on the foundation of socialist parties are imprecise; there were often earlier efforts to form working-class parties. See Sassoon, *One Hundred Years of Socialism*, 10. On Germany, see Michielsen, *Geschiedenis van de Europese Arbeidersbeweging*, 1:93. On France, see Michielsen, *Geschiedenis van de Europese Arbeidersbeweging*, 1:135. See also Lucien van der Walt, "Anarchism and Syndicalism in an African Port City: The Revolutionary Traditions of Cape Town's Multiracial Working Class, 1904–1931," *Labor History* 52, no. 2 (2011): 137–71; "Japan Socialist Party," in *Chambers Dictionary of World History*, ed. Hilary Marsden and Bruce Lenman (Chambers, 2005), 451; Fritjof Tichelman, *Socialisme in Indonesië: De Indische Sociaal-Democratische Vereeniging*, deel 1: *1897–1917* (Foris Publications, 1985), 6; Godio, *Historia del movimiento obrero de argentino*, 78.

196. Hobsbawm, *Age of Empire*, 117; Sassoon, *One Hundred Years of Socialism*, 10; Stefano Bartolini, *The Political Mobilization of the European Left, 1860–1980: The Class Cleavage* (CUP, 2000), 55.

197. Brepoels, *Wat zoudt gij zonder 't werkvolk zijn?*, 1:36; Sassoon, *One Hundred Years of Socialism*, 10, 37; and Hobsbawm, *Age of Empire*, 117.

198. Anahide Ter Minassian, "The Role of the Armenian Community in the Foundation and Development of the Socialist Movement in the Ottoman Empire and Turkey: 1876–1923," in *Socialism and Nationalism in the Ottoman Empire, 1876–1923*, ed. Mete Tunçay and Erik J. Zürchers (British Academic Press, 1994), 118; Ibrahim Yalimov, "The Bulgarian Community and the Development of the Socialist Movement in the Ottoman Empire During the Period 1876–1923," in Tunçay and Zürchers, *Socialism and Nationalism in the Ottoman Empire*, 95; Fikret Adanïr, "The National Question and the Genesis and Development of Socialism in the Ottoman Empire: The Case of Macedonia," in Tunçay and Zürchers, *Socialism and Nationalism in the Ottoman Empire*, 37; and Godio, *Historia del movimiento obrero de argentino*, 78.

199. Trinkaus, *Arbeiterexistenzen und Arbeiterbewegung*, 251, 312, 402.

200. The quote appears as cited in Trinkaus, *Arbeiterexistenzen und Arbeiterbewegung*, 386. See also Bürgermeisterei Amt Völklingen an den Vorsitzenden der königlichen Bergwerksdirektion, Herrn Geheimen Bergrath von Veten, 22 May 1891, in Bewegung unter den Bergleuten, 1891–1893, LRA, SB, 1838, LAS; and Kesternich, *Aufstieg und Wandel*, 120.

201. Trinkaus, *Arbeiterexistenzen und Arbeiterbewegung*, 438.

202. For the quotes, see the surveillance report in Bürgermeisterei Völklingen an den königlichen Landrath Herrn Bake, Völklingen, 22 August 1892, in Bewegung unter den Bergleuten, 1891–1893, LRA, SB, 1838, LAS.

203. For the quotes, see *Saarbrücker Gewerbeblatt*, March 30, 1890, 50.

204. Acta pec., betr. Streik der Burbacher Eisenhütten Arbeiter, Juni 1906, LRA.SB. 1843, LAS; Harald Glaser, *Auf Schicht: Hüttenarbeit und Alltagsleben in Völklingen von der Gründerzeit der Hütte bis in die Sechziger Jahre* (Initiative Völklinger Hütte E.V., 1996), 36; and Seibold, *Röchling*, 165.

205. "Stenographischer Bericht über die gestern Abend im Lokal 'Zum Karlsberg' hierselbst stattgefundene öffentliche Hüttenarbeiter-Versammlung, einberufen von der christlichen Gewerkschaft, Völklingen," 3 May 1912, Gemeinnützige Vereine per procurationem Gemeinnütziger Bauverein, A 1590, SAV.

206. On the Employers' Committee for Combating Social Democracy (Committee der Arbeitgeber zur Bekämpfung der Sozialdemokratie), see Kesternich, *Aufstieg und Wandel*, 1:50.

207. Kesternich, *Aufstieg und Wandel*, 1:119. See, for example, Beobachtung von Sozialdemokraten und Anarchisten, A 2397, SAV; Regierungsbezirk Trier, Kreis Saarbrücken, Bürgermeistereien Völklingen, Acta Generalia betreffend Socialdemokratie, A 2586, SAV. For the quote, see the reports of 1889–1891 in Bewegung unter den Arbeitern, 1889–1891, LRA, SB, 1837, LAS.

208. On police surveillance, see the many reports in Bewegung unter den Bergleuten, 1891–1893, LRA, SB,

1838, LAS; and Montgomery, *Fall of the House of Labor*, 5.

209. "Aufrechterhaltung der Ruhe und Ordnung." See letter of the Minister des Innern, Berlin, 4 March 1899, Acta Generali betr. Bewegung unter den Arbeitern, 1889–1920, LRA, SB, 1833, LAS.

210. Hermann Röchling to M. Kollmann, Gauleiter des Gau VII des Deutschen abstinenten Arbeiterbundes, Völklingen, 7 June 1907, RESW GmbH, Abstinenz Bestrebung: Schriftwechsel, 1907–1910 D/K-21/94, Alter Bestand, VH.

211. Kesternich: *Aufstieg und Wandel*, 181. The word *Hetzer* (agitator) is frequently used in observations of the labor movement. See, for example, Bürgermeisterant Völklingen an den Königlichen Landrath Herrn Rake, Völklingen, 22 May 1891, in Bewegung unter den Bergleuten, 1891–1893, LRA, SB, 1838, LAS; Brief der Burbacher Hütte, an den Landrat Boetticher, Buchbach, 4 June 1906, Acta pec., betr. Streick der Burbacher Eisenhütten Arbeiter, June 1906, LRA, SB, 1843, LAS; Brüggemeier, Farrenkopf, and Grütter, *Das Zeitalter der Kohle*, 164; Stenographischer Bericht über die gestern Abend im Lokal "Zum Karlsberg" hierselbst stattgefundene öffentliche Hüttenarbeiter-Versammlung, einberufen von der christlichen Gewerkschaft, Völklingen, 3 May 1912, Gemeinnützige Vereine per procurationem Gemeinnütziger Bauverein, A 1590, SAV; and Trinkaus, *Arbeiterexistenzen und Arbeiterbewegung*, 498, 516.

212. Massimo De Angelis, "Separating the Doing and the Deed: Capital and the Continuous Character of Enclosures," *Historical Materialism* 12, no. 2 (2004): 73; Werner Sombart, "Die Wandlungen des Kapitalismus," *Weltwirtschaftliches Archiv* 28 (1928): 253; Mary Hilson, Silke Neunsinger, and Greg Patmore, eds., *Global History of Consumer Co-Operation Since 1850* (Brill, 2017), 7; G. D. H. Cole, *A History of Socialist Thought*, vol. 2 (Macmillan, 1957), 112; Brepoels, *Wat zoudt gij zonder 't werkvolk zijn?*, 1:46; Peter Scholliers, "The Social-Democratic World of Consumption: The Path-Breaking Case of the Ghent Cooperative Vooruit Prior to 1914," *International Labor and Working-Class History* 55 (1999): 71–91, here 74; Brepoels, *Wat zoudt gij zonder 't werkvolk zijn?*, 1:48, 1:46.

213. Minsun Ji, "The Worker Cooperative Movement in South Korea: From Radical Autonomy to

State-Sanctioned Accommodation," *Labor History* 59, no. 4 (2018), 415–36; and Van der Walt, "Anarchism and Syndicalism in an African Port City," 137–71. See, in general, Hilson, Neunsinger, and Patmore, *Global History of Consumer Co-Operation*, 12.

214. Hobsbawm, *Age of Empire*, 131; James Riordan, "The Worker Sports Movement," in *The International Politics of Sport in the Twentieth Century*, ed. James Riordan and Arnd Kruger (E. & F. N. Spon, 2002), 107; James Riordan, "Amateurism, Sport and the Left: Amateurism for All Versus Amateur Elitism," *Sport in History* 26, no. 3 (2006): 474; Internationaal Instituut voor Sociale Geschiedenis, "Archief Stem des Volks (Amsterdam) 1898–1940, 1945–1998, 2002–2003, 1898–1940," accessed February 12, 2021, https://search.iisg.amsterdam/Record/ARCH01951; and Roy Rosenzweig and Elizabeth Blackmar, *The Park and the People: A History of Central Park* (Cornell UP, 1992), 359–62.

Chapter 13: Enclosures

1. Charles Maier, *Leviathan 2.0: Inventing Modern Statehood* (HUP, 2012).

2. Pierre Bourdieu, *Über den Staat: Vorlesungen am Collège de France 1989–1992* (Suhrkamp, 2014), 38.

3. Alvaro Sevilla-Buitrago, "Capitalist Formations of Enclosure: Space and the Extinction of the Commons," *Antipode* 47, no. 4 (2015): 999–1020.

4. Charlie Maier periodizes the Leviathan 2.0 as lasting from ca. 1850 to ca. 1970. See Maier, *Leviathan 2.0*, 79, 83, 93, 98, 101.

5. Giovanni Arrighi, *The Long Twentieth Century: Money, Power and the Origins of Our Times* (Verso, 1994), 59; Rudolf Hilferding, *Das Finanzkapital. Eine Studie zur jüngsten Entwicklung des Kapitalismus* (Verlag der Wiener Volksbuchhandlung Ignaz Brand & Co., 1910); Werner Sombart, "Die Wandlungen des Kapitalismus," *Weltwirtschaftliches Archiv* 28 (1928): 250. See also Eric Hobsbawm, *The Age of Empire* (Pantheon, 1987), 40; Charles Tilly, *Coercion, Capital, and European States, AD 990–1990* (Basil Blackwell, 1990), 183.

6. Maier, *Leviathan 2.0*, 80.

7. Pia M. Jolliffe, "Forced Labour in Imperial Japan's First Colony: Hokkaido," *Asia-Pacific Journal* 18, no. 20 (October 2020): 3; Katsuya Hirano, "Thanatopolitics in the Making of Japan's Hokkaido: Settler Colonialism and Primitive Accumulation," *Critical Historical Studies* 2, no. 2 (Fall 2015): 192.

8. For one of many mentions of Hokkaido as Japan's first colony, see, for example, Michele M. Mason, *Dominant Narratives of Colonial Hokkaido and Imperial Japan: Envisioning the Periphery and the Modern Nation-State* (Palgrave Macmillan, 2018), 13.

9. David L. Howell, *Capitalism from Within: Economy, Society, and the State in a Japanese Fishery* (University of California Press, 1995), 2, 18, 19; Mason, *Dominant Narratives of Colonial Hokkaido and Imperial Japan*, 8; Fumiko Fujita, *American Pioneers and the Japanese Frontier: American Experts in Nineteenth-Century Japan* (Greenwood Press, 1994), 1; Capron to Kuroda Chokan, Kaitakushi, Tokei, 29 September 1874, as reprinted in Horace Capron, *Reports and Official Letters to the Kaitakushi* (Massachusetts: Kaitakushi, 1875), 264. For the same argument, see also Horace Capron, "Memoirs," vol. 2, "Expedition to Japan, 1871–1875," unpublished typescript, circa 1884, Special Collections, USDA National Agricultural Library, 92–94. There are widely divergent estimates of the Ainu population, but fifteen thousand seems to be the most reliable. For a much higher estimate, see Hirano, "Thanatopolitics in the Making of Japan's Hokkaido," 204. That fertilizer was important to raising Honshu agricultural productivity, see Kären Wigen, *The Making of a Japanese Periphery, 1750–1920* (University of California Press, 1995), 139, 158.

10. Hirano, "Thanatopolitics in the Making of Japan's Hokkaido," 198. The project played an important role in the formation of the Japanese nation-state, as explained in Jolliffe, "Forced Labour in Imperial Japan's First Colony," 2.

11. Sydney Xu Lu, *The Making of Japanese Settler Colonialism: Malthusianism and Trans-Pacific Migration, 1868–1961* (CUP, 2019), 54. On Hokkaido as an example for settler colonialism, see Mason, *Dominant Narratives of Colonial Hokkaido and Imperial Japan*, 16.

12. Fukuzawa Yukichi, *Sekai Kunizukushi* (1869), as cited in Fujita, *American Pioneers and the Japanese Frontier*, 5–6; and Richard Siddle, *Race, Resistance, and the Ainu of Japan* (Routledge, 1996), 56.

13. As cited in Hirano, "Thanatopolitics in the Making of Japan's Hokkaido," 200.

14. Mori Arinori, as cited in Fujita, *American Pioneers and the Japanese Frontier*, 6.

15. Mason, *Dominant Narratives of Colonial Hokkaido and Imperial Japan*, 25; Fujita, *American Pioneers and the Japanese Frontier*, 3, 5; Lu, *Making of Japanese Settler Colonialism*, 44; Fukuzawa, *Sekai Kunizukushi* (1869), as cited in Fujita, *American Pioneers and the Japanese Frontier*, 6; Siddle, *Race, Resistance, and the Ainu of Japan*, 56; Mori Arinori, as cited in Fujita, *American Pioneers and the Japanese Frontier*, 6; and Hirano, "Thanatopolitics in the Making of Japan's Hokkaido," 200. See also J. Austin Schaefer, "'Go West, [Old] Man': Horace Capron, Gilded Age Capitalism, and the Development of Hokkaido," *Vanderbilt Historical Review*, Spring 2016, 14. See, for example, K. Kuroda to Horace Capron, Shiba, 4 March 1874, as reprinted in Capron, *Reports and Official Letters to the Kaitakushi*, 228.

16. Horace Capron, "Memoirs," vol. 1, "Autobiography," unpublished typescript, circa 1884, Special Collections, USDA National Agricultural Library, 92–93; and Schaefer, "'Go West, [Old] Man,'"14.

17. See "Copy of article furnished by press by Governor Kuroda," March 1874, in folder 128, box 4, Horace Capron Papers, Yale University, New Haven, Connecticut; and Capron, "Autobiography," 5, 19, 42, 67, 81, 130, 142–43.

18. Letter of Capron to Colonel Warren, 25 February 1872, as cited in Fujita, *American Pioneers and the Japanese Frontier*, 22.

19. Capron, "Expedition to Japan, 1871–1875," 43; Horace Capron's receipt of Arinori Mori's overture, 17 April 1871, folder 99, box 4, Capron Papers, Yale University, New Haven, Connecticut; and Capron to Kiroda Dikan, Sapporo, 13 August 1873, as reprinted in Capron, *Reports and Official Letters to the Kaitakushi*, 92.

20. Katsuya Hirano, "Settler Colonialism and the Making of Japan's Hokkaidō," in *The Routledge Handbook of the History of Settler Colonialism*, ed. Edward Cavanagh and Lorenzo Veracini (Routledge, 2017), 328; and Capron to Kuroda Dikan, Sapporo, 22 July 1872, as reprinted in Capron, *Reports and Official Letters to the Kaitakushi*, 59. See, for example, "Abstract of First Annual Report of Horace Capron, Commissioner and Adviser of Kaitakushi of Hokaido, Tokio, Japan, for 1871" (Tokei: Kaitakushi, 1874), as re-

printed in Capron, *Reports and Official Letters to the Kaitakushi*, 41.

21. Capron, "Expedition to Japan, 1871–1875," 33.

22. Capron, "Expedition to Japan, 1871–1875," 135. See, for example, Horace Capron to Kuroda Kiyotaka, Sapporo, 24 June 1874, as reprinted in Capron, *Reports and Official Letters to the Kaitakushi*, 242. On timber, see also Capron, "Expedition to Japan, 1871–1875," 103.

23. "Abstract of First Annual Report of Horace Capron," 43, 44.

24. Capron, "Expedition to Japan, 1871–1875," 22, 89, 187, 192. See, for example, "Abstract of the Report of William P. Blake, Geologist and Mining Engineer, November 20, 1871" (Tokei: Kaitakushi, 1874), as reprinted in Capron, *Reports and Official Letters to the Kaitakushi*, 9–10, 11; Capron, "Expedition to Japan, 1871–1875," 240; Kuroda Kiyotaka, councilor to the Emperor, to Capron, June 5, Year 8 (Meiji), as reprinted in Capron, "Expedition to Japan, 1871–1875," 270; and Fujita, *American Pioneers and the Japanese Frontier*, ix.

25. "Report of A. G. Warfield, Engineer in Chief of Kaitakushi of Hokkaido, Tokei, Japan, December 29, 1871," as reprinted in Capron, *Reports and Official Letters to the Kaitakushi*, 31.

26. "Abstract of First Annual Report of Horace Capron," 47. See, for example, receipt from Mt. Hope Nurseries, folder 101, box 4, Horace Capron Papers, Yale University, New Haven, Connecticut; Capron, "Expedition to Japan, 1871–1875," 232; Michael Thornton, "A Capitol Orchard: Botanical Networks and the Creation of a Japanese 'Neo-Europe,'" *AHR* 127, no. 2 (June 2022): 575; T. Kikuchi, "The Beet Sugar Industry in Japan," in *Sugar*, vol. 24 (November 1922): 610; Ohara Keishi, ed., *Japanese Trade and Industry in the Meiji-Taisho Era* (Obunsha, 1957), 521.

27. Airnu Minzoku Teikoshi Shinya, as cited in Hirano, "Thanatopolitics in the Making of Japan's Hokkaido," 191.

28. Hirano, "Thanatopolitics in the Making of Japan's Hokkaido," 56, 198, 202, 207; Siddle, *Race, Resistance, and the Ainu of Japan*, 56; Mason, *Dominant Narratives of Colonial Hokkaido and Imperial Japan*, 2; and Howell, *Capitalism from Within*, 95, 97, 98, 105, 183. Production increased from 208,000 tons in 1871 to 969,000 tons in 1897.

29. "Abstract of the Report of William P. Blake," 2; Hirano, "Thanato-

politics in the Making of Japan's Hokkaido," 198, 199, 200, 209, 214; David L. Howell, "Early 'Shizoku' Colonialization of Hokkaidô," *Journal of Asian History* 17 (1983): 40–67, esp. 41, 53, 61.

30. Siddle, *Race, Resistance, and the Ainu of Japan*, 59; Jolliffe, "Forced Labour in Imperial Japan's First Colony," 1, 6, 77; Jesús Solís, "From 'Convict' to 'Victim': Commemorating Laborers on Hokkaido's Central Road," *Asia-Pacific Journal* 17, no. 6 (March 2019): 6, 7, as cited in Jolliffe, "Forced Labour in Imperial Japan's First Colony," 8.

31. Jolliffe, "Forced Labor in Imperial Japan's First Colony," 9, 10; and Tessa Morris-Suzuki, "Long Journey Home: A Moment of Japan-Korea Remembrance and Reconciliation," *Asia-Pacific Journal: Japan Focus* 13, no. 36 (2015). See also Tom Arents and Norihiko Tsuneishi, "The Uneven Recruitment of Korean Miners in Japan in the 1910s and 1920s: Employment Strategies of the Miike and Chikuhô Coalmining Companies," *International Review of Social History* 60, no. S1 (December 2015): 121–43; Miyamoto Takashi, "Convict Labor and Its Commemoration: The Mitsui Miike Coal Mine Experience," *Asia-Pacific Journal: Japan Focus* 15, no. 1 (2017); Kobayashi Takiji, *The Crab Cannery Ship and Other Novels of Struggle* (University of Hawai'i Press, 2013); Michael Weiner, *Race and Migration in Imperial Japan* (Routledge, 1994); Tabata Etsuko, "Yūbari to chôsen jin," in *Waga Yûbari, Shirarezaru yama no rekishi*, ed. Yûbari hataraku mono no rekishi wo kiroku suru kai (Kikanshi insatsu shuppan kikaku-shitsu, 1982); 국민대학교 신문방송사, "북해도(北海道) 역사와 韓國人," 국민대학교, October 15, 2004, accessed July 7, 2024, https://press.kookmin.ac.kr/news/articleView.html?idxno=3876.

32. Siddle, *Race, Resistance, and the Ainu of Japan*, 63, 65, 66, 74; Hirano, "Thanatopolitics in the Making of Japan's Hokkaido," 197, 204, 206; Katsuya Hirano, "Settler Colonialism and the Making of Japan's Hokkaidô," 327, 332.

33. Jolliffe, "Forced Labor in Imperial Japan's First Colony," 4.

34. "Abstract of the Report of William P. Blake," 3, 4.

35. Yukie Chiri, preface to *Ainu Shin'yôshû*, 1 March 1922, trans. Sarah Mehlhop Strong, *Ainu Spirits Singing: The Living World of Chiri Yukie's Ainu Shin'yôshû* (University of Hawai'i Press, 2011), 195.

36. Hirano, "Thanatopolitics in the Making of Japan's Hokkaido," 210, 214; and "Abstract of the Report of William Blake," 3, 4.

37. Sevilla-Buitrago, "Capitalist Formations of Enclosure," 1014.

38. This paragraph and the text to page 708 is almost taken verbatim from Sven Beckert. See "American Danger: United States Empire, Eurafrica, and the Territorialization of Industrial Capitalism, 1870–1950," in *AHR* 122, no. 4 (October 2017): 1137–70. Reprinted here with the publisher's permission. "Deutschlands Weltstellung und der Weiterbau am deutschen Nationalstaat," *Alldeutsche Blätter*, January 7, 1894, 5–8. See also, among many others, Ragnhild Fiebig-von Hase, "The United States and Germany in the World Arena, 1900–1917," in *Confrontation and Cooperation: Germany and the United States in the Era of World War I, 1900–1924*, ed. Hans-Jürgen Schröder (Oxford, 1993), 33–68; Fritz Blaich, *Der Trustkampf 1901–1915: Ein Beitrag zum Verhalten der Ministerialbürokratie gegenüber Verbandsinteressen im Wilhelminischen Deutschland* (Duncker & Humblot, 1975), 38; Alfred Vagts, *Deutschland und die Vereinigten Staaten in der Weltpolitik*, vol. 1 (Macmillan, 1935), 345; Frank A. Vanderlip, *Amerikas Eindringen in das Europäische Wirtschaftsgebiet* (Springer, 1903); Hugo von Knebel-Doeberitz, *Besteht für Deutschland eine amerikanische Gefahr?* (Kessinger, 1904); Franz Erich Junge, *Amerikanische Wirtschaftspolitik: Ihre ökonomischen Grundlagen, ihre sozialen Wirkungen und ihre Lehren für die deutsche Volkswirtschaft* (Springer, 1910); Paul Lefébure, "Y a-t-il lieu de modifier la situation actuelle?," in *Les états-unis d'Europe: Congrès des sciences politiques de 1900* (Société Française d'Imprimerie et de Librairie, 1901), 130; Hartmut Kaelble, *Europäer über Europa: Die Entstehung des europäischen Selbstverständnisses im 19. und 20. Jahrhundert* (Campus Verlag, 2001), 62, 70–72; Augustin Léger, "L'américanisation du monde," *Le Correspondant*, April 25, 1902, 221–53, here 221; Édouard Reyer, "L'américanisation de l'Europe," *Revue bleue*, April 19, 1902, 484–88; W. Wendlandt, "Die amerikanische Gefahr, mit besonderer Berücksichtigung des deutschen Zolltarif-Entwurfs," in *Jahresbericht des Bundes der Industriellen für das Geschäftsjahr 1900/1* (Berlin, 1901), 45–84, here 45, 46, 47–48, 52, 66–67; Rudolf Harms, "Weltwirtschaftliche Aufgaben Deutschlands,"

Veröffentlichungen des BdI 1 (1912): 19; Alphonse de Haulleville, *Les aptitudes colonisatrices des Belges, et la question coloniale en Belgique* (Brussels, 1898), 393–97; Egisto Rossi, *Gli Stati Uniti e la concorrenza americana* (Firenze, 1884); "La marcia degli stati," *Il Sole*, August 31, 1900; "Diario: Lotta di continenti," *Il Sole*, July 13, 1901; "Letter to the Editor," *Il Sole*, October 23, 1901; Jean Finot, "Français et Anglais devant l'anarchie européenne," *Revue des Revues* 24 (1903): 493–515; "Has Europe Abandoned Its Plan of Combining Against Us?," *Literary Digest* 23, no. 6 (August 1901): 171–73; Monika Grucza, "Bedrohtes Europa: Studien zum Europa-Gedanken bei Alfons Paquet, André Suarès und Romain Rolland in der Periode zwischen 1890 und 1914" (PhD diss., Justus-Liebig Universität Giessen, 2008), 46; Richard Calwer, *Die Meistbegünstigung der Vereinigten Staaten von Nordamerika* (Berlin, 1902), 9; and German Ambassador in St. Petersburg, v. Schön, to Chancellor von Bülow, St. Petersburg, 24 February 1906, in vol. 5, R 16379 (1906) Generalia no. 13, Amerika, Politisches Archiv des Auswärtigen Amts, Berlin, Germany. "For United Europe Not to Oppose Us," *NYT*, September 20, 1908.
39. Louis Bosc, "Unions douanières et projets d'unions douanières: Essai historique et critique" (PhD diss., Université d'Aix-Marseille, 1904), 237–39, 240, 243, 431. For similar statements, see the Bund der Industriellen (BdI) quoted in Ragnhild Fiebig-von Hase, "Die deutsch-amerikanischen Wirtschaftsbeziehungen, 1890–1914, im Zeichen von Protektionismus und internationaler Integration," *Amerikastudien* 33, no. 3 (1988): 329–57, here 353; Federigo Flora, "Il pericolo americano," *La riforma sociale* 12 (1902): 444–68, here 444.
40. Quote from Gavin Wright and Jesse Czelusta, "Resource-Based Growth Past and Present," in *Natural Resources: Neither Curse nor Destiny*, ed. Daniel Lederman and William F. Maloney (Stanford Economics and Finance, 2007), 183–211, here 184. For the general argument, see also A. Paul David and Gavin Wright, "Increasing Returns and the Genesis of American Resource Abundance," *Industrial and Corporate Change* 6, no. 2 (1997): 203–45; and Michael Barnhart, *Japan Prepares for Total War: The Search for Economic Security, 1919–1941* (Cornell UP, 1991), 50. On the first great divergence, see Kenneth Pomeranz, *The Great Divergence:*

China, Europe, and the Making of the Modern World Economy (PUP, 2000). On the age of empire, see Hobsbawm, *Age of Empire*.
41. Walther Rathenau, "Deutsche Gefahren und neue Ziele," *Neue Freie Presse*, December 25, 1913, as collected in Gesammelte Schriften: Zur Kritik der Zeit (S. Fischer, 1912), 1:268. This discussion is taken almost verbatim from Sven Beckert. See "American Danger: United States Empire, Eurafrica, and the Territorialization of Industrial Capitalism, 1870–1950," in *AHR* 122, no. 4 (October 2017): 1137–1170. Reprinted here with the publisher's permission.
42. D. W. Meinig, *The Shaping of America: A Geographical Perspective on 500 Years of History*, vol. 3, *Transcontinental America, 1850–1915* (Yale UP, 1998); Thomas G. Andrews, *Killing for Coal: America's Deadliest Labor War* (HUP, 2008); Steven Hahn, *A Nation Without Borders: The United States and Its World in an Age of Civil Wars, 1830–1910* (Penguin Books, 2016); Noam Maggor, *Brahmin Capitalism: Frontiers of Wealth and Populism in America's First Gilded Age* (HUP, 2017); US Bureau of the Census with William Mott Steuart, *Special Report: Mines and Quarries, 1902* (US Government Printing Office, 1905), 417, 730; William Rush Merriam, dir., *1900 Census Reports: Agriculture* (US Government Printing Office, 1902), including vol. 5, part 1, "Farms, Live Stock and Animal Products," clxii, and vol. 6, part 2, "Crops and Irrigation," 80, 92, 425, 473, 528; David T. Day, *Mineral Resources of the United States, Calendar Year 1900* (US Government Printing Office, 1901), 144, 287; Gavin Wright and Jesse Czelusta, "Why Economies Slow: The Myth of the Resource Curse," *Challenge* 47, no. 2 (2004): 6–38, here 9; and Edward Barbier, *Scarcity and Frontiers: How Economics Have Developed Through Natural Resource Exploitation* (CUP, 2011), 399. In 1800, the thirteen original colonies and the Northwest Territory occupied around eight hundred thousand square miles; in 1850, the United States occupied nearly three million square miles. See "Expansion of Our Territory" (table), in Oscar Austin, *Steps in the Expansion of Our Territory* (D. Appleton, 1903), 249–50.
43. Sven Beckert, *The Monied Metropolis: New York City and the Consolidation of the American Bourgeoisie, 1850–1896* (CUP, 2001); and Eli Cook, *The Pricing of Progress: Eco-*

nomic Indicators and the Capitalization of American Life (HUP, 2017). For import and export series, which includes both goods and services, see Series U1-25, "Balance of International Payments: 1790 to 1970," in *Historical Statistics of the United States: Colonial Times to 1970*, vol. 2 (US Government Printing Office, 1975), 864–65. For GNP, see Series F1-5, "Gross National Product, Total and Per Capita, in Current and 1958 Prices: 1869–1970," in *Historical Statistics of the United States: Colonial Times to 1970*, vol. 1 (US Government Printing Office, 1975), 216.
44. Richard White, *"It's Your Misfortune and None of My Own": A New History of the American West* (University of Oklahoma Press, 1991); William Cronon, *Nature's Metropolis: Chicago and the Great West* (W. W. Norton, 1992); Noam Maggor, *Brahmin Capitalism*; Pekka Hämäläinen, *The Comanche Empire* (Yale UP, 2008); Richard Franklin Bensel, *The Political Economy of American Industrialization, 1877–1900* (CUP, 2000); Megan Black, *The Global Interior: Mineral Frontiers and American Power* (HUP, 2018), 17, 20; Jürgen Osterhammel has perceptively described the United States as an unusually early case for the administrative and scientific integration of a very large and expanding territory. See Jürgen Osterhammel, *Die Verwandlung der Welt: Eine Geschichte des 19. Jahrhunderts* (C. H. Beck, 2009), 169. The American state, of course, also showed notable weaknesses, but it is still remarkable how successful its project of territorial growth and territorial incorporation was compared with other parts of the world.
45. Black, *Global Interior*, 7, 27. For that story, see the terrific work by Black, *Global Interior*.
46. For a more detailed account, see Claudio Saunt, "Financing Dispossession: Stocks, Bonds, and the Deportation of Native Peoples in the Antebellum United States," *JAH* 106, no. 2 (September 2019): 315–37; and Richard White, *Railroaded: The Transcontinentals and the Making of Modern America* (W. W. Norton, 2011). See Frederick Jackson Turner, "The Significance of the Frontier in American History," in *Annual Report of the American Historical Association for the Year 1893* (US Government Printing Office, 1894), 197–227; Louis A. Pérez, *Cuba in the American Imagination: Metaphor and the Imperial Ethos* (University of North Carolina Press, 2008), 11; and Anna M. Agathangelou and L. H. M.

Ling, *Transforming World Politics: From Empire to Multiple Worlds* (Routledge, 2009), 73.

47. Julius Wolf, "Die Erspriesslichkeit des wirtschaftspolitischen Zusammenschlusses der mitteleuropäischen Staaten u. a. mit Hinblick auf Amerika," speech, Vienna, May 19, 1903, as reprinted in *Materialien betreffend den Mitteleuropäischen Wirtschaftsverein*, 2nd ed. (G. Reimer Puttkammer & Mühlbrecht, 1904), 31.

48. John Darwin, *The Empire Project: The Rise and Fall of the British World-System, 1830–1970* (CUP, 2011); Duncan Bell, *The Idea of Greater Britain: Empire and the Future of World Order, 1860–1900* (PUP, 2007); and Andrew S. Thompson, *Imperial Britain: The Empire in British Politics, c. 1880–1932* (Longman, 2000). Richard White might be entirely right when he argues in *Railroaded* that although building vast transcontinental railroads did not make "sense" economically, from a broader perspective, it was crucial to national territorial integration.

49. Andreas Etges, *Wirtschaftsnationalismus: USA und Deutschland im Vergleich (1815–1914)* (Campus, 1999), 275, 282. See Tony Smith, *The Pattern of Imperialism: The United States, Great Britain, and the Late-Industrializing World Since 1815* (CUP, 1981), 35; and Alfred Thayer Mahan, *The Influence of Sea Power upon History, 1660–1793* (Boston: Little, Brown and Company, 1890), 41–42, 247, 276. There is a huge literature on that new imperialism, with many disagreements over the question of what motivated it. See, for example, A. G. Hopkins, *American Empire: A Global History* (PUP, 2018), 267–81. For a range of very different interpretations of the new imperialism, see, for example, Hans-Ulrich Wehler, *Bismarck und der Imperialismus* (Kiepenheuer und Witsch, 1969); Hans-Ulrich Wehler, *Der Aufstieg des amerikanischen Imperialismus: Studien zur Entwicklung des Imperium Americanum 1865–1900* (Vandenhoeck & Ruprecht, 1974); Rosa Luxemburg, *Die Akkumulation des Kapitals: Ein Beitrag zur ökonomischen Erklärung des Imperialismus* (Buchhandlung Vorwärts Paul Singer, 1913); V. I. Lenin, *Imperialism, the Highest Stage of Capitalism: A Popular Outline* (International Publishers, 1939); Wolfgang J. Mommsen, *Imperialismustheorien: Ein Überblick über die neueren Imperialismusinterpretationen* (Vandenhoeck &

Ruprecht, 1980); Niall Ferguson, *Empire: How Britain Made the Modern World* (Penguin, 2004); Edward Said, *Culture and Imperialism* (Alfred A. Knopf, 1993); and Hobsbawm, *Age of Empire*; Gerhard L. Weinberg, *Germany, Hitler, and World War II: Essays in Modern German and World History* (CUP, 1995); and Hans-Ulrich Wehler, *Das Deutsche Kaiserreich, 1871–1918* (Vandenhoeck & Ruprecht, 1973). See also Alan S. Milward, *The European Rescue of the Nation-State* (University of California Press, 1992); and Desmond Dinan, ed., *Origins and Evolution of the European Union* (OUP, 2006).

50. Peter Duus, *The Abacus and the Sword: The Japanese Penetration of Korea, 1895–1910* (University of California Press, 1998), 2; Klas Rönnbäck and Oskar Broberg, *Capital and Colonialism: The Return on British Investments in Africa, 1869–1969* (Palgrave Macmillan, 2019), 22; David Killingray, "The War in Africa," in *The Oxford Illustrated History of the First World War*, 2nd ed., ed. Hew Strachan (OUP, 1998), 101; Alexander Morrison, *Russian Rule in Samarkand 1868–1910: A Comparison with British India* (OUP, 2008); Seymour Becker, "The 'Great Game': The History of an Evocative Phrase," *Asian Affairs* 43, no. 1 (2012): 61–80; Gerald Morgan, "Myth and Reality in the Great Game," *Asian Affairs* 4, no. 1 (1973): 55–65. Jeff Sahadeo, *Russian Colonial Society in Tashkent, 1865–1923* (Indiana UP, 2007).

51. For the original quote ("pour soustraire nos industries au joug dangereux de l'étranger, nous tournons vers no colonies"), see "Colonie du Niger, les irrigations du Niger et la culture cotonnière au Soudan, octobre 1921," in Series R, Agriculture, Culture du Coton, 1889–1943, 1R/00035, ANS. On the great importance to secure raw materials for national industry, see also "Le coton soudanais: production — outillage — colonisation, rapport," 4, Series R, Agriculture, Culture du Coton, 1889–1943, 1R/00035, ANS, which makes that point explicitly.

52. Harry Denicke, "Ein kolonialpolitisches Nachwort zur Reichstagsrede des Reichskanzlers vom 10. 'Dezember 1891," *Deutsche Kolonialzeitung* 1, no. 9 (January 1892): 3.

53. "Why Not Another America?," *African World*, February 11, 1905, 15.

54. For the newspaper quote ("à nos portes, une espèce Amérique" in the

original French), see "Une politique immigration à Madagascar," *La Dépêche*, June 3, 1926. For similar such statements, see Karl Dove, "Der Sinn einer künftigen Kolonialpolitik," *Deutsche Kolonialzeitung* 33, no. 10 (1916): 156–58, here 158; G. N. Sanderson, "The European Partition of Africa: Origins and Dynamics," in *The Cambridge History of Africa*, vol. 6, *1870–1905*, ed. Roland Oliver and G. N. Sanderson (CUP, 1985), 96–158, here 126; Octave Noël, *Le péril américain* (Paris: Imprimerie de Soye et Fils, 1899), 144. See also Herward Sieberg, *Eugène Étienne und die französische Kolonialpolitik, 1887–1904* (Westdeutscher Verlag, 1968), 77–90; *Journal officiel de la République française: Débats parlementaires*, Chambre des Députés 10 (July–December 1885): 1665; and Heiko Körner, *Kolonialpolitik und Wirtschaftsentwicklung: Das Beispiel Französisch Westafrikas* (G. Fischer, 1965), 41.

55. As cited in Körner, *Kolonialpolitik und Wirtschaftsentwicklung*, 41.

56. Körner, *Kolonialpolitik und Wirtschaftsentwicklung*, 42; and Robert Aldrich, *Greater France: A History of French Overseas Expansion* (St. Martin's Press, 1996), 100.

57. Paul Leroy-Beaulieu, *De la colonisation chez les peuples modernes*, 2nd ed. (Paris, 1882). See also David Todd, "A French Imperial Meridian, 1814–1870," *Past & Present* 210 (February 2011): 155–86, here 183; and H. L. Wesseling, *Divide and Rule: The Partition of Africa, 1880–1914*, trans. Arnold J. Pomerans (Praeger, 1996), 14.

58. Charles Gide, "À quoi servent les colonies?," *Revue de géographie* 18 (January–June 1886): 36–52, 141–47.

59. Robert Aldrich, *Greater France: A History of French Overseas Expansion* (St. Martin's Press, 1996), 100–102, 171; Körner, *Kolonialpolitik und Wirtschaftsentwicklung*, 42; Sieberg, *Eugène Étienne*, 91; and François Caron, *Frankreich im Zeitalter des Imperialismus, 1851–1918* (Deutsche Verlags-Anstalt, 1991), 458. Another important organization was the Union Coloniale Française, founded in 1893 by more than four hundred French entrepreneurs. It published the magazine *La quinzaine coloniale*.

60. For the slogan ("mise en valeur des colonies" in the original French), see Sieberg, *Eugène Étienne*, 78.

61. Cited in Sieberg, *Eugène Étienne*, 79, 92. See also Caron, *Frankreich im Zeitalter des Imperialismus, 1851–1918*, 458.

62. Körner, *Kolonialpolitik und Wirtschaftsentwicklung*, 35–36; Capo de Feuillide (pseud.), *L'Algérie française* (Paris, 1856), 281, 294; and Augustin Bernard, *L'Algérie* (Paris, 1930), 521.

63. Victor Hugo, as quoted in Charles-Robert Ageron, "L'idée d'Eurafrique et le débat colonial franco-allemand de l'entre-deux guerres," *Revue d'histoire moderne et contemporaine* 22, no. 3 (1975): 446–75, here 446.

64. B. Maraini, typescript, "FIAT—Corso per ispettori commerciali all'estero, le Marche esistenti e loro caratteristiche principali," October 1918, 41, in L'Industria Automobilistica Americana, Libro Maraini, box MSC 0100, CSF, Torino, Italy.

65. Quote from Friedrich Naumann, *National-Sozialer Katechismus: Erklärung der Grundlinien des National-Sozialen Vereins* (Berlin, 1897), 7–8. See also A. Stapff, comments at the Dritte Generalversammlung des Mitteleuropäischen Wirtschaftsvereins, Munich, October 14, 1911, as quoted in *Berliner Börsen-Courier*, January 9, 1912.

66. "Veröffentlichungen der Gesellschaft, Bericht über Tagung der Deutschen Kolonialgesellschaft zu Karlsruhe i. B.," Vorstandssitzung am 4. Juni, *Deutsche Kolonialzeitung* 20, n.s. 16, no. 24 (1903): 235–37. There were also efforts to secure oil from Cameroon. See "Exploration of the possibilities of oil drilling in Cameroon," note, 8 April 1907, in Deutsche Kolonialgesellschaft, Akten zur Petroleumgewinnung in den Kolonie, 1907–1914, Reichskolonialamt, R 8023, f443, BA Berlin.

67. Rathenau, "Deutsche Gefahren und neue Ziele."

68. Nautilus (pseud.), "Le coton au Soudan français," *Revue des cultures coloniales* 12–13 (1903): 302; Ed.-C. Achard, "Le coton en Cilicie et en Syrie," *Documents économiques, politiques, et scientifiques*, supplément, *L'Asie française* 203, no. S3 (June 1922): S19–S64, here S21–S23; Claude Malon, *Le Havre colonial de 1880 à 1960* (Presses Universitaires de Rouen et du Havre, 2006), 184; Paul Bourdarie, "La lutte pour le coton colonial," *Bulletin de la société de géographie commerciale du Havre*, 3–4e trimestres 1905 (1906): 418–35; and Peter Grupp, *Deutschland, Frankreich und die Kolonien: Der französische "Parti colonial" und Deutschland von 1890 bis 1914* (J. C. B. Mohr, 1980), 57–58. The "American yoke" is also a trope in Hugo von Knebel-Doeberitz, *Besteht für*

Deutschland eine amerikanische Gefahr? (E. S. Mittler und Sohn, 1904), iv, 1.

69. Sven Beckert, "From Tuskegee to Togo: The Problem of Freedom in the Empire of Cotton," *JAH* 92, no. 2 (2005): 498–526; Karl Supf, "Zur Baumwollfrage," *Deutsche Kolonialzeitung* 17, n.s. 13, no. 20 (1900): 215–18, here 216–18; "Der Verbrauch der Rohbaumwolle der Vereinigten Staaten von Nordamerika," *Deutsche Kolonialzeitung* 18, n.s. 14, no. 33 (1901): 327–28; "Deutsch-koloniale Baumwoll-Unternehmungen 1902–1903," *Deutsche Kolonialzeitung* 20, n.s. 16, no. 31 (1903): 311–13, here 311; Erich Prager, "Kolonialwirtschaft und Nationalvermögen," *Deutsche Kolonialzeitung* 20, n.s. 16, no. 23 (1903): 223–24; "Baumwollbau in den deutschen Kolonien," *Deutsche Kolonialzeitung* 27, no. 17 (1910): 271–72; Dr. Warnack, "Die Baumwollnot," *Deutsche Kolonialzeitung* 27, no. 49 (1910): 816–17; "Der koloniale Baumwollbau und Handel und Industrie [*sic*]," *Deutsche Kolonialzeitung* 30, no. 13 (1913): 214; and Hans-Peter Ullmann, *Der Bund der Industriellen: Organisation, Einfluss und Politik klein- und mittelbetrieblicher Industrieller im Deutschen Kaiserreich, 1895–1914* (Vandenhoeck & Ruprecht, 1976), 172.

70. Alphonse de Haulleville, *Les aptitudes colonisatrices des Belges et la question colonial en Belgique* (J. Lebègue, 1898), 396. See also E. M. de Vogüé, *Spectacles contemporains* (Paris: A. Colin et Cie, 1891), 343.

71. Lothar Wackerbeck, "Die deutschen Kolonialgesellschaften: Ihre Entstehung, Entwicklung und Sonderstellung im Gesellschaftsrecht" (PhD diss., Universität Münster, 1977), 8; Erich Prager, ed., *Die deutsche Kolonialgesellschaft, 1882–1907* (Dietrich Reimer, 1908); "Der Kongreß der drei Amerikas," *Deutsche Kolonialzeitung* 6, n.s. 2, no. 35 (1889): 311; Sanderson, "European Partition of Africa," 51–54, 101, 103.

72. Sanderson, "European Partition of Africa," 98, 126; and Vincent Viaene, "King Leopold's Imperialism and the Origins of the Belgian Colonial Party," *Journal of Modern History* 80, no. 4 (December 2008): 750–57. See also Gustav Schmoller, "Die Wirtschaftliche Zukunft Deutschlands und die Flottenvorlage," in *Handels- und Machtpolitik*, vol. 1, ed. Gustav von Schmoller, Max Sering, and Adolph Wagner (Cotta, 1900), 1–38.

73. Naumann, *National-Sozialer Katechismus*, 10.

74. Wackerbeck, "Die deutschen Kolonialgesellschaften," 8; Prager, ed., *Die deutsche Kolonialgesellschaft*; "Der Kongreß der drei Amerikas," 311; and Sanderson, "European Partition of Africa," 51–54, 101, 103. The concept of a "commodity frontier" and its definition are from Jason W. Moore, "Sugar and the Expansion of the Early Modern World-Economy: Commodity Frontiers, Ecological Transformation, and Industrialization," *Review* (Fernand Braudel Center) 23, no. 3 (2000): 409–33.

75. Cyrus C. Adams, "Foundations of Economic Progress in Tropical Africa," *Journal of Race Development* 2 (July 1911): 1–17.

76. "Protokoll Nr. 1, Sitzung vom 15. November 1884," in *Protokolle und Generalakte der Berliner Afrika-Konferenz, 1884–1885*, ed. Frank Thomas Gatter (Übersee-Museum Bremen, 1984), 101.

77. On the history of European colonialism in Africa, especially its economic dimensions, see, among others, Hopkins, *An Economic History of West Africa*; Gareth Austin, *Labour, Land and Capital in Ghana: From Slavery to Free Labour in Asante, 1807–1956* (University of Rochester Press, 2005); Herbert S. Frankel, *Capital Investment in Africa: Its Course and Effects* (H. Fertig, 1938); Jane I. Guyer, *Money Matters: Instability, Values, and Social Payments in the Modern History of West African Communities* (Heinemann, 1992); Joseph C. Miller, "The Dynamics of History in Africa and the Atlantic Age of Revolutions," in *The Age of Revolutions in Global Context, c. 1760–1840*, ed. David Armitage and Sanjay Subrahmanyam (Palgrave Macmillan, 2010), 101–24; Jane I. Guyer, *Marginal Gains: Monetary Transactions in Atlantic Africa* (University of Chicago Press, 2004); G. N. Sanderson, "The European Partition of Africa," 98, 99, 100; Michael Ralph, *Forensics of Capital* (University of Chicago Press, 2015), 63; Ralph A. Austen and Jonathan Derrick, *Middlemen of the Cameroons Rivers: The Duala and Their Hinterland, c. 1600–c. 1960* (CUP, 1999); Klaus J. Bade, "Imperial Germany and West Africa: Colonial Movement, Business Interests and Bismarck's 'Colonial Policies,'" in *Bismarck, Europe, and Africa: The Berlin Africa Conference, 1884–1885, and the Onset of Partition*, ed. Stig Förster, Wofgang J. Mommsen, and Ronald Robinson (OUP, 1988),

121–47, here 131; Frank Thomas Gatter, ed., *Protokolle und Generalakte der Berliner Afrika-Konferenz, 1884–1885* (Übersee-Museum Bremen, 1984), 103; "Protokoll Nr. 1, Sitzung vom 15. November 1884," in *Protokolle und Generalakte der Berliner Afrika-Konferenz, 1884–1885*, ed. Frank Thomas Gatter (Übersee-Museum Bremen, 1984), 98–117, here 101, 111; *Annuaire statistique de la France* 21 (1901): 265–66; Francesca Schinzinger, *Die Kolonien und das Deutsche Reich: Die wirtschaftliche Bedeutung der deutschen Besitzungen in Übersee* (F. Steiner Verlag Wiesbaden, 1984), 120, 126; G. N. Uzoigwe, "The Results of the Berlin West Africa Conference: An Assessment," in Förster et al., *Bismarck, Europe, and Africa*, 541–52, here 543. On preemption, see Jane Burbank and Frederick Cooper, *Empires in World History* (PUP, 22011), chap. 10; Cyrus C. Adams, "Foundations of Economic Progress in Tropical Africa," *Journal of Race Development* 2 (July 1911): 1–17; and Richard White, *The Middle Ground: Indians, Empires, and Republics in the Great Lakes Region, 1650–1815* (CUP, 2011). In addition to Sanderson, the increasing importance of the state in securing raw materials (though, in this case, during World War II) is also emphasized by William G. Clarence-Smith, "The Battle for Rubber in the Second World War: Cooperation and Resistance," Commodities of Empire Working Paper no. 14 (November 2009), 1–19, here 13.

78. Cited in Uzoigwe, "Results of the Berlin West Africa Conference," 543.

79. See Chikouna Cissé, "Grand-Bassam dans l'expansion du capitalisme européen dans la colonie de Côte d'Ivoire, 1893–1930," unpublished paper (in author's possession) presented at the Colonial Cities in Global Perspective Conference, Saint-Louis, Sénégal, December 2018.

80. For the quote ("cette pénétration méthodique de territoires maintenant acquis à notre domination" in the original French), see letter of Secrétaire d'État aux colonies à Binger, 18 July 1893, ANSOM, CI, 1, 10, as cited in Cissé, "Grand-Bassam dans l'expansion du capitalisme européen."

81. For the first quote ("je me suis montré partisan de la pénétration") in the original French, see Louis Faidherbe, *Le Sénégal: La France dans l'Afrique occidentale* (Hachette, 1889), 2. For the second ("expériences que

le gouverneur Faidherbe, avec la ténacité et la généreuse ardeur qu'il apportait à faciliter, encourager et récompenser tout ce qui pouvait contribuer au développement des richesses du Sénégal, ne perdait pas de vue un seul instant"), see "Culture du coton au Sénégal, 1900/1924," Series R, Agriculture, Culture du Coton, 1889–1943, 1R/00035, ANS.

82. Jenna Nigro, "Colonial Logics: Agricultural, Commercial & Moral Experiments in the Making of French Senegal, 1763–1870" (PhD diss., University of Illinois, 2014), 232; and Catherine Boone, *Merchant Capital and the Roots of State Power in Senegal, 1930–1985* (CUP, 1992), 40–41.

83. Rodolphe Darricau, *Le Sénégal sera-t-il une colonie ou un simple comptoir?* (Paris: Didot Frères, 1850).

84. As cited in Nigro, "Colonial Logics," 244. The original quote in French reads: "Ils subissaient de la part de chefs indigènes, des humiliations, des violences, et des exactions de toute nature."

85. As cited in Nigro, "Colonial Logics," 247. See also Nigro, 250. The original quote in French reads: "Les peuplades arrogates qui ont osé vous provoquer au combat, sont aujourd'hui tremblantes à nos pieds. Elles sollicitent la paix et la protection de la France."

86. Nigro, "Colonial Logics," 235, 239, 240, 241, 256.

87. As cited in Nigro, "Colonial Logics," 258.

88. Nigro, "Colonial Logics," 236, 250, 252–262, 265; Kleoniki Alexopoulou and Dácil Juif, "Colonial State Formation Without Integration: Tax Capacity and Labour Regimes in Portuguese Mozambique (1890s–1970s), *International Review of Social History* 62, no. 2 (2017), 221. For examples of mapping and surveying land and people, see the questionnaire sent out to Senegal in 1890, requesting data on production. See "Direction de l'intérieur": Culture et production dans la colonie du Sénégal, 1887–1890," Agriculture, Series R, 1 R/00240, ANS.

89. Faidherbe as quoted in Nigro, "Colonial Logics," 271. The importance of the US example is also emphasized by Alexis Bois, *Sénégal et Soudan, travaux publics et chemins de fer* (Paris: Challamel Aîné, 1886), 39.

90. For the quote ("vous avez brisé les barrières que la barbarie opposait à la civilisation" in the original French), see *Moniteur*, May 2, 1865, 81, as cited in Nigro, "Colonial Logics," 280. See also Nigro, "Colonial Logics," 332.

91. Louise Young, *Japan's Total Empire: Manchuria and the Culture of Wartime Imperialism* (University of California Press, 1999), 23, 24.

92. As cited in Han-Yu Chang and Ramon H. Meyers, "Japanese Colonial Development Policy in Taiwan, 1895–1906: A Case of Bureaucratic Entrepreneurship," *Journal of Asian Studies* 22, no. 4 (August 1963): 436.

93. "Reimeiki no Tōa burokku," *Ekonomisuto*, April 1, 1938, 35, as cited in Young, *Japan's Total Empire*, 229. Similar statements can be found on 228–31.

94. As cited in Duus, *Abacus and the Sword*, 17.

95. Duus, *Abacus and the Sword*, 432.

96. Young, *Japan's Total Empire*, 32.

97. Duus, *Abacus and the Sword*, 1, 12, 19, 20, 28; Young, *Japan's Total Empire*, 28, 32. For a contemporary perception of continental-scale enclosures, see Young, *Japan's Total Empire*, 229.

98. Jack F. Williams, "Sugar: The Sweetener in Taiwan's Development," in *China's Island Frontier: Studies in the Historical Geography of Taiwan*, ed. Ronald G. Knapp (University of Hawai'i Press, 1980), 220, 221, 223; Hirai Kensuke, *Satō no teikoku: Nihon shokuminchi to Ajia shijō [Empire of Sugar: External Forces of Change in the Economy of Japanese Colonies]* (Tōkyō Daigaku Shuppankai, 2017), 19; and Hirai, *Satō no teikoku*, 12.

99. Williams, "Sugar," 224, 226; Chang and Meyers, "Japanese Colonial Development Policy in Taiwan," 443.

100. Inazo Nitobe, "Japan as a Colonizer," *Journal of Race Development* 2, no. 4 (April 1912): 348.

101. Chang and Meyers, "Japanese Colonial Development Policy in Taiwan," 44, 440; and Williams, "Sugar," 226, 227, 232.

102. On splitting "cane supply regions," see Hirai, *Satō no teikoku*, 18, 19; Williams, "Sugar," 227, 229, 231, 232–33; and Hopkins, *Economic History of West Africa*, 242.

103. Nitobe, "Japan as a Colonizer," 359.

104. Werner Sombart, *Der Moderne Kapitalismus*, vol. 3 (Drucker & Humblot, 1927), 69.

105. Doreen Lustig, *Veiled Power: International Law and the Private Corporation, 1886–1981* (OUP, 2020), 15–30, 25.

106. See Thomas Pakenham, *The Scramble for Africa, 1876–1912* (Weidenfeld & Nicolson, 1991), 245–47. See also Travers Twiss, as cited in United States Senate, 48th Congress, 1st Session, The Commit-

tee of Foreign Relations, Report No. 393, March 26, 1884, 24.

107. Arntz, as cited in United States Senate, 48th Congress, 1st Session, The Committee of Foreign Relations, Report No. 393, March 26, 1884, 33.

108. United States Senate, 48th Congress, 1st Session, The Committee of Foreign Relations, Report No. 393, March 26, 1884, 4, 29.

109. Lea Haller, *Transithandel: Geld- und Warenstroeme im globalen Kapitalismus* (Suhrkamp, 2019), 72; and Lustig, *Veiled Power*, 2.

110. See, for example, the treaty between the Hudson Bay Company Teechamitsa Tribe, as printed in *Papers Connected with the Indian Land Question, 1850–1875* (Victoria: R. Wolfenden, 1875), 5–11.

111. Kumari Jayawardena and Rachel Kurian, *Class, Patriarchy and Ethnicity on Sri Lankan Plantations: Two Plantations: Two Centuries of Power and Protest* (Orient Blackswan, 2015), 2, 23; Julie Tomiak and Justin Paulson, "Original and Ongoing Dispossessions: Settler Capitalism and Indigenous Resistance on British Columbia," unpublished paper presented at the Past and Future of Primitive Accumulation Conference, International Institute for Social History, Amsterdam, 2019, 2, 5; Ho Hai Quang, *Histoire économique de l'ile de La Réunion, 1849–1881* (L'Harmattan, 2004), 183; David Gilmartin, *Blood and Water: The Indus River Basin in Modern History* (University of California Press, 2015), 146; Paul W. Paustin, *Canal Irrigation in the Punjab: An Economic Inquiry Relating to Certain Aspects of the Development of Canal Irrigation by the British in the Punjab* (AMS Press, 1968), 122; R. Gerard Ward, "Land Use and Land Alienation in Fiji to 1885," *Journal of Pacific History* 4 (1969): 5, 6, 8; Matthias van Rossum, "Building Maritime Empire: Shipbuilding and Networks of Coercion Under the Verenigde Oost-Indische Compagnie (VOC) in South and Southeast Asia," *International Journal of Maritime History* 31, no. 3 (2019) 465–80, 468; Chris Baker and Pasuk Phongpaichit, *A History of Thailand* (OUP, 2014), 89; and James C. Ingram, *Economic Change in Thailand Since 1850* (Stanford UP, 1955), 96. For the story of British taxation of Punjabi peasants, see Navyug Gill, "Accumulation by Attachment Revenue, Culture and the Rule of Capital in Colonial Panjab," unpublished paper presented at the International Institute for Social History, 2019. For more on British

killing, see the excellent dissertation by David Avilés Espinoza, "Spatial Political Economy, Uneven Development, and the Production of Nature in Chole" (PhD diss., University of Sydney, 2022), 163.

112. Gagan Preet Singh, "Property's Guardians, People's Terror: Police Avoidance in Colonial North India," *Radical History Review* 137 (May 2020): 55, 57, 59; and Singh as cited in David Gilmartin, "Cattle, Crime and Colonialism: Property as Negotiation in North India," *Indian Economic and Social Review* 40, no. 1 (January 2003): 35, 58.

113. Singh, "Property's Guardians, People's Terror," 64.

114. Joanne S. Liu, *Barbed Wire: The Fence That Changed the West* (Mountain Press Publishing Company, 2009), 34–35, 37, 40, 50; Reviel Netz, *Barbed Wire: An Ecology of Modernity* (Wesleyan UP, 2004), 44.

115. Peter Delius, *The Land Belongs to Us: The Pedi Polity, the Boers and the British in the Nineteenth-Century Transvaal* (Heinemann, 1984), 49–52, 151, 184; and Jeremy Krikler, *Revolution from Above, Rebellion from Below: The Agrarian Transvaal at the Turn of the Century* (Clarendon Press, 1993), 5, 76.

116. Leonard Thompson, *A History of South Africa* (Yale UP, 2001), 123; and Krikler, *Revolution from Above, Rebellion from Below*, 82, 128.

117. Krikler, *Revolution from Above, Rebellion from Below*, 82, 83; and Hirano, "Thanatopolitics in the Making of Japan's Hokkaido," 216.

118. Stacie A. Kent, *Coercive Commerce: Global Capital and Imperial Governance at the End of the Qing Empire* (Hong Kong UP, 2025), 13, 20, 26, 114, 149.

119. Thomas H. Stanton, "Law and Economic Development: The Cautionary Tale of Colonial Burma," *Asian Journal of Law and Society* 1, no. 2 (May 2014), 2, 3, 4, 5, 7, 9, 10, 11, 14.

120. On British Columbia, see Tomiak and Paulson, "Original and Ongoing Dispossessions," 1.

121. Irfan Habib, "Colonialization of the Indian Economy," *Social Scientist* 3 (March 1975): 25–53; Amiya Kumar Bagchi, *The Political Economy of Underdevelopment* (CUP, 1982); and Aditya Mukherjee, "The Return of the Colonial in Indian Economic History," *Social Scientist* 36 (March 2008): 3–44. Despite challenges from Dharma Kumar, *The Cambridge Economic History of India, 1757–1970* (CUP, 1983), and Tirthankar Roy, "Economic History and Modern India: Redefining the Link," *Journal of*

Economic Perspectives 16, no. 3 (Summer 2002): 109–30; it was recently powerfully supported by Pilar Nogues-Marco, "Measuring Colonial Extraction: The East India Company's Rule and the Drain of Wealth, 1757–1858," *Capitalism* 2 (Winter 2021): 154–195. See also Aditya Mukherjee, "Empire: How Colonial India Made Modern Britain," *Economic and Political Weekly* 45, no. 50 (2010): 73–82; Amiya Kumar Bagchi, *Perilous Passage: Mankind and the Global Ascendancy of Capital* (Rowman & Littlefield Publishers, 2005), 241–42; "British Raj Siphoned Out $45 Trillion from India: Utsa Patnaik," *Guardian*, November 19, 2018; Thomas Piketty, *Capital and Ideology*, trans. Arthur Goldhammer (HUP, 2020), 279, 280, 284, 287; Albert Schrauwers, *Merchant Kings: Corporate Governmentality in the Dutch Colonial Empire, 1815–1870* (Berghahn Books, 2021), 20, 75, 80, 173; Kevin Narizny, "The Political Economy of Alignment: Great Britain's Commitments to Europe, 1905–1939," *International Security* 27 (Spring 2003): 194; and Rönnbäck and Broberg, *Capital and Colonialism*, 109, 382. The "drain of wealth" debate has been a mainstay of Indian nationalism and Indian historiography. See, among many others, Dinyar Patel, *Naoroji: Pioneer of Indian Nationalism* (HUP, 2020), 65; and Narendra Krishna Sinha, *The Economic History of Bengal: From Plassey to the Permanent Settlement* (Firma K. L. Mukhopadhyay, 1956–1970).

122. See Angus Maddison, *The World Economy*, vol. 1, *A Millennial Perspective*, and vol. 2, *Historical Statistics* (OECD, 2006), 173, 184, 214.

123. Patrick O'Brien, "Industrialization," in *Oxford Handbook of World History*, ed. Jerry H. Bentley (OUP, 2011), 309. O'Brien used the term "third world economies." See also Frantz Fanon, *The Wretched of the Earth*, trans. Richard Philcox (Grove Press, 2005), 58.

124. Dinyar Patel, *Naoroji: Pioneer of Indian Nationalism* (HUP, 2020), 69, 227, 251, 332.

125. For a review of this argument, see William J. Novack, "The Myth of the 'Weak' American State," *AHR* 113 (June 2008): 752–72.

126. Jeremy Adelman, "Extra-European Origins of European Revolutions," presented at the University of Freiburg for the conference Making Europe: The Global Origins of the Old World, May 27–29, 2010. Another important feedback loop was the production of epidemiological

knowledge from colonial settings into the metropole, as powerfully charted by Jim Downs, *Maladies of Empire: How Colonialism, Slavery, and War Transformed Medicine* (HUP, 2021); and Wigen, *The Making of a Japanese Periphery*, 218. The importance of expansionism to the forging of the modern United States state (and society) is also emphasized in Hahn, *A Nation Without Borders*.

127. Maier, *Leviathan 2.0*, 5, 6, 11.

128. Michael Mann, *The Sources of Social Power*, vol. 2, *The Rise of Classes and Nation States, 1760–1914* (CUP, 2012), 366; E. Sydney Crawcour, "Industrialization and Technological Change, 1885–1920," in *The Economic Emergence of Modern Japan*, ed. Kozo Yamamura (CUP, 1997), 52.

129. Mann, *Sources of Social Power*, 2:363, 365, 393; and as argues Maier, *Leviathan 2.0*, 79.

130. James Scott, *Seeing Like a State: How Certain Schemes to Improve the Human Condition Have Failed* (Yale UP, 1998). On social classifications, see Bourdieu, *Über den Staat*, 29.

131. Vanessa Ogle, *The Global Transformation of Time: 1870–1950* (HUP, 2015), 26.

132. Maier, *Leviathan 2.0*, 112. On the Tokugawa state, see E. Sydney Crawcour, "Economic Change in the Nineteenth Century," in *The Cambridge History of Japan*, ed. John W. Hall, Marius B. Jansen, Madoka Kanai, and Denis Twitchett, vol. 5, *The Nineteenth Century*, ed. Marius B. Jansen (CUP, 2008), 7–11, 42–43, 60, 61, 97, 112, 113; Mason, *Dominant Narratives of Colonial Hokkaido and Imperial Japan*, 13. The prevalence and mechanisms of that alliance are detailed in Shunsuke Nakaoka, "A Gateway to the Business World? The Analysis of Networks in Connecting the Modern Japanese Nobility to the Business Elite," *Business History* 64, no. 2 (January 2022): 434–55.

133. Charles Maier, *Once Between Borders: Territories of Wealth, Power and Belonging Since 1500* (HUP, 2016), 89, 195, 201.

134. Crawcour, "Industrialization and Technological Change." See also Kenneth Pomeranz, "Scale, Scope and Scholarship: Regional Practices and Global Economic Histories," in *Global History, Globally: Research and Practice Around the World*, eds. Sven Beckert and Dominic Sachsenmaier (Bloomsbury Academic, 2018). On regulation in the Ottoman Empire, see Can Nacar, "Negotiating Railroad Safety in the Late Ottoman

Empire: The State, Railroad Companies, Trainmen, and Trespassers," *New Perspectives on Turkey* 60 (2019): 61–84.

135. Massimo De Angelis, "Separating the Doing and the Deed: Capital and the Continuous Character of the Enclosures," *Historical Materialism* 12 (2004): 57–87; J. R. Seeley, *The Expansion of England: Two Courses of Lectures* (Macmillan, 1883), 67; and Steven Hahn, *The Roots of Southern Populism: Yeoman Farmers and the Transformation of the Georgia Upcountry, 1850–1890* (OUP, 1983), 174, 180, 193, 239, 241, 242, 243, 246.

136. Emma Teitelman, "The Properties of Capitalism: Industrial Enclosures in the South and West after the American Civil War," *JAH* 106, no. 4 (March 2020): 885, 886, 889.

137. Teitelman, "Properties of Capitalism," 880, 885, 891, 892. On Dodge, see also Beckert, *Monied Metropolis*, 17–45.

138. Achille Loria, *La terra ed il sistema sociale: Prolusione al corso di economia politica nella R. Università di Padova 21 novembre 1891* (Verona: Fratelli Drucker, 1892), 28, as quoted in (and translated by) Maier, *Once Between Borders*, 176.

139. Alexia Yates, "The Double Life of Property: Mobilizing Land and Making Capitalism in Modern France," *Critical Historical Studies* 6 (2019): 247–78, esp. 249.

140. Angelis, "Separating the Doing and the Deed," 66.

141. Maier, *Leviathan 2.0*, 114; and Stefano Musso, *Le Regole e l'elusione: Il governo del mercato del lavoro nell'industrializzazione italiana, 1888–2003* (Rosenberg and Sellier, 2004), 9; and Tilly, *Coercion, Capital, and European States*, 187.

142. Theda Skocpol, *Protecting Soldiers and Mothers: The Political Origins of Social Policy in the United States* (HUP, 1992), 162–68. For more on American social benefits during the Civil War, see the brilliant Skocpol, *Protecting Soldiers and Mothers*, esp. 1. Skocpol's core argument can be found at Skocpol, *Protecting Soldiers and Mothers*. See esp. 525–40.

143. See the works of Michel Callon.

144. As cited in Thomas McCraw, *Prophets of Innovation: Joseph Schumpeter and Creative Destruction* (Belknap Press of HUP, 2007), 51. See also Sophus A. Reinert, *The Academy of Fisticuffs: Political Economy and Commercial Society in Enlightenment Italy* (HUP, 2018); Quinn Slobodian, "How to See the World Economy: Statistics, Maps, and Schumpeter's Camera in the First

Age of Globalization," *JGH* 10, no. 2 (July 2015): 323.

145. T. W. Hutchison, *On Revolutions and Progress in Economic Knowledge* (CUP, 1978), 94; Alessandro Roncaglia, *The Wealth of Ideas: A History of Economic Thought* (CUP, 2005), 170; and Dimitris Milonakis and Ben Fine, *From Political Economy to Economics: Method, the Social and the Historical in the Evolution of Economic Theory* (Routledge, 2009), 116, 117.

146. Ernesto Screpanti and Stefano Zamagni, *An Outline of the History of Economic Thought* (OUP, 2005), 167, 171.

147. Roncaglia, *Wealth of Ideas*, 278. There is debate about whether it really constituted a revolutionary break with what came before.

148. Eli Cook, *The Pricing of Progress: Economic Indicators and the Capitalization of American Life* (HUP, 2017), 37–38, 243; Roncaglia, *Wealth of Ideas*, 279, 289; William Stanley Jevons, *The Theory of Political Economy* (Palgrave Macmillan, 2013), 49–111.

149. Screpanti and Zamagni, *Outline of the History of Economic Thought*, 167; Milonakis and Fine, *From Political Economy to Economics*, 110; Roncaglia, *Wealth of Ideas*, 279; James Livingston, *Pragmatism and the Political Economy of Cultural Revolution, 1850–1940* (University of North Carolina Press, 1994), 50; Piero Sraffa, *Production of Commodities by Means of Commodities* (CUP, 1960), 93, as cited in Roncaglia, *Wealth of Ideas*, 279.

150. "Political Economy," in *Encyclopedia Britannica*, 9th edition, 1885, vol. 19, 399.

151. Roncaglia, *Wealth of Ideas*, 359.

152. Roncaglia, *Wealth of Ideas*, 360.

153. Gianni Vaggi and Peter Groenewegen, *A Concise History of Economic Thought* (Palgrave Macmillan, 2003), 227, 228.

154. Cook, *Pricing of Progress*, 243.

155. Cook, *Pricing of Progress*, 246.

156. Roncaglia, *Wealth of Ideas*, 366, 367.

157. Roncaglia, *Wealth of Ideas*, 366, 367; Jan Sapp, *Genesis: The Evolution of Biology* (OUP, 2003), 75; Walther Flemming, "Zur Kenntnis der Zelle und ihrer Theilungs-Erscheinungen," *Schriften des Naturwissenschaftlichen Vereins für Schleswig-Holstein* 3 (1878): 23–27; James Clerk Maxwell, "Molecules," *Nature* (September 1873): 437–41; and Alan J. Rocke, "It Began with a Daydream: The 150th Anniversary of the Kekulé Benzene Structure,"

Angewandte Chemie International Edition 54, no.1 (2015): 46–50.

158. Hopkins, *Economic History of West Africa*, 251.

159. Hopkins, *Economic History of West Africa*, 251, 253. On "race," see Karen E. Fields and Barbara J. Fields, *Racecraft: The Soul of Inequality in American Life* (Verso, 2012).

160. See, among many similar documents, "Note, Röchling'schen Eisen- und Stahlwerke, Aufträge in Kriegsmaterial," 17 July 1916, im B/K-276 RESW GmBH: Aufstellung über Aufträge an Kriegsmaterial von 1915/10–1918/02, Saarstahl Archive, Völklingen Germany. See also "Aufstellung über unsere derzeitigen hauptsächlichen Aufträge in Kriegsmaterial," 25 February 1918, and "Aufstellung über unsere derzeitigen hauptsächlichen Aufträge in Kriegsmaterial," 17 December 1917.

161. Richard Nutzinger, Hans Boehmer, and Otto Johannsen, eds., *50 Jahre Röchling Völklingen: Die Entwicklung eines Rheinischen Industrie-Unternehmens* (Gebr. Hofer A. G., 1931), 34.

162. Hubert Kesternich, *Aufstieg und Wandel: 140 Jahre Völklinger Hütte* (Blattlausverlag, 2015), 25; Gerhard Seibold, *Röchling: Kontinuität im Wandel* (Thorbecke Verlag, 2001), 116; and Nutzinger, Böhmer, and Johannsen, *50 Jahre Röchling*, 74.

163. Nutzinger, Böhmer, and Johannsen, *50 Jahre Röchling Völklingen*, 30; and Seibold, *Röchling*, 169.

164. Hermann Röchling to the Staatssekretär des Innern in Berlin, Flin near Luneville, 31 August 1914, in Völklinger Hütte, Röchling, Alter Bestand, Saarstahl, Dillinger Hütte, VH. See also Inge Plettenberg, "Hermann Röchling—der Cherusker," in *Die Röchlings und die Völklinger Hütte*, ed. Meinrad Maria Grewenig (Springpunkt Verlag, 2014), 55.

165. This paragraph draws heavily and partly quotes verbatim Sven Beckert, "American Danger: United States Empire, Eurafrica, and the Territorialization of Industrial Capitalism, 1870–1950," in *AHR* 122, no. 4 (October 2017): 1137–70. For the sources see Vom Abgeordneten Erzberger überreichte Denkschrift des August Thyssen, Mülheim a.Ruhr an den Staatssekretär des Innern in Berlin, Abschrift, C.B. 2258, undated, in Eingaben von Hermann Röchling, Freiherr von Gemmingen und August Thyssen vom Februar 1915 wegen der Erzbecken von Longwy und Briey an den Staatssekretaer des Innern in Berlin, A/K54/439, Alter Bestand, VH.

166. Eingaben von Hermann Röchling, Freiherr von Gemmingen und August Thyssen vom Februar 1915 wegen der Erzbecken von Longwy und Briey an den Staatssekretaer des Innern in Berlin, A/K54/439, Alter Bestand, VH; Reinhard Opitz, *Europastrategien des deutschen Kapitals, 1900–1945* (Pahl-Rugenstein, 1977), 26; Denkschrift Hermann Röchlings an den Statthalter von Elsass-Lothringen, v. Dallwitz, betreffend französischer Erzgebiete, Flin, August 31, 1914, reproduced in Opitz, *Europastrategien des deutschen Kapitals*, 211–15; Kriegzieldenkschrift Walter Rathenaus an Bethmann Hollweg, 7 September 1914, reproduced in Opitz, *Europastrategien des deutschen Kapitals*, 221–25; Denkschrift von August Thyssen, überreicht durch den Abgeordneten Erzberger, September 1914, Antwortschreiben Carl Duisbergs an Gustav Stressemann betr. Belgien, 3 March 1915, reproduced in Opitz, *Europastrategien des deutschen Kapitals*, 299–301; Gemeinsame Denkschrift von Hermann Schumacher und Hugo Stinnes, 16 November 1914, cited in Opitz, *Europastrategien des deutschen Kapitals*, 282; and Wirklicher Geheimrat Szerenyi, Staatssekretär, speech at Konferenz der Mitteleuropäischen Wirtschaftsvereine in Dresden, 17 and 18 January 1916, Protokolle der Verhandlungen, copy in Auswärtiges Amt, Akten betreffend den Mitteleuropäischen Wirtschaftsverein, 1916–1918, R 901, f2502, BABerlin. See also Paul Rohrbach, *Die Bagdadbahn* (Wiegandt, 1902); and Barnhart, *Japan Prepares for Total War*, 23. This discussion is taken almost verbatim from Sven Beckert. See "American Danger: United States Empire, Eurafrica, and the Territorialization of Industrial Capitalism, 1870–1950," in *AHR* 122, no. 4 (October 2017): 1137–1170. Reprinted here with the publisher's permission.

167. On Eisenrat, the iron council, see Seibold, *Röchling*, 170–71; and Plettenberg, "Hermann Röchling—der Cherusker," 26, 55.

168. Röchling to James W. Miller (Pittsburg), letter, Völklingen, April 23, 1898, C/K/64, 1897 bis 1900, Mappe 1, VH.

169. Hermann Röchling, Aktennotiz, 19 December 1913, RESW GmbH: Aktennotizen von Hermann Röchling (zum Teil streng vertraulich), 1912/11 bis 1917/07, E/K37, 162, Alter Bestand, VH.

170. Seibold, *Röchling*, 173, 174,

176–77; Nutzinger, Böhmer, and Johannsen, *50 Jahre Röchling Völklingen*, 36.

171. Erich Mühsam, "Barbaren," in Erich Mühsam, *Ausgewählte Werke*, vol. 1, *Gedichte, Prosa, Stücke* (Volk und Welt, 1978), 99–100.

172. Antonio Gramsci, *Quaderni del carcere*, vol. 1, *Quaderni 1 (16)–5 (9)* (Giulio Einaudi, 1975), 311. The translation is from Slavoj Žižek, "Living in the Time of Monsters," *Counterpoints* 422 (January 2012): 43.

Chapter 14: A Time of Monsters: Industrial Capitalism, 1918–1945

1. Gouverneur Général de l'Afrique Occidentale Française [G. Angoulvant] to Monsieur le Ministre des Colonies, 1 May 1919, in Grève des Cheminots, 1919–1920, Esclavage et Travail, 1807–1920, Sériés K, K 35, ANS; and Workers of the Dakar-Saint-Louis Railway to the Gouverneur Général, Saint-Louis, telegram, 8 April 1919, in Grève des Cheminots, 1919–1920, Esclavage et Travail, 1807–1920, Sériés K, K 35, ANS.

2. Letter from the Cheminots [Railway Workers] to the Gouverneur Général, 8 April 1919, in Grève des Cheminots, 1919–1920, Esclavage et Travail, 1807–1920, Sériés K, K 35, ANS, as cited in Iba Der Thiam, *Les origines du mouvement syndical africain, 1790–1929* (Éditions L'Harmattan, 1993), 126, 128, 133. A further unsigned letter, penciled by the railroad workers in Rufisque, arrived on April 9, amplifying the ultimatum as cited in Thiam, *Les origines du mouvement syndical africain*, 128.

3. Thiam, *Les origines du mouvement syndical africain*, 128; Paul Edward Pheffer, "Railroads and Aspects of Social Change in Senegal, 1878–1933 (PhD diss., University of Pennsylvania, 1975), 318. The importance of the war experience to political mobilizations in the 1920s is also argued by Olivier Sagna, "Les mouvements anti colonialistes africains dans la France de l'entre-deux-guerres, 1919–1939," *Historiens géographes du Sénégal*, vol. 6 (L'Association, 1991), 4.

4. Thiam, *Les origines du mouvement syndical africain*, 127. Africans were gradually hired to fill skilled positions, most notably locomotive engineers, for the simple reason that they could be paid less for work that Europeans would not suffer for long. See Pheffer, "Railroads and Aspects of Social Change in Senegal," 310, 316. The percentage of Africans in

the workforce is taken from Birame Ndour, "Luttes laborieuses en 'situation coloniale': Cheminots du Dakar-Niger, 1919–1951," in *Historiens et géographes du Sénégal*, 6:45.

5. Thiam, *Les origines du mouvement syndical africain*, 133.

6. Thiam, *Les origines du mouvement syndical africain*, 130.

7. Général de Division Bonnier Commandant Supérieur des Troupes du Groupe de l'Afrique Occidentale Française, to Monsieur le Gouverneur Général de l'Afrique Occidentale Française, letter, 10 April 1919, and Inspector General of Public Works (French West Africa) [M. Mouneyres] to the Superior General Commander of the Troupes (French West Africa group), letter, 10 April 1919, both in Grève des Cheminots, 1919–1920, Esclavage et Travail, 1807–1920, Sériés K, K 35, ANS.

8. Gouverneur Général de l'Afrique Occidentale Française [G. Angoulvant] to Monsieur le Ministre des Colonies, 1 May 1919, ANS.

9. Telegram, Giraud to Lachèze, Directeur of the Dakar–Saint-Louis Railway, 15 April 1919, in Grève des Cheminots, 1919–1920, Esclavage et Travail, 1807–1920, Sériés K, K 35, ANS.

10. Giraud, Gouvernement Général de l'Afrique Occidentale Française, to Gouverneur Général, Rufisque, telegram, 14 April 1919, in Grève des Cheminots, 1919–1920, Esclavage et Travail, 1807–1920, Sériés K, K 35, ANS; and telegram from Giraud, Rufisque, 15 April 1919, in Grève des Cheminots, 1919–1920, Esclavage et Travail, 1807–1920, Sériés K, K 35, ANS.

11. Thiam, *Les origines du mouvement syndical africain*, 134; "Liste nominative du personnel journalier du service de la traction," Grève des Cheminots, 1919–1920, Esclavage et Travail, 1807–1920, Sériés K, K 35, ANS. For the quote, see Giraud to Lachèze, Directeur of the Dakar–Saint-Louis Railway, 15 April 1919, in Grève des Cheminots, 1919–1920, Esclavage et Travail, 1807–1920, Sériés K, K 35, ANS; Chamber of Commerce to [G. Angoulvant?], telegram, 15 April 1919, in Grève des Cheminots, 1919–1920, Esclavage et Travail, 1807–1920, Sériés K, K 35, ANS; G. Angoulvant to President of the Chamber of Commerce, 14 April 1919, in Grève des Cheminots, 1919–1920, Esclavage et Travail, 1807–1920, Sériés K, K 35, ANS; and Pheffer, "Railroads and Aspects of Social Change in Senegal," 170. There were a total of 585 workers on the road: 101 Europeans,

449 Africans, and another 45 workers of unspecified origins. See Pheffer, "Railroads and Aspects of Social Change in Senegal," 528.

12. Iba Der Thiam, "Les origines du mouvement syndical sénégalais: La grève des cheminots du Dakar–Saint-Louis, du 13 au 15 avril 1919," in *Annales de la Faculté des Lettres et sciences humaines*, ed. Université de Dakar, Faculté des Lettres et Sciences Humaines, vol. 7 (Presses Universitaires de France, 1977), 229–30.

13. Thiam, "Les origines du mouvement syndical sénégalais," 230.

14. Thiam, "Les origines du mouvement syndical sénégalais," 231.

15. Telegram, Didelot [?] to the Gouverneur Général, 13 April 1919, in Grève des Cheminots, 1919–1920, Esclavage et Travail, 1807–1920, Sériés K, K 35, ANS; and Pheffer, "Railroads and Aspects of Social Change in Senegal," 330.

16. Thiam, "Les origines du mouvement syndical sénégalais," 232.

17. For the quote, see G. Angoulvant to the Ministère de Colonie, Paris, telegram, April 15, 1919, in Grève des Cheminots, 1919–1920, Esclavage et Travail, 1807–1920, Sériés K, K 35, ANS.

18. G. Angoulvant to the Minister of Colonies, 15 April 1919, in Grève des Cheminots, 1919–1920, Esclavage et Travail, 1807–1920, Sériés K, K 35, ANS; Thiam, *Les origines du mouvement syndical africain*, 138–39; Pheffer, "Railroads and Aspects of Social Change in Senegal," 316, 330–31; and Gouverneur Général de l'Afrique Occidentale Française [G. Angoulvant] to Monsieur le Ministre des Colonies, 1 May 1919, ANS. The governor-general even estimates that wages rose in total by more than 30 percent. See also Gouverneur Général de l'Afrique Occidentale Française [G. Angoulvant] to Monsieur le Ministre des Colonies, 1 May 1919, ANS; Chamber of Commerce to the Gouverneur Général, telegram, 25 April 1919, in Grève des Cheminots, 1919–1920, Esclavage et Travail, 1807–1920, Sériés K, K 35, ANS; Babacar Fall, "Le mouvement syndical en Afrique occidentale francophone, de la tutelle des centrales métropolitaines à celle des partis nationaux uniques, ou la difficile quête d'une personnalité (1900–1968)," *Matériaux pour l'histoire de notre temps* 4, no. 84 (2006): 50; Frederick Cooper, *Decolonization and African Society: The Labor Question in French and British Africa* (CUP, 1996), 94; Ndour, "Luttes laborieuses en 'situation coloniale,'" 46. For wages, see "Liste nominative

du personnel journalier du service de la traction," ANS.

19. Calvin Winslow, "Longshoremen's Strikes, 1900–1920," in Aaron Brenner, Benjamin Day, and Immanuel Ness, eds., *The Encyclopedia of Strikes in American History* (Routledge, 2015), 553–56; Douglas E. Haynes, *Rhetoric and Ritual in Colonial India: The Shaping of Public Culture in Surat City, 1852–1928* (University of California Press, 1991), 175–99; Corpo de Investigação e Segurança Pública do Distrito Federal, "Anarchists Under Arrest," trans. Amy Chazkel, in *The Rio De Janeiro Reader: History, Culture, and Politics*, eds. Daryle Williams, Amy Chazkel, and Paolo Knauss de Mendonça (Duke UP, 2016), 174–78; Ann B. Irish, *Hokkaido: A History of Ethnic Transition and Development on Japan's Northern Island* (McFarland & Company Publishers, 2009), 218; and "Bericht über die durch die Kommunisten einberufene Öffentliche Versammlung in der Turnhalle am 20. 10. 1920 7 Uhr," in D-K/45, 199–200, RESW GmbH, Streik, 1921, Mappe 1–2, VH.

20. Deutscher Metallarbeiter Verband, *An die Einwohnerschaft Völklingens!*, pamphlet, undated, in D-K/45, 199–200, RESW GmbH, Streik, 1921, Mappe 1–2, VH; "An Unsere Belegschaft," poster, in B/K-387: RESW GmbH (Streik 1924) Verluste infolge Stilllegung 1924, VH. See "Der Röchlingblock Gesprengt," *Arbeiter-Zeitung*, September 13, 1920; *Volksstimme*, November 12, 1924. See also the documents in B-K, 271: RESW GmbH 1924 und Streik, Alter Bestand, VH, and in B-K, 387: RESW GmbH (Strelk, 1924) Verluste infolge Stilllegung 1924, Alter Bestand, VH.

21. For the quote see "Report on Labour Strikes Received from Various Departments of the Government of India," Industries, Labour, File No. L-811 (i), January 1921, Serial Nos. 1–3, NAI.

22. Extract from His Excellency the Viceroy to the Secretary of State, telegram No. 461, 4 June 1920, in Report on Labour Strikes, NAI.

23. Phillip S. Foner, *History of the Labor Movement in the United States*, vol. 8, *Postwar Struggles, 1918–1920* (International Publishers, 1988), 1; copied extract from Viceroy (Home Department) to the Secretary of State, telegram No. 17, 14 January 1920, in "Report on Labour Strikes," NAI; copied extract from Viceroy (Home Department) to the Secre-

tary of State, telegram No. 472, 19 February 1920, in "Report on Labour Strikes," NAI; copied extract from Viceroy (Home Department) to the Secretary of State, telegram No. 232, 12 March 1920, in "Report on Labour Strikes," NAI; and Howard Spodek, *Ahmedabad: Shock City of Twentieth-Century India* (Indiana UP, 2011), 59–61.

24. Stefano Bartolini, *The Political Mobilization of the European Left, 1860–1980: The Class Cleavage* (CUP, 2000), 55. The number is an average for the years 1921 and 1925 and adds up electoral participation in thirteen European countries. See also Antony G. Hopkins, *An Economic History of West Africa*, 2nd ed. (Routledge, 2020), 312; Pheffer, "Railroads and Aspects of Social Change in Senegal," 353; and Secretary's Report to Congress of the International Federation of Textile Workers, Ghent, 28 May–2 June 1928, copy in N. M. Joshi Papers, 1st Installment, File No. 32, Correspondence About a National and International Textile Union, 1927–28, NMML.

25. Philip Bonner, "South African Society and Culture, 1910–1948," in *The Cambridge History of South Africa* vol. 2, *1885–1994*, ed. Robert Ross, Anne Kelk Mager, and Bill Nasson (CUP, 2011), 269; Franz-Josef Brüggemeier, *Grubengold: Das Zeitalter der Kohle von 1750 bis Heute* (Verlag C. H. Beck, 2018), 173; Gordon J. Barclay, "'Duties in Aid of the Civil Power': The Deployment of the Army to Glasgow, 31 January to 17 February 1919," *Journal of Scottish Historical Studies* 38, no. 2 (November 2018): esp. 285–87; Steven Brocklehurst, "The Battle of George Square: How a Strike Led to Fears of a Workers' Revolt," BBC News, January 30, 2019, https://www.bbc.com/news/uk-scotland-46884527; and Stefano Musso, *Gli operai di Torino, 1900–1920* (Feltrinelli Editore, 1980), 170, 185.

26. As quoted in S. A. Smith, *Russia in Revolution: An Empire in Crisis, 1890 to 1928*, 1st ed. (OUP, 2017), 150.

27. Giovanni Arrighi, *The Long Twentieth Century: Money, Power and the Origins of Our Times* (Verso, 1994), 64; Smith, *Russia in Revolution*, 101; Sheila Fitzpatrick, *The Russian Revolution* (OUP, 1982), 6; and Smith, *Russia in Revolution*, 61.

28. See, for example, Thomas Piketty, *Capital and Ideology* (HUP, 2020), 466.

29. Erez Manela, *The Wilsonian Moment: Self-Determination and the International Origins of Anticolonial Nationalism* (OUP, 2007); David V. C. Browne, *Race, Class, Politics and the Struggle for Empowerment in Barbados, 1914–1937* (Ian Randle Publishers, 2012), 31–41, 43, 55; Durba Ghosh, *Gentlemanly Terrorists: Political Violence and the Colonial State in India, 1919–1947* (CUP, 2017), 44.

30. Arrighi, *Long Twentieth Century*, 64.

31. Antonio Gramsci, *Quaderni del carcere* (Einaudi, 1975), 311, translated by Žižek. See also Arno Mayer, *The Persistence of the Old Regime: Europe to the Great War* (Pantheon, 1981), 3. For political scientist Jeffry Frieden, "almost everything that came after 1914 was bad, or ended badly, for almost all the people almost all the time." See Jeffry A. Frieden, *Global Capitalism: Its Fall and Rise in the Twentieth Century* (W. W. Norton, 2006), 128.

32. Robert Musil, *Der Mann ohne Eigenschaften* (Anaconda, 2019), 560. Originally published in 1930.

33. Werner Sombart, "Die Wandlungen des Kapitalismus," *Weltwirtschaftliches Archiv* 28 (1928): 255.

34. Katya Gianotti: "Mito e realtà di un grande imprenditore: Giovanni Agnelli, tra storiografia e pubblicistica," in *La capitale dell'automobile: Imprenditori, cultura e società a Torino*, ed. Paride Rugafiori (Marsilio, 1999), 143–45.

35. Gianotti, "Mito e realtà di un grande imprenditore," 142, 150.

36. As cited in Gianotti, "Mito e realtà di un grande imprenditore," 165.

37. Musso, *Gli operai di Torino*, 27; Duccio Bigazzi, "The Fiat Works at Lingotto (Turin)," unpublished manuscript, in Stabilimenti FIAT di Produzione Automobilistica, 4, Lingotto, MSC 0023, 1, CSF, Torino, Italy; and Bigazzi, "Fiat Works at Lingotto," 9. A detailed description of that process can be found in Duccio Bigazzi, "Gli operai della catena di montaggio: la FIAT 1922–1943," in *Annali della Fondazione Giangiacomo Feltrinelli 1979/1980*, ed. Fondazione Giangiacomo Feltrinelli (Feltrinelli, 1981), 907–14; and Bigazzi "Fiat Works at Lingotto," 1.

38. Archivio Storico Fiat, *L'industria italiana nel mercato mondiale dalla fine dell'800 alla metà del '900* (Archivio Storico Fiat, 1993), 339; Musso, *Gli operai di Torino*, 18, 28–33, 57; and Ivan T. Berend: *An Economic History of Twentieth-Century Europe: Economic Regimes from Laissez-Faire to Globalization* (CUP, 2006), 37.

39. For a complete list, see Archivio Storico Fiat, *L'industria italiana nel mercato mondiale*, 236–51, 339; and "La Fiat negli Stati Uniti d'Amer-ica," typescript, undated, in MSC 0095, Fiat all'estero, Stati Uniti d'America, CSF, Torino, Italy.

40. Musso, *Gli operai di Torino*, 33; Valerio Castronovo, "I frutti della lezione americana," *Il Sole 24 Ore*, May 17, 2010; Claudia Bocca, *Torino capitale* (Newton Compton Editori, 2010), n.p.; Joshua Freeman, *Behemoth: A History of the Factory and the Making of the Modern* (W. W. Norton, 2018), 136.

41. Freeman, *Behemoth*, 123.

42. Freeman, *Behemoth*, 126.

43. Freeman, *Behemoth*, 118; John Dos Passos, *The Big Money* (Houghton Mifflin, 2000), 38. Originally published in 1936.

44. Freeman, *Behemoth*, 118, 120, 123–25; Stephan J. Link, *Forging Global Fordism: Nazi Germany, Soviet Russia and the Contest over Industrial Order* (PUP, 2020), 30–33.

45. Duccio Bigazzi, *La grande fabbrica, organizzazione industriale e modello americano alla Fiat dal Lingotto a Mirafiori* (Ed. Feltrinelli, 2000), 21e.

46. Jennifer Clark, *Mondo Agnelli: Fiat, Chrysler, and the Power of a Dynasty* (Wiley, 2012), 42; "Fiat Centro e Sezioni Automobili," in Fondo Sepin, Operai in Forza, PER 005, CSF, Torino, Italy.

47. Ing. Maraini della Direzione Fiat, "Studio dei progressi della costruzione americana," 30 September 1918, in L'Industria Automobilistica Americana, Libro Maraini, Box MSC 0100, CSF, Torino, Italy. See also Bigazzi, *La grande fabbrica*, 22.

48. Maraini, "Studio dei progressi della costruzione americana," 2.

49. For the first quote, see Maraini, typescript, introduction, "Fiat, D, Relazione Tecnica," 1919, 3, in L'Industria Automobilistica Americana, Libro Maraini, Box MSC 0100. See also Maraini, "Studio dei progressi della costruzione americana," 22. For the second quote, see Maraini, "Studio dei progressi della costruzione americana," 24.

50. For the first quote, see Maraini, "Studio dei progressi della costruzione americana," 25. For the last quote, see "Relazione Generale—Fascicolo 1," undated but after 1922, 10, in L'Industria Automobilistica Americana, Libro Maraini, Box MSC 0100, CSF, Torino, Italy.

51. Maraini, "Studio dei progressi della costruzione americana," 28.

52. B. Maraini, typescript, "FIAT—Corso per ispettori commerciali all'estero, le Marche esistenti e loro caratteristiche principali," October 1918, 42–48, in L'Industria Automobilistica Americana, Libro Maraini, Box MSC 0100, CSF, Torino,

Italy; and Maraini, "FIAT—Corso per ispettori commerciali all'estero," 44–60. For the quote, see Maraini, "FIAT—Corso per ispettori commerciali all'estero," 55.

53. Maraini, "Fiat, D, Relazione Tecnica," 5; and Bigazzi, *La grande fabbrica*, 28.

54. "Relazione Generale—Fascicolo 1," 6, 10.

55. "Relazione Generale—Fascicolo 1, 11.

56. Giuseppe Volpato, "Produzione e mercato: Verso l'automobilismo di massa," in *Mirafiori*, ed. Carlo Olmo (Umberto Allemandi, 2007), 39; Bigazzi, *La grande fabbrica*, 22.

57. Bigazzi, *La grande fabbrica*, 40.

58. Volpato, "Produzione e mercato," 124, 131; and Bigazzi, *La grande fabbrica*, 28. See also Duccio Bigazzi, "Management Strategies in the Italian Car Industry 1906–1945: Fiat and Alfa Romeo," in *The Automobile Industry and Its Workers: Between Fordism and Flexibility*, ed. Steven Tolliday and Jonathan Zeitlin (Polity in Association with B. Blackwell, 1986), 81, 85; and Volpato, "Produzione e mercato," 137.

59. Volpato, "Produzione e mercato," 126, 131–32, 136; John Foot, *Modern Italy* (Palgrave Macmillan, 2003), 134–35; and Bigazzi, "Management Strategies in the Italian Car Industry," 76.

60. Vera Zamagni, *The Economic History of Italy 1860–1990* (Clarendon Press, 1993), 98; Fiat, Consiglio di Amministrazione, *Fiat 1915–1930: Verbali del consiglio di amministrazione*, vol. 1 (Fabbri, 1991), 487; Valerio Castronovo, *Giovanni Agnelli: La Fiat dal 1899 al 1945* (Einaudi, 1977); Fiat, *Fiat 1915–1930*, 303, 323, 503.

61. Bigazzi, "Management Strategies in the Italian Car Industry," 79, 80. Yet highly skilled workers did not completely disappear from the factory floor.

62. Bigazzi, "Management Strategies in the Italian Car Industry," 80.

63. "Il re tra i soldati e gli operai," *La Stampa*, May 23, 1923, 3.

64. Maraini, "Fiat, D, Relazione Tecnica," 91.

65. Maraini, "Fiat, D, Relazione Tecnica," 5.

66. Maraini, "Fiat, D, Relazione Tecnica," 5.

67. Maraini, "Fiat, D, Relazione Tecnica," 4.

68. Maraini, conclusion to "Fiat, D, Relazione Tecnica," 91.

69. Maraini, "Fiat, D, Relazione Tecnica," 4.

70. Maraini, introduction to "Fiat, D, Relazione Tecnica," 9.

71. See Berta, untitled, in Fiat, *Fiat 1915–1930*, 141. See also Maraini, conclusion to "Fiat, D, Relazione Tecnica," 91–92. And finally, see Bigazzi, *La grande fabbrica*, 27, 51.

72. Bigazzi, *La grande fabbrica*, 55; Freeman, *Behemoth*, 127, 129; and Link, *Forging Global Fordism*, 39. The number of immigrants streaming into the factory is for 1914.

73. Freeman, *Behemoth*, 131.

74. Antonio Gramsci, "Americanism and Fordism," in *Selections from the Prison Notebooks* (International Publishers, 1971), 286, 302.

75. Bigazzi, "Gli operai della catena di montaggio," 945.

76. Paolo Alatri, "La Fiat dal 1921 al 1926," *Belfagor* 29, no. 3 (1974): 298–317. In 1925, 299 workers left, and 302 were newly employed. See Fondo Sepin, Situazione Personale, Anno 1925, PER 008, busta 1, n. corda 8, CSF, Torino, Italy; and Clark, *Mondo Agnelli*, 56.

77. Bigazzi, "Management Strategies in the Italian Car Industry," 81. See, for example, the files in Fondo Sepin 29, Statistiche Varie, 1930A–1940A, PER 029, Ripartizione dei Turni di Lavoro, CSF, Torino, Italy; and Maraini, "Fiat, D, Relazione Tecnica," introduction.

78. Alejo G. Sison: *Corporate Governance and Ethics: An Aristotelian Perspective* (Edward Elgar, 2010), 103; and Clark, *Mondo Agnelli*, 46.

79. For the quotes, see Fiat, *Fiat 1915–1930*, 141.

80. Gianotti, "Mito e realtà di un grande imprenditore," 167; Valerio Castronovo, *Fiat, 1899–1999: Un secolo di storia italiana* (Rizzoli, 1999); Castronovo, *Giovanni Agnelli*, 418; and Volpato, "Produzione e mercato," 134.

81. Bigazzi, "Gli operai della catena di montaggio," 898. On Citroën, see Volpato, "Produzione e mercato," 129. See also Giuseppe Berta, "Uomini e organizzazione," in Olmo, *Mirafiori*, 103.

82. Link, *Forging Global Fordism*, 7, 47, 53, 59–60; Henry Ford, "Why I Am Helping," interview by William A. McGarry, *Nation's Business*, June 1930, 20–24.

83. As cited in Freeman, *Behemoth*, 147.

84. Link, *Forging Global Fordism*, 9, 28, 48, 69.

85. For the first part of the quote, see Bigazzi, *La grande fabbrica*, 56. For the second part, see Angelo Tasca, *I consigli di fabbrica e la rivoluzione mondiale* (Alleanza Coop Torinese, 1921), 4.

86. Frieden, *Global Capitalism*, 157; and John Dos Passos, *U.S.A.* (Mod-

ern Library, 1937); Virginia Woolf, *Mrs. Dalloway* (Hogarth Press, 1925); Virginia Woolf, *To the Lighthouse* (Hogarth Press, 1927).

87. This number is cited in "Everyday Life 1929–1941," Encyclopedia .com, accessed December 2024, https://www.encyclopedia.com/education/news-and-education-magazines/everyday-life-1929-1941. See also Marcel van der Linden and Magaly Rodriguez Garcia, eds., introduction to *On Coerced Labor: Work and Compulsion After Chattel Slavery* (Brill, 2016), 6; and David Love, "From 15 Million Acres to 1 Million Acres: How Black People Lost Their Land," *Atlantic Black Star*, no. 39, June 2017.

88. T. Shaw, "The International Position in the Textile Trade," undated and unsigned (but probably 1928), copy of a secretarial speech to the Twelfth International Textile Workers' Congress, Ghent, 28 May–2 June 1928, in N. M. Joshi Papers, 1st Installment, File 32, Correspondence About a National and International Textile Union, 1927–28, NMML.

89. Thomas Piketty, *Capital in the Twenty-First Century*, trans. Arthur Goldhammer (Belknap Press of HUP, 2014), 298; Facundo Alvaredo, *World Inequality Report 2018* (HUP, 2018), 214. See also records in box 17, Record Group 39, Records of the Bureau of the Treasury, Records Related to Government Agencies or Functions, Correspondence and Other Records Relating to Fiscal Relationships Between the United States and Other Nations, 1918–1941, National Archives and Records Administration, Washington, DC.

90. Frieden, *Global Capitalism*, 134–35, 139, 140, 141, 166; and Arrighi, *Long Twentieth Century*, 282.

91. Adam Tooze, *The Deluge: The Great War, America and the Remaking of the Global Order, 1916–1931* (Penguin Books, 2014), 298; Arrighi, *Long Twentieth Century*, 279.

92. Diego Olstein, *A Brief History of Now* (Palgrave Macmillan, 2021), 79; and Arrighi, *Long Twentieth Century*, 58.

93. Alexander D. Noyes, *The War Period in American Finance, 1908–1925* (G. Putnam's Sons, 1925), 436.

94. As cited in Charles Kindleberger, *World in Depression, 1929–1939* (University of California Press, 1986), 210. See also Kindleberger, 289.

95. Sahadeo Basdao, "The 'Radical' Movement Towards Decolonization in the British Caribbean in the Thir-

ties," *Canadian Journal of Latin American and Caribbean Studies* 22, no. 44 (1997): 128–37; F. K. Donnelly, "Clement Payne and the Barbados Riots of 1937," *Labour History Review* 55, no. 1 (Fall 1990): 35–37; Mary Chamberlain, introduction to *Empire and Nation-Building in the Caribbean: Barbados, 1937–66* (Manchester UP, 2012), 1–10; Sebastian Siebel-Achenbach, *Lower Silesia from Nazi Germany to Communist Poland, 1942–1947* (Palgrave Macmillan, 1994), 16–17; Adeline Alonso Ugaglia, Alessandro Corsi, and Jean-Marie Cordebat, eds., *The Palgrave Handbook of Wine Industry Economics* (Springer International Publishing, 2019), 367; Mary Renda, *Taking Haiti: Military Occupation and the Culture of U.S. Imperialism* (University of North Carolina Press, 2001), 34; Clifton Hood, *In Pursuit of Privilege: A History of New York City's Upper Class and the Making of a Metropolis* (Columbia UP, 2017), 271; Samita Sen, "Labour, Organization and Gender: The Jute Industry in India in the 1930s," in *Routes into the Abyss: Coping with the Crisis in the 1930s*, ed. Helmut Konrad and Wolfgang Maderthaner (Berghahn Books, 2013), 152–65; Gerhard Seibold, *Röchling: Kontinuität im Wandel* (Thorbecke Verlag, 2001), 207; Daniel Vaxelaire, *Le grande livre de l'histoire de La Réunion*, vol. 2, *De 1848 à l'an 2000* (Orphie, 1999), 564; Tomohiro Okada, "The Great Depression and Rural Development in Japan: On the Public Works Program for Relief to Farmers in the 1930s," *Kyoto University Economic Review* 61, no. 2 (Summer 1991), 35–41; David Nelson, "Defining the Urban: The Construction of French-Dominated Colonial Dakar, 1857–1940," *Historical Reflections / Réflexions Historiques* 33, no. 2 (Summer 2007): 240, 255; Robert Cribb, "Convict Exile and Penal Settlement in Colonial Indonesia," *Journal of Colonialism and Colonial History* 18, no. 3 (Winter 2017); Boris Fausto, *A Concise History of Brazil* (CUP, 2014), 206; "22,000 Railway Men Walk Out in Brazil," *NYT*, April 8, 1934; Volpato, "Produzione e mercato," 139; and Matt Gasnier, "Italy 1928–1950: Annual Sales Volumes," *Best Selling Cars Blog*, accessed December 28, 2021, https://bestsellingcarsblog.com/1951/01/italy-1928-1950-annual-sales-volumes-now-available/.

96. Isaac Joshua, *La crise de 1929 et l'émergence américaine* (Presse Universitaire Française, 1999), 7; Frieden, *Global Capitalism*, 176, 178,

186; Robert A. Margo, "Employment and Unemployment in the 1930s," *Journal of Economic Perspectives* 7, no. 2 (1993), 43; Frances Fox Piven and Richard A. Cloward, *Poor People's Movements: Why They Succeed, How They Fail* (Pantheon: 1977), 46; Eric D. Weitz, *Weimar Germany: Promise and Tragedy* (PUP, 2007), 161; Andrew Gordon, "The Right to Work in Japan: Labor and the State in the Depression," *Social Research* 54, no. 2 (Summer 1987), 247, 250; Mark Metzler, *Lever of Empire: The International Gold Standard and the Crisis of Liberalism in Prewar Japan* (University of California Press, 2006), 222; Bill Freund, "South Africa: The Union Years, 1910–1948—Political and Economic Foundations," in *The Cambridge History of South Africa*, vol. 2, *1885–1994*, ed. Robert Ross, Anne Kelk Mager, and Bill Nasson (CUP, 2011), 219; Nicoli Nattrass and Jeremy Seekings, "The Economy and Poverty in the Twentieth Century," in Ross, Mager, and Nasson, *Cambridge History of South Africa*, 2:525; Charles H. Feinstein, *An Economic History of South Africa: Conquest, Discrimination, and Development* (CUP, 2005), 122–23; and Aaron Jakes and Ahmad Shokr, "Capitalism in Egypt, Not Egyptian Capitalism," in *A Critical Political Economy of the Middle East and North Africa*, ed. Joel Beinin, Bassam Haddad, and Sherene Seikaly (Stanford UP, 2021), 133. This is in terms of 1990 international Geary-Khamis dollars. See Angus Maddison, *The World Economy: Historical Statistics*, Development Centre Studies (OECD, 2003), 50, 51, table 1b; and C. H. Feinstein, Peter Temin, and Gianni Toniolo, *The World Economy Between the World Wars* (OUP, 2008), 95.

97. Jakob B. Madsen, "Trade Barriers and the Collapse of World Trade During the Great Depression," *Southern Economic Journal* 67, no. 4 (April 2001): 848; Kindleberger, *World in Depression*, 189; Feinstein, Temin, and Toniolo, *World Economy Between the World Wars*, 95; Esteban Ortiz-Ospina and Diana Beltekian, "Trade and Globalization," *Our World in Data*, accessed November 16, 2021, https://ourworldindata.org/trade-and-globalization; and Barry Eichengreen and Richard Portes, "The Interwar Debt Crisis and Its Aftermath," *The World Bank Research Observer* 5, no. 1 (January 1990): 74.

98. Frieden, *Global Capitalism*, 181; and Elmus Wicker, *The Banking Panics of the Great Depression* (CUP, 1996), 1.

99. Frieden, *Global Capitalism*, 172, 174, 176, 177, 184.

100. Frieden, *Global Capitalism*, 154, 184, 187; and Barry Eichengreen, *Golden Fetters: The Gold Standard and the Great Depression, 1919–1939* (OUP, 1992).

101. For the snippet, see Hans Fallada, *Kleiner Mann, was nun?* (Aufbau Verlag, 2017), 458. For Fallada's description of the protagonist, see letter to his editor, Ernst Rowohlt, as cited in Urs Bitterli, "Hans Fallada," Journal21.ch, December 12, 2014.

102. Piven and Cloward, *Poor People's Movements*, 48.

103. George Orwell, *The Road to Wigan Pier* (Harcourt, Brace, Jovanovich, 1958), 5, 49, 59, 79, 81, 85, 95–96, 173. First published in 1937.

104. Melissa Teixeira, "Making a Brazilian New Deal: Oliveira Vianna and the Transnational Sources of Brazil's Corporatist Experiment," *Journal of Latin American Studies* 50, no. 3 (2018): 623; Kiran Klaus Patel, *The New Deal: A Global History* (PUP, 2016), 63; Jesús Antonio Bejarano, "El despegue cafetero," in J. Ocampo, *Historia económica de Colombia* (Planeta, 2007), 208; Marco Palacios, *El Café en Colombia, 1850–1970* (Colegio de México, 2009), 413; Ian Brown, *A Colonial Economy in Crisis: Burma's Rice Cultivators and the World Depression of the 1930s* (Routledge Curzon, 2005), 37.

105. United States Congress, House of Representatives, Special Committee on Un-American Activities (1938–1944), *Investigation of Un-American Propaganda Activities in the United States* (US Government Printing Office, 1938), 3156.

106. Ferdinand Fried (pseud. for Ferdinand Zimmermann), *Das Ende des Kapitalismus* (Diederichs, 1931), 184.

107. See Jean Fourastié, *Les Trente Glorieuses, ou La révolution invisible de 1946 à 1975* (Fayard, 1979), 182.

108. Lawrence Dennis, *Is Capitalism Doomed?* (Harper & Brothers, 1932), 3.

109. James Burnham, *The Managerial Revolution: What Is Happening in the World* (John Day Co., 1941), 39.

110. Leon Trotsky, "The Death Agony of Capitalism and the Tasks of the Fourth International," in *The Transitional Program for Socialist Revolution* (Pathfinder Press, 1972), 73.

111. United States Congress, House of Representatives, Committee on Banking and Currency, *Hearings Before the Committee on Banking and Currency: Seventy-Fourth Congress First Session on H.R. 5357; A Bill to Provide for the Sound, Effective, and*

Uninterrupted Operation of the Banking System (US Government Printing Office, 1935), 418.

112. United States Congress Senate Committee on Finance, *Investigation of Economic Problems*, vol. 2 (US Government Printing Office, 1933), 891.

113. Joseph A. Schumpeter, *Capitalism, Socialism and Democracy* (Harper & Brothers, 1942; repr., George Allen & Unwin, 1976), 156. Citation here refers to the George Allen & Unwin edition.

114. John Katz, *The Will to Civilization: An Inquiry into the Principles of Historic Change* (Secker and Warburg, 1938), 334.

115. Link, *Forging Global Fordism*, 16; and Karl Polanyi, *The Great Transformation: The Political and Economic Origins of Our Time* (Amereon House, 1944), 41.

116. Link, *Forging Global Fordism*, 9, 16, 18.

117. Link, *Forging Global Fordism*, 17.

118. John Maynard Keynes, "National Self-Sufficiency," *Yale Review*, no. 22, June 1933, 755–69.

119. Keynes, "National Self-Sufficiency," 758.

120. Keynes, "National Self-Sufficiency," 760, 762.

121. Keynes, "National Self-Sufficiency," 755–69.

122. Patel, *New Deal*, 57.

123. Benoy Kumar Sarkar, *Economic Development* (B. G. Paul, 1926), 255.

124. Mark Robson, *Italy: The Rise of Fascism 1915–1945*, 3rd ed. (Hodder Education, 2008), 88; and Frieden, *Global Capitalism*, 213.

125. Frieden, *Global Capitalism*, 195, 203–4; and Ulrich Herbert, *Geschichte Deutschlands im 20. Jahrhundert* (C. H. Beck, 2014), 346–47, 371–72.

126. The quote is from the government's ten-point program, as cited in Metzler, *Lever of Empire*, 200.

127. Metzler, *Lever of Empire*, 210–11. For these connections, see the graph in Takeda Haruhito, *Shinpan Nihon Keizai no jikenbo: Kaikoku kara baburu hōkai made* (Nihon Keizai Hyōronsha, 2009), 172.

128. Louise Young, *Japan's Total Empire: Manchuria and the Culture of Wartime Imperialism* (University of California Press, 1999), 4.

129. Yosano Akiko, *Travels in Manchuria and Mongolia: A Feminist Poet from Japan Encounters Prewar China*, trans. Joshua Fogel (Columbia UP, 2001), 103.

130. Young, *Japan's Total Empire*, 4, 24, 42–44, 183–240; and Michael Barnhart, *Japan Prepares for Total War: The Search for Economic Security, 1919–1941* (Cornell UP, 1991), 18.

131. Fujiwara Ginjirō, president of Oji Paper, as cited in Young, *Japan's Total Empire*, 230.

132. As cited in Young, *Japan's Total Empire*, 228.

133. Young, *Japan's Total Empire*, 42, 192, 194, 198, 203, 208, 213–14, 216, 220.

134. As cited in Young, *Japan's Total Empire*, 183–184, 186, 188, 187, 190, 203, 224.

135. This discussion (to page 793) is taken almost verbatim from Sven Beckert, "American Danger: United States Empire, Eurafrica, and the Territorialization of Industrial Capitalism, 1870–1950," *AHR* 122, no. 4 (October 2017): 1137–70. Reprinted here with the publisher's permission.

136. René Goepfert, "Les phosphates algériens et l'agriculture françaises: L'exploitation du gisement du Djebel-Onk" (PhD diss., Université de Paris, 1925); and Richard N. Coudenhove-Kalergi, *Pan-Europa* (Vienna, 1923). For translations and sales, see Anita Prettenthaler-Ziegerhofer, "Richard Nikolaus Coudenhove-Kalergi, Founder of the Pan-European Union, and the Birth of a 'New' Europe," in *Europe in Crisis: Intellectuals and the European Idea, 1917–1957*, ed. Mark Hewitson and Matthew D'Auria (Berghahn, 2012), 89–109. On Coudenhove-Kalergi, see also Voir Antoine Fleury, "Paneurope et l'Afrique," in *L'Europe unie et l'Afrique: De l'idée d'Eurafrique à la convention de Lomé 1: Actes du colloque international de Paris, 1er et 2 avril 2004*, ed. Marie-Thérèse Bitsch and Gérard Bossuat (Bruylant, 2005).

137. Coudenhove-Kalergi, *Pan-Europa*, 13–16.

138. Coudenhove-Kalergi, *Pan-Europa*, 68–69. This discussion is taken almost verbatim from Sven Beckert. See "American Danger: United States Empire, Eurafrica, and the Territorialization of Industrial Capitalism, 1870–1950," *AHR* 122, no. 4 (October 2017): 1137–70. Reprinted here with the publisher's permission.

139. Richard N. Coudenhove-Kalergi, "Afrika," in *Pan-Europa* 5, no. 2 (1929): 4, 23.

140. Coudenhove-Kalergi, "Afrika," 3.

141. Coudenhove-Kalergi, *Pan-Europa*, 13, 19.

142. Coudenhove-Kalergi, *Pan-Europa*, 8.

143. Coudenhove-Kalergi, *Pan-Europa*, 156–57; and Coudenhove-Kalergi, "Afrika," 19, 29.

144. Coudenhove-Kalergi, "Afrika,"

3. This is also emphasized by Fleury, "Paneurope et l'Afrique," 40.

145. See, among others, Charles-Robert Ageron, "L'idée d'Eurafrique et le débat colonial franco-allemand de l'entre-deux-guerres," *Revue d'histoire moderne et contemporaine* 22, no. 3 (1975): 457, 460; and Joseph Caillaux, *D'Agadir à la grande pénitence*, as quoted in Ageron, "L'idée d'Eurafrique," 463. There are others who thought along similar lines, including Henry de Jouvenel, a publicist. See Jouvenel, "Bloc africain et Fédération européenne," *La Revue des vivants* 1 (January 1930): 1–7, here 2–3; Eugène Guernier, *L'Afrique, champ d'expansion de l'Europe; Avec 14 cartes et graphiques* (A. Colin, 1933); and Herman Sörgel, *Die drei grossen "A": Grossdeutschland und italienisches Imperium, die Pfeiler Atlantropas* (Piloty & Loehle, 1938), xii, 10, 22, 41, 55, 96. On Sörgel, see also Philipp Nicolas Lehmann, "Infinite Power to Change the World: Hydroelectricity and Engineered Climate Change in the Atlantropa Project," *AHR* 121, no. 1 (February 2016): 70–100; and Dirk van Laak, *Weiße Elefanten: Anspruch und Scheitern technischer Großprojekte im 20. Jahrhundert* (Stuttgart, 1999).

146. "Discorso di Francesco Orestano, presidente del convegno," in *Convegno di scienze morali e storiche, 4–11 ottobre 1938—XVI: Tema: l'Africa*, vol. 1 (Reale Accademia d'Italia, 1939), 38–50.

147. Jacopo Mazzei, *Italia e Africa settentrionale nel problema economico mediterraneo* (Firenze, 1942), 19.

148. Adam Tooze, *Wages of Destruction* (Allen Lane, 2007), xxiv, 10.

149. As quoted in Ageron, "L'idée d'Eurafrique," 473.

150. See the essays in Gregor Thum, ed., *Traumland Osten: Deutsche Bilder vom östlichen Europa im 20 Jahrhundert* (Vandenhoeck & Ruprecht, 2006).

151. Ferdinand Fried (pseud.), "Antrittsvorlesung Uni Prag," November 19, 1941, reproduced in Reinhard Opitz, *Europastrategien des Deutschen Kapitals, 1900–1945* (Pahl-Rugenstein, 1994), 835; and Ferdinand Fried (pseud.), *Der Aufstieg der Juden* (Blut und Boden, 1937).

152. Gerhard L. Weinberg, *Hitlers zweites Buch: Ein Dokument aus dem Jahr 1928* (Deutsche Verlags-Anstalt, 1961), 120, 122.

153. Adolf Hitler, "June 13, 1943," in Adolf Hitler, *Monologe im Führerhauptquartier, 1941–1944*, ed. Werner Jochmann (Bindlach, 1980), 398. See also Timothy Snyder, *Black*

Earth: The Holocaust as History and Warning (Tim Duggan Books, 2015), 12–21.

154. Tooze, *Wages of Destruction*, 469–70. On Native Americans, see "Conversation with Dr. Todt and Gauleiter Sauckel, *Führerhauptquartier*, October 17, 1941," in Hitler, *Monologe im Führerhauptquartier*, 90–92, here 91.

155. Hitler, "September 17, 1941," in Jochmann, *Monologe im Führerhauptquartier*, 62–63.

156. For the snippet, see Seibold, *Röchling*, 184–85.

157. On the leather industry, see Sven Beckert, *Bis zu diesem Punkt und nicht weiter: Arbeitsalltag während des Zweiten Weltkriegs in einer Industrieregion Offenbach-Frankfurt* (VAS, 1990). On the Saar, see Seibold, *Röchling*, 181–82; "Die Erzreserven des Minettegebietes nach dem Stande von Ende 1929 nach Gebieten, Sorten, Lagern und Besitzern in Gebrauchsstonnen, signed by Hermann Röchling," A/K7/ 296, Alter Bestand, VH.

158. Seibold, *Röchling*, 184, 209; and "Die Erzreserven des Minettegebietes nach dem Stande von Ende 1929 nach Gebieten, Sorten, Lagern und Besitzern in Gebrauchsstonnen, signed by Hermann Röchling," A/K7/ 296, Alter Bestand, VH; and "Verluste infolge Stillegung, 1924," in B/K-387: RESW GmbH (Streik 1924), VH.

159. Frieden, *Global Capitalism*, 206; Kleoniki Alexopoulou, "An Anatomy of Colonial States and Fiscal Regimes in Portuguese Africa: Long-term Transformations in Angola and Mozambique, 1850s–1970s" (PhD diss., Wageningen University, 2018); Alexandre Quintanilha, introduction to *Esboço do reconhecimento ecológico-agrícola de Moçambique*, vol. 1 (Imprensa Nacional de Moçambique, 1955), 3–30; and Greg Grandin, *Fordlandia: The Rise and Fall of Henry Ford's Forgotten Jungle City* (Metropolitan Books, 2009).

160. Link, *Forging Global Fordism*, 15.

161. Frieden, *Global Capitalism*, 221–26; Jakes and Shokr, "Capitalism in Egypt, Not Egyptian Capitalism," 34.

162. Emine Asli Odman, "Ursprünge, Erscheinungen und Wandel des Ökonomischen Nationalismus in der Peripherie: Etatismus in der Türkei und Populismus in Mexiko im Vergleich, 1910–1940," (unpublished thesis, University of Vienna, 2002), 3–5, 22, 40, 48; *Iktisadiyyat Mecmuast* 1 (February 21, 1916), as cited in Odman, "Ursprünge, Erscheinungen und Wandel des Ökonomischen Nationalismus," 23; and Şevket Pamuk, *Uneven Centuries: Economic Development of Turkey Since 1820* (PUP, 2018), 174–75, 187.

163. Odman, "Ursprünge, Erscheinungen und Wandel des Ökonomischen Nationalismus," 3–4; Stephen H. Haber, "Assessing Obstacles to Industrialization: The Mexican Economy, 1830–1940," in *Journal of Latin American Studies* 24, no. 1 (February 1992): 28; and Joseph L. Love, "Raúl Prebisch and the Origins of the Doctrine of Unequal Exchange," *Latin American Research Review* 15, no. 3 (1980): esp. 54–60. See also League of Nations, Economic, Financial, and Transit Department, "Industrialization and Foreign Trade," in Series of League of Nations Publications, Series II, Economic and Financial, 1945, II. A. 10, 91.

164. Cited in and translated by Link, *Forging Global Fordism*, 22; see also 21.

165. Link, *Forging Global Fordism*, 89.

166. Volpato, "Produzione e mercato," 143.

167. Volpato, "Produzione e mercato," 141.

168. Freeman, *Behemoth*, 144; Link, *Forging Global Fordism*, 3, 12; Volpato, "Produzione e mercato," 148. The number of workers refers to the year 1929.

169. Patel, *New Deal*, 67, 91, 94. On the rise of planning in the United States, see Patrick D. Reagan, *Designing a New America: The Origins of New Deal Planning, 1890–1943* (University of Massachusetts Press, 1999). On Portugal's planning efforts, see Secretariado da Propaganda Nacional, *Portugal: The New State in Theory and in Practice* (New York World's Fair, 1939), 46.

170. Hugh S. Johnson, *The Blue Eagle from Egg to Earth* (Doubleday, Doran, 1935), 169.

171. Patel, *New Deal*, 242; and Charles Maier, *Recasting Bourgeois Europe: Stabilization in France, Germany, and Italy in the Decade After World War I* (PUP, 1975), 581.

172. For the German case, see Timothy Mason, *Social Policy in the Third Reich: The Working Class and the "National Community"* (Berg, 1993); and Götz Aly, *Hitler's Beneficiaries: Plunder, Racial War, and the Nazi Welfare State* (Henry Holt, 2007).

173. Gordon, "Right to Work in Japan," 247–72, esp. 250.

174. As cited in Gordon, "Right to Work in Japan," 251.

175. Piven and Cloward, *Poor People's Movements*, 48–60.

176. As cited in Piven and Cloward, *Poor People's Movements*, 109.

177. Piven and Cloward, *Poor People's Movements*, 41, 107–9, 121, 123–25, 134, 137; and Freeman, *Behemoth*, 165–66, 168.

178. Eric D. Weitz, *Weimar Germany: Promise and Tragedy* (PUP, 2007), 161; Ralf Hoffrogge and Norman LaPorte, *Weimar Communism as Mass Movement 1918–1933* (Lawrence & Wishart, 2017), 171, 174; and Gordon, "Right to Work in Japan," 254, 256.

179. *Seventh Annual Report of the Bombay Textile Labour Union*, 1932/33, 3, copy in N. M. Joshi Papers, 1st Installment, File 58, NMML.

180. Edward Hallett Carr, *Nationalism and After* (Macmillan, 1945), 19.

181. Gordon, "Right to Work in Japan," 268–70; Gregory J. Kasza, "War and Welfare Policy in Japan," *Journal of Asian Studies* 61, no. 2 (May 2002): 417, 424–26. On working-class activities, see the brilliant Gordon, "Right to Work in Japan," 255.

182. Patel, *New Deal*, 74, 81, 117, 194.

183. Nattrass, and Seekings, "Economy and Poverty," 525; Jeremy Seekings, "The Broader Importance of Welfare Reform in South Africa," *Social Dynamics* 28, no. 2 (2002): 12–13; Jeremy Seekings, "Workers and the Beginnings of Welfare State-Building in Argentina and South Africa," *African Studies* 66, no. 2–3 (2007): 259–60; Jeremy Seekings, "'Not a Single White Person Should Be Allowed to Go Under': Swartgevaar and the Origins of South Africa's Welfare State, 1924–1929," *Journal of African History* 48, no. 3 (2007): 530; Jeremy Seekings, "The Carnegie Commission and the Backlash Against Welfare State-Building in South Africa, 1931–1937," *Journal of Southern African Studies* 34, no. 3 (2008): 528; and Jeremy Seekings, "The Social Question in Pre-*Apartheid* South Africa: Race, Religion and the State," in *One Hundred Years of Social Protection: The Changing Social Question in Brazil, India, China, and South Africa*, ed. Lutz Leisering (Palgrave Macmillan–Springer Nature, 2021), 204, 209, 212–13.

184. Ravi Ahuja, "A Beveridge Plan for India? Social Insurance and the Making of the Formal Sector," *International Review of Social History* 64, no. 2 (2019): 207–48; Ravi Ahuja, "'Produce or Perish': The Crisis of the Late 1940s and the Place of

Labour in Post-Colonial India," *Modern Asian Studies* 54, no. 4 (2019): 42–43; Jibran Anand, "In Sickness and in Wealth: Social Insurance in Late Colonial Bombay, 1918–1945," paper presented at the Moturi Satyanarayana Centre seminar series, Krea University, August 2023.

185. Duncan Kennedy, "Three Globalizations of Law and Legal Thought, 1850–2000," in *The New Law and Economic Development: A Critical Reappraisal*, ed. David M. Trubek and Alvaro Santos (CUP, 2006), 19, 38–39.

186. Keynes, "National Self-Sufficiency," 755–69.

187. Keynes, "National Self-Sufficiency," 755–69.

188. Keynes, "National Self-Sufficiency," 755–69.

189. John Maynard Keynes, "The World's Economic Outlook," *Atlantic Monthly* 149, no. 5 (May 1932), 521–26, quote on 525.

190. Keynes, "World's Economic Outlook," 525.

191. C. N. Biltoft, "On a Certain Blindness in Economic Theory: Keynes's Giraffes and the Ordinary Textuality of Economic Ideas," in *New Perspectives on the History of Political Economy*, ed. Robert Fredona and Sophus Reinert (Springer International, 2018), 320.

192. Robert L. Heilbroner, *The Worldly Philosophers: The Lives, Times, and Ideas of the Great Economic Thinkers* (Simon & Schuster, 1972), 254–59.

193. Heilbroner, *Worldly Philosophers*, 256–59.

194. Heilbroner, *Worldly Philosophers*, 260.

195. John Maynard Keynes, *The General Theory of Employment, Investment, and Money* (Harcourt, Brace and Company, 1936). 4.

196. Keynes, *General Theory*, 27.

197. Peter A. Hall, ed., introduction to *The Political Power of Economic Ideas: Keynesianism Across Nations* (PUP, 1989), 6.

198. Alan W. Booth, "New Revisionists and the Keynesian Era in British Economic Policy," *EHR* 54, no. 2 (May 2001): 359–60; and Bradley W. Bateman, "Keynes and Keynesians," in *The Cambridge Companion to Keynes*, ed. Roger E. Backhouse and Bradley W. Bateman (CUP, 2006), 283.

199. Keynes, *General Theory*, 4–22, 27–32; Heilbroner, *Worldly Philosophers*, 262; Frieden, *Global Capitalism*, 237; Biltoft, "On a Certain Blindness in Economic Theory," 333.

200. Eric Hobsbawm, *The Age of Extremes: A History of the World, 1914–1991* (Vintage Books, 1994), 268–74.

201. For a survey, see Jürgen Kocka, "Kapitalismus und Demokratie," *Archiv für Sozialgeschichte* 56 (2016): 50.

202. Piketty, *Capital and Ideology*, 467; Sheri Berman, *The Social Democratic Moment: Ideas and Politics in the Making of Interwar Europe* (HUP, 1998), 151; Peter Alexis Gourevitch, "Breaking with Orthodoxy: The Politics of Economic Policy Responses to the Depression of the 1930s," *International Organization* 38, no. 1 (1984): 95–129; Margaret Weir and Theda Skocpol, "State Structures and the Possibilities for 'Keynesian' Responses to the Great Depression in Sweden, Britain, and the United States," in *Bringing the State Back In*, ed. Peter B. Evans, Dietrich Rueschemeyer, and Theda Skocpol, 1st ed. (CUP, 1985), 108, 131; Walter Korpi, *The Working Class in Welfare Capitalism: Work, Unions, and Politics in Sweden*, International Library of Sociology (Routledge & Kegan Paul, 1978), 81, 320; Frieden, *Global Capitalism*, 233; and Carl Marklund, "The Social Laboratory, the Middle Way and the Swedish Model: Three Frames for the Image of Sweden," *Scandinavian Journal of History* 34, no. 3 (2009): 267–68.

203. Patel, *New Deal*, 230; and Frieden, *Global Capitalism*, 245, 249.

204. Frieden, *Global Capitalism*, 209, 215; Stanley G. Payne, *A History of Fascism, 1914–1945* (University of Wisconsin Press, 1995), 132–33, 282, 324, 327; and Bobi Bobev, "The Dictatorship of Ahmet Zogou in Albania," *Études balkaniques*, no. 2 (1993): 22; and Joseph Fronczak, "The Fascist Game: Transnational Political Transmission and the Genesis of the U.S. Modern Right," *JAH* 105, no. 3 (December 2018): 563–88.

205. Secretariado da Propaganda Nacional, *Portugal*, 8.

206. Secretariado da Propaganda Nacional, *Portugal*, 9.

207. Secretariado da Propaganda Nacional, *Portugal*, 12.

208. Teixeira, "Making a Brazilian New Deal," 613–41. See also John Wirth, *The Politics of Brazilian Development, 1930–1954* (Stanford UP, 1970).

209. Teixeira, "Making a Brazilian New Deal," 614.

210. As cited in Teixeira, "Making a Brazilian New Deal," 640.

211. Teixeira, "Making a Brazilian New Deal," 622.

212. Teixeira, "Making a Brazilian

New Deal," 615, 623, 625, 632; and Juan Manuel Palacio, "The Rise of Labor Courts in Argentina," in *Labor Justice Across the Americas*, ed. Leon Fink and Juan Palacio (University of Illinois Press, 2017), 191.

213. Secretariado da Propaganda Nacional, *Portugal*, 13, 14.

214. Secretariado da Propaganda Nacional, *Portugal*, 16.

215. Secretariado da Propaganda Nacional, *Portugal*, 38; and Teixeira, "Making a Brazilian New Deal," 633.

216. Palacio, "Rise of Labor Courts in Argentina," 191.

217. *La Stampa*, March 11, 1923; Angelo Forgione, *Dov'è la vittoria. Le due Italie nel pallone. Aspetti sportivi della malaunità politico-economica* (Magenes, 2019); Ivan Berend, *An Economic History of Twentieth-Century Europe: Economic Regimes from Laissez-Faire to Globalization* (CUP, 2006); Clark, *Mondo Agnelli*, 49; Castronovo, *Giovanni Agnelli*; Giancarlo Galli, *Gli Agnelli: Il tramonto di una dinastia* (Mondadori, 2003); and Marco Ferrante, *Casa Agnelli* (Mondadori, 2007).

218. Kocka, "Kapitalismus und Demokratie," 42.

219. Kocka, "Kapitalismus und Demokratie," 42.

220. Frieden, *Global Capitalism*, 210.

221. Inge Plettenberg, "Hermann Röchling—der Cherusker," in *Die Röchlings und die Völklinger Hütte*, ed. Meinrad Maria Grewenig (Springpunkt Verlag, 2014), 56. See also Seibold, *Röchling*, 239.

222. Seibold, *Röchling*, 244.

223. Plettenberg, "Hermann Röchling—der Cherusker," 56; and Seibold, *Röchling*, 240, 245.

224. For the quote, see Seibold, *Röchling*, 246.

225. Seibold, *Röchling*, 204.

226. Inge Plettenberg, *Zwangsarbeit in der Völklinger Hütte* (Edition Völklinger Hütte, 2016), 385.

227. As cited in Plettenberg, *Zwangsarbeit in der Völklinger Hütte*, 388. For FÜR DEN FÜHRER!, see Seibold, *Röchling*, 241.

228. As cited in Plettenberg, "Hermann Röchling—der Cherusker," 57.

229. Plettenberg, "Hermann Röchling—der Cherusker," 57.

230. Plettenberg, "Hermann Röchling—der Cherusker," 56; and Seibold, *Röchling*, 229. See the draft in B/K-2 Deckung des deutschen Eisenerzbedarfs aus heimischen Vorkommen, Zur Führerede vom 1937/02/20, Alter Bestand, VH.

231. Hermann Röchling, as cited in Plettenberg, *Zwangsarbeit in der Völklinger Hütte*, 379.

232. Christiane Eifert, "Antisemit und Autokönig: Henry Ford's Autobiographie und ihre deutsche Rezeption in den 1920er-Jahren," *Zeithistorische Forschungen* 6, no. 2 (2009), 228.

233. For Japan, see Jeremy Yellen, *The Greater East Asia Co-Prosperity Sphere: When Total Empire Met Total War* (Cornell UP, 2019), 15.

234. Yellen, *Greater East Asia Co-Prosperity Sphere*, 4–5, 31, 35.

235. Yellen, *Greater East Asia Co-Prosperity Sphere*, 17, 30, 47, 71, 87, 88. See, for example, Ōsawa Kichigrō, *Beikoku no yashin to teikoku no zento* [*America's ambitions and the future of imperialism*] (Meirin Shoin, 1924); Higushi Reiyō, *Beika kuru: Nihon kiki* [*The Arrival of the American Peril: Japan's Crisis*] (Nihon Shoin, 1924).

236. Aristotle A. Kallis, *Fascist Ideology: Territory and Expansionism in Italy and Germany, 1922–1945* (Routledge, 2000), 126; and Christopher Duggan, *A Concise History of Italy*, 2nd ed. (CUP, 2013), 240.

237. Ludwig Max Goldberger, *Das Land der unbegrenzten Möglichkeiten: Beobachtungen über das Wirtschaftsleben der Vereinigten Staaten von Amerika* (Berlin, 1905).

238. Hermann Röchling, as cited in Plettenberg, *Zwangsarbeit in der Völklinger Hütte*, 379.

239. Seibold, *Röchling*, 248–49, 255, 258, 261; Plettenberg, *Zwangsarbeit in der Völklinger Hütte*, 37, 365, 368–71, 373, 395–96; and Plettenberg, "Hermann Röchling—der Cherusker," 248.

240. Seibold, *Röchling*, 247; David Palmer, "Foreign Forced Labor at Mitsubishi's Nagasaki and Hiroshima Shipyards: Big Business, Militarized Government, and the Absence of Shipbuilding Workers' Rights in World War II Japan," in Van der Linden and García, *On Coerced Labor*, 159, 169, 175, 426; David Palmer, "The Straits of Dead Souls: One Man's Investigation into the Disappearance of Mitsubishi Hiroshima's Korean Forced Labourers," *Japanese Studies* 26, no. 3 (December 2006): 338, 351; and Thomas Havens, *Valley of Darkness: The Japanese People and World War Two* (UP of America, 1986), 104.

241. Plettenberg, *Zwangsarbeit in der Völklinger Hütte*, 51.

242. Karl Heinz Roth, "Unfree Labour in the Area Under German Hegemony, 1930–1945," in *Free and Unfree Labour: The Debate Continues*, ed. Tom Brass and Marcel van der Linden (Peter Lang, 1997), 137;

Plettenberg, *Zwangsarbeit in der Völklinger Hütte*, 24, 47, 400. The snippet is as cited in Plettenberg, *Zwangsarbeit in der Völklinger Hütte*, 404. See also Plettenberg, "Hermann Röchling—der Cherusker," 58.

243. As cited in Inge Plettenberg, *Zwangsarbeit in der Völklinger Hütte* (Edition Völklinger Hütte, 2016), 229.

244. Plettenberg, *Zwangsarbeit in der Völklinger Hütte*, 263.

245. See also the documents in D-K10/41: RESW GmbH, Fremdarbeiter 1939–1945, Mappe 2, Alter Bestand, VH; Plettenberg, *Zwangsarbeit in der Völklinger Hütte*, 9, 39, 128, 141, 168, 172, 251, 258, 430–31. Grewenig, *Die Röchlings und die Völklinger Hütte*, 64; and Seibold, *Röchling*, 248.

246. See the "Foreign Workers and Forced Labour" section of "BMW in the Age of National Socialism," BMW Group, accessed November 26, 2021, https://www.bmwgroup .com/en/company/history/BMW -during-the-era-of-national-socialism.html.

247. Neil Gregor, *Daimler-Benz in the Third Reich* (Yale UP, 1998), 195.

248. Henning Bleyl, "Nähe zum Massenmord," *Taz*, December 12, 2015; "Foreign Workers and Forced Labour" section of "BMW in the Age of National Socialism," BMW Group; "75th Anniversary of the End of World War II," accessed November 26, 2021, https:// www.daimler.com/magazine /culture/75th-anniversary-of-the -end-of-world-war-ii.html; "Audi Comes Clean About Its Nazi Past," *Deutsche Welle*, accessed November 26, 2021, https://www.dw.com/en /audi-comes-clean-about-its-nazi -past/a-17664050; Dietmar Hawranek, "Porsche and Volkswagen's Nazi Roots," *Spiegel International*, accessed November 26, 2021, https://www.spiegel.de/interna tional/business/designing-cars-for -hitler-porsche-and-volkswagen-s-n azi-roots-a-637368.html; and United Nations War Crimes Commission, ed., *Law Reports of Trials of War Criminals*, vol. 10, *The I.G. Farben and Krupp Trials* (His Majesty's Stationery Office, 1949). The list of companies comes from Anita Ramasastry, "Corporate Complicity: From Nuremberg to Rangoon: An Examination of Forced Labor Cases and Their Impact on the Liability of Multinational Corporations," *Berkeley Journal of International Law* 20, no. 1 (2002): 124. Note that I slightly corrected the spellings of some of the

company names and also left out some that she mentions.

249. See M1923: OMGUS Finance Division Records Regarding Investigations and Interrogations, 1945–1949, National Archives, Washington, DC; and United Nations War Crimes Commission, *Law Reports of Trials of War Criminals*, vol. 10.

250. Primo Levi, *The Drowned and the Saved*, trans. Raymond Rosenthal (Michael Josephs, 1988), 167.

251. See "Oberstes Gericht der Militärregierung der französischen Besatzungszone in Deutschland," Urteil vom 25 Januaar 1949, in Sachen Hermann Röchling und Genossen, 56–57, T1 NL Drischel Nr. 41, Landesarchiv Baden-Württemberg, Staatsarchiv Freiburg, Germany.

252. Werner Sombart, "Die Wandlungen des Kapitalismus," *Weltwirtschaftliches Archiv* 28 (1928): 245.

253. Sombart, "Die Wandlungen des Kapitalismus," 246.

Chapter 15: Insurgents

1. David Arnold, "The Rise of the Indian Typewriter," in *With Great Truth & Regard: The Story of the Typewriter in India*, ed. Sidharth Bhatia (Roli Books, 2016), 19.

2. P. G. Hubert Jr., "The Typewriter: Its Growth and Uses," *North American Review* 146, no. 379 (1888); David Arnold, *Everyday Technology: Machines and the Making of India's Modernity* (University of Chicago Press, 2013), 48; *Annual Statement of the Sea-Borne Trade and Navigation of British India with the British Empire and Foreign Countries* (Office of the Superintendent of Government Printing, 1900); and Arnold, "Rise of the Indian Typewriter," 18, 28–29.

3. Unsigned memo, 9 September 1952, 2, 4, GAM.

4. B. K. Karanjia, *Godrej: A Hundred Years, 1897–1997*, vol. 1, *Life's Flag Is Never Furled* (Penguin, 1997), 115, 119; Arnold, "Rise of the Indian Typewriter," 32; and Sidharth Bhatia, "Making the Indian Typewriter: The Godrej Story," in Bhatia, *With Great Truth & Regard*, 63.

5. Arnold, "Rise of the Indian Typewriter," 31–32; Karanjia, *Godrej: A Hundred Years*, 1:115; and Bhatia, "Making the Indian Typewriter," 61. On the technical problems of producing the first typewriters, see unsigned memo, 9 September 1952, GAM. See also Karanjia, *Godrej: A Hundred Years*, 1:114–15; and Bhatia, "Making the Indian Typewriter," 63.

6. Unsigned memo, September 9, 1952, GAM.

7. As cited in Bhatia, *With Great Truth & Regard*, 56–57. See also Bhatia, "Making the Indian Typewriter," 65.

8. Karanjia, *Godrej: A Hundred Years*, 1:119; and Rama Lakshmi, "The World of Steno Stereotypes," in Bhatia, *With Great Truth & Regard*, 158. On "government orders," see Godrej and Boyce, circular to "all branches," 20 June 1957, GAM. For these orders, see also, for example, circular to "all branches," 29 January 1960, in GAM; Government of India Stationery Office, Calcutta, to Godrej and Boyce, Calcutta, 19 February 1960, GAM; and circular to "all branches," 16 August 1967, GAM.

9. Karanjia, *Godrej: A Hundred Years*, 1:121. On the creation of the sales network, see circular to "all stockists," 14 July 1954, GAM. See also Bhatia, "Making the Indian Typewriter," 59, 69, 75. For complaints about lackluster performance by his sales agents, see circular of Godrej and Boyce to "all branches," 10 September 1962, GAM. See also Karanjia, *Godrej: A Hundred Years*, 1:121. Additionally, see Arnold, "Rise of the Indian Typewriter," 32. For the numbers of typewriters sold, see MS15-55-1-1, BD1501686, Centenary Collection, GAM.

10. Arnold, "Rise of the Indian Typewriter," 7, 15–16, 18, 23, 25. The precise proportion of women typists and stenographers is 96 percent.

11. Eric Hobsbawm, *The Age of Extremes: The Short Twentieth Century, 1914–1992* (Michael Joseph, 1994), 222; UN Geospatial Information Section, "The World in 1945," No. 4135, Rev. 3, May 2010; "List of Former Trust and Non-Self-Governing Territories," United Nations, accessed February 25, 2023, https://www.un.org/dppa/decolonization/en/history/former-trust-and-nsgts; "Growth in United Nations Membership," United Nations, accessed February 25, 2023, https://www.un.org/en/about-us/growth-in-un-membership; and "Land Area (Sq. Km)—World," CSV file, World Bank, accessed December 17, 2021, https://data.worldbank.org/indicator/AG.LND.TOTL.K2?locations=1W.

12. The author calculated the number by adding up the data for Western Europe, Eastern Europe, the USSR, and Western offshoots. See Angus Maddison, *The World Economy: Historical Statistics*, Development Centre Studies (OECD, 2003), 233. The number on world industrial output is for 1950 and taken from Patrick Karl O'Brien, "Industrialization," in *The Oxford Handbook of World History*, ed. Jerry H. Bentley (OUP, 2011), 309. The numbers for 1975 and 2000, as well as the number for the 2020s, are generated from two separate data sources: the Maddison Project Database for the earlier years and the World Bank for the later year. Because the Maddison Project ends with data in 2001, a different source was needed for the 2020s. For the extrapolation and calculation of GDP, the Maddison Project uses PPP (purchasing-power parity) data derived from an earlier 1990 International Comparison Project (ICP) exercise. For the sake of consistency, GDP based on PPP (current international dollar) published by the World Bank is used for the 2020s data. It should be recognized that there can be minor differences between data generated from the Maddison Project and data generated from the World Bank. Take 2000, for instance: Based on Maddison's data, Europe and the Western offshoots accounted for 50.7 percent of world GDP, while calculations based on data from the World Bank gave a slightly lower number of 50.0 percent. For corresponding data of the Maddison Project, see Maddison, *World Economy*, 233. For corresponding data of the World Bank, see "GDP, PPP (Current International $)," World Bank, accessed August 9, 2022, https://data.worldbank.org/indicator/NY.GDP.MKTP.PP.CD. For a World Bank blog that includes deliberations over the different ways of calculating GDP and discussions on how Maddison dealt with GDP, see Branko Milanovic, "The End of a Long Era," *Let's Talk Development* (blog), July 19, 2013, https://blogs.worldbank.org/developmenttalk/end-long-era.

13. For this argument, see also Tom G. Forrest, *The Advance of African Capital: The Growth of Nigerian Private Enterprise* (University of Virginia Press, 1994), 5.

14. Tirthankar Roy, "Beyond Divergence: Rethinking the Economic History of India," *Economic History of Developing Regions* 27, no. S1, (2012), S57–65; and Gareth Austin, Carlos Dávila, and Geoffrey Jones, "The Alternative Business History: Business in Emerging Markets," *Business History Review* 91, no. 3 (2017): 540.

15. Werner Sombart, "Die Wandlungen des Kapitalismus," *Weltwirtschaftliches Archiv* 28 (1928): 245.

16. Ardeshir Godrej, "The Man Who Makes the Godrej Safes," interview by *Indian National Herald*, April 17, 1927; B. K. Karanjia, *Vijitatma: Founder-Pioneer Ardeshir Godrej* (Viking, 2004), xxxiii, 1, 33; and Vrunda Pathare, "Business Archives: A Window into the Corporate Past," in *NMML Occasional Paper / Perspectives in Indian Development*, New Series 19 (Nehru Memorial Museum and Library, 2013), 6.

17. Godrej, "Man Who Makes the Godrej Safes"; and Karanjia, *Vijitatma*, xxxv.

18. Karanjia, *Vijitatma*, xxiv, 7, 197.

19. Godrej, "Man Who Makes the Godrej Safes."

20. Ardeshir Godrej, "Romantic Story of an Indian Industry," interview by *Indian National Herald*, April 27, 1927, 1; and *Bombay Chronicle*, July 7, 1921, 5.

21. Gandhi, "My Notes," 9 October 1921, *Collected Works of Mahatma Gandhi*, vol. 21 (Publications Division, Ministry of Information and Broadcasting, 1966), 268–74.

22. Karanjia, *Vijitatma*, xxx, xxxi, xxxv; Karanjia, *Life's Flag Is Never Furled*, 1:47, 50, 61, 73.

23. "A Staunch Nationalist," *Bombay Chronicle*, January 13, 1936, 5.

24. Circular, 1 July 1954, MS08-01-419-306, 111, Circular Collection, GAM. For the quote on his upbringing, see Karanjia, *Godrej: A Hundred Years*, 1:164. See also Godrej and Boyce, letter to "all branches," 1 July 1954, Bombay, GAM.

25. B. K. Karanjia, *Godrej: A Hundred Years, 1897–1997*, vol. 2, *The Builder Also Grows* (Penguin, 1997), 5.

26. Karanjia, *Godrej: A Hundred Years*, 2:3, 102

27. Karanjia, *Godrej: A Hundred Years*, 1:70.

28. Karanjia, *Godrej: A Hundred Years*, 1:88.

29. Karanjia, *Godrej: A Hundred Years*, 1:97.

30. Karanjia, *Godrej: A Hundred Years*, 1:69–70, 72–73, 90, 132–33, 142; Godrej and Boyce, "Ballot Boxes," draft circular to all branches, 8 February 1952, GAM; Shiweta Jadhav, "As EVMs Are Debated, This Is How the First Ballot Box Was Made for India's First 1952 Election," *Print*, January 2019. See also *Bombay Chronicle*, December 15, 1951; and Pathare, "Business Archives," 8–9.

31. Pathare, "Business Archives," 89; and Karanjia, *Godrej: A Hundred Years*, 1:79, 85, 87, 94, 99, 156.

32. Karanjia, *Godrej: A Hundred Years*, 1:91, 163–64.

33. See Godrej's ad, "Freedom Wears a Smile," in *Times of India*, January 26, 1962, 9.

34. As cited in Sanya Jain, "For Anand Mahindra, Seeing the East India Company in Indian Hands Is . . . ," NDTV, February 9, 2022, https://www.ndtv.com/offbeat/for -anand-mahindra-seeing-the-east-i ndia-company-in-indian-hands -is-2757926.

35. As cited in Samuel C. Chu, *Reformer in Modern China: Chang Chien, 1853–1926* (Columbia UP, 1965), 45–46.

36. Yat-sen Sun, *The International Development of China* (Commercial Press, 1920); and Babacar Fall, "Le mouvement syndical en Afrique occidentale francophone, de la tutelle des centrales métropolitaines à celle des partis nationaux uniques, ou la difficile quête d'une personnalité (1900–1968)," *Matériaux pour l'histoire de notre temps* 4, no. 84 (2006): 50.

37. J. Ayodele Langley, *Ideologies of Liberation in Black Africa: 1856–1970: Documents on Modern African Political Thought from Colonial Times to the Present* (Rex Collings, 1979), 260; and David Murphy, "No More Slaves! Lamine Senghor, Black Internationalism and the League Against Imperialism," in *The League Against Imperialism: Lives and Afterlives*, ed. Michele Louro et al. (Leiden UP, 2020), 211–36.

38. Langley, *Ideologies of Liberation in Black Africa*, 236.

39. As cited in Robert L. Tignor, "Bank Miṣr and Foreign Capitalism," *International Journal of Middle East Studies* 8, no. 2 (April 1977): 164, 165.

40. A. G. Hopkins, "Economic Aspects of Political Movements in Nigeria and the Gold Coast, 1918–1939," *Journal of African History* 7 (1966): 133–52.

41. National Archives of the UK, Kew, Parliamentary Papers, 1873, vol. 61, Correspondence Respecting Sir Bartle Frere's Mission to the East Coast of Africa, 1872–73, enclosure 1 in No. 51, 102, as cited in Pedro Machado, *Ocean of Trade: South Asian Merchants, Africa and the Indian Ocean, c. 1750–1850* (CUP, 2014), 268.

42. For the quote, see French Consul in Lourenço Marques to Minister of Foreign Affairs, letter, 8 April 1930, Main d'œuvre: Madagascar et Réunion, Recrutement de travailleurs dans l'Inde, dans l'Indo-Chine, dans la Chine, dans le Japon / Rapport Geismar, FM/7AFFECO/19, Travail, Réunion, Recrutements, Extérieur, 1866–1939, ANOM.

43. Sudev Sheth, *Bankrolling Empire: Family Fortunes and Political Transformation in Mughal India* (CUP, 2024), 295, 296; Sven Beckert, *Empire of Cotton: A Global History* (Alfred A. Knopf, 2014); and Chinmay Tumbe, "Transnational Indian Business in the Twentieth Century," *Business History Review* 91, no. 4 (Winter 2017): 662. For this argument on postcolonial history, see also Andre Liu, "Notes Toward a More Global History of Capitalism: Reading Marx's Capital in India and China," *Spectre*, July 6, 2020, https://spectrejournal.com/notes-toward-a -more-global-history-of-capitalism/.

44. Mircea Raianu, *Tata: The Global Corporation That Built Indian Capitalism* (HUP, 2021), 17, 13, 28, 39; Beckert, *Empire of Cotton*; *Statistical Tables Relating to Indian Cotton: Indian Spinning and Weaving Mills, Their Production and Its Distribution, with a List of the Steam Presses in the Country* (Bombay: Times of India Steam Press, 1889), 95; Bhubanes Misra, "The Cotton Mill Industry of Eastern India in the Late Nineteenth Century: Constraints on Foreign Investment and Expansion," *Social Scientist* 15, no. 3 (1987): 5; R. E. Enthoven, *The Cotton Fabrics of the Bombay Presidency* (n.p., approx. 1897), 4, in NAI; Arno S. Pearse, *The Cotton Industry of India: Being the Report of the Journey to India* (Taylor, Garnett, Evans, 1930), 22; Members of the Staff of the Gokhale Institute of Politics and Economics, Poona, India, "Notes on the Rise of the Business Communities in India" (Institute for Pacific Studies, April 1951), 13. On the growth of the Indian cotton industry, see also Department of Commercial Intelligence and Statistics, *Monthly Statistics of Cotton Spinning and Weaving in India Mills* (n.p., 1929). On the roots of swadeshi, see also Dinyar Patel, "To Revive India's Industries: The Global and Imperial Roots of Swadeshi in the Nineteenth Century," in *Modern Asian Studies* (2024), 3–21.

45. FICCI, *Proceedings of the Sixth Annual Meeting, Delhi, 15–16 April 1933*, 5.

46. Naoroji, as cited in Dinyar Patel, *Naoroji: Pioneer of Indian Nationalism* (HUP, 2020), 65.

47. Raianu, *Tata*, 24; Patel, *Naoroji*, 47, 83.

48. Keshav Malhar Bhat, "Address to the Twenty-Third Annual Convention of the Free Religious Association," as printed in *The New Ideal* 3 (July–August 1890): 334.

49. See *India Today*, September 16, 2017.

50. Copy of Communication No. F 146/467, Sir Akbar Hydari, 17 January 1945, as reprinted in FICCI, *Proceedings of the 19th Annual Session, May 1946*, 123.

51. FICCI, *Proceedings of the Fourth Annual Meeting, Delhi, 7–9 April 1933*, 13.

52. Dinyar Patel, "The Transnational Career of the 'Indian Edison': Shankar Abaji Bhisey and the Nationalist Promotion of Scientific Talent," in *Bombay Before Mumbai: Essays in Honor of Jim Masselos*, ed. Prashant Kidambi, Manjiri Kamat, and Rachel Dwyer (Hurst, 2019), 245; Hobsbawm, *Age of Extremes*, 202; Patel, "Transnational Career of the 'Indian Edison,'" 246; Raianu, *Tata*, 110, 111, 112, 175; Claude Markovits, *Indian Business and Nationalist Politics 1931–39* (CUP, 2009); Aditya Mukherjee, *Political Economy of Colonial and Post-Colonial India* (Primus Books, 2022), 211–13.

53. "Our Prosperous Mill Industry," *Bombay Chronicle*, May 21, 1918; Mukherjee, *Political Economy*, 173–74.

54. Raianu, *Tata*, 12, 34; Mukherjee, *Political Economy*, 172–73. See also Members of the Staff of the Gokhale Institute of Politics and Economics, Poona, India, "Notes on the Rise of the Business Communities in India," 11.

55. G. K. Gokhale, "East and West in India," in *Speeches of Gopal Krishna Gokhale*, 3rd ed. (Madras, 1920), 1013.

56. Members of the Staff of the Gokhale Institute of Politics and Economics, Poona, India, "Notes on the Rise of the Business Communities in India," 32.

57. FICCI, *Proceedings of the Third Annual Meeting, 14–16 February 1930*, 15.

58. Raianu, *Tata*, 18, 44–46, 77, 79, 81, 101.

59. Benoy Kumar Sarkar, *Economic Development: Snapshots of World-Movements in Commerce, Economic Legislation, Industrialism and Technical Education* (B. G. Paul, 1926), ix.

60. Sarkar, *Economic Development*, 1–21, 254, 263–67.

61. Sarkar, *Economic Development*, 349.

62. Sarkar, *Economic Development*, 349.

63. Bipan Chandra, Mridula Mukherjee, and Aditya Mukherjee, *India After Independence, 1947–2000* (Penguin, 2002), 48–49, 172–73, 339.

64. Mukherjee, *Political Economy*, 191, 204–5; Raianu, *Tata*, 108–10; Vivek Chibber, *Locked in Place: State-Building and Late Industrialization in India* (PUP, 2003), 92–93, chap. 5.

65. Here my emphasis differs from Chibber, *Locked in Place*. See, for example, 86.

66. Rajnarayan Chandavarkar, *The Origins of Industrial Capitalism in India: Business Strategies and the Working Classes in Bombay, 1900–1940* (CUP, 1994), 414, 416–17. On the estimate of Indian industrial proletariat, see Rajani Kanta Das, *Wartime Labor Conditions in India*, Bulletin No. 755 of the US Bureau of Labor Statistics (US Government Printing Office, 1943), 4; V. B. Karnik, *Strikes in India* (Manaktalas, 1967), 323–25; Ravi Ahuja, "'Produce or Perish': The Crisis of the Late 1940s and the Place of Labour in Post-Colonial India," *Modern Asian Studies* 54, no. 4 (2019): 36; List No. 18 in File 1, Correspondence re Cooperation with Congress etc., All-India Trade Union Congress Papers, NMML.

67. Bombay Girni Kangar Union to the General Secretary of the AITUC, Bombay, letter, 26 November 1936, in List No. 18, File 1, Correspondence re Cooperation with Congress etc, All-India Trade Union Congress Papers, NMML.

68. Letter by the Lalbavta Press Kamgar Union to the General Secretary of the AITUC, Bombay, 21 March 1936, in All-India Trade Union Congress Papers, List No. 18, File 1, Correspondence re Cooperation with Congress etc, NMML.

69. Chandavarkar, *Origins of Industrial Capitalism in India*, 414, 416; Vasant Bhagwant Karnik, *Strikes in India* (Manaktalas, 1967), 285–86; and Raianu, *Tata*, 174.

70. A. G. Hopkins, *An Economic History of West Africa*, 2nd ed. (Routledge, 2020), 326, 328; M. M. Fadakinte, "The Political Economy of Capitalist State Formation in Nigeria: An Analysis of the Fragility of an Emergent State," *International Journal of Modern Social Sciences* 3, no. 2 (2014): 103; Taiwo Ojoye, "Old Money: 10 Super-Rich Men of Independence Era," in *Punch* (Nigeria), October 1, 2017, https://punchng.com /old-money-10-super-rich-men-of -independence-era/; Forrest, *Advance of African Capital*, 16; "The Rich and the Famous: Old Money vs. New Money," *Vanguard Nigeria Newspaper* (online), November 26, 2011, https://www.vanguardngr.com /2011/11/the-rich-and-the-famous -old-money-vs-new-money/; Eromo Egbejule, "The Small Town of the Super Rich," *Forbes Africa*, 2017, https://www.forbesafrica.com /wealth/2017/08/07/small-town -super-rich/; "Sir, Louis Odumegwu

Ojukwu, First Nigerian Billionaire," *Newswire Nigeria*, July 18, 2022, https://newswirengr.com/2022 /07/18/sir-louis-odumegwu -ojukwu-first-nigerian-billionaire/; Ernie Onwumere, "In Quest of Perpetuity: The Ojukwu Nigerians Didn't Know," *This Day* (online), October 26, 2022, https://www.this daylive.com/index.php/2016/05/08 /in-quest-of-perpetuity-the-ojukwu -nigerians-didnt-know/; *London Gazette*, Supplement 42051, June 3, 1960, S3974, https://www.thegazette .co.uk/London/issue/42051/supple ment/3974; Anthony G. Hopkins, "Economic Aspects of Political Movements in Nigeria and in the Gold Coast 1918–1939," *Journal of African History* 7, no. 1 (1966): 146; and Irving Leonard Markovitz, *Power and Class in Africa: An Introduction to Change and Conflict in African Politics* (Prentice Hall, 1977), 244. On the continuities and discontinuities of this group of Nigerian entrepreneurs, see A. G. Hopkins, *Capitalism in the Colonies* (PUP, 2024); and James S. Coleman, *Nigeria: Background to Nationalism* (University of California Press, 1958), 253.

71. For an analysis of these processes, see D. K. Ologbenla, "The Development of Capitalism in Nigeria 1886–1980" (PhD diss., University of Lagos, 1990), https://www.proquest .com/docview/2672746447?parent -SessionId=sufG61%2Fq0QdsY UNli5iYCWI0EzUkzafhw3zPLSX EcX8%3D&pq-origsite=primo& accountid=11311; and Hopkins, *Capitalism in the Colonies*.

72. Nnamdi Azikiwe, *Zik: A Selection from the Speeches of Nnamdi Azikiwe* (CUP, 1961), 155.

73. Azikiwe, *Zik*, 212–13.

74. Azikiwe, *Zik*, 159.

75. Thomas J. Biersteker, *Multinationals, the State and Control of the Nigerian Economy* (PUP, 2014), 53; Ologbenla, "Development of Capitalism in Nigeria," 296; Forrest, *Advance of African Capital*, 16, 83; Markovitz, *Power and Class in Africa*, 245; Richard L. Sklar, *Nigerian Political Parties: Power in an Emergent African Nation* (PUP, 1963), 263; Olakunle A. Lawal, "British Commercial Interests and the Decolonization Process in Nigeria, 1950–60," *African Economic History* 22 (1994): 97; Biersteker, *Multinationals*, 53.

76. As cited in Biersteker, *Multinationals*, 53–54.

77. Coleman, *Nigeria*, 252; Markovitz, *Power and Class in Africa*, 244, 246; Coleman, *Nigeria*, 252; and Forrest, *Advance of African Capital*, 24, 64, 83. On the economic oppor-

tunities, see A. Olukoju, "'Buy British, Sell Foreign': External Trade Control Policies in Nigeria During World War II and Its Aftermath, 1939–1950," *International Journal of African Historical Studies* 35, no. 2/3 (2002): 381.

78. *East Nigerian Guardian*, October 11, 1946.

79. Biersteker, *Multinationals*, 54.

80. N. J. Westcott, "An East African Radical: The Life of Erica Fiah," *Journal of African History* 22, no. 1 (1981): 88.

81. *Kwetu*, May 24, 1940, as cited in Westcott, "East African Radical," 97.

82. Chambi Seithy Chachage, "A Capitalizing City: Dar es Salaam and the Emergence of an African Entrepreneurial Elite (c. 1862–2015)" (PhD diss., Harvard University, 2018); and Westcott, "East African Radical," 86. For a full account of Kleist Sykes's life, see the excellent Mohamed Said, *The Life and Times of Abdulwahid Said, 1924–1968: The Untold Story of the Muslim Struggle Against British Colonialism in Tanganyika* (Minerva Press, 1998), esp. 41, 80. On Fiah, see Westcott, "East African Radical," 85–101.

83. Minutes by Northcote, Scupham, and MacMichael, TNA SMP 22444/1/66-9, as cited in Westcott, "East African Radical," 89.

84. Robert L. Tignor, *Capitalism and Nationalism at the End of Empire: State and Business in Decolonizing Egypt, Nigeria, and Kenya, 1945–1963* (PUP, 2015), 32.

85. Aaron Jakes and Ahmad Shokr, "Capitalism in Egypt, Not Egyptian Capitalism," in *A Critical Political Economy of the Middle East and North Africa*, ed. Joel Beinin, Bassam Haddad, and Sherene Seikaly (Stanford UP, 2021), 130, 132. See also Robert Vitalis, *When Capitalists Collide: Business Conflict and the End of Empire in Egypt* (University of California Press, 1995), 29–62.

86. Vitalis, *When Capitalists Collide*, xi–xix, 1–62; Jakes and Shokr, "Capitalism in Egypt, Not Egyptian Capitalism," 132; Robert L. Tignor, "Nationalism, Economic Planning, and Development Projects in Interwar Egypt," *International Journal of African Historical Studies* 10, no. 2 (1977): 188; and Tignor, *Capitalism and Nationalism at the End of Empire*, 33, 36.

87. Jakes and Shokr, "Capitalism in Egypt, Not Egyptian Capitalism," 124; Vitalis, *When Capitalists Collide*, 1–62, 104–217; Joel Beinin, introduction to *A Critical Political Economy of the Middle East and North Africa*, 18; and Liat Spiro, "Drawing

Capital: Depiction, Machine Tools, and the Political Economy of Industrial Knowledge, 1824–1914" (PhD diss., Harvard University, 2019).

88. Jeffry A. Frieden, *Global Capitalism: Its Fall and Rise in the Twentieth Century* (W. W. Norton, 2006), 209, 226–27, 303–6, 309.

89. Victor Bulmer-Thomas, *La historia económica de América Latina desde la independencia* (Fondo de Cultura Económica, 2017), 187.

90. Jorge Raúl Colva, *El oro blanco en la Argentina* (Editorial Claridad, 1946), 142.

91. Kemal Karpat, "Statism—Devletçilik—and Economic Development," in *Turkey's Politics: The Transition to a Multi-Party System* (PUP, 1959), 294; Şevket Pamuk, *Uneven Centuries: Economic Development of Turkey Since 1820* (PUP, 2018), 222, 233; and Korkut Boratav, "Import Substitution and Income Distribution Under a Populist Regime: The Case of Turkey," *Development Policy Review* 4, no. 2 (1986): 125, 135.

92. Frieden, *Global Capitalism*, 302, 305–6; Celso Furtado, *Economic Development of Latin America: Historical Background and Contemporary Problems* (CUP, 1970), 117; Austin, Dávila, and Jones, "Alternative Business History," 542, 562; Bulmer-Thomas, *La historia económica de América Latina*, 231, 260; Jeremy Adelman, "Global Inequality and the Search for Justice," unpublished paper (in author's possession), 23; and Javier Moreno Lázaro, "The Economic Cycle, Social Capital, Management and Growth of the Mexican Family Business: An Historical Perspective," *EmTHYMÓS, Revista de Estudios Empresariales* 1, no. 4 (2020): 219–41, here 221.

93. Frieden, *Global Capitalism*, 305; Pamuk, *Uneven Centuries*, 222, 231.

94. Bulmer-Thomas, *La historia económica de América Latina*, 229, 283; Beatriz Rodriguez-Satizabal, "Only One Way to Raise Capital? Colombian Business Groups and the Dawn of Internal Markets," *Business History* 63, no. 8 (2021): 1375; Furtado, *Economic Development of Latin America*, 112; Frieden, *Global Capitalism*, 303; and Luis Bértola and José Antonio Ocampo, *El desarrollo económico de América Latina desde la independencia* (Fondo de Cultura Económica, 2012).

95. This changes a historiography that has universalized business history from the center. See Austin, Dávila, and Jones, "Alternative Business History," 538, 554; and Beatriz

Elena Rodriguez-Satizabal, "Pathways from Deglobalisation: Colombian Business Groups, 1950–1985," *Journal of Evolutionary Studies in Business* 5, no. 2 (2020): 178, 187, 200.

96. Rodriguez-Satizabal, "Only One Way to Raise Capital?," 72, 75–76, 81, 84; Rodriguez-Satizabal, "Pathways from Deglobalisation," 179, 183, 188–90, 192–93, 196, 198, 209; and Benedicte Bull, Fulvio Castellacci, and Yuri Kasahara, eds., *Business Groups and Transnational Capitalism in Central America: Economic and Political Strategies* (Palgrave Macmillan, 2014), 1, as cited in Rodriguez-Satizabal, "Pathways from Deglobalisation," 183–84.

97. Lázaro, "Economic Cycle, Social Capital, Management and Growth of the Mexican Family Business," 220–21, 225–26.

98. José Lannes, "The Gerdau Group: The Creation of a Global Competitor," *Apuntes* 41, no. 75 (2014): 143; Austin, Dávila, and Jones, "Alternative Business History," 556; Pamuk, *Uneven Centuries*, 233; and Ian Talbot, *Pakistan: A New History* (OUP, 2015), 79.

99. A concept that US economist Alexander Gerschenkron popularized, building on work by Austrian economist Rudolf Hilferding. See Alexander Gerschenkron, *Economic Backwardness in Historical Perspective: A Book of Essays* (Belknap Press of HUP, 1962). On Gerschenkron's intellectual biography, see Marcel van der Linden, "Gerschenkron's Secret: A Research Note," *Critique* 40 (2012): 553–62.

100. Ngũgĩ wa Thiong'o, *Birth of a Dreamweaver: A Writer's Awakening* (New Press, 2016), 222.

101. Alessandro Iandolo and Chris Miller, "Rethinking the State in the State of the Field: Markets and Governments in Development Historiography," unpublished paper (in author's possession), August 28, 2018, 11.

102. Kwame Nkrumah, *Ghana: The Autobiography of Kwame Nkrumah* (T. Nelson, 1957), x.

103. Fodéba Keita, February 1959, as quoted in Iandolo and Miller, "Rethinking the State in the State of the Field," 12.

104. Hobsbawm, *Age of Extremes*, 350; and Iandolo and Miller, "Rethinking the State in the State of the Field," 13.

105. Hobsbawm, *Age of Extremes*, 350.

106. Kwame Nkrumah, *Africa Must Unite* (Mercury Books, 1965), 108.

107. Modibo Keita, September 1962,

as cited in Iandolo and Miller, "Rethinking the State in the State of the Field," 13.

108. Gunnar Myrdal, *Rich Lands and Poor: The Road to World Prosperity* (Harper, 1957), 7.

109. Myrdal, *Rich Lands and Poor*, 81

110. Myrdal, *Rich Lands and Poor*, 95, 130.

111. Jeremy Adelman, "Global Inequality and the Search for Justice," unpublished paper (in the author's possession), 11, 12, 21, 25, in author's possession. The argument that there exists a link between colonialism and developmentalist thinking more generally is widely made. See, among many others, Uma Kothari, "From Colonial Administration to Development Studies: A Post-Colonial Critique of the History of Development Studies," in *A Radical History of Development Studies: Individuals, Institutions and Ideologies*, ed. Uma Kothari (Zed Books, 2005); Andreas Eckert, "Regulating the Social: Social Security, Social Welfare and the State in Late Colonial Tanzania," *Journal of African History* 45, no. 3 (November 2004): 467–89; Joseph M. Hodge, *Triumph of the Expert: Agrarian Doctrines of Development and the Legacies of British Colonialism* (Ohio UP, 2007); and Joanna Lewis, *Empire State-Building: War and Welfare in Kenya, 1925–52* (OUP, 2000).

112. Hobsbawm, *Age of Extremes*, 203; Purshotamdas Thakurdas et al., *Memorandum Outlining a Plan of Economic Development for India* (Penguin Books, 1945).

113. M. Visvesvaraya, *Planned Economy for India* (Bangalore Press, 1936), vi, 178–83, 193, 239. Originally published in 1934.

114. FICCI, *Proceedings of the Seventh Annual Meeting, April 1934, Delhi*, 21.

115. As cited in Chandra, Mukherjee, and Mukherjee, *India After Independence*, 341.

116. A. C. Ramalinga, Secretary of the Indian Merchants' Chamber, to the Secretary to the Government of India, Department of Industries and Supplies, New Delhi, in the Expansion of Indian Cotton Textile Industry, Report of the Postwar Planning Committee, Bombay, 30 October 1946, Indian Merchants Chamber, Bombay, S. Planning of Cotton Textile Industry, 1946, No. 1673/ File No. 85, NMML.

117. As cited in Aditya Mukherjee, "Jawaharlal Nehru in Our Past, Present and Future," General President's Address, India History Congress, 82nd Sess., December 2023, 45.

118. Thakurdas et al., *Memorandum Outlining a Plan*.
119. Thakurdas et al., *Memorandum Outlining a Plan*, 7.
120. Thakurdas et al., *Memorandum Outlining a Plan*, 8, 65.
121. Thakurdas et al., *Memorandum Outlining a Plan*, 92.
122. Raianu, *Tata*, 124.
123. Thakurdas et al., *Memorandum Outlining a Plan*, 92.
124. Thakurdas et al., *Memorandum Outlining a Plan*, 9, 18–25, 29, 36–37, 58; Minoo Masani, *Picture of a Plan* (OUP, 1945), 18, 58; *Economist*, May 13, 1944, 636.
125. Masani, *Picture of a Plan*, 90.
126. Masani, *Picture of a Plan*, 151–52.
127. Masani, *Picture of a Plan*, 141, 143.
128. Masani, *Picture of a Plan*, 164.
129. Masani, *Picture of a Plan*, 60.
130. Masani, *Picture of a Plan*, 61. On planning, see also Medha Kudaisya, "'A Mighty Adventure': Institutionalising the Idea of Planning in Post-Colonial India," *Modern Asian Studies* 43, no. 4 (2009): 939–78.
131. A. D. Shroff, "The Future of India as an Industrial Nation," record of general meeting held at Chatham House on June 12, 1945, 3, Chatham House Archives, London.
132. J. R. D. Tata, "A Fifteen-Year Plan of Economic Development for India," address delivered at the Bombay Rotary Club on February 15, 1944, in JRDT—SPEE-2, R. D. Tata Papers, Pune, India.
133. Raianu, *Tata*, 27.
134. Tata, "A Fifteen-Year Plan of Economic Development for India." For an appreciative account of Nehru's economic strategy, see also Mukherjee, "Jawaharlal Nehru in Our Past, Present and Future."
135. Tata, "A Fifteen-Year Plan of Economic Development for India."
136. Raianu, *Tata*, 179. For opposition to the Bombay plan, see Chibber, *Locked in Place*, 106.
137. Chandra, Mukherjee, and Mukherjee, *India After Independence*, 2, 9. For the quote, see Mukherjee, *Political Economy*, chapter 6. See also the excellent book by Nikhil Menon, *Planning Democracy: Modern India's Quest for Development* (CUP, 2022), 1.
138. "Statement of Government's Industrial Policy," in FICCI, *Proceedings of the 19th Annual Session, May 1946*, 125.
139. Chandra, Mukherjee, and Mukherjee, *India After Independence*, 16; "India at 70: The Good and Bad of India's Growth Story," *Hindustan Times*, August 15, 2017; B. S. Minhas, "Rural Poverty, Land Re-

distribution and Development Strategy: Facts and Policy," *Indian Economic Review*, n.s., 5, no. 1 (April 1970): 102; Aprameya Rao, "Here's How India's Economy Has Fared in the Last 75 Years," NDTV Profit, August 13, 2021, https://www.ndtv.com/business/indian-economy-since-independence-heres-how-indias-economy-has-fared-in-the-last-75-years-2509759; R. A. Gopalaswami, *Census of India, 1951*, vol. 1, *Part 1-A—Report* (Government of India Press, 1953), 41; and "India at 70: The Good and Bad of India's Growth Story."
140. Chandra, Mukherjee, and Mukherjee, *India After Independence*, 14, 179.
141. Jawaharlal Nehru, *Selected Works of Jawaharlal Nehru*, vol. 7 (Jawaharlal Nehru Memorial Fund, 1997), 598–614.
142. Frieden, *Global Capitalism*, 313; and Raianu, *Tata*, 120.
143. Chandra, Mukherjee, and Mukherjee, *India After Independence*, 179–80.
144. Chandra, Mukherjee, and Mukherjee, *India After Independence*, 177; and Menon, *Planning Democracy*, 12.
145. Chandra, Mukherjee, and Mukherjee, *India After Independence*, 87, 343; and Menon, *Planning Democracy*, 18. On the importance of import substitution and protectionism to the business community, see Chibber, *Locked in Place*, 129.
146. FICCI, *Proceedings of the 26th Annual Session, February 1953*, 268; Chandra, Mukherjee, and Mukherjee, *India After Independence*, 344–45, 347, 349; and Frieden, *Global Capitalism*, 314, 315.
147. Proceedings of the Meeting Between the Representatives of the Federation and the Minister of Commerce and Industry, May 16, 1952, as reprinted in FICCI, *Proceedings of the 26th Annual Session, February 1953*, 56.
148. Staff of the Gokhale Institute of Politics, "Notes on the Rise of the Business Communities in India," 20.
149. "Statement of Government's Industrial Policy," in FICCI, *Proceedings of the 19th Annual Session, May 1946*, 131.
150. D. D. Anklesaria to the Editor, *Times of India*, undated, GAM.
151. Chibber, *Locked in Place*, chap. 5; Raianu, *Tata*, 129–30, 138, 153; and Ahuja, "'Produce or Perish,'" 4, 8–9, 13, 15, 26, 36, 40–41, 60, 69.
152. Menon, *Planning Democracy*, 7.
153. Birla to Prime Minister's Secretary, 26 February 1952, G. D. Birla and Nehru Correspondence, List

No. 296, 31 March 1948 to 18 December 1953, NMML.
154. See G. D. Birla and Nehru Correspondence, List No. 296, 31 March 1948 to 18 December 1953, NMML.
155. Government of India, Ministry of Labour, Industrial Committee on Cotton Textiles, first session, held in New Delhi on 12–14 January 1948, summary of proceedings, in File No. 207, p. 6, NMML.
156. S. R. Vasavada, in Government of India, Ministry of Labour, Industrial Committee on Cotton Textiles, NMML.
157. Summary of the proceedings of the second meeting of the Central Advisory Board, set up under the Minimum Wages Act, 1948, held in Bombay on 8–9 April 1954, in S. No. 849, File 27: All-India Organisation of Industrial Employers, 1954, NMML; and Government of India, Ministry of Labour, Industrial Committee on Cotton Textiles, first session, held in New Delhi on 12–14 January 1948, summary of proceedings, NMML.
158. Government of India, Ministry of Labour, Industrial Committee on Cotton Textiles, first session, held in New Delhi on 12–14 January 1948, summary of proceedings.
159. Government of India, Ministry of Labour, Industrial Committee on Cotton Textiles, first session, held in New Delhi on 12–14 January 1948, summary of proceedings.
160. Government of India, Ministry of Labour, Industrial Committee on Cotton Textiles, first session, held in New Delhi on 12–14 January 1948, summary of proceedings.
161. N. M. Joshi, conference speech on the economic conditions of the country (undated but probably late 1940s), N. M. Joshi Papers, 2nd Installment, File No. 15, NMML.
162. Raianu, *Tata*, 126, 128, 131; and FICCI, *Proceedings of the Twenty-Ninth Annual Meeting, Held at New Delhi on the 4th and 5th of March 1956* (New Delhi, 1956), 13. For the importance of disagreements and divisions, see also Shahid Amin, *Alternative Histories: A View from India* (Centre for Studies in Social Sciences, 2002).
163. FICCI, *Proceedings of the Twenty-Ninth Annual Meeting*, 18.
164. FICCI, *Proceedings of the Twenty-Ninth Annual Meeting*, 99, 102.
165. N. M. Joshi Papers, 2nd Installment, File No. 2, a speech dealing with some problems related to the Indian Trade Union Movement delivered at the Madras Provincial La-

bour Conference, 26–27 July 1927, NMML. See also Joshi, speech, File No. 15, N. M. Joshi Papers, NMML. 166. As cited in Ramachandra Guha, *India After Gandhi* (Ecco, 2019), 201. 167. Mukherjee, *Political Economy of Colonial and Post-Colonial India*, 226, 228–31. On the tensions, see Chibber, *Locked in Place*, 2003. On India's history of democracy, see also the brilliant Ornit Shani, *How India Became Democratic* (CUP, 2017).

168. Jakes and Shokr, "Capitalism in Egypt, Not Egyptian Capitalism," 135.

169. Vitalis, *When Capitalists Collide*, 141–217; Joel Beinin, "Labor, Capital, and the State in Nasserist Egypt, 1952–1961," *International Journal of Middle Eastern Studies* 21 (1989): 73, 79; Tignor, *Capitalism and Nationalism at the End of Empire*, 136–37, 160, 163, 165, 184; Patrick O'Brien and Royal Institute of International Affairs, *The Revolution in Egypt's Economic System: From Private Enterprise to Socialism, 1952–1965* (OUP, 1966), 100; Abdalla Nazem, "Egypt's Absorptive Capacity During 1960–1972," *International Journal of Middle East Studies* 16, no. 2 (1984): 177–98; and Jakes and Shokr, "Capitalism in Egypt, Not Egyptian Capitalism," 136. For an analysis of this land reforms process, see Mahmoud Abdel-Fadil, *Development, Income Distribution and Social Change in Rural Egypt, 1952–1970* (CUP, 1975).

170. Beinin, "Labor, Capital, and the State in Nasserist Egypt," 71–73, 74–76, 82, 85; Tignor, *Capitalism and Nationalism at the End of Empire*, 66.

171. Sayre Schatz, *Nigerian Capitalism* (University of California Press, 1977), 3.

172. Biersteker, *Multinationals*, 54; Lawal, "British Commercial Interests and the Decolonization Process," 97.

173. *West African Pilot*, June 5, 1957, as cited in Samuel Okafor Idemili, *The West African Pilot and the Movement for Nigerian Nationalism 1937–1960* (University of Wisconsin Press, 1980), 341.

174. E. O. Akeredolu-Ale, "Private Foreign Investment and the Underdevelopment of Indigenous Entrepreneurship in Nigeria," in *Nigeria: Economy and Society*, ed. Gavin Williams (Rex Collings, 1976), 112, 118, 330; and "Corruption a Delicate Subject," *Financial Times*, September 30, 1980.

175. Biersteker, *Multinationals*, 58; and Eskor Toyo, "The Cause of the Depression in the Nigerian Economy," *Africa Development* 9, no. 3

(1984): 34–36; and J. O. Odufalu, "Indigenous Enterprise in Nigerian Manufacturing," *Journal of Modern African Studies* 9, no. 4 (1971): 597.

176. Ola Oni, "Gradualist Approach Not Appropriate," *Daily News*, April 15, 1972, 7.

177. Akeredolu-Ale, "Private Foreign Investment," 106, 108; J. S. Ovadia, "The Making of Oil-Backed Indigenous Capitalism in Nigeria," *New Political Economy* 18, no. 2 (2012): 259.

178. Catherine Boone, *Merchant Capital and the Roots of State Power in Senegal, 1930–1985* (CUP, 1992), 24, 41, 104; Akeredolu-Ale, "Private Foreign Investment," 109–10; and Boone, *Merchant Capital and the Roots of State Power*, 104.

179. Boone, *Merchant Capital and the Roots of State Power*, xii, 1, 5, 118–19, 133, 136, 147, 163.

180. Boone, *Merchant Capital and the Roots of State Power*, xii, 10, 31, 78.

181. Boone, *Merchant Capital and the Roots of State Power*, 4, 11, 28–29, 85, 97, 104, 106, 109–10, 126, 129–30.

182. Vanessa Ogle, "'Funk Money': The End of Empires, the Expansion of Tax Havens, and Decolonization as an Economic and Financial Event," *Past & Present* 249, no. 1 (2020): 214, 217; and Sarah Stockwell, "Trade, Empire, and the Fiscal Context of Imperial Business During Decolonization," *EHR* 57 (2004): 151, 156, 158.

183. Claude Sissao, "Histoire coloniale: L'économie de la Haute-Volta à la veille de l'indépendance (1947–1960)," in *Burkina Faso: Cent ans d'histoire, 1895–1995*, ed. Georges Madiéga Yénouyaba and Oumarou Nao, vol. 2 (Karthala, 2003), 1599; Ernest Harsch, *Burkina Faso: A History of Power, Protest, and Revolution* (Zed Books, 2017), 24; "Population, Total—Burkina Faso," World Bank, accessed December 15, 2022, https:// data.worldbank.org/indicator/SP .POP.TOTL?locations=BF; and Ram Christophe Sawadogo, "La politique agricole de la Haute-Volta coloniale et post-coloniale: Appréciations contrastées et interrogations," in Yénouyaba and Nao, *Burkina Faso*, 2:1467. See, in particular, Sissao, "Histoire coloniale," in Yénouyaba and Nao, *Burkina Faso*, 1497. Sissao writes: "Les principaux produits exportés par ordre d'importance: les animaux vivants, plus de la moitié des exportations; l'arachide, les amandes de karité et leur dérivé; le coton et quelques minerais dont l'exploitation industrielle était inexistante (CAOM 200mi 2055). . . . La part de la France dans ses importa-

tions était de 71,2%, alors que pour les exportations cette part était très faible."

184. See K. S. Ouali, "L'économie burkinabè depuis 1960: Du sous-développement à la pauvreté," in Yénouyaba and Nao, *Burkina Faso*, 2:1274–75. Ouali writes: "[L]e poids de l'État dans l'économie en fait une économie dirigée dont le développement et les priorités sont fixées dans un plan. La planification est un indicateur. Les premières expériences sont faites en 1962 et 1963 sans succès. De 1967 à 1982, près de quatre plans quinquennaux sont élaborés et/ou mis en œuvre."

185. Harsch, *Burkina Faso*, 71, 74, 150–51; and Ouali, "L'économie burkinabè depuis 1960," 1265–88, here 1271.

186. Harsch, *Burkina Faso*, 3.

187. Fanny Pigeaud and Sylla Ndongo, *Africa's Last Colonial Currency, The CFA Franc Story* (Pluto Press, 2021); Harsch, *Burkina Faso*, 19; Fanny Pigeaud and Ndongo Samba Sylla, *L'arme invisible de la Françafrique: Une histoire du franc CFA* (La Découverte, 2018); and Harsch, *Burkina Faso*, 30.

188. Frieden, *Global Capitalism*, 317, 320; Hobsbawm, *Age of Extremes*, 345.

189. Maddison, *World Economy*, 182.

190. Ramon H. Myers, "The Economic Transformation of the Republic of China on Taiwan," *China Quarterly* 99 (1984): 513–14; Neil H. Jacoby, *U.S. Aid to Taiwan: A Study of Foreign Aid, Self-Help, and Development* (Frederick A. Praeger, 1966), 153. For Korea, see Charles Raphael Frank, Kwang Suk Kim, and Larry E. Westphal, *South Korea* (National Bureau of Economic Research, 1975), 12; and Jaewoong Jeon, "Sweet Returns: Sugar Capitalism in South Korea and Taiwan," paper presented at the Weatherhead Initiative on Global History Seminar, Harvard University, January 24, 2022.

191. Robert E. Baldwin, Tain-Jy Chen, and Douglas R. Nelson, *Political Economy of U.S.-Taiwan Trade* (University of Michigan Press, 1995), 6–7.

192. Dani Rodrik, Gene Grossman, and Victor Norman, "Getting Interventions Right: How South Korea and Taiwan Grew Rich," *Economic Policy* 10 (1995): 57, 85–87; Myers, "Economic Transformation," 500; Angel J. Ubide and Toms J. T. Balio, *The Korean Financial Crisis of 1997: A Strategy of Financial Sector Reform* (International Monetary Fund, 1999), 11.

193. Myers, "Economic Transforma-

tion," 513; Gary S. Fields, "Employment, Income Distribution and Economic Growth in Seven Small Open Economies," *Economic Journal* 94, no. 373 (March 1984): 80.

194. Maddison, *World Economy*, 184; IMF, World Economic Outlook Database, 2022, accessed August 26, 2022, https://www.imf.org/en/Publications/SPROLLS/world-economic-outlook-databases#sort=%40imfdate%20descending. For Taiwan's GDP in 1975, see https://countryeconomy.com/gdp?year=1975.

195. Gareth Austin, "The State and Business in Ghana: Pre-Colonial, Colonial, Post-Colonial, 1807–2000," unpublished paper, presented at the VI Annual Meeting of the African Economic History Network: New Approaches to African Economic History: History, Methods and Interdisciplinarity," October 21–22, 2016, 14.

196. FICCI, *Proceedings of the 26th Annual Session, February 1953*, 267.

197. Jeon, "Sweet Returns." In 1953, the Indian Merchants' Chamber in Bombay, for example, urged the government of India to remove the "tolerance clause" in cotton contracts that allowed for a certain variability of the underlying cotton. See S. No. 1141 / File No. 42: Matters Regarding Cotton, 1953, Indian Merchants' Chamber, Bombay, NMML; Ministry of Commerce and Industry Notification, New Delhi, 23 October 1952, Indian Merchants' Chamber, Bombay, Matters Regarding Cotton, 1953, S. No. 1141/ File No. 42, NMML; *Sénégal d'aujourd'hui* 1 (October 1968), 20f; and Boone, *Merchant Capital and the Roots of State Power*, 79, 112.

198. Salma Abouelhossein, "Sugar Towns: Urban Ecology, Planning, and the Shifting Geographies of Labor in the Making of Egypt's Sugar Belt" (PhD diss., Harvard University, forthcoming).

199. Hobsbawm, *Age of Extremes*, 352f, 354; Beinin, "Labor, Capital, and the State in Nasserist Egypt," 76–77; *Census of India, 1951*, vol. 4, *Bombay, Saurashtra and Kutch, Part II-A—Tables*, 5; *Census of India, 1971, Series 11: Maharashtra*, part 2, supplement, 10; and Jeffrey D. Sachs, *Ages of Globalization: Geography, Technology, and Institutions* (Columbia UP, 2019), 8. In this paragraph, 1950s refers to the years 1951 to 1961. Figures were calculated based on the raw data provided in International Labour Office, *Year Book of Labour Statistics: Retrospective*

Edition on Population Census, 1945–89 = Annuaire des statistiques du travail: Édition rétrospective sur les recensements de population, 1945–89 (International Labour Office, 1990), 174, 262, 264, 266. On Jakarta, see *Sensus Penduduk 1961*, 4, at https://www.bps.go.id/publication/1962/06/06/ba0319372bf4767645160a8c/sensus-penduduk-1961-republik-indonesia.html, as well as the data at https://www.macrotrends.net/cities/21454/jakarta/population. On São Paulo, see *Censo Demográfico de 1960*, Brasil, VII recenseamento Geral do Brasil, Série Nacional, vol. 1, Fundação Instituto Brasileiro de Geografia e Estatística e População Departamento de Estatísticas, 90, at https://biblioteca.ibge.gov.br/visualizacao/periodicos/68/cd_1960_v1_br.pdf. Regarding labor in the informal sector, see "Informal Employment as Percentage of Total Employment in Latin America and the Caribbean in 2016, by Subregion," Statista, accessed December 3, 2022, https://www.statista.com/statistics/1037179/informal-employment-share-latin-america-caribbean-subregion/. See also European Parliament, "Briefing: Latin America's Informal Economy, Some Formalisation Strategies," September 2016.

200. Adom Getachew, *Worldmaking After Empire: The Rise and Fall of Self-Determination* (PUP, 2020), 2, 5; Walter Rodney, *A History of the Guyanese Working People, 1881–1905* (Johns Hopkins UP, 1981); and Walter Rodney, *How Europe Underdeveloped Africa* (L'Ouverture Publications, 1972).

201. Getachew, *Worldmaking After Empire*, 7, 15, 21; and C. L. R. James, *The Black Jacobins: Toussaint L'Ouverture and the San Domingo Revolution* (Vintage, 1989).

202. Explaining that unequal development was, in his own words, the center of his life's work. See Samir Amin, *L'eurocentrisme: Critique d'une idéologie* (Anthropos, 1988), 11.

203. Samir Amin, *L'accumulation à l'echelle mondiale* (Anthropos, 1970).

204. Samir Amin, *The Implosion of Capitalism* (Pluto Press, 2014), 29, 44.

205. Getachew, *Worldmaking After Empire*, 142–43, 146; and Frieden, *Global Capitalism*, 312. On Lewis, see Robert L. Tignor, *W. Arthur Lewis and the Birth of Development Economics* (PUP, 2005), esp. 45.

206. Tignor, *W. Arthur Lewis*, 45. The citations are taken by Tignor from a document submitted by the

League of Coloured Peoples, in PRO CO 318/445/47, National Archives of the United Kingdom, Kew.

207. Getachew, *Worldmaking After Empire*, 161.

208. Raúl Prebisch, *The Economic Development of Latin America* (United Nations Department of Economic Affairs, 1950), 1, 16. See also J. F. J. Toye and Richard Toye, "The Origins and Interpretation of the Prebisch–Singer Thesis," *History of Political Economy* 35, no. 3 (Fall 2003): 437–67.

209. Christy Thornton, "A Mexican International Economic Order? Tracing the Hidden Roots of the Charter of Economic Rights and Duties of States," *Humanity* 9 (Winter 2018): 390, 395, 401.

210. Ramón Beteta, "Mexico's Foreign Relations," *Annals of the American Academy of Political and Social Science* 208 (March 1940): 170, as cited in Thornton, "A Mexican International Economic Order?," 408.

211. As cited in Getachew, *Worldmaking After Empire*, 23. See also 18, 212. Getachew, *Worldmaking After Empire*, 159.

213. Getachew, *Worldmaking After Empire*, 5; Nehru at FICCI, *Proceedings of the Twenty-Ninth Annual Meeting*, 27; Homer A. Jack, *Bandung: An On-the-Spot Description of the Asian-African Conference* (Toward Freedom, n.d.), 2, 27; and C. Fitzgerald, *The Facts of the Bandung Conference*, ed. D. W. Baker, 27–29.

214. Jack, *Bandung*, 10.

215. Jack, *Bandung*, 10.

216. "Revisiting the 1955 Bandung Asian-African Conference and Its Legacy," South Centre, May 15, 2015, https://www.southcentre.int/question/revisiting-the-1955-bandung-asian-african-conference-and-its-legacy/; and "Non-Aligned Movement," *Britannica*, accessed February 19, 2022, https://www.britannica.com/topic/Non-Aligned-Movement.

217. "Discurso pronunciado por el C. Presidente Constitucional de la República Mexicana, Lic. Luis Echeverría Alvaraez," 126–27, as cited in Thornton, "A Mexican International Economic Order?," 403.

218. Getachew, *Worldmaking After Empire*.

219. Michael Goebel, "'The Capital of Men Without a Country': Migrants and Anticolonialism in Interwar Paris," *AHR* 121, no. 5 (December 2016): 1445, 1461; Hue-Tam Ho Tai, *Radicalism and the Origins of the Vietnamese Revolution* (HUP, 1996), 232–33; and B. H. Ed-

wards, "The Shadow of Shadows," *Positions: East Asia Cultures Critique* 11, no. 1 (March 2003): 23. For similar developments in London, see Jonathan Schneer's *London 1900* and Priyamvada Gopal's *Insurgent Empire.*

220. Ismay Milford et al., "Another World? East Africa, Decolonisation, and the Global History of the Mid-Twentieth Century," *Journal of African History* 62, no. 3 (2021): 2; Hugh Springer, "Federation in the Caribbean: An Attempt That Failed," *International Organization* 16, no. 4 (1962): 760; Erasmus Kloman, "African Unification Movements," *International Organization* 16, no. 2 (1962): 390; and Getachew, *Worldmaking After Empire,* 5, 10.

221. This calculation is based on data found in "World Population Prospects 2022," United Nations, Department of Economic and Social Affairs, Population Division, accessed September 12, 2023, https://population.un.org/wpp/.

222. Zhaojin Zeng, "Nourishing Shanxi: Indigenous Entrepreneurship, Regional Industry, and the Transformation of a Chinese Hinterland Economy, 1907–2004" (PhD diss., University of Texas at Austin, 2018).

223. Jack Werner, "Global Fordism in 1950s Urban China," *Frontiers of History in China* 7 (2012): 415; William C. Kirby, "Continuity and Change in Modern China: Economic Planning on the Mainland and in Taiwan, 1943–1958," *Australian Journal of Chinese Affairs* 24 (1990): 121–41; and Zeng, "Nourishing Shanxi."

224. Werner, "Global Fordism in 1950s Urban China," 421, 425, 434; Nicholas R. Lardy, "Economic Recovery and the 1st Five-Year Plan," in *The Cambridge History of China* (CUP, 1987), 155–57, 174, 395.

225. Hanchao Lu, "Bourgeois Comfort Under Proletarian Dictatorship: Home Life of Chinese Capitalists Before the Cultural Revolution," *Journal of Social History* 52 (2018): 74–100, here 87.

226. Quinn Slobodian, *Globalists: The End of Empire and the Birth of Neoliberalism* (HUP, 2018), 10, 12, 14, 156, 264.

Chapter 16: Taming Industrial Capitalism, 1945–1973

1. Jean Fourastié, *Les Trente Glorieuses, ou La révolution invisible de 1946 à 1975* (Fayard, 1979).

2. Kate A. Baldwin, *The Racial Imaginary of the Cold War Kitchen: From Sokol'niki Park to Chicago's South Side* (Dartmouth College Press, 2016), 3.

3. "The Kitchen Debate," transcript, 24 July 1959, Vice President Richard Nixon and Soviet Premier Nikita Khrushchev, US Embassy, Moscow, Soviet Union, accessed February 28, 2024, via the FOIA Electronic Reading Room, https://www.cia.gov/readingroom/docs/1959-07-24.pdf.

4. Rick Perlstein and Richard M. Nixon, *Richard Nixon: Speeches, Writings, Documents* (PUP, 2008), 88–96.

5. As cited in Ruth Oldenziel and Karin Zachmann, eds., *Cold War Kitchen: Americanization, Technology, and European Users* (MIT Press, 2009), 100. On the debate, see also Sarah T. Phillips and Shane Hamilton, *The Kitchen Debate and Cold War Consumer Politics: A Brief History with Documents* (Bedford / St. Martin's, 2014).

6. M. Hashim Gazdar, "The Havana Conference on International Trade and Employment," *Pakistan Horizon* 1 (March 1948): 26.

7. Guiliano Muzzioli, *Modena* (Editorio Laterza, 1993), 323.

8. Charles Maier, *The Project-State and Its Rivals: A New History of the Twentieth and Twenty-First Centuries* (HUP, 2023), 193.

9. Eric Hobsbawm, *The Age of Extremes* (Michael Joseph, 1994), 258–59, 261, 264, 267; Andrew Glyn et al., "The Rise and Fall of the Golden Age," in *The Golden Age of Capitalism: Reinterpreting the Postwar Experience,* ed. Stephen A. Marglin and Juliet B. Schor (Clarendon Press, 1990), 46.

10. Anthony Crosland, *The Future of Socialism* (Jonathan Cape, 1956), 517.

11. Charles Merriam, *On the Agenda of Democracy* (HUP, 1941), 124.

12. Simon Kuznets, *Shares of Upper Income Groups in Income and Savings* (National Bureau of Economic Research, 1953); Simon Kuznets, "Economic Growth and Income Inequality," *American Economic Review* 45, no. 1 (1955): 1–28; Simon Kuznets, "Quantitative Aspects of the Economic Growth of Nations: VIII. Distribution of Income by Size," *Economic Development and Cultural Change* 11, no. 2 (1963): 1–80.

13. Kuznets, "Economic Growth and Income Inequality," 4.

14. Anders Houltz, "Den stora skalan: Volvo Torslandaverken och massproduktion som mål och mening i 1960-talets Sverige," *Bebyggelsehistorisk tidskrift* 68 (2014): 73; Statens Offentliga Utredningar (SOU) 1972:26, *Förskolan. Del 1: Betänkande avgivet av 1968 års barnstugeutredning,* 17–18; Gunilla Carlstedt and Annika Forssén, *Arbete för livet: Kvinnor berättar om svenskt 1900-tal* (Carlssons, 2018), 74, 78.

15. Tofte Frykman, "Boendeförhållanden 1968–1981," in *Välfärd i förändring: Levnadsvillkor i Sverige 1968–1981,* ed. Robert Erikson and Rune Åberg (Prisma / Institutet för Social Forskning, 1984), 227, 229; Thord Strömberg, "The Politicization of the Housing Market: The Social Democrats and the Housing Question," in *Creating Social Democracy: A Century of the Social Democratic Labor Party in Sweden,* ed. Klaus Misgeld, Karl Molin, and Klas Åmark (Pennsylvania State UP, 1992), 237ff; Micael Nilsson, *Från barnrikehus till sociala hyreshuset. Den selektiva bostadspolitikens ursprung och förändring 1933–1994* (Nordic Academic Press, 2021), 133–35; Hans Rosling, *Hur jag lärde mig förstå världen* (Natur & Kultur, 2017), 23, 35.

16. Sten Carlsson, *Yrken och samhällsgrupper. Den sociala omgrupperingen i Sverige efter 1866* (Almqvist & Wiksell, 1968), 254, table 1, 274.

17. Carlstedt and Forssén, *Arbete för livet,* 73–74. The quote comes from a woman who recollected being a mother during the mid-1900s.

18. SOU 1972:26, *Förskolan,* 95. On working-class life in 1960s Sweden, see also Gunnar Lindstedt, *Stålår* (Natur & Kultur 2020), 32.

19. Janne Jonsson, "Utbildningsresurser," in Erikson and Åberg, *Välfärd i förändring,* 50, 188; Svenåke Kjellström and Olle Lundberg, "Hälsa och vårdkonsumtion," in Erikson and Åberg, *Välfärd i förändring,* 76–79; Björn Ohlsson, "Det räcker nu'—om Volvoarbetares syn på arbetet i olika faser av livet," *Arbetsmarknad & arbetsliv* 16, no. 1 (2010): 62–63; Hugh Heclo and Henrik Madsen, *Policy and Politics in Sweden: Principled Pragmatism* (Temple UP, 1987), 7–8; "Socialförsäkringens historia," Försäkringskassan, accessed September 15, 2022, http://sakringskassan.se/om-for sakringskassan/vart-uppdrag /socialforsakringens-historia.

20. Rosling, *Hur jag lärde mig förstå världen,* 50.

21. "Studiestödets och CSN:s historia," CSN, accessed September 21, 2022, https://www.csn.se/om-csn

/vart-uppdrag/studiestodets-och -csns-historia.html#h-Ar19191974; Jenny Andersson, *Between Growth and Security: Swedish Social Democracy from a Strong Society to a Third Way*, trans. Mireille L. Key (Manchester UP, 2006), 30; ATP information gathered from Agneta Kruse and Åke Elmér, "ATP," *Nationalencyklopedin*, accessed March 9, 2022, https://www-ne-se.ezproxy.its.uu .se/uppslagsverk/encyklopedi /l%C3%A5ng/atp-(allm%C3%A4n -till%C3%A4ggspension); Rune Åberg, Jan Selén, and Henrik Tham, "Ekonomiska resurser," in Erikson and Åberg, *Välfärd i förändring*, 154–55; Mårten Martos Nilsson, "Trots höjningen—a-kassan lägre än på 90-talet," *Arbetet*, June 15, 2020, https://arbetet.se/2020/06/15/trots -hojningen-a-kassan-lagre-an-pa-90 -talet/.

22. *Statens offentliga utredningar 2000:7* and *Långtidsutredningen 1999/2000*, app. 1, 19; Lennart Schön, *En modern svensk ekonomisk historia: Tillväxt och omvandling under två sekel* (Studentlitteratur, 2014), 16–17; and data gathered June 8, 2022, from "Historisk BNP-utveckling," Ekonomifakta, last updated October 9, 2024, by Jacob Öljemark, https://www.ekonomi fakta.se/Fakta/Ekonomi/globala -utvecklingstrender/historisk-bnp -utveckling/. The web page's source is the Maddison Project Database, version 2020. See also Jutta Bolt, Robert Inklaar, Herman de Jong, and Jan Luiten van Zanden, "Rebasing 'Maddison': New Income Comparisons and the Shape of Long-Run Economic Development," Maddison Project Working Paper No. 10 (2018). Sweden's GDP increased from $8,201 in international dollars in 1945 to $21,509 in 1973.

23. Lennart Schön, *An Economic History of Modern Sweden* (Routledge, 2012), 243.

24. Schön, *An Economic History of Modern Sweden*, 239, 245, 267; Sten Carlsson, *Yrken och samhällsgrupper: Den sociala omgrupperingen i Sverige efter 1866* (Almqvist & Wiksell, 1968), 267, table 2; Statistiska Centralbyrån (National Central Bureau of Statistics), *Statsanställda 1954–1981. Del 2: En historisk översikt samt uppgifter om utbildning, tjänstebenämning m.m.* (Stockholm, 1986), 58; United Nations Population Division, Department of Economic and Social Affairs, Population Division (2022). World Population Prospects 2022, Online edition at https://pop ulation.un.org/wpp, accessed November 13, 2022.

25. Sten Carlsson, *Yrken och samhällsgrupper: Den sociala omgrupperingen i Sverige efter 1866* (Almqvist & Wiksell, 1968), 188; Mats Larsson, *Hundra år av ojämlikhet—löner och löneutveckling efter klass och kön* (Landsorganisationen i Sverige, 2014), 31–32.

26. Sheri Berman, *The Primacy of Politics: Social Democracy and the Making of Europe's Twentieth Century* (CUP, 2006), 198–99; Henrik Berggren and Lars Trägårdh, *Är svensken människa? Gemenskap och oberoende i det moderna Sverige* (Norstedt, 2015), 51–54; Gøsta Esping-Andersen, *Politics Against Markets: The Social Democratic Road to Power* (PUP, 1985), 227–36; Heclo and Madsen, *Policy and Politics in Sweden*, 7–8; Gøsta Esping-Andersen, "The Making of a Social Democratic Welfare State," in Misgeld, Molin, and Åmark, *Creating Social Democracy*, 35–66; Ann-Sofie Ohlander, "The Invisible Child? The Struggle over Social Democratic Policy," in Misgeld, Molin, and Åmark, *Creating Social Democracy*, 213–36; Strömberg, "The Politicization of the Housing Market," 237–69; Bo Lindensjö, "From Liberal Common School to State Primary School: A Main Line in Social Democratic Educational Policy," in Misgeld, Molin, and Åmark, *Creating Social Democracy*, 308–37.

27. Strömberg, "Politicization of the Housing Market, 237–38, 252, 254, 260–62.

28. Åke Elmér, "barnbidrag," in *Nationalencyklopedin*, accessed March 17, 2022, https://www-ne-se.ezproxy .its.uu.se/uppslagsverk/encyklopedi /lång/barnbidrag; "Barnbidragets historia," Barnbidrag.info, accessed September 28, 2022, https://barn bidrag.info/barnbidragets-historia/; "moderskapspenning" in *Nationalencyklopedin*, accessed March 17, 2022, http://www-ne-se.ezproxy.its.uu.se /uppslagsverk/encyklopedi/lång /moderskapspenning; Riksdagens protokoll 1976/1977 and Regeringens proposition 1976/77, 90; Riksdagens protokoll 1976/1977 and Regeringens proposition 1976/77, 90, 24; Ohlander, "The Invisible Child?," 228.

29. Esping-Andersen, "Making of a Social Democratic Welfare State," 47–48; Andersson, *Between Growth and Security*, 30; ATP information gathered from Agneta Kruse and Åke Elmér, "ATP," in *Nationalencyklopedin*, accessed March 9, 2022, https://www-ne-se.ezproxy.its.uu .se/uppslagsverk/encyklopedi /l%C3%A5ng/atp-(allm%C3%A4n-till%C3%A4ggspension); Per Gun-

nar Edebalk, "Arbetsgivarna, sjukförsäkringen och sjuklönen—en historik," *Arbetsmarknad & Arbetsliv* 16, no. 3 (2010): 30–32; and Ylva Hasselberg, *Vem vill leva i kunskapssamhället? Essäer om universitetet och samtiden* (Gidlunds Förlag, 2009), 25–26, 134–35.

30. Defined as "the sum of the state and local marginal income tax rates and employee-paid Social Security Contributions." See Gunnar Du Rietz, Dan Johansson, and Mikael Stenkula, "Swedish Labor Income Taxation (1862–2013)," in *Swedish Taxation: Developments Since 1862*, ed. Magnus Henrekson and Mikael Stenkula (Palgrave Macmillan, 2015), 68–75.

31. Statistiska Centralbyrån (National Central Bureau of Statistics), *Historisk statistik för Sverige. Del 1: Befolkning: 1720–1967*, 2nd ed. (Stockholm, 1969), 117–18; Schön, *En modern svensk ekonomisk historia*, 356–57; "Medellivslängden i Sverige," Statistiska Centralbyrån (Nation Central Bureau of Statistics), accessed September 28, 2022, https://www.scb.se/hitta-statistik /sverige-i-siffror/manniskorna-i -sverige/medellivslangd-i-sverige/; and Bo Werner, "Growth in Sweden: Surveillance of Growth Patterns and Epidemiological Monitoring of Secular Changes in Height and Weight Among Children and Adolescents" (PhD diss., Stockholm: Karolinska Institutet, 2007), 17, 23. The height of conscripts increased from 174.7 centimeters to 178.3 centimeters. On social mobility, see Anders Bjorklund and Markus Janth, "Intergenerational Income Mobility in Sweden Compared to the United States," *American Economic Review* 87 (1997): 1008–1009; and Bashkar Mazumder, "Fortunate Sons: New Estimates of Intergenerational Mobility in the United States Using Social Security Earnings Data," *Review of Economics and Statistics* 87, no. 2 (2005): 235–55.

32. Andersson, *Between Growth and Security*, 1–2.

33. Esping-Andersen, *Politics Against Markets*, 64; Hugh Heclo and Henrik Madsen, *Policy and Politics in Sweden: Principled Pragmatism*, (Temple UP, 1987), 25.

34. Andersson, *Between Growth and Security*, 29.

35. Esping-Andersen, *Politics Against Markets*, 52, 56, 108; Esping-Andersen, "Making of a Social Democratic Welfare State," 47–53.

36. Ulf Olsson, *Att förvalta sitt pund: Marcus Wallenberg 1899–1982* (Ekerlids Förlag, 2001), 335, 339.

37. "Sweden Military Spending/Defense Budget 1960–2024," at https://www.macrotrends.net/global-metrics/countries/SWE/sweden/military-spending-defense-budget; and Olsson, *Att förvalta sitt pund*, 335, 338.

38. Marcus Wallenberg to Arne Geijer, telegram, 10 June 1969, as cited in Olsson, *Att förvalta sitt pund*, 339.

39. Andersson, *Between Growth and Security*, 33. Jenny Andersson, *Mellan tillväxt och trygghet: Idéer om produktiv socialpolitik i socialdemokratisk socialpolitisk ideologi under efterkrigstiden* (PhD diss., Uppsala Universitet, 2003), 35.

40. Andersson, *Between Growth and Security*, 61. The original can be found in Andersson, *Mellan tillväxt och trygghet*, 189.

41. Andersson, *Between Growth and Security*, 39. The original can be found in Andersson, *Mellan tillväxt och trygghet*, 35.

42. Benny Andersson and Björn Ulvaeus, "Super Trouper," *Super Trouper* (Polar Music, 1980).

43. Considering that each country has its own way of accounting for social expenditure, there is some variation among published data. The numbers here are drawn from "Public Social Spending as a Share of GDP," Our World in Data, accessed October 6, 2024, https://ourworldindata.org/grapher/social-spending-oecd-longrun?tab=table&time=1960..1973&showSelectionOnlyInTable=1. See also the OECD's website, accessed October 6, 2022, https://www.oecd.org/social/expenditure.htm. According to the Social Security Administration's report for fiscal year 1974: "The old-age, survivors, disability, and health insurance (OASDHI) program alone disbursed $8.5 billion more in 1974 than in 1973." For the complete report, see Alfred M. Skolnik and Sophie R. Dales, "Social Welfare Expenditures in Fiscal Year 1974," *Social Security Bulletin* 38, no. 1 (1975): 3–19.

44. Şevket Pamuk, *Uneven Centuries: Economic Development of Turkey Since 1820* (PUP, 2018), 12; Jeffry A. Frieden, *Global Capitalism: Its Fall and Rise in the Twentieth Century* (W. W. Norton, 2006), 278; Stephen A. Marglin, "Lessons of the Golden Age: An Overview," in Marglin and Schor *Golden Age of Capitalism*, 1; Glyn et al., "Rise and Fall of the Golden Age," 49; Hobsbawm, *Age of Extremes*, 259, 261.

45. John Dower, *Embracing Defeat: Japan in the Wake of World War II* (W. W. Norton / New Press, 1999), 45; Mizutani Michikazu, *Sengo nihon keizai shi: Seisan, ryūtsū, shōhi*

kōzō no henka (Dōbunkan, 1991), 68; Nakamura Takafusa, *The Postwar Japanese Economy: Its Development and Structure, 1937–1994*, 2nd ed. (University of Tokyo Press, 1995), 53, 55, 57, 78–81; Takeda Haruhito, *Nihon keizai shi* (Yūhikaku, 2019), 344; and Glyn et al., "Rise and Fall of the Golden Age," 53.

46. "Fiat Centro e Sezioni Automobili," in Fondo Sepin, Operai in Forza, PER 005, CSF. The figures are calculated based on the raw data provided in Angus Maddison, *The World Economy: Historical Statistics*, Development Centre Studies (OECD, 2003), 56–57. The GDPs of Canada and the US are taken from 85–86. The GDPs of the six Western European countries are taken from 50–53. The GDP of Japan is taken from 172 and 174. See also Frieden, *Global Capitalism*, 288; Glyn et al., "Rise and Fall of the Golden Age," 42.

47. Glyn et al., "Rise and Fall of the Golden Age," 45.

48. Haruhito, *Nihon keizai shi*, 356–60.

49. Haruhito, *Nihon keizai shi*, 361.

50. Glyn et al., "Rise and Fall of the Golden Age," 47, 54; Takafusa, *Postwar Japanese Economy*, 100–101; Lionel Frost and Tony Dingle, "Sustaining Suburbia: An Historical Perspective on Australia's Growth," in *Australian Cities: Issues, Strategies and Policies for Urban Australia in the 1990s*, ed. Patrick Troy (CUP, 1995), 34; and Humphrey McQueen, *Social Sketches of Australia, 1888–2001*, 3rd ed. (University of Queensland Press, 2004), 218.

51. Miguel Martín-Retortillo and Vicente Pinilla, "Patterns and Causes of the Growth of European Agricultural Production, 1950 to 2005," *Agricultural History Review* 63, no. 1 (2015): 144–45; Giovanni Federico, *Feeding the World: An Economic History of Agriculture* (PUP, 2008), 101; Franz-Josef Brüggemeier, "Umweltgeschichte," in *Umwelt und Geschichte in Deutschland und Großbritannien* (K. G. Saur, 2006), chap. 8; Frank Uekötter, *Im Strudel: Eine Umweltgeschichte der modernen Welt* (Campus, 2020), 588; Ulrich Kluge, *Ökowende: Agrarpolitik zwischen Reform und Rinderwahnsinn* (Siedler, 2001), 38.

52. Hobsbawm, *Age of Extremes*, 266; and Jack Werner, "Global Fordism in 1950s Urban China," *Frontiers of History in China* 7, no. 3 (2012): 416. See also Glyn et al., "Rise and Fall of the Golden Age," 55; and "Number of TV Households in America 1950–1978," American Century (website), archived March 28, 2022, at https://

web.archive.org/web/2022032 8173633/https://americancentury.omeka.wlu.edu/items/show/136.

53. Steven Tolliday, "From 'Beetle Monoculture' to the 'German Model': The Transformation of Volkswagen, 1967–1991," *Business and Economic History* 24, no. 2 (1995): 111.

54. Glyn et al., "Rise and Fall of the Golden Age," 56; Patrick Fridenson, "Fordism and Quality: The French Case, 1919–93," in *Fordism Transformed: The Development of Production Methods in the Automobile Industry*, ed. Haruhito Shiomi and Kazuo Wada (OUP, 1995), 163; Henrik Glimstedt, "Non-Fordist Routes to Modernization: Production, Innovation, and the Political Construction of Markets in the Swedish Automobile Industry Before 1960," *Business and Economic History* 24, no. 1 (1995): 249–50; Stephan J. Link, *Forging Global Fordism: Nazi Germany, Soviet Russia and the Contest over Industrial Order* (PUP, 2020), 6. See also Douglas Kellner, "The Frankfurt School and British Cultural Studies: The Missed Articulation," in *Rethinking the Frankfurt School: Alternative Legacies of Cultural Critique*, ed. Jeffrey T. Nealon and Caren Irr (SUNY Press, 2002), 33.

55. Max Horkheimer, *Notizen 1950 bis 1969 und Dämmerung: Notizen in Deutschland* (S. Fischer, 1974), 265, as translated in Douglas Kellner, "The Frankfurt School Revisited: A Critique of Martin Jay's *The Dialectical Imagination*," *New German Critique* 4 (Winter 1975): 134.

56. Hobsbawm, *Age of Extremes*, 263, 266; David C. Mowery, "The Boundaries of the U.S. Firm in R&D," in *Coordination and Information: Historical Perspectives on the Organization of Enterprise*, ed. Naomi R. Lamoreaux and Daniel M. G. Raff (University of Chicago Press, 1995), 153; Arthur Daemmrich, "Synthesis by Microbes or Chemists? Pharmaceutical Research and Manufacturing in the Antibiotic Era," *History and Technology* 25, no. 3 (2009): 238, 248–49; Jeffrey Sturchio, "*Festschrift*: Experimenting with Research: Kenneth Mees, Eastman Kodak and the Challenges of Diversification," *Science Museum Group Journal*, no. 13 (Spring 2020), n.p.; D. Eleanor Westney, "The Evolution of Japan's Industrial Research and Development" in *The Japanese Firm: The Sources of Competitive Strength*, ed. Masahiko Aoki and Ronald Dore (OUP, 1994), 157, 163; Pierre-Yves Donzé, "The Hybrid Production System and the Birth of the Japanese Specialized Industry: Watch Production at Hattori & Co.

(1900–1960)," *Enterprise & Society* 12, no. 2 (June 2011): 377–79.

57. "Enrollment in Institutions of Higher Education, by Sex, Attendance Status, and Type and Control of Institution: 1869–70 to Fall 1991," in Roger L. Geiger, *American Higher Education Since World War II* (PUP, 2019), 129; Martin A Trow, "Reflections on the Transition from Elite to Mass to Universal Access: Forms and Phases of Higher Education in Modern Societies Since WW2," in *International Handbook of Higher Education*, part 1, ed. James J. F. Forest and Philip G. Altbach (Springer, 2006), 245–46; T. J. Pempel, "The Politics of Enrollment Expansion in Japanese Universities," *Journal of Asian Studies* 33, no. 1 (November 1973): 67, 68.

58. Thomas Piketty, *Capital and Ideology*, trans. Arthur Goldhammer (HUP, 2020), 237, 423, 493; Fourastié, *Les Trente Glorieuses*, 165.

59. Ann-Kristin Bergquist, "Renewing Business History in the Era of the Anthropocene," *Business History Review* 93, no. 1 (Spring 2019): 5; and John R. McNeill and Peter Engelke, *The Great Acceleration: An Environmental History of the Anthropocene Since 1945* (HUP, 2014).

60. John Maynard Keynes, "National Self-Sufficiency," *Yale Review*, no. 22, June 1933, 755–69.

61. Simon Avenell, "Japan's Long Environmental Sixties and the Birth of a Green Leviathan," *Japanese Studies* 32, no. 3 (December 2012): 427.

62. Asahi Shinbun Keizaibu, ed., *Kutabare GNP: Kōdo keizai seichō no uchimaku* [*To Hell with GNP: The Lowdown on High Economic Growth*] (Asahi Shinbunsha, 1971), 121.

63. Brüggemeier, "Umweltgeschichte," 241.

64. Brüggemeier, "Umweltgeschichte," 242.

65. Rachel Carson, *Silent Spring* (Penguin Books, 1965), 21–23, 168.

66. Uekötter, *Im Strudel*, 587.

67. Donella H. Meadows et al., *The Limits to Growth: A Report for the Club of Rome's Project on the Predicament of Mankind* (Potomac Associates, 1972).

68. Meadows et al., *Limits to Growth*, 23.

69. Meadows et al., *Limits to Growth*, 87, 25.

70. Meadows et al., *Limits to Growth*, 25, 69, 73.

71. Tsuru Shigeto, *Gendai shihon shugi to kōgai* [*Modern Capitalism and Pollution*] (Iwanami Shoten, 1968), 57–58.

72. Marten Boon, "A Climate of Change? The Oil Industry and Decarbonization in Historical Perspective," *Business History Review* 93, no. 1 (Spring 2019): 101–25. See also Alfred D. Chandler, "Industrial Revolution and Institutional Arrangements," *Bulletin of the American Academy of Arts and Sciences* 33 (1980): 33–50; Hobsbawm, *Age of Extremes*, 262; Timothy Mitchell, "Ten Propositions on Oil," in *A Critical Political Economy of the Middle East and North Africa*, ed. Joel Beinin, Bassam Haddad, and Sherene Seikaly (Stanford UP, 2021), 84. For a related argument, see the important Alessandro Stanziani, *Capital Terre: Une histoire longue du monde d'après (XIIe–XXIe siècle)* (Éditions Payot, 2021).

73. Mitchell, "Ten Propositions on Oil," 71.

74. Mitchell, "Ten Propositions on Oil," 72.

75. Donald Horne, *The Lucky Country: Australia in the Sixties* (Penguin Books, 1964), 21.

76. Richard White, "'The Australian Way of Life,'" *Australian Historical Studies* 18, no. 73 (1979): 540–42.

77. Commonwealth Housing Commission, *First Interim Report, 21 October 1943* (Government Printer, 1943), 3.

78. "Cumberland Plan Explained," *Sydney Morning Herald*, May 30, 1951, 3; Ruth Park, *The Harp in the South* (Angus and Robertson, 1948), 1; "Master Plan 'in Operation,'" *Sydney Morning Herald*, July 28, 1951, 2.

79. Frank Bongiorno, *Dreamers and Schemers: A Political History of Australia* (La Trobe UP, 2022), 207–8, 212; Stuart Macintyre, *Australia's Boldest Experiment: War and Reconstruction in the 1940s* (NewSouth Publishing, 2015), 209–39; John Murphy, "The Commonwealth-State Housing Agreement of 1956 and the Politics of Home Ownership in the Cold War," Working Paper No. 50 (ANU Urban Research Program, December 1995), 1; Frost and Dingle, "Sustaining Suburbia," 31; and Greg Whitwell, *Making the Market: The Rise of Consumer Society* (McPhee Gribble Publishers, 1989), 40.

80. Advertisement for Hardie's Fibrolite asbestos-cement, *Bulletin*, March 13, 1957, 17; Lenore Layman, "Asbestos in the Built Environment," in *Asbestos in Australia: From Boom to Dust*, ed. Lenore Layman and Gail Phillips (Monash UP, 2019), 49, 56; Robin Boyd, *The Australian Ugliness*, 2nd ed. (Penguin Books, 1980), 98; "Homemakers' contest," *Australian Women's Weekly*, April 27, 1955, 76; "Peanut Recipe Contest," *Australian Women's Weekly*, March 4, 1959, 50; "Christmas Seal Contest," *Australian Women's Weekly*, June 2, 1951, 23; "Our Cookery Contest Winners," *Australian Women's Weekly*, November 23, 1955, 15; Stuart Macintyre, *A Concise History of Australia* (CUP, 1999), 216; and Anne Maree Payne, *Stolen Motherhood: Aboriginal Mothers and Child Removal in the Stolen Generations Era* (Lexington, 2021), 55, 556, 59.

81. Fourastié, *Les Trente Glorieuses*, 11–29.

82. For the quote, see Fourastié, *Les Trente Glorieuses*, 28–29.

83. Fourastié, *Les Trente Glorieuses*, 98, 109.

84. Fourastié, *Les Trente Glorieuses*, 36, 49, 88, 92, 109, 115.

85. Fourastié, *Les Trente Glorieuses*, 27, 36, 130–31, 139, 160.

86. For the quote, see Fourastié, *Les Trente Glorieuses*, 118.

87. Fourastié, *Les Trente Glorieuses*, 125.

88. Fourastié, *Les Trente Glorieuses*, 38, 57, 64–65, 74, 121, 127.

89. Fourastié, *Les Trente Glorieuses*, 97.

90. Gary Gerstle and Steve Fraser, *The Rise and Fall of the New Deal Order* (PUP, 1989).

91. Hobsbawm, *Age of Extremes*, 272–73.

92. Christian Democratic Union, Ahlener Programm: Zonenausschuß der CDU für die britische Zone, Ahlen, Westfalen, February 3, 1947, https://www.kas.de/c/document_li brary/get_file?uuid=76a77614-6803 -0750-c7a7-5d3ff7c46206&groupId =252038.

93. German Basic Law, Article 14, para. 1.

94. Manifeste, Mouvement Républicain Populaire (MRP), 24 November 1944, as cited in Donald Sassoon, *One Hundred Years of Socialism: The West European Left in the Twentieth Century* (New Press, 1996), 140. Lebret is cited in Giuliana Chamedes, "The Catholic Origins of Economic Development After World War II," *French Politics, Culture & Society* 33, no. 2 (2015): 64. See also Claire Toupin-Guyot, *Les intellectuels catholiques dans la société française: Le Centre catholique des intellectuels français, 1941–1976* (Presses Universitaires de Rennes, 2002), 201–22.

95. Eveline M. Burns, "The Beveridge Report," *American Economic Review* 33, no. 3 (1943): 513.

96. Brian Abel-Smith, "The Beveridge Report: Its Origins and Outcomes," *International Social Security*

Review 45, no. 1–2 (1992): 5. The citation refers to the English edition.

97. Hobsbawm, *Age of Extremes*, 269.

98. On the Milk and Fat Law (Milch- und Fettgesetz), see Veronika Settele, "Mensch, Kuh, Maschine: Kapitalismus im westdeutschen Kuhstall, 1950–1980," *Mittelweg 36*, no. 1 (2017), 48; OECD, *Collective Bargaining and Government Policies* (OECD, 1979); Gary Gerstle, *The Rise and Fall of the Neoliberal Order: America and the World in the Free Market Era* (OUP, 2022), 25, 43; and Piketty, *Capital and Ideology*, 31.

99. Hobsbawm, *Age of Extremes*, 269; Malcolm Sawyer, "Income Distribution and the Welfare State," in *The European Economy: Growth and Crisis*, ed. Andrea Boltho (OUP, 1982), 191, 192.

100. Hobsbawm, *Age of Extremes*, 270.

101. See, for example, Bradley W. Bateman, "Keynes and Keynesianism," in *The Cambridge Companion to Keynes*, ed. Roger E. Backhouse and Bradley W. Bateman (CUP, 2006), 271–74; Neil Brenner and Nik Theodore, "Cities and the Geographies of 'Actually Existing Neoliberalisms,'" *Antipode* 34, no. 3 (2002), 358; and Hobsbawm, *Age of Extremes*, 272. See also Ivo Maes, "The Spread of Keynesian Economics: A Comparison of the Belgian and Italian Experiences (1945–1970)," *Journal of the History of Economic Thought* 30, no. 4 (December 2008): 492.

102. "Assemblea generale ordinaria e straordinaria degli azionisti 10 aprile 1951," *Relazioni del Consiglio d'Amministrazione e dei Sindaci*, CSF, 7.

103. H. C. Coombs, *Trial Balance: Issues of My Working Life* (Sun Books, 1983), 3.

104. Coombs, *Trial Balance*, 3.

105. Peter A. Hall, ed., introduction to *The Political Power of Economic Ideas: Keynesianism Across Nations* (PUP, 1989), 4; and Alfred D. Chandler Jr., *The Visible Hand: The Managerial Revolution in American Business* (HUP, 1977), 495. See also Marglin, "Lessons of the Golden Age," 7; Hobsbawm, *Age of Extremes*, 282; and Bradley W. Bateman, "What Has Become of Keynesian Economics?," *Review of Keynesian Studies* 1, no. 1 (2019): 23–34.

106. Bateman, "What Has Become of Keynesian Economics?," 29.

107. On "military Keynesianism," see Timothy Barker, "'Don't Discuss Jobs Outside This Room': Reconsidering Military Keynesianism in the 1970s," in *The Military and the Market*, ed. Jennifer Mittelstadt and Mark R. Wilson (University of Pennsylvania Press, 2022), 135–49. On the "permanent war economy," see T. N. Vance (pseud. for Edward L. Sard), "The Permanent War Economy," *New International* 146 (1951): 29–45; and for a critical discussion, Marcel van der Linden, "Edward L. Sard (1913–1999), Theorist of the Permanent War Economy," in *Critique* 46, no. 1 (2018): 117–30.

108. Military expenditure by country from 1949 onward can be accessed at https://milex.sipri.org/sipri. For definitions of military expenditure and information about sources of original historical data, see https://www.sipri.org/databases/milex/sources-and-methods. Social expenditure as a share of GDP can be accessed at https://www.oecd.org/social/expenditure.html (accessed February 20, 2023). See also Timothy Barker, "'Don't Discuss Jobs Outside This Room,'" 138; and Takafusa, *Postwar Japanese Economy*, 46.

109. As cited in Charles Maier, *In Search of Stability* (CUP, 1987), 129.

110. "Décret No. 46-2 du 3 Janvier 1946," *Journal officiel de la République française*, January 4, 1946, 130–31, here 131. For Monnet and the agency, see Marie-Laure Djelic, "Genèse et fondements du plan Monnet: l'inspiration américaine," *Revue Française d'Études Américaines*, no. 68, March 1996: 77–86, here 81. See also Philippe Mioche, "The Origins of the Monnet Plan: How a Transitory Experiment Answered to Deep-Rooted Needs," EUI Working Paper No. 079 (European University Institute, Florence, 1984), 11.

111. Chalmers Johnson, *MITI and the Japanese Miracle: The Growth of Industrial Policy, 1925–1975* (Stanford UP, 1982), 114, 236, 265; and Takafusa, *Postwar Japanese Economy*, 89–90.

112. As cited in Takafusa, *Postwar Japanese Economy*, 90.

113. Takafusa, *Postwar Japanese Economy*, 91, 94.

114. As cited in Takafusa, *Postwar Japanese Economy*, 88.

115. Emmanuel Chadeau, "The Rise and Decline of State-Owned Industry in Twentieth-Century France," in *The Rise and Fall of State-Owned Enterprise in the Western World*, ed. Pier Angelo Toninelli (CUP, 2000), 185–86, 188–89; Ulrich Wengenroth, "The Rise and Fall of State-Owned Enterprise in Germany," in Toninelli, *Rise and Fall*, 119; Jesse B. Bump, "The Long Road to Universal Health Coverage: Historical Analysis of Early Decisions in Germany, the United Kingdom, and the United States," *Health Systems and Reform* 1, no. 1 (2015): 34; and T. R. Gourvish and N. Blake, *British Railways, 1948–73: A Business History* (CUP, 1986), 16. The French banks were Société Générale, Crédit Lyonnais, Comptoir National d'Escompte de Paris, and Banque Nationale pour le Commerce et l'Industrie.

116. "Political Deadlock in Italy," *Economist*, November 30, 1946.

117. Analysis generated from the table in Bernhard Ebbinghaus and Jelle Visser, "When Institutions Matter: Union Growth and Decline in Western Europe, 1950–1995," *European Sociological Review* 15, no. 2 (June 1999): 138, https://doi.org/10.1093/oxfordjournals.esr.a018257; Bob Hancke, "Trade Union Membership in Europe, 1960–1990: Rediscovering Local Unions," *British Journal of Industrial Relations* 31, no. 4 (1993): 594, https://doi.org/10.1111/j.1467-8543.1993.tb00415.x; and John Kenneth Galbraith, *American Capitalism: The Concept of Countervailing Power* (Houghton Mifflin, 1956), 146–48. See also the important book by Andrew Gordon, *The Evolution of Labor Relations in Japan: Heavy Industry, 1853–1955* (HUP, 1985).

118. Data on election results in Australia, France, the Netherlands, UK, Italy, Belgium, Sweden and Germany can be accessed at https://dataverse.harvard.edu/file.xhtml?fileId=6191736&version=1.1, last accessed November 1, 2022.

119. Maier, *Project-State and Its Rivals*, chap. 5; Glyn et al., "Rise and Fall of the Golden Age," 57; Werner, "Global Fordism in 1950s Urban China," 416; Gerstle, *Rise and Fall of the Neoliberal Order*, 24–25; and Christian Testorf, *Ein heisses Eisen: Zur Entstehung des Gesetzes über die Mitbestimmung der Arbeitnehmer von 1976* (Dietz, 2017).

120. Gerstle, *Rise and Fall of the Neoliberal Order*, 29, 38, 42–44; and Piketty, *Capital and Ideology*, 35.

121. Piketty, *Capital and Ideology*, 36; John Kenneth Galbraith, *The Affluent Society* (Houghton Mifflin, 1958); Daniel Bell, *The End of Ideology: On the Exhaustion of Political Ideas in the Fifties* (Free Press, 1960); Michael Denis Biddiss, *The Age of the Masses: Ideas and Society in Europe Since 1870* (Humanities Press, 1977); Salvador Giner, *Mass Society* (Martin Robertson, 1976); Gunnar Myrdal,

Beyond the Welfare State: Economic Planning and Its International Implications (Yale UP, 1960).

122. Daniel Bell, "The End of Ideology Revisited—Part I," *Government and Opposition* 23, no. 3 (1988): 131–50; and Ralf Dahrendorf, *Class and Class Conflict in Industrial Society* (Routledge, 1959).

123. Harold L. Wilensky, *The Welfare State and Equality: Structural and Ideological Roots of Public Expenditures* (University of California Press, 1974), 27; and Myrdal, *Beyond the Welfare State*, 66.

124. This is an argument also made by Maier, *Project-State and Its Rivals*, chap. 5. See also Joseph Schumpeter, *Capitalism, Socialism and Democracy* (Harper & Brothers, 1942), 61.

125. David Hamilton, "The Entrepreneur as Cultural Hero," *Social Science Quarterly* 39, no. 3 (1957): 250. For Schumpeter's celebration of entrepreneurship, see, for example, Schumpeter, *Capitalism, Socialism and Democracy*, 132.

126. "Managerial Prophet: Fleet Street, Monday Might," *Manchester Guardian*, October 14, 1958.

127. Louis M. Hacker, "Revolution (Made in U.S.A.)," *NYT*, May 14, 1950.

128. Maria Mies, *Patriarchy and Accumulation on a World Stage: Women in the International Division of Labour* (Zed Books, 1985), 101, 103.

129. Mies, *Patriarchy and Accumulation on a World Stage*, 110.

130. Lynn Karlsson, "Perspectives on Gendered Labour Legislation in Sweden During the 20th Century," in *Work Life, Work Environment and Work Safety in Transition: Historical and Sociological Perspectives on the Development in Sweden During the 20th Century*, ed. Annette Thörnquist (Arbetslivsinstitutet, 2001), 154, 157–58; Sten Carlsson, *Yrken och samhällsgrupper. Den sociala omgrupperingen i Sverige efter 1866* (Almqvist & Wiksell, 1968), 274; and Yvonne Hirdman, "Kvinnornas Eva," in *Gränslöst knivskarp. En bok om Eva Moberg*, ed. Cecilia Zadig (Leopard Förlag, 2017), 35–36.

131. Karen Schönwälder, "Why Germany's Guestworkers Were Largely Europeans: The Selective Principles of Post-War Labour Recruitment Policy," *Ethnic and Racial Studies* 27, no. 2 (2004): 250.

132. John Lie, "Zainichi: The Korean Diaspora in Japan," *Education About Asia* 14, no. 2 (Fall 2009): 17; David Chapman, *Zainichi Korean Identity and Ethnicity* (Routledge, 2007), 35; Robert Manduca, "In-

come Inequality and the Persistence of Racial Economic Disparities," *Sociological Science* 5, no. 8 (2018): 182; and Kennetta Hammond Perry, *London Is the Place for Me: Black Britons, Citizenship, and the Politics of Race* (OUP, 2015), 231–32.

133. Antina von Schnitzler, "Disciplining Freedom: Apartheid, Counterinsurgency, and the Political Histories of Neoliberalism," in *Market Civilizations: Neoliberals East and South*, ed. Quinn Slobodian and Dieter Plehwe (Zone Books, 2022), 169, 170.

134. Hobsbawm, *Age of Extremes*, 238, 275; and Maddison, *World Economy*, 50–51, 85.

135. Leon Fraser, "Trade Barriers and World Peace," *Proceedings of the Academy of Political Science* 19, no. 1 (May 1940): 56.

136. As cited in Frieden, *Global Capitalism*, 263–65.

137. Frieden, *Global Capitalism*, 263; and Hobsbawm, *Age of Extremes*, 271.

138. "Report by the Policy Planning Staff," Top Secret PPS/23 [Washington], 24 February 1948, as printed in *Foreign Relations of the United States, 1948*, vol. 1, part 2, *General; the United Nations*, ed. Neal H. Petersen, Ralph R. Goodwin, Marvin W. Kranz, and William Z. Slany (US Government Printing Office, 1976), annex, https://history.state.gov/historicaldocuments/frus1948v01p2/d4.

139. On the role of the United States, see, for example, Hilde Eliassen Restad, *U.S. Foreign Policy Traditions: Multilateralism vs. Unilateralism Since 1776* (Norwegian Institute for Defense Studies, 2010), 71–91; Matthias Schmelzer, *Freiheit für Wechselkurse und Kapital: Die Ursprünge neoliberaler Währungspolitik und die Mont Pèlerin Society* (Metropolis-Verlag, 2010), 41; Frieden, *Global Capitalism*, 257, 275; and Julian Germann, *Unwitting Architects: German Primacy and the Origins of Neoliberalism* (Stanford UP), 80.

140. Frieden, *Global Capitalism*, 255–56; Gerstle, *Rise and Fall of the Neoliberal Order*, 353.

141. Frieden, *Global Capitalism*, 258, 268; Hobsbawm, *Age of Extremes*, 276. On US GNP, see https://fred.stlouisfed.org/series/GNP. On the Marshall Plan, see Frieden, *Global Capitalism*, 267.

142. Jonathan Kirshner, "Keynes, Capital Mobility and the Crisis of Embedded Liberalism," *Review of International Political Economy* 6, no. 3 (1999): 314.

143. Robert G. Gilpin, *The Political Economy of International Relations* (PUP, 2016), 355. See also "Keynes, Capital Mobility and the Crisis of Embedded Liberalism," *Review of International Political Economy* 6, no. 3 (Autumn 1999): 314; David Harvey, *A Brief History of Neoliberalism* (OUP, 2005), 10; Germann, *Unwitting Architects*, 81; and Mark Blyth, *Great Transformations: Economic Ideas and Institutional Change in the 20th Century* (CUP, 2002), 127.

144. On hegemony, see Giovanni Arrighi, *The Long Twentieth Century: Money, Power, and the Origins of Our Time* (Verso, 2010), 28. On the economic effects of the order, see Frieden, *Global Capitalism*, 300.

145. L. Bosc, *Zollalliancen und Zollunionen in ihrer Bedeutung für die Handelspolitik der Vergangenheit und Zukunft*, trans. S. Schilder (E. Staude, 1907), 314; Thomas Lenschau, *Die amerikanische Gefahr* (F. Siemenroth, 1902), 47.

146. This paragraph is partly drawn (and cites verbatim) from Beckert, "American Danger," 1169. See also Auswärtiges Amt, Akten betreffend den Mitteleuropäischen Wirtschaftsverein, R 901, f2501, BA Berlin; Roger Battaglia, *Ein Zoll- und Wirtschaftsbündnis zwischen Österreich-Ungarn und Deutschland (Geschichte - Konstruktion - Einwendungen)* (W. Braumüller, 1917), 22–25. See also Paul von Lusse, *Der Frieden mittelst des Deutsch-französischen Zollvereins* (Bussenius, 1888); Guillaume de Molinari, "Union douanière de l'Europe centrale," *Journal des Économistes* 5 (February 1879): 309–18; Albert Schäffle, "Mitteleuropa und Weltbritannien," *Die Zukunft* 7 (May 1894): 252–63; and Frieden, *Global Capitalism*, 285. There is by now a vast literature on these themes, including Ian Kershaw, *Roller-Coaster: Europe, 1950–2017* (Allen Lane, 2018); Richard Swedberg, "The Idea of 'Europe' and the Origin of the European Union—A Sociological Approach," *Zeitschrift für Soziologie* 23, no. 5 (1994): 378–87; Werner Weidenfeld, Wolfgang F. Stolper, and Michael Hudson, "Economic Factors in the Origins of European Integration After the Second World War: A Political Scientist's View," *Zeitschrift für die gesamte Staatswissenschaft / Journal of Institutional and Theoretical Economics* 137, no. 3 (1981): 434–49; Nicholas Crafts, "West European Economic Integration Since 1950," in *Routledge Handbook of the Economics of Euro-*

pean Integration, ed. Harald Badinger and Volker Nitsch (Routledge, 2015), 3–21; Martin J. Dedman, *The Origins and Development of the European Union, 1945–1995* (Routledge, 1996); and Harold James, "The History of European Economic and Monetary Union," in *Routledge Handbook of the Economics of European Integration*, ed. Harald Badinger and Volker Nitsch (Routledge, 2015), 27; "Histoire du marché intérieur," https://www.touteleurope.eu/histoire/histoire-du-marche-interieur/.

147. Christof Van Mol and Helga de Valk, "Migration and Immigrants in Europe: A Historical and Demographic Perspective," in *Integration Processes and Policies in Europe: Contexts, Levels and Actors*, ed. Blanca Garcés-Mascareñas and Rinus Penninx (Springer International Publishing, 2016), 32.

148. Van Mol and De Valk, "Migration and Immigrants in Europe," 31.

149. Hobsbawm, *Age of Extremes*, 276; Knuth Dohse, "Foreign Workers and Workforce Management in West Germany," *Economic and Industrial Democracy* 5, no. 4 (1984): 498; and William M. Spellman, *Uncertain Identity: International Migrations Since 1945* (Reaktion Books, 2008), 25.

150. "Will Migrants Become the Victims Again?," *Time* (international ed.), December 3, 1973, title, 12.

151. Guido Tintori, "Italy: The Continuing History of Emigrant Relations," in *Emigration Nations: Policies and Ideologies of Emigrant Engagement*, ed. Michael Collyer (Palgrave Macmillan, 2013), 128, 132, 139; Philip L. Martin, *Unfinished Story: Turkish Labour Migration to Western Europe, with Special Reference to the Federal Republic of Germany* (ILO, 1991), 3, 25, 33, 44; Rossetos Fakiolas and Russell King, "Emigration, Return, Immigration: A Review and Evaluation of Greece's Postwar Experience of International Migration," *International Journal of Population Geography* 2, no. 2 (1996): 171–90; "Migration of Spain," *Britannica*, accessed October 9, 2022, https://www.britannica.com/place/Spain/Migration; Leszek A. Kosiński, "Yugoslavia and International Migration," *Canadian Slavonic Papers / Revue Canadienne Des Slavistes* 20, no. 3 (1978): 320; Nermin Abadan-Unat, *Turkish Workers in Europe 1960–1975: A Socio-Economic Reappraisal* (Brill, 1976), 21–22; Marcel Heiniger, "Einwanderung," in *Historisches Lex-*

ikon der Schweiz, July 12, 2006, https://hls-dhs-dss.ch/de/articles/007991/2006-12-07; Talip Küçükcan and Güngör Veyis, *Turks in Europe: Culture, Identity and Integration* (Turkevi Research Centre, 2009), 72.

152. Omar S. Valerio-Jiménez, "The United States–Mexican Border as Material and Cultural Barrier," in *Migrants and Migrations in Modern North America: Cross-Border Lives, Labor Markets, and Politics*, ed. Dirk Hoerder and Nora Faires (Duke UP, 2011), 240; Filiz Garip, *On the Move: Changing Mechanisms of Mexico–U.S. Migration* (PUP, 2017), 23, 51–53; Jaime R. Aguila and Brian Gratton, "Mirando atrás: Mexican Immigration from 1876 to 2000," in Hoerder and Faires, *Migrants and Migrations in Modern North America*, 64; Mary C. Waters, Reed Ueda, Helen B. Marrow, eds., *The New Americans: A Guide to Immigration Since 1965* (HUP, 2007), 510; Marie-Claude Blanc-Chaléard, "Transnationalism and Migration in the Colonial and Postcolonial Context. Emigrants from the Souf Area (Algeria) to Nanterre (France) (1950–2000)," in *A Century of Transnationalism: Immigrants and Their Homeland Connections*, ed. Nancy L. Green and Roger Waldinger (University of Illinois Press, 2016), 239; James F. Hollifield, *Immigrants, Markets, and States: The Political Economy of Postwar Europe* (CUP, 2006), 61; Pierre Milza and Marianne Amar, *L'immigration en France au XXe siècle* (Armand Colin, 1990), 42, 272–73; Margaret Byron and Stéphanie Condon, *Migration in Comparative Perspective: Caribbean Communities in Britain and France* (Routledge, 2008), 35, 56; and Ian R. G. Spencer, *British Immigration Policy Since 1939: The Making of a Multi-Racial Britain* (Routledge, 1997), 18.

153. Takeda Haruhito, *Kōdo seichō* (Iwanami Shoten, 2010), 96; Mizutani Michikazu, *Sengo nihon keizai shi: Seisan, ryūtsū, shōhi kōzō no henka* (Dōbunkan, 1991), 93, tables 3–20; and Ryohei Kada and Junko Goto, "Present Issues of Sustainable Land Use Systems and Rural Communities in Japan," in *Japanese and American Agriculture: Tradition and Progress in Conflict*, ed. Luther Tweeten, Cynthia L. Dishon, Wen S. Chert, Naraomi Imamura, and Masaru Morishima (Routledge, 2019), 44. See the important article by Tessa Morris-Suzuki, "Invisible Immigrants: Undocumented Migration and Border Controls in

Early Postwar Japan," *Journal of Japanese Studies* 32, no. 1 (Winter 2006): 119–53.

154. Sven Beckert, *Monied Metropolis: New York City and the Consolidation of the American Bourgeoisie, 1850–1896* (CUP, 2001), 43; John K. Walton, *The British Seaside: Holidays and Resorts in the Twentieth Century* (Manchester UP, 2000), 57–59; H. Spode, "Ein Seebad für zwanzigtausend Volksgenossen," in *Reisekultur in Deutschland: Von der Weimarer Republik zum Dritten Reich*, ed. Peter J. Brenner (Niemeyer, 1997), 7–47.

155. International Labour Office, *Working Conditions Laws Report 2012: A Global Review* (ILO, 2013), 18, https://labordoc.ilo.org/permalink/41ILO_INST/oti1e7/alma994838083402676.

156. Christopher M. Kopper, "The Breakthrough of the Package Tour in Germany After 1945," *Journal of Tourism History* 1, no. 1 (March 2009): 74.

157. Kopper, "Breakthrough of the Package Tour in Germany," 75.

158. United Nations World Tourism Organization, UN World Tourism Barometer, https://www.unwto.org/un-tourism-world-tourism-barometer-data; Luciano Segreto, Carles Manera, and Manfred Pohl, *Europe at the Seaside* (Berghahn Books, 2009), 22; and HC Deb. (6th ser.) (10 February 1983) (36) cols. 422–23W, https://api.parliament.uk/historic-hansard/written-answers/1983/feb/10/average-weekly-wage.

159. Marie Huber, "Creating Destinations for a Better Tomorrow: UN Development Aid for Cultural Tourism in the 1960s," *Journal of Contemporary History* 57, no. 2 (April 2022): 325, https://doi.org/10.1177/002200 9420974765.

160. Eric G. E. Zuelow, *A History of Modern Tourism* (Palgrave Macmillan, 2015), 149, 154.

161. Kopper, "Breakthrough of the Package Tour in Germany," 71–72; Thomas Kaiserfeld, "From Sightseeing to Sunbathing: Changing Traditions in Swedish Package Tours: From Edification by Bus to Relaxation by Airplane in the 1950s and 1960s," *Journal of Tourism History* 2, no. 3 (2010): 149–63.

162. Kopper, "Breakthrough of the Package Tour in Germany," 81.

163. Segreto, Manera, and Pohl, *Europe at the Seaside*, 38, 45–48.

164. Huber, "Creating Destinations for a Better Tomorrow," 317–40; and Robert J. Dunphy, "Why the Computer Chose Cancun," *NYT*, March 5, 1972.

165. Dunphy, "Why the Computer Chose Cancun."
166. Linda M. Ambrosie, "Myths of Tourism Institutionalization and Cancún," *Annals of Tourism Research* 54 (2015): 65–83; and María Bianet Castellanos, *A Return to Servitude: Maya Migration and the Tourist Trade in Cancún* (University of Minnesota Press, 2010), 82.
167. Hilary M. Beckles, *A History of Barbados: From Amerindian Settlement to Caribbean Single Market*, 2nd ed. (CUP, 2006), 147–51, 153–58; Christine Toppin-Allahar, "'De Beach Belong to We!' Socio-Economic Disparity and Islanders' Rights of Access to the Coast in a Tourist Paradise," *Oñati Socio-Legal Series* 5, no. 1 (2015): 308–9; interview with Professor Christian Cwik, University of Trinidad and Tobago, Barbados, November 14, 2016; Denise Brennan, "Women Work, Men Sponge, and Everyone Gossips: Macho Men and Stigmatized/ing Women in a Sex Tourist Town," *Anthropological Quarterly* 77, no. 4 (Fall 2004): 705–33; Reinaldo Funes Monzote, "The Greater Caribbean: From Plantation to Tourism," *Rachel Carson Center Perspectives* 7 (2013): 17–24; Lauren N. Duffy et al., "Tourism Development in the Dominican Republic," *Tourism and Hospitality Research* 16, no. 1 (January 2016): 36, 46; and Carlton Pomeroy and Steve Jacob, "From Mangos to Manufacturing: Uneven Development and Its Impact on Social Well-Being in the Dominican Republic," *Social Indicators Research* 65, no. 1 (2004), 78; for the information on Barbadian beaches I draw on an interview with Christian Cwik, Bridgetown, November 14, 2016.
168. Katie Rawson and Elliott Shore, *Dining Out: A Global History of Restaurants* (Reaktion Books, 2019); and Christoph Ribbat, *Im Restaurant: Eine Geschichte aus dem Bauch der Moderne* (Suhrkamp, 2016).
169. "Who 'Invented' the TV Dinner?," Library of Congress, November 19, 2019, https://www.loc.gov/everyday-mysteries/food-and-nutrition/item/who-invented-and-tv-dinner/; Robert G Phipps, *The Swanson Story: When the Chickens Flew Over the Coop* (Carl and Caroline Swanson Foundation Inc., 1977).
170. Ada Louise Huxtable, "Pow! It's Good-Bye History, Hello Hamburger," *NYT*, March 21, 1971.
171. Rawson and Shore, *Dining Out*, 191.
172. Steve Penfold, "Fast Food," in *The Oxford Handbook of Food History*,

ed. Jeffrey M. Pilcher (OUP, 2012), 287.
173. Penfold, "Fast Food," 287.
174. Ray Kroc, *Grinding It Out: The Making of McDonald's* (H. Regnery, 1977), 123.
175. On the company's history, see the terrific Marcia Chatelain, *Franchise: The Golden Arches in Black America* (Liveright Publishing, 2021); Penfold, "Fast Food," 291; and Robert L. Emerson, *The New Economics of Fast Food* (Van Nostrand Reinhold, 1990), 62.
176. Penfold, "Fast Food," 283.
177. Michelle Saksena, *America's Eating Habits: Food Away from Home* (USDA, Economic Research Service, 2018), 22.
178. "Wife Savers," KFC ad in *Better Homes & Gardens*, November 1968.
179. United Nations, *Economic Survey of Europe in 1971*, part 1, *The European Economy from the 1950s to the 1970s* (United Nations, 1972), 125.
180. Esping-Andersen, *Politics Against Markets*, 229–30; Charles S. Maier, "Consigning the Twentieth Century to History: Alternative Narratives for the Modern Era," *AHR* 105, no. 3 (June 2000), 823.
181. Glyn et al., "Rise and Fall of the Golden Age," 61, 72–73, 77, 81–83. For Giersch's quote, see Herbert Giersch, "Anmerkungen zum weltwirtschaftlichen Denkansatz," *Weltwirtschaftliches Archiv* 125 (1989): 10.
182. Kevin Gallagher, *Ruling Capital: Emerging Markets and the Reregulation of Cross-Border Finance* (Cornell UP, 2015), 31–33; Maurice Obstfeld and Alan M. Taylor, "International Monetary Relations: Taking Finance Seriously," *Journal of Economic Perspectives* 31, no. 3 (Summer 2017), 10–11; and Vanessa Ogle, "Archipelago Capitalism: Tax Havens, Offshore Money, and the State, 1950s–1970s," *AHR* 122, no. 5 (December 2017), 1446; and Blyth, *Great Transformations*, 128–29.
183. Blyth, *Great Transformations*, 129; Schmelzer, *Freiheit für Wechselkurse und Kapital*, 51, 52, 54; Barry Eichengreen, *Exorbitant Privilege: The Rise and Fall of the Dollar and the Future of the International Monetary System* (OUP, 2011), 49–50; Germann, *Unwitting Architects*, 80–82; and William Glenn Gray, "Floating the System: Germany, the United States, and the Breakdown of Bretton Woods, 1969–1973," *Diplomatic History* 31, no. 2 (2007), 296.
184. Blyth, *Great Transformations*, 127; Schmelzer, *Freiheit für Wechselkurse und Kapital*, 14, 56, 181, 189–90; Barry J. Eichengreen, *Glo-*

balizing Capital: A History of the International Monetary System (PUP, 1996), 49–50; Peter Isard, *Globalization and the International Financial System: What's Wrong and What Can Be Done* (CUP, 2005), 126–91; Ronald MacDonald, *Floating Exchange Rates: Theories and Evidence* (Routledge, 1988); and Maurice Obstfeld and Alan Taylor, *Global Capital Markets: Integration, Crisis, and Growth* (CUP, 2004).
185. Schmelzer, *Freiheit für Wechselkurse und Kapital*, 15, 191, 204, 206; Eichengreen, *Globalizing Capital*, 49–50; Robert Leeson, *Ideology and the International Economy: The Decline and Fall of Bretton Woods* (Palgrave Macmillan, 2003), 63–90; Obstfeld and Taylor, "International Monetary Relations," 11; Christoph Scherrer, *Globalisierung wider Willen: Durtchsetzung liberaler Außenwirtschaftspolitik in den USA* (Edition Sigma, 1999), 323; Jörg Huffschmid, *Politische Ökonomie der Finanzmärkte* (VSA, 2002), 106–32.
186. Jonas Kreienbaum, "Der verspätete Schock: Sambia und die erste Ölkrise von 1973/74," *Geschichte und Gesellschaft* 43, no. 4 (2017): 613; Fiona Venn, *The Oil Crisis* (Pearson Education Limited, 2002), 1, 154–62; Marino Auffant, "Globalizing Oil, Unleashing Capital: An International History of the 1970s Energy Crisis" (PhD diss., Harvard University, 2022), 112, 155; G. John Ikenberry, *Reason of State: Oil Politics and the Capacities of American Government* (Cornell UP, 1988), 1; and Fiona Venn, "The October 1973 Energy Crisis," H-Energy, https://networks.h-net.org/october-1973-energy-crisis-fiona-venn-h-energy-1973-energy-crisis-anniversary-discussion.
187. Christopher Dietrich, *Oil Revolution: Anti-Colonial Elites, Sovereign Rights, and the Economic Culture of Decolonialization* (CUP, 2017); Venn, "October 1973 Energy Crisis"; Venn, *Oil Crisis*, 1; Auffant, "Globalizing Oil, Unleashing Capital," 180, 237; Ikenberry, *Reason of State*, 7; Timothy Mitchell, *Carbon Democracy: Political Power in the Age of Oil* (Verso, 2013), 173–99, esp. 191, 192.
188. Mitchell, "Ten Propositions on Oil," 89.
189. See "Impact of Energy Crisis on LDC Balance of Payment," Department of State Airgram, 7 September 1974, and "The Energy Crisis and the Developing Countries: The Need for Additional Financing," July 1974, Bureau for Program and Police Coordination, AID, 49, both in folder IND—Power (Energy Crisis),

box 7, USAID Mission to Chile, Executive Office, Entry #P 189, RG 286, NARA CP.

190. C. Eduardo Altamura, "A New Dawn for European Banking: The Euromarket, the Oil Crisis and the Rise of International Banking," *Zeitschrift für Unternehmensgeschichte / Journal of Business History* 60, no. 1 (2015): 30; Willard R. Johnson and Ernest J. Willson III, "The 'Oil Crisis' and African Economies: Oil Wave on a Tidal Flood of Industrial Price Inflation," *Daedalus* 111, no. 2 (1982): 211–41; Edith Penrose, "Africa and the Oil Revolution: An Introduction," *African Affairs* 75 (1976): 277–83; K. A. Hammeed, "The Oil Revolution and African Development," *African Affairs* 75 (1976): 349–58; Giuliano Garavini, "Completing Decolonization: The 1973 'Oil Shock' and the Struggle for Economic Rights," *International History Review* 33, no. 3 (2011): 473–78; Altamura, "New Dawn for European Banking," 51; Kreienbaum, "Der verspätete Schock," 613; Venn, *Oil Crisis*, 629; and Auffant, "Globalizing Oil, Unleashing Capital," 7, 20.

191. Quinn Slobodian, "World Maps for the Debt Paradigm: Risk Ranking the Poorer Nations in the 1970s," *Critical Historical Studies* 8, no. 1 (Spring 2021): 9; Frieden, *Global Capitalism*, 283. See also https://www.ford.de/ford-entdecken/highlights-und-aktuelles/unser-erbe; https://www.wheelworldreviews.co.uk/motoring-news/ford-celebrates-100-years-in-great-britain; https://www.ford.com.ar/acerca-de-ford/institucional/corporativo/; https://www.ford.co.za/proudly-sa/, all accessed October 10, 2022; and Mira Wilkins, *The Maturing of Multinational Enterprise* (HUP, 1974), 374. On IBM, see *International Business Machines Corporation Annual Report—1957* (IBM Corporation, 1957), 21. On Newmont, see *Newmont Mining Corporation Annual Report—1957* (Newmont Mining Corporation, 1957), 6.

192. Hideki Yoshihara, "The Japanese Multinational," *Long Range Planning* 10, no. 2 (April 1977): 41. In later work, Yoshihara revised the number of Japanese multinationals in 1974 to thirty-seven, not the thirty-six listed in his initial workings. See Hideki Yoshihara, "Belated Changes in International Management of Japanese Multinationals," *Rikkyo Business Review*, no. 1 (2008): 4–15. See also Hideki Yoshihara, "Global Operations Managed by Japanese and in Japanese," in *Multi-*

nationals in a New Era, ed. J. H. Taggart, M. Berry, and M. McDermott (Palgrave Macmillan, 2001), 153–65; Hideki Yoshihara, *Kokusai keiei ron* (Housou Daigaku Kyouiku Sinkoukai, 2006); M. Y. Yoshino, "The Multinational Spread of Japanese Manufacturing Investment Since World War II," *Business History Review* 48, no. 3 (Autumn 1974): 361; M. Y. Yoshino, *Japan's Multinational Enterprises* (HUP, 2014), 1; Milan Balaban, "From European Periphery to Imperial Calcutta: The Story of a Czech Enterprise in Late Colonial India," unpublished paper presented at the Colonial Cities in Global Perspective Conference, Saint-Louis, Senegal, December 2019; and Tolliday, "From 'Beetle Monoculture' to the 'German Model,'" 123–24. For the original source cited by Tolliday, see *Volkswagenwerk Aktiengesellschaft Wolfsburg: Report for the Year 1970*, 17. The full document can be downloaded at https://www.volkswagenag.com/presence/konzern/images/teaser/history/chronik/annual-report/1970-Annual-Report.pdf. *Volkswagenwerk Aktiengesellschaft Wolfsburg:* Report for the Year 1975, 39, 42, https://www.volkswagen-group.com/en/publications/corporate/annual-report-1975-2293.

193. As cited in D. Elson and R. Pearson, "'Nimble Fingers Make Cheap Workers': An Analysis of Women's Employment in Third World Export Manufacturing," *Feminist Review* 7, no. 1 (1981): 93.

194. Hobsbawm, *Age of Extremes*, 277; Folker Fröbel, Jürgen Heinrichs, and Otto Kreye, *Die neue internationale Arbeitsteilung* (Rororo, 1977), 22, 23–28, 30, 33, 34, 52, 61.

195. Brenner and Theodore, "Cities and the Geographies of 'Actually Existing Neoliberalisms,'" 359.

196. Michel Aglietta, *Accumulation et régulation du capitalisme en longue période: L'exemple des États-Unis, 1870–1970* (Insee, 1974); Michel Aglietta, *Régulation et crises du capitalisme* (Calmann-Lévy, 1976; repr., 1997); *A Theory of Capitalist Regulation: The US Experience*, trans. David Fernbach (New Left Books, 1979); Mike Davis, *Prisoners of the American Dream: Politics and Economy in the History of the US Working Class* (Verso, 1986); David M. Gordon, Richard Edwards, and Michael Reich, *Segmented Work, Divided Workers: The Historical Transformation of Labour in the United States* (CUP, 1982); Alain Lipietz, *Mirages and Miracles: Crisis in Global Fordism* (La Découverte, 1985; repr., Verso, 1987); Alain Lipietz, "Towards

Global Fordism?," *New Left Review* 132 (March–April 1982): 33–47; Alain Lipietz, "Behind the Crisis: The Exhaustion of a Regime of Accumulation: A 'Regulation School Perspective' on Some French Empirical Works," *Review of Radical Political Economy* 18, no. 1–2 (1986): 13–32; Larry Hirschhorn, "The Post-Industrial Labor Process," *New Political Science* 2, no. 3 (1981): 11–32.

197. Jennifer Ferreira, "Post-Fordism," in Frederick F. Wherry, Juliet B. Schor, eds., *Encyclopedia of Economics and Society* (Sage, 2016), 1301.

198. Daniel Bell, *The Coming of Post-Industrial Society* (Basic Books, 1973).

199. Michael Piore and Charles Sabel, *The Second Industrial Divide: Possibilities for Prosperity* (Basic Books, 1984).

200. J. Lovering, "Fordism, Post-Fordism and Flexible Specialization," in *International Encyclopedia of Human Geography*, ed. Rob Kitchin and Nigel Thrift (Elsevier, 2009), 232–42. See also Herman Kahn, *The Emerging Japanese Superstate: Challenge and Response* (Prentice Hall, 1970); Satochi Kamata, *Toyota, l'usine du désespoir* (Editions Ouvrières, 1976); *Japan in the Passing Lane: Insider's Account of Life in a Japanese Auto Factory*, trans. Tatsuru Akimoto (Unwin Hyman, 1984); Satochi Kamata, *L'envers du miracle* (Maspero, 1980); Michio Morishima, *Why Has Japan "Succeeded"?* (CUP, 1982); Taiichi Ono, *The Toyota Production System: Beyond Large-Scale Production* (Productivity Press, 1988).

201. Vanessa Ogle, "'Funk Money': The End of Empires, the Expansion of Tax Havens, and Decolonization as an Economic and Financial Event," *Past & Present* 249, no. 1 (2020): 219–20, 229, 239, 248; Ogle, "Archipelago Capitalism," 1433, 1435; Gabriel Zucman, Teresa Lavender Fagan, and Thomas Piketty, *The Hidden Wealth of Nations: The Scourge of Tax Havens* (University of Chicago Press, 2015), 35. On the importance of the difference in legal structures, see Ogle, "Archipelago Capitalism," 1432; Patrick Neveling, "The Global Spread of Export Processing Zones, and the 1970s as a Decade of Consolidation," in *Contesting Deregulation*, eds. Knud Andresen and Stefan Müller (Berghahn, 2017), 23–40.

202. For France, see "Unemployment Rate: Aged 15–74: All Persons for France," at https://fred.stlouisfed.org/series/LRUN74TTFRA156S.

For Germany, see "Arbeitslosenquote der Bundesrepublik Deutschland in den Jahren 1950 bis 2021," accessed January 23, 2023, https://de.statista.com/statistik/daten/studie/1127090/umfrage/arbeitslosenquote-der-bundesrepublik-deutschland/. See also the data collected by the OECD. For unemployment, see https://data.oecd.org/unemp/unemployment-rate.html (accessed January 23, 2023). For price inflation, see https://data.oecd.org/price/inflation-cpi.htm (accessed November 20, 2022).

203. Daniel Stedman Jones, *Masters of the Universe: Hayek, Friedman, and the Birth of Neoliberal Politics* (PUP, 2012), 215; and HC DEB (5th ser.) (17 November 1965) (720) cols. 1165–67, https://hansard.parliament.uk/Commons/1965-11-17/debates/06338c6d-ebdd-4876-a782-59cbd531a28a/EconomicAffairs?highlight=stagflation.

204. "Britain's Struggle with Stagflation," *Time*, September 14, 1970.

205. "Britain's Struggle with Stagflation," *Time*, September 14, 1970; "Stagflation," Google Books N-Gram Viewer, accessed November 7, 2022, https://books.google.com/ngrams/graph?content=stagflation&year_start=1800&year_end=2019&corpus=26&smoothing=3. Michael Szenberg et al., "Introduction: The Significance of Paul A. Samuelson in the Twenty-First Century," in *Samuelsonian Economics and the Twenty-First Century*, ed. Michael Szenberg et al. (OUP, 2006), 12; Richard G. Lipsey, "The Philips Curve and an Assumed Unique Macroeconomic Equilibrium in Historical Context," *Journal of the History of Economic Thought* 38, no. 4 (December 2016): 420; and Aurélien Goutsmedt, "From the Stagflation to the Great Inflation: Explaining the US Economy of the 1970s," *Revue d'économie politique* 131, no. 3 (May–June 2021): 559.

206. Joseph J. Minarik, "The Distributional Effects of Inflation and Their Interpretation," in *Stagflation: The Causes, Effects and Solutions* (Joint Economic Committee, US Congress, 1980), 225–77; Leon Lindberg and Charles Maier, *The Politics of Inflation and Economic Stagnation: Theoretical Approaches and International Case Studies* (Brookings Institution, 1985). As argued in Melinda Cooper, *Family Values: Between Neoliberalism and the New Social Conservatism* (Zone Books, 2017), 27.

207. George Gilder, *Wealth and Poverty* (Basic Books, 1981), chap. 9.

208. Arthur F. Burns, "The Anguish of Central Banking," the 1979 Per Jacobsson Lecture, Belgrade, Yugoslavia, September 30, 1979; and Leo Panitch and Sam Gindin, *The Making of Global Capitalism: The Political Economy of American Empire* (Verso, 2012), 164–72.

209. Javier Blas and Jack Farchy, *The World for Sale: Money, Power, and the Traders Who Barter the Earth's Resources* (Random House, 2021); and Peter Koerner, "Zaire: Indebtedness and Kleptocracy," in *The Poverty of Nations: A Guide to the Debt Crisis—From Argentina to Zaire*, ed. Elmar Altvater et al. (Zed Books, 1991), 230–33.

210. Panitch and Gindin, *Making of Global Capitalism*, 215–16; and Raúl Rojas, "Mexico: Five Years of Debt Crisis," in Altvater et al., *Poverty of Nations*, 169–80.

211. Marglin, "Lessons of the Golden Age," 2, 17, 19; and Armstrong and Glyn (1986) as cited in Marglin, "Lessons of the Golden Age," 18.

212. Thomas B. Edsall, *The New Politics of Inequality* (W. W. Norton, 1984), 128; Kim Phillips-Fein, "Business Conservatives and the Mont Pèlerin Society," in *The Road from Mont Pèlerin: The Making of the Neoliberal Thought Collective*, ed. Philip Mirowski and Dieter Plehwe (HUP, 2009), 281.

213. François Denord, "French Neoliberalism and Its Divisions: From the Colloque Walter Lippmann to the Fifth Republic," in Mirowski and Plehwe, *Road from Mont Pèlerin*, 53.

214. Diane Kunz, *Butter and Guns: America's Cold War Economic Diplomacy* (Free Press, 1997); William Bundy, *A Tangled Web: The Making of Foreign Policy in the Nixon Presidency* (Hill and Wang, 1998); Paul Volcker and Toyoo Gyohten, *Changing Fortunes: The World's Money and the Threat to American Leadership* (Times Books, 1992); John S. Odell, *U.S. International Monetary Policy: Markets, Power, and Ideas as Sources of Change* (PUP, 1982), 324; Eric Helleiner, *States and the Reemergence of Global Finance: From Bretton Woods to the 1990s* (Cornell UP, 1994), 115; Robert Leeson, *Ideology and International Economy: The Decline and Fall of Bretton Woods* (Palgrave Macmillan, 2003); and Schmelzer, *Freiheit für Wechselkurse und Kapital*, esp. 323.

215. John Carson-Parker, "Commentary: The Options Ahead for the Debt Economy," *Business Week*, October 12, 1974, 120.

216. Gerstle, *Rise and Fall of the Neoliberal Order*, 110; Ben Jackson, "The Think-Tank Archipelago: Thatcherism and Neo-Liberalism," in *Making Thatcher's Britain*, ed. Ben Jackson and Robert Saunders (CUP, 2012), 46–47; and Neil Rollings, "Cracks in the Post-War Keynesian Settlement? The Role of Organized Business in the Rise of Neoliberalism Before Margaret Thatcher," *Twentieth Century British History* 24, no. 4 (2013): 641.

217. Mircea Raianu, *Tata: The Global Corporation That Built Indian Capitalism* (HUP, 2021), 182.

218. Raianu, *Tata*, 182.

219. Diego Maiorano, *Autumn of the Matriarch: Indira Gandhi's Final Term in Office* (OUP, 2015), 17. For Tata's support, see Sanjaya Baru, *India's Power Elite: Class, Caste and Cultural Revolution* (Penguin Books India, 2021), 144.

220. Baru, *India's Power Elite*, 144.

221. J. R. D. Tata, "A Myth," in *Keynote: Excerpts from His Speeches and Chairman's Statements to Shareholders*, ed. S. A. Sabavala and R. M. Lala (Tata Press, 1986), 63.

222. Karin Fischer, "The Influence of Neoliberals in Chile Before, During, and After Pinochet," in Mirowski and Plehwe, *Road from Mont Pèlerin*, 311–14; Marion Fourcade-Gourinchas and Sarah L. Babb, "The Rebirth of the Liberal Creed: Paths to Neoliberalism in Four Countries," *American Journal of Sociology* 108, no. 3 (November 2002): 544.

223. Jeanette Hartmann, "Le capital privé en Tanzanie (1962–1982)," *Politique africaine* 26 (1987): 85–86. On the demands of businesspeople, see the list in Jeanette Hartmann, "Development Policy-Making in Tanzania 1962–1982: A Critique of Sociological Interpretations" (PhD diss., University of Hull, 1983), 335–56.

224. As cited in Thomas David and Pierre Eichenberger, "'A World Parliament of Business?' The International Chamber of Commerce and Its Presidents in the Twentieth Century," *Business History* 65, no. 2 (2023): 260; Quinn Slobodian, *Globalists: The End of Empire and the Birth of Neoliberalism* (HUP, 2018), 21.

225. Eva Moberg, "Kvinnans villkorliga frigivning," in *Unga liberaler. Nio inlägg i idédebatten*, ed. Hans Hederberg (Bonnier, 1961), 70.

226. Moberg, "Kvinnans villkorliga frigivning," 72.

227. Moberg, "Kvinnans villkorliga frigivning," 72. It should be noted

that *villkorlig frigivning* is also the Swedish term for "parole."

228. Hirdman, "Kvinnornas Eva," 37–38; Lisbeth Larsson, "Eva Moberg," *Svenskt kvinnobiografiskt lexicon*, accessed April 25, 2022, https://www.skbl.se/sv/artikel/Eva Moberg; and Moberg, "Kvinnans villkorliga frigivning" 76–77.

229. Hirdman, "Kvinnornas Eva," 39.

230. Hirdman, "Kvinnornas Eva," 40.

231. Giandomenica Becchio, *A History of Feminist and Gender Economics* (Routledge, 2020), 124.

232. Nancy Fraser, *Fortunes of Feminism: From State-Managed Capitalism to Neoliberal Crisis* (Verso, 2013), 3–4, 215–16; Nanette Funk, "Contra Fraser on Feminism and Neoliberalism," *Hypatia* 28, no. 1 (Winter 2013): 179.

233. Judy Klemesrud, "Women on the March," August 30, 1970, *NYT*, 125.

234. Lucy Delap, *Feminisms: A Global History* (University of Chicago Press, 2020), 281–82; Klemesrud, "Women on the March," 125; Maud Anne Bracke, *Women and the Reinvention of the Political: Feminism in Italy, 1968–1983* (Routledge, 2014), 13, 70, 79; Dorothy Kaufmann-McCall, "Politics of Difference: The Women's Movement in France from May 1968 to Mitterrand," *Signs* 9, no. 2 (Winter 1983): 283; and Finn Mackay, *Radical Feminism: Feminist Activism in Movement* (Palgrave Macmillan, 2015), 46.

235. Cecilia Conrad, "Feminist Economics: Second Wave, Tidal Wave, or Barely a Ripple?," in *The Legacy of Second-Wave Feminism in American Politics*, ed. Angie Maxwell and Todd Shields (Palgrave Macmillan, 2018), 107.

236. Camila Orozco Espinel and Rebeca Gomez Betancourt, "A History of the Institutionalization of Feminist Economics Through Its Tensions and Founders," *New Historical Perspectives on Women and Economics*, supplement to *History of Political Economy* 54, no. S1 (2022): S160; and Espinel and Betancourt, "A History of the Institutionalization of Feminist Economics," 160.

237. Conrad, "Feminist Economics," 98; Becchio, *History of Feminist and Gender Economics*, 135–37, 142.

238. Mies, *Patriarchy and Accumulation on a World Stage*, xvi.

239. Becchio, *History of Feminist and Gender Economics*, 122–23; Ann Chadeau and Annie Fouquet, "Peut-on mesurer le travail domestique?," *Économie et Statistique* 136 (1981), no. 1, 29–42; Margaret Benston, "Political Economy of Wom-en's Liberation," *Monthly Review* 21, no. 4 (September 1969): 13–27; and Mariarosa Dalla Costa and Selma James, *The Power of Women and the Subversion of Community* (Falling Wall Press, 1972).

240. Gerstle, *Rise and Fall of the Neoliberal Order*, 9, 54–56.

241. Students for a Democratic Society (US), *Port Huron Statement* (1962), Sixties Project, accessed April 20, 2023, http://www2.iath.virginia.edu/sixties/HTML_docs/Resources/Primary/Manifestos/SDS_Port_Huron.html.

242. As cited in Gerstle, *Rise and Fall of the Neoliberal Order*, 100.

243. "Mario Savio Speech on the Steps of Sproul Hall," December 2, 1964, Bay Area Television Archive, MP4 file, accessed April 20, 2023, https://diva.sfsu.edu/collections/sfbatv/bundles/238941.

244. Caroline Hoefferle, "Great Expectations: Sloman's Essex and Student Protest in the Long Sixties," in *Utopian Universities: A Global History of the New Campuses of the 1960s*, ed. Miles Taylor and Jill Pellew (Bloomsbury Academic, 2020), 112.

245. Hoefferle, "Great Expectations," 113.

246. Kristin Ross, *May '68 and Its Afterlives* (University of Chicago Press, 2002), 3–4.

247. Bertram Gordon, "The Eyes of the Marcher: Paris, May 1968—Theory and Consequences," in *Student Protest: The Sixties and After*, ed. Gerard J. DeGroot (Routledge, 2014), 40–41; and Ben Mercer, *Student Revolt in 1968: France, Italy and Germany* (CUP, 2020), 6.

248. Adam Rome, "'Give Earth a Chance': The Environmental Movement and the Sixties," *JAH* 90, no. 2 (September 2003): 535–38; and Simon Avenell, "From Fearsome Pollution to Fukushima: Environmental Activism and the Nuclear Blind Spot in Contemporary Japan," *Environmental History* 17, no. 2 (2012): 248.

249. Andersson, *Between Growth and Security*, 65–67.

250. Esping-Andersen, *Politics Against Markets*, 230–32; Jonas Pontusson, "Behind and Beyond Social Democracy in Sweden," *New Left Review* 143, no. 1 (1984); Jonas Pontusson, "Radicalization and Retreat in Swedish Social Democracy," *New Left Review* 165, no. 1 (1987); and Marcus Wallenberg to L. Amundsen, transcript of handwritten note (undated, but in November 1969), as cited in Olsson, *Att förvalta sitt pund*, 356–57. See also Jonas Pontusson and Peter Swenson, "Labor Markets, Production Strategies, and Wage Bargaining Institutions: The Swedish Employer Offensive in Comparative Perspective," *Comparative Political Studies* 29, no. 3 (1996): 223–250; and Andersson, *Between Growth and Security*, 1–2.

251. Glyn et al., "Rise and Fall of the Golden Age," 40.

Chapter 17: Riding the Tiger: A Neoliberal Age, 1973–2008

1. US Embassy Santiago to the Department of State, "What's Wrong with Chile's Economic Policies," 27 December 1974, in folder Economic Matters GEN, Foreign Service Posts of the Department of State, Chile, US Embassy Santiago, box 58, Classified Central Subject Files, 1964–1974, entry no. P 161, RG 84, NARA CP, declassified under authority NND 989625. The report was signed by Ambassador Popper but most likely drafted by Samuel S. Hart, the economic attaché of the embassy.

2. Handwritten note on "Political Section" stationery, n.d., in folder Economic Matters GEN, Foreign Service Posts of the Department of State, Chile, US Embassy Santiago, box 58, Classified Central Subject Files, 1964–1974, entry no. P 161, RG 84, NARA CP, declassified under authority NND 989625.

3. Neoliberalism unfolded under a wide variety of political regimes, some democratic, others not. See Quinn Slobodian and Dieter Plehwe, eds., *Market Civilizations: Neoliberals East and South* (Zone Books, 2022), 18.

4. Peter Winn, "The Pinochet Era," in *Victims of the Chilean Miracle: Workers and Neoliberalism in the Pinochet Era, 1973–2002*, ed. Peter Winn (Duke UP, 2004), 17. For evidence, and the quote, see "Chile—1972—Debt Rescheduling," confidential memorandum, undated, from Mr. Kleine AA/LA to Mr. Kubisch, in Materials Taken from Mr. Fischer's Safe, September 1973, box 13, Department of State, Bureau of Inter-American Affairs, Office of Bolivia-Chilean Affairs, Records Relating to Chile, 1965–1975, entry no. A 1-5757, Record Group 59, NARA CP; Claudia Kedar, "The International Monetary Fund and the Chilean Chicago Boys, 1973–7: Cold Ties Between Warm Ideological Partners," *Journal of Contemporary History* 54 (2019): 199; Charles A. Meyer and Willis C. Armstrong to the Secretary, Secret Action Memorandum, in Materials Taken

from Mr. Fischer's Safe, September 1973, box 13, Department of State, Bureau of Inter-American Affairs, Office of Bolivia-Chilean Affairs, Records Relating to Chile, 1965–1975, Entry A 1-5757, Record Group 59, NARA CP. There are many debates swirling around the issue of the precise nature of US involvement in Chilean politics, but it is beyond doubt and exceedingly well documented that the United States government played an important role.

5. Angela Vergara, *Copper Workers, International Business, and Domestic Politics in Cold War Chile* (Penn State Press, 2010), 1, 3, 11, 13, 18, 35, 66, 87, 90, 97, 128, 148, 153, 155–56; K. Ross Toole, "A History of the Anaconda Copper Mining Company: A Study in the Relationship Between a State and a Corporation, 1880–1950" (PhD diss., UCLA, 1954), 1. On Frei, see Theodore H. Moran, *Multinational Corporations and the Politics of Dependence: Copper in Chile* (PUP, 1975), 119, 146.

6. Pablo Pryluka, "Advertising Pinochet: The Cold War Limits to a Neoliberal Crusade," *International History Review* 45, no. 2 (2023): 416–17; Víctor Herrero, *Agustín Edwards Eastman: Una Biografía Desclasificada del Dueño de El Mercurio* (Debate, 2014), 257–58, 396; Johanna Gautier Morin and Thierry Rossier, "The Interaction of Elite Networks in the Pinochet Regime's Macroeconomic Policies," *Global Networks* 21 (2021): 340; and US Embassy Santiago, "What's Wrong with Chile's Economic Policies."

7. Department of State Airgram, US Embassy Santiago, 31 August 1973, box 732, General Records of the Department of State, Subject Number Files, 1970–73, Economic, RG 59, entry no. 1613, NARA CP.

8. Morin and Rossier, "Interaction of Elite Networks," 349. For "the Brick," see Eduardo Silva, "Capitalist Coalitions, the State, and Neoliberal Economic Restructuring: Chile, 1973–88," *World Politics* 45, no. 4 (1992): 539–40. For the quotation, see Department of State Airgram, US Embassy Santiago.

9. Pablo Neruda, "Cuándo de Chile," in Pablo Neruda, *Obras Completas*, 4th ed., vol. 1, trans. Franco Paz (Editorial Losada, 1973), 846.

10. Vergara, *Copper Workers*, 180–81; Biblioteca del Congreso Nacional de Chile, Diarios de Sesiones, Junta de Gobierno (11 September 1973 to 16 June 1974), Acta no. 18 (October 9, 1973); "Labor Conditions and Relations in Chile's Big Three Copper Mines," report to Department of State by US Embassy Santiago, 24 May 1974, folder LAB 1—General—1974, Foreign Service Posts of the Department of State, Chile, US Embassy Santiago, box 58, Classified Central Subject Files, 1964–1974, entry no. P 161, RG 84, NARA CP; and Winn, "Pinochet Era," 22.

11. Airgram, US Embassy Santiago, 30 October 1973, in box 732, General Records of the Department of State, Subject Number Files, 1970–73, Economic, entry no. 1613, RG 59, NARA CP.

12. Biblioteca del Congreso Nacional de Chile, Diarios de Sesiones, Junta de Gobierno (11 September 1973 to 16 June 1974), Acta no. 13 (October 2, 1973); Biblioteca del Congreso Nacional de Chile, Diarios de Sesiones, Acta no. 18.

13. On this division, see Winn, "Pinochet Era," 25; Karin Fischer, "The Influence of Neoliberals in Chile Before, During, and After Pinochet," in *The Road from Mont Pèlerin: The Making of the Neoliberal Thought Collective*, ed. Philip Mirowski and Dieter Plehwe (HUP, 2009), 317, 337; US Embassy Santiago to Department of State, memo, 18 January 1974; folder E 2, General Reports and Statistics, 1974, Foreign Service Posts of the Department of State, Chile, US Embassy Santiago, box 58, Classified Central Subject Files, 1964–1974, entry no. P 161, RG 84, NARA CP; Economic Trends Report for Chile, US Embassy Santiago, 14 June 1974, folder E 2: General Reports and Statistics, 1974, Foreign Service Posts of the Department of State, Chile, US Embassy Santiago, box 58, Classified Central Subject Files, 1964–1974, entry no. P 161, RG 84, NARA CP; Report, US Embassy Santiago, "Chile's Economy One Year After Allende," 2 October 1974, signed by David H. Popper, Ambassador, folder E 2: General Reports and Statistics, 1974, Foreign Service Posts of the Department of State, Chile, US Embassy Santiago, Classified Central Subject Files, 1964–1974, entry no. P 161, RG 84, NARA CP, declassified under authority MWD 989625, 8 December 2022; and Airgram, Embassy Santiago, 30 October 1973. See also Sebastian Edwards, "Estabilización con liberalización: Diez años del experimento chileno con políticas de mercado libre 1973–1983," *Revista de Estudios Públicos* 14 (1984): 17; Kedar, "International Monetary Fund and the Chilean Chicago Boys," 186; US Embassy Santiago, confidential report, "Chile's New Economic Policies," 5 October 1973, in folder Economic Matters, Foreign Service Posts of the Department of State, Chile, US Embassy Santiago, box 58, Classified Central Subject Files, 1964–1974, entry no. P 161, RG 84, NARA CP.

14. Telegram, US Embassy Santiago to Department of State, Congressional Presentation, 1 March 1974, in Folder Economic Matters GEN, Foreign Service Posts of the Department of State, Chile, US Embassy Santiago, box 58, Classified Central Subject Files, 1964–1974, entry no. P 161, RG 84, NARA CP, declassified under authority NND 989625.

15. "Memo, Department of State, US Embassy Santiago, 23 January 1974, "Foreign Credits to Chile in 1973 and Plans for 1974," folder FN 14, Foreign Debt, 1974, Foreign Service Posts of the Department of State, Chile, US Embassy Santiago, box 58, Classified Central Subject Files, 1964–1974, entry no. P 161, RG 84, NARA CP.

16. US Economic Trends Report for Chile, Embassy Santiago, 14 June 1974; Department of State telegram, US Embassy Santiago, 15 July 2024, Subject: Chilean Foreign Investment Statute, folder ECIN 1, General Policy, Plans, 1974, Foreign Service Posts of the Department of State, Chile, US Embassy Santiago, box 58, Classified Central Subject Files, 1964–1974, entry no. P 161, RG 84, NARA CP; and Kedar, "International Monetary Fund and the Chilean Chicago Boys," 187, 188.

17. US Embassy Santiago, "Chile's New Economic Policies."

18. Confidential report, "Economic Program Goes Forward," US Embassy Santiago, 17 October 1973, folder Economic Matters, Foreign Service Posts of the Department of State, Chile, US Embassy Santiago, box 58, Classified Central Subject Files, 1964–1974, entry no. P 161, RG 84, NARA CP.

19. For the presence of, and importance of, economists in the deliberations of the junta, see, for example, Biblioteca del Congreso Nacional de Chile, Diarios de Sesiones, Junta de Gobierno (11 September 1973 to 16 June 1974), Acta No. 5 (19 September 1973); Biblioteca del Congreso Nacional de Chile, Diarios de Sesiones, Acta No. 18; Kedar, "International Monetary Fund and the Chilean Chicago Boys," 179–201; Samuel Hart, "Ambassador Samuel F. Hart," interview with Charles Stuart Kennedy, June 12, 1992, Association for Diplomatic Studies and

Training Foreign Affairs Oral History Project, 76–77.

20. Hart, "Ambassador Samuel F. Hart," 77.

21. Morin and Rossier, "Interaction of Elite Networks," 340.

22. On the homegrown traditions, see also Kedar, "International Monetary Fund and the Chilean Chicago Boys," 181; and Bernhard Walpen, *Die offenen Feinde und ihre Gesellschaft. Eine hegemonietheoretische Studie zur Mont Pèlerin Society* (VSA, 2004), 178. For Peru, in particular, see Cesar Castillo-Garcia, "Waves of Neoliberalism: Revisiting the Authoritarian Patterns of Capitalism in South America," part 1, Working Paper 05/2022 (Department of Economics, New School for Social Research, New York, 2022). The argument about the Indigenous roots of neoliberalism is made by Johanna Bockman, "Democratic Socialism in Chile and Peru: Revisiting the 'Chicago Boys' as the Origin of Neoliberalism," *Comparative Studies in Society and History* 61, no. 3 (2019): 654–79. See also US Embassy Santiago to Department of State, mailing and note, 31 August 1971, in box 734, General Records of the Department of State, Subject Number Files, 1970–73, Economic, entry no. 1613, RG 59, NARA CP.

23. Kedar, "International Monetary Fund and the Chilean Chicago Boys," 180, 186, 190; Winn, "Pinochet Era," 26–27, 188; Sebastian Edwards and Leonidas Montes, "Milton Friedman in Chile: Shock Therapy, Economic Freedom, and Exchange Rates," *Journal of the History of Economic Thought* 42, no. 1 (2020): 108; Vergara, *Copper Workers*, 183; Dieter Plehwe, introduction to Mirowski and Plehwe, *Road from Mont Pèlerin*, 2, 32; Fischer, "Influence of Neoliberals in Chile," 337–38; and Edwards, "Estabilización con liberalización," 5–6. On the local roots of neoliberalism and its break with a very long tradition in Chilean economic policymaking, see Peter Winn, ed., introduction to Winn, *Victims of the Chilean Miracle*, 4, 10; and Morin and Rossier, "Interaction of Elite Networks," 2.

24. Edwards, "Estabilización con liberalización," 12, 14–16; Winn, *Victims of the Chilean Miracle*, 3; Kedar, "International Monetary Fund and the Chilean Chicago Boys," 197; and Edwards and Montes, "Milton Friedman in Chile," 118. On the textile industry, see Peter Winn, "'No Miracle for US': The Textile Industry in the Pinochet Era, 1973–1998," in Winn, *Victims of the Chilean Mira-*

cle, 125–63. See also Fischer, "Influence of Neoliberals in Chile," 321–25; and Simon Collier and William F. Sater, *A History of Chile, 1808–2002* (CUP, 2004), 366, 371. See, too, the earlier discussions in the 1 March 1974 telegram, US Embassy Santiago; Frank Adamson and Björn Åstrand, "Privatization or Public Investment? A Global Question," in *Global Educational Reform: How Privatization and Public Investment Influence Education Outcomes*, ed. Frank Adamson, Björn Åstrand, and Linda Darling-Hammond (Routledge, 2016), 6; Abelardo Castro-Hidalgo and Lilian Gómez-Álvarez, "Chile: A Long-Term Neoliberal Experiment and Its Impact on the Quality and Equity of Education," in Adamson et al., *Global Educational Reform*, 36; and Winn, "Pinochet Era," 31–38.

25. Vergara, *Copper Workers*, 180. See also Airgram, US Embassy Santiago, 10 October 1973. In the embassy's summary, the plan acknowledged that "[t]he real income of all Chileans would be reduced during an initial period." See US Embassy Santiago,"Chile's New Economic Policies," NARA; Edwards, "Estabilización con liberalización," 9; US Embassy Santiago, "Chile's Economy One Year After Allende," NARA; and Kedar, "International Monetary Fund and the Chilean Chicago Boys," 198.

26. Confidential Memorandum, from Fred M. Shaver, Valparaiso, to James Halsema, March 22, 1974, in File Pol Chile—Political General 1974, box 14, Department of State, Bureau of Inter-American Affairs, Office of Bolivia-Chilean Affairs, Records Relating to Chile, 1965–1975, Entry A 1-5757, Record Group 59, NARA CP.

27. Secret Letter, Ambassador David H. Popper to Harry W. Shlaudeman, Department of State, Santiago, March 25, 1974, in File Pol Chile—Political General 1974, box 14, Department of State, Bureau of Inter-American Affairs, Office of Bolivia-Chilean Affairs, Records Relating to Chile, 1965–1975, Entry A 1-5757, Record Group 59, NARA CP.

28. US Embassy Santiago, "Chile's New Economic Policies."

29. Airgram, US Embassy Santiago, 10 October 1973.

30. Airgram, US Embassy Santiago, 19 December 1973, box 733, General Records of the Department of State, Subject Number Files, 1970–73, Economic, entry no. 1613, RG 59, NARA CP; and Airgram, US Em-

bassy Santiago, 12 December 1973, box 733, General Records of the Department of State, Subject Number Files, 1970–73, Economic, entry no. 1613, RG 59, NARA CP.

31. Hart, "Ambassador Samuel F. Hart," 74.

32. Morin and Rossier, "Interaction of Elite Networks," 358; and Fischer, "Influence of Neoliberals in Chile," 338.

33. On the performance of the Chilean economy after 1980, see Collier and Sater, *History of Chile*, 395; Ricardo French-Davis, *Economic Reforms in Chile: From Dictatorship to Democracy*, 2nd ed. (Palgrave Macmillan, 2010), 237–39; and Winn, *Victims of the Chilean Miracle*, 4.

34. As cited in Bruce Caldwell and Leonidas Montes, "Friedrich Hayek and His Visits to Chile," *Review of Austrian Economics* 28, no. 3 (2015): 298.

35. As cited in Alessandro Santoni y Sebastián Sanchez, "Los 'amigos de Chile': El régimen de Pinochet y la Gran Bretaña de Thatcher (1979–1988)," *Revista de historia (Concepción)* 29, no. 1 (2022), 412.

36. Edwards and Montes, "Milton Friedman in Chile," 105–6, 125–27. Though in private correspondence, interviews, and writings from around the time of his second visit, Friedman emphasized the importance of political freedom. "Milton Friedman elogió la política monetaria chilena." See archived copy of *La Nación*, 20 November 1981, caja 146, Sociedad Mont Pèlerin, Recortes de Prensa, Viña del Mar noviembre 1981, Folletos y Newsletters, 1977–1980, Bibliotecas Universidad Adolfo Ibáñez, UAI Digital Repository.

37. US Government Memorandum from Economic Counselor Moorhead Kennedy, 10 June 1977, container 10, folder EOF 3-Economic Analysis FY 77, USAID Mission to Chile, Executive Office, entry no. P 189, RG 286, NARA CP. The memo reports on a lecture by Arnold Harberger, director of the Economic Institute of the University of Chicago.

38. Friedrich Hayek, *The Constitution of Liberty* (University of Chicago Press, 1960); and Walpen, *Die offenen Feinde und ihre Gesellschaft*, 176.

39. Pryluka, "Advertising Pinochet," 416–30. See "Report on a Visit to Chile from the 13th to the 16th of November 1973," box 27, Chile 3/3, JWT Collections, David M. Rubenstein Rare Books and Manuscripts Library, Duke University, as cited in Pryluka, "Advertising Pinochet," 418.

40. Letter from Jack Webster to Don Johnston, 23 July 1974, in Johnston Papers, box 24, Chile, 1973m 2/2, JWT Collections, as cited in Pryluka, "Advertising Pinochet," 420.

41. On Chile's role as a vanguard of the neoliberal revolution, see also Robert A. Packenham and William Ratliff, "What Pinochet Did for Chile: The Late Strongman Ruled Harshly but Left Behind the Most Successful Country in Latin America," *Hoover Digest*, January 30, 2007.

42. As Charles S. Maier has pointed out in a brilliant essay. See Charles S. Maier, "Cosigning the Twentieth Century to History: Alternative Narratives for the Modern Era," *AHR* 105, no. 3 (June 2000): 825. See also, for example, Gary Gerstle, *The Rise and Fall of the Neoliberal Order: America and the World in the Free Market Era* (OUP, 2022).

43. Karl Marx and Friedrich Engels, *The Communist Manifesto*, trans. Paul Sweezy (Monthly Review Press, 1964), 7.

44. Per H. Hansen, "From Finance Capitalism to Financialization: A Cultural and Narrative Perspective on 150 Years of Financial History," *Enterprise & Society* 15, no. 4 (December 2014): 627.

45. For these numbers, see International Labour Organization, "Employment in Industry (% of Total Employment) (Modeled ILO Estimate)—China," World Bank Group, accessed August 8, 2023, https://data.worldbank.org/indicator/SL.IND.EMPL.ZS?locations=CN. See also International Labour Organization, "Employment in Agriculture (% of Total Employment) (Modeled ILO Estimate)—China," World Bank Group, accessed August 8, 2023, https://data.worldbank.org/indicator/SL.AGR.EMPL.ZS?locations=CN.

46. Michigan Employment Security Commission, *Michigan Statistical Abstract 1996* (University of Michigan Press, 1996), 461. "World Production of Motor Vehicles, by Selected Country: 1959–1994," Table XIV-1, Organisation Internationale des Constructeurs d'Automobiles, accessed August 10, 2023, https://www.oica.net/category/production-statistics/2010-statistics/; World Semiconductor Trade Statistics, *Historical Billings Report*, https://www.wsts.org/67/Historical-Billings-Report, accessed August 10, 2023; "Number of Smartphones Sold to End Users Worldwide from 2007 to 2023," accessed August 10, 2023, https://www.statista.com/statistics/263437

/global-smartphone-sales-to-end-users-since-2007/; Hamilton Moses, E. Ray Dorsey, David H. M. Matheson, and Samuel O. Thier, "Financial Anatomy of Biomedical Research," *JAMA* 294, no. 11 (2005): 1333–42; and International Economics Division, Economic Research Service, US Department of Agriculture, *World Indices of Agricultural and Food Production*, 1973–82. (See also *Statistical Bulletin No. 697*, 1983.)

47. Author's calculations.

48. Eric Hobsbawm, *The Age of Extremes: The Short Twentieth Century, 1914–1992* (Michael Joseph, 1994), 362, 364.

49. Numbers refer to value added in manufacturing. The statistics are from the United Nations Statistics Division, accessed June 3, 2023, https://unstats.un.org/unsd/snaama/Downloads. On the world-historical importance of the rise of China, see also Pablo Pryluka, "We Can't Go Back to a Golden Age of Capitalism: An Interview with Branko Milanovic," *Jacobin*, February 2021.

50. James Heintz, "Low-Wage Manufacturing and Global Commodity Chains: A Model in the Unequal Exchange Tradition," *Cambridge Journal of Economics* 30, no. 4 (2006): 507–20.

51. Jesus Felipe and Aashish Mehta, "Deindustrialization? A Global Perspective," *Economics Letters* 149 (2016): 148–51.

52. For population of each year, see Shenzen Statistics Office, *Shenzhen Statistical Yearbook* 4, Fig. 1–3, Line "Year-end Permanent Population," (Shenzhen: China Statistics Press, 2020), accessed January 15, 2023, https://web.archive.org/web/20210727043152/http://tjj.sz.gov.cn/attachment/0/736/736628/8386382.pdf; Andrew Liu (Villanova), "Hong Kong and the Neoliberal World Economy," paper presented at the Global History Seminar, Harvard University, March 8, 2021, 6, 17, 19, 24; Tao Yitao and Lu Zhiguo, *China's Economic Zones: Design, Implementation and Impact* (Paths International, 2015), 7; and Paul Cheney, "István Hont, the Cosmopolitan Theory of Commercial Globalization, and Twenty-First Century Capitalism, paper (in author's possession) presented at Global History Seminar, Harvard University, April 5, 2021, 9, 11.

53. For population of each year, see Shenzen Statistics Office, *Shenzhen Statistical Yearbook*, 3–5. See also Yitao and Zhiguo, *China's Economic Zones*, 14, 22, 34; Pun Ngai,

"Women Workers and Precarious Employment in Shenzhen Special Economic Zone, China," *Gender and Development* 12, no. 2 (2004): 29; Douglas Zhihua Zeng, *Building Engines for Growth and Competitiveness in China: Experience with Special Economic Zones and Industrial Clusters* (World Bank, 2010), 58–60.

54. Chusheng Lin, *Red Capitalism in South China: Growth and Development of the Pearl River Delta* (UBC Press, 1997); Zeng, *Building Engines for Growth and Competitiveness in China*, 58; David Harvey, *A Brief History of Neoliberalism* (OUP, 2005), 139; Joshua Freeman, *Behemoth: A History of the Factory and the Making of the Modern World* (W. W. Norton, 2019), 271.

55. Jan Luiten van Zanden and Daan Marks, *An Economic History of Indonesia, 1800–2010* (Routledge, 2012), 188, 190.

56. Makoto Ikedo, director of Minebea Thai Ltd., as cited in Peter Janssen, "Minebea on a Roll," *Asian Business* 25, no. 3 (1989): 18.

57. Chris Baker and Pasuk Phongpaichit, *A History of Thailand* (OUP, 2014), 204, 209; Edith Terry, *How Asia Got Rich: Japan, China, and the Asian Miracle* (Routledge, 2015), 148; Yongyuth Chalamwong, "Thailand: The Economic Concentration, the Labour Market and Migration," in *Labour Migration and the Recent Financial Crisis in Asia* (OECD Publishing, 2000), table 16.

58. Robert B. South, "The Flying Geese Metaphor: Export-Oriented Manufactures in Mexico," *Regional Studies* 50, no. 9 (2016): 1483–95.

59. Janet Abu-Lughod, "Urbanization in the Arab World and the International System," in *The Urban Transformation of the Developing World*, ed. J. Gugler (OUP, 1996), 200. See also the stimulating discussion in Salma Abouelhossein, "Sugar Towns: Urban Ecology, Planning, and the Shifting Geographies of Labor in the Making of Egypt's Sugar Belt" (PhD diss., Harvard University, forthcoming).

60. Abouelhossein, "Sugar Towns."

61. José Lannes, "The Gerdau Group: The Creation of a Global Competitor," *Apuntes* 41, no. 75 (2014): 141, 143–44, 148–49, 160, 163.

62. Lourdes Casanova and Julian Kassum, *The Political Economy of an Emerging Global Power: In Search of the Brazil Dream* (Palgrave Macmillan, 2014), 76; "Saudi Arabian Oil Company," in *International Directory of Company Histories*, ed. Steven

Long, Derek Jacques, and Paula Kepos (St. James Press, 2016), 447–49; and David Fig, "The State of Extraction: The New Scramble for Africa," in *The State of Power*, ed. Nick Buxton (Transnational Institute, 2014), 2. See "Our History," Saudi Aramco, accessed August 22, 2023, https://www.aramco.com/en/who-we-are/overview/our-history; "Tata Group Heritage," Tata Group, accessed August 22, 2023, https://www.tata.com/about-us/tata-group-our-heritage/Our-Timeline-The-Expansion-Years-1969–2017; Dr. Reddy's "Journey So Far," accessed August 22, 2023, https://www.drreddys.com/who-we-are#Journey-so-far; and Jack Ma, 《马云：活着就是为了颠覆世界》[Jack Ma: To Live Is to Turn the World Upside Down] (Nanfang Chubanshe, 2014), 129, 136.

63. On some of its implications, see the excellent Richard Freeman, "China, India and the Doubling of the Global Labor Force: Who Pays the Price of Globalization," *Asia Pacific Journal* 3 (August 2005); "Labour Force, Total—China," World Bank Group: World Development Indicators Database, accessed August 15, 2023, https://data.world bank.org/indicator/SL.TLF.TOTL .IN?locations=CNm; International Labour Organization, "Employment in Industry (% of Total Employment) (Modeled ILO Estimate)—China"; and Eli Friedman and Ching Kwan Lee, "Remaking the World of Chinese Labour: A 30-Year Retrospective," *British Journal of Industrial Relations* 48 (September 2010): 508, 516.

64. Isabella M. Weber, *How China Escaped Shock Therapy: The Market Reform Debate* (Routledge, 2021), 109; Lin, *Red Capitalism in South China*, 98; Friedman and Lee, "Remaking the World of Chinese Labour," 516; and Harvey, *A Brief History of Neoliberalism*, 138.

65. Ngai, "Women Workers and Precarious Employment," 97.

66. Friedman and Lee, "Remaking the World of Chinese Labour," 507, 509, 510, 513, 515, 518; Cing Kwan Lee, "Rights Activism in China in Context," in *Contexts* 7 (August 2008), 14–39.

67. Alan Emery, "Privatization, Neoliberal Development, and the Struggle for Workers' Rights in Post-Apartheid South Africa," *Social Justice* 33, no. 3 (2006): 6–19; and A. Wilson, C. de Jager, L. Gcabashe, and J. B. Sibanyoni, "Amnesty Decision AC/99/0349," in *Truth and Rec-*

onciliation Commission of South Africa Report (1999).

68. Hwasook Nam, *Women in the Sky: Gender and Labor in the Making of Modern Korea* (Cornell UP, 2022), 3, 125, 141, 144.

69. As cited in Hwasook Nam, *Women in the Sky*, 149.

70. Nam, *Women in the Sky*, 153.

71. Nam, *Women in the Sky*, 157.

72. Nam, *Women in the Sky*, 155.

73. Nam, *Women in the Sky*, 156.

74. Nam, *Women in the Sky*, 162.

75. Hagen Koo, *Korean Workers: The Culture and Politics of Class Formation* (Cornell UP, 2001), 1.

76. For a flavor of that discussion, see David Harvey, *The Condition of Post-Modernity: An Enquiry into the Origins of Cultural Change* (Blackwell, 1989).

77. Andrew Smith and Kirsten Greer, "Uniting Business History and Global Environmental History," *Business History* 59, no. 7 (2017): 987–1009.

78. For this argument, see also Jim Glassman, *Drums of War, Drums of Development: The Formation of a Pacific Ruling Class and Industrial Transformation in East and Southeast Asia, 1945–1980* (Brill, 2018), 625–26.

79. Andrew B. Bernard, Valerie Smeets, and Frederic Warzynski, "Rethinking Deindustrialization," *Economic Policy* 32, no. 89 (January 2017): 15, https://doi.org/10.1093 /epolic/eiw016; and Robert Rowthorn and Ramana Ramaswamy, *Deindustrialization: Its Causes and Implications*, Economic Issues No. 10 (International Monetary Fund, 1997), 7.

80. Rowthorn and Ramaswamy, *Deindustrialization: Its Causes and Implications*, 2, 11.

81. Rowthorn and Ramaswamy, *Deindustrialization: Its Causes and Implications*, 2; European Foundation for the Improvement of Living and Working Conditions, *ERM REPORT 2008: More and Better Jobs: Patterns of Employment Expansion in Europe* (Office for Official Publications of the European Communities, 2008), 56; Our World in Data, "Manufacturing Jobs as a Share of Total Employment, 2007," accessed August 18, 2024, https://www.euro found.europa.eu/en/publica tions/2009/erm-report-2009 -restructuring-recession; and Stephen Bazen and Tony Thirlwall, *Deindustrialization*, Studies in the UK Economy (Heinemann Educational, 1992), 15.

82. Margaret Cowell, *Dealing with Deindustrialization: Adaptive Resil-*

ience in American Midwestern Regions (Routledge, 2015), 52. In 1980, 125,716 manufacturing workers labored in the central city of Detroit; twenty years later, fewer than half as many did. See "SOCDS Census Data: Output for Detroit City, MI," State of the Cities Data System, accessed 10 August 2023, https:// socds.huduser.gov/CEnsus/jobind .odb?msacitylist=2160.0*260002200 0*1.0&metro=msa; *Employment and Earnings, States and Areas, 1939–72*, Bulletin 1370-10 (US Department of Labor Statistics, 1974), 317; Fran Shor, "Auto De(Con)Struction: The Spatial Fixes and Racial Repercussions of Detroit's Deindustrialization," *Perspectives on Global Development and Technology* 15, no. 1–2 (2016): 86, 88.

83. Eminem, "So Far . . ."

84. Eminem, "Detroit vs. Everybody."

85. "Top 100 Biggest Cities in the US | 2022 Population Data," Biggest US Cities, accessed May 31, 2023, https://www.biggestuscities.com/; Nate Cohn, "New Republic—the Decline of Detroit in Five Maps," *Geography Bulletin* 47, no. 2 (n.d.): 22–24; Thomas J. Sugrue, *The Origins of the Urban Crisis: Race and Inequality in Postwar Detroit*, rev. ed. (PUP, 2014), 261–62; and Monica Davey and Mary Williams Walsh, "Plan to Exit Bankruptcy Is Approved for Detroit," *NYT*, November 7, 2014.

86. Kenth Lärk, "Bilfabriken där Volvo avskaffade löpande bandet," *Industrihistoria i Väst* 13, no. 1 (2017): 9–11; Paul Bernstein, "The Learning Curve at Volvo," *Columbia Journal of World Business* 23, no. 4 (Winter 1988), 87–95; Steven Tolliday, "The Diffusion and Transformation of Fordism: Britain and Japan Compared," in *Between Imitation and Innovation: The Transfer and Hybridization of Productive Models in the International Automotive Industry*, ed. Robert Boyer (OUP, 1998), 75.

87. Larry Summers, quoted in Hansen, "From Finance Capitalism to Financialization," 624.

88. Crédit Mobilier, assemblées générales procès verbaux, 29 April 1854, as cited in Charlotte Robertson, "Governing Finance: Public Credit and the Interventionist State, 1852–1860," paper (in author's possession) presented at Harvard Business School, November 14, 2023.

89. Gerald A. Epstein, ed., introduction to *Financialization and the World Economy* (Edward Elgar, 2005), 3. See also Greta Krippner, "The Fi-

nancialization of the American Economy," *Socio-Economic Review* 3 (May 2005): 174; Gerald A. Epstein and Arjun Jayadev, "The Rise of Rentier Incomes in OECD Countries: Financialization, Central Bank Policy and Labor Solidarity," in Epstein, *Financialization and the World Economy*, 54; Melinda Cooper, *Family Values: Between Neoliberalism and the New Social Conservativism* (Zone Books, 2017), 124; Jürgen Kocka, "Kapitalismus und Demokratie," *Archiv für Sozialgeschichte* 56 (2016): 45; Aled Davies, "The Roots of Britain's Financialised Economy," in *The Neoliberal Age? Britain Since the 1970s*, ed. Aled Davies, Ben Jackson, and Florence Sutcliffe-Braithwaite (UCL Press, 2021), 300; and Hobsbawm, *Age of Extremes*, 278.

90. Gerard O'Regan, *A Brief History of Computing* (Springer, 2008), 185–88, 190–212, 217, 226; Janet Abbate, *Inventing the Internet* (MIT Press, 1999), 203; and Luis Andrés et al., "Diffusion of the Internet: A Cross-Country Analysis," Policy Research Working Paper No. 4420 (World Bank, Latin America and the Caribbean Region, Sustainable Development Department, December 2007), 2–3; "Number of Internet Users Worldwide from 2005 to 2023," Statista, accessed February 5, 2025, https://www.statista.com/statistics/273018/number-of-internet-users-worldwide/.

91. Lea Haller, *Transithandel: Geld- und Warenstroeme im globalen Kapitalismus* (Suhrkamp, 2019), esp. 23–24, 375–98; and Haller, "Globale Geschäfte," *NZZ Geschichte* 4 (January 2016): 94.

92. Patrick Neveling, "Export Processing Zones / Special Economic Zones," in *International Encyclopedia of Anthropology*, ed. H. Callan (John Wiley & Sons, 2018), 2180, 2181.

93. Patrick Neveling, "Sonderwirtschaftszonen und globale Warenketten," in *Globale Warenketten und ungleiche Entwicklung Arbeit, Kapital, Konsum, Natur*, ed. K. Fischer, C. Reiner, and C. Staritz (Mandelbaum Verlag, 2021), 51; Neveling, "Export Processing Zones / Special Economic Zones," 2179, 2180; Patrick Neveling, "The Global Spread of Export Processing Zones, and the 1970s as a Decade of Consolidation," in *Contesting Deregulation: Debates, Practices and Developments in the West Since the 1970s*, ed. Knud Andresen and Stefan Müller (Berghahn Books, 2017), 23–40; and Christopher Müller, "From Foreign Concessions to Special Economic Zones: Decolonial-

ization and Foreign Investment in Twentieth-Century Asia," in *Decolonization and the Cold War: Negotiating Independence*, ed. Leslie James and Elisabeth Leake (Bloomsbury, 2015), 239–53.

94. Hobsbawm, *Age of Extremes*, 281; and Quinn Slobodian, *Globalists: The End of Empire and the Birth of Neoliberalism* (HUP, 2018), 236.

95. William Leach, *Country of Exiles: The Destruction of Place in American Life* (Pantheon Books, 1999), 36.

96. Leach, *Country of Exiles*, 49–50, 53.

97. Barry Eichengreen, *Globalizing Capital: A History of the International Monetary System* (PUP, 1996); Arjun Appadurai, *Modernity at Large: Cultural Dimensions of Globalization* (University of Minnesota Press, 1996); Thomas L. Friedman, *The Lexus and the Olive Tree: Understanding Globalization* (Farrar, Straus and Giroux, 1999); Joseph Stiglitz, *Globalization and Its Discontents* (W. W. Norton, 2002); Peter Singer, *One World: The Ethics of Globalization* (Yale UP, 2004); Martin Wolf, *Why Globalization Works* (Yale UP, 2005); and Dani Rodrik, *The Globalization Paradox: Democracy and the Future of the World Economy* (W. W. Norton, 2011).

98. Kofi Annan, "Address to World Economic Forum in Davos," speech, Davos, Switzerland, January 31, 1999, United Nations; Anne O. Krueger (first deputy managing director of the IMF), "Supporting Globalization," speech, International Monetary Fund, Washington DC, September 26, 2002; and Pascal Lamy (director general of the World Trade Organization), "Humanising Globalization," speech, World Trade Organization, Santiago, Chile, January 30, 2006, transcript at https://www.wto.org/english/news_e/sppl_e/sppl16_e.htm.

99. Herbert Giersch, "Freer Trade for Higher Employment and Price Level Stability," in *Toward a New World Trade Policy: The Maidenhead Papers*, ed. C. Fred Bergsten (Lexington Books, 1975), 53; Dieter Plehwe and Quinn Slobodian, "Landscapes of Unrest: Herbert Giersch and the Origins of Neoliberal Economic Geography," *Modern Intellectual History*, 2017, 1–31.

100. Herbert Giersch, "Anmerkungen zum weltwirtschaftlichen Denkansatz," in *Weltwirtschaftliches Archiv* 125 (1989): 2, 15.

101. Giersch, "Anmerkungen zum weltwirtschaftlichen Denkansatz," 1, 6. On the cosmopolitanism of much of the neoliberal "thought col-

lective," see also Plehwe, introduction to Mirowski and Plehwe, *Road from Mont Pèlerin*, 3; Giersch, "Freer Trade for Higher Employment and Price Level Stability," 49–59; and Plehwe and Slobodian, "Landscapes of Unrest," 24.

102. Pierre Bourdieu, *Acts of Resistance Against the Tyranny of the Market* (New Press, 1988), 91.

103. Samir Amin, *The Implosion of Capitalism* (Pluto Press, 2014), 51.

104. Neil Brenner and Nik Theodore, "Cities and the Geographies of 'Actually Existing Neoliberalisms,'" *Antipode* 34, no. 3 (2002): 350, 354, 364–66, 373.

105. Gerstle, *Rise and Fall of the Neoliberal Order*, 10. See Jan Breman and Marcel van der Linden, "Informalizing the Economy: The Return of the Social Question at a Global Level," in *Development and Change* 45 (2015): 923; and Pryluka, "We Can't Go Back to a Golden Age of Capitalism."

106. Gerstle, *Rise and Fall of the Neoliberal Order*, 1, 11, 15. On Germany, see Neil Brenner, "'Building Euro-Regions': Locational Politics and the Political Geography of Neoliberalism, in Postunification Germany," *European Union and Regional Studies* 7 (2000): 324.

107. William J. Clinton, "Address Before a Joint Session of the Congress on the State of the Union," speech, Washington, DC, January 27, 2000, American Presidency Project.

108. Friedrich August von Hayek, "The Intellectuals and Socialism," *University of Chicago Law Review* 16, no. 3 (1949): 417–33, reprinted in *The Intellectuals: A Controversial Portrait*, ed. George B. de Huszar (Free Press, 1960), 384.

109. Walpen, *Die offenen Feinde und ihre Gesellschaft*, 277.

110. Slobodian, *Globalists*, 83.

111. On von Mises, see also Plehwe, introduction to Mirowski and Plehwe, *Road from Mont Pèlerin*; and Slobodian, *Globalists*, 11.

112. Milton Friedman, *Capitalism and Freedom* (University of Chicago Press, 2002). See, for example, 202.

113. Slobodian, *Globalists*, 107.

114. Slobodian, *Globalists*, 12, 57.

115. Slobodian, *Globalists*, 9.

116. Plehwe, introduction to Mirowski and Plehwe, *Road from Mont Pèlerin*, 47, 105, 115; Quinn Slobodian and Dieter Plehwe, "Neoliberals Against Europe," in *Mutant Neoliberalism: Market Rule and Political Rupture*, ed. William Callison and Zachary Manfredi (Fordham UP, 2020), 105; and Jennifer Bair,

"Taking Aim at the New International Economic Order," in Mirowski and Plehwe, *Road from Mont Pèlerin*, 347–85. For ambivalence, see Quinn Slobodian, "Demos Veto and Demos Exit: The Neoliberals Who Embraced Referenda and Secession," *Journal of Australian Political Economy* 86 (2020): 19–36.

117. Jamie Peck, *Constructions of Neoliberal Reason* (OUP, 2010); Slobodian, *Globalists*, 2, 6, 92–93, 95, 100, 112, 267, 273, 284; and Philip Mirowski, "The Zero Hour of History: Is Neoliberalism Some Sort of 'Mode of Producton'?," *Development and Change* 47 (2016): 588–89. On the insulation from politics, see Gerstle, *Rise and Fall of the Neoliberal Order*, 88. There is disagreement in the literature regarding the relationship between classical liberalism and neoliberalism, but both draw on the state to create what they deem "natural" or "efficient." For the debate, see, for example, Gerstle, *Rise and Fall of the Neoliberal Order*, 6; and Mirowski, "Zero Hour of History," 588.

118. Ludwig von Mises, *Liberalismus* (Gustav Fischer, 1927), 51.

119. Plehwe, "Looking Back to the Future of Neoliberalism Studies," in *Market Civilizations: Neoliberals East and South*, ed. Slobodian and Plehwe (Zone Books, 2022), 246, 342. The quote is on p. 344.

120. François Denord, "French Neoliberalism and Its Division: From the Colloque Walter Lippmann to the Fifth Republic," in Mirowski and Plehwe, *Road from Mont Pèlerin*, 49.

121. Ronald M. Hartwell, *A History of the Mont Pèlerin Society* (Liberty Fund, 1995), 41–42.

122. Walpen, *Die offenen Feinde und ihre Gesellschaft*, 283, 284.

123. Plehwe, introduction to *Road from Mont Pèlerin*, 11–12; Slobodian, *Globalists*, 3, 126–27; Walpen, *Die offenen Feinde und ihre Gesellschaft*, 36, 283–84; and Denord, "French Neoliberalism and Its Division," 45. For the quotation, see von Hayek, "Intellectuals and Socialism," 417–33, reprinted in de Huszar, *Intellectuals*, 384.

124. Plehwe, introduction to Mirowski and Plehwe, *Road from Mont Pèlerin*.

125. B. R. Shenoy, "Free Market Economy for India" (1959), 5, as cited in Aditya Balasubramanian, "From Socialism to Swatantra: Market Liberalism in India, 1943–1970" (senior thesis, Harvard University, 2013), 65.

126. Plehwe, introduction to Mirowski and Plehwe, *Road from*

Mont Pèlerin, 4. See also Dieter Plehwe and Katja Walther, "In the Shadows of Hayek and Friedman: Quantitative Analysis as an Exploratory Instrument in Socio-Historic Network Research," in *Re-Inventing Western Civilisation: Transnational Reconstructions of Liberalism in Europe in the Twentieth Century*, ed. Hagen Schulz-Forberg and Niklas Olsen (Cambridge Scholars Publishing, 2014), 41–68.

127. Plehwe, introduction to Mirowski and Plehwe, *Road from Mont Pèlerin*, 5, 7; Walpen, *Die offenen Feinde und ihre Gesellschaft*, 22–23, 170; and John Zmirak, as quoted in Mirowski and Plehwe, *Road from Mont Pèlerin*, 15; Edwin J. Feulner Jr., *Intellectual Pilgrims: The Fiftieth Anniversary of the Mont Pèlerin Society* (Edwin J. Feulner Jr., 1999), 42.

128. Plehwe, introduction to Mirowski and Plehwe, *Road from Mont Pèlerin*, 4; and Friedrich August von Hayek, "Freie Wirtschaft und Wettbewerbsordnung," in *Individualismus und wirtschaftliche Ordnung (Erlenbach-Zürich*, 1952), 141.

129. William E. Simon, *A Time for Truth* (Reader's Digest Press, 1978), 229–33.

130. On the spread of neoliberal institutions and that institutional labor more generally, see Plehwe, introduction to Mirowski and Plehwe, *Road from Mont Pèlerin*, 6–7; Walpen, *Die offenen Feinde und ihre Gesellschaft*, 189, 191, 212, 225; and Dieter Plehwe and Matthias Schmelzer, "Marketing Marketization: The Power of Neoliberal Expert, Consulting, and Lobby Networks," *Zeithistorische Forschungen* 3 (2015): 488–99.

131. Plehwe, "Looking Back to the Future of Neoliberalism Studies," 335; and Walpen, *Die offenen Feinde und ihre Gesellschaft*, 220–24. For member institutions, see the amazing research being done at Think Tank Network, thinktanknet workresearch.net. For neoliberalism's spread, see the essays in Slobodian and Plehwe, *Market Civilizations*.

132. Slobodian and Plehwe, *Market Civilizations*, 9; Jimmy Casas Klausen and Paulo Chamon, "Neoliberalism Out of Place: The Rise of Brazilian Ultraliberalism," in Slobodian and Plehwe, *Market Civilizations*, 221, 223, 227, 229.

133. Klausen and Chamon, "Neoliberalism Out of Place," 221.

134. Esra Elif Nartok, "Constructing Turkey's 'Magic Political Formula': The Association for Liberal Thinking's Neoliberal Intellectual

Project," in Slobodian and Plehwe, *Market Civilizations*, 79, 83.

135. Reto Hofmann, "Japan and Neoliberal Culturalism," in Slobodian and Plehwe, *Market Civilizations*, 29–52, 38, 45; Balasubramanian, "From Socialism to Swatantra," 3, 60, 86; and Nartok, "Constructing Turkey's 'Magic Political Formula,'" 80, 81, 83, 86, 90, 99.

136. J. A. Lombard, *Freedom, Welfare and Order: Thoughts on the Principles of Political Co-Operation in the Economy of Southern Africa* (Benbo, 1978), 69.

137. Antina von Schnitzler, "Disciplining Freedom: Apartheid, Counterinsurgency, and the Political Histories of Neoliberalism," in Slobodian and Plehwe, *Market Civilizations*, 173, 181.

138. Plehwe, introduction to Mirowski and Plehwe, *Road from Mont Pèlerin*, 2; Plehwe, "Looking Back to the Future of Neoliberalism Studies," xiii; Mirowski, "Zero Hour of History," 590; Walpen, *Die offenen Feinde und ihre Gesellschaft*," 145–46, 154, 240, 249; Slobodian, *Globalists*, 150, 269; and Adam Tooze, "Neoliberalism's World Order," *Dissent*, Summer 2019, 135.

139. Milton Friedman, "A Friedman Doctrine—the Social Responsibility of Business Is to Increase Its Profits," *NYT*, September 13, 1970; and Wolfgang Streeck, *Buying Time: The Delayed Crisis of Democratic Capitalism* (Verso, 2014), 3.

140. Jelle Visser, "Trade Unions in the Balance," *ILO ACTRAV* Working Paper No. 722482 (Geneva, International Labour Organization, 2019); and Shor, "Auto De(Con)-Struction," 85.

141. "Belfast Comes to Blidworth, Nottinghamshire," *Miner*, June 15, 1984, International Institute of Social History, United Kingdom Social and Political Developments Collection, COLL00275–23.

142. National Union of Mineworkers, "Coal Not Dole, Part 1: Not Just Tea and Sandwiches," Miners' Campaign Tape Project (1984).

143. Martin Adeney and John Lloyd, *The Miners' Strike, 1984–1985: Loss Without Limit* (Routledge, 2022, orig. pub. 1986), 71–72.

144. Trade Union Act, 1984, chap. 49, United Kingdom, https://www .legislation.gov.uk/ukpga /1984/49/enacted; Trades Union Congress, *Put Your Employer on the Spot* (TUC Publications, April 1982), 4.

145. International Labour, Trade & Aid Project, "Fact Sheet. The 'Illegal' Tebbit Laws ~ The M.N.C. Link

~ and the Threat to World Labour," *International Institute of Social History, Miners' International Federation Archives*, ARCH00897–285.

146. Department for Energy Security and Net Zero and Department for Business Energy & Industrial Strategy, "Historical Coal Data: Coal Production, Availability and Consumption 1853–2022," Digest of UK Energy Statistics, January 22, 2013. For toy-gun class-war caption, "Thirty Years After the Miners' Strike: Evocative Images from the Bitter Industrial Dispute That Tore Britain Apart," *Daily Mail*, March 3, 2014, https://www.dailymail.co.uk /news/article-2571744/The-miners -strike-30-years-Amazing-photo graphs-industrial-dispute-tore-Brit ain-apart.html.

147. James M. Pierce as quoted in Joseph A. McCartin, *Collision Course: Ronald Reagan, the Air Traffic Controllers, and the Strike That Changed America* (OUP, 2011), 339.

148. Paul L. Butterworth, James T. Schultz, and Marian C. Schultz, "More Than a Labor Dispute: The PATCO Strike of 1981," *Essays in Economic and Business History* 23, no. 1 (2005): 125–26, 130; and Ruth Milkman and Joseph A. McCartin, "The Legacy and Lessons of the PATCO Strike After 30 Years: A Dialogue," *Labor History* 54, no. 3 (2013): 136.

149. Alex Bryson, Bernhard Ebbinghaus, and Jelle Visser, "Introduction: Causes, Consequences and Cures of Union Decline," *European Journal of Industrial Relations* 17, no. 2 (2011): 97–105; Michael Wallerstein and Bruce Western, "Unions in Decline? What Has Changed and Why," *Annual Review of Political Science* 3 (2000): 355–77; Visser, "Trade Unions in the Balance," 15; and Marcel van der Linden, *Workers of the World: Essays Toward a Global Labor History* (Brill, 2008), 208.

150. In 2023, *Vorwärts* became a membership magazine for the SPD, published just six times a year. See Frauke Steinhäuser, *Die Neue Heimat: Eine sozialdemokratische Utopie und ihre Bauten* (Landeszentrale für Politische Bildung, 2019), 28–29, 32–33; and "Neue Heimat—Das Desaster des Immobilienkonzerns," *Focus Online*, April 9, 2013.

151. James Vernon, *Modern Britain, 1750 to the Present* (CUP, 2017), 479–80.

152. Mairi Maclean, *Economic Management and French Business: From de Gaulle to Chirac* (Routledge, 2002), 157, 161–62; Pier Angelo Toninelli,

"Between State and Market: The Parabola of Italian Enterprise in the 20th Century," *Entreprises et Histoire* 37 (2004): 74; Vernon, *Modern Britain*, 482; and Walpen, *Die offenen Feinde und ihre Gesellschaft*, 256.

153. Andrew R. Goetz and Timothy M. Vowles, "The Good, the Bad, and the Ugly: 30 Years of U.S. Airline Deregulation," *Journal of Transport Geography* 17 (2009): 251; Harvey, *A Brief History of Neoliberalism*, 99–101, 104, 106–10, 116; and Timothy Mitchell, "No Factories, No Problems: The Logic of Neo-Liberalism in Egypt," *Review of African Political Economy* 26, no. 82 (December 1999): 455–68.

154. Jonathan Bradshaw and Alan Deacon, "Social Security," in *In Defence of the Welfare State*, ed. Paul Wilding (Manchester UP, 1986), 94.

155. Neil Rollings, "Between Business and Academia in Postwar Britain: Three Advocates of Neoliberalism at the Heart of the British Business Community," in *Liberalism and the Welfare State: Economists and Arguments for the Welfare State*, ed. Roger E. Backhouse et al. (OUP, 2017), 107. On Shenfield, see Rollings, "Between Business and Academia in Postwar Britain," 102–3.

156. "Selsdon Declaration," adopted by the Selsdon Group's inaugural members at their first official meeting, which took place at the Selsdon Park Hotel in September 1973, as cited in Richard Cockett, *Thinking the Unthinkable: Think-Tanks and the Economic Counter-Revolution, 1931–1983* (Harper Collins, 1995), 212–13.

157. Walpen, *Die offenen Feinde und ihre Gesellschaft*, 210; Cooper, *Family Values*, 62, 64; Jonathan Boswell and James Peters, *Capitalism in Contention: Business Leaders and Political Economy in Modern Britain* (CUP, 1997), 164; and Wendy Brown, "Der Totale Homo oeconomicus," *Blätter für Deutsche und Internationale Politik*, December 2015, 75.

158. Vernon, *Modern Britain*, 488; and Peter Sloman, "Welfare in a Neoliberal Age: The Politics of Redistributive Market Liberalism," in Davies, Jackson, and Sutcliffe-Braithwaite, *Neoliberal Age?*, 83.

159. Bernhard Rieger, "British Varieties of Neoliberalism: Unemployment Policy from Thatcher to Blair," in Davies, Jackson, and Sutcliffe-Braithwaite, *Neoliberal Age?*, 124–27.

160. Jim Tomlinson, "The Failures of Neoliberalism in Britain Since the

1970s: The Limits on 'Market Forces' in a Deindustrializing Economy and a 'New Speenhamland," in Davies, Jackson, and Sutcliffe-Braithwaite, *Neoliberal Age?*, 106; and Rieger, "British Varieties of Neoliberalism," 117–20.

161. Jenny Andersson, *Between Growth and Security: Swedish Social Democracy from a Strong Society to a Third Way*, trans. Mireille L. Key (Manchester UP, 2006), 96, 129–30; and Assar Lindbeck, *Nya villkor för ekonomi och politik: Ekonomikommissionens förslag* (Statens Offentliga Utredningar, 1993), 8, 15. For similar developments in another Nordic country, Denmark, see Jesper Vestermark Køber and Niklas Olsen, "Privatizing the Welfare State: Danish Libertarianism from the 1980s to the 2000s," *Journal of Political Ideologies* 28 (2023): 355–72.

162. Cooper, *Family Values*, 66, 69, 70, 102, 190, 217. See also Hanming Fang and Michael Keane, "Assessing the Impact of Welfare Reform on Single Mothers," Brookings Papers on Economic Activity, 2004, No. 1, 1–95, https://www.brookings.edu /articles/assessing-the-impact-of -welfare-reform-on-single-mothers/; Gary S. Becker, "Altruism in the Family," in *A Treatise in the Family*, rev. ed. (HUP, 1993), 277–306; and Sandy Baum, "The Evolution of Student Debt in the U.S.: An Overview," W. E. Upjohn Institute for Employment Research, October 2013. For the quotation, see Cooper, *Family Values*, 218.

163. A related observation on the welfare state can be found in Pryluka, "We Can't Go Back to a Golden Age of Capitalism"; see also Vernon, *Modern Britain*, 488; Sloman, "Welfare in a Neoliberal Age," 76; John Hills, "The Changing Architecture of the UK Welfare State," *Oxford Review of Economic Policy* 27, no. 4 (Winter 2011): 591–92; and Cooper, *Family Values*, 314.

164. Walpen, *Die offenen Feinde und ihre Gesellschaft*, 209; "Prison Population over Time," Sentencing Project, accessed August 17, 2023, https:// www.sentencingproject.org /research/; Elizabeth Hinton, *America on Fire: The Untold History of Police Violence and Black Rebellion Since the 1960s* (Liveright Publishing, 2021); and J. G. Ballard, *Super-Cannes* (Harper Collins, 2000).

165. David M. Gordon, Richard Edwards, and Michael Reich, *Segmented Work, Divided Workers: The Historical Transformation of Labor in the United States* (CUP, 1982).

166. Slobodian, *Globalists*, 219, 220, 223, 242–45; Jeremy Walker, "Freedom to Burn: Mining Propaganda, Fossil Capital, and the Australian Neoliberals," in Slobodian and Plehwe, *Market Civilization*, 198; Vanessa Ogle, "State Rights Against Private Capital: The 'New International Economic Order' and the Struggle over Aid, Trade, and Foreign Investment, 1962–1981," *Humanity* 5 (Summer 2014): 217, 220, 221; and Mark Mazower, *Governing the World: The History of an Idea* (Penguin Press, 2012), 304.

167. Quinn Slobodian, "World Maps for the Debt Paradigm: Risk Ranking the Poorer Nations in the 1970s," *Critical Historical Studies* 8, no. 1 (2021): 9.

168. Slobodian, "World Maps for the Debt Paradigm," 7, 19.

169. Robert McNamara, as quoted in Patrick Sharma, "Bureaucratic Imperatives and Policy Outcomes: The Origins of World Bank Structural Adjustment Lending," *Review of International Political Economy* 20, no. 4 (2013): 677.

170. McNamara, as quoted in Sharma, "Bureaucratic Imperatives and Policy Outcomes," 677.

171. James Conrow, as quoted in Sarah Babb, *Behind the Development Banks: Washington Politics, World Poverty, and the Wealth of Nations* (University of Chicago Press, 2009), 88.

172. Ogle, "State Rights Against Private Capital," 221, 225; Walpen, *Die offenen Feinde und ihre Gesellschaft*, 238; Slobodian, "World Maps for the Debt Paradigm," 20, Sharma, "Bureaucratic Imperatives and Policy Outcomes," 669, 674; and Plehwe, introduction to Mirowski and Plehwe, *Road from Mont Pèlerin*, 7; and Harvey, *Brief History of Neoliberalism*, 90–93.

173. Slobodian, *Globalists*, 131, 145; Slobodian, "World Maps for the Debt Paradigm," 1–22; Dieter Plehwe, "The Development of Neoliberal Measures of Competitiveness," in *Competition in World Politics: Knowledge, Strategies, and Institutions*, ed. Daniela Russ and James Stafford (Transcript Verlag, 2021), 155–82; Harold James, *Die Deutsche Bank und die « Arisierung »*, trans. Karl Heinz Silber (C. H. Beck, 2001), 216–18; Lauren N. Duffy et al., "Tourism Development in the Dominican Republic," *Tourism and Hospitality Research* 16 (January 2016): 38; Carlton Pomeroy and Steve Jacob, "From Mangos to Manufacturing: Uneven Development and Its Impact on Social Well-Being in the Dominican Republic," *Social Indicators Research* 65, no. 1 (2004): 85; and Beatriz Elena Rodriguez-Satizabal, "Pathways from Deglobalisation: Colombian Business Groups, 1950–1985," *Journal of Evolutionary Studies in Business* 5, no. 2 (2020): 178. Harold James, *Die Deutsche Bank und die "Arisierung,"* trans. Karl Heinz Silber (C. H. Beck, 2001), 216–18.

174. Adom Getachew, *Worldmaking After Empire: The Rise and Fall of Self-Determination* (PUP, 2020), 29; and Şevket Pamuk, *Uneven Centuries: Economic Development of Turkey Since 1820* (PUP, 2018), 224.

175. Pirojsha Godrej, Diwali Speech, 1969, MS-06-01-94, GAM.

176. Aditya Balasubramanian, "(Is) India in the History of Neoliberalism?," in Slobodian and Plehwe, *Market Civilizations*, 61; Balasubramanian, "From Socialism to Swatantra," 3, 86. Mircea Raianu, *Tata: The Global Corporation That Built Indian Capitalism* (HUP, 2021), 190; Bipan Chandra, Mridula Mukherjee, and Aditya Mukherjee, *India After Independence, 1947–2000* (Penguin, 2002), 351, 352, 358; B. K. Karanjia, *Godrej: A Hundred Years, 1897–1997*, vol. 1, *Life's Flag Is Never Furled* (Penguin Books, 1997), 104, 219; and Nikhil Menon, *Planning Democracy: Modern India's Quest for Development* (CUP, 2022), 198, 199.

177. Ravinder Kaur, "'I Am India Shining': The Investor-Citizen and the Indelible Icon of Good Times," *Journal of Asian Studies* 75, no. 3 (2016): 14; Balasubramanian, "(Is) India in the History of Neoliberalism?," 56, 64, 66.

178. As quoted in Kemal Karpat, "Statism—Devletçilik—and Economic Development," in *Turkey's Politics: The Transition to a Multi-Party System* (PUP, 1959), 298.

179. Korkut Boratav, "Import Substitution and Income Distribution Under a Populist Regime: The Case of Turkey," *Development Policy Review* 4 (1986): 124, 137; Pamuk, *Uneven Centuries*, 232, 234, 237, 238; Karpat, "Statism—Devletçilik—and Economic Development," 295, 296, 299, 302.

180. T. Ademola Oyejide, "Adjustment with Growth: Nigerian Experience with Structural Adjustment Policy Reform," *Journal of International Development* 3, no. 5 (1991): 487, 488, 490–93. On the crisis, see also Afeikhena Jerome, "Privatization and Enterprise Performance in Nigeria: Case Study of Some Privatized Enterprises," AERC Research Paper 175 (African Economic Research Consortium, Nairobi, January 2008), 5; Kenneth Nweke and Vincent Nyewusira, "The Political Economy of Privatization Policy in Nigeria," in *Journal of Educational Management* 4, no. 4 (2007): 22–23; Bureau of Public Enterprises (Nigeria), accessed August 20, 2023, https://www.bpe.gov.ng/about/history/#:~:text=As%20government%20could%20no%20longer,and%20political%20conditions%20but%20unfortunately%2C; Matthew Etinosa Egharevba, "Neo-Liberal Socio-Economic Policy and Human Development in the Informal Sector of Lagos State" (PhD diss., Covenant University, 2008), 2; Adekola Abdulazeez Alao and Raheem T. Kazeem, "Privatization of Public Enterprises in Nigeria: Challenges and Prospects," *Entrepreneurial Journal of Management Sciences* 5, no. 1 (2016).

181. Ronald Reagan, "Statement at the First Plenary Session of the International Meeting on Cooperation and Development in Cancún, Mexico," speech, October 22, 1981, Ronald Reagan Presidential Library. On the meeting, see Ogle, "State Rights Against Private Capital," 224.

182. Mila Jonjić and Nenad Pantelić, "The Mediterranean Tiger: How Montenegro Became a Neoliberal Role Model," in Slobodian and Plehwe, *Market Civilizations*, 280.

183. Tobias Rupprecht, "The Road from Snake Hill: The Genesis of Russian Neoliberalism," in Slobodian and Plehwe, *Market Civilizations*, 128, 131. See also Janos Kornai, *The Road to the Free Economy* (W. W. Norton, 1990); and Anders Åslund, *How Russia Became a Market Economy* (Brookings Institution, 1995).

184. Rupprecht, "Road from Snake Hill," 109–38, esp. 111, 121, 125; Jonjić and Pantelić, "The Mediterranean Tiger," 273; Andrzej Chwalba, *Kurze Geschichte der Dritten Republik Polen 1989 bis 2005* (Harrassowitz-Verlag, 2010), 72; and Weber, *How China Escaped Shock Therapy*, 2, 6. For life expectancy data, see "Life Expectancy at Birth," Organisation for Economic Co-Operation and Development, accessed August 10, 2023, https://data.oecd.org/health stat/life-expectancy-at-birth.htm#indicator-chart.

185. On Hungary, see Indeed Editorial Team, "10 Deutsche Firmen in Ungarn: Anzahl Der Mitarbeitenden, Standort, Aktivitäten," Indeed

Karriere-Guide, September 16, 2024; Ivan T. Berend, *From the Soviet Bloc to the European Union: The Economic and Social Transformation of Central and Eastern Europe Since 1973* (CUP, 2009), 3–6; Philipp Ther, *Die Neue Ordnung auf dem Alten Kontinent: Eine Geschichte des Neoliberalen Europa* (Suhrkamp, 2014), 5; Chwalba, *Kurze Geschichte der Dritten Republik Polen*, 73. For a sense of the contemporary excitement of such developments, see Giersch, "Anmerkungen zum weltwirtschaftlichen Denkansatz," 13, 14.

186. Weber, *How China Escaped Shock Therapy*, 89, 90.

187. Weber, *How China Escaped Shock Therapy*, 47, 104–5; and Rupprecht, "Road from Snake Hill," 148. See also the excellent Isabella Weber, "The Ordoliberal Roots of Shock Therapy: The German 'Economic Miracle' in China's 1980s Reform Debate," in Slobodian and Plehwe, *Market Civilizations*, 139–61.

188. Deng Xiaoping, "Emancipate the Mind, Seek Truth from Facts, and Unite as One in Looking to the Future," December 13, 1978, speech at the closing session of the Central Working Conference in Preparation for the Third Plenary Session of the Eleventh Central Committee of the Communist Party, in *Selected Work of Deng Xiaoping* (Foreign Language Press, 1984), 173, as cited in Weber, *How China Escaped Shock Therapy*, 117.

189. Rupprecht, "Road from Snake Hill," 153; and Weber, *How China Escaped Shock Therapy*, 1, 7, 10.

190. Weber, *How China Escaped Shock Therapy*, 18.

191. Weber, *How China Escaped Shock Therapy*, 18, 19, 21–23, 27, 69–84.

192. Weber, *How China Escaped Shock Therapy*, 146.

193. Weber, *How China Escaped Shock Therapy*, 261.

194. Weber, *How China Escaped Shock Therapy*, 120.

195. Weber, *How China Escaped Shock Therapy*, 77, 145.

196. Weber, *How China Escaped Shock Therapy*, 153, 154, 157, 164, 173, 368.

197. Weber, *How China Escaped Shock Therapy*, 177.

198. Weber, *How China Escaped Shock Therapy*, 185, 203, 209.

199. Weber, *How China Escaped Shock Therapy*, 220, 229.

200. Weber, *How China Escaped Shock Therapy*, 227, 238.

201. Weber, *How China Escaped Shock Therapy*, 258, 268.

202. There is a long and important debate on whether China itself should be considered under the neoliberal rubric. I am siding here with Weber in the belief that China's economic development follows "a logic of governance that is distinct from that of neoliberalism." See Isabella M. Weber, "China and Neoliberalism: Moving Beyond the China Is/Is Not Neoliberal Dichotomy," in *The Sage Handbook of Neoliberalism*, ed. Damien Cahill, Martijn Konings, Melinda Cooper, and David Primrose (Sage Reference, 2018), 229. See, for example, Niall Ferguson, "The Trillion-Dollar Question: China or America?," *Telegraph*, June 1, 2009.

203. Marcel van der Linden, "How Some Workers Benefit from the Exploitation of Other Workers," *Revlat: Revista Latinoamericana de Trabajo y Trabajadores* 1 (November 2020–April 2021), 223–39. See also Ulrich Brand and Markus Wissen, *The Imperial Mode of Living: Everyday Life and the Ecological Crisis of Capitalism* (Verso, 2021).

204. Ignacio Flores, Claudia Sanhueza, Jorge Atria, and Ricardo Mayer, "Top Incomes in Chile: A Historical Perspective on Income Inequality, 1964–2017," *Review of Income and Wealth* 66, no. 4 (2020): 850–74. See also Thomas Piketty, *Capital in the Twenty-First Century* (Belknap Press of HUP, 2014), 291, 316–17, 323. Total income figures include capital gains.

205. Thomas Piketty, *Capital and Ideology*, trans. Arthur Goldhammer (Belknap Press of HUP, 2020), 423; and Piketty, *Capital in the Twenty-First Century*, 244, 340, 344, 348, 438. For the quotation, see Piketty, *Capital in the Twenty-First Century*, 244.

206. Lisa McGirr, *Suburban Warriors: The Origins of the New American Right* (PUP, 2001), 238; Cooper, *Family Values*, 102, 129; Michael J. Graetz and Ian Shapiro, *Death by a Thousand Cuts: The Fight over Taxing Inherited Wealth* (PUP, 2006), 12–14; and Piketty, *Capital in the Twenty-First Century*, 443.

207. Martha M. Burt, *Over the Edge: The Growth of Homelessness in the 1980s* (Urban Institute Press, 1992), 211; U.S. Department of Housing and Urban Development, *The 2008 Annual Homeless Assessment Report to Congress*, July 2009; Dale Maharidge, "How the United States Chose to Become a Country of Homelessness," *Nation*, January/February 2021; and Don Mitchell, *Mean Streets: Homelessness, Public Space,*

and the Limits of Capital (University of Georgia Press, 2020), 57–62.

208. Olugbenga Olatunde, "Life Expectancy at Birth and at Age 65 by Local Areas in the United Kingdom: 2004–06 to 2008–10," Office for National Statistics, October 19, 2011. For non-BA white women, from approximately 25 out of 100,000 to approximately 90 out of 100,000. For non-BA white men, from approximately 55 out of 100,000 to over 150 out of 100,000. See Anne Case and Angus Deaton, *Deaths of Despair and the Future of Capitalism* (PUP, 2020); and Raj Chetty et al., "The Association Between Income and Life Expectancy in the United States, 2001–2014," *Journal of the American Medical Association* 315, no. 16 (2016): 1753–57.

209. Nancy Fraser, "After the Family Wage: Gender Equity and the Welfare State," in *Political Theory* 22 (1994): 591; and Cooper, *Family Values*, 9. For the quotation, see Margaret Thatcher, interviewed by Douglas Keay, *Women's Own*, September 23, 1987, 29–30.

210. On neoliberalism as a form of enclosure, see Massimo De Angelis, "Separating the Doing and the Deed: Capital and the Continuous Character of Enclosures," *Historical Materialism* 12 (2004): 57–87; and Gillian Hart, "Denaturalizing Dispossession: Critical Ethnography in the Age of Resurgent Imperialism," *Antipode* 38, no. 5 (2006): 988.

211. Abir Saksouk-Sasso, "Making Spaces for Communal Sovereignty: The Story of Beirut's Dalieh," *Arab Studies Journal* 23 (Fall 2015): 296–318; Mona Fawaz, Ahmad Gharbieh, Abir Saksouk-Sasso, and Nadine Bekdache, "Mumārasat al-'Ām: 'An al-Masāhāt al-Mushtaraka fī Beirut" [Practicing the Public: On Shared Spaces in Beirut], Beirut Urban Lab, https://beiruturbanlab.com/en/Details/569/practicing-the-public accessed October 11, 2022; Hadi Makarem, "Actually Existing Neoliberalism: The Reconstruction of Downtown Beirut in Post–Civil War Lebanon" (PhD diss., London School of Economics and Political Science, 2014); and Brenner and Theodore, "Cities and the Geographies of 'Actually Existing Neoliberalisms,'" 351. On the urban restructuring process in Germany, see Oliver Brüchert, "Werbung für den Strafenden Staat: Beobachtungen anlässlich der WM 2006," in *Kontrollierte Urbanität*, ed. Volker Eick, Jens Sambale, and Eric Töpfer (Transcript Verlag, 2007), 227–44.

212. Fig, "State of Extraction," 1–8; Ernst & Young, *Africa 2013: Getting Down to Business* (Ernst & Young, 2013), 34; and Jimena Durán and Sérgio Chichava, "Resisting South-South Cooperation? Mozambican Civil Society and Brazilian Agricultural Technical Cooperation," in *South-South Cooperation Beyond the Myths: Rising Donors, New Aid Practices?*, ed. Isaline Bergamaschi, Phoebe Moore, and Arlene B. Tickner (Palgrave Macmillan, 2017), 272, 278, 280–83, 288–89. See Uche Usim, "Ex-Naval Boss Hits Gold in Farming," *Daily Sun*, July 8, 2024; United Nations Office for Coordination of Humanitarian Affairs, "Obasanjo Says Farming, Not Corruption, Makes Him Rich," *New Humanitarian*, November 25, 2004. On resistance, see also J. G. N. Onyekpe, "Agrarian Crises in West Niger Igbo Land, 1880–1970" (PhD diss., University of Lagos, 1997); and J. G. N. Onyekpe, *Ownership and Use of Land in Twentieth-Century Nigeria: A Survey and Critique* (University of Lagos Faculty of Arts, 2009).

213. Alan Greenspan, *The Age of Turbulence: Adventures in a New World* (Allen Lane, 2007), 463.

214. Alina Brad, *Der Palmölboom in Indonesien: Zur Politischen Ökonomie einer umkämpften Ressource* (Transcript Verlag, 2019), 9, 101.

215. Brad, *Der Palmölboom in Indonesien*, 9, 10, 11, 12, 16, 18, 106–7, 110, 112, 125, 128. Plantations grew by exactly 278 percent.

216. Brad, *Der Palmölboom in Indonesien*, 76, 78, 80, 111, 114, 118–19, 120, 123, 156–60.

217. Josef C. Brada, "Privatization Is Transition—or Is It?," *Journal of Economic Perspectives* 10, no. 2 (1996): 71; Eva Kiss, "Foreign Direct Investment in Hungary: Industry and Its Spatial Effects," *Eastern European Economics* 45, no. 1 (2007): 9, 11–12; and United Nations Conference on Trade and Development, "FDI Inflows by Host Region, 1985–2003 (millions of dollars)," in Karl P. Sauvant, ed., *World Investment Report 2004: The Shift Towards Services* (United Nations, 2004), 72, https:// digitallibrary.un.org/record/545508 /files/dite4volxiii_en.pdf.

218. Frank Uekötter, *Im Strudel: Eine Umweltgeschichte der Welt* (Campus, 2020), 619; and Laurie Parsons, *Carbon Colonialism: How Rich Countries Export Climate Breakdown* (Manchester UP, 2023).

219. Jason W. Moore, *Capitalism in the Web of Life: Ecology and the Accumulation of Capital* (Verso, 2015); Jason W. Moore, ed., *Anthropocene or Capitalocene? Nature, History, and the Crisis of Capitalism* (PM Press, 2016); and Andreas Malm, *Fossil Capital: The Rise of Steam Power and the Roots of Global Warming* (Verso, 2016).

220. Brown, "Der totale Homo oeconomicus," 69.

221. Brown, "Der Totale Homo oeconomicus," 71.

222. Brown, "Der Totale Homo oeconomicus," 71, 74–75, 79; Daniela Bachelder, *How to Brand Yourself: A Guide to Branding Yourself & Using Personal Branding Strategies to Promote Yourself* (CreateSpace Independent Publishing Platform, 2014); and Rachel Greenwald, *Find a Husband After 35: (Using What I Learned at Harvard Business School)* (Ballantine Books, 2004).

223. Karl Polanyi, *The Great Transformation: The Political and Economic Origins of Our Time* (Beacon Press, 2001), 60. Originally published in 1944.

224. Brown, "Der totale Homo oeconomicus," 73; Brenner, "Building Euro-Regions,'" 319–45; and Kaur, "I Am India Shining," 1, 2.

225. Debora L. Spar, *Work, Mate, Marry, Love: How Machines Shape Our Human Destiny* (Farrar, Straus and Giroux, 2020), 95.

226. Lisbeth N. Trallori, *Der Körper als Ware: Feministische Interventionen*, Kritik & Utopie (Mandelbaum, 2015). On the trade in young children, see Choe Sang-Hun, "World's Largest 'Baby Exporter' Confronts Its Painful Past," *NYT*, September 17, 2023. See also Spar, *Work, Mate, Marry, Love*, 132, 237–54; Eva Illouz, *The End of Love: A Sociology of Negative Relations* (OUP, 2019), 5, 21; Clare Ungerson, "Commodified Care Work in European Labour Markets," *European Societies* 5, no. 4 (2003): 377–96; Rajani Naidoo and Ian Jamieson, "Knowledge in the Marketplace: The Global Commodification of Teaching and Learning in Higher Education," in *Internationalizing Higher Education*, ed. Peter Ninnes and Meeri Hellstén (Springer Verlag, 2005), 37–51.

227. Branko Milanovic, *Capitalism, Alone: The Future of the System That Rules the World* (HUP, 2019), 2, 196.

228. Neil Harvey, *The Chiapas Rebellion: The Struggle for Land and Democracy* (Duke UP, 1998).

229. Mona Fawaz, Ahmad Gharbieh, Abir Saksouk-Sasso, and Nadine Bekdash,"Mumārasat al-'Ām: 'An al-Masāhāt al-Mushtaraka fī Beirut" [Practicing the Public: On Shared Spaces in Beirut], Beirut Urban Lab, accessed October 11, 2022, at https://cdn-5e344ff7f911c80ca0d f760f.closte.com/wp-content/up loads/sites/102/2022/07/00_FINAL _practicingthepublicinbeirut_com pressed.pdf; Hart, "Denaturalizing Dispossession," 986; Friedman and Lee, "Remaking the World of Chinese Labour," 519–21; and Fig, "State of Extraction," 7. For details on these protests, see Han Dongfang, "Police Attack Miners' Demonstration in Hebei," *China Labour Bulletin*, September 15, 1999; "Large-Scale Protest Reported in Nanjing," *China Labour Bulletin*, April 19, 2001; "Not So Sweet— Sugar Workers Demand Wages," *China Labour Bulletin*, July 11, 2001; and "Daqing Oilfield Works Struggle," *China Labour Bulletin*, March 5, 2002. On opposition to land grabbing in Nigeria, see, for example, Onyekpe, "Agrarian Crises in West Niger Igbo Land"; Onyekpe, "Ownership and Use of Land in Twentieth-Century Nigeria"; Miles Larmer, *Mineworkers in Zambia: Labour and Political Change in Post-Colonial Africa* (Palgrave Macmillan, 2007); Peter Alexander, "Marikana Commission of Inquiry: From Narratives Towards History," *Journal of Southern African Studies* 42, no. 5 (2016): 815–39; Peter Alexander, "Marikana, Turning Point in South African History," *Review of African Political Economy* 40, no. 138 (2013): 605–19; Crispen Chinguno, "Marikana: Fragmentation, Precariousness, Strike Violence and Solidarity," *Review of African Political Economy* 40, no. 138 (2013): 639–46; Crispen Chinguno, "The Unmaking and Remaking of Industrial Relations: The Case of Impala Platinum and the 2012–2013 Platinum Strike Wave," *Review of African Political Economy* 42, no. 146 (2015): 577–90; Benjamin Rubbers, *Le paternalisme en question: Les anciens ouvriers de la Gécamines face à la libéralisation du secteur minier katangais (RD Congo)* (L'Harmattan, 2013); and T. Ademola Oyejide, "Adjustment with Growth: Nigerian Experience with Structural Adjustment Policy Reform," *Journal of International Development* 3, no. 5 (1991): 496–97.

230. Michał Wenzel, "Od Samoobrony do Agrounii. Wiejskie ruchy społeczne po 1989 roku," *Teoria Polityki* 7 (2023): 168; Stuart Shields, "Opposing Neoliberalism? Poland's Renewed Populism and Post-Communist Transition," *Third World Quarterly* 33, no. 2 (2012):

359–81; Kai-Olaf Lang, "Bauernre-volte zwischen Oder und Bug? An-drzej Lepper und der Bauernbund Samoobrona," *Aktuelle Analysen / Bundesinstitut für ostwissenschaftliche und internationale Studien* 46 (1999): 1–7; Mateusz Piskorski, "Samoo-brona RP w polskim systemie party-jnym" (PhD diss., Uniwersytet im Adama Mickiewicza, 2010); Natalia Mamonova and Jaume Franquesa, "Populism, Neoliberalism and Agrarian Movements in Europe. Understanding Rural Support for Right-Wing Politics and Looking for Progressive Solutions," *Sociologia Ruralis* 60, no. 4 (2020): 710–31; La-rissa Deppisch, "Die AfD und das 'Dornröschenschloss'—über die (Be-)Deutung von Peripherisierung für den Rechtspopulismuszuspruch," in *Lokal Extrem Rechts*, ed. Daniel Mullis and Judith Miggelbrink (Ver-lag, 2022), 48, 103–21; and Daniel Mullis, "Urban Conditions for the Rise of the Far Right in the Global City of Frankfurt: From Austerity Urbanism, Post-Democracy and Gentrification to Regressive Collec-tivity," *Urban Studies* 58, no. 1 (2021): 131–47.

231. Adam J. Tooze, *Crashed: Wie zehn Jahre Finanzkrise die Welt verändert haben* (München: Siedler, 2018), 63.

232. Yalman Onaran, "Can We Sur-vive the Next Financial Crisis?," Bloomberg, September 10, 2018.

233. Adam J. Tooze, *Crashed: How a Decade of Financial Crises Changed the World* (Penguin Books, 2019), 57, 71, 81, 84, 185.

234. Neil Irwin, *The Alchemists: Three Central Bankers and a World on Fire* (Penguin Press, 2013), 2, as cited in Tooze, *Crashed*, 144.

235. Tooze, *Crashed*, 73, 76, 78; Asha Bangalore, "US Housing Market: Share of Underwater Homes Trend-ing Down," *Market Oracle*, July 13, 2012; Carolin Würfel, "Der Tag an dem die Welt fast Unterging," *Zeit Magazin*, September 6, 2018, 49.

236. M. Fackler, "Toyota Expects Its First Loss in 70 Years," *NYT*, De-cember 22, 2008. The quote is from Tooze, *Crashed*, 158.

237. Yolande Barnes, "Around the World in Dollars and Cents," Savills World Research, 2016; Tooze, *Crashed*, 63, 188; Bruno Martorano, "Pre-Crisis Conditions and Govern-ment Policy Responses: Chile and Mexico During the Great Reces-sion," Innocenti Working Paper No. 2014–15 (Florence, UNICEF Office of Research, 2014), 8; Centro Estu-dios Internationale, "Chile a 10 años de la crisis subprime," Working Pa-per No. 10, April 6, 2018, 4; Claudio Lara Cortés, "The Global Crisis and the Chilean Economy," in *Latin America After the Financial Crisis: Economic Ramifications from Hetero-dox Perspectives*, ed. Juan E. Sant-arcángelo, Orlando Justo, and Paul Cooney (Palgrave Macmillan, 2016), 120–21; Fernando Baeza, Francisca González, Tarik Benmarhnia, and Alejandra Vives Vergara, "Effects of the Great Recession on Suicide Mor-tality in Chile and Contributing Factors," *SSM—Mental Health* 2 (2022): 1; Ángela Vergara, "Writing About Workers, Reflecting on Dic-tatorship and Neoliberalism: Chil-ean Labor History and the Pinochet Dictatorship," *International Labor and Working-Class History* 93 (2018): 52–73; and Gonzalo Durán and Kar-ina Narbona, "Precarising Formal-ity: Understanding Current Labour Developments in Chile," *Global La-bour Journal* 12, no. 3 (2021): 206–26. For the quotation, see Ariel Miranda, "UPDATE 2—Thousands March in Chile for Job Security," Reuters, April 16, 2009.

238. Würfel, "Der Tag an dem die Welt fast Unterging."

Epilogue: The Possibilities of an Island and the Future of Capitalism

1. This paragraph is based upon the author's observations in Phnom Penh in February 2023. See also Laurie Parsons, *Carbon Colonialism: How Rich Countries Export Climate Break-down* (Manchester UP, 2023), 35.

2. Michael Aliprandini, "Cambo-dia," *Salem Press Encyclopedia*, 2022; and Laurie Parsons, interview with the author, February 14, 2023, Phnom Penh. On room rental costs, see also Ngay Nai, "Garment Ex-ports Expected to Ease Amid Global Pressures," *VOD English*, January 25, 2023; May Kummakara, "Apex Tex-tile Sector Lobby Rebranded as TAFTAC," *Phnom Penh Post*, No-vember 20, 2022. For slightly differ-ent numbers, see "Cambodia, Garment, Footwear and Travel Goods Sector Brief," EuroCham Cambodia, November 1, 2022, 12; and Parsons, *Carbon Colonialism*, 34. Figures are noted as $1.07 billion in US dollars to $12.4 billion between 2000 and 2018, as cited in Vichet Sam, *High but Fragile Growth: Fos-tering SMEs Development to Improve Cambodia's Economic Resilience*, MPRA Paper No. 104935 (Univer-sity Library of Munich, Germany, 2020), 6. Slightly different numbers can be found in Jie Shuyi, "Cambo-dia Is Adidas' Biggest Apparel Sup-plier as Sportswear Giant Shifts Production Out of China," *YICAI Global*, February 8, 2023.

3. Svay Chrum (pseudonym), inter-view with the author, February 24, 2023, Phnom Penh.

4. Garment worker (anonymous), in-terview with the author, February 24, 2023, Phasar Daek village, Ponhea Lueu District, Kandal Province; and Parsons, *Carbon Colonialism*, 37, 38.

5. Employment termination of preg-nant women is frequently reported by workers. See, for example, garment worker (anonymous), interview with the author, February 24, 2023; and Svay Chrum (pseudonym), interview with the author, February 24, 2023. On wages, see "Cambodia, Gar-ment, Footwear and Travel Goods Sector Brief," 3; Massimiliano Tro-peano (EuroCham Cambodia), Feb-ruary 25, 2023, Phnom Penh; and Laurie Parsons, interview with the author, February 14, 2023. On room rental costs, see Nai, "Garment Ex-ports Expected to Ease Amid Global Pressures." On overcrowding, see Parsons, *Carbon Colonialism*, 34; and Sokuntheta Hang, interview with the author, February 14, 2023, Phnom Penh.

6. On this strike, see Christopher Kelly, *A Cambodian Spring* (Dart-mouth Films, 2017), 121 min, Feb-ruary 16, 2023, Phnom Penh. For "authoritarian capitalism," see Joel Buckey, interview with the author, February 14, 2023, Solidarity Cen-ter, Phnom Penh; and Brad Adams, *Cambodia's Dirty Dozen: A Long His-tory of Rights Abuses by Hun Sen's Generals* (Human Rights Watch, 2018), https://www.hrw.org/report /2018/06/27/cambodias-dirty -dozen/long-history-rights-abuses -hun-sens-generals.

7. See Museum of the Economy, Phnom Penh, visited February 2023.

8. Brett Atkinson et al., *Southeast Asia on a Shoestring* (Lonely Planet, 1992), 111.

9. Sven Hansen, "Casino-Kapitalismus in Kambodscha: Nichts geht mehr," *Taz*, March 31, 2023. On the number of people liv-ing there, see Atkinson et al., *South-east Asia on a Shoestring*, 111. This account is based on an authorial in-terview with Savmit Chea (pseu-donym) on February 20, 2023, in Kampong Saom (Sihanoukville).

10. Hansen, "Casino-Kapitalismus in Kambodscha"; Yi Lim (pseudonym), interview with the author, February 18, 2023, Kampong Saom (Siha-noukville); Savmit Chea (pseud-onym), interview with the author, February 20, 2023; Zhao Shulan,

"Advantages and Disadvantages of the Phnom Penh Special Economic Zone and the Sihanoukville Special Economic Zone from a Comparative Perspective," in *Cambodia-China Comprehensive Strategic Partnership Towards a Community with a Shared Future*, ed. Sok Touch et al. (Springer, 2023), 123–37; Vannarith Chheang, *The Political Economy of Chinese Investment in Cambodia*, Trends in Southeast Asia, ebook no. 16 (ISEAS–Yusof Ishak Institute, 2017), 1–32, https://bookshop.iseas.edu.sg/publication/2277; Sophal Ear and Sigfrido Burgos, "Cambodia: Growth with a Red Flag," in *Southeast Asia and the ASEAN Economic Community*, ed. Roderick Macdonald (Palgrave Macmillan, 2019), 313–31.

11. Adrian Levy and Cathy Scott-Clark, "Country for Sale," *Guardian*, April 26, 2008; and Sangeetah Amarthalingam, "Purging Sihanoukville's Past with a New Masterplan," *Phnom Penh Post*, September 16, 2021.

12. Levy and Scott-Clark, "Country for Sale."

13. Savmit Chea (pseudonym), interview with the author, February 20, 2023.

14. Nicholas Farrelly, Alice Dawkins, and Patrick Deegan, "Sihanoukville: A Hub of Environmental Crime Convergence," Global Initiative Against Transnational Organized Crime, September 2, 2022, 3, 7, https://globalinitiative.net/analysis/sihanoukville-hub/. Worker figures are as cited in Hansen, "Casino-Kapitalismus in Kambodscha"; and Aliprandini, "Cambodia."

15. Yann Socheata, "Preah Sihanouk Administration Welcomes Development Plans," *Phnom Penh Post*, February 14, 2023.

16. Adrian and Scott-Clark, "Country for Sale." On land grabbing, see also David Koh, *Chinese Investments in Cambodia: View of Chinese Soft Power from the Ground Up* (Selected CICP Publications, 2016), 79–89.

17. Parsons, *Carbon Colonialism*, 43.

18. Michiel Verver, *"Old" and "New" Chinese Business in Cambodia's Capital*, Trends in Southeast Asia, ebook no. 17 (ISEAS–Yusof Ishak Institute, 2019), 17, https://bookshop.iseas.edu.sg/publication/2418; May Kummakara, "Peppercorn Exports to China Get Green Light," *Phnom Penh Post*, November 30, 2022; Wittaya Kreangkriwit and Poohrich Sinwat, interview with the author, February 16, 2023, Phnom Penh. On Cambodian tourism, see Pierre Walter and Vicheth Sen, "A Geography of Ecotourism in Cambodia: Regions, Pat-

terns, and Potentials," *Asia Pacific Journal of Tourism Research* 23, no. 3 (2018): 297–311; Lei Tin Jackie Ong and Russel Arthur Smith, "Perception and Reality of Managing Sustainable Coastal Tourism in Emerging Destinations: The Case of Sihanoukville, Cambodia," *Journal of Sustainable Tourism* 22, no. 2 (2014): 156–278.

19. For a detailed and exceptionally insightful account of this process, see Yuko Shimazaki, *Human Trafficking and the Feminization of Poverty: Structural Violence in Cambodia* (Lexington Books, 2021).

20. On the mechanisms of this trade, this time in Vietnam, see Appellate Trial Panel, High People's Court in Ho Chi Minh City, case against Le Thi Kieu T, February 25, 2020, in author's possession. On surrogate motherhood, see Hannah Beech, "When Surrogacy Becomes a Crime," *NYT*, November 27, 2022.

21. Sarah Hupp Williamson, "Neoliberal Colonialism and the Case of Cambodia," in *Human Trafficking in the Era of Global Migration: Unraveling the Impact of Neoliberal Economic Policy* (Bristol UP, 2022), 45–64; Vichita Ly, interview with the author, Phnom Penh, February 14, 2023; "Cambodia's Pedophiles and the Internet," *ASEAN Post*, September 3, 2019; David Pearson, "'I Was a Slave': Up to 100,000 Held Captive by Chinse Cybercriminals in Cambodia," *Los Angeles Times*, November 1, 2022; Helen Davidson and Chi-hui Liu, "Hundreds of Taiwanese Trafficked to Cambodia and Held Captive by Telecom Scam Gangs," *Guardian*, August 23, 2022; Rebecca Ratcliffe, Nhung Nguyen, and Navaon Siradapuvadol, "Sold to Gangs, Forced to Run Online Scams: Inside Cambodia's Cybercrime Crisis," *Guardian*, October 10, 2022; Lindsey Kennedy, Nathan Paul Southern, and Huang Yan, "Cambodia's Modern Slavery Nightmare: The Human Trafficking Crisis Overlooked by Authorities," *Guardian*, November 2, 2022; Tessa Wong, Bui Thu, and Lok Kee, "Cambodia Scams: Lured and Trapped into Slavery in South East Asia," *BBC News*, September 21, 2022; and Yi Lim, interview with the author, February 19, 2023.

22. W. Nathan Green, "Financial Inclusion or Subordination? The Monetary Politics of Debt in Cambodia," *Antipode* 55 (4) (2023): 1172–92; Scott Hipsher, "Cambodia: Background, Economic Conditions, and Tourism," in *Poverty Reduction, the Private Sector, and Tourism in

Mainland Southeast Asia* (Palgrave Macmillan, 2017), 111–26. Maryann Bylander, "Credit as Coping: Rethinking Microcredit in the Cambodian Context," *Oxford Development Studies* 43, no. 4 (2015): 533–53. See also Parsons, *Carbon Colonialism*, 53; and International Monetary Fund Country Report No. 22/371, "Cambodia: 2022 Article IV Consultation—Press Release; Staff Report; and Statement by the Executive Director for Cambodia," December 2022, 25.

23. As cited in Manoj Mathew, "Cambodia's Ballooning Private Debt a Risk or a a Sign of Growth?," *Khmer Times*, February 27, 2023.

24. Laurie Parsons, interview with the author, February 14, 2023.

25. See "Cambodia GDP Constant Prices," Trading Economics, accessed April 4, 2024, https://tradingeconomics.com/cambodia/gdp; Farrelly, Dawkins, and Deegan, "Sihanoukville: A Hub of Environmental Crime Convergence," 21.

26. Hansen, "Casino-Kapitalismus in Kambodscha."

27. Sokunthea Hang, "Urban Witness 001: Phnom Pen," *Thea Literature Blog*, November 15, 2017.

28. The person interviewed requested anonymity, interview with the author, February 17, 2023, Phnom Penh.

29. Massimiliano Tropeano and Sara Monti (EuroCham Cambodia), interview with the author, February 25, 2023, Phnom Penh. On Chinese investments in Cambodia, see, for instance, Sigfrido Burgos and Sophal Ear, "China's Strategic Interests in Cambodia: Influence and Resources," *Asian Survey* 50, no. 3 (2010): 615–39. See also Koh, *Chinese Investments in Cambodia*, 79–89, and reference to Chan Cheuk Yin and Holly Robertson, "Chinese Factory Owners Living in a World Apart," *Cambodian Daily*, 31 July 2014; Siem Pichnorak, "The High Cost of Effective Sovereignty: Chinese Resource Access in Cambodia," in *In China's Backyard: Policies and Politics of Chinese Resource Investments in Southeast Asia*, ed. Jason Morris-Jung (Singapore: ISEAS—Yusof Ishak Institute, 2017), 182–203, here 191, and as reported in Soth Koernsoeun, "China-Cambodia 'Share Future,'" *Khmer Times*, February 13, 2023.

30. For this argument, see also Thomas Piketty, *Capital and Ideology*, trans. Arthur Goldhammer (Belknap Press of HUP, 2020), 22.

31. Anis Shivani, "This Is Our Neoliberal Nightmare: Hillary Clinton,

Donald Trump, and Why the Market and the Wealthy Win Every Time," *Salon*, June 6, 2016; and Harvey Cox, *The Market as God* (HUP, 2019), 20. See also Jean-Pierre Dupuy, *Economy and the Future: A Crisis of Faith* (Michigan State UP, 2014), x.

32. The brutality of today's sugar frontier, for example, is illustrated in Megha Rjagopalan and Qadri Incamam, "The Brutality of Sugar Debt, Child Marriage and Hysterectomies," *NYT*, March 24, 2024. On the claims of fifteen hundred Kenyan tea workers, see "James Finlay: Why a Scots Firm Faces a Negligence Claim from Up to 1500 Kenyan Workers," *Herald*, January 28, 2022. For an account of the abysmal conditions on the world's mining frontier, see Johannes Dieterich, "Die Klaffenden Wunden des Kongos," *Badische Zeitung*, July 21, 2023, 3. For the efforts of various powers to gain access to maritime mining grounds, see Andreas Rinke and Christian Schwägerl, "Deutschlands 17. Bundesland," *Cicero* 8 (2012): 77–82. On space, see Kristin Ciupa, "Expanding Extractive Frontiers: Space Mining as Response to Capitalist Crisis," unpublished paper (in author's possession), presented at Rethinking Global Capitalism Conference, Rio de Janeiro, March 14, 2024.

33. Achille Mbembe, Holberg Prize Speech, 2024, https://holbergprize.org/news/holbergforelesningen-2024-av-achille-mbembe/.

34. For the commodification of sports, see, for example, Colin Damms, "Different Class: The Creation of the Premier League and the Commercialization of English Football" (master's thesis, University of Southern Mississippi, 2021). For an excellent history of attention as commodity, see Shoshana Zuboff, *The Age of Surveillance Capitalism: The Fight for a Human Future at the New Frontier of Power* (Public Affairs, 2019). For brain waves, see Johnathan Moens, "Your Brain Waves Are Up for Sale: A New Law Wants to Change That," *NYT*, April 17, 2024.

35. Christina Bain and Joseph Mari, "Organ Trafficking: Unseen Form of Human Trafficking," *ACAMS Today*, June 26, 2018; Adam Nossiter and Najim Rahim, "In Afghanistan, a Booming Kidney Trade Preys on the Poor," *NYT*, February 8, 2021; Elif Batuman, "Japan's Rent-a-Family Industry," *New Yorker*, April 23, 2018.

36. Pope Francis, *Laudato si'* [encyclical on care for our common home], Holy See, May 24, 2015.

37. Ruth Whippman, "Everything Is for Sale Now. Even Us," *NYT*, November 24, 2018.

38. Whippman, "Everything Is for Sale Now. Even Us."

39. Lea Haller, "Aufwachen!," *NZZ Geschichte*, June 2015; and Christoph Fleischmann, "Wem gehört die Zeit? Der Mensch im Takt des Kapitalismus," *Blätter für deutsche und internationale Politik*, January 2014, 111; Hartmut Rosa, *Beschleunigung: Die Veränderung der Zeitstrukturen in der Moderne* (Suhrkamp, 2005); Wendy Brown, "Der Totale Homo oeconomicus," *Blätter für Deutsche und Internationale Politik* (December 2015): 81.

40. The numbers are in constant 2021 international dollars; for the data, see https://data.worldbank.org/indicator/NY.GDP.MKTP.PP.KD.

41. Matthew Carr, "How Dark Factories Are Changing Manufacturing (and How to Profit)," Investment U, October 1, 2019.

42. Martín Arboleda, *Planetary Mine: Territories of Extraction Under Late Capitalism* (Verso, 2020), 48, 49.

43. As Thomas Piketty has shown in Thomas Piketty, *Capital in the Twenty-First Century*, trans. Arthur Goldhammer (Belknap Press of HUP, 2014) and as has been confirmed in Òscar Jordà, Katharina Knoll, Dmitry Kuvshinov, Moritz Schularick, Alan M. Taylor, "The Rate of Return on Everything, 1870–2015," *The Quarterly Journal of Economics* 134 (August 2019), 1225–98.

44. Pablo Pryluka, "We Can't Go Back to a Golden Age of Capitalism: An Interview with Branko Milanovic," *Jacobin*, February 2021. See also Jacob S. Hacker and Paul Pierson, *Winner-Take-All Politics: How Washington Made the Rich Richer—and Turned Its Back on the Middle Class* (Simon & Schuster, 2010), 11; and Suresh Naidu, Dan Rodrick, and Gabriel Zucman, "Economics After Neoliberalism," *Boston Review*, February 15, 2019.

45. Lucas Chancel et al., *World Inequality Report 2022* (World Inequality Lab, 2021), 90. Other estimates suggest an even smaller group of individuals owning half the world's wealth. See Larry Elliott, "World's 26 Richest People Own as Much as Poorest 50%, Says Oxfam," *Guardian*, January 21, 2019; Axel Lehmann, Anthony Shorrocks, and Nannette Hechler-Fayd'herbe, "The Global Wealth Pyramid in 2022," *Global Wealth Report 2023*, Credit Suisse, September, 20, 2022, based

on data from James Davies, Rodrigo Lluberas, and Anthony Shorrocks, *Global Wealth Databook 2023*; and Hindu Data Team, "Top 1% Indians Income Share Is Higher Now Than Under British Rule," *Hindu*, March 23, 2024.

46. The five firms control between 70 and 90 percent of the grain trade. See Vincent Kiezebrink, *Hungry for Profits* (SOMO, 2024); and Hope Shand, Kathy Jo Wetter, and Kavya Chowdhry, *Food Barons 2022: Crisis Profiteering, Digitalization and Shifting Power* (ETC Group, 2022), 7. On market concentration, see Axel Ochsenfels and Martin Schmalz, "Die stille Gefahr für den Wettbewerb," *Frankfurter Allgemeine Zeitung*, July 29, 2016, 18. See also Omri Wallach, "The Top 50 Companies Proportion of World GDP," Visual Capitalist, July 19, 2021; and Rajesh Mascarenhas, "Apple's M-Cap Bigger Than Most Countries' GDP," *Economic Times*, July 7, 2023.

47. Naidu et al., "Economics After Neoliberalism."

48. OECD, *Growing Unequal? Income Distribution and Poverty in OECD Countries* (OECD, 2008); Joseph E. Stiglitz, "Die Wirtschaft, die wir brauchen," *Blätter für deutsche und internationale Politik*, October 2019, 80; Wolfgang Streeck, "Wie wird der Kapitalismus enden? Teil II," *Blätter für deutsche und internationale Politik*, April 2015, 111.

49. Jan Breman and Marcel van der Linden, "Informalizing the Economy: The Return of the Social Question at a Global Level," *Development and Change* 45 (2015): 921.

50. "The Jobs We Need," *NYT*, July 5, 2020; Breman and Van der Linden, "Informalizing the Economy," 920–40; Marcel van der Linden, "At the End of a Very Long Cycle: Why the Global Labor Movement Is in Crisis," unpublished paper (in author's possession) presented at the Global History Workshop organized by the Consortium of Global History Centers, Zoom, 2020, 2.

51. Van der Linden, "At the End of a Very Long Cycle," 1; Arboleda, *Planetary Mine*, 55.

52. Carr, "How Dark Factories Are Changing."

53. Birgit Mahnkopf, "Produktiver, Grüner, Friedlicher? Die falschen Versprechen des digitalen Kapitalismus," *Blätter für deutsche und internationale Politik*, October 2019, 89–98; Arboleda, *Planetary Mine*, 2.

54. Van der Linden, "At the End of a Very Long Cycle," 1; Marcel van der Linden, "San Precario: A New Inspiration for Labor Historians," *Labor*

11 (2014), 10; Breman and Van der Linden, "Informalizing the Economy," 924, 926, 928.

55. Arboleda, *Planetary Mine*, 89; Breman and Van der Linden, "Informalizing the Economy," 937–38.

56. Frederic Mousseau, *The Highest Bidder Takes It All: The World Bank's Scheme to Privatize the Commons* (Oakland Institute, 2019), 3.

57. Eman Abdelhalim Lasheen, "Against the Grain: A History and Policy Analysis of Rice, Water, and the Edible Landscape in Egypt" (PhD diss., MIT, 2022); Stephanie McCrummen, "The Great Serengeti Land Grab," *Atlantic*, May 2024, 21–32; Michael McDonald and Tatiana Freitas, "Harvard Land Ownership in Brazil Scrutinized in Title Dispute," Bloomberg, April 24, 2018; Alex Chou and Aryumi Nagatomi, "Stop Harvard Land Grabs Coalition Demands Reparations for Former Harvard Farmland Purchases in Brazil," *Harvard Crimson*, November 9, 2023; Fabio Pitta et al., *Land Grabbing and Ecocide: How Bunge, TIAA, and Harvard Fuel the Destruction of the Brazilian Cerrado* (Friend of the Earth, 2023), 5; Arboleda, *Planetary Mine*, 99; and Lizzie Presser, "Kicked Off the Land: Why So Many Black Families Are Losing Their Property," *New Yorker*, July 22, 2019.

58. Presser, "Kicked Off the Land"; Hannah Allam, "Sapelo Islanders Have Survived Persecution and Slavery. Can They Survive Tourism?," *BuzzFeed News*, August 9, 2018; and David Love, "From 15 Million Acres to 1 Million: How Black People Lost Their Land," *Atlanta Black Star*, June 30, 2017. For quotation, see Pitta et al., *Land Grabbing and Ecocide*, 3, 9.

59. Randy Ziegenhorn, "The Commodification of Hybrid Corn: What Farmers Know," in *Commodities and Globalization: Anthropological Perspectives*, ed. Angelique Haugerud (Rowman & Littlefield, 2000), 135–50; David Harvey, "The Art of Rent: Globalization, Monopoly and Commodification of Culture," *Socialist Register* 38 (2002): 98; and Daniel Robinson, *Confronting Biopiracy: Challenges, Cases and International Debates* (Earthscan, 2010), 63–65.

60. Zuboff, *Age of Surveillance Capitalism*; David Harvey, "The Future of the Commons," *Radical History Review* 109 (Winter 2011): 103. For quotations, see RELX, *2023 Annual Report Including Financial Statements and Corporate Responsibility Report* (RELX, 2023), 23; Brian Resnick and Julia Belluz, "The War to Free Science," *Vox*, July 10, 2019.

61. Parsons, *Carbon Colonialism*, 26; and Jason Hickel, Christian Dorninger, Hanspeter Wieland, and Intaan Sawandi, "Imperialist Appropriation in the World Economy: Drain from the Global South Through Unequal Exchange, 1990–2015," *Global Environmental Change* 73 (2022): 5. Machinery increased from $17 billion in US dollars in 2002 to $65 billion in 2012. See Arboleda, *Planetary Mine*, 3; Stephanie Pappas, "Human-Made Stuff Now Outweighs All Life on Earth," *Scientific American*, December 5, 2020; and Emily Elhacham et al., "Global Human-Made Mass Exceeds All Living Biomass," *Nature* (London) 588, no. 7838 (2020): 442.

62. See interview with Wolfgang Schütz in *Augsburger Allgemeine*, October 5, 2018.

63. Damian Carrington, "Plummeting Insect Numbers 'Threaten Collapse of Nature,'" *Guardian*, February 10, 2019.

64. Isabella Grullón Paz, "PFAS: The 'Forever Chemicals' You Couldn't Escape If You Tried," *NYT*, April 12 2022; Kyle Bagenstose, "Drinking Water of Millions of Americans Contaminated with 'Forever Chemicals,'" *Guardian*, August 17, 2023; Hannah Ritchie, Veronika Samborska, and Max Roser, "Plastic Pollution," Our World in Data, accessed April 22, 2024, https://our worldindata.org/plastic-pollution; Sarah Kaplan, "By 2050, There Will Be More Plastic Than Fish in the World's Oceans, Study Says," *Washington Post*, January 20, 2016; Stephanie Nolen, "Climate Change Drives New Cases of Malaria, Complicating Efforts to Fight the Disease," *NYT*, December 1, 2023; and Priya Joi, "Global Warming Means That One in Two of Us Are Now at Risk of Dengue," Gavi, the Vaccine Alliance, May 2, 2023. For the quotation, see Pope Francis, *Laudato Si'*.

65. Hannah Ritchie and Pablo Rosado, "Fossil Fuels," Our World in Data, accessed August 2, 2024, https://ourworldindata.org/fossil -fuels; Thorfinn Stainforth and Bartosz Brzezinski, "More Than Half of All CO$_2$ Emissions Since 1751 Emitted in the Last Thirty Years," Institute for European Environmental Policy, April 29, 2020; Amitav Ghosh, *The Nutmeg's Curse: Parables for a Planet in Crisis* (University of Chicago Press, 2021), 122; and David Wallace-Wells, "Post-Normal," *NYT Magazine*, September 24, 2023, 16–17. For current emissions, see "Historical GHG Emissions," Climate Watch, accessed May 14, 2024,

https://www.climatewatchdata.org /ghg-emissions?end_year=2020&re gions=TOP&start_year=1990.

66. Simon Black, Ian Parry, and Nate Vernon-Lin, "Fossil Fuel Subsidies Surged to Record $7 Trillion," *IMF Blog*, August 24, 2023.

67. Bryan Walsh, "Silicon Valley Is Chasing the Fountain of Youth," *Axios*, September 25, 2012; Parsons, *Carbon Colonialism*, 18, 82, 83; Wallace-Wells, "Post-Normal," 17; Elmar Altvater, "Zerstörung und Flucht," *Blätter für deutsche und internationale Politik*, January 2016: 83, 93. For quotation, see Hickel et al., "Imperialist Appropriation in the World Economy," 1.

68. Jonathan Watts, "Climate and Economic Risks Threaten 2008-Style Systemic Collapse," *Guardian*, February 12, 2019.

69. Günther Tallinger, "Climate Risk, Insurance: The Fall of Capitalism," as posted on LinkedIn, March 25, 2025. Brad Werner, "Is Earth F**ked? Dynamical Futility of Global Environmental Management and Possibilities for Sustainability via Direct Action Activism," paper presented at the American Geophysical Union meeting, San Francisco, December 5, 2012.

70. Anthony D. Barnosky, et al., "Approaching a State Shift in Earth's Biosphere," *Nature* 486, no. 7401 (June 2012): 52; and Dipesh Chakrabarty, "The Climate of History: Four Theses," *Critical Inquiry* 35 (2009): 200.

71. Arboleda, *Planetary Mine*, 46. The number for Asia's share of manufacturing in 2022 is calculated from "Manufacturing, Value Added (Current US$)," World Bank Group, accessed April 18, 2024, https://data .worldbank.org/indicator/NV.IND .MANF.CD. See also "Real GDP (Purchasing Power Parity)," World Factbook, accessed April 12, 2024, https://www.cia.gov/the-world -factbook/field/real-gdp-purchasing -power-parity/country-comparison/; C. Textor, "China's Share of Global Gross Domestic Product (GDP) Adjusted for Purchasing-Power-Parity (PPP) from 1980 to 2022 with Forecasts Until 2028," accessed April 12, 2024, https://www.statista.com/sta tistics/270439/chinas-share-of -global-gross-domestic-product-gdp/; Devesh Kapur et al., eds., introduction to *The Oxford Handbook of Higher Education in the Asia-Pacific Region* (OUP, 2023), 6; Li Angran, "What Happened When China Expanded Its Higher Education System?," *Sixth Tone*, January 11, 2023; Wing Kit Chan and Jiayu Zhang,

"Can University Qualification Promote Social Mobility? A Review of Higher Education Expansion and Graduate Employment in China," *International Journal of Educational Development* 84 (July 2021): 1; World Intellectual Property Organization, *World Intellectual Property Indicators Report* (World Intellectual Property Organization, 2023); and "China Widens Lead over US in AI Patents After Beijing Tech Drive," *Bloomberg News*, October 24, 2023.

72. Amy Hawkins, "Have We Reached Peak China? How the Booming Middle Class Hit a Brick Wall," *Guardian*, September 10, 2023; "How the Middle Class Will Play the Hero in India's Rise as World Power," *Economic Times*, July 9, 2023; "Global and Regional Poverty Estimates, 1990–2022," in R. Andrés Castañeda Aguilar et al., "March 2024 Global Poverty Update from the World Bank: First Estimates of Global Poverty Until 2022 from Survey Data," *World Bank Blogs*, March 26, 2024; Pryluka, "We Can't Go Back to a Golden Age of Capitalism"; Jason Hickel, "A Letter to Steven Pinker (and Bill Gates, for That Matter) About Global Poverty," *Jason Hickel* (blog), February 4, 2019; and Jason Hickel, "Bill Gates Says Poverty Is Decreasing. He Couldn't Be More Wrong," *Guardian*, January 29, 2019.

73. For counterexamples on neo-Marxist predictions, see Paul A. Baran, *Unterdrückung und Fortschritts: Essays* (Suhrkamp, 1969), 99–128; Ernest Mandel, "Die Marxsche Theorie der ursprünglichen Akkumulation und die Industrialisierung der Dritten Welt," in *Folgen einer Theorie: Essays über "Das Kapital" von Karl Marx*, 5th ed., ed. Ernst Theodor von Mohl (Suhrkamp, 1972), 71–93; Martin Franke, "Afrika liefert, Peking bezahlt," *Frankfurter Allgemeine Zeitung*, February 22, 2021; United Nations, Economic Commission on Latin America and the Caribbean, *Latin America and the Caribbean and China: Towards a New Era of Cooperation* (United Nations, 2015), 44; and Arboleda, *Planetary Mine*, 14.

74. Calculated in constant 2021 international dollars, PPP. See World Bank Group, "GDP, PPP (constant 2021 international $)—China, United States, European Union," accessed February 11, 2025, https://data.worldbank.org/indicator/NY.GDP.MKTP.PP.KD?end=2023&locations=CN-US-EU&start=2019.

75. Achille Mbembe, *Critique of Black Reason* (Duke UP, 2017), 1.

76. Arboleda, *Planetary Mine*, 5.

77. For US share of the global GDP, see Govind Bhutada, "The U.S. Share of the Global Economy over Time," *Visual Capitalist*, January 14, 2021. On the history of economic thought in China, see Isabella Weber, *How China Escaped Shock Therapy: The Market Reform Debate* (Routledge, 2021). For the quotation, see Kishore Mahbubani, interview, *Frankfurter Allgemeine Sonntagszeitung*, April 1, 2012, 11.

78. Maurizio Lazzarato, "From Capital-Labor to Capital-Life," *Ephemera: Theory and Politics in Organization* 4 (2004): 187–208.

79. Van der Linden, "At the End of a Very Long Cycle," 12.

80. Herman Mark Schwartz, "Wealth and Secular Stagnation: The Role of Industrial Organization and Intellectual Property Rights," *Russell Sage Foundation Journal of the Social Sciences* 2, no. 6 (October 2016): 228. Schwartz, "No Growth and No Equality," 3.

81. For Nike, see "Nike Manufacturing Map," accessed September 25, 2024, https://manufacturingmap.nikeinc.com/; and *Moving Together: FY23 Nike, Inc. Impact Report*, accessed September 25, 2024, https://about.nike.com/en/impact. See also Schwartz, "Wealth and Secular Stagnation," 237.

82. For a critical analysis of these trends, see François Chesnais, *Finance Capital Today: Corporations and Banks in the Lasting Global Slump* (Brill, 2016).

83. Margaret O'Mara, *The Code: Silicon Valley and the Remaking of America* (Penguin, 2020); Jerry Hirsch, "Elon Musk's Growing Empire Is Fueled by $4.9 Billion in Government Subsidies," *Los Angeles Times*, May 30, 2015; and Jason Lalljee, "Elon Musk Is Speaking Out Against Government Subsidies. Here's a List of the Billions of Dollars His Businesses Have Received," *Business Insider*, December 15, 2021; Julia Kollewe, "Elon Musk's Tesla Has Received Almost £200m in UK Grants Since 2016," *Guardian*, January 8, 2025; Chris Isidore, "How Much of Musk's Wealth Comes from Tax Dollars and Government Help?," *CNN Business*, November 20, 2024; Eric Lipton et al., "U.S. Agencies Fund, and Fight With, Elon Musk. A Trump Presidency Could Give Him Power over Them," *NYT*, October 30, 2024.

84. Herman Mark Schwartz, "American Hegemony: Intellectual Property Rights, Dollar Centrality, and Infrastructural Power," *Review of International Political Economy* 26, no. 3 (June 2019): 492, 507.

85. Robert Fredona and Sophus A. Reinert, "Leviathan and Kraken: States, Corporations, and Political Economy," *History and Theory: Studies in the Philosophy of History* 59, no. 2 (June 2020): 167–87; Aram Roston, "Private War: Erik Prince Has His Eye on Afghanistan's Rare Metals," *BuzzFeed News*, December 7, 2017; Kristin Ciupa, "Expanding Extractive Frontiers: Space Mining as Response to Capitalist Crisis," paper presented at the Rethinking Global Capitalism Conference, Rio de Janeiro, Brazil, March 13–15, 2024.

86. Alan S. Binder, "Financial Entropy and the Optimality of Over-Regulation," paper (in author's possession) presented at the 17th Annual International Banking Conference, Chicago, November 2014, 4.

87. Gary Gerstle, *The Rise and Fall of the Neoliberal Order: America and the World in the Free Market Era* (OUP, 2022), 260.

88. "Where It Went Wrong—and How the Crisis Is Changing It," *Economist*, July 18, 2009. See also Paul Krugman, "How Did Economists Get It So Wrong?," *NYT*, September 2, 2009; and Andrew Boughton and Michael West, "Wanted: A New Economic Theory," *Sydney Morning Herald*, February 6, 2009. For India, see "Meltdown Result of Faulty Economic System," *Times of India*, February 7, 2009.

89. Joseph Vogl, "Die Vergötzung des Marktes," *Blätter für deutsche und internationale Politik*, September 2017, 97, 103; and Heather Stewart, "This Is How We Let the Credit Crunch Happen, Ma'am . . . ," *Guardian*, July 26, 2009.

90. Harvard Political Review Editorial Board, "An Open Letter to Greg Mankiw," *Harvard Political Review*, November 2, 2011. See also "Wie die Ökonomen ihre eigene Krise beenden wollen," *Frankfurter Allgemeine Zeitung*, September 7, 2016; and International Student Initiative for Pluralism in Economics Editorial Board, "Open Letter—an International Student Call for Pluralism in Economics," International Student Initiative for Pluralism in Economics, May 5, 2014.

91. International Student Initiative for Pluralism in Economics Editorial Board, "ISIPE, One Year Later," In-

ternational Student Initiative for Pluralism in Economics, May 5, 2015; Rethinking Economics International, "About," accessed November 13, 2023, https://www.rethinkeconomics.org/about/; Rethinking Economics International, "Governance," accessed November 13, 2023, https://www.rethinkeconomics.org/about/governance; Liliann Fisher et al., *Rethinking Economics: An Introduction to Pluralist Economics* (Routledge, 2018), 3; Rethinking Economics International, "UNILAG Students Encourage Profs to Expand Econ Curriculum to Real-World Issues," October 5, 2023, accessed November 13, 2023, https://www.rethinkeconomics.org/impact-stories/unilag-students-encourage-profs-to-expand-econ-curriculum-to-real-world-issues/; Rethinking Economics International, "RE Lugano Gets New HET Course Now 5-Years in the Running on the Back of a Powerful Regional Campaign," October 4, 2023, accessed November 13, 2023, https://www.rethinkeconomics.org/impact-stories/lugano-het-course/; and Università della Svizzera italiana, "Storia critica del pensiero economico," accessed November 13, 2023, https://search.usi.ch/it/corsi/35263260/storia-critica-del-pensiero-economico.

92. Naidu et al., "Economics After Neoliberalism."

93. Stiglitz, "Die Wirtschaft, die wir brauchen," 87. See also Kenneth Rogoff, "Wir waren auf dem falschen Pfad," as cited in *Handelsblatt*, January 25, 2012, 17.

94. As cited in "Wenn das Vertrauen fehlt," *Handelsblatt*, January 25, 2012, 17. For the call for historical study, see the influential Carmen Reinhart and Kenneth Rogoff, *This Time Is Different: Eight Centuries of Financial Folly* (PUP, 2009). See also "Wie die Ökonomen ihre eigene Krise beenden wollen; and Patrick Gernau, "Warum ist Wirtschaftsgeschichte plötzlich sexy?," *Frankfurter Allgemeine Sonntagszeitung*, November 23, 2012, 30. For this argument, see also Vogl, "Die Vergötzung des Marktes," 107.

95. Ian Smith, "Civil Unrest Overtakes Terrorism in Insurance Claims," *Financial Times*, April 9, 2023.

96. Neeraj Chauhan, "Protests & Riots Due to Agrarian Distress Almost Doubled in 2016," *Times of India*, December 2, 2017. On social movements in the countryside, see EJAtlas, "Global Atlas of Environmental

Justice," accessed February 1, 2024, https://ejatlas.org/; Allison Goebel, "'Our Struggle Is for the Full Loaf': Protests, Social Welfare and Gendered Citizenship in South Africa," *Journal of Southern African Studies* 37 (2011), 369; and Arundhati Roy, *Capitalism: A Ghost Story* (Haymarket Books, 2014).

97. Quinn Slobodian, "The Backlash Against Neoliberal Globalization from Above: Elite Origins of the Crisis of the New Constitutionalism," *Theory, Culture & Society* 38, no. 6 (2021): 51–69.

98. Edmund Burke Foundation, "National Conservatism: A Statement of Principles," accessed November 3, 2023, https://nationalconservatism.org/national-conservatism-a-statement-of-principles/.

99. Lauren R. Rublin, "2017 Roundtable, Part 1," *Barron's*, January 16, 2017, 54.

100. See Moritz Schularick, interview, *Frankfurter Allgemeine Zeitung*, March 3, 2023. The quote is probably from Edward N. Luttwak, "From Geopolitics to Geo-Economics: Logic of Conflict, Grammar of Commerce," *National Interest*, no. 20 (Summer 1990): 17–23.

101. For the COVID-19 crisis, see, for example, Mike Davis, *The Monster Enters: COVID-19, Avian Flu, and the Plagues of Capitalism* (Verso, 2022); and Quinn Slobodian and Dieter Plehwe, "Neoliberals Against Europe," in *Mutant Neoliberalism: Market Rule and Political Rupture*, ed. William Callison and Zachary Manfredi (Fordham UP, 2020), 92, 100.

102. See, for example, Nancy Fraser, "Legitimation Crisis? On the Political Contradictions of Financialized Capitalism," *Critical Historical Studies* 2, no. 2 (Fall 2015): 158; Stiglitz, "Die Wirtschaft, die wir brauchen," 87; and Schütz, interview. For the quotation, see Robert Kuttner, "Can Democracy Survive Global Capitalism?," *Boston Globe*, April 12, 2018. See also Steven Levitsky and Daniel Ziblatt, *How Democracies Die* (Crown, 2018).

103. Quinn Slobodian, *Crack-Up Capitalism: Market Radicals and the Dream of a World Without Democracy* (Metropolitan Books, 2023), 202; Quinn Slobodian, *Globalists: The End of Empire and the Birth of Neoliberalism* (HUP, 2018), 178–79, 236–37, 277. See also the discussion in chapter 17 of this book.

104. Lauren Collins, "Sark Spring," *New Yorker*, October 22, 2012; Simon Bowers and Helen Pidd, "Brecqhou: How Windswept Eyesore

Became Barclays' Getaway," *Guardian*, June 27, 2012; Jonathan Parry, "Life on Sark," *London Review of Books* 45, no. 10 (May 2023): https://www.lrb.co.uk/the-paper/v45/n10/jonathan-parry/life-on-sark.

105. Conal Walsh, "Barclays Attack Sark as Europe's 'Last Bastion of Feudalism,'" *Guardian*, March 27, 2005; Collins, "Sark Spring"; and Parry, "Life on Sark."

106. This part is also based on personal observations by the author and conversations with the islanders in the summer of 2009. See Pippa Bailey, "How the Barclay Brothers Built and Wrecked an Empire," *New Statesman*, October 25, 2023; Collins, "Sark Spring"; Graham Rowley and Doreen Carvajal, "Masterpieces Tucked Away to Appreciate, Not to Be Appreciated," *NYT*, May 26, 2016; "Buried Treasure: A New Study Details the Wealth Hidden in Tax Havens," *Economist*, October 7, 2017; and Knut Krohn, "1000 Millionäre Ziehen ins Meer," *Badische Zeitung*, August 4, 2021.

107. Slobodian, *Crack-Up Capitalism*, 3, 8; François Bost, "Special Economic Zones: Methodological Issues and Definition," *Transnational Corporations* 26, no. 2 (June 2019): 143.

108. The Seasteading Institute, "Who We Are," accessed May 6, 2024, https://www.seasteading.org/about/.

109. Slobodian, *Crack-Up Capitalism*, 14, 186–210. On exiting capital owners, see also Raymond Craib, *Adventure Capitalism: A History of Libertarian Exit, from the Era of Decolonization to the Digital Age* (PM Press/Spectre, 2022).

110. See tweet by Elon Musk, September 7, 2024, https://x.com/elonmusk/status/18325503222938 37833.

111. Julie Turkewitz, "For Sale: A Chance to Beat Doomsday, and It Has a Water Slide," *NYT*, August 14, 2019; Anna Fifield, "New Zealand Decided It Was in the Public Interest to Make Peter Thiel a Citizen," *Washington Post*, February 1, 2017; and Molly Redden, "Which Tech Bro Is Fleeing Coronavirus on This 'Lord of the Rings' Plane?," *Huffington Post*, March 16, 2020.

112. Jean-Pierre Dupuy, *Economy and the Future: A Crisis of Faith* (Michigan State UP, 2014), xv.

113. As Charles Maier did beautifully for the end of communism. See Charles Maier, *Dissolution: The Crisis of Communism and the End of East Germany* (PUP, 1999).

114. Samir Amin, *The Implosion of Capitalism* (Pluto Press, 2014), 8; Fraser, "Legitimation Crisis," 159; Wolfgang Streek, "Wie wird der Kapitalismus Enden? Teil 1," *Blätter für deutsche und internationale Politik*, March 2015, 99–111.

115. Jason Moore, "The End of Cheap Nature, or How I Learned to Stop Worrying About 'the' Environment and Love the Crisis of Capitalism," in *Structures of the World Political Economy and the Future of Global Conflict and Cooperation*, ed. Christian Suter and Christopher Chase-Dunn (Lit, 2014), 285–314, here 308; and Paul Mason, *Postcapitalism: A Guide to Our Future* (Allan Lane, 2015), x.

116. Barbara Fields uses this trope to talk about slavery. See Barbara Jeanne Fields, "The Advent of Capitalist Agriculture: The New South in a Bourgeois World," in *Essays on the Postbellum Southern Economy*, vol. 18, ed. Thavolia Glymph, Harold D. Woodman, Barbara Jeanne Fields, and Armstead L. Robinson (Texas A&M UP, 1985), 77.

117. Erik Olin Wright, "Untergraben wir den Kapitalismus!," *Blätter für deutsche und internationale Politik*, October 2017, 77; and Kyosuke Inoue, "Satoyama Capitalism 2024," *Japan Times*, October 28, 2023. On Satoyama capitalism, see also Saori Tanaka and Evonne Yiu, "From Money Capitalism to Satoyama Capitalism," *Our World*, January 14, 2016.

118. Corrado Mornese, *Rima— Rimmu: Ieri oggi domani* (Millenia, 1995), 58–59.

119. See Anthony B. Atkinson, *Inequality: What Can Be Done?* (HUP, 2015). Joseph Stiglitz calls for a "progressive capitalism." See Stiglitz, "Die Wirtschaft, die wir brauchen," 79–87; and Wright, "Untergraben wir den Kapitalismus!," 69.

Illustration Credits

Page xi: Copyright The National Gallery, London, all rights reserved; bought 1871. David Teniers the Younger, *The Rich Man Being Led to Hell*, oil on oak, circa 1647.

Page 1: Lindenau-Museum, Altenburg, inventory no. G 1973 164. Elisabeth Voigt, *Der Maschinenmann* [The Machine Man], woodcut, 1932.

Page 29: Bibliothèque nationale de France. Abu Muhammad al-Qasim ibn 'Ali al-Hariri, *Al-Makamat al-Hariri*, circa 1236–1237, folio 119v.

Page 44: Bibliothèque nationale de France. Abu Muhammad al-Qasim ibn 'Ali al-Hariri, *Al-Makamat al-Hariri*, circa 1236–1237, folio 31r.

Page 45: Map by Martin Jan Månsson.

Page 46: Courtesy of the author.

Page 53, both images: Courtesy of the Ministero della Cultura, Musei del Bargello, Florence.

Page 58: Gary Lee Todd, courtesy of Flickr. Held by Liaoning Museum, Shenyang.

Page 63: Bequest of Benjamin Altman, 1913, Metropolitan Museum of Art, New York. Hans Memling, *Maria Portinari (Maria Maddalena Baroncelli, Born 1456)*, oil on wood, circa 1470.

Page 67: Bibliothèque nationale de France. Abraham Cresques, *Atlas de cartes marines*, also known as *Atlas Catalan*, circa 1370–1380.

Page 70: Images from the collections of the National Library of Spain. Diego Durán, *Historia de las Indias de Nueva España e Islas de la Tierra Firme*, 1579.

Page 73: National Library of China, courtesy of Wikimedia commons. Woodblock print, Zhang Xian 張憲 and Zhang Yanghui 張陽輝, eds., Zhang shi tong zong shi pu 張氏統宗世譜, 1535.

Page 79, left: Bibliothèque nationale de France. Abu Muhammad al-Qasim ibn 'Ali al-Hariri, *Al-Makamat al-Hariri*, circa 1236–37, folio 105r.

Page 79, center: Bequest of Benjamin Altman, 1913, Metropolitan Museum of Art, New York. Hans Memling, *Tommaso di Folco Portinari (1428–1501)*, oil on wood, circa 1470.

Page 79, right: National Library of China, courtesy of Wikimedia commons. Woodblock print, Zhang Xian 張憲 and Zhang Yanghui 張陽輝, eds., Zhang shi tong zong shi pu 張氏統宗世譜,1535.

Page 90: Afrasiyab Museum. Artist unknown.

Page 101: Bildarchiv Foto Marburg / Max Hirmer, *Sockelrelief: Legende vom betrügerischen Tuchhändler* [Bas-Relief: Legend of the Dishonest Cloth Merchant], photo of circa 1230 carving on Cathédrale Notre-Dame de Reims.

Page 103, both images: Courtesy of the author. San Marco Monastery.

Page 105: Nationaal Archief, The Hague, Netherlands. Drawings of the forts of St. George del Mina and Nassau along the gold coast of Guinea, by the firm of Van Keulen, eighteenth century.

Page 107: Courtesy of Biblioteca Casanatense, Rome, MiC, MS1889C49. Artist unknown, "Album di disegni, illustranti usi e costumi dei popoli d'Asia e d'Africa con brevi dichiarazioni in lingua portoghese" [Album of Drawings, Illustrating the Uses and Customs of the People of Asia and Africa with Brief Descriptions in Portuguese Language].

Page 109: Smithsonian Libraries and Archives. Philippus Baldaeus and Awnsham Churchill, *A True and Exact Description of the Most Celebrated East-India Coasts of Malabar and Coromandel*, vol. 3 (London, 1703).

Page 111: Bayerische Staatsbibliothek, Munich. Jacob Peeters, *Description des principales Villes.*

Page 113: Courtesy of the Palace Museum. Portrait by Fang Shishu (1692–1791), "Ma Yueguan, the leader of salt merchants from Anhui Province in Yangzhou."

Page 114: Art Collection 2 / Alamy Stock Foto. Artist unknown, portrait of merchant Zheng Chenggong 鄭成功.

Page 116: Biblioteca Geral Digital da Universidade de Coimbra. D. João de Castro, *Tavoas dos lugares da costa da India*, sixteenth century.

Page 122: Library of Congress, Rare Book and Special Collections Division. Theodor de Bry, ed. *Dritte Buch Americae: Darinn Brasilia durch Johann Staden auss eigener Erfahrung in teutsch beschrieben. Item Historia der Schiffart Ioannis Lerij in Brasilien, welche er selbst publiciert hat, jetzt von newem verteutscht, durch Teucrium Annaeum Priuatum, C.*, 1593.

Page 123: Courtesy of Galata Museo del Mare, Genova. Ridolfo Bigordi detto (del) Ghirlandaio, *Ritratto di Cristoforo Colombo.*

Page 124: Rijksmuseum, Amsterdam, object no. SK-A-4282. Hendrik van Schuylenburgh, *The Trading Post of the Dutch East India Company in Hooghly, Bengal*, oil on canvas, 1665.

Page 125: Rijksmuseum, Amsterdam, object no. SK-A-2350. Attributed to circle of Aelbert Cuyp, *VOC Senior Merchant with His Wife and an Enslaved Servant*, oil on canvas, circa 1650–1655.

Page 130: Courtesy of the Hispanic Museum & Library, New York. Artist unknown.

Page 134: Courtesy of the author.

Page 137: Rijksmuseum, Amsterdam, on loan from the City of Amsterdam. Rembrandt van Rijn, *The Sampling Officials of the Amsterdam Drapers' Guild, Known as "The Syndics,"* oil on canvas, circa 1662.

Page 140: Amsterdam Museum, on loan from Vereniging Hendrik de Keyser, 2007, object no. SK-C-6. Philips (II) Vinckboons, *Courtyard of the Bourse*, oil on canvas, 1634.

Page 142: Rijksmuseum, Amsterdam, gift of J. H. Willink van Bennebroek, Oegstgeest, object no. SK-A-1972. Abraham van den Tempel, *David Leeuw and Cornelia Hooft with Their Children*, oil on canvas, 1671.

Page 143: Noord-Hollands Archief, 1477, Collectie van Prenten van C. G. Voorhelm Schneevoogt te Haarlem, inventory no. 158. Maarten van Heemskerck and Dirck Volkertszoon Coornhert, *De Deugdzame vrouw bedient haar gezin* [The Virtuous Woman Serves Her Family], from Maarten van Heemsckerck, *Praise of the Virtuous Wife* series, 1555.

Page 146: Rijksmuseum, Amsterdam, on loan from the Broere Charitable Foundation, object no. SK-C-6. Willem van de Welde, *Dutch Ships in a Calm Sea*, oil on canvas, circa 1665.

Page 155: Fototeca Musei Civici Fiorentini.

Page 162: British Library Collection, MS Add. 15217. Hieronymus Köler the Elder, *Gouverneur Georg Hohermuth von Speyer (Rechts) und Philipp von Hutten (Mitte) anläßlich der Musterung der Welser-Armada in Sanlúcar de Barrameda vor der Einschiffung nach Venezuela* [Governor Georg Hohermuth of Speyer (Right) and Philipp von Hutten (Center) on the Occasion of the Mustering of the Welser Armada in Sanlúcar de Barrameda Before Embarkation for Venezuela], drawing, 1560.

Page 165: Copyright the Trustees of the British Museum. Artist unknown.

Page 177: Library of Congress Prints and Photographs Division. John Hinton, *A Representation of the Sugar-Cane and the Art of Making Sugar*, engraving, 1749.

Page 193: Provided by Harvard University. Johann Baptist Homann, *Prospect Grundris und Gegend der polnischen vesten Reichs und Handels-Stadt Dantzig und ihrem Werder*, map, circa 1720.

Page 199: Courtesy of Wikimedia Commons. Joseph Vivien, *Portrait of Samuel Bernard Comte de Coubert*, pastel on paper.

Page 201: William L. Clements Library, University of Michigan. I. M. Beck, *Tilforladelig kort over eylandet St. Croix udi America: Saaledes som det ved en acurat udmaaling er befunden met quarterernes nayne og enhver plantagies nummer estler hvilke de udi matriculen findes indeforte og til enhver kiöber cederet beliggende paa 17 grader 38 minuter norder brefe*, 1754.

Page 205: Amsterdam Museum, on loan from Koninklijk Oudheidkundig Genootschap, Amsterdam. Artist unknown, *Gevelsteen 'D. Cormandelse Catoen Baalen*, sandstone.

Page 207: Collection Westfries Museum, Hoorn, Netherlands. Jacques Waben, *Portrait of Jan Pieterszoon Coen*, oil on panel, 1623.

Page 208: Rijksmuseum, Amsterdam, object no. SK-A-4476. Attributed to Johannes Vinckboons, *Gezicht op Banda, zuidelijke Molukken*, oil on linen, circa 1662–1663.

Page 218, both images: courtesy of the Diocesi Patriarcato di Venezia. Monument to Doge Giovanni Pesaro, Basilica di Santa Maria Gloriosa dei Frari, sculpture, circa 1665–1669.

Page 219: Archives national d'Outre-mer, Aix-en-Provence, France, 164 APOM 1, Le Gentil de Paroy. Jacques Dion, *Le Gentil de Paroy, Plantation on Saint Domingue*.

Page 245: Copyright SLUB Dresden / Technol.A.222-6. Friedrich Kohl, Franz Luckenbacher, and Hermann Rentzsch, *Die mechanische Bearbeitung der Rohstoffe* (Berlin: Otto Spamer 1867), 207.

Page 247: Sächsisches Staatsarchiv, Dresden. Image taken from Bruno E. H. Gerstmann, "Beiträge zur Kulturgeschichte Schlesiens."

Page 249: Courtesy of the author.

Page 254: Rijksmuseum, Amsterdam. "Bord uit V.O.C.-schip de 'Witte Leeuw,'" porcelain.

Page 259: Purchase, bequest of George Blumenthal and gift of Indjoudjian Freres, by exchange, and the Friends of the Islamic Department Fund, 1982, object no. 1982.66, Metropolitan Museum of Art, New York. Bed cover (palampore), attributed to Coromandel Coast, India, cotton, plain weave, mordant painted and dyed, resist-dyed, eighteenth century.

Page 267: Li Zhaoxiang, *History of the Longjiang Shipyard* (Jiangsu Ancient Books, 1999). Original 1553.

Page 271: Stadsarchief, Amsterdam. Johannes Davidsz Vingboons and Justus Vingboons, *Kloveniersburgwal 29, Ontwerp van het Trippenhuis, Afbeelding in spiegelbeeld*, engraving, 1662.

Page 272: Amsterdam Museum, inventory. no. 1426. Credited to Jacob Gerritsz Cuyp, *Mansportret, traditioneel geidentificeerd als Louis de Geer (1587–1652)* [Portrait of a Man, Traditionally Identified as Louis de Geer (1587–1652)], 1632.

Page 273: Rijksmuseum, Amsterdam, object no. SK-A-1510. Allaert van Everdingen, *Hendrick Trip's Cannon Foundry in Julitabruk, Sweden*, oil on canvas, 1650–1675.

Page 283: Yale Center for British Art, Paul Mellon Collection. Thomas Luny, *The Port of London*, oil on canvas, 1798.

Page 284: Bibliothèque nationale de France, département Estampes et photographie. Yves-Marie Le Gouaz, engraving after Nicolas-Marie Ozanne, *Le port de Bordeaux // Vu devant le Château Trompette sur la Garonne*, 1776.

Page 285: Courtesy of the Bethmann family. Image from Wolfgang Henninger, *Johann Jakob von Bethmann, 1717–1792: Kaufmann, reeder und kaiserlicher Konsul in Bourdeaux*, vol. 2 (Universitätsverlag Dr. N. Brockmeyer, 1993), 703.

Page 288: Courtesy of the John Carter Brown Library, Providence, Rhode Island. Nicolas Ponce, M. Phelipeau, and M. L. E. Moreau de Saint-Méry, *Recueil de vues des lieux principaux de la colonie françoise de Saint-Domingue*, 1791.

Page 291: Graph by Angela Yan. Source: Marion Johnson, *Anglo-African Trade in the Eighteenth Century: English Statistics on African Trade, 1699–1808* (Centre for the History of European Expansion, 1990), pp. 54–55.

Page 320: Wellcome Collection, London. J. Hinton, *Spinners and Stocking Makers: Interior View, a Spinning Wheel and a Stocking Machine*, engraving, 1750.

Page 325: Bomann-Museum, Celle, Germany, inventory no. BM00273. August Dankworth, *Porträt der Celler Kaufmannsfamilie Jacobs* [Portrait of the Merchant Family Jacobs from Celle], 1852.

Page 327: history_docu_photo / Alamy Stock Foto. Cotton mill at Walter Evans and Company, Derby, England, nineteenth century.

Page 329: Balfron Heritage Group.

Page 335: Copyright CSG CIC Glasgow Museums and Libraries Collection: The Mitchell Library, Special Collections. D. O. Hill, untitled view of the Garnkirk & Glasgow Railway, 1831.

Page 338: Graph by Angela Yan. Source: Seymour Shapiro, *Capital and the Cotton Industry in the Industrial Revolution* (Cornell University Press, 1967), 253.

Page 339: Graph by Angela Yan. Source: Seymour Shapiro, *Capital and the Cotton Industry in the Industrial Revolution* (Cornell University Press, 1967), 23.

Page 352: Courtesy of Wikipedia. Unknown artist, portrait of John Cockerill.

Page 364: Bibliothèque nationale de France. "Scènes dans les mines de houille, en Angleterre—Le Trapper," *Le Magasin pittoresque*, 1843.

Page 371: Graph by Angela Yan. Source: Seymour Shapiro, *Capital and the Cotton Industry in the Industrial Revolution* (Cornell University Press, 1967), 23.

1258 | ILLUSTRATION CREDITS

Page 375: Graph by Angela Yan. Source: Paul Bairoch, "International Industrialization Levels from 1750 to 1980," *Journal of European Economic History* 11, no. 2 (1982): 296, 304.

Page 377: Marc Ferrez / Coleção Gilberto Ferrez / Acervo Instituto Moreira Salles. Unknown photographer, *Departure for the Coffee Harvest by Ox Cart, Vale do Paraíba, Brazil*, circa 1885.

Page 380: Copyright Mairie de Bordeaux, Musée d'Aquitaine. Unknown artist, *Représentation de l'idée que, dans la colonie française de Saint Domingue . . .* , paper, 1797.

Page 386: Graph by Angela Yan. Source: "Hay, Cotton, Cottonseed, Shorn Wool, and Tobacco—Acreage, Production, and Price: 1790 to 1860—Con," in U.S. Department of Commerce, Historical Statistics of the United States, 517–18.

Page 393: Graph by Angela Yan. Sources: Aurora Gómez-Galvarriato, "Premodern Manufacturing," in *Cambridge Economic History of Latin America*, vol. 1, ed. Victor Bulmer-Thomas, John Coatsworth, Roberto Cortes-Conde (Cambridge University Press, 2005), 368; Pierre de Sornay, *Isle de France, Ile Maurice* (General Printing and Stationery, 1950), 367; Ulbe Bosma and Jonathan Curry-Machado, "Two Islands, One Commodity: Cuba, Java, and the Global Sugar Trade (1790–1930)," *New West Indian Guide* 86 (Brill, KITLV, Royal Netherlands Institute of Southeast Asian and Caribbean Studies, 2012): 238; Ulbe Bosma, *The Sugar Plantation in India and Indonesia: Industrial Production, 1770–2010* (Cambridge University Press, 2016), 19, 29; Willem G. Wolters, "Sugar Production in Java and in the Philippines During the Nineteenth Century," *Philippine Studies* 40, no. 4 (1992): 412; J. H. Galloway, *The Sugar Cane Industry: An Historical Geography from Its Origins to 1914* (Cambridge University Press, 1989), 212.

Page 395: Yale Center for British Art, Paul Mellon Collection. William A. V. Austin, *Ten Views in the Island of Antigua: In Which Are Represented the Process of Sugar Making, and the Employment of the Negroes, in the Field, Boiling-House and Distillery*, from drawings made by William Clark (London: Thomas Clay, 1823).

Page 396: Justo Germán Cantero, *Los ingenios: Colección de vistas de los principales ingenios de azúcar de la Isla de Cuba*, illus. Eduardo Laplante (Havana: L. Marquier, 1857), 94. Images taken from the 2005 reprint by Centro de Estudios y Experimentación de Obras Públicas (Madrid).

Page 397: Justo Germán Cantero, *Los ingenios: Colección de vistas de los principales ingenios de azúcar de la Isla de Cuba*, illus. Eduardo Laplante (Havana: L. Marquier, 1857), 37. Images taken from the 2005 reprint by Centro de Estudios y Experimentación de Obras Públicas (Madrid).

Page 398: Courtesy of Fundación Antonio Núñez Jiménez, Havana, Cuba, Fondo de agrimensores Serafín Sánchez Govín. Juan Augusto Dulong, "Plano del reparto de las haciendas Banagüises, Jigüe y Rio de Piedras, según las operaciones realizadas en los años de 1839 y 1840," August 2, 1842.

Page 399: Courtesy of the author. John Morley, *The Life of William Ewart Gladstone*, vol. 1, *1809–1859* (Macmillan, 1903).

Page 403: Graph by Angela Yan. Sources: M. R. Fernando, "Coffee Cultivation in Java, 1830–1917," in *The Global Coffee Economy in Africa, Asia, and Latin America, 1500–1989*, ed. William Gervase Clarence-Smith and Steven Topik (Cambridge University Press, 2003); Michel-Rolph Trouillot, "Motion in the System: Coffee, Color, and Slavery in Eighteenth-Century Saint-Domingue," *Review* (Fernand Braudel Center) 5, no. 3 (1982): 337; Rafael Marquese, "Compulsory Labor and the Reconfiguration of the Coffee World Economy in the Age of Revolutions, c. 1760–1840," unpublished paper (in author's possession), 4; Mario Samper and Radin Fernando, "Appendix: Historical Statistics of Coffee Production and Trade from 1700 to 1960," in *The Global Coffee Economy in Africa, Asia, and Latin America, 1500–1989*, ed. William Gervase Clarence-Smith and Steven Topik (Cambridge University Press, 2003); C. F. van Delden Laërne, *Brazil and Java: Report on Coffee-Culture* (London: W.H. Allen, 1885), 413–18, 428; V. L. Baril, *L'Empire du Brésil* (Paris: Ferdinand Sartorius, 1862), 189.

Page 405: Getty Research Institute, Los Angeles, 2897-629. Johann Rugendas, *Voyage pittoresque dans le Brésil* (Paris: Engelmann, 1835).

Page 417: National Army Museum, London, 1971-02-33-488-2. *The Taking of the Island of Chusan by the British, 5th July 1840*, lithograph after Lieutenant-Colonel Sir Harry Darell (1814–1853), 7th Dragoon Guards, published by Day and Son, 1852.

Page 418: Image courtesy of Martyn Gregory Gallery, London.

Page 420: Graph by Angela Yan. Sources: Romesh Chunder Dutt, *The Economic History of India Under Early British Rule* (K. Paul, Trench, Trübner, 1908), 295; Lewis Ceil Gray and Esther Katherine Thompson, *History of Agriculture in the Southern United States* (Carnegie Institution, 1933), 1024; Robert S. Smith, "Indigo Production and Trade in Colonial Guatemala," *Hispanic American Historical Review* 39, no. 2 (1959): 196–97; José Gemán Pacheco Troconís, *El añil: Historia de un cultivo olvidado en Venezuela, 1767–1870* (Universitat Autònoma de Barcelona, 2009), 479, 487, 851; Dauril Alden, "The Growth and Decline of Indigo Production in Colonial Brazil: A Study in Comparative Economic History," *Journal of Economic History* 25, no. 1 (1965): 35–60; John

Garrigus, "Blue and Brown: Contraband Indigo and the Rise of a Free Colored Planter Class in French Saint Domingue," *Americas* 50, no. 2 (1993): 239.

Page 422: From the British Library Collection, shelfmark X 108, 76. William Simpson and John William Kaye, *India, Ancient and Modern: A Series of Illustrations of the Country and People of India and Adjacent Territories*, vol. 2 (London: Day and Son, 1867).

Page 424: From the British Library Collection, shelfmark 10057.e.38, 116. Colesworthey Grant, *Rural Life in Bengal; Illustrative of Anglo-Indian Suburban Life, Etc.* (1860), 116.

Page 426: Graph by Angela Yan. Source: B. R. Mitchell, *European Historical Statistics, 1750–1970* (Macmillan Press, 1975), 199–277.

Page 431: Photographer unknown.

Page 433: Graph by Angela Yan. Sources: Maurice J. Bric, "Patterns of Irish Emigration to America, 1783–1800," *Éire-Ireland* 36, no. 1 (2001): 26; William P. Dillingham, *Reports of the Immigration Commission*, vol. 3 (Government Printing Office, 1911), 14–27; Patrick Fitzgerald and Brian Lambkin, *Migration in Irish History, 1607–2007* (Palgrave Macmillan, 2008), 175; Joel Mokyr, *Why Ireland Starved: A Quantitative and Analytical History of the Irish Economy, 1800–1850* (Routledge, 2013), e-book, ch. 8.1; William Forbes Adams, *Ireland and Irish Emigration to the New World* (Yale University Press, 1932), 413–26; Jeffrey G. Williamson, "The Impact of the Irish on the British Labor Market During the Industrial Revolution," *Journal of Economic History* 46, no. 3 (1986): 697.

Page 436: From the British Library Collection, P.P.7611, 380. *Illustrated London News*, December 16, 1848.

Page 445: Instituto Moreira Salles, São Paulo. Photographer unknown, *Lady in the Litter with Two Slaves, Bahia, Brazil*, circa 1860.

Page 448: The Metropolitan Museum of Art, New York. Artist unknown, drawing, *Daily Graphic*, March 30, 1880.

Page 451: Courtesy of the Peabody Essex Museum, Salem, Massachusetts. Milton M. Miller, *Family of a Chinese Merchant, 1860–1863*, albumen print.

Page 457: Upplandsmuseet, Uppsala, Sweden. August Fredrik Schagerström, photograph, July 28, 1915.

Page 459: Acervo Museu da República / IBRAM / Ministério da Cultura. Emil Bauch, *António Clemente Pinto, primeiro barão de Nova Friburgo, e sua esposa* [António Clemente Pinto, first baron of Nova Friburgo, and his wife], 1867.

Page 460: Courtesy of Ulrich Mücke. Photographer unknown, circa 1860s.

Page 462: Courtesy of Tata Central Archives, Pune, India.

Page 467: Courtesy of Ministero della Cultura, Musei del Bargello, Florence.

Page 469: Archives of the National Library Foundation, Brazil.

Page 471: Photographer unknown, taken from Mona Abaza, "The Cotton Plantation Remembered: An Egyptian Family Story" (American University in Cairo Press, 2013), 108. Courtesy of Laura Staut.

Page 472: Courtesy of the Bethmann family. 1864.

Page 474: Courtesy of Zemaria Pinto. Photo, circa 1900, palavradofingidor.blogspot.com/2014/12/manaus-amor-e-memoria-clxxxix.html.

Page 477: Collection of Museu Paulista da Universidade de São Paulo, José Rosael / Hélio Nobre.

Page 482: Manchester Libraries, Information and Archives, identifier GB127.m53434. Photographer unknown, 1856.

Page 484: Manchester Libraries, Information and Archives, identifier GB127.m19377. W. H. Farrow, 1895.

Page 485: From the British Library Collection, Evan.5095. Anglo-American Drug Co. / Henry Evanion, "Mrs. Winslow's soothing syrup. Oldest and safest remedy for children teething soothes the child gives rest to the mother. Price 1s/1 1/2 per bottle . . . Anglo-American Drug Co., Ltd. registered design," 1892.

Page 492: Wikimedia Commons. Messieurs de Balzac, Roger de Beauvoir, and Raymond Brucker, *Les Belles Femmes de Paris et de la Province* (Paris: Au Bureau, 1839–1840), microfilm, History of Women, reel 154, no. 980.

Page 495: Wikimedia Commons. John Jabez Edwin Mayall, *Portrait of Karl Marx*, date unknown but before August 24, 1875.

Page 509: Wikimedia Commons. *Combat et prise de la Crête-à-Pierrot* (*Attack and Take of the Crête-à-Pierrot*) (March 4–24, 1802). Ernst Hébert, engraving after Auguste Raffet, from M. de Norvins, *Histoire de Napoleon* (1839), 239.

Graphische Sammlung, erworben 1924, beschlagnahmt 1937, Rückkauf 1948. Otto Dix, *Sturmtruppe geht unter Gas vor* [Shock Troops Advance Under Gas], etching, aquatint, and drypoint, 1924.

Page 734: San Diego Air & Space Museum. Photographer unknown, AEG (Allgemeine Elektricitäts-Gesellschaft) G II 1915 Nowarra.

Page 735: Bibliothèque nationale de France. Agence Rol, Kattowitz (now Katowice), 1921.

Page 737: Courtesy of Centro Storico Fiat, Torino, Italy.

Page 738: Wikimedia Commons. Postcard, 1905.

Page 743: Photographer unknown, 1920.

Page 745: Copyright 1970 by Frank Cass. Clements Kadalie, *My Life and the ICU: The Autobiography of a Black Trade Unionist in South Africa.*

Page 746: From Hans Spethmann, *Die Rote Armee an Rhein und Ruhr, mit einem Charakterbild von Hans Severing*, 6th ed. (R. Hobbing, 1932), tafel 4.

Page 747: Transnet Heritage Library Magazine Collection, drisa.co.za.

Page 748: Collection International Institute of Social History, Amsterdam. Corn Leenheer, photograph, 1904.

Page 752, top and bottom: Stabilimenti FIAT di Produzione Automoblistica, 4, Lingotto, MSC 0023. Courtesy of Centro Storico Fiat, Torino, Italy.

Page 753: Courtesy of Centro Storico Fiat, Torino, Italy.

Page 754: ales Department, Poughkeepsie, in MSC 0095, La Fiat all' estero, Stati Uniti d'America. Courtesy of Centro Storico Fiat.

Page 755: Courtesy of Centro Storico Fiat, Torino, Italy.

Page 760: SPS 19354-755, photography collection. Courtesy of Centro Storico, Fiat, Torino, Italy.

Page 762: Österreichisches Gesellschafts- und Wirtschaftsmuseum, inventory no. INV-00001-059. "Kraftwagenbestand der Erde," from *Gesellschaft und Wirtschaft.*

Page 765: Staatliche Kunsthalle Karlsruhe. Georg Scholz, *Zeitungsträger* [Newspaper Carrier], lithograph, 1924.

Page 766: Graph by Angela Yan. Source: Records of the Bureau of the Treasury, Records Related to Government Agencies or Functions, Correspondence and Other Records Relating to Fiscal Relationships Between the United States and Other Nations, 1918–1941, record group 39, box 117, U.S. National Archives and Record Administration, Washington, DC.

Page 771: Oskar Morgenstern, in *Monatsberichte des österreichischen Instituts für Konjunkturforschung* 7, no. 11 (November 1933): 183.

Page 780: Courtesy of National Diet Library, Japan. dl.ndl.go.jp/pid/3514946/1/39. Photographer unknown.

Page 782: Copyright SLUB Dresden / 2011 8 025873. Herman Sörgel, *Atlantropa* (Fretz & Wasmuth, 1932).

Page 784: Deutsches Museum, Munich, Archive, CD_78659. Herman Sörgel, "Atlantropa-Projekt, Schaubild zur Energiegewinnung und zum Schienenverkehr" [Atlantropa Project, Diagram of Energy Generation and Rail Transport], 1932.

Page 786: Courtesy of the Röchling Group. Hermann Röchling, *Wir halten die Saar* [We Hold the Saar] (Volk und Reich Verlag, 1934).

Page 805: Copyright Archives Nationales, France. Photographer unknown.

Page 808: Courtesy of Centro Storico Fiat, Torino, Italy.

Page 811: Saarstahlarchiv, Völklingen, Germany. Photographer unknown.

Page 812: BMW Group Archives. Photographer unknown, circa early 1940s.

Page 815: Reproduced with permission of © Oxford University Press India. Copyright Oxford University Press India, 1940. From Minoo Masani, *Our India*, illus. C. H. G. Moorhouse (Oxford University Press, 1940).

Page 817: PH Collection - Pandit Jawaharlal Nehru, the First Prime Minister of India, typing on the all-Indian Typewriter made by Godrej & Boye, at the Congress session in Avadi, Chennai, circa 1955, DIG2021601800, PH06-01-96-93, Photographs Collection, Godrej Archives.

Page 818: PH Collection—Test typists working on the Godrej M-12 typewriter at typewriter plant at Godrej & Boyce, Vikhroli, Mumbai, circa 1960, PH10-20-17-13, Photographs Collection, Godrej Archives.

Page 822: PH Collection—Ardeshir B. Godrej, Founder, Godrej Group, undated, DIG 201702935, PH06-01-96-1, Photographs Collection, Godrej Archives.

created. Social expenditure as a share of GDP can be accessed at web-archive.oecd.org/2024-06-24/63248 -expenditure.htm.

Page 914: Source: Hagen Lesch, "Trade Union Density in International Comparison." CESifo Forum 5 (2004), 13.

Page 915: Graph by Angela Yan. Sources: For Japan, see Brian Mitchell, *International Historical Statistics: Africa, Asia & Oceania, 1750–1988*, 2nd rev. ed. (Palgrave Macmillan UK, 1995), 131, accessed at doi.org/10.1007/978 -1-349-24069-2. For the US, see Brian Mitchell, *International Historical Statistics: The Americas, 1750–1988*, 2nd ed. (Palgrave Macmillan, 1993), 126, accessed at doi.org/10.1007/978-1-349-13071-9. For the UK, see Brian Mitchell, *International Historical Statistics: Europe 1750–1988*, 3rd ed. (Stockton Press, 1992), 186–87. For West Germany, see Brian Mitchell, *International Historical Statistics: Europe 1750–1988*, 3rd ed. (Stockton Press, 1992), 185, 187.

Page 916: Courtesy of Centro Storico FIAT, Torino, Italy.

Page 928: Table by Angela Yan. Source: UNWTO (2024), processed by Our World in Data. "International Tourist Trips by Region of Departure" (dataset). UNWTO, "145 Key Tourism Statistics" (original data), ourworldin data.org/grapher/international-tourist-arrivals-by-region-of-origin.

Page 929: Wirtschaftswundermuseum, Rheinberg, Germany. Artist unknown.

Page 934: U.S. Department of Agriculture.

Page 935: AP Images / Marty Lederhandler, 1984.

Page 936: Graph by Angela Yan. Source: US Department of Agriculture, "Total food spending reached $2.6 trillion in 2023," June 27, 2024, http://www.ers.usda.gov/data-products/chart-gallery/gallery/chart-detail/?char tId=58364.

Page 937: KFC.

Page 945: Graph by Angela Yan. Source: Office for National Statistics, "GDP Growth Rate and Unemployment Rate, seasonally adjusted, 1971 to 2018," ons.gov.uk/economy/economicoutputandproductivity/output/arti cles/changesintheeconomysincethe1970s/2019-09-02; Office for National Statistics, "Bank Rate and Infla- tion, UK, Seasonally Adjusted, 1970 to 2018," ons.gov.uk/economy/economicoutputandproductivity/output /articles/changesintheeconomysincethe1970s/2019-09-02.

Page 957: "Fac-similé de la 4ème couverture," *Cahiers du GRIF*, no. 2 (1974).

Page 961: Copyright Larry Gonick, 2018.

Page 963: Chas Gerretsen / Nederlands Fotomuseum.

Page 973: Graph by Angela Yan. Source: World Inequality Database, wid.world/data/#countrytimeseries/sptinc _p90p100_992_j;sptinc_p0p50_992_j;sptinc_p99p100_z/CL/1820/2021/eu/k/p/yearly/s.

Page 979: Graph by Angela Yan. Source: United Nations Statistics Division, "GDP and Its Breakdown at Constant 2015 Prices in U.S. dollars: All Countries for All Years—Sorted Alphabetically," unstats.un.org/unsd/amaapi /api/file/6.

Page 986: Copyright Eric Miller, 1987.

Page 992: Wikimedia Commons. Photographer unknown, 2009.

Page 995: Graph by Angela Yan. Source: World Bank, Global Financial Development Database, databank.world bank.org/reports.aspx?source=global-financial-development#.

Page 998: Graph by Angela Yan. Source: World Trade Organization, "Evolution of Trade Under the WTO: Handy Statistics," wto.org/english/res_e/statis_e/trade_evolution_e/evolution_trade_wto_e.htm.

Page 999: Graph by Angela Yan. Source: Statista, "International Seaborne Trade Carried by Container Ships from 2017 to 2024," statista.com/statistics/253987/international-seaborne-trade-carried-by-containers/.

Page 1,011: PA Images / Alamy Stock Foto. Photographer unknown.

Page 1,029, left: Courtesy of Fu Shuaixiong.

Page 1,029, right: China Image Group via Wikimedia Commons. Chen Yun Research Group of the Literature Re- search Office of the Central Committee of the Chinese Communist Party, ed., *Photos of Chen Yun* (Xinhua, 1996).

Page 1,031: Graph by Angela Yan. This is a graph reproduced using data downloaded via piketty.pse.ens.fr/files /capital21c/en/Piketty2014FiguresTablesSuppLinks.pdf. The original graph can be found in Thomas Piketty, *Capital in the Twenty-First Century*, trans. Arthur Goldhammer (Harvard University Press, 2018), 291.

Page 1,032: Graph by Angela Yan. Sources: For trade union percentage dataset, see stats.oecd.org/Index.aspx?Data SetCode=TUD; for GDP level, see stats.oecd.org/Index.aspx?QueryId=117275#; for wage share of GDP, see stats.oecd.org/index.aspx?queryname=345&querytype=view#.

Index

Italicized page numbers indicate material in tables or illustrations.